M ANAGERIAL ACCOUNTING

Accounting Textbooks from West Educational Publishing

Listed Alphabetically by author

Jesse T. Barfield, Cecily A. Raiborn, and Michael R. Kinney: *Cost Accounting, Traditions and Innovations, 2E*

Leonard J. Brooks: *Professional Ethics in Accounting*

John G. Burch: *Cost and Management Accounting: A Modern Approach*

Janet Cassagio, Dolores Osborn & Beverly Terry: *College Accounting*

James Doak and Christine Kloezeman: *Computerized Accounting Principles*

James A. Hall: *Accounting Information Systems*

Bart P. Hartman, Robert M.J. Harper, Jr., James A. Knoblett, and Philip M. Reckers: *Intermediate Accounting*

William H. Hoffman, Jr., William A. Raabe, James E. Smith and David M. Maloney: *West's Federal Taxation: Corporations, Partnerships, Estates and Trusts, 1996 Edition*

William H. Hoffman, Jr., James E. Smith, and Eugene Willis: *West's Federal Taxation: Individual Income Taxes, 1996 Edition*

Michael C. Knapp: *Contemporary Auditing: Issues and Cases, 2E*

Michael C. Knapp: *Financial Accounting: A Focus on Decision Making*

Larry F. Konrath: *Auditing Concepts and Applications: A Risk Analysis Approach, 3E*

Joseph G. Louderback, G. Thomas Friedlob, and Franklin J. Plewa: *Survey of Accounting*

Kevin Murphy with Rick L. Crosser and Mark Higgins: *Concepts in Federal Taxation, 2E*

William A. Raabe, Gerald E. Whittenburg, and John C. Bost: *West's Federal Tax Research, 3E*

Cecily A. Raiborn, Jesse T. Barfield, and Michael R. Kinney: *Managerial Accounting, 2E*

James E. Smith: *West's Internal Revenue Code of 1986 and Treasury Regulations: Annotated and Selected, 1996 Edition*

Gerald E. Whittenburg and Martha Altus-Buller: *Income Tax Fundamentals, 1996 Edition*

CHAPTER NINE:
RELEVANT COSTING

CHAPTER THIRTEEN:
CONTROLLING INVENTORY AND
PRODUCTION COSTS

CHAPTER TEN:
MANAGERIAL ASPECTS OF BUDGETING

CHAPTER FOURTEEN:
CAPITAL ASSET SELECTION
AND CAPITAL BUDGETING

CHAPTER ELEVEN:
THE MASTER BUDGET

CHAPTER FIFTEEN:
RESPONSIBILITY ACCOUNTING AND TRANSFER
PRICING IN DECENTRALIZED OPERATIONS

Ochsner Medical Institutions

CHAPTER TWELVE:
CONTROLLING NONINVENTORY COSTS

CHAPTER SIXTEEN:
MEASURING AND REWARDING PERFORMANCE

MANAGERIAL ACCOUNTING

SECOND EDITION

Cecily A. Raiborn
LOYOLA UNIVERSITY—NEW ORLEANS

Jesse T. Barfield
LOYOLA UNIVERSITY—NEW ORLEANS

Michael R. Kinney
TEXAS A&M UNIVERSITY

WEST PUBLISHING COMPANY

MINNEAPOLIS/SAINT PAUL

NEW YORK

LOS ANGELES

SAN FRANCISCO

COPYEDITOR	Beverly Peavler and Sheryl Rose
COMPOSITION	Parkwood Composition
TEXT DESIGN	Kristen Weber for Metiér
PHOTO RESEARCHER	Michelle Oberhoffer
PAGE LAYOUT	Gary Hespenheide
COVER DESIGN	Tracy Trost/Fish Bone Design
COVER PHOTO	© Jeff Greenberg/PhotoEdit

PRODUCTION, PREPRESS, PRINTING AND BINDING BY WEST PUBLISHING COMPANY

PHOTO CREDITS FOLLOW THE INDEX

British Library Cataloguing-in-Publication Data. A catalogue record for this book is available from the British Library.

Material from Uniform CPA Examination, Questions and Unofficial Answers, copyright © 1977–1979, 1981–1985, and 1988 by American Institute of Certified Public Accountants, Inc., is reprinted (or adapted) with permission.

Material from Certified Management Accountant Examination, copyright © 1972, 1974, 1976–1988, and 1990–1994 by Institute of Certified Management Accountants, is reprinted (or adapted) with permission.

WEST'S COMMITMENT TO THE ENVIRONMENT

In 1906, West Publishing Company began recycling materials left over from the production of books. This began a tradition of efficient and responsible use of resources. West recycles nearly 22 million pounds of scrap paper annually—the equivalent of 181,717 trees. Since the 1960s, West has devised ways to capture and recycle waste inks, solvents, oils and vapors created in the printing process. We also recycle plastics of all kinds, wood, glass, corrugated cardboard, and batteries, and have eliminated the use of Styrofoam book packaging. We at West are proud of the longevity and the scope of our commitment to the environment.

Library of Congress Cataloging-in-Publication Data

Raiborn, Cecily A.
    Managerial accounting / Cecily A. Raiborn, Jesse T. Barfield, Michael R. Kinney. --2nd ed.
    p. cm.
    Includes bibliographical references and index.

    ISBN 0-314-05826-5 (alk. paper)
    1. Managerial accounting. I. Barfield, Jesse T. II. Kinney, Michael R. III. Title.
HF657.4.R34   1996
658.15'11—dc20   95-33105
    ISBN 0-314-07591-7 (loose leaf edition)   CIP
    ISBN 0-314-07014-1 (annotated instructor's edition)

CONTENTS IN BRIEF

CONTENTS

CHAPTER 4   INCLUDING OVERHEAD IN PRODUCT AND SERVICE
                COSTS   129

CHAPTER 5   ACTIVITY-BASED MANAGEMENT   191

PART II: USING MANAGERIAL ACCOUNTING INFORMATION IN COSTING   000

CHAPTER 7   PROCESS COSTING   315

PART III   USING MANAGERIAL ACCOUNTING INFORMATION FOR PLANNING   367

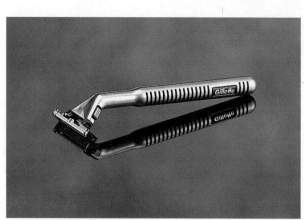

CHAPTER 11   THE MASTER BUDGET   547

PART IV   USING MANAGERIAL ACCOUNTING INFORMATION FOR CONTROLLING   367

CHAPTER 12   CONTROLLING NONINVENTORY COSTS   599

PREFACE

Accounting is often referred to as the "language of business." However, managers must be able to communicate their information needs to accountants and understand the resulting answers. This text provides a context for dialogue among all of the business disciplines and emphasizes the practical rather than the theoretical. Thus, it stresses the techniques and procedures of greatest managerial importance. The perspective taken by *Managerial Accounting* is that managers and accountants must have a common understanding of the organizational role of accounting information, what techniques are available to provide that information, what details are needed to perform the techniques, and the benefits and limitations of the information provided by the various techniques in response to the manager's needs. An integrated approach to information flow will create an atmosphere of trust, sharing, and cooperation.

We believe that it is critical for readers to understand that accounting is a cross-functional discipline that provides information useful to all management areas. It is also essential that readers recognize that managerial accounting information is necessary in all types of businesses (manufacturing, service, and not-for-profit), regardless of size. Substantial effort has been taken to illustrate all of these types of enterprises, in both domestic and international operations. Rapid changes in the global business environment, such as the introduction in previously communist countries of profit-making operations, will create new demands for management information, and this information will be prepared in the international language of business: accounting.

AUDIENCE

This text is primarily directed toward students who have a basic familiarity with the informational content of financial statements. It may be used in a course under either the semester or the quarter system.

PEDAGOGY

This text is extremely student-oriented. The following text features have been designed to promote an ease of learning and provide a high interest level.

Learning Objectives Each chapter provides an orderly framework for the material to be covered. Margin annotations indicate the text coverage of the learning objectives. Margin annotations that identify the learning objective(s) to which each exercise, problem, and case item relates are also included.

On-Site Openers Each chapter begins with a vignette about a relevant aspect of a real-world organization. These openers show students how the chapter topics affect a business on a daily basis. The On-Sites feature organizations such as Rubbermaid, Motorola, Levi Strauss & Co. (Canada) Inc., DeBourgh Manufacturing, the Minnesota Twins, Ochsner Hospital, Southwire Company, and many more.

News Notes News Notes in the chapters provide current selections from the popular business press and reflect the contemporary world of business activity. Four themes (general business, international, quality, and ethics) are used in the News Notes to illustrate how managerial accounting concepts affect various aspects of business. Logos are used to inform the reader of the News Note theme. There are over 80 references to organizations such as Honda, the Girl Scouts, Stewart Pet Products, the City of Mississauga, European Union Commission, Northwest Airlines, and Kerrygold.

Key Terms When a new term is introduced in a chapter, it is listed in boldface type and defined at that point. These terms are also indicated in margin annotations.

Site Analysis This chapter section continues discussion of the On-Site company's reaction to, or resolution of, the opening topic.

Cross-Functional Applications Strategies These strategies follow the Site Analysis section and indicate how chapter tools are applicable to the business disciplines of accounting, economics, finance, management, and marketing. For example, the application strategies section in the cost-volume-profit chapter indicates that CVP is important in marginal analysis for economists, in indicating profit impacts of volume changes for financial analysts, in identifying the effects of cost and pricing strategies for managers, and in justifying appropriate advertising budgets for marketers.

Chapter Summary Each chapter includes a summary to promote student retention of primary chapter points.

Glossary An end-of-chapter glossary is provided so students are aware of the new terms and definitions included in the chapter. The terms are cross-referenced with the page number containing the definition. Additionally, there is a complete end-of-text glossary.

Solution Strategies In this section, students are provided with all relevant formulas and major computational formats from the chapter. These strategies may be used as guides to work end-of chapter materials or to refresh the memory.

Demonstration Problem At the end of appropriate chapters, a demonstration problem and solution are given so that students can check their understanding of chapter computations before doing end-of-chapter assignments.

End-of-Chapter Materials Each chapter contains a variety of end-of-chapter materials (at different levels of difficulty) that include questions, exercises, communication activities, problems, cases, ethics and quality discussions, and suggested projects. The communication activities provide the opportunity for students to utilize their writing skills and, in some instances, these activities focus on the skills of the various business disciplines and the need for interaction among these disciplines in a business environment. Many of the ethics and quality discussions are taken from the popular business press and relate to actual business situations. These items provide the dual benefit of indicating that ethical and quality choices are important to an organization's current and future existence as well as providing an additional avenue for written expression and logical thought. (A brief overview of the various ethical theories is provided in Appendix B.) The projects section includes two to four opportunities for students to interact with members of the business community and/or to work in teams to develop the interpersonal skills that are crucial in the business world. The numerical end-of-chapter materials that are computer-solvable are indicated with a computer icon. Cross-functional and team activities are also indicated by appropriate icons.

MAJOR CHANGES IN SECOND EDITION

Although the first edition of this text was very well received, the authors gathered comments from adopters and reviewers and made numerous changes to increase its teachability and student orientation. In addition, the Accounting Education Change Commission has also been instrumental in providing guidance on improving and adding to the text's pedagogical features. The AECC has indicated that it is essential for students in accounting courses to possess strong communication, intellectual, and interpersonal skills as well as to understand ethics and make value-based judgments. Thus, to encourage students to improve their communication and intellectual skills, we have expanded the quantity of essay and logic problems in end-of-chapter materials, student study guide, and test bank. To improve the process of analyzing and making ethical decisions and value-based judgments, we have included more real-world discussion questions in the end-of-chapter materials. Additionally, to promote interpersonal skills, projects that can be used by teams are presented for each chapter; these may be assigned for oral or written presentation. Teamwork is essential in today's business environment because flattened organization structures result in the empowerment of employee teams with the authority, responsibility, and accountability for making positive changes and rational decisions.

The organizational and pedagogical changes to the second edition are listed below. Changes in the supplements are provided in the appropriate Instructor and Student Support Materials sections.

Organization

- Chapter 1 introduces the discipline of management accounting and then focuses on the global environment in which businesses operate. This chapter is designed to help students understand the numerous forces that must be considered by business people today and how those forces affect accounting and decision making.
- Chapter 2 addresses the demand for quality in products and services, the need for reduced cycle time, the increased technological abilities available to businesses, and the desire of management to focus on strategy-based cost management practices.
- Chapter 4 discusses cost flow issues and uses job order costing to illustrate product cost accumulation.
- The absorption/variable costing material has been shortened and is included at the beginning of Chapter 8 on breakeven and cost-volume-profit analysis. The cash breakeven appendix has been deleted. The relevant costing chapter has been placed as Chapter 9 for a continuation of short-run decision-making information.
- The chapter on controlling noninventory costs has been placed after the budgeting chapters to allow students to consider the issues of cost and revenue relationships (variable costing, cost-volume-profit, and relevant costing) with the issues of planning (budgeting) and cost control.
- The capital budgeting chapter has been reorganized to address payback period and then discounted cash flow methods. Accounting rate of return has been moved to an appendix. Future value tables are included in the end-of-chapter appendix in addition to the previously provided present value tables.
- The previous chapter on decentralization and responsibility accounting has been split into two chapters. The first chapter covers decentralized operations, including transfer pricing; the second covers the processes of measuring and rewarding performance.

- The pricing and legal requirements/ethical behavior chapters have been deleted and information from these chapters has been included at appropriate points throughout the text.
- An end-of-text Appendix A has been developed that addresses issues related to professional management accountants in both the United States and Canada.

Pedagogy

- There is increased discussion throughout the text on quality and international issues. Where appropriate, each chapter contains a specific quality and/or international section. Because of the need for businesses to compete in international markets, some examples and end-of-chapter materials use alternative currency units and quantity measurements. There is also greater inclusion of issues related to service companies.
- The themes of the opening vignettes are carried through the chapter using a fictitious company in a related industry. Because of the need to maintain confidentiality of proprietary information, the On-Site company's actual data have not been used, but example data are reflective of reality.
- The end-of-chapter materials include discussion questions on both ethics and quality. As mentioned earlier, many of these questions address actual business situations. The quality discussion questions focus on the impacts of introducing (or choosing not to introduce) quality techniques on company costs, employee and customer behavior, and production/service processes.
- Journal entries are, in many places, presented separately in chapter appendices. This placement allows faculty to include or exclude this accounting process information without interrupting the flow of the chapters.
- Approximately 25 percent of the end-of-chapter material is new and there are typically at least two exercises for each key concept in the chapter. An emphasis to illustrate the cross-functional interactions of business disciplines has been included in some end-of-chapter materials; such materials promote discussion of who can provide necessary information and how different disciplines would react to problem situations. These cross-functional items are indicated with a logo in margin annotations.
- As indicated in the Pedagogy: End-of-Chapter Materials section above and in response to the guidelines of the Accounting Education Change Commission, there is increased emphasis in the end-of-chapter materials on written and oral communication skills and team projects.

INSTRUCTOR SUPPORT MATERIALS

The text is accompanied by a full range of support materials for the instructor.

Annotated Instructor's Edition This special edition of the text was prepared by the authors and contains a variety of margin notes to improve and enhance teaching effectiveness and efficiency. These notes include the following:

- Teaching Notes—provide additional facts or explanations for use by the instructor.
- Points to Emphasize—provide some logical "check points" to ensure student clarity on subject matter.

- Points to Consider—indicate questions that can be asked to generate student response to evaluate understanding of the material or critical thinking skills; some of these points also provide alternative examples to those given in the text.
- Teaching Transparencies—refer to points at which selected teaching transparencies can be used. The masters for these transparencies are in the Instructor's Manual and are not duplicates of textual exhibits, but rather provide additional perspectives on the text materials.
- Video Vignette Icons—identify points at which it would be appropriate to show one or more of the videos supplied by West Publishing.
- Check Figures—present answers for all numerical end-of-chapter exercises, problems, and cases.

Solutions Manual This volume, prepared by the authors, has been independently reviewed and checked for accuracy. It contains complete solutions to each question, exercise, problem, and case in the text. This volume also contains a copy of the Student Check Figures. This list is available free of charge when ordered by faculty to be shrink-wrapped with the textbook.

Solution Transparency Acetates Acetates are provided from the solutions manual for all numerical end-of-chapter materials.

Test Bank The test bank (prepared by Chandra Schorg at Texas Woman's University) contains over one thousand multiple-choice, short exercise, and short discussion questions with related solutions.

WesTest™ This supplement is a computerized version of the multiple-choice and short problem portions of the hard-copy test bank. WesTest includes edit and word processing features that allow test customization through the addition, deletion, or scrambling of test selections.

Instructor's Manual This manual (developed by Gregory K. Lowry) contains sample syllabi, a listing of chapter terminology, chapter lecture outlines, an assignment classification table indicating the level of difficulty of all end-of-chapter materials, and some CMA exam multiple-choice questions for use as additional test materials or for quizzes. Also included are masters for the teaching transparencies referenced in the Annotated Instructor's Edition as well as for some of the text exhibits.

Astound™ This package (prepared by Donna Dietz at Concordia College) is a state-of-the-art, CD-ROM graphics package program. It provides entertaining and informative graphics and text for full-color electronic presentations. PowerPoint files are also available on disk.

Videos This text is accompanied by a wide selection of videos that illustrate text concepts. For example, one tape provides the students with a tour that illustrates a basic production process by showing a walk-through of the highly automated West Publishing facility. Other videos are tied directly to text examples and relate to companies (such as the Minnesota Twins and First Bank) introduced in the On-Site vignettes. A variety of tapes produced by the Association for Manufacturing Excellence (AME) are available to qualified adopters. These tapes feature companies such as Hewlett-Packard, Motorola, Spectra-Physics, Whirlpool, Northern Telecom, and Oregon Cutting Systems. These videos illustrate automated processes, just-in-time/total quality management philosophies, manufacturing excellence at small and mid-sized companies, global business strategies, and teamwork skills. Short videos are also available featuring some companies that have been designated "Blue Chip Enterprises." This program for small businesses is sponsored by Connecticut Mutual Life Insurance Company, the U.S. Chamber of Commerce, and *Nation's Business* magazine. Three videos are also available that illustrate ethical issues related to job order costing, budgeting, and quality/performance. These videos were produced by Arthur Andersen and Co., SC, Chicago, Illinois (© 1991) and are used with this organization's permission.

Video Guide A video guide provides a brief overview of each segment, indicates segment length, discusses each segment's key points, and provides some questions for classroom discussion about each segment.

STUDENT SUPPORT MATERIALS

Students are also provided with a comprehensive support package to enhance their learning experience.

Working Papers This student supplement contains a set of forms for all numerical end-of-chapter problems and cases. These working papers are partially completed and help structure problem solutions.

Study Guide The student study guide (prepared by Alan Campbell at University of Southwestern Louisiana) contains chapter learning objectives, chapter overviews, detailed chapter notes, and self-test questions.

Student Check Figures For instructors who wish to provide students with answers to end-of-chapter materials, this list has been prepared by the authors from the solutions contained in the solutions manual. These are available free of charge upon instructor request to be shrink-wrapped with text.

Spreadsheet Applications for Managerial Accounting Prepared by Christina Moorcroft (at Luther College), this package allows students to use Lotus 1-2-3® to solve many in-text problems (which have been indicated with a computer disk icon).

Practice Sets Two practice sets are available for the text.

■ Pennsylvania Containers: An Activity-Based Costing Case, developed by Mark Bettner of Bucknell University, illustrates activity-based costing using a manufacturing company that produces garbage dumpsters and customized trash receptacles. This practice set concentrates on determination of cost drivers and their use in assigning overhead costs to products. It can be used when teaching Chapter 5 (Activity-Based Management) or in conjunction with several chapters from the text to show the student the impact of activity-based costing on decision making. A solutions manual is available for instructors.

■ Pet Polygon Manufacturing Company is an IBM-compatible computerized practice set that was written by L. Murphy Smith of Texas A&M University and Dana Forgione of the University of Baltimore. It provides students with the opportunity to develop a complete master budget and make managerial decisions. A solutions manual indicates how the practice set can be used in conjunction with the master budgeting chapters (10 and 11) or as a continuing problem for the entire term.

Student Solutions Manual This student supplement, prepared from the instructor's Solutions Manual, provides complete solutions to alternate end-of-chapter exercises and problems.

Insights: Readings in Managerial Accounting This readings book is available for those faculty who wish to supplement text assignments with articles that discuss contemporary issues in managerial accounting and the related business environment. This soft-cover book contains 20 selections from sources such as *Fortune*, *Management Accounting*, and *The Journal of Cost Management*.

Student Notetaking Guide This unique supplement includes copies of the transparencies provided to instructors. They are printed at fifty percent normal size on full sheets, with space for students to take lecture notes. Detailed outlines are also provided.

ESL Supplement Prepared by Luis Guillen, this supplement is a Spanish glossary of the key terms to aid those students for whom English is a second language.

ACKNOWLEDGMENTS

We would like to thank the many people who have helped us during the revision of this text. The constructive comments and suggestions made by the following reviewers were instrumental in developing, rewriting, and improving the quality and readability of this book.

Janice Ammons	New Mexico State University
Mark S. Bettner	Bucknell University
Marvin L. Bouillon	Iowa State University
G. Robert Cluskey, Jr.	Bradley University
Michael F. Cornick	University of North Carolina—Charlotte
Johan DeRooy	University of British Columbia
Lee Dexter	Moorhead State University
Michael Dole	Marquette University
Craig Emby	Simon Fraser University
James R. Emore	University of Akron
Micah P. Frankel	California State University—Hayward
G. Richard French	Indiana University—Southeast
Lawrence J. Gramling	University of Connecticut
Jane Hall	Murray State University
Jan Richard Heier	Auburn University—Montgomery
Richard Houser	North Arizona University
Mohamed E. Ibrahim	Concordia University
Fred Jex	Macomb Community College
Gregory K. Lowry	Consultant
Jim Makofske	Fresno City College
Margaret D. McCrory	Marist College
Laurie McWhorter	Austin Peay State University
Christina Moorcroft	Luther College
Bob Picard	Idaho State University
Peter J. Poznanski	Cleveland State University
Frederick W. Schaeberle	Western Michigan University
Chandra A. Schorg	Texas Women's University
William A. Stahlin	Drexel University
Tom Tolleson	University of North Texas
Y. Joseph Ugras	LaSalle University

Special mention must be given to Margie Boldt at the University of Oklahoma for her hard work as a problem checker, to Joel Ridenour for gaining the appropriate permissions, and to the many individuals who provided information related to the On-Sites and Site Analyses. Special thanks must also be made to the Institute of Management Accountants. This organization has been extremely generous in its permission to use numerous CMA problems and excerpts from its *Management Accounting* periodical and other publications. We also want to acknowledge the many publishers who granted permission for use of their materials as On-Site/Site Analysis/News Note excerpts.

Lastly, the authors thank all the people at West Publishing (especially Rick Leyh, Jayne Lindesmith, Tom Modl, Jessica Evans, and Cathy Story) who have helped us on this project and to our families and friends who have encouraged and supported us in this endeavor.

Cecily Raiborn
Jesse Barfield
Mike Kinney

I

BASICS OF
MANAGERIAL
ACCOUNTING

MANAGEMENT ACCOUNTING IN A GLOBAL BUSINESS ENVIRONMENT

LEARNING OBJECTIVES

1. Compare financial, management, and cost accounting.

2. Explain why management accounting information is important to managers.

3. Relate management accounting to the various managerial functions.

4. Differentiate among the stages of production.

5. Distinguish between product and period costs.

6. Explain how markets have become international in scope and how this has affected the way firms compete.

7. (Appendix) Discuss organizational structure relationships.

In today's business environment, any company that overlooks foreign markets is risking obsolescence.
—James E. Denny, "Tapping Foreign Markets," *Journal of Accountancy* (May 1994)

ON SITE

Rubbermaid: Lowered Prices Don't Mean Lowered Profits

Rubbermaid's sales are derived from the broad line of plastic and rubber products it manufactures for the home and commercial markets under the Rubbermaid, Little Tikes, Con-Tact, SECO, Eldon, and Gott names. The products range from food storage containers and plastic garbage cans to bird feeders, toys, and modular office furniture.

So dominant are the company's brand names that Rubbermaid is the market share leader in all five of its businesses, usually controlling over 50%. The remainder is fragmented into several segments. This allows Rubbermaid to leverage more effectively any innovations made in materials and product development, market investments, and promotions.

Forced to lower prices in 1993 for the third year in a row, Rubbermaid's chairman and CEO, Wolfgang Schmitt, was still able to generate 15% earnings growth during the third quarter. He achieved that by boosting Rubbermaid's operating margins. Some of this improvement has come by way of higher productivity. But most of the increase has come from lower raw material prices and from trimming selling, general, and administrative (SG&A) expenses.

For example, the types of resin Rubbermaid uses, such as high-density polyethylene, have fallen in price from a peak of 51¢ a pound in 1988 to 29¢ [in 1994]. In 1992, the company cut SG&A costs from 18.5% to 17.2% of sales. According to Rubbermaid's annual report, this reduction came as a result of "lower amounts spent on advertising, strict controls on selling and administrative spending, and lower bad debt provisions."

[Because the company has an ironclad policy of not increasing prices,] at this point, Schmitt has three possible ways in which he can achieve growth: increase productivity, acquire other companies, and expand internationally. He is doing all three.

In 1992, for example, Rubbermaid spent $134.5 million on capital expenditures. "What we have done is streamlined our factories to make them more productive," says Schmitt. "We want to have factories that have very high velocity, high technology, high throughput, and high flexibility. Things that are more job shop–oriented we now outsource to smaller organizations that are more nimble and efficient."

The big challenge for Schmitt will be boosting Rubbermaid's international sales. Rubbermaid currently gets only about 11% of its consolidated revenues from outside the U.S., almost all from Canada. Schmitt would like to see that more than double, to 25%, by 2000. "What we really are working hard on is globalizing the business," says Schmitt.

SOURCES: Alexandra Ourusoff, "Valuing the Rubbermaid Brands," *Financial World* (February 1, 1994), p. 38; and Michael K. Ozanian and Alexandra Ourusoff, "Never Let Them See You Sweat," *Financial World* (February 1, 1994), pp. 34, 35, 38. Both items excerpted from FINANCIAL WORLD 1328 Broadway, New York, NY 10001. © Copyrighted 1994 by Financial World Partners. All rights reserved.

Rubbermaid may be a corporate giant, but its managers need the same basic information as those in a business of any other size. Wolfgang Schmitt needs information about the relationship between sales and costs to determine organizational profitability. He needs information about cash and credit availability to assess whether funds will be available to acquire plant assets or corporate entities. He needs information about global markets and customer desires. Much of the information managers need is provided by the accounting information system.

This chapter discusses how financial, management, and cost accounting relate to one another and to the information needs of management. In addition, managerial functions are addressed because it is by performing these functions that the need for information arises. Last, the environment in which businesses operate is discussed since information needs are affected by the type of organization (manufacturer, service, or retail) and by the necessity of operating in a global economy.

RELATIONSHIP OF FINANCIAL, MANAGEMENT, AND COST ACCOUNTING

All accounting information tends to rely on the same basic accounting system and set of accounts. Accounting information is expected to address four functions: (1) provide information to external parties (stockholders, creditors, and various regulatory bodies); (2) help estimate the costs of products and services; (3) help control operations; and (4) help in product/service pricing. Each function requires different information and could possibly justify a different accounting information system. Harvard professor Robert S. Kaplan noted that "systems designed mainly to value inventory for financial and tax statements are not giving managers the accurate and timely information they need to promote operating efficiencies and measure product costs."[1]

Although existing technology would allow companies to design different accounting systems for different purposes, most companies still rely on a single system to supply the basic accounting information. Thus, financial accounting and management accounting use a common database to provide external and internal information, respectively. The accounting system is typically focused on providing information for financial accounting purposes, and its informational output must be adapted to meet most internal management requirements.

> ■ **LEARNING OBJECTIVE 1**
> Compare financial, management, and cost accounting.

Financial Accounting

Financial accounting focuses on external users and so must comply with generally accepted accounting principles. The information used in financial accounting is typically historical, quantifiable, monetary, and accurate. These characteristics are essential to the consistency, verifiability, and uniformity needed for external financial statements. Financial accounting information is usually quite aggregated and relates to the entire organization. In some cases, a regulatory agency (such as the Securities and Exchange Commission) or an industry commission (such as in banking or insurance) may mandate certain financial accounting practices. In other cases, financial accounting information is required for obtaining loans, preparing tax returns, and understanding how well or poorly the business is performing.

Management Accounting

Management accounting can be used in all types of organizations to provide information for internal users. **Management accounting** refers to the "process of

management accounting

---

[1]Robert S. Kaplan, "One Cost System Isn't Enough," *Harvard Business Review* (January–February 1988), p. 61.

identification, measurement, accumulation, analysis, preparation, interpretation, and communication of financial information used by management to plan, evaluate, and control within an organization and to assure appropriate use of and accountability for its resources."[2] Exhibit 1–1 details the differences between financial and management accounting.

Managers are often concerned with individual parts or segments of the business rather than the organization as a whole. Therefore, management accounting information commonly focuses on particular segmental aspects of an entity rather than the "big picture" of financial accounting. For example, Rubbermaid needs information about the profitability of each of its different products in addition to determining the company's overall profitability.

Management accounting is not generally required by any organization or regulatory body. Except for rules set forth by the Cost Accounting Standards Board (discussed in Appendix A to the text), management accounting is not externally influenced. Accountants do not have to adhere to generally accepted accounting principles in providing internal information and, thus, can be more flexible in preparing that information. Often, these accountants provide forecasted, qualitative, and nonmonetary information. For instance, a manager debating whether to sell a piece of land now or in three years is not likely to use the land's historical cost to make the decision. Instead, he or she will need estimates about expected changes in land prices for the next three years as well as information about expected events, such as the possibility that a shopping center will be built on property that adjoins the land.

A primary criterion for internal information is that it serve management's needs. A related criterion is the cost/benefit consideration that information should be developed and provided only if the cost of producing it is less than the benefit gained from using the information. These two criteria, however, must be considered in light of the criteria for financial accounting information that were noted earlier: verifiability, uniformi-

■ LEARNING
OBJECTIVE 2
Explain why management
accounting information is
important to managers.

■ **EXHIBIT 1–1**

Financial and Management Accounting Differences

	FINANCIAL	**MANAGEMENT**
Primary users	External	Internal
Primary organizational focus	Whole (aggregated)	Parts (segmented)
Information characteristics	Must be	May be
	Historical	Forecasted
	Quantitative	Quantitative or qualitative
	Monetary	Monetary or nonmonetary
	Accurate	Timely and, at a minimum, a reasonable estimate
Overriding criteria	Generally accepted accounting principles	Situational relevance (usefulness)
	Consistency	Benefits in excess of cost
	Verifiability	Flexibility
Record keeping	Formal	Combination of formal and informal

---

[2]Institute of Management Accountants (formerly National Association of Accountants), *Statements on Management Accounting Number 2: Management Accounting Terminology* (New York: National Association of Accountants, June 1, 1983), p. 65.

ty, and consistency. These three characteristics are also important for management accounting because it would be counterproductive to base *any* document simply on whim or flexibility. But from a management accounting perspective, meeting managerial needs involves much more than satisfying financial accounting requirements.

Cost Accounting

Some organizations are involved in changing raw materials or supplies from one form into another in a process called **conversion.** Exhibit 1–2 compares the conversion activities of different types of organizations. Although all manufacturers engage in high levels of conversion activities, so do some service companies.[3] For example, firms of professionals (such as accountants, architects, attorneys, engineers, and surveyors) convert labor and other resource inputs (materials and overhead) into completed jobs (audit reports, building plans, contracts, blueprints, and property survey reports).

Companies that engage in conversion activities have a distinct need for **cost accounting,** a part of management accounting that is used to determine the cost of making products or performing services. Cost accounting information creates an overlap between financial accounting and management accounting and integrates with financial accounting by providing product cost measurements for inventories and cost of goods sold on the financial statements. As part of management accounting, cost accounting provides some of the quantitative, cost-based information managers need to assess product profitability, prepare budgets, and make decisions about investments. Exhibit 1–3 (page 8) depicts the relationship of cost accounting to the larger systems of financial and management accounting.

Regardless of whether information is provided by financial, management, or cost accounting, managers use it to make decisions. As indicated in the accompanying

conversion

cost accounting

■ **EXHIBIT 1–2**
Degrees of Conversion in Firms

LOW DEGREE OF CONVERSION	**MODERATE DEGREE OF CONVERSION**	**HIGH DEGREE OF CONVERSION**
(adding only the value of having merchandise when, where, and in the assortment needed by customers)	(washing, testing, packaging, labeling, etc.)	(causing a major transformation from input to output)
Retailing companies that act as mere conduits between suppliers and consumers (department stores, gas stations, jewelry stores, travel agencies)	Retailing companies that make small visible additions to the output prior to sale or delivery (florists, meat markets, oil change businesses)	Manufacturing, mining, construction, agricultural, and printing companies; architectural, engineering, legal, and accounting firms; restaurants

[3]For convenience, the term *manufacturer* refers to a company engaged in a high degree of conversion of raw material input into other tangible output. Manufacturers typically convert inputs to outputs through the use of people and machines to produce large quantities of output that can be physically inspected. The term *service company* refers to an individual or firm engaged in a high or moderate degree of conversion using few raw material inputs and, often, a significant amount of effort (either human or machine). Service output may be tangible (an audit report) or intangible (health care) and normally cannot be inspected prior to its use. Service firms may be profit-making businesses or not-for-profit organizations.

■ **EXHIBIT 1–3**
Financial, Management, and Cost Accounting Overlap

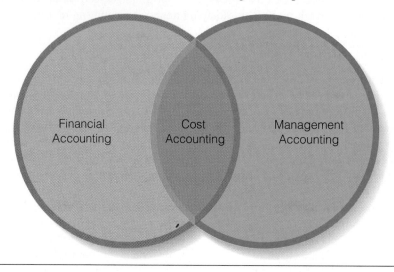

News Note, different information may be needed at different times. Some information may be estimated and reflect the contents of a plan prepared before certain activities are begun. Other quantitative, factual information may provide answers during the activities to questions such as "Where are we?" "How did we get here?" and "How are we doing?" Still other information may report the results of activities, so that these results can be analyzed, evaluated, and used in future planning. Some of the needed information may be historical, monetary, or based on generally accepted accounting principles, but managers also often require forecasted, qualitative information.

relevant information

Whatever form the information takes, it must be relevant to the decision being made and the possible solutions available so managers can make the most valid choices and analyses. **Relevant information** satisfies three conditions: it is logically related to the decision under consideration; it is important to a decision maker; and it has a connection to or bearing on some future endeavor. Thus, relevance exists if information is useful to the managers who employ it in fulfilling their organizational functions, which include planning, controlling, evaluating, and decision making.

MANAGEMENT FUNCTIONS

goals
objectives

Managers set goals and objectives for the future. **Goals** are desired results or conditions expressed in qualitative terms. **Objectives,** on the other hand, are quantitatively expressed results that can be achieved during a preestablished period or by a specified date. Objectives should logically result from goals. For example, one goal cited by Wolfgang Schmitt is to increase Rubbermaid's international sales. He translated this goal into an objective when he indicated that he wanted 25 percent of company revenues to be generated outside the United States by the year 2000.

■ **LEARNING OBJECTIVE 5**
Distinguish between product and period costs.

planning

Translating goals and objectives into the specific activities and resources required for achievement is **planning.** Planning allows managers to make choices about future

What Information Is Needed?
How Is It Obtained?

Although the role of accounting has expanded greatly in recent years, the importance of precise, reliable financial reporting—the "bean counter's forté"—hasn't diminished. Businesses still need accountants with strong technical skills who can keep accurate records, maintain effective control systems, and produce financial reports that meet legal and ethical requirements.

But organizations have come to expect even more from their accountants. Top managers want access to powerful information that will help them to make better business decisions. They have turned to the accounting profession to provide such information.

The need for more complete internal management information surfaced in the 1980s, when many U.S. businesses were besieged by non-U.S. competition. But even though accounting wasn't the cause of all problems, most of our cost accounting systems were not capable of delivering the kind of information required for good internal cost management. That's because they were designed to accommodate external financial reporting. They were never intended to be used as internal management tools.

The concept of separate systems for external reporting and internal management information made good business sense. But before the internal systems could be developed, top management had to define and articulate long-term business strategies. Given a solid vision, an understanding of the firm's critical success factors that needed to be addressed to achieve the vision, specific long- and short-term objectives, and clearly assigned accountability, the management accountant had a blueprint for developing effective internal management tools and systems.

SOURCE: Lou Jones, "Management Accounting in the '90s and Beyond," *Management Accounting Campus Report* (Spring 1993), pp. 1–2. Copyright © 1993 IMA (formerly NAA).

Careful planning and an eye toward costs were essential in Rubbermaid's creating new square and rectangle container designs for the EZ Topps food container line. Rubbermaid uses business teams to make product design decisions as well as analyze effective distribution channels.

The Japanese Plan-Do-Check-Action System

According to Hiromoto, Japanese accounting and control systems are subservient to corporate strategy; they are used to influence behavior. In the United States, on the other hand, accounting and control systems have been used mainly to inform management about the company's performance. In Japan, planning and control are based on a bottom-up approach through which workers and lower-level managers participate in developing goals and receive considerable feedback as the plans are implemented.

In the United States, planning and control are based on a top-down approach. The financial budget is rolled down into the organization. The view that the Japanese are highly committed to planning and feedback is supported by their almost fanatical use of a system called plan-do-check-action (PDCA). In this system (which is frequently used by quality control circles), the *plan* step includes identifying the problem and the underlying cause, plus developing a plan for the problem's solution. The *do* step involves a trial run to determine if the plan works. In the *check* step, the trial run is evaluated and revisions are made if necessary. The final *action* step is to implement the plan. The PDCA approach is a never-ending activity for the Japanese, who are meticulous about providing documentation for nearly every decision.

SOURCE: James R. Martin, et al., "Comparing U.S. and Japanese Companies: Implications for Management Accounting," *Journal of Cost Management* (Spring 1992), p. 11. Reprinted with permission from The Journal of Cost Management for the Manufacturing Industry, © 1992 Warren, Gorham & Lamont, 31 St. James Ave., Boston, MA 02116. All rights reserved.

activities. Companies develop short-term, intermediate-term, and long-term plans. Short-term plans are prepared in the greatest detail and are used by managers as one basis for controlling and evaluating performance. In the past, many managers tended to focus solely on short-term results (such as annual profits) because they could be easily measured against detailed plans. This tendency is changing as managers begin to realize that, since companies are expected to be in business for the long term, the true measures of performance should capture long-term accomplishments. This new outlook produces better long-range planning and additional performance measurements.

controlling

Exerting managerial influence on operations so that they will conform to plans is called **controlling.** The control process uses norms against which actual results are compared. Control involves setting performance standards, measuring performance, periodically comparing actual performance with standards, and taking corrective action when operations do not conform with established standards. For instance, Rubbermaid's standard time to produce a laundry basket is 45 seconds. A longer time might indicate equipment problems; a shorter time might indicate quality problems. Unless Rubbermaid managers knew that production should take 45 seconds, they could not know that any other quantity of time could indicate problems. Thus, control cannot be exercised unless a plan has been made. The degree of planning and control activities varies by manager and, as indicated in the accompanying News Note, by country.

performance evaluations

Using management accounting information, managers can conduct **performance evaluations** to determine if operations are proceeding according to plan or if actual results differ significantly from those expected. In the latter case, adjustments to operating activities may be needed. The best performance maximizes both effectiveness

effectiveness

and efficiency. Successfully accomplishing a task reflects **effectiveness,** while performing a task to produce the best outcome at the lowest cost from the resources used reflects **efficiency.**

For example, it is effective to mass market test a new product, but it is more efficient to test in a small group. Using focus groups significantly reduces sampling and advertising expenditures. Many companies could not handle new product rollouts without mass market testing, but Rubbermaid can. Its new products are so carefully designed that 90 percent of them succeed, whereas the general rule is that 90 percent of new consumer products fail.[4]

Managers are information users and accountants are information providers. A manager's ability to manage depends on good **decision making**—using information to choose the best alternative from the options available to reach a particular goal or objective:

> In today's corporations, oceans of data drown most decision makers. Eliminating irrelevant information requires the knowledge of what is relevant, the knowledge of how to access and select appropriate data, and the knowledge of how best to prepare the data by sorting and summarizing it to facilitate analysis. This is the raw material of decision making.[5]

The quantity of information needed by managers is related both to the expected consequences of the decision and to the complexity of activities performed by the organization. More important decisions and more complex activities require more information. For instance, decisions about which products to carry or make are critical to retailers and manufacturers, respectively. But these decisions will require different kinds and quantities of information about selling prices, sales volumes, and operating expenses. An operating expense of prime importance is cost of goods sold. Managers of retail businesses can gain this cost information by reviewing product purchase prices. In manufacturing and service concerns, managers must accumulate numerous pieces of cost information throughout the various stages of the production or service process.

STAGES OF PRODUCTION

Most retail or merchandising companies do not have stages of production because products are purchased ready for sale to customers or in the form of finished goods. Manufacturers and service companies, however, convert raw materials and/or supplies into different forms. This conversion process requires a production flow that, for accounting purposes, must be traced through the organization.

In making a product or performing a service, processing or performance flows through three stages: (1) work not started (raw materials and supplies), (2) **work in process** (goods or services that have been started, but are not yet complete), and (3) finished work. Costs are associated with each stage. The stages and related costs of production in a manufacturing firm are shown in Exhibit 1–4 (page 12).

A manufacturer first incurs costs during the beginning stage of processing. These costs reflect the prices paid for purchasing raw materials and/or supplies. To begin the second stage, raw materials or supplies are issued into the conversion portion of a production process. Additional costs are then incurred to convert the raw materials into finished products. These costs include the wages paid to people producing the goods as well as factory **overhead** charges. Factory overhead costs are the indirect or

efficiency

decision making

■ LEARNING OBJECTIVE 4
Differentiate among the stages of production.

work in progress

overhead

---

[4]Seth Lubove, "Okay, Call Me a Predator," *Forbes* (February 15, 1993), p. 152.
[5]Edward G. Mahler, "Perform as Smart as You Are," *Financial Executive* (July/August 1991), p. 18.

■ EXHIBIT 1–4
Stages and Costs of Production

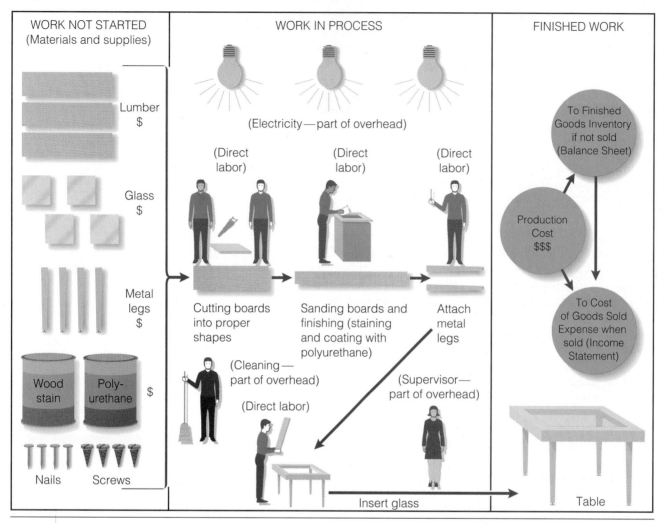

supporting costs of converting raw materials into finished products. These costs include amounts paid or incurred for items such as electricity, machinery and building depreciation, cleanup, supervision, and equipment maintenance incurred in the production or manufacturing function.

The total accumulated production costs for raw materials, labor, and overhead equal the cost of goods in the third stage (finished work). Thus, the primary inventory accounts involved in the cost accumulation process of a manufacturer are: (1) Raw Materials Inventory, (2) Work in Process Inventory, and (3) Finished Goods Inventory. These accounts relate to the three stages of production shown in Exhibit 1–4.

Technically, all organizations convert inputs (materials, labor, and overhead) into outputs although the conversion process in merchandising businesses is less significant in terms of time, effort, or cost than it is in manufacturing or service companies. For example, conversion in a merchandising company would include tagging merchandise with sales tickets and adding store-name labels to goods as is done at some department stores. Similarly, when employees in a grocery store cut open shipping containers and stock individual packages on shelves, a labor cost for conversion has been incurred. The costs of such activities theoretically should be treated as additional costs of merchandise. Department and grocery stores, however, do not try to attach the stockpeople's wages to inventory; such labor costs are treated as expenses as they are incurred. Firms engaging in only a limited degree of conversion can expense any labor and overhead costs related to the conversion process if they are insignificant. The clerical cost saved by expensing these costs outweighs the value of any slightly improved information that might result from assigning them to products or services.

Service firms also do not have as high a degree of cost and process complexity as manufacturers. For service firms, costs in the work-not-started stage normally consist only of the costs of supplies that are inventoried until work is begun on them. At that point, labor and overhead are added to achieve finished results. Service firms may accumulate conversion costs for work in process, but they do not normally maintain an inventory of finished work. Such an inventory is usually unnecessary because service is commonly rendered and delivered to the client in a single step.

In contrast, in high-conversion manufacturing firms, the informational benefits gained from assigning conversion labor and overhead costs to the output produced significantly exceed the clerical costs of maintaining the necessary accounting system. For instance, no one would presume to expense the labor costs incurred for workers constructing a bridge. Rather, these costs would be treated as part of the cost of the construction job and retained in an inventory account until the bridge was completed and accepted by the client.

Exhibit 1–5 (page 14) compares the input/output relationships of a merchandiser with those of a manufacturer/service company. This exhibit shows that the primary difference between these types of companies is the absence or presence of an area labeled "the production center." This center involves the conversion of physical inputs to final products. Input factors flow into the production center and are transformed to completed goods or services. If the output is a product, it can be warehoused or displayed (or both) after it is completed until it is sold to a customer. Service outputs are simply provided to the client who commissioned the work.

The input/output relationships shown in Exhibit 1–5 are merely one piece of an organization's value chain. A **value chain** is "the linked set of value-creating activities all the way from basic raw material sources for component suppliers through to the ultimate end-use product delivered into the final consumers' hands."[6] Costs are incurred for all activities within the value chain and where they are incurred affects their classification as product or period costs.

value chain

PRODUCT COSTS AND PERIOD COSTS

Costs associated with making or acquiring inventory are **product costs;** all other costs are **period costs.** In general, product costs are incurred in the production or conversion portion of the value chain, and period costs are incurred outside the production or conversion areas.[7]

product costs
period costs

■ LEARNING
OBJECTIVE 5
Distinguish between product and period costs.

---

[6]John K. Shank and Vijay Govindarajan, *Strategic Cost Management* (New York: The Free Press, 1993), p. 13.

[7]Although less common, it is possible for a cost to be physically incurred outside the production area but still directly support production and therefore be considered a product cost. An example of this situation is the salary of a product cost analyst who is based at company headquarters.

■ **EXHIBIT 1–5**
Business Input/Output Relationships

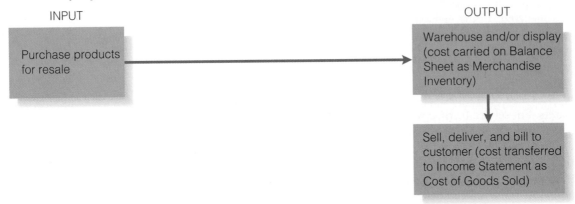

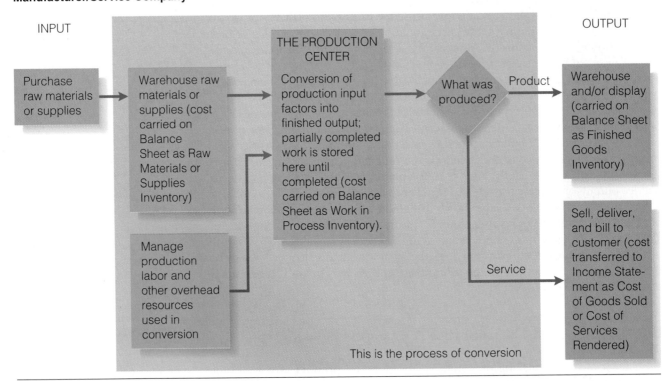

Product Costs

inventoriable costs

Product (or **inventoriable**) **costs** for a merchandising company are fairly easy to determine. Most retailers buy goods in finished or almost finished condition and do not have significant conversion activities. The only significant product cost is the purchase cost (including any associated freight charges) of the merchandise that has been bought for resale. Such firms ordinarily have only a single inventory account, called Merchandise Inventory, which represents the unexpired product cost (an asset). As the merchandise is sold, the product cost is transferred to Cost of Goods Sold, which represents an expired product cost (or expense).

In contrast, manufacturers and service companies engage in many value chain activities involving the physical change of inputs into finished products and services. The costs of these activities must be gathered and assigned to the outputs as product costs. This assignment allows the company to determine inventory costs and the cost of goods sold or services rendered.

If control is to be maintained over the production process, manufacturers must account for raw materials and supplies, work in process for partially completed goods, and finished goods inventory. Each type of inventory requires its own account. Costs are considered unexpired until the goods are sold. As indicated earlier, service firms will have an inventory account for the supplies used in the conversion process and may have a Work in Process account for the cost of jobs not yet completed, but these firms would rarely have Finished Goods Inventory accounts. Services are not normally warehoused and, upon completion and acceptance, their product costs are expensed on the income statement in a Cost of Services Rendered account.

Resin plastic is the primary product cost in this Little Tikes Party Kitchen. When Rubbermaid achieves significant savings in material, labor, or overhead costs (through suppler sourcing, relocation, or product redesign), these savings are passed along to customers through reduced selling prices.

Period Costs

Period costs are noninventoriable and are associated with periods of time rather than with making or acquiring a product or performing a service. These costs are related to business operations other than production, such as in the selling and administrative areas. Period costs that have been incurred and have future benefit are unexpired and are classified as assets. Period costs that have no determinable future benefit (such as secretaries' salaries and current period advertising) are expensed as incurred. For example, prepaid insurance on an administration building represents an unexpired period cost; as the premium period passes, the insurance becomes an expired period cost (insurance expense).

Note that insurance on an administrative building, such as one of Rubbermaid's, is considered a period cost. In contrast, if the insurance cost were for one of Rubbermaid's manufacturing buildings, it would be considered factory overhead and, therefore, a product cost. Thus, the distinction between product and period cost is made primarily on the basis of *where* the cost was incurred rather than *what kind* of cost was incurred. Exhibit 1–6 provides some additional examples of product and period costs.

distribution cost

Mention must be made of one specific type of period cost, that associated with distribution. A **distribution cost** is any cost incurred to fill an order for a product or service. Distribution costs include all amounts spent on warehousing, delivering, and/or shipping products to customers. Total distribution cost changes with changes in product or service volume. Although these costs directly relate to products and services, distribution costs must be expensed as incurred for financial accounting purposes.

When making decisions, managers cannot take an "out of sight, out of mind" attitude about these costs simply because they have been charged off in a selling or general expense category for financial accounting purposes. Distribution is an expensive and definitely essential part of an organization's operating environment, as indicated in the accompanying News Note.

■ **EXHIBIT 1–6**
Cost Classifications for Financial Reporting

Product Costs* (Production)	Period Costs** (Nonproduction)
■ Raw materials ■ Factory labor (production workers, supervisors, maintenance staff, janitorial staff) ■ Factory insurance premiums ■ Factory utility costs ■ Depreciation or rent on factory buildings and equipment ■ Property taxes on factory buildings ■ Maintenance supplies used on factory buildings and equipment	■ Salaries, wages, and commissions for office/sales personnel ■ Depreciation or rent on office/sales buildings and equipment ■ Shipping expenses ■ Insurance premiums on office/sales buildings ■ Property taxes on office/sales buildings ■ Legal and accounting fees ■ Advertising/promotion expenses ■ Recruiting costs for office/sales personnel

*(Unexpired) Assets (Raw Materials, Work in Process, and Finished Goods Inventories and all other unexpired production assets)	*(Expired) Expenses (Cost of Goods Sold or Cost of Services Rendered)	**(Unexpired) Assets (Prepaid Expense or other nonproduction asset)	**(Expired) Expenses (Expenses shown below Gross Margin on the Income Statement; functionally shown in selling and administrative categories)

You Can Sell It, But Can You Get It There?

Call it distribution or logistics or supply-chain management. By whatever its name, it is the sinuous, gritty, and cumbersome process by which companies move materials, parts, and products to customers. Says Robert Sabath, a vice president with Mercer Management Consulting in Chicago: "Logistics, long an unsung, operations-intensive area, has suddenly become very strategic."

Just how strategic? Compaq Computer, the white-hot company that recently became the world's No. 1 producer of PCs, estimates it has lost $500 million to $1 billion in sales [in 1994] because its laptops and desktops weren't available when and where customers were ready to buy them.

Compaq's executives are hurrying to overhaul a logistics system that is creaking under the strain of the company's growth. The company wants to drastically improve the way it gets computers from its factories to distributors, wholesalers, and retailers, whose ranks have swelled tenfold to 31,000 [from 1991 to 1994]. When it comes to deliveries, Compaq, like most computer companies, has an on-time arrival record that would land it in bankruptcy court if it were an airline. On average, only 40% of Compaq's computers reach the customer on time.

Logistics. It may not be cool. But it's flush with potential. Says the Boston Consulting Group's Hal Sirkin: "We're miles ahead of where we were [in 1989], but we've only just begun to tap the savings we can get out of the system." May your trucks run full, your warehouses stay empty, and your supply chains come alive with the sound of cooperative suppliers and truly delighted customers.

SOURCE: Ronald Henkoff, "Delivering the Goods," *Fortune* (November 28, 1994), pp. 64ff. © 1994 Time Inc. All rights reserved.

Similar types of costs are classified as product or period for merchandising, manufacturing, and service companies, although some of the account titles differ. Exhibit 1–7 (page 18) compares these costs and account titles. Information from these accounts can be used to analyze company profitability and answer a variety of managerial questions. For instance, a manager might want to know how much it costs to purchase the raw materials needed to make a product. An answer to this question can be obtained by reviewing information in the Raw Materials Inventory account, but that answer is based on historical information and may not reflect current or future conditions. Raw materials costs change for a variety of factors, including where the purchase was made. Fifty years ago, "where the purchase was made" generally would have referred to which domestic firm sold the product. Now, that phrase relates to which international seller.

THE GLOBAL ENVIRONMENT OF BUSINESS

One important influence in the contemporary business environment is the concept of globalization, as was emphasized by Wolfgang Schmitt. The **globalization** of markets involves a changeover in market focus from competition among national or local suppliers to competition among international suppliers. Companies large and small as well as consumers have realized that alternative choices exist for the sale and purchase of products and services. Thus, businesses are viewed as operating in a global economy.

globalization

global economy

■ LEARNING
OBJECTIVE 6
Explain how markets have
become international in scope
and how this has affected the
way firms compete.

The **global economy** includes the international trade of goods and services, the international movement of labor, and international flows of capital and information.[8] Essentially, the world has become smaller through improved modes of communication and transportation. Also contributing to a global economy are trade agreements among countries, the establishment of standards for international trade, and a trend toward reducing the fiscal barriers that impede the international movement of goods and services. As a result, markets have become substantially more globalized. The implications of globalization are many.

■ **EXHIBIT 1–7**
Comparison of Product and Period Costs

	COST CLASSIFICATION ON	
MERCHANDISING COMPANY	**BALANCE SHEET (UNEXPIRED COSTS)**	**INCOME STATEMENT (EXPIRED COSTS)**
Product Costs (Inventoriable)— incurred through purchases of merchandise for resale	Merchandise Inventory ⟶	Cost of Goods Sold
Period Costs (Noninventoriable)— incurred through payment or accrual for variety of nonmerchandise-related costs	Prepaid Expenses ⟶	Selling, General, & Administrative (SG&A) Expenses
MANUFACTURING COMPANY		
Product Costs (Inventoriable)— incurred through purchase of raw materials; converted through incurrence of direct labor and factory overhead costs; completed and transferred out of the factory; sold	Raw Materials Inventory to Work in Process Inventory to Finished Goods Inventory ⟶	Cost of Goods Sold
Period Costs (Noninventoriable)— incurred through payment or accrual for a variety of nonproduction-related costs	Prepaid Expenses; Nonproduction Assets ⟶	SG&A Expenses
SERVICE COMPANY		
Product Costs (Inventoriable)— incurred through using direct labor and overhead to convert supplies into services; acceptance of service by customers	Supplies Inventory possibly to Work in Process Inventory possibly to Completed Services Inventory* ⟶	Cost of Services Rendered
Period Costs (Noninventoriable)— incurred through payment or accrual for a variety of nonservice-revenue-related costs	Prepaid Expenses; Nonproduction Assets ⟶	SG&A Expenses

*It is possible for service companies to have WIP Inventory and Completed Services Inventory on the balance sheet, although generally these accounts would not appear because services usually cannot be warehoused.

---

[8]Paul Krugman, *Peddling Prosperity*, quoted by Alan Farnham in "Global—or Just Globaloney," *Fortune* (June 27, 1994), p. 98.

Globalization has not only created marketing opportunities for goods and services, it has also created new vendor sources for production inputs. No longer is a domestic producer compelled to deal only with domestic vendors. Many large firms have international operations that span both the production and marketing functions. With globalization, manufacturing operations can be situated in the geographical location offering the greatest cost and quality advantages, and production inputs can be purchased from vendors offering the most reasonable worldwide price for a given level of quality and service.

For any business, globalization creates two major considerations. First, the company must devise a business strategy that considers both domestic and international competitors. Second, the company must be aware of conditions in the various markets around the world so that the markets can be identified in which the company has the strengths and the desire to compete.

Global Business Strategy

Companies seeking to expand to global markets should not do so without careful planning. A variety of factors need to be considered in setting corporate strategy relative to globalization endeavors. These factors can be political (stability of government and guarantees against expropriation or nationalization), monetary (levels of interest rates, inflation, and taxes as well as possible currency restrictions), and "hygiene" (availability of resources such as materials, labor, and utilities). Exhibit 1–8 provides some strategy guidelines from a recent Conference Board survey on U.S. manufacturers in the global marketplace; many of these guidelines could be equally applicable to non-U.S. companies.

Another strategy consideration is the manner in which the globalization will occur. Some companies such as the washing machine manufacturing division of Whirlpool (in Clyde, Ohio), may simply want to export their goods or services to foreign countries. Other companies may wish to engage in licensing arrangements with foreign

---

■ **EXHIBIT 1–8**
Strategy Guidelines for Multinational Operations

Firms that engage in the global marketplace tend to be more profitable, especially when measured by return on equity, than those which limit their competition geographically. Operating globally may create an organizational challenge and a corresponding problem-solving capability that benefits the performance of the business itself. There are many paths to expanding operations and making critical choices for maximizing sales and profits. Some important guidelines suggested by the survey (of 1,250 U.S. manufacturing companies) are:

- Firms moving into the international market with either licenses or limited production achieve rapid sales growth but earn only an 8% return on assets compared with a 12% return on assets for the full-scale multinational.
- Geographic diversification may be more important to profitability than the specific country location.
- The importance of multinational presence intensifies as corporate size grows; firms without foreign plants or joint ventures experience a sharp erosion in profitability as sales move above $1 billion.
- Even a small firm with annual sales below $500 million may sacrifice its prospects for expansion by remaining domestic. Not only is size no obstacle to international expansion, but early entry to the global market may be a clear sign of success.
- Companies active in Eastern Europe, Central Europe, Latin America, and the Middle East achieve higher profits than the larger group involved in Western Europe and North America.
- Majority-owned subsidiaries are not more profitable than joint ventures.
- Investment in high technology does not automatically translate into competitive advantage. High-tech firms do achieve double the sales growth of low-tech firms, but profitability for high-tech firms lags that for low-tech firms—irrespective of the scope of international presence.

SOURCE: "U.S. Manufacturers in the World Market," *Deloitte & Touche Review* (April 18, 1994).

companies. Still others are establishing plants and extensive sales infrastructures in other countries or engaging in international joint-venture arrangements. Rubbermaid, for example, had a joint venture with DSM, a Netherlands-based conglomerate, to produce housewares under the name of Curver Rubbermaid from 1990 to 1994. The joint venture was discontinued because of "disappointing" sales and earnings figures as well as differences on management and strategy issues. Rubbermaid still has a joint venture with Richell Corp. of Japan.[9]

Businesses often find the easiest way to establish a presence in foreign markets is to buy an existing business that serves those markets. But differences among international financial accounting practices may create some difficulties in the global merger market. For example, the United States has the most complete and comprehensive financial accounting regulations of any nation in the world. This situation could place U.S. businesses attempting to purchase foreign businesses at a disadvantage for two reasons.

First, prior to an acquisition, a company will examine its target's financial statements. Because of the detail required in the annual reports of U.S.-based businesses, foreign investors can learn more about publicly-traded U.S. corporate merger targets than U.S. businesses can glean from examining the financial statements of foreign merger targets. Thus, it is often easier for foreign firms to gain access to U.S. markets than it is for U.S. firms to gain access to foreign markets. Second, U.S. firms have less flexibility than their foreign counterparts in accounting for mergers because U.S. generally accepted accounting principles (GAAP) are strictly prescribed in this area. For instance, U.S. GAAP require goodwill arising from a merger to be expensed in no more than 40 years, which reduces future earnings. Japan's write-off period is only five years. Alternatively, the United Kingdom and Germany allow goodwill to be written off directly against stockholders' equity so that future income statements show no effect from the merger.[10]

In 1994, Rubbermaid opened a new production facility in Differdange, Luxembourg, to make juvenile products for the European market. This state-of-the-art molding machine was installed to make the production of Little Tikes toys faster and with higher quality.

In assessing its globalization strategy, a company needs to be aware that operating in foreign markets may create some risks not found domestically. Some of these (such as the potential for expropriation or nationalization of assets) should have been considered prior to any global move. Others, such as cultural differences, are more subtle. Also, what might have appeared originally to be a strength (high availability of labor) may become, as indicated in the accompanying News Note, a difficulty.

Legal and Ethical Considerations

An austere reality for businesses today is the legal responsibilities they bear for all facets of their operations. Increasingly, courts are holding firms responsible for both

---

[9]Raju Narisetti, "Rubbermaid Ends Venture in Europe, Signaling Desire to Call Its Own Shots," *Wall Street Journal* (June 1, 1994), p. A4.

[10]Nancy Anderson, "The Globalization GAAP," *Management Accounting* (August 1993), p. 53.

Risks of the New Global Enterprise

Suzuki Motor Corp. has accumulated losses of approximately $140 million over the past four years in its Linares, Spain, truck factory. The company estimates that the Spanish plant requires five times as many workers as its Iwata plant in Japan and building a Samurai truck costs 46% more than in the Iwata plant. Under the weight of its losses, the company has decided to close the plant. However, closing the plant has proved costly and difficult because of Spain's strict labor laws.

Until about mid-April 1994, the plant employed 2,400 Spanish workers. The Japanese owners, in an effort to keep the plant open, appealed to the workers for wage cuts and limited layoffs. The workers refused to make any concessions, and Suzuki was forced to close the plant. Even then, workers blocked the factory gates and refused to allow finished vehicles to be removed from the factory for shipment.

Suzuki's experience in Spain is similar to those of many other global enterprises. The unemployment rate in Spain now approaches 25%. The country has no more jobs now than it did in 1964, despite a 25% growth in population. Even companies that are doing well in Spain hesitate to expand their operations there because they fear that they will be unable to lay off employees in an economic downturn.

SOURCE: Adapted from Judith Valente and Carlta Vitzthum, "With Boom Gone Bust, Spain's Social Agenda Still Haunts Economy," *Wall Street Journal* (June 13, 1994), pp. A1, A8. Reprinted by permission of The Wall Street Journal, © 1994 Dow Jones and Company, Inc. All Rights Reserved Worldwide.

product and process quality. Further, global businesses are aware that legal and ethical standards differ from one country to another. Although, in general, the standards for business conduct are higher in most industrialized and economically developed countries than in less developed countries, legal standards vary greatly from one industrialized country to another.

Laws represent codified rules for a society. Violators of laws may be subject to both civil and criminal penalties. Laws are not constants; they change over time as the society for which they are established changes. For example, the former Soviet Union is now having to change many of its laws because of the fall of communism.

Government, especially in the United States, is heavily involved with regulation of business activities. Although early government regulations in the United States were primarily concerned with controlling pricing and profitability, government regulation is currently focusing on other issues. More laws are being written to assure fair disclosure of corporate information to third parties, protect consumers, and safeguard natural resources.

Among the obligations imposed by regulation are those associated with periodic reporting. In the United States, all firms are subject to filing periodic reports with the Internal Revenue Service (IRS), and firms whose stock is publicly traded must provide periodic financial reports to the Securities and Exchange Commission. In addition, many companies must provide similar reports to both state and foreign governments. For example, it is becoming more common for U.S. firms to raise capital in both domestic and foreign capital markets. When U.S. firms raise capital in foreign markets, they subject themselves to the reporting requirements that apply to the capital markets in the other countries. Additionally, the firms will likely be required to report to the foreign country's equivalent of the IRS for purposes of determining the tax owed to the foreign jurisdiction.

Product and environmental liability are two important legal considerations. Companies, especially in the food and health-related products industries, are increasingly being held accountable when their products adversely affect consumers. Similarly, manufacturing and extraction operations are particularly capable of harming the environment. Product or environmental liability has bankrupted at least two large multinational businesses: Manville, a producer of asbestos, and A. H. Robbins, producer of the Dalkon shield birth control device. The highest-profile environmental case in recent years concerned an oil spill by an Exxon tanker off the shore of Alaska. Although Exxon is one of the largest industrial companies in the United States, the oil spill may substantially impair its financial status. At this time, lawsuits are pending from a diverse group of firms and individuals claiming to have been harmed by the spill.

Concern about product safety and the environment are two areas in which consumers and regulators are increasingly scrutinizing the way businesses fulfill their social responsibilities. Corporations are becoming more active in defining responsible social behavior, and this trend is likely to continue. Irresponsible social behavior tends to be perceived by government as an invitation to increase its monitoring and regulation. Furthermore, consumers are becoming more concerned about the social policies of firms. Those with undesirable policies may be shunned by the consumer in the marketplace.

Foreign Corrupt Practices Act (FCPA)

One aspect of undesirable social behavior led the United States to pass the **Foreign Corrupt Practices Act (FCPA).** The FCPA was passed in 1977 after Americans discovered that hundreds of U.S. corporations had been giving bribes and other improper payments in connection with foreign and domestic business activities. This law was enacted to prevent businesses from offering or giving bribes (directly or indirectly) to foreign officials to influence those individuals (or cause them to use their influence) to help businesses obtain or retain business. The act is directed at payments that cause officials to act in a way specified by the firm rather than in a way prescribed by their official duties.

grease payments

Grease payments (or facilitating payments) to minor employees (such as payments made to customs officials to expedite the processing of goods on the dock) are excluded from the act.

ethical standards

In contrast to laws, **ethical standards** are less formally acknowledged in society. Such standards represent beliefs about what behaviors are moral or immoral. Since beliefs are inherently personal, some differences in moral perspectives exist among individuals. However, as indicated in the accompanying News Note, the moral perspective is generally more homogeneous within a given society than it is across societies.

It should be noted that ethical standards have meaning only at the individual, not at the organizational, level. Ethics are involved in choices made or actions taken; thus, although they affect the broader organization, they are associated with events involving individuals. Accordingly, ethical standards are simply standards for individual conduct in making decisions and engaging in business transactions. Thus, because of varying individual standards of ethical behavior and varying international laws, a company should develop internal norms for conduct (such as a code of ethics) to ensure that behavior is consistent in all of its geographical operating segments.

Trade Agreements

To encourage a global economy, government and business leaders around the world have made reduction of fiscal and physical barriers to trade a paramount concern of the 1990s. Remarkable progress has been achieved, as evidenced by the European Union, the North American Free Trade Zone, and the GATT renegotiations.

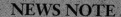
NEWS NOTE

There's No Such Thing as Multinational Ethical Behavior

In a number of important respects, the increased globalization of the economies of the United States, Western Europe, and Japan is making business practices more uniform. The structure and organization of companies, manufacturing technologies, the social organization of production, customer relations, product development, and marketing—all are becoming increasingly similar throughout the advanced industrial economies. One might logically think that a similar trend would be taking place with respect to the principles and practices of business ethics.

But business ethics have not yet globalized; the norms of ethical behavior continue to vary widely in different capitalist nations. During the past decade, highly publicized incidents of misconduct on the part of business managers have occurred in virtually every major industrial economy. Yet, while interest in business ethics has increased substantially in a number of countries in Europe, and to a lesser extent in Japan, no other capitalist nation approaches the United States in the persistence and intensity of public concern with the morality of business conduct.

Not only are many American legal norms and standards of corporate conduct being adopted in other capitalist nations, but as globalization proceeds and world commerce increasingly is driven by multinational corporations, these companies may well come to adopt common ethical standards. These developments are important. But they continue to be overshadowed by the persistence of fundamental differences in the ways in which business ethics are defined, debated, and judged.

SOURCE: David Vogel, "Is U.S. Business Obsessed with Ethics?" *Across the Board* (November/December 1993), pp. 31, 33.

The **European Community (EC)** was created in 1957 as the European Economic Community. It originally was comprised of six member nations (France, Germany, Italy, Belgium, the Netherlands, and Luxembourg) and eventually added six more (the United Kingdom, Ireland, Denmark, Spain, Portugal, and Greece).[11] Through trade initiatives, the EC eliminated virtually all barriers to the flow of capital, labor, goods, and services among member nations, creating the world's largest single market (prior to the establishment of the North American Free Trade Zone). In fact, the EC is sometimes referred to as "the Single Market."

European Community (EC)

> With the coming of the Single Market, a German from Aachen is now free to travel to Liège in Belgium to buy a new car, and to drive it home without paying excessive taxes or fees. Likewise, the Dutch residents of Heerlen can drive to the nearby city of Cologne in Germany to shop, much faster than they could journey to Rotterdam or Amsterdam. With the dropping of countless border checks, tariffs, duties, and import controls, the nearly 350 million consumers of the EC have formed an internal market where goods, services, people, and capital can move across national borders unhindered by physical, technical, or other trade restrictions.[12]

The European Community became the **European Union (EU)** when the Maastricht Treaty became effective in late 1993. More European market integration is likely to occur in the future and may include countries in the former Soviet Bloc in Eastern Europe.

European Union (EU)

---

[11]Turkey and Austria are also considering membership in the EU.
[12]Peter Wiggin, "Road to Unification," *Sky* (June 1993), p. 35.

North American Free Trade Agreement (NAFTA)

Following Europe's lead, Canada, Mexico, and the United States have formed the North American Free Trade Zone market alliance through the 1994 enactment of the **North American Free Trade Agreement (NAFTA).** When implemented in its entirety, the trade zone will encompass approximately 370 million people having a combined economic output of over $6.5 trillion.[13]

While not as comprehensive as the EU agreement, NAFTA nevertheless establishes a new level of market integration in the three bordering countries. NAFTA essentially provides for the duty-free transfer of goods if the following conditions are met: (1) the goods are 100 percent grown, mined, and/or produced in a NAFTA country, or (2) components made in a NAFTA country comprise at least 60 percent of the product's retail price or 50 percent of its manufacturing cost. Duties will be retained for up to 15 years, however, to protect certain industries (such as shoes and glassware) that are extremely sensitive to import competition.

NAFTA also removes barriers for investment purposes and profit/payment transfers. Many businesses will quickly move to take advantage of the NAFTA trade provisions, as did Dawn Food Products, which provides ingredients to the bakery industry. This company, with annual sales of $350 million, expects to reap significant benefits from the adoption of NAFTA as described in the accompanying News Note.

General Agreement on Tariffs and Trade (GATT)

A significant world-wide trade agreement is the **General Agreement on Tariffs and Trade (GATT).** The objective of the GATT is to provide a "level playing field" for trade among the many nations. When the GATT was originally signed in 1947, 23 countries participated, and the average tariff was almost 40 percent. This accord has been revised seven times, and the average tariff has been reduced to approximately 3 percent.[14] At the time this text went to press, 116 countries were participating in an eighth round of trade talks. In addition to reducing and standardizing the tariffs on goods traded among the signees, the eighth GATT discussions also considered provisions related to intellectual property, technical standards, import licenses, customs regulations, exchanges of services, and product dumping. (**Dumping** refers to selling products abroad at prices lower than the ones charged in the home country or in other national markets.) If the eighth round of talks succeeds, the results shown in Exhibit 1–9 will be effective.

dumping

Although the GATT will likely lead to even more reductions and eliminations in trade barriers on a truly global scale, the eighth round discussions included one obstacle that delayed (but did not ultimately preclude) U.S. congressional approval: a provision that replaced the GATT with a World Trade Organization (WTO) as the arbiter of global trade. The WTO gives "each country one vote, no matter what its size—making Slovakia theoretically equal to the U.S. Critics worry that the WTO's beefed-up powers will be used to challenge environmental and health laws."[15]

The reduction in trade barriers means that consumers have the freedom to choose from a significantly larger selection of goods than in the past. As companies become more globally competitive, consumers have the option of purchasing either domestic or foreign goods, and they are often making these choices on the bases of price, quality, access (time of availability), and design rather than on the question of domestic or foreign production.

---

[13]Charles P. Heeter, Jr., "NAFTA Opens New Markets for CPAs," *Journal of Accountancy* (March 1994), p. 70.

[14]"A Guide to GATT," *The Economist* (December 4, 1993), p. 25.

[15]Bob Davis, "Unexpected Obstacles Are Threatening to Delay or Derail Congressional Approval of GATT Pact," *Wall Street Journal* (April 8, 1994), p. A14.

How NAFTA Has Influenced One Michigan Company

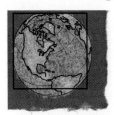

[Peter J. Staelens, CFO, describes management's reaction to NAFTA:] Our Mexican sales are about $3 million a year. But we're not in Mexico now as an importer. Under NAFTA, we'll probably want to set up a sales office there fairly soon.

We've decided to expand our presence in Mexico not only to increase sales but to support and service our customers. Being very close to our customers to determine their needs is a great part of Dawn's success. We certainly can't do that as a U.S. exporter relying on a Mexican distributor.

What's good about NAFTA is that it enables Dawn Food Products to compete far more favorably in the early stages of business development, when we're building our market. Of course, that's the time when your marketing expenses are the highest and when you can least afford to have a high import cost. So, even though we're not the importer [the customers will be], under NAFTA our customers will have a lower-cost product coming into Mexico, and that certainly will build the market.

Our competition in Mexico now is composed of producers, not importers. They're using ingredients of Mexican origin, so they're not subject to the current duties. On the other hand, our duties [going into Mexico] average about 12%, so we're at a 12% disadvantage right from the start.

SOURCE: Peter J. Staelens, "Neighbors, Yes—But Partners?" *Financial Executive* (March/April 1993), p. 17. Reprinted with permission from Financial Executive, March/April 1993, copyright 1993 by Financial Executives Institute, 10 Madison Avenue, P. O. Box 1938, Morristown, NJ 07962-1938. (201) 898-4600.

■ **EXHIBIT 1–9**
Who Gets What from GATT

AGRICULTURE—Europe will gradually reduce farm subsidies, opening new opportunity for such U.S. farm exports as wheat and corn. Japan and Korea will begin to import rice. But growers of U.S. sugar, citrus fruits, and peanuts will have their subsidies trimmed.

AUTOMOTIVE PRODUCTS—The U.S. will be permitted to protect just one industry with a "voluntary" restraint agreement that limits imports. Detroit fears it will not be that one industry and will lose its ability to restrict Japanese exporters' share of U.S. car sales.

ENTERTAINMENT, PHARMACEUTICALS, AND SOFTWARE—New rules will protect patents, copyrights, and trademarks. But many developing nations will have a decade to phase in patent protection for drugs, and France refused to liberalize market access for the U.S. entertainment industry.

FINANCIAL, LEGAL, AND ACCOUNTING SERVICES—Freer trade in services comes under international trading rules for the first time, potentially creating a vast opportunity for these competitive U.S. industries. But specific terms of market access remain to be worked out, mainly with developing countries.

TEXTILES AND APPAREL—Strict quotas limiting imports from developing countries will be phased out over ten years, causing further job loss in the rag trade. But U.S. retailers and consumers will be big winners, since quotas add $15 billion a year to clothing prices.

SOURCE: Louis S. Richman, "What's Next after GATT's Victory?" *Fortune* (January 10, 1994), p. 66. © 1994 Time Inc. All rights reserved.

[While in the running for eight years, it was not until 1994 (and again in 1995) that Rubbermaid was designated as America's Most Admired Company in an annual Fortune magazine survey. CEO Schmitt has set some impressive goals and objectives for the company, including] entering a new product category every 12 to 18 months (hardware cabinets and garden sheds, most recently), and getting 33% of sales from products introduced in the past five years.

[Rather than depending on a single product, the company works] on making small improvements to some 5,000 unspectacular products: mailboxes, window boxes, storage boxes, toys, mops, dust mitts, spatulas, and more. Famous for fecundity, Rubbermaid is known as a new product machine. In 1993, it churned out new (not just improved) products at the rate of one a day. Nine out of ten hit their commercial targets. The company habitually pumps 14% of profits into R&D.

Rubbermaid's success rate in introducing more than 365 new products a year seems more incredible when you consider that the company does no market testing. None. Focus groups, yes. Twelve bass fishermen critiqued a new tacklebox. But actual market testing, no. Schmitt doesn't believe in it. "We don't want to be copied. It's not that much riskier to just roll it out. Plus, it puts pressure on us to do it right the first time."

[Rubbermaid's success in both earnings and product development rests largely on the company's substantial planning, controlling, and decision-making activities. All of these activities have to be supported by solid information on costs, quality, and production activities. Such information is generated through a management accounting system that uses, but is not restricted to, financial accounting data. As products flow through Rubbermaid's manufacturing processes, product costs must be gathered and accounted for. In addition, those costs must be analyzed for ways to make the products and processes more effective and efficient so that Rubbermaid will be an even more successful, internationally recognized company in the future.]

SOURCE: Alan Farnham, "America's Most Admired Company," *Fortune* (February 7, 1994), pp.

CHAPTER SUMMARY

There are two primary variations of the accounting language: financial accounting and management accounting. Financial accounting is focused on external users and has the primary criteria of verifiability, uniformity, and consistency. Management accounting involves the development, analysis, and presentation of information used by managers in performing their functions of planning, controlling, evaluating, and decision making. The information provided by management accounting can be quantitative, qualitative, factual, and/or estimated. The overriding criterion of management accounting information is that it meet the needs of its users. Cost accounting is a part of management accounting that interacts with financial accounting through its focus on accumulating production costs to determine measurements for external financial statement presentations. While all types of accounting information are used in the managerial functions of planning, controlling, performance evaluation, and decision making, management accounting information is best suited for these purposes.

The three basic stages of production are: work not started (materials and supplies), work in process, and finished work. Labor and overhead are added to raw materials to convert those inputs to finished outputs. The costs that flow through these stages are accumulated to determine the cost of making a product or performing a service.

The process of converting inputs to finished goods is what distinguishes manufacturers and service companies from merchandising companies. The conversion process is a primary portion of a business's value chain.

Organizational costs can be classified as product or period. Product costs include inventory, raw materials, labor, and overhead. These costs are unexpired until goods are sold. Period costs are those costs incurred outside the production or conversion area for selling and administrative functions. These costs are expensed when they expire, which is often in the period in which they were incurred.

From regional or national competition, markets have evolved in most industrialized countries to global competition. Global competition has meant that organizations have had to change their strategies and their perspectives to be successful. While legal and ethical standards vary on an international basis, governments have worked diligently to establish trade agreements among governments to standardize some practices and foster global competition. Among the most notable agreements are the initiatives established by the European Union, the North American Free Trade Agreement, and the General Agreement on Tariffs and Trade.

APPENDIX

Organizational Structure

An organization is made up of humans, nonhuman resources, and commitments that are configured to achieve certain explicit and implicit goals and objectives. This appendix provides some general information regarding organizational structure. An entity's structure normally evolves from its nature, policies, and goals because certain designs are more conducive to certain types of operations. For example, a manufacturer will have an organizational segment known as the production center, while a wholesaler will not.

An **organization chart** illustrates the functions, divisions, and positions in a company and how they are related. An important part of reviewing an organization chart is determining line and staff employees. **Line employees** are directly responsible for achieving the organization's goals and objectives; **staff employees** are responsible for providing advice, guidance, and service to line personnel. In some organizations, accountants may be viewed as line personnel and part of the management group. Such a classification depends on the firm's size and structure. Accountants are more often considered staff employees. As such, they are responsible for providing line managers with timely, complete, and relevant information to improve decision making and reduce uncertainty. The News Note (page 28) discusses the importance of making sure that accountants—especially management accountants—are part of the management team.

The organization chart also indicates the lines of authority and responsibility. The right (usually by virtue of position or rank) to use resources to accomplish a task or achieve an objective is called **authority.** It differs from **responsibility,** which is the obligation to accomplish a task or achieve an objective. Authority can be delegated or assigned to others; ultimate responsibility cannot be delegated.

Although organization charts permit visualization of a company's structure, they do not present all factors necessary for understanding how an organization functions. At any given organizational level, it is impossible to see from the organization chart who wields more power, has more status, or has more informal authority and responsibility.

■ **LEARNING OBJECTIVE 7**
Discuss organizational structure relationships.

organization chart

line employees
staff employees

authority

responsibility

NEWS NOTE

Moving into a Line Position

The number one complaint of management accountants with 10 or more years of experience is that "Management doesn't listen to us. We have a lot of knowledge about the company, but when it comes to the key business decisions we are not 'in the loop.' We are thought of as green eyeshade types or bean counters. If given the chance, we could really add value!"

Alfred King, former IMA managing director, explains that in too many organizations one of two things is happening. Management does not expect anything other than financial reports from its accounting staff—very low expectation levels in fact are being met. Or, management would like to have active participation in business decisions using both the knowledge and skills of their management accountants, but the individuals are not perceived as being able to deliver.

[According to Nathan Weaks, treasurer of Automatic Feed,] management accountants should be teachers within the company. They should educate managers about what data are available and how to access those data directly. Most important, he advises, they should not wait for managers to come to them. Management accountants should be walking the shop floor, talking to marketing and advertising managers to find out what data these departments need and then fulfilling those needs.

If the management accountant's objective is to gain increased respect, the solution has to come from working on and then improving real-world business problems, King notes. As one author says, "Management accountants must understand the operating environment of their company. Knowing and applying the latest FASB pronouncement or calculating the cost of capital to the third decimal place may be necessary to perform today's narrowly defined job description. They are not sufficient to make you a player on tomorrow's management team."

SOURCE: Susan Jayson, "Playing on the Management Team," *Management Accounting* (March 1993), p. 24. Published by Institute of Management Accountants, Montvale, NJ.

Nonetheless, an organization chart does provide a basic diagram of certain official chains of command and channels of communication.

Exhibit 1–10 presents an organization chart for the Klaus Corporation, a firm that constructs and operates sporting goods stores. This chart shows two positions under the vice-president of finance: treasurer and controller. The duties of these two individuals are often confused. A corporation's **treasurer** generally handles organizational resources but does not have access to the accounting records, although he or she receives many accounting reports. The treasurer is normally responsible for handling cash receipts, disbursements, and balances; managing credit and collections; maintaining bank relations and arranging financing; managing investments; and insuring company assets. In contrast, the **controller** supervises operations of the accounting system but does not handle or negotiate changes in actual resources.

In many organizations, the controller is the chief accountant and is responsible for maintaining and reporting on both financial and managerial information. Job functions include overseeing the budgeting process, tax planning, and investment evaluations. The controller should ensure that the accounting system provides the maximum amount of detail needed for external and internal purposes while having the minimum amount of data redundancy. The controller is also responsible for designing and maintaining the company's internal control system and for helping management interpret accounting information. This latter function allows the controller to

treasurer

controller

■ **EXHIBIT 1–10**
Organization Chart for Klaus Corporation

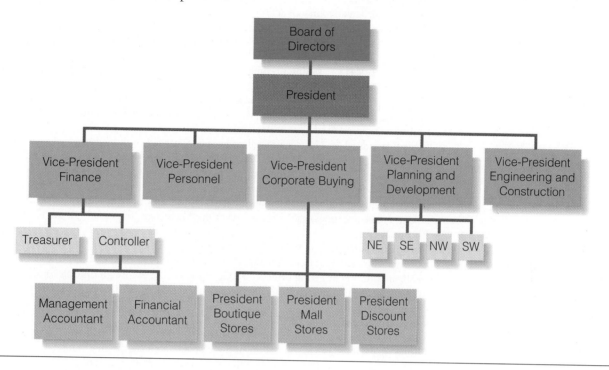

exercise his or her technical abilities by assisting managers in determining the relevance of certain information to a decision, the need for additional accounting data, and the financial consequences of potential actions.

In addition to the traditional hierarchical (rank order) line-staff organization structure just discussed, some companies have adopted **matrix structures.** In these organizational structures, functional departments (based on traditional areas such as accounting, marketing, and production) and multidisciplinary project teams (set up for special projects such as quality review) exist simultaneously. Thus, an individual reports to two managers (one in the functional area and one in the project team), which provides a dual authority system. This structure is often used in organizations, such as R&D companies and consulting firms, that require significant personnel coordination and that must respond to rapidly changing environments.

matrix structures

GLOSSARY

Authority (p. 27)   the right (usually by virtue of position or rank) to use resources to accomplish a task or achieve an objective (from appendix)

Controller (p. 28)   the person who supervises operations of the accounting system, but does not handle or negotiate changes in actual resources (from appendix)

Controlling (p. 10)   the exerting of managerial influence on operations so that they will conform to plans

Conversion (p. 7)   the process of changing raw materials and supplies into a different form

Cost accounting (p. 7)   an area of management accounting that focuses on determining the cost of making products or performing services

Decision making (p. 11)   the process of choosing among the alternative solutions available for a particular course of action

Distribution cost (p. 16)   any cost incurred to fill an order for a product or service; includes all money spent on warehousing, delivering, and/or shipping products and services to customers

Dumping (p. 24)   selling products abroad at lower prices than those charged in the home country or in other national markets

Effectiveness (p. 10)   the successful accomplishment of a task

Efficiency (p. 11)   the performance of a task to produce the best outcome at the lowest cost from the resources used

Ethical standard (p. 22)   a moral code of conduct for an individual

European Community (EC) (p. 23)   an economic alliance originally created in 1957 as the European Economic Community by France, Germany, Italy, Belgium, the Netherlands, and Luxembourg and later joined by the United Kingdom, Ireland, Denmark, Spain, Portugal, and Greece; has eliminated virtually all barriers to the flow of capital, labor, goods, and services among member nations; under the terms of the Maastricht Treaty (1993), the EC became the European Union

European Union (EU) (p. 23)   see European Community

Foreign Corrupt Practices Act (FCPA) (p. 22)   a law designed to prevent U.S. companies from offering or giving bribes (directly or indirectly) to foreign officials for the purpose of influencing those officials (or causing them to use their influence) to help the companies obtain or retain business

General Agreement on Tariffs and Trade (GATT) (p. 24)   a treaty among many nations setting standards for tariffs and trade for signees

Global economy (p. 18)   an economy characterized by the international trade of goods and services, movement of labor, and flows of capital and information

Globalization (p. 17)   a changeover in market focus from competition among national or local suppliers to competition among international suppliers

Goal (p. 8)   a desired result or condition, contemplated in qualitative terms

Grease payment (p. 22)   a facilitating payment to a minor employee

Inventoriable cost (p. 14)   see product cost

Line employee (p. 27)   a person who is directly responsible for achieving an organization's goals and objectives (from appendix)

Management accounting (p. 5)   the process of identification, measurement, accumulation, analysis, preparation, interpretation, and communication of financial information used by management to plan, evaluate, and control within an organization and to assure appropriate use of and accountability for its resources

Matrix structure (p. 29)   an organizational structure in which functional departments and project teams exist simultaneously, so that the resulting lines of authority resemble a grid (from appendix)

North American Free Trade Agreement (NAFTA) (p. 24)   an agreement among Canada, Mexico, and the United States establishing the North American Free Trade Zone, with a resulting reduction in trade barriers

Objective (p. 8)   a target that can be expressed in quantitative terms to be achieved during a preestablished period or by a specified date

Organization chart (p. 27)   an illustration of the functions, divisions, and positions in a company and how they are related (from appendix)

Overhead (p. 11)   the indirect or supporting costs of converting materials or supplies into finished products or services

Performance evaluation (p. 10)   the process of determining the degree of success in accomplishing a task; relates to both effectiveness and efficiency

Period cost (p. 13)   any cost other than those associated with making or acquiring inventory

Planning (p. 8)   the process of translating goals and objectives into the specific activities and resources required to achieve those goals and objectives

Product cost (p. 13)   any cost associated with making or acquiring inventory; also called inventoriable cost

Relevant information (p. 8)   information that is logically related to the decision under consideration, is important to a decision maker, and has a connection to or bearing on some future endeavor; information that is useful to managers in fulfilling their organizational functions

Responsibility (p. 27)   the obligation to accomplish a task or achieve an objective (from appendix)

Staff employee (p. 27)   a person who is responsible for providing advice, guidance, and service to line personnel (from appendix)

Treasurer (p. 28)   the person who generally handles the actual resources in an organization but who does not have access to the accounting records (from appendix)

Value chain (p. 13)   the linked set of value-creating activities beginning with the basic raw material sources and concluding with delivery of the ultimate end-use product to the final consumer

Work in process (p. 11)   goods or services that have been started, but are not yet complete

END OF CHAPTER MATERIALS

■ QUESTIONS

1. An organization typically has only one accounting system. Why may having only one system limit the generation of accounting information that supports managerial functions?

2. What criteria are used to evaluate the worthiness of financial accounting information? How do these differ from the primary criteria for management accounting?

3. Define *management accounting*. How is it related to financial and cost accounting?

4. Why is flexibility in management accounting important to managers? How can management accounting provide such flexibility?

5. What are the three characteristics that information must have to be relevant? Why are these characteristics important?

6. What are the primary management functions, and how are they supported by management accounting?

7. Distinguish between goals and objectives. What goals do you hope to achieve by taking this course? What objectives can you establish to measure the degree to which you achieve the goals?

8. Differentiate between effectiveness and efficiency. Give an example related to your life as a college student.

9. What is the role of information in decision making? How does decision making cause interactions between accountants and managers?

10. What are the stages of production? What kinds of costs are incurred in each stage, and why do such costs need to be accumulated?

11. Which type of company (service or manufacturing) can produce output at a level that differs significantly from the level of current demand for its output? Explain.

12. What are the major differences between a merchandising firm and a manufacturing firm? How are these differences reflected in the cost accumulation process?

13. Why do manufacturing companies need three different inventory accounts? What costs are accumulated in each account?

14. What is the distinction between product and period costs? Provide examples of period costs.

15. Why would operating in a global (rather than a strictly domestic) marketplace create a need for additional information? Discuss some of the additional information you think managers would need and why such information would be valuable.

16. What do legal standards represent? What do ethical standards represent? How are they the same and how do they differ?

17. Why should businesses concern themselves about a clean environment when it might be substantially less expensive to pollute, thus making their products cheaper for consumers?

18. What factors might hinder the implementation of a single market in Europe? What factors might hinder the implementation of NAFTA? Which hindrances do you believe would be most difficult to overcome, and why?

19. *(Appendix)* Describe your reaction to the following statement: "An organization chart represents the manner in which a company operates."

20. *(Appendix)* Differentiate between authority and responsibility. Can you have one without the other? Explain.

21. *(Appendix)* Briefly explain the duties of the controller and the treasurer.

22. *(Appendix)* An individual in a matrix organization has two "bosses." Discuss the problems that such an organizational structure might create.

■ EXERCISES

23. (LO 3, 6; *Terminology*) Match the following lettered items on the left with the appropriate numbered description on the right.

a. WTO	**1.**	A target expressed in quantitative terms
b. GATT	**2.**	The European Union
c. Goal	**3.**	A trade agreement among Canada, Mexico, and the United States
d. Dumping	**4.**	Selling products abroad for prices lower than those charged at home
e. Objective	**5.**	The arbiter of global trade
f. NAFTA	**6.**	A change in market focus from domestic to international
g. Effectiveness	**7.**	A desired result, expressed qualitatively
h. Single market	**8.**	A measure of success of an endeavor
i. Globalization	**9.**	The international trade agreement that provides a level playing field for international trade
j. Efficiency	**10.**	A measure of output achieved relative to resources consumed

24. (LO 1; *Difference between financial and management accounting*) The words and phrases below describe or are associated with either financial or managerial accounting. Indicate for each item whether it is most closely associated with financial (F) or managerial (M) accounting.

    a. verifiable
    b. historical
    c. relevant
    d. internally focused
    e. FASB
    f. SEC
    g. CASB
    h. focus on organizational segments
    i. cost/benefit analysis
    j. focus on serving external users
    k. emphasis on timeliness
    l. emphasis on consistency
    m. future oriented
    n. flexible

25. (LO 1, 3; *Degree of conversion*) Next to each of the following descriptions of firms, indicate whether the firm is best described as engaging in a high (H), moderate (M), or low (L) degree of conversion. Also indicate whether the firm is best described as a manufacturing (M), merchandising (MD), or service (S) enterprise.

    a. firm engaged in the extraction of silver ore
    b. commercial lending department of a bank
    c. fast-food franchise
    d. university bookstore
    e. hair salon
    f. city street cleaning department
    g. labor union
    h. freight company
    i. insurance company
    j. vegetable cannery
    k. cotton farm
    l. street newspaper vendor
    m. flower shop
    n. butcher shop
    o. airline

26. (LO 3, 4, 5; *Type of organization*) Indicate whether each of the following accounts is likely to be associated with a manufacturing (M), merchandising (MD), or service (S) business. Note that there may be more than one correct answer for each item.

    a. Selling Expenses
    b. Raw Materials Inventory
    c. Cost of Goods Sold
    d. Finished Goods Inventory
    e. Administrative Expenses
    f. Work in Process Inventory
    g. Shipping Expenses
    h. Merchandise Inventory
    i. Cost of Services Rendered
    j. Rent Expense

27. (LO 3, 4; *Inventory types*) Manufacturing firms typically have three different types of inventory: raw materials (RM), work in process (WIP), and finished goods (FG).

For each of the following items, indicate which inventory would be affected by the given transaction. Note that some transactions may involve more than one type of inventory.

  a. A clothes manufacturer purchases denim cloth.
  b. A clothes manufacturer sells 1,000 pairs of denim slacks.
  c. A contractor installs fence posts in a customer's commercial parking lot.
  d. A hose manufacturer completes the production of 2,000 feet of custom-made hose.
  e. A lamp manufacturer purchases 3,000 light bulbs.
  f. A lamp manufacturer installs 400 electric-cord sets in lamps on the production floor.
  g. A lamp manufacturer ships 500 lamps from the production floor to a warehouse pending shipment to wholesalers.
  h. A restaurant chain purchases 3,000 pounds of ground beef.
  i. A farmer sprays his corn crop with insecticide to prevent insect damage.
  j. A commercial bakery adds yeast to its bread mix.

28. (LO 5; *Product or period cost*) For each of the following, indicate whether the transaction involves a product (PR) or period (PD) cost.

  a. A retail firm pays $1,200 to advertise its special winter clothes sale.
  b. An engineering firm pays salaries of $100,000 to engineers who are working on four different design contracts.
  c. A manufacturing firm incurs $48,000 of conversion costs in its factory.
  d. An accounting firm incurs $62,000 of administrative costs.
  e. A grocer pays $25 to repair a display shelf.
  f. A manufacturer records $98,000 of depreciation on its factory building.
  g. A restaurant pays $400 in electricity costs to operate its stoves and other cooking equipment.
  h. A hardware store pays $200 to have its windows cleaned.
  i. A marketing executive pays $3,000 to entertain prospective clients.
  j. An ice cream company buys milk from a local dairy for $2,100.
  k. A California fruit farm pays $18,000 to ship fruit to the east coast.
  l. A tire manufacturer records $40,000 of depreciation on its finished goods inventory warehouse.

■ COMMUNICATION ACTIVITIES

29. (LO 2, 3; *Cross-functional management*) "Every manager must think cross-functionally because every department has to play a strategic role, understanding and contributing to other facets of the business."

SOURCE: Rosabeth Moss Kanter, "The New Managerial Work," *Harvard Business Review* (November–December 1989), p. 89.

  Prepare a five-minute oral presentation in which you identify your business major and discuss why you will need to understand all the other business disciplines. Place particular emphasis on conveying how individuals with your major interact in business settings with individuals having other majors.

30. (LO 2, 3; *Corporate strategy and information*) Find the latest annual report for a major industrial company. Read the annual report and review the financial data presented. Use the textual information to identify the firm's basic strategies for a specific product line or organizational segment. (Frequently, the Management Discussion Letter is useful for this purpose.) Write a brief essay describing the corporate strategy and the information that managers will need to be successful in competing under such a strategy.

31. (LO 6; *Pro/con FCPA*) The FCPA prohibits U.S. firms from giving bribes in foreign countries, although giving bribes is customary in some countries and non-U.S. companies operating in foreign countries may not be similarly restricted. Thus, adherence to the FCPA could make competing with non-U.S. firms more difficult in foreign countries. Do you think that bribery should be considered so ethically repugnant to Americans that companies are asked to forego a foreign custom and, thus, the profits that could be obtained through observance of the custom? Prepare both a pro and a con position for your answer, assuming you will be asked to defend one position or the other.

32. (LO 2; *Environmental protection*) You have just been elected president of the United States. One of your most popular positions was that you would reduce the costs of doing business in the United States. When asked how you intended to accomplish this, you replied, "By seeking to repeal all laws that create unnecessary costs. Repealing these laws will be good not only for business but also for the consumer, since product prices will be reduced." Congress heard the message and has decided to repeal all environmental protection laws. Write an essay that discusses the short-term and long-term implications of such a policy.

33. (LO 6; *Cost of complying with regulations*) The complex set of laws and regulations in effect in the United States imposes extraordinary costs on U.S. businesses. For example, one study found that the Fortune 500 companies spent, in total, about $1.06 billion to comply with federal and state income tax laws. That amounts to approximately $2.1 million per company. This amount reflects simply the compliance cost; the actual taxes paid are significantly more.

SOURCE: Based on "Tax Report," *Wall Street Journal* (December 1, 1993), p. A1.]

   a. Much of the tax compliance cost for U.S. businesses is associated with foreign operations. The U.S. tax system subjects all income earned by U.S.-based companies to income taxation, whether that income is earned in a domestic or a foreign operation. Why must the U.S. tax system subject the foreign operations of U.S. businesses to the same taxes imposed on domestic operations?
   b. How will increasing globalization and the global economy likely affect future tax compliance costs of large U.S. multinational businesses?

34. (LO 6; *Globalization*) The United States provides an ethnically, racially, and culturally diverse workplace. It has been argued that this plurality may be a competitive handicap for U.S. businesses. For example, communicating may be difficult because some workers do not speak English, motivating workers may be complicated because workers have diverse work ethics, and work scheduling may be difficult because of differing religions and ethnic holidays. Conversely, it has been argued that Japan has a competitive advantage because its population is much more homogeneous.

   Prepare a presentation that addresses each of the following issues:

   a. What are the advantages of a pluralistic society in the global marketplace?
   b. On balance, does America's plurality give it a competitive advantage or place it at a competitive disadvantage? Discuss.

35. (LO 6; *Global trade*) *To see the future of Daewoo Group, take a look at the windshield stickers on the newest generation of Espero and Le Mans sedans assembled at the Daewoo Motor Co. plant just outside Seoul. Almost every car is heading for a developing country—the Philippines,*

Columbia, Pakistan. Chairman Kim Woo Choong is committing some $8 billion to make and sell Daewoo goods in Eastern Europe, Central Asia and Latin America.

[SOURCE: Steve Glain, "Daewoo Group Shifts Its Focus to Markets in the Third World," *Wall Street Journal* (October 11, 1993), p. A1.]

a. Through enhanced engineering, Daewoo has shed its image as a producer of substandard cars. Why would the company want to aim at markets in developing countries rather than developed countries?

b. "When hard currency is scarce, Daewoo accepts barter." Discuss this out-of-the-ordinary business strategy from two perspectives: first, as a businessperson in an industrialized country and second, as a businessperson in a developing nation.

36. (LO 6; *NAFTA*) Ross Perot once said that the approval of NAFTA would create a "great sucking sound" as American jobs were pulled into Mexico. Others said that NAFTA would create more jobs for American workers than it would eliminate.

a. Discuss the negative effects the ratification of NAFTA has had or may have on the U.S. economy and U.S. products.

b. Discuss the positive effects the ratification of NAFTA has had or may have on the U.S. economy and U.S. products.

c. Discuss the negative effects the ratification of NAFTA has had or may have on the Mexican economy.

d. Discuss the positive effects the ratification of NAFTA has had or may have on the Mexican economy.

37. (LO 7; *Appendix*) Coordination is the organizational integration of tasks and activities. In general, effective coordination can be attained by the proper assignment of responsibility and delegation of authority within the context of the formal organizational structure.

a. Discuss some basic principles that you think would allow the delegation of authority to be effective.

b. Identify some actions of a superior that would undermine the effectiveness of the delegation of authority.

c. Identify some actions of subordinates that would undermine the effectiveness of the delegation of authority.

(*CMA adapted*)

■ CASES

38. (LO 7; *Appendix*) Rockelle Inc. is a holding company with three major divisions as depicted on the accompanying organizational chart. The three division presidents report directly to Martin Willis, the vice president of corporate operations. In general, Rockelle has preferred a decentralized relationship with these three divisions; however, the managers of planning for each division have an indirect reporting relationship to Anne Kleine, the vice president of corporate finance, who is responsible for coordinating the corporate planning process.

The organizational chart also displays the internal reporting relationships within Leenkin Co. A description of each vice president's area follows.

■ Joan Rogert's responsibilities as vice president of finance include financial planning, general accounting, and cost accounting. Roger Mellon reports to Rogert and manages the planning function for the division.

Rockelle Inc. Organizational Chart

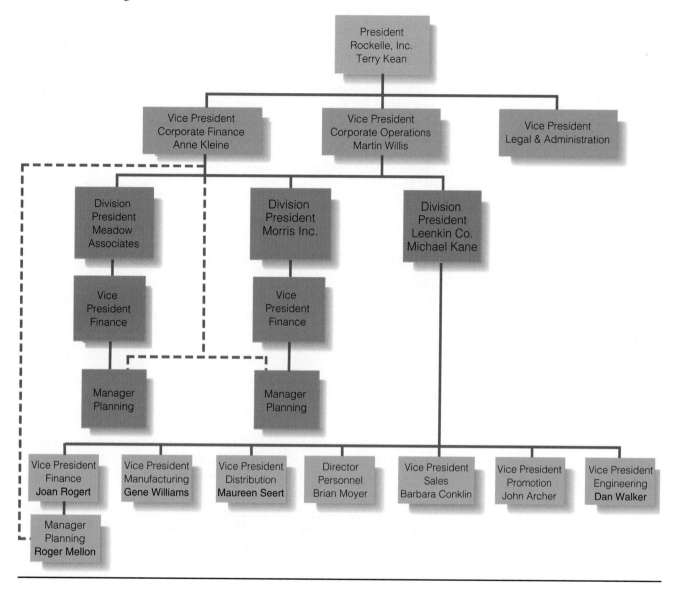

- Gene Williams, vice president of manufacturing, oversees the production of Leenkin's main product, office furniture.

- Maureen Seert, vice president of distribution, handles the packaging and distribution of the office furniture through a network of wholesalers.

- As director of personnel, Brian Moyer is responsible for the sales relationships with retail outlets.

- John Archer, vice president of promotion, produces all advertising material including a bimonthly catalog of Leenkin's products.

- Dan Walker, vice president of engineering, is responsible for product development and design, machine implementation, time study analysis, and quality control.

a. Define line and staff functions in an organization.

b. Describe any potential conflicts that may occur between line and staff employees in this organization based only on your understanding of the organizational chart and descriptions of job responsibilities.

c. Discuss the benefits and disadvantages of the indirect reporting relationship of Roger Mellon.

d. Identify the job function of each of the following individuals at Leenkin Co. as a line or a staff function, and explain why.

   1. Gene Williams

   2. Joan Rogert

   3. Maureen Seert

   4. Dan Walker

(CMA adapted)

■ ETHICS AND QUALITY DISCUSSIONS

39. Assume that you need legal services because you have been named as a defendant in a lawsuit. The plaintiff in the lawsuit seeks to recover damages from you for injuries sustained in a car accident in which you were a driver. You are now facing the onerous task of selecting an attorney to represent you. A listing from the local bar association indicates that there are five thousand attorneys that practice locally.

Describe the process that you would use to identify which of these five thousand attorneys is best for your case. Describe your objectives in the search process and the criteria and information that you would use to discriminate among the lawyers.

Next, assuming that you are a typical consumer of legal services, explain to the internal management of law firms the criteria that you used to select an attorney. Describe why each criterion that you used to select a lawyer should be of importance to law firm managements.

40. Harbour and Associates recently released a report regarding the relative competitive positions of the "Big Three" U.S. automakers. According to the report Ford Motor Company is the most efficient U.S. auto producer in the assembly of vehicles. The following table indicates the number of workdays required to assemble a vehicle in the firms' North American plants. Data are given for both 1989 and 1993:

	Workdays per vehicle assembled	
	1989	*1993*
General Motors	4.88	3.94
Chrysler	4.58	3.52
Ford Motor	3.25	2.99

SOURCE: Douglas Lavin, "GM Would Have to Cut 20,000 Workers to Match Ford Efficiency, Report Says," *Wall Street Journal* (June 24, 1994), p. A3.]

a. Based on the data in the table, which firm would apparently incur the lowest costs per vehicle for assembly? Conjecture (without calculations) how much higher General Motors' annual profit would be if it could assemble vehicles with the same efficiency as Ford Motor.

b. Discuss reasons why Ford Motor Company would not necessarily have the highest profit per car produced.

c. Describe the relationship between the quality of assembly operations and the efficiency of the operations.

41. Broadstreet Deli and Bakery is known countrywide for its excellent bread and donuts. Sales have been falling, however, because of small but continuous price increases. The increases have been warranted because of increased costs for ingredients. The vice president of marketing wants to substitute low-grade animal fat for 95 percent of the vegetable shortening currently used and reduce the selling prices of the products to their old levels. She does not, however, want to change the slogan on the package ("Made with Pure Vegetable Shortening") since some vegetable shortening will still be used. You are the marketing manager for the bakery. How would you react to this proposal? Why? What suggestions would you make to management?

42. A primary area of expansion for Wal-Mart is small-town U.S.A. But when Wal-Mart moves in, many local retailers are forced to close their doors because they cannot compete. According to the *Wall Street Journal*, "more than 80% of Wal-Mart's sales can come at the expense of other local businesses, which can mean a loss of as much as $8 million in sales to area stores."

SOURCE: Barbara Marsh, "Merchants Mobilize to Battle Wal-Mart in a Small Community," *Wall Street Journal* (June 5, 1991), p. A1.

a. Explain Wal-Mart's reasoning in expanding to small towns.

b. Assume that you are a senior citizen on a fixed income. Write a short letter to your local small-town newspaper on your feelings about a new Wal-Mart opening in your town.

c. Assume that you are the owner of Small Town Pharmacy. Since the new Wal-Mart opened, your customers have almost disappeared. Discuss your feelings about the Wal-Mart store.

d. Do the benefits received by the members of the local community outweigh the costs to the local retailers? Explain the reasons for your answer.

43. "Few trends could so thoroughly undermine the very foundation of our free society," writes Milton Friedman in *Capitalism and Freedom*, "as the acceptance by corporate officials of a social responsibility other than to make as much money for their shareholders as possible."

a. Discuss your reactions to this quote from a legal standpoint.

b. Discuss your reactions to this quote from an ethical standpoint.

c. How would you resolve any conflicts that exist between your two answers?

44. EraTech Corporation, a developer and distributor of business applications software, has been in business for five years. The company's sales have increased steadily to the current level of $25 million per year.

Andrea Nolan joined EraTech about one year ago as accounting manager. Her duties include supervision of the company's accounting operations and preparation of the company's financial statements. Nolan has noticed that in the past six months, EraTech's sales have ceased to rise and have actually declined in the two most recent months. This unexpected downturn has resulted in cash shortages. Compounding these problems, EraTech has had to delay the introduction of a new product line because of delays in documentation preparation.

EraTech contracts most of its printing requirements to Web Graphic, Inc., a small company owned by Ron Borman. Borman has dedicated a major portion of his printing capacity to EraTech's requirements because EraTech's contracts represent approximately 50 percent of Web Graphic's business. Andrea Nolan has known Borman for many years; in fact, she learned of EraTech's need for an accounting manager from Borman.

While preparing EraTech's most recent financial statements, Nolan became concerned about the company's ability to maintain steady payments to its suppliers; she estimated that payments to all vendors, normally made within thirty days, could exceed seventy-five days. Nolan is particularly concerned about payments to Web Graphic; she knows that EraTech had recently placed a large order with Web for printing the new product documentation.

Nolan is considering telling Borman about EraTech's cash problems; however, she is aware that a delay in the printing of the documentation would jeopardize EraTech's new product.

   a. Describe Andrea Nolan's ethical responsibilities in the previous situation. Refer to specific standards of the IMA's Code of Ethics (shown in Exhibit A–1 Appendix A to the text, "The Management Accouning Professional.") to support your answer.

   b. Without prejudice to your answer in part (a), assume that Andrea Nolan learns that Ron Borman has decided to postpone the special paper order for EraTech's printing job; Nolan believes that Borman must have heard rumors about EraTech's financial problems from some other source because she has not talked with Borman. Should Andrea Nolan tell the appropriate EraTech officials that Borman has postponed the paper order? Explain your answer using the IMA Code of Ethics for support.

   c. Without prejudice to your answers in parts (a) and (b), assume that Ron Borman has decided to postpone the special paper order for EraTech's printing job because he has learned of EraTech's financial problems from some source other than Nolan. In addition, Nolan realizes that Jim Grason, EraTech's purchasing manager, knows of her friendship with Ron Borman. Now Nolan is concerned that Grason may suspect she told Borman of EraTech's financial problems when Grason finds out Borman postponed the order. Describe the steps that Andrea Nolan should take to resolve this situation. Use the IMA Code of Ethics to support your answer.

(CMA)

■ PROJECTS

45. Form a team to investigate some primary differences between a foreign country's accounting practices and U.S. generally accepted accounting principles. Prepare a presentation to explain these differences to your peers. Be sure to address (a) how each of these differences would affect the financial statements and (b) whether these differences would make the financial statements of a company domiciled in that country more or less appealing to a U.S. company targeting the foreign company for acquisition?

46. Your company produces a variety of electronic products and has decided to locate a new production facility in Eastern Europe. The new facility will produce mother boards for the firm's line of computers and also supply electronic components to a variety of consumer product manufacturers in the U.S. and Europe. Production processes in the new facility will be highly automated, using very sophisticated production equipment. The Vice President of Manufacturing-Europe is assigned the responsibility of plant oversight. This person maintains an office and staff in Paris; she is a native, French-speaking citizen of Canada.

The criteria to be used in selecting the location of the new plant is the subject of the project. Your class should be divided into teams, preferably of four member each. One member of each team should represent each of the following functional areas: marketing, manufacturing, finance, and accounting. Each team member should develop a list discussing the important criteria for determining the location of the new production site. The individual member lists should then be discussed by the team and coordinated into a five to ten minute oral report.

47. *(Appendix)* Obtain the annual reports of three companies and compare their organization charts. Which companies have treasurers and/or controllers? To whom do these individuals report, and who reports to them? Does there appear to be anything unusual about the lines of responsibility or authority in the charts? If so, what?

2

MANAGEMENT ACCOUNTING IN A QUALITY-ORIENTED ENVIRONMENT

The way to control your destiny in a global environment of change and uncertainty is simple: Be the highest-value supplier in your marketplace.

Jack Welch, in Noel M. Tichy and Stratford Sherman, *Control Your Destiny or Someone Else Will*, 1993.

LEARNING OBJECTIVES

1. Discuss how companies are addressing the demand for product and service quality.

2. Explain the underlying factors supporting the concept of total quality management.

3. Differentiate between process and results benchmarking.

4. Discuss how a company's move along the quality continuum could be assessed.

5. Explain why a company needs to reduce cycle time and how that objective can be achieved.

6. Identify and discuss recent changes in technology that are affecting current business practices.

7. Discuss why a strategically based management accounting system is needed in addition to a financial accounting system.

Motorola: It's Electronics Manufacturing with a Major Competitive Edge

Mention Motorola, the company that almost everyone loves to love, and the accolades fairly gush: titan of TQM (total quality management), epitome of empowerment, tribune of training, icon of innovation, prince of profits. A leader in the worldwide revolution in wireless communications, this manufacturer of cellular telephones, pagers, two-way radios, semiconductors, and other electronic gadgets has become that most unusual of creatures—a big company that sizzles.

Motorola's transformation from a slowly declining American electronics company to a world-beating, Baldrige Award–winning powerhouse has become the stuff of industrial legend. Management books and business school cases have chronicled the company's fanatic pursuit of six sigma quality (3.4 mistakes per million), its high-profile battles with the Japanese, and its pioneering advances in self-directed work teams, training, and business process reengineering. Consultants marvel at the way Motorola decentralizes decision making, breaks down organizational boundaries, and promotes cooperation between labor and management.

Sales of cellular phones—the company's flagship product—are booming, up 43% in the U.S. [in 1993]. Motorola, which commands a 45% share of the worldwide market, continues to attract new customers as it makes phones smaller, lighter, cheaper, and easier to use.

Increasingly multinational, Motorola—which generated 56% of its revenues overseas [in 1993]—is spreading the wonders of wireless communication to Asia, Eastern Europe, and Latin America. Countries with archaic state-run phone systems have seized on wireless networks as a relatively inexpensive means of quickstepping into the future. [In 1993], Motorola sold more than four million pagers in China, the company's biggest foreign market. That's four times as many as it sold there in 1992.

As part of its quality drive, Motorola has invested new meaning in the phrase "team spirit." At the cellular equipment plant in Arlington Heights, Illinois, self-directed teams hire and fire their co-workers, help select their supervisors, and schedule their own work (in consultation with other teams). [In 1993,] the factory's 1,003 workers were also mustered into no fewer than 168 special teams dedicated to improving quality, cutting costs, and reducing cycle time.

In what must be a boon to the international airline industry, managers and professionals at all levels routinely meet to swap [information on] best practices in manufacturing, R&D, quality, cycle time, supplier relations, and environmental protection.

SOURCE: Ronald Henkoff, "Keeping Motorola on a Roll," *Fortune* (April 18, 1994), pp. 67, 68, 72, 77. © 1994 Time Inc. All rights reserved.

Contemporary business is distinguished from that of the past by its rapid pace of change and by a redirection of focus from short-run profits to long-run market success. The way business is conducted is constantly developing and evolving, as evidenced by the discussion about Motorola. New markets and competitors emerge; customer satisfaction standards increase; different management styles and organizational structures are introduced.

To understand the role of management accounting in business, it is necessary to understand how business is practiced. As business practices change and evolve, so must the discipline of management accounting. Changes in the business environment affect the information needed by managers to fulfill their organizational functions. Management accounting's goal is to provide managers with information that is relevant to their decisions in the contemporary business climate. Thus, accounting practices must be devised or changed so that the information generated is what managers need. Indeed, many of the concepts and practices discussed in subsequent chapters received little or no mention in management accounting texts written 10 to 15 years ago: These emerging practices have been developed as the demand for them has arisen.

This chapter provides a portrait of the business environment in which management accounting is currently practiced and identifies some major forces of change in organizations. This introduction should allow the concepts presented in later chapters to be better understood because those concepts can be related to the circumstances in which they are to be applied. More and more frequently, changes in business practices are being driven by the demand for quality, the need for reduced cycle time, and the increased abilities provided by technology. All of these factors affect an organization's potential for long-run market success and its need to introduce strategically based cost management practices.

THE DEMAND FOR QUALITY

In the 1970s and 1980s, managers focused on fostering market growth and creating company strengths to differentiate their firms from all the others. Today, managerial emphasis has shifted, and managers are focusing on product and service quality and the creation of customer value. This new viewpoint refines, blends, and extends prior competitive strategies. A quality perspective merges the concepts of increased market share and differentiated products by using a customer focus as the key integrating factor. This focus causes managers to keep one eye on their processes and the other on their customers. By satisfying the wants and needs of specific customers, firms create customer value.

Because a firm is part of an extensive value chain, all participants in that firm's internal processes should add value to the chain. With increased attention being given to the design and flow of internal processes, firms are constantly searching for ways to improve their process quality, decrease their process costs, eliminate any processes or costs that fail to provide customer value, and increase a product's or service's value to customers by modifying design or adding features.

Total Quality Management

The current challenge to improve quality in products and processes has led many firms to look closely at their fundamental business practices. Some companies have concluded that quality must be the key focus in every facet of operations for improvements in profitability to be realized. Thus, Motorola and many other companies have adopted total quality management as their basis for operating activity.

Total quality management (TQM) is a philosophy of organizational management and change. It is defined as "a structural system for creating organization-wide participation in planning and implementing a continuous improvement process that exceeds the expectations of the customer/client."[1] The objective of TQM is contin-

■ LEARNING OBJECTIVE 1
Discuss how companies are addressing the demand for product and service quality.

■ LEARNING OBJECTIVE 2
Explain the underlying factors supporting the concept of total quality management.

Total Quality Management (TQM)

---

[1]L. Edwin Coate, "Implementing Total Quality Management in a University Setting," *Oregon State University* (July 1990), p. 5.

uous improvement, and the underlying principles are customer focus, process improvement, and total organizational involvement. It is management's responsibility to provide employees with the necessary resources to support the achievement of this objective and these principles. These factors are shown in the model presented in Exhibit 2–1.

All members of a company striving for total quality management must view the objective of continuous improvement as a routine part of the work environment: It must become a way of life. Improvements should be expected rather than viewed as unusual. As targets are met, new ones should be established. For example, in 1981, Motorola set a goal of reducing defects 90 percent by 1986; in 1987, another 90 percent improvement goal was set for 1989; and yet another similar goal was set for 1991.[2] It was only with this kind of dedication to continuous improvement that the company was able to pursue its overall corporate goal of six sigma quality (or 3.4 mistakes per million).

The concept of continuous improvement is different from the concept of innovation. **Continuous improvement** refers to small, but ongoing efforts to make positive adjustments in the status quo; **innovation** involves a dramatic improvement in the status quo caused by radical new ideas, technological breakthroughs, or large investments in new technology or equipment. Both concepts are necessary for long-run survival, but continuous improvement efforts can be accomplished at all organizational levels, and innovation is typically a function of top management or research and development efforts.

continuous improvement
innovation

Customer Focus

Pursuing quality requires chasing a moving target because customer expectations continue to rise, and customer expectations have been designated as the ultimate

---

■ **EXHIBIT 2–1**
Concepts Underlying TQM

SOURCE: Arthur R. Tenner and Irving J. DeToro, *Total Quality Management* (Reading, MA: Addison-Wesley, 1992), p. 32. © 1992 by Addison-Wesley Publishing Company, Inc. Reprinted by permission of the publisher.

---

[2]Jeremy Main, "How to Win the Baldrige Award," *Fortune* (April 23, 1990), pp. 104, 108.

arbiters of quality in a total quality management approach to business. TQM focuses attention on the relationship between the production/service process and the customer. (**Customer** is a generic term for an external or internal recipient or beneficiary of a process's output.)[3] Customer-driven quality first requires a recognition of who the customers of the process are and an identification of their needs and expectations for the product or service. Exhibit 2–2 (page 48) illustrates eight stages of a customer-oriented quality improvement program implemented by Alcoa of Australia.

customer

Although external customers are crucial to organizational survival, companies may not be able to afford to consider all groups of individuals as potential customers. Most companies must perform some amount of market segmentation or classification and then address the needs and expectations of particular groups of customers. Some companies may want to consider eliminating some customers because they simply cost more than they add in profits. For example, Nypro (a custom injection molder) eliminated all customers that could not purchase at least $1 million of goods per period. The concept that shedding one or more sets of customers is good for business may be difficult to accept at first, but most organizations have some clients who drain, rather than improve, their ability to provide high-quality products and services.

> Smart businesses pick customers—and learn from them. While some customers consistently add value along several dimensions, other customers are value-subtractors: What they cost in time, money and morale outstrips the prices they pay. Having the courage to identify, and then "fire" low-value customers is a healthy first step. It helps assure that valued customers receive the best possible service and that potential customers recognize that the company cares about quality.[4]

After determining who its value-adding customers are, a company must understand what they want. The primary characteristics currently desired by customers appear to be quality, value, and "good" service. Good service is an intangible; it means different things to different people. But most customers would agree that it reflects the interaction between themselves and organizational employees. Frequently, only service quality separates one product from its competition. Poor service can be disastrous. Data indicate that "70 percent of customers stop doing business with companies because of perceived rude or indifferent behavior by an employee—over three times the total for price or product quality (20 percent)."[5]

A firm should constantly monitor its customers and their needs for two reasons. First, the needs and expectations of external customers change throughout the product or service life. For instance, after purchase and delivery, customers focus their needs and expectations more on areas such as durability, reasonably priced preventive maintenance and parts, and/or prompt and efficient service availability. Second, as a product or product group matures, customer needs and expectations rise. For instance, Model T automobiles were available only in black and that satisfied customer expectations. Consider how unsatisfied today's customers would be if there were no choice in automobile color. Additionally, features that were previously viewed as new or innovative tend to become seen as basic needs, with expectations being set considerably higher. Finding out what customers want is discussed in the News Note on page 49.

In addition to focusing on external customers, a company engaging in total quality management must also consider the organization's internal customers. If the qual-

---

[3]Jack Hagan, *Management of Quality* (Milwaukee: ASQC Quality Press, 1994), p. 73.
[4]Michael Schrage, "Fire Your Customers!" *Wall Street Journal* (March 16, 1992), p. A12.
[5]Scott J. Simmerman, "Improving Customer Loyalty," *B&E Review* (April-June 1992), p. 4.

■ **EXHIBIT 2–2**

Customer-Oriented Quality Improvement Program Flow Chart

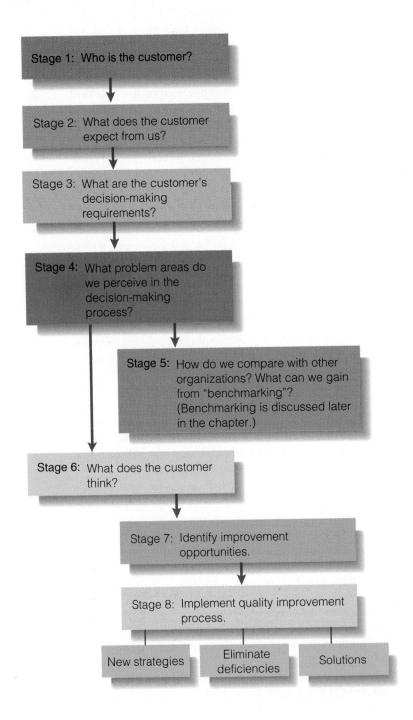

SOURCE: Malcom Smith, "Improving Management Accounting Reporting Practices: A 'Total Quality Management' Approach (Part 1)," *Journal of Cost Management* (Winter 1994), p. 51. Reprinted with Permission from The Journal of Cost Management for the Manufacturing Industry, © 1994, Warren, Gorham & Lamont, 31 St. James Avenue, Boston, MA 02116. All rights reserved.

If You Want to Know, Just Ask!

NEWS NOTE

Know thy customer! [Increasing customer awareness] begins with the basics. Rule No. 1: Don't overlook the most obvious way to get to know your customers—talk to them. Companies are exploring new ways of doing this. Rule No. 2: Mine the data about your customers that are already in your computers. Rule No. 3: Don't let focus group results overwhelm your common sense.

Honda uses all the standard research tools, including focus groups and customer surveys. The company even videotapes drivers as they test new cars. In response to all this customer input, Honda has made thousands of changes in the Accord since introducing it in 1976. The new wrinkles range from installing a suspension system used on racing cars for improved handling to changing the shape of the rear window so that a large soft drink can be passed into the car without spilling. In the process Honda just happened to produce the best-selling car in America from 1989 until 1992, when the Ford Taurus edged it out. Says Ben Knight, vice president for R&D of Honda North America: "We believe that the market and the customer will always find the truth."

Honda's manufacturing unit kicked off its most extensive customer research effort yet, the E.T. Phone Home Project, in November 1992. (The name and the notion were lifted from the film *E.T.*) Over the following three months, factory workers who actually bolt and bang the Accord together called over 47,000 recent Accord buyers, or about half the owners who registered their cars with the company the previous spring. Honda's goal: to find out if customers were happy with their autos and to get ideas for improvements. Given the long lead times in the auto industry, you can expect to see the impact of E.T. on the 1995 and 1996 Accords.

SOURCE: Terence P. Paré, "How to Find Out What They Want," *Fortune* (Autumn/Winter 1993), p. 39. © 1993 Time Inc. All rights reserved.

ity of the output provided to an internal customer is flawed, there is no way that external customers will be satisfied. In partial recognition of this idea of internal customers, managers in TQM companies have begun instituting higher degrees of decentralization and employee empowerment.

Decentralization refers to the downward delegation, by top management, of decision-making authority. This process has eliminated tiers of middle managers and, in general, has caused organizational structures to become flatter. Decentralization can work in TQM-based organizations because employees are given greater rights and responsibilities or are empowered. **Empowerment** refers to the process of giving workers the training and authority they need to manage their own jobs. The TQM philosophy supports the concept that the individuals who are closest to a process are the ones who are most able to know when things go wrong and, often, the best ways to fix the problems. The concept of empowerment was born in 1961 when Taiichi Ono (a Toyota self-taught engineer) "installed a cord above every work station and instructed workers—all workers—to stop the [production] line immediately if they spotted a problem." His rationale was that if the errors were allowed to continue uncorrected to downstream internal customers, they would simply multiply and

decentralization

empowerment

become more expensive to fix.[6] Exhibit 2–3 shows how employee empowerment is enacted at some large and small organizations.

For empowerment to be effective, empowered employees must: (1) understand how their jobs fit into the "big picture"; (2) recognize the needs of their customers; (3) have the knowledge, skills, and resources to properly perform their jobs; (4) be educated to make appropriate judgments; (5) be held responsible for the outcomes of their decisions; and (6) believe that they are trusted by and can trust management. If these conditions are met, empowered employees can effect valuable changes in their organizations, especially in the area of process improvement. For instance, at Ford, an executive estimated that employee ideas related to the manufacturing process for the Taurus often were "worth more than $300,000 each."[7]

quality circles

Empowered workers within a given organizational area establish self-managed teams to set their own goals and interact on issues with a common purpose. Workers may also form intra- or interdepartmental teams to solve quality-related problems. These teams are sometimes referred to as **quality circles.** Many of the problems addressed in these teams focus on ways to improve process quality.

Process Improvement and Benchmarking

Evaluating customer needs and expectations allows managers and workers to better understand the organization's value chain and to assess the contribution of each internal process to that value chain. Using this information, managers can estimate the cost of each process and compare the cost with the customer value created by that process. They can then devote more attention to processes that have poor value-to-cost relationships.

■ EXHIBIT 2–3

Employee Empowerment

	PERCENT WHO SAY THEY ARE AUTHORIZED TO TAKE THIS ACTION	
Action	*Small-business employees*	*Large-business employees*
Stop work in progress to correct a problem	90%	80%
Intervene on a customer's behalf	86%	81%
Rework a product or redo a service	66%	64%
Make an exception to procedures	66%	60%
Replace merchandise	48%	32%
Refund money or authorize credit	33%	23%

SOURCE: Gallup Organization for the American Society for Quality Control, "Employer Attitudes on Teamwork, Empowerment, and Quality Improvement," cited in "So This Is Empowerment," *Inc.* (July 1994), p. 96. Reprinted with permission of Inc. magazine. © 1994 by Goldhirsh Group, Inc.

---

[6]Jerry Bowles and Joshua Hammond, *Beyond Quality* (New York: Berkley Books, 1991), p. 31.

[7]James W. Dean, Jr., and James R. Evans, *Total Quality* (Minneapolis/St. Paul: West Publishing Company, 1994), p. 199.

Before an ability to improve can exist, the company's processes and procedures must be defined and standardized. The definition should indicate the process's inputs and outputs as well as its beginning and end. Standardization is necessary so that variations can be identified. Statistics indicate that processes will have natural variations over time, but that "errors" are typically produced at points of uncommon variations. These errors typically take the form of defective goods or poor service.

To analyze process variations, a variety of **control charts** can be prepared by recording the occurrences of selected performance measure(s). Possible performance measures include things such as number of defective products, errors in tolerance levels, and unexpected work slowdowns or stoppages. The charts display the results of actual processes on a graph that indicates upper and lower control limits. A process is in or out of control depending on how well results remain within these established limits, as illustrated in Exhibit 2–4. Company personnel who prepare the charts must do so consistently and accurately so that an intelligent analysis can be made about the items that are out of control.

control charts

After processes have been defined, standardized, and stabilized, workers can seek to make significant, practical improvements. All processes cannot be improved at once, so specific targets for improvement should be chosen. The selection of targets can be based on ease of or critical need for improvement. Some companies may want to make basic "housekeeping" improvements that would build confidence in the quality movement before addressing more difficult process variations. Other companies may find that a particular process variation is critical to organizational success. For example, improvements to the wiring process at Saturn Corp. were probably put on the "critical need" list after the General Motors subsidiary had to voluntarily recall all 352, 768 Saturns built before April 15, 1992, for a problem that could cause engine fires.[8]

Companies can determine how to improve processes by relying on employee suggestions or by looking to others for information and assistance in the form of bench-

■ **EXHIBIT 2–4**
Control Chart

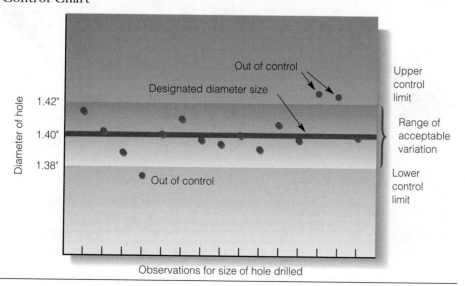

[8]"GM Recalling Saturns for Wiring Defect," *Dallas Morning News* (August 11, 1993), p. 1D.

benchmarking

■ **LEARNING OBJECTIVE 3**
Differentiate between process and results benchmarking.

process benchmarking

marking. Simply put, **benchmarking** means learning from others. More completely, it is the process of investigating, comparing, and evaluating the company's products, processes, and/or services against those of companies (or other organizational divisions) believed to be the "best in class." Such comparisons allow a company to understand other production and performance methods, so that it can identify its own strengths and weaknesses. The success of benchmarking efforts is frequently gauged by progress in key measurable dimensions or indicators of a process. For example, a key indicator for a particular production process might be the pounds of scrap produced by the process relative to the number of good units produced.

There are two types of benchmarking: process and results. **Process benchmarking** refers to assessing the quality of key internal processes by comparing them with those of other firms. The key dimensions of process benchmarking are (1) focusing on individual processes or internal functions rather than the entire operations of the organization and (2) selecting as the quality standard those firms that have established the highest quality results for a given practice or process, regardless of whether they compete in the same industry. For example, Motorola studied the First National Bank of Chicago's electronic data transfer techniques. Adopting the bank's methods saved Motorola 8,000 hours auditing its books during a period when the company's sales increased 50 percent.[9]

Process benchmarking helps companies learn about their own strengths and weaknesses and those of their competitors. For example, Xerox's benchmarking efforts indicated that the company had nine times as many suppliers as the best companies, ten times as many assembly line rejects, and seven times as many defects per hundred machines—and Xerox's unit manufacturing cost equaled the Japanese selling price of

L.L. Bean's distribution center has been hailed as world-class. Stock selection (or "picking") and shipping techniques have been so well defined that a variety of companies have chosen to process benchmark against this facility.

---

[9]Jesse Cole, "Bettering the Best," *Sky* (January 1993), p. 20.

a similar unit in the United States.[10] Armed with benchmarked information, companies can adapt the best practices to their own operations.

In **results benchmarking,** the company examines the end product or service and focuses on product/service specifications and performance results. Results benchmarking helps companies determine which other companies are the "best in class." Also, by the use of "reverse engineering" (disassembling a product), one company can often ascertain another company's product design, process, and costs.

results benchmarking

Because benchmarking can be an expensive and time-consuming procedure, it should be used primarily on the internal processes that are most critical to organizational success. A step-by-step approach to benchmarking is given in Exhibit 2–5. The final step of the process (striving for continuous improvement) is critical: If a company strives only to be as good as another firm, it limits its ability to succeed and will never be a competitive leader.

Benchmarking is consistent with the customer-oriented focus of business and its concept of market-defined quality. By identifying the fundamentals of success of the firms that are achieving the highest quality in specific processes, companies can reengineer and adapt the benchmark practices in their own processes to achieve greater quality. Although benchmarking against direct competitors is often necessary, it can create a risk of "industry stagnation." To illustrate:

> General Motors, Chrysler, and Ford have historically done a lot of competitive benchmarking among themselves. Over time, their processes became similar. But then came the import competition, which had totally different processes and which blew the Big Three

■ **EXHIBIT 2–5**

Step-by-Step Approach to Benchmarking

1.	Identify and describe the organization's mission and goals. If necessary, translate these goals into a consumer's perspective.
2.	Identify and describe all significant internal processes of the organization.
3.	Determine which of the processes identified in Step 2 are most essential to achieving the mission and goals identified in Step 1.
4.	For each process identified in Step 3, select an appropriate organization to benchmark.
5.	Identify those practices of the bench-mark organization that may foster an improvement in quality and that are adaptable to the organization's culture.
6.	Identify critical success factors that can be used to gauge improvement in the quality of each process.
7.	Measure progress in quality initiatives by monitoring changes in critical success factors.
8.	Use feedback regarding success of initiatives to design additional quality programs.

---

[10]James R. Evans and William M. Lindsay, *The Management and Control of Quality* (Minneapolis/St. Paul: West Publishing Company, 1993), p. 144.

away. It was like [there were] three club tennis players who all had similar levels of skill and who knew each other's games inside and out—and then Bjorn Borg walked on the court.[11]

Since each company has its own unique philosophy, products, and people, "copying" is neither appropriate nor feasible. Therefore, each company should attempt to imitate those ideas that are readily transferable but, more importantly, to upgrade its own effectiveness and efficiency by improving on methods in use by others.

Although the concept of benchmarking may superficially appear to benefit only one party, the flow of information should, in the long run, be two-directional. To illustrate, assume that Company B benchmarks itself against Company A, the "best in class." After Company B implements process improvements, it becomes the "best in class." It is only appropriate that Company B share its improvements with Company A. Thus, as indicated in the accompanying News Note, benchmarking helps companies keep up with the competition.

Benchmarking has risen in popularity partly because it benefits organizational quality and profitability. However, another reason for the emphasis on benchmarking has been the establishment of various quality awards, one of which specifically features benchmarking in its criteria.

Quality Awards

■ **LEARNING OBJECTIVE 4**
Discuss how a company's move along the quality continuum could be assessed.

Baldrige Award

The ultimate affirmation of TQM in the United States is the 1987 Malcolm Baldrige National Quality Improvement Act, which established a program to encourage U.S. businesses to pursue quality initiatives. The program is administered by the U.S. Department of Commerce. At the heart of the program is the Malcolm Baldrige Quality Award or **Baldrige Award,** named after the late Malcolm Baldrige, a former Secretary of Commerce. Awards are given annually to winners in manufacturing, service, and small business. The winners have demonstrated quality achievements in the seven categories listed in Exhibit 2–6. Throughout the categories are questions related to an organization's benchmarking efforts.

■ **EXHIBIT 2–6**
Baldrige Quality Award Categories

- **Leadership**—examines top management's *personal* leadership and involvement in creating quality values and how those values are included in the way the company operates
- **Information and analysis**—examines the scope and effectiveness of the company's information related to external and internal quality improvements
- **Strategic quality planning**—examines the company's short- and long-term plans and planning process relative to quality requirements
- **Human resource development and management**—examines the success of the company's efforts to develop and realize the full potential of the work force relative to quality objectives
- **Management of process quality**—examines the company's systematic processes to pursue ever-higher quality and company performance
- **Quality and operational results**—examines the company's quality levels and improvement trends in quality, operating performance, and supplier quality; also examines current quality and performance levels relative to those of competitors
- **Customer focus and satisfaction**—examines the effectiveness of the company's systems to determine customer requirements, customer satisfaction, and marketplace competitiveness as well as how the company's results compare to those of competitors

SOURCE: Adapted from Earl Naumann, *Creating Customer Value* (Cincinnati: Thomson Executive Press, 1994), pp. 222-235.

---

[11]Beth Enslow, "The Benchmarking Bonanza," *Across the Board* (April 1992), p. 20.

If You're Not the Best, You Might Not Be Anything Soon

Are you as good as the best in the world? You'd better be. GE chief Jack Welch warns, "If you can't meet a world standard of quality at the world's best price, you're not even in the game." Ram Charan, a consultant to many of the world's largest companies, including Citicorp and Du Pont, goes further: "If you're not *better* than the best on a worldwide basis, you're not going to make a living."

With global champions ranging the world seeking opportunity, many competitive advantages no longer last long. Today Chrysler is admired as the world leader in new-car development: It brought the small, affordable Neon to market in just 31 months at a cost of $1.3 billion, peanuts by industry standards. But Maryann N. Keller, car industry expert, believes that all major carmakers will soon catch up. She says: "That standard is going to be a given for everyone, and I doubt there'll be significant advantage in getting it down 5% more. The enduring advantages will come from making better use of people."

The need to ask whether you're as good as the best in the world applies to national economies as well as businesses. The leading candidate for reengineering is Germany which, as a Volkswagen executive puts it, has "the highest unit production costs on the face of the earth." The typical hourly wage for automotive employees there is $21 vs. roughly $16 in Japan or the U.S. The country's famous social contract has become a nightmare: a 35-hour workweek, six weeks' annual vacation, typical absentee rates over 20%. VW's response: eliminating 30,000 jobs—25% of the total—and proposing a four-day workweek and a 20% wage reduction.

Let's face it: Few people anywhere can say they're as good as the best in the world. Regard that fact as a large opportunity. It's just that you have to take advantage of it—because quite soon, being as good as the best will be a matter of survival.

SOURCE: Stratford Sherman, "Are You as Good as the Best in the World?" *Fortune* (December 13, 1993), pp. 95-96. © 1993 Time Inc. All rights reserved.

Applicants for the Baldrige Award undergo a quality evaluation by a review board composed of experts from both the public and the private sector. One significant benefit of the evaluation process, other than the possibility of winning the award, is the feedback received from the review board. This benefit is described by Patrick Mene of the Ritz-Carlton, a Baldrige Award winner in 1992:

> We thought we were doing a very good job when we submitted our application. When the Baldrige team came in, they left us a report that mentioned 75 areas where we could make improvements. From the point of view of improving your business, how could you ask for more than that?[12]

The evaluation process for the Baldrige Award is modeled after the **Deming Prize,** an award instituted in Japan in 1950. This award, named for the late W. Edwards Deming, is the highest form of industrial recognition in Japan. The Deming Prize places its primary emphasis on conformity of products to standard whereas the

Deming Prize

---

[12]Ronald Fink, "Group Therapy—Not a Fad or a Quick Fix, but a Way of Managing Change: That's Benchmarking," *Financial World* (September 28, 1993), p. 46.

Baldrige Award is more focused on customers. In fact, there is no category in the Deming Prize related to customer satisfaction.

To compete effectively in the global market, companies must recognize and willingly comply with a variety of standards outside their domestic borders. Standards are essentially the international language of trade; they are formalized agreements that define the various contractual, functional, and technical requirements that ensure that products, services, processes, and/or systems perform as they are expected. Global quality standards have also been set, although they are not considered as demanding as those embodied by the Baldrige Award and the Deming Prize.

ISO 9000

The most notable among the international quality initiatives is the **ISO 9000** series, developed in 1987 by the International Organization for Standardization, based in Geneva, Switzerland. This organization is comprised of members of quality standards boards from more than 90 countries. The ISO series of five standards are written in a general manner and prescribe the design, material procurement, production, quality control, and delivery procedures necessary to produce high-quality products and services.[13] These standards address *process* quality, not *product* quality. Exhibit 2–7 outlines the coverage of the five standards.

Beginning in 1993, companies must have an approved quality system in order to sell certain products in Europe—and the system described in the ISO series is the only one that meets the European Economic Area requirements.[14] For example, firms selling toys, weighing machines, gas appliances, and certain medical equipment must meet ISO standards. Over 40 countries have adopted the ISO standards as either a component of or a stand-alone national quality standard.[15]

An individual firm can become ISO certified through a registration process in which the firm hires a third-party accredited registrar to examine or audit the quality of its processes. No international organization administers the program. Thus, companies seeking ISO registration must qualify under an internationally accepted registration program that is administered by a national registrar.

The ISO standards are also becoming a part of certain U.S. federal rules and regulations. For example, in revising the 1978 Good Manufacturing Practices, the Food and Drug Administration is aligning those standards with ISO 9001 standards by making certain design control and service elements mandatory. In addition, "in Canada, some of the provincial governments and certainly the federal government are seriously considering a requirement for ISO 9000 certification by their suppliers."[16]

Currently, the ISO 9000 standards are undergoing some revisions that will ultimately lead to greater consistency in the registration process and remove some ambiguities in the individual standards. Additionally, "comparisons show ISO at best meets 40% of the criteria used by the U.S. Baldrige Award. So companies are pressuring the International Standards Organization to upgrade the guidelines by 1996."[17]

The Malcolm Baldrige National Quality Award has served to raise the quality consciousness of U.S. manufacturing, service, and small businesses, and its standards provide a framework for measuring quality efforts of those businesses.

---

[13]The ISO 9000 standards are equivalent to the American Society for Quality Control (ASQC) Q-90 quality series, issued in 1987. Companies that currently meet the Q-90 standards also meet the ISO 9000 standards.

[14]The European Economic Area includes the twelve countries belonging to the European Economic Union (Belgium, Denmark, France, Germany, Greece, Ireland, Italy, Luxembourg, the Netherlands, Portugal, Spain, and the United Kingdom) and the seven countries that belong to the European Free Trade Association (Austria, Finland, Iceland, Liechtenstein, Norway, Sweden, and Switzerland).

[15]Gary Spizizen, "The ISO 9000 Standards: Creating a Level Playing Field for International Quality," *National Productivity Review* (Summer 1992), p. 333.

[16]William J. L. Swirsky, "Focus on: ISO 9000," *Journal of Accountancy* (February 1994), p. 61.

[17]Jonathan B. Levine, "Want EC Business? You Have Two Choices," *Business Week* (October 19, 1992), p. 59.

■ **EXHIBIT 2–7**
Content of ISO 9000 Standards

STANDARD NUMBER	CONTENT
9000	Provides a model for assuring quality in product design and development; covers contracts, organizational structure, purchasing data, processing controls, and production, installation, and servicing
9001	Covers requirements for conformance during product design, production, installation, and servicing; applicable to engineering, construction, and manufacturing companies
9002	Provides a model for assuring quality when only production and installation conformance is required; applicable to companies in which product requirements are stated relative to established designs or specifications (like chemical, food, and pharmaceutical companies)
9003	Provides a model for assuring quality when only final inspection and testing conformance is required; applicable to companies (or internal organizational units) that inspect and test the products they supply (like laboratories)
9004	Provides guidelines related to a company's internal quality management and the development and implementation of a quality system; discusses the technical, administrative, and human factors that affect product and service quality

Total Involvement

Because all processes in a firm are interdependent, a company will not be able to earn the Baldrige Award or the Deming Prize or be ISO certified without total employee involvement. TQM recognizes that everyone in an organization shares the responsibility for product/service quality. Thus, all members of the organization must accept a personal role and participate in continuously improving their work efforts.

Consistent and committed top management leadership is the catalyst for moving the company culture toward an *esprit de corps* in which all individuals feel compelled to meet and exceed customer expectations. Such an attitude should also permeate everything a company does, including customer relations, marketing, research and development, product design, production, and information processing. Upper-level management must be involved in the quality process, develop an atmosphere that is conducive to quality improvements, and set an example of commitment to TQM. Workers should be made to feel that they are part of the process of success, not the creators of the problems. A primary initiative is to instill employees with the basic tenets of total quality management listed in Exhibit 2–8 on page 58.

In addition, a management information system for planning, controlling, and decision making must exist. This system should be capable of providing information about process quality to both managers and workers. Historically, the consideration of quality has not been part of the planning process but rather has involved an after-the-fact measurement of errors. Action was not triggered until a predetermined threshold was exceeded. In contrast, a total quality system should be designed to promote a reorientation of thinking from an emphasis on inspection to an emphasis on prevention. The system should indicate any existing quality problems so that managers

■ **EXHIBIT 2–8**
Basic Tenets of TQM

1. Design quality into products and processes.
2. Make consumer preferences the focus for change in products and processes.
3. Develop tools that measure progress in improving quality. Measures should reflect quality as perceived by the consumer.
4. Empower employees to make changes to improve the performance of their jobs. Avoid imposing changes on employees; let them lead the initiatives. Continual education and job training is necessary to support the process of change.
5. Bring the power of expertise to bear through the use of teams and teamwork.
6. Use benchmarking to define quality in processes and procedures.

SOURCE: Adapted from Arleen M. Heiss, "Quality as Change Management," *Public Manager—The New Bureaucrat* (Fall 1993), pp. 57-59.

can set goals and methods for improving quality. The system should also be capable of measuring quality and providing feedback on quality improvements. Last, the system should encourage teamwork in the quality improvement process. In other words, a TQM system should move an organization away from product inspection (finding and correcting problems at the end of the process) to process control (designing and monitoring the process so that problems do not occur).

Another part of the management information system should address the issue of supplier relationships. Suppliers are an integral part of an organization's value chain and can directly affect production costs and process and product quality. Therefore, managers should carefully screen suppliers, standardize and reduce the number and variety of components needed from suppliers, and reduce the total number of suppliers. For example, Ford Motor Company announced a substantial restructuring of its global operations in 1994 to try to reduce operating costs by $2 billion to $3 billion per year by the end of the decade. The greatest cost savings are expected to come from a reduction in the cost of purchased components, where Ford spends $37 billion a year. Ford expects to achieve cost reductions by "scouring the world looking to buy more common parts from fewer suppliers at lower prices."[18] The accompanying News Note provides an international perspective on this issue.

Exhibit 2–9 depicts the quality continuum along which companies move in achieving world-class status. At the most basic level, a company simply opts for quality assurance and inspects products for defects or monitors employees and surveys customers to find poor service. When a company implements quality assurance techniques to eliminate the possibility of defective products or poor service, the company has become quality conscious. When an organization's quality system has progressed to a high level of sophistication, that organization may choose to compete against others for quality honors. Finally, when the concept of quality has become a distinct element of the organizational culture and tolerances for defective products or poor service are set at zero percent, the company has achieved world-class status and can be viewed as the benchmark for others. But achieving world-class status does not mark an ending point. TQM is not a static concept; when one problem has been solved, there is always another problem waiting for a solution.

---

[18]Neal Templin, "Ford's Trotman Gambles on Global Restructuring Plan," *Wall Street Journal* (April 22, 1994), p. B3.

Reduce the Number of Suppliers, Reduce the Costs

Well over half of the ex-factory value of a car is generated by materials, components, and systems bought from the supply sector. Individual car makers have already taken drastic action to cut the number of their direct suppliers from around 1,250 on average in 1988 to 900 at present, according to a report produced by the Boston Consulting Group (BCG) for the European Commission. The number is expected to drop again to around 400 by 1997.

The European motor industry still has more suppliers than it really needs," claims Eckhard Jokisch, vice-president of supply at Ford of Europe. "A lot have already fallen by the wayside, because they could not even meet today's challenges and others will follow. Changing our philosophy from buying nationally to buying globally has already led to a reduction in numbers."

Ford has more than 700 suppliers—all in North America—for its U.S.-built Ford Tempo/Mercury Topaz range. The successor Ford Contour/Mercury Mystique models due to be launched later [in 1994] will have only 227 suppliers drawn from around the world.

Valeo, the leading French automotive components producer, was served by 3,500 suppliers in Europe in mid-1991, but this number has been cut to 1,800, and the aim is to reach around 1,000 by the end of 1995.

Chrysler's president Bob Lutz views "suppliers as an integral part of a value-added chain—a chain that leads not to us, but through us to the real boss, the customer. We work with pre-selected 'supplier-partners' to arrive at mutually agreed costs for a vehicle's parts and components." Chrysler maintains that it has made savings of $400 million a year during the last four years through a programme designed to reduce supplier costs. "Those savings came from waste reductions, not from cutting suppliers' profit margins," insists Mr. Lutz.

SOURCE: "The Challenge Is Clear: Change or Die," *(London) Financial Times* (July 12, 1994), p. i.

■ **EXHIBIT 2–9**
Quality Continuum

SOURCE: Grant Thornton, *Survey of American Manufacturers* (New York: Grant Thornton, 1992), p. 20.
© 1992 Grant Thornton.

THE NEED FOR REDUCED CYCLE TIME

■ **LEARNING OBJECTIVE 5**
Explain why a company needs to reduce cycle time and how that can be achieved.

At Motorola, there are still production quality efforts to be pursued, but the company is also looking at doing things faster. Speed is an element of quality, so Motorola management makes certain the company engages continuous improvement efforts in this direction also. Consider the following:

> [By 1990,] the company had cut the time it took to fill an order for portable radios from 55 days to 15; [the 1991] goal was seven days. Not even the corporate legal department was exempt. Motorola's patent lawyers used to take 18 to 36 months to write and file a patent claim. That leisurely pace was cut in many cases to two months. The eventual six sigma goal: one-day service for getting the information about an invention from the engineers and filing the claim.[19]

cycle time

How long something takes depends on an individual perspective. **Cycle time** can be viewed as the time elapsed from when a customer places an order to the time that product or service is delivered. Alternatively, the definition of cycle time could take a full life-cycle approach and be seen as the time elapsed from the conceptualization of a product or service to the time the product is delivered to the customer. Regardless of which definition is selected, there is one irrefutable fact: Time is money and, the longer something takes, the greater is the cost.

Companies are recognizing this fact and striving to reduce total cycle time for at least three primary reasons. First, reducing cycle time means that companies can react more rapidly to customer requirements and, thus, are engaging in a total quality management focus. Shortening cycle time increases an organization's flexibility or its ability to respond to market changes. Companies are not held to long-range production or performance projections that may be found to be inaccurate. This factor is especially important in industries, such as clothing and toys, that are significantly affected by popular trends. Cycle time reduction helps to eliminate stockpiling of inventory in anticipation of future demand. Stockpiling inventory leads to additional costs for items such as building rental or depreciation and insurance as well as the cost of obsolescence. General Motors recognizes this situation, as discussed in the accompanying News Note.

Second, a reduction in cycle development time allows a company to bring a product to market more rapidly and, thus, be more competitive. For example, a survey of 553 global manufacturers found that Japanese companies take an average of 17.7 months "to introduce a product, compared with 19.7 months in the U.S. and 20.6 months in Europe. Companies grow faster and grab a bigger market share when they 'bring the right innovative products to market ahead of the pack.'"[20] Time to market is an effective organizational benchmark.

Third, cycle time reduction creates a need to reduce waste in all processes. Production activities that are wasteful create additional cycle time; therefore, efforts at cycle time reduction focus on making quality improvements that eliminate the need for procedures such as inspections, rework, and defects. Reducing cycle time forces companies to do things right the first time.

A variety of methods can be used to reduce cycle time. Analyzing the development or production process will indicate the activities that are being performed and these

---

[19]Jeremy Main, "How to Win the Baldrige Award," *Fortune* (April 23, 1990), p. 108.

[20]Joann S. Lublin, "Best Manufacturers Found to Triumph by Fostering Cooperation of Employees," *Wall Street Journal* (July 20, 1993), p. A2.

NEWS NOTE

Cadillac Buyers Can Now Get Their Cars Faster

A General Motors Corp. test program in Florida could reduce the amount of time Cadillac buyers must wait for new cars and whittle down the inventory dealers currently carry.

If the test is successful, the program could spread to Cadillac dealerships nationwide. And GM's other divisions are looking closely at the test as a way to slash delivery times, say dealers and company officials.

Under the program, which begins in mid-September 1994, about 1,500 Cadillacs will be parked at a regional distribution center in Orlando, Fla., to await delivery to dealers statewide within 24 hours. In some areas of Florida, many buyers currently wait two days for popularly equipped cars, say dealers. Additionally, GM's Cadillac factory in Detroit will speed up production of specially ordered Cadillacs as well as reduce shipping time. Made-to-order Cadillacs will arrive at dealerships in about three weeks, compared with eight to 12 weeks now, say GM officials.

GM hopes improving customer service will boost sales of Cadillacs. Cadillac loses a substantial number of sales when customers are put off by lengthy delivery times, says Charles Carridine, Cadillac's director of product distribution and fleet sales. "Research shows we lose 10% to 11% because the car's not available," he says. GM says the test program will increase Cadillac's sales [in Florida] by 10%.

SOURCE: Gabriella Stern, "Cadillac Will Test Distribution Method to Cut Delivery Time and Dealer Stock," *Wall Street Journal* (August 16, 1994), p. A5. Reprinted by permission of the Wall Street Journal, © 1994 Dow Jones & Company, Inc. All Rights Reserved Worldwide.

can be designated as either adding or not adding customer value. Minimizing or eliminating the activities within the value chain that do not increase the worth of a product or service to a customer can substantially reduce cycle time and costs as well as increase productivity.

Working more effectively with suppliers is another way to reduce cycle time. Companies can establish supplier certification programs that demand that purchased materials and components be guaranteed as to quality. Thus, inspection of these goods and the related time would be eliminated. In addition, the companies can interact on packaging techniques. Suppliers could reduce packaging or pack in reusable containers. Suppliers may also be asked for input on helping the company implement **design for manufacturability** concepts for its products. Such concepts focus on reducing the number of parts in a product, using standard (rather than special order) parts when possible, and simplifying the assembly process.

design for manufacturability

One final technique for reducing cycle time is the implementation of a just-in-time inventory system. **Just-in-time (JIT)** is a philosophy about when to do something. The *when* is "as needed" and the *something* is a production, purchasing, or delivery activity. The JIT philosophy is applicable to all departments of all types of organizations. Its three primary goals are:

just-in-time (JIT)

1. eliminating any production process or operation that does not add value to the product/service
2. continuously improving production/performance efficiency
3. reducing the total cost of production/performance while increasing quality

In a JIT inventory system, a firm does not buy or make a product until a customer has demanded it. This system depends on accurate market data, since a tight linkage is required between sales and production volume. In addition, high-quality production processes are required so that defects can be avoided. JIT production promotes flexibility in production processes, short lead times, short production runs, quick setups, and greatly reduced inventory levels.

Cutting cycle time requires that all business functions (design, development, production, ordering, shipping, and billing) be speeded up. Continuous improvement efforts will reduce cycle time slowly, but innovation is essential to making substantial cycle time reductions rapidly. Often, these innovations are caused by changes in technology.

INCREASED TECHNOLOGICAL ABILITIES

■ **LEARNING OBJECTIVE 6**
Identify and discuss recent changes in technology that are affecting current business practices.

In the current business environment, the firm having the highest level of technology *and* the employees with the skill to employ that technology to its fullest often finds itself one step ahead of its competitors. For instance, Montague Corp. designs its mountain bikes in Cambridge, Massachusetts, makes them in Taiwan, and sells most of them in Europe—a situation that would be impossible without modern modes of technology and communication.[21] An advance in technology frequently foreshadows a change in business practices—even, as indicated in the accompanying News Note, for rock groups.

Information Systems

Companies have entered what could be termed the Information Revolution. Exhibit 2–10 (p. 64) indicates the effect on productivity of this revolution and compares it with the effects of two important revolutions of the past, the Agricultural and Industrial Revolutions. New information technologies are becoming less and less expensive and, at the same time, more and more powerful. It is estimated that there is an improvement of 15 to 25 percent in the cost-to-performance ratio annually.[22]

Technological innovations have dramatically advanced accounting and other information systems. Even in the smallest companies, accounting, customer, and supplier records are regularly computerized. Computerized record keeping reduces the error rate in recorded data and enhances data usage for a variety of applications. For example, the time and effort dedicated to preparing financial statements, filing tax documents, or preparing budgets is substantially reduced when data are recorded electronically.

In addition, investments in technology for the sake of systems integration may be needed. The trend is to integrate all fundamental business systems, such as accounting, production, inventory, marketing, and product design. Such systems integration provides a more accurate and complete picture of organizational operations. It also provides the ability to obtain and retain important market information and stay informed about customer requirements. Furthermore, systems integration eliminates duplicate systems, allows managers to identify and respond to problems more quickly, and facilitates more rapid decision making. As new technology is developed, this systems integration trend is likely to accelerate.

---

[21]Alan Farnham, "Global—or Just Globaloney," *Fortune* (June 27, 1994), p. 97.

[22]R. C. Heterick, "Paradigms and Paradoxes," *Higher Education Product Companion* (Vol. 3, Number 1, 1993), p. 10.

Aerosmith Spins Out on the Information Highway

The number of personal computers in American homes increased dramatically in the late 1980s and early 1990s. Along with the proliferation of personal computers came new computer services designed to serve the needs of home computing. Among them are on-line computing services accessed via phone lines and computer modems. One of the largest on-line services is CompuServe, which has approximately 2,000,000 subscribers. CompuServe offers an array of on-line services including bulletin boards, news, sports, weather, travel services, computer games, market news, movie reviews, consumer product ratings, and home shopping.

Early in 1994, CompuServe pioneered a new alliance with the entertainment industry involving CD technology. Specifically, CompuServe announced that it would be retailing computer CDs containing movie previews, music albums, photographs, and music videos. CompuServe also intends to use the CD technology to market other goods and services in the future.

In late June 1994, the rock group Aerosmith recorded a milestone in both the personal computing and music industries. The group released a new single, *Head First*, on CompuServe rather than through the usual retail music markets. This represented an advance over prior technologies because customers were not required to obtain any physical storage medium beyond their personal computers. CompuServe customers could simply download the 3-minute, 14-second recording onto 4.3 megabytes of hard disk storage in their computers (about the equivalent of 1,300 pages of text). To successfully download the recording, the personal computer merely had to be equipped with Windows software and a sound card. The time to download the single was estimated at a minimum of an hour for consumers with the fastest modems. Although the release of the recording on CompuServe may be an initially awkward marriage between two previously disparate technologies, it indicates that a new era has dawned for the music recording industry, the retail music industry, and industries involved in the production and sale of stereos and other sound equipment.

SOURCES: Jeffrey A. Trachtenberg, "Compuserve to Sell CD-ROM as Tool to Market Goods, Entertainment, Itself," *Wall Street Journal* (May 27, 1994), p. B8; David Landis, "Aerosmith Jumps onto Info Highway 'Head First,'" USA Today (June 15, 1994), p. 1. Copyright 1994, USA TODAY. Reprinted with permission.

Electronic Data Interchange

Technology has greatly benefited various modes of communication. The most noteworthy recent advances in information technology are those that have made it possible to integrate one company's information system with the electronic systems of other companies. For example, retail firms now commonly use point-of-sale devices to record a sale in accounting records, update inventory and customer records, and, if necessary, order additional inventory from suppliers. These systems reflect electronic data interchange (EDI) capability.

Electronic data interchange (EDI) refers to the almost instantaneous computer-to-computer transfer of information. EDI systems allow firms to eliminate paperwork and communicate with their suppliers and customers electronically. Typical communications involve ordering goods and services and acknowledging receipt of orders for

electronic data interchange (EDI)

■ **EXHIBIT 2–10**

Productivity Leverage of the Great Revolutions

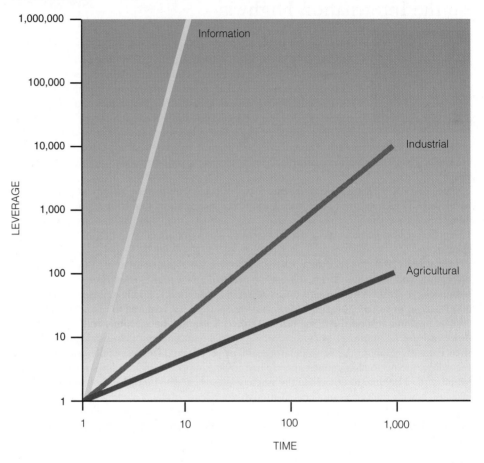

- The Agricultural Revolution increased the productivity of our fields by about a factor of a hundred.
- The Industrial Revolution gave us a leverage of about a thousand to one—three orders of magnitude.
- The Information Revolution has computers doing things at least a million times better than we used to do with our hands.

[Leverage would be defined in this circumstance as the magnification power to increase productivity of the several revolutions over time.]

SOURCE: R. C. Heterick, "Paradigms and Paradoxes," *Higher Education Product Companion* (Vol. 3, Number 1, 1993), p. 14.

goods and services. Frequently, these communications are triggered by external information systems that monitor and control inventory levels, record sales, and account for purchases and sales.

Electronic communication reduces the likelihood of errors in communication, decreases the time needed to prepare and send written communication through traditional modes such as the postal services, and eliminates the manual data entries that

EDI Savings Are Substantial

In a race to cash checks, three helicopters land in rapid succession at the airport [in Burbank, California]. Workers scramble to unload hundreds of thousands of bundled checks, hurl them into carts and run them out to a waiting Learjet. On board are $600 million in checks that must get to banks in 46 cities by 8 A.M. or payment will be delayed a day—a costly proposition.

In contrast, Barbara Woollett, an accountant at Chevron U.S.A., Inc., has no doubt about the delivery time for an $11,637 payment she authorized that same day for parts used in one of the Chevron Corp. unit's oil refineries. Instead of telling her accounts-payable clerk to write a check, Ms. Woollett zapped the payment electronically from Chevron's bank to the parts manufacturer's bank.

After years of promise but little action, more and more companies are adopting that no-muss, no-fuss approach. [In 1993,] they paid more than 35 million invoices electronically, up 59% from 1992. After targeting large vendors [in mid-1993,] Chevron now is making more than 5,800 electronic payments a month to suppliers, nearly 14% of the checks it once wrote.

Beating the drums the loudest for electronic funds transfer is the National Automated Clearing House, the bank-owned electronic-payment system. Elliott McEntee, its president, predicts growth of 100% a year in usage for the foreseeable future. He speaks of the "absurdities" of checks in an age of computers, estimating that printing, mailing and clearing the 60 billion or so checks written by individuals and companies each year in the U.S. cost more than $50 billion.

Companies save about 75 cents each time they do not print, handle, and mail checks. And knowing precisely which day payments will be debited and credited gives companies more flexibility in managing their cash. Of even greater interest to corporate treasurers is the precision, thoroughness, and uniformity of remittance information arriving in a standard electronic format.

SOURCE: Fred R. Bleakley, "Electronic Payments Now Supplant Checks at More Large Firms," *Wall Street Journal* (April 13, 1994), p. A1. Reprinted with by permission of The Wall Street Journal, © 1994 Dow Jones & Company, Inc. All Rights Reserved Worldwide.

would otherwise be required to update inventory records and related accounting records. As indicated in the accompanying News Note, paying for goods and services by electronic transfer rather than bank drafts or checks is becoming common. "In fact, any company that plans to remain aggressive and profitable—and in business— [in 1999] had better start looking at what it needs to become EDI-capable."[23]

Production Systems and Management

In a customer-focused manufacturing environment, each product or service should be defect-free. A starting point for this objective is to demand that all material inputs and conversion processes be virtually flawless. Employee training and empowerment,

---

[23]Allan Snow, "EDI: Made to Order," *CMA Magazine* (November 1994), p. 22.

strong supplier relationships, and technologically advanced production equipment are important factors in helping an organization attain total quality.

bar codes

Bar coding is probably the technology with which people are most familiar. **Bar codes** are groups of lines and spaces arranged in a special machine-readable pattern. These codes, which revolutionized retailing, appear on almost every product-related item in a store and are scanned to transmit information to a computer. Manufacturers can also use bar codes to gain information about raw material receipts and issuances, products as they move through an assembly area, and quality problems. Bar codes have reduced clerical costs, paperwork, and inventory, and simultaneously made processing faster, less expensive, and more reliable.

Conventional bar codes carry information in a single dimension: the width. But one company, Symbol Technologies of Bohemia, New York, has developed a two-dimensional bar code that can store even more information in a very small space. "The entire Gettysburg Address, for example, can be stored in less than a two-inch square on one of Symbol's PDF 417s."[24] These codes have been put to use in all economic sectors: Military personnel will soon have identification cards with two-dimensional bar codes that will not be able to be forged and will contain their entire medical history; and Volvo is using the PDF in its electronic data interchange applications.

Bar code scanners have made product receiving, sales recording, and inventory control substantially easier. These bar codes are also inserted into pets using Avid microchips, allowing immediate identification of lost or stolen pets via a national registry.

Bar coding is only the most visible of the many technologies used in manufacturing. Modern manufacturing equipment often uses computerized technology to schedule, control, and monitor production with little or no human intervention. In highly integrated systems, computer programs oversee each production process and develop statistical data on both the component and process reliability. These data are used to evaluate the reliability of components obtained from internal and external suppliers as well as to aid in the design of new products and processes.

Because of this intense oversight process, production defects should be promptly discovered and their causes identified and corrected. Sometimes the computer-generated statistical data are used to identify problem situations. Other times, elements of the production system are designed to be self-checking. In Japan, such techniques are called *poka-yoke*, a phrase meaning "mistake proofing."

If possible, devices should be devised to discover disorders automatically, without the worker's having to attend to minute details and measurements. Examples of *poka-yoke* are the following:

■ If operation A was to machine a diameter, the fixture at operation B would receive the part as machined in operation A. If the diameter was undersized or oversized, the part would not fit on the fixture at operation B.
■ Socket wrenches are dipped in red paint so that torqued parts are seen visually. Untorqued parts are thus easily spotted at subsequent operations.
■ A machine does not start if a part is not mounted properly on a fixture.[25]

[24]Srikumar S. Rao, "Tomorrow's Rosetta Stones," *Financial World* (November 22, 1994), p. 71.

[25]Mark C. DeLuzio, "The Tools of Just-in-Time," *Journal of Cost Management* (Summer 1993), p. 19.

Solutions Don't Necessarily Need to Be Expensive

The poka-yoke method essentially builds the function of a checklist into an operation so we can never "forget what we have forgotten." For example, if an operator needs to insert a total of nine screws into a subassembly, modify the container so it releases nine at a time. If a screw remains, the operator knows the operation is not complete.

Shigeo Shingo, who taught production engineering to a generation of Toyota managers, recommends four principles for implementing poka-yoke:

1. *Control upstream, as close to the source of the potential defect as possible.* For example, attach a monitoring device that will detect a material abnormality or an abnormal machine condition and will trigger shutdown before a defect is generated and passed on to the next process.
2. *Establish controls in relation to the severity of the problem.* A simple signal or alarm may be sufficient to check an error that is easily corrected by the operator, but preventing further progress until the error is corrected is even better.
3. *Think smart and strive small.* Strive for the simplest, most efficient, and most economical intervention. Don't overcontrol—if operator errors result from a lack of operations, improve methods before attempting to control the results. Similarly, if the cost of equipment adjustment is high, improve equipment reliability and consider how to simplify adjustment operations before implementing a costly automated-inspection system.
4. *Don't delay improvement by overanalyzing.* Poka-yoke solutions are usually the product of decisiveness and quick action. While design improvements can reduce manufacturing defects in the long run, you can implement many poka-yoke ideas at very low cost within hours of their conception, effectively closing the quality gap until you develop a more robust design.

SOURCE: Reprinted by permission of *Harvard Business Review*. An excerpt from "On-Line Quality: Shigeo Shingo's Shop Floor," by Connie Dyer (January–February 1990). Copyright © 1990 by the President and Fellows of Harvard College; all rights reserved.

Many poka-yoke techniques are low-cost and relate to a primary checklist of functions needed to perform an activity. The accompanying News Note provides some additional discussion on poka-yoke concepts.

New high-technology equipment has raised quality levels on two fronts. It has provided substantial opportunities to reduce defective production as well as to attain a higher level of satisfaction of customer wants and expectations. A global economy has made consumers more aware of the breadth and depth of the competition vying for their attention in the market and to be more discriminating in their purchases. In the customer-oriented market, firms have tried to distinguish their products and services from those of competitors by offering the prices and features that appeal to specific consumer profiles. One of the predictable consequences of this type of competition is that it leads firms to focus on needs and wants of individual consumers rather than the market as a whole.

As firms develop products and services to meet the needs of specific customer groups, variety has increased dramatically. In addition, to remain cost-competitive, firms must produce this diverse product/service line while maintaining efficient production and service systems. In the manufacturing sector, accomplishing this task requires that firms be able to change rapidly from one production run to another and use standard components to produce the variety and quality of products desired by consumers.

flexible manufacturing system (FMS)

Rapid changeover is a feature of a **flexible manufacturing system (FMS).** These systems allow a single factory to produce numerous variations of products through the use of computer-controlled robots. As indicated in Exhibit 2–11, industrial robots are becoming a new kind of labor force.

■ **EXHIBIT 2–11**
Robots in Use

INDUSTRIAL ROBOTS
per 100,000 people (1991)

SOURCE: Robots in Use: World Economic Forum, in Thomas A. Stewart, "The Information Age in Charts," *Fortune* (April 14, 1994), p. 76. © 1994 Time Inc. All rights reserved.

A 1992 survey of 900 American and Japanese companies by Deloitte & Touche consultants indicated that "Japanese manufacturers are about a third more likely than Americans to say increased flexibility figures importantly in their plans."[26] But flexibility reflects a definitive commitment to total quality in the form of meeting customer wants and expectations. Nissan, a firm believer in flexible manufacturing, "describes its strategy as 'five anys': to make anything in any volume anywhere at any time by anybody."[27]

Flexible manufacturing systems require a high level of investment in equipment as well as in research and development. Additionally, increased product variety causes manufacturers to incur substantial overhead costs for ordering and stocking components. This situation is reflected in the fact that Nissan's "five anys" philosophy resulted in over 28 different kinds of chassis on which it assembled automobiles. In 1994, the company announced that it wanted to reduce that number by a third, which would provide a savings of up to ¥100 billion (or over $950 million).[28] Although some costs rise when flexible manufacturing systems and product variability are installed, total profits may increase because of shorter setup times, fewer errors, and higher sales volumes caused by the satisfaction of customer wants and expectations.

A firm's success in a global, quality-based competitive environment will reflect consumers' perceptions of the value-to-price relationship for the firm's products and services. Customers perceive a product or service to have high value relative to that item's price if it meets most of their needs at the lowest possible price. When that relationship occurs, the product or service is likely to be a market success. Alternatively, if consumers perceive a product to have a low ratio of value to price, then the product is likely to be a market failure, regardless of how the product measures up on a singular scale of quality, such as lack of defects.

Companies that have shifted their focus to customers and quality have been forced to take a longer-run perspective on their business operations. This perspective has necessitated an in-depth review of the types and timing of information provided by the management accounting system.

STRATEGY-BASED COST MANAGEMENT PRACTICES

Today's business strategy of focusing on customers and quality requires a firm to manage organizational costs so a reasonable value-to-price relationship can be achieved. Although prices are more commonly set by the competitive market than necessarily by internal organizational costs, companies lacking appropriate cost management skills cannot expect to succeed for the long run. Thus, it can be said that organizations need to engage in **strategic cost management (SCM)**.

SCM can be viewed as the managerial use of management accounting information for the purpose(s) of setting and communicating organizational strategies; establishing, implementing, and monitoring the success of methods to accomplish the strate-

strategic cost management (SCM)

---

[26]Thomas A. Stewart, "Brace for Japan's Hot New Strategy," *Fortune* (September 22, 1992), p. 63.

[27]Stewart, "Brace for Japan's Hot New Strategy," p. 72.

[28]"Nissan Will Reduce Varieties of Chassis in Cost-Cutting Bid," *Wall Street Journal* (March 3, 1994), p. A12.

■ LEARNING
OBJECTIVE 7
Discuss why a strategically based
management accounting system
is needed in addition to a
financial accounting system.

gies; and assessing the level of success in meeting the promulgated strategies.[29] Thus, an organization's management accounting system should be designed and used to accumulate and report information related to organizational success in meeting customer- and quality-related goals and objectives. Managers can analyze and interpret such information in order to plan and control current activities and to make decisions about future courses of action, including expansion of the company's market base and/or technology installation.

In designing such a management accounting system, consideration must be given to cost accumulation and process measurement activities. Costs that are accumulated for financial accounting purposes may be inadequate for strategy-based decisions. For example, financial accounting requires that research and development costs be expensed as incurred. However, a product's cost is largely determined during design. Design has implications for a product's perceived value, the complexity and variety of components required for its production, its manufacturability, and its durability and likelihood of failure. Consequently, strategy-based cost management would suggest that design cost be accumulated as part of product cost. It is not necessary that this cost appear on the financial accounting statements, but that the cost exist in the management accounting system for decision making.

On the other hand, financial accounting accumulates all production costs as inventoriable and makes no distinction as to whether they add value in the eyes of the customer. A strategically based cost management system would provide a way to distinguish costs that add value from those that do not so that managers and employees alike could work to reduce such costs. In this way, the objective of continuous improvement would be enhanced.

Another example of the abilities of a strategically based management accounting system is in the area of process measurement rather than cost accumulation. Financial accounting is monetarily based and, therefore, does not measure nonfinancial organizational activities. However, as indicated earlier in the chapter, many activities critical to success in a quality-oriented, global marketplace are related to time—a nonmonetary characteristic. A useful management accounting system would ensure that information related to nonmonetary occurrences (such as cycle time or defect rates) would be available. Such information could then, if necessary, be translated into financial terms so that its significance to the company's profitability could be objectively analyzed.

Finally, financial accounting reflects a short-term perspective of operating activity. An organizational goal of continuous improvement is not short term; it is ongoing. Gathering monetary information and forcing it into a particular annual period of time does not necessarily provide managers with a clear indication of how today's decisions will affect the organization's long-run financial success. For example, not investing in research and development would cause a company's short-run profitability to improve, but could be disastrous in the long run.

Thus, a strategically based management accounting system would report a greater number of the costs and benefits of organizational activities. Having this information in a form designed to meet managerial needs would allow managers to make informed assessments of the company's performance in the value chain, position of competitive advantage (or disadvantage), and progress toward organizational goals.

---

[29]The term *strategic cost management* was coined by Professors John K. Shank and Vijay Govindarajan of Dartmouth College. A full discussion of the concept is provided in their book, *Strategic Cost Management* (New York: The Free Press, 1993).

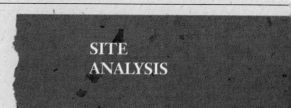

Big and sprawling, empowered and reengineered, trained and TQMed, Motorola [a 1988 Baldrige winner] now faces a whole new set of challenges—most of them brought on by its own explosive growth. As the company, which has long been dominated by engineers, makes its products more affordable to ordinary consumers (not just on-the-move executives), it must become more adept at marketing. As it ventures into more countries—managers expect three-fourths of sales to come from abroad by the end of the decade—it must tailor its approaches to cultures unfamiliar and uncomfortable with concepts like empowerment, decentralization, and cycle time. Above all, Motorola must struggle to keep its workers energized, motivated, and *dissatisfied*—even in the face of their company's storied success.

Warns Gary Tooker, vice chairman and CEO: "Fame is a fleeting thing. When the alarm clock rings tomorrow morning, you'd better get up and understand that your customers expect more from you than they did the day before. You'd better finds ways to be better."

This company strives to measure every task performed by every one of its 120,000 employees, and calculates that it saved $1.5 billion by reducing defects and simplifying processes [in 1993]. While that figure is hard to verify, here's one that isn't: Since 1986, productivity (sales per employee) has increased 126%, even though Motorola has expanded its work force.

At some Motorola factories quality is so high that they've stopped counting defects per million and started working on defects per billion. Overall, the company aims to reduce its error rate tenfold every two years and to increase the speed of its processes—cut its cycle time—tenfold every five years.

[In February 1994 and March 1995 *Fortune's* annual Corporate Reputations Survey, which included more than 10,000 senior executives, outside directors, and financial analysts, placed Motorola in the top ten of America's most admired corporations. It was number one in both years in the field of electronics and electrical equipment.]

SOURCE: Ronald Henkoff, "Keeping Motorola on a Roll," *Fortune* (April 18, 1994), pp. 68,70, 72.
© 1994 Time Inc. All Rights Reserved.

CHAPTER SUMMARY

Modern managers are now trying to balance both short-run and long-run considerations in conducting their planning, controlling, performance-evaluating, and decision-making functions. Globalization of business has increased competition, which, in turn, has led managers to find ways to improve quality and lower costs. The quality movement focuses on meeting or exceeding customer expectations and promotes a long-run continuous improvement effort. It requires total employee involvement. TQM has also fostered decentralization through worker empowerment. Empowerment challenges all employees to be involved, manage their own jobs, and work in teams to solve group problems.

In focusing on the quality of internal processes, firms have established benchmarking practices. Benchmarking requires identifying firms having the highest-quality processes in specific operational areas. Managers then try to emulate and improve the successful practices of the benchmark organizations in their own companies.

Governments have also encouraged a focus on quality by establishing awards for achievements in quality. The premier quality awards in the United States and Japan, respectively, are the Baldrige Award and the Deming Prize. International quality standards are established by the ISO 9000 standards. Such increased scrutiny places even greater importance on controlling the quality of internal processes and the quality of products and services produced.

Another thrust of modern managers is to reduce production cycle time or the interval between the customer placing an order and the delivery of the product or service. Customers are better served and costs are reduced when cycle time is shorter. Inventory levels are also decreased, which allows a company to dispose of unneeded resources or divert resources to worthwhile pursuits.

Technological innovations are also having a continuing impact on business operations. Advances in technology have substantially enhanced the abilities of firms to process information and have allowed electronic linkages among firms and the linkage of production and control systems within companies. Electronic data interchange systems diminish paperwork and speed up communications with suppliers and customers. Bar codes, robotics, and other forms of automation can enhance the quantity and quality of business output and the value-to-price relationship of a company's goods and services for customers.

Strategically based cost management views management accounting as a means of assisting managers in setting and communicating organizational strategies and establishing and monitoring methods of accomplishing the intended results of those strategies. This type of cost management system differs from financial accounting by taking a longer-range perspective, including an alternative view of product costs. For instance, a strategically based cost management system would include research and development costs in total product cost, but would exclude costs of activities that create no value in the value chain.

GLOSSARY

Baldrige Award (p. 54)   an award program administered by the U.S. Department of Commerce to recognize quality achievements by U.S. businesses

Bar code (p. 66)   a group of lines and spaces arranged in a special machine-readable pattern

Benchmarking (p. 52)   the process of investigating, comparing, and evaluating the company's products, processes, and/or services against those of companies believed to be the "best in class" so that the investigating company can imitate, and possibly improve on, their techniques

Continuous improvement (p. 46)   the process of small but ongoing positive adjustments in the status quo

Control chart (p. 51)   a graphical presentation of the results of a specified activity; indicates the upper and lower control limits and the results that are out of control

Customer (p. 47)   a generic term for the recipient or beneficiary of a process's output; can be internal or external

Cycle time (p. 60)   the time from when a customer places an order to the time that product or service is delivered or, using a full life-cycle approach, the time from the conceptualization of a product or service to the time the product or service is delivered to the customer

Decentralization (p. 49)   the downward delegation by top management of authority and decision making to the individuals who are closest to internal processes and customers

Deming Prize (p. 55)   Japan's premier quality award

Design for manufacturability (p. 61)   the process of reducing the number of parts in a product, using standard (rather than special order) parts when possible, and simplifying the assembly process

Electronic data interchange (EDI) (p. 63)   the almost instantaneous computer-to-computer transfer of information

Empowerment (p. 49)   the process of giving workers the training and authority they need to manage their own jobs

Flexible manufacturing system (FMS) (p. 68)   a production system in which a single factory manufactures numerous variations of products through the use of computer-controlled robots

Innovation (p. 46)   a dramatic improvement in the status quo caused by radical new ideas, technological breakthroughs, or large investments in new technology or equipment

ISO 9000 (p. 56)   a set of standards established by the international community to define the minimum acceptable quality for processes that generate products and services offered in international trade

Just-in-time (JIT) (p. 61)   a philosophy about when to do something; the *when* is "as needed" and the *something* is a production, purchasing, or delivery activity

Malcolm Baldrige Quality Award (p. 54)   see Baldrige Award

Process benchmarking (p. 52)   benchmarking in which the quality of internal processes are assessed by comparing them with similar processes of firms identified as having the highest-quality processes globally; also involves subsequent efforts to emulate and improve on the quality achievements of the benchmark firms

Quality circle (p. 50)   an intra- or interdepartmental team of empowered workers who meet to identify and solve quality-related problems

Results benchmarking (p. 53)   benchmarking in which an end product or service is examined; the focus is on product/service specifications and performance results

Strategic cost management (SCM) (p. 69)   the managerial use of cost information for the purpose(s) of setting and communicating organizational strategies; establishing, implementing, and monitoring the success of methods to accomplish the strategies; and assessing the level of success in meeting the promulgated strategies

Total quality management (TQM) (p. 45)   a philosophy for organizational management and organizational change that seeks ever-increasing quality or continuous improvement

---

END OF CHAPTER MATERIALS

■ QUESTIONS

1. What is Total Quality Management? Why does adoption of TQM require a fundamental change in the way a company considers quality in its operations?

2. Why must a quality standard be regarded as a moving target rather than a static objective?

3. For the sake of protecting profitability, why would a business be willing to stop serving certain groups of customers?

4. Top managers at Global Manufacturing Company are considering the possibility of decentralizing control of all foreign operating divisions. The firm has traditionally maintained very tight control over these operations. What are some of the major benefits that the company stands to gain from decentralization?

5. Many companies are now "empowering" their employees. What is employee empowerment? What additional costs might a company incur to empower employees?

6. How can statistical process controls be utilized to monitor quality?

7. How does benchmarking allow a company to evaluate the quality of its products and services?

8. How do process benchmarking and results benchmarking differ? How are they similar?

9. Describe the nine steps in benchmarking that can be used to improve a specific production process.

10. What is the Baldrige Award? What are the award categories?

11. Why do countries establish quality standards? Why is it desirable to have a common set of global quality standards?

12. What role is served by the International Organization for Standardization?

13. What are the advantages and disadvantages of having only one (or a few) supplier sources?

14. What are the four stages or levels on the quality continuum? Where is TQM located on the continuum?

15. What is cycle time for a product or service? Why are many companies concerned with reducing cycle time?

16. Why would using design for manufacturability concepts reduce cycle time?

17. "Philosophically, JIT is aimed at minimizing time, space, and energy." Discuss what you think the person making this statement meant.

18. How has the evolution of technology dramatically affected the processing of information?

19. Why should businesses be concerned about electronic data interchange? Wouldn't it be better for them to continue to use paper transactions and checks? Discuss the advantages and disadvantages of each type of system.

20. What is *poka-yoke*? Provide three examples not given in the text of how such a concept could be used. The examples can be related to home, business, or school.

21. Choose any product that is produced in at least ten varieties (such as calendars). What kinds of additional costs would a company incur to produce such variety?

22. What is a flexible manufacturing system? How do such systems provide greater capability to produce a variety of products quickly?

23. How does strategic cost management link information management to corporate strategies?

■ EXERCISES

24. (LO 1, 2, 3, 4, 7; *Terminology*) Match each numbered item on the right with a lettered item on the left.

a. Deming Prize	**1.** Assessing the quality of end products or services
b. Baldrige Award	**2.** A quality-oriented team of empowered workers
c. ISO 9000	**3.** Machine-readable lines and spaces
d. Bar codes	**4.** Assessing the quality of internal procedures and techniques
e. Electronic data interchange	**5.** Aligning information system to report on organizational strategies
f. Flexible manufacturing system	**6.** Giving workers the training and authority to manage their own jobs
g. Process benchmarking	**7.** The primary Japanese quality award
h. Results benchmarking	**8.** A set of international quality standards
i. Strategic cost management	**9.** Computer-to-computer transfer of information
j. Empowering	**10.** Production using computer-controlled robots
k. Quality circle	**11.** The primary U.S. quality award

25. (LO 1, 2, 3, 4, 5; *True/false*) Mark each of the following statements as true or false and explain why the false statements are incorrect.

   a. Adoption of TQM leads to more stability in organizational processes.
   b. Accounting practices, like laws, once created remain in effect forever.
   c. A focus on quality allows companies to engage in economies of scale by producing the best of a single type of product.
   d. By reducing the number of suppliers, companies should achieve better relations with the suppliers that are retained.
   e. Smart companies are willing to drop some customers.
   f. The information revolution has allowed computers to do things at least a million times better than people can do them manually.
   g. Benchmarking is the same as copying another company's products or processes.
   h. TQM requires participation by everyone in the organization and can only be successful with top management support.
   i. Reducing cycle time allows firms to rely less on long-term production planning.

26. (LO 1, 2, 5; *Work restructuring*)

To build a factory of the future, Sony Corp. is taking a page from the workshops of the past.

At a plant [in Japan] men are dismantling conveyor belts on which as many as 50 people assembled camcorders. Nearby, Sony has set up tables to form a snail-shaped shop for four people. Walking through this "spiral line," workers assemble an entire camera themselves, doing everything from soldering to testing.

This is progress, Sony says. Output per worker on the experimental line is 10% higher than on a conventional one. The spiral performs better, Sony says, because it frees efficient assemblers to churn out more product instead of limiting them to a conveyor belt's speed. It reduces handling time, the seconds consumed as goods under production are passed from worker to worker. And if something goes wrong, only a small section of the plant is affected.

"There is no future in conventional conveyor lines," says Hitoshi Yamada, a consultant to Sony and other companies. "They are a tool that conforms to the person with the least ability."

With the spiral line reducing assembly time to 15 minutes per camera from 70, the plant is moving closer to a goal sought by many manufacturers: Making goods only as customers order them, instead of basing output on estimates. That change would slash inventory close to zero.

[SOURCE: Michael Williams, "Some Plants Tear Out Long Assembly Lines, Switch to Craft Work," *Wall Street Journal* (October 24, 1994), pp. A1, A4. Reprinted by permission of The Wall Street Journal, © 1994 Dow Jones & Company, Inc. All Rights Reserved Worldwide.]

   a. If craft-type work or small-group manufacturing is more efficient than mass manufacturing, why did mass manufacturing evolve in the industrial revolution as a (presumably) more efficient replacement for craft work?
   b. Is the small group work cell approach described at Sony likely to be the most efficient work configuration for all types of products? Explain.
   c. Why does the emerging emphasis on quality favor small-group production over mass manufacturing?
   d. How does the evolution of computer-based manufacturing, including flexible manufacturing systems, provide a competitive edge for small group manufacturing over mass manufacturing?

27. (LO 1, 2; *Sourcing*) *Nothing is certain yet, but it increasingly looks like Texas Municipal Power Agency [in east-central Texas] will change its power contract to Western coal [mined in Wyoming], at the expense of Navasota Mining Co. lignite [a local Texas coal. The benefits include the following.]*

The Wyoming fuel, 35,000 tons of which [was] test burned Dec. 26-31, 1994, burns stronger and has less sulphur and ash than Navasota Mining's locally produced fuel.

The coal's heat is good, its power is more intense, [and] the TMPA furnace would not require major modification if a fuel switch took place.

[While there may be transportation delays since the mine is about 1,500 miles from the power plant,] triple [railroad] tracks are under construction to alleviate train bottlenecks leaving the mine.

[SOURCE: David Howell, "Power Company Considering Fuel Change," *Bryan-College Station Eagle* (January 13, 1995), p. A9. Reprinted courtesy of the Bryan-College Station Eagle.]

a. As stated or implied in the article, what are the apparent important dimensions of coal quality to the Texas power plant?

b. As manager of the Texas power plant, what would be your greatest concern in purchasing the Wyoming coal?

c. Should the potential loss of income and jobs at the Texas Navasota Mining Co. affect this sourcing decision? Why or why not?

d. What factors favor sourcing the coal locally, even if it is of "lower quality"?

28. (LO 6; *Technological change*) Although technological change has dramatically affected practices in many industries, its impact on the entertainment industry is extraordinary. Paul Tagliabue, commissioner of the National Football League (NFL), describes how technological change has affected the NFL:

"Sports was still local in the '40s and '50s. It started to become national in the '60s and '70s, and then in the '80s, it started to become really international. The evolution is now the information technology, really. We can't stand still. I think it's more competitive now. There's more and more sports and more and more programming chasing fewer network viewers and fewer network advertisers."

[Even so,] the popularity of the NFL has continued under Tagliabue. At last year's Super Bowl in Pasadena, for example, there were 2,164 media credentials issued to 652 news organizations, 372 of which were for international media from 21 countries. The game was shown on television in a record 100 countries, including live telecasts for the first time to China and Brazil.

At their recent meeting in Chicago, the NFL team owners decided to set up a football league based solely in Europe beginning in 1995.

[SOURCE: Manny Topol, "In a League of His Own," *Sky*, (January 1994), pp. 49-57. Reprinted through the courtesy of Halsey Publishing, publishers of Delta Air Lines' *Sky* magazine.]

a. Why has technology affected the NFL more than other organizations?

b. Which specific technologies have had the greatest impact on the growing popularity of the NFL?

c. What would be major impediments to "globalizing" the NFL?

d. Are all parts of the American entertainment industry likely to enjoy the same market benefits from technology as the NFL? Explain.

■ COMMUNICATION ACTIVITIES

29. (LO 6; *Technology changes*) *A lot of people would just as soon stay behind as America charges full speed into the electronic information age. Surveys show that substantial minorities of people are still uncomfortable with videocassette recorders, answering machines, compact disc players and even digital alarm clocks—not to mention home computers. The thought of trying to send mail, consult an encyclopedia, order a movie or chat with strangers over a computer network leaves them scared, hostile or indifferent.*

[SOURCE: Robert S. Boyd, "Technology: Fear Keeps Some Living in Past," *(New Orleans) Times-Picayune* (May 3, 1994), p. A-10.]

Assume you are the manager of a medium-sized business. Prepare a report that addresses the following issues:

a. Why are some people experiencing "technophobia"?

b. If several people in your organization were "technophobes," how would you attempt to eliminate this fear?

c. If technophobia could not be eliminated, what problems might arise in the areas in which the technophobes worked? (Assume that one was in production operations, one in accounting, and one in marketing.)

30. (LO 3; *Benchmarking*) *Oregon, a perennial innovator among the states, has come up with an inventive way to measure how well it's doing. The approach, borrowed from the corporate world, is called "Benchmarks." Benchmarks began in 1988. Hundreds of Oregonians—from business, labor, education, environmental groups, state and local government, the health care system and grass-roots organizations—developed the official set of benchmarks for the state.*

Then, in 1991, the legislature enacted the benchmarks into law. The lawmakers also created an Oregon Progress Board to make sure the process stays alive and on target. Each two years, the board has to report publicly on progress toward each benchmark goal.

Altogether, Oregon has 272 benchmarks. For practicality, they've been divided into two classes—priority standards related to acute questions (health care access, drugs, reducing teenage pregnancy, for example) and "core" benchmarks (for more long-term fundamental issues such as the base of the state's economy and basic literacy of the population). All are, however, based on measurable outcomes.

[SOURCE: Neal Peirce, "Benchmarks for State, Local Governments Good Idea," *(New Orleans) Times-Picayune* (April 11, 1994), p. B-5.]

You are a politician running for office in Oregon. Your future constituency wants information about the use of benchmarking in a political setting. Develop a presentation for a paid political announcement that would address the following questions.

a. Why are benchmarks as useful in government as they are in business?

b. What benefits might (1) the Oregon government and (2) Oregonians expect from the use of benchmarks?

c. What potential hazards might exist in using benchmarks in a governmental setting?

■ CASES

31. (LO 1, 2; *Change in competitive environment*) *[There are two major producers of railroad locomotives for the U.S. market: General Motors (GM) and General Electric (GE). For most of the recent past, GM has dominated the market with a market share of about 70%. However, in the late 1980s, 39-year-old Michael Lockhart became head of GE's locomotive division.]*

Before Mr. Lockhart arrived in January 1989, he attended GE's annual Christmas dinner for railroad presidents. At the dinner, "I asked them what I could do to help them. They told me I could make our locomotives work." Subsequent visits to railroads confirmed that GE had a problem. At CSX [railway], Mr. Taylor [vice-president of CSX] recounts he told Mr. Lockhart: "I need help. I've got this installed fleet that's killing me."

Shocked, Mr. Lockhart returned to the production plant. He moved the locomotive headquarters from the perimeter of the sprawling plant to a building in the middle of assembly operations. He set up a task force of 100 engineers to fix a dozen problems, drawing experts from around GE's empire. GE's locomotive marketing manager, who had antagonized some railroad officials, left the company.

"Lockhart shook things up," says Michael Iden, director of motive power engineering at the Chicago & Northwestern. "At General Electric it used to be, 'Here's my product,' but now the company's listening to customers and building more reliable units."

[After making many changes, GE has cut the time to build a locomotive from 92 days to 46 days and has earned a 60% market share.]

Just as General Electric began improving its performance, GM was encountering setbacks. Having dominated the locomotive business, some GM officials became arrogant, rail executives say. Mimicking a GM official, one rail official juts his jaw out and says: "I'm here to take orders."

With the world's biggest locomotive plant in LaGrange, GM also was stuck with costly overcapacity when orders fell. And because the parent has suffered huge losses on autos in recent years, the corporation isn't giving the locomotive unit funds to make its plants smaller and more efficient. In fact, GM has put a majority stake in its locomotive business for sale, with no takers thus far.

[SOURCE: William M. Carley, "GE Locomotive Unit, Long an Also-Ran, Overtakes Rival GM," *Wall Street Journal* (September 3, 1993), pp. A1, A4. Reprinted by permission of The Wall Street Journal, © 1993 Dow Jones & Company, Inc. All Rights Reserved Worldwide.]

a. Identify changes that were made in the GE locomotive plant that are consistent with changes occurring in business today as described in the chapter.

b. Why would GM be so (apparently) complacent about its position in the locomotive market?

c. What actions do you recommend that the GM locomotive unit consider in its efforts to return to its market dominance?

d. After GE's Lockhart assembled a significant number of engineers to resolve problems in GE's locomotives, the ultimate output of the engineers' efforts was a new locomotive design. Carl Taylor, vice president of CSX Railway, described the new locomotives: "They work." What does the story suggest about the importance of product design and engineering to product quality and perceived customer value?

32. (LO 6; *Coping with technological innovations*) *In 10 years, Hopper Specialty Co. had grown from a small storefront into the biggest distributor of industrial hardware in northwest New Mexico, catering especially to oil and gas drillers. In May 1988, NCR Corp.'s highly touted Warehouse Manager computer package promised even better things to come. When up and running, the computer system would track the thousands of items in a huge inventory, keep prices current, warn when items were running low, punch up invoices in seconds and even balance the monthly books—all at the touch of a few keystrokes. Particularly for drilling customers who lose money every minute their equipment isn't working, anything that could get orders for parts filled faster would indeed be cause for celebration.*

NCR began installing hardware and countertop terminals for Hopper. During sales demonstrations, Mr. Hopper had been impressed that the terminals could punch up a customer invoice in a fraction of a second. But when Hopper Specialty actually switched on its new system in September 1988, the response time ranged from half a minute to several minutes, leaving Hopper's customers waiting in increasingly long lines. Additional delays were caused by 20 to 30 terminal lockups a day.

At Hopper, Warehouse Manager couldn't even be relied on to keep prices straight. A piece of industrial hose that should have been listed at $17 a foot showed up as costing $30 a foot.

By far the most damaging problem stemmed from huge gaps between what the computer told Hopper Specialty was in stock and what actually was there. The Warehouse Manager might show 50 parts in stock, for instance, when in fact Hopper needed to order 50. Other times, it would show that items were on order when they were sitting on the shelf.

The chaos seemed to compound itself. Six times in two months during 1989, Hopper employees hand-counted every item in the building, only to find the tally didn't match what NCR's computer said was there.

NCR kept records of complaints from Hopper and the nearly identical ones from many others using Warehouse Manager. But at Hopper and other locations, users say NCR told them that their problems were isolated. When he called for technical help, Mr. Hopper says, NCR blamed his employees' inexperience in using the system. In one instance, Mr. Hopper says, NCR technicians blamed problems on static electricity from office manager Tracy Irwin's nylon stockings.

Ms. Irwin, the office manager, began logging 14-hour days and coming in on weekends with her children to work out problems with the system. But she couldn't keep customers from taking their business two doors down, to Advance Supply Pump Co., which now was boasting superior inventory and service. As Hopper Specialty's customer base eroded, it couldn't afford to carry as big an inventory. The shrinking inventory and confusion over what was in stock in turn further hurt Hopper's reputation for reliability. "The whole thing just snowballed," says Mr. Hopper.

[SOURCE: Milo Geyelin, "How an NCR System for Inventory Turned into a Virtual Saboteur," *Wall Street Journal* (August 8, 1994), pp. A1, A4. Reprinted by permission of The Wall Street Journal, © 1994 Dow Jones & Company, Inc. All Rights Reserved Worldwide.]

a. What procedures could Mr. Hopper have used to evaluate Warehouse Manager before purchasing the system?

b. In general, how can managers reduce uncertainty about whether an emerging technology is appropriate for use in their companies?

c. What internal factors are likely to affect the success of adopting a new technology? What external factors?

d. How can the quality of a new technology be assessed by nonexpert managers?

33. (LO 2, 5, 6; *Report on plant modernization*) The Arvee Corporation has manufactured recreational vehicles for nearly ten years. During this time Arvee bought existing older buildings near the founder's home to expand the facilities as needed. Now, new competition and rapid sales growth to an annual level of nearly $300 million have made management realize that the company needs to consolidate its locations, reorganize its operations, and modernize its equipment to bring costs into line and to maintain traditional profit margins.

Five existing plant locations service the three operating divisions: Van Division (small motorized travel vans), Home Division (large motorized homes), and Trailer Division (nonmotorized hitch-on trailers). Several warehouses service the various plant locations, and the corporate office is at a location separate from the production and warehouse facilities. All buildings are within a five-mile radius. Some plant locations include production facilities for two divisions; the overlap that has developed is creating inefficiencies and additional costs. Corporate management has decided that it should take one of the following two courses of action:

■ Alternative 1 is to consolidate the facilities into fewer existing locations.

■ Alternative 2 is to consolidate all facilities into one new location.

With either of these two alternatives, each division would have exclusive management, production, and warehouse areas. A central warehouse would house common production materials and components; each division's production locations would house other inventories unique to its vehicle models.

The manufacturing operations at most plant locations need to be reorganized for greater production efficiency. Frequently, the plans for the production facilities needed to meet the increased sales were not well conceived. This poor planning is now adversely affecting current work activities as well as materials and production flow. Moreover, the technology for this kind of production is changing. Thus, much equipment needs to be replaced because it is obsolete or worn out. In general, management has come to realize that a complete plant modernization is needed to survive the emerging market challenges.

Tony Pratt, corporate controller, is responsible for presenting a summary report on the proposed plant modernization at an upcoming meeting of the Modernization Committee, which will oversee project implementation.

      a. Discuss what types of information Tony needs to prepare his report and from what sources such information can be obtained.

      b. Design a report format that you think would provide the information to the committee in an understandable and useful way.

(CMA adapted)

■ ETHICS AND QUALITY DISCUSSIONS

34. *Grumman Corp., in a move to avert criminal charges of defrauding the Navy, has agreed to a precedent-setting $20 million civil settlement that greatly expands federal supervision of the company's ethics compliance programs.*

    The agreement . . . mandates the most extensive involvement yet by federal agencies in a major defense contractor's internal compliance efforts. It also is expected to allow the Bethpage, N.Y., contractor to avoid being suspended or barred from receiving new federal contracts.

    Law enforcement officials said that the settlement, which gives Justice Department and Pentagon officials a direct say in sensitive legal and personnel decisions facing Grumman's top management, is likely to serve as a model for future agreements with other companies.

    The settlement . . . ends a five-year criminal investigation of the company that was part of the nationwide Pentagon corruption inquiry dubbed Operation III Wind. The investigation . . . uncovered a pattern of overcharges, fraud and other violations involving some $17 million in business. . . .

[SOURCE: Andy Pasztor, "U.S., Grumman Reach Accord in Pentagon Case," *Wall Street Journal* (November 23, 1993), pp. A3, A4. Reprinted by permission of The Wall Street Journal, © 1993 Dow Jones & Company, Inc. All Rights Reserved Worldwide.]

    a. What does this story suggest about the costs of legal and ethical compliance relative to the costs of legal and ethical noncompliance?

    b. Discuss whether the federal government should have the right to monitor compliance with ethical codes in addition to federal laws.

    c. What does the story suggest about the importance of both compliance with ethical codes and compliance with laws in governing organizations?

35. *A senior Toyota Motor Corp. official sharply criticized U.S. auto-parts suppliers [because] American suppliers still produce lower-quality parts than their Japanese competitors. In addition, U.S. suppliers are slower than Japanese suppliers. For instance, Japanese suppliers met every deadline when producing part prototypes for the Avalon sedan. U.S. suppliers, however, met their deadlines just 47% of the time. Toyota said it was forced to modify its product-development schedule to accommodate the slower U.S. suppliers.*

[SOURCE: Krystal Miller, "Toyota, Alleging Low Quality, Says It Won't Expand U.S. Parts Purchases," *Wall Street Journal* (June 17, 1994), p. A2. Reprinted by permission of The Wall Street Journal, © 1994 Dow Jones & Company, Inc. All Rights Reserved Worldwide.]

    a. Why would a delay in Toyota's product-development schedule be of extreme concern to the company?

    b. What reasons might a U.S. company give for the lower quality and time delays?

    c. What techniques might the American companies employ to raise quality and reduce lead times?

36. *A new voice-activated robot could enable quadriplegics and other severely disabled people to work at office jobs, researchers at Southwestern Pennsylvania Human Services said.*

    The researchers, led by K. G. Engelhardt and others formerly associated with Carnegie Mellon University, spent three years designing a version of the robot for use in the customer service department at Pittsburgh National Bank [PNC], a unit of Pittsburgh Financial Corp.

    PNC hired Scott Ferguson, a 31-year-old who became quadriplegic after a motorcycle accident 10 years ago, to use the robot to answer customers' questions about credit card accounts.

The technology is timely, since the Americans with Disabilities Act required businesses with 25 or more employees to provide "reasonable accommodation" to disabled workers by July 26, 1992. It's unclear what "reasonable" means. But companies that can employ quadriplegics will be easily able to accommodate employees "with less severe disabilities," Ms. Engelhardt said.

It's too early to tell how important the robot will be to PNC. The company planned to test the robot for a year before deciding whether to buy more, at an estimated cost of $50,000 each.

[SOURCE: Joan E. Rigdon, "Robot Could Help Quadriplegics Work at Jobs in Offices," *Wall Street Journal* (January 22, 1992), p. B6. Reprinted by permission of The Wall Street Journal, © 1992 Dow Jones & Company, Inc. All Rights Reserved Worldwide.]

a. What ethical obligation do business firms bear to employ disabled workers, given the assumption that the cost to employ a disabled worker will exceed the cost to employ other workers?

b. In your opinion is $50,000 per employee a "reasonable" cost to incur to accommodate a disabled employee? Explain.

c. What do companies stand to gain by hiring disabled workers? What do they stand to lose in doing so?

■ PROJECTS

37. Your college of business has been attempting to integrate some total quality management processes into its structure. The dean has requested ideas from you as to how students could be empowered. Prepare a written report listing at least five empowerment ideas, how they could be implemented, and why they would improve the college.

You may choose to conduct this project as a team exercise. If so, one or more students on each team should be assigned responsibility for developing empowerment ideas on the areas of: college and university administration; coursework design and development; and development of student evaluation criteria.

38. Find out what organizations have won the Baldrige Award from 1988 to the present. Select one company from this list and investigate it further. Prepare a report on that company and what you believe contributed to its winning the Baldrige.

39. Many colleges and universities are striving to become more consumer-focused. One of the most common consumer-based performance measures for teaching effectiveness is the student teaching evaluation. Substantial literature exists discussing the positive and negative aspects of student evaluations. Find several articles that offer arguments on both sides of this controversial issue. Summarize the pro and con positions and discuss your own viewpoint. Also, discuss differences between businesses and academic institutions that make consumer-based evaluations more appropriate for the former than the latter.

40. Intel Corp. is known worldwide for its Pentium chip, used in computers made by IBM, Compaq, Dell, Gateway 2000, and others. In late 1994, a flaw was discovered in the chip when it was making calculations involving more than five significant digits. Intel's original response was that the company "did not believe the chip needed to be recalled, asserting that the typical user would have but one chance in more than 9 billion of encountering an inaccurate result as a consequence of the error."

[SOURCE: "Flaw Found in Intel's Pentium Chips," *Dallas Morning News* (November 24, 1994), p. 2D.]

Do a library search and prepare a report on what has occurred relative to Intel's Pentium chips since late 1994. Discuss your perceptions of whether this incident was significant in terms of TQM to the organization, taking the different positions of a college student, a business executive, and a research scientist.

3

COST TERMINOLOGY AND COST FLOWS

Understanding the classification and flow of costs in a manufacturing environment is essential. Marketing uses cost information for product planning and production forecasting. Management uses cost trends to highlight situations that require executive intervention. Finally, tomorrow's strategies are often based on yesterday's experience—it is wise to look behind when planning ahead.

Paul Swift "Cost Calculation and Flow in the Manufacturing Environment," *P&IM Review* (November 1989)

LEARNING OBJECTIVES

1. Understand the assumptions accountants make about cost behavior and why these assumptions are necessary.

2. Understand the relationship between cost objects and direct costs.

3. Classify product costs into direct materials, direct labor, and factory overhead categories.

4. Differentiate between the quality costs of conformance and costs of nonconformance.

5. Calculate cost of goods manufactured.

6. (Appendix) Understand the differences in income statements of merchandising, manufacturing, and service businesses.

ON SITE — Jubilations, Inc.: Big Orders Change the Cost Picture

In Columbus, Mississippi, Tamara Craddock found that the desire and ability to make a product people wanted were far from the only ingredients she needed to establish a cheesecake bakery that would grow and be profitable. She faced a formidable challenge in finding financing and suppliers. After banks spurned her loan application (she had no credit in her own name, just her husband's), she finally found an individual who would cosign a bank note with her and invest in the business, called Jubilations, Inc. Suppliers only wanted to sell in huge quantities: a dairy wanted to sell butter in railroad boxcar loads; container companies wanted to sell in lots of 10,000 units! But customers came much more easily—probably because of the care she and her five employees take in manufacturing the company's 37 different flavors of cheesecake. How many cheesecakes can Jubilations' six workers make in a month? Amazingly, about 23,000!

In 1992, Jubilations received an order from Cracker Barrel restaurants for 10,000 Cheesecakes Supreme. After agreeing to produce the cheesecakes, Ms. Craddock asked herself, "How in the world are we going to do this?" To answer that question and to be certain that accepting the order would benefit the company's bottom line, Ms. Craddock needed to understand what items created costs for the company and how (or if) those costs would change because of this particular order. She must have had a fairly comprehensive picture of her business because she decided she needed to increase the size of her work force and incur costs for additional equipment. Ms. Craddock's good business sense allowed her to produce the Cracker Barrel order on time and profitably.

SOURCES: Adapted from Blue Chip Enterprise Initiative, *Real-World Lessons for America's Small Businesses* (Nation's Business: 1992), p. 22; and Mary Fonseca, "A Sweet Business," *Mississippi Magazine* (November/December 1993).

Everyone is concerned about costs. A student is concerned about the cost of a Saturday night dinner and movie. Parents are concerned about the cost of their child's college education. Airline managers are concerned about the monthly meal cost for scheduled flights. Tamara Craddock is concerned about the costs of ingredients, equipment, and product quality assurance. However, simply referring to "the cost" is inappropriate because numerous conditions must be specified before "the cost" can be determined. Is the student considering a fast-food or a four-star restaurant? Will the child want to attend a public or private college, in-state or out-of-state? Are the flights serving breakfast, lunch, or dinner, and in what cabin? At Jubilations, how many cheesecakes are to be produced and how well are the employees trained?

cost

Effective managers must be able to understand and communicate about costs using common management accounting terms. **Cost** is an often-used word and reflects a monetary measure of the resources given up to acquire a good or service. But the term cost is seldom used without a preceding adjective to specify the type of cost being considered. Different types of costs are used in different situations. For instance, an asset's historical or acquisition cost is used to prepare a balance sheet, but its replacement cost is used to estimate insurance value.

A cost can be viewed in many ways, depending on the information desired. Exhibit 3–1 presents a number of different cost categories and the types of costs included in each. These categories are not mutually exclusive; a cost may be included in different categories at different times. A variety of costs will be discussed throughout the text. At this time, it is merely important to understand that the term *cost* can have many different meanings. This chapter focuses on the product costs incurred in manufacturing a good or performing a service.

COST BEHAVIOR

In any period, a cost may change from a prior period because of changes in activity. The way a cost responds to a change in activity is known as its **cost behavior.** Activity measures can include sales and/or production volume, machine hours, number of purchase orders sent, or number of grocery stores selling cheesecakes. The way a *total* (rather than unit) cost reacts to a change in activity reflects that cost's behavior pattern. Every cost will change if a long enough time passes or if extreme shifts in activity occur. Therefore, for cost behavior information to be properly identified, analyzed,

cost behavior

■ LEARNING
OBJECTIVE 1
Understand the assumptions accountants make about cost behavior and why these assumptions are necessary.

■ **EXHIBIT 3–1**
Cost Classification Categories

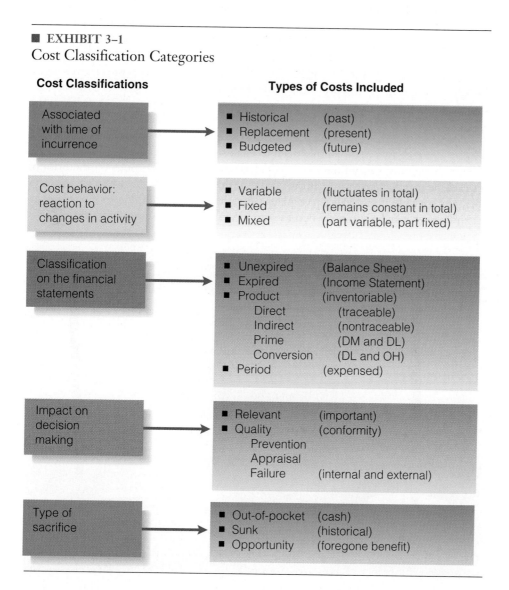

relevant range

cost driver

and used, a time frame must be specified to indicate how far into the future a cost should be examined, and a particular range of activity must be assumed. The time frame generally encompasses the operating cycle or a year, whichever is longer. The assumed activity range usually reflects the company's normal operating range and is referred to as the **relevant range.**

To understand how costs will behave under various conditions, accountants need to find the underlying cost driver for cost changes. A **cost driver** is an activity or occurrence that has a direct cause-effect relationship with a cost. For example, production volume has a direct effect on the total cost of raw materials used and so can be said to "drive" that cost. A change in production volume causes a similar change in the cost of raw materials. The accompanying News Note illustrates the idea of a cost driver: IBM determined that the method of laser mirror construction, rather than production quantity, caused testing costs. Changing the way the mirrors were constructed dramatically changed the cost associated with the product. Thus, knowing the underlying drivers of costs was extremely important to IBM.

In most situations, the cause-effect relationship is less clear because costs are commonly affected by multiple factors. For example, quality assurance costs are affected by volume of production, quality of materials used, skill level of workers, and level of automation. While determining which factor actually *caused* a specific change in quality assurance cost might be difficult, managers could choose any one of these factors to *predict* that cost if they were confident about the factor's relationship with cost changes. When a change in an activity measure is accompanied by a consistent, observable change in a cost item, that activity measure is a **predictor.** To be used as a predictor, the activity measure need only change with the cost in a foreseeable manner.

predictor

In contrast to a cost driver, a predictor does not necessarily *cause* the change in the related item; the two items simply need to change in the same manner. For instance, assume that almost every time one particularly avid football fan pulls on the brim of his cap, the team's quarterback throws a pass. If this behavior is consistent and observable, you may use it to predict pass plays—but the gesture itself does not cause passes, and passes may be thrown when the fan wears no cap or is not in attendance!

This dome in Lakeville, Minnesota is used for indoor golf practice. Utility costs per month vary with number of users and with weather conditions. It would be easier for dome management to predict utility costs by selecting number of users as the independent variable—however, this factor may not be the most appropriate cost driver.

Change the Process—Change the Cost

NEWS NOTE

International Business Machines Corp. said it developed a low-cost way to make tiny lasers, a technology now dominated by Japanese electronics companies.

[The new process] allows IBM to test the lasers in batches of as many as 20,000 units; testing is a major expense in laser-making. IBM estimated that its method will be 50% cheaper than current processes, and said it will also be faster and more efficient.

IBM said it used a chip-making process to etch small trenches into 3-inch-diameter wafers of laser material. Then it covered the trenches with a reflective material that turned them into tiny mirrors. After each wafer was tested, it was cut into as many as 20,000 separate lasers.

By contrast, current laser-making methods form mirrors by breaking the wafer into tiny pieces; the broken edges then act as reflecting surfaces. Since the lasers aren't finished until their mirrors are made, devices must then be tested one at a time.

Daniel Wilt, a technical supervisor at AT&T's Bell Laboratories, estimated that IBM's method, if done well, could cut the cost of each semiconductor laser from $10 to $1.

SOURCE: Laurence Hooper, "IBM Finds Way to Reduce Costs of Small Lasers," *Wall Street Journal* (January 31, 1991), p. B5. Reprinted by permission of The Wall Street Journal, © 1991 Dow Jones & Company, Inc. All Rights Reserved Worldwide.

The difference between a cost driver and a predictor is important. A cost driver reflects the *actual* cause-effect relationship; a predictor reflects a *possible* relationship or perhaps even a totally random occurrence that simply *seems* to be related. However, managers often use both cost drivers and predictors to estimate how changes in activity will influence cost behavior.

Variable and Fixed Costs

Cost behavior patterns will be referred to throughout the text because they are so helpful in many management accounting situations requiring analysis and decision making. The two most common types of cost behaviors are variable and fixed. The respective total cost and unit cost definitions for variable and fixed cost behaviors are presented in Exhibit 3–2 on page 88.

A cost that varies *in total* in direct proportion to changes in activity is classified as a **variable cost.** Since the total cost varies in direct proportion to the changes in activity, a variable cost is a constant amount *per unit*.[1] Examples of variable costs and their drivers include raw materials costs and production volume, units-of-production

variable cost

---

[1]An accountant's view of a variable cost is, in fact, a slight distortion of reality. Variable costs usually increase at a changing rate until a range of activity is reached in which the marginal variable cost rate per unit becomes fairly constant. Within this range, the slope of the cost line becomes less steep because the firm benefits from operating efficiencies such as price discounts on materials, improved worker skills, and increased productivity. Beyond this range, the slope becomes quite steep as the firm enters an activity range in which some operating inefficiencies (such as worker crowding and material shortages) cause the marginal variable cost rate to trend sharply higher. Because of the curves on each end of the variable cost spectrum, accountants choose as the relevant range that range of activity in which the variable costs are constant per unit.

■ **EXHIBIT 3–2**

Comparative Total and Unit Cost Behavior Definitions

	Total Cost	**Unit Cost**
Variable Cost	varies in direct proportion to changes in activity throughout the relevant range	remains constant throughout the relevant range
Fixed Cost	remains constant throughout the relevant range	varies inversely with changes in activity throughout the relevant range

depreciation and production volume, sales commissions and number or price of products sold, and gasoline cost and miles driven. Variable costs are extremely important to a company's total profit picture because every time a particular activity takes place, a specific amount of variable cost is incurred.

In contrast, a cost that remains constant *in total* within the relevant range of activity is a **fixed cost.** Such a cost varies inversely on a per-unit basis with changes in activity: the per-unit fixed cost decreases with increases in activity and increases with decreases in activity. Fixed costs include supervisors' monthly salaries, annual straight-line depreciation, and biannual insurance premiums on factory assets. Each of these costs is independent of production or sales volume as long as a relevant range is specified. However, if production or sales volume were to rise to a point at which additional supervisors, plant space, or equipment were needed, the related salaries, depreciation, and insurance costs would also rise.

The need to define a relevant range of activity in order to determine variable and fixed cost levels can be illustrated as follows. Assume that Jubilations, Inc., has the cost structures for cream cheese and building rent shown in the graphs in Exhibit 3–3. The exhibit indicates that actual cost for cream cheese is curvilinear rather than linear and that, over a wide range of activity, several levels of fixed cost will actually exist for rent.

The curves on the cream cheese cost graph (Graph A) reflect suppliers' pricing policies. If Jubilations' purchasing agent buys cream cheese in less than 2,000-pound lots, the price per pound is $1.10. If cream cheese is purchased in lots between 2,000 and 10,000 pounds, the price is $.95 per pound. Quantities over 10,000 pounds may be purchased for $.85 per pound. The company always buys cream cheese in quantities of 2,000 to 10,000 pounds; therefore, this activity level becomes the relevant range for cream cheese purchases. The cream cheese cost is variable because total cost varies in direct proportion to the quantity purchased within the relevant range. If Jubilations buys 4,000 pounds, it will pay $3,800 for its purchases; if it buys 8,000 pounds, the cost will be $7,600. In each instance, the volume is within the relevant range and, thus, the cost remains constant at $.95 per pound. Under these circumstances, the per-pound cost of cream cheese is a truly linear variable cost.

A decision about the relevant range of activity must also be made for fixed costs. Rent is the fixed cost shown in Exhibit 3–3. Jubilations' management has determined that a building that can be rented for $1,000 per month is large enough to house the equipment needed to produce between 1 and 15,000 cheesecakes per month. However, if monthly production exceeds 15,000 cheesecakes, additional facilities will

fixed cost

■ **EXHIBIT 3–3**

Relevant Range of Activity for Jubilations, Inc.

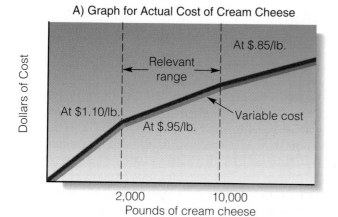

A) Graph for Actual Cost of Cream Cheese

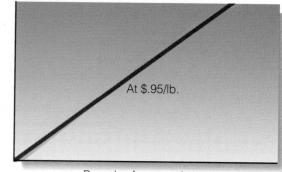

B) Accounting Graph for Cost of Cream Cheese

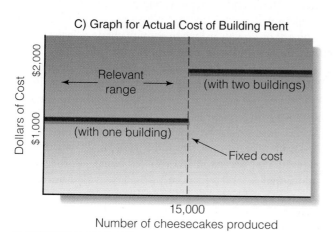

C) Graph for Actual Cost of Building Rent

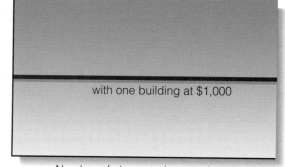

D) Accounting Graph for Cost of Building Rent

be required. If another similar building is acquired, an additional $1,000 of monthly building rent will be incurred. The company always produces between 2,000 and 5,000 cheesecakes per month, so the fixed cost for building rent is $1,000 per month.

In some businesses and for some items, managers can decide to "trade" variable and fixed costs for one another. For instance, a company may reduce the variable cost of postage by investing in a fixed cost for a machine to presort mail. Or a company may reduce the fixed cost of salaried employees by hiring part-time workers who are paid an hourly wage. Shifting from costs exhibiting one type of cost behavior to costs exhibiting a different type of behavior changes a company's basic cost structure and can significantly affect profits.

Companies may decide to **outsource,** or hire external providers to perform certain tasks that were previously done in-house. This situation occurred when Cracker Barrel decided to buy cheesecakes from Jubilations, Inc., rather than make them at each restaurant. Companies that outsource will realize additional profit if the costs paid to external providers are less than the costs that were incurred internally. As indicated in

outsource

the accompanying News Note, Dial Corporation decided to trade substantial fixed costs for lower variable costs when it decided to outsource its mainframe computer operations.

Mixed and Step Costs

mixed cost

Some costs are not strictly variable or fixed. For example, a **mixed cost** (also called a semivariable cost) has both a variable and a fixed component. This type of cost does not fluctuate in direct proportion with changes in activity, nor does it remain constant with changes in activity. Electricity is a good example of a mixed cost. Electricity bills are commonly computed as a flat charge (the fixed component) for basic service plus a stated rate for each kilowatt hour (kwh) of electricity used (the variable component). Exhibit 3-4 shows a graph for Jubilations' electricity charge, which consists of a flat rate of $100 per month plus $.018 per kwh. If Jubilations uses 20,000 kwhs of electricity in a month, its total electricity bill is $460 [$100 + ($.018 x 20,000)]. If the company uses 30,000 kwhs, the electricity bill is $640. Management accountants generally separate mixed costs into their variable and fixed components so that the behavior of these costs is more readily apparent.[2]

step costs

Another type of cost shifts upward or downward when activity changes by a certain interval or step. **Step costs** can be variable or fixed. Step variable costs have small steps and are treated for analysis purposes as variable costs. A water bill computed at $.002 per gallon for 1 to 1,000 gallons, $.003 per gallon for 1,001 to 2,000 gallons, $.005 per gallon for 2,001 to 3,000 gallons, and so on, is an example of a step variable cost. In contrast, step fixed costs have large steps and are commonly treated as fixed costs. An example of a step fixed cost would be salaries for telephone operators. Assume that each operator can handle 150 calls per day and is paid $2,500 per month. For each additional 150 calls per day that occur (on an extended basis), another operator is needed, requiring an additional $2,500 per month in salary. A relevant range of activity must be specified for step variable and step fixed costs to allow their treatment, respectively, as variable or fixed.

■ **EXHIBIT 3–4**
Graph of a Mixed Cost

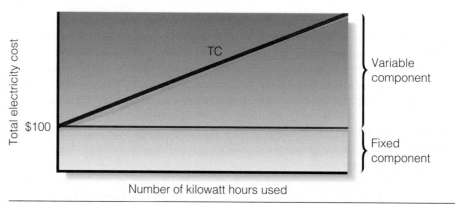

---

[2]Methods for analyzing mixed costs are discussed in Chapter 4.

Outsourcing Can Definitely Be Cost-Beneficial

[One of the reasons Dial Corporation hired Andersen Consulting was to provide] mainframe computer operations, systems software maintenance, and telecommunications support of Dial's operating locations.

Andersen Consulting's charges for services rendered include a set rate per Central Processing Unit (CPU) hour of processing time and a rate per gigabyte per month for storage of Dial Corporation files on disk packs at Andersen's Dallas facility. These rates will be adjusted annually for inflation, but they are not subject to renegotiation during the contract period. Andersen charges Dial on a cost-plus basis both for telecommunications between Dallas and Dial's end-user facilities and for systems software acquired after the effective date of the contract.

Andersen's fees for processing time and file storage are based on equivalent pricing benchmarks developed jointly by the two parties. The rates were computed to save Dial 10% of the out-of-pocket costs that the company would incur to provide the services internally, based on expected processing volumes. (Included are such items as operators' salaries, overtime charges, utility costs, repair and maintenance expenditures, and office supplies, among others.) Dial's managers also expect telecommunications costs to be lower due to Andersen's use of state-of-the-art technology in configuring channels from Dallas to Dial business unit locations.

Dial's management expects [an initial] overall savings of several million dollars from outsourcing. [The arrangement with Andersen Consulting converted the structure of costs from primarily fixed to variable.]

SOURCE: Michael A. Robinson, "Dial's Approach to MIS Improvement," *Management Accounting* (September 1991), pp. 30-31. Published by Institute of Management Accountants. Montvale, NJ.

Separating mixed costs and specifying a relevant range for step costs allows accountants to *treat their perceptions of the cost behaviors that occur in the relevant range as if they were fact*. A variable cost is assumed to be perfectly linear and equal to the average variable unit cost within the relevant range, while a fixed cost is assumed to be constant in total within the relevant range. These treatments of variable and fixed costs are justified for two reasons. First, the assumed conditions approximate reality: if the company operates only within the relevant range of activity, the cost behaviors reflect the expected and actual cost patterns. Second, selection of a constant variable cost per unit and a fixed cost total provides convenient, stable measurements for use in planning and decision making.

Although all costs do not strictly conform to the categories just described, the categories represent the types of cost behavior typically encountered in business. Managers who understand cost behavior can better estimate total costs at various levels of activity.

COMPONENTS OF PRODUCT COST

In addition to being given a designation as to cost behavior, costs are classified as either product or period costs. Product costs relate to the products or services that generate an entity's revenues. These costs are either direct or indirect to a particular cost object. A **cost object** is anything to which management desires to attach costs or

cost object

direct costs
indirect costs
allocated
■ LEARNING
OBJECTIVE 2
Understand the relationship between cost objects and direct costs.

direct material

to which costs are related. A cost object can be a product or service, a department, a division, or a territory. Any costs that are clearly traceable to the cost object are called **direct costs.** Costs that cannot be traced are **indirect** (or common) **costs** and these costs can only be **allocated,** or assigned, to cost objects by use of one or more appropriate drivers, predictors, or arbitrarily chosen bases.[3] Product cost components can be designated as direct materials, direct labor, or factory overhead (an indirect cost).

Direct Materials

Any readily identifiable, physical part of a product that is clearly, conveniently, and economically traceable to that product is a **direct material.** Direct materials may be purchased raw materials or manufactured subassemblies.[4] Direct materials cost should theoretically include the cost of all materials used in manufacturing a product or performing a service. For example, the costs of the cream cheese, graham cracker crumbs, sugar, sour cream, butter, eggs, lemon juice, and vanilla would theoretically make up the direct materials cost for Jubilations' cheesecakes.

However, management may decide that the benefit of treating an insignificant cost as direct is not worth the clerical cost involved. Such costs are treated and classified as indirect costs. For instance, most accountants would agree that the cost of the

■ LEARNING
OBJECTIVE 3
Classify product costs into direct materials, direct labor, and factory overhead categories.

A primary direct material in Welch's grape juice is grapes. The cost of the grapes is a significant part of total product cost and can be conveniently traded to the output of the production process.

---

[3]Different cost objects may be designated for different decisions. As the cost object changes, the direct and indirect costs may also change. For instance, if a production division is specified as the cost object, the division manager's salary is direct. If, instead, the cost object is a sales territory and the production division operates in more than one territory, the division manager's salary is indirect.

[4]Outside processing cost may also be considered a direct material cost. For example, a furniture manufacturer may want a special plastic laminate on tables. Rather than buying the necessary equipment, the manufacturer may send the tables to another company that specializes in this process. The amount paid for this process may be considered a direct material cost by the manufacturer.

lemon juice is neither economically traceable nor monetarily significant to the cheesecake's production cost. Thus, this cost would probably be deemed an indirect material and included as a part of overhead.

Similarly, in a service business, some materials that could be traced to a cost object may have such an insignificant cost that they are not considered direct. For instance, a marketing firm needs to separately accumulate costs of each advertising campaign for each of its clients. When dummy boards (or mock-ups) of possible ads are created, artists use a variety of colored pens and pencils for design purposes. But the firm would probably not attempt to trace the costs of these items to a particular advertising campaign. The costs would be too insignificant and would be treated as overhead.

Direct Labor

Direct labor refers to the individuals who work specifically on manufacturing a product or performing a service. Their labor transforms raw materials or supplies into finished goods or completed services. Another perspective on direct labor is that it directly adds value to the final product or service. The crust former and mixer operator at Jubilations represent direct labor.

direct labor

Direct labor cost consists of wages or salaries paid to employees who work on a product or perform a service. Direct labor cost should include basic compensation, production efficiency bonuses, and the employer's share of social security taxes. In addition, when a company's operations are relatively stable, direct labor cost should include all employer-paid insurance costs, holiday and vacation pay, and pension and other retirement benefits.[5]

Direct labor cost is commonly viewed as a variable cost in Western cultures, but not necessarily in others. For example, in Japan, many workers have life-long employment contracts; thus, companies often treat direct labor costs as fixed. Because of a downturn in the Japanese economy, some companies are trying to modify this situation and trade these fixed costs for variable ones, as indicated in the News Note on page 94.

While direct labor cost is clearly traceable to a particular cost object, to be considered direct the cost must also be conveniently and economically traceable to the product or service. As with some materials, some labor costs that should theoretically be considered direct are treated as indirect for two reasons.

First, it might be cost-inefficient to trace the labor costs. For example, some employee fringe benefits should conceptually be treated as direct labor cost, but many companies do not have stable work forces and cannot develop a reasonable estimate of fringe benefit cost. Thus, the time, effort, and cost of trying to trace the fringe benefit costs might not be worth the additional accuracy that would be provided. In contrast, when fringe benefit costs are extremely high (such as for professional staff in a service organization), tracing them to products and services may provide more useful management information.

Second, erroneous information about product or service costs might result from handling such costs in the "theoretically" correct manner. An assumed payroll for one week at Jubilations, Inc., can illustrate this possibility. If each of Jubilations' six employees earns $6 per hour, time-and-a-half overtime pay would be $9 per hour. One week prior to a holiday, the employees worked a total of 300 hours, including 60

---

[5]Institute of Management Accountants (formerly National Association of Accountants), *Statements on Management Accounting Number 4C: Definition and Measurement of Direct Labor Cost* (Montvale, N.J.: National Association of Accountants, June 13, 1985), p. 4.

Lifetime Contracts Make Labor Cost Fixed

Recent business publications contend that Japan's current economic woes are compounded by the inability of companies to reduce their work forces due to lifetime employment practices.

Most Japanese companies understand the nature of their current problem. The typical Japanese company still views almost all of its costs, including labor, as fixed. To steer their way through the current recession, however, Japanese companies must focus on reducing all costs, which means changing their view on the fixed nature of personnel expenses.

One manufacturer is toying with the idea of putting everyone in its Japanese operations on a temporary contract. That is, anyone in the work force could be laid off as economic conditions dictate. To make this work, at the end of five months and 29 days, a worker would be dismissed for a day, then re-employed under a new five-month, 29-day contract. (Under Japanese labor practices, at the end of six months a worker becomes a "permanent" employee.) The company concedes that this would be easiest to apply to factory-floor workers. At any rate, the company says it will probably not be able to implement such a program because it is "too American" and it would be impossible to recruit and retain quality workers.

SOURCE: Douglas T. Shinsato, "Japan Tries to Get the Size Right," *Wall Street Journal* (June 28, 1993), p. A16. Reprinted by permission of The Wall Street Journal, © 1993 Dow Jones & Company, Inc. All Rights Reserved Worldwide.

hours of overtime to complete all the orders. Exhibit 3–5 presents the determination of how much of Jubilations' weekly payroll is direct labor and how much is overhead.

Cheesecake production is scheduled based on the size and flavor of the cakes. If the $3 per hour overtime premium were assigned to the cheesecakes produced during the overtime hours, the labor cost for these cakes would appear to be 50 percent greater than that for cakes manufactured during regular working hours. Since scheduling is

---

■ **EXHIBIT 3–5**

Payroll Analysis for Direct Labor and Overhead

Week's payroll information:

- 300 hours worked, of which 60 hours are overtime at time-and-a-half pay
- $6 per hour regular pay rate; applies to all hours worked (considered direct labor cost)
- $3 per hour overtime premium; applies only to the overtime hours (considered overhead)

Total hours for week	300	Overtime hours for week	60
× Regular pay rate per hour	× $6	×Overtime premium rate per hour	× $3
Direct labor cost (1)	$1,800	Factory overhead (2)	$180

Total payroll = $1,800 + $180 = $1,980

(1) The $1,800 direct labor cost is assigned directly to all cheesecakes made during the week, regardless of whether they were made during regular hours or overtime hours.

(2) The $180 of factory overhead cost is considered overhead and will be assigned, by indirect means that are described later, to all products made by Jubilations, Inc., over a longer period.

random, the cakes made during overtime hours should not be forced to bear the overtime charges. Therefore, amounts incurred for costs such as overtime or shift premiums are usually considered overhead rather than direct labor cost and are allocated to all cakes.

There are occasions, however, when allocating costs such as overtime to all units is not appropriate. If a customer requests a job to be scheduled during overtime hours or is in a rush and requests that overtime be worked, overtime or shift premiums should be considered direct labor and be attached to the job that created the costs.

The proportion of direct labor cost to total product cost has been slowly declining in many industries, especially over the past 25 years.[6] Now, in many highly automated production environments, "[i]t is not uncommon to find that direct labor accounts for only 8%-12% of total cost at many manufacturers. This trend is even more pronounced when one considers current forecasts relating to the factory of the future."[7] Eventually, managers may find that almost all direct labor cost is replaced with a new cost of production—the cost of robots and other fully automated machinery. Thus, while labor may still be an essential element of production in some industries, managers should resist overstating the importance of labor cost in a technically advanced setting.

Factory Overhead

Factory overhead is any factory or production cost that is not directly or conveniently traceable to manufacturing a product or providing a service.[8] Factory overhead costs are essential to the conversion process. "The great part of most companies' costs (other than those for purchased materials) typically occurs in overhead categories. Even in manufacturing, more than two-thirds of all nonmaterial costs tend to be indirect or overhead expenses."[9]

While direct materials and direct labor are generally variable in relation to production volume, factory overhead costs may be variable, mixed, or fixed. Variable factory overhead includes the cost of indirect materials and indirect labor paid on an hourly basis, such as wages for forklift operators, material handlers, and others who support the production, assembly, and/or service process. Also included in variable factory overhead are the costs of oil and grease used for machine maintenance, paper towels used in the factory rest rooms, and the variable portion of utility charges (or any other mixed cost) for the conversion area. Depreciation calculated using the units-of-production method is a variable factory overhead cost.

Fixed factory overhead comprises costs such as straight-line and declining-balance depreciation and insurance and property taxes on production/service-providing assets. Fixed indirect factory labor cost includes salaries for production supervisors, shift superintendents, and service managers. The fixed portion of mixed costs (such as maintenance and utilities) incurred in the conversion area is also part of fixed factory overhead.

---

[6]Germain Böer, "Five Modern Management Accounting Myths," *Management Accounting* (January 1994), p. 22, 24.

[7]James A. Brimson, "How Advanced Manufacturing Technologies Are Reshaping Cost Management," *Management Accounting* (March 1986), p. 27.

[8]Another term used for overhead is burden. The authors believe that this term is unacceptable, as it connotes costs that are extra, unnecessary, or oppressive.

[9]James Brian Quinn et al., "Beyond Products: Services-based Strategy," *Harvard Business Review* (March-April 1990), p. 65.

prevention costs

appraisal costs

failure costs

Customer satisfaction is an important measure of quality. The money spent to determine the level of customer satisfaction is an appraisal cost to a company. Appraisal costs are incurred to assess areas in which the company may need to increase prevention and/or to eliminate potential future areas of failure.

Quality Costs

An important category of factory overhead cost is that related to quality. There are two basic categories of quality costs: the costs of conformance and the cost of non-comformance. Exhibit 3–6 lists specific examples of these quality costs.

The costs of conformance include prevention and appraisal costs. **Prevention costs** are incurred to improve quality by preventing defects and dysfunctional processing from occurring. Amounts spent on training programs, researching customer needs, and improved production equipment are considered prevention costs. Amounts spent for monitoring or inspection are called **appraisal costs;** these costs are intended to discover the mistakes that were not eliminated through prevention activities. Prevention and appraisal costs are incurred with the intention of eliminating the present costs of failure and maintaining that zero level in the future; thus, they are proactive on management's part. Furthermore, effective use of prevention costs can minimize the costs of appraisal.

In contrast, costs of nonconformance are the *results* of production imperfections that have occurred. This category encompasses all **failure costs,** which may be internal (such as scrap and rework) or external (such as product returns caused by quality problems, warranty costs, and complaint department costs). As indicated in the News Note on page 98, the size of failure costs can be substantial.

In trying to determine the cost of quality, companies must develop actual or estimated costs for each item listed in Exhibit 3–6. If these costs were plotted on a graph, they would look similar to the cost curves shown in Exhibit 3–7 (page 98). If the firm spends larger amounts on prevention and appraisal costs, the number of defects are lower and the costs of failure are smaller. If less is spent on prevention and appraisal, the number of defects are greater and failure costs are larger. The external failure costs curve begins moving toward vertical when a certain number of defects are encountered by customers. The ultimate external failure cost is reached when customers will no longer buy a given product or any other products made by a particular firm because it produces such poor-quality work.

It has been estimated that the price of conformance for a well-run company is 2 to 3 percent of sales, while the price of nonconformance is 20 to 25 percent of sales.[10] Exhibit 3–8 (page 99) contrasts the traditional and emerging views of quality costs. The traditional view argues that, from a cost control perspective, the optimal level of quality to achieve is the one that generates the lowest cost. This optimal level may be below the highest attainable quality level. Accordingly, the quality cost curve is U-shaped. The alternative, emerging view of quality is that higher quality always leads to lower costs. Thus, the more current view depicts quality costs as a constantly decreasing function of quality; as the achieved quality level increases, costs are reduced.

By developing a system in which quality costs are readily available or determinable, the management accountant is able to provide useful information. Managers who are trying to make spending decisions by pinpointing the areas that provide the highest cost-benefit relationships need information on quality costs. Additionally, quality cost information indicates how a shift in one or more curves will affect the others.

[10]Philip B. Crosby, *Quality Without Tears* (New York: McGraw-Hill, 1984), p. 86.

■ **EXHIBIT 3–6**

Types of Quality Costs

COSTS OF CONFORMANCE		COSTS OF NONCONFORMANCE	
Prevention Costs	*Appraisal Costs*	*Internal Failure Costs*	*External Failure Costs*
Employees: ■ Hiring for quality ■ Training and establishing awareness ■ Establishing participation programs *Customers:* ■ Surveying needs ■ Researching needs ■ Conducting field trials *Machinery:* ■ Designing to detect defects ■ Arranging for efficient flow ■ Arranging for monitoring ■ Implementing preventive maintenance ■ Testing and adjusting equipment ■ Fitting machinery for mistake-proof operations *Suppliers:* ■ Arranging for quality ■ Educating suppliers ■ Involving suppliers *Product Design:* ■ Developing specifications ■ Engineering and modeling ■ Testing and adjusting for conformity, effective and efficient performance, durability, ease of use, safety, comfort, appeal, and cost	*Before Production:* ■ Receiving inspection for parts and materials *Production Process:* ■ Monitoring and inspecting ■ Keeping the process consistent, stable, and reliable ■ Using procedure verification ■ Automating *During and After Production:* ■ Performing quality audits *Information Process:* ■ Recording and reporting defects ■ Measuring performance *Organization:* ■ Administering quality control department	*Product:* ■ Reworking ■ Producing defects or waste ■ Storing and disposing of spoilage and waste ■ Reinspecting rework *Production Process:* ■ Reprocessing ■ Having unscheduled interruptions ■ Experiencing unplanned downtime	*Organization:* ■ Staffing complaint departments ■ Staffing warranty claims departments *Customers:* ■ Losing future sales ■ Losing reputation ■ Losing goodwill *Product:* ■ Repairing ■ Replacing ■ Reimbursing ■ Recalling ■ Litigating *Service:* ■ Providing unplanned service ■ Expediting ■ Following up on nonconforming prior service

Peeling Paint Peels Away Profits

Ford Motor Co. executives say they want to bond with their customers. But many Ford owners say they wish the company had bonded the paint to their vehicles.

F-Series pickups are currently the best-selling vehicle in the U.S. But peeling paint on 1985-91 models and on other Ford vehicles could cost the auto maker as much as $1.5 billion over two years, according to former employees, dealers and industry experts.

Ford has traced the paint problem to a new process for eliminating corrosion, which caused certain exterior paint colors to peel if exposed to too much sunlight. Ford says several years ago it reformulated the paint to provide greater protection against sunlight. But sources say there have been complaints about peeling paint on recent-model vehicles. Ford says repainting costs $1,500 to $2,000 a truck.

[As of January 1, 1994, Ford decided] to give customers just 60 days to claim a new paint job once they receive a customer survey. The response time was formerly open-ended.

Industry analysts say Ford has good reason to put a cap on its exposure to claims on paint jobs. The company has already spent $800 million repainting F-Series pickups and Bronco sport utility vehicles in the 1993 model year, individuals familiar with the program say. That cut per-vehicle profits on the new vehicles Ford sold [in 1993] by an average of $231 each. Ford is expected to spend at least another $800 million in the [1994] model year for paint repairs—more than it spent to develop the new Mustang.

SOURCE: Jacqueline Mitchell, "Peeling Paint on Ford Trucks Becomes Costly," *Wall Street Journal* (March 15, 1994), p. B1. Reprinted by persmission of The Wall Street Journal, ©1994 Dow Jones & Company, Inc. All Rights Reserved Worldwide.

■ **EXHIBIT 3–7**
Relationships Among Quality Costs

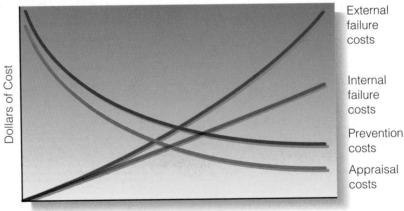

SOURCE: William R. Pasewark, "The Evolution of Quality Control Costs in U.S. Manufacturing, *Journal of Cost Management* (Spring 1991), p. 48. Reprinted with permission from the Journal of Cost Management for the Manufacturing Industry, © 1991, Warren, Gorham & Lamont, 31 St. James Avenue, Boston, MA 02116. All rights reserved.

Exhibit 3–9 (page 100) shows the location in the production-sales cycle where each type of quality cost is usually incurred. Note in this exhibit that an information feedback loop should link appraisal and failure costs to prevention costs. Through this feedback loop, alert managers and employees continuously monitor the nature of nonconformities to discover their causes and adjust prevention activities to close the gaps that allowed the nonconformities to occur. These continuous rounds of action, reaction, and action are essential to continuous improvement initiatives.

In manufacturing, quality costs may be variable in relation to the quantity of defective output, step fixed with increases at specific levels of defective output, or fixed. For example, scrap and rework costs are almost zero if almost no defective output is

■ **EXHIBIT 3–8**

Comparison of Traditional and Emerging Views of Quality Costs

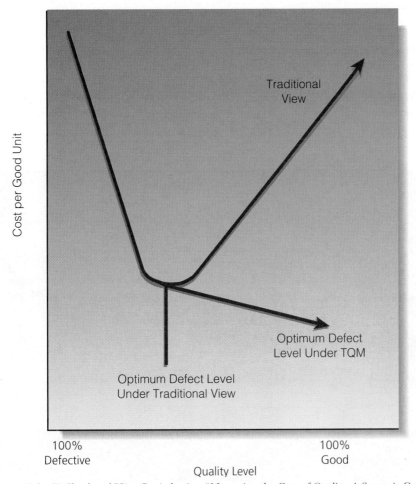

SOURCE: John K. Shank and Vijay Govindarajan, "Measuring the Cost of Quality: A Strategic Cost Management Perspective," *Journal of Cost Management* (Summer 1994), p. 6. Reprinted with permission from the Journal of Cost Management for the Manufacturing Industry, © 1994, Warren, Gorham & Lamont, 31 St. James Avenue, Boston, MA 02116. All rights reserved.

■ **EXHIBIT 3–9**

Time-Phased Model for Quality Costs

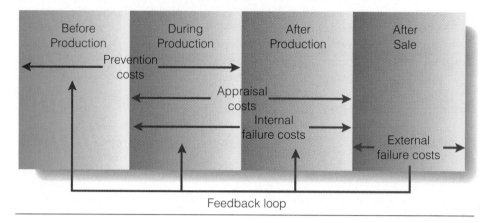

produced. However, these costs would be extremely high if defective production was also quite high. "Training expenditures, on the other hand, would not vary regardless of the quantity of defective output produced in a given time period."[11] Regardless of the type of cost behavior, companies are learning that spending money on prevention is easier than having to pay to correct problems later.

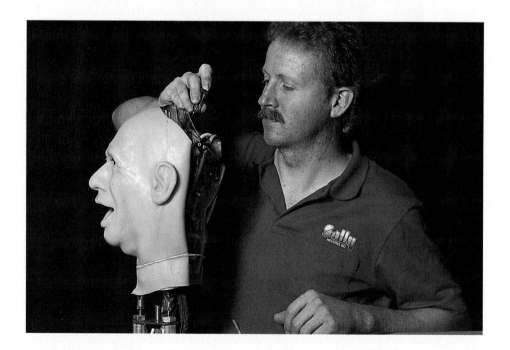

At Sally Industries in Jacksonville, Florida, a substantial portion of both prime and conversion cost is the cost of direct labor. It takes skilled craftspeople to design and produce the wide variety of robotic (animatronic) characters for companies such as MCA Universal.

---

[11]Lawrence A. Poneman, "Accounting for Quality Costs," *Journal of Cost Management* (Fall 1990), p. 46.

The sum of direct materials, direct labor, variable overhead, and fixed overhead costs comprises total product cost.[12] Product costs can also be classified as either prime or conversion costs. According to generally accepted accounting principles, product costs are inventoriable until the products are sold or otherwise disposed of.

Prime and Conversion Costs

The total cost of direct materials and direct labor is referred to as **prime cost** because these costs are most convincingly associated with and traceable to a specific product. **Conversion cost** is defined as "the sum of direct labor and factory overhead which is directly or indirectly necessary for transforming raw materials and purchased parts into a salable finished product."[13] Since direct labor is included as part of both prime cost and conversion cost, prime cost plus conversion cost does not sum to product cost. Exhibit 3–10 shows the typical components of product cost for a manufacturing company in terms of prime and conversion costs.

prime cost

conversion cost

■ **EXHIBIT 3–10**
Components of Product Cost

PRIME COST

CONVERSION COST

Direct Materials

Direct Labor

Factory Overhead
    Variable Overhead Components
        Indirect materials
        Indirect labor (hourly wages)
        Variable portion of mixed costs
            (including quality costs)
        Other variable factory costs
    Fixed Overhead Components
        Rent
        Depreciation
        Indirect labor (salaried employees)
        Licenses
        Taxes
        Insurance
        Fixed portion of mixed costs
            (including quality costs)
        Other fixed factory costs

[12]This definition of product cost is traditionally accepted and is also referred to as absorption costing. Another product costing method, called variable costing, excludes the fixed factory overhead component from inventories. Absorption and variable costing are compared in Chapter 8.

[13]Institute of Management Accountants (formerly National Association of Accountants), *Statements on Management Accounting Number 2: Management Accounting Terminology* (Montvale, N.J.: National Association of Accountants, June 1, 1983), p. 24.

ACCUMULATION OF PRODUCT COSTS

The financial accounting concept of periodicity requires that financial statements be prepared at regular intervals. The balance sheet lists all assets owned by an entity, while the income statement reflects income for a specified period of time. Assets are items of future benefit, having either an exchange value or an ability to generate revenues or reduce costs. Because of the financial accounting requirement to produce financial statements, costs must be designated as unexpired (assets) or expired (expenses or losses). As assets (unexpired costs) are exchanged, consumed, or lost, they become expenses or losses (expired costs). Such costs must be properly classified on the financial statements. Unexpired period costs are typically shown as prepaid assets or plant and equipment. Expired period costs are operating expenses and comprise the selling and administrative expense categories. Unexpired product costs that reflect raw materials, goods in process, or completed goods must be shown as inventory; upon sale, these assets become expired product costs and are shown as cost of goods sold in determination of gross profit or gross margin. Other unexpired product costs may be shown as prepaid expenses (for example, prepaid insurance or taxes on a factory building) or as plant and equipment costs.

Product costs may be accumulated for inventory purposes and expensed to Cost of Goods Sold using either a periodic or a perpetual inventory system. In either system, all product costs flow through Work in Process Inventory to Finished Goods Inventory and, ultimately, to Cost of Goods Sold. The periodic system provides beginning-of-the-period information in the inventory accounts during the period; information is updated only after physical inventories have been taken (or estimates of these quantitites made) at financial statement dates. In contrast, the perpetual system continuously provides current inventory and cost of goods sold information for financial statement preparation and for inventory planning, cost control, and decision making. Because the costs of maintaining a perpetual system have fallen significantly as computerized production, bar-coding, and information processing have become more pervasive, this text will assume that all companies discussed use the perpetual inventory method.

Hypothetical information for Jubilations, Inc., is used to illustrate the flow of product costs in a manufacturing organization. The May 1, 1996, inventory account balances for the company are as follows: Raw Materials (all direct), $2,500; Work in Process, $1,040; and Finished Goods, $1,890. The company uses separate variable and fixed accounts to record the incurrence of overhead. Such separation of information improves the accuracy of tracking and controlling costs. Actual overhead costs are transferred at the end of the month to the Work in Process Inventory account. The following transactions, keyed to the journal entries in Exhibit 3–11, represent Jubilations' activity for a month.

During May, Jubilations' purchasing agent bought $22,400 of direct materials on account (entry 1), and $18,800 of materials were transferred into the production area (entry 2). Production wages for the month totaled $6,500; direct labor accounted for $5,000 of that amount (entry 3). May salary for the production supervisor was $3,000 (entry 4). The total utility cost for May was $520; analyzing this cost indicated that $410 of this amount was variable and $110 was fixed (entry 5). Indirect materials costing $1,300 were removed from the inventory of factory supplies and placed into the production process (entry 6). Jubilations also paid $600 for May's food licenses (entry 7), depreciated the factory assets $22,500 (entry 8), and recorded the expiration of $1,000 of prepaid insurance on the factory assets (entry 9). Entry 10 shows the trans-

■ **EXHIBIT 3-11**

Flow of Product Costs Through Accounts

(1) Raw Materials Inventory	22,400	
Accounts Payable		22,400
To record cost of direct materials purchased on account.		
(2) Work in Process Inventory	18,800	
Raw Materials Inventory		18,800
To record direct materials transferred to production.		
(3) Work in Process Inventory	5,000	
Variable Factory Overhead	1,500	
Salaries and Wages Payable		6,500
To accrue factory wages for direct and indirect labor.		
(4) Fixed Factory Overhead	3,000	
Salaries and Wages Payable		3,000
To accrue production supervisor's salary.		
(5) Variable Factory Overhead	410	
Fixed Factory Overhead	110	
Utilities Payable		520
To record mixed factory utility cost in its variable and fixed proportions.		
(6) Variable Factory Overhead	1,300	
Factory Supplies Inventory		1,300
To record indirect materials used.		
(7) Fixed Factory Overhead	600	
Cash		600
To record payments for food licenses for the period.		
(8) Fixed Factory Overhead	22,500	
Accumulated Depreciation-Factory Equipment		22,500
To record depreciation on factory assets for the period.		
(9) Fixed Factory Overhead	1,000	
Prepaid Factory Insurance		1,000
To record expiration of prepaid insurance on factory assets.		
(10) Work in Process Inventory	30,420	
Variable Factory Overhead		3,210
Fixed Factory Overhead		27,210
To record the transfer of actual overhead costs to Work in Process Inventory.		
(11) Finished Goods Inventory	52,450	
Work in Process Inventory		52,450
To record the transfer of work completed during the period.		
(12) Accounts Receivable	74,670	
Sales		74,670
To record the sale of goods on account during the period.		
(13) Cost of Goods Sold	51,315	
Finished Goods Inventory		51,315
To record cost of goods sold for the period		

fer of actual overhead to Work in Process Inventory. During May, $52,450 of goods were completed and transferred to Finished Goods (entry 11). Sales on account of $74,670 were recorded during the month (entry 12); the goods that were sold had a total cost of $51,315 (entry 13).

As illustrated in the T-accounts in Exhibit 3–12, the perpetual inventory system provides detailed information about the cost of raw materials used, goods completed, and goods sold. From this information, formal financial statements can be prepared.

COST OF GOODS MANUFACTURED AND SOLD

■ LEARNING OBJECTIVE 5
Calculate cost of goods manufactured.

cost of goods manufactured (CGM)

In merchandising businesses, cost of goods sold (CGS) is presented as beginning merchandise inventory plus net purchases minus ending merchandise inventory. Manufacturing businesses cannot use such a simplistic approach to calculate cost of goods sold. The production costs incurred during the period relate both to goods that were completed and to goods that are still in process. Therefore, a manufacturer prepares a schedule of **cost of goods manufactured (CGM)** as a preliminary step to the presentation of CGS. CGM represents the total production cost of the goods that were completed and transferred to Finished Goods Inventory during the period. This amount does not include the cost of work still in process at the end of the period. The schedule of cost of goods manufactured allows managers to see the relationships among the various production costs and to know the results of the cost flows through the inventory accounts. It is prepared only as an internal schedule and is not provided to external parties.

■ EXHIBIT 3–12
Selected T-Accounts for Jubilations, Inc.

Raw Materials Inventory

Beg. Bal.	2,500	(11)	18,800
(1)	22,400		
End. bal.	6,100		

Variable Factory Overhead

(3)	1,500	(10)	3,210
(5)	410		
(6)	1,300		

Work in Process Inventory

Beg. bal.	1,040	(11)	52,450
(2)	18,800		
(3)	5,000		
(10)	30,420		
End bal.	2,810		

Fixed Factory Overhead

(4)	3,000	(10)	27,210
(5)	110		
(7)	600		
(8)	22,500		
(9)	1,000		

Finished Goods Inventory

Beg. bal.	1,890	(13)	51,315
(11)	52,450		
End. bal.	3,025		

Cost of Goods Sold

(13)	51,315	

Using the information given in the previous section, the CGM and CGS schedules based on the information given in the previous section for Jubilations, Inc., are shown in Exhibit 3–13. The schedule of cost of goods manufactured reflects the manufacturing activity as summarized in the Work in Process Inventory account. It first presents the beginning balance of Work in Process Inventory; the details of all product cost components added during the period (direct materials, direct labor, variable

---

■ **EXHIBIT 3–13**

Cost of Goods Manufactured and Cost of Goods Sold Schedules

Jubilations, Inc.
Schedule of Cost of Goods Manufactured
For Month Ended May 31, 1996

Beginning balance of Work in Process, 5/1/96			$ 1,040
Manufacturing costs for the period:			
Raw Materials (all direct)			
Beginning balance	$ 2,500		
Purchases of materials	22,400		
Raw materials available for use	$24,900		
Ending balance	(6,100)		
Total raw materials used		$18,800	
Direct labor		5,000	
Variable overhead			
Indirect labor	$ 1,500		
Utilities	410		
Supplies	1,300	3,210	
Fixed overhead			
Supervisor's salary	$ 3,000		
Utilities	110		
Food licenses	600		
Factory asset depreciation	22,500		
Factory insurance	1,000	27,210	
Total current period manufacturing costs			54,220
Total costs to account for			$55,260
Ending balance of Work in Process, 5/31/96			(2,810)
Cost of goods manufactured			$52,450

Jubilations, Inc.
Schedule of Cost of Goods Sold
For Month Ended May 31, 1996

Beginning balance of Finished Goods, 5/1/96	$ 1,890
Cost of Goods Manufactured	52,450
Cost of Goods Available for Sale	$54,340
Ending balance of Finished Goods, 5/31/96	(3,025)
Cost of Goods Sold	$51,315

overhead, and fixed overhead) are shown next. Following are brief descriptions of each element of the CGM schedule.

The cost of direct materials used in production during the period is equal to beginning balance of Raw Materials Inventory plus raw materials purchased minus the ending Raw Materials Inventory. Direct labor cost is determined from payroll records of the period and is added to the cost of direct materials used. Since direct labor cannot be warehoused, all charges for direct labor during the period become part of Work in Process Inventory. Variable and fixed overhead costs are added to the prime costs of production to represent total current period manufacturing costs.

Adding beginning Work in Process Inventory and total current period manufacturing costs provides a subtotal that can be referred to as "total costs to account for." The value of ending Work in Process Inventory is calculated (through techniques discussed later in the text) and subtracted from the subtotal to provide the cost of the goods that were manufactured during the period.

To calculate Cost of Goods Sold, Cost of Goods Manufactured is first added to the beginning balance of Finished Goods Inventory to determine the cost of goods available for sale during the period. Ending Finished Goods Inventory is subtracted next to yield Cost of Goods Sold. The ending finished goods inventory amount is calculated by multiplying a physical unit count times a unit cost. Under a perpetual inventory system, the balance shown in Finished Goods Inventory at the end of the period should be compared with the inventory that is actually on hand. Any differences can be attributed to loss factors such as theft, breakage, or recording errors. Major differences between the amount of inventory shown in the accounting records and the actual amount of inventory on hand should be investigated.

SITE ANALYSIS

In her entrepreneurial role, Ms. Craddock took advantage of information from Mississippi State University's Food and Fiber Center. The center helped her locate contacts and supplies and put together a workable business plan. Because she chose to use only fresh ingredients (never any prepackaged mixes or powders), Ms. Craddock recognized that her direct materials costs would be slightly higher than if she used lower-quality materials. But she believes the quality is worth the cost. Her all-female crew is hard-working and ready to provide ideas for ways to improve either the recipes or the processes. Good ideas are rewarded monetarily to encourage a continual flow of them.

Overhead costs must be kept under control at Jubilations, Inc., if the company is to provide a large enough gross margin to cover the numerous selling and administrative costs. As order quantities rise, the need to acquire additional equipment emerges, creating higher depreciation costs. At some point, Ms. Craddock may find that "Sweet 8" of Building 7 is too small to accommodate the increasing production volume and that a larger space at a higher rent is needed. Ms. Craddock has invested in prevention and appraisal quality costs by having the right equipment and training employees so that internal and external failure costs are minimized.

In her roles as salesperson, advertising person, bookkeeper, and personnel manager, Tamara Craddock has learned to intimately understand the details of her business operations. She is aware of what costs are incurred in her business, how they react to production volume changes, and what their underlying drivers are. This knowledge has served Ms. Craddock well—her profitable business has expanded to all fifty states.

SOURCE: Interview with Tamara Craddock, 1994.

CHAPTER SUMMARY

This chapter introduces terminology used by managers and management accountants and presents the flow of costs in a manufacturing environment. Variable costs are constant per unit but fluctuate in total with changes in activity levels within the relevant range. Fixed costs are constant in total as activity levels change within the relevant range, but vary inversely on a per-unit basis with changes in activity levels. The relevant range is generally the company's normal operating range. Step variable costs have small steps and are treated as variable costs; step fixed costs have large steps and are treated as fixed costs. Mixed costs have both a variable and a fixed element.

A predictor is an activity measure that changes in a consistent, observable way with changes in a cost. A cost driver is an activity measure that has a direct causal effect on a cost.

Direct costs are so defined because they are traceable to a specific cost object. Because indirect costs cannot be explicitly traced to a cost object, allocation techniques can be used to assign such costs to related cost objects. Materials and labor may be directly or indirectly related to particular products, but factory overhead costs are indirect and must be allocated to the products produced.

Quality costs are part of overhead. There are two broad categories of quality costs: conformance and nonconformance. Conformance costs include costs of prevention and of appraisal. Nonconformance costs are separated into internal and external failure costs. Businesses incur quality conformance costs to eliminate, to the extent possible, the current costs of quality failure and to strive for a zero level of failure in the future.

Cost of goods manufactured is the total cost of the goods completed and transferred to finished goods during the period. This computation is prepared for internal management information and is presented on a schedule that supports the cost of goods sold computation on the income statement.

APPENDIX

Income Statement Comparisons

The income statements of merchandising, manufacturing, and service businesses are basically the same except for differences in the cost of goods sold section. A merchandising company has only one inventory account and, thus, Cost of Goods Sold reflects only changes within the Merchandise Inventory account. A manufacturing organization has three inventory accounts, and the cost of goods sold section of its income statement depicts the changes in Finished Goods Inventory. A manufacturer supports its cost of goods sold computation with an internal schedule of cost of goods manufactured (CGM) for the period. The CGM replaces the purchases amount used by merchandisers. A service company computes the Cost of Services Rendered instead of Cost of Goods Sold. Illustrations of income statements for each type of business follow using assumed amounts. Balance sheets are not shown because the only differences are in the number and titles of inventory accounts.

■ **LEARNING OBJECTIVE 6**
(Appendix) Understand the differences in income statement of merchandising, manufacturing, and service businesses.

CATLETT DEPARTMENT STORE
Income Statement
For the Year Ended December 31, 1996

Net Sales		$5,840,000
Cost of Goods Sold		
Merchandise inventory, 1/1/96	$ 922,000	
Cost of purchases	4,040,000	
Total merchandise available for sale	$4,962,000	
Less: Merchandise inventory, 12/31/96	(900,000)	
Cost of goods sold		(4,062,000)
Gross Margin on Sales		$1,778,000
Operating Expenses		
Selling expenses	$ 898,000	
Administrative expenses	628,000	(1,526,000)
Income from Operations		$ 252,000
Other Income		
Dividend income	$ 17,000	
Rental income	5,820	$ 22,820
Other Expenses		
Interest on bonds and notes	(52,120)	(29,300)
Income before Income Taxes		$ 222,700
Income Taxes		(86,680)
Net Income		$ 136,020
Earnings per share (assume 100,000 shares outstanding)		$1.36

GERALD MANUFACTURING COMPANY
Income Statement
For the Year Ended December 31, 1996

Sales		$9,000,000
Cost of Goods Sold		
Beginning inventory of finished goods	$ 180,000	
Cost of goods manufactured (see below)	6,000,000	
Cost of goods available for sale	$6,180,000	
Less: Ending inventory of finished goods	(164,000)	
Cost of goods sold		(6,016,000)
Gross Margin on Sales		$2,984,000
Operating Expenses		
Selling expenses (similar to items detailed for merchandising company)	$ 900,000	
Administrative expenses (similar to items detailed for merchandising company)	540,000	(1,440,000)
Income from Operations		$1,544,000
Other Expenses		
Interest on notes		(44,000)

Income before Income Taxes		$1,500,000
Income Taxes		(680,000)
Net Income		$ 820,000
Earnings per share (assume 500,000 shares outstanding)		$1.64

Schedule of Cost of Goods Manufactured
For the Year Ended December 31, 1996

Beginning Work in Process			$ 600,000
Manufacturing costs for the period			
Raw Materials (all direct)			
Beginning inventory	$ 350,000		
Purchases	3,400,000		
Total materials available	$3,750,000		
Ending inventory	400,000		
Raw materials used		$3,350,000	
Direct Labor		1,800,000	
Variable Overhead		400,000	
Fixed Overhead		350,000	5,900,000
Total Cost to Account For			$6,500,000
Ending Work in Process			(500,000)
Cost of Goods Manufactured			$6,000,000

REEVES ADVERTISING AGENCY
Income Statement
For the Year Ended December 31, 1996

Service Revenue		$3,600,000
Cost of Services Rendered		
Direct labor	$1,350,000	
Supplies used	67,500	
Service department overhead	355,500	(1,773,000)
Gross Margin on Services		$1,827,000
Operating Expenses		
Selling expenses (similar to items detailed for merchandising company)	$ 262,500	
Administrative expenses (similar to items detailed for merchandising company)	780,000	(1,042,500)
Income from Operations		$ 784,500
Interest Expense		(123,000)
Income before Income Taxes		$ 661,500
Income Taxes		(185,220)
Net Income		$ 476,280
Earnings per share (assume 100,000 shares outstanding)		$4.76

GLOSSARY

Allocate (p. 92)   assign based on the use of a cost predictor or an arbitrary method

Appraisal cost (p. 96)   a quality control cost incurred for monitoring or inspection; compensates for mistakes not eliminated through prevention

Conversion cost (p. 101)   the sum of direct labor and factory overhead costs; the cost incurred in changing direct materials or supplies into finished products or services

Cost (p. 84)   a monetary measure of the resources given up to acquire a good or a service

Cost behavior (p. 85)   the manner in which a cost responds to a change in a related level of activity

Cost driver (p. 86)   a factor that has a direct cause-effect relationship to a cost

Cost object (p. 91)   anything to which costs attach or are related

Cost of goods manufactured (CGM) (p. 104)   the total cost of the goods that were completed and transferred to Finished Goods Inventory during the period

Direct cost (p. 92)   a cost that is clearly, conveniently, and economically traceable to a particular cost object

Direct labor (p. 93)   the time spent by individuals who work specifically on manufacturing a product or performing a service and whose efforts are conveniently and economically traceable to that product or service

Direct material (p. 92)   a readily identifiable, physical part of a product that is conveniently and economically traceable to that product

Failure cost (p. 96)   a quality control cost associated with goods or services that have been found not to conform or perform in accordance with the required standards, as well as all related costs (such as that of the complaint department); may be internal or external

Fixed cost (p. 88)   a cost that remains constant in total within a specified range of activity

Indirect cost (p. 92)   a cost that cannot be clearly traced to a particular cost object; a common cost; a cost that must be allocated to a cost object

Mixed cost (p. 90)   a cost that has both a variable and a fixed component; it does not fluctuate in direct proportion to changes in activity, nor does it remain constant with changes in activity

Outsource (p. 89)   use a source external to the company to provide a service or manufacture a needed product or component

Predictor (p. 86)   an activity measure that changes in a consistent, observable manner with changes in another item

Prevention cost (p. 96)   a quality control cost incurred to improve quality by preventing defects from occurring

Prime cost (p. 101)   the sum of direct materials costs and direct labor costs

Relevant range (p. 86)   the specified range of activity over which a variable cost remains constant per unit or a fixed cost remains fixed in total

Step cost (p. 90)   a variable or fixed cost that shifts upward or downward when activity changes by a certain interval or step

Variable cost (p. 87)   a cost that varies in total in direct proportion to changes in activity

SOLUTION STRATEGIES

Cost of Goods Manufactured

Beginning balance of Work in Process Inventory		XXX
Manufacturing costs for the period		
Raw Materials (all direct)		
Beginning balance	X	
Purchases of materials	+ XX	
Raw materials available for use	XXX	

Ending balance	- XX	
Total raw materials used		XXX
Direct labor	+ XX	
Variable factory overhead	+ XX	
Fixed factory overhead	+ XXX	
Total current period manufacturing costs		+ XXXX
Total costs to account for		XXXX
Ending balance of Work in Process Inventory		- XX
Cost of Goods Manufactured		XXXX

Cost of Goods Sold

Beginning balance of Finished Goods Inventory	XX
Cost of goods manufactured	+ XXXX
Cost of goods available for sale	XXXX
Ending balance of Finished Goods Inventory	- X
Cost of Goods Sold	XXXX

FLOW OF COSTS

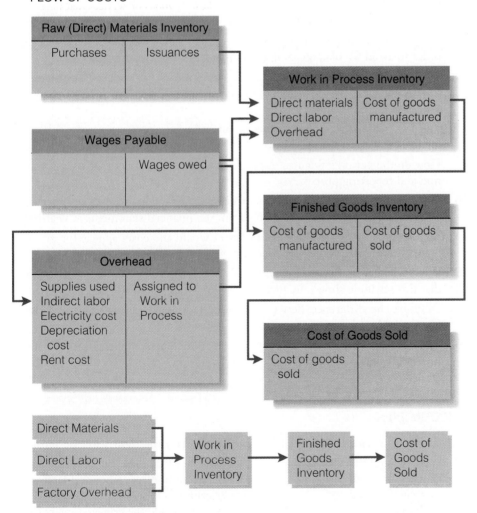

END-OF-CHAPTER MATERIALS

■ QUESTIONS

1. Why must the word *cost* be accompanied by an adjective to be meaningful?
2. Why is the relevant range important to managers?
3. How do predictors and cost drivers differ? Why is the distinction important?
4. What is the distinction between a fixed cost and a variable cost?
5. What is a mixed cost? How do mixed costs behave with changes in the activity measure?
6. What is a step cost? Explain the distinction between a step fixed and a step variable cost.
7. With respect to a specific cost object, what is the difference between a direct cost and an indirect cost?
8. What is a product cost? What are the three general categories of product costs?
9. What specific costs are usually included in direct labor cost?
10. Over the past decade or so, which product cost category has been growing most rapidly? Why?
11. What are the two basic categories of quality costs, and how are they related?
12. Discuss why a company might logically prefer to incur $X of prevention costs in order to avoid $Y of external failure costs, if $X were greater than $Y.
13. "Prime costs and conversion costs are components of product cost; therefore, the sum of these two cost categories is equal to product cost." Is this statement true or false? Explain.
14. What is meant by the term *conversion cost* and what product costs does the term include?
15. How do the periodic financial reporting requirements affect the cost accumulation and reporting process?
16. What is the difference between an expired and an unexpired product cost? Where would each type of cost appear in the financial statements at year-end?
17. At year-end, where on the Balance Sheet would the costs appear for products that had been placed into production but were not finished?
18. What is included on the Cost of Goods Manufactured schedule? Why is it said that this schedule shows the flow of costs in a manufacturing company?
19. Describe the difference between Cost of Goods Manufactured and Cost of Goods Sold.
20. *(Appendix)* Describe the major differences in income statement formats among merchandising, manufacturing, and service businesses.

■ EXERCISES

21. (LO 1, 2, 3; *Terminology*) Match the definitions on the right with the terms on the left. Definitions may be used more than once or not at all.

   a. Cost of goods manufactured
   b. Expired cost

   1. The sum of direct labor and factory overhead
   2. A cost outside the conversion area

c. Overhead

d. Conversion cost

e. Mixed cost
f. Unexpired cost

g. Indirect cost

h. Product cost
i. Period cost

j. Direct cost

k. Prime cost

l. Outsource
m. Cost driver

3. A factor that causes a cost to be incurred
4. A cost that has both a variable and a fixed component
5. The process of using external suppliers
6. The sum of direct materials and direct labor
7. A cost that cannot be traced to a particular cost object
8. A cost that has no future benefit
9. The total cost of products finished during the period
10. A cost that is clearly traceable to a particular object
11. The total of all nontraceable costs necessary to make a product or perform a service
12. An expense or a loss
13. An inventoriable cost

22. (LO 1; *Cost behavior*) Indicate whether each of the following items is a variable (V), fixed (F), or mixed (M) cost with respect to production volume; and whether it is a product or service (PT) cost or a period (PD) cost. If some items have alternative answers, indicate the alternatives and the reasons for them.

   a. Wages of forklift operators who move materials along an assembly line
   b. Hand soap used in factory restrooms
   c. Utility costs incurred at manufacturing company headquarters
   d. Drafting paper used in an architectural firm
   e. Cost of company labels attached to shirts made by a firm
   f. Wages of quality control inspectors at a factory
   g. Insurance premiums on raw materials warehouses
   h. Salaries of staff auditors in a CPA firm
   i. Cost of clay to make pottery
   j. Wages of carpenters in a construction company

23. (LO 1, 2, 3; *Cost behavior, product cost category*) Classify the following factory costs incurred in manufacturing bicycles as direct materials, direct labor, or factory overhead; and indicate whether each cost is most likely fixed, mixed, or variable (using number of units produced as the activity measure).

   a. Factory supervision
   b. Aluminum tubing
   c. Rims
   d. Emblem
   e. Gearbox
   f. Crew supervisor's wages
   g. Fenders
   h. Inventory clerk's wages
   i. Quality inspector's salary
   j. Handlebars
   k. Metal worker's wages
   l. Roller chain
   m. Spokes
   n. Paint

24. (LO 1; *Cost behavior*) Old World Products Co. produces croquet sets. The company incurred the following costs to produce 2,000 sets last month:

Wooden cases (1 per set)	$ 4,000
Balls (6 per set)	6,000
Mallets	12,000
Wire hoops (12 per set including extras)	4,800
Straight-line depreciation	2,400
Supervisors' salaries	4,400
Total	$33,600

   a. What did each croquet set component cost? What did each croquet set cost?
   b. What type of behavior would you expect each of these costs to exhibit?
   c. This month, the company expects to produce 2,500 sets. Would you expect each type of cost to increase or decrease relative to last month? Why? What will be the total cost of 2,500 sets?

25. (LO 1; *Cost behavior*) A small municipality pays $300 per month for a photocopy machine maintenance contract. In addition, variable charges average $.04 per page copied.

   a. Determine the total cost and the cost per page if the municipality makes the following number of photocopies (pages):

   1. 1,000
   2. 2,000
   3. 4,000

   b. Why is the cost per page different in the three previous cases?

26. (LO 2; *Direct versus indirect costs*) Northwest State University's College of Business has five departments: Accounting, Finance, Management, Marketing, and Decision Sciences. Each department chairperson is responsible for the department's budget preparation. The following costs are incurred in the Management Department:

   a. Management faculty salaries
   b. Chairperson's salary
   c. Cost of computer time of campus mainframe used by members of the department
   d. Cost of equipment purchased by the department from allocated state funds
   e. Cost of travel by department faculty paid from externally generated funds contributed directly to the department
   f. Cost of secretarial salaries (secretarial salaries are shared by the entire college)
   g. Depreciation allocation of the college building cost for the number of offices used by department faculty
   h. Cost of periodicals and books purchased by the department
      Indicate whether each of these costs is direct or indirect to the Management Department.

27. (LO 3; *Product cost category*) Classify the following factory costs incurred in manufacturing potato chips as direct materials, direct labor, or manufacturing overhead.

   a. Wages of a packaging machine operator
   b. Wages of maintenance and clean-up personnel
   c. Potato costs

    d. Cooking oil costs

    e. Seasoning costs

    f. Packaging material costs

    g. Packing carton costs

    h. Heating and energy costs

    i. Potato storage costs

    j. Production supervisor's salary

28. (LO 3; *Product cost category*) Camp Creek Company makes aluminum canoes. Following are some costs incurred in the factory in 1996:

MATERIAL COSTS

Aluminum	$471,000
Oil and grease for equipment	5,000
Chrome rivets to assemble canoes	23,600
Wooden ribbing and braces	18,400

LABOR COSTS

Equipment operators	$220,000
Equipment mechanics	54,000
Factory supervisors	28,000

    a. What is the total direct material cost for 1996?

    b. What is the total direct labor cost for 1996?

    c. What are the indirect labor and indirect materials costs for 1996?

29. (LO 3; *Direct labor cost*) Four Star Restaurant Supply operates two shifts, paying a late-shift premium of 10 percent and an overtime premium of 50 percent. Labor premiums are included in service overhead. The June 1997 factory payroll is as follows:

Total wages for June for 7,000 hours	$66,000
Normal hourly wage for early-shift employees	$8
Total regular hours worked, split evenly	
between the early and late shifts	5,000

All overtime was worked by the early shift during June.

    a. How many overtime hours were worked in June?

    b. How much of the total labor cost should be charged to direct labor? To service overhead?

    c. What amount of service overhead was for late-shift premiums? For overtime premiums?

30. (LO 4; *Cost of quality*) Southland Ceramic Tableware is evaluating its quality control costs for 1996 and preparing plans and budgets for 1997. The 1996 quality costs incurred in the Consumer Products Division follow:

Prevention	$ 300,000
Appraisal	100,000
Internal failure costs	400,000
External failure costs	200,000
Total	$1,000,000

    a. Which category or categories of failure costs would be affected by the decision to spend $150,000 on a new computer-controlled ceramic kiln (which would replace an older manual kiln)? Explain.

b. Assume that projected external failure costs for 1997 can be reduced 50 percent (relative to 1996 levels) by either spending $80,000 more on appraisal or $120,000 more on prevention. Why might the firm rationally opt to spend the $120,000 on prevention rather than the $80,000 on appraisal?

31. (LO 3; *Prime cost and conversion cost*) A small manufacturing company's accounting records showed the following manufacturing costs and operating costs for the year 1996:

Direct materials	$518,000
Direct labor	321,000
Indirect materials	102,000
Indirect labor	129,000
Factory utilities	103,000
Selling and administrative expenses	317,000

a. What amount of prime cost was incurred in 1996?
b. What amount of conversion cost was incurred in 1996?
c. What was total product cost for 1996?

32. (LO 3; *Expired and unexpired costs*) Plastic Containers, Inc., purchased a plastics extruding machine for $400,000 to make plastic pill bottles. During its first operating year, the machine produced 500,000 bottles and depreciation was calculated to be $50,000 on the machine. The company sold 450,000 bottles.

a. What part of the $400,000 machine cost is expired?
b. Where would all amounts related to this machine appear on the financial statements?

33. (LO 3; *Expired and unexpired costs*) In 1997, Pacific Fashions completed its first year of operations. The company generated sales of $4,000,000 and net income of $600,000. For this same period, the firm's gross margin was $2,100,000. Total manufacturing cost incurred in 1997 was $3,200,000.

a. How much period cost did this firm incur in 1997?
b. How much product cost did this firm charge against its revenues in 1997?
c. How much unexpired manufacturing cost would be shown on the balance sheet from 1997?

34. (LO 5; *CGM and CGS*) Midwest Metal Customworks had the following inventory balances at the beginning and end of June 1996:

	6/1/96	6/30/96
Raw Materials Inventory	$16,000	$18,000
Work in Process Inventory	94,000	72,000
Finished Goods Inventory	36,000	22,000

All raw materials are direct to the production process. The following information is also available about manufacturing costs incurred during June:

Costs of raw materials used	$ 94,000
Direct labor costs	181,000
Factory overhead	258,000

a. Calculate the cost of goods manufactured for June.
b. Determine the cost of goods sold for June.

35. (LO 5; *Cost of services rendered*) The following information is related to the American Dog Clinic for June 1996, the firm's first month in operation:

Veterinary salaries for June	$22,000
Assistants' salaries for June	6,200
Medical supplies purchased in June	3,200
Utilities for month (80% related to animal treatment)	900
Office salaries for June (50% related to animal treatment)	3,400
Medical supplies at June 30	1,800
Depreciation on medical equipment for June	2,100
Building rental (80% related to animal treatment)	1,700

Compute the cost of services rendered.

36. (LO 5; *CGM and CGS*) Seattle Custom Mirror's July 1997 Cost of Goods Sold was $900,000. July 31 work in process was 80 percent of the July 1 work in process. Overhead was 100 percent of direct labor cost. During July, $220,000 of raw materials were purchased. All raw materials are direct to the production process. Other July information follows:

	JULY 1	JULY 31
Raw Materials Inventory	$108,000	$ 95,400
Work in Process Inventory	180,000	?
Finished Goods Inventory	419,000	411,200

a. Prepare a schedule of the cost of goods sold for July.
b. Prepare the July cost of goods manufactured schedule.
c. What was the amount of prime costs incurred in July?
d. What was the amount of conversion costs incurred in July?

37. (LO 6; *Appendix*) For each of the following accounts, indicate whether the account is associated with a manufacturing (M), merchandising (MD), or service (S) business. There may be more than one correct answer for each item.
a. Gross margin
b. Cost of goods sold
c. Merchandise inventory
d. Selling expenses
e. Income taxes
f. Cost of goods manufactured
g. Raw materials
h. Work in process inventory
i. Administrative expenses
j. Service revenue
k. Interest expense
l. Cost of services rendered

■ **COMMUNICATION ACTIVITIES**

38. (LO 1; *Cost drivers and cost predictors*) To explain or predict the behavior of costs, accountants often use factors that change in a consistent pattern with the costs in question. What are some factors you might select to predict or explain the behavior of the following costs? Would these same factors be considered cost drivers as well as predictors? If not, why not and what other items could be used as cost drivers?

a. Inspection costs
b. Equipment maintenance
c. Salesperson's travel expenses
d. Indirect factory labor

39. (LO 4; *Quality costs*) The following summary numbers have been taken from a quality cost report of Metro Landscaping Supply Co. for 1997. The firm produces and sells a variety of plants, sod, and other landscaping products.

Prevention costs	$ 600,000
Appraisal costs	200,000
Internal failure costs	400,000
External failure costs	600,000
Total quality costs	$1,800,000

The company is now actively seeking to identify ways to reduce total quality costs. The company's current strategy is to increase spending in one or more quality cost categories in hopes of achieving greater spending cuts in other quality cost categories.

Write a memorandum to the president of Metro Landscaping and discuss ways to reduce spending on quality-related costs. Your memo should address:

a. which of the spending categories are more susceptible to control by managers;
b. why it is more logical for the company to increase spending in the prevention cost and appraisal cost categories than in the failure cost categories;
c. which cost category is the most likely target for spending reductions; and
d. how the adoption of a TQM philosophy would affect the focus in reducing quality costs.

40. (LO 1; *Cost drivers and changing technology*) *Consumers are demanding new diversified products in short intervals. Due to factory automation, robots and computer-controlled manufacturing systems are replacing the conventional production lines. What all these changes mean is the traditional standard costing systems, which emphasize cost control in the manufacturing phase of the product life cycle, are no longer effective. With a one-year product life, controlling costs in the manufacturing phase simply doesn't accomplish much. Once the product is developed and designed, there is a limit to how much cost cutting companies can do in the manufacturing stage.*

[SOURCE: John Y. Lee, "Use Target Costing to Improve Your Bottom Line," *CPA Journal* (January 1994), p. 68.]

With the preceding article in mind, discuss the following propositions:

a. Why is determining the cost to manufacture a product a quite different activity from determining how to control such costs.
b. Does the advancement of technology appear to make costs more difficult to control? Discuss.
c. For many production costs, why should "number of units produced" not be considered a cost driver even though it may certainly be a valid cost predictor?

■ PROBLEMS

41. (LO 1; *Cost predictors*) The following are graphical representations of the relationships between four different costs and production volume. Briefly discuss for each cost why, production volume is, or is not, a good predictor for the cost. Also, identify a specific cost item that may be represented by each graph.

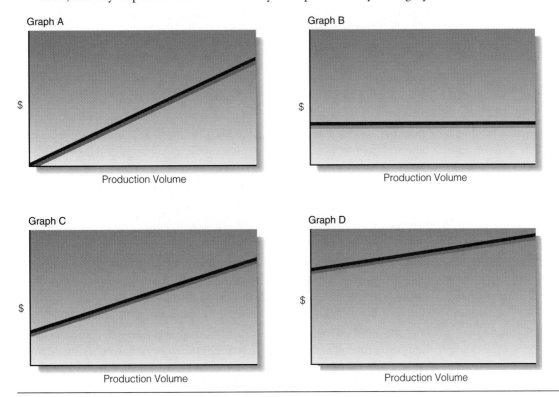

Graph A

$

Production Volume

Graph B

$

Production Volume

Graph C

$

Production Volume

Graph D

$

Production Volume

42. (LO 1; *Cost behavior*) A company's cost structure may contain many different cost behavior patterns. Descriptions of several different costs are on the following page. Identify, by letter, the graph that illustrates each of the described cost behavior patterns. Graphs may be used more than once. On each graph, the vertical axis represents cost and the horizontal axis represents level of activity or volume.

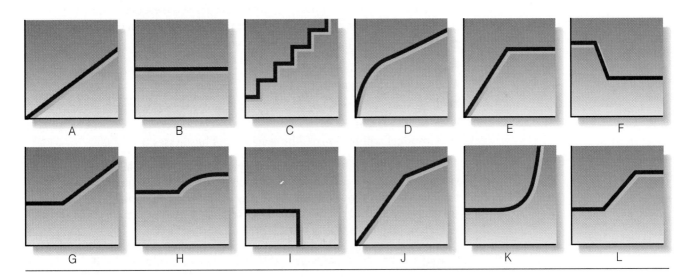

A   B   C   D   E   F

G   H   I   J   K   L

1. Cost of raw materials, where the cost decreases by $.06 per unit for each of the first 150 units purchased, after which it remains constant at $2.75 per unit.

2. City water bill, which is computed as follows:
First 750,000 gallons or less	$1,000 flat fee
Next 15,000 gallons	$.002 per gallon used
Next 15,000 gallons	$.005 per gallon used
Next 15,000 gallons	$.008 per gallon used
Etc.	Etc.

3. Rent on a factory building donated by the city, where the agreement provides for a fixed-fee payment unless 250,000 labor hours are worked, in which case no rent needs to be paid.

4. Cost of raw materials used.

5. Electricity bill which is a flat fixed charge of $250 plus a variable cost after 150,000 kilowatt hours are used.

6. Salaries of maintenance workers if one maintenance worker is needed for every 1,000 hours or less of machine time.

7. Depreciation of equipment using the straight-line method.

8. Rent on a factory building donated by the county, where the agreement provides for a monthly rental of $100,000 less $1 for each labor hour worked in excess of 200,000 hours. However, a minimum rental payment of $20,000 must be made each month.

9. Rent on a machine that is billed at $1,000 for up to 500 hours of machine time. After 500 hours of machine time, an additional charge of $1 per hour is paid up to a maximum charge of $2,500 per period.

   (AICPA adapted)

43. (LO 1; *Cost behavior*) Marla Staples has been elected to handle the local little theater summer play. She is trying to determine the price to charge little theater members for attendance at this year's presentation of *The Lady is a Tramp*. She has developed the following cost estimates associated with the play:

    ■ Cost of printing invitations will be $260 for 100 to 500; cost to print between 500 and 600 will be $280.

    ■ Cost of readying and operating the theater for three evenings will be $1,000 if attendance is below 500; this cost rises to $1,016 if attendance is 500 or above.

    ■ Postage to mail invitations will be $.30 each.

    ■ Cost of building stage sets will be $1,215.

    ■ Cost of printing up to 1,000 programs will be $250.

    ■ Cost of security will be $110 per night plus $30 per hour; five hours will be needed each night.

    ■ Costumes will be donated by several local businesses.

    The little theater has 200 members, and each member is allowed two guests. Ordinarily, only 75 percent of the members attend the summer offering, each bringing the two allowed guests. The play will be presented from 8 P.M. to 11 P.M. Invitations are mailed to those members calling to say they plan to come and also to each of the guests they specify.

    a. Indicate the type of behavior exhibited by all the items Marla needs to consider.

b. If the ordinary attendance occurs, what will be the total cost of the summer offering of the play?

c. If the ordinary attendance occurs, what will be the cost per person attending?

d. If 90 percent of the members attend and each invites two guests, what will be the total cost of the play? The cost per person? What primarily causes the difference in the cost per person?

44. (LO 1; *Cost behavior*) Airline Service Co. prepares dinners for several airlines, and sales average 300,000 meals per month. The significant costs of each dinner prepared are for the meat, vegetables, and plastic trays and utensils. (No desserts are provided, because passengers are more calorie-conscious than in the past.) The company prepares meals in batches of 1,000. The following data are shown in the company's accounting records for June 1997:

Cost of meat for 1,000 dinners	$900
Cost of vegetables for 1,000 dinners	360
Cost of plastic trays and utensils	
for 1,000 dinners	120
Direct labor for 1,000 dinners	950

Overhead charges total $1,200,000 per month; these are considered fully fixed for purposes of cost estimation.

a. What is the cost per dinner based on average sales and June prices?

b. If sales increase to 400,000 dinners per month, what will be the cost per dinner (assuming that cost behavior patterns remain the same as in June)?

c. If sales are 400,000 dinners per month but the company does not want the cost per dinner to exceed its current level (based on part a), what amount can the company pay for meat, assuming all other costs are the same as in June?

d. The company's major competitor has bid a price of $10.96 per dinner to the airlines. The profit margin in the industry is 100 percent of total cost. If Airline Service Co. is to retain the airlines' business, how many dinners must the company produce each month to reach the bid price of the competitor and maintain the 100 percent profit margin? Assume June cost patterns will not change and dinners must be produced in batches of 1,000.

45. (LO 2; *Cost classification, cost object*) Ahmad Olibe, a painter, incurred the following costs during April 1997 when he painted three houses. He spent $600 on paint, $50 on mineral spirits, and $65 on brushes. He also bought two pairs of coveralls for $12 each; he wears coveralls only while he works. During the first week of April, Ahmad placed a $10 ad for his business in the classifieds. Ahmad had to hire an assistant for one of the painting jobs; he paid her $8 per hour, and she worked 25 hours.

   Being a very methodical person, Ahmad keeps detailed records of his mileage to and from each painting job. His average operating cost per mile for his van is $.25. He found a $15 receipt in his van for a Mapsco that he purchased in April; he uses it to find addresses when he is first contacted to give an estimate on a painting job. He also had $6 in receipts for bridge tolls ($1 per trip) for a painting job he did across the river.

   Near the end of April, Ahmad decided to go camping, and he turned down a job on which he had bid $1,800. He called the homeowner long-distance (at a cost of $3.60) to explain his reasons for declining the job.

Using the following headings, indicate how each of the April costs incurred by Ahmad would be classified. Assume that the cost object is a house-painting job.

COST	VARIABLE	FIXED	DIRECT	INDIRECT	PERIOD	PRODUCT

46. (LO 4; *Cost of quality*) Below are selected cost data taken from records of the Milnar Technology Company for 1996 and 1997:

	1996	1997
Defect prevention costs		
Quality training	$ 8,000	$ 9,500
Quality technology	6,000	8,000
Quality production design	4,000	9,000
External failure costs		
Warranty handling	$15,000	$10,000
Customer reimbursements	11,000	7,200
Customer returns handling	7,000	4,000

a. Compute the percentage change in the two quality cost categories from 1996 to 1997.

b. Write a brief explanation for the pattern of change in the two categories.

47. (LO 3; *Cost flows, prime costs and conversion costs*) Custom Fiberglass Products had the following inventory balances at the beginning and end of October 1996:

	OCTOBER 1	OCTOBER 31
Raw Materials Inventory	$16,900	$21,700
Work in Process Inventory	32,100	29,600
Finished Goods Inventory	25,800	22,600

During October, the company purchased $90,000 of raw materials. All raw materials are considered direct materials. Total labor payroll for the month was $78,000. Direct labor employees were paid $9 per hour and worked 6,800 hours in October. Total factory overhead charges for the period were $109,300.

a. Determine the prime cost added to production during October.

b. Determine the conversion cost added to production in October.

c. Determine the cost of goods manufactured in October.

d. Determine the cost of goods sold in October.

48. (LO 3; *Journal entries*) Smith-Barnes manufactures a single product: mailboxes. The following data represent transactions and balances for May 1997, the company's first month of operations.

Direct materials purchased on account	$124,000
Direct materials issued to production	93,000
Direct labor payroll accrued	67,000
Factory insurance expired	1,800
Factory utilities accrued	8,100
Factory depreciation recorded	7,900
Ending work in process inventory (6,000 units)	18,000
Sales on account ($12 per unit)	324,000
Ending finished goods inventory (3,000 units)	?

a. How many units were sold in May? How many units were completed?

b. What was the total cost of goods manufactured in May?

c. What was the per unit cost of goods manufactured in May?

d. Prepare the journal entries to record the flow of costs in the company for May using the perpetual inventory system.

49. (LO 5; *CGM and CGS*) Barnes, Inc. produces American flags for department stores. The raw materials account includes both direct and indirect materials. The account balances at the beginning and end of August 1997 are as follows:

	AUGUST 1	AUGUST 31
Raw Materials Inventory	$18,000	$16,700
Work in Process Inventory	24,500	19,200
Finished Goods Inventory	8,000	9,200

During the month, Barnes purchased $92,000 of raw materials; direct materials consumption in August was $47,900. Factory payroll costs for August were $95,000, of which 87 percent was related to direct labor. Factory overhead charges for depreciation, insurance, utilities, and maintenance were $69,400 for the month.

a. Determine total overhead for August. (Hint: include indirect material.)

b. Prepare a schedule of the cost of goods manufactured.

c. Prepare a schedule of the cost of goods sold.

50. (LO 5; *CGM and CGS*) The Electric Trimmer Co. began business in October of last year and makes electric lawn mowers. Following are data taken from the firm's accounting records that pertain to its first year operations.

Direct materials purchased on account	$213,000
Direct materials issued to production	192,000
Direct labor payroll accrued	114,000
Indirect labor payroll paid	45,300
Factory insurance expired	2,700
Factory utilities paid	8,900
Factory depreciation recorded	18,700
Ending work in process inventory	32,000
Ending finished goods inventory (80 units)	12,800
Sales on account ($210 per unit)	442,050

a. How many units did the company sell in its first year? How many units were manufactured in the first year?

b. What was the total cost of goods manufactured?

c. What was the per unit cost of goods manufactured?

d. What was the cost of goods sold in the first year?

e. Did the company have a positive gross margin in its first year of operations?

51. (LO 5; *Missing figures*) For each of the following cases, compute the missing figures:

	CASE 1	CASE 2	CASE 3
Sales	$9,300	$?	$112,000
Direct materials used	1,200	?	18,200
Direct labor	?	4,900	?
Prime cost	3,700	?	?
Conversion cost	4,800	8,200	49,300
Factory overhead	?	?	17,200
Cost of goods manufactured	6,200	14,000	?

	CASE 1	CASE 2	CASE 3
Beginning work in process inventory	500	900	5,600
Ending work in process inventory	?	1,200	4,200
Beginning finished goods inventory	?	1,900	7,600
Ending finished goods inventory	1,200	?	?
Cost of goods sold	?	12,200	72,200
Gross profit	3,500	?	?
Operating expenses	?	3,500	18,000
Net income (loss)	2,200	4,000	?

■ CASES

52. (LO 3; *Direct labor cost*) Some of the costs incurred by businesses are designated as "direct labor costs." As used in practice, the term *direct labor cost* has a wide variety of meanings. Unless the meaning intended in a given context is clear, misunderstanding and confusion are likely. A user who does not understand the elements included in direct labor cost may interpret the numbers incorrectly, and poor management decisions may result.

In addition to understanding the conceptual definition of *direct labor cost,* management accountants must understand how direct labor cost should be measured.

a. Distinguish between direct labor and indirect labor.

b. Discuss why some nonproductive labor (such as coffee breaks and personal time) can be and often is treated as direct labor, while other nonproductive time (such as downtime or training) is treated as indirect labor.

c. Following are three labor cost categories used by a company and some costs it has included in each category:

■ Direct labor: Included in the company's direct labor cost are cost production efficiency bonuses and certain benefits for direct labor workers, such as FICA (employer's portion), group life insurance, vacation pay, and workers' compensation insurance.

■ Manufacturing overhead: Included in the company's overhead are costs for wage-continuation plans in the event of illness, the company-sponsored cafeteria, the personnel department, and recreational facilities.

■ Direct labor or manufacturing overhead depending on the situation: Included in the "situational" category are maintenance expense, overtime premiums, and shift premiums.

Explain the rationale used by the company in classifying these costs in the three categories.

d. The two aspects of measuring direct labor costs are (1) the quantity of labor effort that is to be included (the types of hours to be counted) and (2) the unit price by which each of these quantities is multiplied to arrive at monetary cost. Why are these considered separate and distinct aspects of measuring labor cost?

(CMA adapted)

53. (LO 3, 5; *Missing data*) The Georgia Textile Co. experienced a flood on May 21 of the current year that destroyed the company's work in process inventory. For the purposes of submitting an insurance claim, the company needs an estimate of the inventory value. Management found the following information in some records that were salvaged:

Raw materials inventory, May 1	$1,000
Work in process inventory, May 1	5,000
Accounts payable, May 1	5,500
Accounts payable, May 20	8,000
Direct labor hours from May 1 to May 20	1,750
Direct labor hourly rate	6
Estimated fixed overhead, May 1 to May 20	3,500
Estimated variable overhead, May 1 to May 20	5,250

On May 22, the company took a physical inventory and found $2,500 of raw materials on hand. The accounts payable account is used only for purchases of raw materials. Payments made on account from May 1 through May 20 were $6,500.

a. Determine the value of Work in Process Inventory that was destroyed by the flood if $16,000 of goods had been transferred to Finished Goods Inventory from May 1 to May 20.

b. What other information might the insurance company require? How would management determine or estimate this information?

54. (LO 2, 3; *Cost management*) Litchfield Inc.'s main business is the publication of books and magazines. Alan Shane is the production manager of the Bridgton Plant which manufactures paper used in all of Litchfield's publications. The Bridgton Plant has no sales staff and limited contact with outside customers as most of its sales are to other divisions of Litchfield. As a consequence, the Bridgton Plant is evaluated by merely comparing its expected costs to its actual costs to determine how well costs were controlled.

Shane perceives the accounting reports that he receives to be the result of a historical number-generating process that provides little information that is useful in performing his job. Consequently, the entire accounting process is perceived as a negative motivational device that does not reflect how hard or effectively he works as a production manager. In discussions with Susan Brady, controller of the Bridgton Plant, Shane said, "I think the cost reports are misleading. I know I've had better production over a number of operating periods, but the cost reports still say I have excessive costs. Look, I'm not an accountant; I'm a production manager. I know how to get a good quality product out. Over a number of years, I've even cut the raw materials used to do it. The cost reports don't show any of this; they're always negative, no matter what I do. There's no way you can win with accounting or the people at headquarters who use these reports."

Brady gave Shane little consolation when she stated that the accounting system and the cost reports generated by headquarters are just part of the corporate game and almost impossible for an individual to change. "Although these reports are used to evaluate your division and the means headquarters uses to determine whether you have done the job they want, you shouldn't worry too much. You haven't been fired yet! Besides, these cost reports have been used by Litchfield for the last 15 years."

From discussions with the operations people at other Litchfield divisions, Shane knew that the turnover of production managers at the company was high, even though relatively few were fired. A typical comment was: "The accountants may be quick with numbers but they don't know anything about production. I wound up completely ignoring the cost reports. No matter what they say about not firing people, negative cost reports mean negative evaluations. I'm better off working for another company."

A copy of the most recent cost report for the Bridgton Plant follows:

BRIDGTON PLANT COST REPORT
FOR THE MONTH OF NOVEMBER 1996
(IN THOUSANDS)

	Expected Cost	Actual Cost	Excess Cost
Raw materials	$ 400	$ 437	$ 37
Direct labor	560	540	(20)
Factory overhead	100	134	34
Total	$1,060	$1,111	$ 51

a. Discuss Alan Shane's perception of the business role of Susan Brady, controller.

b. Discuss Alan Shane's perception of corporate headquarters' reasons for issuing cost reports.

c. Discuss Alan Shane's perception of himself, as a production manager.

d. How could the cost report be changed to make it more useful to Mr. Shane?
(CMA)

■ ETHICS AND QUALITY DISCUSSIONS

55. For a benchmark, assume that the typical U.S. firm incurs quality costs in the following proportions:

Prevention	25%
Appraisal	25%
Internal failure	25%
External failure	25%
Total costs	100%

Explain why the following industries might be inclined to have a spending pattern on quality costs that differs from the benchmark:

a. health care profession

b. lawn fertilizer production

c. rug and carpet production

d. used car retailing

56. *We Dalkon survivors [users of the Dalkon shield - a contraceptive device] are the female equivalent of the Agent Orange Viet Nam vets—gravely, often permanently damaged by a new technology promoted by a bottom-line-bent company ignoring known dangers for the sake of corporate greed. [The technology] had tragic ripple effects down to the second generation in never-born, stillborn, and severely handicapped children. In 1984, 300,000 Agent Orange vets won a settlement of only $180 million, which interest payments have since swelled to $240 million. That's less than 10 percent of what we Dalkon claimants stand to collect, maybe sooner than the vets. Yet some women, and lawyers, backing the legal appeals in this enormously complex case argue, among other things, that $2.475 billion isn't enough.*

[SOURCE: Catherine Breslin, "Day of Reckoning," *Ms.* (June 1989), p.52.]

a. How does the Dalkon shield case provide evidence that the potential cost of external quality failure varies in magnitude across businesses and industries?

b. Does a $2.475 billion liability claim against a company indicate the company was "bottom-line-bent"? Explain.

    c. Discuss the author's implication that a profit-oriented company would, in the interest of profit, intentionally place a flawed product on the market.

    d. Should companies determine the optimal quality of their products and services based on both ethical and cost considerations? Explain.

57. *[In the early 1990s, Chambers Development Inc. appeared to be a company on the rise.] Then, on March 17 [1992], the developer of landfills dropped a bombshell. Chambers said it would start expensing indirect costs related to developing landfill sites. The company had been capitalizing these costs, which include public relations and legal costs to obtain permits for landfills.*

    The change resulted in a $27 million charge to earnings, wiping out more than half the company's 1991 net income - and more than $1.4 billion of Chambers' market valuation.

    [SOURCE: Roula Khalaf, "Fuzzy Accounting," *Forbes* (June 22, 1992), p. 96. Reprinted by persmission of Forbes magazine. © Forbes Inc., 1992.]

    a. How does the issue of capitalizing versus expensing relate to the conceptual difference between expired and unexpired cost?

    b. Why would a company's market value drop because of a simple change in an accounting practice?

    c. What ethical obligations do accountants and managers bear in deciding whether to "expense" or "capitalize" a cost item?

58. You are the chief financial officer for a small manufacturing company that has applied for a bank loan. In speaking with the bank loan officer, you are told that two minimum criteria for granting loans are (1) a 40 percent gross margin and (2) income of at least 15 percent of sales. Looking at the last four months' income statements, you find that gross margin has been between 30 and 33 percent and income has ranged from 18 to 24 percent of sales. You discuss these relationships with the company president, who suggests that some of the product costs included in Cost of Goods Sold be moved to the selling, general, and administrative categories so that the income statement will conform to the bank's criteria.

    a. Which types of product costs might be most easily reassigned to period cost classifications?

    b. Since the president is not suggesting that any expenses be kept off the income statement, do you see any ethical problems with the request? Discuss.

    c. Write a short memo to convince the banker to loan the company the funds in spite of its noncompliance with the loan criteria.

59. A cost of operating any organization in the contemporary business environment is computer software. Most software can be purchased on either a per-unit basis (making it a variable cost) or a site license basis (making it a fixed cost). You are a manager in a marketing company that engages in a great deal of market research. You have asked the company to acquire a copy of a statistical analysis package that would cost $400 per package for each of the 20 people in your department. Alternatively, the software company will give a site license at a cost of $12,000. The package is essential to the organization's ability to perform research, but the controller does not have funds in the budget for 20 copies. Therefore, the controller purchases 4 copies and tells you to duplicate the other necessary copies. You resist, saying that to do so would violate the copyright law, which allows only one copy to be made for backup purposes.

    a. Since the fixed cost for the site license exceeds the cost for 20 copies, can you think of any reason to incur that $12,000 cost? Discuss.

b. Assume you are currently working on a marketing research project for Mighty Midget Toy Company. Proper analysis requires the use of this software package. Is the cost of the software a direct or an indirect cost to the Mighty Midget project? If direct, what amount do you believe could be attached to the project? If indirect, should the cost be allocated to the project in some way? If so, how?

c. How would you handle this situation? What might be the consequences of your actions?

■ PROJECTS

60. Choose one of the following projects or one of your own:

a. Mowing the lawn

b. Changing the oil in a car

c. Preparing a meal or a dessert

d. Cleaning your dorm room or apartment

Determine the cost of goods produced or cost of services rendered, estimating as well as you can the cost of materials, cost of labor (assume a pay scale of $5.75 per hour for all labor time), and overhead cost. Based on your estimated cost, what would you consider a reasonable sales price for your product or service? Justify your answer.

61. It is well known that obtaining a college education is an expensive undertaking. Consider your college education to be a cost object; and as completely as possible, identify all costs you and/or your parents have incurred for your education. Then separate the costs you identified into two categories: direct and indirect. Last, estimate the total direct and total indirect costs of your education.

62. You and three of your classmates have decided to form a new business venture. The business will provide a variety of in-house and on-site computer training programs. Your clients will be local businesses and individuals who want to enhance their understanding of and ability to use computer software applications.

As a first step in the financial management of the new business, you have decided it is necessary to develop a quantitative financial plan that will cover all aspects of the start-up of the business. For example, this plan should include the financing of and expenditures for acquiring a business site and necessary equipment, training employees, and so on.

Your business partnership team must explicitly state any assumptions that need to be made in developing the financial plan, including the size and scope of the business. Your team may divide the planning effort among the members in any optimal way. At the conclusion of the planning process, a written report must be prepared by the team. At a minimum the report must contain the following: estimates of the service volume or other measures that were used as the basis for the financial plan; important assumptions that were made about the business and its clients; a description of all resources that need to be acquired according to the financial plan; estimates of all start-up expenditures; and a plan for obtaining the financial resources needed to meet the expenditures.

INCLUDING OVERHEAD IN PRODUCT AND SERVICE COSTS

Overhead is like your front lawn. It just keeps growing back.
Mark F. Blaxill, "Can Corporate America Get Out from Under Its Overhead?"
Business Week (May 18, 1992)

LEARNING OBJECTIVES

1. Explain the different product costing systems and measurement methods.

2. Discuss why the use of predetermined factory overhead rates provides better information than applying actual factory overhead to production.

3. Analyze mixed costs using the high-low method and (Appendix 1) least-squares regression analysis.

4. Explain the usefulness of flexible budgeting to managers.

5. Develop predetermined factory overhead rates, use those rates to apply overhead, and understand the impact of the capacity measure selected.

6. Account for underapplied or overapplied factory overhead at year-end.

7. (Appendix 2) Allocate service department costs to revenue-producing departments using the direct and step methods.

ON SITE · Starbucks Coffee: Company Turns Up the Heat on Overhead Costs

On the far side of the glass behind Howard Schultz, multicolored boxes of coffee move like rush-hour traffic on a miniature freeway, winding their way on a conveyor belt that runs through the center of the building. The air is gently infused with the warm, fresh-brewed scent of today's blend. From where he sits, Schultz can see the tasting room, a kitchen-cum–laboratory complete with Bunsen burners, that's located just outside his office. High-gloss snapshots of the coffee-brewing process decorate the walls, along with the current prices per pound of each of the 30 blends Starbucks Coffee Co. sells.

After the beans arrive in Seattle, trained roasters brown them almost black. Within two hours of leaving the roaster, the coffee is packed in vacuum-sealed bags and shipped to mail-order customers around the country and to Starbucks' growing network of stores and airport kiosks. Starbucks' stringent calendar requires the coffee to be sold or served in seven days. In 1993, over 100,000 pounds of "Eighth Day Beans" (past-date coffee) were given to charities in the locales of the stores and kiosks.

At the end of 1993, Seattle-based Starbucks was the leading retailer and roaster of specialty coffee in North America with over 250 stores in 10 different markets. Boston, New York, and Minneapolis were added to the list in 1994. Through it all, Schultz runs a tight ship. Although the company spends, by his estimate, $1,000 to train each new employee, his overhead is dropping as a percentage of sales, even as the number of stores climbs. The figure fell from 12.3% in 1989 to a scant 9% in 1992.

SOURCES: Matt Rothman, "Into the Black," *Inc.* (January 1993), p. 59; reprinted with permission of *Inc.* magazine © 1993 by Goldhirsh Group, Inc. Starbucks Coffee Co. *1993 Annual Report*; Richard S. Teitelbaum, "Companies to Watch," *Fortune* (August 24, 1992), p. 133, © 1992 Time Inc., all rights reserved.

All organizations, whether manufacturers, retailers, or service organizations, are concerned with overhead costs. There are two primary types of overhead: production and nonproduction. In manufacturing operations, factory overhead is generated in the conversion area and, like direct materials and direct labor, is a product cost. Retail and service organizations cannot incur factory overhead because they manufacture no goods; however, these companies do create overhead by performing their services. This overhead is, like factory overhead in a manufacturer, also a product cost and should be assigned to them.

Production overhead can be viewed as being "above the line overhead" (that is, above gross margin) and included in the cost of goods manufactured or cost of services rendered. In contrast, nonproduction overhead is "below the line overhead" and must be covered by a company's gross margin if a company is to be profitable. Nonproduction overhead is incurred outside the production or sales area of a company and is a period, rather than a product, cost. These overhead costs are incurred in every business for functions such as upper-level management, accounting and legal services, marketing, distribution, and human resources.

In a business such as Starbucks Coffee, the types of overhead costs tend to blur. Obviously, the location at which coffee beans are roasted for shipment to mail-order customers or franchise locations is a manufacturing plant, and overhead incurred there is a product cost. What about the overhead incurred at retail stores and kiosks? Such costs would appear to be period costs because they are being incurred at a sales location. However, these retail outlets are really additional manufacturing sites. Each pound of coffee beans or cup of coffee sold must be bagged or perked prior to sale. Thus, each store is essentially a mini-manufacturing plant where materials, labor, and overhead costs are incurred for each item sold.

This chapter describes the methods of product costing and discusses the process of assigning overhead costs to products and services. Because of the variety and monetary significance of overhead costs, managers need to understand what overhead exists in their business and what drives (or causes) that overhead to occur. This information will allow managers to better manage and control product and period overhead costs, determine individual product profitability, and make good decisions about product pricing, optimal product mix, and long-run company strategies.

METHODS OF PRODUCT COSTING

One accounting function is to determine the cost of the products made or the services performed by an organization. Product costing is concerned with identifying, assigning, and managing costs. Just as a variety of methods (first-in, first-out; last-in, first-out; average; specific identification) exist to assign costs to inventory and cost of goods sold in a retail company, different methods are available to calculate product cost in a manufacturing or service environment. The method chosen depends on the nature of the product or service and the company's production or service process.

Before products can be costed, the type of product costing system and the method of cost measurement to be used must be determined. The product costing system used specifies what is to be the cost object and how costs are to be assigned to production. The method of measurement specifies how product costs will be determined. Companies must have both a cost system and a method of measurement. Six possible combinations exist as shown in Exhibit 4–1.

■ **EXHIBIT 4–1**
Costing Systems and Inventory Measurement

COST SYSTEM	METHOD OF MEASUREMENT		
	Actual	**Normal**	**Standard**
Job Order	Actual DM Actual DL Actual OH assigned to job after end of period	Actual DM Actual DL OH applied at completion of job or end of period (predetermined rate x actual input)	Standard DM and/or Standard DL OH applied when goods are completed or at end of period (predetermined rate x standard input)
Process	Actual DM, DL, and OH costs using FIFO or weighted average cost flow	Actual DM and DL and predetermined OH rates using FIFO or weighted average cost flow	Standard DM, DL and OH; always FIFO cost flow

KEY: DM (direct materials); DL (direct labor); OH (production overhead); FIFO (first-in, first-out)

Costing Systems

job order costing

Job order and process costing are the two basic costing systems. **Job order costing** is used by entities that produce limited quantities of custom-made goods or services that conform to specifications designated by the purchaser. Job order costing is appropriate for a printing firm that prepares advertisements for numerous clients, a research firm that performs product development studies, and an attorney who has her own practice. In general, services are highly user-specific so job order costing systems are usually appropriate for such businesses. Job order costing is discussed in the next section of this chapter.

■ **LEARNING OBJECTIVE 1**
Explain the different product costing systems and measurement methods.

process costing

Process costing, the other primary product costing system, is used by entities engaged in the continuous mass production of large quantities of homogeneous goods. For example, companies manufacturing bricks, saltwater taffy, and breakfast cereal would use a process costing system. The output of a single process in a company using process costing is homogeneous; thus, specific units of output cannot be readily identified with specific input costs within a given time frame. This characteristic necessitates the use of a cost flow assumption. Cost flow assumptions provide a way for accountants to assign costs to products without relying on the actual physical flow of units. Process costing systems use either the weighted average or first-in, first-out cost flow assumption. These systems are discussed in depth in Chapter 7.

A company that engages in different types of productive activity may use a hybrid of these two types of primary costing systems. If the firm needs job order costing in some areas and process costing in other areas, use of a hybrid system is necessary. For example, process costing would be appropriate for the coffee bean roasting activity at Starbucks. However, if Starbucks accepts orders from customers who want a particular roasted mix of beans (such as Sumatra *Boengie* and espresso), the company could use job order costing for these special orders.

Measurement Methods

The three basic methods of measurement are actual, normal, and standard costing. A company that accumulates the actual costs of direct materials, direct labor, and over-

The various types of Starbucks' coffee are manufactured in continuous mass production processes. To account for the costs of direct materials, direct labor, factory overhead, and properly assign these costs to individual bags of coffee Starbucks would use a process costing system.

head to determine the cost of Work in Process (WIP) Inventory is employing an **actual cost system.** Actual overhead costs are accumulated separately from materials and labor and are assigned to WIP Inventory at the end of a period. Actual cost systems are less than desirable because they require that all overhead cost information for the period be known before any cost assignment can be made to products or services. Waiting for the information reduces management's ability to make timely operating decisions.

actual cost system

Instead of using actual overhead costs, many companies use predetermined overhead rates to assign factory overhead costs to inventory. A **predetermined overhead rate** (or overhead application rate) is an average constant charge per unit of activity for a group of related overhead amounts. If the predetermined rate is substantially equivalent to what the actual rate would have been, using a predetermined overhead rate provides an acceptable and useful costing system. The method of measurement that combines actual direct materials and labor costs with predetermined production overhead rates is called a **normal cost system.**

predetermined overhead rate

Rather than using actual costs, companies may employ **standards** (or predetermined benchmarks) for costs to be incurred and/or quantities to be used. In a **standard cost system,** unit norms are developed for direct material and direct labor quantities and/or costs. Overhead is applied to products and services according to a predetermined rate, which is considered the standard. In a standard cost system, both actual and standard costs are recorded in the accounting records to provide an essential element of cost control—having norms against which actual costs of operations can be compared. These standards are used to plan for future activities and costs and to measure inventories. Standard costing is discussed in depth in Chapter 6.

normal cost system
standards
standard cost system

JOB ORDER COSTING

Actual, normal, or standard costing can be used in a job order costing environment. In a job order system, costs are accumulated individually by **job.** The output of a given job can be a single unit[1] or group of units identifiable as being produced to distinct customer specifications. Each job in a job order system is treated as a unique cost object.

job

If a job's output is a single product, the total costs of the job are assigned to that product. If the job results in multiple outputs, a unit cost may only be computed if the units are similar. In such a case, the total job cost is averaged over the number of units produced to determine a cost per unit. If the output consists of dissimilar units, no cost per unit can be determined, although it is still possible to know the total cost of the job. Costs of different jobs are maintained separately.

When materials are needed for a job, a **materials requisition** is prepared so that raw materials can be released from the warehouse and sent to the production area. This source document links the types and quantities of materials to be placed into production (or used in performing a service) to specific jobs and provides a way to trace responsibility for materials cost. Material requisitions release warehouse personnel from further responsibility for the issued materials and assign responsibility to the department that issued the requisition. As materials are issued, their costs are transferred from Raw Materials Inventory and, if the materials are direct to the job,

materials requisition

---

[1] *Units* should be read to mean either products or services, since job order costing is applicable to both manufacturing and service companies. For the same reason, *produced* can mean manufactured or performed.

are added to Work in Process Inventory. If Raw Materials Inventory also contains indirect materials, costs for issuances of those materials are transferred to an overhead account.

job order cost sheet

When direct materials are first issued to production, a job is considered to be "in process." At this time it is necessary to begin to accumulate product costs on a **job order cost sheet.** This source document provides virtually all financial information about a particular job. The set of all job order cost sheets for uncompleted jobs provide the details underlying the Work in Process Inventory account. A job order cost sheet includes the job number, a description of the job, customer identification, scheduling information, delivery instructions, and contract price. Details about the accumulated product costs are provided on the cost sheet with separate sections for direct materials, direct labor, and factory overhead. The job order cost sheet might also include budgeted cost information, especially if such information was used to estimate the job's selling price.

employee time sheets

Production workers, both direct and indirect, may keep track of the jobs they work on each day and the time they spend on each job using **employee time sheets** (or time tickets). Alternatively, in today's highly automated factories, machine time can be tracked on machine clocks or counters. As jobs are transferred from one machine to another, the machine's clock or counter can be reset to record the start and stop times. Another convenient way to track employee time is through bar coding. Bar coding also allows the company to trace machine depreciation to specific products by using

Car repairs are customer-specific. The time spent on each job by a mechanic is detailed on his or her time sheet and then added to the cost of parts and a charge for overhead on a job order cost sheet, which is the basis for the customer's bill.

Bar Coding: Not Just for Grocery Stores Anymore

NEWS NOTE

Bar coding is among the most accurate data collection technologies. As cost systems are revised to meet management's need for timely information, bar coding often becomes the data collection method of choice from both a price and performance perspective.

Aside from point-of-sale applications, bar code systems were initially implemented to track and control product movement through the receipt, storage, and shipping functions of large warehouse facilities. More and more firms are adopting the JIT philosophy and are seeking to reduce inventories, improve quality, and eliminate waste. Many of these firms realize that having ready access to timely, accurate information is the key to maintaining *total* control of the business and that bar code systems are best able to supply this information to management.

Carefully designed pilot projects in visible, highly successful applications enable bar coding to reveal its many benefits to management and systems users. For example, one large plumbing manufacturer in the Midwest recently implemented time-and-attendance and shop-floor-control systems that use bar coding. The pilot project was begun in a rather simple two-stage labor process involving furnace heating and quality inspection. In less than two years, the company eliminated eleven different forms that were used when time and inspection data were recorded manually. Inspector efficiency improved by 10 to 12 percent, in part because the inspector never touched a piece of paper other than a bar code label.

SOURCE: Thomas Tyson, "The Use of Bar Coding in Activity-Based Costing," *Journal of Cost Management* (Winter 1991), pp. 52–53. Reprinted with permission from The Journal of Cost Management for the Manufacturing Industry, © 1991, Warren, Gorham & Lamont, 31 St. James Avenue, Boston, MA 02116. All rights reserved.

a time-related depreciation measure (such as depreciation per hour of use). The accompanying News Note indicates the versatility of this tool.

Labor information is recorded on the job order cost sheet in both time and cost amounts. Labor cost equals the time spent on a job multiplied by the employee's wage rate. If total actual labor costs for the job differ significantly from the original estimate, the manager responsible for labor cost control can be asked to clarify the reasons underlying the situation.

Actual factory overhead of a period is accumulated in a factory overhead control account. If actual overhead is applied to jobs, the management accountant must wait until after the end of the period to assign overhead costs. Actual overhead incurred would be divided by some related measure of activity or cost driver to obtain the actual overhead rate. Then, that rate would be multiplied by the actual measure of activity associated with each job to calculate the amount of overhead to assign to each job. More commonly, under normal costing, factory overhead is applied to jobs by use of predetermined overhead application rates.

PREDETERMINED OVERHEAD RATES

To calculate a predetermined overhead rate, the budgeted annual overhead cost is divided by a related budgeted measure of volume. A single predetermined overhead rate can be calculated using total plantwide or department production overhead costs, or separate rates can be calculated for variable and fixed overhead. The general formula to compute a predetermined overhead rate is:

$$\text{Predetermined OH rate} = \frac{\text{Budgeted overhead cost}}{\text{Budgeted level of related volume or activity}}$$

The time frame over which the factory overhead cost and level of activity are budgeted is typically one year "unless the production/marketing cycle of the entity is such that the use of a longer or shorter period would clearly provide more useful information."[2] For example, the use of a longer period of time would be appropriate in companies such as Avondale Shipyards (which builds military ships) and Boh Bros. Construction Company (which constructs roads, bridges, and office buildings).

To illustrate the calculation of a predetermined OH rate, consider Espressoly Yours, a specialty coffee manufacturer. The owner estimates that 1,372,800 one-pound cans of coffee will be prepared in 1996. Total budgeted factory overhead costs for 1996 are $560,560. To provide the most useful information to managers, these factory overhead costs should be separated into distinct **cost pools** or groupings of all costs that are associated with the same activity or cost driver. Cost pools should be selected by cross-functional management teams based on judgment as to usefulness and upon analysis of the major cross-functional activities that occur in the company.

Assume that the cost driver of brewing-related overhead costs is total number of cans of coffee produced and that the total cost pool for this cost driver is $54,912. The predetermined OH rate for brewing-related costs is $.04 per can ($54,912 ÷ 1,372,800 cans). The remaining $505,648 of factory overhead costs should be divided into other related cost pools, and appropriate drivers should be used to establish predetermined rates.

There are three primary reasons for using predetermined OH rates rather than actual overhead costs for product costing. First, a predetermined overhead rate allows overhead to be assigned to the goods produced or services rendered during the period rather than at or after the end of a period. If actual factory overhead costs are to be assigned to products and services, total overhead cost cannot be determined until all overhead transactions of the period have occurred. Thus, using a predetermined rate increases the availability of timely information for planning, controlling, and decision-making purposes.

Second, predetermined OH rates can compensate for fluctuations in actual overhead costs that are unrelated to activity levels. Overhead may vary on a monthly basis because of seasonal or calendar factors. For instance, production-related utility costs may be higher during the summer than at other times of the year. If production were constant each month and actual overhead were assigned to production, the increase in utilities would cause product cost per unit to be greater during the summer months than in other months.

Assume that Espressoly Yours has factory overhead costs of $45,000 per month, excluding utilities. Utility costs for two months (March and July) are $45,760 and $48,048, respectively. Assume, for purposes of this calculation, that Espressoly Yours only makes one type of coffee and defines activity in terms of one-pound cans. Production each month is 114,400 cans of coffee. The actual utility cost per unit is calculated as follows:

cost pools

■ LEARNING
OBJECTIVE 2
Discuss why the use of predetermined factory overhead rates provides better information than applying actual factory overhead to production.

---

[2]Institute of Management Accountants (formerly National Association of Accountants), *Statements on Management Accounting number 4G: Accounting for Indirect Production Costs* (Montvale, N.J.: National Association of Accountants, June 1, 1987), p. 11.

	March	**July**
$\dfrac{\text{Actual fixed utility cost}}{\text{Actual units produced}}$	$\dfrac{\$45{,}760}{114{,}400}$ = \$.40 per can	$\dfrac{\$48{,}048}{114{,}400}$ = \$.42 per can

The \$.02 cost differential between these two months is related solely to the \$2,288 difference in the numerators—not to any difference in the product itself.

Third, predetermined overhead rates can overcome a problem created by fixed costs. Total fixed overhead costs are unaffected by changes in activity, but fluctuations in activity cause actual per-unit fixed overhead to vary. Activity levels may vary because of seasonal or monthly calendar differences, including holiday periods. Even if total overhead costs were exactly equal each period, changes in activity would cause a per-unit change in cost because of the fixed-cost element of overhead.

Suppose that Espressoly Yours has \$19,260 of actual fixed overhead cost in both January and August. The company produces 113,294 cans of coffee in January and 96,300 cans of coffee in August. Actual fixed overhead per unit increases by \$.03 from January to August:

	January	**August**
$\dfrac{\text{Actual fixed overhead}}{\text{Actual units produced}}$	$\dfrac{\$19{,}260}{113{,}294}$ = \$.17 per can	$\dfrac{\$19{,}260}{96{,}300}$ = \$.20 per can

Because costs are caused by different factors, separate predetermined rates should be developed for the various cost pools of an organization. Additionally, since variable and fixed overhead costs behave differently, separate predetermined overhead rates should be developed for the variable and fixed elements of overhead cost.

ANALYZING MIXED COSTS

The first step in computing separate variable and fixed predetermined overhead rates is to examine the behavior of each production overhead cost incurred by the company.

■ **LEARNING OBJECTIVE 3**
Analyze mixed costs using the high-low method and (Appendix 1) least-squares regression analysis.

Cost Behavior

As discussed in Chapter 3, the most common accounting classifications of costs are variable, fixed, and mixed. Behavior may be related to the type of cost being incurred; for example, costs such as indirect materials and indirect labor are typically variable, and costs of supervision, building occupancy, and depreciation are typically fixed. But behavior may also depend on the type of business rather than the type of cost. For instance, tooling, quality control, and energy costs may be variable, mixed, or fixed depending on whether the company is highly automated and whether it manufactures homogeneous or heterogeneous products.

All costs are treated by accountants as linear rather than curvilinear. Because of this treatment, the general formula for a straight line is used to describe any type of cost (variable, fixed, or mixed) within a relevant range of activity. The straight-line formula is:

$$y = a + bX$$

where y = total cost
        a = fixed portion of total cost
        b = variable portion of total cost (the rate at which total cost changes in
              relation to changes in X; if a graph were prepared to depict the
              straight line, b would represent the slope of the line)
        X = activity base (or cost driver) to which y is being related

Exhibit 4–2 illustrates the use of the straight-line formula for each type of cost behavior. An entirely variable cost is represented as y = $0 + bX. Zero is shown as the value for the a term because there is no fixed cost. A purely fixed cost is formulated as y = a + $0X. Zero is the b term in the formula since no cost component varies with activity. A mixed cost has formula values for both the a and b unknowns. Thus, mixed costs must be separated into their variable and fixed components before separate variable and fixed overhead rates can be calculated. The simplest method of separation is the high-low method.

■ **EXHIBIT 4–2**
Uses of the Straight Line Cost Formula

Variable Cost

To explain or predict a variable cost such as indirect materials when the cost per unit is $2:

$$y = 0 + \$2X$$

where y = total indirect materials cost
      X = number of units produced

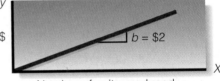

Number of units produced

Fixed Cost

To explain or predict a fixed cost such as building rent of $80,000 per year:

$$y = \$80,000 + 0X$$

where y = total annual building rent

Any measure of activity

Mixed Cost

To explain or predict a mixed cost such as repairs and maintenance when the fixed element is $14,000 per year and the variable element is $.60 per machine hour:

$$y = \$14,000 + \$.60X$$

where y = total annual repairs
            and maintenance cost
      X = number of machine
            hours incurred

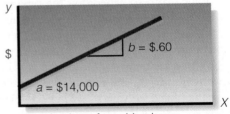

Number of machine hours

High-Low Method

The **high-low method** is a cost estimation technique for separating a mixed cost into its variable and fixed components. The high-low method uses activity and cost information from an actual set of cost observations to calculate the variable and fixed cost estimates. The highest and lowest activity levels are selected from the data set *if* these two levels are within the relevant range. The reason for selecting the high and low activity levels rather than high and low costs is that the analysis is undertaken to estimate how *costs* change in relation to *activity* changes. Activities cause costs to change; costs do not cause activities to change.

The high-low method is used to develop an equation that predicts the unknown values of a dependent variable (y term) from the known values of one or more independent variables (X term). An **independent variable** is an amount that, when changed, will cause consistent, observable changes in another variable. A **dependent variable** is an unknown amount that is to be predicted by the use of one or more independent variables.

Total mixed cost increases or decreases with changes in activity. The change in cost is equal to the change in activity multiplied by the unit variable cost; the fixed cost element does not fluctuate with changes in activity. The variable cost per unit of activity reflects the average change in cost for each additional unit of activity. Finding the changes in activity and cost simply involves subtracting the low observation values from the high values. These differences are then used to calculate the b term in the y = a + bX formula as follows:

$$b = \frac{\text{Change in total cost}}{\text{Change in activity level}}$$

The b term represents the unit variable cost per measure of activity. At either the low or high level of activity, the b value can be multiplied by the activity level to determine the amount of total variable cost contained in the total mixed cost.

Since a mixed cost has both a variable and a fixed component, the latter is found by subtracting total variable cost from total cost: y − bX = a. Either the high or the low level of activity can be used to determine the fixed portion of the mixed cost. Both activity levels are assumed to be on the same straight line and, thus, fixed cost would be constant at all activity levels within the relevant range.

The high-low method is illustrated in Exhibit 4–3 (page 140) using Espressoly Yours' data on cans produced and utility cost. The company's normal operating range of activity is 80,000 to 116,000 cans of coffee per month. For Espressoly Yours, the variable cost is $.01 per can of coffee and the fixed cost is $569 per month.

Note that the July data for Espressoly Yours are outside the relevant range; this high activity was analyzed and found to occur during a competitor's temporary production shutdown. A nonrepresentative point that falls outside of the relevant range of activity or that is a distortion of normal costs within the relevant range is known as an **outlier.** Outliers should be disregarded in analyzing mixed costs under the high-low method.

Regression analysis is another technique used to separate mixed costs into their variable and fixed cost elements. Regression (discussed in Appendix 1 to this chapter) often results in a better estimate of the cost formula than does the high-low method. Although performing it by hand is tedious, many software packages are available to do regression analysis.

Regardless of which method is used to separate mixed costs, it is important to recognize the following three points. First, high-low and regression are simply cost esti-

high-low method

independent variable
dependent variable

outlier

■ **EXHIBIT 4-3**
High-Low Analysis of Utility Cost

The following information on cans of coffee and utility cost is available from the prior year:

MONTH	LEVEL OF ACTIVITY IN CANS OF COFFEE	UTILITY COST
January	113,000	$1,712
February	114,000	1,716
March	90,000	1,469
April	115,000	1,719
May	112,000	1,698
June	101,000	1,691
July	122,000	1,989

Step 1: Select the highest and lowest levels of activity within the relevant range and obtain the costs associated with those levels. These levels and costs are 115,000 and 90,000 cans of coffee and $1,719 and $1,469, respectively.

Step 2: Calculate the change in activity and the change in cost.

	CANS OF COFFEE	ASSOCIATED UTILITY COST
High activity - April	115,000	$1,719
Low activity - March	90,000	1,469
Changes	25,000	$ 250

Step 3: Determine the relationship of cost change to activity change to find the variable cost element.

$$b = \frac{\text{Change in total cost}}{\text{Change in activity volume}} = \frac{\$250}{25,000} = \$.01 \text{ per can}$$

Step 4: Compute total variable cost (TVC) at either level of activity.

High level of activity: TVC = $.01 (115,000) = $1,150
or
Low level of activity: TVC = $.01 (90,000) = $ 900

Step 5: Subtract total variable cost from total cost at either level of activity to determine fixed cost.

High level of activity: a = $1,719 − $1,150 = $569
or
Low level of activity: a = $1,469 − $ 900 = $569

Step 6: Substitute the fixed and variable cost values in the straight-line formula to get an equation that can be used to estimate total cost at any level of activity within the relevant range.

$$y = \$569 + \$.01X$$

where   X = number of cans of coffee

mation techniques; neither provides exact costs of future activities. Second, the appropriateness of the cost formula depends on the validity of the activity measure chosen to predict the variable cost. The activity base selected should be logically related to the incurrence of overhead cost and should reflect significant correlation. (**Correlation** is a statistical measure of the strength of relationship between two variables.) Third, when significant changes are occurring in a business (such as the introduction of new production techniques or new product lines or expansion into new locales), historical information may not be extremely useful in attempting to predict future costs.

correlation

PREPARING FLEXIBLE BUDGETS

After all overhead costs are analyzed as to their cost behavior, managers can use the various y = a + bX cost formulas to prepare a flexible budget. A **flexible budget** is a series of individual financial plans that detail the individual costs comprising total cost and present those costs at different levels of activity.[3] In a flexible budget, all costs are treated as either variable or fixed; thus, mixed costs must be separated into their variable and fixed components.

flexible budget

■ LEARNING OBJECTIVE 4
Explain the usefulness of flexible budgeting to managers.

The activity levels shown on a flexible budget usually cover management's contemplated range of activity for the upcoming period. If all activity levels are within the relevant range, costs at each successive level should equal the amount of the previous level plus a uniform dollar increment for each variable cost factor. The increment is the variable cost per unit of activity multiplied by the quantity of additional activity.

An analysis of historical data for individual overhead costs for Espressoly Yours has generated the information shown in Exhibit 4–4 (page 142). This information is used to illustrate the preparation of a flexible budget. The company's activity base is cans of coffee, and its contemplated range of activity for the upcoming year is between 1,000,000 and 1,500,000 cans of coffee.

All cost factors are presented in terms of the a (fixed) and b (variable) values of the straight-line formula. Note that the information in Exhibit 4–4 indicates that both supervision and machine maintenance contract costs increase at an activity level of 1,400,000 cans of coffee. These costs are said to be step fixed or long-term variable costs. Espressoly Yours needs two flexible budget formulas (given at the bottom of the exhibit), since the analysis indicates the existence of changes in the fixed costs within the contemplated range of activity.

With the formulas derived in Exhibit 4–4, a flexible budget (shown in Exhibit 4–5, page 143) can be prepared for Espressoly Yours' factory overhead costs. Preparing a flexible budget is a good way to see any steps that exist for the categories of expected fixed costs. Exhibit 4–5 also illustrates the stable behavior of variable cost per can of coffee compared with the irregular behavior of fixed cost per can.

Two factors cause the irregular behavior of Espressoly Yours' fixed cost per can of coffee: a change in activity level and the steps in the fixed costs. As cans of coffee increase, fixed cost per can should decrease, assuming total fixed cost does not change. However, in this company, total fixed cost increases by $36,000 at 1,400,000 cans of coffee. The irregular behavior of fixed cost per unit requires that a specific level be chosen to calculate a predetermined fixed overhead rate per unit for product costing purposes.

---

[3]Flexible budgets can be prepared for all types of costs (both product and period), not just for overhead.

■ EXHIBIT 4–4
Analysis of Overhead Costs

The formulas are based on cans of coffee as the independent variable (X).

	a = FIXED COST	b = VARIABLE COST
PURELY VARIABLE COSTS		
Indirect materials		$.11
Indirect labor:		
Support workers		.07
Idle time		.02
Fringe benefits		.03
Total variable cost per can		$.23
PURELY FIXED COSTS		
Supervision	$ 90,000*	
Depreciation	100,000	
Maintenance contract	30,000**	
Insurance	4,256	
Total fixed cost per can	$224,256	
MIXED COST		
Utilities	6,832	.01
Totals for flexible budget formula		
(for X < 1,400,000 cans)	$231,088	$.24

*Supervision is expected to be $120,000 when $X \geq 1,400,000$ cans.

**Machine maintenance contract will increase to $36,000 when $X \geq 1,400,000$ cans.

Flexible budget formulas (where y = total manufacturing overhead):

(If X < 1,400,000 cans of coffee)   y = $231,088 + $.24X
(If X ≥ 1,400,000 cans of coffee)   y = $267,088 + $.24X

DEVELOPING AND USING PREDETERMINED OVERHEAD RATES

■ LEARNING
OBJECTIVE 5
Develop predetermined factory
overhead rates, use those rates to
apply overhead, and understand
the impact of the capacity
measure selected.

With the information provided in the flexible budget, a company can compute separate overhead rates for variable and fixed overhead costs.

Variable Overhead Rate

Variable overhead (VOH) changes proportionately in total with some measure of volume or activity. A predetermined overhead rate should be computed for each variable overhead cost pool. The information needed for these computations can be taken from any level of activity shown on the flexible budget that is within the relevant range. Total cost for each cost pool is then divided by the level of activity on which the estimate was based. Variable factory overhead is applied to production using the related activity base.

■ **EXHIBIT 4–5**
Overhead Flexible Budget

	CANS OF COFFEE			
	1,000,000	*1,100,000*	*1,372,800*	*1,400,000*
VARIABLE OVERHEAD COSTS				
Indirect materials	$110,000	$121,000	$151,008	$154,000
Indirect labor:				
Support workers	70,000	77,000	96,096	98,000
Idle time	20,000	22,000	27,456	28,000
Fringe benefits	30,000	33,000	41,184	42,000
Utilities	10,000	11,000	13,728	14,000
Total variable costs	$240,000	$264,000	$329,472	$336,000
Variable cost per can	$ .24	$ .24	$ .24	$ .24
FIXED COSTS				
Supervision	$ 90,000	$ 90,000	$ 90,000	$120,000
Depreciation	100,000	100,000	100,000	100,000
Maintenance contract	30,000	30,000	30,000	36,000
Insurance	4,256	4,256	4,256	4,256
Utilities	6,832	6,832	6,832	6,832
Total fixed costs	$231,088	$231,088	$231,088	$267,088
Fixed cost per can (rounded)	$ .23	$ .21	$ .17	$ .19
Total cost	$471,088	$495,088	$560,560	$603,088
Total cost per can of coffee	$ .47	$ .45	$ .41	$ .43

Since VOH is constant per unit at all activity levels within the relevant range, the activity level chosen for budgeting total variable cost is unimportant. For example, Espressoly Yours' owner budgets $121,000 of indirect materials cost at 1,100,000 cans of coffee. These budget amounts give a predetermined variable overhead rate for indirect materials of $.11 per unit ($121,000 ÷ 1,100,000). Correspondingly, if indirect materials cost is truly variable, the company would budget a total cost of $143,000 for 1,300,000 cans, or the same $.11 per can.

The activity measure selected to apply overhead to production should provide a logical relationship between the measure and the overhead cost incurrence. The activity measure that generally first comes to mind is production volume. However, unless a company makes only one type of output (such as Espressoly Yours), production volume is not really a feasible activity measure for any overhead cost. If multiple products or services are produced, overhead costs are incurred because of numerous factors, including the differing nature of the items, product variety, and product complexity.

The concept of homogeneity underlies all cost allocation. Some measure of activity that is common to all costs in a given cost pool must be used to allocate overhead to heterogeneous products. The most frequently used volume-based allocation measures include direct labor hours, direct labor dollars, machine hours, production orders, and production-related physical measures such as pounds and gallons. In addition, companies often use only a single total overhead cost pool or two overhead cost pools (total variable and total fixed). Alternatively, some companies apply overhead to products separately in each department and develop predetermined departmental overhead rates for this purpose.

As technology and the manufacturing environment change, companies must recognize that they may need to change their cost information systems. Using a less-than-appropriate allocation base and a minimal number of cost pools can result in poor managerial information. The failure of traditional labor-based allocation systems, with a small number of cost pools, to accurately assign costs is becoming more apparent as companies automate, increase the number and variety of product lines, and incur higher overhead costs than ever before. An alternative viewpoint is, however, presented in the accompanying News Note.

In Chapter 2, an emerging production environment is presented in which new manufacturing methods based on computer-driven, automated machinery and information technology is changing a number of accounting practices. For example, using direct labor to allocate overhead costs in highly automated plants results in extremely large overhead rates because the costs are applied over an ever-decreasing number of labor hours (or dollars). When automated plants allocate overhead on the basis of labor, managers are frequently concerned about the high rates per labor hour. On occasion, some managers have concluded that the way to reduce overhead is to reduce labor. This conclusion is erroneous. The overhead charge is high because labor is low; further reducing labor will simply increase the overhead rate!

If only a single type of activity base is to be used for overhead allocations in highly automated plants, machine hours are a more appropriate base than either direct labor hours or direct labor dollars. However, machine hours and overhead costs should be accumulated by machine type to develop a predetermined overhead rate per machine. In this way, overhead can be assigned in a cause-and-effect manner to products as they move through the various machine processes.

Many companies are looking at multiple cost pools and new activity measures for overhead allocation, including number or time of machine setups, number of different parts, material handling time, and quantity of product defects.[4] But regardless of how many cost pools are created or which activity base is chosen, the *method* of overhead application is the same. In a normal cost system, overhead is assigned to Work in Process Inventory using the predetermined rate multiplied by the actual quantity of the activity base. For simplicity, at this time, separate cost pools for variable and fixed overhead will be assumed, as will a single activity measure for allocating each.

Espressoly Yours's total predetermined variable overhead rate was given in Exhibit 4–5. As indicated earlier, the owner selected 1,372,800 cans of coffee as the estimated production volume. At that level of activity, estimated variable overhead costs of $329,472 were shown in the flexible budget. Dividing this cost estimate by the production volume estimate gives the predetermined variable overhead rate of $.24 as follows:

$$\text{Predetermined VOH rate} = \frac{\text{Budgeted VOH cost}}{\text{Budgeted output in cans}} = \frac{\$329,472}{1,372,800} = \$.24$$

This computation produces the necessary information for product costing purposes, but it does not provide the detail needed by managers to plan or control variable overhead costs. For these purposes, managers need individual costs per type of activity, as shown in Exhibit 4–6. This information allows the actual and budgeted costs

[4]Use of such nontraditional activity measures to allocate overhead and the resultant activity-based costs are discussed in Chapter 5.

In Japan, Direct Labor is Still a Good Allocation Base

American executives have been barraged with criticism about how long-accepted techniques for allocating manufacturing overhead can distort product costs and paint a flawed picture of the profitability of manufacturing operations. Accounting experts challenge direct labor hours as an overhead allocation base since direct labor represents only a small percentage of total costs in most manufacturing operations. They argue that a logical and causal relationship should exist between the overhead [costs] and the assignment of costs to individual products. They believe that an allocation system should capture as precisely as possible the reality of shop-floor costs.

Japanese companies are certainly aware of this perspective, but many companies don't seem to share it. Consider the practices of the Hitachi division that operates the world's largest factory devoted exclusively to videocassette recorders. The Hitachi VCR plant is highly automated yet continues to use direct labor as the basis for allocating manufacturing overhead. Overhead allocation doesn't reflect the actual production process in the factory's automated environment. [When accountants were asked] whether that policy might lead to bad decisions, they responded with an emphatic no. Hitachi, like many large Japanese manufacturers, is convinced that reducing direct labor is essential for ongoing continuous improvement. The company is committed to aggressive automation to promote long-term competitiveness. Allocating overhead based on direct labor creates the desired strong pro-automation incentives throughout the organization.

The perspective offered by Hitachi managers seems to be shared by their counterparts at many other companies. It is more important, they argue, to have an overhead allocation system (and other aspects of management accounting) that motivates employees to work in harmony with the company's long-term goals than to pinpoint production costs. Japanese managers want their accounting systems to help create a competitive future, not quantify the performance of their organizations at this moment.

SOURCE: Reprinted by permission of Harvard Business Review. An excerpt from "Another Hidden Edge—Japanese Management Accounting" by Toshiro Hiromoto (July-August 1988). Copyright © 1988 by the President and Fellows of Harvard College; all rights reserved.

of each activity to be compared. Significant **variances** (or deviations) from budgets can be investigated and their causes determined.

variances

Remember that predetermined overhead rates are always calculated in advance of the year of application. So the 1996 rate for Espressoly Yours was computed in 1995, on the basis of budgeted variable overhead costs and production volume for 1996. As

■ **EXHIBIT 4–6**

Detailed Predetermined Variable Overhead Rate Calculation

Estimated indirect materials	$151,008 ÷ 1,372,800 =	$.11
Estimated indirect labor		
Support workers	$ 96,096 ÷ 1,372,800 =	.07
Idle time	$ 27,456 ÷ 1,372,800 =	.02
Fringe benefits	$ 41,184 ÷ 1,372,800 =	.03
Estimated utilities	$ 13,728 ÷ 1,372,800 =	.01
Total variable overhead rate		$.24

production occurs in 1996, overhead will be assigned to the Work in Process Inventory account. The process of making this assignment is described after the discussion of fixed overhead rates.

Fixed Overhead Rate

Fixed overhead (FOH) is that portion of total overhead that remains constant in total with changes in activity within the relevant range. For product costing purposes, all fixed factory overhead costs must be budgeted and assigned to appropriate cost pools to comprise the numerators of the predetermined fixed factory overhead rate calculations.

Since fixed overhead is constant in total, it varies inversely on a per-unit basis with changes in activity. Therefore, a different unit cost is associated with each different level of activity. For this reason, calculating the predetermined FOH rate per unit requires that a specific activity level be chosen for the denominator. The level of activity selected is usually the firm's expected activity. **Expected capacity** is a short-run concept representing the anticipated level of activity of the firm for the upcoming year. If actual results are close to expected or budgeted results (in both dollars and volume), this measure of **capacity** (production volume or volume of another specified cost driver) should result in product costs that most closely reflect actual costs. Except where otherwise indicated throughout the text, the expected activity level has been chosen as the basis to calculate the predetermermined fixed factory overhead rate because it is believed to be the most prevalent practice.[5]

expected capacity

capacity

Even retail stores incur overhead costs. But open-air markets (such as this one in Charlotte Amalie, St. Thomas) allow merchants to eliminate the many fixed overhead costs associated with capital facilities—depreciation, utilities, property taxes, and so forth.

---

[5]Although many firms use expected activity to compute their predetermined fixed overhead rates, this choice of activity level may not be the most effective for planning and control purposes because it ignores the effects of unused capacity. This issue is discussed further in Chapter 6 in regard to standard cost variances.

Companies may choose to use an activity level other than expected capacity to compute their predetermined fixed overhead rates. Alternative measurement bases include theoretical, practical, and normal capacity. The estimated maximum productive activity that could occur in an organization during a specified time frame is the ideal or **theoretical capacity.** This measure assumes that all production factors are operating perfectly and, as such, disregards probable occurrences such as machinery breakdowns and reduced or halted plant operation on holidays.

theoretical capacity

These assumptions were traditionally considered unrealistic and, until recently, theoretical capacity has generally been considered an unacceptable basis for overhead application. Reducing theoretical capacity by factors such as unused resources and ongoing, regular operating interruptions (such as holidays, downtime, and start-up time) provides the **practical capacity** that could be efficiently achieved during normal working hours. The News Note on page 148 provides a perspective on valid reasons why practical capacity (rather than expected activity) may be a more appropriate base to calculate a predetermined overhead rate.

practical capacity

Sometimes managers wish to consider historical and estimated future production levels as well as cyclical and seasonal fluctuations in the computation of a predetermined fixed overhead rate. In such an instance, a **normal capacity** measure that encompasses the long-run average production activity (over five to ten years) may be used. This measurement does represent a reasonably attainable level of activity, but does not generally provide estimates that are most similar to actual costs in a given annual period. When normal capacity is used, distortions of cost would arise when activity levels vary significantly within the long-run period.

normal capacity

The budgeted fixed overhead costs for Espressoly Yours were given in Exhibit 4–5. Because Espressoly Yours is highly automated, the company's accountant has determined that fixed costs are more appropriately related to machine hours (MHs) than to production volume. To produce the budgeted 1,372,800 cans of coffee in 1996 will require 114,400 machine hours. Based on these budgeted figures, the predetermined fixed overhead rate is calculated as $2.02 per machine hour:

$$\frac{\text{Budgeted FOH to produce 1,372,800 cans of coffee}}{\text{Budgeted MHs to produce 1,372,800 cans of coffee}} = \frac{\$231,088}{114,400} = \$2.02 \text{ per MH}$$

OVERHEAD APPLICATION

Once the predetermined variable and fixed overhead rates have been calculated, they are used throughout the following year to apply (or assign) overhead to Work in Process Inventory. Factory overhead is assigned to goods being transferred from one processing department to another or as goods are transferred to Finished Goods Inventory so that a complete product cost can be obtained. Additionally, overhead must be applied at the end of each period so that the Work in Process Inventory account contains costs for all three product elements (direct materials, direct labor, and factory overhead).

Applied overhead is the amount of overhead assigned to Work in Process Inventory as a result of the occurrence of the activity that was used to develop the application rate. Application is based on the predetermined overhead rates and the actual level of activity. For example, assume that during January 1996, Espressoly Yours produces 108,000 cans of coffee and its factory machines run 9,100 hours. The previously calculated rates of $.24 for variable factory overhead and $2.02 for fixed factory overhead result in the following applications to Work in Process Inventory: $25,920 of variable factory overhead (108,000 cans X $.24 per can) and $18,382 of

applied overhead

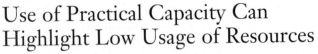
Use of Practical Capacity Can Highlight Low Usage of Resources

Practical capacity should be used as the relevant capacity level because it reveals the cost of unused resources. The concept of unused resources makes a distinction between the cost of resources *available* for manufacturing and the cost of resources acually used for that purpose.

The cost of supplying the productive resources is largely fixed in the short-run, does not vary with usage, and provides information relevant for predicting near-term spending. The cost of resources used provides information relevant for predicting changes in resource requirements as a function of changes in demand, technology, and product design. The difference between these two costs is called the cost of unused resources.

By using the practical capacity available in determining the fixed [overhead] rate, the cost of each unit produced contains only the cost of the resource used and, unlike the cost computed using [expected activity], does not include the cost of unused resources. Hence, each identical item of production is assigned the same cost, regardless of the number of such items produced or the number of changes in the product mix.

In addition, using practical capacity highlights the fact that some capacity is idle. Since world-class manufacturing must be flexible enough to respond to changing market conditions, corporate management must be informed when its facilities are not being used efficiently so that appropriate action can be taken. [Note: Idle capacity is indicated by the size of the underapplied overhead at the end of the period. This concept is discussed later in the chapter.]

SOURCE: Marinus DeBruine and Parvez R. Sopariwala, "The Use of Practical Capacity for Better Management Decisions," *Journal of Cost Management* (Spring 1994), pp. 26-27. Reprinted with permission from The Journal of Cost Management for the Manufacturing Industry, © 1994, Warren, Gorham & Lamont, 31 St. James Avenue, Boston MA 02116. All rights reserved.

fixed factory overhead (9,100 MHs X $2.02 per MH). The journal entry to record this overhead application is:

Work in Process Inventory	44,302	
Variable Factory Overhead		25,920
Fixed Factory Overhead		18,382
To apply factory overhead to production in January		

Underapplied and Overapplied Overhead

Although companies may be able to budget future overhead costs and expected activity with some degree of accuracy, it simply is not humanly possible to precisely project future events. Thus, actual overhead incurred during a period probably never equals applied overhead. The difference between the two total amounts represents underapplied or overapplied overhead. When the amount of overhead applied to Work in Process Inventory is less than actual overhead, overhead is **underapplied.** When the amount applied is more than actual overhead, overhead is **overapplied.**

It is important to note that the incurrence of actual factory overhead costs does *not* affect the process of overhead application. Actual factory overhead costs may be recorded to an overhead account on a daily, weekly, or monthly basis. Those overhead costs are created because activity takes place in the production area of the company.

underapplied overhead
overapplied overhead

That same actual activity causes overhead to periodically be applied to Work in Process Inventory and that application is based on the *predetermined* overhead rate multiplied by the *actual* quantity of activity. Thus, applied overhead is directly related to the amount of actual activity that took place, but only indirectly related to the amount of actual overhead cost incurred by a company.

The factory overhead accounts used for recording actual and applied overhead amounts are temporary accounts. Any balances in these accounts are closed at year-end because an annual period was used to develop the predetermined overhead rates.

Disposition of Underapplied and Overapplied Overhead

In a normal costing system, actual overhead costs are debited to the variable and fixed overhead accounts and credited to the various sources of overhead costs. (These entries are presented in Chapter 3.) Applied overhead is debited to Work in Process Inventory using predetermined rates multiplied by actual activity levels, and credited to the variable and fixed overhead accounts. Applied overhead is added to actual direct materials and direct labor costs in the computation of cost of goods manufactured. The end-of-period balance in each overhead account represents underapplied (debit) or overapplied (credit) overhead.

■ LEARNING
OBJECTIVE 6
Account for underapplied or overapplied factory overhead at year-end.

VARIABLE OR FIXED OVERHEAD		WORK IN PROCESS INVENTORY	
Actual OH costs XXX*	Applied OH costs YYY	DM √√√	
		DL √√√	
		Applied OH costs	YYY

*Offsetting these debits are credits to various sources of overhead costs, such as Accumulated Depreciation, Accounts Payable, Supplies Inventory, and Wages Payable.

Disposition of underapplied or overapplied overhead depends upon the materiality of the amount involved. If the amount of the variance is immaterial, it is closed to Cost of Goods Sold in a manufacturing firm or to Cost of Services Rendered in a service firm. When underapplied overhead is closed, it causes Cost of Goods Sold (or Cost of Services Rendered) to increase since not enough overhead was applied to production during the year. Alternatively, closing overapplied overhead causes Cost of Goods Sold (or Cost of Services Rendered) to decrease because too much overhead was applied to production during the year.

If the amount of underapplied or overapplied overhead is material, it should be allocated among the accounts containing applied overhead (Work in Process Inventory, Finished Goods Inventory, and Cost of Goods Sold or Cost of Services Rendered). Allocation to the accounts may be based on the relative amounts of overhead contained in the accounts or the relative account balances. A material amount of underapplied or overapplied overhead means that the balances in these accounts vary significantly from what they would have been if actual overhead costs had been assigned to production. The underapplied or overapplied amount is allocated among the affected accounts so that their balances conform more closely with actual historical costs as required by generally accepted accounting principles for external financial statements.

Exhibit 4–7 (page 150) uses assumed amounts for Espressoly Yours to illustrate the technique of apportioning overapplied variable overhead among the necessary accounts. Had the amount been underapplied, the accounts debited and credited in

■ EXHIBIT 4–7
Apportioning Overapplied Overhead

Variable overhead		Amount of VOH in account balances:	
Actual	$73,400	Work in Process Inventory	$ 58,500
Applied	94,400	Finished Goods Inventory	97,500
Overapplied OH	$21,000	Cost of Goods Sold	234,000

1. Add overhead amounts in accounts and determine proportional relationships:

	VOH BALANCE	PROPORTION	PERCENTAGE
Work in Process Inventory	$ 58,500	$ 58,500 ÷ $390,000	15%
Finished Goods Inventory	97,500	$ 97,500 ÷ $390,000	25%
Cost of Goods Sold	234,000	$234,000 ÷ $390,000	60%
Total	$390,000		100%

2. Multiply percentages times overapplied variable overhead amount to determine the amount of adjustment needed:

	PERCENTAGE	×	OVERAPPLIED VOH	= ADJUSTMENT AMOUNT
Work in Process Inventory	15%	×	$21,000	=	$ 3,150
Finished Goods Inventory	25%	×	$21,000	=	5,250
Cost of Goods Sold	60%	×	$21,000	=	12,600

3. Prepare journal entry to close variable overhead account and assign adjustment amount to appropriate accounts:

Variable Overhead	21,000	
Work in Process Inventory		3,150
Finished Goods Inventory		5,250
Cost of Goods Sold		12,600

the journal entry would have been reversed. The computational process would be the same if the overhead were fixed rather than variable.

If predetermined overhead rates are based on valid cost drivers, those rates provide a rational and systematic way for accountants to assign overhead costs to products for external financial statement preparation. Separate cost pools as well as separate variable and fixed overhead rates should be used to obtain the most refined information for planning, controlling, and decision making. In spite of this fact, companies may (and commonly do) choose to use combined overhead rates rather than separate ones for variable and fixed overhead.

COMBINED OVERHEAD RATES

Combined overhead rates are traditional in businesses for three reasons: clerical ease, clerical cost savings, and absence of any formal requirement to separate overhead costs by cost behavior. The process of computing a combined predetermined overhead rate is essentially the same as that of computing separate rates. The difference is that only one type of activity can be selected for the cost pool (rather than different activities for the variable and fixed components). Once the activity base is chosen, management specifies the level of activity at which costs are to be budgeted. Variable and fixed costs are computed for that activity using the appropriate cost formulas and the costs are totaled and divided by the activity level to yield the single overhead application rate.

Assume that Espressoly Yours decides to use a combined predetermined factory overhead rate based on expected production volume. With the previously specified 1,372,800 cans of coffee as its expected activity level, the company's combined predetermined overhead rate is calculated as follows:

Total budgeted VOH at 1,372,800 cans of coffee (from Exhibit 4–5)	$ 329,472
Total budgeted FOH (from Exhibit 4–5)	231,088
Total budgeted overhead cost	$ 560,560
Divided by expected activity in cans of coffee	÷ 1,372,800
Predetermined overhead rate per can of coffee (rounded)	$.41

Note that this single rate is equal to the sum of the variable and fixed rates calculated earlier in Exhibit 4–5.

For each can of coffee produced by Espressoly Yours in 1996, the company's Work in Process Inventory account will be charged with $.41 of overhead. If Espressoly Yours produces 108,000 cans of coffee in January, $44,280 (108,000 × $.41) of overhead would be added to the Work in Process Inventory account as follows:

Work in Process Inventory	44,280	
Factory Overhead		44,280
To apply January factory overhead to production		

Although achieving the necessary function of assigning factory overhead costs to production, the use of a combined overhead rate reduces a manager's ability to determine the causes of underapplied or overapplied overhead.

Progressive die metal stamping presses produce thousands of parts per minute at Masco Industries, with minimal operator involvement. It is highly unlikely that direct labor is an appropriate basis upon which to assign overhead costs to products in such a situation.

When companies use a single overhead application rate, the rate can be related to a particular cost pool (such as machine-related overhead) or to overhead costs in general. As more cost pools are combined, the underlying cause-effect relationships between activities and costs are blurred. This factor may contribute to an inability to reduce costs, improve productivity, or discover the causes of underapplied or overapplied overhead. The lack of detailed information hinders managers' abilities to plan operations, control costs, and make decisions. Thus, although some clerical cost savings may be achieved, the ultimate costs of poor information are probably significantly greater than the savings generated.

Using separate departmental and cost pool activity bases is superior to using a combined plantwide base. Since most companies produce a wide variety of products or perform a wide variety of services, different activity measures should be used to calculate overhead rates for different departments and for different types of overhead costs. Machine hours may be the most appropriate activity base for many costs in a department that is highly automated. Direct labor hours may be the best basis for assigning the majority of overhead costs in a labor-intensive department. In the quality control area, number of defects may provide the best allocation base.

Separate bases for overhead computations allow management to accumulate and apply costs for distinct homogeneous groups of activities rather than a heterogeneous set of plantwide activities. Different rates provide better information for planning, control, performance evaluation, and decision making.

SITE ANALYSIS

Coffee lovers are happy to shell out from 95 cents to $2.25 for a cup of Starbucks' potent brew because they think it's wonderful. Mail-order customers around the country pay anywhere from $6.95 to $14.95 per pound. Starbucks has made these customers happy by making certain that the best coffee beans and processes are used. And the company is equally interested in its employees.

Two primary overhead costs for many companies are training and employee fringe benefits. At Starbucks, each new employee receives 25 hours of classroom training—even though over 50 percent of the retail sales force is part-time. Management trainees attend 8 to 12 weeks of classes with titles like Coffee Knowledge 101. As to fringe benefits, Schultz is adamant that his employees be provided with a generous and comprehensive package that includes health care, stock options, career counseling, and product discounts for all workers—full-time and part-time. Giving employees a stake in the outcome of the business helps to imbue them with a sense of loyalty and corporate culture and encourages attentive service to customers. Quality is high; attrition and inventory shinkage are low. (Pilferage—a tremendous cost in business—is less than half of one percent.)

Since they cannot control the cost of direct materials (green coffee beans), Schulz and his managers must control overhead costs in the roasting operations and in the retail stores. But at Starbucks, control does not mean making certain that all overhead costs are as low as they can be. Control means making certain that the dollars spent for overhead costs are in some way contributing to business profitability. And this often means spending more to improve the well-being of employees who, in turn, contribute to successfully operating in a coffee-bean-and-beverage market that totaled $6.5 billion in 1991.

Discipline	Application	CROSS-FUNCTIONAL APPLICATIONS STRATEGIES
Accounting	Using predetermined OH rates allows timely financial statement valuations; provides more stable product costs; and assists managers in making plans, controlling costs, and solving problems.	
Economics	Using predetermined OH rates helps in analyzing and predicting costs in the quest for efficiency in a competitive market environment; and provides a real-world measure of the economic concept of marginal cost in decision making.	
Finance	Using predetermined OH rates helps in estimating costs for future periods; and provides more timely knowledge of gross profit margins.	
Management	Using predetermined OH rates helps in OH cost analysis and control; provides a basis for planning, controlling, and decision making; provides an indication of product/service profitability; and forces recognition of cause-effect relationships between costs and activities or cost drivers.	
Marketing	Using predetermined OH rates allows bid prices to be estimated more easily because underlying costs are understood.	

CHAPTER SUMMARY

In costing products, companies must first select a costing system. A job order costing system is used by companies making a limited quantity of products or providing services uniquely tailored to customer specifications. Process costing is used in companies making large quantities of homogeneous items.

Next, companies must choose a cost measurement method. Actual costing assigns the actual costs of direct materials, direct labor, and/or overhead to products (or services). Normal costing uses actual direct materials and direct labor costs, but uses predetermined rates to assign overhead to products and services. A standard cost system uses norms for all cost elements.

If separate variable and fixed overhead rates are to be calculated, mixed costs must be separated into their variable and fixed components. One technique that can be used to make this separation is the high-low method. The high-low method uses two points of actual activity data (the highest and lowest) to determine the change in cost and activity. Dividing the cost change by the activity change gives the per-unit variable cost portion of the mixed cost. Fixed cost results from subtracting total variable cost from total cost at either the high or the low level of activity.

After mixed costs have been separated into their variable and fixed elements, flexible budgets that indicate costs at various activity levels can be prepared. All costs in the flexible budget can be calculated by use of the formula $y = a + bX$, where y = total cost, a = fixed cost, b = variable cost per unit of activity, and X = the level of activity.

Given the overhead cost formulas, accountants can calculate predetermined overhead rates by dividing budgeted overhead costs by a selected level of activity. Such rates assign overhead cost to goods or services based on the actual quantity of activity used to produce the goods or services. The use of predetermined rates eliminates the delays and distortions that occur when actual overhead is applied. Separate rates computed according to cost behavior and for different cost pools yield costs that best reflect the resources sacrificed to make a product or perform a service.

Since unit variable costs remain constant over the relevant range of activity, total variable overhead for each cost pool can be divided by any level of activity to compute the predetermined rate. The predetermined fixed overhead rate is computed as budgeted fixed overhead at a specific level of activity divided by that level of activity. Most companies select the expected annual capacity level as the activity measure.

Using predetermined rates normally results in either underapplied or overapplied overhead at year-end. If the total amount of underapplied or overapplied overhead is small, it is closed to Cost of Goods Sold or Cost of Services Rendered. If the amount is large, it is allocated to Work in Process Inventory, Finished Goods Inventory, and Cost of Goods Sold/Services Rendered.

APPENDIX

Least-Squares Regression Analysis

least-squares regression analysis

The chapter illustrates the high-low method of separating mixed costs into their variable and fixed elements. A potential weakness of the high-low method is that outliers may be inadvertently used in the calculation. Outliers are not representative of actual costs and are generally not good predictors of future costs. Thus, a cost formula derived from outlier data will probably not be very useful.

This appendix introduces a statistical technique known as **least-squares regression analysis** as another method of mixed cost analysis. The least-squares method makes it possible to mathematically determine the cost formula of a mixed cost by considering the best fit to all representative data points rather than only two points.

■ **LEARNING OBJECTIVE 3**

Analyze mixed costs using the high-low method and (Appendix 1) least-squares regression analysis.

Like the high-low method, least-squares separates the variable and fixed cost elements of any type of mixed cost. When multiple independent variables exist, least-squares regression also helps managers to select the independent variable that has the strongest correlation with and, thus, is the best predictor of the dependent variable. For example, least-squares can be used by managers trying to decide if machine hours, direct labor hours, or number of parts per product best explain and predict changes in a certain factory overhead cost pool.

All chapter examples assume that a linear relationship exists between the independent and dependent variables. Thus, each one-unit change in an independent variable produces a specific unit change in the dependent variable. When only one independent variable is used to predict the dependent variable, the process is known as **simple regression** analysis.[6]

simple regression

Simple linear regression employs the same straight-line formula ($y = a + bX$) used in the high-low method. First, the available data set consisting of the actual values of the independent variable (X) and actual values of the dependent variable (y) is analyzed for outliers, which are eliminated from consideration. Next, a **regression line** is mathematically developed that represents the line that best fits the data observations. This line minimizes the sum of the squares of the vertical deviations between the line and the actual observation points.

regression line

Exhibit 4–8 graphically illustrates least-squares regression. Graph A of the exhibit presents a set of actual observations. Actual observation values from the data set are designated as y values. Graph B indicates that many lines could be drawn through the data set, but most would provide a poor fit. The y values are used, along with the actual activity levels (X values), to mathematically determine the regression line of best

---

[6]In multiple regression, two or more independent variables are used.

fit. This regression line represents values computed for the dependent variable for all actual activity levels. The dependent values that comprise the regression line are designated as y_c values.

The vertical line segments from the actual observation points (y values) to the regression line (y_c values) in Graph B of Exhibit 4–9 are deviations. The amount of a deviation is determined by subtracting the y_c value at an activity level from its related y value. Deviations above the regression line are positive amounts, while deviations below the line are negative. By squaring the deviations, the negative signs are eliminated. These positive sum of the squared deviations $[(y - y_c)^2]$ can be mathematically manipulated to yield the regression line of best fit. This regression line minimizes the sum of the squared deviations (hence, the name least-squares). The least-squares regression line can then be used to estimate cost formula values for fixed (a) and variable (b) terms. This equation can then be used by the cost analyst to make predictions and analyses.

The Espressoly Yours data for cans of coffee and utility cost from Exhibit 4–3 are used here to illustrate the calculation of the least-squares regression line. The equations necessary to compute b and a values using the method of least squares are as follows:[7]

$$b = \frac{\Sigma\, xy - nxy}{\Sigma\, x^2 - nx^2}$$

$$a = y - bx$$

where
  x = value of independent variable
  y = value of dependent variable
  n = number of observations
  x = mean (or arithmetic average) of the independent variable
  y = mean (or arithmetic average) of the dependent variable

■ **EXHIBIT 4–8**
Illustration of Least-Squares Regression Line

Graph A   Assumed set of data points

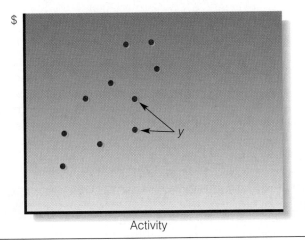

Graph B   Trend lines with deviations

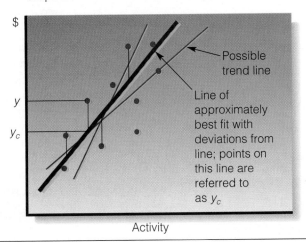

[7]These equations are derived from mathematical computations beyond the scope of this text but found in many statistics books. The symbol Σ means "the summation of."

The Espressoly Yours data must be restated in an appropriate form for substitution into the equations for b and a. Because of the magnitude of the X values, calculations are made for each one-thousand cans of coffee to avoid working with extremely large numbers. At the completion of the calculations, the resulting values are converted to a per-unit b value by dividing by 1,000. These restatements are as follows:

	x	y	xy	x^2
January	113	$ 1,712	$ 193,456	12,769
February	114	1,716	195,624	12,996
March	90	1,469	132,210	8,100
April	115	1,719	197,685	13,225
May	112	1,698	190,176	12,544
June	101	1,691	170,791	10,201
	645	$10,005	$1,079,942	69,835

The mean value for the data in the x column is 107.5 (or 645 ÷ 6) and the mean value for the data in the y column is $1,667.5 (or $10,005 ÷ 6). (Note that the outlier for July of 122,000 cans of coffee has once again been ignored.)

Substituting appropriate amounts into the formulas yields the b (variable) and a (fixed) cost values. The b value is calculated first, since it is used to compute a.

$$b = \frac{\Sigma\, xy - n\bar{x}\bar{y}}{\Sigma\, x^2 - n\bar{x}^2}$$

$$= \frac{\$1,079,942 - 6\,(107.5)\,(\$1,667.5)}{69,835 - 6\,(107.5)\,(107.5)}$$

$$= \frac{\$4,404.5}{497.5} = \$8.85 \text{ per thousand or \$.009 per can}$$

$$a = \bar{y} - b\bar{x}$$

$$= \$1,667.50 - \$8.85(107.5)$$
$$= \$1,667.50 - \$951.38$$
$$= \$716.12$$

Thus, the cost formula under least-squares regression is:

Total utility cost = $716.12 + $.009 per can of coffee

Notice that the least-squares method gives a different cost formula than did the high-low method demonstrated in Exhibit 4–3. Regression information yields more reliable results—a characteristic that is very important to managers seeking to understand and control costs based on changes in activity. Because of the many computer packages that are able to do least-squares regression quickly and accurately, it has become virtually costless to do this type of analysis using a variety of possibilities as the independent variable.

APPENDIX

Allocation of Service Department Costs

Organizations incur costs for two basic types of activities: those that generate revenue (products and services) and those that do not. Organizational support areas consist of

Administration Costs Take Big Bite From Cookie Profits

The annual cookie sale—the Girl Scouts' main funding source—generates about an estimated $400 million in revenue. But many in this volunteer cadre—the Scouts, troop leaders and parents who provide the free labor [and generate the revenues]—are starting to question the annual cookie drive, saying the troops simply don't see enough of the profits. Tax-free cookie proceeds mainly support the Girl Scouts' sprawling bureaucracy, critics say, while the girls themselves are left with the crumbs.

[For example, most of the profits from 1993 cookie sales in Connecticut were] kept by Connecticut Trails Council, the Girl Scouts' local administrative office in North Haven. The council, which trains volunteer troop leaders and plans events, relied on cookie sales to fund fully 66% of its $3.5 million 1992 budget, including $1.6 million in salaries and benefits for 42 employees.

There are 332 such regional Scout councils scattered around the U.S., each one with an office and a paid staff overseen by a volunteer board. Some larger councils—serving 12,000 girls or more—have dozens of employees. Together they spend about $357 million a year.

SOURCE: Ellen Graham, "Sprawling Bureaucracy Eats Up Most Profits of Girl Scout Cookies," *Wall Street Journal* (May 13, 1993), p. A1. Reprinted by permission of The Wall Street Journal, © 1993 Dow Jones & Company, Inc. All Rights Reserved Worldwide.

both service and administrative departments. **Service departments** (such as central purchasing and central computing) perform one or more specific functional tasks for other internal units; **administrative departments** (including top management and organization headquarters personnel) perform management activities that benefit the entire organization. Costs of service and administrative departments are referred to collectively as service department costs, since company administration provides service to the rest of the company. As can be seen from the accompanying News Note, service and administrative departments can be extremely expensive.

If an organization is to make a profit, the selling prices it charges for its goods or services must cover both the costs of revenue-generating activities and the costs of support activities. Since non-revenue-producing activities are conducted to support revenue-producing activities, in essence service department costs are simply another form of overhead.

Service department costs are often allocated or charged to revenue-producing departments so that their managers are made aware that their activities are responsible for covering all organizational costs. A rational and systematic allocation base for service department costs should reflect consideration of four criteria: (1) the benefits received by the revenue-producing department from the service department; (2) a cause-and-effect relationship between factors in the revenue-producing department and costs incurred in the service department; (3) the fairness of the service department allocations between or among revenue-producing departments; and (4) the ability of revenue-producing departments to bear the allocated costs.

Benefits received and causal relationships are the criteria used most often to select allocation bases. These criteria are reasonably objective and produce rational allocations. Fairness, although a valid theoretical basis for allocation, is difficult to implement since people may disagree about what is fair or equitable. The ability-to-bear criterion

service departments

administrative departments

■ LEARNING OBJECTIVE 7
Allocate service department costs to revenue-producing departments using the direct and step methods.

is not normally used to allocate service department costs to revenue-producing departments because it often results in unrealistic or profit-detrimental actions. For example, departmental managers might employ financial and logistical manipulations in an attempt to minimize the basis on which costs are to be allocated to their departments.

Applying the two primary criteria (benefits and cause-effect) to the allocation of service department costs can help to specify some acceptable allocation bases. The allocation base selected must be a valid one because an improper base always yields improper information regardless of how complex or precise the allocation process appears to be.

Methods of Service Department Cost Allocation

When service department costs are allocated to revenue-producing areas, the basic cost pools are the direct costs of each revenue-producing and service department. These costs can be gathered and specified in terms of cost behavior (variable and fixed) or in total. The service department cost pools are then allocated to the revenue-producing departments. The allocation process may require one or more steps to complete depending on the allocation method selected. In each revenue-producing department, the allocated service department costs may be combined with that department's direct costs if a combined predetermined rate is to be computed. Alternatively, the allocated service department costs may be left in a separate cost pool in the revenue-producing department if multiple predetermined rates are to be calculated using different measures of activity. The single or multiple predetermined overhead rates are then used to allocate all overhead costs (from the revenue-producing department and allocated service-departments) to final cost objects (such as products, programs, or salable services).

direct method

Two basic methods of allocating the pooled costs of the service departments to revenue-producing departments are the direct method and the step method.[8] The **direct method** of allocation is the easier method. Service department costs are assigned directly to the revenue-producing areas with one specific allocation basis used for each service department. For example, personnel department costs might be assigned to production departments based on the number of people in each production department. Because costs are allocated directly, there are no intermediate cost pools (temporary groups of allocated costs). Also, no service department cost is allocated to any other service department.

step method

The **step method** of cost allocation assigns service-department costs to revenue-producing departments in a multiple step process. Relationships among departments are considered in this method based on the quantity of services provided by each service department to other areas. These relationships are listed in a **benefits-provided ranking** that begins with the service department providing service to the most organizational areas (both non-revenue-producing and revenue-producing) and ends with the department that provides service primarily to revenue-producing areas. The ranking sequence provides a partial recognition of the reciprocal relationships among the service departments. For example, since the personnel department provides services for all areas of the company, it might be the first department listed in the ranking. All other areas would receive a proportionate allocation of the personnel department's costs. Once costs have been assigned from the personnel department, no additional costs are charged back to that department in subsequent allocations.

benefits-provided ranking

[8]A third method, the algebraic or reciprocal approach to service department cost allocation, considers all interrelationships of departments and reflects them in simultaneous equations. This technique is covered in standard cost accounting texts.

After the ranking is developed, a specific allocation base for each department is indicated. Service department costs are allocated down the list until all costs have been assigned to the revenue-producing areas.

Illustration of Service Department Cost Allocation

Assume that Wanna-Cuppa is a manufacturing company that has two production divisions (Coffee Beans and Tea Leaves) and three service departments (Administration, Personnel, and Public Relations). Budgeted costs for all departments are as follows:

Administration	$ 600,000
Personnel	280,000
Public Relations	320,000
Total service department costs	$1,200,000
Coffee Beans departmental overhead	940,000
Tea Leaves departmental overhead	1,125,000
Total overhead costs	$3,265,000

Wanna-Cuppa's management has decided that number of employee hours, number of employees, and dollars of assets employed in a department are the three best available measures of departmental activity. The managers have gathered these statistics for each department and have composed the following list in the benefits-provided ranking:

	NUMBER OF EMPLOYEE HOURS	NUMBER OF EMPLOYEES	DOLLARS OF ASSETS EMPLOYED
Administration	9,400	4	$380,000
Personnel	6,240	3	140,000
Public Relations	4,160	2	90,000
Coffee Beans	11,250	5	400,000
Tea Leaves	16,875	6	600,000

Company management believes that administration costs should be allocated on the basis of employee hours, personnel costs on the basis of number of employees, and public relations costs on the basis of dollars of assets employed. When all service department costs are allocated to the revenue-producing departments, alternative activity measures will be used to assign costs to departmental output.

Exhibit 4–9 (page 160) shows the direct method of service department allocation. This allocation produces $1,434,000 of total overhead costs for the Coffee Beans Department and $1,831,000 for the Tea Leaves Department. These costs will be attached to each department's output through an additional allocation process. The allocation of service department costs to revenue-producing departments allows those departments to better monitor, control, and evaluate their use of services.

Step allocation of Wanna-Cuppa's service costs is shown in Exhibit 4–10 (page 161). The costs are assigned in the benefits-provided ranking order and using the selected measures of activity. This method of allocation results in $1,437,600 of total overhead costs for the Coffee Beans Department and $1,827,400 in the Tea Leaves Department. As under the direct method, these costs will be attached to departmental output using an additional allocation process.

For simplicity, cost behavior in all departments has been ignored. A more appropriate allocation process would specify different bases for the variable and for the

■ **EXHIBIT 4–9**
Direct Method of Allocating Service Department Costs

	BASE	PERCENT OF TOTAL BASE	AMOUNT TO ALLOCATE	AMOUNT ALLOCATED
Administration costs				
(employee hours) assigned to:				
Coffee Beans	11,250	40	$600,000	$ 240,000
Tea Leaves	16,875	60	600,000	360,000
Totals	28,125	100		$ 600,000
Personnel costs				
(number of employees)				
Coffee Beans	5	45	$280,000	$ 126,000
Tea Leaves	6	55	280,000	154,000
Totals	11	100		$ 280,000
Public Relations Costs				
(dollars of assets employed)				
Coffee Beans	$ 400,000	40	$320,000	$ 128,000
Tea Leaves	600,000	60	320,000	192,000
Totals	$1,000,000	100		$ 320,000

Revenue-Producing Departments Total Overhead Costs:

	COFFEE BEANS	TEA LEAVES	TOTAL
Allocated overhead			
From Administration	$ 240,000	$ 360,000	$ 600,000
From Personnel	126,000	154,000	280,000
From Public Relations	128,000	192,000	320,000
Direct overhead	940,000	1,125,000	2,065,000
Total overhead	$1,434,000	$1,831,000	$3,265,000

fixed costs in each department. Costs would then be assigned in a manner more reflective of their behavior. Such differentiation would not change the process of allocation but would change the results for each of the two methods (direct and step). The computer makes this process significantly more practical than it was in the past.

GLOSSARY

Actual cost system (p. 133)   a method of accumulating product or service costs that uses actual direct materials, actual direct labor, and actual overhead costs

Administrative department (p. 157)   an organizational unit that performs management activities that benefit the entire organization (from appendix)

Applied overhead (p. 146)   the amount of overhead assigned to Work in Process Inventory as a result of the occurrence of the activity that was used to develop the application rate; the result of multiplying the quantity of actual activity by the predetermined rate

Benefits-provided ranking (p. 158)   a listing of service departments in an order that begins with the one providing the most service to all other organizational areas; the ranking ends with the service department that provides the least service to all but the revenue-producing areas (from appendix)

■ **EXHIBIT 4–10**
Step Method of Allocating Service Department Costs

	BASE	PERCENT OF TOTAL BASE	AMOUNT TO ALLOCATE	AMOUNT ALLOCATED
Administration Costs				
(employee hours)				
Personnel	6,240	16	$600,000	$ 96,000
Public Relations	4,160	11	600,000	66,000
Coffee Beans	11,250	29	600,000	174,000
Tea Leaves	16,875	44	600,000	264,000
Totals	38,525	100		$ 600,000
Personnel Costs				
(number of employees)				
Public Relations	2	15	$376,000*	$ 56,400
Coffee Beans	5	39	376,000	146,640
Tea Leaves	6	46	376,000	172,960
Totals	13	100		$ 376,000
Public Relations Costs				
(dollars of assets employed)				
Coffee Beans	$ 400,000	40	$442,400**	$ 176,960
Tea Leaves	600,000	60	442,400	265,440
Totals	$1,000,000	100		$ 442,400

Revenue-Producing Departments Total Overhead Costs:

	COFFEE BEANS	TEA LEAVES	TOTAL
Allocated overhead			
From Administration	$ 174,000	$ 264,000	$ 438,000
From Personnel	146,640	172,960	319,600
From Public Relations	176,960	265,440	442,400
Direct overhead	940,000	1,125,000	2,065,000
	$1,437,600	$1,827,400	$3,265,000

*The $376,000 of personnel costs to be allocated is the sum of the $280,000 budgeted personnel costs plus the $96,000 allocated from administration.

**The $442,400 of public relations costs is the sum of the $320,000 budgeted public relations costs plus the $66,000 allocated from administration and the $56,400 allocated from personnel.

Capacity (p. 146)   a measure of production volume or of some other cost driver related to plant production capability during a period

Correlation (p. 141)   a statistical measure of the strength of relationship between two variables

Cost pool (p. 136)   a grouping of all costs that are associated with the same activity or cost driver

Dependent variable (p. 139)   an unknown variable that is to be predicted by use of one or more independent variables

Direct method (of service department cost allocation) (p. 158)   a method that uses a specific base to assign service department costs directly to revenue-producing departments with no intermediate cost allocations (from appendix)

Employee time sheet (time ticket) (p. 134)   a source document that indicates, for each employee, what jobs were worked on and for what amount of time

Expected capacity (p. 146)   a short-run concept representing the anticipated level of activity for the upcoming year

Flexible budget (p. 141)   a series of financial plans that detail the individual variable and fixed cost factors comprising total cost and present those costs at different levels of activity according to cost behavior

High-low method (p. 139)   a technique for separating mixed costs that uses actual observations of a total cost at the highest and lowest levels of activity and calculates the change in both activity and cost; the levels chosen must be within the relevant range

Independent variable (p. 139)   a variable that, when changed, will cause consistent, observable changes in another variable; a variable used as the basis of predicting the value of a dependent variable

Job (p. 133)   a single unit or group of like units identifiable as being produced to distinct customer specifications

Job order costing (p. 132)   the product costing system used by entities that produce tailor-made goods or services in limited quantities that conform to specifications designated by the purchaser of those goods or services

Job order cost sheet (p. 134)   a source document that provides virtually all the financial information about a particular job; the set of all job order cost sheets for uncompleted jobs provides supporting information about Work in Process Inventory

Least-squares regression analysis (p. 154)   a statistical technique for mathematically determining the cost line of a mixed cost that best fits the data set by considering all representative data points; allows the user to investigate the relationship between or among dependent and independent variables (from appendix)

Materials requisition (p. 133)   a source document that indicates the types and quantities of materials to be placed into production or used in performing a service; causes materials and their costs to be released from the raw materials warehouse and sent to Work in Process Inventory

Normal capacity (p. 146)   a firm's long-run average activity (over five to ten years) which considers historical and estimated future production levels as well as cyclical and seasonal fluctuations

Normal cost system (p. 133)   a method of accumulating product or service costs that uses actual direct materials and direct labor costs but assigns overhead costs to Work in Process Inventory using a predetermined overhead rate

Outlier (p. 139)   a nonrepresentative point that either falls outside the relevant range or is a distortion of typical cost-volume relationship within the relevant range

Overapplied overhead (p. 148)   the excess of overhead applied to Work in Process Inventory above actual overhead incurred for a period

Practical capacity (p. 146)   the activity level of a firm that could be achieved during normal working hours given unused capacity and ongoing, regular operating interruptions, such as holidays, downtime, and start-up time

Predetermined overhead rate (p. 133)   a budgeted constant charge per unit of activity used to assign overhead costs to production or services

Process costing system (p. 132)   the product costing system used by entities that produce large quantities of homogeneous goods in continuous mass production

Regression line (p. 154)   a line representing the cost formula for a set of cost observations which has been fit to those observations in a mathematically determined manner (from appendix)

Service department (p. 157)   an organizational unit that performs one or more functional support or assistance tasks for other internal units (from appendix)

Simple regression (p. 154)   a method in which only one independent variable is used to predict a dependent variable in least-squares regression (from appendix)

Standard (p. 133)   a benchmark or norm against which actual results may be compared

Standard cost system (p. 133)   a system in which budgeted costs for direct materials, direct labor, and/or factory overhead are used to account for manufacturing a single unit of product or performing a single service; the budgeted costs represent the estimated expenditures that should be incurred to achieve a specific objective

Step method (of service department cost allocation) (p. 158)   a method in which service department costs are assigned to cost objects by use of a specific base after the most important interrelationships of the service departments and the revenue-producing departments have been considered (from appendix)

Theoretical capacity (p. 146)   the estimated maximum potential production activity of a firm for a specific time

Underapplied overhead (p. 148)   the excess of actual overhead above the overhead applied to Work in Process Inventory for a period

Variance (p. 145)   any difference between an actual and an expected (or a budgeted) cost

---

SOLUTION STRATEGIES

HIGH-LOW METHOD (example using assumed amounts)

	ACTIVITY (INDEPENDENT VARIABLE)	ASSOCIATED TOTAL COST (DEPENDENT VARIABLE)	=	TOTAL VARIABLE COST (RATE × ACTIVITY)	+	TOTAL FIXED COST
High level of activity	28,000	$36,000		$22,400	+	$13,600
Low level of activity	18,000	28,000		14,400	+	13,600
Differences	10,000	$ 8,000				

$.80 variable cost per unit of activity

FLEXIBLE BUDGET (at any activity level within the relevant range)

$$y = a + bX$$

or

Total cost = Total fixed cost + (Variable cost per unit of activity × Level of activity)

PREDETERMINED OVERHEAD RATE

Predetermined OH rate = Budgeted overhead ÷ Budgeted level of activity

(Should be separated into variable and fixed rates and by related cost pools)

UNDERAPPLIED AND OVERAPPLIED OVERHEAD

Variable/Fixed Production Overhead	XXX	
Various accounts		XXX

Actual overhead is debited to the overhead general ledger account and credited to the sources of the overhead costs

Work in Process Inventory*	YYY	
Variable/Fixed Production Overhead		YYY

Applied overhead is debited to WIP Inventory and credited to the overhead general ledger account

*Can be debited directly to Cost of Services Rendered (CSR) in a service company

A debit balance in Variable/Fixed Production Overhead at the end of the period is underapplied overhead; a credit balance is overapplied overhead. An immaterial underapplied or overapplied balance in the OH account is closed at the end of the period to CGS or CSR; a material amount is prorated to Work in Process Inventory, Finished Goods Inventory, and CGS or CSR.

SERVICE DEPARTMENT COST ALLOCATION

Direct method:

1. Determine rational and systematic allocation base for each service department.
2. Assign costs from each service department directly to revenue-producing areas using specified allocation bases.

Step method:

1. Determine rational and systematic allocation base for each service department.
2. List service departments in order (benefits-provided ranking) from the one that provides the most service to all other areas (both revenue-producing and non-revenue producing) to the one that provides service only to revenue-producing areas.
3. Beginning with the first service department listed, allocate the costs from that department to all remaining departments; repeat the process until only revenue-producing departments remain.

DEMONSTRATION PROBLEM

Precision Metalworks builds towers for equipment used in radio, television, and communications transmission. Each tower is custom-engineered based on site conditions and height requirements. The towers are built in sections in the firm's factory and then hauled by rail or truck to the site location, where they are assembled.

The firm has two revenue-producing departments: Construction and Assembly. The construction department is responsible for engineering and manufacturing each tower; the assembly department assembles and erects the towers.

In its first year of operations (1996), Precision Metalworks obtained contracts for the construction of three towers:

- Tower 1: a 1,500-foot tower for public television in Boise
- Tower 2: a 300-foot radio tower in Cleveland
- Tower 3: a 500-foot radio tower in Atlanta

The firm uses a job order costing system based on normal costs. Overhead is applied in the construction department at the predetermined factory overhead rate of $40 per ton of metal processed. In the assembly department, factory overhead is applied at the predetermined rate of $100 per foot of tower height.

During 1995, the firm's management accountant devised the following budget figures for 1996 overhead costs and production activity:

	CONSTRUCTION	ASSEMBLY	TOTAL
Budgeted overhead:			
Variable	$32,400	$120,450	$152,850
Fixed	39,600	44,550	84,150
Total	$72,000	$165,000	$237,000

Budgeted activity:

Tons of metal processed	1,800	0	1,800
Feet of tower constructed	0	1,650	1,650
Direct labor hours	26,000	34,000	60,000
Machine hours	6,000	2,000	8,000

Significant transactions for 1996 are summarized as follows:

1. Raw material (metal) was purchased on account: 2,000 tons at $100 per ton.

2. Materials were requisitioned for use in the three towers (all materials used are regarded as direct materials): Tower 1—1,300 tons; Tower 2—200 tons; and Tower 3—300 tons. All of the materials were issued to the Construction Department.

3. The time sheets and payroll summaries for each department indicated the following direct labor costs were incurred:

	CONSTRUCTION	PERCENT COMPLETE	ASSEMBLY	PERCENT COMPLETE
Tower 1	$200,000	100%	$300,000	100%
Tower 2	25,000	100%	40,000	50%
Tower 3	30,000	40%	0	0%

4. Indirect manufacturing costs were incurred in each department:

	CONSTRUCTION	ASSEMBLY
Indirect labor	$20,000	$ 40,000
Utilities	10,000	5,000
Depreciation	40,000	110,000

5. Factory overhead was applied based on the predetermined overhead rates in effect in each department.

6. Tower 1 was completed and sold at a price equal to cost plus $400,000.

7. Underapplied or overapplied overhead was assigned to Cost of Goods Sold.

   a. Using the budgeted data for 1996, demonstrate how the predetermined departmental overhead rates of $40 for Construction and $100 for Assembly were calculated.

   b. Using the budgeted data for 1996, calculate a separate variable and fixed rate for Construction using tons of metal processed and a separate variable and fixed rate for Assembly using feet of tower erected.

   c. Using the budgeted data for 1996, determine a company-wide predetermined overhead rate using direct labor hours as the activity base. Also, compute departmental rates using direct labor hours.

   d. Using the budgeted data for 1996, determine a company-wide predetermined overhead rate using machine hours as the activity base. Also, compute departmental rates using machine hours.

   e. Given the large number of predetermined overhead rates calculated above, provide some guidelines the company might use to select the appropriate rate or set of rates.

   f. Record the journal entries for items 1 through 7.

   g. As of the end of 1996, determine the total cost assigned to Tower 2 and Tower 3.

■ SOLUTION TO DEMONSTRATION PROBLEM

a. Construction predetermined OH rate = $72,000 ÷ 1,800 tons = $40 per ton
Assembly predetermined OH rate = $165,000 ÷ 1,650 feet = $100 per foot

b. Construction variable OH rate = $32,400 ÷ 1,800 tons = $18 per ton
Construction fixed OH rate = $39,600 ÷ 1,800 tons = $22 per ton
Assembly variable OH rate = $120,450 ÷ 1,650 feet = $73 per foot
Assembly fixed OH rate = $44,550 ÷ 1,650 feet = $27 per foot

c. Companywide predetermined OH rate = $237,000 ÷ 60,000 DLHs = $3.95 per DLH
Construction predetermined OH rate = $72,000 ÷ 26,000 DLHs = $2.77 per DLH
Assembly predetermined OH rate = $165,000 ÷ 34,000 DLHs = $4.85 per DLH

d. Companywide predetermined OH rate = $237,000 ÷ 8,000 MHs = $29.63 per MH
Construction predetermined OH rate = $72,000 ÷ 6,000 MHs = $12 per MH
Assembly predetermined OH rate = $165,000 ÷ 2,000 MHs = $82.50 per MH

e. A company should choose the rate or rates that help management most effectively plan, control, problem solve, and evaluate performance of cost objects. The activity base chosen should make it possible to assign overhead to cost objects (in this problem, jobs) in a manner that reflects causation of the overhead by the cost objects and benefits received from the overhead by the cost objects. The activity base selected should demonstrate a high correlation with the overhead costs and should preferably be a cost driver. Departmental rates are usually better than companywide rates, and rates based on cost behavior (variable or fixed) are usually better than combined rates because the more refined rates result in more accurate information. (Improving accuracy of overhead assignment to cost objects is further addressed in Chapter 5.)

f. **1.** Raw Materials Inventory 200,000
  Accounts Payable 200,000
  To record purchase of materials

  2. WIP Inventory—Construction (Tower 1)* 130,000
  WIP Inventory—Construction (Tower 2) 20,000
  WIP Inventory—Construction (Tower 3) 30,000
  Raw Materials Inventory 180,000
  To record requisition and issuance of materials

  3. WIP Inventory—Construction (Tower 1) 200,000
  WIP Inventory—Construction (Tower 2) 25,000
  WIP Inventory—Construction (Tower 3) 30,000
  WIP Inventory—Assembly (Tower 1) 300,000
  WIP Inventory—Assembly (Tower 2) 40,000
  Wages Payable 595,000
  To record direct labor costs

  4. Manufacturing Overhead—Construction 70,000
  Manufacturing Overhead—Assembly 155,000
  Wages Payable 60,000
  Utilities Payable 15,000
  Accumulated Depreciation-Plant 150,000
  To record indirect manufacturing costs

5. WIP Inventory—Construction (Tower 1)   52,000
    WIP Inventory—Construction (Tower 2)   8,000
    WIP Inventory—Construction (Tower 3)   12,000
        Manufacturing Overhead—Construction   72,000
      To record application of Construction
      Department manufacturing overhead
    WIP Inventory—Assembly (Tower 1)   150,000
    WIP Inventory—Assembly (Tower 2)   15,000
      Manufacturing Overhead—Assembly   165,000
      To record application of Assembly Department
      manufacturing overhead; Tower 1, 15,000 feet
      $\times$ \$100; Tower 2, 300 feet $\times$ 50% complete
      $\times$ \$100

6. Finished Goods Inventory   832,000
      WIP Inventory—Construction (Tower 1)   382,000
      WIP Inventory—Assembly (Tower 1)   450,000
      To record completion of Tower 1
    Cost of Goods Sold   832,000
      Finished Goods Inventory   832,000
      To record cost of tower sold
    Accounts Receivable   1,232,000
      Sales   1,232,000
      To record sale of Tower 1

7. Manufacturing Overhead—Construction   2,000
    Manufacturing Overhead—Assembly   10,000
        Cost of Goods Sold   12,000
        To close OH to CGS

*Note: For simplicity, a separate account for departmental Work in Process Inventory for each job is presented in these entries. More commonly in practice, a company will keep a general ledger account for work in process for each department that is supported by a subsidiary ledger of work in process by job accounts.

g.

	TOWER 2	TOWER 3
Direct materials—Construction	$ 20,000	$30,000
Direct labor—Construction	25,000	30,000
Manufacturing overhead—Construction	8,000	12,000
Direct materials—Assembly	0	0
Direct labor—Assembly	40,000	0
Manufacturing overhead—Assembly	15,000	0
Totals	$108,000	$72,000

END-OF-CHAPTER MATERIALS

■ QUESTIONS

1. What are the two major types of overhead cost? Which of these categories has been increasing in recent years? Why?

2. What are the overhead implications of expanding automation and product variety in American industry?

3. What are the major distinctions between the production environments that would be appropriate for job order costing and process costing?

4. Identify the three methods of measuring the cost of inventory. Discuss the differences among the three methods with regard to overhead.

5. Would normal or standard product costing provide the greater opportunity to evaluate the control of costs for a period? Explain.

6. For identical products produced in different periods, which costing method (actual, normal, or standard) is likely to show the greatest interperiod fluctuation in the costs assigned to the products? Why?

7. What are the major documents that support the cost flows in a job order costing system?

8. Why would the question of whether factory overhead was assigned using actual rates or predetermined rates make a difference in costing a product?

9. List three reasons to use predetermined overhead rates rather than actual costs to apply indirect costs to products. Why would these reasons be of importance to managers? To marketers? To accountants?

10. Why is it necessary to separate mixed costs into their variable and fixed cost elements for product costing purposes?

11. What is a flexible budget? Why is it necessary to separate mixed costs into fixed and variable components to prepare a flexible budget?

12. Why must a particular level of activity be specified to calculate a predetermined fixed overhead rate? Why is such specificity not required to calculate a predetermined variable overhead rate?

13. What is the primary criterion for selecting an overhead application base? Explain.

14. Why do some companies use multiple cost pools, rather than a single cost pool, to allocate overhead costs?

15. What are the four capacity measures that may be used for overhead application? Which one is most commonly used? Which capacity measure will result in the greatest underapplication of overhead? Why?

16. Why may overhead for a given period be underapplied or overapplied? What are the alternative methods for disposing of the underapplied or overapplied overhead?

17. (Appendix 1) How does the least-squares regression method improve upon the high-low method for separating mixed costs into their fixed and variable components?

18. (Appendix 1) Differentiate between an independent and a dependent variable.

19. (Appendix 1) You are trying to project your total college expenses for next year. If you use simple regression analysis, which variable would you choose as the independent variable? If you used multiple regression analysis, which six variables might you choose as the independent variables? Which method would provide better information and why?

20. (Appendix 2) What are service departments? Why are service department costs often allocated to revenue-producing departments?

21. (Appendix 2) What criteria are used to select a base for allocating service department costs?

22. (Appendix 2) What are two primary methods of allocating service department costs, and what are their relative strengths?

■ EXERCISES

23. (LO 1; *Job order vs. process costing*) The following is a list of different types of firms. Indicate for each firm, based on the type of production process and the nature of the product or service, whether its costing system would more likely be based on job order costing (JOC) or on process costing (PC).

  a. A firm that manufactures jet airplanes to customer specifications.
  b. A firm that manufactures household paints.
  c. A firm that produces three types of soft drinks.
  d. A firm that is an automobile repair shop.
  e. A firm that is a corporate law firm.
  f. A firm that manufactures hair spray and hand lotion.
  g. A firm that is a hospital.
  h. A firm that cans salmon and tuna.
  i. A firm that provides lawn care services.
  j. A firm that is a commercial freight company.
  k. A firm that cleans and dries grain and seeds for commercial growers.

24. (LO 1; *Job order costing*) Berkowitz Studio specializes in painting custom murals in office lobbies and other commercial sites. The firm uses a job order costing system. During July, the company worked on jobs for the following companies:

	TIMBERLAND	KINSCO	REALTY PLUS
Direct labor hours	80	250	500
Direct materials cost	$1,560	$6,200	$12,600

Berkowitz is able to trace direct materials to each job since most costs associated with materials are related to paint and other supplies. The firm's accountant has set the annual production overhead application rate at $30 per direct labor hour. The normal labor cost is $25 per hour.

  a. Determine the total cost for each of the accounts for July.
  b. Is the firm using an actual costing system or a normal costing system? Explain.

25. (LO 3; *High-low method*) Mercury Retail Electronics incurred the following expenses for maintenance during the first six months of 1995:

MONTH	SALES VOLUME	MAINTENANCE COST
January	$60,000	$600
February	35,000	350
March	40,000	400
April	50,000	450
May	30,000	150
June	42,500	425

  a. Using the high-low method, develop a budget formula for maintenance expense.
  b. Describe any unusual features of your solution in part a. Give a probable explanation for the result.

26. (LO 3; *High-low method*) The staff of LaFrance Restaurant wants to estimate a cost function for its supplies expense. The restaurant has been operating for six months and has had the following activity (customer volume) and costs:

MONTH	CUSTOMER VOLUME	SUPPLIES COST
March	3,400	$6,100
April	3,100	5,850
May	3,400	6,200
June	3,600	6,400
July	3,000	5,500
August	2,800	5,400

    a. In a restaurant, what types of supplies are in the variable expense category? The fixed expense category?

    b. Using the high-low method, estimate the cost equation for supplies expense.

    c. What amount of supplies expense would the company expect to incur in a month in which 3,300 customers were served?

27. (LO 4; *Flexible budget*) Motor City Trax Co. used the following formula to prepare its flexible budget for selling and administrative expense in the past year: $y = \$3,500 + \$1.85X$, where X = number of records sold. The company is expecting to expand into a new relevant range in the coming year. Accordingly, fixed costs are expected to remain at $3,500 for volumes under 6,000 units; at volumes equal to or exceeding 6,000 units, fixed costs are expected to increase to $5,200. Variable costs will remain at $1.85 per unit for volumes at or below 7,000 units. Above 7,000 units, variable costs are expected to decline to $1.75 per unit.

    a. Prepare a flexible budget for the following activity levels: 5,000, 7,000 and 9,000 units of sales.

    b. Calculate the unit costs at each level of sales.

28. (LO 4; *Flexible budget*) The Healthy Hound Pet Salon is in the dog grooming business. It has determined the following formulas for its costs:

Grooming supplies (variable):	$y = \$0 + \$4.00X$
Direct labor (variable):	$y = \$0 + \$12.00X$
Overhead (mixed):	$y = \$8,000 + \$1.00X$

Willie Coyote, the owner, has determined that direct labor is the cost driver for all three cost categories.

    a. Prepare a flexible budget for each of the following activity levels: 550, 600, 650, and 700 direct labor hours.

    b. Determine the total cost per direct labor hour at each of the levels of activity.

    c. Groomers at Healthy Hound normally work a total of 650 direct labor hours during a month. Each grooming job typically takes a groomer one and one-quarter hours. Willie wants to earn a profit equal to 40 percent of the costs incurred. What should she charge each pet owner for grooming?

29. (LO 5; *Predetermined OH rates with different bases*) Sara Johnson Enterprises prepared the following 1996 abbreviated flexible budget:

MACHINE HOURS			
10,000	*11,000*	*12,000*	*13,000*

FACTORY COSTS				
Variable	$40,000	$44,000	$48,000	$52,000
Fixed	15,000	15,000	15,000	15,000

The company has set 11,000 machine hours as the 1996 expected annual capacity and expects to operate at one-twelfth of the expected annual capacity each month. It takes two machine hours to produce each product.

a. Calculate separate variable and fixed overhead rates using (1) machine hours and (2) units of products.

b. Calculate the combined overhead rate using (1) machine hours and (2) units of products.

c. Assume that in April 1996, the company produced 442 units. During April, $3,360 of variable overhead and $1,310 of fixed overhead were incurred, and 884 actual machine hours were recorded. Based on the preceding information and your answers in parts a and b, determine:

1. the amount of fixed factory overhead to be applied to production in April 1996.

2. the amount of variable factory overhead to be applied to production in April 1996.

3. the overapplied or underapplied variable and fixed overhead amounts for April 1996.

30. (LO 5; *Overhead application with multiple rates*) Momar Electronics has determined that a single overhead application rate no longer results in a reasonable allocation of overhead to its diverse products. Accordingly, the company has restructured its overhead application. It has established six cost pools and identified appropriate cost drivers. The new cost pools and allocation bases and rates follow:

COST POOL	APPLICATION RATE
Setup costs	$37 per setup
Machine costs	$15 per machine hour
Labor-related costs	$ 7 per direct labor hour
Material handling costs	$ 1 per pound of material received
Quality costs	$80 per customer return
Other	$ 4 per machine hour

During 1996, the company experienced the following volume for each cost application base:

Setups	300
Machine hours	9,000
Direct labor hours	8,000
Pounds of material received	100,000
Customer returns	250

a. Determine the amount of overhead applied in 1996.

b. Assuming the company incurred $362,000 in actual overhead costs in 1996, compute the company's underapplied or overapplied overhead.

c. Why are more firms adopting multiple application rates to apply overhead?

31. (LO 5, 6; *Predetermined OH rates and underapplied/overapplied OH*) Custom Printing Co. had the following cost information in its Work in Process Inventory account for April 1997:

WORK IN PROCESS INVENTORY

Beginning balance	5,000	Transferred out	167,500
Materials added	75,000		
Labor (10,000 DLHs)	45,000		
Applied overhead	60,000		
Ending balance	17,500		

All workers are paid the same rate per hour. Factory overhead is applied to Work in Process Inventory on the basis of direct labor hours. The only job left in process at the end of the month had a total of 1,430 direct labor hours accumulated to date.

   a. What is the total predetermined overhead rate per direct labor hour?
   b. What amounts of material, labor, and overhead are included in the ending Work in Process Inventory balance?
   c. If actual total overhead for April is $59,350, what is the amount of underapplied or overapplied overhead?

32. (LO 5; *Selecting capacity measure*) Green Paper Supply Company manufactures recycled paper. The company has decided to use predetermined factory overhead rates to apply factory overhead to its products. To set such rates, the company has gathered the following budgeted data:

Variable factory overhead at 12,000 machine hours	$72,000
Variable factory overhead at 14,000 machine hours	84,000
Fixed factory overhead at all levels between 12,000 and 20,000 machine hours	72,000

Practical capacity is 20,000 machine hours; expected capacity is 75 percent of practical capacity.

   a. What is the company's predetermined variable factory overhead rate?
   b. Compute the company's fixed factory overhead rate based on expected capacity. Using practical capacity, compute the company's predetermined fixed factory overhead rate.
   c. If the company incurred a total of 13,500 machine hours during a period, what would be the total amount of applied factory overhead assuming fixed factory overhead was applied based on expected capacity? Practical capacity? If actual factory overhead during the period was $155,000, what was the amount of underapplied or overapplied factory overhead, assuming fixed factory overhead was applied based on expected capacity? Practical capacity? (Use your answers to parts a and b.)
   d. Based on your answers in part c, explain why most firms use expected capacity as the factory overhead allocation base. What is the benefit of using practical capacity?

33. (LO 6; *Disposition of underapplied/overapplied OH*) Dozier Research and Testing Services Company has an overapplied overhead balance of $31,000 at the end of 1996. The amount of overhead contained in other selected account balances at year-end are:

Work in Process Inventory	$ 27,000
Finished Goods Inventory	60,000
Cost of Goods Sold	213,000

a. Prepare the necessary journal entries to close the overapplied overhead balance assuming that:

   1. the amount is material.
   2. the amount is immaterial.

b. Which approach is the better choice, and why?

34. (LO 1, 5; *Total cost and sales price*) Metal Art is a small firm whose specialty is the production of custom metal products. The firm employs a job order costing system based on normal costs. Overhead is applied to production at the rate of $6 per direct labor hour. During August, the firm finished Job 129, a batch of ornamental railings. The total direct material and direct labor costs assigned to Job 129 were $14,000 and $18,000, respectively. The firm's direct labor rate is $9 per hour.

   a. Compute the total cost of Job 129.
   b. Record the journal entry to transfer the job to the Finished Goods Inventory.
   c. Compute the sales price of Job 129 assuming the job is priced to yield a gross margin equal to 60 percent of the sales price.

35. (LO 1; *Journal entries*) Westin Industries is a newly formed firm that manufactures various items of equipment used in handling granular materials. For its first month of operations, it recorded the following activity:

   ▪ Purchased $800,000 of direct materials on account.
   ▪ Used $650,000 of the purchased materials in production operations.
   ▪ Incurred direct labor costs: 16,000 hours at $12 per hour.
   ▪ Incurred manufacturing overhead costs: indirect labor, $400,000; utilities, $300,000; rent, $200,000; and depreciation, $300,000. All costs, except depreciation, were paid in cash.

   The firm employs a job order costing system based on actual costs.

   a. Prepare the journal entries to record the previous transactions.
   b. Prepare the journal entry that would be recorded at the end of January to charge production for the overhead costs.
   c. Assuming no products were completed during the period, compute the ending balances in the Raw Material Inventory and Work in Process Inventory accounts.

36. (LO 3; *Appendix 1*) In your examination of the 1995 financial statements of Sterling Mfg. Co., you wish to determine the relationship between total production costs incurred and total direct labor hours worked. From the financial statements and accompanying notes you gather the following data:

MONTH	LABOR HOURS (IN HUNDREDS)	PRODUCTION COST (IN THOUSANDS)
January	25	$ 20
February	35	25
March	45	30
April	32	23
May	27	21

Using the least squares method, determine the following:

a. fixed monthly production cost.
b. variable production cost.
c. estimated production cost when 3,100 labor hours are worked.

37. (LO 3; *High-low method; Appendix 1*) Better Cheddar specializes in making cheese. Management wants to improve its budgeting of overhead costs and provides you with the following data:

MONTH	MONTHLY PRODUCTION IN POUNDS OF CHEESE	CHEESE-MAKING FACILITY OVERHEAD
January	1,000	$12,000
February	1,250	10,900
March	2,000	13,300
April	1,500	12,100
May	2,125	16,500
June	1,750	13,000
July	1,800	13,700

a. Determine the a and b values for the equation $y = a + bX$ using the high-low method.
b. Determine the a and b values for the equation $y = a + bX$ using the regression formula.
c. Provide four other possible independent variables that management might consider using to forecast overhead costs. When might each of these bases provide better information than the others?

38. (LO 7; *Appendix 2*) Jones Cookware Corp. allocates its service department costs to its producing departments using the direct method. For September 1996, the Personnel Department incurred $69,000 of costs and the Maintenance Department incurred $50,000 of costs. Other information for the month follows:

	PERCENTAGE OF SERVICES PROVIDED TO OTHER DEPARTMENTS	
	Personnel	*Maintenance*
Personnel		50%
Maintenance	10%	
Fabricating	30%	30%
Finishing	60%	20%

a. What amount of Personnel and Maintenance costs should be assigned to Fabricating for September?
b. What amount of Personnel and Maintenance costs should be assigned to Finishing for September?
c. Why would the step method of allocating service department costs be preferred for this company?

 39. (LO 7; *Appendix 2*) FirstBank has three revenue-generating areas: checking accounts, savings accounts, and loans. The bank also has three service areas: administration, personnel, and accounting. The direct costs per month and the interdepartmental service structure are shown below in a benefits-provided ranking.

PERCENT OF SERVICE USED BY

Department	Direct Costs	Admin.	Pers.	Acctg.	Check.	Sav.	Loans
Administration	$ 40,000	—	10	10	40	20	20
Personnel	60,000	10	—	10	20	40	20
Accounting	60,000	10	10	—	20	20	40
Checking accounts	60,000						
Savings accounts	50,000						
Loans	100,000						

a. Compute the total cost for each revenue-generating area using the direct method.

b. Compute the total cost for each revenue-generating area using the step method.

■ COMMUNICATION ACTIVITIES

40. (LO 1, 2, 5; *Designing an overhead allocation system*) You have been assigned to install a cost system for Midwest Electrical Fixtures Co. You have discovered the following facts regarding this company:

■ The company makes a line of lighting fixtures and lamps. The cost for material for any item ranges from 15 to 60 percent of total factory cost, depending on the kinds of metal and fabric used in making the product.

■ The business is subject to wide cyclical fluctuations, since the sales volume follows new housing construction.

■ About 60 percent of the manufacturing activity is normally performed in the first quarter of the year.

■ For the whole plant, the wages range from $9.25 to $18.75 per hour. However, within each of the eight individual departments, the spread between the high and low wage rate is less than 7 percent.

■ Each of the products made uses all eight of the manufacturing departments, but not proportionately.

■ Within the individual manufacturing departments, factory overhead ranges from 30 percent to 80 percent of conversion cost.

Based on the preceding information, prepare a written statement to the company president with recommendations for the following items. Discuss the rationale for your recommendations.

a. Should the company use a normal or actual costing system?

b. Should a single, companywide overhead application rate or departmental application rates be used?

c. Should the allocation rate (or rates) be based on direct labor hours, direct labor cost, or prime cost?

41. (LO 2, 4; *Control of overhead costs*) *Upward cost pressures and less support from state governments have financially squeezed public and private institutions of higher education. Such institutions are increasingly asking their researchers to cover overhead costs. In fact most universities attach a fixed percentage onto direct research costs to cover overhead costs. For example, at Harvard, the Medical School asks for 88 cents for each dollar of direct research cost; similarly, Yale asks for 60 cents and MIT asks for 57.5 cents. The U.S. government, as the predominant fund-*

ing source for most research conducted by universities, ultimately foots much of the bill for overhead costs.

[SOURCE: Sharon Begley et al., "Milking the Laboratories for Dollars," *Newsweek* (May 6, 1991), p. 58.)]

Write a brief memo to one of your federal congressional representatives. In the memo, describe why the practice of automatically reimbursing overhead costs results in universities having little incentive to control overhead costs and in noncompetitive pricing for performing research services.

42. (LO 1, 3; *Decisions affecting overhead cost*) Your employer, a major international truck freight company, is considering entering the competitive car hauling industry. Most of the business in this industry is generated from contracts with automakers to haul cars from manufacturing plants to dealers. Other business is generated by used-car dealers and automobile auctions. One of the most crucial competitive decisions to be made by car haulers involves whether they should own or lease the expensive trucks and equipment that are required. Prepare a five minute oral presentation discussing the kinds of costs that would be incurred by a firm that owned rather than leased the required trucks and equipment. Also, address the relative competitive cost advantages of both alternatives.

■ PROBLEMS

43. (LO 1, 6; *Job order costing*) Thunder Valley Racing Products uses a job order costing system and applies factory overhead to jobs using a predetermined rate of 250 percent of direct labor cost. At the beginning of June 1996, Job #218 was the only job in process. Costs of Job #218 included direct materials of $6,500, direct labor of $5,400, and applied factory overhead of $13,500. During June, Thunder Valley Racing Products began work on Jobs #219, #220, and #221, and issued $14,700 of direct materials. Direct labor cost for the month totaled $15,600. Job #220 had not been completed at the end of June, and its direct materials and direct labor charges were $2,700 and $1,900, respectively. All the other jobs were completed in June.

a. What was the total cost of Job #220 as of the end of June 1996?

b. If actual overhead for June was $36,700, was the overhead underapplied or overapplied for the month? By how much?

44. (LO 3, 5; *Mixed cost analysis and predetermined OH rate*) Southwest Manufacturing's predetermined total factory overhead rate is $6.70 per machine hour, of which $6.30 is variable. Costs at two production levels are:

FACTORY OVERHEAD ITEMS	8,000 MH	10,000 MH
Indirect materials	$12,800	$16,000
Indirect labor	27,000	33,000
Maintenance	3,700	4,500
Utilities	4,000	5,000
All other	6,700	8,300

a. Determine the variable and fixed values for each item, and give the total factory overhead formula.

b. What is Southwest's expected capacity level if the predetermined rate given is based on expected capacity?

c. Determine the expected factory overhead costs at the expected activity level.

d. Assuming the firm raises its expected capacity level by 2,375 machine hours over that found in part b, calculate a new predetermined total factory overhead rate. Draft a memo to management to explain why the rate has changed.

45. (LO 3, 5; *Analyzing OH costs*) Electric Motor Corp.'s predetermined total factory overhead rate for product costing purposes is $23 per unit. Of this amount, $18 is the variable portion. Cost information for two levels of activity follows:

OVERHEAD COMPONENTS	800 UNITS	1,200 UNITS
Indirect materials	$4,000	$6,000
Indirect labor	5,600	8,400
Handling	2,600	3,800
Maintenance	800	1,200
Utilities	2,000	2,800
Supervision	4,000	4,000

a. Determine the fixed and variable values for each of the preceding components of factory overhead and determine the total factory overhead cost formula.

b. What is the company's budgeted volume level if the predetermined rate is based on expected capacity?

c. Determine the budgeted factory overhead costs at the expected capacity level.

d. Electric Motor's management decides to raise its expected capacity level 80 units over the present level. Determine the new total predetermined factory overhead rate for product costing purposes.

46. (LO 3, 4; *High-low method and flexible budget*) Portland Industries tests prospective employees for its management team with the following flexible factory overhead budget at several levels of activity. Some of the amounts are intentionally missing.

	DIRECT LABOR HOURS (X)				
Overhead Accounts	*8,000*	*10,000*	*12,000*	*14,000*	*16,000*
Indirect materials	$2,400			$4,200	
Indirect labor		$50,000			$80,000
Insurance	600			600	
Depreciation	3,000				3,000
Repairs and maintenance		3,800	$4,300		
Utilities			2,700	3,100	

a. Using the high-low method, determine the a and b values for the formula $y = a + bX$, where X is direct labor hours for each item presented.

b. Complete the factory overhead flexible budget presented in the problem.

c. Assume that the expected capacity is 10,000 direct labor hours.

Determine the following:

1. predetermined variable factory overhead application rate.
2. predetermined fixed factory overhead application rate.
3. total predetermined factory overhead application rate.

47. (LO 3, 4, 5; *Mixed cost analysis and capacity measures*) Pennsylvania Upholstery has two departments: Framing and Covering. Framing is highly automated, and machine hours are used as the factory overhead allocation activity base in that department. Covering is labor-intensive, so it uses direct labor hours as the activity base. A flexible budget is provided below for each department:

	MACHINE HOURS (MHs)			
Framing Overhead	3,000	4,000	5,000	6,000
Variable	$ 6,600	$ 8,800	$11,000	$13,200
Fixed	4,200	4,200	4,200	4,200
Total	$10,800	$13,000	$15,200	$17,400

	DIRECT LABOR HOURS (DLHs)			
Covering Overhead	9,000	12,000	15,000	18,000
Variable	$45,000	$60,000	$75,000	$90,000
Fixed	3,000	3,000	3,000	3,000
Total	$48,000	$63,000	$78,000	$93,000

The firm produces one style of sofa, which can be covered in a variety of fabrics. Each sofa requires one hour of machine time and three hours of direct labor. Next year, Pennsylvania Upholstery plans to produce 6,000 sofas, which is 1,000 more than normal capacity.

a. Give the a and b values for the cost formula for each department.
b. Predict next year's factory overhead for each department.
c. Using normal capacity, calculate the predetermined total factory overhead per sofa. Using expected capacity, calculate the predetermined total factory overhead per sofa.
d. Management wants to earn a gross margin of 50 percent on cost. Which of the two capacity measures used in part c would you select to determine total cost per sofa, and why?

48. (LO 3, 5, 6; *Capacity measures and underapplied/overapplied OH*) Boulton Enterprises makes only one product. It has a theoretical capacity of 50,000 units annually. Practical capacity is 80 percent of theoretical capacity, and normal capacity is 80 percent of practical capacity. The firm is expecting to produce 36,000 units next year. The company president, Michael Howington, has budgeted the following factory overhead costs for the coming year:

- Indirect materials: $2.00 per unit
- Indirect labor: $144,000 plus $2.50 per unit
- Utilities for the plant: $6,000 plus $.04 per unit
- Repairs and maintenance for the plant: $20,000 plus $.34 per unit
- Material handling costs: $16,000 plus $.12 per unit
- Depreciation on plant assets: $.06 per unit
- Rent on plant building: $50,000 per year
- Insurance on plant building: $12,000 per year

a. Determine the cost formula for total factory overhead.
b. Assume that Boulton produces 35,000 units during the year and that actual costs are exactly as budgeted. Calculate the overapplied or underapplied overhead for each possible capacity base.
c. Which information determined in part b would be the most beneficial to management, and why?

49. (LO 5; *Plantwide vs. departmental OH rates*) Dickerson Manufacturing is composed of a Cutting Department and an Assembly Department. The Cutting Department is staffed by one person who runs fifteen machines. The Assembly Department is highly labor-intensive, with twenty direct laborers and three machines. All products manufactured by Dickerson pass through both departments. Product KL85 uses the following quantities of machine time and direct labor hours:

	CUTTING	ASSEMBLY
Machine hours	9.00	.12
Direct labor hours	.03	3.00

Dickerson has estimated the following total factory overhead costs and activity levels for each department for 1996:

	CUTTING	ASSEMBLY
Budgeted factory overhead	$862,200	$432,000
Budgeted machine hours	72,000	14,280
Budgeted direct labor hours	5,200	40,000

a. Dickerson Manufacturing's accountant uses a plantwide rate based on machine hours for factory overhead application. What rate will be used for 1996?

b. How much factory overhead is assigned to each unit of Product KL85 under the method currently in use?

c. The company's auditors inform Dickerson that the method being used to apply factory overhead is inappropriate. They indicate that machine hours should be used for an application base in Cutting and direct labor hours should be used in Assembly. Using these bases, determine the departmental rates for 1996. How much factory overhead would be assigned to each unit of Product KL85 if departmental rates were used?

50. (LO 5; *Multiple OH allocation rates*) Ralph Dudley, marketing manager for International Hydraulic Systems had become increasingly discontented over his firm's competitive position in the market for custom hydraulic systems. Recently, he discovered that his bids for relatively simple custom projects were not competitive with those of other firms in the industry; however, his bids on more complex projects were almost always acceptable. An example of two recent bids follows:

	BID #134	BID #1372
Direct materials	$18,000	$27,000
Direct labor	12,000	18,000
Factory overhead*	21,000	21,000
Total cost	$51,000	$66,000
Markup (40% of costs)	20,400	26,400
Bid price	$71,400	$92,400

*Applied at the rate of $30 per machine hour

In attempting to find a solution to the competitive pricing problem, Mr. Dudley sent the information on the two bids to the company's new cost accountant, Liz Smolly. Ms. Smolly was somewhat surprised at the relative amounts of factory overhead costs assigned to the two projects. She believed that Project

#1372 was much more complex to manufacture and should bear a greater share of the overhead burden. As a result, she decided to investigate whether the use of a single factory overhead rate was appropriate. With the aid of production managers and engineers, she determined that it was possible to separate the overall application rate into several rates based on different application bases and cost pools. A summary of the proposed new cost pools, application bases, and application rates follows:

COST POOL	APPLICATION BASE	APPLICATION RATE
Setup costs	Number of setups	$120
Material handling	Number of parts	9
Quality costs	Number of inspections	60
Machine costs	Number of machine hours	10
Other costs	Dollars of direct labor	20% of DL cost

Ms. Smolly then wanted to examine how the new application rates would affect the bid prices on the two projects. She gathered the following additional information:

	BID #1341	BID #1372
Number of setups	10	70
Number of parts	400	1,200
Number of quality inspections	5	15

a. Determine the amount of overhead cost assigned to each of the two projects using the new application rates.
b. Determine the new bid price for each project.
c. Which factory overhead costs were distorted most in the allocations that used the single overhead application rate?

51. (LO 5; *Determining product cost; Note: This problem is a companion problem to Chapter 5's Problem 40.*) Thuston Chemical Products Company produces two products: A and B. The company's expected factory overhead costs for the coming year are as follows:

OVERHEAD ITEMS	AMOUNTS
Utilities	$ 300,000
Setup	250,000
Materials handling	800,000
Total	$1,350,000

The company's expected production and related statistics follow:

	PRODUCT A	PRODUCT B
Machine hours	35,000	15,000
Direct labor hours	20,000	25,000
Direct materials (pounds)	75,000	125,000
Number of units produced	10,000	5,000

Additional data: One direct labor hour costs $10, and the 200,000 pounds of material were purchased for $360,000.

a. Determine the total cost for each product and the cost per unit under the following assumptions:

  1. overhead is applied based on direct labor hours.

  2. overhead is applied based on machine hours.

b. Explain why your answers to parts a and b differ.

52. (LO 5; *Determining product cost Note: This problem is a companion problem to Chapter 5's Problem 41.*) Bowling Green Custom Lumber Products has three product lines: A, B, and C. The company is considering two alternative bases to be used in applying factory overhead costs to products in 1997. The budgeted factory overhead costs for 1997 are as follows:

OVERHEAD ITEMS	AMOUNTS
Utilities	$ 300,000
Scheduling and setup	272,000
Materials handling	640,000
Total	$1,212,000

The company's budgeted production statistics for 1997 follow:

	PRODUCTS		
	A	*B*	*C*
Machine hours	30,000	10,000	20,000
Direct labor hours	32,000	18,000	50,000
Number of units produced	40,000	20,000	60,000
Direct costs	$80,000	$80,000	$90,000

a. Assuming the company applies factory overhead based on machine hours, compute the total cost of making each product.

b. Assuming the company applies factory overhead to products on the basis of direct labor hours, compute the total cost of making each product.

c. The company sets selling prices of its products by adding 20 percent to production cost. Determine the per-unit sales price assuming:

  1. the product costs are based on the overhead allocation in part a.

  2. the product costs are based on the overhead allocation in part b.

d. What are the implications of your answers in part c?

e. How could this company use multiple factory overhead application rates to refine its product costing system?

53. (LO 1; *Journal entries*) Mechanical Man Inc. custom-manufactures robots that are used in repetitive production tasks. At the beginning of 1996, three jobs were in process. The costs assigned to the jobs as of January 1, 1996, are as follows:

	JOB 114J	JOB 117N	JOB 128P
Direct materials	$200,000	$1,400,000	$100,000
Direct labor	150,000	800,000	60,000
Overhead	100,000	600,000	42,000
Totals	$450,000	$2,800,000	$202,000

During the course of 1996, two more jobs were started, 133I and 134P, and the following transactions occurred:

■ Materials were purchased on account: $1,200,000.
■ Direct materials were issued to production:

Job 114J	$212,000
Job 117N	158,000
Job 128P	410,000
Job 133I	160,000
Job 134P	125,000

- Indirect materials were issued to production: $111,900.

- Labor costs were incurred as follows:

Job 114J	$175,000
Job 117N	302,000
Job 128P	450,000
Job 133I	205,000
Job 134P	110,000
Indirect labor	300,000

- Other factory overhead costs were incurred, $500,000. Assume these costs were paid in cash.

- Actual factory overhead costs were applied to jobs on the basis of machine hours. The machine hours consumed on the jobs were as follows:

Job 114J	1,200
Job 117N	1,800
Job 128P	3,400
Job 133I	900
Job 134P	700

a. Prepare the journal entries to record the events listed above.

b. Assume that Jobs 114J and 117N were completed during the year. Prepare the journal entries to record the completion of these jobs.

c. Assume Job 117N was sold during the year for $3,600,000. Prepare the necessary journal entries to record the sale.

54. (LO 1, 5; *Flow of costs*) After preparing for your managerial accounting exam, you confidently turn to your roommate and declare, "I think I've finally figured out how product costs flow through the various accounts and how they are reflected on income statements and balance sheets."

On hearing this wonderful news, your roommate responds, "Hey, if you really want to test your understanding of product costing, try working a problem my old prof gave me." After rummaging for 15 minutes through various files, folders, and shelves, your roommate slaps a sheet of paper in front of you and explains that it contains information for one year of operations for Elios Manufacturing Company. The sheet contains the following information:

Beginning Direct Material Inventory,	$ 20,000
Ending Direct Material Inventory,	40,000
Direct material used	400,000
Sales	900,000
Beginning Work in Process Inventory	100,000
Ending Work in Process Inventory	160,000
Cost of products completed during the year	800,000
Actual factory overhead costs incurred	190,000
Selling and administrative expenses	140,000
Beginning Finished Goods Inventory	200,000
Ending Finished Goods Inventory	170,000
Beginning balance—Property, Plant and Equipment	450,000
Ending balance—Property, Plant, and Equipment	480,000
Applied factory overhead = 60% of direct labor cost	

At the bottom of the sheet was the following information: Elios uses a normal costing system.

Using the information just given, compute the following:

a. cost of direct materials purchased.
b. cost of direct labor.
c. applied factory overhead.
d. Cost of Goods Sold before closing underapplied or overapplied factory overhead.
e. net income or net loss before closing underapplied or overapplied factory overhead.

55. (LO 3; *Appendix 1*) Levine Enterprises has compiled the following data to analyze its utility costs in an attempt to improve cost control:

MONTH	MACHINE HOURS	UTILITY COST
January	200	$150
February	325	220
March	400	240
April	410	245
May	525	310
June	680	395
July	820	420
August	900	450

a. Determine the a and b values for the utility cost formula using the high-low method.
b. Determine the a and b values for the utility cost formula using least-squares regression analysis.
c. Assuming September's machine hours are expected to be 760, what is the expected utility cost for September based on your answers to part a? Based on your answer to part b? Why do these answers differ?
d. Which answer (the one to part a or to part b) is preferable, and why?
e. As a manager, what questions might you ask about the data just compiled?

56. (LO 7; *Appendix 2*) Briarcrest Hospital is a small country hospital that wants to determine the full costs of operating its three revenue-producing programs: Surgery; In-Patient Care; and Out-Patient Services. The hospital wants to allocate budgeted costs of Administration, Public Relations, and Maintenance to the three revenue-producing programs. The costs budgeted for each service department are as follows: Administration, $872,500; Public Relations, $210,000; and Maintenance, $326,500. Total assets employed is chosen as the allocation base for Administration; number of employees is to be used for Public Relations; and number of square feet assigned is used for Maintenance. The expected utilization of these activity bases is as follows:

	DOLLARS OF ASSETS EMPLOYED	NUMBER OF EMPLOYEES	SQUARE FEET ASSIGNED
Administration	$ 767,800	15	12,000
Public Relations	188,000	7	2,200
Maintenance	372,200	16	3,500
Surgery	2,800,000	8	2,160
In-Patient Care	1,750,000	32	32,400
Out-Patient Services	1,050,000	24	19,440

a. Using the direct method, allocate the expected service department costs to the revenue-producing areas.

b. Assuming that the areas are listed in a benefits-provided ranking, allocate the expected service department costs to the revenue-producing areas using the step method.

57. (LO 7; *Appendix 2*) Philadelphia Realty generates revenue through three departments: Commercial Sales, Residential Sales, and Property Management. The owner, Buster Cooper, wants to determine the total costs (including support department costs) of each revenue-generating department. Departmental direct costs and several allocation bases are presented below.

AVAILABLE ALLOCATION BASES

Department	Direct Costs	Number of Employees/ Salespersons	Dollars of Assets Employed	Dollars of Revenue
Administration	$ 980,000	12	$1,760,000	N/A
Accounting	477,000	6	682,000	N/A
Promotion	381,000	6	470,000	N/A
Commercial Sales	5,245,000	36	620,000	$6,760,000
Residential Sales	4,589,510	108	968,750	8,450,000
Property Management	199,200	36	348,750	1,690,000

Mr. Cooper has listed the service departments in their benefits-provided ranking. He has decided to allocate service department costs according to the following allocation bases: number of employees/salespersons for Administration; dollars of assets employed for Accounting; and dollars of revenue for Promotion.

a. Using the direct method, allocate the service department costs to the revenue-generating departments.

b. Using the step method, allocate the service department costs to the revenue-generating departments.

c. Under each method, which department is most profitable?

■ CASES

58. (LO 4; *Flexible budget*) Martin Charity Hospital wants to budget its expected costs for each month of the upcoming year in its psychiatric ward. The hospital's management accountant has determined that bed occupancy is the best predictor of cost behavior. The ward has a total of 100 beds, which are generally 70 percent occupied. At 70 percent occupancy, the following costs are incurred:

	COST PER PATIENT DAY	PER-DAY COST	TOTAL FIXED COST PER MONTH
Variable Costs			
Linens	$ 4.00	$ 280	
Food	7.50	525	
Drugs	30.00	2,100	
Doctors	60.00	4,200	
Mixed Costs			
Orderlies (one full-time)		768	$2,880
Nurses (two full-time)		2,700	8,000
Maintenance		100	4,000
Fixed Costs			
Depreciation			1,800
Utilities			960

Except for the three full-time employees, nurses and orderlies are hired from a hospital pool by the ward; this is the reason their salaries can be computed on a daily basis. If such hirings are made, they will result in the costs shown in the "per-day cost" column. One additional full-time nurse and orderly will be necessary if occupancy reaches 85 percent.

Utilities generally cost a fixed $960 per month; this will, however, increase to approximately $1,140 if occupancy reaches 85 percent. Depreciation charges are computed on a straight-line basis at $1,800 per month.

Doctors' charges are entirely variable, based on number of patients and assuming one visit for 30 minutes per day. Variable costs are based on a 30-day month.

a. What costs are expected for the ward for a month at 60 percent, 80 percent, and 90 percent occupancy?

b. What criticisms might be leveled at the 90 percent occupancy budget? Because of the organizational type, what criticisms might be leveled at any of the expected budgets?

59. (LO 5; *Overhead allocation and cost control*) Rose Bach has recently been hired as controller of Empco, Inc. Empco has been in the sheet metal business for many years and is currently investigating ways to modernize its manufacturing process. At Bach's first staff meeting, Bob Kelley, chief engineer, presented a proposal for automating the Drilling Department. Kelley recommended that Empco purchase two robots to replace the eight direct labor workers in the department.

The cost savings outlined in Kelley's proposal included the elimination of direct labor cost in the Drilling Department and a reduction of manufacturing overhead cost in the department to zero, because Empco charges manufacturing overhead on the basis of direct labor dollars using a plantwide rate.

The president of Empco was puzzled by Kelley's explanation of cost savings, believing it made no sense. Bach agreed, explaining that as firms become more automated, they should rethink their manufacturing overhead systems. The president then asked Bach to look into the matter and prepare a report for the next staff meeting.

Bach reviewed articles on manufacturing overhead allocation for an automated factory and discussed the matter with her peers. Bach also gathered the following historical data on Empco's manufacturing overhead rates over the years.

DATE	AVERAGE ANNUAL DIRECT LABOR COST	AVERAGE ANNUAL MANUFACTURING OVERHEAD COST	AVERAGE MANUFACTURING OVERHEAD APPLICATION RATE
1940s	$1,000,000	$ 1,000,000	100%
1950s	1,200,000	3,000,000	250%
1960s	2,000,000	7,000,000	350%
1970s	3,000,000	12,000,000	400%
1980s	4,000,000	20,000,000	500%

Bach also wanted to have some departmental data to present at the meeting. Using Empco's accounting records, she was able to estimate the following annual averages for each manufacturing department in the 1980s.

	CUTTING DEPARTMENT	GRINDING DEPARTMENT	DRILLING DEPARTMENT
Direct labor	$ 2,000,000	$1,750,000	$ 250,000
Manufacturing overhead	11,000,000	7,000,000	2,000,000

a. Disregarding the proposed use of robots in the Drilling Department, describe the shortcomings of the system for applying overhead that is currently used by Empco, Inc.

b. Explain the misconceptions underlying Bob Kelley's statement that manufacturing overhead cost in the Drilling Department would be reduced to zero if the automation proposal was implemented.

c. Recommend ways to improve Empco's method for applying overhead by describing how it should revise its overhead accounting system:

  1. in the Cutting and Grinding Departments; and
  2. to accommodate the automation of the Drilling Department.
  (CMA)

60. (LO 2, 5; *Quality costs and overhead application*) Moss Manufacturing has just completed a major change in its quality control (QC) process. Previously, products were reviewed by QC inspectors at the end of each major process, and the company's ten QC inspectors were charged as direct labor to the operation or job. In an effort to improve efficiency and quality, the company purchased a computerized video QC system for $250,000. The system consists of a minicomputer, 15 video cameras, other peripheral hardware, and software.

The new system uses cameras stationed by QC engineers at key points in the production process. Each time an operation changes or there is a new operation, the cameras are moved, and a new master picture is loaded into the computer by a QC engineer. The camera takes pictures of the units in process, and the computer compares them with the picture of a "good" unit. Any differences are sent to a QC engineer, who removes the bad units and discusses the flaws with the production supervisors. The new system has replaced the ten QC inspectors with two QC engineers.

The operating costs of the new QC system, including the salaries of the two QC engineers, have been included as factory overhead in calculating the company's plantwide factory overhead rate, which is based on direct labor dollars.

The company's president is confused. His vice-president of production has told him how efficient the new system is, yet there is a large increase in the factory overhead rate. The computation of the rate before and after automation is as follows:

	BEFORE	**AFTER**
Budgeted overhead	$1,900,000	$2,100,000
Budgeted direct labor	1,000,000	700,000
Budgeted overhead rate	190%	300%

"Three hundred percent," lamented the president. "How can we compete with such a high factory overhead rate?"

a. **1.** Define factory overhead, and cite three examples of costs typically included in factory overhead.

   2. Explain why companies develop factory overhead rates.

b. Explain why the increase in the overhead rate should not have a negative financial impact on Moss Manufacturing.

c. Explain, in the greatest detail possible, how Moss Manufacturing could change its overhead accounting system to eliminate confusion over product costs.
   (CMA)

■ ETHICS AND QUALITY DISCUSSIONS

61. According to William J. Fife, Jr., chairman of Giddings & Lewis, Inc.: "The labor content of a product today is probably less than 15%. So, I don't care how much I cut [direct] labor, it's not going to get to the bottom line. We have to get at overhead costs."

Today, U.S. firms have some of the highest overhead burdens among global companies. Much of the higher overhead cost is associated with the tiered management structures prevalent in the United States. The layers of white collar managers create a tremendous cost disadvantage. The redundant layers of management are associated with the traditional notion that companies need to supervise employees to maintain productivity and control quality.

[SOURCE: Based on Thane Peterson, "Can Corporate America Get Out From Under Its Overhead?" *Business Week* (May 18, 1992), p. 102.]

a. With appropriate training of blue-collar workers in American industry, how can layers of white-collar managers be eliminated and productivity and quality increased?

b. How does the traditionally hostile relationship between white collar managers and blue collar workers place American firms at a disadvantage in the global market relative to countries that have traditionally fostered cooperation among all employees?

62. *[Phelps County Bank (PCB), in Rolla, Missouri, has taken the road less traveled in competing in the financial services industry. Unlike its big-city contemporaries, PCB's prices are high, and its line of products and services are limited. For example, its interest rate on residential mortgages may exceed by a full point the rates charged by its competition.*

The company competes by delivering only the highest quality services to its customers.] The lobby opens five minutes before 9 a.m. and closes five minutes after 3 p.m.—there are no disgruntled customers peering in and looking angrily at their watches. If people knock on the door after closing, customer-service reps have been trained to invite them into a secure room and ask how they can help. Reps have the authority to resolve most customer's complaints on the spot.

In the loan department, lending officers typically sit down with prospective borrowers for most of an hour, just to get to know them, before even beginning on the loan application. The bank's newspaper ads carry lending officers' home phone numbers, as do the officers' business cards. Customers are encouraged to call nights or weekends on urgent matters.

Service is partly a matter of systems, and PCB monitors its services by sending surveys to new borrowers (after three months) and customers opening new accounts (after six). The surveys alert the bank to bottlenecks—and to unmet customer needs.

[SOURCE: John Case, "Total Customer Service, " *Inc.* (January 1994). Reprinted with permission of Inc. magazine. © 1994 by Goldhirsh Group, Inc.]

a. One of the key ingredients in PCB's success is a willingness to pay employees for delivering high-quality service to customers. How would PCB's focus on delivering high quality services affect its overhead costs?

b. An employee stock ownership plan (ESOP) is central in the compensation structure of the bank. How can employee ownership of the bank enhance the quality of the services it delivers?

c. In the 10 years ending 1992, the market value of the bank's stock more than quadrupled. In light of the high prices charged for the bank's services, what does the increase in market value suggest about the relationship between quality and profitability?

d. Do you think a large bank with interstate operations could easily duplicate the success of PCB?   Explain.

63. "Stanford gets some $175 million a year in direct research funding from the federal government. Like other schools that receive these grants, it also gets reimbursed by Uncle Sam for overhead or indirect costs associated with the research. In Stanford's case, that's an additional $85 million or so a year, or roughly 20% of its operating budget." Some of the items that were charged to the government for research included:

- $2,000 a month in floral arrangements;
- $2,500 to refurbish a grand piano;
- $3,000 for a cedar-lined closet; and
- $184,000 in depreciation on a yacht donated to Stanford's sailing program.

After investigations, Stanford returned almost $700,000 to the government for inappropriate charges.

[SOURCE: Based on Maria Shao, "The Cracks in Stanford's Ivory Tower," *Business Week* (March 11, 1991), p. 64.]

a. Discuss the rationale for allowing colleges and universities to charge the government for overhead costs related to research grants.
b. Discuss the ethical implications of allowing colleges and universities to "liberally" decide what overhead costs should be included in research-related overhead.
c. Discuss the budgetary implications of allowing colleges and universities to "liberally" decide what costs should be included in research-related overhead.
d. What is your reaction as a taxpayer to a college or university's inclusion of costs such as those listed earlier in "research-related overhead"?
e. What if Stanford were a research firm rather than a university and you had engaged it to perform a research task for your company. Discuss how you would want to set policy for what costs could be considered part of research-related overhead, for which you could be charged.

64. Assigning overhead costs to products is necessary to more accurately estimate the cost of producing a good or performing a service. One "product" that takes on an exceptional number of additional charges for overhead is an aspirin dose (two units) in a hospital. Following is an estimate of why a patient is charged $7 for a dose of aspirin. Some costs are referred to as "shared and shifted costs"; others are called overhead. In all cases, this simply means that these costs are not covered by revenue dollars elsewhere and so must be covered for the hospital to do all of the things a hospital charges for—including administering aspirin.

COUNTY COMMUNITY HOSPITAL PRODUCT COSTING SHEET

	Unit	Unit Cost	Total Units	Total Cost
Raw Material				
Aspirin	each	$ 0.006	2	$0.012
Direct Labor				
Physician	hour	60.000	0.0083	0.500
Pharmacist	hour	30.000	0.0200	0.603
Nurse	hour	20.000	0.0056	0.111
Indirect Labor				
Orderly	hour	12.000	0.0167	0.200
Recordkeeping	hour	12.000	0.0167	0.200

Supplies

Cup	each	0.020	1	0.020

Shared and Shifted Costs

Unreimbursed Medicare	0.200	1	0.200
Indigent Care	0.223	1	0.223
Uncollectible Receivables	0.084	1	0.084
Malpractice Insurance*	0.034	2	0.068
Excess Bed Capacity	0.169	1	0.169
Other Operating Costs	0.056	1	0.056
Other Administrative Costs	0.112	1	0.112
Excess Time Elements	0.074	1	0.074
HOSPITAL OVERHEAD COSTS @32.98%			.868
FULL COST (including Overhead)			$3.500
PROFIT (@ 50%)			3.500
PRICE (per dose)			$7.000

*Note that the dose is charged twice for malpractice insurance—once for each aspirin!

[SOURCE: Based on David W. McFadden, "The Legacy of the $7 Aspirin," *Management Accounting* (April 1990), p. 39. Published by Institute of Management Accountants, Montvale, N. J.]

a. Discuss the reasons why such cost shifting is necessary.

b. What other kinds of costs might be included in the additional "overhead" charge at the rate of 32.98 percent?

c. Discuss the ethical implications of shifting costs such as those for indigent care, uncollectible receivables, and excess bed capacity to a patient receiving a dose of aspirin.

d. Are you willing to accept a $7 charge for a dose of aspirin, knowing what costs are considered in developing such a charge if you are (1) a paying customer or (2) the hospital manager? Discuss the reasons behind your answers.

65. Tom Savin has recently been hired as a cost accountant by the Offset Press Company, a privately-held company that produces a line of offset printing presses and lithograph machines. During his first few months on the job, Savin discovered that Offset has been underapplying factory overhead to the Work in Process Inventory account while overstating expense through the general and administrative accounts. This practice has been going on since the start of the company six years ago. The effect in each year has been favorable and has materially improved the company's tax position. No internal audit function exists at Offset, and the external auditors have not yet discovered the underapplied factory overhead.

Prior to the sixth-year audit, Savin points out the practice and its effect to Mary Brown, the corporate controller, and asks her to let him make the necessary adjustments. Brown directs him not to make adjustments but to wait until the external auditors have completed their work and see what they uncover. Brown directs him not to make adjustments but to wait until the external auditors have completed their work and see what they uncover.

The sixth-year audit is completed, and the external auditors once again fail to discover the underapplication of factory overhead. Savin again asks Brown if he can make the required adjustments and is again told not to make them. Savin, however, believes that the adjustments should be made and that the external auditors should be informed of the situation.

Since there are no established policies at Offset Press Company for resolving ethical conflicts, Savin is considering three alternative courses of action:

■ Follow Brown's directive and do nothing further.

- Attempt to convince Brown to make the proper adjustments, and advise the external auditors of her actions.
- Tell the Audit Committee of the Board of Directors about the problem and give them the appropriate accounting data.

  a. For each of these three alternative courses of action, explain whether the action is appropriate. You may want to refer to the "Standards of Ethical Conduct for Management Accountants" given in Appendix A at the end of the text.

  b. Without prejudice to your answer in part a, assume that Tom Savin again approaches Mary Brown to make the necessary adjustments and is unsuccessful. Describe the steps that Tom Savin should take in resolving this situation.

  (CMA adapted)

■ PROJECTS

66. Invite to your class an alumnus who has worked in the controller's function in a given manufacturing industry for 20 years or more. Ask this individual to discuss changes in how overhead is applied to production that he or she has observed during his or her career. Specifically ask the individual to address the following points:

  a. how technology has affected the amount of overhead cost incurred relative to the amount of other product costs incurred;

  b. how technology has affected the application of overhead to production; and

  c. any changes that have occurred in the way overhead costs have been recorded and accounted for over the years.

67. *For some low-cost, point-to-point carriers like Southwest Airlines, turning planes around in 15 minutes is how they have done business for years. But, for others, particularly airlines that have both connecting flights and short-hop commuter routes, the approach is new. Continental Airlines started using quick turns on some flights [in 1993] as part of its Continental Lite operation. And UAL Corp. plans to use them on its United Shuttle when it starts service on the West Coast in October [1994].*

  In Baltimore on a recent afternoon, 12 USAir High Ground flights arrived between 3 p.m. and 5 p.m. When USAir flight 2243 from Tampa, Fla., landed at 3:40, ramp agents opened the plane's cargo doors within seconds and began unloading baggage. At any given time, six or seven employees worked to turn around the plane, up from three or four for a regular USAir flight.

  [SOURCE: Carl Quintanilla, "New Airline Fad: Faster Airport Turnaround," *Wall Street Journal* (August 4, 1994), p. B1. Reprinted by permission of The Wall Street Journal, © 1994 Dow Jones & Company, Inc. All Rights Reserved Worldwide.]

  Obtain current financial statements of several prominent airline carriers. Use the financial statements as a basis to write a report that answers the following questions.

  This project is best suited to be accomplished in teams. Optimally, each team should have three members: one to examine marketing costs, one to examine financing costs, and one to examine costs of service provision including costs of plant and equipment.

  a. What are the major costs incurred by airline companies?

  b. Which major costs are likely to be fixed and which are likely to be variable?

  c. Based on your answers to parts a and b, why do airlines strive to have quick turnarounds for flights?

5

ACTIVITY-BASED MANAGEMENT

Virtually all of a company's activities exist to support the production and delivery of today's goods and services. They should therefore all be considered product costs.

Robin Cooper and Robert S. Kaplan, "Measure Costs Right: Make the Right Decisions" *Harvard Business Review* (September-October 1988)

LEARNING OBJECTIVES

1. Discuss how reasonably accurate product and service cost information can be developed.

2. Differentiate between and provide examples of value-added and non-value-added activities.

3. Identify the causes of decreased manufacturing cycle efficiency.

4. Designate cost drivers in an activity-based costing system.

5. Distinguish between activity-based costing and conventional overhead allocation methods.

6. Determine when the use of activity-based costing is appropriate.

7. Recognize the benefits and limitations of using activity-based costing.

AT&T: The Big Breakup Forced Management, Not Allocation, of Costs

Throughout its history, North America's telephone business has been regulated. The Federal Communications Commission developed its methods for establishing tariffs (prices) on the basis of cost plus an allowable profit. To satisfy regulators that the cost of a tariffed service was correct, AT&T had to develop sophisticated cost allocation procedures. Thus, an important management process was concerned with how to allocate cost to satisfy the political/legal process.

AT&T's breakup into smaller, more focused business units, combined with the advent of price-cap regulation (instead of the predefined return on investment regulation) made managing, rather than allocating, costs critical. The company's business units compete in an open market, and the need for accurate cost and profit information by service is vital.

[Allocation methods did exist to assign costs to business units.] Initially, however, costs were allocated most often on the basis of "convenient," high-level volume drivers. They were not allocated according to service, customer segment, or actual activity being performed.

[The company decided to implement an activity-based costing (ABC) pilot project in the business billing center.] Product managers with profit and loss responsibility wanted better insight into the center's operations and an identification of specific activities that added value. A process-focused, team-based approach was used to achieve the following objectives:

- Integrate financial management results (economic value added) with operational management and customer results (customer value added).
- Identify operational cost improvements and quantify cost savings from proposed initiatives (for example, cost of rework). Identify and manage costs according to process.
- Analyze productivity increases or decreases in the business billing center.
- Establish a fact-based process for business planning and budget negotiations. The process should focus on the benefit/cost of specific activities. It should not result in emotional disagreements over allocations.
- Benchmark the business billing center's costs with other billing centers and internal business billing center groups.

SOURCE: Terrence Hobdy, Jeff Thomson, and Paul Sharman, "Activity-Based Management at AT&T," *Management Accounting* (April 1994), pp. 35-36. Published by Institute of Management Accountants, Montvale, NJ.

Like many other companies, AT & T has numerous, complex processes that generate a wide variety of products and services. Overhead costs in such organizations should be allocated to products and services through the use of multiple predetermined overhead rates rather than a single one. Management accountants should develop these rates using a reasonable number of cost pools and should base the allocations on the underlying cost drivers.

AT&T's original allocation methods worked well when the company could simply add a profit margin to its costs and charge that amount to customers. But when forced to compete with other telecommunications companies in an open market, AT&T managers decided they needed to understand the nature of organizational costs and to exercise control over them. For AT&T to be able to meet the competition's prices and remain profitable, the most "convenient" method of overhead allocation would no longer provide adequate product or service cost information.

Therefore, AT&T managers and accountants implemented a new costing system to help managers obtain the best possible estimates of product or service costs. The new system is called activity-based costing (ABC), which comes under the umbrella heading of activity-based management (ABM). The simple difference between ABC and ABM has been defined as follows: "ABC is about gathering cost information. ABM shows you how to do something about it."[1] This chapter examines the need for ABM and the process of analyzing organizational activities and cost drivers. The information gained from such an analysis can be used in ABC to more appropriately allocate overhead costs to products and services. The chapter also discusses when ABC systems will provide better information than traditional overhead allocations and how the resulting costs can be used by managers.

DEVELOPING PRODUCT/SERVICE COST INFORMATION

■ **LEARNING OBJECTIVE 1**
Discuss how reasonably accurate product and service cost information can be developed.

Product or service costs are developed for three purposes: (1) to have information that enables management to report to stockholders and various regulatory bodies; (2) to help management make product decisions such as pricing and product line expansions or deletions; and (3) to allow management to monitor and control operations. In many organizations, the first purpose has often overwhelmed the other two. This circumstance has arisen partially because the external parties (the Securities and Exchange Commission, the Internal Revenue Service, and other regulatory agencies) to which companies report have established rules about what should be included in determining cost. For instance, the Financial Accounting Standards Board has mandated that research and development costs be expensed as incurred. Therefore, those costs cannot be considered product costs for audited financial statements.

Generally accepted accounting principles have been developed to provide comparability and consistency in external reporting, but no one has mandated how product costs should be developed for the other two purposes. Thus, it is often easier to use the same product costing system for all three purposes. However, this approach may directly diminish the usefulness of resulting decisions. The following quote summarizes the dissatisfaction of many managers with traditionally determined cost information: "Today's management accounting information, driven by the procedures and cycles of the organization's financial reporting system, is too late, too aggregated, and too distorted to be relevant for managers' planning and control decisions."[2]

While it is impossible to determine exact product costs, managers should try to develop the best possible cost estimates. The best estimate occurs when the largest amount of production or service costs can be traced directly to the resulting products or services. Direct tracing requires the use of valid measures of resource consumption (cost drivers). Direct materials and direct labor costs have always been traced easily to products because these costs are readily determined by material requisitions and employee time sheets. The volume of production or service is a valid measure of direct materials and direct labor consumption.

If the best estimate arises when the most costs are traced directly, it is equally true that the best estimate will be obtained when the fewest costs are assigned arbitrarily.

---

[1]Daniel J. McConville, "Start with ABC," *Industry Week* (September 6, 1993), p. 33.

[2]H. Thomas Johnson and Robert S. Kaplan, *Relevance Lost* (Boston: Harvard Business School Press, 1987), p. 1.

■ LEARNING
OBJECTIVE 2
Differentiate between and
provide examples of value-added
and non-value-added activities.

Overhead, by its very nature, is an indirect or common cost and, thus, cannot be directly traced to individual products or services. Some allocation method must be selected to distribute overhead costs: that method can use a valid cost predictor or driver or the method can be arbitrary. In the past, factory overhead was often attached to products by use of a direct labor hour base. While this base may not have been the *most accurate* measure of resource consumption, it was generally considered a reasonable, rather than arbitrary, allocation base.

The modern manufacturing environment is more machine-intensive, with low direct labor costs and high overhead costs. Attempts to use direct labor hours as the overhead allocation base in such an environment could lead to significant product cost distortions. Most overhead costs in these environments are machine-related: depreciation on high-cost machinery; power costs to run the machinery; repair and maintenance to keep the machinery operating. Overhead allocation rates based on direct labor hours would be very high and would assign primarily machine-related overhead costs to products that used relatively high amounts of direct labor. Products using a great deal of machine time and relatively little direct labor would be assigned only minimal overhead costs. Thus, more sophisticated measures of overhead cost allocation are needed.

Machine hours are often an important overhead allocation base in the modern manufacturing environment. But even machine hours may not be adequate as the sole allocation base for overhead costs. If overhead is created by factors such as product variety, product complexity, or other cost drivers, multiple allocation bases will result in more accurate estimates of product or service cost. Fortunately, companies now have the technology to collect, process, analyze, and use a much greater quantity of information than in the past. This ability means that it is possible to obtain greater accuracy in product costing by using multiple cost drivers to rationally allocate, rather than arbitrarily assign, overhead costs.

ACTIVITY ANALYSIS

Although specifically designated as an accounting function, the development of product or service cost concerns all managers. Because they will be using the cost information in a variety of ways, managers need to be assured that the costs have been developed in a systematic and rational manner and that they are as accurate as possible so that they may be relied on for planning, controlling, and decision making purposes. For example, product costs affect decisions on corporate strategy (Is it profitable to be in a particular market?), marketing (What is the relationship between product cost and product price?), production (Should a component be made or purchased?), and finance (Should money be invested in additional plant assets to manufacture this product?).

In theory, it would not matter how much it cost to make a product or perform a service if enough customers were willing to buy that product or service at a price set by the company. This price would cover costs and provide a reasonable profit margin. In reality, there are two problems with this concept. First, customers usually only purchase a product or service that provides acceptable value for the price being charged. Second, companies often do not set their own prices. The prices are set by competitive forces in the market. Thus, management should be concerned about whether customers perceive selling price and value to be equal. This concern is normally addressed through making certain that the product meets customer expectations in the areas of quality and service. Additionally, management must be concerned about whether the company can make a reasonable profit given external prices and internal costs. If the market price is considered a given, then costs become the controlling variable creating profitability.

Activity-Based Management

Managers can use **activity-based management (ABM)** to help them improve the customer value and the profit created by providing a product or service. ABM can help companies make products or perform services more efficiently, determine costs more accurately, and control and evaluate operations more effectively. ABM overlaps in many respects with other disciplines. Depending on one's perspective, ABM could be viewed as part of a total quality management (TQM) or a business process reengineering effort. Alternatively, TQM and BPR (discussed later in the chapter) could result from implementing activity-based management. Some concepts that can be considered parts of activity-based management are shown in Exhibit 5–1.

Any efforts to use activity-based management first require an analysis of what the organization does: its activities. An **activity** is any repetitive action, movement, or work sequence performed to fulfill a business function. Each activity should be describable with a verb and a noun. For example, "lift material," "open door," "start machine" are all activities.

The activities performed in making or doing something can be detailed on a flow chart or grid called a **process map.** These maps should include *all* activities performed to accomplish a specific task or process, not just the obvious ones. For example, storing newly purchased parts would not be on a typical list of "Steps in Making Product X." However, when materials and supplies are purchased, they are commonly warehoused

activity-based management (ABM)

activity

process map

■ **EXHIBIT 5–1**
The Activity-Based Management Umbrella

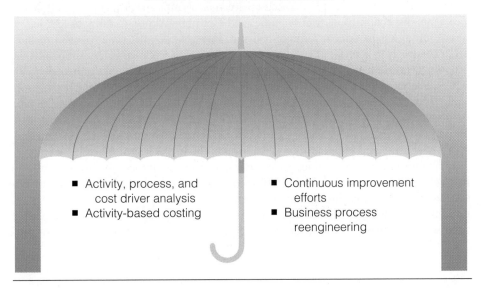

ACTIVITY-BASED MANAGEMENT

- Activity, process, and cost driver analysis
- Activity-based costing
- Continuous improvement efforts
- Business process reengineering

until needed. Storing parts requires both people and time (and, therefore, costs), even though storage is not essential to the primary process of making Product X.

By detailing all activities, the process map "makes it possible to identify duplication, waste, and unnecessary work. The map can also be used for intraorganizational benchmarking to ensure that best practices are identified and adopted throughout all divisions of the business."[3]

Value-Added and Non-Value-Added Activities

value charts

value-added (VA) activity

Some process maps are called **value charts** because they indicate the time spent in each activity from the beginning to end of a process and assess the value of each activity. Activities may be value-added, non-value-added, or business-value-added. A **value-added (VA) activity** increases the worth of a product or service to customers and customers are willing to pay for the activities. VA activities are undertaken to perform the functions necessary to manufacture a product or perform a service. The time spent in these activities is the value-added **processing** (or **service**) **time**. For example, AT&T's process of connecting calls between telephone users is a value-added activity and the time spent in making the connections is value-added service time.

processing (or service) time

Other activities simply increase the time spent on a product or service but do not increase its worth to the customer; these are **non-value-added (NVA) activities.** The time spent in performing NVA activities creates unnecessary additional costs. If these activities were eliminated, costs would decrease without affecting the market value or quality of the product or service. NVA activities exist throughout an organization, and they are costly regardless of where they are located.

non-value-added (NVA) activities

Some NVA activities are essential to business operations, but customers would not willingly choose to pay for these activities. These activities are known as **business-value-added activities.** For instance, AT&T must prepare telephone bills for its customers. Customers know this activity must occur, that it creates costs, and that telephone rates must be set to cover the cost of this activity. However, because preparation of the bill adds no direct value to telephone calls made, customers would prefer not to have to pay for this activity. The accompanying News Note discusses some business-value-added and NVA activities that occur before manufacturing processes even begin.

business-value-added activities

The time spent engaged in NVA activities can be classified as NVA processing or service time, inspection time, transfer time, and idle time. Although most processing or service time is value-added, some of it is not. For example, the time spent in making products simply to keep people and machines busy is non-value-added. Additionally, the processing time spent in packaging is essential for some products but unnecessary for others. For example, customers are willing to pay for the processing time spent packaging medicines for health and safety reasons. But customers may not consider the time spent packaging a man's dress shirt into its cellophane package equally as value-added. To help reduce time and cost as well as to be environmentally-conscious, many companies are focusing attention on minimizing or eliminating packaging.

inspection time
transfer time
idle time

In manufacturing companies, performing quality assurance activities results in **inspection time,** and moving products or components from one place to another constitutes **transfer time.** Storage time and time spent waiting at the production operation for processing are referred to as **idle time.** Although inspection time and transfer time are non-value-added from a customer's perspective, very few companies can com-

---

[3]Takeo Yoshikawa, John Innes, and Falconer Mitchell, "Functional Analysis of Activity-Based Cost Information," *Journal of Cost Management* (Spring 1994), p. 41.

Cut NVA Costs to Cut Overhead

NEWS NOTE

Improving productivity in pre-manufacturing translates into improving customer impact while improving profits. If your "improvement" to an activity does not provide value to the customer or reduce your overhead, there is no need to be doing it.

[To analyze these activities,] the first thing management must do is set up teams for each of the critical processes. Next, a company must assign individuals to be the "process owners," and take responsibility for leading each team in flowcharting a process and its sub-processes and eventually documenting the detailed activities involved in the process.

The team must then perform a value assessment of the activities to determine which are adding value that the customer will pay for, which are not, and which are needed to operate the business.

In increasing front office productivity, the goal is to eliminate all the non-value-added activities and make the business-value-added activities more effective and efficient.

Manufacturers are amazed by how much useless time and money they expend on activities that do nothing for themselves or their customers. In studies of four manufacturers, [the accounting firm] Grant Thornton found that in the best case, only 30% of the company's pre-manufacturing activities added value for the customer. For two companies, the figure was 15%. And, for the fourth, the figure was 12%.

In picking the activities to start reorganizing, choose those where you are spending the most money but not adding any value to the customer.

In one case, a manufacturer found that the total cost of quoting a job was $17,000. Of that, $10,000 was non-value-added: the company was reviewing the quote eight times before it was released, with many of the reviews being rubber stamps of the previous approval.

These savings add up. One company identified in a three-to-five-month period, 33,000 hours of administrative time spent on useless activities that could be eliminated.

Another company set a goal of reducing non-value-added costs by 40% and business-value-added costs by 25%. Out of a total annual administrative cost of $10 million, that meant savings of $2.4 million. Now that's productivity improvement worth aiming for.

SOURCE: Dan Seidner, "In Improving Productivity, Don't Neglect Your Front Office," reprinted from [*Grant Thornton*] *Manufacturing Issues* (Fall 1992), pp. 8-9. © Grant Thornton 1992.

pletely eliminate their quality control functions, and elimination of all transfer time is impossible. However, understanding the non-value-added nature of these functions should motivate managers to minimize such activities to the extent possible.

These same types of NVA time are found in service companies. For instance, when AT&T reviewed the activities in its billing center, the company found that substantial time was spent on order comparisons (inspection time) and filing (transfer time). When AT&T employees were given new computers, the employees were able to make faster comparisons and eliminate over 19,000 paper copies of service orders. The change saved approximately $42,000 per month and reduced filing time substantially.[4] Although AT&T continued to perform some order comparisons and file some documents, employees did so more efficiently and effectively.

The value chart in Exhibit 5–2 (page 198) illustrates the various manufacturing activities of Walker Corporation. Note the excessive amounts of time consumed in

---

[4] Terrence Hobdy, Jeff Thomson, and Paul Sharman, "Activity-Based Management at AT&T," *Management Accounting* (April 1994), p. 38.

■ **EXHIBIT 5–2**
Value Chart

Compounding									
Operations	Receiving	Quality control	Storage	Move to production facility	Wait for use	Set up machine	Compounding	Quality control	Move to packaging
Average Time (Days)	1	2	15-20	.5	5	.5	3.5	1	.5

Packaging												
Operations	Receiving	Storage	Move to production facility	Wait for use	Set up machine	Packaging	Quality control	Move to finished goods warehouse	Storage	Move to shipping dock	Sit on shipping dock	Ship to customer
Average Time (Days)	.5	5-15	.5	5	.5	.5	2	.5	0-20	1	.5	1-3

Total time in compounding:	29.0 - 34.0 days	Total value-added time:	3.5 days
Total time in packaging:	17.0 - 49.0 days	Total value-added time:	.5 days
Total processing time:	46.0 - 83.0 days	Total value-added time:	4.0 days
	Non-value-added time:	42–79 days	

Non-Value-Added Activities

Value-Added Activities

■ **LEARNING OBJECTIVE 3**
Identify the causes of decreased manufacturing cycle efficiency.

storing and moving materials. Only four days of value-added processing time are needed in the entire sequence; even within this sequence, as mentioned earlier, the company may question the time spent in packaging.

Manufacturing Cycle Efficiency

manufacturing cycle efficiency (MCE)

In a manufacturing company, the total cycle time reflects the time from the receipt of an order to completion of a product. Thus, cycle time is equal to value-added processing time plus total non-value-added time. Dividing value-added processing time by total cycle time gives **manufacturing cycle efficiency (MCE),** a measure of how well a firm's manufacturing capabilities use time resources. In a manufacturing environment,

[t]ypically, cycle time efficiency at most companies is 10%. In other words, value is added to the product only 10% of the time from receipt of the parts until shipment to the customer. Ninety percent of the cycle time is waste. A product is much like a magnet. The longer the cycle time, the more the product attracts and creates cost.[5]

[5]Tom E. Pryor, "Activity Accounting: The Key to Waste Reduction," *Accounting Systems Journal* (Fall 1989), p. 34.

In a retail environment, cycle time refers to the time from the ordering of an item to the sale of that item to a customer. Non-value-added activities in retail include shipping time from the supplier, receiving department delays for counting merchandise, and any storage time between receipt and sale. In a service company, cycle time refers to the time between the service order and completion of the service. All activities other than actual service performance and nonactivity (such as delays in beginning a job) are considered non-value-added *for that job*.

The following example illustrates non-value-added activities in a service environment. On Monday at 9:00 A.M., the telephone company is asked to install a telephone line for a customer. The job is scheduled for Tuesday at 3:30 P.M. Upon arriving at the customer's house, the service technician spends 20 minutes installing the telephone jack, 5 minutes writing an invoice, and 5 minutes chatting with the homeowner. The total cycle time is 31 hours (9:00 A.M. Monday to 4:00 P.M. Tuesday) or 1,860 minutes—of which only 20 to 25 minutes is value-added time for that particular job! (The 5 minutes spent writing the invoice could be perceived as value-added by the customer because if there is a problem with the installation, the invoice will provide evidence that the work was performed by a telephone company employee.) Thus, the maximum service cycle efficiency for this job is a mere 1.3 percent (25 minutes ÷ 1,860 minutes.

Non-value-added activities can be attributed to systemic, physical, and human factors. For example, a system may require that products be manufactured in large batches to minimize costs of setting up machinery or that service jobs be taken in order of importance. Physical factors contribute to non-value-added activities since, in many instances, building layouts do not provide for the most efficient transfer of products. This factor is especially apparent in multistory buildings in which receiving and shipping must be on the ground floor while storage and production are on other floors. People may be responsible for non-value-added activities because of improper skills or training or because of their need to be sociable (as when workers discuss weekend sports events on Monday morning). Attempts to reduce non-value-added activities should be directed at all of these causes and should focus on those activities that create the most unnecessary costs.

In a perfect environment, the manufacturing or service cycle efficiency would be 100 percent because all non-value-added time would be eliminated. Such an environment will never exist, but companies are moving toward higher cycle efficiencies. One means by which companies can move toward such an optimized environment is through the use of just-in-time (JIT) inventory management. As discussed in Chapter 2, the idea behind JIT is to manufacture or purchase inventory only as the need for it arises or in time to be sold or used. Using JIT eliminates a significant portion of the idle time consumed in storage and wait processes. If inventory is not stored, it will not have to be moved into and out of storage, thus reducing non-value-added transfer activity and saving more time.

Preparing process maps or constructing value charts for each product or service could be quite time-consuming. Making a few such charts, however, can quickly indicate where a company is losing time through NVA activities. An estimate of the cost of that time can be made by totaling costs for items such as depreciation on storage

As robots replace direct labor at this Chrysler plant in Fenton, Missouri, the manufacturing cycle efficiency rises. However, an MCE of 100% will never be reached because even robots have downtime—usually related to repairs and maintenance.

Non-value-added time occurs in service as well as manufacturing areas. The idle time you spend on telephone "hold" is not only frustrating, but it precludes the accomplishment of your value-added organizational functions.

facilities, wages for employees who handle warehousing, and an "interest charge" on tied-up working capital funds. Having this information would allow managers to make informed decisions about how much cost could be reduced through the elimination of non-value-added activities and, therefore, how to improve company profitability.

Level of Cost Incurrence

As companies engage in their various activities, company resources are consumed and, in turn, costs are incurred. All activities have related cost drivers, or factors that have direct cause-effect relationships to costs. It may be possible to identify many cost drivers for an individual business unit. For example, cost drivers for a purchasing area include number of purchase orders, number of supplier contacts, and number of shipments received. Some of the cost drivers in a billing center identified by AT&T include service orders, change requests, bill groups (customer locations), and pages printed.[6]

The number of cost drivers that can be identified is not necessarily the number that should be used in the process of overhead allocation. Obviously, the more cost drivers and cost pools developed, the greater is the degree of accuracy of reported product costs. But, as indicated in the accompanying News Note, the benefits provided by increased cost accuracy should be greater than the cost of defining, accumulating, and maintaining the data.

Thus, management should use a reasonable number of cost drivers and be certain that the cost of measuring them is not excessive. For instance, a company might find that determining and using eight cost drivers increases organizational costs by one percent but provides enough data to reduce total costs by five percent, for a net cost reduction of four percent. Adding another eight drivers to the system might reduce costs another five percent but the incremental cost of those additional eight drivers may be more than the incremental five percent saved. Thus, the company should expend its efforts only where significant rewards are possible.[7] The cost drivers selected should also be easy to understand, directly related to the activity being performed, and appropriate for performance measurement.

Manufacturing overhead has traditionally been accumulated into one or two cost pools (total overhead or variable and fixed overhead), either by department or plant wide. Furthermore, one or two drivers (direct labor hours and/or machine hours) have been used to assign costs to products. However, the use of single cost pools and single cost drivers may produce illogical product or service costs in complex production or service environments.

To reflect the more complex environments, the accounting system must recognize that costs are created at different levels. This recognition requires that managers and accountants investigate, quantify, and explain the level at which activities and, thus, their related costs are incurred. Traditionally, activities and costs were assessed only in relation to volume. Some costs are in fact **unit-level costs** that are strictly variable and created by the production or acquisition of a single unit of product or the delivery of a single unit of service. Costs that do not change with unit-based activity have traditionally been viewed, from an accounting standpoint, as fixed.

■ **LEARNING OBJECTIVE 4**
Designate cost drivers in an activity-based costing system.

unit-level costs

---

[6]Hobdy et al., "Activity-Based Management at AT&T," p. 37.

[7]Ilene K. Kleinsorge and Ray D. Tanner, "Activity-Based Costing: Eight Questions to Answer Before You Implement," *Journal of Cost Management* (Fall 1991), p. 87.

Limit the Cost Drivers

Unfortunately, the number of activities performed in a typical facility is so great that it is not economically feasible to use a different cost driver for each activity. Instead, many activities have to be aggregated and a single driver used to trace the costs of the activities to products. For example, every time a new batch is run in a metal-cutting operation, new tools have to be drawn from the tool room, inserted, and qualified. The feeds and speeds of the machine must be altered, parts moved from inventory storage to the shop floor, the first part has to be inspected, the batch scheduled, and so on. Despite this complexity, a well-designed [accounting] system might use only one or two cost drivers to trace the setup costs of associated activities to products.

Using only two drivers to trace the cost of so many different activities generally introduces distortions into reported product costs. The difficulty of designing good cost systems lies in achieving a system that is economical to maintain yet does not introduce excessive distortions.

The art of designing [the] system can thus be viewed as making two separate but interrelated decisions about the number of cost drivers needed and which cost drivers to use.

The minimum number of cost drivers required depends on the desired accuracy of reported product costs and on the complexity of the product mix being produced. [Greater accuracy requires a larger number of drivers. Higher complexity also requires more drivers to minimize cost distortions. But, the objective of the system designer] is to design a cost system that provides the most benefit for the lowest overall cost.

Source: Robin Cooper, "The Rise of Activity-Based Costing—Part Three: How Many Cost Drivers Do You Need, and How Do You Select Them?" *Journal of Cost Management* (Winter 1989), p. 34, 45. Reprinted with permission from The Journal of Cost Management for the Manufacturing Industry, © 1989 Warren, Gorham, & Lamont, 31 St. James Avenue, Boston, MA 02116. All rights reserved.

But, an activity-based system recognizes that costs may vary at levels of activity "higher" than the unit level. These higher levels include batch, product or process, and organizational or facility levels.[8] Some examples of the kinds of costs that occur at the various levels are given in Exhibit 5–3 (page 202).

A cost created when a group of similar things are made, handled, or processed at the same time is called a **batch-level cost.** A good example of a batch level cost is setup cost. Assume that setting up a printer to run invoices costs AT&T $100. Two different types of invoices (residential and business) are to be run during the day; therefore, two setups will be needed, at a total cost of $200. The first run will generate 500 residential invoices, and the second run will generate 100 business invoices. If a unit-based cost driver (such as number of invoices run) were used to allocate the setup cost, the total setup cost of $200 would be divided by 600 invoices, giving a cost per invoice of $.33 (rounded). This method would assign the majority of the cost to residential invoices (500 × $.33 = $165). However, because the setup cost is actually a batch-level cost, $100 should be spread over the 500 residential invoices for a cost

batch-level costs

---

[8]This hierarchy of costs was introduced by Robin Cooper in "Cost Classification in Unit-Based and Activity-Based Manufacturing Cost Systems," in the *Journal of Cost Management* (Fall 1990).

of $.20 per invoice, and $100 should be spread over 100 business invoices for a cost of $1 per invoice. Using a batch-level perspective shows the commonality of the cost to the units within the batch and better indicates the relationship between the activity (setup) and the driver (different invoice runs).

product- or process-level cost

A cost incurred in support of different products or processes in a company is called a **product-** or **process-level cost.** These costs are created by activities such as developing products, processing engineering change orders, or maintaining production specifications. "The costs of these activities can be assigned to individual products, but the costs are independent (i.e., fixed) of the number of batches or the number of units of each product produced."[9] Product/process-level costs will vary, however, with increases in the number of products or processes that need to be sustained in an organization.

To illustrate a product/process-level cost, assume that the billing department of AT&T revised ten forms during May. Of these revisions, eight related to Customer Group One, two related to Customer Group Two, and none related to Customer Group Three. Each form revision costs $2,700 to issue. During May, the company produced 2,000 forms for Customer Group One, 3,000 forms for Customer Group

■ **EXHIBIT 5–3**

Levels of Costs

Classification Levels	Types of Costs	Necessity of Cost
Unit-Level Costs	■ Direct materials ■ Direct labor ■ Some machine costs, if traceable	Cost is incurred for each unit produced
Batch-Level Costs	■ Purchase orders ■ Setup ■ Inspection ■ Movement ■ Scrap, if related to the batch	Cost is incurred for each batch produced
Product- or Process-Level Costs	■ Engineering change orders ■ Equipment maintenance ■ Product development ■ Scrap, if related to product design	Cost supports different product types or processes
Organizational- or Facility-Level Costs	■ Building depreciation ■ Plant or division manager's salary ■ Organizational advertising	Cost supports the physical equipment used in overall production or service processes

[9]Robin Cooper, "Cost Classification in Unit-Based and Activity-Based Manufacturing Cost Systems," *Journal of Cost Management* (Fall 1990), p. 6.

Two, and 10,000 forms for Customer Group Three. If forms-revision costs were treated as unit-level costs, the total cost of $27,000 would be spread over the 15,000 forms produced at a cost per form of $1.80. However, this method inappropriately assigns $18,000 of form-revision cost to Customer Group Three, which had no form revisions for the month! Treating form-revision costs as product/process level costs would result in the assignment of $21,600 of costs to Customer Group One and $5,400 to Customer Group Two. These amounts should not be assigned only to the revised forms produced in the current month, but to all the revised forms produced while the revisions are in effect. The current period revision cost theoretically benefits all current and future issuances.

Organizational- or **facility-level costs** are incurred only to support and sustain a business unit. The unit can be a department, a division, or organizational headquarters. If the unit is one that has identifiable output, costs may be attachable to that output in a reasonable allocation process. For example, one department at AT&T might be responsible for handling only residential customers or one division of an automobile manufacturer might make only one type of automobile. Any facility-level costs are then reasonably attachable to the output of that facility. Alternatively, if the costs incurred at this level are common to many different activities, products, or services, those costs can only be assigned to products on an arbitrary basis. For instance, the president's salary, the cost of the annual corporate audit, and the costs of stockholder meetings are company-wide organizational costs and could not be allocated to individual products or services in any rational manner. While these costs may appear on the surface to be fixed, they will actually change as the organization grows: more vice-presidents will be added; audit costs will become more expensive; and stockholder meetings will require larger space and greater costs.

Thus, batch-level, product/process-level, and organizational/facility-level costs are all variable, but they vary with causes other than changes in production or service volume. Accounting has traditionally assumed that costs that did not vary with changes in activity at the unit level were fixed rather than variable. This assumption is detrimental to rigorous cost analysis because it is too narrowly conceived. In contrast, activity-based systems often refer to fixed costs as being **long-term variable costs.** Essentially, long-term variable costs are step fixed costs. However, rather than ignoring the steps as is often the case, ABC acknowledges their existence. Professor Robert Kaplan of Harvard University analyzes the ability of fixed costs to rise using the "Rule of One." According to this rule, any time there is more than one unit of a resource, that resource is variable and the appropriate cost driver simply needs to be identified. Knowledge of the driver may help to eliminate the source of the cost change.

To accurately estimate product or service cost, the company should accumulate costs at each successively higher activity level. Then, cost assignment should be made relative to the activities causing the costs. Unit-, batch-, and product/process-level costs all relate to units of products, merely at different levels. Thus, after assigning these costs to products at the appropriate activity level, a total cost for the product can be developed and matched with revenues from product sales.

In contrast, organizational- and facility-level costs may not be product-related. Organizational-level costs that cannot be associated with a particular product or service should be subtracted in total from net product margin. An activity-based system will normally not try to assign organizational-level costs to products, because the allocation base would be too arbitrary.

Exhibit 5–4 (page 204) indicates how cost accumulation at the various levels can be used to determine a total unit cost. Each product's total unit cost is multiplied by the number of units sold, and that product's cost of goods sold is subtracted from its total revenues, yielding a net product margin. These margins are summed to determine a

organizational- or facility-level costs

long-term variable costs

■ **EXHIBIT 5–4**

Determining Product Profitability and Company Profits

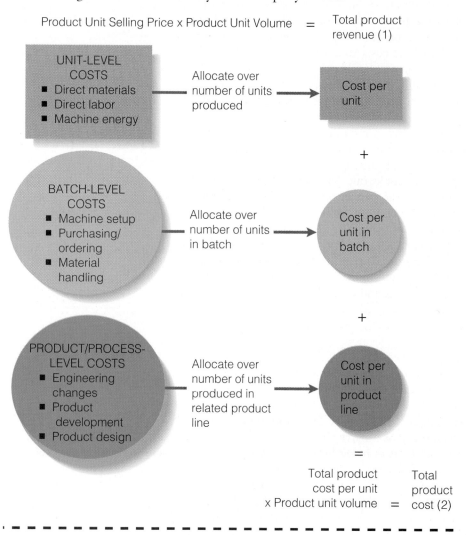

Product Unit Selling Price x Product Unit Volume = Total product revenue (1)

UNIT-LEVEL COSTS
- Direct materials
- Direct labor
- Machine energy

Allocate over number of units produced → Cost per unit

+

BATCH-LEVEL COSTS
- Machine setup
- Purchasing/ordering
- Material handling

Allocate over number of units in batch → Cost per unit in batch

+

PRODUCT/PROCESS-LEVEL COSTS
- Engineering changes
- Product development
- Product design

Allocate over number of units produced in related product line → Cost per unit in product line

=

Total product cost per unit
x Product unit volume = Total product cost (2)

- -

    Total product revenue (1 above)
− Total product cost (2 above)

= Net product margin
+ All other net product margins*

= Total margin provided by products

    ORGANIZATIONAL- or FACILITY-LEVEL COSTS**
    - Corporate/divisional administration
    - Facility depreciation

−

= Company profit or loss

total company margin. Then, the unassigned organizational-level (or common) costs are subtracted to find company profit or loss. In this model, the traditional distinction between product and period costs is not visible, because the emphasis is on analyzing product profitability for internal management rather than financial statement presentation.

Data for Ring-Ring Telephone Co.'s billing department (Exhibit 5–5) are used to illustrate the effect of recognizing multiple activity and cost levels on the information available to management. Before recognizing that some costs were incurred at the batch-, product/process-, and organizational/facility-levels, Ring-Ring totaled its service overhead costs and allocated them among its three lines of business (residential service, commercial service, and mobile telephones) on a computer access hour (CAH) basis. The company assumes that each customer averages two CAHs of service per month, but the mobile phone customer group is extremely low-volume. As shown in

---

■ **EXHIBIT 5–5**

Profitability Analysis for Ring-Ring Telephone Co.

Total OH cost = $8,113,000
Total CAHs = 1,330,000
OH rate per CAH = $8,113,000 ÷ 1,330,000 = $6.10
Per unit amounts reflect revenue or cost per customer.

	RESIDENTIAL (600,000 CUSTOMERS)		COMMERCIAL (50,000 CUSTOMERS)		MOBILE (15,000 CUSTOMERS)		
	Unit	Total	Unit	Total	Unit	Total	Total
Service Revenue	$20.00	$12,000,000	$25.00	$1,250,000	$60.00	$900,000	$14,150,000
Service Costs							
Direct	$ 3.80	$ 2,280,000	$ 4.60	$ 230,000	$32.00	$480,000	$ 2,990,000
OH per 2 CAHs	12.20	7,320,000	12.20	610,000	12.20	183,000	8,113,000
Total	$16.00	$ 9,600,000	$16.80	$ 840,000	$44.20	$663,000	11,103,000
Profit or (loss)		$ 2,400,000		$ 410,000		$237,000	$ 3,047,000

	RESIDENTIAL (600,000 CUSTOMERS)		COMMERCIAL (50,000 CUSTOMERS)		MOBILE (15,000 CUSTOMERS)		
	Unit	Total	Unit	Total	Unit	Total	Total
Service Revenue	$20.00	$12,000,000	$ 25.00	$1,250,000	$60.00	$900,000	$14,150,000
Service Costs							
Direct	$ 3.80	$ 2,280,000	$ 4.60	$ 230,000	$32.00	$480,000	$ 2,990,000
Overhead							
Unit-level	6.00	3,600,000	7.20	360,000	24.00	360,000	4,320,000
Batch-level	2.00	1,200,000	4.00	200,000	8.00	120,000	1,520,000
Product/ process-level	1.20	720,000	1.20	60,000	2.40	36,000	816,000
Total	$13.00	$ 7,800,000	$ 17.00	$ 850,000	$66.40	$996,000	$ 9,646,000
Service line margin		$ 4,200,000		$ 400,000		$ (96,000)	$ 4,504,000
Organizational/ facility-level costs							1,457,000
Company profit							$ 3,047,000

the first section of the exhibit, cost information indicated that mobile phone customers were a profitable customer group for Ring-Ring. After analyzing its activities, the company began accumulating costs at different levels and assigning them to products based on appropriate drivers. While the individual details for this overhead assignment are not shown, the final assignments and resulting product profitability figures are presented in the second section of Exhibit 5–5. This more refined approach to assigning costs shows that the mobile phone customer group is unprofitable. Such information may mean that Ring-Ring should increase the selling prices it charges to mobile phone users or find ways to reduce the costs of having and serving mobile phone users.

ACTIVITY-BASED COSTING

activity-based costing (ABC)

■ LEARNING
OBJECTIVE 5
Distinguish between activity-based costing and conventional overhead allocation.

Recognizing that various activity and cost levels exist, gathering costs into related cost pools, and using multiple cost drivers to assign costs to products and services are the three underlying elements of **activity-based costing (ABC)**. ABC is an accounting information system that identifies the various activities performed in an organization and collects costs on the basis of the underlying nature and extent of those activities. Activity-based costing focuses on attaching costs to products and services based on the activities used to produce, perform, distribute, or support those products and services.

Two-Step Allocation

activity center

After initial recording, costs are accumulated in activity center cost pools. An **activity center** is a segment of the production or service process for which management wants a separate report of the costs of the activities performed. In defining these centers, management should consider the following issues: geographical proximity of equipment; defined centers of managerial responsibility; magnitude of product costs; and a need to keep the number of activity centers manageable. Costs having the same driver are accumulated in pools reflecting the appropriate level of cost incurrence (unit, batch, or product/process). The fact that a relationship exists between a cost pool and a cost driver indicates that, if the cost driver can be reduced or eliminated, the related cost should also be reduced or eliminated.

Gathering costs in pools having the same cost drivers allows managers to recognize any cross-functional activities in an organization. In the past, some companies may have accumulated overhead in smaller-than-plantwide pools, but this accumulation was typically performed on a department-by-department basis. Thus, the process reflected a vertical-function approach to cost accumulation. But production and service activities are horizontal by nature. A product or service flows *through* an organization, affecting numerous departments as it goes. Using a cost driver approach to develop cost pools allows managers to more clearly focus on the various cost effects created by making a product or performing a service than was possible traditionally.

For example, assume that Colleen Tilden, a telephone repairwoman, has been assigned a schedule for the day. While Colleen is on her way to her first client, the telephone company is contacted by a business customer whose phone line has been hit by lightning. The telephone company considers this a priority job, so the scheduler phones Colleen and changes her schedule. The scheduler must then call the other scheduled customers to inform them of the delay. In addition, Colleen may have to return to the office to obtain different parts and an invoice must be sent to the new customer. On a vertical-function basis, everyone in the organization is working the regular number of hours and performing the regular functions. On a cross-functional basis, however, a particular cost driver (an emergency telephone call) causes additional activity and creates additional costs. ABC focuses on these additional activities and costs. In contrast, an accounting system using a conventional cost driver (such as repairperson labor hours) would not recognize the added activities or costs because, from a vertical-function perspective, nothing has changed.

After accumulation, costs are allocated out of the activity center cost pools and assigned to products and services by use of a second driver. These drivers are often referred to as activity drivers. An **activity driver** measures the demands placed on activities and, thus, the resources consumed by products and services. The activity driver selected often indicates an activity's output. The process of cost assignment is the same as the overhead application process illustrated in Chapter 4. Exhibit 5–6 illustrates this two-step process of tracing costs to products and services in an ABC system and Exhibit 5–7 (page 208) provides some common activity drivers.

As noted in Exhibit 5–6, the cost drivers for the collection stage may differ from the activity drivers used for the allocation stage because some activity center costs are not traceable to lower levels of activity. Costs at the lowest (unit) level of activity should be allocated to products by use of volume- or unit-based drivers. Costs

activity driver

■ **EXHIBIT 5–6**

Tracing Costs in an Activity-Based Costing System

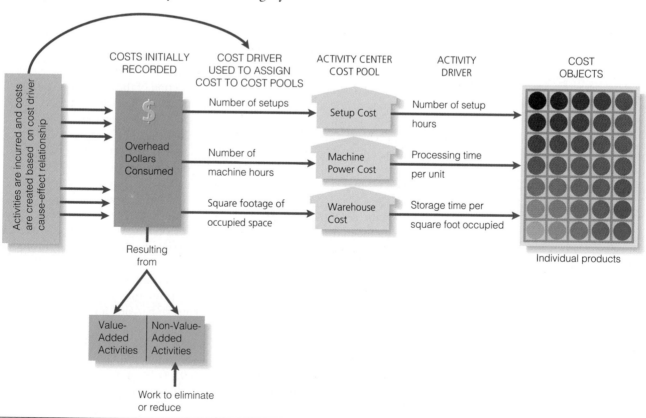

■ **EXHIBIT 5–7**
Activity Drivers

ACTIVITY CENTER	ACTIVITY DRIVERS
Accounting	Reports requested; dollars expended
Personnel	Job change actions; hiring actions; training hours; counseling hours
Data processing	Reports requested; transactions processed; programming hours; program change requests
Production engineering	Hours spent in each shop; job specification changes requested; product change notices processed
Quality control	Hours spent in each shop; defects discovered; samples analyzed
Plant services	Preventive maintenance cycles; hours spent in each shop; repair maintenance actions
Material services	Dollar value of requisitions; number of transactions processed; number of personnel in direct support
Utilities	Direct usage (metered to shop); space occupied
Production shops	Fixed per-job charge; setups made; direct labor; machine hours; number of moves; material applied

SOURCE: Michael D. Woods, "Completing the Picture: Economic Choices with ABC," *Management Accounting* (December 1992), p. 54. Published by Institute of Management Accountants, Montvale, NJ.

incurred at higher (batch and product/process) levels may also be allocated to products by use of volume-related drivers, but the volume measure should include only those units associated with the batch or the product/process—not total production or service volume.

Activity-Based Costing Illustrated

Exhibit 5–8 provides a brief illustration of overhead allocation in the Printing Department of Ring-Ring Telephone Co. The first section of the exhibit shows the traditional allocation of departmental overhead costs among the outputs of the department (telephone bills, regular telephone books, and yellow-page telephone books). This assignment provides an allocated overhead cost of $.03, $.29, and $.25, respectively, for each telephone bill, regular telephone book, and yellow-page telephone book.

The second section of the exhibit assigns the departmental overhead costs using activity-based costing. Under ABC, the costs of activities are first pooled by related cost drivers. Ring-Ring's printing department has determined that overhead costs are pooled among the three departmental activities (setup, printing, and distribution/handling) based on the number of employees (the cost driver). Next, these costs are transferred from the cost pools to specific products or services based on appropriate activity drivers. The department has decided that the activity drivers for cost pool assignment are best stated in number of occurrences of primary activities. The following activity drivers have been selected: number of print runs for setup; number of printing hours for printing; and tons of printed material handled for distribution/handling. Each type of overhead cost is assigned to output using the cost per unit of the activity driver multiplied by the number of occurrences of that driver. The total assigned overhead cost for each output is divided by units of output to determine the following approximate overhead costs per unit: $.02, $.28, and $.44, respectively, for each telephone bill, regular telephone book, and yellow-page telephone book.

■ **EXHIBIT 5–8**

Activity-Based Costing Illustration

- ■ 3 departmental activities: setup (5 employees); printing (3 employees); and distribution/handling (2 employees)
- ■ $555,000 total budgeted annual departmental overhead cost related to activities
- ■ Departmental outputs: telephone bills (7,000,000); regular telephone bills (750,000); yellow page telephone books (500,000)
- ■ 222,000 total budgeted printing hours (PHs): telephone bills (84,000 PHs); regular telephone books (88,000); and yellow-page telephone books (50,000)

TRADITIONAL ALLOCATION SYSTEM—BASED ON PHs

$555,000 ÷ 222,000 PHs = $2.50 per PH

	Bills	Regular Books	Yellow Pages
PHs needed	84,000	88,000	50,000
Multiplied by overhead rate per PH	× $2.50	× $2.50	× $2.50
Total allocated OH per activity	$210,000	$220,000	$125,000
Divided by production output	÷ 7,000,000	÷ 750,000	÷ 500,000
OH allocated per bill/book	$.03	≈$.29	$.25

ACTIVITY-BASED COSTING ALLOCATION SYSTEM

	Setup	Printing	Distrib./Handl.
Total printing department OH: $555,000			
Step 1: Assign OH to cost pools based on cost driver (number of employees):			
Setup (5 of 10 employees): 50% × $555,000	$277,500		
Printing (3 of 10 employees): 30% × $555,000		$166,500	
Distribution/handling (2 of 10 employees): 20% × $555,000			$111,000
Step 2: Assign OH cost in cost pool to cost objects using activity drivers			
Setup (number of print runs)	50		
Printing (number of printing hours)		222,000	
Distribution/handling (tons of material handled)			2,500
Cost allocation per unit of activity driver	$5,550	$.75	$44.40

Activity Information for Cost Allocation to Products

Bills: 7,000,000 bills require 12 runs, 84,000 PHs, and 16 tons of handling.

Regular telephone books: 750,000 books require 14 runs, 88,000 printing hours, and 1,420 tons of handling.

Yellow-page telephone books: 500,000 books require 24 runs, 50,000 printing hours, and 1,064 tons of handling.

Cost Allocations	Bills	Regular Books	Yellow Pages
Print runs (12; 14; and 24) @ $5,550	$ 66,600	$ 77,700	$133,200
Printing hours (84,000; 88,000; and 50,000) @ $.75	63,000	66,000	37,500
Tons of material (16; 1,420; and 1,064) @ $44.40	710	63,048	47,242
Total OH assigned to product	$130,310	$206,748	$217,942
Divided by number of units of product	÷ 7,000,000	÷ 750,000	÷ 500,000
OH cost per unit of product	≈$.02	≈$.28	≈$.44

Using activity-based costing caused the overhead cost for telephone bills to decline substantially (33 percent) from that calculated under a traditional system. Telephone bills are rather simple to produce (basically requiring little more than the use of an accumulated data base) and they are produced in high volumes. The overhead allocated to regular telephone books was only minimally affected. In contrast, the overhead cost for yellow-page telephone books increased approximately 76 percent. Yellow-page telephone books are produced in relatively low volumes and are more complex (setting and sizing advertisements, multiple listings under different headings, and so on). In addition, yellow-page books require almost half of all setups, a factor ignored under traditional allocations. Because setup cost is extremely high, ABC allocates substantially more cost to those books.

A primary consequence of relying on the inaccurate traditional cost figures might be that the cost of billings would be overstated, while advertising rates for the yellow-pages might be understated. Such improper information might cause company management to make poor decisions regarding how to price services and whether to outsource the printing work or change the charges for telephone service or advertising rates. Planning, control, and evaluation should also be more effective with the better information generated under ABC.

Discrepancies in costs between traditional and activity-based costing are not uncommon. Activity-based costing systems indicate that significant resources are consumed by low-volume products and complex production operations. Studies have shown that, after the implementation of activity-based costing, companies have found that their traditional costing systems have assigned too much cost to high-volume, standard products. Using ABC, costs assigned to these products have declined anywhere from 10 to 30 percent. Low-volume, complex specialty product costs tend to increase from 100 to 500 percent, although in some cases these costs have risen by 1,000 percent to 5,000 percent![10] Thus, activity-based costing typically shifts a substantial amount of overhead cost from the standard, high-volume products to which those costs have been assigned under more traditional methods to premium special-order, low-volume products, as shown in Exhibit 5–9. The ABC costs of moderate products and services (those that are neither extremely simple nor complex, nor produced in extremely low or high volumes) tend to remain approximately the same as the costs calculated using traditional costing methods.

DETERMINING IF ABC IS APPROPRIATE

■ LEARNING OBJECTIVE 6
Determine when the use of activity-based costing is appropriate.

The preceding illustration indicates that an accounting system that ignores activity and cost relationships may lose vital information. Not every accounting system that uses direct labor or machine hours as the cost driver is providing inadequate or inaccurate cost information. Activity-based costing is a useful tool, but not necessarily one that is appropriate for all companies. Consideration of the following factors helps provide a means to judge whether ABC will be advantageous for a particular business.

For a given organization, is it likely that ABC will produce costs that are significantly different from those that are generated with conventional accounting, and does it seem likely that those costs will be "better"? The factors involved here include:

■ the number and diversity of products or services produced,
■ the diversity and differential degree of support services used for different products,

---

[10]Peter B. B. Turney, *An Introduction to Activity-based Costing* (ABC Technologies, Inc.: 1990), video.

■ **EXHIBIT 5–9**

Traditional Versus ABC Overhead Allocations

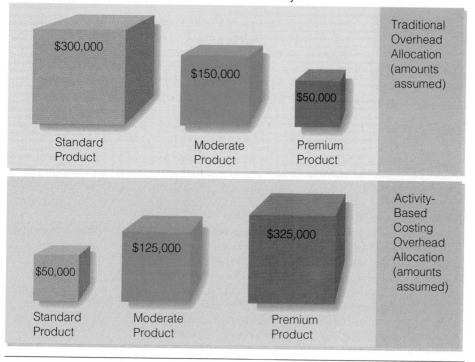

■ the extent to which common processes are used,
■ the effectiveness of current cost allocation methods,
■ and the rate of growth of period costs.

If information that is considered "better" is generated by ABC, will the new information change the dependent decisions made by the management? The factors involved here are:

■ management's freedom to set prices,
■ the ratio of period costs to total costs,
■ strategic considerations,
■ the climate and culture of cost reduction in the company,
■ and the frequency of analysis that is desirable or necessary.[11]

The News Note on the following page discusses the underlying assumptions that companies must consider before adopting this system.

With Product Variety and Product Complexity

Two factors commonly associated with a need to consider activity-based costing are product variety and product complexity. **Product variety** refers to the number of different types of products produced. The products may be variations of the same prod-

product variety

---

[11]T. L. Estrin, Jeffrey Kantor, and David Albers, "Is ABC Suitable for Your Company?" *Management Accounting* (April 1994), p. 40.

ABC Is Only Appropriate IF ...

Although ABC systems often provide better product cost data than volume-based systems, they are based on a number of assumptions that should be evaluated before ABC costs are considered superior. If the data do not satisfy the assumptions, ABC costs may not be any more reliable than the costs provided by simpler volume-based systems.

Two assumptions underlying activity-based costing are:

1. The costs in each cost pool are driven by homogeneous activities.
2. The costs in each cost pool are strictly proportional to the activity.

The homogeneity assumption will be violated if the costs in a cost pool are driven by two or more not highly correlated activities but only one of the activities is used to assign all costs in the cost pool to products. Under these conditions, some costs are assigned to products on an arbitrary basis. The arbitrarily assigned costs are those caused by an activity or activities not used as the cost driver.

The second assumption, proportionality, will be violated by several conditions, including the presence of nonlinear costs. For example, costs that are subject to the learning curve phenomenon will violate the proportionality assumption. [A learning curve exists when people become more proficient at their tasks the longer those tasks are performed.] The assumption will also be violated if both fixed and variable costs are included in the same cost pool and they are assigned to products as if they were strictly variable. Finally, joint costs [which are incurred in making multiple kinds of products at the same time] will violate this assumption when they are not strictly proportional to the activity.

SOURCE: Harold P. Roth and A. Faye Borthick, "Are You Distorting Costs by Violating ABC Assumptions?" *Management Accounting* (November 1991), pp. 39–40. Published by Institute of Management Accountants, Montvale, NJ.

uct line (such as Hallmark's different types of greeting cards), or they may be in numerous product families (such as Proctor & Gamble's detergents, diapers, fabric softeners, and shampoos). In either case, product additions causes numerous overhead costs to increase. Exhibit 5–10 illustrates the potential for increased overhead with an increase in product variety.

In addition, the changes in overhead costs resulting from increased product variety make it clear that seemingly fixed costs are in fact long-term variable costs. Long-term variable costs tend to increase with increases in the number and types of products because of the need for additional overhead support, such as warehousing, purchasing, setups, and inspections. The News Note (page 214) discusses the idea that simply packaging a product differently is the same as introducing another product.

mass customization

In the quest for product variety, many companies are striving for **mass customization** of products through the use of flexible manufacturing systems. Such personalized production can often be conducted at a relatively low-cost. For example, Dell Computer Company in Austin, Texas, allows customers to phone in an order for a computer with the exact features desired to be delivered to the customer's home in one week. While such customization may please some customers, it does have some drawbacks.

First, there may simply be too many choices. For instance, at GE Fanuc (a Charlottesville, Virginia, manufacturer), customers had to look through several four-inch-thick binders of components in order to design a custom-made product—an extremely time-consuming project.[12] Nissan reportedly had 87 different varieties of steering wheels, but customers did not want many of them and disliked having to choose from so many options.[13] Second, mass customization creates a tremendous opportunity for errors. And third, most companies have found that customers, given the wide variety of choices, typically make selections from a rather small percentage of the total. At Toyota, investigation of purchases revealed that 20 percent of the product varieties accounted for 80 percent of the sales.[14] This 20:80 ratio is a fairly common one and is referred to as the **Pareto principle,** after the Italian economist Vilfredo Pareto.[15]

Pareto principle

Product complexity refers to the number of components in a product or the number of processes or operations through which a product flows. Management can minimize product complexity by reviewing the design of the company's products and processes to standardize them and reduce the number of different components, tools, and processes required.

product complexity

Products should be designed to consider the Pareto principle and take advantage of commonality of parts. Analyzing components will generally reveal that 20 percent

---

■ **EXHIBIT 5–10**

Product Variety Creates Overhead Costs

ORIGINAL PRODUCT LINE

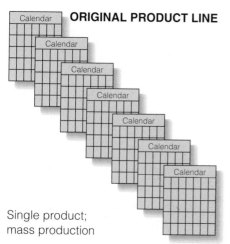

Single product; mass production

ADDITIONS TO PRODUCT LINE

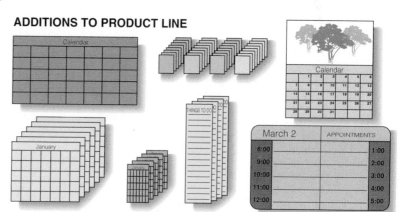

Still make original product in mass quantities; additional products are each made in extremely limited quantities.

WITH WHICH PRODUCT SET WOULD THE COMPANY HAVE MORE:

- Inventory carrying costs?
- Purchasing costs?
- Scheduling costs?
- Setup and changeover costs?
- Expediting costs?
- Quality control costs?
- Scrap costs?
- Rework costs?

TO WHICH PRODUCTS DO THESE INCREASED COSTS RELATE?

BUT *which product would bear most of the costs?*

---

[12]Joe Pine, "Customers Don't Want Choice," *Wall Street Journal* (April 18, 1994), p. A12.

[13]B. Joseph Pine II, Bart Victor, and Andrew C. Boynton, "Making Mass Customization Work," *Harvard Business Review* (September-October 1993), p. 110.

[14]Pine et al., "Making Mass Customization Work," p. 108.

[15]Pareto found that about 85 percent of Milan's wealth was held by about 15 percent of the people. The term *Pareto principle* was coined by Joseph Juran in relationship to quality problems. Juran found that a high proportion of such problems were caused by a small number of process characteristics (the *vital few*), while the majority of process characteristics (the *trivial many*) accounted for only a small proportion of quality problems.

Same Product, Two Sets of Costs

When a company has excess capacity, adding one new product does not add much [cost], but continuing to add new products on an ongoing basis does. As product families grow, sooner or later incremental investments in both people and equipment are required—another accountant, an additional product manager, another purchasing agent, new equipment, etc. Before long, these incremental investments become significant. Since many companies find it difficult to eliminate members of product families that are no longer needed or economical, products and product lines tend to proliferate.

Components of the service offerings contribute to product proliferation and can be as difficult and costly to handle as direct additions to the product line. The effects of adding a new service may seem deceptively simple and low in cost, but consider what it really means (for example), to offer customers the option of products delivered on a pallet or in a case:

■ Manufacturing must be set up to package the product in two different formats;
■ The warehouse operation needs two different storage arrangements; and
■ Two separate inventories need to be maintained.

In effect, these two packaging options make two separate products out of one. In other words, if this delivery option were offered for every product, the company's product line would effectively be doubled.

SOURCE: Elizabeth Haas Edersheim and Joan Wilson, "Complexity at Consumer Goods Companies: Naming and Taming the Beast," *Journal of Cost Management* (Fall 1992), p. 27. Reprinted with permission from the Journal of Cost Management for the Manufacturing Industry, © 1992, Warren, Gorham, & Lamont, 31 St. James Avenue, Boston, MA 02116. All rights reserved.

of the components are used in 80 percent of the products. If this is the case, then companies need to consider two other factors. First, are the remaining components used in key products? If so, could equal quality be achieved by using the more common parts? If not, can the products be sold for a premium price to cover the costs associated with the use of low-volume components? Second, are the parts specified for use in products purchased by important customers who are willing to pay a premium price for the products? If so, the benefits from the complexity may be worth the cost. However, would customers be equally satisfied if more common parts were used and the product price were reduced? Parts complexity is acceptable only if it is value-added from the customer's point of view.

Process complexity may develop over time, or it may exist because of a lack of sufficient planning in product development. Processes are complex when they create difficulties for the people attempting to perform production operations (physical straining, awkwardness of motions, or wasted motions) or for the people using manufacturing machinery (multiple and/or detailed setups, lengthy transfer time between machine processes, recalibration of instruments, and so on). Process complexity reflects numerous non-value-added activities and thus causes time delays and cost increases.

simultaneous (or concurrent) engineering

A company can employ simultaneous engineering to reduce both product and process complexity. **Simultaneous** (or **concurrent**) **engineering** refers to a process

Yogurt—a fairly simple product—until you consider the wide variety produced by a company such as Yoplait. The numerous added ingredients (fruits and flavorings) as well as the diverse packaging can create large increases in overhead costs—possibly indicating a need for activity-based costing.

of continuously involving all primary functions and personnel contributing to a product's origination and production from the beginning of a project. Multifunctional teams design the product by considering customer expectations, vendor capabilities, parts commonality, and production process compatibility. Such an integrated design effort is referred to as a design-for-manufacturability approach. Simultaneous engineering helps companies to shorten the time to market for new products and minimize complexity and cost.

Even when simultaneous engineering is used in process development, processes may develop complexity over time. One way to overcome such process complexities is **business process reengineering (BPR)** or process innovation and redesign. BPR's goal is to find and implement radical changes in how things are made or how tasks are performed to achieve substantial cost, service, or time reductions. Emphasizing continuous improvement, BPR ignores "the way it is" and looks instead for "the way it should be." For instance, AT&T took two years to reengineer its Global Business Communication Systems. In the process, the company rewrote hundreds of job descriptions, revised the performance evaluation and reward systems, upgraded the computer system, retrained personnel, and made extensive changes in financial reporting, proposals and contracts writing, supplier relationships, and the manufacturing, shipping installation, and billing functions.[16] As indicated in the News Note on page 217, BPR may redesign old processes or design new ones to eliminate complexity.

business process reengineering (BPR)

Many traditional cost systems are not designed to account for information such as how many different parts are used in a product, so management cannot identify prod-

---

[16]Thomas A. Steward, "Reengineering: The Hot New Managing Tool," *Fortune* (August 23, 1993), p. 42.

ucts made with low-volume or unique components. Activity-based costing systems are flexible and are intended to gather such details and provide important information about relationships among activities and cost drivers to persons involved in reengineering efforts. Armed with this data, these people can focus reengineering efforts on the primary causes of process complexity and those that create the highest level of waste.

With Lack of Commonality in Overhead Costs

Certain products and services create substantially more overhead costs than others. While some of these additional overhead costs may be caused by product variety or process complexity, others may be related to a variety of support services. For example, some products require substantially more advertising than others; some use higher cost distribution channels; and some necessitate the use of high-technology machinery. In addition, some companies' output volumes differ significantly among its products and services. Each of these differences creates additional overhead costs.

If only one or two overhead pools are used, overhead related to specific products will be spread over all products. The result will be increased costs for products that are not responsible for the increased overhead. To illustrate, it has been noted (concerning the use of traditional allocation methods) that when "production volumes are fairly similar—say, volume of one product is no more than five times that of any other—product costs will probably be accurate. Accuracy falls off rapidly as the range grows to more than 10 to 1."[17] Similar decreases in accuracy would occur with the other mentioned differences.

With Problems in Current Cost Allocations

If a company has undergone one or more significant changes in its products or processes (such as increased product variety or business process reengineering), managers and accountants need to investigate whether the existing cost system still provides a reasonable estimate of product or service cost. Many companies that have automated their production processes have experienced large reductions in labor and large increases in overhead costs. In such companies, the use of direct labor as an overhead allocation base will produce extraordinarily high application rates. Products made using automated equipment will tend to be charged an insufficient amount of overhead, while products made using high proportions of direct labor will tend to be overcharged.

Another problem with traditional cost allocations is that they generally emphasize the assignment of product costs to products while expensing the majority of period costs when incurred. Activity-based costing recognizes that some period costs may be distinctly and reasonably associated with specific products and thus should be traced and allocated to those products. This recognition changes the traditional view of product versus period cost.

With Changes in Business Environment

A change in the competitive environment in which a company operates may also require better cost information. Increased competition may occur for several reasons:

---

[17]Robin Cooper, "You Need a New Cost System When ...," *Harvard Business Review* (January-February 1989), p. 80.

Redesign or Replace?

Process redesign takes the present process and removes waste while reducing cycle time and improving the effectiveness of the process. Process redesign (which is also called focus improvement, since it focuses its efforts on the present process, or process reengineering) can lead to improvements that range from 300 to 1000 percent. Process redesign is the right choice for approximately 70 percent of the business processes.

[In contrast, new process design] takes a fresh look at the objectives of the process. It completely ignores the present process and organizational structure. The approach takes advantage of the latest mechanization, automation, and information techniques available. New process design can lead to improvements that range from 700 to 2000 percent. New process design provides the biggest improvement, though it costs more and takes more time to implement than process redesign. It also has the highest degree of risk; often the new process design approach includes departmental restructuring and is very disruptive to the organization. Most organizations can effectively implement only one change of this magnitude at a time.

SOURCE: H. James Harrington, "Process Breakthrough: Business Process Improvement," *Journal of Cost Management* (Fall 1993), pp. 36, 38. Reprinted with permission from The Journal of Cost Management for the Manufacturing Industry, © 1989, Warren, Gorham, & Lamont, 31 St. James Avenue, Boston, MA 02116. All rights reserved.

(1) other companies have recognized the profit potential of a particular product or service; (2) the product or service has become cost-feasible to make or perform, or (3) an industry has been deregulated. If many new companies are competing for old business, the best estimate of product or service cost must be available to management so that profit margins and prices can be reasonably set.

Changes in management strategy can also signal a need for a new cost system. For example, if management wants to begin new operations, the cost system must be capable of providing information on how costs will change. Confirming management's view of costs in the traditional variable versus fixed classifications may not allow such information to be effectively developed. Viewing costs as short-term variable versus long-term variable focuses on cost drivers and the changes the planned operations will have on activities and costs.

Many companies are currently engaging in kaizen or continuous improvement efforts. As discussed in Chapter 2, kaizen relates to improving the way employees perform their tasks, the level of quality achieved in a product, and the level of service generated by the company. Continual improvement recognizes the concept of eliminating non-value-added activities to reduce cycle time, making products (or performing services) with zero defects, reducing product costs on an ongoing basis, and simplifying products and processes. Activity-based costing, by promoting an understanding of cost drivers, allows the non-value-added activities to be identified and their causes eliminated or reduced.

The choice to implement activity-based costing should mean that management is willing to accept the new information and use it to plan, control, and evaluate operating activities. If this is the case, then management must have some ability to set prices relative to cost changes, accept alternative business strategies (such as eliminating or expanding product or service offerings) if the new costs should so indicate, and reduce waste where necessary (including downsizing or job restructuring).

Regardless of the reason or reasons behind the need for a change in costing systems, companies now have the ability to implement ABC systems. In the past, such implementation would not have been technologically feasible. Introduction of the personal computer, bar coding, and other advanced technologies means that significantly more information can be readily and cost-effectively supplied.

OPERATIONAL CONTROL UNDER ABC

■ **LEARNING OBJECTIVE 7**
Recognize the benefits and limitations of using activity-based costing.

The list of companies using activity-based costing is large and impressive and includes Hewlett-Packard, Cal Electronic Circuits, Hughes Aircraft, IBM, Tektronix, GenCorp Polymer Products, and Owens Corning Fiberglass. Most companies use activity-based costing as a stand-alone system to supplement the information provided by their conventional cost accounting systems—although some companies have partially integrated ABC with their conventional systems. Exhibit 5–11 indicates the results of a recent survey on the usage of ABC systems.

Although activity-based costing can be used to generate product costs for financial statements, this system is more often employed as a tool to improve performance and enhance management's ability to make better analyses of product profitability. Activity-based costing should be perceived as a means to provide additional, more accurate information.

Activity-based management and costing provide many benefits for both production and service organizations. While ABC information is often more appropriate for long-term decisions, it can still be useful for short-term decisions. Since ABC systems more accurately assign overhead costs to products and services, the information generated from such systems should allow companies to better control costs; adjust product, process, or marketing strategy; affect behavior; and evaluate performance.

To control costs, managers must understand where costs are being incurred and for what purpose. This understanding is provided by more appropriate tracing of overhead costs to products and services. Viewing fixed costs as long-term variable costs provides useful information for assessing the cost-benefit relationship of obtaining more customers or providing more goods and services. And, as indicated in the

■ **EXHIBIT 5–11**
Companies Using ABC

Based on a 27% response from 1,500 members of the IMA's Cost Management Group.

	PERCENT OF LEADING INDUSTRIAL COMPANIES USING ACTIVITY-BASED COSTING SYSTEMS	
	1993	*1994*
Use ABC		
As main system	23	29
As supplemental (stand-alone) system	59	56
For both purposes	16	15

SOURCE: "ABC Beats Old-Style Costing, Survey Finds," *Accounting Today* (June 6, 1994), p. 14.

The Costs of NVA Activities Are Really Important

Traditional cost accounting measures what it costs to *do* a task, for example, to cut a screw thread. Activity-based costing also records the cost of *not doing*, such as the cost of machine downtime, the cost of waiting for a needed part or tool, the cost of inventory waiting to be shipped, and the cost of reworking or scrapping a defective part. The costs of not doing, which traditional cost accounting cannot and does not record, often equal and sometimes even exceed the costs of doing. Activity-based costing therefore gives not only much better cost control, but increasingly, it also gives *result* control.

Traditional cost accounting assumes that a certain operation—for example, heat treating—has to be done and that it has to be done where it is being done now. Activity-based costing asks: Does it have to be done? If so, where is it best done? Activity-based costing integrates what were once several activities—value analysis, process analysis, quality management, and costing—into one analysis.

Using that approach, activity-based costing can substantially lower manufacturing costs—in some instances by a full third or more. Its greatest impact, however, is likely to be in services. In most manufacturing companies, cost accounting is inadequate. But service industries—banks, retail stores, hospitals, schools, newspapers, and radio and television stations—have practically no cost information at all.

Activity-based costing shows—or at least attempts to show—the impact of changes in costs and yields of every activity on the results of the [company as a] whole.

SOURCE: Reprinted by permission of Harvard Business Review. An excerpt from "The Information Executives Truly Need" by Peter F. Drucker, January–February 1995. Copyright © 1995 by the President and Fellows of Harvard College.

accompanying News Note, differentiating between value-added and non-value-added activities helps managers visualize what needs to be done to control those costs, to implement cost reduction activities, and to plan resource utilization.

Traditional accounting systems concentrate on controlling cost incurrence, while ABC focuses on controlling the cause of the cost incurrence. Concentrating on the *causes* of costs makes cost reduction efforts more successful because they can be directed at specific cost drivers. It is "important to note, however, that a reduction in drivers, which results in a reduced dependency on activities, does not lower costs until the excess resources are reduced or redeployed into more productive areas."[18] But armed with ABC information, managers are more likely to understand the activity-cost relationships and be able to reduce the costs of inefficiency.

Managers who have a better understanding of the underlying cost of making a product or performing a service can obtain new insight into product or service profitability:

Often managers can see, for the first time, the cost of nonconformance, the cost of design activities, the cost of new product launches, and the cost of administrative activities, such as processing customer orders, procurement, and handling special requests. The high cost of

---

[18]Michael R. Ostrenga, "Activities: The Focal Point of Total Cost Management," *Management Accounting* (February 1990), p. 43.

these activities can stimulate companies to adopt the TQM, JIT, and business process improvement programs that will produce a leaner and more responsive enterprise.[19]

This improvement in information can result in management decisions about expanding or contracting product variety, raising or reducing prices, and entering or leaving a market. For example, managers may decide to raise selling prices or discontinue production of low-volume specialty output, since that output consumes disproportionately more resources than does high-volume output. Managers may decide to discontinue manufacturing products that require complex operations. For instance, one soft-drink company found that the costs of its array of brands varied as much as 400 percent from the costs provided by traditional cost accounting methods. This information was crucial to decisions on discontinuing some brands while increasing advertising on others.[20]

ABC information can even affect decisions about plant and equipment investments. Managers may also find that benefits can be obtained from low-volume or complex production if high-technology processes are implemented. Installing computerized equipment may reduce non-value-added production activities and increase efficiency. Activity-based costing, in a variety of ways, helps managers understand the effects of the various activities that are needed in the changing business environment (especially relative to technology) and be flexible in designing systems that are able to cope with this environment. Although activity-based costing only *indirectly* changes the cost accumulation process, it *directly* changes the cost assignment process, making it more realistic regarding how and why costs are incurred.

CRITICISMS OF AND CONCLUSIONS ABOUT ABC

■ LEARNING
OBJECTIVE 7
Recognize the benefits and limitations of using activity-based costing.

New models and approaches to accounting must always be realistically judged for what they can help managers accomplish. No currently existing accounting technique or system can provide management with exact cost information for every product or with all the information needed to make consistently perfect decisions. Activity-based costing, while it can provide better information than a traditional overhead allocation process, is not a panacea for all managerial difficulties. The following points should be noted as some of this method's shortcomings.

First, implementing ABC requires a significant investment in terms of time and cost. If implementation is to be successful, substantial support is needed throughout the firm. An environment for change must be created, and creating such an environment requires overcoming a variety of individual, organizational, and environmental barriers. Individual barriers are typically related to fear of (1) the unknown or a shift in the status quo, (2) a possible loss of status, or (3) the need to learn new skills. Organizational barriers may be related to "territorial," hierarchical, or corporate-culture issues. Environmental barriers are often built by employee groups (including unions), regulatory agencies, or other stakeholders.

To overcome barriers, managers first must recognize that those barriers exist; second, managers need to investigate the causes of the barriers; and third, managers must communicate information about ABC to all concerned parties. It is essential that top

---

[19]Robert S. Kaplan, "In Defense of Activity-Based Cost Management," *Management Accounting* (November 1992), p. 60.

[20]Kevin Kelly, "A Bean-Counter's Best Friend," *Business Week/Quality 1991*, p. 43.

management be involved with and support the implementation process. Lack of commitment or involvement by top management will make achieving meaningful progress very slow and difficult. Additionally, employees and managers must be educated in some nontraditional techniques, including new terminology, concepts, and performance measurements. Such an educational process cannot occur overnight. And assuming that top management supports the changes in the internal accounting system and employees are educated about the system, additional time will be required to analyze the activities taking place in the activity centers, trace costs to those activities, and determine the appropriate cost drivers.

Another shortcoming of ABC is that it does not conform specifically with generally accepted accounting principles. ABC would suggest that some nonproduct costs (such as research and development costs and some service department costs) be allocated to products and that certain traditionally-designated product costs (such as factory building depreciation) not be allocated to products. Therefore (as indicated in Exhibit 5–11), most companies that have implemented ABC use it as a supplemental system for internal reporting while continuing to use a more traditional system to account for product and period costs, allocate indirect costs, and prepare external financial statements. By using two costing systems, these companies are incurring more clerical costs than if only one system were used. It is possible that, as ABC systems become more widely accepted, more companies will choose to refine how ABC and GAAP determine product cost to make the two systems more compatible and thereby eliminate the need for two costing systems.

One final criticism that has recently been leveled at activity-based costing is that it does not promote total quality management and continuous improvement. Dr. H. Thomas Johnson (a professor of quality management at Portland State University) has provided the following cautions:

> [T]he decade of the 1970s ushered in a new competitive environment—call it the global economy—in which accounting information is not capable of guiding companies toward competitiveness and long-term profitability.
>
> Activity-based prescriptions for improved competitiveness usually entail steps that lead to selling more or doing less of what should not be sold or done in the first place. Indeed, activity-based cost information does nothing to change old remote-control, top-down management behavior. Simply because improved cost information becomes available, a company does not change its commitment to mass-produce output at high speed, to control costs by encouraging people to manipulate processes, and to persuade customers to buy output the company has produced to cover its costs. American businesses will not become long-term global competitors until they change the way managers think. No cost information, not even activity-based cost management information, will do that.[21]

Companies attempting to implement ABC as a cure-all for product failures, volume declines, or financial losses will quickly recognize that Professor Johnson is correct. However, companies can implement ABC and its related management techniques in support of and in conjunction with TQM, BPR, JIT, and other world-class methodologies. Companies doing so will provide the customer with the best variety, price, quality, service, and cycle time of which they are capable. Not coincidently, they should find their businesses booming. Activity-based costing and activity-based management can effectively support continuous improvement, short cycle times, and flexible manufacturing by helping managers to do the following:

---

[21]H. Thomas Johnson, "It's Time to Stop Overselling Activity-Based Concepts," *Management Accounting* (September 1992), pp. 31, 33.

- Identify and monitor significant technology costs
- Trace many technology costs directly to products
- Promote achievement of market share through use of target costing (discussed in Chapter 6)
- Identify the cost drivers that create or influence costs
- Identify activities that do not contribute to perceived customer value (i.e., non-value-added activities or waste)
- Understand the impact of new technologies on all elements of performance
- Translate company goals into activity goals
- Analyze the performance of activities across business functions
- Analyze performance problems
- Promote standards of excellence

Activity-based costing, in and of itself, does not change the amount of overhead costs incurred; however, it does distribute those costs in a more equitable manner. ABC does not change the cost accumulation process, but it makes that process more realistic about how and why costs are incurred. Finally, activity-based costing provides a more appropriate means of charging overhead costs to products than has been possible under traditional methods. In summary, ABC is an improved cost accounting tool that helps managers know how the score is kept so that they can play the game more competitively.

SITE ANALYSIS

[A year after the activity-based costing pilot was implemented in AT&T's business billing center, the "customers" were satisfied and the information generated from the project was used to improve management of the center's operations. For instance, the system:]

- Performs a fact-based risk assessment of the cost of performing special projects at the business billing center.
- Measures associates' productivity in completing certain activities (monthly volume of service orders processed).
- Conducts benchmark studies among the center's functional groups. Specifically, functional workgroups are organized by customer type (for example, 10th of the month bill cycle) and are responsible for performing activities such as bill verification in support of these customers.
- Allocates resources and performs workload balancing.
- Supports the budget process by providing profit and loss managers with fact-based business choices driven by the identification of activities, [the value they add] and related cost drivers.

Not only was the final output an innovative tool to better manage costs, but it was an education to enhance the operation of the business. Management learned it is possible to determine unit cost information for the outputs of its organization and could determine the costs associated with servicing each business segment. Management's understanding of the relationships among processes, drivers, and transactions improved. This insight provided management with the knowledge that old allocation methods could be improved upon dramatically. Finally, ABC has taught management how to manage the business proactively with the objective of increasing productivity and profits. It has led to improvements in internal processes, supplier relationships, and customer satisfaction.

SOURCE: Terrence Hobdy, Jeff Thomson, and Paul Sharman, "Activity-Based Management at AT&T," *Management Accounting* (April 1994), pp. 38-39. Published by Institute of Management Accountants, Montvale, NJ.

Discipline	Application
Accounting	Use of cost drivers provides natural accumulation and allocation technique; more realistic costs help indicate what products should be "outsourced" (purchased rather than produced).
Economics	More realistic costs provide better indication of marginal costs and marginal revenues; cost reduction efforts of non-value-added activities are facilitated to create higher profits; more realistic costs help determine elasticity of demand if low-volume product/service prices increase.
Finance	More realistic costs help in evaluating true profitability of products or services for decisions such as elimination or expansion of products, product lines, or services.
Management	Higher awareness of causes of costs are created; closer relationships with suppliers and customers are promoted; standardized product designs are encouraged; cross-functional processes are promoted; more relevant performance measurements can be used.
Marketing	More realistic bid prices can be generated because of knowledge of more realistic costs; more realistic costs help to plan market strategies for product promotion; activity-based costing highlights the costs of product variety and product complexity.

CROSS-FUNCTIONAL APPLICATIONS STRATEGIES

CHAPTER SUMMARY

In a highly competitive business environment, companies need to reduce costs to make profits. One way to reduce costs without reducing quality is to decrease the number of non-value-added organizational activities. Value is added to products only during production (manufacturing company), performance (service company), or display (retail company). All other activities, such as inspecting, moving, storing, and waiting, are considered non-value-added.

Activity-based management views organizational processes as value-added and non-value-added activities. Process mapping can be performed to see all the activities that take place in the production of a product or the performance of a service. Each activity is designated as value-added or non-value-added on a value chart. Management should strive to minimize or eliminate non-value-added activities because they create unnecessary costs and longer cycle times without providing extra "worth" for customers.

A third category of activities, known as business-value-added activities, also exists. While customers would not want to pay for these activities, they are necessary to conduct business operations.

Activity-based management is also concerned with finding and selecting an appropriate number of activity cost pools and identifying the set of cost drivers that best represent the firm's activities and are the underlying causes of costs. The activities chosen by management are those judged to reflect the major and most significant processes conducted by the company. These activities normally overlap several functional areas or departmental lines.

Traditional costing systems often accumulate costs in one cost pool (or a very few cost pools) and allocate those costs to products using one cost driver (generally related to direct labor or machine hours). Activity-based costing accumulates costs for activity centers in multiple cost pools at a variety of levels (unit, batch, product/process, and organizational). ABC then allocates these costs using multiple cost drivers (both volume-related and non-volume-related). Thus, overhead costs are assigned more accurately, and managers can focus on controlling activities that create costs rather than trying to control the resulting costs.

Product and process variety and complexity often cause a business's costs to increase because of unobserved increases in non-value-added activities. Simultaneous engineering (using multifunctional teams to design-for-manufacturability) can help firms to accelerate the time to market of new products and reduce the complexity and costs of these new products and the processes by which they are made.

Business process reengineering is a method of improving or replacing complex processes that already exist. BPR finds and implements radical changes in the way things are made or the way tasks are performed to achieve cost, service, or time reductions.

GLOSSARY

Activity (p. 195)   a repetitive action, movement, or work sequence performed to fulfill a business function

Activity-based costing (p. 206)   an accounting information system that identifies the various activities performed in an organization and collects costs on the basis of the underlying nature and extent of those activities

Activity-based management (p. 195)   a discipline that focuses on how the activities performed during the production/performance process can improve the value received by a customer and the profit achieved by providing this value

Activity center (p. 206)   a segment of the production or service process for which management wants a separate report of the costs of activities performed

Activity driver (p. 207)   a measure of the demands placed on activities and, thus, the resources consumed by products and services; often indicates an activity's output

Batch-level cost (p. 201)   a cost that is created by a group of similar things being made, handled, or processed at a single time

Business process reengineering (BPR) (p. 215)   process innovation and redesign aimed at finding and implementing radical changes in how things are made or how tasks are performed to achieve substantial cost, service, or time reductions

Business-value-added activity (p. 196)   an activity that is necessary for the operation of a business but for which a customer would not want to pay

Facility-level cost (p. 203)   see *organizational-level cost*

Idle time (p. 196)   the time spent waiting at a production operation for processing or in storage

Inspection time (p. 196)   the time taken to perform quality control

Long-term variable cost (p. 203)   a cost that has traditionally been viewed as fixed, but which will actually react to some significant change in activity; a step fixed cost

Manufacturing cycle efficiency (MCE) (p. 198)   value-added processing time divided by total cycle time; provides a measure of processing efficiency

Mass customization (p. 212)   relatively low-cost mass production of products to the unique specifications of individual customers; requires the use of flexible manufacturing systems

Non-value-added activity (p. 196)   an activity that increases the time spent on a product or service but does not increase its worth to the customer

Organizational-level cost (p. 203)   a cost incurred to support ongoing operations to provide available facilities

Pareto principle (p. 213)   a rule which states that the greatest effects in human endeavors are traceable to a small number of causes (the *vital few*), while the majority of causes (the *trivial many*) collectively yield only a small impact; this relationship is often referred to as the 20-80 rule

Processing time (p. 196)   the time taken to perform the functions necessary to manufacture a product

Process-level cost (p. 202)   a cost created by the need to implement or support a specific process

Process map (p. 195)   a flowchart or diagram that indicates every step in making a product or providing a service

Product complexity (p. 213)   an assessment about the number of components in a product or the number of process (p. 202)   a cost that is caused by the development, production, or acquisition of a type of product

Product variety (p. 211)   the number of different types of products produced (or services rendered) by a firm

Service time (p. 196)   the time taken to perform all necessary service functions for a customer

Simultaneous (concurrent) engineering (p. 214)   an integrated approach in which all primary functions and personnel contributing to a product's origination and production are involved continuously from the beginning of a project

Transfer time (p. 196)   the time it takes to move products or components from one place to another

Unit-level cost (p. 200)   a cost created by the production or acquisition of a single unit of product or the delivery of a single unit of service

Value-added activity (p. 196)   an activity that increases the worth of a product or service to the customer and for which the customer is willing to pay

Value chart (p. 196)   a visual representation of the value-added and non-value-added activities and the time spent in all of these activities from the beginning to the end of a process

SOLUTION STRATEGIES

MANUFACTURING CYCLE EFFICIENCY

$$\text{Manufacturing cycle efficiency} = \frac{\text{Value-added processing time}}{\text{Total cycle time}}$$

ACTIVITY-BASED COSTING

1. Determine the activity centers of the organization.
2. Determine the activities and the efforts needed to conduct those activities—the cost drivers.
3. Determine the resources the organization consumes in conducting its activities and the level at which those resources are consumed (unit, batch, product/process, organizational).
4. Allocate the resources to the activity centers based on the cost drivers.
5. Allocate unit-, batch-, and product/process-level costs to products and services based on activities and activity drivers involved.
6. Treat organizational-level costs as nonattachable to products.

DEMONSTRATION PROBLEM

Thelma's Thermostats uses a traditional approach to overhead allocation. The company produces a regular (Model R) and a programmable (Model P) thermostat. For 1996, the company incurred $300,000 of factory overhead and produced 40,000 units of Model R and 20,000 units of Model P. The predetermined factory overhead rate used was $10 per direct labor hour. Based on this rate, the cost per unit of each product in 1996 was as follows:

	MODEL R	MODEL P
Direct materials	$ 6	$10
Direct labor	5	5
Factory overhead	5	5
Total	$16	$20

The market is becoming more competitive, so the firm is considering the use of activity-based costing in 1997. Analysis of the 1996 data revealed that the $300,000 of overhead could be assigned to three activities as follows:

	SETUPS	MATERIALS HANDLING	EQUIPMENT OPERATIONS	TOTAL
1996 Overhead	$20,000	$60,000	$220,000	$300,000

Management determined that the following activity drivers were appropriate for each overhead category:

	ACTIVITY DRIVER	1996 ACTIVITY VOLUME
Setups	Number of setups	160 setups
Materials handling	Pounds of material	120,000 pounds
Equipment operations	Machine hours	40,000 MHs

Activity drivers and units produced in 1996 for each product are:

	MODEL R	MODEL P
Number of units	40,000	20,000
Number of setups	100	60
Pounds of material handled	60,000	60,000
Machine hours	14,000	26,000

Required:

a. In 1996, the company used the traditional allocation based on direct labor hours. How much total factory overhead was allocated to the Model R product line and to the Model P product line?

b. For 1996, how much total factory overhead would have been allocated to each product line if ABC had been used? Calculate a unit cost for Model R and Model P.

c. Assuming that Thelma's Thermostats has a policy of setting selling prices with the unit costs in mind, what direction do you think the prices of Model R and Model P will take if the company begins using activity-based costing? Why?

■ SOLUTION TO DEMONSTRATION PROBLEM

a. Model R: 40,000 units × $5 $200,000
    Model P: 20,000 units × $5   100,000
        Total allocated overhead $300,000

b. Cost per setup: $20,000 ÷ 160 = $125
    Cost per pound: $60,000 ÷ 120,000 = $.50
    Cost per machine hour: $220,000 ÷ 40,000 = $5.50

	Model R		**Model P**
100 setups × $125	$ 12,500	60 setups × $125	$ 7,500
60,000 pounds × $.50	30,000	60,000 pounds × $.50	30,000
14,000 MHs × $5.50	77,000	26,000 MHs × $5.50	143,000
Assignable factory OH	$119,500	Assignable factory OH	$180,500
Divided by units	÷ 40,000	Divided by units	÷ 20,000
Factory OH per unit	≈$2.99	Factory OH per unit	≈$9.03

	Model R	**Model P**
Direct materials	$ 6.00	$10.00
Direct labor	5.00	5.00
Factory overhead	2.99	9.03
Total activity-based product cost	$13.99	$24.03

c. Since the cost of Model R is $13.99 under ABC and $16 under traditional costing, the price of Model R should be reduced; this pricing decision will probably make Model R more competitive and increase its sales volume. In contrast, because the cost of Model P is $20 based on the traditional approach and $24.03 using ABC, Model P's price should be raised. Because ABC provides management with more accurate information, management's planning, control, problem solving, and evaluation should be enhanced.

END-OF-CHAPTER MATERIALS

■ QUESTIONS

1. Why does management need product cost information?

2. Describe the system known as activity-based management. What cost management tools fall under the activity-based management umbrella?

3. Define value-added activity and non-value-added activity. Compare these types of activities and give examples of each.

4. Why is the concept of value-added activities a customer-oriented notion?

5. To what factors can non-value-added activities be attributed? Why would customers perceive these factors as not adding value?

6. Define *manufacturing cycle efficiency* (MCE) and explain how it is calculated. In an optimized manufacturing environment, where MCE is equal to 100 percent, what would be the level of non-value-added activities?

7. Explain what cost drivers are and how they are used.

8. Does traditional cost accounting use cost drivers? If so, explain how. If not, explain why.

9. What are the four levels of cost drivers? Which level is the focus in traditional costing systems?

10. What is the "Rule of One," and how is it related to the concept of long-term variable costs?

11. Briefly describe the cost accumulation and assignment process in an ABC system.

12. Why do the more traditional methods of overhead assignment "overload" standard, high-volume products with overhead costs, and how does ABC improve overhead assignments?

13. What operating characteristics of a company might indicate that ABC could provide improved information to the company's managers?

14. The chapter identified several underlying causes of a company's need for a new cost system. List and discuss some symptoms that might be visible reflections of these underlying causes.

15. Why can control in an activity-based management system be more effective than control in a traditional costing system?

16. Explain this comment: "Identifying non-value-added activities provides management with a distinct control opportunity."

17. Describe the Pareto principle and its application to controlling profitability and costs.

18. What is the comparative advantage of simultaneous engineering in the design of products and processes? What costs are likely to be reduced if this approach is adopted successfully?

19. Why is ABC often adopted as a stand-alone control system rather than as the main product costing system?

20. Should ABC be considered for adoption by all firms? Why or why not? Can some firms expect to benefit more than others from adopting ABC? Why or why not?

■ EXERCISES

21. (LO 2, 5, 6; *Terminology*) Match each item in the right-hand column with a term in the left-hand column.

a. Activity-based costing
b. Pareto principle
c. Process map
d. Activity driver
e. Manufacturing cycle efficiency
f. Long-term variable cost
g. Value-added activity
h. Simultaneous engineering
i. Non-value added activity
j. Mass customization

1. Increases the worth of a product to a customer
2. A measure of the demands placed on an activity
3. Relatively low-cost mass production of products to customer specifications
4. Increases the time and cost of production, but not worth of a product to a customer
5. A measure of processing efficiency
6. Involvement of all design and production personnel from the beginning of a project
7. A cost that has traditionally been viewed as fixed
8. A flowchart indicating all steps in producing a product or performing a service
9. An item often referred to as the 20:80 rule
10. A system that collects costs according to the nature and extent of activities

22. (LO 1, 4, 6 *Terminology*) Match each item in the right-hand column with a term in the left-hand column.

a. Activity center
b. Value chart
c. Product complexity

1. Process innovation and redesign
2. A focus on activities to improve the value delivered to customers

d. Transfer time
e. Activity-based management
f. Business process reengineering
g. Batch level cost
h. Activity
i. Idle time
j. Product variety

3. The number of components, operations, or processes needed to produce a product
4. A cost created by a group of things being processed at a single time
5. Storage time and time waiting for processing
6. The time it takes to move products or components from one place to another
7. A repetitive action performed to fulfill a business function
8. A part of the organization for which management wants a separate reporting
9. The number of different types of products produced
10. A representation of the value-added and non-value-added activities and the time spent in these activities from the beginning to the end of a process

23. (LO 2; *VA and NVA activities*) Smith, Edberg, and Johnson is a law firm that is considering implementing activity-based costing. Following is a list of the activities performed by one of the attorneys in a typical day.

ACTIVITY	TIME (HOURS)
Taking depositions	1.0
Doing research	3.0
Making conference calls	0.5
Travelling to/from court	1.0
Litigating case	1.5
Writing correspondence	1.0
Eating lunch	0.5
Contemplating litigation strategy	2.0

a. List the value-added activities and explain why they are value-added.
b. List the non-value-added activities and explain why they are non-value-added.

24. (LO 2; *VA and NVA activities*) Viking Construction Company constructs alpine-style homes in the Catskill Mountains for its customers. As its consultant, you have developed the following value chart:

OPERATION	AVERAGE NUMBER OF DAYS
Receiving materials	1
Storing materials	5
Measuring and cutting materials	4
Handling materials	4
Setting up and moving scaffolding	5
Assembling materials	7
Building fireplace	4
Framing structure	3
Cutting and framing doors and windows	2
Attaching siding and sealing joints	4
Inspecting home (by county inspectors)	1

   a. What are the value-added activities and their total time?

   b. What are the non-value-added activities and their total time?

25. (Lo 2, 3, 4; *VA and NVA activities*) Rockport Manufacturing Company is investigating the costs of schedule changes in its factory. Following is a list of the activities, estimated times, and average costs required for a single schedule change.

ACTIVITY	ESTIMATED TIME	AVERAGE COST
Review impact of orders	30 min.−2 hrs.	$ 300
Reschedule orders	15 min.−24 hrs.	800
Lost sales		
Unreliable customer service		
Contact production supervisor	5 min.	5
Reschedule production orders	15 min.−1 hr.	75
Stop production and change over		
Generate paperwork to return materials		
Return excess inventory and		
locate new materials	20 min.−6 hrs.	1,500
Generate new production paperwork	15 min.−4 hrs.	500
Change routings		
Change bill of materials		
Change procurement schedule	10 min.−8 hrs.	2,100
Collect paperwork from the floor	15 min.	75
Review new line schedule	15 min.−30 min.	100
Account for overtime premiums	3 hrs.−10 hrs.	1,000
Total		$6,455

   a. Which of the previous activities, if any, are value-added?

   b. What is the cost driver in this situation?

   c. How can the cost driver be controlled and the activities eliminated?

26. (LO 2, 3; *Cycle time and MCE*) Bud Adams is the manager of the Rice House Brewery. Rice House employees perform the following functions when making the company's nonalcoholic beer:

FUNCTION	TIME (HOURS)
Receiving and transferring ingredients	1
Mixing ingredients and cooking	3
Bottling beer	6
Transferring bottled beer to trucks	2

   a. Calculate the cycle time of this manufacturing process.

   b. Calculate the manufacturing cycle efficiency of this process.

27. (LO 4; *Cost drivers*) CCC Copy is a self-service photocopy store. The store maintains 15 photocopy machines for use by its customers. A manager is always on duty in the store to handle complaints or problems and monitor the machines. Determine whether each of the costs that follow is a unit-level (U), batch-level (B), product/process-level (P), or organizational-level (O) cost for CCC Copy.

   a. Store manager's salary

   b. Cost of paper

   c. Cost of toner

   d. Electricity expense

   e. Depreciation on the photocopy machines

  f. Property taxes on the building
  g. Repairs expense
  h. Cost of labor to place paper and toner in machines
  i. Advertising and promotion expense
  j. Insurance expense on photocopy machines
  k. Order costs for purchasing paper and toner

28. (LO 4; *Cost drivers*) Following is a list of important costs in a manufacturing company. For each of these costs, identify a cost driver and explain why it is appropriate.

  a. Equipment maintenance
  b. Building utilities
  c. Computer operations
  d. Quality control
  e. Material handling
  f. Material storage
  g. Factory depreciation
  h. Setup cost
  i. Engineering changes
  j. Advertising expense
  k. Freight costs for materials

29. (LO 5; *Activity-based costing*) Resource Publishing Company is concerned about the profit generated by its regular dictionaries. Company managers are considering producing only the top-quality, hand-sewn dictionaries with gold-edged pages. Resource is currently assigning the $1,000,000 of overhead costs to both types of dictionaries based on production hours. Some additional data follow.

	REGULAR	HAND-SEWN
Revenues	$3,200,000	$2,800,000
Direct costs	$2,500,000	$1,200,000
Number produced	1,000,000	700,000
Production hours	85,000	15,000
Inspection hours	5,000	25,000

  The $1,000,000 of overhead is composed of $400,000 of utilities and $600,000 of quality control inspectors' salaries.

  a. Determine the overhead cost that should be assigned to each type of dictionary, using activity drivers appropriate for each type of overhead cost.
  b. Should Resource Publishing stop producing the regular dictionaries? Explain.

30. (LO 5; *Activity-based costing*) Canadian Shipworks is attempting to institute an activity-based accounting system to cost products. The Purchasing Department incurs costs of $473,500 per year and has five employees. Because finding the best supplier takes the majority of effort in the department, most of the costs are allocated to this area.

ACTIVITY	ALLOCATION MEASURE	NUMBER OF PEOPLE	TOTAL COST
Find best suppliers	Number of telephone calls	3	$300,000
Issue purchase orders	Number of purchase orders	1	100,000
Review receiving reports	Number of receiving reports	1	73,500

During the year, 150,000 telephone calls are made in the Purchasing Department, 10,000 purchase orders are issued, and 7,000 shipments are received and reports filed. Often, many of the purchase orders are received in a single shipment.

A complex product manufactured by the company required the following activities in the Purchasing Department over the year: 118 telephone calls, 37 purchase orders, and 28 receipts.

a. What amount of Purchasing Department cost should be assigned to the manufacturing of this product?

b. If 200 units of the product are manufactured during the year, what is the Purchasing Department cost per unit?

31. (LO 5; *Activity-based costing*) For the past 20 years, Mega Manufacturing Company has maintained an internal research and development (R&D) department. The department provides services only to in-house manufacturing departments. In recent years, the costs of operating this department have been rising dramatically. Management has determined that to control costs, it will institute an activity-based costing system and charge the in-house users of the department for services it provides in developing products and processes. The principal expense in the department is salaries of professional workers, including marketing consultants and product and process engineering specialists. Activities in the R&D department fall into three major categories. The categories follow, along with the estimated cost of professional salaries associated with each activity:

Evaluation of Market Opportunities	$1,200,000
Product Development	3,600,000
Process Design	4,800,000

Management has determined that the appropriate cost allocation base for evaluation of market opportunities is hours of professional time; for product development, the allocation base is the number of products developed; and for process design, the allocation base is the number of engineering process changes. For 1997, the R&D department worked 30,000 hours evaluating market opportunities, aided in the development of 200 new products, and responded to 1,000 engineering process change requests.

a. Determine the allocation rate for each activity in the R&D department.

b. How can the developed rates be used for evaluating output relative to cost incurred in the R&D department? What alternative does the firm have to maintaining an internal R&D department?

c. How much cost would be charged during the year to a manufacturing department that had consumed 2,000 hours of market research time, received aid in developing 25 new products, and requested aid for 150 engineering process changes?

32. (LO 5, 6; *Product profitability*) Westfield Security Systems manufactures two products: security lights and security cameras. Security lights are relatively simple to produce and are made in large quantities. Security cameras are more complicated to produce because they must be more customized to individual customer sites. Westfield sells 50,000 security lights annually and 25,000 security cameras. The costs incurred for each product are as follows:

	SECURITY LIGHTS	SECURITY CAMERAS
Revenue	$8,000,000	$8,000,000
Direct labor	3,000,000	5,000,000
Direct materials	2,000,000	1,000,000
Overhead	?	?

Both products require the same amount and kind of material. Labor is paid $20 per hour. Overhead consists of $2,000,000 of depreciation and $1,500,000 of headquarters expenses.

a. Calculate the profit (loss) on each product if overhead is assigned according to direct labor hours.

b. Calculate the profit (loss) on each product if headquarters expenses are deducted from total company income rather than being allocated to products.

c. Does your answer in part a or part b provide the better representation of the profit contributed by each product? Explain.

■ COMMUNICATION ACTIVITIES

33. (LO 2; *Value chart*) You are the new controller of a small job shop that manufactures special-order desk nameplate stands. As you review the records, you find that all the orders are shipped late; the average process time for any order is three weeks; and the time actually spent in production operations is two days. The president of the company has called you in to discuss missed delivery dates. Prepare an oral presentation for the executive officers in which you address:

a. Possible causes of the problem.

b. How a value chart could be used to address the problem.

34. (LO 4; *Controlling overhead*) Industrial Paints Inc. has engaged you to help the company analyze and update its costing and pricing practices. The company product line has changed over time from general paints to specialized marine coatings. Although some large orders are received, the majority of business is now generated from products designed and produced in small lot sizes to meet specifically detailed environmental and technical requirements.

The company has experienced tremendous overhead growth, including costs in customer service, production scheduling, inventory control, and laboratory work. Factory overhead has essentially doubled since the shift in product lines. Management believes that large orders are being penalized and small orders are receiving favorable cost (and therefore selling price) treatment.

a. Indicate why the shift in product lines would have caused such major increases in overhead.

b. Is it possible that management is correct in its belief about the costs of large and small orders? If so, why?

c. Write a memo to management suggesting how it should change the cost accounting system to reflect the changes in the business.

35. (LO 5; *Traditional vs. ABC methods*) Many companies now recognize that their cost systems are inadequate in the context of today's powerful global competition. Managers in companies selling multiple products are making important product decisions based on distorted cost information, as most cost systems designed in the past focused on inventory measurement. To elevate the level of management information, current literature suggests that companies should have as many as three cost systems for (1) inventory measurement, (2) operational control, and (3) activity-based costing.

   a. Discuss why the traditional cost information system, developed to measure inventory, distorts product cost information.

   b. Identify the purpose and characteristics of each of the following cost systems:

      1. Inventory measurement

      2. Activity-based costing

   c. **1.** Describe the benefits that management can obtain from using activity-based costing.

      2. List the steps that a company using a traditional cost system would take to implement activity-based costing.

(CMA adapted)

■ PROBLEMS

36. (LO 2, 3; *VA and NVA activities; MCE*) Jeff Watson, a newly elected big-city mayor, is concerned about deficit spending by his city. As a manager of the city's road construction workers, you have been asked to evaluate their performance in an effort to reduce costs. After spending some time secretly observing your workers, you noted the following activities.

ACTIVITY	TIME (HOURS)
Driving to the work location	1
Blocking off the road	2
Setting up the road stripper	3
Drinking coffee	13
Stripping the road	10
Setting up the asphalt layer	7
Talking to each other	4
Laying asphalt on the road	5
Unblocking the road	3
Loading equipment and leaving area	2

   a. What are the value-added activities and times?
   b. What are the non-value-added activities and times?
   c. Calculate the manufacturing cycle efficiency. Discuss the result.

37. (LO 4, 5; *Using ABC to set price*) The budgeted manufacturing overhead costs of Beaver Window Company for 1997 are as follows.

TYPE OF COST	COST AMOUNT
Electric power	$ 500,000
Work cells	3,000,000
Materials handling	1,000,000
Quality control inspections	1,000,000
Product runs (machine setups)	500,000
Total budgeted overhead costs	$6,000,000

   For the last five years, the cost accounting department has been charging overhead production costs based on machine hours. The estimated budgeted capacity for 1997 is 1,000,000 machine hours.

Phil Stolzer, president of Beaver Window, recently attended a seminar on activity-based costing. He now believes that ABC results in more reliable cost data that, in turn, will give the company an edge in pricing over its competitors. On the president's request, the production manager provided the following data regarding expected 1997 activity for the cost drivers of the preceding budgeted overhead costs.

TYPE OF COSTS	ACTIVITY DRIVERS
Electric power	100,000 kilowatt hours
Work cells	600,000 square feet
Materials handling	200,000 material moves
Quality control inspections	100,000 number of inspections
Product runs (machine setups)	50,000 product runs

Linda Ryan, the VP of Marketing, received an offer to sell 5,000 doors to a local construction company. Linda asks the management accountant to prepare cost estimates for producing the 5,000 doors. The management accountant accumulated the following data concerning production of 5,000 doors:

Direct materials cost	$100,000
Direct labor cost	$300,000
Machine hours	10,000
Direct labor hours	15,000
Electric power—kilowatt hours	1,000
Work cells—square feet	8,000
Number of material handling moves	100
Number of quality control inspections	50
Number of product runs (setups)	25

a. What is the predetermined overhead rate if the traditional measure of machine hours is used?
b. What is the manufacturing cost per door under the present cost accounting system?
c. What is the manufacturing cost per door under the proposed ABC method?
d. If the prior two cost systems will result in different cost estimates, which cost accounting system is preferable as a pricing policy and why?

[SOURCE: Adapted from Nabil Hassan, Herbert E. Brown, and Paula M. Saunders, "Management Accounting Case Study: Beaver Window Inc.," *Management Accounting Campus Report* (Fall 1990). Copyright © 1990 IMA (formerly NAA).]

38. (LO 4, 5; *Activity driver analysis and decision making*) Playpen Manufacturing is concerned about its ability to control factory labor-related costs. The company has recently finished an analysis of these costs for 1996. Following is a summary of the major categories of labor costs identified by the Playpen Accounting Department:

CATEGORY	AMOUNT
Base wages	$42,000,000
Health care benefits	7,000,000
Payroll taxes	3,360,000
Overtime	5,800,000
Training	1,250,000
Retirement benefits	4,600,000
Workers' compensation	800,000

Listed below are some of the potential cost drivers identified by the company for labor-related costs, along with their 1996 volume levels.

POTENTIAL ACTIVITY DRIVER	1996 VOLUME LEVEL
Average number of factory employees	1,400
Number of new hires	200
Number of regular labor hours worked	2,100,000
Number of overtime hours worked	192,000
Total factory wages	$47,800,000
Volume of production in units	8,000,000
Number of production process changes	400
Number of production schedule changes	250

a. For each cost pool, determine the cost per unit of the activity driver using the activity driver that you believe has the closest relationship with the cost pool.

b. Based on your judgments and calculations in part a, which activity driver should receive the most attention from company managers in their efforts to control labor-related costs? How much of the total labor-related cost is attributable to this activity driver?

c. In the contemporary environment, many firms are asking their employees to work record levels of overtime. What activity driver does this practice suggest is a major contributor to labor-related costs? Explain.

39. (LO 4, 5; *Activity-based costing and pricing*) Barsdale Community Hospital has found itself under increasing pressure to be accountable for the charges it assesses its patients. Its current pricing system is ad hoc, based on pricing norms for the geographical area, and it only explicitly considers direct costs for surgery, medication, and other treatments. Barsdale's controller, Marsha Dent, has suggested that the hospital try to improve its pricing policies by seeking a tighter relationship between costs and pricing. This approach would make prices for services less arbitrary. As a first step, Ms. Dent has determined that most costs can be assigned to one of three cost pools. The three cost pools follow along with the estimated amounts and activity drivers.

ACTIVITY CENTER	AMOUNT	ACTIVITY DRIVER	QUANTITY
Professional salaries	$900,000	professional hours	30,000 hours
Building costs	450,000	square feet used	15,000 square feet
Risk management	320,000	patients served	1,000 patients

The hospital provides service in three broad categories. The services are listed below with their volume measures for the activity centers.

SERVICE	PROFESSIONAL HOURS	SQUARE FEET	NUMBER OF PATIENTS
Surgery	6,000	1,200	200
Housing patients	20,000	12,000	500
Outpatient care	4,000	1,800	300

a. Determine the allocation rates for each activity center cost pool.

b. Allocate the activity center costs to the three services provided by the hospital.

c. What bases might be used as cost drivers to allocate the service center costs among the patients served by the hospital? Defend your selections.

40. (LO 4, 5; *Determining product cost*) Thuston Chemical Products Company has identified activity centers to which overhead costs are assigned. The cost pool amounts and activity drivers for these centers are as follows:

ACTIVITY CENTER	COSTS	ACTIVITY DRIVER
Utilities	$300,000	50,000 machine hours
Setup	250,000	1,000 setups
Materials handling	800,000	200,000 pounds of material

The company's products and related statistics follow:

	PRODUCT A	PRODUCT B
Machine hours	35,000	15,000
Direct materials (pounds)	75,000	125,000
Direct labor hours	20,000	25,000
Number of setups	200	800
Number of units produced	10,000	5,000

Additional data: One direct labor hour costs $10, and the 200,000 pounds of material were purchased for $360,000.

Determine the total cost for each product and the cost per unit.

41. (LO 4, 5, 6, 7; *Determining product cost*) Bowling Green Custom Lumber Products has identified activity centers to which overhead costs are assigned. The cost pool amounts for these centers and their selected cost drivers for 1997 are as follows.

ACTIVITY CENTERS	COSTS	ACTIVITY DRIVERS
Utilities	$300,000	60,000 machine hours
Scheduling and setup	272,000	800 setups
Materials handling	640,000	1,600,000 pounds of material

The company's products and other operating statistics follow:

	PRODUCTS		
	A	**B**	**C**
Direct costs	$80,000	$80,000	$90,000
Machine hours	30,000	10,000	20,000
Number of setups	130	400	270
Pounds of materials	500,000	300,000	800,000
Number of units produced	40,000	20,000	60,000
Direct labor hours	32,000	18,000	50,000

a. Determine unit product cost using the appropriate cost drivers for each of the products.

b. Before it installed an ABC system, the company used a conventional costing system and allocated factory overhead to products using direct labor hours. The firm operates in a competitive market and product prices were set as cost plus a 20 percent markup.

   1. Calculate unit costs based on conventional costing.

   2. Determine selling prices based on unit costs for conventional costing and for ABC costs.

c. Discuss the problems related to setting prices based on conventional costing and explain how ABC improves the information.

42. (LO 4, 5, 6; *Cost assignment*) Count D. Cash, CPA, was not entirely convinced that his fees for different types of services were based on accurate costs. His son, Petty, was home for the summer and had just completed his managerial accounting course where he learned about ABC. Count and Petty were discussing costing for the firm's services (accounting and auditing, tax, and management services) and they decided to apply ABC to find more accurate costs for these services. That summer, they identified the following activity centers, assigned costs to cost pools, and selected cost drivers for the second-stage assignment of costs to services for the fiscal year ended May 31:

ACTIVITY CENTER	COSTS	QUANTITIES	COST DRIVERS
Planning and review	$ 65,240	93,200	Billable time (hours)
EDP	72,000	7,200	Computational time (hours)
Clerical	56,160	52	Number of professionals
Library	21,948	186	Books and periodicals purchased
Programming	56,160	4,160	Programmer time (hours)
Building costs	87,000	15,000	Square feet
Administration	150,000	500	Number of clients
Total	$508,508		

Also, the Cashs compiled the following statistics for each of the services provided clients during the past year:

	A&A	TAX	MANAGEMENT
Direct costs	$1,952,000	$1,610,000	$732,000
Billable time (hours)	48,800	32,200	12,200
EDP (hours)	4,320	2,400	480
Clerical (number of professionals)	30	16	6
Library (new purchases)	51	99	36
Programming (hours)	1,200	520	2,440
Building (square feet)	8,800	4,875	1,325
Administration (number of clients)	170	280	50

a. Make a second-stage assignment of cost pools to the cost of services.
b. Determine the total cost of each class of service.
c. Prior to this year, Mr. Cash applied overhead based only on professional labor hours (billable time). The overhead rate was found simply by dividing total budgeted overhead by total budgeted professional hours. Using the original information, (1) what overhead rate would Mr. Cash have used for the current year, and (2) how much overhead would have been assigned to each service area? Assuming Mr. Cash bases his service prices on the cost of rendering the services, in general how would the relative prices of services differ using the traditional overhead allocations instead of the ABC allocations obtained in part b?

43. (LO 4, 5, 6; *Activity-based costing*) Smith's Home & Office Products uses a traditional overhead allocation scheme in its manufacturing plant. The company produces three products: TV trays, lamp stands, and printer stands. For 1997, the company incurred $1,000,000 of manufacturing overhead costs and produced 200,000 TV trays, 20,000 lamp stands and 60,000 printer stands. The company's overhead application rate was $10 per direct labor hour. Based on this rate, the cost per unit for each product group in 1997 was as follows.

	TV TRAYS	LAMP STANDS	PRINTER STANDS
Direct materials	$ 2.00	$20.00	$ 2.00
Direct labor	3.00	22.50	7.50
Factory overhead	2.00	15.00	5.00
Total	$ 7.00	$57.50	$14.50

Because profitability has been lagging and competition has been growing, the company is considering the implementation of an activity-based costing system for 1998. In analyzing the 1997 data, management determined that all $1,000,000 of factory overhead could be assigned to four basic activities: quality control, setups, materials handling, and equipment operation. Data from 1997 on the costs associated with each of the four activities follows:

	QUALITY CONTROL	SETUPS	MATERIALS HANDLING	EQUIPMENT OPERATION	TOTAL
Costs	$50,000	$50,000	$150,000	$750,000	$1,000,000

Management has determined that it will use the following activity drivers; the total 1997 volume for each driver is also given:

ACTIVITY	ACTIVITY DRIVERS	QUANTITY
Quality control	Number of units produced	140,000
Setups	Number of setups	500
Materials handling	Pounds of material used	1,000,000
Equipment operation	Number of machine hours	500,000

Volume measures for 1997 for each product and each activity driver were as follows:

	TV TRAYS	LAMP STANDS	PRINTER STANDS
Number of units	200,000	20,000	60,000
Number of setups	100	200	200
Pounds of material	200,000	500,000	300,000
Number of machine hours	100,000	200,000	200,000

a. For 1997, determine the total amount of overhead allocated to each product group using the traditional allocation based on direct labor hours.

b. For 1997, determine the total overhead allocated to each product group using the activity-based costing allocation measures. Compute the cost per unit for each product group.

c. If the company sets prices based on product costs, how would the sales prices using activity-based costing differ from those using the traditional overhead allocation?

44. (LO 4, 5, 6, 7; *Activity-based costing*) Classic Design Company produces office desks. The desks typically produced are five-drawer desks made of gray metal. However, Classic Design does take custom orders for desks. The company's overhead costs for a month in which no custom desks are produced are as follows:

Purchasing costs for raw materials and supplies
    (10 purchase orders) $ 5,000

Setting up machines for production runs (4 times per month after maintenance checks)	400
Utilities (based on 3,200 machine hours)	160
Supervisors (2)	8,000
Machine and building depreciation	5,500
Quality control and inspections (performed on random selection of desks each day; one quality control worker)	2,500
Total overhead costs	$21,560

Classic Design's factory operations are highly automated, and the management accountant is allocating factory overhead to products based on machine hours. This allocation process has resulted in a factory overhead allocation rate of $6.7375 per machine hour ($21,560 ÷ 3,200 MHs).

In June 1997, six orders were filled for custom desks. The sales prices were based on charges for actual direct materials, actual direct labor, and the $6.7375 per machine hour for an estimated 200 hours of machine time. During that month, the following costs were incurred for 3,200 hours of machine time.

Purchasing costs for raw materials and supplies (22 purchase orders)	$ 6,200
Setting up machines for production runs (18 times)	1,800
Utilities (based on 3,200 machine hours)	160
Supervisors (2)	8,000
Machine and building depreciation	5,500
Quality control and inspections	2,980
Engineering design and specification costs	3,000
Total overhead costs	$27,640

a. What part of the purchasing costs are variable and what part is fixed? Indicate what types of purchasing costs would fit into each of these categories.

b. Why might the number of machine setups have increased from 4 to 18 when only six custom orders were received?

c. Why might the cost of quality control and inspections have increased?

d. Why were engineering design and specification costs included during June but did not appear in the original overhead cost listing?

e. If Classic Design were to adopt activity-based costing, what should the management accountant consider as the cost drivers for each of the previous items?

f. Do you think the custom orders should have been priced using an overhead rate of $6.7375 per machine hour? Indicate the reasoning behind your answer.

■ CASES

45. (LO 4, 5, 6; *Activity-based costing and pricing*) Steven Haws owns and manages a commercial cold-storage warehouse. He stores a vast variety of perishable goods for his customers. Historically, he has charged customers using a flat rate of $.04 per pound per month for goods stored. His cold storage warehouse has 100,000 cubic feet of storage capacity.

In the past two years, Mr. Haws has become dissatisfied with the profitability of the warehouse operation. Despite the fact that the warehouse remains relatively full, revenues have not kept pace with operating costs. Recently, Mr. Haws approached his accountant, Jill Green, about using activity-based costing to improve his understanding of the causes of costs and revise the pricing formula. Ms. Green has determined that most costs can be associated with one of four activities. Those activities and their related costs, volume measures, and volume levels for 1995 follow:

ACTIVITY	COST	MONTHLY VOLUME MEASURE
Send/receive goods	$6,000	Weight in pounds—500,000
Store goods	4,000	Volume in cubic feet—80,000
Move goods	5,000	Volume in square feet—5,000
Identify goods	2,000	Number of packages—500

a. Based on the activity cost and volume data, determine the amount of cost assigned to the following customers, whose goods were all received on the first day of last month.

CUSTOMER	WEIGHT OF ORDER	CUBIC FEET	SQUARE FEET	NUMBER OF PACKAGES
Jones	40,000	3,000	300	5
Hansen	40,000	2,000	200	20
Assad	40,000	1,000	1,000	80

b. Determine the price to be charged to each customer under the existing pricing plan.
c. Determine the price to be charged using ABC, assuming Mr. Haws would base the price on the cost determined in part a plus a markup of 40 percent.
d. How well does Mr. Haws' existing pricing plan capture the costs incurred to provide the warehouse services? Explain.

[SOURCE: Adapted from Harold P. Roth and Linda T. Sims, "Costing for Warehousing and Distribution," *Management Accounting* (August 1991), pp. 42-45. Published by Institute of Management Accountants, Montvale, NJ.]

46. (LO 4, 5, 6; *Activity-based costing*) Roth and Borthick Company manufactures two products. Following is a production and cost analysis for each product for the year 1996.

COST COMPONENT	PRODUCT A	PRODUCT B	BOTH PRODUCTS	COST
Units produced	10,000	10,000	20,000	
Raw materials used (units)				
Material X	50,000	50,000	100,000	$ 800,000
Material Y		100,000	100,000	$1,200,000
Labor used (hours)				
Department 1				$ 681,000
Direct labor ($375,000)	20,000	5,000	25,000	
Indirect labor				
Inspection	2,500	2,500	5,000	
Machine operations	5,000	10,000	15,000	
Setups	200	200	400	
Department 2				$ 462,000
Direct labor ($200,000)	5,000	5,000	10,000	

Indirect labor				
Inspection	2,500	5,000	7,500	
Machine operations	1,000	4,000	5,000	
Setups	200	400	600	
Machine hours used				
Department 1	5,000	10,000	15,000	$ 400,000
Department 2	5,000	20,000	25,000	$ 800,000
Power used (kwh)				$ 400,000
Department 1			1,500,000	
Department 2			8,500,000	
Other activity data				
Building occupancy				$1,000,000
Purchasing				$ 100,000
Number of purchase orders				
Material X			200	
Material Y			300	
Square feet occupied				
Purchasing			10,000	
Power			40,000	
Department 1			200,000	
Department 2			250,000	

Faye Harold, the management accountant, has just returned from a seminar on activity-based costing. To apply the concepts she has learned, she decides to analyze the costs incurred for Products A and B from an activity basis. In doing so, she specifies the following first and second allocation processes.

FIRST STAGE: ALLOCATIONS TO DEPARTMENTS

Cost pool	Cost object	Activity allocation base
Building occupancy	Departments	Square feet occupied
Purchasing	Materials	Number of purchase orders
Power	Departments	Kilowatt hours

SECOND STAGE: ALLOCATION TO PRODUCTS

Cost pool	Cost object	Activity allocation base
Departments		
Indirect labor	Products	Hours worked
Power	Products	Machine hours
Machinery related	Products	Machine hours
Building occupancy	Products	Machine hours
Materials		
Purchasing	Products	Materials used

a. Determine the total overhead for Roth and Borthick Company.
b. Determine the plantwide overhead rate for the company, assuming the use of direct labor hours.
c. Determine the cost per unit for Product A and for Product B using the overhead application rate found in part b.
d. Using activity-based costing, determine the cost allocations to departments (first-stage allocations). Allocate in the following order: building occupancy, purchasing, and power.

e. Using the allocations found in part d, determine the overhead cost allocations to products (second-stage allocations).

f. Determine the cost per unit for Product A and Product B using the overhead allocations found in part e.

[SOURCE: Adapted from Harold P. Roth and A. Faye Borthick, "Getting Closer to Real Product Costs," *Management Accounting* (May 1989), pp. 28-33. Published by Institute of Management Accountants, Montvale, NJ.]

47. (LO 4, 5, 6, 7; *Activity-based costing*) CarryAll Company produces briefcases from leather, fabric, and synthetic materials in a single production department. The basic product is a standard briefcase made from leather and lined with fabric. CarryAll has a good market reputation because its standard briefcase is of high quality and has been well produced for many years.

Last year, CarryAll decided to expand its product line and produce briefcases for special orders. These briefcases differ from the standard in that they vary in size, contain both leather and synthetic materials, and are imprinted with the buyer's logo. Synthetic materials are used to hold down the materials cost. To reduce labor cost per unit, most of the cutting and stitching on the specialty briefcases is done by automated machines that are used sparingly in the production of the standard briefcases. Because of these changes in the design and production of the specialty briefcases, CarryAll believed that they would cost less to produce than the standard briefcases. However, because they are specialty items, they were priced slightly higher—standards are priced at $30, specialty briefcases at $32.

After reviewing last month's results of operations, CarryAll's president became concerned about the profitability of the two product lines. The standard briefcase showed a loss while the specialty briefcases showed a greater profit margin than expected. The president is considering dropping the standard briefcase and focusing entirely on specialty items. The cost data for last month's operations are as follows:

	STANDARD		**SPECIALTY**	
Units produced		10,000		2,500
Direct materials				
Leather	1.0 square yard	$15.00	0.5 square yard	$ 7.50
Fabric	1.0 square yard	5.00	1.0 ssquare yard	5.00
Synthetic				5.00
Total materials		$20.00		$17.50
Direct labor	0.5 hours @ $12	6.00	0.25 hours @ $12	3.00
Factory overhead	0.5 hours @ $8.98	4.49	0.25 hours @ $8.98	2.25
Cost per unit		$30.49		$22.75

Factory overhead is applied on the basis of direct labor hours. The rate of $8.98 per DLH was calculated by dividing $50,500 of total overhead for the month by 5,625 direct labor hours. As the data indicate, a standard briefcase costs $30.49 to produce, whereas the specialty briefcase costs $22.75. These costs, however, do not accurately reflect the activities involved in manufacturing each product.

Activity-based costing would provide better product costing data to help managers gauge the actual profitability of each product line. To develop the activity-based costing information, factory overhead costs must be analyzed to determine the activities causing the costs.

Assume that the following costs and activity drivers have been identified.

- The purchasing department cost is $6,000, primarily created by the number of purchase orders processed. During the month, the purchasing department prepared 20 purchase orders for leather, 30 for fabric, and 50 for synthetic material.

- Receiving and inspecting materials cost is $7,500. This cost is driven by the number of deliveries. During the month, 30 deliveries were made for leather, 40 for fabric, and 80 for synthetic materials.

- The cost of setting up the production line to produce the different types of briefcases is $10,000. A setup for production of the standard briefcases requires one hour, while setup for the specialty briefcases requires two hours. Standard briefcases are produced in batches of 200; specialty briefcases are produced in batches of 25. During last month, there were 50 setups for the standard items and 100 setups for the specialty items.

- The cost of inspecting finished goods is $8,000. All briefcases are inspected to ensure that quality standards are met. The inspection of standard briefcases takes very little time because the employees identify and correct quality problems as they do the hand-cutting and stitching. Inspection personnel indicated that, during the month, they spent 150 hours inspecting standard briefcases and 250 hours inspecting specialty cases.

- Equipment-related costs are $6,000 for repairs, depreciation, and utilities. These costs are assigned to products using machine hours. A standard briefcase requires 1/2 hour of machine time, and a specialty briefcase requires 2 hours. During the last month, 5,000 hours of machine time related to the standard line, and 5,000 hours related to the specialty line.

- Plant-related costs are $13,000 for items such as property taxes, insurance, and administration. These costs are assigned to products using machine hours.

  a. Using activity-based costing concepts, what overhead costs are assigned to the two units?

  b. What is the unit cost of the two products using activity-based costing concepts?

  c. Reevaluate the president's concern about the profitability of the two product lines.

(IMA adapted)

■ QUALITY AND ETHICS DISCUSSION

48. An activity-based approach to management and product costing may frequently cause managers to restructure the operations of their firms. For example, Amoco recently announced plans to eliminate an entire layer of decision makers. The elimination of a management layer will reduce costs and push decision making to lower organizational levels, resulting in faster decisions. Amoco has also moved to consolidate certain activities that were redundantly performed by various operating units. To illustrate, the company intends to consolidate functions such as human resources, government affairs, health, environment, and safety.

[SOURCE: Based on Caleb Solomon, "Amoco to Cut More Jobs, Radically Alter Its Structure," *Wall Street Journal* (July 22, 1994), p. B4.]

  a. What is the likely short term impact on quality of eliminating a layer of decision makers?

b. What is the likely long-term impact on quality of eliminating a layer of decision makers?

c. How does ABM with its cost control focus, implicitly, or explicitly, give consideration to effects of activities on quality?

49. *Phyllis Coleman, a single mother and assembly-line worker at GM's complex in Flint, Mich., has put her son in counseling and just learned that her 18-year-old daughter is pregnant. Coleman's children are mad they never see her.*

"I keep thinking that maybe if I'd been able to spend more time with them this wouldn't have happened," she said. "But there's this constant pressure to be at work."

Coleman and 11,500 other unionized workers at General Motors Corp. have been on strike in a dispute that illustrates a trend in the American workplace of late: forced overtime.

[SOURCE: Lisa Genasci, "Workers Singing the Overtime Blues," *Bryan-College Station Eagle* (September 30, 1994), p. A3.]

a. What costs are GM managers trying to control by using overtime hours for production rather than hiring additional workers?

b. How can asking existing workers to work longer hours instead of hiring additional workers affect the quality of work performed, both positively and negatively?

c. What are the ethical considerations in asking employees to work overtime hours?

50. *In the course of maintaining its military edge, America contaminated billions of gallons of water and millions of tons of soil with the waste from its bomb-building plants. The Department of Energy, which is responsible for the cleanup effort, initially estimated its cost at between $35 billion and $64 billion. [Between 1988 and 1992,] however, the DOE estimate has nearly tripled, and many of those involved now concede that the final bill could go much higher than $200 billion, though just how high no one seems to know.*

The cost of the job would be daunting enough, but a detailed review of the effort to date indicates billions of dollars of waste, inefficiency and corruption.

For every $1 budgeted for materials and labor on what is known as "environmental remediation" work in Fernald, Ohio, nearly $2 more goes to administrative costs and other "landlord" activities. The dollars add up. In 1993 at Fernald, the DOE has budgeted $105 million for the cleanup; $203 million will go for contractor overhead and related costs. A review of DOE contracts by the White House Office of Management and Budget (OMB) has found that agency-approved overhead rates were more than twice as high as those on similar contracts let by the Army Corps of Engineers, which also uses commercial contractors for much of its work. According to the OMB review, the DOE's Albuquerque field office could save $51 million and the Savannah River [waste processing] plant $151 million—on overhead alone.

[SOURCE: Douglas Pasternak and Peter Cary, "A $200 Billion Scandal," excerpted from *U.S. News & World Report* (December 14, 1992) pp. 34, 36.]

a. What indications can you find that waste and corruption may be occurring with these contracts?

b. What can the DOE do to address the problem?

c. What are some possible implications of the fact that DOE-approved overhead rates are more than twice as high as those on similar contracts signed by the Army Corps of Engineers?

51. Many manufacturers are deciding to no longer service small retailers. For example, some companies have policies to serve only customers who purchase $10,000 or more of their products annually. The companies defend such policies on the basis that it allows them to better serve their larger outlets, which handle more volume and more diverse product lines.

    a. Relate the concepts in the chapter to the decision of manufacturers to drop small customers.
    b Are there any ethical implications of eliminating groups of customers that may be less profitable than others?
    c. Does activity-based costing adequately account for all costs that are related to a decision to eliminate a particular customers base? (Hint: Consider opportunity costs such as those related to reputation.)

■ PROJECTS

52. Obtain copies of annual reports for several companies that have recently adopted activity-based costing. Typically the adoption of such techniques are discussed in the president's letter or the management discussion and analysis section. Read these portions of the annual reports. Write a paper that describes the objectives that company officers commonly give for adopting activity-based costing and describe any other innovative techniques that are typically adopted along with activity-based costing.

53. Invite an expert on activity-based costing systems to address your class. Ask this individual about problems and successes he or she has observed following implementation of such systems.

54. Your firm has been experiencing increased costs associated with banking activities in recent years. The corporate treasurer asked for your team's help in identifying the activities that account for the majority of the firm's banking costs. Your team met and decided that the best way to proceed was to assign one member of the team to each of the two important banking functions: cash deposits and cash payments. Each person will identify the costs associated with his or her function and the respective cost drivers. Then, each member should make recommendations about changes that could be made to reduce the overall banking costs for the firm.

II USING MANAGERIAL ACCOUNTING INFORMATION IN COSTING

6

INTRODUCTION TO A STANDARD COST SYSTEM

Without standard costs the battle against waste must be fought in the dark and without weapons.

Stanley B. Henrici, *Standard Costs for Manufacturing*, 1947

LEARNING OBJECTIVES

1. Explain why standard cost systems are used.

2. Compare target and kaizen costing.

3. Understand how standards for material and labor are set.

4. Calculate material, labor, and factory overhead variances.

5. Analyze variances for purposes of control and performance evaluation.

6. Recognize how organizational evolution and desired level of attainability affect standard setting.

7. Understand how standard setting and standard usage are changing in modern business.

8. (Appendix) Prepare journal entries for a standard cost system.

Levi Strauss & Co. (Canada) Inc.: Sturdy Pants, Sturdy Values

Blue jeans typify the pioneering spirit in Canada—tough, durable, and adaptable to any weather. The first jeans in Canada were made in 1911 by the Great Western Garment (GWG) Company in Edmonton, Alberta. A majority interest in GWG was acquired by the American jeans manufacturer Levi Strauss and Co. in the early 1960s. Levi Strauss had begun his jeans business in 1853 in San Francisco by making pants for gold miners from rolls of canvas intended for tents and wagon covers. He later used a heavy cotton fabric called *serge de Nîmes*—later shortened to denim.

Levi Strauss & Co. now has three other locations based in Ontario. Today, Levi Strauss & Co. is the world's largest apparel manufacturer, making and marketing Levi's jeans, jeans-related products, and casual sportswear in 60 countries. Levi Strauss & Co. employs about 36,000 people worldwide, including more than 2,000 in Canada.

In the apparel industry, cost control and product quality are both extremely important. To support both functions, Levi Strauss & Co. (Canada) Inc. changed from assembly line to team manufacturing in its domestic production facilities in 1990. This $5 million conversion improved product quality and production flexibility as well as shortened the overall production process (from 10 days to 1–3 days). The new production method also required about 20,000 hours at each plant for training so that workers could perform multiple (rather than single) job functions.

Product quality is enhanced at Levi Strauss & Co. by use of manufacturing standards that are enforced worldwide. Each pair of any style of jeans—regardless of production location—should contain the same quality and quantity of material and go through the same processing steps.

Just as it has established production values for in-house manufacturing, the company also establishes and enforces strict guidelines for its worldwide contractors. Contractor issues include environmental requirements, ethical standards, health and safety standards, legal requirements, and responsible employment practices.

SOURCES: Adapted from Levi Strauss & Co. (Canada) Inc., *Corporate Backgrounder* and various corporate *Factsheets*.

Three of Levi Strauss & Co. (Canada) Inc.'s goals are to produce and sell high-quality products, to deliver outstanding customer service, and to provide financial and personal recognition for employees. To aid in attaining these goals, the company establishes production standards that allow management to monitor and reward performance, determine causes of variations, and take corrective action. Performance can be evaluated by comparing actual results against a predetermined measure or criterion. Thus, standards (or benchmarks) must exist to ensure product quality and consistency. Without such standards, no one can know what is expected. Without the actual-to-standard comparison, no one can know if expectations were met or whether problems exist. Such lack of knowledge makes managerial control impossible.

Almost all organizations develop and use standards in some manner. For example, charities set a standard for the amount of annual contributions to be raised; sales managers set standards against which employee business expenses are compared. Because of the variety of production methods and information objectives existing in organizations, no single form of standard cost system is appropriate for all situations. Thus, many forms of standard cost systems are in use. Some systems use standard prices, but not standard quantities; other systems (especially in service entities) use labor, but not material, standards. Traditional standard cost systems require price and quantity standards for both material and labor.

This chapter discusses a traditional standard cost system using standards for the three product cost components: direct materials (DM), direct labor (DL), and factory overhead (OH). Chapter examples assume the use of only one material and one labor category in production activities. The chapter provides information on how material and labor standards are developed, how deviations (or variances) from standard are calculated, why standard cost systems are used, and what information can be gained from detailed variances analysis. Innovative trends in the use of standard costing systems are also discussed. Journal entries used in a standard cost system are presented in the chapter appendix.

STANDARD COST SYSTEMS

Standard costs can be used with either job order or process costing systems. These costs provide important information for managerial planning, controlling, and decision-making functions. In planning, standards are building blocks used to coordinate activities more quickly and easily than otherwise would be possible. For example, if the Cornwall plant of Levi Strauss & Co. (Canada) Inc. plans to produce 200,000 pairs of pants in June, plant management can project materials, labor, and overhead costs by reviewing the standard costs established for each of these cost elements.

Standards can also be used for motivation and control purposes. One requirement for control is that managers be aware of differences between actual activities and actual resource consumption and expected activities and expected resource consumption. A standard cost system helps companies recognize variances from expected production costs and correct problems resulting from excess costs or usage. (A **variance** is any deviation between actual and standard costs or quantities.) Actual costing systems do not provide these benefits, and normal costing systems cannot provide them in relation to materials and labor.

If the variances from standard are significant, managers need to investigate what caused the difference. For example, suppose the actual cost for denim for the 200,000 pairs of pants was $10,000 less than expected. Based on management's investigation, several possibilities could exist: the price paid per bolt of denim might have been less than expected, or new technology or employee cross-training and team efforts might have made production more efficient by generating less scrap and, thus, lowering cost. In both cases (assuming the quality of denim was satisfactory), the variance would be viewed positively and no corrective action would be taken.

Note that the explanations of the $10,000 difference suggest that there are two possible underlying causes of the variance. One relates to the cost of the material, while the other relates to the quantity of the material used. These causes can exist separately or together. To properly evaluate organizational and personnel performance, managers need to be able to determine which part of the total variance relates to which cause.

The availability of standards speeds up and improves decision making because managers have a predetermined, rigorous set of expectations upon which to base decisions, such as setting prices. Performance evaluation is also improved through the comparison of actual costs of operations to standard costs and the highlighting of significant differences.

LEARNING OBJECTIVE 1
Explain why standard cost systems are used.

variance

DEVELOPMENT OF A STANDARD COST SYSTEM

Standard cost systems were initiated by manufacturing companies, but they can also be used in service entities. In any organization, however, it is critical that the standards development process is handled in a knowledgeable and thorough manner.

Target Costing and Kaizen Costing

■ **LEARNING OBJECTIVE 2**
Compare target and kaizen costing.

target costing

cost tables

In developing products to market, Western manufacturers have traditionally confined their approach to the following sequence. A product is designed; its costs are determined; and a selling price is set, based to some extent, on the costs involved. If the market will not bear the resulting selling price, either the company does not make as much profit as it hoped or it attempts to lower production costs. This process is illustrated on the left side of Exhibit 6–1. As an alternative, some manufacturing companies are now beginning to employ a technique known as **target costing** before a product is ever designed, engineered, or produced. This technique, discussed in the News Note on page 254, was developed in Japan but has begun to make some inroads in the West.

As indicated on the right side of Exhibit 6–1, a company employing target costing first uses market research to estimate what the market will pay for a product with specific characteristics. "This sales price generally reflects not current, but future, market conditions and reflects the team's best forecasting efforts, although the price may change over the product's life cycle."[1] Next, the company determines as "allowable" product cost by subtracting an acceptable profit margin rate from the estimated selling price. The resulting difference is an implied maximum per-unit product cost.

The implied maximum, or target cost, is compared with the expected product cost. If the target cost is less than the expected cost, the company has several alternatives. First, the product design and/or production process can be changed to reduce costs. Preparation of **cost tables** helps in determining how such adjustments can be made. These tables are data bases that provide information about how using different input resources, manufacturing processes, and design specifications would affect product costs. Second, a less-than-desired profit margin can be accepted. Third, the company can decide that it does not want to enter this particular product market at the current time because it cannot generate the profit margin it desires.

By designing a product to meet a specified, allowable cost, a company can work to eliminate as many non-value-added activities (and, therefore, costs) from the production process as possible. In addition, suppliers can provide valuable input into the target costing process, as indicated in the News Note on page 255. For instance, engineering may find that, with a few modifications to the original design, regularly-stocked supplier components rather than more costly, special-order items can be used in production.

The degree to which target costing techniques are used is affected by the type of product being manufactured. As product cost and complexity increase and as product life cycle is shortened because of changing consumer preferences, target costing becomes more important because proper design can generate greater potential savings.[2]

---

[1]John Y. Lee, Rudolph Jacob, and Michael Ulinski, "Activity-Based Costing and Japanese Cost Management Techniques: A Comparison," *Advances in Management Accounting* (1994), pp.183, 185.

[2]Robin Cooper, *When Lean Enterprises Collide: Competing through Confrontation* (Boston: Harvard Business School Press, in press), draft page 143.

Once the target cost has been determined, standards can be set that indicate the allowable costs and quantities specified by the target cost. Actual production costs and activities can then be monitored so that their level of conformity to the target standards can be determined. But some Japanese companies are not content to "leave well enough alone." Once the product enters the manufacturing stage, kaizen costing is often employed.

■ **EXHIBIT 6–1**
Developing Product Costs

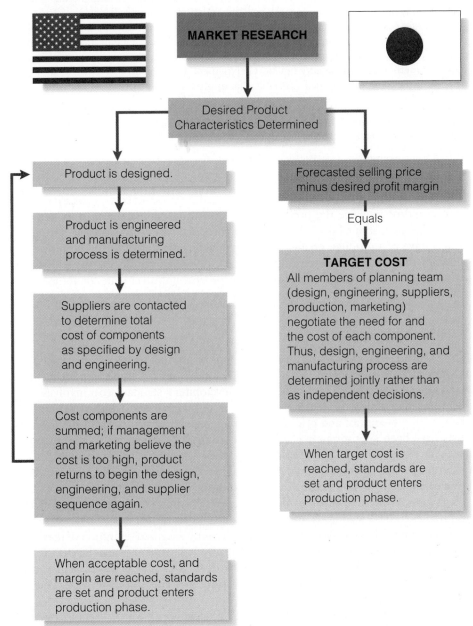

MARKET RESEARCH

Desired Product Characteristics Determined

Product is designed.

Product is engineered and manufacturing process is determined.

Suppliers are contacted to determine total cost of components as specified by design and engineering.

Cost components are summed; if management and marketing believe the cost is too high, product returns to begin the design, engineering, and supplier sequence again.

When acceptable cost, and margin are reached, standards are set and product enters production phase.

Forecasted selling price minus desired profit margin

Equals

TARGET COST
All members of planning team (design, engineering, suppliers, production, marketing) negotiate the need for and the cost of each component. Thus, design, engineering, and manufacturing process are determined jointly rather than as independent decisions.

When target cost is reached, standards are set and product enters production phase.

The Need for Target Costing

Target costing will be a key to competitive advantage in the future. The effective application of the process requires a sound competitive business strategy, broad cultural changes, and a deep understanding of customers and competitors. It requires fundamental shifts in focus and business processes. Foremost among these changes are acquiring quality customer and competitive information to drive simultaneous product and process design and applying a robust multifunctional profit and cost planning process. Equally important, because they are essential to profit and cost planning, are new methods and data to predict cost.

The target costing process is more than merely setting new cost targets. It also includes the means necessary to achieve cost and quality goals. Excellence in application will require changes to methods and processes throughout the firm. For some practitioners, supporting tools and methods include quality function deployment, cost-up and cost-down analysis, benchmarking, multidimensional cost tables, [and] product and process cost analysis.

SOURCE: Remarks by John J. Dutton from a presentation on target costing, cited in Julian M. Freedman, "Target Costing," *Management Accounting* (April 1994), pp. 72–73. Published by Institute of Management Accountants, Montvale, NJ.

kaizen costing

Kaizen costing involves ongoing efforts to reduce product costs, increase product quality, and/or improve the production process after manufacturing activities have begun. Because about 80 to 90 percent of product cost is determined during the design stage of a product, greater monetary benefits are derived from target costing activities than from kaizen costing activities. However, kaizen costing efforts can reduce costs and provide useful insight into process improvements for future products. Exhibit 6–2 (page 256) compares target and kaizen costing.

Setting Standards

standard cost

The estimated cost to manufacture a *single unit* of product or to perform a service is the **standard cost.** Standards are traditionally established for each component (material, labor, and overhead) of product cost. Developing a standard cost involves judgment and practicality in identifying the types of material and labor to be used and their related quantities and prices. Developing standards for overhead requires that costs have been appropriately classified according to cost behavior, valid allocation bases have been chosen, and a reasonable level of activity has been specified.

Target costing can be used to develop original estimates for production standards, which may later be modified by kaizen costing procedures. However, the standards set in most Western companies do not generally reflect these innovative Japanese techniques. These standards are often as valid as those generated from target or kaizen costing. The only difference is that there is no specified definition of maximum allowable cost and pressure for downward cost adjustment. Levi Strauss & Co. (Canada) Inc. does, however, employ initiatives such as activity-based management and value analysis to continuously improve processes and eliminate costs from the value chain.

Target costing emphasizes that the level of efficiency with which "a company *should* be able to build a product is less important than how efficiently [the company] *must*

Let the Suppliers Do It!

The next manufacturing revolution is under way, and U.S. companies are bringing airplanes, cars, even kitchen stoves to market faster and cheaper by leaning on their suppliers to help engineer . . . new projects.

To succeed in this new world, big companies are abandoning some cherished assumptions. Absolute control is no longer paramount, and the common practice of pitting suppliers to bid against each other is being abandoned in favor of long-term commitments to single suppliers. Manufacturers are also bringing suppliers on board much earlier in the design process, at times even inviting them to help dream up a new product.

[Such alliances can be illustrated by a $450 million contract for wing sections between Rockwell International Corp. and Seattle-based Boeing.] Rockwell engineers spent months in Seattle co-designing the parts. The roots of Rockwell's new intimacy with Boeing were put down [in 1990] when Boeing began developing its all-new 777. The 300-passenger airliner, designed entirely on computers, is the first commercial jet devised by Boeing "design-build teams" that included suppliers and airline managers.

When the first 777 came off the assembly line [in 1993], parts snapped together so neatly that its nose-to-tail measurement was off less than 23/1000 of an inch from design goals. Boeing believes it has eliminated up to half the costly parts "rework" that, in the past, has plagued new planes. And suppliers note that many key parts are being built in half the order-to-delivery "cycle time" of earlier Boeing models.

Manufacturers are betting that this esprit de corps will translate into real savings. Manufacturers that properly incorporate suppliers into their product development process can cut their bills for purchased parts and services by as much as 30%, according to A. T. Kearney Inc., a Chicago consulting firm. That's a huge savings, for purchased parts and services typically account for 50% to 70% of manufacturers' total costs.

SOURCE: Neal Templin and Jeff Cole, "Manufacturers Use Suppliers to Help Them Develop New Products," *Wall Street Journal* (December 19, 1994), pp. A1, A6. Reprinted by permission of The Wall Street Journal, © 1994 Dow Jones & Company, Inc. All Rights Reserved Worldwide.

be able to build [the product] for maximum marketplace success."[3] Therefore, variances from the target cost may not indicate inefficiencies or waste, but merely an inability to compete effectively in the market.

A primary objective in manufacturing a product or performing a service is to minimize unit cost while achieving certain quality specifications. Almost all products can be manufactured with a variety of inputs (material, labor, and overhead) that would generate the same basic output. This is true even after output quality has been specified. The input choices ultimately made affect the standards that are set.

Once management has established the design and manufacturing process that will produce the desired output quality and has determined which input resources will be used, quantity and price standards can be developed. As in the determination of target costs, standards should be developed by representatives from the following areas: management accounting, product design, industrial engineering, personnel, data processing, purchasing, and production management. It is especially important to involve

---

[3]Toshiro Hiromoto, "Another Hidden Edge—Japanese Management Accounting," *Harvard Business Review* (July-August 1988), p. 26.

■ **EXHIBIT 6–2**

Differences Between Target Costing and Kaizen Costing

	TARGET COSTING	**KAIZEN COSTING**
WHAT?	A procedural approach to determining a maximum allowable cost for an identifiable, proposed product assuming a given target profit margin	A mandate to reduce costs, increase product quality, and/or improve production processes through continuous improvement efforts
USED FOR?	New products	Existing products
WHEN?	Design and development stages	Production stage
HOW?	Works best through aiming at a specified cost reduction objective; used to set original production standards	Works best through aiming at a specified cost reduction objective; reductions are integrated into original production standards to sustain improvements and provide new challenges
WHY?	Extremely large potential for cost reduction because 80%-90% of a product's life-long costs are embedded in the product during the design and development stages	Limited potential for reducing cost of existing products, but may provide useful information for future target costing efforts
FOCUS?	All product inputs (materials, labor, and overhead elements) as well as production processes and supplier components	Depends on where efforts will be most effective in reducing production costs; generally begins with the most costly component and (in the more mature companies) ends with overhead components

managers and, to some extent, employees whose performance will be compared with the standards in the process of standard setting. This involvement helps assure the credibility of the standards and helps motivate personnel to operate as closely as possible to the standards. Information from suppliers can also be useful, especially in the area of setting material price standards.

MATERIAL STANDARDS

■ **LEARNING OBJECTIVE 3**
Understand how standards for materials and labor are set.

The first step in developing material standards is to identify and list the specific direct material components used to manufacture the product or to perform the service. It is essential that four things be known about the materials: what inputs are needed; what the quality of those inputs must be; what quantities of inputs of the specified quality are needed; and what price is to be paid for each input.

The determination of what inputs are needed is a design specification. For example, to make a pair of jeans, Levi Strauss & Co. must have denim and thread. However, some jeans' design call for metal zippers and a snap, while others require buttons. In making quality decisions, managers should consult materials experts, engineers, accountants, and marketing personnel. Many cost-benefit trade-offs are involved in making quality decisions. In most cases, as the grade of raw material rises, so does the cost. Decisions about material input components usually attempt to balance the interrelationships of cost, quality, quantity, and selling prices.

The ingredients and bottle shape for Coca-Cola are standardized worldwide and, thus, would not be candidates for target costing. But at this Japanese bottling plant, workers might engage in Kaizen costing relative to efforts to make the production process more effective and efficient. Such efforts would then be reflected in revised labor and/or overhead standards.

Given the quality selected for each necessary component, physical quantity estimates can be made in terms of weight, size, volume, or other measures. These estimates can be based on results of engineering tests, opinions of people using the materials, or historical data. Information about direct material components, their specifications (including quality), and the quantities needed are compiled on a document called **the bill of materials.** Even companies that do not have formal standard cost systems are likely to develop a bill of materials for each of their products simply as a guide for production activity.

bill of materials

Exhibit 6–3 illustrates a bill of materials for a pair of Pure Country (PC) jeans produced by an illustrative company, Thunder Bay Clothing. Although Levi Struass &

■ **EXHIBIT 6–3**
Bill of Materials

Product: PC Jeans: Waist 70 cm.;   Revision Date: 8/1/95
              Length 82.5 cm.   Standard Contract Size: 400
Product Number: Stock Keeping Unit (SKU) #262

Component ID#	Quantity Required	Description of Component	Comments
F-15	2 square meters	Black denim fabric	Highest quality
Z-7	1	18.5 centimeter zipper	Brass
S-2	1	1.9 centimeter snap	Brass; imprinted with PC jeans logo

Co. (Canada) Inc. considers thread to be a direct material, Thunder Bay management has chosen to view thread as indirect and includes it in variable overhead. Thus, thread is not shown on the bill of materials.

After the standard quantities of material components have been developed, prices are determined for each component. The purchasing agent is the person most likely to have the expertise to establish standard prices. Prices should reflect factors such as desired quality, reliability and physical proximity of the supplier, and quantity and purchase discounts allowed. If purchasing agents are involved in setting reasonable price standards for materials, these individuals are more likely to be able to explain causes of future variations from the standards.

When all quantity and price information has been gathered, component quantities are multiplied by unit prices to yield the total cost of each component. These totals are summed to determine the total standard materials cost of one unit of product. The total standard materials cost, along with other total costs, for one pair of PC jeans produced by Thunder Bay Clothing will be shown later, in Exhibit 6–5.

LABOR STANDARDS

■ **LEARNING OBJECTIVE 3**
Understand how standards for materials and labor are set.

The basic procedures for developing labor standards are the same as those used for materials. Each worker operation, such as bending, reaching, lifting, moving materials, cutting and sewing fabric, attaching sundry items (such as zippers, snaps, and patches), and packaging, should be identified. When operations and movements are specified, activities such as setup must be considered because they are performed during the production process. All unnecessary movements by workers and of materials as well as any rework activities should be disregarded when time standards are set and should be minimized or eliminated as they represent non-value-added activities.

Each production operation must be converted to quantitative information to be a usable standard. Time and motion studies, discussed in the accompanying News Note, may be performed by the company.[4] Alternatively, times developed from industrial engineering studies or from historical data may be used.[5] Historical data, however, may incorporate past inefficiencies or may not consider technologically advanced machinery that was recently

In developing labor time standards at Levi Strauss and Co. (Canada) Inc., consideration is given to the time necessary to set up sewing machines for a production run. Although efforts are being made to minimize such non-value-added time, it is still a part of the production process.

added or training that workers recently received. For example, after Levi Strauss & Co. (Canada) Inc. installed new equipment and cross-trained employees, labor time was reduced and standards were revised.

[4]In performing internal time and motion studies, observers need to be aware that employees may engage in slowdown tactics when they are being clocked. The purpose of such tactics is to have a relatively long time set as the standard, so that the employees will appear more efficient when actual results are measured.

[5]An employee time sheet indicates what jobs were worked on and for what period of time. "Time sheets" can also be prepared for machines by use of machine clocks or counters. Bar coding is another way to track work flow through an organization.

The Beginning of Time and Motion Studies

Frederick Winslow Taylor [was born] in 1856 to a prominent Philadelphia family. Taylor nevertheless went to work in a steel factory, first as a machinist and then as a foreman. There he began to develop his ideas about ways to reorganize factory work to increase efficiency, minimize waste, and encourage laborers to work harder.

As a foreman, Taylor was upset when employees slacked off and [he] became obsessed with finding ways to speed up their work. Beginning in 1882, Taylor and his associates began time-and-motion studies. They would break down complex factory tasks into smaller motions, and time these as they were performed by workers considered efficient. Using the results as a norm, and factoring in time for delays and rest, Taylor came up with a set of instructions for work to be efficiently performed. Workers were expected to meet the standard rate, with bonuses paid for faster work and penalties for slower.

Eventually, Bethlehem Steel and other business owners hired Taylor to improve efficiency in their own shops. Shovel makers used his name as a seal of approval in their advertising. His theories laid the groundwork for the creation of the assembly line and were exported to Germany and the Soviet Union. Later, Taylor's disciples suggested that his management principles could be applied to non-industrial bureaucracies, such as government and schools.

[Not everyone was happy with Taylor's ideas, however.] For much of his career, Taylor was virulently opposed by worker's groups, unions, and muckraking journalists who contended that his management system dehumanized workers.

SOURCE: Scott Heller, "Taking Taylor's Measure: Book Weighs Cultural Impact of Efficiency Expert's Ideas," *Chronicle of Higher Education* (July 21, 1993), p. A12. This is an excerpt of the condensed version.

After the labor tasks have been analyzed, an **operations flow** (or routing) **document** can be prepared. This document lists all the tasks necessary in making a product or performing a service and the time allowed for each task. All specified activities should be analyzed as to their ability to add value to the product or service. Any non-value-added activities that are included in the operations flow document should be targeted for reduction or elimination. Exhibit 6–4 on the next page presents a simplified operations flow document that reflects the manufacturing process for a pair of PC jeans #262 at Thunder Bay Clothing. This document shows 4 minutes (1.50 + 2.50) of move time which is non-value-added.

operations flow document

Labor rate standards should reflect the wages and fringe benefits paid to employees who perform the various production tasks. All personnel doing the same job in a given department may be paid the same wage rate. In addition, to promote a team rather than individualistic perspective, hourly workers at Levi Strauss & Co. (Canada) Inc. receive a weekly bonus if the entire facility meets its production volume and quality targets. This bonus is considered in determining standard cost variances for direct labor.

In contrast, if employees within a department performing the same or similar tasks are paid different wage rates, a weighted average rate must be computed and used as the standard. The average rate is computed as the total wage cost per hour divided by the number of workers.

As the composition of a labor team changes, the time needed to make a product may also change. For instance, workers who have been doing a job longer may be paid

■ **EXHIBIT 6–4**
Operations Flow Document

| Product: PC Jeans: Waist 70 cm.; Length 82.5 cm. | | Revision Date: 8/1/95 | |
| Product Number: Stock Keeping Unit (SKU) #262 | | Standard Contract Size: 400 | |

Operation ID#	Department	Standard Labor Minutes per Pair	Description of Task
27	Cutting	3.50	Align fabric for cutting (actual machine time, 6 minutes)
29	Cutting	2.50	Cut fabric (actual machine time, 4 minutes)
		1.50	*Move to Sewing Department*
33	Sewing	6.00	Stitch fabric pieces together (actual machine time, 5.5 minutes)
35	Sewing	1.50	Attach zipper (actual machine time, 2 minutes)
37	Sewing	.50	Attach snap (actual machine time, 1 minute)
		2.50	*Move to Finishing Department*
45	Finishing	2.00	Wash to soften and pre-shrink (actual processing time in machine, 16 minutes)
48	Finishing	4.00	Dry and fold (actual processing time in machine, 14 minutes)

more and be able to do the job more quickly than those who were just hired. Often trade-offs must be made between rates and times for labor just as trade-offs are made between price and quality for material.

OVERHEAD STANDARDS

■ **LEARNING OBJECTIVE 3**
Understand how standards for materials and labor are set.

Overhead standards are simply the predetermined factory overhead application rates discussed in Chapter 4. Separate variable and fixed rates or a combined overhead rate can be computed from the information in the overhead flexible budget. Management may consider the use of either a standard plantwide rate or standard departmental rates. Alternatively, as indicated in the accompanying News Note, activity-based costing concepts employing multiple cost pools and multiple cost drivers may be used to determine standard overhead cost rates.

The predetermined variable factory overhead rate for the Cutting and Sewing Departments at Thunder Bay Clothing is $11.10 per direct labor hour. As shown in Exhibit 6–4, the two departments work a total of 14 (6 + 8) minutes on each pair of jeans, so the total variable factory overhead applied per pair is $2.59 [(14 ÷ 60) × $11.10]. The fixed overhead rate for these two departments is $9.60 per machine hour. As indicated in the task description section of Exhibit 6–4, the departments have a total of 18.5 (6 + 4 + 5.5 + 2.0 + 1.0) machine minutes of machine time. Thus, $2.96 [(18.5 ÷ 60) × $9.60] of fixed factory overhead will be applied to the jeans in these two departments. The Finishing Department is machine-intensive, and the predetermined total overhead rate (variable and fixed) has been set at $5.80 per machine hour. Each pair of jeans requires 30 (16 + 14) machine minutes in Finishing, indicating that $2.90 [(30 ÷ 60) × $5.80] of overhead should be applied in that department.

ABC and Standard Costing Are Compatible, Not in Conflict

NEWS NOTE

Some people may incorrectly perceive activity-based costing as a replacement for standard costing. This was probably never the intent of those who first wrote about activity-based costing.

First the concept of standard costing: Measuring performance of any kind, whether in manufacturing, on a golf course, or in track and field requires comparing actual performance to some baseline measurement: a standard, a par, or a world record.

The concept of activity-based costing is also relatively straightforward. Companies have recognized that the activities performed by their employees consume the costs the companies incur. The products manufactured consume the activities that are performed. The concept of activity-based costing, therefore, suggests that, by managing activities and eliminating non-value-added activities, costs can be managed so that product and service costs are optimized.

Now bring the two concepts together. Activity-based costing is both a tool for developing a standard and for measuring actual performance. From a systems perspective, activity-based costing is the way the system is developed and designed structurally and mechanically. Standard costing is the way the system is used to manage costs.

In typical manufacturers today, the emphasis is shifting sharply away from labor. Instead, overhead is now the cost component emphasized in developing accurate standards. To a large degree, this is the motivation behind the development of activity-based costing. The development and maintenance of accurate standards, therefore, hinges on the degree to which overhead can be analyzed and overhead rates adjusted for more fair distributions.

The concepts of activity-based costing and standard costing are compatible. Standard costing, when effectively applied, can be a powerful management tool. Activity-based costing, when effectively applied, results in far more accurate standards.

SOURCE: Robert A. Bonsack, "Does Activity-Based Costing Replace Standard Costing?" *Journal of Cost Management* (Winter 1991), pp. 46–47. Reprinted with permission from The Journal of Cost Management for the Manufacturing Industry, © 1991, Warren, Gorham & Lamont, 31 St. James Avenue, Boston, MA 02116. All rights reserved.

The costs associated with the 4 minutes of move time are considered part of factory overhead and the overhead costs caused by move time are included in the predetermined factory overhead rates.

After the bill of materials, operations flow document, and standard overhead costs have been developed, a **standard cost card** is prepared. This document (shown in Exhibit 6–5, page 262) summarizes all the standard quantities and costs needed to complete one pair of Pure Country jeans #262.

Standard costs and quantities are used during the period to assign costs to inventory accounts. In actual or normal cost systems, actual material and labor costs are charged to Work in Process Inventory as production occurs. In most standard cost systems, standard (rather than actual) costs of production are charged to Work in Process Inventory.[6] The difference between actual and standard costs or quantities is the variance.

standard cost card

---

[6]The standard cost of each cost element (direct material, direct labor, variable overhead, and fixed overhead) is said to be applied to the goods produced. This terminology is the same as that used when overhead is applied to inventory based on a predetermined rate.

Standards often use either direct labor hours or machine hours as the measure of inputs. These measures are used and referred to in the models that follow for illustrative purposes. Alternative cost drivers such as setup time, pounds of material moved, or number of defective units may be more appropriately related to cost incurrence. If such drivers exist, using them will result in better information than would direct labor hours or machine hours.

■ **EXHIBIT 6–5**
Standard Cost Card

Product: PC Jeans: Waist 70 cm. ; Length 82.5 cm.
SKU: 262

| | | DIRECT MATERIALS | | | | | |
| | | _Departments_ | | | | | |
ID#	Unit Cost	Total Quantity	Cutting Cost	Sewing Cost	Finishing Cost	Total Cost
F-15	$5.50/sq. meter	2 sq. meters	$11.00			$11.00
Z-7	$ .70 each	1 per pair		$ .70		.70
S-2	$ .20 each	1 per pair		.20		.20
Direct Materials Totals			$11.00	$ .90		$11.90

| | | DIRECT LABOR | | | | |
ID#	Avg. Wage per Minute*	Total Minutes	Cutting Cost	Sewing Cost	Finishing Cost	Total Cost
27	$.24	3.5	$ .84			$ .84
29	.24	2.5	.60			.60
33	.30	6.0		$1.80		1.80
35	.32	1.5		.48		.48
37	.26	0.5		.13		.13
45	.16	2.0			$0.32	.32
48	.19	4.0			.76	.76
Direct Labor Totals			$1.44	$2.41	$1.08	$4.93

| | PRODUCTION OVERHEAD | | | |
Cost Driver	Standard Time	Standard Departmental Rate	Total Cost
Cutting and Sewing Departments:			
Direct Labor Hours	14.0 minutes	$11.10 per DLH for VOH	$2.59
Machine Hours	18.5 minutes	$ 9.60 per MH for FOH	2.96
Finishing Department:			
Machine Hours	30.0 minutes	$ 5.80 per MH for all OH	2.90
Overhead Total			$8.45

Total cost = $11.90 + $4.93 + $8.45 = $25.28
*Note: Labor cost per minute equals hourly rates divided by 60.

VARIANCE COMPUTATIONS

total variance

■ LEARNING
OBJECTIVE 4
Calculate material, labor, and
factory overhead variances.

The most basic variance computation is the **total variance,** or the difference between total actual cost incurred and total standard cost allowed for the output of the period. This variance can be diagrammed as follows:

Actual cost of actual
production inputs

Standard cost of actual
production outputs

Total Variance

A total variance can be computed for each production cost element; however total variances do not provide useful information for determining why such differences occurred. To help managers in their control objectives, total variances for materials and labor are subdivided into price and quantity elements.

A **price variance** reflects the difference between what was paid and what should have been paid for inputs during the period. A **quantity variance** provides a monetary measure of the difference between the quantity of actual inputs and the standard quantity of inputs allowed for the actual output of the period. Quantity variances focus on the efficiency of results—the relationship of inputs to outputs. Quantity can be measured as pounds of material, hours of direct labor time, number of setups, or any other specified and reasonable indicator of output.

price variance
quantity variance

The basic diagram used to calculate a total variance can be expanded to provide a general model indicating the subvariances:

Actual price of
actual inputs

Standard price of
actual inputs

Standard price of standard
inputs for actual outputs

Price (or Rate) Variance

Quantity (or Efficiency) Variance

Total Variance

The middle column is a budget column and indicates what costs should have been incurred for actual inputs. The far-right column uses a measure of output known as the **standard quantity allowed.** This quantity measure translates actual output into the standard quantity of input that *should have been used* to achieve the actual level of output. The right-hand measurement is computed as the standard quantity allowed multiplied by the standard price of the input resources.

standard quantity allowed

The diagram can be simplified by use of the abbreviated notations shown in Exhibit 6–6 (page 264). This model progresses from the *actual* price of *actual* input on the left to the *standard* price of *standard* input allowed on the right. The middle measure of input is a hybrid of *actual* quantity and *standard* price. The price variance portion of the total variance is measured as the actual input quantity multiplied by the difference between the actual and standard prices:

$$\text{Price Variance} = \text{AQ} (\text{AP} - \text{SP})$$

■ **EXHIBIT 6–6**
Simplified Variance Model

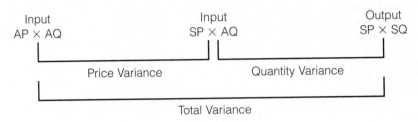

Input	Input	Output
AP × AQ	SP × AQ	SP × SQ

Price Variance   Quantity Variance

Total Variance

where   AP = actual material price or average actual labor rate
AQ = actual quantity of materials or actual labor hours
SP = standard price or rate
SQ = standard quantity of materials or standard labor hours

The quantity portion of the total variance is determined as the standard price multiplied by the difference between the actual quantity and the standard quantity allowed for the actual output:

$$\text{Quantity Variance} = SP\,(AQ - SQ)$$

Production of Pure Country jeans #262 in the Cutting Department of Thunder Bay Clothing Company is used to illustrate variance computations. The standard costs in this department are taken from the standard cost card in Exhibit 6–5 and are repeated at the top of Exhibit 6–7. Also shown in the exhibit are the actual quantity and cost data for the week of June 10-14, 1996. This information is used in computing the materials, labor, and overhead variances for the week. Variance computations must indicate whether the amount of the variance is favorable (F) or unfavorable (U).

Material Variances

Using the model and inserting information concerning material quantities and prices provides the following computations. (Note that the standard quantity for denim is taken from the bottom of Exhibit 6–7.)

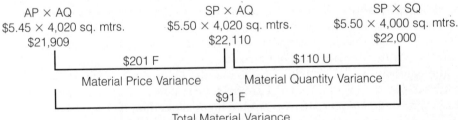

AP × AQ	SP × AQ	SP × SQ
$5.45 × 4,020 sq. mtrs.	$5.50 × 4,020 sq. mtrs.	$5.50 × 4,000 sq. mtrs.
$21,909	$22,110	$22,000

$201 F $110 U

Material Price Variance   Material Quantity Variance

$91 F

Total Material Variance

material price variance (MPV)

The subvariances for materials are known as the material price and material quantity variances. The **material price variance (MPV)** indicates the amount of money spent below (F for favorable) or above (U for unfavorable) the standard price for the quantity of materials purchased. For Thunder Bay Clothing Company, the actual price paid for denim was $5.45 per square meter, while the standard price was $5.50, giving a favorable material price variance of $201. This variance can also be calculated as [4,020 ($5.45 − $5.50) = 4,020 (−$.05) = −$201]. The sign of the favorable variance is negative because the actual price is *less* than the standard price.

The **material quantity variance (MQV)** indicates the cost saved (F) or expended (U) because of the difference between the actual quantity of material used and the standard quantity of material allowed for the goods produced or services rendered during the period. If the actual quantity used is less than the standard quantity allowed, the company has been more efficient than expected; if a greater quantity has been used than allowed, the company has been less efficient. Thunder Bay Clothing Company used 20 square meters of denim more than the standard allowed for the production of 2,000 pairs of jeans. This inefficient usage resulted in an unfavorable materials quantity variance [$5.50 (4,020 − 4,000) = $5.50 (20) = $110]. In this

material quantity variance (MQV)

■ **EXHIBIT 6–7**

Standard Actual Cost Data for Week of June 10–14, 1996 (Cutting Department)

Standards for 1 pair of PC Jeans SKU #262:

2 square meters of black denim fabric at $5.50 per square meter	$11.00
6 minutes of labor at $14.40 per hour	1.44
Applied variable factory overhead (based on 6 minutes of direct labor time at $11.10 per DLH)	1.11
Applied fixed factory overhead (based on 10 minutes of machine time at $9.60 per MH)*	1.60
Total standard Cutting Department cost per pair	$15.15

* The $9.60 rate per machine hour is based on a total expected fixed overhead amount of $199,680 for the year and an expected total number of machine hours of 20,800 related to the production of these jeans. This product is expected to be produced evenly at the rate of 2,496 pairs per week for 50 weeks of the year or 124,800 pairs for the year.

Actual data for June 10-14, 1996:

Number of pairs produced	2,000
Square meters of denim used	4,020
Price per square meter of denim used	$5.45
Direct labor hours incurred	208
Average direct labor wage per hour	$14.50
Total variable factory overhead cost	$2,500
Machine hours used	350
Total fixed factory overhead	$3,850

STANDARD QUANTITIES ALLOWED

Direct Materials: Standard quantity allowed for denim = 2,000 pairs × 2 square meters per pair = 4,000 square meters

Direct Labor: Standard quantity allowed for direct labor hours = 2,000 pairs × 6 minutes per pair = 12,000 minutes or 200 hours

Variable Factory Overhead: Applied on the basis of direct labor hours = 2,000 pairs × 6 minutes per pair = 12,000 minutes or 200 hours

Fixed Factory Overhead: Standard quantity allowed for machine hours = 2,000 pairs × 10 minutes per pair = 20,000 minutes or 333 ⅓ hours

instance, the variance sign is positive (and, thus, unfavorable) because the actual quantity used is greater than the standard quantity allowed.

The total material variance ($91 F) can be calculated by taking the difference between $21,909 (the total actual cost of inputs) and $22,000 (the total standard cost of the outputs). The total variance also represents the summation of the individual material variances. Thus, an alternative way to compute the total material variance is to add the price and quantity subvariances (−$201 F + $110 U = −$91, a favorable variance).

Point of Purchase Material Variance Model

A total variance for a cost component *generally* equals the sum of the price subvariance and the quantity subvariance. An exception to this rule occurs when the quantity of material purchased is not the same as the quantity of material placed into production. In such cases, the general model is altered slightly to provide information more rapidly for management control purposes.

Because the material price variance relates to the purchasing (not production) function, the altered model calculates the material price variance at the point of purchase and bases that calculation on the quantity of materials *purchased* rather than the quantity of materials *used*. This variation in the model allows the material price variance to be isolated or pinpointed as close to the variance source and as quickly as possible.

Assume that Thunder Bay Clothing Company had purchased 4,400 square meters of black denim for Pure Country jeans #262 but had only used 4,020 during the week of June 10–14, 1996. The point of purchase material price variance is calculated as follows:

```
AP × AQ                                              SP × AQ
$5.45 × 4,400                                        $5.50 × 4,400
  $23,980                                              $24,200
       |_____|
                          $220 F
                  Material Price Variance
```

This change in the general model is shown below, with subscripts to indicate actual quantity purchased (p) and used (u).

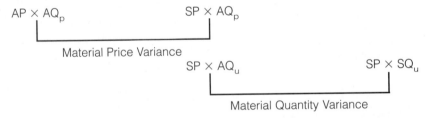

```
AP × AQ_p                      SP × AQ_p
    |_____|
        Material Price Variance
                          SP × AQ_u                      SP × SQ_u
                              |_____|
                               Material Quantity Variance
```

The material quantity variance is still calculated as presented earlier because the actual quantity of denim used in production is not determined by the amount purchased. Thus, the MQV would remain at $110 U. A point of purchase variance computation results in the material price and quantity variances being computed from different bases. For this reason, these variances should not be summed; and thus, no total material variance can be determined.

Labor Variances

The price and usage elements of the total labor variance are called the labor rate and labor efficiency variances. The model for computing these variances and computations for Thunder Bay Clothing Company follow. The standard quantity allowed is taken from the bottom of Exhibit 6–7 for direct labor hours.

The **labor rate variance (LRV)** shows the difference between the actual rate (or actual weighted average rate) paid to the direct labor workers for the period and the standard rate for all hours actually worked during the period. The labor rate variance can also be computed as [208 × ($14.50 − $14.40) = 208 ($.10) = $20.80 U].

The **labor efficiency variance (LEV)** compares the number of actual direct labor hours worked with the standard hours allowed for the actual number of jeans produced. The difference is multiplied by the standard labor rate to establish a dollar value for the efficiency (F) or inefficiency (U) of the direct labor workers. The labor efficiency variance can also be calculated as [$14.40 × (208 − 200) = $14.40 (8) = $115.20 U].

The total labor variance ($136 U) can be determined by subtracting the total standard labor cost for the actual production ($2,880) from the total actual labor cost ($3,016). Alternatively, the total labor variance can be found by adding the labor rate and efficiency variances ($20.80 U + $115.20 U).

The News Note on page 268 provides a slightly different perspective on efficiency variances. It suggests that the efficiency variance is truly composed of two elements—quality problems and efficiency problems—that should be accounted for separately.

As the News Note points out, it is possible that a company may achieve reductions in labor time (and, thus, have favorable efficiency variances) by producing defective or poor-quality units. For example, assume that workers at a company who are earning $15 per hour can produce one unit of product in two hours. During a period, 1,500 units are made in 2,610 hours. (Of these, 80 were defective.) The standard quantity of time allowed for total actual production is 3,000 hours. The labor efficiency variance is [$15 × (2,610 − 3,000)] or $5,850 F. However, this variance fails to include the impact of the 80 defective units. The quality variance is computed as follows: 80 defective units × 2 hours per unit × $15 per hour or $2,400 U. Subtracting this unfavorable quality variance from the $5,850 favorable efficiency variance provides a net true efficiency variance for the 1,420 good units of $3,450 F. This restated efficiency variance can be shown as follows:

1,420 good units × 2 hours per unit = 2,840 standard hours allowed (SHA)
2,840 SHA − 2,610 actual hours = 230 hours less than standard (F)
230 hours × $15 standard cost per hour = $3,450 F efficiency variance

Factory Overhead Variances

The use of separate variable and fixed factory overhead application rates and accounts allows the computation of separate variances for each type of overhead. These separate computations provide managers with the greatest detail and, thus, the greatest

labor rate variance (LRV)

labor efficiency variance

NEWS NOTE

Separating Quality Problems from Efficiency Problems

Historically, efficiency variances have been computed by multiplying excess inputs by the standard price. In recent years, this approach has been criticized for motivating managers to ignore quality concerns to avoid unfavorable efficiency variances. In other words, there is an incentive to produce a low-quality product by minimizing the amount of material used or the time spent in production.

[An approach could be taken that] separates the efficiency variance from the quality variance. Inputs consisting of conversion time or material used in defective units [would be] captured in the quality variance.

Separating the two variances allows production decision makers to evaluate the trade-offs between efficiency and quality. They can minimize production time to gain a favorable efficiency variance but this probably will increase the number of defective units and result in an unfavorable quality variance. Likewise, trying to minimize the number of defective units may result in investing more time and more material and therefore having an unfavorable efficiency variance.

SOURCE: Carole Cheatham, "Updating Standard Cost Systems," *Journal of Accountancy* (December 1990), pp. 59–60.

flexibility for control and performance evaluation purposes. Also, because of increased use of nonsimilar bases for various overhead allocations, each different cost pool for variable and fixed factory overhead may require separate price and usage computations. In the Cutting Department for Thunder Bay Clothing, variable and fixed factory overhead calculations are based, respectively, on direct labor hours and machine hours.

As with materials and labor, total variable and total fixed factory overhead variances can be divided into specific price and quantity subvariances for each type of overhead. The overhead subvariances are referred to as follows:

Variable overhead price element   ⟶   Variable overhead spending variance
Variable overhead quantity element   ⟶   Variable overhead efficiency variance
Fixed overhead price element   ⟶   Fixed overhead spending variance
Fixed overhead quantity element   ⟶   Volume variance

VARIABLE OVERHEAD The total variable overhead (VOH) variance is the difference between actual variable factory overhead costs incurred for the period and standard variable factory overhead cost applied to the period's actual production or service output. The difference at year-end is the total variable factory overhead variance, which is also the amount of underapplied or overapplied variable factory overhead. The following diagram illustrates the computation of the total variable overhead variance.

Actual Variable   Variable Overhead Cost
Overhead Cost   Applied to Production

Total Variable Overhead (VOH) Variance
(Underapplied or Overapplied Variable Overhead)

The variable factory overhead variance computations for the Cutting Department of Thunder Bay Clothing use the June 10–14, 1996, data. The actual variable factory overhead cost for the week was $2,500 for 208 direct labor hours of work; this is an approximate cost of $12.02 per DLH. Two hundred standard direct labor hours were allowed for that period's production and each direct labor hour was expected to cost the company $11.10 in variable factory overhead. The variable overhead variances for the Cutting Department are computed as follows:

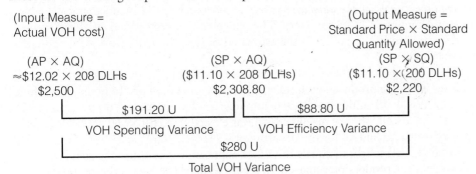

The **variable overhead spending** (or budget) **variance** is the difference between actual variable factory overhead and budgeted variable factory overhead based on actual input. The **variable overhead efficiency variance** is the difference between budgeted variable factory overhead at the actual input activity and budgeted variable factory overhead at standard input (such as DLHs) allowed. This variance quantifies the effect of using more or less actual input than the standard allowed for the actual output. When actual input exceeds standard input allowed, operations appear inefficient. Excess input also means that more variable overhead is needed to support the additional input.

variable overhead spending variance

variable overhead efficiency variance

FIXED OVERHEAD   The total fixed overhead (FOH) variance is the difference between actual FOH cost incurred and standard FOH cost applied to the period's actual production. This difference is also the amount of underappplied or overapplied fixed overhead for the period. The following model shows the computation of the total fixed overhead variance.

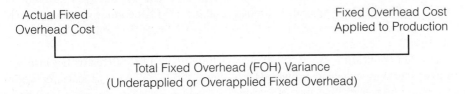

The total fixed overhead variance is subdivided into its price and quantity elements by the insertion of *budgeted* fixed overhead as a middle column into the model.

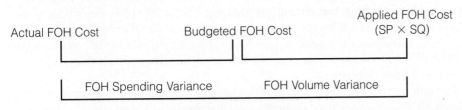

In the model, the left column is simply labeled "actual FOH cost" and is not computed as a price times quantity measure, because fixed overhead is generally acquired in lump-sum amounts rather than on a per-unit input basis. The **fixed overhead spending** (or budget) **variance** is the difference between actual and budgeted fixed overhead. The fixed overhead **volume variance** is the difference between budgeted and applied fixed overhead. Budgeted fixed overhead is a constant amount throughout the relevant range; thus, *the middle column is a constant figure regardless of the actual quantity of input or the standard quantity of input allowed.* This concept is a key element in computing FOH variances. The budgeted amount of fixed overhead is equal to the standard FOH rate times the estimated capacity measure used to compute the standard rate.

The Cutting Department of Thunder Bay Clothing had estimated that 2,496 pairs of jeans would be produced each week, amounting to a total of 416 hours of machine time (2,496 × 10 minutes = 24,960 minutes; 24,960 minutes ÷ 60 minutes = 416 hours). Since each hour of machine time was expected to cost $9.60, the weekly fixed factory overhead budget for the department is (416 × $9.60) or $3,993.60.

Applied fixed overhead equals the FOH application rate times the standard input allowed for the production achieved. In regard to fixed factory overhead, the standard input allowed for the production achieved measures capacity utilization for the period. The standard input for Thunder Bay Clothing's Cutting Department is 10 minutes of machine time per pair of jeans; thus, since 2,000 pair of jeans were produced, the standard machine time allowed is 333 1/3 hours, as shown at the bottom of Exhibit 6–7.

Inserting the data for the Cutting Department into the model gives the following:

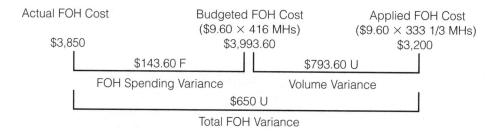

The week's actual fixed overhead cost is $3,850, while the budgeted amount is $3,993.60. The $143.60 favorable difference is the FOH spending variance, which could be related to a variety of causes such as decreased rent payments for machinery or decreased insurance premiums.

The FOH application rate is $9.60 per machine hour. This rate exists because the company chose an expected annual capacity level of 124,800 pairs of jeans, or 2,496 per week for 50 weeks. Had any other capacity level been chosen, the rate would have been different, even though the total amount of budgeted fixed overhead ($199,680) would have been the same. *If any level of capacity is experienced other than that which was used in determining the application rate, a volume variance will occur.* For example, if Thunder Bay Clothing had chosen 100,000 pairs (or 2,000 pairs per week) as the denominator level of activity for setting the predetermined FOH rate, there would be no volume variance for the week of June 10–14, 1996. If any number of pairs less than 2,000 had been chosen as the denominator level of activity, the volume variance would have been favorable.

The difference between the $3,993.60 budgeted FOH and the $3,200 applied FOH gives the $793.60 unfavorable volume variance for the week. This variance is also equal to the difference of 496 pairs of jeans (2,496 − 2,000) that the company expected to make but did not produce multiplied by the $1.60 standard fixed overhead rate per pair of jeans. The variance is unfavorable because fewer jeans were produced this week than budgeted. The $650 unfavorable total fixed factory overhead variance is the underapplied amount of fixed factory overhead for the week.

COST CONTROL AND VARIANCE RESPONSIBILITY

Cost control focuses on the variances between actual costs incurred for a period and the standard costs that should have been incurred based on actual output. To exercise any type of effective control, managers first must be provided with detailed information on the various cost components. Second, a well-designed system of cost control and variance analysis should capture variances as early as possible.

Variance analysis is the process of categorizing the nature (favorable or unfavorable) of the differences between standard and actual costs and seeking the reasons for those differences. The cost control and variance analysis system should help managers determine who or what is responsible for the variance and who is best able to explain it. When variances reflect poor performance, an early measurement system may allow operational performance to be improved. The longer the reporting of a variance is delayed, the more difficult it becomes to determine its cause.

Material price and labor rate variances are not as controllable at the production or service level as are material quantity and labor efficiency variances. Price and rate standards tend to be predictive in nature and are more dependent on outside forces than are usage standards.

Material Variances

Material price variances are normally determined at the point of purchase. Purchasing agents cannot always *control* prices, but given adequate lead time and resources, these individuals should be able to *influence* those prices. They exert this influence through knowing what suppliers are available and choosing suppliers that provide the appropriate material in the most reasonable time span at the most reasonable cost. The purchasing agent can also influence material prices by purchasing in quantities that provide price discounts or by engaging in contractual arrangements such as long-term purchase contracts, such as Levi Strauss & Co. (Canada) Inc. does with some of its preferred suppliers.

The purchasing agent is usually the person who is best able to explain why a material price variance occurs. Also, as part of the team that originally set the material price standard, the purchasing agent is usually the individual to whom responsibility for material price variances is assigned.

Material quantity variances can be determined when materials are issued or used. Such variances are considered the responsibility of the person in charge of the job or department. Materials are ordinarily requisitioned based on the number of actual units to be produced times the standard quantity per unit. When additional materials are taken out of inventory, material requisition slips of a different color may be used. These color-coded excess requisition slips allow control to occur while work is under way rather than at the end of the period or when production is completed. Monitoring requisition slips for significant excess material withdrawals alerts managers to seek causes for the excesses and, if possible, take timely corrective action.

Some production settings, such as chemical and petroleum processing, involve a continuous flow of material. In these cases, it may not be practical or reasonable to

■ **LEARNING OBJECTIVE 5**
Analyze variances for purposes of control and performance evaluation.

variance analysis

isolate quantity variances when materials are placed into production. The material quantity variance is more feasibly measured when production is complete and the total quantity of production is known. Measuring usage for relatively short time periods and reporting quantity variances after production is complete can still assist management in controlling operations. (Labor efficiency variances are also more appropriately measured at the end of production in these types of manufacturing operations.)

There are exceptions to the normal assignment of responsibility for material price and quantity variances. Assume that the manager in the Cutting Department at Thunder Bay Clothing asks the purchasing agent to acquire, without adequate lead time, additional quantities of denim. She makes this request because the marketing manager has just told her that the demand for jeans has unexpectedly increased. Making a spur-of-the-moment acquisition of this kind could result in paying a price higher than standard. Price variances resulting from these types of causes should be assigned to production (or marketing/merchandising for inadequate predictions), not to purchasing.

In contrast, assume the purchasing agent acquires inferior-quality denim that results in excess consumption and an unfavorable quantity variance. This quantity variance should be assigned to purchasing rather than to production. Such situations are likely to be identified from continuous, rather than end-of-period, reporting.

Labor Variances

Labor rate and labor efficiency variances are commonly identified as part of the payroll process and assigned to the person in charge of the production or service area. This assignment assumes that the manager has the ability to influence the type of labor personnel used. For instance, the Cutting Department manager could use skilled or unskilled workers to align, mark, and cut material. Using highly skilled, highly paid individuals for lower-level jobs could cause an unfavorable labor rate variance, accompanied by a favorable labor efficiency variance. Thus, as with material variances, correlations may exist between labor variances.

Sometimes a common factor may influence both material and labor and thereby cause both a material and a labor variance. For instance, in a manufacturing situation, the purchase of inferior-quality materials could result in a favorable material price variance, an unfavorable material quantity variance, and an unfavorable labor efficiency variance. The efficiency variance could reflect increased production time, since many units were rejected as substandard because of the inferior materials. In another common situation, the use of lower-paid, less-skilled workers might result in a favorable rate variance but could cause excessive material usage.

The probability of detecting relationships among variances is improved, but not assured, by timely variance reporting. The accounting and reporting process should highlight interrelationships of variances, and managers should be aware of the possibility of such relationships when reviewing variance reports.

Factory Overhead Variances

The difference between actual and applied overhead is the amount of underapplied or overapplied overhead or the total overhead variance that must be explained. Control purposes differ for variable and fixed overhead because of the types of costs that make up the two categories as well as the ability of managers to influence those costs.

VARIABLE OVERHEAD   Variable overhead costs are incurred on a continual basis as work is performed and are directly related to that work. Because of this direct relationship to activity, control of VOH costs is similar to that for materials and labor. Companies control variable overhead by (1) keeping actual costs in line with planned costs for the actual level of activity and (2) getting the planned output yield from the overhead resources placed into production.

Variable overhead spending variances are commonly caused by price differences— paying average actual prices that are higher or lower than the standard prices allowed. Such fluctuations often occur because price changes have not been reflected in the standard rate. For instance, average indirect labor wage rates, supply costs, or utility rates may have increased or decreased since the standard VOH rate was computed. In such instances, the standard rate should be adjusted.

If managers have no control over prices charged by external parties, they should not be held accountable for variances arising because of such price changes. In contrast, if managers could influence prices—for example through long-term purchase arrangements—such options should be investigated as to their long-term costs and benefits before a decision is made to change the standard. Waste or spoilage of resources, such as indirect materials, is another possible cause of the VOH spending variance.

The VOH efficiency variance reflects the managerial control implemented or needed in regard to the yield of output as related to input. VOH represents a variety of resources that, like direct materials and direct labor, bear a known and measurable relationship to the activity base used to represent production activity. These resources are managed by monitoring and measuring their actual use in conformity with standard usage, promptly investigating any variances, and adjusting resource usage when necessary. Control of the variable overhead resource elements can only be achieved if the variance from standard for each VOH component is analyzed rather than attempting to analyze and control variable overhead in total. The cost and usage of each component of VOH could react independently of one another.

If variable factory overhead is applied on the basis of direct labor hours, the signs (favorable or unfavorable) of the variable overhead and direct labor efficiency variances will be the same, since the actual and standard hours compared in the two calculations are the same. However, when alternative overhead application bases are used, the signs of these two variances may no longer be related to one another, and this is often the case. Use of any alternative basis, including those provided under activity-based costing, does not affect the implementation of a standard costing system.

FIXED OVERHEAD   Control of fixed factory overhead is distinctly different from control of variable factory overhead because fixed overhead may not be directly related to current activity. Since many types of fixed factory costs must be committed to in lump-sum amounts before current period activity takes place, managers may have only limited ability to control FOH costs in the short run. Once managers commit to a fixed cost, it becomes unchangeable for some period of time *regardless of whether actual work takes place.* Thus, control of many fixed overhead costs must occur at the *time of commitment* rather than at the *time of activity.*

The FOH spending variance normally represents a variance in the costs of fixed overhead components, although this variance can also reflect mismanagement of resources. Control over the FOH spending variance often must take place on a transaction-by-transaction basis when managers arrange for facilities. Many fixed overhead costs are uncontrollable in the short run. For example, depreciation expense is based on the factory's historical cost, salvage value, and expected life. Utility costs (which are partially fixed) are set by rate commissions and are influenced by the size and type of the physical plant. Even a "turn-off-the-lights" program can only reduce utility costs by a limited amount. Repair and maintenance costs (which are also partially fixed) can be controlled to some extent but are highly affected by the type of operation involved. Salaries are contractual obligations that were set at the time of employment or salary review.

The information provided by a total FOH spending variance amount would not be specific enough to allow management to decide whether corrective action was possible or desirable. Individual cost variances for each component need to be reviewed. Such a review will help managers determine the actual causes of and responsibility for the several components of the total fixed overhead spending variance.

In addition to controlling spending, utilizing capacity is another important aspect of managerial control. Capacity utilization is reflected in the volume variance because the volume variance is a direct function of the capacity level chosen for the computation of the standard fixed overhead application rate. Although utilization is controllable to some degree, the volume variance is the variance over which managers have the least influence and control, especially in the short run. But it is important that managers exercise what ability they do have to influence and control capacity utilization.

An unfavorable volume variance indicates less-than-expected utilization of capacity and a favorable volume variance indicates greater-than-expected utilization. If available capacity is currently being used at a level below (or above) that which was anticipated, managers should recognize that condition, investigate the reasons for it, and (if possible and desirable) initiate appropriate action. The degree of capacity utilization should always be viewed in relation to inventory and sales. If capacity is overutilized and inventory is stockpiling, managers should decrease capacity utilization. A favorable volume variance could, however, be due to increased sales demand with no stockpiling of inventory—in which case no adjustments should be made to reduce utilization.

If capacity is underutilized and sales are back-ordered or going unfilled, managers should try to increase capacity utilization. However, managers must understand that underutilization of capacity is *not* always undesirable. In a manufacturing company, it is more appropriate for managers not to produce goods that would simply end up in inventory stockpiles. Unneeded inventory production, although it serves to utilize capacity, generates substantially more costs for materials, labor, and overhead (including storage and handling costs and the high-risk costs of inventory spoilage and write downs). The positive impact that such unneeded production will have on the fixed overhead volume variance is unimportant because it is outweighed by the unnecessary costs of accumulating excess inventory.

Managers can sometimes influence capacity utilization by modifying work schedules, taking measures to relieve production constraints, eliminating non-value-added activities, and carefully monitoring the movement of resources through the production or service process. Such actions should be taken during the period rather than after the period has ended. Efforts made after work is completed may improve next period's operations but will have no impact on current work.

Expected annual capacity (rather than practical or theoretical) is commonly selected as the denominator level of activity by which to compute the predetermined fixed factory overhead application rate. Use of this base does, however, ignore an important management concern: that of unused capacity. Having, but not using, capacity creates additional non-value-added organizational costs. The only way these costs can be highlighted is through the selection of practical or theoretical capacity to compute the fixed factory overhead application rate.

Rather than using the traditional fixed overhead computations, companies may want to compute fixed overhead variances in a manner that could provide additional information. This innovative process is described in Exhibit 6–8, using Thunder Bay Clothing Company's production of PC Jeans. In this example, the fixed factory overhead rate is computed on the basis of practical capacity rather than expected annual capacity. This computation allows managers to focus on the cost of unused capacity so that it can be accounted for and, therefore, analyzed and controlled.[7]

CONVERSION COST AS AN ELEMENT IN STANDARD COSTING

Conversion cost consists of both direct labor and manufacturing overhead. The traditional view separates the elements of product cost into three categories: direct material, direct labor, and overhead. This practice is appropriate in labor-intensive production settings; however, in more highly automated factories, direct labor cost generally represents an extremely small part of total product cost. In such circumstances, one worker may oversee a large number of machines and may deal with troubleshooting machine malfunctions more often than converting raw materials into finished products. These new conditions mean that workers' wages are more closely associated with indirect labor than direct labor.

Many companies have responded to having large overhead costs and small direct labor costs by adapting their standard cost systems to provide for only two elements of product cost: direct materials and conversion. In these situations, conversion costs are likely to be separated into their variable and fixed components. Conversion costs are also likely to be separated into direct and indirect categories based on their ability

■ **LEARNING OBJECTIVE 6**
Recognize how organizational evolution and desired level of attainability affect standard setting.

■ **EXHIBIT 6–8**
Analyzing the Volume Variance

Total fixed factory overhead costs (from Exhibit 6-7)	$199,680
Total practical capacity of factory in MHs (assumed)	24,960
Total expected annual capacity of factory in MHs (from Exhibit 6-7)	20,800

Predetermined fixed factory overhead rate based on
practical capacity = $199,680 ÷ 24,960 = $8.00 per MH

Practical capacity	24,960 MHs
Expected annual capacity	20,800 MHs
Unused capacity	4,160 MHs
Multiplied by the cost per MH	× $ 8
Cost of unused capacity	$33,280

If 20,000 MHs are the standard hours allowed for actual production, the company would have a capacity utilization variance of $6,400 U [(20,800 − 20,000) × $8].

If 21,000 MHs are the standard hours allowed for actual production, the company would have a capacity utilization variance of $1,600 F [(20,800 − 21,000) × $8].

---

[7]This discussion is based on the work of Robert S. Kaplan in "Flexible Budgeting in an Activity-Based Costing Framework," *Accounting Horizons* (June 1994), p. 104–109.

Standards also exist in service companies such as Delta Air Lines. The preflight checklist can be viewed as a type of "operations flow document" with each activity requiring a specific amount of time. As a target level of performance, would you want the airline to set standards for these activities at an expected, practical, or theoretical level of attainability?

to be traced to a machine rather than to a product. Overhead may be applied by use of a variety of cost drivers, including machine hours, cost of materials, number of production runs, number of machine setups, and throughput time.

Variance analysis for conversion cost in automated plants normally focuses on the following: (1) spending variances for overhead costs; (2) efficiency variances for machinery and production costs rather than labor costs; and (3) the traditional (or more control-focused) volume variance for production. In an automated system, managers are likely to be able to better control not only the spending and efficiency variances but also the volume variance. The idea of planned output is essential in a just-in-time system. Variance analysis under a conversion cost approach is illustrated in Exhibit 6–9. Regardless of the method by which variances are computed, it is essential that managers analyze those variances and use them for cost control purposes as much as possible.

CONSIDERATIONS IN ESTABLISHING STANDARDS

■ LEARNING OBJECTIVE 6
Recognize how organizational evolution and desired level of attainability affect standard setting.

When standards are established, appropriateness and attainability should be considered. Appropriateness, in relation to a standard, refers to the basis on which the standards are developed and how long they are expected to last. Attainability refers to the degree of difficulty or rigor that should be instilled in achieving the standard.

Appropriateness

While standards are developed from past and current information, they should reflect technical and environmental factors expected for the period in which the standards are to be applied. Factors such as materials quality, normal ordering quantities, employee wage rates, degree of plant automation, facility layout, and mix of employee skills should be considered. Management should not think that standards, once set, will remain useful forever. Standards must evolve over the organization's life to reflect

■ **EXHIBIT 6–9**

Variances Under Conversion Approach

$$\text{Conversion Rate per Machine Hour} = \frac{\text{Budgeted Labor} + \text{Budgeted Factory Overhead Costs}}{\text{Budgeted Machine Hours}}$$

(should be separated into variable and fixed costs)
If variable and fixed conversion costs are separated:

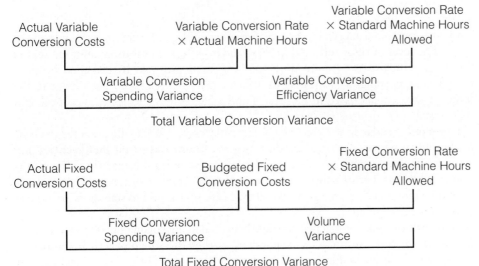

its changing methods and processes. Current operating performance cannot be compared against out-of-date standards because to do so would produce variances that were illogical for planning, controlling, decision making, or evaluating performance.

To illustrate this point, suppose that Levi Strauss & Co. (Canada) Inc. sets time standards for labor before its factory reorganization and does not change those standards after the reorganization takes place. The new equipment and change in factory layout caused labor times to decline drastically, in part because of the elimination of many non-value-added labor movements. Consistently favorable labor efficiency variances result, and managers should become aware that these efficiency variances are not relevant to evaluating worker performance, determining inventory valuation, or making product pricing decisions. Rather, the new time reductions would make the standard obsolete and worthless.

In some Japanese firms, standards are changed quite frequently, especially if kaizen costing techniques are in effect. For example, at Citizen Watch Company, Ltd., standards are changed every three months to accomodate the effects of continuous improvement efforts. The standard is adjusted the month after the kaizen change is implemented. For instance, suppose a worker who had been standing on the right side of a production line to perform a task found that he could reduce the time to perform that task by 15 seconds if he stood on the left side of the line. This change is implemented in March, but the standard is not be adjusted until April. The delay in changing the standard is made so that the worker will have time to get used to the new procedure. By April, company management expects no labor time variance to occur.

Citizen measures its success in meeting standards using an "achievement ratio," which is expected to be 100 percent (that is, no variance). If a 1 percent unfavorable variance occurs, a review of the process is triggered. Such a low tolerance for non-conformance is not unusual in Japanese firms and indicates how tightly Japanese production processes are controlled.[8]

Levi Strauss & Co. (Canada) Inc. makes adjustments to standards similar to those made at Citizen. After company managers investigate variance causes, and if the variance was above a specified allowable deviation, standards may be changed if the circumstance creating the variance is of a long-term nature. Thus, standards are more likely to reflect current, rather than past, conditions.

Attainability

Standards provide a target level of performance and can be set at various levels of rigor. The level of rigor reflected in the standard affects motivation, and one reason for using standards is to motivate employees. Standards can be classified by their degree of rigor, ranging from easy to difficult. The classifications are similar to the levels of capacity discussed in Chapter 4 and are as follows: expected, practical, and theoretical.

expected standards

Expected standards are set at a level that reflects what is actually expected to occur in the future period. Such standards anticipate future waste and inefficiencies and allow for them. As such, expected standards are not of significant value for motivation, control, or performance evaluation. Any variances from expected standards should be minimal and managers should take care that expected standards are not set to be too easy to achieve.

practical standards

Standards that can be reached or slightly exceeded approximately 60 percent to 70 percent of the time with reasonable effort by workers are called **practical standards.** These standards allow for normal, unavoidable time problems or delays such as machine downtime and worker breaks. Practical standards represent an attainable challenge and have traditionally been thought to be the most effective at inducing the best worker performance and at determining how effectively and efficiently workers are performing their tasks. Both favorable and unfavorable variances result from the use of moderately rigorous standards such as these.

theoretical standards

Standards that allow for no inefficiencies of *any* type are called **theoretical standards.** Theoretical standards encompass the highest level of rigor and do not allow for normal operating delays or human limitations such as fatigue, boredom, or misunderstanding. It has been traditionally thought it was impossible for theoretical standards to be attained. Even in a plant that is entirely automated, there is still the possibility of human or machine failure. Most attempts to use such standards in the past resulted in discouraged and resentful workers who ultimately ignored the standards. Variances from theoretical standards were always unfavorable and these variances were not considered useful for constructive cost control or performance evaluation. This traditional perspective has, however, begun to change, as the following section explains.

management by exception

Depending on the type of standard in effect, the acceptable ranges used to apply the **management by exception** principle differ. (Management by exception allows managers to set upper and lower limits of tolerance for deviations and investigate only deviations that fall outside those tolerance ranges.) This difference is especially notable for deviations on the unfavorable side. If a company uses expected standards, the ranges of acceptable variances should be extremely small, since actual cost should

---

[8]Robin Cooper, *When Lean Enterprises Collide: Competing through Confrontation* (Boston: Harvard Business School Press, in press), draft pages 260–261.

closely conform to the standard. In contrast, a company using theoretical standards would expect variances to fall within very wide ranges of acceptability, since managers would know that the standards could not be met. The News Note on page 280 about a recent study of manufacturing company controllers provides some reasons why managers are using more formalized methods of judging when to investigate variances than those used in the past.

Variances large enough to fall outside the ranges of acceptability generally indicate trouble. The variances themselves, though, do not reveal the cause of the trouble or the person or group responsible. To determine causes of variances, managers must investigate problems through observation, inspection, and inquiry. Such investigations involve the time and effort of people at the operating level as well as accounting personnel. Operations personnel should be alert in spotting variances as they occur and should record the reasons for the variances to the extent that those causes can be determined. For example, operating personnel can readily detect and report causes such as machine downtime or material spoilage.

How well a company determines the causes of variances is often proportional to how much time, effort, and money it spends in gathering information about variances during the period. Managers must be willing and able to accumulate variance information regularly and consistently to evaluate the evidence, isolate the causes, and (if possible) influence performance to improve the process. If variances are ignored when they occur, it is often impossible or extremely costly to determine the relevant data and to take corrective action at a later time.

CHANGES IN THE USE OF STANDARDS

■ **LEARNING OBJECTIVE 7**
Understand how standard setting and standard usage are changing in modern business.

Sometimes, in using variances from standards for control and performance evaluation purposes, accountants (and, to a certain extent, businesspeople in general) believe that an incorrect measurement is employed. For example, material standards often include a factor for waste and labor standards are commonly set at the expected level of attainment, even though this level allows for downtime and human error. The practice of using standards that are not aimed at the highest possible theoretical level of attainment is now being questioned in a business environment concerned with world-class operations, especially continuous improvement.

Use of Theoretical Standards For Quality Improvement

Japanese influence on American management philosophy and production techniques has been substantial in the recent past. Just-in-time (JIT) production systems and total quality management (TQM) concepts were both imported to this country as a result of an upsurge in Japanese productivity. These two world-class concepts are notable departures from the traditional view that ideals should not be used in standards development and application. Rather than including waste and inefficiency in the standards and then accepting additional waste and spoilage deviations under a management by exception principle, both JIT and TQM begin from the premises of zero defects, zero inefficiency, and zero downtime. Under such a system, theoretical standards become expected standards. There is no acceptable level of deviation from standard (or only a minimal allowable level).

While workers may, at first, resent the introduction of standards set at a "perfection" level, it is in their and management's best long-run interest to have such standards. When a standard permits a deviation from the ideal, managers are allowing for less than perfectly efficient uses of resources. Setting standards at the tightest possible

When to Investigate Variances

Variance investigation policies [for materials and labor at large companies] are moving away from pure judgment and toward the use of structured or formalized exception procedures.

[One] explanation is that the results are being driven by manufacturing innovations that lead to shorter production runs and shorter product life cycles. In such an environment, monthly variance reports may be so untimely as to be virtually useless. In a flexible manufacturing environment, production runs can be extremely short—only days or perhaps even hours. To provide timely feedback in an environment where the nature of operations and the products being produced change rapidly, more accounts and greater reporting frequency are required.

[Another] explanation relates to the increasing globalization of markets rather than to the characteristics or individual operating policies of the firm. When competing internationally, companies face more competitors, are less likely to be the lowest-cost producers, and face more uncertainties than in domestic markets. . . . By reducing production cost surprises, intensified management accounting (in the frequency of reports and the details of variance composition) can compensate for these additional uncertainties.

SOURCE: Bruce R. Gaumnitz and Felix P. Kollaritsch, "Manufacturing Variances: Current Practice and Trends," *Journal of Cost Management* (Spring 1991), pp. 63-64. Reprinted with permission from The Journal of Cost Management for the Manufacturing Industry, © 1991, Warren, Gorham & Lamont, 31 St. James Avenue, Boston, MA 02116. All rights reserved.

(theoretical) level is intended to produce the most useful information for managerial purposes as well as the highest-quality products and services at the lowest possible cost. If no inefficiencies are built into or tolerated in the system, deviations from standard should be minimized and overall organizational performance improved.

If theoretical standards are to be implemented, management must be prepared to go through a four-step "migration" process. First, teams should be established to determine where current problems lie and identify the causes of those problems. Second, if the causes relate to equipment, facility, or workers, management must be ready to invest in plant and equipment items, equipment rearrangements, or worker training so that the standards are amenable to the operations. (Training is essential if workers are to perform at the high levels of efficiency demanded by theoretical standards.) If the causes are related to external sources (such as poor-quality materials), management must be willing to change suppliers and/or pay higher prices for higher-quality input. Third, since management has given the workers the responsibility for quality, management must also give workers the authority to react to problems as discussed in the accompanying News Note. "The key to quality initiatives is for employees to move beyond their natural resistance-to-change mode to a highly focused, strategic, and empowered mind-set. This shift unlocks employees' energy and creativity, and leads them to ask 'how can I do my job even better today?'"[9] Fourth, requiring people to work at their maximum potential demands recognition, meaning that management must provide rewards for achievement.

---

[9]Sara Moulton, Ed Oakley, and Chuck Kremer, "How to Assure Your Quality Initiative Really Pays Off," *Management Accounting* (January 1993), p. 26.

Empowering Employees Is an Ethical Business Practice

Making employees more involved in and responsible for their work activities increases the value of those individuals not only to the organization, but also to themselves and to society as a whole. The organizational benefits gained from empowerment are that employees have a sense of ownership of and work harder toward goals they have set for themselves. Thus, employee involvement automatically promotes a higher degree of effort on the part of the work force. We avoid the basis of the Marxist critique of capitalism: the exploitation and subsequent alienation and rebellion of the worker. Problems will be solved more quickly and, therefore, the cost of errors will be reduced.

Providing training to employees for improving skills and/or decision making results in a person who is a more valuable and productive member of the company and society. Additionally, empowered employees are less likely to become bored and should experience more job satisfaction. Lastly, empowering employees provides a valuable means by which people's 'timeless quest to express [themselves] and establish [their] individuality be furthered in the face of a world that is becoming more complex and more dependent on technology.' Maslow's pinnacle of his hierarchy of need is achieved as well: self-actualization.

SOURCE: Cecily Raiborn and Dinah Payne, "TQM: Just What the Ethicist Ordered," *Journal of Business Ethics* (forthcoming 1995).

Whether setting standards at the theoretical level will become the norm of Western companies cannot be determined at this time. However, the authors believe that the level of attainability for standards will move away from the expected and closer to the ideal. This conclusion is based on the fact that a company whose competitor produces goods based on the highest possible standards must also use such standards to compete on quality and to meet cost (and, thus, profit margin) objectives. Higher standards for efficiency automatically mean lower costs because of the elimination of non-value-added activities such as waste, idle time, and rework.

Basing Price Variance on Purchases Rather Than Usage

Traditionally, the material price variance computation has been more commonly based on purchases than on usage. This choice allows management to calculate the variance as near as possible to the time of cost incurrence. Although a point-of-purchase calculation allows managers to see the impact of buying decisions more rapidly, such information may not be highly relevant in a just-in-time environment. Buying materials that are not needed currently requires that the materials be stored and moved—both non-value-added activities. Any price savings from such purchases should be measured against the additional costs of such a purchase.

Additionally, a point-of-purchase price variance may reduce a manager's ability to recognize a relationship between a favorable material price variance and an unfavorable material usage variance. If a favorable price variance results from the purchase of lower quality materials, the effects of that purchase are not known until the materials are actually used.

Long-term versus Short-term Standards

Standards have traditionally been set after prices and quantities for the various cost elements were comprehensively investigated. These standards were almost always retained for at least one year and, sometimes, for many years. The current business environment (which includes supplier prices, contractual relationships, technology, competition, product design, and manufacturing methods) changes so rapidly that a standard may no longer be useful for management control purposes throughout an entire year. Company management needs to consider whether to incorporate rapid changes in the environment into the standards during a year in which *significant* changes occur. The two obvious choices are to ignore the changes or to reflect those changes in the standard.

Ignoring the changes is a simplistic approach that allows the same type of cost to be recorded at the same amount all year. Thus, for example, any material purchased during the year is recorded at the same standard cost regardless of when the purchase was made. This approach, while making record keeping easy, eliminates any opportunity to adequately control costs or evaluate performance. Additionally, such an approach could create large differences between standard and actual costs, making standard costs unacceptable for external reporting.

Changing the standards to reflect price or quantity changes makes some aspects of management control and performance evaluation more effective and others more difficult. For instance, financial plans prepared under the original standards must be adjusted before appropriate actual comparisons can be made against them. Changing the standards also creates a problem for record keeping and inventory measurement. At what standard cost should products be reported—the standard in effect when they were produced or the standard in effect when the financial statements are prepared? If the standards are changed, the standards are more closely related to actual costs but many of the benefits discussed earlier in the chapter might be compromised.

Management may consider combining these two choices in the accounting system. Plans prepared by use of original and new standards can be compared; any variances reflect changes in the business environment. These variances can be designated as uncontrollable (such as those related to changes in the market price of raw materials) or internally initiated (such as changes in standard labor time resulting from employee training or equipment rearrangement) or internally controllable (such as excess usage of materials and/or labor time caused by the purchase of inferior-quality materials).

Although Levi Strauss & Co. "cuts and sews pants," the company has taken a "leap into technology" that has improved every aspect of business. According to CEO Robert Haas, "Computers help us identify trends, plan work flow, and control our broad-based businesses. In our most advanced facilities, transporters move materials from station to station and robots link our transporters to automatic sewing equipment. Instead of making pants based on what consumers bought in the past, we're using computers to design and market-test products before we buy the first bolt of cloth. This way, we can tell what the 'hot' items will be before they arrive in stores. You've heard of supply-side economics; we're engaged in demand-side manufacturing."

Most recently, the company made the news through the innovative use of technology to manufacture custom-fit jeans for women. "We are moving from an era of mass production to one of mass customization," says Gordon D. Shank, president of Levi Strauss & Co. (Canada) Inc. In partnership with an entrepreneur who developed the technology, the company has taken advantage of a dedicated channel of distribution through Levi's® Only Stores in addition to its domestic manufacturing capacity.

As well, the company has been on the forefront of electronic data interchange (EDI) technology that communicates information both up and down the supply chain. EDI reduces lead times, allows Levi Strauss & Co. to manufacture products closer to market demands, and keeps the company closely in tune with requirements of both consumers and retailers.

In addition to reengineering efforts, Levi Strauss already has globalized its manufacturing process, a feat Haas calls "a triumph over old geographic limitations. Our company buys denim in North Carolina, ships it to France where it is sewn into jeans, launders these jeans in Belgium, and markets them in Germany using TV commercials developed in Britain."

Levi Strauss & Co. is engaged in concentrated efforts to reduce cycle time in all of the company's activities. For example, Levi Strauss & Co. (Canada) Inc. is investigating the use of bar coding for fabric entering the receiving area. Company management recognizes that counting receipts, comparing receipts with orders, and manually entering receiving information into the computer system is time-consuming and non-value-added from the customer viewpoint. Scanning bar coded purchases will reduce time as well as increase accuracy of recorded information.

Most recently, Levi Strauss & Co. was honored in *Fortune's* 1994 ranking of American businesses as the most admired company in the apparel industry and the sixteenth most admired company overall. In part, this honor was related to the privately held company's commitment to environmental protection. For example, company stationery is made from 100 percent recycled denim, which reduces shipping and disposal of denim scraps to landfills while also saving trees. But the honor is also due simply to the kind of company that Levi Strauss is—intensely dedicated to producing consistently high-quality garments and producing them to standard, to rewarding employees based on merit (rather than politics or background), and to maintaining a work environment that is safe, efficient, and forward-focused. In sum, Levi's standards aren't set just for materials, labor, and overhead; they are set for an ethically based corporate culture.

SOURCES: Walter Roessing, "Blue Jean Boss," *Sky* (August 1994), pp. 67-68 (this excerpt has been reprinted through the courtesy of Halsey Publishing Co., publisher of Delta Air Lines' Sky magazine) ; Chris Lee, "The Vision Thing," *Training* (February 1993), p. 29; Jennifer Reese, "America's Most Admired Corporations," *Fortune* (March 6, 1995), p. 66, 90; and 1995 discussion with Desmond Rodrigues, CMA, Cornwall Plant Controller.

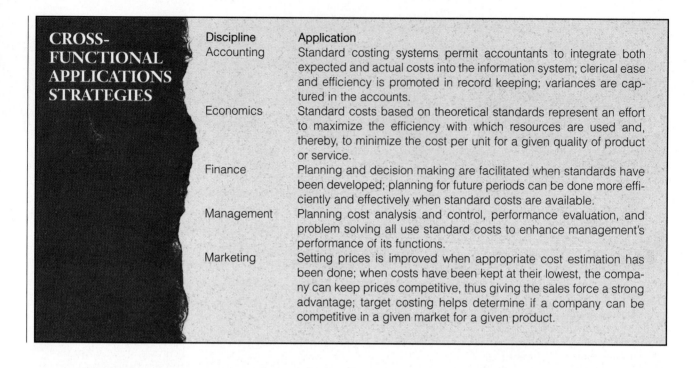

CROSS-FUNCTIONAL APPLICATIONS STRATEGIES	Discipline	Application
	Accounting	Standard costing systems permit accountants to integrate both expected and actual costs into the information system; clerical ease and efficiency is promoted in record keeping; variances are captured in the accounts.
	Economics	Standard costs based on theoretical standards represent an effort to maximize the efficiency with which resources are used and, thereby, to minimize the cost per unit for a given quality of product or service.
	Finance	Planning and decision making are facilitated when standards have been developed; planning for future periods can be done more efficiently and effectively when standard costs are available.
	Management	Planning cost analysis and control, performance evaluation, and problem solving all use standard costs to enhance management's performance of its functions.
	Marketing	Setting prices is improved when appropriate cost estimation has been done; when costs have been kept at their lowest, the company can keep prices competitive, thus giving the sales force a strong advantage; target costing helps determine if a company can be competitive in a given market for a given product.

CHAPTER SUMMARY

Target costing was developed in Japan. It is a technique that helps management determine the maximum cost feasible for a product at the point of its conception. The target cost is calculated as the estimated life cycle selling price minus an acceptable profit margin. Target costing is an important first step in developing a product's standard cost. Once production activity has begun on the product, kaizen costing can be implemented to improve quality and reduce costs. As costs are decreased from continuous improvement efforts, standard costs must be amended to reflect the process and product improvements.

A standard cost is a budget for one unit of product or service output. Standards provide norms against which actual costs can be compared so that cost can be controlled and performance evaluated. In a true standard cost system, standards are computed for prices and quantities of each product component (materials, labor, variable overhead, and fixed overhead). Standards should be developed by a team composed of professional staff and managers as well as employees whose performance will be evaluated by such standards. A standard cost card is used to accumulate and record specific information about the components, processes, quantities, and costs that form the standard for a product. The material and labor sections of the standard cost card are derived from the bill of materials and the operations flow document, respectively.

In a standard costing system, actual and standard costs are accumulated; then, variances are computed and analyzed. Each total variance is separated into subvariances relating to price and quantity (or efficiency) elements.

Variance analysis provides a basis for management planning, control, and performance evaluation. Using standard costs, managers can forecast what costs should be at various levels of activity and can compare these forecasts with actual results. When large variances are observed, the responsible manager attempts to determine the causes and, if possible, takes corrective action. Variances should be recorded as early in the production/service process as is feasible so that their causes will more likely be discoverable.

Standards should be established that are appropriate and attainable. Standards should be current and up-to-date to reflect the relevant technical and operational expectations for the period in which the standards are to be applied. Attainability refers to the degree of rigor built into the standards. The level of rigor chosen should be based on realistic expectations and motivational effects on employees. The practical level has typically been thought to have the best motivational impact; however, some Japanese firms use theoretical standards to indicate their goals of minimum cost and zero defects.

Management has begun to change the way standards are set and are used. Traditionally, standards have been set by including some level of waste and spoilage and, regarding fixed overhead, have been based on expected activity levels. These standards were commonly held constant for a year or longer. Recently, many firms have discovered that their standards have not been useful in implementing process, quality, or cost improvements. Thus, managers are revising the way standards are set and how they are used because of technology advances, process improvements, and global market competitiveness.

APPENDIX

Standard Cost System Journal Entries

Journal entries for the information contained in the chapter related to Thunder Bay Clothing Company Cutting Department are given in Exhibit 6–10. The material price variance in this exhibit is accounted for based on the secondary information that 4,400 square meters of denim were purchased. Note that unfavorable variances have debit balances and favorable variances have credit balances. Unfavorable variances represent excess costs, while favorable variances represent cost reductions. Since standard costs are shown in Work in Process Inventory (a debit-balanced account), it is reasonable that excess costs are also debits.

While standard cost systems are useful for internal reporting, such costs are not acceptable for external reporting unless they are *substantially equivalent* to those that would have resulted from using an actual cost system.[10] If standards are achievable and updated periodically, this equivalency should exist. Using standard cost for financial statements should provide fairly conservative inventory valuations because the effects of excess prices and/or inefficient operations are minimized.

If actual costs are used in financial statements, the standard cost information shown in the accounting records must be adjusted at year-end to approximate actual cost information. The nature of the year-end adjusting entries depends on whether the variance amounts are significant or not.

All manufacturing variances (materials, labor, and overhead) are considered together in determining the appropriate year-end disposition. If the combined impact of these variances is considered insignificant, standard costs are approximately the same as actual costs, and the variances are closed to Cost of Goods Sold (or Cost of Services

■ **LEARNING OBJECTIVE 8**
Prepare journal entries for a standard cost system.

---

[10]Actual product costs should not include extraordinary charges for such items as waste, spoilage, and inefficiency. Such costs should be written off as period expenses.

■ **EXHIBIT 6–10**

Journal Entries for Cutting Department, Week of June 10–14, 1996

	Raw Materials Inventory	24,200.00	
	Materials Price Variance		220.00
	Accounts Payable		23,980.00
	To record the purchase of 4,400 square meters of denim at $5.45 per square meter.		
	Work in Process Inventory—Cutting Dept.	22,000.00	
	Materials Quantity Variance	110.00	
	Raw Materials Inventory		22,110.00
	To record the issuance and usage of 4,020 square meters of denim for 2,000 pairs of jeans.		
	Work in Process Inventory—Cutting Dept.	2,880.00	
	Labor Rate Variance	20.80	
	Labor Efficiency Variance	115.20	
	Wages Payable		3,016.00
	To record the usage of 208 direct labor hours at a wage rate of ≈$14.50 per DLH.		
During period:	Variable Overhead—Cutting Dept.	2,500.00	
	Various accounts		2,500.00
	To record actual variable overhead costs.		
During period:	Fixed Overhead—Cutting Dept.	3,850.00	
	Various accounts		3,850.00
	To record actual fixed overhead costs incurred for depreciation, insurance, repairs and maintenance, etc.		
At end of period (or upon completion of production):	Work in Process Inventory—Cutting Dept.	5,420.00	
	Variable Overhead— Cutting Dept.		2,220.00
	Fixed Overhead— Cutting Dept.		3,200.00
	To apply overhead at $11.10 per DLH (variable) and $9.60 per MH (fixed) for actual production of 2,000 pairs of jeans.		
At year-end: (assuming the variances for June 10–14 were the only ones for the year)	VOH Spending Variance—Cutting Dept.	191.20	
	VOH Efficiency Variance—Cutting Dept.	88.80	
	Variable Overhead—Cutting Dept.		280.00
	To close the variable overhead account.		
	FOH Volume Variance—Cutting Dept.	793.60	
	FOH Spending Variance—Cutting Dept.		143.60
	Fixed Overhead—Cutting Dept.		650.00
	To close the fixed overhead account.		

Rendered in a service organization). Unfavorable variances are closed by being credited; favorable variances are closed by being debited. In a manufacturing company, although all production of the period has not yet been sold, this treatment of insignificant variances is justified on the basis of the immateriality of the amounts involved.

In contrast, if the total variance amount is significant, the overhead variances are prorated at year-end to ending inventories and Cost of Goods Sold in proportion to the relative size of those account balances. This proration disposes of the variances and presents the financial statements in a way that approximates the use of actual costing. The disposition of significant variances is similar to the disposition of large amounts of underapplied or overapplied overhead shown in Chapter 4. The material price variance (based on purchases) is prorated among Raw Materials Inventory, Work in Process Inventory, Finished Goods Inventory, and Cost of Goods Sold (or Cost of Services Rendered). All other variances occur as part of the conversion process and are prorated only to the Work in Process Inventory, Finished Goods Inventory, and Cost of Goods Sold (or Cost of Services Rendered) accounts.

GLOSSARY

Bill of materials (p. 257)   a document that contains information about product material components, their specifications (including quality), and the quantities needed for production

Cost table (p. 252)   a data base that provides information about how using different input resources, manufacturing processes, and product designs will affect product costs

Expected standard (p. 278)   a standard that reflects what is actually expected to occur in a future period

Fixed overhead spending variance (p. 270)   the difference between actual and budgeted fixed overhead

Kaizen costing (p. 254)   a costing technique to reflect continuous efforts to reduce product costs, improve product quality, and/or improve the production process after manufacturing activities have begun

Labor efficiency variance (p. 267)   the difference between the number of actual direct labor hours worked and the standard hours allowed for the actual output multiplied by the standard labor rate per hour

Labor rate variance (p. 267)   the difference between the total actual direct labor wages for the period and the standard rate multiplied by all hours worked during the period

Management by exception (p. 278)   a technique in which managers set upper and lower limits of tolerance for deviations and investigate only deviations that fall outside those tolerance ranges

Material price variance (p. 264)   the amount of money spent under (favorable) or over (unfavorable) the standard total price for a given quantity of materials; may be calculated for quantity purchased or quantity used

Material quantity variance (p. 265)   the cost saved (favorable) or expended (unfavorable) because of the difference between the actual quantity of material used and the standard quantity of material allowed for the goods produced during the period

Operations flow document (p. 259)   a listing of all tasks necessary to make a unit of product or perform a service and the time allowed for each operation

Practical standard (p. 278)   a standard that allows for normal, unavoidable time problems or delays, such as machine downtime and worker breaks; can be reached or slightly exceeded approximately 60 to 70 percent of the time with reasonable effort by workers

Price variance (p. 263)   the difference between what was paid and what should have been paid for inputs during the period

Quantity variance (p. 263)   the difference between the quantity of actual inputs and the standard quantity of inputs for the actual output of the period multiplied by a standard price or rate

Standard cost (p. 254)   a budgeted or estimated cost to manufacture a single unit of product or perform a single service

Standard cost card (p. 261)   a document that summarizes the direct material and direct labor standard quantities and prices as well as the overhead allocation bases and rates needed to complete one unit of product

Standard quantity allowed (p. 263)   a measure of quantity that translates the actual output achieved into the standard input quantity that should have been used to achieve that output

Target costing (p. 252)   a Japanese method of determining the maximum allowable cost of a product before it is designed, engineered, or produced by subtracting an acceptable profit margin rate from a forecasted selling price

Theoretical standard (p. 278)   a standard that allows for no inefficiency of any type and, therefore, is sometimes also called a perfection or theoretical standard

Total variance (p. 263)   the difference between total actual cost incurred and total standard cost applied for the output produced during the period; can also be designated by cost components (direct materials, direct labor, variable factory overhead, and fixed factory overhead)

Variable overhead efficiency variance (p. 269)   the difference between budgeted variable overhead at actual input activity and budgeted variable overhead at standard input activity allowed

Variable overhead spending variance (p. 269)   the difference between actual variable overhead and budgeted variable overhead based on actual input

Variance (p. 251)   any difference between actual and standard costs or quantities

Variance analysis (p. 271)   the process of categorizing the nature (favorable or unfavorable) of the differences between standard and actual costs and seeking the reasons for those differences

Volume variance (p. 270)   the difference between budgeted and applied fixed overhead

SOLUTION STRATEGIES

VARIANCES IN FORMULA FORMAT

Material price variance = AQ (AP − SP)
Material quantity variance = SP (AQ − SQ)
Labor rate variance = AQ (AP − SP)
Labor efficiency variance = SP (AQ − SQ)
Variable overhead spending variance = Actual VOH − (SR × AQ)
Variable overhead efficiency variance = SR (AQ − SQ)
Fixed overhead spending variance = Actual FOH − Budgeted FOH
Fixed overhead volume variance = Budgeted FOH − (SR × SQ)

VARIANCES IN DIAGRAM FORMAT

Actual Price ×
Actual Quantity Purchased

Standard Price ×
Actual Quantity Purchased

Material Price Variance
(calculated at point of purchase)

Standard Price ×
Actual Quantity Used

Standard Price ×
Standard Quantity Allowed

Material Quantity Variance

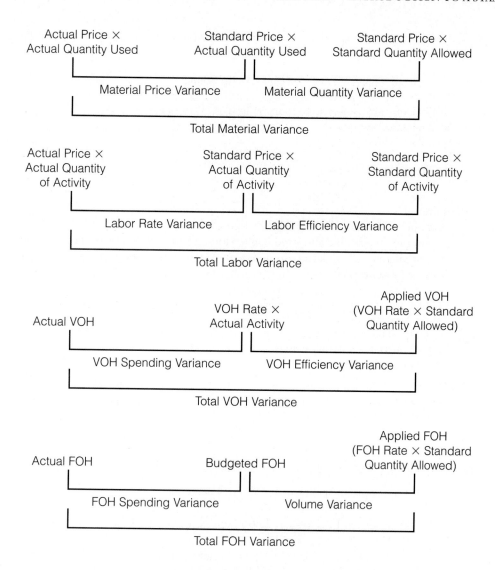

DEMONSTRATION PROBLEM

Squeaky Clean manufactures large rubber erasers. The production operation is a simple process requiring only one material and very little labor. Variable factory overhead is applied on a machine hour (MH) basis. Fixed factory overhead is applied on a per-unit basis; the predetermined rate was based on a production budget of 100,000 erasers per month. The following standard costs and quantities have been developed for one eraser:

Direct material (1 ounce of rubber)	$ 1.60 per pound	$.10
Direct labor (1 minute of direct labor time)	$ 6.00 per DLH	.10
Variable factory overhead (15 seconds of machine time per eraser)	$ 12.00 per MH	.05
Fixed factory overhead (per eraser)		.10
Total cost per eraser		$.35

For May, company records give the following actual cost and production information:

Purchases of rubber: 4,000 pounds at $1.58 per pound
Usage of rubber: 6,480 pounds
Direct labor: 1,750 hours at $6.10 per hour
Machine time: 384 hours
Variable overhead: $5,150
Fixed overhead: $9,900
Production: 102,000 erasers

Required:
a. Compute all material, labor, and overhead variances.
b. Compute the variable and fixed conversion cost variances. For purposes of this requirement, the standard costs and quantities for one eraser are rearranged for ease of presentation:

Direct material (one ounce of rubber)	$.10 per ounce	$.10
Variable conversion cost (15 seconds of machine time per eraser)*	$36 per MH	.15
Fixed conversion cost (per eraser)		.10
Total cost per eraser		$.35

*($.15 variable conversion cost for 15 seconds of machine time) × 4 units per machine minute = $.60 per minute; $.60 × 60 minutes = $36 variable conversion cost per MH

■ SOLUTION TO DEMONSTRATION PROBLEM

Determine appropriate standards for all cost elements.

102,000 erasers × 1 ounce = 102,000 ounces; 102,000 ÷ 16 = 6,375 pounds of DM
102,000 erasers × 1 minute = 102,000 minutes; 102,000 ÷ 60 = 1,700 hrs. of DL time
102,000 erasers × 15 seconds = 1,530,000 seconds; 1,530,000 ÷ 60 = 25,500 minutes; 25,500 ÷ 60 = 425 hours of machine time
Total budgeted FOH = 100,000 erasers × $.10 per eraser = $10,000

a. Direct Materials:

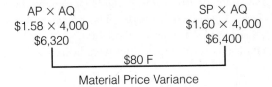

```
   AP × AQ              SP × AQ
$1.58 × 4,000        $1.60 × 4,000
   $6,320               $6,400
        |_____$80 F_____|
          Material Price Variance
```

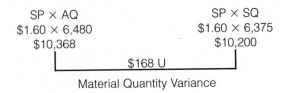

```
        SP × AQ              SP × SQ
     $1.60 × 6,480        $1.60 × 6,375
        $10,368              $10,200
             |_____$168 U_____|
             Material Quantity Variance
```

Direct Labor:

AP × AQ	SP × AQ	SP × SQ
$6.10 × 1,750	$6 × 1,750	$6 × 1,700
$10,675	$10,500	$10,200

$175 U	$300 U
Labor Rate Variance	Labor Efficiency Variance

$475 U

Total Labor Variance

Variable Factory Overhead:

Actual VOH	SP × AQ	SP × SQ
	$12 × 384	$12 × 425
$5,150	$4,608	$5,100

$542 U	$492 F
VOH Spending Variance	VOH Efficiency Variance

$50 U

Total VOH Variance

Fixed Factory Overhead:

Actual FOH	Budgeted FOH	SP × SQ
		$.10 × 102,000
$9,900	$10,000	$10,200

$100 F	$200 F
FOH Budget Variance	Volume Variance

$300 F

Total FOH Variance

b. Variable Conversion:

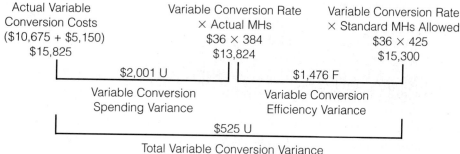

Actual Variable Conversion Costs ($10,675 + $5,150)	Variable Conversion Rate × Actual MHs	Variable Conversion Rate × Standard MHs Allowed
	$36 × 384	$36 × 425
$15,825	$13,824	$15,300

$2,001 U	$1,476 F
Variable Conversion Spending Variance	Variable Conversion Efficiency Variance

$525 U

Total Variable Conversion Variance

Fixed Conversion:

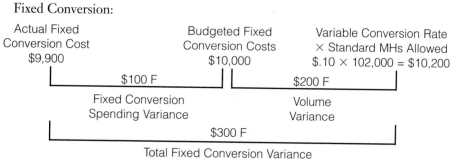

Actual Fixed Conversion Cost	Budgeted Fixed Conversion Costs	Variable Conversion Rate × Standard MHs Allowed
$9,900	$10,000	$.10 × 102,000 = $10,200

$100 F	$200 F
Fixed Conversion Spending Variance	Volume Variance

$300 F

Total Fixed Conversion Variance

END-OF-CHAPTER MATERIALS

■ QUESTIONS

1. Why is a standard costing system regarded as both a planning and a control tool?

2. Would an actual or a standard product costing system provide the better opportunity to evaluate the control of costs for a period? Explain.

3. What is target costing and how does it help decision makers evaluate the market potential of prospective new products?

4. How is target costing used to reduce the cost of producing products?

5. Why would a cost table be a valuable tool to use in designing a new product or service?

6. What is kaizen costing? How is it different from target costing?

7. What is a bill of materials and how is it used in a standard cost system?

8. What is an operations flow document? How is it used in a standard cost system?

9. In a standard costing system, is it standard cost or actual cost that is charged to Work in Process Inventory for direct material, direct labor and manufacturing overhead? Explain. How are actual costs reflected in a standard costing system?

10. What is a variance and what does it measure?

11. What is variance analysis? Why do managers conduct variance analysis?

12. For the following list of variances indicate (a) when each variance should be calculated and (b) to whom responsibility for the variance should be assigned and why.
    a. Material price variance
    b. Material quantity variance
    c. Labor rate variance
    d. Labor efficiency variance
    e. Variable factory overhead spending variance
    f. Volume variance

13. Why is the computation of the material price variance frequently based on the quantity of material purchased, rather than the quantity consumed, during the period?

14. Roger Johnson, manufacturing vice-president of Turner Controls, has noticed that one manufacturing plant experienced several large unfavorable material quantity variances during the prior quarter. Before starting his probe of the matter, he has requested that you list some possible reasons for this type of variance.

15. Is fixed factory overhead controlled by management on a per-unit basis? Explain your answer.

16. Of what importance is capacity utilization to managers? When managers control utilization, are they always controlling costs? Explain.

17. Why is a "conversion cost" category emerging in some companies to replace the traditional cost categories of direct labor and manufacturing overhead?

18. Why is it important for managers to update standards periodically?

19. What is the likely behavioral effect of setting standards too high to be achieved? Why will this effect occur?

20. What is management by exception, and what is its role in a management control system that uses standard costing?

21. (Appendix) If the variances incurred in a given period are not significant in amount, how are they typically closed out at the end of the period?

■ **EXERCISES**

22. (LO 2, 3, 6; *Terminology*) Match each item in the right-hand column with a term in the left-hand column.

a. Operations flow document	**1.** A data base that provides information about cost of alternative inputs
b. Practical standard	**2.** A difference between budgeted and applied fixed overhead
c. Kaizen costing	**3.** A process of identifying maximum production cost that starts with sales price
d. Cost table	**4.** A document specifying the materials required for a product
e. Labor rate variance	**5.** A process of identifying causes of variances
f. Target costing	**6.** A listing of tasks required to make a product
g. Volume variance	**7.** Integrates continuous improvement efforts to reduce product cost after manufacturing activities have begun
h. Standard cost card	**8.** A standard of performance that has a reasonable probability of attainment
i. Variance analysis	**9.** A labor variance caused by a difference between standard and actual labor rates
j. Bill of materials	**10.** A document listing standard costs of all inputs for a product

23. (LO 2; *Target costing*) Allison Manufacturing is considering introducing a new product, a residential flagpole. According to the market research conducted by the firm, the type of flagpole Allison Manufacturing would produce could be sold for $175 per unit. The firm estimates that variable selling costs would be $25 per unit; fixed selling and administrative costs would be $400,000 per year. The firm has capacity to produce 5,000 flagpoles annually. The firm will produce the flagpoles only if it can generate a profit of $20 per unit.

a. Compute the target cost to manufacture the flagpole.
b. Assume the company estimates that it will actually cost $80 per unit to produce the flagpole. What action should the company take?

24. (LO 4, 5; *Material variances*) Bill Neeman and Company makes large bronze statues of endangered animals. Several wildlife and environmental groups purchase and then resell the statues to raise funds. In June 1996, the purchasing agent, Jill Keene, bought 52,800 pounds of scrap copper and tin at an average price of $2.40 per pound in the correct proportions to make bronze. In June, the company used 49,700 pounds and produced 225 statues. Each statue requires a standard quantity of 210 pounds of scrap at a standard cost of $2.25 per pound.

a. Calculate the material price variance, based on quantity purchased, and indicate who has responsibility for it.

   b. Calculate the material quantity variance and indicate who has responsibility for it.

25. (LO 4, 5; *Material variances*) Eagleton Canvas Shop experienced the following costs related to direct materials during August 1996:

Actual quantity purchased	45,500 pounds
Actual quantity used	43,500 pounds
Standard quantity allowed	44,300 pounds
Actual unit price	$22.00
Standard unit price	$22.50

   The company president has requested that you determine the material price variance and the material quantity variance. Compute the material price variance based on (a) quantity purchased and (b) quantity used.

26. (LO 4, 6; *Material variances*) Harold's Print Shop incurred the following direct material costs in November 1997 for high-volume routine printing jobs:

Sheets of paper purchased in November	500,000
Sheets of paper used in November	390,000
Standard quantity allowed for good production	397,000
Actual unit purchase price per sheet	$.035
Standard unit price per sheet	$.032

   a. Calculate the material price variance based on the quantity purchased and the material quantity variance.
   b. Does this company employ standards based on theoretical performance? Explain.
   c. As the vice-president of manufacturing, why might you desire to move to a more rigorous standard than the one presently used?

27. (LO 4; *Labor variances*) Wilson Fabrics uses a standard cost system. The company experienced the following results related to direct labor in December 1997:

Actual hours worked	27,500
Standard hours allowed for production	27,000
Actual direct labor rate	$7.25
Standard direct labor rate	$6.75

   Calculate the:

   a. total actual payroll.
   b. labor rate variance.
   c. labor efficiency variance.

28. (LO 4; *Labor variances*) Hooked-On-Rugs makes a one-design residential four-by-six foot rug. The firm uses a standard costing system. During February 1997, the firm experienced the following direct labor hours and costs:

Standard hours	1,350
Actual hours	1,275
Standard wage rate per hour	$12.00
Actual wage rate per hour	$12.10

   Determine:

   a. total actual labor cost.

    b. standard labor cost.

    c. the labor rate and efficiency variance.

29. (LO 4; *Labor variances*) Jack's Cabinets builds kitchen cabinets in uniform sets. Each set requires a standard quantity of 23.5 direct labor hours. The average standard hourly wage of the crew of cabinetmakers is $16.50. During October 1997, the company built 150 sets. Production required 3,400 hours, and direct labor pay was $58,650. Jack has asked you to analyze direct labor for him.

30. (LO 4; *Overhead variances*) Better Manufacturing Company employs a standard costing system. In the company's Delaware plant, factory overhead is applied to production based on machine hours. The following information is from the Delaware plant's records pertaining to October:

Standard variable factory overhead rate per machine hour	$12
Standard fixed factory overhead rate per machine hour	$10
Standard machine hours for month	2,100
Actual machine hours for month	2,200
Total budgeted monthly fixed factory overhead	$20,000
Actual fixed factory overhead	$21,000
Actual variable factory overhead	$25,850

    Calculate the:

    a. total actual overhead cost.

    b. total applied overhead.

    c. variable overhead variances.

    d. fixed overhead variances.

31. (LO 4; *Overhead Variances*) Office Innovations manufactures a table-top office filing system. The company uses a standard cost system and applies factory overhead to production using direct labor hours. For 1997, budgeted fixed factory overhead was $160,000; budgeted direct labor hours were 20,000; and the standard variable factory overhead rate was set at $12 per direct labor hour. The standard direct labor time per unit is .5 hours. The following data pertain to 1997:

Number of units produced	41,000
Actual direct labor hours	21,000
Actual variable factory overhead cost	$257,250
Actual fixed factory overhead cost	$172,000

    a. Compute the amount of total applied factory overhead.

    b. Compute the total actual cost of factory overhead.

    c. Calculate the variable factory overhead variances.

    d. Calculate the fixed factory overhead variances.

32. (LO 5, 6; *Conversion cost variances*) After automating its facilities in Louisiana, Super Hot Sauce Co. decided to change its standard costing system. The most significant change was to combine direct labor and variable overhead into a single conversion-cost pool. In its first year of implementing the new system, the company set the following standards:

Variable conversion costs per machine hour	$9
Fixed conversion costs (based on 40,000 budgeted machine hours) per machine hour	$8

The following data reflect actual results for the year:

Actual machine hours worked	38,000
Standard machine hours allowed	39,000
Variable conversion costs	$331,500
Fixed conversion costs	$318,000

a. Compute the variable conversion cost variances for the year.

b. Compute the fixed conversion cost variances for the year.

c. Assume this firm only produces goods as they are ordered by customers. What manager in the firm has the greatest control over the fixed conversion cost volume variance? Why?

33. (LO 8; *Appendix*) The following information pertains to 1996 operations of CoolCo., a maker of roof coatings.

Purchase of materials (at standard cost)	$200,000
Standard cost of materials issued to production	184,000
Direct labor (at standard cost)	96,000
Material price variance	3,700 F
Material quantity variance	9,100 U
Direct labor rate variance	2,100 U
Direct labor efficiency variance	3,900 F

a. Record the journal entry for purchasing direct materials on account.

b. Record the journal entry for issuing direct materials into production.

c. Record the journal entry to accrue direct labor costs.

d. Record the year-end journal entry to close the variance accounts. Assume the variances are not material in amount.

■ COMMUNICATION ACTIVITIES

34. (LO 2, 5, 7; *Continuous cost improvement*) *In the brave new world of procurement, customers are treating their suppliers almost like their own employees.*

Vendor sales representatives have desks next to the factory floor. Their badges let them roam wherever they choose, attend production-status meetings, stop by the research lab and click computers onto sales forecasts. Then, they can write a sales order for which the customer is billed.

It's called JIT II, the 1990s version of just-in-time inventory control. The original just-in-time practice can stir up hostility by putting pressure on suppliers; JIT II is designed to create harmony and efficiencies for both sides. Based on sharing of previously guarded data, such as up-to-the-minute sales forecasts, JIT II relies heavily on trust since the companies could face serious conflicts of interest.

Golden Valley [Honeywell's Minnesota plant] now has on hand 15 representatives from 10 suppliers, ranging from printed materials to metals to electronics, who have their own cubicles just off the production floor. Some are technicians working on new product designs. But most are overseeing purchases for existing products, and they think more like a Honeywell employee and look around for ways to trim costs. Honeywell's payoff so far has been inventory levels measured in days rather than weeks or months, 25% fewer purchasing agents, and tips on ways to standardize some parts so they are cheaper to make.

[SOURCE: Fred R. Bleakley, "Strange Bedfellows: Some Companies Let Suppliers Work on Site and Even Place Orders," *Wall Street Journal* (January 13, 1995), pp. A1, A6. Reprinted by permission of The Wall Street Journal, © 1995 Dow Jones & Company, Inc. All Rights Reserved Worldwide.]

a. Does JIT II sound like an effective kaizen costing tool? Explain.

b. Discuss risks that customers bear when they allow suppliers to have access to critical inside information.

c. What types of costs would customers expect to save by having representatives of suppliers on-site? Explain.

d. How would responsibility for purchase price variances be established when vendors are allowed to submit their own purchase orders?

35. (LO 5, 6; *Controlling difficult costs*) Many manufacturing costs are easily controlled by use of a standard costing system and traditional variance analysis. Other organizational costs have historically been more difficult to control. Foremost among costs in this category are costs associated with legal work—both by inside and outside counsel. Adding to the difficulty of controlling costs are certain practices that have evolved in the legal industry, especially those used to account for how time is spent. For example:

■ In an audit of a bill from a New York law firm, an analyst found that one attorney who attended an internal meeting charged for four hours of time; another attorney attending the same meeting charged for two hours.

■ A New York law firm billed a client for an item listed as HVAC on the client billing. Upon inquiry, it was learned that HVAC is an acronym for "heating, ventilation and air conditioning."

■ Attorneys frequently use a time-spent category called "attention to." This category is often a catch-all category for time spent thinking—perhaps while playing golf or driving home from work.

■ Some firms bill for the time spent preparing bills or bill clients for the time it takes to explain why it billed for time spent billing.

■ Other law firms submit bills to clients in which the billed items simply sum to a total different from that which appears on the bill.

[SOURCE: Based on Amy Stevens, "Ten Ways (Some) Lawyers (Sometimes) Fudge Bills," *Wall Street Journal* (January 13, 1995), pp. B1, B10. Reprinted by permission of The Wall Street Journal, © 1995 Dow Jones & Company, Inc. All Rights Reserved Worldwide.]

a. What differences between legal costs and costs such as direct material and direct labor make them more difficult to control?

b. How could concepts used in standard product costing be applied to other costs such as those incurred for legal work?

c. Other than changing costing techniques, what can firms do to control legal costs?

36. (LO 1, 3, 5; *Standard setting*) Mark-Wright, Inc. (MWI) is a specialty frozen food processor located in the midwestern states. Since its founding in 1982, MWI has enjoyed a loyal local clientele that is willing to pay premium prices for the high quality frozen foods it prepares from specialized recipes. In the last two years, the company has experienced rapid sales growth in its operating region and has had many inquiries about supplying its products on a national basis. To meet this growth, MWI expanded its processing capabilities, which resulted in increased production and distribution costs. Furthermore, MWI has been encountering pricing pressure from competitors outside its normal marketing region.

As MWI desires to continue its expansion, Jim Condon, CEO, has engaged a consulting firm to assist MWI in determining its best course of action. The consulting firm concluded that, while premium pricing is sustainable in some areas, if sales growth is to be achieved, MWI must make some price concessions. Also, in order to maintain profit margins, costs must be reduced and controlled. The consulting firm recommended the institution of a standard cost system to better accommodate the changes in demand that can be expected when serving an expanded market area.

Condon met with his management team and explained the recommendations of the consulting firm. Condon then assigned the task of establishing standard costs to his management team. After discussing the situation with their respective staffs, the management team met to review the matter.

Jane Morgan, purchasing manager, advised at that meeting that expanded production would necessitate obtaining basic food supplies from other than MWI's traditional sources. This would entail increased raw material and shipping costs and may result in lower quality supplies. Consequently, these increased costs would need to be made up by the processing department if current cost levels are to be maintained or reduced.

Stan Walters, processing manager, countered that the need to accelerate processing cycles to increase production, coupled with the possibility of receiving lower grade supplies, can be expected to result in a slip in quality and a greater product rejection rate. Under these circumstances, per-unit labor utilization cannot be maintained or reduced, and forecasting future unit labor content becomes very difficult.

Tom Lopez, production engineer, advised that if the equipment is not properly maintained, and thoroughly cleaned at prescribed daily intervals, it can be anticipated that the quality and unique taste of the frozen food products will be affected. Jack Reid, vice-president of sales, stated that if quality cannot be maintained, MWI cannot expect to increase sales to the levels projected.

When Condon was apprised of the problems encountered by his management team, he advised them that if agreement could not be reached on appropriate standards, he would arrange to have them set by the consulting firm, and everyone would have to live with the results.

a. **1.** Describe the major advantages of using a standard cost system.

   2. Describe disadvantages that can result from using a standard cost system.

b. **1.** Identify those who should participate in setting standards and describe the benefits of their participation in the standard-setting process.

   2. Explain the general features and characteristics associated with the introduction and operation of a standard cost system that make it an effective tool for cost control.

c. What would be the consequences if Jim Condon has the standards set by the outside consulting firm?

(CMA)

37. (LO 1, 3, 5; *Implementing a standard cost system*) Some executives believe that it is extremely important to manage "by the numbers." This form of management requires that all employees with departmental or divisional responsibilities spend time understanding the company's operations and how they are reflected by the company's performance reports. Managers are then expected to transmit to their employees a need to be attuned to important signposts that can be detected in performance reports. One of the various numerical measurement systems used by companies is standard costs.

a. Discuss the characteristics that should be present in a standard cost system to encourage positive employee motivation.

b. Discuss how a standard cost system should be implemented to positively motivate employees.

c. The use of variance analysis often results in "management by exception." Discuss the meaning and behavioral implications of "management by exception." Explain how employee behavior could be adversely affected when "actual to standard" comparisons are used as the basis for performance evaluation.

(CMA adapted)

38. (LO 1, 3, 7; *Benefits of a standard cost system*) Standard cost accounting is a powerful concept that is important in finance and marketing. The marketing application of the concept is to develop and manage a balanced portfolio of products. Market share and market growth can be used to classify products for portfolio purposes, and the product classifications are often extended to the organizational units that make the product. The market share/growth classifications can be depicted in the following manner.

		MARKET SHARE	
		High	Low
MARKET GROWTH RATE	High	Rising Star	Question Mark
	Low	Cash Cow	Dog

Question marks are products that show high growth rates but have relatively small market shares, such as new products that are similar to their competitors. Rising stars are high-growth, high-market share products that tend to mature into cash cows. Cash cows are slow-growing, established products that can be "milked" for cash to help the question marks and introduce new products. The dogs are low-growth, low-market share items that are candidates for elimination or segmentation.

Understanding where a product falls within this market share/growth structure is important when applying a standard cost system.

a. Discuss the major advantages of using a standard cost accounting system.

b. Describe the kinds of information that are useful in setting standards and the conditions that must be present to support the use of standard costing.

c. Discuss the applicability or nonapplicability of using standard costing for a product classified as a

    1. cash cow.

    2. question mark.

(CMA)

■ **PROBLEMS**

39. (LO 4; *Material variances*) Wolfe Supply Co. manufactures electrical supply boxes. The company uses a standard costing system. Its standard quantities and costs for one electrical supply box follow:

Direct materials	3 square feet at $1.10 per square foot
Direct labor	6 minutes at $14.00 per hour

In May 1997, 60,000 boxes were produced. The company's purchasing agent bought 195,000 square feet of material in May at $1.11 per square foot. The

May factory payroll reflected $87,420 of direct labor cost for 6,200 hours. In May, 179,000 square feet of direct materials were placed in production.

Calculate material and labor variances. Base the material price variance on the quantity purchased.

40. (LO 4; *Material and labor variances*) Betty's Brooches manufactures brooches using a variety of stock molds. One-eighth of a pound of direct material and 15 minutes of direct labor are required to produce a brooch. Direct material cost $5.20 per pound at standard, and the standard direct labor rate is $12.00 per hour.

During April, 32,000 brooches were made, and the company experienced a $130 unfavorable material quantity variance. The purchasing agent had purchased 800 pounds of material more than the company used, incurring a favorable price variance of $965. Total direct labor hours worked were 8,200, and a total unfavorable labor variance of $1,580 was incurred.

Determine the following:

a. Standard quantity of material allowed
b. Actual quantity of material used
c. Actual quantity of material purchased
d. Actual price of material purchased
e. Standard hours allowed for production
f. Labor efficiency variance
g. Labor rate variance
h. Actual labor rate paid

41. (LO 4; *Labor variances*) For each of the following independent cases, supply the missing amounts:

	CASE 1	CASE 2	CASE 3	CASE 4
Units produced	600	(d)	310	215
Standard hours per unit	2	.3	(g)	(j)
Standard hours allowed	(a)	1,200	930	(k)
Standard rate per hour	$5	(e)	$9.50	$8
Actual hours worked	1,230	1,170	(h)	450
Actual labor cost	(b)	(f)	$3,230	$3,645
Labor rate variance	$62 U	$117 U	$475 F	(l)
Labor efficiency variance	(c)	$360 F	(i)	$160 U

42. (LO 4, 5; *Overhead variances*) Carroll Industries makes a very popular 36-inch window shade. Standard time and costs per stock window shade follow:

Machine time (hours)	.20
VOH rate per machine hour	$8.50
FOH rate per machine hour	$6.50

During 1995, the following operating statistics were compiled:

Total fixed factory overhead applied to production	$715,000
Actual variable factory overhead	937,400
Actual fixed factory overhead	709,000
Volume variance	17,000 F
Variable factory overhead spending variance	10,900 U

a. For fixed factory overhead, calculate the following:

1. Standard machine hours allowed

2. Number of window shades produced

3. Budgeted FOH

4. Expected annual capacity in machine hours

5. Fixed factory overhead spending variance

6. Fixed factory overhead total variance

b. For variable factory overhead, calculate the following:

1. Total applied variable factory overhead

2. Total variable factory overhead variance

3. Actual machine hours incurred

4. Variable factory overhead efficiency variance

c. Assume you are the president of Carroll Industries and you are curious about the causes of the variable factory overhead spending variance. Who would you call to explain the variance? Defend your answer.

43. (LO 4, 5; *All variances*) Patio Solutions manufactures picnic table kits that are sold in various large discount department stores. The standard cost card indicates the following costs are incurred to produce a single picnic table kit:

60 board feet of pine lumber	$54
2 pipe frame units	18
1 package of fasteners	8
.5 hours of direct labor at $14 per hour	7
Variable factory overhead at $20 per machine hour	4
Fixed factory overhead at $15 per machine hour*	3
Total	$94

*Based on budgeted annual FOH of $30,000 and expected annual capacity of 2,000 hours.

During 1997, the firm had the following actual data related to the production of 11,000 picnic table kits:

PURCHASE AND USAGE OF MATERIALS

Lumber	690,000	board feet at $.85 per board foot
Pipe frame units	22,250	units at $9.10 per unit
Packages of fasteners	11,120	packages at $6.90 per package

DIRECT LABOR USED

5,600 hours at $14.20 per hour

FACTORY OVERHEAD COSTS

Actual machine hours recorded	2,000
Actual variable factory overhead incurred	$38,000
Actual fixed factory overhead incurred	$32,300

a. Calculate materials, labor, and overhead variances.

b. Provide a possible explanation for each variance computed.

44. (LO 4, 5, 7; *Material and labor standards*) As part of its cost control program, Tracer Company uses a standard cost system for all manufactured items. The standard cost for each item is established at the beginning of the fiscal year, and the standards are not revised until the beginning of the next fiscal year. Changes

in costs, caused during the year by changes in material or labor inputs or by changes in the manufacturing process, are recognized as they occur by the inclusion of planned variances in Tracer's monthly operating budgets.

The following labor standard was established for one of Tracer's products, effective June 1, 1996, the beginning of the fiscal year.

Assembler A labor (5 hours at $10 per hour)	$ 50
Assembler B labor (3 hours at $11 per hour)	33
Machinist labor (2 hours at $15 per hour)	30
Standard cost per 100 units	$113

The standard was based on the assumption that the labor would be performed by a team consisting of five persons with Assembler A skills, three persons with Assembler B skills, and two persons with machinist skills; this team represents the most efficient use of the company's skilled employees. The standard also assumed that the quality of material that had been used in prior years would be available for the coming year.

For the first seven months of the fiscal year, actual manufacturing costs at Tracer have been within the standards established. However, the company has received a significant increase in orders, and there is an insufficient number of skilled workers available to meet the increased production. Therefore, beginning in January, the production teams will consist of eight persons with Assembler A skills, one person with Assembler B skills, and one person with machinist skills. The reorganized teams will work more slowly than the normal teams, and as a result, only 80 units will be produced in the time in which 100 units would normally be produced. Faulty work has never been a cause for units to be rejected in the final inspection process, and it is not expected to be a cause for rejection with the reorganized teams.

Furthermore, Tracer has been notified by its material supplier that a lower-quality material will be supplied beginning January 1. Normally, one unit of raw material is required for each good unit produced, and no units are lost because of defective material. Tracer estimates that 6 percent of the units manufactured after January 1 will be rejected in the final inspection process because of defective material.

a. Determine the number of units of lower-quality material that Tracer Company must enter into production to produce 35,720 good finished units.

b. Without regard to your answer in part a, assume that Tracer must manufacture a total of 50,000 units in January to have sufficient good units to fill the order received.

   1. Determine how many hours of each class of labor will be needed to manufacture a total of 50,000 units in January.

   2. Determine the amount that should be included in Tracer's January operating budget for the planned labor variance caused by the reorganization of the labor teams and the lower-quality material, and indicate how much of the planned variance can be attributed to (a) the change in material and (b) the reorganization of the labor teams.

(CMA adapted)

45. (LO 4, 5; *Multiple variances*) Lieto Stamping Company manufactures a variety of products made of plastic and aluminum components. During the winter months, substantially all production capacity is devoted to the production of lawn sprinklers for the following spring and summer seasons. Because a variety of products are made throughout the year, factory volume is measured by direct labor hours rather than units of product.

The company has developed the following standards for the production of a lawn sprinkler:

Direct materials:		
Aluminum	.2 pounds at $.40 per pound	$ .08
Plastic	1.0 pounds at $.38 per pound	.38
Direct labor	.3 hours at $4.00 per hour	1.20
Factory overhead:		
Variable	.3 hours at $1.60 per hour	.48
Fixed*	.3 hours at $1.20 per hour	.36

*Based on expected annual capacity of 30,000 direct labor hours.

During February 1997, 8,500 good sprinklers were manufactured, and the following costs were incurred and charged to production:

MATERIALS REQUISITIONED FOR PRODUCTION:

Aluminum	1,900 pounds at $.40 per pound	$ 760
Plastic		
Regular grade	6,000 pounds at $.38 per pound	2,280
Low grade*	3,500 pounds at $.38 per pound	1,330

DIRECT LABOR:

Regular time	2,300 hours at $4.00 per hour	9,200
Overtime	400 hours at $6.00 per hour	2,400

FACTORY OVERHEAD

Variable	5,200
Fixed	3,100
Total costs charged to production	$24,270

*Because of plastic shortages, the company was forced to purchase lower-grade plastic than called for in the standards. This increased the number of sprinklers rejected on inspection.

Material price variances are charged to a material price variance account at the time the invoice is entered. All materials are carried in inventory at standard prices. Material purchases for February were:

Aluminum	1,800 pounds at $.48 per pound	$ 864
Plastic		
Regular grade	3,000 pounds at $.50 per pound	1,500
Low grade*	6,000 pounds at $.29 per pound	1,740

a. What is the total difference between standard and actual cost for production in February?

b. Compute the labor rate variance.

c. Compute the fixed factory overhead spending variance.

d. Compute the volume variance.

e. The standard material quantities already include an allowance for acceptable material scrap loss. In this situation, what is the likely cause of the material usage variance?

(CMA adapted)

46. (LO 6; *Conversion cost variances*) Otterdam Resources, Inc., uses a standard costing system in its pipe manufacturing facility in central Mexico. Because the company is automated and direct labor costs are relatively low compared with machine-related expenses, the company uses a conversion cost pool instead of separate cost pools for direct labor and overhead. For 1997, standards were set as follows:

Variable conversion cost rate	$14 per machine hour
Fixed conversion cost rate*	$20 per machine hour

*Based on 5,000 expected machine hours.

At standard, one machine hour is required to produce 50 feet of pipe. For 1997, the company actually produced 300,000 feet of pipe, worked 5,800 machine hours, and incurred the following costs:

Variable conversion costs	$ 75,400
Fixed conversion costs	102,500

For 1997, compute the following:

a. the two variable conversion costs variances; and
b. the two fixed conversion cost variances.

47. (LO 4, 8; *All variances; Appendix*) Garden Mills Inc. established the following standards for 1997 for its principal product, a kit to convert ordinary lawn mowers into mulching mowers:

DIRECT MATERIALS

Mower blades	2 blades at $13 per blade	$26
Universal adapter kit	1 kit at $6 per kit	6

DIRECT LABOR

Grinding process	1/2 hour at $14 per hour	7
Finishing and testing	2/3 hour at $12 per hour	8

FACTORY OVERHEAD

Variable	$8 per machine hour	4
Fixed*	$12 per machine hour	6
Total cost per kit		$57

* Based on expected production of 5,000 mulching mower kits.

Actual results for producing 5,400 kits in 1997 follow:

Mower blades purchased	11,300 blades at $12.75 per blade
Mower blades used	10,900 blades
Universal adapter kits purchased	5,900 kits at $5.60 per kit
Universal adapter kits used	5,650 kits
Grinding process actual labor cost	$42,000 based on 2,800 DLHs
Finishing and testing actual labor cost	$45,325 based on 3,700 DLHs
Actual machine hours worked	2,900 MHs
Actual variable factory overhead	$22,910
Actual fixed factory overhead	$33,000

   a. Prepare the journal entries to recognize the following:

      1. Purchase of direct materials on account.

      2. Issuance of direct materials to production.

      3. Incurrence of direct labor cost (credit wages payable).

      4. Incurrence of manufacturing overhead cost.

      5. Application of manufacturing overhead cost to production.

      6. Closing of any year-end balance in factory overhead.

      7. Transfer of completed production to finished goods.

      8. Sale of 4,000 kits for $425,000.

   b. Close all variances; assume they are not significant in amount.

   c. If, collectively, the variances were significant in amount, how would your closing entry have differed from that shown for part b?

48. (LO 4, 5; *Direct labor variances*) Day-Mold was founded several years ago by two designers who had developed several popular lines of living room, dining room, and bedroom furniture for other companies. The designers believed that their design for dinette sets could be standardized and would sell well. They formed their own company and soon had all the orders they could complete in their small plant in Dayton, Ohio.

   From the beginning, the firm was successful. The owners bought a microcomputer and software that produced financial statements, which an employee prepared. The owners thought that the information they needed was contained in these statements.

   Recently, however, the employees have been requesting raises. The owners wonder how to evaluate the employees' requests. At the suggestion of Day-Mold's CPA, the owners have hired a consultant to implement a standard cost system. The consultant believes that the calculation of variances will aid management in setting responsibility for labor's performance.

   The supervisors believe that, under normal conditions, a dinette set can be assembled with five hours of direct labor costing $20 per hour. The consultant has assembled labor cost information for the most recent month and would like your advice in calculating direct labor variances.

   During the month, the actual direct labor wages paid were $127,600 to employees who worked 5,800 hours. The factory produced 1,200 dinette sets during the month.

   a. Using the previous information, prepare variance computations for management's consideration. (Hint: Under the conventional approach, there will be a direct labor efficiency variance, a direct labor rate variance, and a total direct labor variance. Under a different logical approach, there will be a direct labor efficiency variance, a direct labor rate variance, a direct labor "joint" variance, and a total direct labor variance.)

   b. Contrast these two approaches and make some recommendations to management.

   [SOURCE: Nabil Hassan and Sarah Palmer, "Management Accounting Case Study: Day-Mold," *Management Accounting Campus Report* (Spring 1990). Copyright © 1990 IMA (formerly NAA).]

49. (LO 4, 7; *Overhead variances*) Fooland Chemicals uses a standard cost system for planning and control purposes. For 1997, the firm expected to produce 4,000 units of product. At that level of production, its expected costs for factory overhead were:

Variable	$ 9,600
Fixed	$24,000

At standard, two machine hours are required to produce a single unit of product. Actual results for 1997 follow:

Units produced	4,200
Machine hours worked	8,600
Actual variable factory overhead	$ 9,460
Actual fixed factory overhead	$24,900

a. Calculate standard hours allowed for actual output.
b. Calculate all overhead variances.
c. For 1998, the firm is considering automating a production process that is currently performed manually. In its standard cost system, which standards would likely be affected by such a change? Explain. What individuals would likely be consulted to assist in revising the standards?

50. (LO 4; *All variances; process costing*) Southerland Company uses standard costs with its process costing system. Standard costs for the molding process are as follows:

Direct material	$4
Direct labor	4
Variable factory overhead	2
Fixed factory overhead*	2

*Based on expected capacity of 20,000 units per month

All direct material is added at the beginning of the process. Conversion costs are added continually throughout the process. Operating results for the month were as follows:

Beginning WIP inventory (60% complete as to labor and OH)	4,000 units
Units started during the month	20,000 units
Ending WIP inventory (40% complete as to labor and OH)	6,000 units
Actual costs incurred during the month:	
Direct material	$75,000
Direct labor	80,000
Variable factory overhead	42,000
Fixed factory overhead	45,000

a. Compute the total direct material and direct labor variances for the month. (Hint: Remember to first compute equivalent units of production; see Chapter 7.)
b. Calculate the standard cost of goods manufactured.
c. Compute the total variance for variable factory overhead and the total variance for fixed factory overhead.
d. What additional information would you need to compute the variable factory overhead spending and efficiency variances?

51. (LO 3, 5, 7; *Material and labor standards*) ColdKing Company is a small producer of fruit-flavored frozen desserts. For many years, ColdKing's products have had strong regional sales on the basis of brand recognition; however, other companies have begun marketing similar products in the area, and price competition has become increasingly important. John Wakefield, the company's controller, is planning to implement a standard cost system for ColdKing and has gathered considerable information from his coworkers on production and material requirements for ColdKing's products. Wakefield believes that the use of standard costing will allow ColdKing to improve cost control and make better pricing decisions.

ColdKing's most popular product is raspberry sherbet. The sherbet is produced in 10-gallon batches, and each batch requires six quarts of good raspberries. The fresh raspberries are sorted by hand before they enter the production process. Because of imperfections in the raspberries and normal spoilage, one quart of berries is discarded for every four quarts of acceptable berries. Three minutes is the standard direct labor time for the sorting that is required to obtain one quart of acceptable raspberries. The acceptable raspberries are then blended with other ingredients; blending requires 12 minutes of direct labor time per batch. During blending, there is some loss of materials. After blending, the sherbet is packaged in quart containers. Wakefield has gathered the following cost information:

- ColdKing purchases raspberries at a cost of $.80 per quart.
- All other ingredients cost a total of $.45 per gallon.
- Direct labor is paid at the rate of $9 per hour.
- The total cost of material and labor required to package the sherbet is $.38 per quart.

a. Develop the standard cost for each direct cost component and the total cost of a 10-gallon batch of raspberry sherbet. The standard cost should identify the

   1. standard quantity,
   2. standard rate, and
   3. standard cost per batch.

b. As part of the implementation of a standard cost system at ColdKing, John Wakefield plans to train those responsible for maintaining the standards on how to use variance analysis. Wakefield is particularly concerned with the causes of unfavorable variances.

   1. Discuss the possible causes of unfavorable material price variances, and identify the individual(s) who should be held responsible for these variances.

   2. Discuss the possible causes of unfavorable labor efficiency variances, and identify the individual(s) who should be responsible for these variances.

c. Assume you have just graduated from college with a degree in accounting and you have been hired by ColdKing. Your first assignment is to develop a new standard for the quantity of raspberries used in production. Your supervisor, the controller, has indicated that a new standard is needed because the year-to-year change in the material quantity variance is simply unpredictable and seems to be unrelated to the effectiveness of production controls. One of your friends who also recently graduated from college has a degree in agronomy; another has a degree in meteorology. How might your two friends assist you in developing a flexible quantity standard?

(CMA adapted)

■ CASES

52. (LO 3, 5, 6; *Revision of standards*) NuLathe Company produces a turbo engine component for jet aircraft manufacturers. A standard cost system has been used for years with good results.

Unfortunately, NuLathe has recently experienced production problems. The source for its direct material went out of business. The new source produces a similar but higher-quality material. The price per pound from the original source had averaged $7, while the price from the new source is $7.77. The use of the new material results in a reduction of scrap. This scrap reduction reduces the actual consumption of direct material from 1.25 to 1 pound per unit. In addition, the direct labor is reduced from 24 to 22 minutes per unit because there is less scrap labor and machine setup time.

At the same time NuLathe was changing its material source, it was also engaging in labor negotiations. The negotiations resulted in an increase of over 14 percent in hourly direct labor costs. The average rate rose from $12.60 per hour to $14.40 per hour. Production of the main product requires a high level of labor skill. Because of a continuing shortage in that skill area, an interim wage agreement had to be signed.

NuLathe started using the new direct material on April 1, the same date on which the new labor agreement went into effect. NuLathe has been using standards that were set at the beginning of the calendar year. The direct material and direct labor standards for the turbo engine component are as follows:

Direct material	1.2 pounds at $6.80 per pound	$ 8.16
Direct Labor	20 minutes at $12.30 per DLH	4.10
Standard prime cost per unit		$12.26

Howard Foster, management accounting supervisor, was examining a performance report that he had prepared at the close of business on April 30. The report follows:

PERFORMANCE REPORT

Standard Cost Variance Analysis for April 1997

	Standard	Price Variance			Quantity Variance			Actual
DM	$ 8.16	($ .97 × 1.0)	=	$.97 U	($ 6.80 × .2)	=	$1.36 F	$ 7.77
DL	4.10	[$2.10 × (22/60)]=		.77 U	[$12.30 × (2/60)]	=	.41 U	5.28
	$12.26							$13.05

Comparison of 1997 Actual Costs

	1st Quarter Costs	April Costs	%Increase (Decrease)
DM	$ 8.75	$ 7.77	(11.2)%
DL	5.04	5.28	4.8 %
	$13.79	$13.05	(5.4)%

Jane Keene, assistant controller, came into Foster's office, and Foster said, "Jane, look at this performance report! Direct material price increased 11 percent, and the labor rate increased over 14 percent during April. I expected greater variances, yet prime costs decreased over 5 percent from the $13.79 we experienced during the first quarter of this year. The proper message just isn't coming through."

"This has been an unusual period," said Keene. "With all the unforeseen changes, perhaps we should revise our standards based on current conditions and start over."

Foster replied, "I think we can retain the current standards but expand the variance analysis. We could calculate variances for the specific changes that have occurred to direct material and direct labor before we calculate the normal price and quantity variances. What I really think would be useful to management right now is to determine the impact the changes in direct material and direct labor had in reducing our prime costs per unit from $13.79 in the first quarter to $13.05 in April—a reduction of $.74."

a. Discuss the advantages of (1) immediately revising the standards and (2) retaining the current standards and expanding the analysis of variances.

b. Prepare an analysis to explain the impact the new direct material source and new labor contract had on reducing NuLathe's prime costs per unit from $13.79 to $13.05. The analysis should show the changes in prime costs per unit that are caused by (1) the use of new direct material and (2) the new labor contract. This analysis should contain sufficient detail to identify the changes caused by direct material price, direct labor rate, the effect of direct material quality on material usage, and the effect of direct material quality on direct labor usage.

(CMA adapted)

53. (LO 4, 5; *Variances and behavior*) Funtime, Inc., manufactures video game machines. Market saturation and technological innovations have created pricing pressures, which have resulted in declining profits. To stem the slide in profits until new products can be introduced, top management has turned its attention to both manufacturing economies and increased production. An incentive program has been developed to reward managers who contribute to an increase in the number of units produced and effect cost reductions.

The production managers have responded to the pressure of improving manufacturing in several ways, which have resulted in an increase in completed units over normal production levels. The video game machines are put together by the Assembly Group, which requires parts from the Printed Circuit Boards (PCB) and Reading Heads (RH) groups. To increase production levels, the PCB and RH groups have begun to reject parts that previously would have been tested and modified to meet manufacturing standards. Preventive maintenance on machines used in the production of these parts has been postponed with only emergency repair work being performed to keep production lines moving. The Maintenance Department is concerned that there will be serious breakdowns and unsafe operating conditions.

The more aggressive Assembly Group production supervisors have pressured maintenance personnel to attend to their machines at the expense of other groups. This has resulted in machine downtime in the PCB and RH groups, which, when coupled with demands for accelerated parts delivery by the Assembly Group, has led to more frequent parts rejections and increased friction among departments.

Funtime operates under a standard cost system. The standard costs for video game machines are as follows:

	STANDARDS PER UNIT		
Cost Item	Quantity	Cost	Total
Direct materials			
Housing unit	1	$20	$ 20
Printed circuit boards	2	15	30
Reading heads	4	10	40
Direct labor			
Assembly group	2 hours	8	16
PCB group	1 hour	9	9
RH group	1.5 hours	10	15
Variable overhead	4.5 hours	2	9
Total standard cost per unit			$139

Funtime prepares monthly reports based on standard costs. The report for May 1997, when production and sales both reached 2,200 units follows.

	BUDGET	ACTUAL	VARIANCE
Units	2,000	2,200	200 F
Variable costs			
Direct materials	$180,000	$220,400	$40,400 U
Direct labor	80,000	93,460	13,460 U
Variable overhead	18,000	18,800	800 U
Total variable costs	$278,000	$332,660	$54,660 U

Funtime's top management was surprised by the unfavorable variances. Janice Rath, management accountant, was assigned to identify and report on the reasons for the unfavorable variances as well as the individuals or groups responsible. After review, Rath prepared the following usage report:

COST ITEM	QUANTITY	ACTUAL COST
Direct materials		
Housing unit	2,200 units	$ 44,000
Printed circuit boards	4,700 units	75,200
Reading heads	9,200 units	101,200
Direct labor		
Assembly group	3,900 hours	31,200
PCB group	2,400 hours	23,760
RH group	3,500 hours	38,500
Variable overhead	9,900 hours	18,800
Total variable cost		$332,660

Rath reported that the PCB and RH groups supported the increased production levels but experienced abnormal machine downtime. This, in turn, caused idle time, which required the use of overtime to keep up with the accelerated demand for parts. The idle time was charged to direct labor. Rath also reported that the production managers of these two groups resorted to parts rejections, as opposed to testing and modification procedures formerly applied. Rath determined that the Assembly Group met management's objectives by increasing production while utilizing fewer hours than standard.

a. For May 1997, Funtime's labor rate variance was $5,660 unfavorable, and the labor efficiency variance was $200 favorable. Calculate the following variances,

    1. Material price variance

    2. Material quantity variance

    3. Variable overhead efficiency variance

    4. Variable overhead spending variance

  b. Using all six variances from part a, prepare an explanation of the $54,660 unfavorable variance between budgeted and actual costs for May 1997.

  c. **1.** Identify and briefly explain the behavioral factors that may promote friction among the production managers and the maintenance manager.

    2. Evaluate Janice Rath's analysis of the unfavorable results in terms of its completeness and its effect on the behavior of the production groups.

(CMA adapted)

■ ETHICS AND QUALITY DISCUSSIONS

54. To remain competitive, manufacturing companies are giving suppliers more responsibility in the design of their new products. A few notable examples follow:

- ■ Whirlpool Corporation is developing its first gas-burning stove and is hiring no engineers to develop the burner. Instead it is relying on Eaton Corporation, its supplier, to design the burner. Eaton already produces components for gas ranges for other appliance makers.

- ■ Chrysler Corporation uses its suppliers to design many components—from drive shafts to car seats.

- ■ McDonnell Douglas is expecting to trim $300 to $500 million from the development cost of its new 100-seat plane. It is doing so by having its suppliers bear much of the research and development effort.

However, it is worth noting the outcome of another experience where one American industry relied extensively on its suppliers: "In the 1960s, the then-dominant U.S. television industry gave the technology to build picture tubes to low-cost Asian suppliers; a few years later, the Asians began manufacturing entire TV sets, and the U.S. industry nearly went out of business."

[SOURCE: Based on Neal Templin and Jeff Cole, "Manufacturers Use Suppliers to Help Them Develop New Products," *Wall Street Journal* (December 19, 1994), pp. A1, A6. Reprinted by permission of The Wall Street Journal, © 1994 Dow Jones & Company, Inc. All Rights Reserved Worldwide.]

  a. What relative advantages do companies gain by involving suppliers in conducting target costing and other analysis for new products?

  b. What quality considerations should be taken into account in turning product design over to suppliers?

  c. What are the risks of involving suppliers in product design?

55. *Vickers PLC is expected to announce that Bayerische Moteren Werke AG [BMW] will become a strategic partner, supplying it with technical advice and parts for new models of Bentley and Rolls-Royce luxury cars, according to a person familiar with the companies.*

*   Vickers, with engineering and aerospace interests, has been seeking a partner because the cost of developing new models—estimated at [$234 million to $312 million]—has become too high to shoulder alone, given the small number of cars made each year by Rolls-Royce.*

Under the cooperation agreement, BMW will provide Rolls-Royce with an array of technical and engineering consulting services. Although Rolls-Royce's design will be kept largely in Rolls-Royce's hands, BMW will provide the company with facilities and engineering know-how to test, refine and adapt the design.

[SOURCE: Audrey Choi and Lawrence Ingrassia, "BMW Is Expected to Help Vickers PLC Develop New Rolls-Royce, Bentley Cars," *Wall Street Journal* (December 19, 1994), p. A10. Reprinted by permission of The Wall Street Journal, © 1994 Dow Jones & Company, Inc. All Rights Reserved Worldwide.]

a. Why would BMW be willing to provide technical advice to a competitor in the luxury car market?

b. How is the agreement likely to benefit Vickers in terms of the quality of its product? In terms of its ability to control costs?

56. Mera O'Brien was hired a month ago at the Jackson Division of the Denver Manufacturing Company. O'Brien supervises plant production and is paid $6,500 per month. In addition, her contract calls for a percentage bonus based on cost control. The company president has defined cost control as "the ability to obtain favorable cost variances from the standards provided."

After one month, O'Brien realized that the standards that were used at the Jackson Division were outdated. Since the last revision of standards, the Jackson Division had undergone some significant plant layout changes and installed some automated equipment, both of which reduced labor time considerably. However, by the time she realized the errors in the standards, she had received her first month's bonus check of $5,000.

a. Since the setting of the standards and the definition of her bonus arrangement were not her doing, O'Brien does not feel compelled to discuss the errors in the standards with the company president. Besides, O'Brien wants to buy a red turbo Porsche. Discuss the ethics of her not discussing the errors in the standards and/or the problems with the definition of cost control with the company president.

b. Assume instead that O'Brien has an elderly mother who has just been placed in a nursing home. The older O'Brien is quite ill and has no income. The younger O'Brien lives in an efficiency apartment and drives a six-year-old car so that she can send the majority of her earnings to the nursing home to provide for her mother. Discuss the ethics of her not discussing the errors in the standards and/or the problems with the definition of cost control with the company president.

c. Assume again the facts in part b. Also assume that the company president plans to review and revise, if necessary, all production standards at the Jackson Division next year. Discuss what may occur if O'Brien does not inform the president of the problems with the standards at the current time. Discuss what may occur if O'Brien informs the president of all the facts, both professional and personal. Can you suggest a way in which she may keep a bonus and still have the standards revised? (Consider the fact that the standard cost has implications for sales prices.)

57. *[Levi Strauss & Co. is a world leader among businesses in the regard it gives to human rights. Its consideration of human rights extends beyond its own employees to evaluation of the policies and practices of governments in countries in which it operates. Based on China's record of human rights violations, Levi Strauss & Co. made the decision to pull out of the country in 1993.]*

The decision could hurt Levi's future sales in China, although the U.S. apparel company said its current sales are minuscule because its clothing isn't being mass-marketed.

The move won't hurt China much economically, because Levi hadn't yet made any direct investment there. Levi intends to phase out its relatively small purchases of about $50 million annually in trousers and shirts from its Chinese sewing and laundry contractors.

Still, the pullout of a highly visible U.S. company, whose trademark jeans are synonymous with Western capitalism, is likely to add to the debate in Washington over whether to continue China's trade status as a most-favored nation for another year. China's MFN status, which qualifies its imports for the lowest U.S. tariffs, [expired June 3, 1993]. China has been accorded the favored status since the Carter years.

[SOURCE: Jim Carlton, "Ties with China Will Be Severed by Levi Strauss," *Wall Street Journal* (May 4, 1993), p. A3. Reprinted by permission of The Wall Street Journal, © 1993 Dow Jones & Company, Inc. All Rights Reserved Worldwide.]

  a. Discuss the Levi Strauss decision to leave China from both an ethical perspective and a cost management perspective.
  b. Why is the U.S. government likely to continue most-favored nation trade status for China?
  c. As a stockholder of Levi Strauss & Co., how would you react to the company's decision to pull out of China?

58. Flower Mound Corporation needs to hire four factory workers who can run robotic equipment and route products through processing. All factory space is on a single floor. Labor standards have been set for product manufacturing.

At this time, the company has had 10 experienced people apply for the available jobs. One of the applicants is David Sima. David is paralyzed and uses a wheelchair. He has several years experience using the robotic equipment, but for him to use the equipment, the controls must be placed on a special panel and lowered. Willie Roberts, the personnel director, has interviewed David and has decided against hiring him because Willie does not believe David can work "up to the current labor standard."

  a. How, if at all, would hiring a person with a physical disability affect labor variances (both rate and hours) if the standards had been set based on workers without physical disabilities?
  b. If a supervisor has decided to hire a worker with a physical disability, how (if at all) should that worker's performance evaluations be affected?
  c. What are the ethical implications of hiring people with physical disabilities in preference to those without physical disabilities? What are the ethical implications of hiring the people without physical disabilities in preference to those with physical disabilities?
  d. On what bases should Willie Roberts make his decision to hire or not hire David Sima? Discuss what you believe to be the appropriate decision process. (Hint: Investigate the implications of the Americans with Disabilities Act before answering this question.)

■ PROJECTS

59. Invite a representative of the accounting department of an industrial firm that uses standard costing to address your class. Ask the representative to discuss in his or her presentation, the following features of his or her company's standard costing system:

  a. How standards are set for materials, labor, and overhead
  b. The frequency and nature of variance analysis
  c. The process for revising standards
  d. How the standard cost system has been affected by technological evolution.

60. *In an industry desperate for a flight plan to profits and obsessed with Southwest Airlines'*
prosperity, Continental seemingly had found the right route. Over the past 18 months,
it turned half its 2,000 flights into a low-fare, short-haul service. Investors, analysts and
even travelers cheered, at first. UAL Corp.'s United Airlines and USAir Group Inc.
quickly followed suit on certain routes, and other carriers lamented that they couldn't
change so easily.

But corporate strategies aren't easily copied. Continental's "Lite" service has cost the
carrier millions of dollars and led to the ousting of its chief executive officer. Another
high-ranking executive apparently is on his way out. Now the airline, which managed
to alienate passengers, frequent fliers, corporate clients and travel agents, is quietly
rescinding many of the changes it made only last year. Its schedule, starting [January 10,
1995], will drop Lite flights that are losing money.

"To try to sit back and say I'm going to be Southwest tomorrow, when you have a dif-
ferent underlying structure, doesn't work," says Jon Ash, managing director of Global
Aviation Associates, a consulting firm in Washington.

[SOURCE: Bridget O'Brian, "Continental CALite Hits Some Turbulence in Battling Southwest,"
Wall Street Journal (January 10, 1995), pp. A1, A4. Reprinted by permission of The Wall Street
Journal, © 1995 Dow Jones & Company, Inc. All Rights Reserved Worldwide.]

Southwest Airlines enjoys a cost advantage in the airline industry that has
given it a competitive edge for a number of years. Divide your class into teams
and develop strategies to launch an airline that will compete against Southwest.
In developing strategies, teams should employ concepts discussed in this chapter, especially target costing. Each team should produce a report summarizing its
strategy.

PROCESS COSTING

> *There must necessarily be, at the close of the period, a general mixture of unfinished work in each department which ranges from work on which manufacture has just begun to that on which it is just about to be completed. Inability to identify each lot and to determine the actual cost expended upon it makes it necessary to rely on some method of estimating the cost of unfinished work.*
>
> W.B. Lawrence, *Cost Accounting* (Prentice-Hall), 1937

LEARNING OBJECTIVES

1. Differentiate process costing from job order product costing.

2. Understand why equivalent units of production are used in process costing.

3. Compute equivalent units of production using the weighted average and FIFO methods of process costing.

4. Calculate unit costs and inventory values using the weighted average and FIFO methods of process costing.

5. Understand how standard costs are used in a process costing system.

6. Determine how multidepartment processing affects the computation of equivalent units of production.

7. Discuss how quality control can minimize spoilage.

8. (Appendix) Prepare journal entries for a process costing system.

Marguerite's Cakes: Bakery Makes Royal Treats

Marguerite's Cakes was started in New Orleans in 1982 by Marlene Schroeder. At that time, the company produced King Cakes only during Carnival season from January 6 (Epiphany) through Mardi Gras (the day before Ash Wednesday). The King Cake tradition was begun in France and originally related to weekly royal balls held to help celebrate Mardi Gras. Now, in New Orleans, King Cake parties take place throughout the city during Carnival. Hidden within each cake is a plastic doll. Whoever finds the doll is responsible for hosting the following week's King Cake party.

To make its King Cakes, Marguerite's buys sweet dough manufactured to specifications from a vendor in 100-pound containers. Small quantities of the dough are passed through a rolling machine that flattens the dough into a 40-inch elongated strip, the edges of which are trimmed straight. The strip is flavored with spices and, if desired, fillings are added. The strip is then halved lengthwise and the two strips are braided. The ends are connected to form an oval. The cake dough is left to rise and then baked. The baked cake is decorated with sugar icing in the traditional Mardi Gras colors (purple, green, and gold), and the doll is inserted in the underside of the cake. Of the total King Cakes produced by the bakery in 1994, 80 percent were plain cinnamon and 20 percent contained other fillings.

Success at this single operation caused Ms. Schroeder to undertake other baking activities, and Marguerite's has grown into a full-line bakery. King Cakes are still produced, but not only at Carnival time. The market area for King Cakes has expanded because tourists to the city have found the cakes to be excellent souvenirs. Approximately 1.3 million King Cakes are produced in the city by 25 bakeries. Nationwide shipments have been made possible by overnight delivery services.

SOURCE: Information provided by Marlene and Ron Schroeder, 1994.

---

process costing

The mass production of King Cakes is totally unlike the job order production process discussed in Chapter 4. Marguerite's Cakes, like many other food producers, uses **process costing** to determine the product cost of its King Cakes. This costing method accumulates and assigns costs to units of production in companies that make large quantities of homogeneous products in a continuous production process. Process costing is also used by manufacturers of bricks, gasoline, steel, paper, automobiles, and appliances.

This chapter illustrates the two methods of calculating unit cost in a process costing system: the weighted average and FIFO methods. Once unit cost is determined, total costs are assigned to the units transferred out of a department and to that department's ending Work in Process Inventory.

INTRODUCTION TO PROCESS COSTING

■ **LEARNING OBJECTIVE 1**
Differentiate process costing from job order product costing.

In some ways, the cost accumulation in a process costing system is similar to job order product costing procedures. In a process costing system, as in a job order system, costs are accumulated by cost component in each production department. As units are transferred from one department to the next, unit costs are also transferred, so that a total production cost is accumulated by the end of production. In a job order system, accumulated departmental costs are assigned to specific jobs, which may be single units or batches of units. In contrast, in a process costing system, accumulated departmental costs are assigned to all the units that flowed through that department during the period. As indicated in Chapter 4 (Exhibit 4–1), the measurement method chosen (actual, normal, or standard) affects which costs are included in the inventory accounts.

The two basic differences between job order and process costing are (1) the quantity of production for which costs are being accumulated at any one time and (2) the cost object to which the costs are assigned. For example, an entrepreneur who bakes cookies at home for specific orders would use a job order product costing system. The costs of the direct materials, direct labor, and factory overhead associated with production of each baking job would be gathered and assigned to the individual jobs. The cost per cookie could be determined if all the cookies baked for the job were similar.

In contrast, bakeries such as Entenmann's, which makes over 2 million cookies a week, would not use a job order system because volume is simply too great and the cookies are reasonably homogeneous. At Entenmann's, direct materials, direct labor, and factory overhead costs could be gathered during the period for each department and each product. Since a variety of cookies are produced in any department during a period, the costs assignable to each type of product must be individually designated and attached to each type of cookie. Costs are then assigned to the products worked on during the period. Production does not have to be complete for costs to be assigned in a process costing system.

As shown in Exhibit 7–1, the costs of inventory components are accumulated in the accounts as the inventory flows through the production process. At the end of production, the accumulated costs must be assigned to all the units produced to determine the cost per unit for purposes of inventory measurement and calculation of cost of goods sold.

■ **EXHIBIT 7–1**
Flow of Costs Through Production

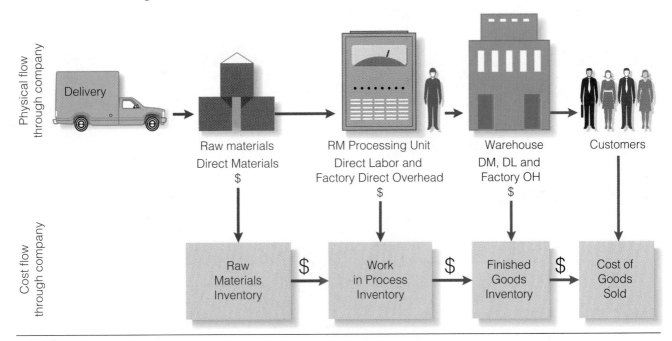

Cost assignment in any process costing environment using actual costing is essentially an averaging process. In general, and in the simplest of situations, a product's actual unit cost is the result of dividing a period's departmental production costs by that period's departmental quantity of production. This average is expressed by the following formula:

$$\text{Unit Cost per Period} = \frac{\text{Sum of Production Costs}}{\text{Quantity of Production}}$$

Production costs include direct materials, direct labor, and factory overhead.

The Numerator

The formula numerator (sum of production costs) is obtained by accumulation of departmental costs incurred for a single time period. Since most companies manufacture more than one product, costs must be accumulated by product, not just by department. For example, Marguerite's Cakes would accumulate the costs of producing King Cakes separately from the costs of producing wedding cakes, apple pies, or chocolate chip cookies.

Exhibit 7–2 presents the source documents and records used to initially assign costs to production departments during a period. The three products in the exhibit are

■ **EXHIBIT 7–2**
Cost Flows and Cost Assignments

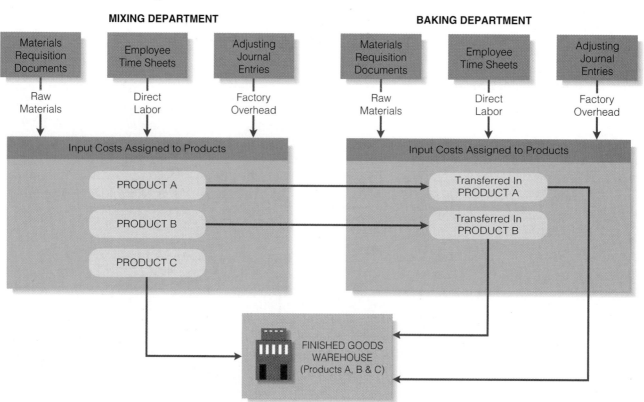

started in the Mixing Department. Products A and B are transferred to Baking so that they form properly. Product C, however, is made of a material that forms without baking and, therefore, does not need to be processed in the second department. Production costs incurred in Mixing for Products A and B are transferred to Baking as the goods are transferred. Additional costs in the Baking Department will attach to the products before they are sent to Finished Goods Inventory. Product C will contain only material, labor, and factory overhead costs from the Mixing Department.

As in job order costing, the direct material and direct labor components of product cost present relatively few problems for cost accumulation and assignment. Direct materials cost can be measured from the materials requisition slips and invoiced prices; direct labor cost can be determined from the employee time sheets and wage rates for the period. These costs are assigned at the end of the period (usually each month) from the departments to the units produced. In contrast to direct material and direct labor, which are easily traced to products, factory overhead must be allocated in some manner to production.

Factory overhead may be assigned to products through the use of predetermined rates, although actual costs are often used for product costing in process costing systems. If total actual overhead costs are relatively constant each period and production volume is relatively steady over time, using actual overhead costs will provide a fairly stable production cost. If such conditions do not exist, application of actual overhead will yield fluctuating product costs, and predetermined overhead rates should be used.

To summarize, the numerator in the average product cost fraction is the sum of the (1) actual direct material cost, (2) actual direct labor cost, and (3) actual or predetermined overhead cost. Costs are accumulated in individual departments and relate to the units of product worked on in those departments during the period.

The Denominator

The unit cost formula denominator represents total departmental production for the period. If all units were 100 percent complete at the end of each accounting period, units could simply be counted to obtain the denominator. But in most production processes, a work in process inventory of partially completed units exists at the end of each period. Any partially completed ending inventory of the current period becomes the partially completed beginning inventory of the next period. Process costing assigns costs to both fully and partially completed units by converting partially completed units to equivalent whole units or equivalent units of production.

Equivalent units of production (EUP) approximate the number of whole units of output that could have been produced during a period from the actual effort expended during that period. Using EUP is necessary because using only completed units to determine unit cost would not clearly reflect all the work accomplished during a period. For instance, if 45 partially completed units were determined to be two-thirds complete, these partially completed units would be counted as $(45 \times \frac{2}{3})$ or 30 whole units. To calculate equivalent units of production for a period, it is necessary to multiply the number of actual, but incomplete, units produced by the percentage of completion and then add the results to the fully completed units for the period.

For example, assume Department One had no beginning inventory. During January, Department One produced 100,000 complete units and 10,000 units that were 20 percent complete. These partially complete units are in ending Work in Process Inventory. The period's EUP are calculated as $[(100,000 \times 100\%) + (10,000 \times 20\%)]$ or 102,000 EUP. This quantity is the denominator of the formula used to calculate departmental equivalent unit product costs.

■ LEARNING OBJECTIVE 2
Understand why equivalent units of production are used in process costing.

equivalent units of production (EUP)

Use of equivalent units of production requires recognition of two factors related to inventory. First, units in beginning WIP Inventory were started last period but will be completed during the current period. This two-period production sequence means that some costs related to these units were incurred last period and additional costs will be incurred in the current period. Second, partially completed units in the ending WIP Inventory will be started in the current period but will not be completed until the next period. Thus, current period production efforts on the ending WIP Inventory will cause costs to be incurred in this period and additional costs to be incurred next period.

Qualified production personnel should inspect ending work in process units to determine what proportion of work was completed during the current period. The mathematical complement to this proportion (or one minus the percentage of work completed in the prior period) represents the amount of work to be performed next period. Physical inspection at the end of last period provided the information about the work to be performed in the current period on the beginning inventory.

INTRODUCING WEIGHTED AVERAGE AND FIFO PROCESS COSTING

A primary purpose of any costing system is to determine product costs for financial statements. When goods are transferred from Work in Process Inventory of one department to another department or to Finished Goods Inventory, a cost must be assigned to those goods. In addition, at the end of any period, a cost amount must be assigned to goods that are only partially complete and still remain in Work in Process Inventory.

weighted average method
FIFO method

There are two primary alternative methods of accounting for cost flows in process costing: the **weighted average method** and the **FIFO** (first-in, first-out) **method.** These methods relate to the way in which physical cost flows are accounted for in the production process. In a very general way, it is helpful to relate these process costing approaches to the cost flow methods used in financial accounting.

In a retail business, the weighted average method is used to determine an average cost per unit of inventory. This cost equals the total cost of goods available divided by total units available. Total cost and total units, respectively, are the sums of cost and unit information, for beginning inventory and purchases. Costs and units of the current period are not distinguished in any way from those of the prior period. In contrast, in retail accounting, the FIFO method separates goods by when they were purchased and what they cost. Unit costs of beginning inventory are the first to be sent to Cost of Goods Sold; units in ending inventory are costed at the most recent purchase prices.

The use of these methods in costing manufactured goods is similar to their use in costing retail purchases. The weighted average method computes an average cost per unit of production, while the FIFO method keeps beginning inventory and current period production and costs separate. The denominator used in the unit cost formula differs depending on which of the two methods is used. Both methods generally result in approximately the same unit costs.

For a production operation to begin, some direct material must be introduced. Without any direct material, there would be no need for labor or factory overhead to be incurred. The material added at the start of production is 100 percent complete throughout the process regardless of the percentage of completion of labor and overhead. For example, when King Cakes are made, the dough must be added in full at the start of production.

Most production processes require more than one direct material. Additional materials may be added at any point or may be added continuously during processing. Materials may even be added at the end of processing. For example, the bags into which King Cakes are placed for local sale are direct materials added at the end of processing. Thus, the King Cake is 0 percent complete as to the bag at any point prior to the end of the production process, although other materials and some labor and overhead may have been incurred. Exhibit 7–3 (page 322) provides the production flow for the King Cake manufacturing process and illustrates the need for separate EUP computations for each cost component.

As the exhibit shows, the material "dough" is 100 percent complete at any point in the King Cake process after the start of production; no additional dough is added later. When labor and factory overhead reach the 60 percent completion point, spices are added. Before the 60 percent point, spices were 0 percent complete; after this point, the spices are 100 percent complete. After more labor and factory overhead costs have been incurred and the cakes have been baked, they are iced and the dolls are inserted. Last, the cakes are bagged and are 100 percent complete. Thus, at the end of a month, the unfinished King Cakes could be anywhere in the production process. If, for example, the cakes were 75 percent complete as to labor and factory overhead, they would be 100 percent complete as to dough and spices but 0 percent complete as to icing and bags.

When different components of a product are at different stages of completion, an EUP calculation is necessary for each cost component. But a single EUP calculation can be made for multiple cost components that are at the same degree of completion. For example, separate EUP calculations would need to be made for the dough, spices, and dolls comprising the King Cakes. But because direct labor and overhead are incurred at the same rate in the King Cake process, these two conversion cost elements may be combined and one EUP calculation made for conversion costs.

If factory overhead is applied to production using direct labor as a base or if a highly automated manufacturer does not account for direct labor cost separately (because it is too insignificant), a single conversion cost EUP calculation can be made. However, as discussed in Chapters 4 and 5, factory overhead may be applied to products by use of machine hours or a variety of non-traditional allocation bases (such as number of machine setups, pounds of material moved, and/or number of material requisitions). The number of equivalent unit computations required depends on the number of different cost pools and overhead allocation bases established in a company. Companies with multiple cost pools and allocation bases will need to make separate computations for each cost pool that is at a different level of completion than the others.

In making scones, the flour, butter and eggs are added at the beginning of the process. After some kneading takes place, liquified brown sugar is added. Until this point, the first group of ingredients is 100% complete, but the sugar is 0%. Recognition of differences in degrees of completion requires the use of equivalent units of production.

EUP CALCULATIONS AND COST ASSIGNMENT

Exhibit 7–4 (page 323) outlines the six steps necessary to determine the costs assignable to units completed and to units still in process at the end of a period in a process costing system. Each of these steps is discussed briefly, and then a complete example is provided for both weighted average and FIFO costing.

1. Calculate the total physical units for which the department is responsible, or the **total units to account for.** This amount is equal to the total number of units

■ LEARNING OBJECTIVE 3
Compute equivalent units of production using the weighted average and FIFO methods of process costing.

total units to account for

■ **EXHIBIT 7–3**
King Cake Manufacturing Process

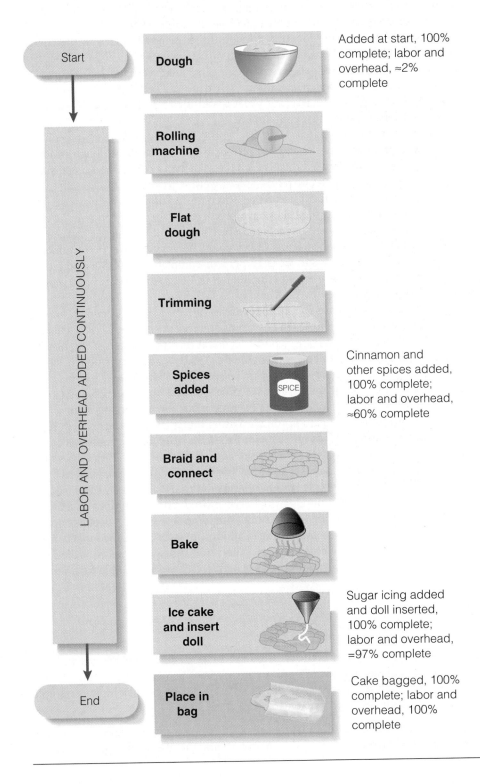

Start

LABOR AND OVERHEAD ADDED CONTINUOUSLY

End

Dough — Added at start, 100% complete; labor and overhead, ≈2% complete

Rolling machine

Flat dough

Trimming

Spices added — Cinnamon and other spices added, 100% complete; labor and overhead, ≈60% complete

Braid and connect

Bake

Ice cake and insert doll — Sugar icing added and doll inserted, 100% complete; labor and overhead, =97% complete

Place in bag — Cake bagged, 100% complete; labor and overhead, 100% complete

worked on in the department during the current period: beginning inventory units plus units started.

2. Determine what happened to the units to account for during the period. This step also requires the use of physical units. Units may fit into one of two categories: (1) completed and transferred or (2) partially completed and remaining in ending Work in Process Inventory.[1]

■ **LEARNING OBJECTIVE 4**
Calculate unit costs and inventory values using the weighted average and FIFO methods of process costing.

■ **EXHIBIT 7–4**

Steps in Process Costing

COMMENTS

(1) Calculate the physical units to account for
Beginning WIP units
+ Units started

Determine the units that are in the process.

(2) Calculate the physical units accounted for
Units transferred out
+ Units in ending inventory

Identify groups of units to be costed (beginning work in process, started & completed, and ending work in process).

Verify that Step 2 equals Step 1

(3) Determine the equivalent units of production — Weighted average — or — FIFO

Identify the related effort incurred for each unit group by cost component (i.e., materials, labor, and overhead).

(4) Determine the total cost to account for — Beginning inventory — + — Current costs

Determine the costs that have been incurred.

(5) Calculate the cost per equivalent unit — Weighted average — or — FIFO

Calculate the cost per cost component to be assigned to each cost element.

(6) Assign the costs to inventories — Transferred out (next department or FG) — and — Ending inventory (WIP)

Verify that the total costs transferred out plus the costs in ending inventory equal Step 4

---

[1]Another category, that of spoilage or damaged units, does exist. One method of accounting for such occurrences is discussed in a later section in the chapter.

total cost to account for

3. Use either the weighted average or the FIFO method to determine the equivalent units of production for each cost component.
4. Find the **total cost to account for,** which includes the balance in Work in Process Inventory at the beginning of the period plus all current costs for direct material, direct labor, and factory overhead.
5. Compute the cost per equivalent unit for each cost component using either the weighted average or the FIFO equivalent units of production calculated in step 3.
6. Use the costs computed in step 5 to assign costs to the units completed and transferred from the production process and to the units remaining in ending Work in Process Inventory.

Royalty Bakery is used to demonstrate the steps involved in the computation of equivalent units of production and cost assignment for both methods of process costing. Royalty uses the same basic process of manufacturing King Cakes as Marguerite's Cakes. The bakery views the production process as consisting of a single department. Dough is purchased from a vendor and is considered the only direct material. For purposes of simplicity, it is assumed that the costs of the spices, icing, dolls, and bags are extremely small; thus, these materials are considered indirect and, as such, part of factory overhead. Since the dough is added at the start of processing, all inventories are 100 percent complete as to material as soon as processing has begun. Labor and overhead are assumed to be added at the same rate throughout the production process. Exhibit 7–5 presents information regarding Royalty's production inventories and costs for February 1996.

While figures are given for both cakes transferred out and cakes in ending inventory, it is not essential to provide both of these figures. The number of cakes remaining in process at February 29 can be calculated as the total cakes to account for minus the cakes completed and transferred during the period. Alternatively, the number of cakes transferred out can be computed as the total cakes to account for minus the cakes in ending inventory.

Weighted Average Method

The weighted average method of computing equivalent units of production adds the units in beginning Work in Process Inventory to the units started during the current period to determine the maximum production for the period. The work performed during the period does not necessarily always result in complete units. The weighted average method is not concerned about what quantity of work was performed in the prior period on the units in beginning inventory. This method focuses only on units that are completed in the current period and units that remain in ending Work in Process Inventory.

Step 1: Calculate the total units to account for.

Beginning inventory	120
Units started during current period	5,500
Total units to account for	5,620

Step 2: Calculate the total units accounted for.

Units completed and transferred out	5,530
Units in ending WIP inventory	90
Total units accounted for	5,620

The items detailed at this point (those transferred out and those in ending inventory) indicate the categories that will be assigned costs in the final step. Notice that the units accounted for in step 2 equal the units to account for in step 1.

Completed units are either (1) beginning inventory units that have been completed during the current period or (2) units started and completed during the period. The number of **units started and completed** (S&C) equals the total units completed during the period minus the units in beginning inventory. For Royalty Bakery, the number of units started and completed in February is 5,410 (5,530 - 120).

Step 3: Determine the equivalent units of production for each cost component.

At the end of the period, the units in beginning inventory and the units that were started and completed this period are 100 percent complete as to all cost components. The units in ending inventory are 100 percent complete as to direct materials, but only 80 percent complete as to labor and factory overhead. Since labor and overhead are at the same degree of completion, a single EUP calculation can be made for both of these cost components and called "conversion."

units started and completed

The weighted average computations for equivalent units of production are as follows:

	DM EUP	CONVERSION (DL AND OH) EUP
BI (whole units × % complete)	120 × 100% = 120	120 × 100% = 120
Units started and completed (whole units × % complete)	5,410 × 100% = 5,410	5,410 × 100% = 5,410
EI (whole units × % complete)	90 × 100% = 90	90 × 80% = 72
EUP	5,620	5,602

Note that the first two lines of this schedule (BI and Units started and completed) are equal to the total units completed and transferred out (5,530) given in step 2 above.

■ **EXHIBIT 7–5**

Royalty Bakery Production and Cost Information—February 1996

Beginning inventory (30% complete as to conversion)		120
Cakes started during current period		5,500
Cakes completed and transferred to finished goods		5,530
Ending inventory (80% complete as to conversion)		90
Cost of beginning inventory:		
Direct material	$ 172.60	
Direct labor	112.04	
Overhead	44.42	$ 329.06
Current period costs:		
Direct material	$5,335.00	
Direct labor	7,450.66	
Overhead	8,078.48	20,864.14

The weighted average method does not distinguish between units in beginning inventory and units entering production and completed during the period. As such, the weighted average method treats beginning inventory units as though they were started and completed in the current period.

Only when all product components are placed into production at the same time and at the same rate will material, labor, and factory overhead all be at equal percentages of completion. Generally, the cost components are at different degrees of completion. In such cases, the completion percentage must be separately determined *for each cost component.* If the percentages of completion differ, separate EUP calculations must be made for each cost component.

Step 4: Determine the total cost to account for.

For Royalty Bakery, the total cost to account for is $21,193.20.

	DM	DL	OH	TOTAL
BI cost	$ 172.60	$ 112.04	$ 44.42	$ 329.06
Current period costs	5,335.00	7,450.66	8,078.48	20,864.14
Total cost to account for	$5,507.60	$7,562.70	$8,122.90	$21,193.20

Information is given on total costs for each element of production: direct material, direct labor, and factory overhead. Total cost will be assigned in step 6 to the goods transferred out to Finished Goods Inventory (or the next department) and to ending Work in Process Inventory in relation to the whole or equivalent whole units contained in each category.

Step 5: Calculate the cost per equivalent unit of production.

A cost per equivalent unit of production must be computed for each cost component for which a separate calculation of EUP is made. Since the weighted average method does not distinguish between units in beginning inventory and units started during the period, neither does it differentiate between beginning inventory costs and current period costs. The costs of beginning inventory and the current period are summed for each cost component and averaged over that component's weighted average equivalent units of production. The calculation of unit cost for each cost component at the end of the period is as follows:

$$\text{Cost per Equivalent Unit} = \frac{\text{Beginning Inventory Cost} + \text{Current Period Cost}}{\text{Weighted Average Equivalent Units of Production}}$$

$$= \frac{\text{Total Cost Incurred}}{\text{Total WA Equivalent Units of Effort}}$$

Under the weighted average method, costs from two different periods are totaled to form the numerator of the unit cost equation, and units from two different periods are used in the denominator. This computation allows total costs to be divided by total units—the common weighted average approach which produces an average component cost per unit. Because a single conversion EUP calculation was made, Royalty Bakery must add the total costs of labor ($7,562.70) and overhead ($8,122.90) to obtain the total conversion cost. The bakery's weighted average calculations for cost per EUP for material and conversion are as follows:

	DM	CONVERSION	TOTAL
Total cost to account for (step 5)	$5,507.60	$15,685.60	$21,193.20
Divided by EUP (step 3)	÷ 5,620	÷ 5,602	
Cost per EUP	= $.98	= $2.80	$3.78

The unit costs for the two product cost components are summed to yield the total production cost for all whole units completed during February. For Royalty Bakery, this cost is $3.78.

Step 6: Assign costs to inventories.

This step assigns total production costs to units of product. Cost assignment in a department involves determining the cost of (1) goods completed and transferred out during the period and (2) units in ending inventory.

The cost of goods transferred out under the weighted average method is the result of multiplying the total number of units transferred by the total cost per EUP, which combines all component costs. Because this method is based on an averaging technique that combines prior and current period work, the period in which the transferred units were started is not important. All units and all costs have been commingled. The total cost transferred out for Royalty Bakery for February is $20,903.40 or (5,530 × $3.78).

Ending WIP Inventory cost is based on the equivalent units of production for each cost component. The EUP are multiplied by the component cost per unit calculated in step 5. Cost of ending inventory under the weighted average method is:

Ending WIP inventory:	
Direct material (90 × 100% × $.98)	$ 88.20
Conversion (90 × 80% × $2.80)	201.60
Total cost of ending inventory	$289.80

The quantities that result from multiplying whole units by the percentage of completion are equal to the equivalent units of production.

The total costs assigned to transferred-out units and units in ending inventory must equal the total cost to account for. For Royalty Bakery, total cost to account for (step 4) was determined as $21,193.20, which equals transferred-out cost ($20,903.40) plus ending work in process cost ($289.80).

The steps just discussed can be combined into a **production and cost report.** This document details all manufacturing quantities and costs, shows the computation of cost per EUP, and indicates the cost assignment to goods produced during the period. Exhibit 7–6 on the next page shows the production and cost report for Royalty Bakery under the weighted average process costing method.

production and cost report

FIFO Method

As mentioned, the FIFO method of determining EUP more realistically reflects the way in which most goods actually physically flow through the production system. The FIFO method does not commingle units and costs of different periods. Equivalent units and costs of beginning inventory are withheld from the computation of average current period cost. FIFO focuses specifically on the work performed during the current period.

Steps 1 and 2 in Exhibit 7–4 are the same for the FIFO method as for the weighted average method because these two steps involve the use of physical units.

■ **EXHIBIT 7–6**

Production and Cost Report (Weighted Average Method)

PRODUCTION DATA		EQUIVALENT UNITS OF PRODUCTION	
	Whole Units	DM	Conversion
BI	120*	120	36
Units started	5,500		
To account for	5,620		
BI completed	120	0	84
S&C	5,410	5,410	5,410
Units completed	5,530		
EI	90**	90	72
Accounted for	5,620	5,620	5,602

COST DATA

	Total	DM	Conversion
BI cost	$ 329.06	$ 172.60	$ 156.46
Current period costs	20,864.14	5,335.00	15,529.14
Total cost to account for	$21,193.20	$5,507.60	$15,685.60
Divided by EUP		5,620	5,602
Cost per EUP	$3.78	$.98	$2.80

COST ASSIGNMENT

Transferred out (5,530 × $3.78)		$20,903.40	
Ending inventory:			
Direct material (90 × $.98)	$ 88.20		
Conversion (72 × $2.80)	201.60	289.80	
Total cost accounted for		$21,193.20	

*Fully complete as to direct material; 30% as to conversion.

**Fully complete as to direct material; 80% as to conversion.

Therefore, based on the data from Exhibit 7–5, the total units to account for and accounted for are 5,620.

Step 3: Determine the equivalent units of production.

Under FIFO, as mentioned, the work performed last period is not commingled with work of the current period. The EUP schedule for FIFO is:

	DM EUP		CONVERSION (DL AND OH) EUP	
BI (whole units × % *not* completed in prior period)	120 × 0% =	0	120 × 70% =	84
Units started and completed (whole units × % complete)	5,410 × 100% = 5,410		5,410 × 100% = 5,410	
EI (whole units × % complete)	90 × 100% =	90	90 × 80% =	72
EUP		5,500		5,566

Cost differences that might result from the use of weighted average of FIFO process costing at Marguerite's Cakes are inconsequential. King Cakes are generally prepared, baked, and sold the same day—either for in-store consumption, take-home, or shipment. Such a situation would not exist at Keebler, General Foods, or Del Monte Foods.

Under FIFO, only the work performed on the beginning inventory *during the current period* is shown in the EUP schedule. This work equals the whole units in beginning inventory multiplied by a percentage equal to (1 - the percentage of work done in the prior period). In the Royalty Bakery example, no additional direct material is needed in February to complete the 120 units in the beginning inventory. Since beginning inventory was only 30 percent complete as to conversion, the company needs to do 70 percent more labor on the cakes during February or the equivalent of 84 units (120 × 70%).

The remaining figures in the FIFO EUP schedule are the same as those for the weighted average method. The *only* difference between the weighted average and FIFO EUP computations is that the work performed in the prior period on beginning inventory is *not* included in current period EUP. This difference is equal to the number of units in beginning inventory multiplied by the percentage of work performed in the prior period. A reconciliation of EUPs determined by the two methods follows:

	DM	CONVERSION
FIFO EUP	5,500	5,566
Plus the EUP in BI (work completed in the prior period: DM, 100%; Conversion, 30%)	120	36
Weighted Average EUP	5,620	5,602

Step 4:   Determine the total cost to account for.

This step is the same as under the weighted average method. The total cost to account for is $21,193.20.

Step 5:   Calculate the cost per equivalent unit of production.

Since cost determination is made on the basis of equivalent units of production, the results of the step differ from those obtained under the weighted average method. The calculations for cost per equivalent unit reflect the difference between the quantities that the methods use for beginning inventory. Because the EUP calculation for FIFO ignores work performed on beginning inventory during the prior period, the FIFO cost per EUP computation also ignores prior period costs and uses only costs incurred in the current period. The FIFO cost per EUP calculation is:

$$\text{Cost per Equivalent Unit} = \frac{\text{Current Period Cost}}{\text{FIFO Equivalent Units of Production}}$$

Calculations for Royalty Bakery are:

	DM	CONVERSION	TOTAL
Current period costs	$5,335.00	$15,529.14	$20,864.14
÷ EUP (Step 3)	5,500	5,566	
Cost per EUP	$.97	$2.79	$3.76

The production cost for each whole unit produced during February under the FIFO method is $3.76.

It is useful to recognize the difference between the two total cost computations. The weighted average total cost of $3.78 is the average total cost of each unit completed during February, *regardless of when production was begun.* The FIFO total cost of $3.76 is the total cost of each unit that was produced *(both started and completed)* during the current period. The $.02 difference results from the difference in treatment of beginning work in process inventory costs.

Step 6: Assign costs to inventories.

The FIFO method assumes that the units in beginning inventory are completed first during the current period and, thus, are the first units transferred out. The remaining units transferred out during the period were both started and completed in the current period. As shown in the production and cost report in Exhibit 7–7, the two-step computation needed to determine the cost of goods transferred out distinctly presents this FIFO logic.

The first part of the cost assignment for units transferred out relates to the beginning inventory units. These units had material and some labor and factory overhead costs attached to them at the start of the period. These prior period costs were *not* included in the cost-per-EUP calculations in step 5 above. Finishing these units required current period work and, therefore, current period costs. To determine the total cost of finished units in beginning inventory, the costs associated with the beginning inventory are added to the current period costs needed to complete those units.

The second part of the cost assignment for units transferred out relates to the units that were started and completed in the current period. The cost of these units is based solely on current period costs.

This two-step transferred-out cost assignment process is shown below using the Royalty Bakery information. The company had 120 units in the beginning February inventory and transferred out a total of 5,530 units during the month.

Transferred out:	
(1) Beginning inventory (prior period costs)	$ 329.06
Completion of beginning inventory:	
Conversion (120 × 70% × $2.79)	234.36
Total cost of beginning inventory transferred	$ 563.42
(2) Units started and completed (5,410 × $3.76)	20,341.60
Total cost of units transferred out	$20,905.02

■ **EXHIBIT 7–7**

Production and Cost Report (FIFO Method)

PRODUCTION DATA

EQUIVALENT UNITS OF PRODUCTION

	Whole Units	DM	Conversion
BI	120*	120	36
Units started	5,500		
To account for	5,620		
BI completed	120	0	84
S&C	5,410	5,410	5,410
Units completed	5,530		
EI	90**	90	72
Accounted for	5,620	5,500	5,566

COST DATA

	Total	DM	Conversion
BI cost	$ 329.06		
Current period costs	20,864.14	$5,335.00	$15,529.14
Total cost to account for	$21,193.20		
Divided by EUP		5,500	5,566
Cost per EUP	$3.76	$.97	$2.79

COST ASSIGNMENT

Transferred out		
Beginning inventory costs	$ 329.06	
Cost to complete:		
Conversion (84 × $2.79)	234.36	
Total cost of BI transferred	$ 563.42	
Started & completed (5,410 × $3.76)	20,341.60	$20,905.02
Ending inventory:		
Direct material (90 × $.97)	$ 87.30	
Conversion (72 × $2.79)	200.88	288.18
Total cost accounted for		$21,193.20

*Fully complete as to direct material; 30% as to conversion. The quantities under EUP for this line are not included in the final EUP summation.

**Fully complete as to direct material; 80% as to conversion.

Since the cakes in beginning inventory were 100 percent complete as to direct material, no additional material was added during the month. At the start of the month, units were only 30 percent complete as to labor and factory overhead, so 70 percent of the conversion work is performed during February at current period costs. The units started and completed are costed at the total current period FIFO cost of $3.76, since all work on these units was performed during the current period.

Calculation of the cost of ending work in process inventory is the same under both the FIFO and weighted average methods. Although cost per unit differs, the number of equivalent units of production is the same under both methods. Ending work in process cost under FIFO is as follows:

Ending inventory:	
Direct material (90 × 100% × $.97)	$ 87.30
Conversion (90 × 80% × $2.79)	200.88
Total cost of ending inventory	$288.18

The total cost of the units transferred ($20,905.02) plus the cost of the ending inventory units ($288.18) equals the total cost to be accounted for ($21,193.20).

The accompanying News Note discusses the use of weighted average and FIFO cost flow methods in a selected groups of companies. It also highlights the fact that the LIFO (last-in, first-out) cost flow method is not generally applicable in manufacturing settings.

Cost assignment is easier for the weighted average method than for the FIFO method. However, simplicity is not the only consideration in choosing a cost flow method. The FIFO method reflects the actual physical flow of goods through production. Furthermore, when period costs fluctuate, the FIFO method gives managers better information with which to control costs and on which to base decisions because it does not combine costs of different periods. In addition, the FIFO method focuses on current period costs, and managerial performance is evaluated on the basis of costs incurred in the current period.

PROCESS COSTING WITH STANDARD COSTS

■ LEARNING
OBJECTIVE 5
Understand how standard costs are used in a process costing system.

All previous discussion in the chapter uses actual historical costs to assign costs to products under either the weighted average method or FIFO method. Companies may prefer to use standard rather than actual costs for inventory measurement purposes. The use of standard costs simplifies process costing and allows variances to be measured during the period. Actual costing requires that a new production cost be computed each production period. Standard costing eliminates such recomputations, although standards do need to be reviewed (and possibly revised) at least once a year to keep the amounts current.

Calculations of equivalent units of production for standard process costing are identical to those for FIFO process costing. Unlike the weighted average method, both standard costing and FIFO emphasize the measurement and control of current production and current period costs. The commingling of units and costs that occurs when the weighted average method is used reduces the emphasis on current effort that standard costing is intended to represent and measure.

In a standard cost process costing system, actual costs of the current period are recorded and are compared with the standard costs of the equivalent units of production. If actual costs are less than standard, there is a favorable variance; unfavorable variances arise if actual costs are greater than the standard. Units are transferred out of a department at the standard cost of each production element.[2]

---

[2]Standard costing and variances are discussed in depth in Chapter 6.

FIFO, Yes; LIFO, No

[T]he results of a recent survey of 112 manufacturing operations indicate that 52% of these companies are using process costing in their basic cost accounting systems. Furthermore, 58% of the companies surveyed are using the FIFO cost flow assumption, whereas only 21% are using average cost. [Note: The remaining companies might use a standard process costing system.]

The major shortcoming of the average cost method is that the costs of different periods are mixed together and, as a result, interperiod variations in unit costs are concealed. The fact that process costing under the FIFO method is more informative than under the average approach reduces the likelihood of incorrect decisions by management with regard to controlling costs.

As an alternative, process cost flows could be based on a LIFO assumption. However, LIFO applications for work-in-process inventories rarely are found in practice. Most companies tend to keep their end-of-period balances in work-in-process inventories at a minimum and, consequently, there are no significant advantages to be gained from using LIFO.

LIFO is not logically defensible as a process cost flow assumption because it is contrary to the actual physical flows of manufacturing activities. The application of LIFO has been confined to raw materials and finished goods inventories.

SOURCE: Rex C. Hauser, Frank R. Urbancic, and Donald E. Edwards, "Process Costing: Is It Relevant?" *Management Accounting* (December 1989), p. 53. Published by Institute of Management Acountants, Montvale, NJ.

PROCESS COSTING IN A MULTIDEPARTMENT SETTING

Most companies have multiple, rather than single, processing facilities. In a multidepartment processing environment, goods are transferred from a predecessor department to a successor department. For example, the production of King Cakes could occur in two departments: Production and Packaging.

As illustrated in Exhibit 7–1, manufacturing costs always follow the physical flow of goods. Therefore, the costs of completed units of predecessor departments are treated as input material costs in successor departments. Such a sequential treatment requires the use of an additional cost component element called "transferred-in" or "prior department cost." This element always has a percentage of completion factor of 100 percent, since the goods would not have been transferred out of the predecessor department if they had not been fully complete. The transferred-in element is handled the same as any other cost element in the calculations of EUP and cost per EUP.

A successor department may add additional raw materials to the units that have been transferred in or may simply provide additional labor, with the corresponding incurrence of overhead. Anything added in the successor department requires its own cost element column for calculating equivalent units of production and cost per equivalent unit (unless the additional elements have the same degree of completion, in which case they can be combined).

Occasionally, successor departments may change the unit of measure used in predecessor departments. For example, when Royalty Bakery produces cookies, the measure in the Mixing Department might be batches of cookie dough; the Baking

Department might use number of cookies as its measure; and the Packaging Department might use number of boxes of cookies. Assume that the Baking Department transferred 650 cookies to the next department. If each box contains a baker's dozen (13) cookies, the Packaging Department would need to record the receipt as 50 boxes (650 ÷ 13) transferred in.

Exhibit 7–8 provides a production and cost report for the Packaging Department at Royalty Bakery. Weighted average unit costs from Exhibit 7–6 are used for the units transferred in from the previous department. In this department, King Cakes are placed either on cardboard rounds in plastic bags for local delivery or in boxes for shipping. Both kinds of packaging have approximately the same cost. The beginning inventory is assumed to be fully complete as to transferred-in units and cost, 0 percent complete as to packaging, and 75 percent complete as to conversion. The ending inventory is assumed to be fully complete as to transferred-in units and cost, 0 percent complete as to packaging, and 40 percent complete as to conversion. The Packaging

---

■ EXHIBIT 7–8
Multidepartment Setting—Packaging Department (Weighted Average Method)

PRODUCTION DATA   **EQUIVALENT UNITS OF PRODUCTION**

	Whole Units	Transferred In	DM	Conversion
BI	100*	100	0	75
Units transferred in	5,530			
To account for	5,630			
BI completed	100	0	100	25
S&C	5,380	5,380	5,380	5,380
Units completed	5,480			
EI	150**	150	0	60
Accounted for	5,630	5,630	5,480	5,540

COST DATA

	Total	Transferred In	DM	Conversion
BI cost	$ 438.35	$ 434.30	$ 0	$ 4.05
Current period costs	22,546.35	20,903.40	1,370.00	272.95
Total cost to account for	$22,984.70	$21,337.70	$1,370.00	$277.00
Divided by EUP		5,630	5,480	5,540
Cost per EUP	$4.09	$3.79	$.25	$.05

COST ASSIGNMENT

Transferred out (5,480 × $4.09)		$22,413.20
Ending inventory:		
Transferred in (150 × $3.79)	$568.50	
Conversion (60 × $.05)	3.00	571.50
Total cost accounted for		$22,984.70

*Fully complete as to transferred in; 75% as to conversion.

**Fully complete as to transferred in; 40% as to conversion.

Department uses the weighted average process costing method. Information is provided in the exhibit for beginning inventory and current period material and conversion costs in this department. Because labor cost is extremely minimal in the department, it is considered indirect and, thus, a part of factory overhead.

REDUCING SPOILAGE BY IMPLEMENTING QUALITY PROCESSES

This chapter has assumed that there is no nonconforming production; but in reality, most businesses do produce some spoiled or defective units. While detailed methods of accounting for spoilage are beyond the scope of this text,[3] managers should always be alert for ways to minimize spoilage in a production process. The control aspect of quality implementation requires knowledge of the answers to three specific questions:

1. What does the spoilage actually cost?
2. Why does the spoilage occur?
3. How can the spoilage be controlled?

Many companies find it difficult, if not impossible, to answer the question of what spoilage (or lack of quality) costs. One cause of this difficulty is a traditional method of handling spoilage in process costing situations. Under a technique called the **method of neglect,** spoiled units are simply excluded from the equivalent units of production schedule. The total cost of producing both good and spoiled units is assigned solely to the good units; and thus, the cost of those units is increased. Because the spoiled units are excluded from the extensions in the equivalent units schedule, the cost of those units are effectively "buried" and hidden in magnitude from managers. In a job order costing environment, an estimate of spoilage cost is often added to total budgeted factory overhead when the predetermined overhead rate is calculated. When this is done, spoilage cost is again hidden and ignored.

In service organizations, the cost of spoilage may be even more difficult to determine because spoilage is, from a customer viewpoint, poor service; the customer simply may not do business with the organization again. Such a cost is not processed by the accounting system. Thus, in all instances, a potentially significant dollar amount of loss from nonconformance to requirements is unavailable for investigation as to its planning, controlling, and decision-making ramifications.

As to the second question, managers may be able to pinpoint the reasons for spoilage or poor service but those managers may have a mindset that condones lack of control. The managers may believe that a particular cause creates only a "minimal" amount of spoilage; because of this attitude, they settle for an "accepted quality level" with some tolerance for error. These error tolerances are built into the system and they become justifications for problems. Production is "graded on a curve" that allows for a less-than-perfect result.

Incorporating error tolerances into the production system and combining such tolerances with the method of neglect discussed earlier result in a situation in which managers do not have the information necessary to determine how much spoilage cost the company is incurring. Therefore, although they believe that the quantity and cost of spoiled goods are "minimal," the managers do not have historical or even estimated accounting amounts on which to base such a conclusion. If managers were

■ LEARNING
OBJECTIVE 7
Discuss how quality control can minimize spoilage.

method of neglect

---

[3]This topic is covered in depth in any cost accounting text.

Make More Only If You Can Make Them Right

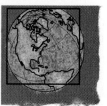

[At Samsung, South Korea's electronics giant, Chairman Lee Kun Hee] wants to shake off what he calls the Samsung diseases, notably a preoccupation with expanding volume regardless of quality. The result, he says, is that some 6,000 Samsung employees are kept busy repairing 20,000 defective products annually produced by 30,000 other Samsung workers. "You can find no comparable inefficiency in the world." Making defective products, adds Lee, "is cancerous and a criminal act on the part of management." Samsung, among other things, has adopted the Japanese practice of stopping assembly lines when defects occur. Workers often stayed as late as 10 P.M., so Samsung decreed that they must leave at 4 P.M., after eight hours. Lee thinks the relatively shorter day will actually improve efficiency and enhance morale.

Standing Samsung on its head to stress quality, says Lee, "was not a premeditated strategy" but evolved from a personal sense of crisis. Samsung faced eroding competitiveness in many fields, he says, and was doing little about it. With Korea steadily opening its protected home market, Lee told his executives that the company would have to compete head-on with [companies known for high quality, such as] Sony, Matsushita, Philips, and General Electric.

SOURCE: Louis Kraar, "Korea Goes For Quality," *Fortune* (April 18, 1994), pp. 156-157. © 1994 Time Inc. All rights reserved.

aware of the cost, they could make more informed decisions about whether to ignore the problem causing the spoilage or try to correct its causes.

In other instances, managers may believe that spoilage is uncontrollable. In some cases, this belief is accurate. For example, when a printing press converts from one job to the next, some pages are consistently misprinted. The number is not large, and process analysis has proved that the cost of attempting to correct this production defect would be significantly greater than the savings resulting from the correction. But in most production situations and almost every service situation, the cause of spoiled goods or poor service is controllable. It is only necessary to determine the cause and institute corrective action. As indicated in the accompanying News Note, the push to understand the causes of quality problems and correct those causes is occurring worldwide.

Spoilage has often been controlled through a process of inspecting goods or, in the case of service organizations, surveying customers. Now, companies are deciding that if quality is *built into* a process to prevent defects or problems, there will be less need for inspections or surveys, because spoilage and poor service will be minimized. The goal is, then, to maintain quality through process *control* rather than output *inspection and observation*. Exhibit 7–9 contrasts the traditional and total quality management viewpoints on quality.

Many companies are now implementing quality programs to minimize defects or poor service. These companies often employ **statistical process control (SPC)** techniques to analyze their processes for situations that are "out of control" and creating spoilage. SPC techniques are based on the theory that a process varies naturally over time from normal, random causes but that some variations occur that fall outside the limits of the natural variations. These uncommon or special-cause variations are typically the points at which the process produces errors, which may be defective goods or poor service. Often, these variations can be—and have been—eliminated by the installation of computer-integrated manufacturing systems, which have internal con-

statistical process control (SPC)

trols to evaluate tolerances and sense production problems. The control charts discussed in Chapter 2 are one of many SPC techniques used to analyze process results relative to a benchmark, or standard, and in relation to the amount of variation expected in a stable (controlled) process.

SPC requires that persons involved in a problem area select a relevant measure of performance and track that performance measurement over time. The measures selected to prepare control charts for manufacturing companies are nonfinancial ones, such as number of defective products, nonconformances in tolerance levels, and unexpected work slowdowns or stoppages. In service organizations, quality measures used to prepare SPC charts often reflect key indicators of "good performance" as indicated in the News Note on page 339.

■ **EXHIBIT 7–9**
Contrasting Quality Paradigms

TRADITIONAL PARADIGM	TQM PARADIGM
Responsibility for Quality	
Worker is responsible for poor quality	Everyone is responsible for poor quality
Quality problems start in operations	Majority of the quality problems start long before the operations stage
Inspect quality in	Build quality in
After-the-fact inspection	Quality at the source
Quality inspectors are the gatekeepers of quality	Operators are responsible for quality reliability
Quality control department has large staff	Quality control department has small staff
The focus of the quality control department is to reject poor quality output	The focus of the quality control department is to monitor and facilitate the process
Managers and engineers have the expertise; workers serve their needs	Workers have the expertise; managers and engineers serve their needs
Linkages with Suppliers	
Procure from multiple suppliers	Procure from a single supplier
Acceptance sampling of inputs at point of receipt	Certify suppliers who can deliver right quantity, right quality, and on time; no incoming inspection
New Product/Service Development	
Separate designers from operations	Use teams with operations, marketing, and designers
Design for performance (with more parts, more features—not to facilitate operations)	Design for performance and ease of processing
Overall Quality Goal	
Zero defects is not practical	Zero defects is the goal
Mistakes are inevitable and have to be inspected out	Mistakes are opportunities to learn and become perfect
It costs too much to make defect-free products	Quality is free
A "reasonable" tradeoff is the key	Perfection is the key; perfection is a journey, not a destination

SOURCE: John K. Shank and Vijay Govindarajan, "Measuring the 'Cost of Quality': A Strategic Cost Management Perspective," *Journal of Cost Management* (Summer 1994), p. 10. Reprinted with permission from The Journal of Cost Management for the Manufacturing Industry, © 1994, Warren, Gorham, Lamont, 31 St. James Avenue, Boston, MA 02116. All rights reserved.

SPC charts are important tools in a total quality environment. They indicate the variations in the process, so that unacceptable deviation can be noted and corrective action taken.

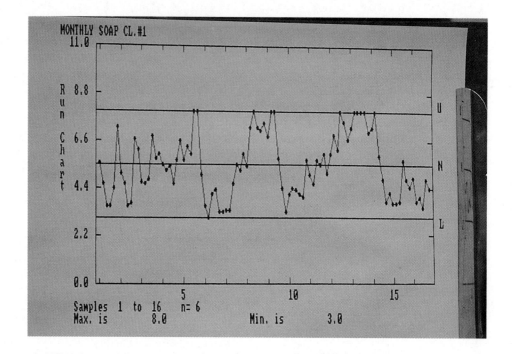

SPC allows the individuals involved in a process to become the quality control monitors and helps to eliminate the need for quality inspections. Thus, the "accepted quality level" can be raised and the defects reduced significantly. For instance, as noted in Chapter 2, Motorola's goal of six sigma defects (no more than 3.4 defects per million—or 99.9997% perfect) is close to being met and the company is now attempting to reduce that defect level to defects per billion. Such goals are not unusual for companies competing in global, world-class environments.

The development, implementation, and interpretation of an SPC system requires a firm grasp of statistics and is well beyond the scope of this text. However, it is essential for managers and accountants to recognize the usefulness of such a tool in determining why problems occur. The important managerial concern regarding spoilage is to *control* it; properly *accounting for* spoilage costs is a first step in helping managers determine how spoilage can be controlled. Quality control programs can be implemented to develop ideas on redesigning products for higher quality, determine where quality control problems exist, measure the costs associated with those problems, and make a more informed cost-benefit analysis of problem correction.

What Will Be Measured in a Service Company?

Service organizations all share common features that differ from manufacturing. These features include direct contact with the customer, large volumes of transactions and processing, and often large amounts of paperwork. It is easy to see that the sources of error are considerable in recording transactions and in processing. It is not unusual to see a newspaper report of a large error in billing that amounts to thousands or hundreds of thousands of dollars.

Although control charts were first developed and used in a manufacturing context, they are easily applied to service organizations. The major difference is the quality characteristic that is controlled. Many of the standards used in service industries form the basis for quality control charts. Listed below are just a few of the many potential applications of control charts for services.

ORGANIZATION	QUALITY MEASURE
Hospital	lab test accuracy
	on-time delivery of meals and medication
Bank	check-processing accuracy
Insurance company	claims-processing accuracy
	billing accuracy
Post office	sorting accuracy
	time of delivery
	percent express mail delivered on time
Ambulance	response time
Police department	incidence of crime in a precinct
	number of traffic citations
Hotel	proportion of rooms satisfactorily cleaned
	number of complaints received
Transportation	proportion of freight cars correctly routed
Auto service	percent of time work completed as promised
	number of parts out of stock

SOURCE: James R. Evans and William M. Lindsay, *The Management and Control of Quality* (St. Paul: West Publishing Company, 1993), pp. 565–566.

SITE ANALYSIS

Marguerite's Cakes grew 10 percent in 1994 and is expected to grow an additional 15 to 20 percent in 1995. Company management believes that the key to success in today's increasingly competitive marketplace is to provide the customer with a high-quality product and a high level of service while continually striving to reduce production costs. The company is achieving some overhead cost reductions by improving the bakery layout to decrease the time it takes to move materials, work in process, and finished products from point to point. Additionally, more efficient equipment has been acquired. The greater machine efficiency has lowered the overall labor cost per King Cake, even though the company has increased wages and benefits to individual workers.

The bakery has faced some difficulties that are common to many smaller businesses—for example, difficulties in obtaining financing and establishing credibility with vendors and equipment manufacturers. The owner decided to face these problems head-on by obtaining an accounting degree. The knowledge she gained from this education has allowed her not only to communicate more effectively with suppliers and other creditors but also to implement a full range of managerial accounting techniques (including product costing, budgeting, and breakeven analysis) for planning and decision making purposes.

Ms. Schroeder's plans for the future are ambitious but attainable. Each strategy and step is supported by sound accounting and focused on the primary goal of maintaining a profitable business—achieved to a great extent because of a thorough knowledge of product costs and of the cost-to-selling price relationship. And when the company implements its plan to serve as a production facility for up to seven sales-only outlets, the substantial increase in output will make sound product costing techniques even more important.

SOURCE: Information provided by Marlene and Ron Schroeder, 1994.

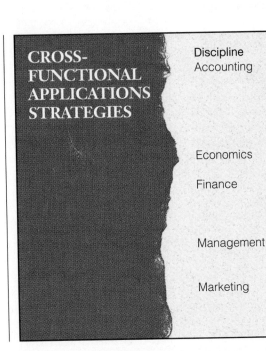

CROSS-FUNCTIONAL APPLICATIONS STRATEGIES

Discipline	Applications
Accounting	Process costing is a costing system used to match accounting results with the true nature of a manufacturing process; process costing systems should be used in mass production processes such as those for fluids and powders; equivalent unit computations are necessary to account for the work performed on goods still in process at the end of a period.
Economics	Process costing can provide reasonably accurate product costs for economic decisions including cost/price relationships.
Finance	Accurate financial reporting for companies engaging in mass production of homogeneous output requires the use of a process costing system; capital analysis is partially dependent upon the ability to generate and predict reasonably accurate unit costs.
Management	Managers must have detailed cost information to conduct their planning, controlling, problem-solving, and evaluating functions and to understand the effects of spoilage on costs.
Marketing	Competitive pricing requires knowledge of product costs; rational promotion decisions are a function of the relative profitability of products, which requires a knowledge of product costs.

CHAPTER SUMMARY

Process costing is used in manufacturing companies producing large quantities of homogeneous products. It is an averaging method used to assign manufacturing costs to units of production for purposes of planning, controlling, decision making, and preparing financial statements.

Either the weighted average or the FIFO method can be used to compute equivalent units of production and assign costs in a process costing system. The difference between the two methods lies solely in the treatment of the work performed in the prior period on the beginning Work in Process Inventory. Under the weighted average method, work performed in the prior period is combined with current period work, and the total costs are averaged over all units. Under the FIFO method, work done in the last period on beginning inventory is not commingled with current period work, nor are costs of beginning inventory added to current period costs to derive unit production cost. With FIFO, current period costs are divided by current period production to generate a unit production cost related entirely to work performed in the current period.

The six basic steps necessary to derive and assign product cost under a process costing system are listed in Exhibit 7–4 and in the Solution Strategies at the end of the chapter. Equivalent units of production must be calculated for each cost component. The cost components include transferred-in costs (in multidepartmental settings), direct material, direct labor, and factory overhead. In cases where multiple materials have different degrees of completion, each material is considered a separate cost component. If factory overhead is applied on a direct labor basis or is incurred at the same rate as direct labor, labor and overhead may be combined as a single cost component and referred to as "conversion cost."

Companies in multidepartment process environments need to track costs continuously as the goods move through departments and from one department to the next. The tracking is handled through the use of a transferred-in cost component for purposes of EUP and cost per EUP computations.

Managers who are aware of spoilage costs can make better decisions as to whether to ignore the causes of spoilage or try to correct them. Impediments to such awareness include using the method of neglect and "burying" the cost of spoilage in predetermined overhead rates rather than accounting for the spoilage separately. Managers may rationalize the existence of these impediments because they believe that a particular cause only creates an insignificant amount of spoilage; thus, tolerances for error are built into the system. Also, managers may believe that spoilage is uncontrollable, when it may actually be controllable.

Many companies now build quality into their processes, which reduces the need for inspections. Often, these companies use statistical process control (SPC) to reduce spoilage. SPC relies on the idea that natural variations occur in a process over time due to random factors and are to be expected. "Out of control" variations also occur, and these commonly produce spoiled units. Control charts are used by workers to record selected nonfinancial performance measures so that process variations can be analyzed.

APPENDIX

Journal Entries Related to Royalty Bakery

Summary journal entries and T-accounts for the Production and Packaging Departments of the Royalty Bakery example given in the chapter (Exhibits 7–5, 7–6, and 7–8) follow. For these entries, the following four assumptions are made: sales for February were 5,470 King Cakes; all sales were on account for $8 per unit; a perpetual weighted average inventory system is used; and Royalty Bakery began February with no Finished Goods Inventory.

■ LEARNING
OBJECTIVE 8
(Appendix) Prepare journal entries for a process costing system.

1. Work in Process Inventory—Production   5,335.00
       Raw Materials Inventory   5,335.00
     To record issuance of direct material
     to production

2. Work in Process Inventory—Production   7,450.66
       Wages Payable   7,450.66
     To accrue wages for direct labor

3. Manufacturing Overhead—Production   8,078.48
       Various accounts   8,078.48
     To record actual overhead costs

4. Work in Process Inventory—Production   8,078.48
       Manufacturing Overhead—Production   8,078.48
     To apply actual overhead to production

5. Work in Process Inventory—Packaging   20,903.40
       Work in Process Inventory—Production   20,903.40
     To transfer completed King Cakes to
     Packaging Department

6. Work in Process Inventory—Packaging   1,370.00
       Raw Materials Inventory   1,370.00
     To record issuance of direct material
     to production

7. Manufacturing Overhead—Packaging   272.95
       Various accounts   272.95
     To record actual overhead costs,
     including indirect labor

8. Work in Process Inventory—Packaging   272.95
       Manufacturing Overhead—Packaging   272.95
     To apply actual overhead to production

9. Finished Goods Inventory   22,413.20
       Work in Process Inventory—Packaging   22,413.20
     To transfer cost of completed units to
     finished goods

10. Cost of Goods Sold   22,372.30
      Finished Goods Inventory   22,372.30
      To transfer cost of units sold from FG
      to CGS (5,470 × $4.09)

11. Accounts Receivable   43,760.00
      Sales   43,760.00
      To record February sales on account
      ($5,470 × $8.00)

SELECTED ROYALTY BAKERY T-ACCOUNTS
(Numbers in parentheses indicate the related journal entry.)

WORK IN PROCESS INVENTORY—Production

Beginning balance	329.06	Transferred out (5)	20,903.40
DM (1)	5,335.00		
DL (2)	7,450.66		
Actual OH (4)	8,078.48		
Ending balance	289.80		

WORK IN PROCESS INVENTORY—Packaging

Beginning balance	438.35	CGM (9)	22,413.20
Transferred in (5)	20,903.40		
DM (6)	1,370.00		
Actual OH (8)	272.95		
Ending balance	571.50		

FINISHED GOODS INVENTORY

Beginning balance	0	CGS (10)	22,372.30
CGM (9)	22,413.20		
Ending balance	40.90		

COST OF GOODS SOLD

February CGS (10)	22,372.30

GLOSSARY

Equivalent units of production (EUP) (p. 319)   an approximation of the number of whole units of output that could have been produced during a period from the actual effort expended during that period

FIFO method (p. 320)   a method of process costing that computes an average cost per equivalent unit of production using only current period production and current cost information; units and costs in beginning inventory are accounted for separately

Method of neglect (p. 335)   a method of treating spoiled units in the equivalent units schedule as if they did not exist

Process costing (p. 316)   a method of accumulating and assigning costs to units of production in companies that make large quantities of homogeneous products

Production and cost report (p. 327)   a document used in a process costing system; details all manufacturing quantities and costs, shows the computation of cost per EUP, and indicates the cost assignment to goods completed during the period and those remaining in ending Work in Process Inventory

Statistical process control (SPC) (p. 336)   any technique that is used to analyze whether processes are in or out of control; based on the theory that a process varies naturally over time but that uncommon variations also occur and are typically the points at which the process produces errors, which may be defective or spoiled goods or poor service

Total cost to account for (p. 324)   the sum of the balance in beginning Work in Process Inventory plus all current costs for direct material, direct labor, and factory overhead

Total units to account for (p. 321)   the total units that were worked on in a department during the period; consists of beginning inventory units plus units started

Units started and completed (p. 325)   the total units completed during the period minus the units in beginning inventory; alternatively, units started minus units in ending inventory

Weighted average method (p. 320)   a method of process costing that computes an average cost per equivalent unit of production; combines beginning inventory units with current production and beginning inventory costs with current costs to compute that average

---

◼◻▭ SOLUTION STRATEGIES

1. Compute whole units to account for:
    Beginning inventory in whole units
    + Units started (or transferred in) during period
2. Compute whole units accounted for:
    Units completed and transferred out
    + Ending inventory in whole units
3. Compute equivalent units of production per cost component:
    a. Weighted average
        Beginning inventory in whole units
        + Units started and completed*
        + (Ending inventory × Percentage complete)
    b. FIFO
        (Beginning inventory × Percentage not complete at start of period)
        + Units started and completed*
        + (Ending inventory × Percentage complete)
4. Compute total costs to account for:
    Costs in beginning inventory
    + Costs of current period
5. Compute cost per equivalent unit per cost component:
    a. Weighted average
        Cost of component in beginning inventory
        + Cost of component for current period
        = Total cost
        ÷ EUP for component
    b. FIFO
        Cost of component for current period
        ÷ EUP for component

---

*Units started and completed = Units transferred out - Units in beginning inventory

6. Assign costs to inventories:
   a. Weighted average
      1. Transferred out
         (Whole units transferred × Total cost per EUP for all components)
      2. Ending inventory
         (EUP for each component × Cost per EUP for each component)
   b. FIFO
      1. Transferred out:
            Beginning inventory costs
         + (Beginning inventory × Percentage not completed at start of period for
            each component × Cost per EUP for each component)
         + (Units started and completed × Total cost per EUP for all components)
      2. Ending inventory:
            (EUP for each component × Cost per EUP for each component)

DEMONSTRATION PROBLEM

The Big Muddy Brick Company, located near St. Louis, Missouri, manufactures a
high-quality brick used in residential and commercial construction. The firm is small
but highly automated and typically produces about 300,000 bricks per month. A brick
is formed in a continuous production operation. In the initial step, a mixture of soils
and water is forced into a brick mold travelling on a continuous conveyor belt. No
other materials are required to produce a brick. Each brick spends about three days
on the conveyor belt. Approximately the last 36 hours on the conveyor belt are spent
in an oven that removes moisture from the product. The actual time each brick
spends on the conveyor depends on the temperature and humidity conditions inside
and outside of the plant. The conveyer speed is controlled and monitored by a computer. The firm uses a process costing system based on actual costs to assign production costs to output. Costs are accumulated in three cost pools: direct materials, direct
labor, and factory overhead. The following are cost and production data for
November 1996.

Beginning Work in Process Inventory	25,000 bricks
This inventory is 100% complete as to materials, 60% complete as to direct labor, and 36% complete as to factory overhead.	
Started this period	305,000 bricks
Ending Work in Process Inventory	30,000 bricks
This inventory is 100% complete as to materials, 50% complete as to direct labor, and 40% complete as to factory overhead.	

Costs:

	MATERIALS	DIRECT LABOR	OVERHEAD
Beginning inventory	$ 1,330	$ 435	$ 852
Costs incurred in November	12,200	15,000	18,180

Required:
a. Determine the cost of the bricks transferred to Finished Goods Inventory and the
   cost of bricks in ending WIP Inventory for November 1996. Assume the company uses the weighted average method.

b. Repeat part a, but assume the company uses the FIFO method.

■ SOLUTION TO DEMONSTRATION PROBLEM

a. Weighted average:

Step 1: Calculate total units to account for:

Beginning inventory	25,000
Units started during current period	305,000
Units to account for	330,000

Step 2: Calculate the total units accounted for:

Units completed and transferred out	300,000
Units in ending WIP Inventory	30,000
Units accounted for	330,000

Step 3: Determine the equivalent units of production:

	MATERIALS	DIRECT LABOR	OVERHEAD
BI (whole units)	25,000	25,000	25,000
Units started and completed	275,000	275,000	275,000
EI (whole units × % complete)	30,000	15,000	12,000
EUP	330,000	315,000	312,000

Step 4: Determine the total cost to account for:

	MATERIALS	DIRECT LABOR	OVERHEAD
BI cost	$ 1,330	$ 435	$ 852
Current period cost	12,200	15,000	18,180
Total cost to account for	$13,530	$15,435	$19,032

Total all cost pools = $13,530 + $15,435 + $19,032 = $47,997

Step 5: Calculate the cost per equivalent unit of production:

	MATERIALS	DIRECT LABOR	OVERHEAD
Total cost	$ 13,530	$ 15,435	$ 19,032
Divide by EUP	330,000	315,000	312,000
Cost per EUP	$.041	$.049	$.061

Total cost per EUP = $.041 + $.049 + $.061 = $.151

Step 6: Assign costs to inventories and goods transferred out:

Cost of goods transferred ($.151 × 300,000)		$45,300
Cost of ending inventory:		
Materials ($.041 × 30,000)	$ 1,230	
Direct labor ($.049 × 15,000)	735	
Overhead ($.061 × 12,000)	732	2,697
Total cost accounted for		$47,997

b. FIFO method:

Step 1: Calculate total units to account for:

Beginning inventory	25,000
Units started during current period	305,000
Units to account for	330,000

Step 2: Calculate the total units accounted for:

Units completed and transferred out	300,000
Units in ending WIP Inventory	30,000
Units accounted for	330,000

Step 3: Determine the equivalent units of production:

	MATERIALS	DIRECT LABOR	OVERHEAD
BI (EUP not completed in October, the prior period)	0	10,000	16,000
Units started and completed	275,000	275,000	275,000
EI (whole units × % complete)	30,000	15,000	12,000
EUP	305,000	300,000	303,000

Step 4: Determine the total cost to account for:

	MATERIALS	DIRECT LABOR	OVERHEAD
BI cost	$ 1,330	$ 435	$ 852
Current period cost	12,200	15,000	18,180
Total cost to account for	$13,530	$15,435	$19,032

Total all cost pools = $13,530 + $15,435 + $19,032 = $47,997

Step 5: Calculate the cost per equivalent unit of production:

	MATERIALS	DIRECT LABOR	OVERHEAD
Current period cost	$ 12,200	$ 15,000	$ 18,180
Divide by EUP	305,000	300,000	303,000
Cost per EUP	$.04	$.05	$.06

Total cost per EUP = $.04 + $.05 + $.06 = $.15

Step 6: Assign costs to inventories and goods transferred out:

Cost of goods transferred:		
Beginning inventory costs	$ 2,617	
Costs to complete beginning WIP:		
Direct labor ($.05 × 10,000)	500	
Overhead ($.06 × 16,000)	960	
Total cost of beginning inventory	$ 4,077	
Started and completed ($.15 × 275,000)	41,250	
Total cost of goods transferred		$45,327
Cost of ending inventory:		
Materials ($.04 × 30,000)	$ 1,200	
Direct labor ($.05 × 15,000)	750	
Overhead ($.06 × 12,000)	720	2,670
Total cost accounted for		$47,997

END-OF-CHAPTER MATERIALS

■ QUESTIONS

1. Describe the characteristics of a production environment in which process costing would likely be found.

2. What is the major difference in the way departmental costs are assigned to products in job order and process costing systems? How does this difference affect product costs?

3. What is the most important source document for determining the cost of direct materials to be assigned to products for a period in a department? What is the most important source document for determining the cost of direct labor? What information does each of these documents provide?

4. What is meant by the term *equivalent units of production* (EUP), and what is the role of EUP in process costing?

5. What are the two methods used in process costing to assign an average cost to products? How do these methods differ?

6. Briefly describe the six steps involved in assigning product costs in a process costing environment.

7. At the end of a period, the total production costs accumulated in a department are assigned to two groups of products. Identify the two groups. Where do the costs in each group appear on the accounting records?

8. What is meant by the term *transferred out costs*? How does calculation of transferred out cost differ under the weighted average and the FIFO methods?

9. Arrange the following four terms in an equation so that each side of the equation contains two terms and the right-hand side is equal to the left-hand side:

Cost of the beginning inventory	(BI)
Costs transferred out	(TO)
Cost of the ending inventory	(EI)
Costs incurred this period	(TP)

10. Arrange the following terms, which relate to a period's production, in an equation so that the two sides are equal, one side represents total units to account for, and the other side represents total units accounted for:

Units in the beginning inventory	(BI)
Units in the ending inventory	(EI)
Units started and completed	(S&C)
Units started but not completed	(SNC)
Units transferred out	(TO)

11. In computing the cost per equivalent unit of production, is one equivalent unit computation sufficient for all of the cost categories (direct material, direct labor, and factory overhead)? Explain.

12. Which process costing method, weighted average or FIFO, provides the better picture of the actual amount of work accomplished in a period? Explain.

13. In an inflationary environment (in which costs are rising from period to period), which process costing method, weighted average or FIFO, would assign the higher cost to the ending Work in Process Inventory in a department? (Assume production is stable from period to period.) Explain.

14. Describe a circumstance (or circumstances) in which the weighted average and FIFO costs per equivalent unit of production would be identical or nearly identical.

15. In a firm in which the process costing system is used as a primary tool to evaluate periodic cost control as well as to assign costs to products, would weighted average or FIFO more likely be used? Explain.

16. What document is used in process costing to detail all manufacturing quantities and costs and indicate cost assignments? Discuss the information provided to managers by this document.

17. When products are assigned a standard cost in a process costing system, does the cost assignment approach more closely resemble the weighted average or FIFO approach? Explain.

18. Under what circumstances will a department have a cost pool called transferred-in costs?

19. Why should companies design process accounting systems to capture costs of spoilage?

20. How are statistical process control techniques used by companies to control quality-related costs?

21. How do suppliers contribute to the presence or absence of quality in production processes?

22. (Appendix) Assume a food processing company transfers $20,000 of products from the Cleaning Department to the Cutting Department. What would the journal entry be for this transfer?

23. (Appendix) In a company that uses a process costing system and is made up of three sequential processing departments (Cutting, Stitching, and Finishing, respectively), what journal entry would identify the cost of the goods manufactured during the period?

■ EXERCISES

24. (LO 3; *FIFO and WA EUP*) For each of the following situations, determine the equivalent units of production using both the FIFO and weighted average methods:

a.	Units started in production	140,000
	Units transferred out	100,000
	Ending inventory (25% complete)	60,000
	Beginning inventory (40% complete)	20,000
b.	Units started in production	120,000
	Units transferred out	100,000
	Ending inventory (60% complete)	60,000
	Beginning inventory (25% complete)	40,000
c.	Units started in production	35,000
	Units transferred out	30,000
	Beginning inventory (40% complete)	15,000
	Ending inventory (70% complete)	?
d.	Units transferred out	80,000
	Units started in production	?
	Beginning inventory (10% complete)	10,000
	Ending inventory (80% complete)	20,000

25. (LO 3; *Total units; WA EUP*) Southwestern Chemical Company uses a process costing system to account for its production costs (based on the weighted average method). All materials are added at the start of the process, while labor and factory overhead costs are incurred evenly throughout the production process. The company's records for September contained the following information:

Beginning inventory	16,000 gallons
Started during September	400,000 gallons
Transferred out	404,000 gallons

As of September 1, the beginning inventory was 40 percent complete as to labor and overhead. On September 30, the ending inventory was 60 percent complete as to labor and overhead.

a. Determine the total number of units to account for.

b. Determine the equivalent units of production for direct materials.

c. Determine the equivalent units of production for direct labor and factory overhead.

26. (LO 3; *Reconciling FIFO and WA EUP*) On November 1, Royal Company had 20,000 units in process in Department 1 that were 100 percent complete as to material costs and 20 percent complete as to conversion costs. During November, 160,000 units were started in Department 1, and 170,000 units were completed and transferred to Department 2. Work in Process Inventory on November 30 was 100 percent complete as to material costs and 40 percent complete as to conversion costs. By what amount would equivalent units for conversion costs for November differ under the FIFO method and the weighted average method?

27. (LO 3, 4; *WA EUP and cost per EUP*) The Rad Tan Company produces tanning gel in a continuous flow production process. The company uses process costing based on the weighted average method to assign production costs to products. Direct labor costs are incurred evenly throughout the process, while all material is added at the beginning of the process. Following is information on the direct labor costs and physical unit activity for July 1996.

	POUNDS OF GEL
Beginning inventory	14,000
Transferred out this period	50,000
Ending inventory	10,000

	DIRECT LABOR COSTS
Beginning inventory	$ 2,000
Incurred this period	12,000

The beginning inventory for July is 75 percent complete as to direct labor costs and the ending inventory is 60 percent complete.

a. Determine the equivalent units of production for direct labor in July.

b. Determine the cost per equivalent unit of production for direct labor in July.

28. (LO 3, 4; *WA; determining cost of ending WIP*) On April 1, Liquid Fertilizer Company had 6,000 gallons in process in Department A—the first stage of its production cycle. The costs attached to these 6,000 gallons were $2,500 for materials and $2,000 for conversion cost. Materials are added at the beginning of the process, and conversion costs are applied evenly throughout the process. Conversion was 50 percent complete on April 1. During April, 14,000 gallons were started. Material costs incurred in April were $5,500, and conversion costs incurred were $3,400. On April 30, Department A had 5,000 gallons in process that were 60 percent complete. Assuming the company uses the weighted average method, how much cost should be assigned to the ending Work in Process Inventory for April?

29. (LO 3, 4; *WA EUP; cost per EUP; cost distribution*) The Supreme Cream Company produces ice cream and employs a process costing system based on the weighted average method to assign costs to production. Various materials are added at discrete stages in the production process, while direct labor and factory overhead are incurred evenly throughout the process. For the first week in May, the company recorded the following results:

Gallons of ice cream in beginning inventory	4,000	
Gallons of ice cream started	30,000	
Gallons of ice cream completed	24,000	

For the same week, the relevant costs were as follows:

	DIRECT LABOR	FACTORY OVERHEAD
Beginning inventory	$ 2,000	$1,800
Costs this period	10,000	4,500

Also for this week, the beginning inventory was 25 percent complete as to direct labor and 30 percent complete as to factory overhead. The ending inventory was 60 percent complete as to direct labor and 75 percent complete as to overhead.

  a. Compute equivalent units of production for direct labor and overhead.

  b. For direct labor and overhead, compute the cost per equivalent unit of production.

  c. Determine the cost of the direct labor and overhead included in ending Work in Process Inventory and the cost of the two cost elements transferred to Finished Goods Inventory.

30. (*LO 3, 4; FIFO EUP; cost per EUP; cost distribution*) The Thirsty Powder Drink Company employs a process costing system based on the FIFO method. For January 1996, the following information was gathered from the company's records for direct labor costs:

Beginning inventory (40% complete as to labor)	10,000 pounds
Direct labor cost in beginning inventory	$ 450
Ending inventory (80% complete as to labor)	20,000 pounds
Total direct labor costs incurred	$20,000
Cost per equivalent unit for direct labor	$ .10

  a. Compute the total equivalent units (pounds) for direct labor in January.

  b. Determine the cost of direct labor in goods completed and transferred out.

  c. Compute the cost of direct labor in the ending WIP Inventory.

31. (*LO 3, 4; WA EUP; cost per EUP; cost distribution*) The Global Oil Refinery uses a process costing system based on the FIFO method. Some summary information for April 1996 on direct labor costs in the Chemical Department follows:

Beginning inventory (40% complete as to labor)	3,000,000 gallons
Units started	15,000,000 gallons
Ending inventory (30% complete as to labor)	5,000,000 gallons
Direct labor cost per equivalent unit	$ .05
Total direct labor costs transferred out	$737,000

Suppose the company used the weighted average method rather than the FIFO method.

  a. Determine the direct labor cost per equivalent unit of production.

  b. Determine the direct labor cost assigned to ending Work in Process Inventory.

32. (*LO 3, 4, 5; FIFO EUP; cost per EUP; cost distribution*) The Magicure Company manufactures a flu vaccine in a single-process production system. The company

352 PART II USING MANAGERIAL ACCOUNTING INFORMATION IN COSTING

uses a process costing system based on standard costs. The company's standard costs for a single vial follow:

	STANDARD COST PER VIAL
Direct materials	$1
Direct labor	6
Manufacturing overhead	2
Total	$9

Materials are added at the beginning of the production process, and conversion costs are applied evenly throughout the process. Production and WIP Inventory information for February 1996 follows:

Beginning inventory	3,000 vials (30% complete)
Started this period	12,000 vials
Ending inventory	2,000 vials (80% complete)

For February 1996, compute the following:

a. equivalent units of production for direct materials and conversion costs. (Hint: Standard cost EUP calculations are the same as FIFO EUP calculations.)

b. the cost of the ending inventory and goods completed and transferred out. (Hint: In a standard cost system, inventory costs are based on standard, not actual, costs.)

33. (LO 6; *Missing numbers; multidepartment production*) The Hybrid Fruit Company produces a limited variety of fruit drinks in a three-stage production process. Each stage of the process is organized as a separate department, and maintains a separate Work in Process Inventory account to track and assign costs to production. Sequentially the departments are Steaming, Mixing, and Packaging. Limited information on the inventory accounts follows for March:

WIP INVENTORY—STEAMING

Beginning	$ 60,000		
DM	180,000		
DL	40,000	?	
OH	50,000		
Ending	$ 36,000		

WIP INVENTORY—MIXING

Beginning	$200,000		
Trans. In	?		
DM	?	$400,000	
DL	?		
OH	?		
Ending	$140,000		

WIP INVENTORY—PACKAGING

Beginning	$180,000		
Trans. In	?		
DM	200,000		
DL	400,000	?	
OH	120,000		
Ending	$220,000		

FINISHED GOODS INVENTORY

Beginning	$330,000		
CGM	?	$960,000	
Ending	?		

a. What was the cost of goods transferred from the Steaming Department to the Mixing Department in March?

    b. What was the sum of direct materials, direct labor, and factory overhead costs in the Mixing Department for March?

    c. What was the cost of the goods manufactured for March?

34. (LO 8; *Appendix*) Following are transactions of the Smithfield Pellet Company for January 1997. The company manufactures alfalfa pellets that are used as animal feed. The company processes alfalfa in a two-department sequential process. The first process, dehydration, removes moisture from raw alfalfa; the second process, pelletizing, compresses the alfalfa into pellets. Provide the journal entry for each transaction.

    a. Alfalfa costing $100,000 was removed from Raw Material Inventory and entered processing in the Dehydration Department.

    b. The Dehydration Department paid labor costs of $120,000; of this amount, $80,000 was considered direct.

    c. Other factory overhead costs amounting to $70,000 were incurred in the Dehydration Department. (Note: credit Accounts Payable.)

    d. Goods costing $330,000 were transferred from the Dehydration Department to the Pelletizing Department.

    e. Labor costs of $81,000 were paid in the Pelletizing Department; $62,000 of this amount was considered direct.

    f. Other overhead costs incurred in the Pelletizing Department amounted to $113,000. (Note: credit Accounts Payable.)

    g. Goods costing $490,000 were transferred from the Pelletizing Department to Finished Goods Inventory.

    h. Goods costing $450,000 were sold for $730,000 cash.

■ COMMUNICATION ACTIVITIES

35. (LO 7; *Statistical process controls*) Assume that the pedals, wheels, chain, and gears on your bicycle are the equivalent of a manufacturing process. Further assume that the bicycle is in perfect working order. Now, consider how many revolutions of the pedals would be required to move the bicycle a distance of 100 yards (one production run), given that the bicycle is always in the same gear. Assume that this process, repeated many times (trials), is equivalent to many production runs.

    a. Even though the bicycle is in perfect working order, why will the number of revolutions required to move the bicycle a distance of 100 yards be expected to vary somewhat from one trial to the next?

    b. Suppose the bicycle is in perfect working order and you conduct 100 trials in which you pedal the bicycle a distance of 100 yards. How could the resulting information be used as a statistical guide in future tests of whether the bicycle is "in control"?

36. (LO 1; *Location of processes*) It is interesting how process-oriented companies organize their activities. For some global industries almost all processing steps for a given product are performed in a single location. For other industries, processing steps are distributed strategically around the globe. Consider the following industries: chemicals, pharmaceuticals, and lumber production. Prepare a short paper that addresses the following questions.

    a. What factors are likely to drive the decision to geographically scatter production activities?

    b. What factors are likely to limit the extent to which a company in one of the three industries mentioned above can geographically distribute activities?

■ PROBLEMS

37. (LO 3; *FIFO and WA methods*) The Fat Cat Food Company produces canned cat food. The company employs a process costing system to assign production costs to the units produced. For the second week in July, the firm had a beginning inventory of 20,000 cans that were 20 percent complete as to materials and 50 percent complete as to conversion costs. During the week, an additional 100,000 cans were started in production. At the end of the week, 25,000 cans were still in process; these cans were 70 percent complete as to materials and 80 percent complete as to conversion costs. For the second week in July, perform the following tasks:

   a. Compute the total units to account for.

   b. Determine how many units were started and completed.

   c. Determine the equivalent units of production for each cost component based on the FIFO method.

   d. Determine the equivalent units of production for each cost component based on the weighted average method.

   e. reconcile your answers in parts c and d.

38. (LO 3, 4; *WA; multidepartment production and cost report*) Mississippi Automotive manufactures bumpers for cars. Its operations comprise a continuous process executed in two departments: Machining and Finishing. For August, company records indicate the following production results:

	MACHINING	FINISHING
Units in beginning inventory	0	0
Units started or transferred in	40,000	20,000
Units completed	20,000	10,000
Units in ending inventory	20,000	10,000

   Percent of completion for units in process at August 31 follow:
Machining: materials, 100 percent; labor, 80 percent; factory overhead, 80 percent
Finishing: materials, 0 percent; labor, 60 percent; factory overhead, 40 percent
   Cost records indicate the following for the month:

	MACHINING	FINISHING
Materials	$ 80,000	$44,600
Labor	144,000	73,600
Factory overhead	36,000	31,920

   a. Prepare a production and cost report for each department for August.

   b. Why was it unnecessary in this instance to specify whether the company uses the FIFO or weighted average method?

39. (LO 3, 4; *WA; cost distribution*) Ellicon Company produces a single product, which is a preservative used in the manufacture of canned food products. The company employs a process costing system based on the weighted average cost flow assumption. The following information pertains to the company's operations for October 1997:

UNIT DATA

Beginning work in process	12,000 gallons
(70% complete as to conversion)	

Started this period   24,000 gallons
Ending work in process   17,000 gallons
  (40% complete as to conversion)

COST DATA	DIRECT MATERIALS	CONVERSION COSTS
Beginning work in process	$ 9,500	$14,700
Incurred this period	35,600	73,080

All materials are introduced at the start of the process.

a. Determine the total number of units to account for.
b. Compute the total costs to account for in each cost pool.
c. Compute the cost per equivalent unit for direct materials and for conversion.
d. Compute the cost assigned to the goods transferred to Finished Goods Inventory and the cost of ending Work in Process Inventory.

40. (LO 3, 4; *FIFO; production and cost report*) LiquidFlo, Inc., manufactures tubular steel products in a three process operation. December information on the first process, Milling, follows:

Units in process, December 1   6,000
Units started in production   45,000
Units in process, December 31   5,000

All materials are added at the start of the milling process. Work in Process Inventory on December 1 was 40 percent complete as to labor and overhead. Work in Process Inventory on December 31 was 30 percent complete as to labor and factory overhead. A summary of costs follows:

	BEGINNING INVENTORY	DECEMBER
Materials	$43,000	$315,000
Labor	13,600	270,000
Factory overhead	9,000	180,400

Prepare a production and cost report for Milling for December, assuming that LiquidFlo, Inc., uses a FIFO process costing system.

41. (LO 3, 4; *FIFO; cost distribution*) AgriGrow Chemical Company produces anhydrous ammonia, which is used as a farm fertilizer. In its plant, the firm accounts for the product costs using a process costing system based on the FIFO method. The following information pertaining to direct labor costs has been extracted from the company's cost records for March:

Beginning inventory (60% complete as to direct labor)   1,000,000 pounds
Beginning inventory cost $108,000
Direct labor costs incurred this period $1,600,000
Direct labor cost per equivalent unit (pound) $.20
Ending inventory (40% complete as to direct labor)   500,000 pounds

a. For March, what was the denominator used in computing the cost per equivalent unit for direct labor?
b. Compute the cost of direct labor in the ending inventory.
c. Compute the cost of direct labor in the goods transferred out.

42. (LO 3, 4, 8; *FIFO method*) Hillsdale Beverages employs a process costing system (based on the FIFO method) in its non-alcoholic beer production plants. In the company's Colorado plant, beer is packaged in 16-gallon kegs. Materials are added at the beginning of the process, and conversion costs are incurred evenly throughout the process. Unit information for a recent period follows:

Beginning inventory	500 kegs (40% complete)
Units started	4,000 kegs
Ending inventory	1,000 kegs (80% complete)

The following are relevant costs for the same period.

	DIRECT MATERIALS	CONVERSION COSTS
Beginning inventory	$ 900	$ 590
Current period costs	7,200	11,685

a. Determine the total units to account for.
b. Determine the equivalent units of production.
c. Determine the cost per equivalent unit.
d. Determine the cost of the ending inventory and the cost of goods completed and transferred out.
e. Prepare the journal entry for the transfer of goods from Work in Process Inventory to Finished Goods Inventory.

43. (LO 3, 4, 6; *FIFO; two materials*) Downtown Bakery produces sheet cakes in mass quantities and uses a process costing system to account for its costs. The bakery production line is set up in one department. Batter is mixed first, with all necessary ingredients added at the start of production. The batter is poured into pans, baked, and cooled. Then the cake is iced with a mixture of confectionary sugar and water. The last step in the process is to let the icing harden and move the cake into a display case. Icing is added when the cakes are at the 85 percent stage of completion.

   Production and cost data for April 1997 follow. Beginning inventory consisted of 20 cakes, which were 80 percent complete as to labor and production overhead. The batter associated with beginning inventory had a cost of $60, and related conversion costs totaled $32. A total of 430 cakes were started during April, and 440 were completed. The ending inventory was 90 percent complete as to labor and production overhead. Costs for the month were: batter, $1,324.40; icing, $31.50; and conversion cost, $857.34.

   a. Using the FIFO method, determine the equivalent units of production for each cost component for April for Downtown Bakery.
   b. Calculate the cost per unit for each cost component for the bakery for April.
   c. Determine the appropriate valuation for April's ending Work in Process Inventory and the units transferred to the display case for sale.
   d. The bakery sells its cakes for $7.75 each. During April, 427 cakes were sold. What was the total gross profit margin on the sale of the cakes?

44. (LO 3, 4; *WA and FIFO; production and cost report*) In a single-process production system, the Spookum Corporation produces wax lips for Halloween. For September 1997, the company's accounting records reflected the following:

Beginning Work in Process Inventory	10,000 units
100% complete as to Material A	
0% complete as to Material B	
40% complete as to direct labor	
60% complete as to factory overhead	

Started during the month   80,000 units
Ending Work in Process Inventory   15,000 units
   100% complete as to Material A
     0% complete as to Material B
    30% complete as to direct labor
    40% complete as to factory overhead

COST DATA	BEGINNING INVENTORY	SEPTEMBER
Material A	$1,900	$ 8,000
Material B	0	37,500
Direct labor	1,195	7,550
Factory overhead	1,530	9,000

a. For September, prepare a production and cost report assuming the company uses the weighted average method.

b. Prepare a production and cost report for September assuming the company uses the FIFO method.

c. How does the weighted average method help disguise what was apparently poor cost control in August?

45. (LO 3, 4, 7; *WA EUP; spoilage*) The Aziz Company manufactures coil springs in a single-step production process. The determination of spoiled goods is made upon inspection at the end of the process, after all costs have been incurred. All material is added at the beginning of the process. Assume the following data:

Beginning inventory units (60% complete as to conversion)	8,000
Units started	41,000
Ending inventory units (30% complete as to conversion)	6,000
Good units completed	40,000
Spoiled units	3,000

	MATERIALS	CONVERSION	TOTAL
Beginning inventory	$ 43,700	$ 17,000	$ 60,000
Current period	207,000	129,300	336,300
Total costs	$250,700	$146,300	$396,300

a. Prepare an EUP schedule using the weighted average method and the method of neglect for the spoiled units.

b. Determine the cost per equivalent unit based on the EUP schedule in part a.

c. Instead of using the method of neglect, prepare an EUP schedule and determine the cost per equivalent unit by extending the spoiled units to the equivalent unit column. (Note: Each spoiled unit was 100% complete upon inspection.)

d. What is the total cost of spoiled production for the period?

e. Why would the use of the method of neglect not encourage managers to decrease spoilage?

46. (LO 3, 4; *Multiproduct*) Gregg Industries manufactures a variety of plastic products including a series of molded chairs. The three models of molded chairs, which are all variations of the same design, are Standard (can be stacked), Deluxe (with arms), and Executive (with arms and padding). The company uses batch manufacturing and has a process costing system.

Gregg has an extrusion operation and subsequent operations to form, trim, and finish the chairs. Plastic sheets are produced by the extrusion operation, some of which are sold directly to other manufacturers. During the forming operation, the remaining plastic sheets are molded into chair seats and the legs are added; the Standard model is sold after this operation. During the trim operation, the arms are added to the Deluxe and Executive models and the chair edges are smoothed. Only the Executive model enters the finish operation where the padding is added. All of the units produced receive the same steps within each operation.

The May production run had a total manufacturing cost of $898,000. The units of production and direct material costs incurred were as follows:

	UNITS PRODUCED	EXTRUSION MATERIALS	FORM MATERIALS	TRIM MATERIALS	FINISH MATERIALS
Plastic sheets	5,000	$ 60,000			
Standard model	6,000	72,000	$24,000		
Deluxe model	3,000	36,000	12,000	$ 9,000	
Executive model	2,000	24,000	8,000	6,000	$12,000
	16,000	$192,000	$44,000	$15,000	$12,000

Manufacturing costs applied during May were:

	EXTRUSION OPERATION	FORM OPERATION	TRIM OPERATION	FINISH OPERATION
Direct labor	$152,000	$60,000	$30,000	$18,000
Factory overhead	240,000	72,000	39,000	24,000

a. For each product produced by Gregg Industries during May, determine the
1. unit cost.
2. total cost.
Be sure to account for all costs incurred during the month, and support your answer with appropriate calculations.
b. Without prejudice to your answer in part a, assume that 1,000 units of the Deluxe model remained in Work in Process Inventory at the end of the month. These units were 100 percent complete in the trim operation. Determine the cost assigned to the 1,000 units of the Deluxe model in Gregg Industries' Work in Process Inventory at the end of May.
(CMA)

47. (LO 3, 4, 6, 8; *WA; second department; appendix*) The Festive Calendar Company produces desktop calendars in a two-process, two-department operation. In the first process (the Printing Department), materials are printed and cut. In the second process (the Assembly Department), materials received from the Printing Department are assembled into individual calendars and then bound. Each department maintains its own Work in Process Inventory account, and costs are assigned by use of the weighted average process costing method. In the Assembly Department, conversion costs are incurred evenly throughout the process, while direct materials are attached to the product at the end of the process. For November 1996, the following costs were recorded in the Assembly Department:

	TRANSFERRED IN	CONVERSION	MATERIALS
Beginning inventory	$19,000	$ 600	$ 0
Incurred this period	85,000	17,000	21,000

For November, the beginning inventory in the Assembly Department contained 20,000 calendars, and an additional 80,000 calendars were transferred in from the Printing Department. The ending inventory consisted of 30,000 calendars that were 60 percent through the conversion process. For November, perform the following tasks:

a. Compute the cost per equivalent unit of production for all three cost pools.
b. Compute the cost transferred to Finished Goods Inventory.
c. Compute the cost of the ending WIP Inventory.
d. Record the journal entries to recognize the activity in the department.

48. (LO 3, 4, 6, 8; *WA and FIFO EUP; two departments; appendix*) In a two-process operation, SunFan Inc. manufactures beach umbrellas. Information for a recent period follows:

	DEPARTMENT	
UNITS	*Assembly*	*Finishing*
Beginning inventory	10,000	12,000
Units started	20,000	
Units transferred	26,000	
Ending inventory	4,000	10,000
CURRENT COSTS		
Materials	$22,000	$14,000
Labor	8,136	9,000

OTHER INFORMATION

Beginning Work in Process Inventory in the Assembly Department was one-half complete with respect to conversion costs. Material is added at the start of production. Beginning inventory includes $11,300 for material costs and $2,000 for direct labor. Factory overhead is applied at the rate of 50 percent of direct labor cost. Ending inventory is 40 percent complete as to conversion.

Beginning Work in Process Inventory in the Finishing Department was 75 percent complete with respect to conversion costs. Material is added at the end of the process. Beginning inventory includes $17,560 for transferred-in costs and $3,200 for direct labor. Factory overhead is applied at the rate of 100 percent of direct labor cost. Ending inventory was estimated to be 25 percent complete as to conversion.

a. Calculate the cost of goods transferred from each department and the cost of ending work in process inventories. Use the FIFO method for Assembly and the weighted average method for Finishing.
b. Record the journal entries necessary to recognize the activity in each department. Assume the following additional facts:
   1. All units completed during the period were sold for 200 percent of cost.
   2. There was no beginning finished goods inventory.
   3. Applied overhead was equal to actual overhead in each department.

■ **CASES**

49. (LO 3, 4; *FIFO and WA*) Safe-T-Light, Inc., manufactures outdoor lights for patios and gardens. The lights are sold to various major department stores under private labels. At the beginning of February 1997, the company had 4,000 lights in beginning work in process inventory, which were 90 percent complete as to

material and 75 percent complete as to conversion. During the month, 22,000 units were started; at the end of February, 5,000 remained in process. The ending work in process inventory was 60 percent complete as to material and 40 percent complete as to conversion.

Actual cost data for the month were as follows:

	MATERIAL	CONVERSION	TOTAL
Beginning inventory	$ 82,200	$ 31,000	$113,200
Current costs	397,800	245,000	642,800
Total costs	$480,000	$276,000	$756,000

a. Prepare EUP schedules under the FIFO and weighted average methods.
b. Prepare production and cost reports under the FIFO and weighted average methods.
c. Discuss the differences in the two reports prepared for part b. Which would provide better information to departmental managers, and why?

50. (LO 3, 4, 6, 8; WA; two departments; appendix) One Deep Well is a small business that provides water to approximately 200 rural households in western Wyoming. The company is organized into two departments. In the Screening Department, water is pulled from a local river and then pushed through a series of screens to remove large particulates. In the Chemical Department, the water is run through a series of fine filters, and then chemicals such as chlorine and fluoride are added. For November, the company experienced the following results:

			PERCENTAGES OF COMPLETION	
Units	Gallons (000s)	Transferred In	Materials	Conversion
Screening Department				
Beginning inventory	100	NA	100%	40%
Transferred out	2,000			
Ending inventory	200	NA	100%	60%
Chemical Department				
Beginning inventory	80	100%	0%	40%
Transferred in	?			
Ending inventory	100	100%	0%	70%

Costs	Transferred In	Materials	Conversion
Screening Department			
Beginning inventory	NA	$ 600	$ 120
November costs	NA	6,000	2,000
Chemical Department			
Beginning inventory	$424	$ 0	$ 90
November costs	?	3,960	3,600

a. Prepare a production and cost report for the Screening Department for November assuming the company uses the weighted average method.
b. Prepare a production and cost report for the Chemical Department for November assuming the company uses the weighted average method.
c. Prepare the journal entries for the transfer of goods in November from the Screening Department to the Chemical Department and from the Chemical Department to the potable water storage tank (Finished Goods Inventory).

51. (LO 6, 8; *Cost flows; multidepartment; appendix*) The Beach Ball Company produces rubberized beach balls in a variety of colors. Each ball passes through
three separate departments before it is complete and ready for shipment to
sporting goods wholesalers. The ball begins in the Molding Department, then
passes into the Vulcanizing Department, and is finished in the Packaging
Department. Product costs are separately tracked by department and assigned
by use of a process costing system. Overhead is applied to production in each
department at a rate of 70 percent of the department's direct labor cost. The following information pertains to departmental operations for the second complete
year of the company's existence.

WIP INVENTORY—MOLDING			
Beginning	$50,000		
DM	80,000		
DL	80,000	?	
OH	?		
Ending	$25,000		

WIP INVENTORY—VULCANIZING			
Beginning	$80,000		
Trans. In	?		
DM	40,000		
DL	?	$320,000	
OH	?		
Ending	$50,000		

WIP INVENTORY—PACKAGING			
Beginning	$120,000		
Trans. In	?		
DM	?		
DL	20,000	?	
OH	?		
Ending	$ 90,000		

FINISHED GOODS INVENTORY			
Beginning	$185,000		
CGM	450,000		
		$520,000	
Ending	?		

   a. What was the cost of goods transferred from the Molding Department to the
Vulcanizing Department for the year?

   b. How much direct labor cost was incurred in the Vulcanizing Department?
How much overhead?

   c. How much direct material cost was charged to products passing through the
Packaging Department?

   d. Prepare the journal entries for all interdepartmental transfers of products,
including the transfer from the Packaging Department to the Finished
Goods Inventory.

52. (LO 3, 4; *FIFO cost assignments*) Wood Glow Manufacturing Company produces
a single product, a wood refinishing kit that sells for $17.95. The final process-
ing of the kits occurs in the Packaging Department. An internal quilted wrap is
applied at the beginning of the packaging process. A compartmentalized outside
box printed with instructions and the company's name and logo is added when
units are 60 percent through the process. Conversion costs, consisting of direct
labor and applied overhead, occur evenly throughout the packaging process.
The following data pertain to the activities of the Packaging Department during
October.

   ■ Beginning Work in Process Inventory was 10,000 units, 40 percent complete
as to conversion costs.

   ■ 30,000 units were started and completed in the month.

■ There were 10,000 units in ending Work in Process Inventory , 80 percent complete as to conversion costs.

The Packaging Department's October costs were:

Quilted wrap	$80,000
Outside boxes	50,000
Direct labor	22,000
Applied factory overhead ($3.00 per direct labor dollar)	66,000

The costs transferred in from prior processing were $3 per unit. The cost of the goods sold for October was $240,000, and the ending Finished Goods Inventory was $84,000. Wood Glow uses the FIFO method of process costing.

Wood Glow's controller, Mark Brandon, has been asked to analyze the activities of the Packaging Department for October. Brandon knows that in order to properly determine the department's unit cost of production, he must first calculate the equivalent units of production.

a. Prepare an equivalent units of production schedule for the October activity in the Packaging Department. Be sure to account for the beginning Work in Process Inventory, the units started and completed during the month, and the ending Work in Process Inventory.
b. Determine the cost per equivalent unit of the October production.
c. Assuming that the actual overhead incurred during October was $5,000 more than the overhead applied, describe how the cost of the ending Work in Process Inventory would be determined.

(CMA)

53. (LO 3, 4; *FIFO and WA*) Kristina Company, which manufactures quality paint sold at premium prices, uses a single production department. Production begins with the blending of various chemicals, which are added at the beginning of the process, and ends with the canning of the paint. Canning occurs when the mixture reaches the 90 percent stage of completion. The gallon cans are then transferred to the Shipping Department for crating and shipment. Labor and overhead are added continuously throughout the process. Factory overhead is applied at the rate of $3.00 per direct labor hour.

Prior to May, when a change in the process was implemented, work in process inventories were insignificant. The change in process enables greater production but results in substantial amounts of work in process for the first time. The company has always used the weighted average method to determine equivalent production and unit costs. Now, production management is considering changing from the weighted average method to the first-in, first-out method.

The following data relate to actual production during May:

UNITS FOR MAY (GALLONS)

Work in Process Inventory, May 1 (25% complete)	4,000
Sent to Shipping Department	20,000
Started in May	21,000
Work in Process Inventory, May 31 (80% complete)	5,000

COSTS AT MAY 1:

Work in Process Inventory, May 1 (4,000 gallons, 25% complete)	
Direct materials—chemicals	$ 45,600
Direct labor ($10 per hour)	6,250
Factory overhead	1,875

Mᴀʏ ᴄᴏꜱᴛꜱ ᴀᴅᴅᴇᴅ

Direct materials—chemicals	$228,400
Direct materials—cans	7,000
Direct labor ($10 per hour)	35,000
Factory overhead	10,500

a. Prepare a schedule of equivalent units for each cost element for May using the
    1. weighted average method.
    2. FIFO method.
b. Calculate the cost (to the nearest cent) per equivalent unit for each element for May using the
    1. weighted average method.
    2. FIFO method.
c. Discuss the advantages and disadvantages of using the weighted average method versus the FIFO method, and explain under what circumstances each method should be used.

(CMA)

■ ETHICS AND QUALITY DISCUSSIONS

54. Hard-driving expansion in the 1970s and 1980s led Groupe Michelin, a French company, to the number-one position in worldwide tire manufacturing. However, the company's organizational structure failed to keep pace with the rate of expansion. More to the point, the company failed to consider local differences in the many new plants it opened:

> *Mr. Michelin simply transferred his French systems to his new plants, often giving processes French code names that U.S. employees didn't understand. Eager for discipline, he sometime hired former military people in the U.S.*
>
>   *. . . by 1991, debt from the expansion had twice plunged the family-controlled company into deep financial trouble. Costs were out of control and proud Michelin was getting slaps in the face from valued customers and distributors. Sears, Roebuck & Co., Michelin's biggest U.S. distributor, complained of too-slow delivery and warned that it was starting to buy more tires from Michelin's archrivals: Goodyear Tire & Rubber Co., Bridgestone Inc. of Japan and Pirelli SpA of Italy.*
>
>   *To protect what it considers superior methods, Michelin guarded secrets even among employees, in France and around the world. Its test tracks, for example, were off-limits even to most senior executives.*
>
>   *Belatedly realizing that he had been too slow to modernize, family patriarch Francois Michelin now is reinventing his own company. He is tearing down strict, inward-looking management systems that he long considered a key to his success. He is slowly, uncomfortably, lifting the secrecy that had kept Michelin from communicating properly even with itself.*

[ꜱᴏᴜʀᴄᴇ: E.S. Browning, "Michelin Is Setting Out on the Road to Transformation," *Wall Street Journal* (September 22, 1994), p. B4. Reprinted by permission of The Wall Street Journal, © 1994 Dow Jones & Company, Inc. All Rights Reserved Worldwide.]

a. How could centralization both promote and impede the pursuit of quality in production processes at Michelin?
b. How could local decision making improve the quality of Michelin's processes.
c. What knowledge would local managers likely have that central managers lack? How would this knowledge relate to the control of quality?

55. GM recently announced a major overhaul of its organizational structure. Perhaps the most stunning announcement involved the Saturn Division, which previously had been a free-standing independent division.

GM has decided that for Saturn to grow and make more money, it must share engineering and manufacturing processes and economies of scale with other GM small cars, both in North America and Europe. As reported, GM is considering having Saturn sell vehicles developed by its German-based Adam Opel AG unit.

"This is a step toward reabsorbing Saturn into the mainstream of GM. It'll be a little less of a fully independent company," said David Healy, an analyst with S. G. Warburg & Co. "Over time, Saturn is going to share more GM products. Instead of independently developing new models, Saturn is going to be linked up with GM in a product sense more than it is right now."

[According to the executive in charge of GM's small car division:] . . . the reorganization will enable [Saturn] to share "technology, ideas and experience" with GM's other small cars.

[SOURCE: Gabriella Stern, "GM Puts Saturn in Small-Car Group, Shakes Up North American Operations," *Wall Street Journal* (October 5, 1994), p. A7. Reprinted by permission of The Wall Street Journal, © 1994 Dow Jones & Company, Inc. All Rights Reserved Worldwide.]

a. Go to your school library and find news articles describing the original formation of the Saturn Division. What were the major reasons given for the establishment of this new GM division?

b. In light of the reasons given, do you think that the integration of the Saturn Division into the GM Small Car Group is a wise move on the part of GM?

c. What will be the likely impact of this restructuring on the quality of other products in the Small Car Group?

d. What will be the likely impact of this restructuring on the quality of the Saturn line?

56. *[In the fall of 1994,] Johnson & Johnson's McNeil Consumer Products Co. unit will launch the Arthritis Foundation Pain Relievers: acetaminophen (both day and nighttime formulas), ibuprofen and coated aspirin. The drugs, chemically, are no different from others of their type.*

Under a royalty arrangement, Johnson & Johnson will guarantee the Arthritis Foundation at least $1 million a year, which the group says it will use to sponsor scientific research on curing arthritis. In exchange, Johnson & Johnson will capitalize on the credibility of the foundation.

"Whether true or false, the perception will be there that this is a good product for arthritis," says Jack Trout, president of Trout & Ries, a Greenwich, Conn., marketing strategy firm. "It isn't as good as the 'Good Housekeeping' seal, but it has the 'Good Housekeeping' cachet."

Still, some donors may be "turned off" by seeing a group they support put its name on a product, says George Annas, director of the law, medicine and ethics program at Boston University. "The real societal question is whether there is any difference between profit and nonprofit organizations in this country anymore," Mr. Annas says.

[SOURCE: Pamela Sebastian, "Nonprofit Group's Name to Go on For-Profit Pills," *Wall Street Journal* (July 13, 1994), p. B1. Reprinted by permission of The Wall Street Journal, © 1994 Dow Jones & Company, Inc. All Rights Reserved Worldwide.]

a. What are the ethical considerations involved in a not-for-profit entity's endorsement of a for-profit entity's products?

b. How does your answer in part a depend on whether the for-profit firm is paying a fee for the endorsement?

c. Is the Arthritis Foundation achieving or undermining its objectives by endorsing products of Johnson & Johnson?

57. FulRange, Inc., produces complex printed circuits for stereo amplifiers. The circuits are sold primarily to major component manufacturers, and any production overruns are sold to small manufacturers at a substantial discount. The small manufacturer segment appears very profitable because the basic operating budget assigns all fixed expenses to production for the major manufacturers, the only predictable market.

A common product defect that occurs in production is a "drift," caused by failure to maintain precise heat levels during the production process. Rejects from the 100 percent testing program can be reworked to acceptable levels if the defect is drift. However, in a recent analysis of customer complaints, George Wilson, the cost accountant, and the quality control engineer have ascertained that normal rework does not bring the circuits up to standard. Sampling shows that about one-half of the reworked circuits will fail after extended, high-volume amplifier operation. The incidence of failure in the reworked circuits is projected to be about 10 percent over one to five years' operation.

Unfortunately, there is no way to determine which reworked circuits will fail, because testing will not detect this problem. The rework process could be changed to correct the problem, but the cost/benefit analysis for the suggested change in the rework process indicates that it is not practical. FulRange's marketing analyst has indicated that this problem will have a significant impact on the company's reputation and customer satisfaction if it is not corrected. Consequently, the board of directors would interpret this problem as having serious negative implications on the company's profitability.

Wilson has included the circuit failure and rework problem in his report for the upcoming quarterly meeting of the board of directors. Due to the potential adverse economic impact, Wilson has followed a long-standing practice of highlighting this information.

After reviewing the reports to be presented, the plant manager and her staff were upset and indicated to the controller that he should control his people better. "We can't upset the board with this kind of material. Tell Wilson to tone that down. Maybe we can get it by this meeting and have some time to work on it. People who buy those cheap systems and play them that loud shouldn't expect them to last forever."

The controller called Wilson into his office and said, "George, you'll have to bury this one. The probable failure of reworks can be referred to briefly in the oral presentation, but it should not be mentioned or highlighted in the advance material mailed to the board."

Wilson feels strongly that the board will be misinformed on a potentially serious loss of income if he follows the controller's orders. Wilson discussed the problem with the quality control engineer, who simply remarked, "That's your problem, George."

a. Discuss the ethical considerations that George Wilson should recognize in deciding how to proceed in this matter.

b. Explain what ethical responsibilities should be accepted in this situation by
   1. The controller.
   2. The quality control engineer.
   3. The plant manager and her staff.

c. What should George Wilson do in this situation? Explain your answer.

(CMA)

■ PROJECTS

58. Refer to Communication Activity #35. This project is intended is be completed by teams. Your team is charged with the task of reducing the amount of variance in the production process (the number of pedal revolutions required to move the bicycle a distance of 100 yards). As specifically as possible, describe actions that could be taken to improve the consistency and reduce the variability of the production process.

59. Make a list of the prominent manufacturing businesses in your area and indicate whether each would more likely use process costing or job order costing. Identify the reasons each business was so classified.

60. Choose a product that is manufactured in your area. Draft an illustration of the manufacturing process of that product and indicate the points at which you assume that the various manufacturing components would be added. By mail, by phone, or in person, contact the manufacturer to see how well your illustration portrayed the actual process.

III USING MANAGERIAL ACCOUNTING INFORMATION FOR PLANNING

VARIABLE COSTING AND COST-VOLUME-PROFIT ANALYSIS

At the beginning of his undertaking, and at every successive stage, the alert business man strives to modify his arrangements so as to obtain better results with a given expenditure, or equal results with less expenditure.

Alfred Marshall, 1890

LEARNING OBJECTIVES

1. Distinguish between absorption (full) and variable (direct) costing.

2. Convert absorption costing information to variable costing information and vice versa.

3. Compute breakeven point and understand what it represents.

4. Perform cost-volume-profit (CVP) analysis for a single product firm on both before-tax and after-tax bases.

5. Perform a CVP analysis for a multiproduct firm.

6. Explain the underlying assumptions of CVP analysis and how these assumptions create a short-run managerial perspective.

7. Discuss how quality decisions affect the components of CVP analysis.

8. Explain how the margin of safety and operating leverage concepts are used in business.

9. (Appendix) Prepare breakeven and profit-volume graphs.

DeBourgh Manufacturing Co.: High Costs Created Red Ink

DeBourgh Manufacturing was founded in 1909 as a metal fabricating business. Like the rest of the companies in this industry, DeBourgh began suffering from declining sales and high costs in the 1980s. After two divisions of the company had been liquidated, President Steven C. Berg decided that the only way the remaining division—producer of All-American Lockers—could be saved was to move from Bloomington, Minnesota, to a lower-cost environment. Thus, the company packed up 80 semitrailer trucks and moved 1,000 miles to La Junta, Colorado.

The firm incurred some high costs to make the move. First, the physical relocation cost approximately $1.2 million. Second, severance benefits were expensive, because bonuses were paid to employees remaining in Minnesota to encourage them to continue production during the move. Third, the new manufacturing plant needed a replacement roof; and during construction, the plant was flooded by rain, all but halting production for weeks. Despite the additional costs, the company reaped substantial benefits in the variable cost area of labor wages because of a change from a union to a nonunion labor force. The tax environment in La Junta was also less onerous than that in Minnesota. These positive cost factors, combined with an increased sales volume, caused profits to soar and allowed all employees to participate in a profit-sharing plan.

SOURCE: Adapted from *Real World Lessons for America's Small Businesses* (published by Nation's Business magazine on behalf of Connecticut Mutual Life Insurance Company and the U.S. Chamber of Commerce, 1992), p. 45.

A s explained in previous chapters, job order and process costing are two specific costing *systems*. Job order costing is appropriate for companies making products or performing services in compliance with customer specifications. Process costing is appropriate for manufacturers producing large quantities of homogeneous output in a continuous production process. DeBourgh Manufacturing generally uses a job order costing system, because the company normally builds lockers to order for a specific customer contracts.

There are also three methods of cost *measurement*: actual, normal, and standard. Actual costing uses actual direct materials, direct labor, and overhead costs to compute product or service cost. Normal costing includes actual direct material and direct labor costs, but uses predetermined overhead rates to apply factory overhead to production. Standard costing assigns direct material, direct labor, and factory overhead to products or services using established per-unit norms. Many of DeBourgh's lockers are made in a common size and with common specifications, so standard costing can be easily used.

A company's costing system and inventory measurement method provide necessary, but not sufficient, information for determining product cost. Two additional dimensions must be considered: cost accumulation and cost presentation. The method of accumulation specifies which manufacturing cost components are recorded as product cost. The method of presentation focuses on how costs are shown on external financial statements or internal management reports. Accumulation and presentation procedures use either absorption or variable costing. These methods are discussed and contrasted in the first part of the chapter. The methods use the same basic data but structure and process those data differently. Either method can be used in job order or process costing and with actual, normal, or standard costs.

Since covering costs is a matter of operational survival (regardless of whether you manage DeBourgh Manufacturing Company, the Dallas Cowboys, Ace of Base's concert tour, or a dental practice), the second part of the chapter uses variable costing information to find an organization's breakeven point. At breakeven, a company experiences neither profit nor loss on its operating activities and total revenues equal total costs. Managers, however, generally do not want to operate at a volume level that merely covers costs; they want to make profits. Cost-volume-profit analysis adds a profit element into breakeven calculations so that managers are better able to plan for volume goals that should generate income rather than losses.

AN OVERVIEW OF ABSORPTION AND VARIABLE COSTING

Knowing the cost to produce a product or provide a service is important to all businesspeople. But, as discussed in Chapter 3, cost may be defined in a variety of ways. The most common approach to product costing is **absorption costing,** which is also known as full costing. This approach treats the costs of all manufacturing components (direct material, direct labor, variable factory overhead, and fixed factory overhead) as inventoriable, or product, costs. Absorption costing considers costs incurred in the nonmanufacturing (selling and administrative) areas of the organization as period costs and it expenses these costs in a manner that properly matches them with revenues. Exhibit 8–1 on page 372 depicts the absorption costing model.

absorption costing

■ LEARNING OBJECTIVE 1
Distinguish between absorption (full) and variable (direct) costing.

An organization incurs costs for direct material (DM), direct labor (DL), and variable factory overhead (VOH) only when goods are produced or services are rendered. Since total DM, DL, and VOH costs increase with each additional product made or unit of service rendered, these costs are considered product costs and are inventoried until the product or service is sold. Fixed factory overhead (FOH) costs, on the other hand, may be incurred even when production or service facilities are idle. Although total FOH cost does not vary with units of production or level of service, this cost provides the basic capacity necessary for production or service to occur. Because production could not take place without the incurrence of fixed factory overhead, absorption costing considers fixed factory overhead costs to be inventoriable.

Thus, when absorption costing is used, the financial statements show the Work in Process Inventory, Finished Goods Inventory, and Cost of Goods Sold accounts as including variable per-unit production costs as well as a per-unit allocation of fixed factory overhead. Absorption costing also presents expenses on an income statement according to their functional classifications. A **functional classification** is a grouping of costs that were all incurred for the same basic purpose. Functional classifications include categories such as cost of goods sold, selling expenses, and administrative expenses.

functional classification

Variable costing is a cost accumulation method that includes only variable production costs (direct material, direct labor, and variable factory overhead) as inventoriable, or product, costs. Thus, variable costing defines product costs solely as costs of *actual production*. Since fixed factory overhead will be incurred even if there is no production, variable costing proponents believe this cost does not qualify as a product cost. Fixed factory overhead costs are therefore treated as period expenses by being charged against revenue as incurred. Variable costing is also known as direct costing and is illustrated in Exhibit 8–2 on page 373.[1]

variable costing

---

[1]Direct costing is, however, a misnomer for variable costing. All variable *manufacturing* costs, whether direct or indirect, are considered product costs under variable costing.

■ **EXHIBIT 8–1**
Absorption Costing Model

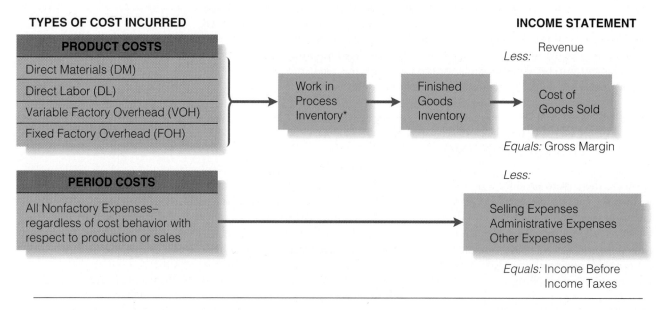

* The actual Work in Process cost that is transferred to Finished Goods is computed as follows:

Beginning Work in Process	XXX
+ Production costs for period (DM + DL + VOH + FOH)	XXX
= Total Work in Process to be accounted for	XXX
− Ending Work in Process (computed using job order, process, or standard costing; also appears on end-of-period Balance Sheet)	XXX
= Cost of Goods Manufactured	XXX

A variable costing income statement or management report separates costs by cost behavior, although it may also present expenses by functional classifications within the behavioral categories. Under variable costing, Cost of Goods Sold is more appropriately called *Variable* Cost of Goods Sold because it is composed only of the variable production costs related to the units sold. Revenue minus variable cost of goods **product contribution margin** sold is called **product contribution margin** and indicates how much revenue is available to cover all period expenses and to provide net income.

Variable nonfactory period expenses (such as a sales commission set at 10 percent of product selling price) are deducted from product contribution margin to determine **total contribution margin** the amount of **total contribution margin.** Total contribution margin is the difference between total revenues and total variable expenses. This amount represents the dollar figure available to "contribute" to the coverage of all fixed expenses, both factory and nonfactory. After fixed expenses are covered, any remaining contribution margin provides income to the company. Variable costing income statements are also known as contribution margin income statements.

Major authoritative bodies of the accounting profession, such as the Financial Accounting Standards Board and Securities and Exchange Commission, apparently believe that absorption costing provides external parties with the most informative picture of earnings. This belief is indicated by the fact that the accounting profession has unofficially disallowed the use of variable costing as a generally accepted inventory measurement method for external reporting purposes since the IRS began requiring absorption costing for tax purposes.[2] The rationale for this position reflects the importance of the matching concept in that absorption costing expenses all product costs in the period that the related revenue is recognized.

On the other hand, managers attempting to use absorption costing information for internal decision making find that combining costs into functional classifications obscures important cost behavior patterns (relative to changes in activity). Therefore,

■ **EXHIBIT 8–2**
Variable Costing Model

TYPES OF COST INCURRED   **INCOME STATEMENT**

Revenue
Less:

PRODUCT COSTS

| Direct Materials (DM) |
| Direct Labor (DL) |
| Variable Factory Overhead (VOH) |

Work in Process Inventory* → Finished Goods Inventory → Variable Cost of Goods Sold

Equals: Product Contribution Margin
Less:

PERIOD COSTS

Variable Nonfactory Expenses →

Variable Nonfactory Expenses (classified as selling, administrative, and other)

Equals: Total Contribution Margin
Less:

| Fixed Factory Overhead |
| Fixed Nonfactory Expenses |

Total Fixed Expenses (classified as factory, selling, administrative, and other)

Equals: Income Before Income Taxes

* The actual Work in Process cost that is transferred to Finished Goods is computed as follows:

Beginning Work in Process	XXX
+ Variable production costs for period (DM + DL + VOH)	XXX
= Total Work in Process to be accounted for	XXX
− Ending Work in Process (computed using job order or process costing; also appears on end-of-period Balance Sheet)	XXX
= Cost of Goods Manufactured	XXX

[2]Robert W. Koehler, "Triple-Threat Strategy," *Management Accounting* (October 1991), p. 34.

while companies must prepare external statements using absorption costing, internal reports are also often prepared to facilitate management analysis and decision making by showing cost behaviors. Variable costs may figure more prominently in short-run decisions because, for ongoing operations, these costs are normally more controllable than fixed costs.

Even with their differences, the two costing methods have some underlying similarities. First, both methods use the same basic cost information. Second, the treatment of direct materials, direct labor, and variable factory overhead is the same under absorption and variable costing; these costs are always considered product costs. Third, selling and administrative expenses are considered period costs under both costing methods. Fourth, there are no differences between accounts other than in Work in Process Inventory, Finished Goods Inventory, and the expense accounts under the two methods. The expense accounts differ only in that, under variable costing, each expense is accounted for relative to its variable or fixed cost behavior. The next section of the chapter provides a detailed illustration of both absorption and variable costing.

ABSORPTION AND VARIABLE COSTING ILLUSTRATIONS

■ LEARNING OBJECTIVE 2
Convert absorption costing information to variable costing information and vice versa.

MetalWorks, Inc., produces high-quality steel school lockers. These lockers are formed in "cabinet units" that have multiple openings. The units are 5 feet long, 6 feet high, and 22 inches deep. The company employs a standard costing system, has negotiated long-term contracts for all material and labor, and has automated the majority of the production processes. For the last two reasons, actual material and labor costs differ little from standard costs in any year. Any variances in variable factory overhead that arise are insignificant in amount and are written off through Cost of Goods Sold as incurred. For purposes of this illustration, the standard and budgeted costs are assumed to remain constant over the years 1995–1997. In addition, actual costs are assumed to be equal to standard costs for each year shown. Exhibit 8–3 provides the standard production costs per unit and the annual budgeted nonproduction costs for MetalWorks, Inc. These costs are used to compare absorption and variable costing procedures and presentations.

MetalWorks, Inc., computes its standard predetermined fixed overhead application rate by dividing budgeted annual fixed factory overhead (FOH) by its budgeted annual capacity in units, as shown in Exhibit 8–3. This calculation provides a standard fixed overhead application rate of $27.50 per unit. An application rate based on units is acceptable for this company because it makes only one type of product.

Actual production and sales information for the years 1995 through 1997 are shown in Exhibit 8–4. Assume that MetalWorks began its 1995 operations with no Finished Goods Inventory. The company also ended 1995 with no Finished Goods Inventory, since all units produced that year were sold. In the other two years, production and sales differ; such a situation is common because production frequently "leads" sales figures as a company stockpiles inventory for a later period.

Absorption Costing

Exhibit 8–5 (page 376) presents absorption costing income statements for MetalWorks, Inc., for 1995–1997. Selling price per unit is $450. The standard absorption cost per unit is $342.50 or the sum of the standard costs of direct materi-

■ **EXHIBIT 8–3**
Metalworks, Inc., Basic Data

Standard variable cost per unit:

Direct material	$185
Direct labor	93
Variable factory overhead	37
Total variable cost per unit	$315

$$\text{Predetermined Fixed Factory Overhead Rate} = \frac{\text{Budgeted Annual Fixed Factory Overhead}}{\text{Budgeted Annual Capacity in Units}}$$

$$= \frac{\$550,000}{20,000} = \$27.50$$

Total absorption cost per unit:

Standard variable cost	$315.00
Standard fixed factory overhead application rate	27.50
Total absorption cost per unit	$342.50

Budgeted nonproduction costs:

Selling expenses (mixed cost)	$210,000 + $18 per unit sold
Administrative expenses (fixed)	$490,000

al ($185), direct labor ($93), variable factory overhead ($37), and fixed factory overhead ($27.50). Cost of goods manufactured is equal to the $342.50 standard production cost per unit multiplied by the number of units produced that year. Ending inventory cost is calculated as the units in ending inventory multiplied by the $342.50 standard cost per unit.

In each year, production volume was not equal to the expected annual volume used to compute the FOH application rate, causing a volume variance to occur. As discussed in Chapter 6, a volume variance is the difference between budgeted and applied fixed overhead. Fixed factory overhead is applied to production based on the actual output of the period. If production is less than expected, the volume variance is unfavorable (U); if production is greater than expected, the volume variance is favorable (F).

In Exhibit 8–5, each year's volume variance is shown as an adjustment to Cost of Goods Sold. An unfavorable volume variance causes Cost of Goods Sold to increase, whereas a favorable volume variance causes Cost of Goods Sold to decrease. Gross

■ **EXHIBIT 8–4**
Actual Production and Sales Information (1995–1997)

YEAR	UNITS PRODUCED	UNITS SOLD
1995	15,000	15,000
1996	21,000	18,000
1997	17,000	20,000
Totals	53,000	53,000

■ EXHIBIT 8–5

Absorption Costing Comparative Income Statements

	1995	1996	1997	TOTAL
Units produced	15,000	21,000	17,000	53,000
Sales volume	15,000	18,000	20,000	53,000
Sales ($450 × number of units sold)	$6,750,000	$8,100,000	$9,000,000	$23,850,000
Cost of Goods Sold:				
Beginning inventory ($342.50 × number of units in BI)	$ 0	$ 0	$1,027,500	$ 0
Cost of goods manufactured ($342.50 × number of units produced)	5,137,500	7,192,500	5,822,500	18,152,500
Cost of goods available	$5,137,500	$7,192,500	$6,850,000	$18,152,500
Ending inventory ($342.50 × number of units in EI)	0	(1,027,500)	0	0
Cost of goods sold ($342.50 × number of units sold)	$5,137,500	$6,165,000	$6,850,000	$18,152,500
Volume Variance*	137,500	(27,500)	82,500	192,500
Adjusted Cost of Goods Sold	$5,275,000	$6,137,500	$6,932,500	$18,345,000
Gross Margin	$1,475,000	$1,962,500	$2,067,500	$ 5,505,000
Operating Expenses:				
Selling [$210,000 + ($18 × number of units sold)]	$ 480,000	$ 534,000	$ 570,000	$ 1,584,000
Administrative (fixed cost)	490,000	490,000	490,000	1,470,000
Total	$ 970,000	$1,024,000	$1,060,000	$ 3,054,000
Income before Tax	$ 505,000	$ 938,500	$1,007,500	$ 2,451,000

*Volume Variance:	1995	1996	1997	TOTAL
Actual production	15,000	21,000	17,000	53,000
×Predetermined FOH rate	× $27.50	× $27.50	× $27.50	× $27.50
Applied FOH	$412,500	$577,500	$467,500	$1,457,500
Budgeted annual FOH (from Exhibit 8–3)	550,000	550,000	550,000	1,650,000
Volume variance	$137,500 U	$ 27,500 F	$ 82,500 U	$ 192,500 U

margin is the difference between sales revenue and the adjusted Cost of Goods Sold. The nonfactory costs shown in Exhibit 8–5 are grouped by functional areas (selling and administrative). As indicated in Exhibit 8–3, selling expenses are mixed costs and contain both a variable and a fixed cost element. The behavior of these different elements are not apparent from the absorption costing income statement.

Variable Costing

Exhibit 8–6 provides the variable costing income statements for MetalWorks, Inc., for the years 1995–1997. Under variable costing, the standard cost per unit is $315 rather than $342.50. This $27.50 difference reflects the fact that fixed factory overhead is included as a period expense in variable costing rather than being allocated on a per-unit basis as part of product cost. Notice also that no volume variance is shown

■ **EXHIBIT 8–6**
Variable Costing Comparative Income Statements

	1995	1996	1997	TOTAL
Units produced	15,000	21,000	17,000	53,000
Sales volume	15,000	18,000	20,000	53,000
Sales ($450 × number of units sold)	$6,750,000	$8,100,000	$9,000,000	$23,850,000
Cost of Goods Sold:				
Beginning inventory ($315 × number of units in BI)	$ 0	$ 0	$ 945,000	$ 0
Cost of goods manufactured ($315 × number of units produced)	4,725,000	6,615,000	5,355,000	16,695,000
Cost of goods available	$4,725,000	$6,615,000	$6,300,000	$16,695,000
Ending inventory ($315 × number of units in EI)	0	945,000	0	0
Variable Cost of Goods Sold ($315 × number of units sold)	$4,725,000	$5,670,000	$6,300,000	$16,695,000
Product Contribution Margin ($135 per unit × number of units sold)	$2,025,000	$2,430,000	$2,700,000	$ 7,155,000
Variable Selling Expenses ($18 × number of units sold)	270,000	324,000	360,000	954,000
Total Contribution Margin ($117 × number of units sold)	$1,755,000	$2,106,000	$2,340,000	$ 6,201,000
Fixed Expenses:				
Factory	$ 550,000	$ 550,000	$ 550,000	$ 1,650,000
Selling	210,000	210,000	210,000	630,000
Administrative	490,000	490,000	490,000	1,470,000
Total	$1,250,000	$1,250,000	$1,250,000	$ 3,750,000
Income before Tax	$ 505,000	$ 856,000	$1,090,000	$ 2,451,000

on the variable costing income statements. A volume variance arises in absorption costing when actual production activity does not equal the activity level used in setting the fixed factory overhead application rate. Since no FOH application rate exists under variable costing, no volume variance can occur.

Cost of goods manufactured in Exhibit 8–6 equals the $315 standard variable production cost multiplied by the number of units produced. Ending inventory is equal to the units *not* sold multiplied by the standard cost of $315 per unit. Product contribution margin each year is a constant amount of $135 multiplied by the number of units sold. The $135 is the difference between the selling price of $450 and the standard variable production cost of $315. Since this per-unit amount is constant, all years having equal sales volumes would also have equal amounts of product contribution margin.

Because of its emphasis on cost behavior, the variable costing income statement also includes the total contribution margin. All variable nonfactory expenses are subtracted from product contribution margin to derive total contribution margin. For MetalWorks, Inc., the only variable nonfactory expense is the selling cost of $18 per unit sold. The contribution margin percentage is equal to total contribution margin divided by total sales. This percentage is constant at 26 percent each year, as shown:

	DOLLARS	PERCENTAGE
Sales price per unit	$450	100%
Variable production costs per unit	315	70%
Product contribution margin per unit	$135	30%
Variable selling expenses per unit	18	4%
Total contribution margin per unit	$117	26%

The contribution margin percentage indicates that $.26 of each $1.00 of sales can be used to cover fixed costs and to generate a profit for the firm.

All fixed expenses are deducted from the total contribution margin to determine income before taxes for the year. The fixed expenses include the fixed factory overhead of $550,000, the fixed selling expenses of $210,000, and the fixed administrative expenses of $490,000.

Note that all nonfactory expenses for each year are always shown as period costs on both sets of income statements. For example, total 1995 selling expenses are shown in Exhibit 8–5 as a single amount of $480,000. Under variable costing, these amounts are merely rearranged on the income statement into their separate variable and fixed component amounts. In Exhibit 8–6, for example, the $480,000 of selling expenses are separated into their variable ($270,000) and fixed ($210,000) amounts. The variable selling expenses are included in determining total contribution margin, while the fixed portion is deducted from total contribution margin.

Variable costing income statements are more useful internally for planning, controlling, and decision making than absorption costing statements are. This benefit exists because, to effectively carry out their various functions, managers need to understand and be able to project how different costs will change in reaction to changes in activity levels. "Systems designed mainly to value inventory for financial and tax statements are not giving managers the accurate and timely information they need to promote operating efficiencies and measure product costs."[3]

Comparing the Two Approaches

The income statements in Exhibits 8–5 and 8–6 show that absorption and variable costing provide different income figures when sales are not equal to production. These income differences arise solely from what components are included in or excluded from product cost for each method rather than from the method of presentation. That is, the differences are caused by including fixed factory overhead as a product cost under absorption costing but considering it a period cost under variable costing.

The amount of fixed factory overhead included in product cost under absorption costing will ultimately be taken into account in computing net income when the products are sold. Product sales, however, may take place in a time period different from the one in which the costs are actually incurred.

To illustrate, in 1995, the $412,500 difference between the $5,137,500 cost of goods manufactured (CGM) under absorption costing and the $4,725,000 CGM under variable costing is equal to 15,000 units produced multiplied by the unit fixed factory overhead application rate of $27.50. Since all units produced in 1995 are also sold, this $412,500 differential is reflected as expense on both methods' income statements in the same period. Under absorption costing, the $412,500 is shown as part of

---

[3]Robert S. Kaplan, "One Cost System Isn't Enough," *Harvard Business Review* (January–February 1988), p. 61.

Cost of Goods Sold, but this amount is expensed on the variable costing income statement as part of the fixed factory overhead period cost. Since all fixed factory overhead is expensed on the 1995 income statements of both methods, there is no difference in income for that year. In a standard costing system, in which standard costs are constant over time and in which production and sales volumes are equal, income under absorption costing is equal to income under variable costing.

In 1996, absorption and variable costing differ in the costs assigned to ending inventories and cost of goods manufactured. In addition, the absorption and variable costing beginning inventories differ in 1997. In both these years, multiplying the fixed factory overhead application rate by the change in the number of units in inventory gives the net income differences between the two methods. Whenever production and sales volumes differ (resulting in increases or decreases in inventory), incomes under the two methods differs. If standard costs are used and variances are expensed as immaterial, the amount of the difference can be computed as follows:

$$\begin{array}{ccc} \text{Change in} & \text{Fixed overhead} & \text{Dollar difference between} \\ \text{number of units} \quad \times & \text{application} \quad = & \text{absorption \& variable} \\ \text{in inventory} & \text{rate} & \text{costing incomes} \end{array}$$

Using this formula for the 1995–1997 data of MetalWorks, Inc., gives the following:

YEAR	UNITS IN EI	−	UNITS IN BI	=	CHANGE IN NUMBER OF UNITS	×	FOH APPLICATION RATE	=	DIFFERENCE IN INCOMES
1995	0		0		0		$27.50		0
1996	3,000		0		+ 3,000		$27.50		+ $82,500
1997	0		3,000		− 3,000		$27.50		− $82,500

If no beginning and ending inventories exist or if there are no changes in beginning and ending inventories, the cumulative total income under both methods are identical. For MetalWorks, Inc., over the three-year period, 53,000 units are produced and 53,000 units are sold. All costs incurred (whether variable or fixed) are expensed in one year or another under both methods. The income difference in any year is caused solely by when fixed overhead is expensed. Whether absorption costing income is greater or less than variable costing income depends on the relationship of production to sales, and on two basic assumptions: (1) unit product costs are constant over time and (2) all variances from standard costs are immaterial.

Because absorption costing uses a process of deferring and releasing fixed overhead costs to and from inventory, income manipulation is possible, as discussed in the News Note on page 380. For this reason, some people believe that variable costing might be more useful than absorption costing for external as well as internal purposes.

Exhibit 8–7 (page 381) summarizes the differences between absorption and variable costing according to four categories: composition of product cost, structure of the chart of accounts, process of accumulating costs, and format of the income statement. Although four categories are presented, only two real differences exist between the methods. The primary difference lies in the treatment of fixed factory overhead:

The difference between absorption and variable costing is simple. In both methods, the wages of this DeBourgh factory employee would be considered product cost. Absorption costing would also include the depreciation of this metal shearing machine, the facility that houses it, and other fixed factory costs as product cost, and variable costing would not.

Income Manipulation Not Possible under Variable Costing

Conceptually, variable costing always has given a more realistic income. Any "full" method of costing (absorption costing or activity-based costing) permits management to manipulate income by adjusting inventory. A company can increase income by producing more units and thus deferring more fixed costs of this period. In this way it even is possible for a company to report a profit when its sales are lower than the breakeven point. If planned income is more than sufficient in the current period, production could be reduced so that fewer fixed costs could be deferred. Accordingly, income can be reported higher or lower than in the previous period even if unit sales, prices, and costs are the same. Variable costing would eliminate this avenue for income manipulation. It is a purer system because costs are charged off as incurred.

SOURCE: Robert W. Koehler, "Triple-Threat Strategy," *Management Accounting* (October 1991), p. 34. Published by Institute of Management Accountants, Montvale, NJ.

FOH is a product cost for absorption costing and a period cost for variable costing. The other difference is that absorption costing ignores cost behavior in presenting information, while variable costing focuses on such behavior. Because of this focus, variable costing requires different charts of accounts, processes of accumulating costs, and formats for income statements.

Information must be gathered and recorded somewhat differently under these two costing methods. Thus, the accounting process is affected, although maintaining two sets of accounting records is unnecessary. Often, the accounting system is kept on a variable costing basis, and working paper entries are made at year-end to convert the internal information to an appropriate external form. These working paper entries increase the Work in Process Inventory, Finished Goods Inventory, and Cost of Goods Sold accounts by the amount of the fixed factory overhead cost multiplied by the number of units in each account. Additionally, a volume variance must be recorded if the actual level of activity differs from the budgeted level of activity.

Keeping the accounting records on a variable costing basis will allow managers to have information available about the behavior of various product and period costs. This information can be used in computing breakeven point and analyzing a variety of cost-volume-profit relationships.

THE BREAKEVEN POINT

breakeven point (BEP)

■ LEARNING OBJECTIVE 6
Explain the underlying assumptions of CVP analysis and how these assumptions create a short-run managerial perspective.

The level of activity, in units or dollars, at which total revenues equal total costs is called the **breakeven point (BEP).** Finding breakeven point requires an understanding of an organization's revenue and cost functions.

Basic Assumptions

As noted in Chapters 3 and 4, certain assumptions are made about cost behavior so that cost information can be used in accounting computations. The following list summarizes these simplifying assumptions about revenue and cost functions.

■ **EXHIBIT 8–7**
Differences Between Absorption and Variable Costing

ABSORPTION COSTING	VARIABLE COSTING
(1) Composition of Product Cost	
Fixed factory overhead is attached, in separate measurable amounts, to units produced. Only if the firm sells all inventory produced in a period as well as all inventory on hand at the beginning of the period will all previously incurred fixed factory overhead be recognized on the income statement as part of Cost of Goods Sold.	Fixed factory overhead is recognized as a period cost (expense) when it is incurred. It does not attach in separate measurable amounts to the units produced. Each period, all fixed factory overhead incurred is recognized on the income statement as an expense, but not through Cost of Goods Sold.
(2) Structure of the Chart of Accounts	
Costs are classified according to functional categories (such as production, selling, and administrative).	Costs are classified according to both type of cost behavior (fixed or variable) and functional categories (factory and nonfactory). Mixed costs are separated into their fixed and variable components.
(3) Process of Accumulating Costs	
Costs are assigned to functional categories without analysis of behavior. All factory costs are considered product costs. All nonfactory costs are considered period costs.	Costs are classified and accumulated by cost behavior. Only variable factory costs are considered product costs. Fixed factory costs are considered period costs. All nonfactory costs are considered period costs.
(4) Format of the Income Statement	
Costs are presented on the income statement by functional categories, which highlights gross margin (as shown in Exhibit 8–1). The various functional categories present costs without regard to cost behavior. Nonfactory period costs are deducted from gross margin to determine income before taxxes.	Costs are presented on the income statement separately by cost behavior, which highlights contribution margin (as illustrated in Exhibit 8–2). Fixed costs are deducted from contribution margin to determine income before taxes. Costs may be further categorized by functional classifications.

Relevant range: A primary assumption is that the company is operating within the relevant range of activity specified in determining the revenue and cost information.

Revenue: Total revenue fluctuates in direct proportion to units sold. Revenue per unit is assumed to remain constant, and fluctuations in per-unit revenue for factors such as quantity discounts are ignored.

Variable costs: Total variable costs fluctuate in direct proportion to level of activity or volume. On a per-unit basis, variable costs remain constant. Variable costs exist in all functional business areas including production, distribution, selling, and administration.

Fixed costs: Total fixed costs remain constant; thus, per-unit fixed cost decreases as volume increases and increases as volume decreases. Fixed costs include both fixed factory overhead and fixed selling and administrative expenses.

Mixed costs: Mixed costs must be susceptible to separation into their variable and fixed elements. Any method (such as high-low or regression analysis) that validly separates these costs in relation to one or more predictors may be used.

Because these basic assumptions treat selling prices and costs as *known* and *constant,* any analysis based on the assumptions is valid for only the short term. Long-range planning must recognize the possibilities of price and cost fluctuations.

contribution margin (CM)

An important amount in breakeven analysis is contribution margin. On a per-unit basis, **contribution margin (CM)** is equal to selling price minus per-unit variable production, selling, and administrative costs. Contribution margin reflects the revenue remaining after all variable costs have been covered. Contribution margin per unit is constant, because both revenue and variable costs per unit have been defined as being constant. Total contribution margin, as described earlier in the chapter, fluctuates in direct proportion to sales volume.

To illustrate the computation of the breakeven point, 1995 income statement information for MetalWorks, Inc., previously given in Exhibit 8–6 is presented in Exhibit 8–8. The current relevant range of production and sales for the company is between 10,000 and 30,000 lockers per year. The costs given in the exhibit are stand-ard costs for all product elements.

Formula Approach

■ **LEARNING OBJECTIVE 3**
Compute breakeven point and understand what it represents.

The formula approach uses an algebraic equation to calculate the breakeven point. However, the answer to the equation is not always acceptable and may need to be rounded to a whole number. For instance, partial units cannot be sold, and some items may be sold only in specified lot sizes.

Algebraic breakeven computations use an equation representing the income statement. This equation groups costs by behavior and shows the relationships among revenue, volume, variable cost, fixed cost, and profit as follows:

$$R(X) - VC(X) - FC = P$$

where

R = revenue (selling price) per unit
X = number of units sold or to be sold
$R(X)$ = total revenue
FC = total fixed cost
VC = variable cost per unit
$VC(X)$ = total variable cost
P = before-tax profit

■ **EXHIBIT 8–8**
Metalworks, Inc., 1995 Income Statement

	TOTAL	PER UNIT	PERCENT OF SALES
Sales (15,000 lockers)	$6,750,000	$450	100%
Variable Costs:			
Production	$4,725,000	$315	70%
Selling	270,000	18	4%
Total variable cost	4,995,000	$333	74%
Contribution Margin	$1,755,000	$117	26%
Fixed Costs:			
Production	$ 550,000		
Selling and administrative	700,000		
Total fixed cost	1,250,000		
Income before Taxes	$ 505,000		

Since the equation represents an income statement, P can be set equal to zero for the formula to indicate a breakeven situation. BEP in units can be found by solving the equation for X.

$$R(X) - VC(X) - FC = \$0$$
$$R(X) - VC(X) = FC$$
$$(R - VC)(X) = FC$$
$$X = FC \div (R - VC)$$

Breakeven volume is equal to total fixed cost divided by the difference between revenue per unit and variable cost per unit. Since revenue minus variable cost equals contribution margin, the formula can be abbreviated as follows:

$$X = FC \div CM$$
where CM = contribution margin per unit or $(R - VC)$

For MetalWorks, Inc., Exhibit 8–8 indicates a unit selling price of $450, a unit variable cost of $333, and total fixed costs of $1,250,000. The company's contribution margin is $117 per unit ($450 − $333). Substituting these values into the equation yields the following breakeven point:

$$\$450X - \$333X = \$1,250,000$$
$$\$117X = \$1,250,000$$
$$X = \$1,250,000 \div \$117$$
$$X = 10,684 \text{ lockers}$$

This answer is rounded up from 10,683.76.

As mentioned, breakeven point can be expressed either in units or in dollars of revenue. One way to convert a unit breakeven point to dollars is to multiply the breakeven point in units by the selling price per unit. For MetalWorks, Inc., the breakeven point in sales dollars is $4,807,800 (10,684 units × $450 per unit). Another method of computing breakeven point in sales dollars requires the computation of a contribution margin ratio.

The **contribution margin ratio (CM%)**, calculated as contribution margin divided by revenue, indicates what proportion of selling price remains after variable costs have been covered. The CM ratio can be computed with either per-unit or total cost information and allows the BEP to be determined even if unit selling price and unit variable cost are not known or if multiple products are involved. Dividing total fixed cost by the CM ratio gives the breakeven point in sales dollars.

contribution margin ratio (CM%)

$$X_\$ = FC \div CM\%$$
where $X_\$$ = breakeven point in sales dollars
$CM\%$ = contribution margin ratio or $(R - VC) \div R$

The contribution margin for MetalWorks, Inc., is given in Exhibit 8–8 as 26 percent ($117 ÷ $450). Thus, based on the CM ratio, the company's breakeven point in dollars equals $1,250,000 ÷ .26 = $4,807,692—virtually the same amount shown in the earlier calculation (rounding caused the slight difference). The breakeven point in units equals the BEP in sales dollars divided by the unit selling price, or $4,807,692 ÷ $450 = 10,684 (rounded up from 10,683.76).

As indicated in the News Note (page 384), knowledge of the BEP can help managers plan for future operations although managers want to earn profits, not just

BEP Helps Businesses Plan for Profits

"Breakeven point." Does the term ring a bell? It should. That's the magic number that tells you when your revenue will cover your expenses. Although entrepreneurers often fail to realize the significance of recognizing and reaching the breakeven point, understanding what it takes to break even is critical to making any business profitable.

Failing to calculate your breakeven point early in your business life is a grave mistake that could lead to an entrepreneurial nightmare. The Dun & Bradstreet Corp. reports that U.S. business failures increased 14.3% in the first nine months of 1992 to 74,715, from 65,368 in the same period in 1991. Poor financial planning is certainly a major culprit in the untimely demise of many of these businesses.

Incorporating accurate and thorough breakeven analysis as a routine part of your financial planning will keep you abreast of how your business is really faring. Determining how much business is needed to keep the door open will help improve your cash-flow management and your bottom line.

Because most [small] businesses remain severely undercapitalized, entrepreneurs have little or no margin for error. If they don't plan for profit early on, their chances of surviving three years are almost nil. After you've determined your breakeven point, adds Louis Hutt, Jr., managing partner of a Columbia, Md., accounting firm, "the profit factor can be built into your business."

SOURCE: Kevin D. Thompson, "Planning for Profit," *Black Enterprise*, pp. 93-94. Copyright April 1993, The Earl Graves Publishing Co., Inc., 130 Fifth Avenue, New York, NY 10011. All rights reserved.

cover costs. Substituting an amount other than zero for the profit (P) term converts the breakeven formula to cost-volume-profit analysis.

CVP ANALYSIS

cost-volume-profit (CVP) analysis

■ LEARNING
OBJECTIVE 4
Perform cost-volume-profit (CVP) analysis for a single product firm on both before-tax and after-tax bases.

Cost-volume-profit (CVP) analysis is the process of examining the relationships among revenues, costs, and profits for a relevant range of activity and for a particular time. This technique is applicable in all economic sectors (manufacturing, wholesaling, retailing, and service industries) because the same types of managerial functions are performed in all types of organizations.

When known amounts are used for selling price per unit, variable cost per unit, volume of units, and fixed costs, the algebraic equation given in the previous section can be solved to give the amount of profit generated under specified conditions. A more frequent and significant application of CVP analysis is to set a desired target profit and focus on the relationships between that target and specified income statement amounts to find an unknown. Volume is a common unknown in such applications because managers want to achieve a particular level of profit and need to know what quantity of sales must be generated for this objective to be accomplished. Managers may want to use CVP analysis to determine how high variable cost can be (given fixed costs, selling price, and volume) and still provide a given profit level. Variable cost may be increased or decreased by modifying product design specifications, the manufacturing process, or grade of material.

Profit may be stated as either a fixed or a variable amount and on either a before-tax or an after-tax basis. The following examples continue the MetalWorks, Inc., example by adding various levels of desired profit.

Fixed Amount of Profit before Tax

If desired profit is stated as a before-tax amount, it is treated in CVP analysis simply as an additional fixed cost to be covered. The following equation yields before-tax profit in units:

$$R(X) - VC(X) - FC = PBT$$
$$R(X) - VC(X) = FC + PBT$$
$$X = (FC + PBT) \div (R - VC)$$
$$OR$$
$$X = (FC + PBT) \div CM$$

where
$$PBT = \text{specified amount of profit before tax}$$

If sales dollars information is desired, the formula is as follows:

$$R(X) = (FC + PBT) \div CM\%$$

Assume that MetalWorks, Inc., wants to generate a before-tax profit of $622,000. To do so, the company must sell 16,000 lockers, which will provide $7,200,000 of revenue. These calculations are shown in Exhibit 8–9.

Fixed Amount of Profit after Tax

Both production costs and income taxes are important in analyzing organizational profitability. Income taxes represent a significant aspect of business decision making, and managers need to be aware of tax effects when specifying a profit amount.

A company desiring a particular amount of after-tax net income must first determine the equivalent amount on a before-tax basis, given the applicable tax rate. The CVP formulas needed to calculate a desired after-tax net income amount are as follows:

■ **EXHIBIT 8–9**

CVP Analysis—Fixed Amount of Profit Before Tax

$$PBT \text{ desired} = \$622,000$$

In Units:

$$R(X) - VC(X) = FC + PBT$$
$$\$450X - \$333X = \$1,250,000 + \$622,000$$
$$X = \$1,872,000 \div \$117$$
$$= 16,000 \text{ lockers}$$

In Sales Dollars:

$$X_\$ = (FC + PBT) \div CM\%$$
$$= \$1,872,000 \div .26$$
$$= \$7,200,000$$

DeBourgh Manufacturing does not want to simply break even on sales of its lockers. Therefore, company president, Steven Berg, makes certain that costs are controlled, quality is high, and selling prices are set competitively enough to generate the sales volume needed to assure profitability.

$$R(X) - VC(X) - FC = PBT$$
$$[(PBT)(TR)] = \text{Tax Expense}$$
$$PBT - [(PBT)(TR)] = PAT$$
$$PBT(1 - TR) = PAT$$
$$PBT = PAT \div (1 - TR)$$

where   PBT = specified amount of profit before tax
         TR = tax rate
         PAT = specified amount of profit after tax

Thus, the profit after tax is equal to the profit before tax minus the applicable tax. Defined as such, PAT can be integrated into the original before-tax CVP formula.

Assume that MetalWorks, Inc., wants to earn $444,000 of profit after taxes and the company's tax rate is 30 percent. The number of lockers and dollars of sales needed are calculated in Exhibit 8–10.

Rather than specifying a fixed amount of profit to be earned, managers may state profit as a variable amount. Then, as units sold or sales dollars increase, profit will increase proportionally. Variable profit may be stated on either a before-tax or an after-tax basis and either as a percentage of revenues or a per-unit amount. If the variable amount is stated as a percentage, it is convenient to convert that percentage into a per-unit amount. When variable profit is used, the CVP formula must be adjusted to recognize that profit is related to volume of activity.

Variable Amount of Profit before Tax

Managers may want desired profit to be equal to a specified variable amount of sales. The CVP formula for computing the unit volume of sales necessary to earn a specified variable rate or per-unit profit before tax is as follows:

$$R(X) - VC(X) - FC = P_uBT(X)$$

■ **EXHIBIT 8–10**
CVP Analysis—Fixed Amount of Profit After Tax

PAT desired = $444,000; tax rate = 30%

In Units:

$$
\begin{aligned}
\text{PBT} \ &= \text{PAT} \div (1 - \text{Tax rate}) \\
&= \$444{,}000 \div (1 - .30) \\
&= \$444{,}000 \div .70 \\
&= \$634{,}286
\end{aligned}
$$

$$
\begin{aligned}
\text{CM}(X) \ &= \text{FC} + \text{PBT} \\
\$117X \ &= \$1{,}250{,}000 + \$634{,}286 \\
\$117X \ &= \$1{,}884{,}286 \\
X \ &= \$1{,}884{,}286 \div \$117 \\
&= 16{,}106 \text{ lockers (rounded)}
\end{aligned}
$$

In Sales Dollars:

$$
\begin{aligned}
X_{\$} \ &= (\text{FC} + \text{PBT}) \div \text{CM}\% \\
&= (\$1{,}250{,}000 + \$634{,}286) \div .26 \\
&= \$1{,}884{,}286 \div .26 \\
&= \$7{,}247{,}254 \text{ (rounded)}
\end{aligned}
$$

where P_uBT = desired profit per unit before tax

Solving for X (or volume) gives the following:

$$
\begin{aligned}
R(X) - VC(X) - P_uBT(X) \ &= FC \\
X \ &= FC \div (R - VC - P_uBT) \\
X \ &= FC \div (CM - P_uBT)
\end{aligned}
$$

The profit is treated in the CVP formula as if it were an additional variable cost to be covered. If the profit is viewed in this manner, the original contribution margin and contribution margin ratio are effectively adjusted downward to reflect the desired net margin or profit per unit.

When the desired profit is set as a percentage of selling price, that percentage cannot exceed the contribution margin ratio. If it does, an infeasible specification is created, since the effective contribution margin is a negative percentage. In such a case, the actual contribution margin percentage plus the desired profit percentage would exceed 100 percent of the selling price—a condition that cannot occur.

Assume that the president of MetalWorks, Inc., wants to know what sales level (in units and dollars) would be required to earn an 8 percent before-tax profit on sales. The calculations in Exhibit 8–11 (page 388) provide the answer.

Variable Amount of Profit after Tax

Adjusting the CVP formula to determine a return on sales on an after-tax basis involves stating profits in relation to both volume and the tax rate.

■ **EXHIBIT 8–11**

CVP Analysis—Variable Amount of Profit Before Tax

$$P_uBT \text{ desired} = 8\% \text{ of revenue} = .08\,(\$450) = \$36$$

In Units:

$$
\begin{aligned}
R(X) - VC(X) - P_uBT(X) &= FC \\
\$450X - \$333X - \$36X &= \$1{,}250{,}000 \\
X &= \$1{,}250{,}000 \div (\$117 - \$36) \\
&= \$1{,}250{,}000 \div \$81 \\
&= 15{,}433 \text{ lockers (rounded)}
\end{aligned}
$$

In Sales Dollars:

The following relationships exist

	PER UNIT	PERCENT OF SALES
Selling price	$450	100%
Variable costs	(333)	(74%)
8% net profit on sales	(36)	(8%)
Effective contribution margin	$ 81	18%

$$
\begin{aligned}
X_\$ &= FC \div \text{Effective CM ratio*} \\
&= \$1{,}250{,}000 \div .18 = \$6{,}944{,}444
\end{aligned}
$$

*Note that it is not necessary to have per-unit data; all computations can be made with percentage information only.

The algebraic manipulations are as follows:

$$
\begin{aligned}
R(X) - VC(X) - FC &= P_uBT(X) \\
[P_uBT(X)](TR) &= \text{Tax Expense}
\end{aligned}
$$

$$
\begin{aligned}
P_uBT(X) - [P_uBT(X)](TR) &= P_uAT \\
P_uBT(X)[(1 - TR)] &= P_uAT \\
P_uBT(X) &= P_uAT \div (1 - TR)
\end{aligned}
$$

$$
\begin{aligned}
R(X) - VC(X) - FC &= P_uBT(X) \\
R(X) - VC(X) - P_uBT\,(X) &= FC \\
CM(X) - P_uBT(X) &= FC \\
X(CM - P_uBT) &= FC \\
X &= FC \div (CM - P_uBT)
\end{aligned}
$$

where P_uAT = desired profit per unit after tax

Assume that MetalWorks, Inc., wishes to earn a profit after tax of 14 percent on revenue and has a 30 percent tax rate. The necessary sales in units and dollars are computed in Exhibit 8–12. Note that the necessary number of units (46,297 lockers) is beyond the current maximum of MetalWorks' relevant range of activity (30,000 lockers). Thus, it is highly unlikely that such a high rate of profit could be generated under the current cost structure.

■ **EXHIBIT 8–12**

CVP Analysis—Variable Amount of Profit After Tax

P_uAT desired = 14% of revenue = .14($450) = $63.

Tax rate = 30%

In Units:

$$P_u BT(X) = [\$63 \div (1 - .3)] (X)$$
$$= [\$63 \div .7]X$$
$$= \$90X$$

$$R(X) - VC(X) - P_u BT(X) = FC$$
$$\$450X - \$333X - \$90X = \$1,250,000$$
$$\$27X = \$1,250,000$$
$$X = \$1,250,000 \div \$27$$
$$= 46,297 \text{ lockers (rounded)}$$

In Sales Dollars:

	PER UNIT	PERCENT OF SALES
Selling price	$450	100%
Variable costs	(333)	(74%)
Net profit on sales before taxes	(90)	(20%)
Effective contribution margin	$ 27	6%

$$X_\$ = FC \div \text{Effective CM ratio}$$
$$= \$1,250,000 \div .06$$
$$= \$20,833,333 \text{ (rounded)}^*$$

*46,297 lockers @ $450 selling price = $20,833,650. The difference between the answer in units and the answer in sales dollars results from rounding in both the unit answer and the contribution margin percentage answer.

All the previous illustrations of CVP analysis used a variation of the formula approach. Solutions were not accompanied by mathematical proofs; however, income statements are effective means of developing and presenting solutions and/or proofs for solutions to CVP applications.

The answers provided by breakeven and CVP analysis are valid only in relation to specific selling prices and cost relationships. Changes in the company's selling price or cost structure will cause changes in the breakeven point and in the sales needed for the company to achieve a desired profit figure. How revenue and cost changes will affect these results can be determined through incremental analysis.

INCREMENTAL ANALYSIS FOR SHORT-RUN CHANGES

The breakeven point may increase or decrease, depending on the particular changes that occur in revenue and cost factors. Other things being equal, the breakeven point will increase if there is an increase in total fixed cost, a decrease in selling price per unit, or an increase in variable costs. A decrease in selling price, an increase in variable costs, or a combination of the two will cause a decrease in unit contribution margin. These relationships are illustrated in Exhibit 8–13. The breakeven point will decrease if there is a decrease in total fixed cost or an increase in unit or percentage contribution margin. Any factor that causes a change in the breakeven point will also cause a shift in total profits or losses at any level of activity.

incremental analysis

Incremental analysis is a process that focuses on factors that change from one course of action or decision to another. As related to CVP situations, incremental analysis is based on changes in revenues, costs, and/or volume. Following are some examples of changes that may occur in a company and the incremental computations that can be used to determine the effects of those changes on the breakeven point or profits.

All of the following examples use before-tax information to simplify the computations. After-tax analysis would require the application of a (1 - tax rate) factor to all profit figures.

Case 1: The company wishes to earn a profit before taxes of $702,000. How many lockers does it need to sell?

Since BEP is known, answering this question requires simply determining how many lockers above the breakeven point are needed to generate $702,000 of before-tax profits. Each dollar of contribution margin generated by product sales goes first to cover fixed costs and then to produce profits. *Thus, after the breakeven point is reached, each dollar of contribution margin is a dollar of profit.* To achieve $702,000 in desired profits requires MetalWorks, Inc., to sell 6,000 units over the breakeven point, with each locker providing $117 of contribution margin:

$$\$702,000 \div \$117 = 6,000 \text{ lockers above BEP}$$
$$BEP = 10,684 \text{ units}$$
$$\text{Total lockers} = 10,684 + 6,000 = 16,684$$

■ **EXHIBIT 8–13**
Effects of Changes From Original Data

Original Data:

Revenue per unit		$450
Variable cost per unit		333
Contribution margin per unit		$117
Fixed costs = $1,250,000		
Breakeven point = 10,684 lockers		

If fixed costs increase to $2,340,000, BEP rises to 20,000 lockers.

$$\$117X = \$2,340,000; \ X = \$2,340,000 \div \$117; \ X = 20,000$$

If revenue per unit falls to $433, BEP rises to 12,500 lockers.

$$\$433 - \$333 = \$100 \text{ new CM}; \ \$100X = \$1,250,000; \ X = 12,500$$

If variable costs rise to $340, BEP rises to 11,364 lockers.

$$\$450 - \$340 = \$110 \text{ new CM}; \ \$110X = \$1,250,000; \ X = 11,364 \text{ (rounded)}$$

Case 2: MetalWorks, Inc., estimates that it can sell an additional 40 lockers if it spends $4,200 more on advertising. Should the company incur this extra fixed cost?

The contribution margin from the additional lockers must cover the additional fixed cost before profits can be generated.

Increase in contribution margin	
(40 lockers × $117 CM per unit)	$4,680
Increase in fixed cost	(4,200)
Net incremental benefit	$ 480

Since there is a net incremental benefit, the advertising campaign would result in an increase in profits and, thus, should be undertaken.

Case 3: The company estimates that, if the selling price of each locker is reduced to $440, an additional 1,000 lockers can be sold per year. Should the company reduce the price of lockers? Current sales volume (given in Exhibit 8–8) is 15,000 units.

If the selling price is reduced, the contribution margin per unit will decrease to $107 per unit ($440 SP − $333 VC). Sales volume is estimated to increase to 16,000 units (15,000 + 1,000).

Total new contribution margin	
(16,000 lockers × $107 CM per unit)	$1,712,000
Total fixed costs (unchanged)	(1,250,000)
New profit before taxes	$ 462,000
Current profit before taxes (from Exhibit 8–8)	(505,000)
Reduction in profit before taxes	$ (43,000)

Since the company will have less profit before taxes than is currently being generated, the company should not reduce its selling price in this instance.

These are just a few examples of changes that might occur in a company's revenue and cost structure. In most situations, the incremental approach is often sufficient to determine the monetary merits of proposed or necessary changes. In making decisions, however, management must also consider the qualitative and long-run effects of the changes.

All examples provided to this point relate to a single product company. Most businesses do not produce and/or sell only one type of product. The next section deals with the more realistic multiproduct entity.

CVP ANALYSIS IN A MULTIPRODUCT ENVIRONMENT

■ **LEARNING OBJECTIVE 5**
Perform a CVP analysis for a multiproduct firm.

Companies typically produce and sell a variety of products or services. To perform CVP analysis in a multiproduct company, it is necessary to assume a constant product sales mix and to use a corresponding average contribution margin ratio. The constant mix assumption can be referred to as the "bag" or "package" assumption. This analogy compares the sales mix to a bag or package of items that are sold together. For example, whenever some of Product A is sold, specified quantities of Products B and C are also sold.

Use of the constant sales mix assumption allows the computation of a weighted average contribution margin ratio. The CM ratio is *weighted* on the basis of the quantity of each item included in the bag. The contribution margin ratio of the item that makes up the largest proportion of the bag has the greatest impact on the average contribution margin of the bag mix. Without the assumption of a constant sales mix, the breakeven point cannot be calculated, nor can CVP analysis be used effectively.[4]

The MetalWorks, Inc., example is continued. Because of the success of the school lockers, company management has decided to begin producing metal jewelry vaults for jewelry stores. The vice-president of marketing estimates that for every five school lockers sold, the company will sell two jewelry vaults. Therefore, the bag of products has a 5:2 ratio. The company must incur $150,000 in additional fixed costs related to plant assets (depreciation, insurance, and so on) to support a higher relevant range of production and additional licensing fees. Exhibit 8–14 provides relevant company information and shows the breakeven computations.

Any shift in the proportion of sales mix of products will change the weighted average contribution margin and the breakeven point. If the sales mix shifts toward products with lower contribution margins, there will be an increase in the BEP; furthermore, there will be a decrease in profits unless there is a corresponding increase in total revenues. A shift toward higher-margin products without a corresponding decrease in revenues will cause increased profits and a lower breakeven point.

It is also possible to calculate the weighted average contribution margin ratio by multiplying the sales mix percentage (relative to sales dollars) by the CM ratio for each product and summing the results. According to the note in Exhibit 8–14, the relationship of dollars of school locker sales to dollars of jewelry vault sales is 90 percent to 10 percent. Based on this information, the CM ratio for the bag of products is computed as follows:

$$
\begin{aligned}
\text{School lockers: } 90\% \times 26\% &= .234 \\
\text{Jewely vaults: } 10\% \times 20\% &= \underline{.020} \\
\text{Total CM ratio} \quad\quad &\ \ \underline{\underline{.254}}
\end{aligned}
$$

To break even at the level indicated, MetalWorks, Inc., must sell the products in exactly the relationships specified in the original sales mix. If sales are at the specified level but not in the specified mix, the company will experience either a profit or a loss, depending on whether the mix is shifted toward the product with the higher or the lower contribution margin ratio.

UNDERLYING ASSUMPTIONS OF CVP ANALYSIS

■ LEARNING
OBJECTIVE 6
Explain the underlying assumptions of CVP analysis and how these assumptions create a short-run managerial perspective.

The CVP model is a useful planning tool that can provide information on how profits are affected when changes are made in the costing system or in sales levels. Like any model, however, it reflects reality but does not duplicate it. Cost-volume-profit analysis is a tool that focuses on the short run, partially because of the assumptions that underlie the computations. Although these assumptions are necessary, they limit the results' accuracy. These assumptions follow; some of them were also provided at the beginning of the chapter.

1. All variable cost and revenue behavior patterns are constant per unit and linear in total within the relevant range.

---

[4]Once the constant percentage contribution margin in a multiproduct firm is determined, all of the situations regarding income points can be treated the same as they were earlier in the chapter—remembering that the answers reflect the "bag" assumption.

■ **EXHIBIT 8–14**
CVP Analysis—Multiple Products

Product cost information:	SCHOOL LOCKERS		JEWELRY VAULTS	
Selling price	$450	100%	$125	100%
Total variable cost	333	74%	100	80%
Contribution margin	$117	26%	$ 25	20%

Total fixed costs ($1,250,000 previous + $150,000 additional) = $1,400,000

	SCHOOL LOCKERS		JEWELRY VAULTS		TOTAL	PERCENT
Number of units	5		2			
Revenue per unit	$450		$125			
Total revenue per bag		$2,250		$250	$2,500	100.0%
Variable cost per unit	333		100			
Total variable per bag		1,665		200	1,865	74.6%
Contribution margin per unit	$117		$ 25			
Contribution margin per bag		$ 585		$ 50	$ 635	25.4%

BEP in units: CM(B) = FC

where   B = bag of products

$635B = $1,400,000
    B = 2,205 bags to break even (rounded)

Note: Each bag is made up of 5 lockers; thus, it will take 11,025 school lockers and 4,410 jewelry vaults to break even, assuming the constant 5:2 sales mix.

BEP in sales dollars: B = FC ÷ CM ratio

where   CM ratio = weighted average for each bag of products

B = $1,400,000 ÷ .254
   = $5,511,811 (rounded)

Note: The breakeven sales dollars also represent the assumed constant sales mix of $2,250 of school locker sales to $250 of jewelry vault sales or a 90% to 10% ratio. Thus, the company must have approximately $4,960,630 ($5,511,811 × 90%) of school locker sales and $551,181 ($5,511,811 × 10%) of jewelry vault sales to break even.

Proof of above computations using the income statement approach:

	SCHOOL LOCKERS	GUN LOCKERS	TOTAL
Sales	$4,960,630	$551,181	$5,511,811
Variable Costs (74%; 80%)	3,670,866	440,945	4,111,811
Contribution Margin	$1,289,764	$110,236	$1,400,000
Fixed Costs			1,400,000
Net Income (Loss)			$ 0

2. Total contribution margin (total revenue − total variable costs) is linear within the relevant range and increases proportionally with output. This assumption follows directly from assumption 1.

3. Total fixed cost is a constant amount within the relevant range.

4. Mixed costs can be accurately separated into their fixed and variable elements. Such accuracy is particularly unrealistic, but reliable estimates can be developed from the high-low method or regression analysis (discussed in Chapter 3 and its appendix).

5. Sales and production are equal; thus there will be no fluctuation in inventory levels. This assumption is necessary because otherwise some fixed overhead costs might be included on the income statement in a different year from that in which they were incurred (because of the use of absorption costing). The assumption is more realistic as more companies begin to use just-in-time inventory systems.

6. There will be no capacity additions during the period under consideration. If such additions were made, fixed (and possibly variable) costs would change. Any changes in fixed or variable costs would invalidate assumptions 1–3.

7. In a multiproduct firm, the sales mix will remain constant. Absent this assumption, no useful weighted average contribution margin could be computed for the company.

8. Either there will be no inflation, or inflation will affect all cost factors equally; or, if factors will be affected unequally, the appropriate effects will be incorporated into the CVP figures.

9. Labor productivity, production technology, and market conditions will not change. If any of these factors changed, costs would change correspondingly, and it is possible that selling prices would change. Such changes would invalidate assumptions 1–3.

These nine premises are the traditional assumptions associated with cost-volume-profit analysis and reflect a basic disregard of possible (and probable) future changes. Accountants have generally assumed that cost behavior, once classified, remained constant over periods of time as long as operations remained within the relevant range and in the absence of evidence to the contrary. Thus, for example, once a cost was determined to be fixed, it would be fixed next year, the year after, and 10 years from now.

As mentioned in Chapter 4, however, it may be more realistic to regard fixed costs as long-term variable costs. Companies can, over the long run and through managerial decisions, lay off supervisors and sell plant and equipment items. Alternatively, companies may grow and increase their fixed investments in people, plant and equipment. Fixed costs are not fixed forever. In many companies, some costs considered to be fixed "have been the most variable and rapidly increasing costs."[5] Part of this cost "misclassification" problem has occurred because of improper specification of cost drivers. As companies become less focused on production and sales volumes as cost drivers, they will begin to recognize that fixed costs only exist under a short-term reporting period perspective.

In addition, certain costs may arise that are variable in the first year of providing a product or service to a customer but will not recur in future years. Differing current and future period costs are very important concerns in various service businesses. Getting new customers requires a variety of one-time costs for things such as advertising, mailing, and checking customers' credit histories. "In credit cards, for exam-

---

[5]Robin Cooper and Robert S. Kaplan, "How Cost Accounting Distorts Product Costs," *Management Accounting* (April 1988), p. 27.

ple, companies spend an average of $51 to recruit a new customer and set up the new account."[6] As companies and customers become more familiar with one another, services can be provided more efficiently or higher prices can be charged for the trusted relationship. Failure to consider such changes in costs can provide a very distorted picture of how profits are generated and, therefore, can lead to an improper analysis of the relationships of costs, volume, and profits.

COSTS AND QUALITY

While cost, price, and volume are the three major factors in determining a company's profits, it is necessary to recognize that these three factors work hand in hand with a fourth factor—quality. A Gallup Poll in 1988 showed that high-quality products are typically able to command higher selling prices,[7] and often sales volume increases simply through quality recognition. For example, a substantial part of the popularity of Häagen-Dazs and Coca-Cola is quality-based. Quality improvements are especially important for companies that wish to compete in export markets, as indicated in the News Note on page 396.

■ **LEARNING OBJECTIVE 7**
Discuss how quality decisions affect the components of CVP analysis.

Achieving higher quality, however, will affect costs. Some costs may decline because products or parts are redesigned to simplify processing or standardize components. Other costs may increase. Some of the increased costs may be variable (such as costs for higher-grade materials and components, training courses for employees, and preventive maintenance), while others (such as costs of supplier certification programs, computer-integrated machines to better monitor quality, and implementation of quality-circle programs) may be fixed or long-term variable.

It would seem that the costs of ensuring quality should, in the long run, outweigh the costs of having poor quality. At DeBourgh Manufacturing, controlling costs does not simply mean "obtaining the lowest cost." For instance, 60 years ago, DeBourgh pioneered the all-welded locker that was fully assembled at the plant in contrast to the then-traditional "knockdown" locker that was shipped flat and assembled at the job site. Although the costs of the all-welded locker were higher than those of the knockdown, DeBourgh believed its approach provided higher quality. Today, the company still chooses to manufacture its products in this manner and to purchase top grade domestic steel, which results in direct material costs that are higher than those of some other manufacturers. Significant variable and fixed costs are also incurred at DeBourgh for training employees, educating distributors about corporate products, purchasing state-of-the-art equipment that improves product quality, and investing in the community in which the company operates. While such practices may create some higher variable and fixed costs currently, they lower other costs (such as those attributable to rework, redesign, and product failure). Thus, DeBourgh management is well aware of the adage: "You get what you pay for."

Breakeven point and the volume levels needed to achieve desired profits do not necessarily rise as a result of quality-enhancing measures. It may be possible to charge higher selling prices for a high-quality product and thus maintain a constant contribution margin. And even if the BEP volume levels do rise, these levels may be more attainable because of the higher quality of the products. All in all, considering the

---

[6]Frederick F. Reichheld and W. Earl Sasser, Jr., "Zero Defections: Quality Comes to Services," *Harvard Business Review* (September–October 1990), pp. 106–107.

[7]George Melloan, "Computers Elevate Product Quality Standards," *Wall Street Journal* (October 11, 1988), p. A25.

When Quality Rises, So Do Export Sales

Most businesses [on the eastern] side of the Berlin Wall spent the past few decades specializing in the production of one thing: junk.

But now, more and more companies in Central and Eastern Europe, no longer content to make shoddy autos and second-rate textiles, are rapidly raising the quality of their products to Western standards.

The far-reaching change is obvious at Petofi Printing & Packaging Co., a maker of cardboard boxes, wrappers and other containers in Kecskemet, Hungary. Only a few years ago, Petofi's employees drank beer at work. Flies buzzing in open windows got stuck in the paint and pressed into the paperboard. Containers were delivered in wrong colors and sizes. If red paint was running low, orange would do. But customers didn't dare complain. Instead, they bribed the state company with chocolates and liquor to take their orders. Not surprisingly, only 7% of Petofi's production was exported, and that went east.

But after being privatized in 1990, Petofi began overhauling itself, leapfrogging Western companies with state-of-the-art machinery. It whipped its work force into shape with a combination of inducements and threats. Now, most of its products are exported, and its customers include multinationals such as Unilever NV of the Netherlands and General Electric Co. and Philip Morris Co. of the U.S. Some are shifting orders from Western suppliers.

Petofi's quality "compares very favorably," says Gerry Flanagan, a purchaser for PepsiCo Inc., which buys Petofi wrappers for some Cheetos and Ruffles snacks. "They have filled the gap between competitive quality and best cost."

Aided by tax breaks and low labor costs, Petofi has gross profit margins of about 30%, one-third higher than most of its competitors. It can undercut Western rivals' prices by 10% to 15%, taking away customers and driving down prices in the industry. Its output is growing 30% annually in a flat European market.

SOURCE: Dana Milbank, "East Europe's Industry Is Raising Its Quality and Taking on West," *Wall Street Journal* (September 21, 1994), p. A1, A4. Reprinted by permission of The Wall Street Journal, © 1994 Dow Jones & Company, Inc. All Rights Reserved Worldwide.

implications of quality changes on cost, price, and volume should help focus managers' attention more on the long run and less on the short run.

MARGIN OF SAFETY AND OPERATING LEVERAGE

■ LEARNING OBJECTIVE 8
Explain how the margin of safety and operating leverage concepts are used in business.

The breakeven point is the lowest level of sales volume at which an organization would want to operate. As sales increase from that point, managers become less concerned about whether decisions will cause the company to lose money. Thus, when making decisions about various business opportunities, managers often consider the company's margin of safety and degree of operating leverage.

Margin of Safety

margin of safety

The **margin of safety** is the excess of a company's budgeted or actual sales over its breakeven point. By reflecting the amount that sales can drop before reaching the breakeven point, the margin of safety allows management to determine how close to a danger level the company is operating and provides an indication of risk. The lower the margin of safety, the more carefully management must watch sales figures and control costs so that a net loss will not be generated. At low margins of safety, managers are less likely to take advantage of opportunities that, if analyzed incorrectly, could send the company into a loss position.

The margin of safety can be expressed as units, dollars, or a percentage. The following formulas are applicable:

$$\text{Margin of safety in units} = \text{Actual units} - \text{Breakeven units}$$
$$\text{Margin of safety in dollars} = \text{Actual sales dollars} - \text{Breakeven sales dollars}$$

$$\text{Margin of safety percentage} = \frac{\text{Margin of safety in units or dollars}}{\text{Actual sales in units or dollars}}$$

The breakeven point for MetalWorks, Inc., is 10,684 lockers or $4,807,692 of sales. The company's income statement for the year ended December 31, 1995 (presented in Exhibit 8–8), showed actual sales of 15,000 units or $6,750,000. The margin of safety for MetalWorks, Inc., is calculated in Exhibit 8–15. The margin is quite high, since the company is operating far above its breakeven point.

Degree of Operating Leverage

The relationship of a company's variable and fixed costs is reflected in its **operating leverage.** Typically, highly labor-intensive organizations, such as McDonald's and Domino's Pizza, have high variable costs and low fixed costs and, thus, have low operating leverage and a relatively low breakeven point. (An exception to this rule is sports teams, which are highly labor-intensive but have labor costs that are fixed rather than variable.) Companies with low operating leverage can show a profit even when they experience wide swings in volume levels. Entrepreneurs Kitson and Julie Logue who own Stewart Pet Products, a small business, explain their philosophy toward operating leverage in the News Note on the following page. That philosophy is to eliminate fixed costs through outsourcing and, therefore, reduce the probability of losses if business volume declines.

Conversely, organizations that are highly capital-intensive, such as Delta Air Lines and Arkansas Power & Light, have a cost structure that includes low variable and high fixed costs. Such a structure reflects high operating leverage. Because fixed costs are high, the breakeven point is relatively high; if selling prices are predominantly set by the market, volume has the primary impact on profitability. As companies become more automated, they will face this type of cost structure and will be increasingly dependent on volume to add profits. Donald Fites, chairman of Caterpillar, noted

operating leverage

Just as a net provides protection for a trapeze artist, a margin of safety provides protection for a business. The margin of safety reflects the cushion by which sales may fall before a company faces injury in the form of income statement losses.

■ **EXHIBIT 8–15**
Margin of Safety

In units:	15,000 actual − 10,684 BEP = 4,316 lockers
In sales dollars:	$6,750,000 actual − $4,807,692 BEP = $1,942,308
Percentage:	(15,000 − 10,684) ÷ 15,000 = .288, or 29% (rounded)
	or
	($6,750,000 − $4,807,692) ÷ $6,750,000 = .288, or 29% (rounded)

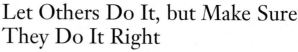

Let Others Do It, but Make Sure They Do It Right

There are no economies of scale to small production runs and micromarkets, so start-up businesses can't afford to sink cash into bricks, sticks, or paychecks. "We want variable costs," says Kitson Logue. "The less fixed cost you have, the more survivable you are." [With this philosophy, the Logue's business is] without a factory, without a warehouse, without a sales force or employees.

From a three-room office in South Bend, Indiana, 10,000-pound shipments of dog biscuits are shuttled around the world with one fax, two phones, and a PC. One vendor ships a premix of the product to the Logues' manufacturer who sends the biscuits on to the packing warehouse, where workers customize orders and send them out to distributors and reps in five countries. A direct-mail house handles samples. A free-lance artist designs the packaging and some advertising.

[However,] outsourcing the bulk of their operations requires vigilance. The Logues police quality closely, talking to vendors every day. "Our job is to put a stick in their ribs and do to some degree what GM does. You have to write specs telling vendors every step of the process. It's an endless sequence of small details."

SOURCE: Anne Murphy, "The Start-Up of the 90s," *Inc.* (March 1992), p. 36. Reprinted with permission of Inc. Magazine. © 1992 by Goldhirsh Group, Inc.

that his company has learned that "the cost structure you put in place in good times is the cost structure you have to live with in hard times."[8]

Companies with high operating leverage also have high contribution margin ratios. While such companies have to establish fairly high sales volumes to cover fixed costs, each unit sold after breakeven produces large profits. Thus, a small increase in sales can have a major impact on a company's profits.

degree of operating leverage (DOL)

The **degree of operating leverage (DOL)** indicates how sensitive the company is to sales increases and decreases by measuring how a percentage change in sales will affect company profits. The computation for the degree of operating leverage factor is:

$$\text{Degree of operating leverage } = \frac{\text{Contribution margin}}{\text{Income before tax}}$$

This calculation assumes that fixed costs do not increase when sales increase.

Assume that MetalWorks, Inc., is currently selling 12,000 school lockers. Using the basic facts from Exhibit 8–8, Exhibit 8–16 provides the income statement that reflects this sales level. As shown in the exhibit, the company has an operating leverage factor of 9.12 at this level of sales. If the company increases sales by 20 percent, the change in profits is equal to the degree of operating leverage multiplied by the percentage change in sales, or 182 percent! If sales decrease by the same 20 percent, there is a negative 182 percent impact on profits.

The degree of operating leverage diminishes as a company moves farther from its breakeven point. When the margin of safety is small, the degree of operating leverage is large. In fact, at breakeven, the degree of operating leverage is infinite, since

[8]Robert L. Rose, "As Economy Grows, Cyclicals Keep Wary Eye on Costs," *Wall Street Journal* (April 18, 1994), p. B4.

■ **EXHIBIT 8–16**
Degree of Operating Leverage

	(12,000 LOCKERS) CURRENT	(14,400 LOCKERS) 20% INCREASE	(9,600 LOCKERS) 20% DECREASE
Sales	$5,400,000	$6,480,000	$4,320,000
Variable costs	3,996,000	4,795,200	3,196,800
Contribution margin	$1,404,000	$1,684,800	$1,123,200
Fixed costs	1,250,000	1,250,000	1,250,000
Income before tax	$ 154,000	$ 434,800	$ (126,800)

Degree of operating leverage:
Contribution margin ÷ Income before tax
($1,404,000 ÷ $154,000)   9.12
($1,684,800 ÷ $434,800)   3.87
[$1,123,200 ÷ $(126,800)]   Can't be calculated

Income increase at 14,400 lockers = $434,800 − $154,000
                                                = $280,800 or 182% of original income
Income decrease at 9,600 lockers = $(126,800) − $154,000
                                                = $(280,800) or −182% of original income

any increase from zero is an infinite percentage change. If a company is operating close to the breakeven point, each percentage increase in sales can make a dramatic percentage impact on net income. As the company moves away from breakeven sales, the margin of safety increases, but the degree of operating leverage declines.

When Steven Berg decided to make the move to La Junta, he did so out of a need to save his business. Selling prices of All-American lockers could not be increased because competitors were lowering their prices. Thus, DeBourgh Manufacturing could pursue one of three options. First, the company could meet the reduced market selling price and achieve profits by reducing costs and controlling them more effectively. Second, the company could hold the selling price at the current level and provide customers with a locker of sufficient quality to justify a higher selling price. Third, the company could control costs, maintain the selling price, and increase quality, which would correspondingly increase volume and profits. Mr. Berg chose the third stategy.

The BEP is used as a starting point in the annual budgeting process. DeBourgh analyzes its variable and fixed costs carefully so that it can position itself to take advantage of opportunities for new products or, in isolated instances, to sell existing products for less. Most of the company's costs are easily defined and fairly stable but difficult to control. For instance, there is little bargaining power with regard to raw materials. Increases in steel prices are simply passed on to the company by suppliers because DeBourgh is not large enough to effectively negotiate prices. Additionally, economies of scale in the production process are limited, because the lockers are virtually assembled one at a time, so larger orders do not translate into significantly less expensive production costs.

Of greatest concern is the lack of control over selling prices. The company sells school lockers to dealers, who sell to the final customer. Thus, the dealer controls the final selling prices, and larger-volume dealers receive larger discounts from list prices. Because of market competition, volume discounts, and the bid process often related to school district business, many of the largest jobs must be priced based on contribution margin—not desired profit margin.

SOURCE: Information provided by Steve Berg and Frank McKenzie, DeBourgh Manufacturing Company, 1994

Discipline	Application
Accounting	Users of cost information need to understand the differences in product costing methods and how those differences will affect analysis. For example, breakeven sales may not result in zero profit on an absorption costing income statement. In variable costing, costs are separated into their fixed and variable elements making flexible budget preparation easier. Breakeven and CVP analysis show relationships among all profitability factors in the relevant range and help managers seek the best combination of those factors; help determine the sales volume needed to meet desired profit figures; help explain how taxes will affect desired profits.
Economics	Absorption costing focuses on short-run profits rather than long-run profit contributions; variable costing provides managers with costs that are close to the economist's notion of marginal costs and, thus, improves decision making. Breakeven and CVP analysis make companies aware of the importance of volume and help pinpoint the volume at which profits will be maximized; allow use of incremental analysis for decision making; promote recognition of the sensitivity of profits to price changes; are useful in decision making about alternative systems of

	production (including automation) by focusing on the effects of differing cost structures; and aid in choosing the optimal price, cost, and output levels for each product.
Finance	Users should compare the information from both absorption and variable costing to standard industry-related financial statement guidelines for normal cost and profit ranges to determine if the company's basic costs and expense structure are reasonable; estimations of a firm's value are generally made by analysts using external financial statements based on absorption costing.
	Breakeven and CVP analysis indicate the profit effects of operating structure (low versus high leverage) before and after new product or service introductions or changes in sales mix; help influence what product lines to emphasize; can be used to determine profit impact of volume changes.
Management	Variable costing provides information necessary for effective operational planning, controlling, and decision making; however, strict reliance on variable costing information might lead to underpricing and lowered profits.
	Breakeven and CVP analysis help identify various cost and pricing strategies and their effects on profits and show dollar-for-dollar effects of contribution margin on profits above BEP; margin of safety and degree of operating leverage help indicate overall company health and the significance of volume increases on total profits.
Marketing	Variable and absorption costing provide different definitions of product cost and, thus, may help in deciding on selling prices for special orders.
	Breakeven and CVP analysis help justify advertising budgets (the higher the CM%, the more dollar-for-dollar benefit of advertising); solutions from these models can be compared with sales forecasts to check for reasonableness (Can sales level be achieved at stated price and with estimated marketing expenditure level? If fixed advertising expenditures are increased, can needed sales increases be achieved based on market share?); cause consideration of unit contribution margin (or %) and capacity utilization to determine which products to emphasize (market, promote, advertise) and which to demarket (raise price, harvest, cut advertising).

CHAPTER SUMMARY

Two methods by which businesses can determine product costs are absorption costing and variable costing. Under absorption costing, all factory costs (both variable and fixed) are treated as product costs. The absorption costing income statement reflects a full production cost approach for cost of goods sold, computes gross margin, and classifies nonfactory costs according to functional areas rather than by cost behavior.

Variable costing computes product cost using only the variable costs of production (direct material, direct labor, and variable factory overhead). Fixed factory overhead charges are considered period costs and are expensed when they are incurred. The variable costing income statement presents cost of goods sold as composed of only the variable production cost per unit, shows product and total contribution margin figures, and classifies costs according to their cost behavior (variable or fixed). While variable costing can provide management with better information for internal purposes than can absorption costing, variable costing is not considered an acceptable method of inventory measurement for external reporting or tax returns.

Income determined under absorption costing differs from that determined under variable costing for any period in which production and sales volumes differ. The difference between the two income amounts reflects the amount of fixed overhead that is attached to, or released from, inventory in absorption costing as opposed to being immediately expensed in variable costing.

Management planning for company success includes planning for price, volume, fixed and variable costs, quality, contribution margin, and breakeven point. The interrelationships of these factors are studied in breakeven point (BEP) and cost-volume-profit (CVP) analysis, both of which use variable costing information.

The BEP is that quantity of sales volume at which the company will experience zero profit or loss. Total contribution margin (sales minus all variable costs) is equal to total fixed costs at the BEP.

Since most companies want to operate above breakeven, CVP analysis extends the BEP computation by introducing a desired profit factor. A company can determine the sales necessary to generate a desired amount of profit by adding the desired profit to fixed costs and dividing that total by contribution margin or contribution margin ratio. After fixed costs are covered, each dollar of contribution margin generated by company sales will produce a dollar of before-tax profit.

In a multiproduct firm, all BEP and CVP analyses are based on an assumed constant sales mix of products or services. This sales mix requires the computation of a weighted average contribution margin (and, thus, contribution margin ratio) for a bag of products. Answers to breakeven or CVP computations are in units or dollars of these bags of products. The number of bags can be converted to individual items by use of the sales mix relationship.

CVP analysis is short-range in focus because it assumes linearity of all functions. Managers need to include in their considerations the effects of changes in quality and other types of changes on both current and future costs to make better, more realistic decisions. While CVP analysis provides one way for a manager to reduce the risk of uncertainty, the model is based on several assumptions that limit its ability to reflect reality.

The margin of safety for a firm indicates how far (in units, sales dollars, or a percentage) a company is operating from its breakeven point. A company's degree of operating leverage shows what percentage change in profit would occur given a specified percentage change in sales.

APPENDIX

breakeven graph

■ LEARNING
OBJECTIVE 9
(Appendix) Prepare breakeven
and profit-volume graphs.

Graphic Approaches to Breakeven Analysis

To graphically depict the relationships among revenues, variable costs, fixed costs, and profits (or losses), a **breakeven graph** may be used. The breakeven point is located at the point where the total cost and total revenue lines cross. The following steps are necessary to preparing a breakeven graph.

Step 1: Label the x-axis as volume and the y-axis as dollars. Plot the variable cost line as a linear function with a slope equal to total variable cost per unit. Next, plot the revenue line with a slope equal to the unit sales price. The area between the variable cost and revenue lines represents total contribution margin at each level of volume. The result of this step is shown in Exhibit 8–17.

Step 2: To graph total cost add a line parallel to the total variable cost line. The distance between the total and variable cost lines is the amount of fixed cost. The total cost line is above and to the left of the total variable cost line. The breakeven point is located where the revenue and total cost lines intersect. If exact readings could be taken on the graph shown in Exhibit 8–18 (page 404), the breakeven point for MetalWorks, Inc., would be shown as $4,807,692 of sales and 10,684 school lockers (both figures are rounded).

The format of this breakeven graph allows the following important observations to be made.

1. Contribution margin is created by the excess of revenues over variable costs. If variable costs are greater than revenues, no quantity of volume will allow a profit to be made.
2. Total contribution margin is equal to total fixed cost plus profit or minus loss.
3. Before profits can be generated, contribution margin must exceed fixed costs.

Another method of visually presenting income statement information is the **profit-volume (PV) graph,** which reflects the amount of profit or loss at each sales level. The horizontal axis on the PV graph represents unit sales volume, and the vertical axis represents dollars. Amounts above the horizontal axis are positive and represent profits, while amounts below the horizontal axis are negative and represent losses.

profit-volume (PV) graph

■ **EXHIBIT 8–17**
Step One in Breakeven Graph Preparation

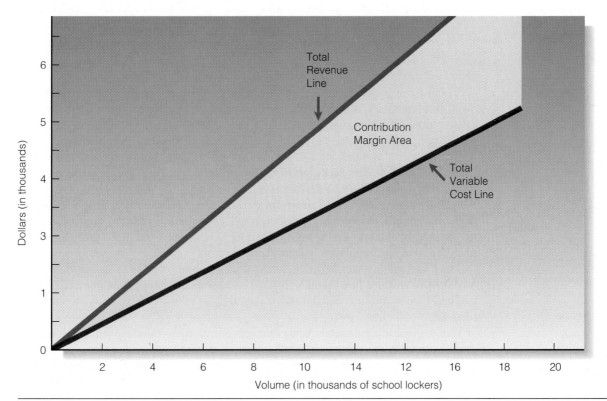

■ **EXHIBIT 8–18**
Breakeven Graph

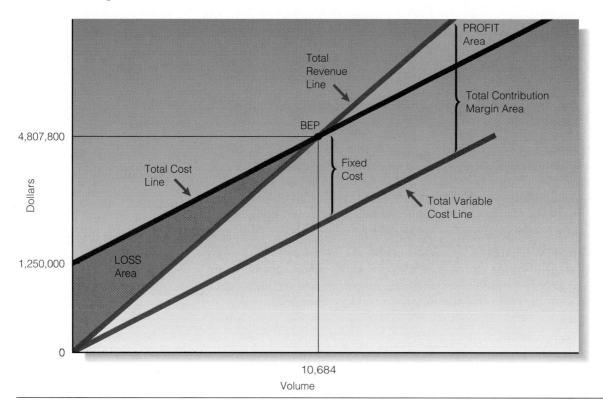

To draw the graph, first locate two points: total fixed costs and breakeven point. Total fixed costs are shown on the vertical axis as a negative amount (or below the sales volume line). If no units were sold, fixed costs would still be incurred, and a loss would result. Location of the breakeven point may be determined either by use of a breakeven graph or algebraically. The breakeven point in units is shown on the horizontal axis because there is no profit or loss at that point. With these two points plotted, a line is drawn that passes between and extends through the breakeven point. This line can be used to read, from the vertical axis, the amount of profit or loss for any sales volume. This line represents total contribution margin, and its slope is determined by the unit contribution margin. The line shows that no profit is earned until the contribution margin covers the fixed costs.

The PV graph for MetalWorks, Inc., is shown in Exhibit 8–19. Total fixed costs are $1,250,000, and the breakeven point is 10,684 lockers. The profit line reflects the original Exhibit 8–8 income statement data that, at sales of 15,000 lockers, the company earns $505,000.

While graphic approaches to breakeven point, cost-volume-profit analysis and profit-volume relationships provide detailed visual displays, they cannot yield precise answers to questions asked by managers. Such solutions must be found using an algebraic formula approach because exact numerical points cannot be read from the graphs.

■ **EXHIBIT 8–19**
Profit Volume Graph

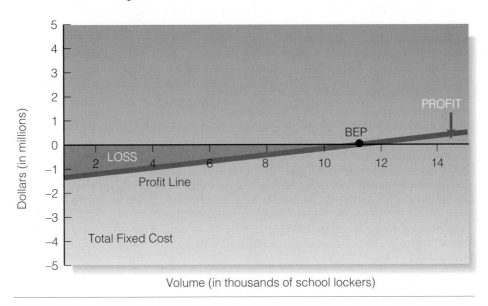

Volume (in thousands of school lockers)

Even in business the statement "A picture is worth a thousand words" is true. Pictures created by this computer-aided design system help DeBourgh Manufacturing staff explain locker configurations and design specifications to clients. Breakeven and profit-volume graphs provide pictures that help managers visualize financial results of operating along a wide spectrum of activity.

GLOSSARY

Absorption costing (p. 371)   a cost accumulation method that includes the costs of all manufacturing components (direct materials, direct labor, variable overhead, and fixed overhead) as inventoriable, or product, costs; also known as full costing

Breakeven graph (p. 402)   a graphical depiction of the relationships among revenues, variable costs, fixed costs, and profits (or losses) (from appendix)

Breakeven point (BEP) (p. 380)   the level of activity, in units or dollars, at which total revenues equal total costs

Contribution margin (CM) (p. 382)   selling price per unit minus all variable production, selling, and administrative costs per unit; the amount that contributes to the coverage of fixed costs and the generation of profits

Contribution margin ratio (CM%) (p. 383)   contribution margin divided by revenue; indicates what proportion of selling price remains after variable costs have been covered

Cost-volume-profit (CVP) analysis (p. 384)   a process of examining the relationships among revenues, costs, volume, and profits for a relevant range of activity and for a particular time frame

Degree of operating leverage (DOL) (p. 398)   a measure of how a percentage change in sales will affect profits; calculated at a specified sales level as contribution margin divided by income before tax

Functional classification (p. 371)   a grouping of costs incurred for the same basic purpose

Incremental analysis (p. 390)   a decision making or computational process that focuses only on factors that change from one course of action or decision to another

Margin of safety (p. 396)   the excess of the budgeted or actual sales of a company over its breakeven point; can be calculated in units or sales dollars, or as a percentage

Operating leverage (p. 397)   a factor that reflects the relationship of a company's variable and fixed costs; measures the change in profits expected to result from a specified percentage change in sales

Product contribution margin (p. 372)   revenue minus total variable production costs

Profit-volume (PV) graph (p. 403)   a graphical presentation of the profit or loss associated with each level of sales (from appendix)

Total contribution margin (p. 372)   revenue minus all variable costs regardless of the area (production or nonproduction) of incurrence

Variable costing (p. 371)   a cost accumulation method that includes only variable production costs (direct material, direct labor, and variable overhead) as product or inventoriable costs and treats fixed overhead as a period cost; also known as direct costing

SOLUTION STRATEGIES

ABSORPTION VERSUS VARIABLE COSTING

1. Which method is being used: absorption or variable?
   a. If absorption:

   - What is the fixed overhead application rate?
   - What capacity was used in the denominator in determining the fixed factory overhead application rate?
   - Is production equal to the denominator capacity used in determining the fixed factory overhead application rate? If not, there is a volume variance, which must be assigned, at least in part, to the income statement.
   - What is the cost per unit of product? (DM + DL + VOH + FOH)

b. If variable:

- What is the cost per unit of product? (DM + DL + VOH)
- How is the total fixed factory overhead accounted for? This amount is assigned to the income statement as a period cost.

2. What is the relationship of production to sales?

   a. Production = Sales

   Absorption costing income = Variable costing income

   b. Production > Sales

   Absorption costing income > Variable costing income

   c. Production < Sales

   Absorption costing income < Variable costing income

3. How is the difference in income measured? Dollar difference between absorption costing income and variable costing income = FOH application rate 3 Change in inventory units

4. How are dollar differences in fixed costs used to explain financial statement difference? Income figures are converted as follows:

	Income Statement	**Balance Sheet**
P = S	AC = VC No difference in PBT as beginning inventory FC equals ending inventory FC	No change in FC from beginning inventory
P > S (Stockpiling inventory)	PBT or AC > PBT of VC by amount of fixed OH in ending inventory minus fixed OH in beginning inventory	Ending inventory FC difference increased (by the amount of fixed OH attached to the increase in inventory produced)
P < S (Selling off beginning inventory)	PBT or AC < PBT of VC by amount of fixed OH released from beginning inventory	Ending inventory FC difference reduced (by the amount of fixed OH from BI that is charged to cost of goods sold)

where P = Production, S = Sales, and FC = Fixed Cost
         AC = Absorption Costing, VC = Variable Costing, and PBT = Profit Before Tax

Note: The effects of the relationships presented here are based on two qualifying assumptions:
(1) that unit costs are constant over time; and
(2) that any fixed cost variances from standard are written off when incurred rather than being prorated to
    inventory balances.

COST-VOLUME-PROFIT

Most CVP problems are solvable by use of numerator/denominator approach. All numerators and denominators and the type of problem to which each relates are listed below. The formulas relate to both single-product and multiproduct firms, but results for multiproduct firms are per bag and must be converted to units of individual products.

Problem Situation	Numerator	Denominator
Simple BEP in units	FC	CM
Simple BEP in dollars	FC	CM%
CVP with lump-sum profit in units	FC + P	CM
CVP with lump-sum profit in dollars	FC + P	CM%
CVP with variable profit in units	FC	CM - P_u
CVP with variable profit in dollars	FC	CM% - P_u%

where   FC = fixed cost
       CM = contribution margin per unit
   CM% = contribution margin percentage
        P = total profit (can be on before-tax or an after-tax basis
           converted to before-tax)
     P_u = profit per unit
   P_u% = profit percentage per unit

To convert after-tax profit to before-tax profit, divide after-tax profit by $(1 - \text{tax rate})$.

MARGIN OF SAFETY

$$\text{Margin of safety in units} = \text{Actual units} - \text{Breakeven units}$$
$$\text{Margin of safety in dollars} = \text{Actual sales \$} - \text{Breakeven sales \$}$$

$$\text{Margin of safety percentage} = \frac{\text{Margin of safety in units or dollars}}{\text{Actual sales in units or dollars}}$$

DEGREE OF OPERATING LEVERAGE

$$\text{Degree of operating leverage} = \frac{\text{Contribution margin}}{\text{Income before tax}}$$

$$\text{Predicted additional income} = \text{Degree of operating leverage} \times \text{Percent change in sales} \times \text{Current income}$$

DEMONSTRATION PROBLEM

TabbyWorld makes and sells scratch posts for cats. Cost information for one scratch post is as follows:

Direct material	$2.00
Direct labor	1.00
Variable factory overhead	.50
Variable selling expenses	.10
Total variable costs	$3.60
Total fixed factory overhead	$388,800

Each scratch post sells for $9. Current annual production and sales volume is 75,000 posts. A predetermined fixed factory overhead rate can be computed based on this activity level.

Required:

a. What is the absorption cost per unit?

b. What is the variable cost per unit?

c. Compute the contribution margin and contribution margin ratio for TabbyWorld's product.

d. Compute the breakeven point in units for TabbyWorld, using contribution margin.

e. Compute the breakeven point in sales dollars for TabbyWorld, using contribution margin ratio.

f. What is TabbyWorld's margin of safety in units? In sales dollars?

g. What is TabbyWorld's degree of operating leverage? If sales increase by 20 percent, by how much will before-tax income increase?

h. If TabbyWorld wants to earn $43,200 of before-tax profits, how many posts will it have to sell?

i. If TabbyWorld wants to earn $40,500 after taxes and is subject to a 25 percent tax rate, how many units will it have to sell?

j. If TabbyWorld's fixed costs increased by $7,560, how many units would it need to sell to break even? (Use original data.)

k. TabbyWorld can sell an additional 6,000 scratch posts overseas for $8.50. Variable costs will increase by $.30 for shipping expenses, and fixed costs will increase by $25,000 because of the purchase of a new machine. This is a one-time-only sale and will not affect domestic sales this year or in the future. Should TabbyWorld sell the additional units?

■ SOLUTION TO DEMONSTRATION PROBLEM

a. Absorption cost = $3.60 + ($388,800 ÷ 75,000) = $3.60 + ≈$5.18 = $8.78

b. Variable cost = $3.60

c. CM = Selling price − Variable cost = $9.00 − $3.60 = $5.40
CM% = (Selling price − Variable cost) ÷ Selling price = $5.40 ÷ $9.00 = 60%

d. BEP = Fixed Cost ÷ CM = $388,800 ÷ $5.40 = 72,000

e. BEP = Fixed Cost ÷ CM% = $388,800 ÷ .6 = $648,000
(Note: This answer is also equal to 72,000 units × $9 per unit selling price.)

f. Margin of safety = Current units of sales − Breakeven sales = 75,000 − 72,000 = 3,000 units
Current revenues = Current sales volume × Unit selling price = 75,000 × $9 = $675,000

Margin of safety = Current revenues − Breakeven revenues = $675,000 − $648,000 = $27,000

g. Current CM = 75,000 × $5.40 = $405,000; current before-tax profit = $405,000 − $388,800 = $16,200

Degree of operating leverage = $405,000 ÷ $16,200 = 25

Increase in income = 25 × 20% = 500%

Proof: 75,000 × 1.2 = 90,000 units; 90,000 × $5.40 = $486,000 CM − $388,800 FC = $97,200 PBT; ($16,200 current PBT × 500%) + $16,200 = $97,200

h. BEP = (FC + Desired Profit) ÷ CM = ($388,800 + $43,200) ÷ $5.40 = 80,000 units

i. Profit after tax ÷ (1 − Tax rate) = Profit before tax

$40,500 ÷ .75 = $54,000

BEP = (FC + Desired Profit) ÷ CM = ($388,800 + $54,000) ÷ $5.40 = 82,000 units

j. Additional units to break even = Increase in FC ÷ CM = $7,560 ÷ $5.40 = 1,400; new BEP = 72,000 + 1,400 = 73,400 units

k. New CM for these units = $8.50 − $3.90 = $4.60; 6,000 × $4.60 = $27,600, which is $2,600 above the additional $25,000 fixed cost. Yes, TabbyWorld should sell the additional units.

END-OF-CHAPTER MATERIALS

■ QUESTIONS

1. Which of the following are defined as product costs when absorption costing is used? When variable costing is used?

   a. Direct material
   b. Variable factory overhead
   c. Selling expenses
   d. Direct labor
   e. Fixed factory overhead
   f. Administrative expenses

2. What is a functional classification of expenses? Give examples of functional classifications.

3. Which approach (absorption or variable) classifies costs by behavior? Which classifies costs by functional categories?

4. For each of the terms that follow, indicate whether the term would be found on an absorption income statement (A), a variable costing income statement (V), or both (B).

   a. Cost of goods sold
   b. Contribution margin
   c. Gross margin
   d. Selling expenses
   e. Variable expenses
   f. Administrative expenses
   g. Fixed expenses

5. What is the difference between absorption and variable costing in the treatment of fixed factory overhead?

6. Define product contribution margin and total contribution margin. What is the difference between the product contribution margin and total contribution margin?

7. Which approach, absorption or variable, is unofficially required by the Financial Accounting Standards Board and the Securities and Exchange Commission for external financial reporting? Why do you think this requirement exists?

8. Would a volume variance ever be found on a variable costing income statement? Explain.

9. For a specific firm in a year in which production and sales volume are equal, both an absorption and a variable costing income statement are prepared. Would you normally expect that the gross margin on the absorption costing statement would be equal to the total contribution margin on the variable costing statement? Explain.

10. Which of the following statements are true?
    a. Net income under absorption costing is a function of both sales volume and production volume.
    b. Net income under absorption costing is a function of sales volume only.
    c. Net income under variable costing is a function of both sales volume and production volume.
    d. Net income under variable costing is a function of sales volume only.

11. Describe a circumstance in which net income computed under absorption costing exceeds net income computed under variable costing. Why does this occur?

12. Since managers in commercial entities aspire to make a profit, why do these managers care about the breakeven point?

13. Why does contribution margin fluctuate in direct proportion to sales volume?

14. How is breakeven analysis related to CVP analysis?

15. If the per-unit variable costs associated with a product increase but selling price and fixed costs remain constant, what will happen to (a) contribution margin and (b) breakeven point? Explain.

16. The CVP model works directly with income before taxes. How can you solve a problem in which income is presented as an after-tax amount?

17. What is incremental analysis? What types of changes are examined in this kind of analysis?

18. What is the bag assumption and why is it necessary in a multiproduct company?

19. What are the basic CVP assumptions? Why do managers who use CVP analysis keep these assumptions in mind when using the answers provided by the model?

20. What effect would specifying the quality of a product be likely to have on each of the CVP factors (selling price, variable costs, fixed costs, volume, and profits)? Why?

21. The president of Henry's Hamburgers has just been informed that the chain is operating at an 8 percent margin of safety with a degree of operating leverage of 52. What should his course of action be and why?

22. Why is it necessary to consider qualitative factors when solving problems using CVP?

23. Why is the perspective of managers using CVP a short-term one, and what are the implications of such a perspective?

24. (Appendix) What is a breakeven graph? How is it similar to and different from a profit-volume graph?

■ EXERCISES

25. (LO 1; *Product cost under AC and VC*) The Blue Suede Shoe Company produced 100,000 pairs of shoes and sold 70,000 in its first year of operations. There was no Work in Process Inventory at year-end. Its costs for that year were:

Direct materials	$ 400,000
Direct labor	300,000
Variable factory overhead	150,000
Variable selling and administrative	210,000
Fixed factory overhead	250,000
Fixed selling and administrative	175,000
Total	$1,485,000

For this company's first year of operations, compute the cost of one unit of product if the company uses (a) variable costing and (b) absorption costing.

26. (LO 1; *Product cost under AC and VC*) The Allison Electric Company is considering switching to variable costing. In an effort to better understand the significance of the possible change, the management team has asked that ending inventories be priced on both an absorption and a variable costing basis. Production for the year was 200,000 units, of which 25,000 units remained in ending inventory. Additional information concerning production follows:

Direct material costs	$600,000
Direct labor costs	450,000
Factory overhead costs	600,000

Factory overhead has not been separated into fixed and variable components, but the fixed factory overhead rate approximates $6 per direct labor hour. The current direct labor rate is $10 per hour. Calculate the total costs to be assigned to ending inventory under both absorption and variable costing.

27. (LO 1; *Volume variance*) Overland Soup Company produces canned vegetable soup and uses an absorption costing system based on standard costs. Factory overhead is applied to production at a rate of $.12 per unit. The standard costs per unit for 1996 were:

Direct materials	$.07
Direct labor	.05
Variable factory overhead	.04
Fixed factory overhead	?

The expected production level for 1996 is 4,000,000 units.

a. For 1996, how much total fixed factory overhead did the company expect to incur?
b. If actual production was 4,200,000 units, what was the volume variance?
c. Prepare the journal entry to dispose of the volume variance.

28. (LO 1; *Profit determination under VC and AC*) During the past year, Ridall Garments, Inc., produced 200,000 units of product and sold 90 percent of everything produced. There was no beginning inventory of finished units.

Production costs consisted of $400,000 direct materials, $600,000 direct labor, $100,000 variable factory overhead, and $160,000 fixed factory overhead. The fixed factory overhead application rate was based on an expected capacity for the plant of 200,000 units. Selling price is $8. Compare income results under variable and absorption costing.

29. (LO 1; *Missing numbers*) Shortly after the end of its first year of operations, thieves stole or destroyed nearly all cost and production records of the Safe Living Products Company, a producer of high-quality burglar alarms. Having been hired to piece together the fragments of the records that were salvaged from the scene, you have determined the following regarding the first-year operations:

Production in units	?
Sales in units	9,500
Total sales	$109,250
Gross margin	54,625
Total fixed factory overhead costs incurred	22,500
Total selling and administrative costs	38,000
Variable production costs (per unit)	3.50

   a. How many units were produced in the first year?
   b. From the previous information, prepare an income statement using absorption costing.

30. (LO 1; *NI under AC and VC*) The following information pertains to the operations of the Plainview Manufacturing Company for 1997:

Sales (1,000 units at $40 per unit)	$40,000
Variable costs of production	$20,000
Fixed costs of production	$10,000
Fixed selling costs	$ 3,000
Variable selling costs (per unit sold)	$5
Beginning WIP and Finished Goods Inventories (units)	0
Ending WIP Inventory (units)	0
Total units produced	1,250

   Assume the company uses an actual costing system. Determine net income for 1997 if

   a. absorption costing is used.
   b. variable costing is used.
   c. Reconcile your answers to parts a and b.

31. (LO 2; *Converting to VC*) Alabama Paper Company produces and sells boxes of assorted stationery. Included with its published 1996 financial statements was the following income statement:

Sales (1,000,000 boxes at $4 per box)	$4,000,000
Cost of goods sold	2,000,000
Gross margin	$2,000,000
Selling & administrative expenses	1,500,000
Net income	$ 500,000

   From carefully scanning the company records, you were able to obtain additional information regarding the company's operations for 1996:

■ The company had no Work in Process Inventory at the beginning or end of the year.

■ The company had no Finished Goods Inventory at the beginning of the year.

■ Production in 1996 was 1,250,000 units.

■ Total fixed production costs were $400,000.

■ Variable selling costs were $1 per unit.

    a. Determine the company's net income for 1996 under variable costing.

    b. Reconcile the net income computed in part a with the net income reported in the previous income statement.

32. (LO 2; *Converting to AC*) The Newark Paint Company has been in operation for two years. It is a privately held firm and produces no external financial information. It employs the variable costing method for preparing internal financial statements. Selected information from its first two years of operations follows:

	YEAR 1	YEAR 2
Gallons of product produced	500,000	500,000
Gallons of product sold	450,000	525,000
Fixed production costs	$2,000,000	$2,000,000
Variable production costs	2,500,000	2,500,000
Net income (variable costing)	500,000	1,600,000

    a. Had the company used absorption costing in year 1, how much net income would it have reported?

    b. Had the company used absorption costing in both years, how much net income would it have reported in year 2?

33. (LO 3; *BEP*) Smith & Forest Enterprises has the following revenue and cost functions:

Revenue = $30 per unit
Fixed costs = $400,000
Variable costs = $22 per unit

What is the breakeven point in units? In dollars?

34. (LO 3; *BEP*) In each of the following situations, how many units must be sold for the company to break even?

    a. Total fixed costs are $90,000, and the unit contribution margin is $5.

    b. Unit selling price is $8, unit variable cost is $5, and total fixed costs are $48,000.

    c. Unit selling price is $10, contribution margin is 25 percent of revenue, and total fixed costs are $30,000.

    d. Unit variable cost is 80 percent of the unit selling price, total fixed costs are $48,000, and unit selling price is $12.

    e. Unit variable cost is $5, contribution margin per unit is $3, and total fixed costs are $24,000. Compute total sales at the breakeven volume in addition to total number of units.

35. (LO 3; *BEP*) Alder-Birch Co. publishes paperback cartoon books. The following operational data relate to a typical month:

Unit sales price	$ 8.00
Unit variable cost	$ 2.60
Fixed costs	$16,200
Current volume of books	3,200

The company is considering an expansion that would increase monthly fixed costs by $2,700. If it does, production and sales will increase by 1,000 books.

a. Without considering the expansion, calculate the firm's breakeven point and its monthly before-tax income.

b. Recalculate breakeven point in books and monthly before-tax income assuming that the company undertakes the expansion.

36. (LO 4; *CVP with before-tax income*) Office Supply Co. is planning to make and sell 10,000 computer disk trays. Fixed costs are $40,000, and variable costs are 60 percent of the selling price. What must the selling price be for the company to earn $10,000 of before-tax income on the trays?

37. (LO 4; *CVP in alternative cost structures*) A large, diversified corporation is considering the acquisition of two firms that manufacture electric razors. Firm A has a variable unit cost of $11 and total fixed costs of $2,500,000. Firm B has a variable unit cost of $14 and total fixed costs of $500,000. The wholesale price for the electric razors is $16, and each firm has an annual capacity of 800,000 razors.

Which firm would you recommend that the corporation acquire if the estimated demand for electric razors is:

a. 400,000 units per year?
b. 600,000 units per year?
c. 800,000 units per year?

38. (LO 4; *CVP with after-tax income*) Boiler Maker, Inc., manufactures home furnaces that sell for $800. The unit costs are:

Direct materials	$275
Direct labor	150
Variable factory overhead	130
Variable selling expense	45

Annual fixed factory overhead is $100,000 and annual fixed selling and administrative expenses are $120,000. The company is in a 30 percent tax bracket.

How many furnaces does the company need to make and sell to earn $140,000 in after-tax income?

39. (LO 4; *CVP analysis*) Compute the number of units that must be sold and the total sales in each of the following situations:

a. The company's income goal is $40,000. Total fixed costs are $80,000, unit contribution margin is $5, and unit selling price is $8.

b. The company's income goal is $25,000 after tax, and its tax rate is 40 percent. Unit variable cost is $6, unit contribution margin is $4, and total fixed costs are $40,000.

c. The company's after-tax income goal is $54,000, and the tax rate is 40 percent. Unit variable cost is 70 percent of the $10 unit selling price, and total fixed costs are $60,000.

d. The company's after-tax income goal is $30,000, and the tax rate is 50 percent. Unit contribution margin is $3, unit variable cost is 70 percent of the unit selling price, and total fixed costs are $60,000.

e. The company's after-tax income goal is $40,000 and the tax rate is 50 percent. Unit variable cost is $9, unit contribution margin is 25 percent of selling price, and total fixed costs are $25,000.

40. (LO 4; *Incremental analysis*) Mid-Plains Furniture Co. has annual sales of $1,800,000, variable expenses of 60 percent of sales, and fixed expenses of $60,000 monthly. How much will sales have to increase so that Mid-Plains Furniture Co. will have before-tax income of 20 percent of sales?

41. (LO 4; *CVP; incremental analysis*) Merlin Jones is an accountant who specializes in consulting. He charges $100 per client hour. His monthly expenses are:

Office rent	$ 800
Office staff	1,200
Utilities	400
Total fixed expenses	$2,400

Monthly variable costs average $20 per client hour, and Mr. Jones is in a 20 percent tax bracket. In addition to the above expenses, Mr. Jones must have 60 hours of continuing education (CE) annually to maintain his certification. He has determined that this CE costs him $400 a month.

a. How many client hours per month must Mr. Jones generate to break even?

b. How many client hours per month must Mr. Jones generate to earn $8,000 per month after tax? Use incremental analysis based on your answer to part a.

c. Mr. Jones enjoys bowling and flying his private plane and wonders if he could work six-hour days and four-day weeks and still earn $8,000 after tax. Could he do this? Show computations and prove your answer (assume that there are four weeks per month). Use incremental analysis based on your answer to part a.

42. (LO 3, 5; *Multiproduct BEP*) College Novelty Products Co. sells flags and sun visors at the entrances to local sporting events. The firm sells two flags for each sun visor. A flag sells for $3 and costs $1. A sun visor sells for $1.50 and costs $1. The company's monthly fixed costs are $4,500. How many flags will the company sell at the BEP? Prove your answer.

43. (LO 3, 5; *Multiproduct CVP*) Erotech Automobile Company manufactures two types of children's electric cars, which are sold to toy stores throughout the country. The compact car is sold for an average price of $2,000 per unit; variable manufacturing costs are $1,800 per unit. The standard-size car is sold for an average price of $3,500 per unit; variable manufacturing costs are $3,000 per unit. Total fixed costs are estimated to be $360 million per year.

a. Determine the breakeven volume for the company if the expected sales mix is one-third compact cars and two-thirds standard cars.

b. Because of a battery shortage, the management team expects the sales mix to shift to 50 percent compact cars and 50 percent standard cars. Determine the breakeven volume based on the new sales mix, and explain why your answer differs from the one you gave in part a.

c. It is expected that if the firm produced more than 50 percent compact cars, fixed costs would increase by $65 million. Determine the breakeven volume based on a sales mix of 60 percent compact cars and 40 percent standard cars.

44. (LO 3, 8; *BEP; margin of safety*) Terri White has a street lunch vending business in which she sells quiche and a soda as a package for $3. The variable costs of each package lunch are $1.20. Her annual fixed costs are $27,000.

a. What is her breakeven point in revenue and number of lunches?

b. If the business is currently selling 18,000 lunches annually, what is Terri's margin of safety in units, percentage, and dollars?

45. (LO 4, 8; *CVP; margin of safety*) Newman Tool and Die Company is considering acquiring new equipment to set up a production line to produce a newly designed locking wrench. Demand for this wrench is estimated at 100,000 units a year, and the selling price is to be $10. One production line being considered uses primarily manual labor. Estimated variable production cost per unit on this line is $7, and total fixed production cost for the line is $150,000. The other possible production line is more automated; its estimated variable production cost per unit is $3, and total fixed production cost for this line is $630,000.

   a. Which production line would you recommend that the firm use? What is the margin of safety for each production line?

   b. If the demand were estimated to be 120,000 units, would your recommendation change?

   c. If the demand were estimated to be 150,000 units, would your recommendation change?

   d. Assume that the firm has an after-tax income goal of $60,000. If the tax rate is 40 percent and estimated demand is 100,000 units, what will the selling price have to be for both production lines?

46. (LO 8; *Margin of safety; operating leverage*) Picante Hot Sauce, Inc., sells its four-ounce bottle of pepper sauce for $2.90. Variable costs are $.52 per bottle, and fixed costs are $288,000 annually. The firm is currently selling 320,000 bottles annually.

   a. What is the company's margin of safety in units?

   b. Calculate the degree of operating leverage.

   c. If the company can increase sales by 25 percent, by what percentage will its income increase? Prove your answer.

47. (LO 3, 8; *BEP; operating leverage*) Fashion Pet Salon specializes in washing and grooming pets. The company charges $10 per pet visit and has the following costs:

Variable costs per visit	
Direct materials	$ .50
Direct labor	2.00
Fixed monthly costs	
Shop rent	$400
Insurance	50
Licenses	25
Equipment depreciation	25
Advertising	100
Utilities	150

   a. How many pet visits does the company need to break even? How many dollars of revenue?

   b. Management wants to earn income equal to 25 percent of revenue before tax. How many pet visits would this require?

   c. If the company averages 140 pet visits per month, what is its operating leverage?

   d. If business increased by 20 percent over the current 140 visits, how much would income increase? What would be the new total income? Prove your answer.

48. (LO 3, 4, 8; *BEP; margin of safety; operating leverage*) In early 1996, Scarlett O'Hara received from her publisher, Tara Press, a $9 million advance for a new book. This advance is against future royalties of 15 percent of retail selling price of $18.95. Should the book fail to sell enough to cover the advance, O'Hara is not liable for repayment. Tara expects the cost of printing 1.5 million hardcover copies of the book to be $3 million. Advertising costs for the book are expected to be $200,000, and other fixed costs are budgeted at $4.5 million. Selling price from Tara Press to booksellers is 60 percent of retail price.

a. To justify the amount of the advance, how many copies of the book will Tara Press need to sell?

b. If the printing costs are considered fixed for the 1.5 million copies, and variable costs of production are $.01 per copy, what is Tara Press's breakeven point?

c. Using the original data, determine how much before-tax income Tara will earn if it sells only the 1.5 million copies from the first run.

d. Using the original data, determine how much Tara Press will earn if the hardback goes into a second printing of 1.5 million copies and if the entire second printing is sold.

e. Using the original data, and assuming that 1,475,000 copies are sold, determine the company's margin of safety in sales dollars and in units. What is the company's degree of operating leverage? If sales increased 1.5 percent above the 1,475,000 copies, what would be the percentage increase in income? Prove your answer.

49. *(Appendix)* Cajun Candy Co. makes and sells boxes of Cajun candies. The firm's income statement for 1997 follows:

Sales (25,000 boxes × $12)		$300,000
Variable costs		
Production (25,000 × $3)	$75,000	
Sales commissions (25,000 × $1.20)	30,000	105,000
Contribution margin		$195,000
Fixed costs		
Production	$58,000	
Selling and administrative	20,000	78,000
Income before tax		$117,000

a. Prepare a cost-volume-profit graph for Cajun Candy Co.

b. Prepare a profit-volume graph for Cajun Candy Co.

■ COMMUNICATION ACTIVITIES

50. (LO 1; *AC versus VC*) Which of the following dimensions of product costing would be affected by a switch from absorption to variable costing: the product costing system, the measurement method, cost accumulation, or financial statement presentation? Why and how?

51. (LO 3; *BEP; revenue and cost curves*) Riverboat gambling has been the new wave in casino development. However, investing in the new casinos has been more risky than playing in them. Much of the risk of these businesses is related to attracting a sufficient volume of players and generating enough dollar volume per player. Three Louisiana riverboats have vastly different experiences in this regard. In early 1994, the *Star* (based in New Orleans) generated an average revenue per passenger of $55.42; the *Queen of New Orleans* generated a mere $30.27 per pas-

e. Assuming Year 3 production was only 45,000 units, compute the Year 3 volume variance.

57. (LO 1, 2; *Income under AC and VC*) Lansing Mfg., Inc., has been developing models to predict its costs and revenues. As a result of its work, the following three models have been developed:

Revenue model: y = $40X
  where y is total revenue and X is number of units sold
Production cost model: y = $50,000 + $12X
  where y is total production cost and X is number of units produced
Period cost (selling and administrative expense) model: y = $30,000 + $5X
  where y is total period costs and X is number of units sold

a. Based on these models, compute projected net income for a period in which the company produces 10,000 units and sells 7,000 units. Assume the company uses absorption costing.
b. Repeat part a, but this time assume that the company uses variable costing.
c. Reconcile your answers in parts a and b.

58. (LO 1; *Product costs under VC and AC; CM; GM*) Golf-Go Equipment Company produces and sells electric golf carts. The company uses a costing system based on actual costs. Selected accounting and production information for fiscal 1996 follows:

Net income (under absorption costing)	$ 400,000
Sales	$3,400,000
Fixed factory overhead cost incurred	$ 600,000
Variable selling and administrative costs	$ 400,000
Fixed selling and administrative costs	$ 500,000
Net income (under variable costing)	$ 310,000
Units produced	2,000
Units sold	?

Golf-Go had no Work in Process Inventory at either the beginning or end of fiscal 1996. The company also did not have any Finished Goods Inventory at the beginning of the fiscal year.
   Compute each of the following:

a. number of units sold.
b. cost of one unit of product under variable costing.
c. cost of one unit of product under absorption costing.
d. total contribution margin under variable costing.
e. gross margin under absorption costing.

59. (LO 2; *Converting AC to VC*) Littlefield Inc. has been recording inventory on an absorption costing basis. There are plans to convert to a variable costing basis for internal reporting purposes. To get an impression of the overall impact of the change, the management team would like to see the effect on the company's income figures since its inception, three years ago. Data for the last three years of the company's operations follow:

	YEAR		
	1	*2*	*3*
Absorption costing income	$80,000	$110,000	$200,000
Units produced	5,000	6,000	7,000
Units sold	4,000	5,000	7,000
Fixed manufacturing costs	$50,000	$ 54,000	$ 70,000

Calculate the variable costing income for each of the three years. Assume the fixed manufacturing overhead application rate is based on actual units produced. If necessary, use a FIFO cost flow assumption.

60. (LO 1, 2; *Income under VC and AC; cost of FG*) Midland Appliance Company manufactures deep fat fryers for use in restaurants, nightclubs, and snack bars. The company employs a standard variable costing system. Because the company has common stock that is publicly traded, it must convert the variable costing data to an absorption basis for external financial statements. The following information pertains to fiscal years 1996 and 1997:

	1996	1997
Average sales price per unit	$40	$41
Production in units	25,000	30,000
Sales in units	25,000	25,000
Beginning Finished Goods Inventory (units)	2,000	?
Work in Process Inventory (beginning and ending; units)	0	0
Standard costs per unit for both 1996 and 1997:		
Materials	$8.00	
Labor	6.50	
Factory overhead	3.50	

Annual fixed costs (actual and budgeted were the same):	
Factory overhead	$240,000
Selling and administrative	100,000

For both 1996 and 1997, variable selling and administrative costs amounted to 20 percent of total sales. In converting the variable costing information to absorption costing information, the company applies the fixed factory overhead based on its practical capacity of 30,000 units. Any resulting volume variance is treated as an adjustment to Cost of Goods Sold. Variable factory overhead is applied based on the actual number of units produced in the period.

a. Prepare a 1997 income statement based on standard variable costing.
b. Prepare a 1997 income statement based on standard absorption costing.
c. Reconcile your answers in parts a and b.
d. Compute the cost assigned to the ending Finished Goods Inventory for 1997 under standard absorption costing.

61. (LO 1; *Missing numbers; VC income statement*) The following information was taken from the cost records of Belden Company for 1998. For 1998, the company had no units in Finished Goods Inventory at the beginning of the year, and no units in Work in Process Inventory at either the beginning or end of the year. Belden uses variable costing.

	VARIABLE COSTS	FIXED COSTS
Direct materials	$3 per unit	
Direct labor	5 per unit	
Factory overhead	2 per unit	$200,000
Selling and administrative	2 per unit	350,000

The product contribution margin in 1998 was $8 per unit, and net income was $200,000.

a. What was the company's sales price per unit?
b. What were total revenues?
c. How many units were sold?
d. Prepare a variable costing income statement for 1998.

62. (LO 1, 3; *AC and VC; BEP*) The Cowboy Log Company manufactures fireplace logs in Laramie County, Wyoming. This firm is unusual in that all of its costs are variable. Sawdust and glue are combined to make the logs; all labor and sales are done on a piecework basis. The logs are manufactured in an open field in molds filled with the sawdust and glue. These molds serve as the outside wrapping for the logs and are also burned with the logs.
The following data relate to the operations of the Cowboy Log Company:

	1996	1997
Sales	5,000 logs	5,000 logs
Production	7,500 logs	2,500 logs
Beginning inventory	0	2,500 logs
Ending inventory	2,500 logs	0
Selling price	$10 per log	$10 per log
Production costs (all variable)	$15,000	$5,000
Selling and administrative expense	$1 per bag	$1 per bag

a. Determine the net income for each year using absorption costing and using variable costing.
b. Determine the cost amounts of the beginning and ending inventories of finished goods for each year using absorption costing and using variable costing. Explain the results.
c. What is the breakeven point in units? In dollars?

63. (LO 1, 3, 4; *AC and VC; BEP*) The Weird Corporation of Somewhere, Pennsylvania, is known throughout the accounting world because all its costs are fixed. It manufactures charcoal made from coal dust that is taken from the atmosphere in Bucks County. All employees are salaried and hired on an annual basis. Output from the plant can be increased or decreased by adjustment of the speed of the intake fan that draws in air to remove the coal dust. Some of the free coal dust is burned to generate power to supply electricity, light, and heat.
The following data relate to the operations of the Weird Corporation:

	1996	1997
Sales	5,000 bags	5,000 bags
Production	7,500 bags	2,500 bags
Beginning inventory	0	2,500 bags
Ending inventory	2,500 bags	0
Selling price	$10 per bag	$10 per bag
Production costs (all fixed)	$15,000	$15,000
Selling and administrative expense	$ 5,000	$ 5,000
Budgeted production*	5,000 bags	5,000 bags

*Any volume variance is charged to Cost of Goods Sold in the current period.

a. Determine the net income for each year using absorption costing and using variable costing.

b. Determine the cost amounts of the beginning and ending inventories for each year using absorption costing and using variable costing.

c. What is the breakeven point in units? In dollars?

d. Compare the cost structures of the Weird Company with the Cowboy Log Company (problem 62). Under what circumstances would you prefer each cost structure?

64. (LO 4; *BEP; CVP before and after tax*) High School Traditions operates a shop that makes and sells class rings for local high schools. Operating statistics follow:

Average selling price per ring	$250
Variable costs per ring	
Rings and stones	$ 90
Sales commissions	18
Variable overhead	8
Annual fixed costs	
Selling expenses	$42,000
Administrative expenses	56,000
Production	30,000

The company's tax rate is 30 percent.

a. What is the firm's breakeven point in rings? In revenue?

b. How much revenue is needed to yield $140,000 before-tax income?

c. How much revenue is needed to yield an after-tax income of $120,000?

d. How much revenue is needed to yield an after-tax income of 20 percent of revenue?

e. The firm's marketing manager believes that by spending an additional $12,000 in advertising and lowering the price by $20 per ring, he can increase the number of rings sold by 25 percent. He is currently selling 2,200 rings. Should he make these changes?

65. (LO 3, 4, 5; *Multiproduct CVP*) Get-In-Line Automobile Company manufactures three types of cars, all of which are sold at wholesale to dealers throughout the world. Compact models manufactured by Get-In-Line sell at an average price of $2,200, and variable costs per unit total $1,900. Standard-size cars sell at an average price of $3,700, and variable costs per unit equal $3,000. Luxury models sell at an average price of $6,000, and the variable costs per unit are $5,000. Total fixed costs for the company are estimated at $1,080,000,000.

a. The company's marketing department estimates that next year's unit sales mix will be 30 percent compact, 50 percent standard, and 20 percent luxury. What is the breakeven point in units and sales for the firm?

b. If the company has an after-tax income goal of $1 billion and the tax rate is 50 percent, how many units of each type of car must be sold for the goal to be reached?

c. Assume the sales mix shifts to 50 percent compact, 40 percent standard, and 10 percent luxury. How does this mix affect your answer to part b?

d. If Get-In-Line sold more luxury cars and fewer compact cars, how would your answers to parts a and b change?

66. (LO 3, 4, 5, 8; *Multiproduct company*) Techno Sounds, Inc., makes portable CD players, CDs, and batteries, which follow a normal sales mix pattern of 1:3:6. The following are the company's costs:

	CD PLAYERS	CDs	BATTERIES
Variable product costs	$ 62	$1.20	$.22
Variable selling expenses	14	.50	.10
Variable administrative expenses	3	.05	.03
Selling prices	140	5.00	.50
Annual fixed factory overhead		$110,000	
Annual fixed selling expenses		60,000	
Annual fixed administrative expenses		16,290	

The firm is in a 40 percent income tax bracket.

a. What is the annual dollar breakeven point?

b. How many CD players, CDs, and batteries are expected to be sold at the breakeven point?

c. If the firm desires a before-tax income of $114,640, how much total revenue is required and how many units of each item must be sold?

d. If the firm desires an after-tax income of $103,176, how much total revenue is required and how many units of each item must be sold?

e. If the firm achieves the revenue determined in part d, what is its margin of safety in dollars and percentage?

67. (LO 3, 4, 5; *Multiproduct company*) Decoy Decorators makes carved wooden mallard hens and ducklings. For every hen the firm sells, it sells two ducklings. The following are the company's revenues and costs:

	HENS	DUCKLINGS
Selling price	$12	$ 6
Variable cost	4	4
Contribution margin	$ 8	$ 2

Monthly fixed costs are $12,000.

a. What is the average contribution margin ratio?

b. Calculate the breakeven point. At the breakeven point, identify the total units of each product sold and sales dollars of each product.

c. If the company wants to earn $24,000 in before-tax income per month, how many hens and how many ducklings must it sell?

d. The company specifies $9,000 of after-tax income as its objective, is in a 40 percent tax bracket, and believes that the mix has changed to five ducklings for every hen. How much total revenue is needed, and in what product proportions, to achieve its income objective?

68. (LO 4; *Multiproduct CVP; incremental analysis*) Laurel Stices owns a travel agency. She receives commission revenue based on the total dollar volume of business she generates for various client-firms in the travel and entertainment industries. Her rates of commission currently are 20 percent of total hotel fees, 15 percent of total car rental fees, and 10 percent of airline ticket fees. Data for a normal month's operations are as follows:

Costs		Fees Generated for Clients	
Advertising	$1,000	Hotel fees	$10,800
Rent	800	Car rental fees	3,600
Utilities	300	Airline ticket fees	14,200
Other expenses	1,400		$28,600

a. Given the stated commission percentages, what is Ms. Stices's normal total monthly commission? The normal monthly before-tax income?

b. Ms. Stices can increase the amount of hotel fees she generates by 40 percent if she spends an additional $200 on advertising. Should she do this?

c. Joe Westin has offered to merge his bookings with Ms. Stices's and become her employee. He would receive a base salary of $600 a month plus 20 percent of the commissions on client fees he generates, which, for a normal month, are:

Hotel fees	$5,000
Car rental fees	2,000
Airline ticket fees	2,000

Should Ms. Stices accept the proposal?

d. Use the information in part c. During Mr. Westin's first month, he generated $10,000 of total fees, but they were as follows:

Hotel fees	$3,000
Car rental fees	2,000
Airline ticket fees	5,000

Will Ms. Stices be pleased? Why or why not?

69. (LO 3, 4, 8; *BEP; CVP; incremental analysis; margin of safety*) Boudreaux Company makes small flat-bottomed boats called pirogues. The president, Bayou Boudreaux, enlists your help in predicting the effects of some changes she is contemplating and gives you the following information:

Variable costs to produce each pirogue:

Direct materials	$ 90
Direct labor	100
Variable factory overhead	20
Average variable selling cost per pirogue	30
Average variable administrative cost per pirogue	10
Annual fixed factory overhead	$660,000
Annual fixed selling expenses	190,000
Annual fixed administrative expenses	300,000

Bayou advises you that each pirogue sells for $400 and that demand for the current year is 14,400 pirogues or $5,760,000 of sales.
The following are some of the changes Bayou is considering:

Proposition 1: The sales staff believes that demand will increase 15 percent if price is reduced 10 percent.

Proposition 2: The engineering design staff believes that spending $30 on each pirogue to strengthen the hull will cause demand to increase 20 percent because this product will be superior to any other product on the market.

Proposition 3: The sales manager believes that increasing advertising by $25,000 will increase demand by 20 percent.

a. Calculate the breakeven point in units and dollars.
b. Calculate the margin of safety in units, in dollars, and as a percentage.
c. Calculate the effects on income and dollar breakeven point of the independent propositions (ignore tax implications). Advise the president about each proposition.

70. (LO 3, 4, 8; *Incremental analysis; operating leverage*) The Earl Davison Cycle Company sells bikes for an average price of $1,000. The average variable cost per bike is $600. At the present time, the company sells 12,500 bikes a year, and its fixed costs are $4 million. An advertising program costing $1 million is being planned. It is estimated that the advertising program will increase sales by 15 percent (over existing sales of 12,500 units) in the year of the program.

a. What is the breakeven volume for the company prior to implementing the advertising program?
b. Should the company undertake the advertising program? Use incremental analysis to determine your answer.
c. How much would volume have to be increased for the firm to consider undertaking the advertising program?
d. How would you answer part c if a tax rate of 40 percent were assumed?
e. Determine the relative operating leverage for the firm at its present sales volume.

71. (LO 3, 8, 9; *Margin of safety; operating leverage; appendix*) You are considering acquiring one of two local firms (VPI and TECH) that manufacture slip rings. VPI employs a considerable amount of labor in its manufacturing processes, and its salespeople all work on commission. TECH employs the latest technology in its manufacturing operations, and its salespeople are all salaried.

You have obtained the following financial information concerning the two firms:

	VPI		TECH	
	1996	*1997*	*1996*	*1997*
Sales	$100,000	$160,000	$100,000	$140,000
Expenses including taxes	88,000	137,200	88,000	111,200
Net income	$ 12,000	$ 22,800	$ 12,000	$ 28,800

After examining cost data, you determine that the fixed costs for VPI are $10,000, while the fixed costs for TECH are $50,000. The tax rate for both firms is 40 percent.

a. Determine breakeven sales for each of the firms in 1996 and 1997.
b. Determine the relative operating leverage for each firm in 1996 and 1997.
c. Suppose you could acquire either firm for $200,000 and you want an after-tax return of 12 percent on your investment. Determine what sales level for each firm would allow you to reach your goal.
d. Assuming the demand for slip rings fluctuates widely, comment on the relative positions of the firm.
e. Prepare a profit-volume graph for each firm.

72. (LO 9; *Appendix*) The Montana Boys Club has enlisted your help in developing a presentation for a group of local business executives who have previously given generously to support the club's efforts. Investigation reveals that each boy pays monthly dues of $8, monthly variable costs per member are $1, and the club's monthly fixed expenses are $2,100. Most of the club's workers are volunteers.

   a. Prepare a breakeven graph for the club.
   b. Prepare a profit-volume graph for the club.
   c. Which graph would you recommend that the club use in its presentation?

CASES

73. (LO 1; *VC and AC*) The Daniels Tool & Die Corporation has been in existence for a little over three years. The company's sales have increased each year as it builds a reputation. The company manufactures dies to its customers' specifications; as a consequence, a job order cost system is employed. Factory overhead is applied to the jobs based on direct labor hours; the absorption (full) costing method is used. Overapplied or underapplied overhead is treated as an adjustment to Cost of Goods Sold. The company's income statements for the last two years are as follows:

DANIELS TOOL & DIE CORPORATION
1996–1997 COMPARATIVE INCOME STATEMENTS

	1996	1997
Sales	$840,000	$1,015,000
Cost of goods sold		
Finished goods inventory, 1/1	$ 25,000	$ 18,000
Cost of goods manufactured	548,000	657,600
Total available	$573,000	$ 675,600
Finished goods inventory, 12/31	18,000	14,000
Cost of goods sold before overhead adjustment	$555,000	$ 661,600
Underapplied factory overhead	36,000	14,400
Cost of goods sold	$591,000	$ 676,000
Gross profit	$249,000	$ 339,000
Selling expenses	$ 82,000	$ 95,000
Administrative expenses	70,000	75,000
Total operating expenses	$152,000	$ 170,000
Operating income	$ 97,000	$ 169,000

DANIELS TOOL & DIE CORPORATION
INVENTORY BALANCES

	12/31/95	12/31/96	12/31/97
Raw Material Inventory	$22,000	$30,000	$10,000
Work in Process Inventory			
Costs	$40,000	$48,000	$64,000
Direct labor hours	1,335	1,600	2,100
Finished Goods Inventory			
Costs	$25,000	$18,000	$14,000
Direct labor hours	1,450	1,050	820

Daniels used the same predetermined overhead rate in applying overhead to production orders in both 1996 and 1997. The rate was based on the following estimates:

Fixed factory overhead	$ 25,000
Variable factory overhead	$155,000
Direct labor hours	25,000
Direct labor costs	$150,000

Actual direct labor hours expended were 20,000 in 1996 and 23,000 in 1997. Raw materials put into production were $292,000 in 1996 and $370,000 in 1997. Actual fixed overhead was $42,300 for 1996 and $37,400 for 1997, and the planned direct labor rate was the direct labor rate achieved.

For both years, all of the reported administrative costs were fixed, while the variable portion of the reported selling expenses resulted from a commission of 5 percent of sales revenue.

a. For the year ended December 31, 1997, prepare a revised income statement for the company using the variable costing method. Be sure to include the contribution margin on your statement.

b. Prepare a numerical reconciliation of the difference in operating income between the 1997 income statement prepared on the basis of absorption costing and the revised 1997 income statement prepared on the basis of variable costing.

c. Describe both the advantages and disadvantages of using variable costing.

(CMA adapted)

74. (LO 2; *Converting AC to VC*) Portland Optics, Inc., specializes in manufacturing lenses for large telescopes and cameras used in space exploration. Because the specifications for the lenses are determined by the customer and vary considerably, the company uses a job order cost system. Factory overhead is applied to jobs on the basis of direct labor hours, and the absorption (full) costing method is used. Portland's predetermined overhead rates for 1997 and 1998 were based on the following estimates:

	1997	1998
Direct labor hours	32,500	44,000
Direct labor cost	$325,000	$462,000
Fixed factory overhead	$130,000	$176,000
Variable factory overhead	$162,500	$198,000

Jim Bradford, Portland's controller, would like to use variable costing for internal reporting purposes, since he believes statements based on variable costing are more appropriate for use in making product decisions. To explain the benefits of variable costing to the other members of Portland's management team, Bradford plans to convert the company's income statement from absorption costing to variable costing. He has gathered the following information for this purpose:

PORTLAND OPTICS, INC.
COMPARATIVE INCOME STATEMENT
FOR THE YEARS 1997 AND 1998

	1997	1998
Net sales	$1,140,000	$1,520,000
Cost of goods sold		
Finished goods inventory on January 1	$ 16,000	$ 25,000
Cost of goods manufactured	720,000	976,000
Total available	$ 736,000	$1,001,000
Finished goods inventory on December 31	25,000	14,000
Cost of goods sold before overhead adjustment	$ 711,000	$ 987,000
Overhead adjustment	12,000	7,000
Cost of goods sold	$ 723,000	$ 994,000
Gross profit	$ 417,000	$ 526,000
Selling expense	$ 150,000	$ 190,000
Administrative expense	160,000	187,000
Total operating expenses	$ 310,000	$ 377,000
Operating income	$ 107,000	$ 149,000

Portland's actual manufacturing data for the two years are as follows:

	1997	1998
Direct labor hours	30,000	42,000
Direct labor cost	$300,000	$435,000
Raw materials used	$140,000	$210,000
Fixed factory overhead	$132,000	$175,000

The company's actual inventory balances were:

	12/31/96	12/31/97	12/31/98
Raw Materials Inventory	$32,000	$36,000	$18,000
Work in Process Inventory			
Costs	$44,000	$34,000	$60,000
Direct labor hours	1,800	1,400	2,500
Finished Goods Inventory			
Costs	$16,000	$25,000	$14,000
Direct labor hours	700	1,080	550

For both years, all administrative costs were fixed, while a portion of the selling expense resulting from an 8 percent commission on net sales was variable. Portland reports any overapplied or underapplied overhead as an adjustment to Cost of Goods Sold.

a. For the year ended December 31, 1998, prepare the revised income statement for Portland Optics, Inc., using the variable costing method. Be sure to include the contribution margin on the revised income statement.

b. Describe two advantages of using variable costing rather than absorption costing.

(CMA adapted)

75. (LO 1, 2; *Cost analysis*) Sun Company, a wholly owned subsidiary of Guardian, Inc., produces and sells three main product lines. The company employs a standard cost accounting system for record keeping purposes. At the beginning of 1996, the president of Sun Company presented the budget to the parent company and accepted a commitment to contribute $15,800 to Guardian's consolidated income in 1996. The president has been confident that the year's income would exceed the budget target, since the monthly sales reports that she has been receiving have shown that sales for the year will exceed budget by 10 percent. The president is both disturbed and confused when the controller presents an adjusted forecast as of November 30, 1996, indicating that income will be 11 percent under budget. The two forecasts are as follows:

	1/1/96	11/30/96
Sales	$268,000	$294,800
Cost of sales at standard*	212,000	233,200
Gross margin at standard	$ 56,000	$ 61,600
(Underapplied) overapplied fixed overhead	0	(6,000)
Actual gross margin	$ 56,000	$ 55,600
Selling expenses	$ 13,400	$ 14,740
Administrative expenses	26,800	26,800
Total operating expenses	$ 40,200	$ 41,540
Earnings before tax	$ 15,800	$ 14,060

*Includes fixed factory overhead of $30,000.

There have been no sales price changes or product mix shifts since the January 1, 1996, forecast. The only cost variance on the income statement is the underapplied fixed factory overhead. This amount arose because only 16,000 standard machine hours were required for the year's production activity. Production was less than the budgeted 20,000 machine hours because of a shortage of raw materials the company experienced while its principal supplier was closed by a strike. Fortunately, Sun Company's Finished Goods Inventory was large enough to fill all sales orders received.

a. Analyze and explain why income has declined in spite of increased sales and good control over costs.

b. What plan, if any, could Sun Company adopt during December to improve its reported income at year-end? Explain your answer.

c. Illustrate and explain how Sun Company could adopt an alternative internal cost reporting procedure that would avoid the confusing effect of the present procedure.

d. Would the alternative procedure described in part c be acceptable to Guardian, Inc., for financial reporting purposes? Explain.

(CMA adapted)

76. (LO 3, 4, 6; *BEP; CVP*) Kalifo Company manufactures a line of electric garden tools that are sold in general hardware stores. The company's controller, Sylvia Harlow, has just received the sales forecast for the coming year for Kalifo's three products: weeders, hedge clippers, and leaf blowers. Kalifo has experienced considerable variations in sales volumes and variable costs over the past two years, and Harlow believes the forecast should be carefully evaluated from a cost-volume-profit viewpoint. The preliminary forecast information for 1997 is as follows:

	WEEDERS	HEDGE CLIPPERS	LEAF BLOWERS
Unit sales	50,000	50,000	100,000
Unit selling price	$28	$36	$48
Variable manufacturing cost per unit	13	12	25
Variable selling cost per unit	5	4	6

For 1997, Kalifo's fixed factory overhead is estimated at $2,000,000, and the company's fixed selling and administrative expenses are forecasted to be $600,000. Kalifo has an effective tax rate of 40 percent.

a. Determine Kalifo Company's forecasted net income for 1997.

b. Assuming the sales mix remains as budgeted, determine how many units of each product Kalifo Company must sell to break even in 1997.

c. Determine the total dollar sales Kalifo Company must have in 1997 to earn an after-tax income of $450,000.

d. After preparing the original estimates, Kalifo Company determined that the variable manufacturing cost of leaf blowers would increase 20 percent, and the variable selling cost of hedge clippers would increase $1 per unit. However, Kalifo has decided not to change the selling price of either product. In addition, Kalifo has learned that its leaf blower has been perceived as the best value on the market; so it can expect to sell three times as many leaf blowers as any other product. Under these circumstances, determine how many units of each product Kalifo Company would have to sell to break even in 1997.

e. Explain the limitations of cost-volume-profit analysis that Sylvia Harlow should consider when evaluating Kalifo Company's 1997 forecast.

(CMA adapted)

77. (LO 3, 4, 7; *BEP*; *CVP*) Mountain Airways is a small local carrier that flies among the northern midcontinent states. All seats are coach, and the following data are available:

Average full passenger fare	$150
Number of seats per plane	120
Average load factor (seats occupied)	70%
Average variable cost per passenger	$40
Fixed operating costs per month	$1,800,000

a. What is the breakeven point in passengers and revenues?

b. What is the breakeven point in number of flights?

c. If Mountain raises its average full passenger fare to $200, it is estimated that the load factor will decrease to 55 percent. What will be the breakeven point in number of flights?

d. The cost of fuel is a significant variable cost to any airline. If fuel charges increase $8 per barrel, it is estimated that variable cost per passenger will rise to $60. In this case, what will be the new breakeven point in passengers and in number of flights? (Refer to original data.)

e. Mountain has experienced an increase in variable cost per passenger to $50 and an increase in total fixed costs to $2,000,000. The company has decided to raise the average fare to $180. What number of passengers is needed to generate an after-tax income of $600,000 if the tax rate is 40 percent?

f. Mountain is considering offering a discounted fare of $120, which the company feels would increase the load factor to 80 percent. Only the additional seats would be sold at the discounted fare. Additional monthly advertising costs would be $100,000. How much before-tax income would the discounted fare provide Mountain if the company has 40 flights per day, 30 days per month? (Use the original data.)

g. Mountain has an opportunity to obtain a new route. The company feels it can sell seats at $175 on the route, but the load factor would be only 60 percent. The company would fly the route 20 times per month. The increase in fixed costs for additional crew, additional planes, landing fees, maintenance, and so on, would total $100,000 per month. Variable cost per passenger would remain at $40.

    1. Should the company obtain the route?

    2. How many flights would Mountain need to earn pretax income of $57,500 per month on this route?

    3. If the load factor could be increased to 75 percent, how many flights would the company need to earn before-tax income of $57,500 per month on this route?

    4. What qualitative factors should Mountain consider in making its decision about acquiring this route?

■ ETHICS AND QUALITY DISCUSSION

78. *[Efficiency in production in automobile manufacturing plants is frequently related to technology. For example,] according to an internal GM analysis, 20 of its car assembly plants require an average of 35.7 worker-hours per vehicle, vs. 21.6 hours for Ford. Worse, GM needs 32.2 hours to 36.3 hours to put together such midsize models as the Chevy Lumina and Pontiac Grand Prix, while Ford can turn out the similarly sized Taurus and Mercury Sable with under 27.2 hours. Figuring labor at $31.50 an hour for wages and fringes, overall Ford has a $441 cost advantage [per car] on the factory floor alone.*

[SOURCE: Alex Taylor III, "Can GM Remodel?" *Fortune* (January 13, 1992), pp. 26-29, 32-34. © 1992 Time Inc. All rights reserved.]

a. Does the labor cost advantage enjoyed by Ford necessarily mean that Ford is more profitable than GM?

b. Assuming the Ford labor advantage is attributable to greater use of machine technology in production, how would Ford's and GM's cost structures likely differ? Which firm would have the highest degree of operating leverage for a given level of production? Explain.

c. How might the differences in the cost and production structures of Ford and GM translate into differences in the quality of processes?

d. In general, do you perceive that there is a relationship between cost structure and quality in the automobile manufacturing industry? Explain.

79. Agricultural operations face unique challenges in CVP analyses. Many volume considerations are linked to uncontrollable factors such as rain, temperature, and sunshine. Consider how Louisiana sugar-grinding mills were affected by a Christmastime freeze, coupled with a summer drought, that cut sugar cane production drastically:

This year's grinding is expected to last only 40 to 60 days in the River Parishes instead of the usual 70, and some mills in areas hit harder by the freeze will operate just 20 days, said Ben Legendre, a researcher with the U.S. Department of Agriculture's sugar cane research station in Houma.

"It's costing us the same amount of money to grind (around $35 a ton) but we're actually producing 25 pounds less [raw sugar] per ton of cane," Legendre said. Normally, he said, an average mill processing 5,500 tons of cane a day needs to process 250,000 to 300,000 tons in a season to break even.

Last year, the Louisiana crop averaged about 208 pounds of sugar per ton of cane. This year, the average will be closer to 183 pounds, Legendre said.

[SOURCE: Rob Cambias, "Sugar Cane Growers Take Their Lumps," *(New Orleans) Times-Picayune* (November 28, 1990), pp. D-1, D-2. © The Times-Picayune Publishing Corporation.]

a. According to the information given, how many days would a sugar grinding mill need to operate to reach the breakeven point? (Provide a range for the breakeven point.)

b. What evidence in this story indicates that not only the quantity but also the quality of the sugar cane crop was affected by the weather?

c. Why would the quality of the sugar cane have such a significant effect on the number of pounds of raw sugar obtained from a ton of sugar cane?

80. Killoway Chemical Company's new president has learned that for the past four years, the company has been dumping its industrial waste into the local river and falsifying reports to authorities about the levels of suspected cancer-causing materials in that waste. His plant manager says that there is no sure proof that the waste causes cancer, and there are only a few fishing towns within a hundred miles downriver. If the company has to treat the substance to neutralize its potentially injurious effects and then transport it to a legal dumpsite, the company's variable and fixed costs would rise to a level that might make the firm uncompetitive. If the company loses its competitive advantage, 10,000 local employees could become unemployed, and the town's economy could collapse.

a. What kinds of variable and fixed costs can you think of that would increase (or decrease) if the waste were treated rather than dumped? How would these costs affect product contribution margin?

b. What are the ethical conflicts the president faces?

c. What rationalizations can you detect that have been devised by plant employees?

d. What options and suggestions can you offer the president?

81. Peter Klein is a sales representative for a heavy construction equipment manufacturer. He is compensated by a moderate fixed salary plus an 8 percent bonus on sales. Klein is aware that some of the higher-priced items earn the company a lower contribution margin and some of the lower-priced items earn the company a higher contribution margin. He learned this information from the variable costing financial statements produced by the company for management-level employees. One of Klein's best friends is a manager at the company.

Klein has recently started pushing sales of the high-priced items (to the exclusion of lower-priced items) by generously entertaining receptive customers and offering them gifts through the company's promotion budget. He feels that management has not given him adequate raises in the 20 years he has been with the company, and now he is too old to find a better job.

a. Are Klein's actions legal?

b. What are the ethical issues involved in the case from Klein's standpoint?

c. Are there ethical issues in the case from company management's standpoint?

d. What do you believe Klein should do? Why?

82. Women often receive reports that their Pap smears showed positive results when, in actuality, these results were negative. Newspaper accounts detail an industry using overworked, undersupervised, and poorly paid technicians to perform Pap smear tests. Some labs allow workers to analyze up to four times as many specimens per year as experts recommend for accuracy. Workers may be paid $.45 to analyze a smear when patients are charged $35.

    a. Discuss the cost-volume-profit relationships that exist in this case.
    b. Discuss the ethics of laboratory owners who allow technicians to be paid piecework for such analysis.
    c. Discuss the ethics of the workers who rush through Pap smear analyses.

83. Assume that, as a service to your community, you have agreed to serve on a community board that is investigating the possibility of opening a day care center and preschool for area children. You are the financial expert on the board. Details follow:

    The Community Club plans to open a child care center in the near future. The center will operate five days a week and 50 weeks each year and charge $25 per week for each child. It has been determined that $20,000 must be spent to upgrade facilities in the club building to meet state standards. These facilities have an estimated life of five years.

    Supplies for each child are estimated to cost $.50 per day, and food is estimated to cost $.75 per day. Each year $1,000 must be spent on new equipment for the center. For every 10 children, one paraprofessional must be included on the staff. For every 20 children, there must be at least one professional on the staff. For the school to operate, there must be a minimum of one professional on the staff. Annual salaries for professionals and paraprofessionals are $9,000 and $4,000 respectively.

    Space limitations in the facility limit the center to accepting 60 children. This would require a staff of three professionals and six paraprofessionals.

    a. Prepare a schedule showing the annual financial results of operating the center with 20, 40, and 60 children.
    b. Discuss some of the problems (including any ethical ones) of employing financial analysis in this type of problem.

■ PROJECTS

84. This team project involves a class debate on the relative merits of variable and absorption costing. The class should be divided into teams of two and each team should prepare to orally debate for either side of the argument. Then, in class, the instructor should select teams to debate the issue. All teams should be asked to submit evidence of sources they have identified and notes of the arguments they have constructed for both sides of the issue.

    In preparing for the debate, students should be encouraged to search for materials to support their arguments. A voluminous amount of literature exists and many materials should be easily obtained.

85. Invite to your class an accountant from a local firm that uses variable costing. Ask the accountant to demonstrate and explain the reconciliation of the variable costing data to an absorption format for external reporting. Also, ask for a separate explanation of the reconciliation required for purposes of computing state and federal income tax obligations.

86. Find a series of annual income statements for two companies. One company should be in a highly capital-intensive industry (with high fixed costs), such as steel production. The other company should have comparably low fixed costs and high variable costs (as do certain service firms). For the two companies, try to answer the following questions:

   a. In which company is annual change in net income more sensitive to annual change in revenues?

   b. Discuss your perception of the differences in risk of owning stock in the two companies because of differences in their cost structures.

9

RELEVANT COSTING

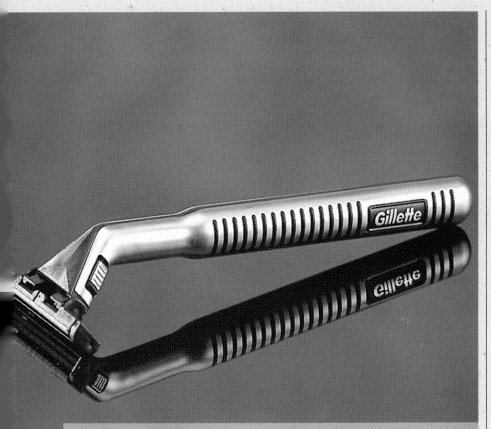

LEARNING OBJECTIVES

1. Determine what constitutes relevance in a decision-making situation.

2. Understand why a sunk cost (such as joint cost) is not relevant in decision making, but an opportunity cost is.

3. Specify the relevant costs and qualitative factors that exist in a make-or-buy situation.

4. Determine how management can best utilize a scarce resource.

5. Relate relevant costing to sales mix, special pricing, compensation changes, and advertising budget decisions.

6. Use product margin to determine whether a product line should be retained or eliminated.

7. (Appendix) Describe the elements of a linear programming problem.

Businesses use information to communicate activities in one part of an organization to decision makers in another part. But information does more than just communicate. The type of information communicated triggers actions that determine a company's performance. Only if CEOs rely on information that is relevant to the goals of global competition will their firms survive in the 1990s and beyond.

H. Thomas Johnson, *Relevance Regained,* 1992

The Gillette Co.: Sharp and Successful

For every 15 product candidates that Gillette identifies, only one actually makes it into development. And, of those, only a third advance from development to eventually reach the market. The others are dropped or "shelved" because manufacturing costs are higher than the company would like. "In our business, pennies matter," says Chairman and CEO Alfred M. Zeien. This statement is the major reason Gillette has outpaced its competition for decades. The company has the ability to consistently reduce manufacturing costs while improving quality. Since the Sensor razor was introduced in 1990, Gillette has produced 1 billion Sensor blade cartridges. "With that kind of volume, when you can incrementally shave a fraction off the manufacturing cost, you're talking big money," says Edward DeGraan, senior vice president of manufacturing and technical operations.

Since 1990, Gillette has cut the manufacturing cost of the Sensor line by 30 percent. "Each year, in all our products, we have the objective of reducing costs to meet or beat the rate of inflation. And we are meeting that objective," declares DeGraan.

Rather than attempting to make big cost reduction breakthroughs, Gillette benchmarks and uses continuous improvement efforts to achieve small, incremental gains. For example, Gillette operates presses in its metal-stamping operations at between 800 and 1,200 strokes a minute. This process rate is twice the speed of 10 years ago despite tighter specifications. Cycle time for molded plastic parts is consistently less than 10 seconds. But quality is so high that reject rates are measured in single-digit parts per million.

Thirty-three percent of the world's annual 20 billion razor blades sales are made by Gillette, even though most nondomestic markets have local manufacturers of double-edged blades. Gillette's marketing technique against those producers is simple. First, the company offers better double-edged blades and, second, it tries to upgrade customers to razors with twin-blade cartridges. The cartridges give Gillette an additional penny profit margin per blade. Gillette keeps its product universal (made in similar factories by similarly-trained employees), but may customize some packaging and sales techniques to local markets.

SOURCES: William H. Miller, "Gillette's Secret to Sharpness" and "The Gillette Advantage," *Industry Week* (January 3, 1994), pp. 26, 28 (reprinted with permission; copyright Penton Publishing, Inc., Cleveland, Ohio); Rita Koselka, "It's My Favorite Statistic," *Forbes* (September 12, 1994), pp. 172, 176 (reprinted by permission of Forbes magazine, © Forbes Inc., 1994).

Gillette has made numerous decisions about which products it will sell, product prices, and product lines to eliminate. In addition, while the company would prefer universality in its products, it occasionally must adapt to a particular foreign market, since approximately 70 percent of its sales come from outside the United States. For instance, in Russia, Sensor razors are selling well but a razor costs almost a month's pay. After buying one, a customer may not be able to afford the five-cartridge pack of replacement blades. So, in Russia, Gillette is selling single-cartridge packs originally made for the Latin American market.[1] In a business where even tenths of pennies are important, many such decisions must be based solely on monetary factors. The company commonly assesses the viability of its decisions using **relevant costs**, which are those costs that are pertinent to or logically associated with a specific problem or decision and that differ between alternatives.

relevant costs

[1]Rita Koselka, "It's My Favorite Statistic," *Forbes* (September 12, 1994), p. 176.

Gillette's business choices reflect a common type of decision: how to competently allocate available but limited organizational resources so that company goals and objectives are achieved. As indicated in the following quote, making decisions in today's business environment is not an easy task.

> Decision making in the 1990s will be more of an art and less of a science. Not only is the world growing more complex and uncertain at a faster and faster pace, but the old decision-making models are failing, and we can expect their failure to accelerate as well.
>
> If executives once imagined they could gather enough information to read the business environment like an open book, they have had to dim their hopes. The flow of information has swollen to such a flood that managers are in danger of drowning; extracting relevant data from the torrent is increasingly a daunting task.[2]

Accounting information can improve, but not perfect, management's understanding of the consequences of resource allocation decisions. To the extent that this information can reduce management's uncertainty about the economic facts, outcomes, and relationships involved in various courses of action, the information is valuable for decision making purposes and necessary for conducting business.

As discussed in Chapter 8, many decisions are made on the basis of incremental analysis. Such analysis encompasses the concept of relevant costing, which allows managers to focus on pertinent facts and disregard extraneous information. This chapter illustrates the use of relevant costing in decisions about making or buying a product or part, allocating scarce resources, and determining the appropriate sales or production mix. While these decisions are often viewed by managers as short-run, each decision also has significant long-run implications that must be considered.

THE CONCEPTS OF RELEVANCE AND RELEVANT COSTING

Managers routinely make decisions concerning alternatives that have been identified as feasible solutions to problems or feasible methods for the attainment of objectives. In doing so, the managers must weigh the relevant costs and benefits associated with each course of action and then determine the best course.

Information is relevant when it logically and significantly relates to a decision about a future endeavor. Costs provide information, and different costs can be used for many different purposes. No single cost can be relevant in all decisions or to all managers. Two general rules are that (1) most variable costs are relevant and (2) most fixed costs are not. The reasoning behind these rules is that, as sales or production volume changes within the relevant range, variable costs change but fixed costs do not. As with most general rules, though, there are some exceptions that must be acknowledged in the decision-making process.

Accountants can assist managers in determining which costs are relevant to the objectives and decisions at hand. To the extent possible and practical, **relevant costing** allows managers to focus on pertinent facts and disregard extraneous information by comparing the differential, incremental revenues and costs of alternative decisions. *Differential* means that the costs differ between or among the choices. *Incremental* means the additional or extra amount associated with some action. Thus, **incremental revenue** is the additional revenue resulting from a contem-

■ **LEARNING OBJECTIVE 1**
Determine what constitutes relevance in a decision-making situation.

relevant costing

incremental revenue

[2]Amitai Etzioni, "Humble Decision Making," *Harvard Business Review* (July-August 1989), p. 122.

incremental cost

■ LEARNING
OBJECTIVE 2
Understand why a sunk cost
(such as joint cost) is not
relevant in decision making, but
an opportunity cost is.

opportunity cost

plated sale or provision of service. An **incremental cost** is the additional cost of producing and/or selling a contemplated quantity of output.

Differential, incremental costs are relevant in a decision. These costs may be variable or fixed. For example, the direct material cost of a product is a relevant incremental variable cost in a decision to make additional units. In contrast, the fixed cost of the available production machinery would not be relevant to the production of additional units. However, the cost of buying new machinery is an incremental fixed cost relevant to the decision to produce a new product line or expand an existing one beyond the current relevant range.

Some relevant costs, such as sales commissions and the prime costs of production (direct materials and direct labor), are easily identified and quantified. These factors are integral parts of the accounting system. Other factors (such as opportunity costs) may be relevant and quantifiable but are not part of the accounting system. (An **opportunity cost** represents the benefits foregone when one course of action is chosen over another.) Such factors cannot be overlooked simply because they may be more difficult to obtain or may require the use of estimates.

The difference between the incremental revenue and incremental cost of a particular alternative is the positive or negative incremental benefit of that course of action. When evaluating alternative courses of action, managers should select the alternative that provides the highest incremental benefit to the company. Such a comparison may superficially appear simple but often is not, because relevance is a concept that is inherently individual. For example, an investment proposal might provide a high rate of return for a company but might also create a future potential environmental hazard. One unit manager might view the potential hazard as very relevant, while another manager might minimize the relevance of that possibility. In some instances, all alternatives result in incremental losses, and managers must choose the one that creates the smallest incremental loss.

One alternative course of action often considered is defensive avoidance, or the "change nothing for the moment" option. While other alternatives have certain incremental revenues and costs associated with them, the "change nothing" alterna-

Sometimes, a company may
choose a "change nothing"
strategy rather than incur costs
currently. But if that strategy
violates government regulations,
the company may find itself
with no concerns about future
cost incurrences.

tive represents current conditions. It may serve as a baseline against which all other alternatives can be measured. However, even the "change nothing" alternative may involve the risk of loss of competitive advantage. If a firm chooses this alternative while its competitors upgrade processes, that firm may incur the ultimate incremental loss—its market. Also, the opportunity costs associated with the status quo may result in less benefit than another alternative.

The "change nothing" alternative should be chosen only when it is perceived to be the best decision choice. Often, however, this alternative is selected only because it is easier than making changes. At other times, this selection is made because decision makers, lacking information, perceive uncertainty to be so great that they consider the risk of making a change to be greater than the risk of continuing the current course of action. When this condition exists, the results achieved from the "change nothing" alternative (current results) are thought to be more advantageous than the potential incremental benefit of any other alternative.

In some situations (such as those involving government regulations or mandates), a "change nothing" alternative does not truly exist. For example, if a company were polluting river water and a governmental regulatory agency issued an injunction against it, the company (assuming it wished to continue in business) would be forced to correct the pollution problem. The company could, of course, delay installation of the pollution control devices at the risk of fines or closure—creating additional incremental cost effects that would have to be considered. Managers in this situation must make decisions using a "now-versus-later" attitude and may determine that "now" is better regardless of the cost.

Since a comprehensive evaluation of all alternative courses of action is part of rational management behavior, the chosen course should be the one that will make the business and its stakeholders better off in the future. This means that managers must provide some mechanism for including all nonmonetary or inherently nonquantifiable considerations in the decision process. Managers can do that by attempting to quantify items or simply by making instinctive value judgments about nonmonetary benefits and costs.

To illustrate this point, consider the factors that should be evaluated when a labor-intensive company analyzes the labor savings that would result from replacing employees with robots or, as discussed in the accompanying News Note, with different employees. Company managers need to weigh potential future cost reductions and increases in productivity against possible short- and long-range negative public reaction toward the company because of unemployment increases resulting from the layoffs. Although public reactions are difficult to measure and quantify and may not be immediately noticeable, such reactions should still be factored into the decision. In addition, there may be very relevant but highly nonquantifiable costs resulting from ethical considerations, such as the moral obligations the firm has toward the displaced workers. Such costs must be estimated in a reasonable manner if the decision to replace workers is to be based on a truly valid analysis.

The need for specificity in information depends on how important that information is relative to management objectives. If all other factors are equal, more precise information is given greater weight in the decision-making process. However, if information is important but qualitative and imprecise, management should find a way to estimate the impact such information may have on known, monetary details and company profits.

Information can be based on past or present data but is relevant only if it relates to a future choice and creates a differential effect in regard to alternative choices. All managerial decisions are made to affect future events, so the information on which

Do the Actual Savings Equal the Opportunity Costs Incurred?

At the gleaming headquarters building of Stride Rite Corp. in [Cambridge, Massachusetts], plaques on the walls honor the shoe company for its good deeds. . . . [But Stride Rite planned to close two plants elsewhere in Massachusetts in 1994, in locales having approximately 30% and 14% unemployment rates, respectively. And, in June of 1992,] Stride Rite closed another plant, in Tipton, Missouri, and laid off 280 workers. The unemployment rate is grim there, too. . . . In the past decade, Stride Rite has prospered partly by closing 15 factories, mostly in the Northeast and several in depressed areas, and moving most of its production to various low-cost Asian countries. The company still employs 2,500 workers in the U.S., but that is down from a peak of about 6,000.

[Such activities create] difficult questions: What makes a company socially responsible? And how far can social responsibility be expected to go? Stride Rite contends that it has been socially responsible but nevertheless has to balance the demands of two masters—shareholders and society. If a company doesn't stay competitive, its executives contend, it can't grow, it would provide even fewer jobs, it would earn too little to afford its community programs, and, at worst, it might jeopardize its survival.

[Stride Rite had to move its production facilities, it says, to survive. Its income plummeted 68% in 1983, and the moves provided huge labor savings.] Skilled workers in China earn $100 to $150 a month, working 50 to 65 hours a week. Unskilled workers get $50 to $70 a month. By comparison, Stride Rite's U.S. workers average $1,200 to $1,400 per month in wages alone, plus modest fringe benefits.

SOURCE: Joseph Pereira, "Social Responsibility and Need for Low Cost Clash at Stride Rite," *Wall Street Journal* (May 28, 1993), pp. A1, A4. Reprinted by permission of The Wall Street Journal, © 1993 Dow Jones & Company, Inc. All Rights Reserved Worldwide.

decisions are based should reflect future conditions. The future may be the short run (two hours from now or next month) or the long run (five years or more from now).[3]

Future costs are the only costs that can be avoided, and the longer into the future a decision's time horizon extends, the more costs are avoidable, controllable, and relevant. *Only information that has a bearing on future events is relevant in decision making.* But people too often forget this basic truth and try to make decisions using inapplicable data. One common error is trying to use a previously incurred, historical cost to make a current decision.

SUNK COSTS AND JOINT PROCESSES

Current costs (such as replacement or budgeted costs) are assumed to be accurate or reasonably accurate at the current time. As such, these costs represent relevant information and should be considered in the decision-making process. In contrast, histor-

sunk costs

ical costs incurred in the past to acquire an asset or a resource—called **sunk costs**—are not recoverable and cannot be changed, regardless of what current circumstances

[3]Short-run decisions typically focus on a measure of accounting income that excludes some past costs, such as depreciation on old assets. Long-range decision analysis commonly uses cash flow as its decision criterion; this topic is covered in Chapter 16.

exist or what future course of action is taken. A current or future selling price may be obtained for an asset, but that is the result of current or future conditions and is not a recouping of an historical cost. The following discussion illustrates why sunk costs are not relevant costs.

Like Gillette, almost every company makes and sells a wide variety of products. Companies often must engage in multiple production processes to produce their products; for instance, Gillette could not manufacture its Sensor razors, Oral-B toothbrushes, and Waterman pens in the same manufacturing operation. However, it is possible for a single process to simultaneously generate several different outputs, as when Tyson Foods processes chickens to produce whole birds, parts, and "nuggets." Industries that produce multiple products from a single process include refineries, lumber mills, and chemical, food, and cosmetics manufacturers. A single process in which one product cannot be manufactured without others' being produced is known as a **joint process.**

A corn processing plant can be used to illustrate the types of outputs resulting from a joint process. Outputs may include corn on the cob and whole-kernel corn (joint products), partial corn kernels (by-products) used for cornmeal, inferior kernels (scrap) for sale to producers of animal food, and cobs (waste) that are discarded. Exhibit 9-1 (page 444) shows the outputs of such a joint process.

The point at which the outputs of a joint process are first identifiable as individual products is called the **split-off point.** A joint process may have one or more split-off points, depending on the number and types of output produced. Output may be sold at the split-off point, if a market exists for products in that condition. Alternatively, some or all of the products may be processed further after exiting the joint process.

The costs incurred for materials, labor, and overhead during a joint process (up to the split-off point) are referred to as the **joint cost** of the production process. For companies to engage in a joint process, total revenues from sales of all resulting products should exceed the total costs of those products. The joint process results in a "basket" of products, and managers must be aware that some output from the joint process may require additional processing to make it salable. However, after the joint process cost has been incurred, it is a sunk cost *regardless* of whether the output is salable at the end of the joint process and *regardless* of how much the output may sell for.

If any of the joint process outputs are processed after the split-off point, additional costs will be incurred. Costs after split-off are assigned to the separate products for which those costs are incurred. Thus, management must consider the total joint costs plus any separate processing or selling costs it expects will be incurred before making the decision to commit resources to the joint process.

At the split-off point, the joint cost is allocated only to the joint products and not to any resulting by-products, scrap, or waste. The rationale for this allocation is that the joint products are the primary reason that management undertook production. Allocation may be made on the basis of a physical measure (such as pounds or units) or a monetary measure (such as final sales value). Joint cost is a necessary and reasonable cost of producing the joint products and, thus, should be attached to those products for external financial statement purposes. However, the amount of joint cost allocated to the joint products is not relevant to decision making because once the joint process costs are incurred, they are historical and, therefore, sunk.

To illustrate, assume that a joint product has a selling price of $10 at split-off, but its selling price after further processing is $16. If the additional processing costs are less than $6 ($16 - $10), then the incremental revenue exceeds the incremental costs and additional processing should occur. Notice that the joint cost is not considered in this decision process. Once the products have reached the split-off point, the joint cost is a sunk cost. Additionally, the joint cost is a common cost of all joint products

LEARNING OBJECTIVE 2
Understand why a sunk cost (such as joint cost) is not relevant in decision making, but an opportunity cost is.

joint process

split–off point

joint cost

■ EXHIBIT 9–1
Illustration of Joint Process Output

Raw Material
Input—
Fresh Corn

Joint Process—
Shucking and
Cleaning

Joint Process Outputs

Corn on the cob
(Joint Product)—
will be bagged and sold.

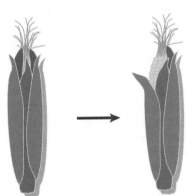

Whole kernels (Joint Product)—
will be added to water and
sugar, canned, and sold.

Partial kernels (By-product)—
will be ground to make corn
meal or grits and sold.

Inferior kernels (Scrap)—
will be sold to manufacturers
of animal food.

Husks, corn silk, and cobs
(Waste)*—
will be discarded.

*Remember, it is up to the judgment of management how joint process output is classified. In
other companies, the cobs and husks could be sold to other companies as filler in those
companies' products.

and is irrelevant to the decision to sell or process a particular joint output further. The only relevant items in the decision whether to sell or process further are the incremental revenues and incremental costs after the split-off point.

This example introduces the difference between relevant and irrelevant costs. The next section shows how the concepts of relevant costing are applied in making some common managerial decisions.

RELEVANT COSTS IN MAKE-OR-BUY DECISIONS

A constant concern in manufacturing is whether components of the right quality will be available at the right time and at a reasonable price. Companies often assure the availability of a component by manufacturing it themselves. (In some cases, this decision may be made because the company is interested in embarking on a vertical integration path, in which one division or subsidiary can serve as a supplier to others within the same company.) Other companies prefer to **outsource,** or purchase some or all components from external parties. "Toyota makes only about 25% of its own parts, vs. 47% at GM";[4] Dell and Zeos computer companies "buy circuit boards, disk drives, and other modules—designed specifically for them—from outside manufacturers and assemble the computers in their own warehouses."[5] This type of **make-or-buy decision** should be made only after proper analysis. Managers should compare the cost of internally manufacturing a product component with the cost of purchas-

■ **LEARNING OBJECTIVE 3**
Specify the relevant costs and qualitative factors that exist in a make-or-buy situation.

outsource

make–or–buy decision

ing it from outside suppliers (or from another division). They should also assess the best uses of the available facilities. (Consideration of a "make" option implies that the company has the available capacity for that purpose.) Relevant information for a make-or-buy decision includes both quantitative and qualitative factors.

Exhibit 9–2 (page 446) presents some of these quantitative and qualitative factors. Many of the quantitative factors (such as incremental production costs per unit and the purchase price quoted by the supplier) are known with a high degree of certainty. Other factors, such as the opportunity cost associated with production facilities, must be estimated. The qualitative factors should be evaluated by more than one individual so that personal biases do not cloud valid business judgments.

Exhibit 9–3 (page 446) provides information about a motor for a ladies' electric shaver produced by Concordia Ltd., which produces a variety of health and beauty aids. The total cost to manufacture one motor is $5. The company can purchase motors from McGill Manufacturing, Inc., for $4.75 per unit. Concordia's accountant is trying to determine whether the company should make the motors or buy them from the outside supplier.

Relevant costs are those costs that are pertinent and avoidable, regardless of whether they are variable or fixed. In a make-or-buy decision, variable costs of pro-

Company managers at Gillette made a significant make-or-buy decision when they decided that, not only would all product be purchased internally, but that the company would also manufacture some of the equipment to be used in production. This decision was required so that the company could maintain the highest control over quality tolerances and specifications.

[4]Alex Taylor III, "The Auto Industry Meets the New Economy," *Fortune* (September 5, 1994), p. 56.
[5]Shawn Tully, "You'll Never Guess Who Really Makes ...," *Fortune* (October 3, 1994), p. 124.

■ **EXHIBIT 9–2**
Make-or-Buy Considerations

RELEVANT QUANTITATIVE FACTORS

Incremental production costs for each unit
Unit cost of purchasing from outside supplier (price less any discounts available plus shipping)
Availability of production capacity to manufacture components
Opportunity costs of using facilities for production rather than for other purposes
Availability of storage space for units and raw materials

RELEVANT QUALITATIVE FACTORS

Relative net advantage given uncertainty of estimates (costs, risks, and so forth)
Reliability of source(s) of supply
Ability to assure quality when units are purchased from outside
Nature of the work to be subcontracted (such as the importance of the part to the whole)
Number of available suppliers
Impact on customers and markets
Future bargaining position with supplier(s)
Perceptions regarding possible future price changes
Perceptions about current product prices (Is the price appropriate or—as may be the case with international suppliers—is product dumping involved?)
Strategic and competitive importance of component to long-run organizational success

duction are relevant. Fixed production costs may be relevant if they can be avoided by discontinuance of production. Production of each shaver motor requires a cost outlay of $4.40 for materials, labor, and variable overhead. In addition, $.20 of the fixed overhead is considered a relevant product cost because it specifically relates to the manufacture of motors. This $.20 is an incremental cost, since it could be avoided if shaver motors were not produced. The remaining $.40 of fixed overhead is not relevant to the decision whether to make or buy the motors. This $.40 is a common cost that cannot be associated with shaver motor production and is incurred because of

■ **EXHIBIT 9–3**
Make-or-Buy Cost Information

	PRESENT MANUFACTURING COST PER MOTOR	RELEVANT MANUFACTURING COST
Direct materials	$1.60	$1.60
Direct labor	2.00	2.00
Variable factory overhead	.80	.80
Fixed factory overhead*	.60	.20
Total unit cost	$5.00	$4.60

Quoted price from McGill Manufacturing Inc. $4.75

*Of the $.60 fixed factory overhead, only $.20 is directly linked to production of the motors. This amount is related to the production supervisor's salary and could be avoided if the firm chose not to produce shaver motors. The remaining $.40 of fixed factory overhead is an allocated indirect (common) cost that would continue even if shaver motor production ceased.

general production activity. Because this portion of the fixed cost would continue under either alternative, it is not relevant.

The relevant cost for the "make" alternative is $4.60—the cost that would be avoided if the product were not made. This amount should be compared with the $4.75 price quoted by the supplier under the "buy" alternative. The $4.60 is the incremental cost of production, and the $4.75 is the incremental cost of purchasing. Based solely on the quantitative information, management should choose to manufacture the motors rather than buy them, since it will save $.15 on each motor produced rather than purchased.

The opportunity cost associated with the facilities being used by production may also be relevant in a make-or-buy alternative. Concordia's management must determine if an alternative purpose exists for the facilities now being used to manufacture the motors. If a more profitable alternative is available, management should consider diverting the capacity to this alternative use.

For example, assume that Concordia Ltd. has an opportunity to rent the building now used to produce motors to an outside tenant for $176,000 per year. Concordia produces 800,000 motors annually. Thus, it incurs an opportunity cost of $.22 per unit ($176,000 ÷ 800,000 motors) by using rather than renting the building. The opportunity cost should be added to the production cost since the company is giving up this amount by choosing to make the motors. The giving up of an inflow is as much a cost as the incurrence of an outflow. Exhibit 9–4 shows calculations relating to this decision on both a per-unit and a total cost basis. Under either format, the comparison indicates that there is a $.07 per unit advantage to purchasing rather than producing.

Concordia Ltd.'s accountant should inform management that, based on the information shown in Exhibit 9-4, it is more economical to buy motors from McGill for $4.75 than to manufacture them. Such information is the typical starting point of the decision process—determining whether an alternative satisfies the quantitative considerations associated with a problem. If it does, managers then use judgment to assess the qualitative aspects of the decision.

Assume that Concordia's purchasing agent recently read in *The Wall Street Journal* that McGill Manufacturing was in poor financial condition and was likely to file for

---

■ **EXHIBIT 9–4**

Opportunity Cost in a Make-or-Buy Decision

PER UNIT:	MAKE	BUY	
Direct production costs	$4.60		
Opportunity cost (revenue foregone)	.22		
Purchase cost		$4.75	
Cost per motor	$4.82	$4.75	

IN TOTAL:	MAKE	BUY	DIFFERENCE IN FAVOR OF PURCHASING
Revenue from renting facility	$ 0	$ 176,000	$176,000
Direct cost for 800,000 motors	(3,680,000)	(3,800,000)	(120,000)
Net (cost) or revenue	$(3,680,000)	$(3,624,000)	$ 56,000*

*The $56,000 represents the net purchase benefit of $.07 per unit multiplied by the 800,000 units to be purchased during the year.

bankruptcy. In this case, Concordia's management will probably decide to continue producing the motors rather than purchasing them from McGill. Even though quantitative analysis supports the purchase of the units, qualitative judgment suggests that this would not be a wise course of action, since the stability of the supplying source is questionable. If Concordia stops motor production and rents out its facilities and McGill Manufacturing, Inc., goes bankrupt, Concordia could be faced with high start-up costs to revitalize its motor production process.

Control over product quality and on-time delivery are two other important factors in decisions to buy from suppliers. As the accompanying News Note illustrates, outsourcing may appear on the surface to be the best answer to cost control; however, if contract manufacturers do not produce properly, it may be less expensive to acquire internal resources.

These additional considerations indicate that there are many potential long-run effects of a theoretically short-run decision. Some companies have taken a more long-range perspective of certain make-or-buy decisions. Gillette, for instance, took a very long-run perspective when it decided to manufacture its razor blades internally rather than purchase them from suppliers. The company believed that there was a competitive advantage to be obtained by determining how to shape and strengthen the blade on internally designed laser welding equipment. This choice was apparently the right one; total razor and blade sales for Gillette have increased 54 percent in the U.S. and 71 percent worldwide since the 1990 introduction of the Sensor.[6] Exhibit 9–5 provides a flow chart to analyze whether outsourcing an activity is in a company's best interest.

Make-or-buy decisions are not confined to manufacturing entities. Many service organizations must make the same kinds of choices. For example, accounting and law firms must decide whether to prepare and present in-house continuing education programs or rely on external sources such as professional organizations and consultants. Private schools must determine whether to own school buses or hire independent contractors. Doctors must investigate the relative merits of having blood drawn and tested in the office or having this work done in separate lab facilities; considerations include cost, quality of results, and convenience to patients. These examples simply indicate that the term *make* in *make-or-buy* does not necessarily mean converting a raw material to a finished component; it can also mean providing an in-house service.

Make-or-buy decisions consider the opportunity costs associated with utilized facilities because those facilities are in limited supply. If capacity is occupied in one way, it cannot be used at the same time for another purpose. Limited capacity is only one type of scarce resource that managers need to consider when making decisions.

RELEVANT COSTS IN SCARCE RESOURCE DECISIONS

scarce resources

Managers are frequently confronted with the short-run problem of making the best use of **scarce resources** that are essential to production activity but are available only in limited quantity. Scarce resources create constraints on producing goods or providing services. These resources may include money, machine hours, skilled labor hours, raw materials, and production capacity. In the long run, management may desire and be able to obtain a greater abundance of a scarce resource—for example,

■ **LEARNING OBJECTIVE 4**
Determine how management can best utilize a scarce resource.

[6]Koselka, "It's My Favorite Statistic," p. 164.

■ **EXHIBIT 9–5**

Steps in Outsourcing Decision Analysis

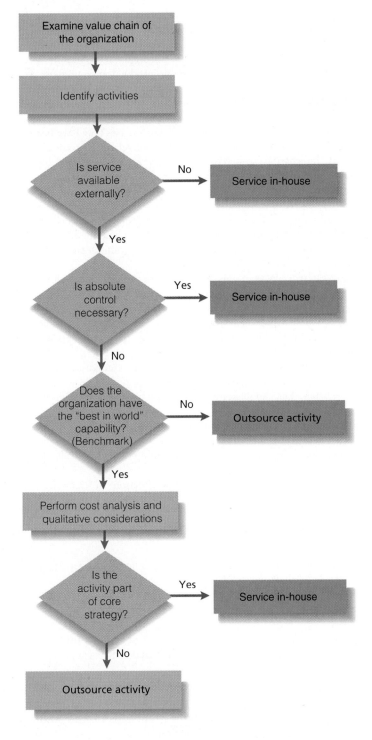

SOURCE: Adapted from Ralph E. Drtina, "The Outstanding Decision," *Management Accounting* (March 1994), p. 62. Published by Institute of Management Accountants, Montvale, NJ.

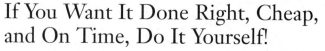

NEWS NOTE

If You Want It Done Right, Cheap, and On Time, Do It Yourself!

[In 1981, AC International was formed to make one type of product. The company opted to become a "virtual corporation" by outsourcing all manufacturing, packaging, distribution, sales, and billing processes and owning no production equipment. According to the owners, this seemingly good idea] began to spawn trouble. "Our customers were constantly on the phone, complaining about late shipments and back orders. We, in turn, were always screaming at our suppliers for not keeping their promises. Their excuses may have been valid, but their always being behind in shipping didn't help customer relations or sales."

[In 1989, AC International purchased a business that manufactured bicycle water bottles and decided to continue to outsource certain processes, such as the blow-molding of the bottle and the injection molding of the caps.] "The blow molder told us he could make a certain quantity of bottles each month, and we took orders based on his number," says one owner. "Incredibly, by the third month, we had two months' worth of back orders. We immediately began looking for our own blow-molding equipment, and within 60 days, we were making the quantity of bottles the job shop had promised and never delivered. The cost was halved.

"Our bottle-cap maker was in Taiwan. Because of the variety of colors we offered and the 70-day lead time to get the caps, we constantly found our inventory out of balance. Our air-freight bill skyrocketed because we had to fly in missing chunks of cap inventory to keep our customers from totally losing their sense of humor. So we bought a second injection-molding machine and started making our own caps. Of course, the cost dropped. This time the savings were 80%.

"Along with all the cost cutting and the control of production timing came dramatic improvements in quality. The outside vendors had always had difficulty controlling color from batch to batch. The cap maker in Taiwan saw neon yellow differently from the way the bottle maker in Los Angeles saw it.

[Since opening, the company has] gone from making a few thousand bottles a month to being the second-largest maker of bicycle water bottles in the world, with shipments of more than 5 million units expected in 1994, including container loads of bottles to customers in 30 countries.

There are certainly business opportunities and situations in which the virtual corporation makes sense. But when it comes to control of quality, delivery, and cost, [the owners of AC International] believe the outmoded and politically incorrect concept of the vertical corporation should be dusted off and included in the list of options for sources of products and services.

SOURCE: Randy W. Kirk, "It's About Control," *Inc.* (August 1994), pp. 25-26. Reprinted by permission of Inc. magazine. © 1994 by Goldhirsh Group, Inc.

by purchasing additional machines to increase availability of machine hours. However, in the short run, management must make the best current use of the scarce resources it has.

Determining the best use of a scarce resource requires that specific company objectives be recognized. If management's objective is to maximize company contribution margin and profits, the best use of a scarce resource is for the production and sale of the product that has the highest contribution margin per unit of the scarce resource. This strategy assumes that the company is faced with only one scarce resource.

Exhibit 9–6 presents information on two products made by Concordia Ltd. on its KF50 plastic molding machines. Only 4,000 machine hours are available per month to make plastic housings for either blow dryers or hot rollers or some combination of both. Demand is unlimited for both products. Assume there are no variable selling or administrative costs related to either product.

The blow dryer's $30 unit selling price minus its $20 unit variable cost provides a contribution margin of $10 per unit. The hot roller's contribution margin per unit is $13 ($24 − $11). Fixed overhead totals $320,000 and is allocated to products on a machine hour basis for purposes of inventory measurement. However, fixed overhead does not change with production levels within the relevant range and, therefore, is not a relevant cost for a decision on scarce resource mix.

Since fixed overhead per unit is not relevant in the present case, unit contribution margin rather than unit gross margin is the appropriate measure of profitability of the two products.[7] Unit contribution margin is multiplied by the number of units of output per unit of the scarce resource (in this case, machine hours) to obtain the contribution margin per unit of scarce resource. The last line in Exhibit 9–6 shows a contribution margin per machine hour of $800 ($10 × 80) for blow dryers compared with $520 ($13 × 40) for hot rollers. Blow dryers are the more profitable items for Concordia Ltd. to produce.

At first, it would appear that hot rollers would be more profitable, since their $13 unit contribution margin is higher than the $10 unit contribution margin for blow dryers. However, since one hour of machine time produces twice as many blow dryers as hot rollers, a greater amount of contribution margin per hour of scarce resource is generated by the production of blow dryers. If Concordia Ltd. wanted to achieve the highest possible profit, it would dedicate all machine time to the production of blow dryers. If all units produced were sold, this strategy would provide a total contribution margin of $3,200,000 per month ($800 per hour × 4,000 available hours).

When one limiting factor is involved, the outcome of a scarce resource decision will always indicate that a single type of product should be manufactured and sold. Most situations, though, involve several limiting factors that compete with one another. One method used to solve problems that have several limiting factors is **linear programming.** Analysts use this method to find the optimal allocation of scarce

linear programming

■ **EXHIBIT 9–6**
Scarce Resource—Machine Hours

	BLOW DRYERS	**HOT ROLLERS**
Selling price per unit (a)	$ 30	$ 24
Variable production cost per unit:		
Direct materials	$6	$5
Direct labor	8	4
Variable overhead	6	2
Total variable cost (b)	20	11
Unit contribution margin [(c) = (a) − (b)]	$ 10	$ 13
Units of output per machine hour (d)	× 80	× 40
Contribution margin per machine hour [(c) × (d)]	$800	$520

resources when there is one objective and multiple restrictions on achieving that objective.[8]

Managers must be concerned about the quantitative effects of scarcity of resources, but they must also remember that not all factors involved in the decision alternatives can be readily quantified. Company management must consider qualitative aspects of the problem in addition to quantitative ones. For example, to achieve the maximum possible profit, Concordia Ltd. would have to produce only blow dryers during the available time on the KF50 molding machines. Before choosing such a strategy, managers would need to assess the potential damage to the company's reputation and image from limiting its market assortment of products by providing one product to the exclusion of another. For instance, suppose Concordia's computations had indicated that hot rollers were the more profitable line to produce. Producing only hot rollers might have limited the company's market segment only to women. Concentrating on a single product might also create market saturation and cause future sales to decline. For example, blow dryers and hot rollers last for a fairly long time, and each person only needs one or two.

Other situations can also make multiple products desirable: the products may be complementary (Gillette's Oral-B toothbrushes and Oral-B dental floss), one product may not be usable without the other (Sensor razors and cartridges), or one product may be the key to high revenue generation in future periods. To illustrate the latter possibility, consider Mattel, Inc., the producer of Barbie dolls. Would it be reasonable for Mattel to produce only Barbie dolls and none of the related accessories (clothes, dream house, car, camper, and so forth)? While the sale of Barbie dolls is profitable, the income flow from the total group of Barbie products is enormous.

For all of the above reasons, management may decide that some less profitable products are necessary components in the company's product mix. Production mix internally translates into sales mix externally. The next section addresses the issue of sales mix.

RELEVANT COSTS IN SALES MIX AND SALES PRICE DECISIONS

sales mix

■ LEARNING
OBJECTIVE 5
Relate relevant costing to sales mix, special pricing, compensation changes, and advertising budget.

Management continuously strives to satisfy a variety of company goals such as maximization of company profit, improvement of relative market share, and generation of customer goodwill and loyalty. These goals are achieved through selling products or performing services. Regardless of whether the company is a retailer, manufacturer, or service organization, **sales mix** refers to "the relative combination of quantities of sales of the various products that make up the total sales of a company."[9] One way a company can achieve its goals is to manage its sales mix effectively. Some important factors affecting the appropriate sales mix are product selling prices, sales force compensation, and advertising expenditures. A change in one or all of these factors may cause a company's sales mix to shift. The Concordia Ltd. data presented in Exhibit 9–7 are used to illustrate the effects on sales mix of the three factors mentioned earlier. The company produces three types of bathroom scales: basic, deluxe, and talking.

---

[8]Linear programming is briefly discussed in the appendix to this chapter and is covered in depth in most management science courses.

[9]Institute of Management Accountants (formerly National Association of Accountants), *Statements on Management Accounting Number 2: Management Accounting Terminology* (Montvale, N.J.: National Association of Accountants, June 1, 1983), p. 94.

■ **EXHIBIT 9–7**

Product Information for Various Sales Mix Decisions

	BASIC SCALE		DELUXE SCALE		TALKING SCALE	
Unit selling price		$100		$130		$150
Variable unit costs:						
Direct materials	$15		$20		$36	
Direct labor	10		15		31	
Variable factory overhead	3		7		17	
Total variable production cost	$28		$42		$84	
Variable selling expense*	10		13		15	
Total variable costs		(38)		(55)		(99)
Contribution margin per unit		$ 62		$ 75		$ 51

*The only variable selling expense is a sales commission, which is always 10% of unit selling price.

Sales Price Changes and Relative Profitability of Products

Managers must continuously monitor the selling prices of company products, in relation to each other as well as to competitors' prices. This process may provide information that causes management to change one or more selling prices. For example, if Concordia Ltd. found that talking scales sold better at the beginning of the year (after the holidays) than at other times, it might increase the sales price of these scales during this period. Factors that might influence price changes include fluctuations in demand, production/distribution costs, economic conditions, and competition. Any shift in the selling price of one product in a multiproduct firm will normally cause a change in the sales mix of that firm because of the economic law of demand elasticity with respect to price.[10]

    Concordia's management has set profit maximization as the primary corporate goal. This strategy does not necessarily mean selling as many units as possible of the product with the highest selling price and as few as possible of the products with lower selling prices. The product with the highest selling price per unit does not necessarily yield the highest contribution margin per unit or per unit of scarce resource. In Concordia Ltd.'s case, talking scales yield the lowest unit contribution margin of the three products. The talking scale also requires more direct labor and machine time, based on the high costs shown for direct labor and variable overhead. But even making the simplistic assumption that no resources are scarce, it is more profit-beneficial to sell deluxe scales than either basic or talking scales, since a deluxe scale provides the highest unit contribution margin of the three products. Even a basic scale is more profitable than a talking scale because, although the basic scale has the lowest unit selling price, its unit contribution margin is greater than that of the talking scale.

    Unit contribution margin and sales volume should be considered together when profitability is evaluated. Total company contribution margin is equal to the combined contribution margins provided by all the products' sales. Exhibit 9–8 (page 453) indicates the respective total contribution margins of Concordia's three types of bathroom scales. While the basic scales do not have the highest unit contribution margin,

---

[10]The law of demand elasticity indicates how closely price and demand are related. Product demand is highly elastic if a small price reduction generates a large demand increase. If demand is less elastic, large price reductions are needed to bring about moderate sales volume increases.

■ EXHIBIT 9–8

Relationship Between Contribution Margin and Sales Volume

	UNIT CONTRIBUTION MARGIN (FROM EXHIBIT 9-7)	CURRENT SALES VOLUME IN UNITS	TOTAL
Basic scales	$62	20,000	$1,240,000
Deluxe scales	$75	13,000	975,000
Talking scales	$51	8,000	408,000
Total contribution margin of product sales mix			$2,623,000

they do generate the largest total product line contribution margin because of their sales volume. To maximize profits, Concordia management must maximize total contribution margin rather than per-unit contribution margin.

The sales volume of a product or service is usually directly related to its selling price. When selling price is increased and demand is elastic with respect to price, demand for that good decreases.[11] Thus, if Concordia management, in an attempt to increase profits, decides to raise the price of the basic scales to $120, there should be some decline in demand. Assume that consultation with marketing research personnel indicates that such a price increase would cause demand for the product to drop from 20,000 to 12,000 scales per period. Exhibit 9–9 shows the effect of this pricing decision on total contribution margin.

Even though the contribution margin per unit of the basic scales increased from $62 to $80, the total dollar contribution margin generated by sales of the product has declined because of the decrease in sales volume. This example assumes that customers did not switch their purchases from basic scales to other Concordia bathroom

■ EXHIBIT 9–9

Relationship Between Sales Price and Demand

	UNIT CONTRIBUTION MARGIN	NEW SALES VOLUME IN UNITS	TOTAL
Basic scales	$80*	12,000	$ 960,000
Deluxe scales	$75	13,000	975,000
Talking scales	$51	8,000	408,000
Total contribution margin of product sales mix			$2,343,000

*Calculated as:

New selling price	$120
Total variable production cost (from Exhibit 9-7)	(28)
Total variable selling expense (10% of selling price)	(12)
Contribution margin	$ 80

---

[11]Such a decline in demand generally does not occur when the product in question has no close substitutes or is not a major expenditure in consumers' budgets.

scales when the price of the basic scale was raised. Price increases normally cause customers to switch from a company's high-priced products to its lower-priced products or to a competitor's product. In this instance, switching within the company was ignored because the basic scales were the company's lowest-priced scales. It is unlikely that customers would stop buying basic scales because of a $20 price increase and begin buying deluxe scales that cost even more—but that situation could occur. Customers might believe that the difference in quality between the basic and deluxe scales is worth the extra $10 (rather than $30) and make such a purchasing switch.

In making decisions to raise or lower prices, the relevant quantitative factors include: prospective or new contribution margin per unit of product; both short-term and long-term changes in product demand and production volume caused by the price increase or decrease; and best use of any scarce resources. Some relevant qualitative factors involved in pricing decisions are: impact of changes on customer goodwill toward the company; customer loyalty toward company products; and competitors' responses to the firm's new pricing structure.[12]

When deciding to change the price of current products or to introduce new products that will compete with current products and may affect their sales volumes, managers need to be certain that their assumptions about consumer behavior are rational. Comparisons are typically made against a "base case" scenario, which estimates how consumers will behave if no changes are made. "Often companies implicitly assume that the base case is simply a continuation of the status quo, but this assumption ignores market trends and competitor behavior. Using the wrong base case is typical of product launches in which the new product will likely erode the market for the company's existing product line."[13] Sometimes the base case is appropriate, as discussed in the accompanying News Note; sometimes—especially in high technology industries such as computers—it is not.

Special Order Pricing

In **special order pricing,** management must determine a sales price to charge for manufacturing or service jobs that are outside the company's normal production or service realm. Special order situations include jobs that require a bid, are taken during slack periods, or are made to a specific buyer's specifications. Typically, the sales price quoted on a special order job should be high enough to cover the variable costs of the job and any incremental (additional) fixed costs caused by the job and to generate a profit. Special order pricing requires knowledge of the relevant costs associated with the specific problem or decision at hand.

Concordia has been given the opportunity to bid on a special order for 1,000 deluxe scales. Company management wants to obtain the order as long as the additional business will provide a satisfactory contribution to profit. The company has machine and labor hours that are not currently being used, and raw materials can be obtained from the supplier. Also, Concordia has no immediate opportunity to use its currently unused capacity in another way, so an opportunity cost is not a factor.

The information necessary to determine a price to bid on the deluxe scales is presented in Exhibit 9–7. Direct materials, direct labor, and variable factory overhead

special order pricing

[12]Patrick Barwise, Paul R. Marsh, and Robin Wensley, "Must Finance and Strategy Clash?" *Harvard Business Review* (September-October 1989), p. 86.

[13]In regard to this last item, consider what occurs when one airline raises or lowers its fares between cities. It typically does not take very long for all the other airlines flying that route to adjust their fares accordingly. Thus, competitive advantage often exists only for a short time.

Marquis Didn't Break Waterford's Market

The shine is returning to Waterford Wedgewood PLC. Four years ago, the future looked grim for the well-known Irish maker of crystal and china. Sales were falling in the U.S.—Waterford's main market—as the economy slowed and customers cooled to prestige products. Competition was heating up from low-cost crystal makers in the former Eastern block.

But today, sales are up for both Waterford crystal and Wedgwood china. The turnabout began with a decision in 1990 to launch Marquis by Waterford, a brand of crystal, the company's first [new brand] in 200 years. It was a calculated risk. Marquis would sell for about 20% less than traditional Waterford. But if Marquis succeeded, it might drain sales from the Waterford line. If it flopped, it could damage the flagship brand's name.

The strategy worked. Marquis has become the sixth largest-selling brand [of premium crystal]. Marquis so far hasn't detracted from the flagship brand. Sales of traditional Waterford were up 16% in 1993, and it's the top-selling premium brand.

Key to the success of Marquis, says Waterford's sales and marketing director P. Redmond O'Donoghue, was to keep it sufficiently different from traditional Waterford, while still allowing the new brand to benefit by association from the Waterford name. That meant Marquis had to be cheaper, but not cheap. [One cost-cutting technique was to reduce] overhead by contracting out the making of the Marquis line to producers in Germany and Slovenia in the former Yugoslavia.

The results of one key aspect of the strategy won't be known for some years: Waterford is counting on customers who buy Marquis to eventually trade up to the more expensive crystal as their buying power increases.

SOURCE: Judith Valente, "A New Brand Restores Sparkle to Waterford," *Wall Street Journal* (November 10, 1994), p. B1. Reprinted by permission of The Wall Street Journal, © 1994 Dow Jones & Company, Inc., All Rights Reserved Worldwide.

costs are relevant to setting the bid price because these variable production costs will be incurred for each additional deluxe scale manufactured. While all variable costs are normally relevant to a special pricing decision, the variable selling expense is irrelevant in this instance because no sales commission will be paid on this sale. Fixed production overhead and fixed selling and administrative expenses are not expected to increase because of this sale, so these expenses are not included in the pricing decision.

Using the available cost information, the relevant cost used to determine the bid price for the deluxe scales is $42 (direct materials, direct labor, and variable overhead). This cost is the minimum price at which the company should sell a deluxe scale. If the existing fixed costs have been covered by regular sales, any price exceeding $42 will provide the company some profit.

Assume that Concordia is currently experiencing a $10,000 net loss. Company managers want to set a bid price that would cover the net loss generated by other sales and create a $3,000 before-tax profit. In this case, Concordia would spread the total $13,000 desired amount over the 1,000 deluxe scales at $13 per scale. This would give a bid price of $55 per scale ($42 variable cost + $13). However, any price above the $42 variable cost will contribute toward reducing the $10,000 loss.

In setting the bid price, management must decide how much profit it would consider reasonable on the special order. As another example, since Concordia's usual selling price for a deluxe scale is $130, each sale provides a normal contribution margin of $75 or approximately 58 percent. Setting the bid price for the special order at $66.36 would cover the variable production costs of $42 and provide a normal 58 percent contribution margin. This computation illustrates a simplistic cost-plus approach to pricing, but ignores both product demand and market competition. Concordia's bid price should also reflect these considerations. In addition, company management should consider the effect that the special order will have on all company activities (purchasing, receiving, warehousing, and so forth) and whether these activities will create additional, unforeseen costs.

Sometimes a company will depart from its typical price-setting routine and "low-ball" bid jobs. A low-ball bid may only cover variable costs or it may be below such costs. The rationale behind low-ball bids is to obtain the job to have the opportunity to introduce company products or services to a particular market segment. Special pricing of this nature may provide work for a period of time, but cannot be continued for the long run. To remain in business, a company must set product or service selling prices to cover total variable costs, to cover an appropriate amount of fixed, selling, or administrative costs, and to provide a reasonable profit margin. An exception to this general rule, however, may occur when a company produces related or complementary products. For instance, a company such as Nintendo might sell video hardware at or below cost and use the ancillary software games programs as the primary source of profit.

Special prices may also be justified when orders are of an unusual nature (because of the quantity, method of delivery, or packaging) or because the products are being tailor-made to customer instructions. Lastly, special pricing can be used when producing goods for a one-time job, such as an overseas order that will not affect domestic sales.

When setting a special order price, management must consider the qualitative issues as well as the quantitative ones. For instance, will a low bid price cause this customer (or others) to feel that a precedent has been established for future prices? Will the contribution margin on a bid, set low enough to acquire the job, earn a sufficient amount to justify the additional burdens placed on management or employees by this activity? How, if at all, will special order sales affect the company's normal sales? If the job is taking place during a period of low business activity (off-season or recession), is management willing to take the business at a lower contribution or profit margin simply to keep a trained work force employed?

Compensation Changes

Many companies compensate their salespeople by paying a fixed commission rate on gross sales dollars. If Concordia Ltd. uses this type of commission structure, sales personnel will be motivated to sell talking scales, rather than basic or deluxe. Emphasizing sales of the talking scales will not help the company achieve its profit maximization objective, however, since these scales provide the lowest unit contribution margin. If management wants to motivate salespeople so that the company is able to achieve its profit maximization objective, a change in the commission compensation structure is needed.

The starting point for a change in the compensation structure is knowledge of product contribution margin, which is equal to selling price minus total variable production (but not variable selling) costs. The per-unit product contribution margins of each of Concordia's products are as follows:

	SELLING PRICE	TOTAL VARIABLE PRODUCTION COST	PRODUCT CONTRIBUTION MARGIN
Basic scales	$100	$28	$72
Deluxe scales	130	42	88
Talking scales	150	84	66

Concordia is considering a new policy of paying salespeople a commission of 15.3 percent on product contribution margin rather than 10 percent on sales price. This policy change should motivate sales personnel to sell more of the product that produces the highest commission, which, in turn, will shift the original sales mix toward sales of products most profitable to the company.

Exhibit 9–10 compares Concordia's total contribution margin based on the original sales mix and commission structure (repeated from Exhibit 9-8) with total contribution margin under the new assumed sales mix and commission structure. The new commission policy is beneficial for the company because it shifts sales mix from the high-priced, low-contribution-margin talking scales toward the lower-priced but more profitable basic scales and deluxe scales.

Fixed costs are not considered in setting sales commissions. All sales and production volumes of the respective products are assumed to be within the relevant range of activity for the company. Therefore, regardless of a shift in activity levels, total fixed costs will remain constant.

For morale purposes, the sales personnel must be shown that the new commissions are expected to slightly exceed the total commissions under the original plan. These computations are shown in Exhibit 9–11. In this instance, the total volume is held constant at 41,000. Sales personnel should be made aware that attempts to increase

■ **EXHIBIT 9–10**

Impact of Change in Commission Structure

Old Policy—Commissions equal 10% of selling price

	PRODUCT CONTRIBUTION MARGIN	COMMISSION	CONTRIBUTION MARGIN AFTER COMMISSION	OLD VOLUME	TOTAL CONTRIBUTION MARGIN
Basic scales	$72	$10 (.1 × $100)	$62	20,000	$1,240,000
Deluxe scales	88	13 (.1 × $130)	75	13,000	975,000
Talking scales	66	15 (.1 × $150)	51	8,000	408,000
Total contribution margin for product sales					$2,623,000

New Policy—Commissions equal 15.3% of product contribution margin per unit

	PRODUCT CONTRIBUTION MARGIN	COMMISSION	CONTRIBUTION MARGIN AFTER COMMISSION	NEW VOLUME	TOTAL CONTRIBUTION MARGIN
Basic scales	$72	$11.02 (.153 × $72)	$60.98	20,500	$1,250,090
Deluxe scales	88	13.46 (.153 × $88)	74.54	17,000	1,267,180
Talking scales	66	10.10 (.153 × $66)	55.90	3,500	195,650
Total contribution margin for product sales					$2,712,920

■ **EXHIBIT 9–11**
Total Effect of Changing Sales Commissions

ORIGINAL PLAN

Product	Commission	Volume	Total Commission
Basic scales	$10.00	20,000	$200,000
Deluxe scales	13.00	13,000	169,000
Talking scales	15.00	8,000	120,000
Total		41,000	$489,000

NEW PLAN

Product	Commission	Volume	Total Commission
Basic scales	$11.02	20,500	$225,910
Deluxe scales	13.46	17,000	228,820
Talking scales	10.10	3,500	35,350
Total		41,000	$490,080

the sales of basic and deluxe scales should be easier than attempts to increase sales of talking scales, and such efforts will result in even higher total commissions and higher company income. The relationships should be stressed so that the sales personnel will work more effectively at accomplishing company profit objectives.

Advertising Budget Changes

Another factor that may cause shifts in the sales mix involves either increasing the total company advertising budget or reallocating the budget among the products the company sells. This discussion uses the original data for Concordia Ltd. and examines a proposed increase in the company's total advertising budget.

Concordia's advertising manager, Leah Donti, has proposed doubling the advertising budget from $30,000 to $60,000 per year. Donti thinks the increased advertising will result in the following additional unit sales during the coming year: basic, 200 scales; deluxe, 500 scales; and talking, 100 scales.

If the company spends the additional $30,000 for advertising, will the additional 800 units of sales raise profits? The original fixed costs as well as the contribution margin generated by the old sales level are irrelevant to the decision. The relevant items are the increased sales revenue, increased variable costs, and increased fixed cost—the incremental effects of the change. The difference between incremental revenues and incremental variable costs is the incremental contribution margin. The incremental contribution margin minus the incremental fixed cost is the incremental benefit (or loss) resulting from the decision.[14]

Exhibit 9–12 shows how the increased advertising expenditures are expected to affect contribution margin. The $55,000 of additional contribution margin far exceeds the $30,000 incremental cost for advertising, so the Concordia Ltd. should definitely increase its advertising budget by $30,000.

---

[14]This same type of incremental analysis is shown in Chapter 8 in relation to CVP computations.

■ **EXHIBIT 9–12**
Incremental Analysis of Increasing Advertising Cost

	BASIC	DELUXE	TALKING	TOTAL
Increase in volume	200	500	100	800
Contribution margin per unit	× $62	× $75	× $51	
Incremental contribution margin	$12,400	$37,500	$5,100	$55,000
Incremental fixed cost of advertising				30,000
Incremental benefit of increased advertising expenditure				$25,000

Increasing advertising may cause changes in the sales mix or the number of units sold. Sales can also be affected by opportunities that allow companies to obtain business at a sales price that differs from the normal price, such as the situations discussed earlier in this chapter.

RELEVANT COSTS IN PRODUCT LINE DECISIONS

■ **LEARNING OBJECTIVE 6**
Use product margin to determine whether a product line should be retained or eliminated.

To facilitate performance evaluations, operating results in multiproduct environments are often presented in terms of separate product lines. In reviewing these disaggregated statements, managers must distinguish relevant from irrelevant information for each product line. If all costs (variable and fixed) are charged to product lines, a product line or segment may be perceived to be operating at a loss when actually it is not. Such perceptions may be caused by the commingling of relevant and irrelevant information on the statements.

Exhibit 9–13 presents basic earnings information for Concordia Ltd.'s Men's Products Division, which manufactures three product lines: Canadian Woods shaving creme, Yukon Gold after-shave, and Grasslands cologne. The format of the information at the top of the exhibit makes it appear that the shaving creme and after-

■ **EXHIBIT 9–13**
Product Line Income Statements

	SHAVING CREME	AFTER-SHAVE	COLOGNE	TOTAL
Sales	$150,000	$85,000	$380,000	$615,000
Total direct variable expenses	(87,500)	(55,250)	(228,000)	(370,750)
Total contribution margin	$ 62,500	$29,750	$152,000	$244,250
Total fixed expenses*	(79,000)	(35,000)	(76,000)	(190,000)
Net income (loss)	$ (16,500)	$(5,250)	$ 76,000	$ 54,250
*Fixed expenses:				
(1) Avoidable fixed expenses	$ 50,000	$32,000	$ 48,000	$130,000
(2) Unavoidable fixed expenses	9,000	1,000	6,000	16,000
(3) Allocated common costs	20,000	2,000	22,000	44,000
Total	$ 79,000	$35,000	$ 76,000	$190,000

shave lines are operating at a net loss ($16,500 and $5,250, respectively). Managers reviewing such results might reason that Concordia's Men's Product Division would be $21,750 ($16,500 + $5,250) more profitable if both of these products were eliminated. This conclusion may be premature, however, because of the mixture of relevant and irrelevant information in the income statement presentations. This problem results from the fact that all fixed expenses have been allocated to the individual product lines.

Fixed cost allocations are traditionally based on one or more measures that are presumed to provide an "equitable" division of costs. These measures might include square footage of the manufacturing plant occupied by each product line, number of machine hours incurred for production of each product line, or number of employees directly associated with each product line. Regardless of the allocation base, allocations may force fixed costs into specific product line operating results even though those costs may not have actually been caused (or driven) by the making or selling of that specific product line. This inequity results from the fact that most cost allocation schemes currently used by managers are arbitrary.

The detail in Exhibit 9–13 separates the Men's Products Division's fixed expenses into three categories: (1) those that could be avoided by elimination of the product line; (2) those that are directly associated with the product line but are unavoidable; and (3) those that are incurred for the division as a whole (common costs) and allocated to the individual product lines. The latter two categories are irrelevant to the question of whether to eliminate a product line.

An unavoidable cost will be shifted to another product line if the product line with which it is associated is eliminated. For example, the division has several senior employees who work in the shaving creme area. If that product line were eliminated, those employees would be transferred to after-shave or cologne. Similarly, depreciation on factory equipment used to manufacture a specific product is an irrelevant cost in product line decisions. If a product line were eliminated but the equipment were kept in service and used to produce other products, its depreciation expense would be unavoidable. However, if the equipment were sold, the depreciation expense would also be irrelevant because it would no longer be incurred. Alternatively, amount recieved from the sale would be relevant because it would increase the marginal benefit of a decision to discontinue the product line.

As to common costs, they will be incurred regardless of which product lines are retained. One example of a common cost is the insurance premium on a manufacturing facility that houses all product lines.

If the division eliminated both shaving creme and after-shave, its total profit would decline by $10,250. This amount represents the combined lost **product margin** of the two product lines, shown in Exhibit 9–14. Product margin represents the excess of revenues over direct variable expenses and avoidable fixed expenses. It is the amount remaining to cover unavoidable direct fixed expenses and common costs and then to provide profits.[15] Product margin is the appropriate figure on which to base a decision to continue or eliminate a product, since that figure measures the product's ability to help cover indirect and unavoidable costs. For the Men's Products Division, the decrease in total income from eliminating both shaving creme and after-shave can be shown in the following alternative computations:

product margin

---

[15]It is assumed here that all common costs are fixed costs; this is not always the case. Some common costs are variable, such as costs of processing purchase orders and computer time-sharing expenses for payroll or other corporate functions.

■ **EXHIBIT 9–14**
Product Line Income Statements

	SHAVING CREME	AFTER-SHAVE	COLOGNE	TOTAL
Sales	$150,000	$ 85,000	$380,000	$615,000
Total direct variable expenses	(87,500)	(55,250)	(228,000)	(370,750)
Product contribution margin	$ 62,500	$ 29,750	$152,000	$244,250
(1) Avoidable fixed expenses	(50,000)	(32,000)	(48,000)	(130,000)
Product margin	$ 12,500	$ (2,250)	$104,000	$114,250
(2) Unavoidable direct fixed expenses (see Exhibit 9-12)				(16,000)
Product line operating results				$ 98,250
(3) Common costs				(44,000)
Net income (loss)				$ 54,250

Current net income	$ 54,250
Increase in income due to elimination of after-shave product line (product margin)	2,250
Decrease in income due to elimination of shaving creme product line (product margin)	(12,500)
New net income	$ 44,000
or	
Product contribution margin of cologne line	$152,000
Minus avoidable fixed expenses of cologne line	(48,000)
Product margin of the cologne line	$104,000
Minus all remaining expenses shown on Exhibit 9–14 ($16,000 + $44,000)	(60,000)
Remaining income with one product line	$ 44,000

Based on the quantitative information in Exhibit 9–14, the Men's Products Division should eliminate only the after-shave line. That product line is generating a negative product margin and thus is not even covering its own costs. If that product line were eliminated, total divisional profit would increase by $2,250, the amount of the negative product margin.

Before making decisions to discontinue a product line or sell a segment, management should carefully also consider what it would take to "turn that product line or division around." Some products, like General Foods' Jell-O, have been turned around through greater investment and advertising. Other product lines (and even segments or divisions of companies) must be abandoned through either discontinuance or sale. For instance, in 1989, Dell Computer Corp. became the first computer producer to sell at "superstore" outlets; in July 1994, it was "the first to pull out as it abandoned its unprofitable retail efforts."[16] Dell now only sells its computers by mail-order. And, Sears, Roebuck and Co. spun off its Allstate Corp. insurance business to shareholders in November 1994 to come full circle back to its retail beginnings by focusing solely on selling merchandise.[17]

---

[16]Scott McCarnety, "Dell Computer Plans to Quit Retail Field and Refocus on Its Mail-Order Business," *Wall Street Journal* (July 12, 1994), p. A2.

[17]Gregory A. Patterson, "Sears to Spin Off Allstate; Brennan to Retire in 1995," *Wall Street Journal* (November 11, 1994), p. A3.

The other decision relative to product lines is expansion or extension. Expansion refers to the introduction of totally new products. Extension refers to the introduction of "off-shoots" of current products because the company decides that the market needs to be more highly segmented. The segmentation might focus on price, size, flavor, or health-consciousness issues; alternatively, extensions might have been necessary to meet competitive pressures.

For example, in 1994, Gillette introduced 20 new products, including Ultra Floss dental floss, the SuperVolume hair dryer, and the SensorExcel razor. A SensorExcel for women is also expected.[18] The dental floss and hair dryer are expansions of Gillette's product lines; the razors are extensions.

Incremental costs of expansions and extensions (other than the variable costs of the product) include market research, product and packaging development, product introduction, and advertising. Extensions have often been viewed as fairly low-cost endeavors—especially if a company has excess capacity. But, as indicated in the accompanying News Note, there are several quantitive and qualitative problems of extending a product line that may not be quite so obvious.

Several techniques are available that could minimize some of the difficulties discussed in the News Note. For example, the use of activity-based costing may make some of the costs of complexity more visible to managers. Just-in-time inventories

Product line expansions and extensions are quite common in the breakfast cereal markets. Such activities, however, typically create numerous incremental production overhead costs relating to purchasing and storing as well as for advertising.

[18]Barbara Carton, "Gillette Looks Beyond Whiskers to Big Hair and Stretchly Floss," *Wall Street Journal* (December 14, 1994), p. B1.

Extra Costs for Extra Products May Be Hard to Recoup

Companies expect and plan for a number of costs associated with a line extension [. . . , including] certain increases in administrative costs: planning the promotion calendar takes more time when an extension is added to the line, as does deciding on the advertising allocations between the core brand and its extensions. But managers may not foresee the following pitfalls:

- Fragmentation of the overall marketing effort and dilution of the brand image.
- Increased production complexity from shorter production runs and more frequent line changeovers. (These are somewhat mitigated by the ability to customize products toward the end of an otherwise standardized production process with flexible manufacturing systems.)
- More errors in forecasting demand and increased logistics complexity, resulting in increased remnants and larger buffer inventories to avoid stockouts.
- Increased supplier costs due to rush orders and the inability to buy the most economic quantities of raw materials.
- Distraction of the research and development group from new product development.

The unit costs for multi-item lines can be 25% to 45% higher than the theoretical cost of producing only the most popular item in the line. The inability of most line extensions to increase demand in a category makes it hard for companies to recover the extra costs through increases in volume. And even if a line extension can command a higher unit price, the expanded gross margin is usually insufficient to recover such dramatic incremental unit costs.

SOURCE: Reprinted by permission of *Harvard Business Review*. An excerpt from "Extend Profits, Not Product Lines," by John A. Quelch and David Kenny, (September-October 1994). Copyright © 1994 by the President and Fellows of Harvard College; all rights reserved.

and long-term supplier contracts may reduce the possibilities of increased buffer inventories or supplier costs. And target costing may improve a company's ability to assess potential profitability as well as determine the design and manufacturing processes necessary to assure that profitability.

Alfred Zeien, Gillette's chairman and CEO, believes in rapid cycle time—getting there first with the highest-quality. "We've had annual earnings growth of 17% on sales growth of only 9%, by changing to a more profitable product mix," Zeien explains. "But over the next five years it will be difficult to repeat [that], so we have to emphasize [sales] growth."

Company profit margins increased nicely as customers began using expensive "shaving systems"—as Gillette calls reusable razors like TracII, Atra, Atra Plus, and Sensor razors—rather than cheap disposable razors. "We don't sell a lot more units or raise prices from year to year, but we earn more from each customer," explains Zeien.

With new products, as with shavers, Gillette tries to move customers up in value rather than to force prices down. In 1991, Braun (a Gillette company) introduced the Flex Control electric razor for $200 in Japan and Europe, a price that was substantially higher than the $70 razors in the upper end of the market. "We're not trying to kill the competition on price; we're trying to create a profit," asserts Jacque Lagarde, the manager responsible for Braun and Oral-B. "We forced competitors to follow us in this price segment and now everybody's actually making more money. That's the name of the game."

Once a product hits the market, however, Gillette isn't afraid to cut its losses if necessary. The company has discontinued 22 product lines from 1979 to 1993. One example was the company's 1985 decision to sell its Cricket disposable-lighter business. "We divest any part of the business we're not happy with," explains Mr. Zeien. "We are very disciplined." Although some firms stay with a losing product, hoping that it might turn around, he says, "we are convinced that the benefits of worldwide leadership are so great that we can't afford to waste time, money, and management talent where that leadership is not achievable."

Whether deciding to introduce a new product, cut or raise a price in a market, or discontinue a product line, Gillette's management must understand the incremental costs and benefits of each alternative. Recognizing how the benefit of cutting fractions of a cent off a variable production cost is compounded when large volumes of that product are sold focuses management attention on controlling costs. Zeien is also concerned with both short- and long-term goals. He follows a 50-50 philosophy. "We're spending 50% for the future [in research and development] and we're giving 50% to our shareholders today," he says.

SOURCES: Rita Koselka, "It's My Favorite Statistic," *Forbes* (September 12, 1994), pp. 164, 166, 170 (reprinted by permission of Forbes magazine, © Forbes Inc., 1994); and William H. Miller, "Gillette's Secret to Sharpness," *Industry Week* (January 3, 1994), pp. 26 (reprinted with permission; copyright Penton Publishing, Inc., Cleveland, Ohio).

CROSS-FUNCTIONAL APPLICATIONS STRATEGIES

Discipline	Applications
Accounting	Relevant costing helps managers to focus on information that is important in decision making; it reinforces the idea that past costs are sunk costs. Accurate costs can improve appropriate product pricing, which must be supportable in cost-plus contracts and fair trade pricing.
Economics	Relevant costing is a form of the economic concept of marginal costing, which holds that rational decisions for short-run problems are made on the basis of marginal revenue versus marginal cost. Understanding the concept of relevant costs will help the decision maker avoid two common pitfalls: ignoring opportunity cost and *not* ignoring sunk costs. Decisions should be based on a comparison of incremental revenues versus incremental (relevant and opportunity) costs.
Finance	Relevant costing helps decision makers to evaluate major financial decisions about expansion or contraction of product lines.
Management	Relevant costing emphasizes the critical nature of differentiating among avoidable fixed, unavoidable fixed, and allocated common costs in making valid product decisions. It helps to differentiate between costs useful for short-run decisions and costs useful for long-run decisions. It helps in the allocation of scarce resources.
Marketing	Relevant costing helps to indicate the reasons behind: basing sales commissions on contribution margin rather than sales price; basing special prices on incremental costs to win business; and justifying additional advertising costs by comparing the increase in fixed costs with the incremental contribution generated by the advertising.

CHAPTER SUMMARY

Management's task is to effectively and efficiently allocate its finite stock of resources to accomplish its chosen set of corporate goals and objectives. Managers should explain how requested information will be used so that accountants can make certain relevant information is provided in an appropriate form. In this way, managers will have a reliable quantitative basis on which to analyze problems, compare viable solutions, and choose the best course of action.

For information to be relevant, it must (1) relate to the decision at hand, (2) be important to the decision, and (3) have a bearing on a future endeavor. Relevant costing compares the incremental, or additional, revenues and/or costs associated with alternative decisions.

Relevant information may be quantitative or qualitative. Variable costs are generally relevant to a decision; they are irrelevant only when they cannot be avoided under any possible alternative or when they do not differ between (or among) alternatives. Direct avoidable fixed costs are also relevant to decision making. Sometimes costs seem relevant when they actually are not. Examples of such irrelevant costs include sunk costs, arbitrarily allocated common costs, and nonincremental fixed costs that have been averaged on a per-unit basis.

Managers use relevant cost information to determine the incremental benefits of alternatives. One option often available is to "change nothing." This option, however, may be strategically risky if competitors gain advantage by upgrading their processes. After rigorous analysis of the quantifiable factors associated with each alternative, a manager must assess the merits and potential risks of the qualitative factors involved so that the best possible course of action is chosen.

Relevant costing is essential in many decision-making situations, including those related to further processing of a product, make-or-buy alternatives, scarce resource allocations, sales mix distributions, and retentions or eliminations of product lines. The following points are important to remember:

1. In deciding whether to engage in further processing of a product at split-off, management should ignore the total or allocated joint cost. The only relevant items are the incremental revenues and costs of processing further.
2. In a make-or-buy decision, management should include the opportunity costs associated with the make alternative; the buy alternative may provide an opportunity to make plant assets and personnel available for other purposes.
3. In a decision involving a single scarce resource, if the objective is to maximize company contribution margin and profits, then production and sales should be focused toward the product with the highest contribution margin per unit of the scarce resource.
4. Changes in selling prices and advertising normally affect a company's sales volume and sales mix, thus changing the company's total contribution margin. Special order prices may be set using variable costs as a starting point. Tying sales commissions to contribution margin will motivate salespeople to sell the products that are most beneficial to the company's profit picture.
5. In a product line decision, product lines should be evaluated on their product margins rather than their income amounts. Product margin considers relevant direct costs and avoidable fixed expenses but excludes unavoidable fixed expenses and allocated common costs.

Quantitative analysis is short-range in perspective. Additional, qualitative factors should be reviewed by management in each case. Some of these qualitative factors may have long-range planning and policy implications. Others may be short-range in nature. Managers must decide the relevance of individual factors based on experience, judgment, knowledge of economic theory, and logic.

Linear Programming

Linear programming (LP) is a method used to solve problems with one objective and multiple limiting factors. LP is used to find the optimal allocation of scarce resources when the objective and restrictions on achieving that objective can be stated as linear equations. This technique is also useful in allocating a scarce resource when the allocation will not be based on which single product would maximize the scarce resource.

The objective in an LP problem is to either maximize or minimize some measure of performance. The mathematical statement expressing that objective is called the **objective function.** For example, Gillette's objective could be to maximize product contribution margin or to minimize product cost. A linear programming problem can have only one goal, expressed as the objective function.

A restriction on management's pursuit of its objective is a **constraint.** There are several types of constraints. Resource constraints involve limited availability of labor time, machine time, raw materials, space, or production capacity. Demand or marketing constraints restrict the quantity of the product that can be sold during a time period. Constraints can also take the form of technical product requirements. For example, management may be constrained in the production requirements for frozen meals by caloric or vitamin content. A final constraint in all LP problems is a nonnegativity constraint. This constraint specifies that physical quantities cannot have negative values. Constraints, like the objective function, represent the limits imposed on optimizing the objective function and are specified in mathematical equations (reflected in equal to, less than, less-than-or-equal-to, greater than, or greater-than-or-equal-to conditions).

Almost every allocation problem has a number of **feasible solutions** that do not violate any of the problem constraints. Different solutions generally give different values for the objective function. In some problems, several solutions provide the same value for the objective function. Solutions may also be generated that contain fractional values. The **optimal solution** to a maximization or minimization goal is the one that provides the best answer to the allocation problem. Some LP problems have more than one optimal solution.

Linear programming problems may be solved by a graphical approach or the simplex method. Graphs are simple to use and provide a visual representation of the problem. However, because it is impossible to accurately draw and interpret graphs in three or more dimensions, graphical approaches to solving LP problems lose their appeal when the number of unknowns exceeds two. In such cases, the computer-adaptable simplex method can be used.

The **simplex method** uses an iterative (sequential) algorithm to solve multivariable, multiconstraint LP problems. (An algorithm is a logical step-by-step problem-solving technique that continuously searches for an improved solution until it achieves the optimal one.) Simplex solutions also provide valuable additional information that may be used in budgeting and production analyses.

■ LEARNING OBJECTIVE 7
(Appendix) Describe the elements of a linear programming problem.

objective function

constraint

feasible solutions

optimal solution

simplex method

GLOSSARY

Constraint (p. 467)   a restriction on the ability to reach an objective (from appendix)

Feasible solution (p. 467)   an answer to a linear programming problem that does not violate any of the problem constraints (from appendix)

Incremental cost (p. 440)   the additional cost of producing and/or selling a contemplated quantity of output

Incremental revenue (p. 439)   the additional revenue resulting from a contemplated sale of a quantity of output

Joint cost (p. 443)   the cost incurred, up to the split-off point, for materials, labor, and overhead in a joint process

Joint process (p. 443)   a process in which one product cannot be manufactured without others' being produced

Linear programming (p. 451)   a method used to solve problems with one objective and multiple limiting factors; finds the optimal allocation of scarce resources when the objective and the restrictions on achieving that objective can be stated as linear equations

Make-or-buy decision (p. 445)   a decision based on comparing the cost of internally manufacturing a product component with the cost of purchasing it from outside suppliers or from another division and, thus, attempting to assess the best uses of available facilities

Objective function (p. 467)   a mathematical equation that states the maximization or minimization goal of a linear programming problem (from appendix)

Opportunity cost (p. 440)   the benefit foregone when one course of action is chosen over another

Optimal solution (p. 467)   the solution to a linear programming problem that provides the best answer to the allocation problem without violating any problem constraints (from appendix)

Outsource (p. 445)   buy a service or component from an external provider

Product margin (p. 461)   the excess of a product's revenues over both its direct variable expenses and avoidable fixed expenses; the amount remaining to cover unavoidable direct fixed expenses and common costs and then to provide profits

Relevant cost (p. 438)   a cost that is pertinent to or logically associated with a specific problem or decision and that differs between alternatives

Relevant costing (p. 439)   a process that allows managers to focus on pertinent facts and disregard extraneous information by comparing, to the extent possible and practical, the differential, incremental revenues and incremental costs of alternative decisions

Sales mix (p. 452)   the relative combination of quantities of sales of the various products that make up the total sales of a company

Scarce resource (p. 448)   an item that is essential to production activity but that is available only in a limited quantity

Simplex method (p. 467)   an iterative technique used to solve multivariable, multiconstraint linear programming problems; usually requires the aid of a computer (from appendix)

Special order pricing (p. 455)   the process of setting a sales price for manufacturing or service jobs that are outside the company's normal production or service realm

Split-off point (p. 443)   the point at which the outputs of a joint process are first identifiable as individual products

Sunk cost (p. 442)   the historical or past cost associated with the acquisition of an asset or a resource; it has no future recovery value

SOLUTION STRATEGIES

General rule of decision making: Choose the alternative that yields the greatest incremental benefit (or the smallest incremental loss).

Incremental (additional) revenues
− Incremental (additional) costs
‾‾‾‾‾‾‾‾‾‾‾‾‾‾‾‾‾‾‾‾‾‾‾‾‾‾‾‾‾‾
= Incremental benefit (positive or negative)

RELEVANT COSTS

Direct materials and direct labor
Variable production overhead
Variable selling expenses related to each alternative (may be greater or less than under the "change nothing" alternative)
Avoidable fixed production overhead
Avoidable fixed selling/administrative costs (if any)
Opportunity cost of choosing some other alternative (can be viewed as either increasing one alternative's cost or reducing the cost of the other)

SINGLE SCARCE RESOURCE

1. Determine the scarce resource.
2. Determine the production per unit of the scarce resource.
3. Determine the contribution margin (CM) per unit of the scarce resource.
4. Multiply units of production times CM per unit of the scarce resource to obtain total CM provided by the scarce resource. Production and sale of the product with the highest CM per unit of scarce resource will maximize profits.

PRODUCT LINES

Sales
− Direct variable expenses
‾‾‾‾‾‾‾‾‾‾‾‾‾‾‾‾‾‾‾‾‾‾‾‾
= Contribution margin
− Avoidable fixed expenses
‾‾‾‾‾‾‾‾‾‾‾‾‾‾‾‾‾‾‾‾‾‾‾‾
= Product margin*

*Make decision to retain or eliminate based on this line item.

DEMONSTRATION PROBLEM

Vancouver Home Products is a firm that manufactures several types of high-quality home appliances. One of the company's product lines consists of electric coffeepots. The company produces three different models of coffeepots. Vancouver is presently considering a proposal from a vendor who wishes to supply the company with glass carafes for the coffeepots.

The company currently produces the carafes it requires. Because customers have differing preferences, Vancouver now offers two alternative carafes for each coffeepot model (therefore, the company now must produce a total of six different types of carafes). The vendor has indicated it would produce three different types of carafes for each coffeepot model, thus expanding the variety of carafes that could be offered to the customer. The vendor would charge Vancouver C$2.60 per carafe.

Vancouver produces its carafes in its factory in Victoria, British Columbia, along with all the other coffeepot components. For the coming year, Vancouver has projected the costs of carafe production as follows (based on projected volume of 100,000 units):

Direct materials	C$ 75,000
Direct labor	65,000
Variable overhead	55,000
Fixed overhead	
Depreciation on equipment[1]	50,000
Property taxes on production space and equipment[2]	15,000
Factory supervision[3]	34,970
Total production costs	C$294,970

[1]The equipment used to produce the carafes has no alternative use and no material market value.
[2]The space occupied by carafe production activities will remain idle if the company purchases rather than makes the carafes.
[3]The factory supervision cost reflects the salary of a production supervisor who oversees carafe production. This individual would be dismissed from the firm if carafe production ceased.

Required:

a. Determine the net advantage or disadvantage of purchasing, rather than producing, the carafes required for the coming year.

b. Determine the level of coffeepot production at which Vancouver would be indifferent between buying and producing the carafes. If the volume of production was expected to increase in the future, would the firm be more likely to make or buy?

c. For this part only, assume that the space presently occupied by carafe production could be leased to another firm for C$45,000 per year. How would this affect the make-or-buy decision?

d. What other factors should the company take into account in determining whether it should make or buy the carafes?

e. Assume that Vancouver Home Products is currently experiencing a C$25,000 loss from operations. The company has an opportunity to sell an additional 10,000 carafes to a foreign distributor. Vancouver has the capacity to produce the additional carafes and no opportunity costs are associated with the order. What is the minimum price per carafe the company should charge for the special order? What price should the company charge if it wants to produce a C$5,000 net income?

■ SOLUTION TO DEMONSTRATION PROBLEM

a. Relevant costs to make 100,000 carafes:

Direct materials (C$.75 per unit)	C$ 75,000
Direct labor (C$.65 per unit)	65,000
Variable overhead (C$.55 per unit)	55,000
Factory supervision	34,970
Total	C$229,970
Cost to buy: 100,000 × C$2.60	(260,000)
Net advantage of in-house production	C$ 30,030

Note that the only fixed cost that is relevant to the decision is the cost of factory supervision. The other fixed costs would be unaffected by the decision.

b. The total relevant cost to make the carafes can be expressed as C$34,970 + C$1.95X, where X represents production volume. The term C$34,970 is the relevant fixed cost and the term C$1.95X represents the total relevant variable costs.

The total relevant cost to buy the required carafes can be expressed as C$2.60X, where X represents production volume.

When the production cost equation is set equal to the purchase cost equation, the point of indifference can be found:

$$C\$34,970 + C\$1.95X = C\$2.60X$$
$$C\$.65X = C\$34,970$$
$$X = 53,800 \text{ units}$$

As production volume goes up, so does the benefit of in-house production, because the average cost per unit will continually decline (due to the fixed cost element) and total cost rises only at a rate of C$1.95 per unit rather than C$2.60 per unit.

c. Referring to the solution to part a, the net advantage of in-house production is C$30,030. The possibility of renting the production space for C$45,000 per year increases the cost of in-house production because an opportunity cost of C$45,000 is incurred. Consequently, the balance shifts to favor the purchase of the carafes:

Original advantage of producing in-house	C$ 30,030
Additional opportunity cost (lost rent)	(45,000)
Net cost of producing the carafes	
(or net advantage of purchasing)	C$(14,970)

d. Among the additional factors that might be considered are the quality of the carafes produced relative to the quality of the carafes purchased, vendor reliability, number of competing vendors, effect of the additional variety of carafes on customer demand, likelihood of vendor price increases in the future, and alternative (cost-reducing or income-generating) uses of the space currently utilized to produce carafes.

e. The minimum selling price per unit would be the C$1.95 variable cost per unit. The price that would allow the company to make C$5,000 would be C$4.95 [(C$25,000 + C$5,000) ÷ 10,000 = C$3.00; C$3.00 + C$1.95 = C$4.95].

END-OF-CHAPTER MATERIALS

■ QUESTIONS

1. What are the three characteristics that a cost must possess to be relevant to a decision? Why are these characteristics important?

2. What is meant by the term *incremental* as it applies to costs and revenues?

3. Are future variable costs always relevant costs? Discuss the rationale for your answer.

4. What category of costs is often relevant in decision making, but is probably never directly recorded in a company's accounting records? Explain.

5. On November 13, 1996, Bill paid Jim $25 for a concert ticket that Jim had originally purchased for $50. On December 15, 1996, Ted offered Bill $30 for the ticket. Which of the costs mentioned are relevant in Bill's decision regarding whether to sell the ticket to Ted or attend the concert? What opportunity cost will Bill incur if he decides to attend the concert? Explain.

6. What is the "change nothing" alternative? Why is it not always a feasible alternative?

7. What is the term used to describe historical costs? Are such costs relevant in making decisions? Explain.

8. What are joint products, and what is the split-off point? Once joint products have reached the split-off point, are joint costs relevant? Are joint costs relevant before joint products reach the split-off point? Explain.

9. What are some qualitative factors that should be considered in make-or-buy decisions?

10. In a make-or-buy decision, could some of the fixed costs associated with the "make" option be relevant? Explain.

11. Evaluate the merit of the following statement: "In the long run, the only binding constraint on a firm's output is capital; in the short run, nearly any resource can be a binding constraint."

12. In production decisions that involve the allocation of a single scarce production resource among multiple products, which of the following is relevant?
    a. Sales demand for each product
    b. Sales price of each product
    c. Fixed production costs
    d. Variable selling costs for each product
    e. Variable production costs for each product
    Explain the reasons for your answers.

13. In allocating a scarce production resource in a multiproduct corporation whose goal is to maximize the total corporate contribution margin, why would management not simply produce the product that generates the highest contribution margin per unit?

14. In a multiproduct company, what is meant by the term *sales mix*?

15. What factors are most likely to be manipulated in managerial attempts to change a company's sales mix?

16. How are special prices set and when are they used?

17. In a special order decision, to avoid losing money on the order, the minimum selling price a company should charge is the sum of all the incremental costs of production and sale. Is this a true statement? Discuss the rationale for your answer.

18. In considering a special order that will enable a company to make use of currently idle capacity, which costs are likely to be relevant? Irrelevant?

19. Why does the compensation structure for marketing personnel have a direct affect on the sales mix?

20. Why are some direct fixed costs irrelevant to the decision to eliminate a product line?

21. What is product margin, and how is it related to the decision to keep or eliminate a product line?

22. In the short run, which of the following must be non-negative in order for management to decide to retain a product line and why?
    a. Product line contribution margin
    b. Product line product margin
    c. Product line net income

23. (*Appendix*) Why is linear programming used in business organizations?

24. (*Appendix*) What is the difference between a feasible solution and an optimal solution?

■ EXERCISES

25. (LO 2; *Process further*) The East Europe Petro-Chemical Company uses a production process that generates joint products. The joint costs associated with the process are $30,000.

PRODUCT ID	UNITS OF OUTPUT	SELLING PRICE AT SPLIT-OFF	ADDITIONAL PROCESSING COSTS	FINAL SELLING PRICE
AA	10,000	$1.00	$ .75	$1.50
BB	20,000	$ .50	$1.00	$3.00
CC	500	$ .75	$ .10	$ .90

a. Compute the incremental revenue and incremental costs associated with further processing of each joint product.

b. Compute the incremental profit generated from further processing of each joint product. Which of the joint products should be processed beyond the split-off point?

26. (LO 2; *Process further*) A certain joint process yields two joint products, A and B. The joint cost for June 1996 is $32,000 and the sales value of the output at split-off is $86,000 for product A and $27,000 for product B. Management is trying to decide whether to process its products further. If the products are processed beyond split-off, the final sales value will be $100,000 for product A and $38,000 for product B. The additional costs of processing are expected to be $16,000 for A and $4,000 for B.

a. Should management process the products further? Show computations.

b. Are there any revenues and/or costs that are not relevant to the decision? If so, what are they and why are they not relevant?

27. (LO 3; *Make-or-buy*) The Sole Company manufactures various types of shoes for sports and recreational use. Several types of shoes require a built-in air pump. The company presently makes all of the air pumps it requires for production, however management is evaluating an offer from Air Supply Company to provide air pumps at a cost of $5 each. Sole's management has estimated that the variable production costs of the air pump amount to $3 per unit. The firm also estimates that it could avoid $50,000 per year in fixed costs if it purchased rather than produced the air pumps.

a. If Sole requires 20,000 pumps per year, should it make them or buy them from Air Supply Company?

b. If Sole requires 30,000 pumps per year, should it make them or buy them?

c. Assuming all other factors are equal, at what level of production would Sole be indifferent between making and buying the pumps? Show computations.

28. (LO 3; *Make-or-buy*) The Quarry Corporation needs 100 rock crushers to use in its gravel production plant. An outside vendor has offered to sell the company the required crushers at a price of $4,000 per crusher. If the company does not manufacture the rock crushers, it can manufacture gravel grinders. The manufacture of gravel grinders would produce $6,000 of additional contribution margin.

Costs for Quarry Corporation to manufacture the crushers follow:

	COST TO MANUFACTURE 100 ROCK CRUSHERS
Direct material	$130,000
Direct labor	150,000
Variable overhead	72,000
Fixed overhead ($70,000 allocated and $50,000 direct)	120,000

a. Identify the relevant out-of-pocket costs to produce the rock crushers.
b. Identify any other relevant costs.
c. Should Quarry Corporation make the rock crushers or purchase them? Show computations.

29. (LO 4; *Scarce resource*) Because of a labor strike in the plant of its major competitor, Langtry Tool Co. has found itself operating at peak capacity. The firm makes two electronic woodworking tools: sanders and drills. At this time, the company can sell as many of either product as it can make. The firm's machines can only be run 90,000 hours per month. Data on each product follow:

	SANDERS	DRILLS
Sales	$45	$28
Variable costs	30	19
Contribution margin	$15	$ 9
Machine hours required per unit	8	6

Fixed costs are $110,000 per month.

a. How many of each product should the company make? Explain your answer.
b. How much profit would the company expect to make based on your recommendation in part a?

30. (LO 4; *Scarce resource*) Merry Melodies manufactures holiday bells. The firm produces three types of bells: jingles, jangles, and tingalings. Because of political turmoil in Africa, a critical raw material, bellinium, is in very short supply thus restricting the number of bells the firm can produce. For the coming year, the firm will be able to purchase only 20,000 pounds of bellinium (at a cost of $5 per pound). The firm needs to determine how to allocate the bellinium to maximize profits. The following information has been gathered for your consideration:

	JINGLES	JANGLES	TINGALINGS
Sales demand in units	200,000	300,000	100,000
Sales price per unit	$15.00	$10.00	$4.00
Bellinium cost per unit	6.25	5.00	2.50
Direct labor cost per unit	6.00	3.00	1.00
Variable overhead cost per unit	2.00	1.00	.25

Fixed production costs total $200,000 per year, fixed selling costs are $28,000, and there are no variable selling costs.

a. How should Merry Melodies allocate the bellinium?
b. Based on the optimal allocation, what is the company's projected contribution margin for the coming year?

31. (LO 5; *Sales mix*) Sara's Hound Pound provides two types of services to dog owners: grooming and training. All company personnel can perform either service equally well. To expand sales and market share, Sara's relies heavily on radio

and billboard advertising. For 1997, advertising funding is expected to be very limited. Information on projected operations for 1997 follows:

	GROOMING	TRAINING
Projected billable hours for 1997	10,000	8,000
Revenue per billable hour	$ 15	$ 25
Variable cost of labor	5	10
Material cost per billable hour	1	2
Allocated fixed costs per year	100,000	90,000

a. What is Sara's projected profit or loss for 1997?

b. If $1 spent on advertising could increase either grooming revenue or training revenue by $20, on which service should the advertising dollar be spent?

c. If $1 spent on advertising could increase grooming billable time or training billable time by one hour, on which service should the advertising dollar be spent?

32. (LO 5; *Sales mix*) Among many products made by Diversified Toy Company is a plastic tricycle. The company's projections for this product for 1996 follow:

Projected volume in units	100,000
Sales price per unit	$ 62
Variable production costs per unit	42
Variable selling costs per unit	8
Total fixed production costs	500,000
Total fixed selling and administration costs	200,000

a. Compute the projected profit to be earned on the tricycle during 1996.

b. Corporate management estimates that unit volume could be increased by 15 percent if the sales price were decreased by $4. How would such a change affect the profit level projected in part a?

c. Rather than cutting the sales price, management is considering holding the sales price at the projected level and increasing advertising by $200,000. Such a change would increase expected volume by 20 percent. How would the level of profit under this alternative compare with the profit projected in part a?

33. (LO 5; *Special order*) Ito Company produces a plastic courtroom set that includes a judge's bench, witness stand, jury box, and 25 people. The set is sold to exclusive children's toy stores for $200. Plant capacity is 20,000 sets per year. Production costs are as follows:

Direct materials cost per set	$20
Direct labor cost per set	30
Variable overhead cost per set	40
Variable selling cost per set	10
Fixed overhead cost per year	$1,100,000

A prominent Los Angeles store, which has not previously purchased from Ito Company, has approached the marketing manager about buying 5,000 sets for $170 each. No selling expenses would be incurred on this offer, but the Los Angeles store wants the set to include five plastic briefcases. This request means that Ito Company will incur an additional $2 cost per set. The company is currently selling 18,000 courtroom sets, so acceptance of this job would require the company to reject some of its current business.

a. What is the current operating income of Ito Company?
b. If the company accepted this offer, what would be its operating income? Should the company accept the offer?
c. If Ito Company were currently selling only 10,000 sets per year and wanted to earn $150,000 of income for the year, what selling price would the company have to quote the Los Angeles store?

34. (LO 5; *Special order*) The manufacturing capacity of Giardella Company's plant is 60,000 units of product per year. A summary of operations for the year ended December 31, 1996, is as follows:

Sales (36,000 units at $75 per unit)		$2,700,000
Variable manufacturing costs	$1,440,000	
Variable selling costs	180,000	(1,620,000)
Contribution margin		$1,080,000
Fixed costs		(990,000)
Operating income		$ 90,000

A Puerto Rican distributor has offered to buy 20,000 units at $60 per unit during 1997. Assume all costs (including variable selling expenses) will be at the 1996 level during 1997. If Giardella accepts this offer and also sells as many units to regular customers as it did in 1996, what would be the total operating income for 1997? Normal variable selling costs will be incurred on this and all transactions as a result of a sales contract.

35. (LO 6; *Product line*) Megatalent Marketing is in the business of hiring celebrities and marketing their services. The firm has three operating segments: rock and roll (R & R) entertainment, after-dinner speakers, and political action speakers. Projected income statements for the fourth quarter of this fiscal year follow:

	R & R	AFTER-DINNER	POLITICAL
Sales	$600,000	$250,000	$300,000
Variable costs of professional services	(200,000)	(150,000)	(162,500)
Variable marketing costs	(100,000)	(37,500)	(50,000)
Direct fixed costs	(200,000)	(75,000)	(62,500)
Allocated fixed costs	(30,000)	(15,000)	(15,000)
Net income	$ 70,000	$ (27,500)	$ 10,000

a. Assuming that $35,000 of the direct fixed costs of the After-Dinner segment can be avoided if the segment is eliminated, what would be the effect of its elimination on Megatalent's overall net income?
b. Before the After-Dinner segment is eliminated, what qualitative factors should be considered?

36. (LO 6; *Product line*) The management of Northern Pipe Company is currently contemplating the elimination of one of its products, product B, because this product is now showing a loss. An annual income statement follows:

NORTHERN PIPE COMPANY
INCOME STATEMENT
FOR YEAR ENDED AUGUST 1, 1995
(IN THOUSANDS)

| | Product | | | |
	A	B	C	Total
Sales	$2,200	$1,400	$1,800	$5,400
Variable cost of sales	(1,400)	(800)	(1,080)	(3,280)
Production contribution margin	$ 800	$ 600	$ 720	$2,120
Avoidable fixed and				
variable marketing costs	$ 630	$ 525	$ 520	$1,675
Allocated fixed costs	90	80	105	275
Total fixed costs	$ 720	$ 605	$ 625	$1,950
Operating profit	$ 80	$ (5)	$ 95	$ 170

a. Should the Norhtern Pipe Company management stop sales of product B? Support your answer with appropriate schedules.

b. How would the net income of the company be affected by the decision?

37. (LO 7; *Appendix*) The contribution margins for three different products of a company are $12.50, $9.00, and $7.30. State, in words, the objective function that would communicate a goal of maximizing the company's contribution margin.

38. (LO 7; *Appendix*) The variable costs for four different products are $.56, $.93, $2.12 and $1.98. State, in words, the objective function that would communicate a goal of minimizing the company's variable costs.

■ COMMUNICATION ACTIVITIES

39. (LO 1, 2; *Relevant vs. sunk costs*) Teddy Edwards and his friend Donald Thump visit several Las Vegas casinos over spring break to gamble. Donald disappears for the entire afternoon but returns to the hotel room around dinnertime looking haggard and dejected. Before Teddy gets a chance to speak, Donald says, "Look, pal, I've been shoving quarters in the same slot machine all afternoon. I've invested $300 in this machine, but I've run out of money. Please loan me $50 so I can get back to the casino. I've got that slot primed, and the odds are now in my favor to win a ton of money."

a. Using concepts from this chapter, briefly describe how Teddy could inform his friend that the $300 should simply be forgotten.

b. If Teddy agrees to loan Donald $50, will the odds of winning go up with each additional quarter placed in the slot machine? Explain.

40. (LO 1, 2; *Time and relevant costs*) The following costs are associated with a product line of Lapland Technologies, Inc. The costs reflect capacity-level production of 18,000 units per year.

Variable production costs	$15
Fixed production costs	13
Variable selling costs	22
Fixed selling and administrative costs	31

Prepare a presentation showing how time, relative to the stage of production, affects relevant costs for a product line. Begin with the point in time at which the above product line is in the planning stage. Then show how the set of relevant costs changes (1) after acquisition of the production facilities but before actual production commences and (2) after production is complete.

41. (LO 1, 2; *Relevant costs*) Bobby B. Wise is about to graduate from Private University. He is currently trying to decide whether he should stay at the university and obtain a master's degree or enter the job market with only a bachelor's degree. He has asked for your help and provided you with the following information:

Costs incurred for the bachelor's degree	$48,000
Out-of-pocket costs to get a master's degree	20,000
Estimated starting salary with B.A.	29,500
Estimated starting salary with M.A.	33,000
Estimated time to complete master's degree	2 years
Estimated time from the present to retirement	40 years

Prepare a classroom presentation in which you answer the following questions:

a. Which of the previous factors are relevant in Bobby's decision?
b. What incremental costs must Bobby incur to obtain the master's degree?
c. What is Bobby's best financial alternative?

■ PROBLEMS

42. (LO 2; *Process further*) Stilson, Inc., produces two final products, C and D, from a joint process. Process 1 yields 400 units of intermediate product A and 600 units of intermediate product B. For this yield, a cost of $15,000 is incurred in process 1. The 400 units of product A are then sent to process 2. Joint costs of $16,000 are incurred in process 2 to produce 800 units of product C and 1,200 units of product D. The final sales price for products C and D are, respectively, $10 and $20. Assuming the 400 units of intermediate product A could have been sold for $18,000, should this intermediate product have been processed further? Explain your answer.

43. (LO 2; *Process further*) North American Textiles produces three products (pre-cut fabrics for hats, shirts, and pants) from a joint process. Rather than sell the products at the split-off, the company can complete each product. Information related to these products is shown below:

	HATS	SHIRTS	PANTS	TOTAL
Number of units produced	5,000	8,000	3,000	16,000
Joint cost allocated	$ 56,250	?	?	$180,000
Sales value at split-off point	?	$129,000	$ 40,000	$300,000
Additional costs of processing further	$ 13,000	10,000	$ 39,000	$ 62,000
Sales value after all processing	$150,000	$134,000	$105,000	$389,000

a. As a management accountant, describe the process you may have used to determine the additional costs of processing further.
b. What sales value for hats at the split-off would make the firm indifferent between completing the hats and selling pre-cut fabric for hats?
c. What amount of joint cost allocated to pre-cut shirts would make it economically infeasible to produce them?
d. What is the effect on corporate profit of completing pants rather than selling pre-cut fabric for pants?

44. (LO 3; *Make-or-buy*) The New Visions Lighting Company manufactures various types of household light fixtures. Most of the light fixtures require 60-watt light bulbs. Historically, the company has produced its own light bulbs. The costs to produce a bulb (based on capacity operation of 3,000,000 bulbs per year) are as follows:

Direct materials	$.10
Direct labor	.05
Variable factory overhead	.01
Fixed factory overhead	.03
Total	$.19

The fixed factory overhead includes $60,000 of depreciation on equipment for which there is no alternative use and no external market value. The balance of the fixed factory overhead pertains to the salary of the production supervisor. The production supervisor of the light bulb operation has a lifetime employment contract; she also has skills that could be used to displace another manager (the supervisor of electrical cord production), who draws a salary of $15,000 per year but is due to retire from the company.

The Specific Electric Company has recently approached New Visions with an offer to supply all the light bulbs New Visions requires at a price of $.18 per bulb. Anticipated sales demand for the coming year will require 2,000,000 bulbs.

a. Identify the relevant costs in this make-or-buy decision.
b. What is the total annual advantage or disadvantage (in dollars) of buying, rather than making, the bulbs?
c. What qualitative factors should be taken into account in this make-or-buy decision?
d. As an accountant, how would you obtain information about the employment contracts of factory managers?
e. As the personnel manager, how might you respond to a suggestion by the accounting staff to fire the supervisor of electrical cord production?

45. (LO 3; *Make-or-buy*) Pacific Active Wear is a large clothing manufacturer. Profitability has gone down in the past few years, and after a bitter internal struggle, Petre McIntyre has been appointed the new CEO. McIntyre's opinion is that the company can increase profitability by discontinuing the Distribution Department and hiring a trucking firm to transport the company's products to retail outlets. You have been given the task of determining if she is correct. The following information (given in thousands) is available for the preceding fiscal year:

	MANUFACTURING	PACKAGING	DISTRIBUTION	TOTAL
Salaries and wages	$4,000	$ 500	$1,950	$ 6,450
Material	2,000	750	0	2,750
Office supplies	500	350	350	1,200
Occupancy costs	420	300	300	1,020
Selling and administrative expense	650	310	450	1,410
Depreciation	200	75	90	365
Total	$7,770	$2,285	$3,140	$13,195

Additional information:

- After a detailed review of personnel, management decides it can transfer the distribution supervisor (who earns a salary of $35,000), an assistant distribution supervisor (who earns a salary of $25,000), and six laborers (who earn average wages of $15,000) to the Packaging Department to prepare goods for shipment.

- Owing to more stringent requirements imposed by trucking companies, an additional $100,000 will have to be expended annually for packaging materials.

- The space of the Distribution Department will be required by the Packaging Department for storage of goods prior to shipment.

- The cost of office supplies for the Packaging Department is expected to increase by $50,000.

- Insurance costs included in selling and administrative expenses are expected to decline by $50,000. Other administrative costs are expected to increase, because of the addition of three staff members in Accounts Payable at an annual rate of $12,000 per employee and two people in the Payroll Department at an annual salary of $15,000 each. In addition, management will need to add four clerical positions at an annual rate of $10,000 each.

- A trucking company has offered to provide shipping for $2.5 million annually.

- No equipment in use in the Distribution Department has alternative applications or external market value.

a. Prepare a statement setting forth in comparative form the costs of product distribution under the present arrangement and under the proposed change in operations. Determine the net savings or cost of accepting the proposal.

b. Assuming the company is functionally organized (that is, Manufacturing, Packaging, Distribution, and Marketing currently all have separate managements), what concerns might these managers have in the restructuring that Petre McIntyre should address?

46. (LO 3; *Make-or-buy*) Sportway Inc. is a wholesale distributor supplying moderately priced sporting equipment to large chain stores. About 60 percent of Sportway's products are purchased from other companies while the rest are manufactured by Sportway. The company's Plastics Department currently manufactures molded fishing tackle boxes. Sportway manufactures and sells 8,000 tackle boxes annually, making full use of its direct labor capacity at available work stations. Following are the selling price and costs associated with Sportway's tackle boxes:

Selling price per box		$86.00
Costs per box		
Molded plastic	$ 8.00	
Hinges, latches, handle	9.00	
Direct labor ($15 per hour)	18.75	
Manufacturing overhead	12.50	
Selling and administrative cost	17.00	65.25
Profit per box		$20.75

Sportway believes it could sell 12,000 tackle boxes if it had sufficient manufacturing capacity. The company has looked into the possibility of purchasing the tackle boxes for distribution. Maple Products, a steady supplier of high-quality products, would be able to provide up to 9,000 tackle boxes per year at a price of $68 per box delivered to Sportway's facility.

Bart Johnson, Sportway's product manager, has suggested that the company could make better use of its Plastics Department by manufacturing skateboards. A market report indicates an expanding skateboard market and a need for additional suppliers. Johnson believes that Sportway could sell 17,500 skateboards per year at $45 per skateboard. Manufacturing cost estimates follow:

Selling price per skateboard		$45.00
Costs per skateboard		
Molded plastic	$5.50	
Wheels, hardware	7.00	
Direct labor ($15 per hour)	7.50	
Manufacturing overhead	5.00	
Selling and administrative cost	9.00	34.00
Profit per skateboard		$11.00

In the Plastics Department, Sportway uses direct labor as the application base for manufacturing overhead. This year, the Plastics Department has been allocated $50,000 of factorywide fixed manufacturing overhead. Every unit of product that Sportway sells, whether purchased or manufactured, is allocated $6 of fixed overhead cost for distribution; this amount is included in the selling and administrative cost. Total selling and administrative costs for the purchased tackle boxes would be $10 per unit.

a. Using the data presented, determine which products Sportway, Inc., should manufacture and which it should purchase. Support your answer with appropriate calculations.

b. Assume that Sportway, Inc., used some formal analysis to determine that the potential market for tackle boxes was 12,000 units annually. Describe the process that Sportway, Inc., may have used to estimate potential demand.

(CMA adapted)

47. (LO 4; *Scarce resource*) The Celebrity Bakery produces three types of cakes: birthday, wedding, and special occasion. The cakes are made from scratch and baked in a special cake oven. During the holiday season (roughly November 15 through January 15), total demand for the cakes exceeds the capacity of the cake oven. The cake oven is available for baking 690 hours per month, but because of the size of the cakes, it can bake only one cake at a time. Management must determine how to ration the oven time among the three types of cakes. Information on costs, sales prices, and product demand follows:

	BIRTHDAY CAKES	WEDDING CAKES	SPECIAL OCCASION CAKES
Required minutes of oven time per cake	10	80	18
Sales price	$25	$100	$40
Variable costs:			
Direct material	5	30	10
Direct labor	5	15	8
Variable overhead	2	5	4
Variable selling	3	12	5
Fixed costs (monthly)			
Factory		$1,200	
Selling and administrative		800	

a. If demand is essentially unlimited for all three types of cakes during the holiday season, which cake or cakes should Celebrity bake during the holiday season? Why?

b. Based on your answer in part a, how many cakes of each type will be produced? What is the projected level of monthly profit for the holiday season?

c. If you were the marketing manager for Celebrity, how would your marketing efforts differ between the holiday season and the rest of the year?

48. (LO 4; *Scarce resource*) Jennie has been studying the role of relevance in making decisions. She has decided that she may be able to employ the concepts she has learned to allocate her limited time to review for final exams. Allowing adequate time for meals and rest, she has estimated that she has 34 hours available to review for final exams. As a first step, she has determined that her goal should be to maximize her semester grade point average. Her grade point average is measured on a four-point scale where an A is worth four points, a B is worth three points, a C is worth two points, and a D is worth one point. She is currently enrolled in six courses (each course is worth three semester credit hours). She has estimated, for each course, the review time that she must spend to maintain her existing semester grade (failure to invest this review time will result in her semester grade dropping by one letter) and the total time that she would have to study to actually raise her semester grade by one letter. The following table summarizes her estimates:

COURSE	EXISTING GRADE	REVIEW TIME REQUIRED TO MAINTAIN EXISTING GRADE	TOTAL REVIEW TIME REQUIRED TO RAISE GRADE BY ONE LETTER
Geology	B	4 hours	9 hours
Accounting	C	3 hours	7 hours
Chemistry	B	4 hours	9 hours
Marketing	B	4 hours	10 hours
Spanish	C	5 hours	12 hours
French	A	7 hours	NA

a. Determine how Jennie should allocate the time she spends reviewing for final exams to maximize her grade point average.

b. Based on your solution to part a, what is Jennie's expected grade point average for the semester?

c. What other factors should Jennie consider in deciding how to allocate her time?

49. (LO 5; *Sales mix*) One year ago, Jim Butler gave up his position as the movie critic and sportswriter of the local paper and purchased the rights (under a five-year contract) to sell concessions at a local municipal football stadium. After analyzing the results of his first-year operations, Jim is somewhat disappointed. His two main products are "dogs" and "burgers." He had expected to sell about the same number of each product over the course of the year. However, his sales mix was approximately two-thirds dogs and one-third burgers. Jim feels this combination is less profitable than a balanced mix of dogs and burgers. He is now trying to determine how to improve profitability for the coming year and is considering strategies to improve the sales mix. His first year operations are summarized below:

DOGS

Sales (100,000 @ $1.50)	$150,000	
Less: Direct materials	(40,000)	
Direct labor	(15,000)	
Fixed costs	(45,000)	
Net profit		$ 50,000

BURGERS

Sales (50,000 @ $2.50)	$125,000	
Less: Direct materials	(55,000)	
Direct labor	(10,000)	
Fixed costs	(15,000)	
Net profit		45,000
Total profit		$ 95,000

If Jim takes no action to improve profitability, he expects sales and expenses in the second year to mirror the first-year results. Jim is considering two alternative strategies to boost profitability.

Strategy 1: Add point-of-sale advertising to boost burger sales. The estimated cost per year for such advertising would be $29,000. Jim estimates the advertising would decrease dog sales by 6,000 units and increase burger sales by 22,000 units.

Strategy 2: Provide a sales commission to his employees. The commission would be paid at a rate of 10 percent of the product contribution margin (sales less variable production costs) generated on all sales. Jim estimates this strategy would increase dog sales by 10 percent and burger sales by 25 percent.

a. Determine what action Jim should take: no action, strategy 1, or strategy 2. Show your supporting calculations.
b. Assuming Jim decided to implement either of the new strategies, what behavioral concerns should he be prepared to address? Explain.

50. (LO 5; *Special order*) Jennifer Chaix makes and sells the "Huggable Brown," her famous stuffed puppy for young children. They are sold to department stores for $50. The capacity of the plant is 20,000 Huggables per year. Costs to make and sell each stuffed animal are as follows:

Direct materials	$ 5.50
Direct labor	7.00
Variable overhead	10.00
Fixed overhead	12.00
Variable selling expenses	3.00

An Australian import/export company has approached Jennifer about buying 2,000 Huggables. She is currently making and selling 20,000 Huggables per year. The Australian firm wants its own label attached to each stuffed animal, which will raise costs by $.50 each. No selling expenses would be incurred on this offer. Jennifer feels she must make an extra $1 on each stuffed animal to accept the offer.

a. What is the opportunity cost per unit of selling to the Australian firm?
b. What is the minimum selling price Jennifer should set?

   c. Predict how much more operating profit Jennifer will have if she accepts this offer at the price specified in part b.

   d. Prove your answer to part c by providing operating profits without and with the new offer.

51. (LO 5; *Special order*) LaKisha Jerome makes wax figurines for various holidays to be sold in gift shops. Her selling price is $1.25 each. Her costs are as follows:

Variable production cost per unit	$.45
Fixed production cost per unit	.15

   Jerome pays her salespeople a 10 percent commission on all sales. Other period expenses are all fixed in total at $20,000 per year. A large department store has asked Jerome to bid on providing 1,000 figurines during the Christmas season. She has sufficient unused capacity to fill the order. Jerome's company has already done sufficient business to be profitable for the year prior to the bid request.

   a. What is the lowest bid price that would not result in a loss on this special order?

   b. What price should Jerome bid to make a 10 percent profit on the order?

   c. What price should Jerome bid if she expects the additional 1,000 figurines to also increase fixed expenses by $200 and she wants 5 percent profit on the order?

52. (LO 6; *Product line*) The Aspen Plastic Co. is now considering eliminating one of its existing products (product C) because decreased sales have resulted in the product's generating a loss. The following information is available for a recent operating year:

	A	B	C
Units produced and sold	1,000	1,500	1,000
Sales price per unit	$2.00	$4.00	$2.10
Cost of goods sold:			
Material per unit	.80	2.00	1.05
Labor per unit	.30	.75	.80
Factory overhead per unit	.35	.45	.35
Selling and administrative expenses			
per unit	.15	.30	.20

The following information is also available:

1. If product C were eliminated, the sales of products A and B would remain the same.

2. Variable factory overhead is charged as follows: product A, $.25 per unit; product B, $.35 per unit; product C, $.20 per unit.

3. Variable selling and administrative expenses are charged as follows: product A, $.10 per unit; product B, $.20 per unit; product C, $.15 per unit.

Prepare a schedule to help Aspen Plastic Co. management decide whether to eliminate product C. Give your choice and the reasons for this choice.

53. (LO 6; *Product line*) Bubba's Big Buckle, a western wear store, is considering dropping its line of boots, which is now showing a loss. The firm's accountant raised the issue and submitted the following operating statement, which is typical for recent operations:

	SHIRTS	HATS	BOOTS	TOTAL
Revenue from sales	$110,000	$60,000	$35,000	$205,000
Variable cost of sales				
Raw material	$ 15,000	$22,000	$13,000	$ 50,000
Direct labor	27,000	10,000	10,000	47,000
Factory overhead	13,000	8,500	7,000	28,500
	$ 55,000	$40,500	$30,000	$125,500
Gross margin on sales	$ 55,000	$19,500	$ 5,000	$ 79,500
Selling and				
administrative expense	(30,000)	(9,700)	(8,000)	(47,700)
Operating profit (loss)	$ 25,000	$ 9,800	$(3,000)	$ 31,800

That accountant is no longer employed by the firm, and the management team would like you to advise them on the issue brought to light. You examine the costs and conclude the following:

■ Variable costs include raw material, direct labor, and factory overhead. Variable factory overhead per product line is as follows: shirts, $6,000; hats, $4,250; boots, $3,500; and variable selling and administrative expenses as follows: shirts, $16,000; hats, $5,000; boots, $6,000.

■ Nonvariable costs include $14,750 factory overhead and $20,700 selling and administrative expenses. These costs are allocated to the product lines.

■ No fixed costs are avoidable if the boot line is dropped.

a. Revise the operating statement so that it provides better information for the management team as it decides whether to continue or eliminate its line of western boots. Give your advice on the decision.

b. As a marketing manager, what concerns that would not be obvious to an accountant might you have about eliminating a product line? Explain.

54. (LO 6; *Product line*) The Canadian Paper Company produces three types of consumer products: sticky note pads, tablets, and custom stationery. The firm has become increasingly concerned about the profitability of the custom stationery line. A segmented income statement for the most recent quarter follows:

	STICKY NOTES	TABLETS	CUSTOM STATIONERY
Sales	$800,000	$400,000	$1,000,000
Variable costs:			
Production	(200,000)	(150,000)	(550,000)
Selling	(150,000)	(100,000)	(200,000)
Fixed costs:			
Production	(160,000)	(80,000)	(300,000)
Selling	(200,000)	(60,000)	(180,000)
Net income	$ 90,000	$ 10,000	$(230,000)

Because of the significance of the loss on custom stationery products, the company is considering the elimination of that product line. Of the fixed production costs, $400,000 are allocated to the product lines based on relative sales value; likewise, $250,000 of fixed selling expenses are allocated to the product lines based on relative sales value. All of the other fixed costs charged to each product line are direct and would be eliminated if the product line was dropped.

Recast the income statements in a format more meaningful for deciding whether the custom stationery product line should be eliminated. Based on the new income statements, determine whether any product line should be eliminated and disuss the rationale for your conclusion.

■ CASES

55. (LO 5; *Sales and profit improvement*) Cathy's Classic Clothes is a retail organization that sells upscale clothing to professional women in the Northeast. Each year store managers, in consultation with their supervisors, establish financial goals. Actual performance is captured by a monthly reporting system.

One sales district of the firm, district A, contains three stores. This district has historically been a very poor performer. Consequently, its supervisor has been searching for ways to improve the performance of her three stores. For May, the district supervisor has set performance goals with the managers of stores 1 and 2, who will receive bonuses if certain performance measures are exceeded. The manager of store 3 has decided not to participate in the bonus scheme. Since the district supervisor is unsure what type of bonus will encourage better performance, the manager of store 1 will receive a bonus based on sales in excess of budgeted sales of $570,000, while the manager of store 2 will receive a bonus based on net income in excess of budgeted net income. The company's net income goal for each store is 12 percent of sales. The budgeted sales for store 2 are $530,000.

Other pertinent data for May follow:

- At store 1, sales were 40 percent of total district A sales while sales at store 2 were 35 percent of total district A sales. The cost of goods sold at both stores was 42 percent of sales.

- Variable selling expenses (sales commissions) were 6 percent of sales for all stores and districts.

- Variable administrative expenses were 2.5 percent of sales for all stores and districts.

- Maintenance cost includes janitorial and repair services and is a direct cost for each store. The store manager has complete control over this outlay; however, this cost should not be below 1 percent of sales.

- Advertising is considered a direct cost for each store and is completely under the control of the store manager. Store 1 spent two-thirds of district A's total outlay for advertising, which was 10 times more than store 2 spent on advertising.

- The rental expenses at store 1 are 40 percent of district A's total, while store 2 incurs 30 percent of district A's total.

- District A expenses are allocated to the stores based on sales.

a. Which store, store 1 or store 2, would appear to be generating the most profit under the new bonus scheme?

b. Which store, store 1 or store 2, would appear to be generating the most revenue under the new bonus scheme?

c. Why would store 1 have incentive to spend so much more on advertising than store 2?

d. Which store manager has more incentive to spend money on regular maintenance? Explain.

e. Which bonus scheme appears to offer more incentive to improve the profit performance of the district in the short term? In the long term?

(CMA adapted)

56. (LO 3; *Make-or-buy*) Lansing Manufactured Products makes three products from three different material inputs. A component on the production line is due for replacement. The machine can be produced in-house or purchased from another firm for $1,010,000. The following is the income statement for last year:

Sales	$6,210,000
Cost of goods sold	(5,047,500)
Selling and administrative expense	(270,000)
Operating profit	$ 892,500

Additional information:

■ Plant capacity is 162,500 machine hours.

■ The material inputs (X, Y, and Z) for products A, B, and C are as follows:

	INPUT (IN UNITS)		
PRODUCT	*X*	*Y*	*Z*
A	7	2	5
B	4	6	3
C	5	3	2

■ Variable overhead is based on machine hours used and is applied at the rate of $12 per hour. Machine hours used for product A are 3.75 hours; for product B, 5 hours; and for product C, 1.875 hours.

■ Per unit costs for material inputs are as follows:

INPUT	**INVENTORY COST**	**REPLACEMENT COST**
X	$5	$6
Y	7	7
Z	3	5

■ Present material inventories are: input X, 2,000 units; input Y, 3,000 units; and input Z, 2,000 units.

■ Part Y is a high-technology part and has become obsolete for most uses. However, it is acceptable for making the new machine. Beginning this year, part Y will be replaced by a new part that will cost $7 per unit. The only alternative use for part Y will be to sell it for scrap at $1 per unit.

■ The requirements for the new machine in terms of materials are: part X, 2,000 units; part Y, 2,000 units; and part Z, 1,000 units. In addition, Lansing will need to purchase materials totaling $150,000 to produce the machine.

■ Sales for last year were: product A, 10,000 units; product B, 15,000 units; and product C, 5,000 units.

■ Fixed production costs of $450,000 are allocated based on units produced.

■ Direct labor hours for product A are 3 hours; for product B, 4 hours; and for product C, 2.5 hours.

- Selling and administrative expenses, fixed and variable, are allocated based on units sold. Fixed selling and administrative expenses are $150,000.

- The selling price for product A is $186; for product B, $248; and for product C, $126.

- If Lansing builds the machine rather than buys it, construction will use 30 percent of the machine hour capacity. If building the machine and producing the three existing products exceeds total capacity, production of the product with the lowest contribution margin will be reduced.

- Constructing the machine will require 10,000 direct labor hours.

- Lansing expects unit sales and contribution margins to remain constant throughout the year.

Determine if Lansing Manufactured Products should purchase the new machine or produce it in-house.

57. (LO 5; *Special pricing*) Glover-Casey Ltd. builds custom motor homes, which range in price from $100,000 to $400,000. For the past twenty-five years, the company's owner, Gil Glover, has determined the selling price of each vehicle by estimating the costs of materials, labor, and prorated overhead, and adding 25 percent to these estimated costs. For example, a recent price quotation was determined as follows:

Direct materials	$ 50,000
Direct labor	80,000
Overhead	20,000
Cost	$150,000
Plus 25%	37,500
Selling price	$187,500

Overhead is allocated to all orders at 25 percent of direct labor. The company has traditionally operated at 80 percent of full capacity. Occasionally, a customer would reject a price quote and, if the company were in a slack period, Glover would often be willing to reduce the markup to as little as 10 percent over estimated costs. The average markup for the year is estimated to be 20 percent.

Glover has recently completed a course on pricing with an emphasis on the contribution margin approach to pricing. He thinks that such an approach would be helpful in determining the selling prices of his custom vehicles.

Total overhead, which includes selling and administrative costs for the year, is estimated to be $1,500,000. Of this amount, $900,000 is fixed and the remainder is variable in direct proportion to direct labor.

a. Assume the customer in the example rejected the $187,500 bid and also rejected a $165,000 bid. The customer countered with a $150,000 offer.

    1. What is the difference in net income for the year (assuming no replacement offer) between accepting and rejecting the customer's offer?

    2. What is the minimum selling price Glover could have quoted the customer without reducing or increasing net income for the year?

b. What advantage does the contribution margin approach to pricing have over the approach Glover is currently using?

c. What pitfalls are there, if any, to contribution pricing?

(CMA adapted)

58. (LO 6; *Product line*) Stac Industries is a multiproduct company with several manufacturing plants. The Clinton Plant manufactures and distributes two household cleaning and polishing compounds, regular and heavy duty, under the
Cleen-Brite label. The forecasted operating results for the first six months of
1997, when 100,000 cases of each compound are expected to be manufactured
and sold, are presented in the following statement:

CLEEN-BRITE COMPOUNDS—CLINTON PLANT
FORECASTED RESULTS OF OPERATIONS
FOR THE SIX-MONTH PERIOD ENDING JUNE 30, 1997
(IN THOUSANDS)

	Regular	Heavy Duty	Total
Sales	$2,000	$3,000	$5,000
Cost of sales	(1,600)	(1,900)	(3,500)
Gross profit	$ 400	$1,100	$1,500
Selling and administrative expenses			
Variable	$ 400	$ 700	$1,100
Fixed*	240	360	600
Total selling and administrative expenses	$ 640	$1,060	$1,700
Income (loss) before taxes	$ (240)	$ 40	$ (200)

*The fixed selling and administrative expenses are allocated between the two products on the basis
of dollar sales volume on the internal reports.

The regular compound sold for $20 per case and the heavy-duty compound
sold for $30 per case during the first six months of 1997. The manufacturing
costs by case of product are presented in the following schedule:

COST PER CASE

	Regular	Heavy Duty
Raw materials	$ 7	$ 8
Direct labor	4	4
Variable manufacturing overhead	1	2
Fixed manufacturing overhead*	4	5
Total manufacturing cost	$16	$19
Variable selling and administrative costs	$ 4	$ 7

*Depreciation charges are 50 percent of the fixed manufacturing overhead of each product.

Each product is manufactured on a separate production line. Annual normal
manufacturing capacity is 200,000 cases of each product. However, the plant is
capable of producing 250,000 cases of regular compound and 350,000 cases of
heavy-duty compound annually.

The following schedule reflects the consensus of top management regarding
the price/volume alternatives for the Cleen-Brite products for the last six
months of 1997. These are essentially the same alternatives management had
during the first six months of 1997.

REGULAR COMPOUND		HEAVY-DUTY COMPOUND	
Alternative prices (per case)	Sales volume (in cases)	Alternative prices (per case)	Sales volume (in cases)
$18	120,000	$25	175,000
20	100,000	27	140,000
21	90,000	30	100,000
22	80,000	32	55,000
23	50,000	35	35,000

Top management believes the loss for the first six months reflects a tight profit margin caused by intense competition. Management also believes that many companies will be forced out of this market by next year and profits should improve.

a. What unit selling price should Stac Industries select for each of the Cleen-Brite compounds for the remaining six months of 1997? Support your answer with appropriate calculations.

b. Without considering your answer to part a, assume that the optimum price/volume alternatives for the last six months are a selling price of $23 and volume level of 50,000 cases for the regular compound and a selling price of $35 and volume of 35,000 cases for the heavy-duty compound.

1. Should Stac Industries consider closing down its operations until 1998 to minimize its losses? Support your answer with appropriate calculations.
2. Identify and discuss the qualitative factors that should be considered in deciding whether the Clinton Plant should be closed down during the last six months of 1997. Who would general managers ask for the information necessary to assess these factors?

(CMA adapted)

■ ETHICS AND QUALITY DISCUSSIONS

59. In Japan, the decision to stop production of a product or to close down a plant has different cost consequences than in the United States. One principal difference is that Japanese managers are much less likely to fire workers who are displaced by an event such as a plant closing. Japanese managers simply try to move the displaced workers to active plants. However, this concept of permanent or lifetime employment can be awkward to manage when economic times become difficult and prudent financial management suggests that activities, including employment, be scaled back to cut costs. One Japanese company has found an interesting solution:

Nissan Motor Co., in a sign that its severe slump may be worsening, is taking the unusual step of loaning some of its idle factory workers to a rival auto maker.

Nissan said it will assign 250 of its production employees to work for six months at factories run by Izuzu Motors Ltd., a 37% owned affiliate of General Motors Corp.

Nissan's spokesman, Koji Okuda, called the move an attempt to deal with the company's sharp drop in auto output in Japan. In May, Nissan's Japanese auto production fell 26% from a year earlier. "Demand is low," Mr. Okuda said. "We have to adjust our operations."

[SOURCE: Michael Williams, "Nissan Will Loan Workers to Rival Amid Low Demand," *Wall Street Journal* (June 24, 1994), p. A4. Reprinted by permission of The Wall Street Journal, © 1994 Dow Jones & Company, Inc., All Rights Reserved Worldwide.]

a. What specific types of costs might Nissan have considered relevant in its decision to loan employees to Izuzu?

b. Why would Izuzu be interested in hiring, on a temporary basis, workers of Nissan?

c. What are the likely impacts of this arrangement on the quality of the output at Izuzu? The quality of output at Nissan?

60. *Federal regulators issued a "Special Fraud Alert" to warn health-care providers and patients about aggressive and possibly illegal pharmaceutical industry marketing tactics.*

In one marketing scheme, a drug company pays pharmacies to persuade physicians to change prescriptions from a competing product to its own drug. Miles Inc. is under criminal investigation by the [Inspector General's] office for a program that paid pharmacists to counsel patients about its heart drug, Adalat CC.

In another scheme, dubbed by the inspector general's office as the "frequent flier" scheme, a drug company awards physicians points toward free airline tickets each time physicians complete paperwork saying they had newly prescribed the company's drug. Last year, Ayerst Laboratories Inc. agreed to a settlement in such a program involving some 20,000 physicians. . . . It agreed to pay $830,000 to settle civil and administrative claims.

In the third scheme, a drug company gives physicians substantial payments as a "research grant" for keeping minor records on a prescription drug's usage, the inspector general's office said.

[SOURCE: Elyse Tanouye, "Drug Marketers May Use Illegal Tactics to Sell," *Wall Street Journal* (August 23, 1994), pp. B1, B6. Reprinted by permission of The Wall Street Journal, © 1994 Dow Jones & Company, Inc., All Rights Reserved Worldwide.]

a. Are the ethical considerations in product promotion different for pharmaceutical companies than for typical manufacturing concerns?

b. Is it ethical behavior on the part of physicians to financially benefit from the prescriptions they write? Explain.

c. Would promotion and advertising by pharmaceuticals be more ethically acceptable if they were directed at patients rather than physicians? Explain.

61. Lundy's Computers manufactures computers and all their components. The purchasing agent recently informed the company owner, George Lundy, that another company has offered to supply keyboards for Lundy's computers at prices below the variable costs at which Lundy can make them. Incredulous, Mr. Lundy hired an industrial consultant to explain how the supplier could offer the keyboards at less than Lundy's variable costs.

The consultant explained that she suspected the supplier of using many illegal aliens to work in its plant. These people are poverty stricken and will take such work at substandard wages. The purchasing agent and the plant manager feel that Lundy should buy the keyboards from the supplier, as "no one can blame us for the supplier's hiring practices, and no one will even be able to show that we knew of those practices."

a. What are the ethical issues involved in this case?

b. What are the advantages and disadvantages of buying from this competitor supplier?

c. What do you think Mr. Lundy should do, and why?

■ **PROJECTS**

62. *The Financial Accounting Standards Board is moving to require more companies to break down sales and profit figures by segments, or individual product or business lines,* *in their annual reports. Financial analysts welcome the initiative by the accounting profession's chief rule-making body because it could help investors figure out how companies fare against their competitors. [One analyst responded] "Companies and accountants have been foot-dragging on this for a long time and denying analysts and investors critical financial data to make their stock-market decisions."*

But many companies oppose the change, saying it would be costly to prepare such data and might give away proprietary information to rivals. [One business executive said] "It would be very expensive, require us to redo our entire accounting system and could give away competitive financial information."

[SOURCE: Lee Berton, "FASB Moves to Require Annual Reports to Divide Sales and Profit by Segments," *Wall Street Journal* (July 28, 1994), p. A2. Reprinted by permission of The Wall Street Journal, © 1994 Dow Jones & Company, Inc., All Rights Reserved Worldwide.]

Select two teams to debate the issue of whether firms should be required by the FASB to disclose segment-level data. The debate should center around the issue of whether investors should have the same access as managers to data useful in evaluating the performance of individual business segments. [Hint: You may want to gather some information on the report issued by the Special Committee on Financial Reporting (aka the Jenkins Committee) from the AICPA in answering this question.]

63. One of the indisputable trends of the 1980s and 1990s is the movement of production facilities and production jobs from the United States to third-world nations. One of the most successful American firms, Hewlett-Packard, has established operations in Malaysia. In moving certain operations to Malaysia, Hewlett-Packard obviously expected to cut costs.

The Malaysian scenario has already played out in more advanced Asian countries like Taiwan, and is just starting in less-developed nations such as China and Indonesia. It means that some of America's most skilled workers are likely to face the same punishing competition and wage pressures from abroad now felt by blue-collar workers.

Of course the creation of one professional or skilled job in Malaysia doesn't necessarily subtract one in the U.S. A robust world economy can be a boon all around. Still, the benefits are spread unevenly because of a shift in investment by industrialized nations.

This shift is sending billions of dollars of capital to countries like Malaysia from the U.S. and Japan, fueling the growth of high-paying jobs overseas. U.S. companies have doubled their annual foreign investment over the past four years, to a record $50 billion in 1993, according to the United Nations' World Investment Report.

[SOURCE: G. Pascal Zachary, "High-Tech Firms Shift Some Skilled Work To Asian Countries," *Wall Street Journal* (September 30, 1994), pp. A1, A2. Reprinted by permission of The Wall Street Journal, © 1994 Dow Jones & Company, Inc., All Rights Reserved Worldwide.]

Visit your school library and read articles on the movement of U.S. production facilities to other countries. Write a report summarizing the major causes for such moves and express your opinion about the long-term effects of such moves on the U.S. economy and the global economy.

The following additional references may be used to begin your library research:

- James C. Cooper and Kathleen Madigan, "All that Corporate Cutting Is Giving Consumers the Creeps," *Business Week* (June 9, 1993), pp. 21-22.

- James Alex, "Mexican Labor's Hidden Costs," *Fortune* (October 17, 1994), p. 32.

- Gary S. Becker, "Down and Out All Over Europe: A Lesson for America," *Business Week* (October 4, 1993), p. 18.°

10 MANAGERIAL ASPECTS OF BUDGETING

To prophesy is extremely difficult, especially with respect to the future.

Chinese proverb

LEARNING OBJECTIVES

1. Understand the importance of the budgeting process.

2. Differentiate between strategic and tactical planning and relate these to the budgeting process.

3. Understand the influence of the operating environment on managerial planning.

4. Explain how product life cycle stages affect sales and costs.

5. Compare the advantages and disadvantages of imposed budgets and participatory budgets.

6. Explain how a budget manual facilitates the budgeting process.

7. Understand how the managerial function of control is related to budgeting.

8. Explain why actual revenue from a product differs from budgeted revenue.

9. Recognize why managers should use achievable budget targets.

10. Understand how budgeting in an international context differs from that in a domestic context.

11. (Appendix) Differentiate traditional budgeting from zero-based budgeting.

Minnesota Twins: Uncertain Revenues, Certain Costs Make Budgeting Tough

There's no doubt about it: professional sports teams are big business. In 1993, total revenues (gate receipts as well as media, stadium, licensing, and merchandising revenues) for the 28 major-league baseball teams were approximately $1,774,500,000, with an average of $63.4 million. Naturally, player costs are the highest single expense faced by most sports teams: in baseball, these costs averaged about 56 percent of total revenues. Other expenses (including travel, advertising, media, depreciation, interest, and general and administrative costs) compose approximately another 34 percent of total revenues— meaning that average income per franchise is 10%. But in 1993, 8 of the 28 teams operated at a loss.

In 1993, the operating statistics of the Minnesota Twins were slightly out of line with those of the other franchises. Total revenues were $15 million less than the average and player costs averaged 63 percent of total revenues. Other expenses were "in the ball park" at 35% of total revenues. But these statistics meant that the team was operating very close to a loss position, with an operating income of only $1 million.

In planning for future operations, the Twins' management staff needed to establish strategies on how to sell more tickets and signage, how to increase concession spending by fans, and how to cut costs without reducing either player quality or Metrodome (the home stadium) ambiance. Then, with strategies in place, estimates could be made for numerous categories of revenues and expenses. In baseball, play-date schedules are set mid-year for the following year. This information tells team management the number of home versus away games and the number of games designated for media coverage, so that forecasts can be made about revenues. These budgeted inflows create the starting point for expenses, beginning with what is affordable for player salaries.

While the process sounds fairly easy, budgeting is extremely difficult for a sports team. The financial and management areas of the organization cannot forecast how well or poorly the team will play during the forecast period. Ticket and media revenues depend heavily on winning, but player salaries continue regardless of the win-loss record.

SOURCES: Michael K. Ozanian, "The $11 Billion Pastime," *Financial World* (May 10, 1994), p. 52 (excerpted from Financial World, 1328 Broadway, New York, NY 10001; © copyrighted 1994 by Financial World Partners; all rights reserved.; interview with Kevin Mather, Vice-President of Finance, Minnesota Twins (July 1994).

Planning is the cornerstone of effective management, and one vital part of good planning is budgeting. Owner Carl Pohlad and his management staff at the Twins project future sales and expenditures so that they can use the plans to guide their actions and compare actual performance against the plans—a process of budgetary control. While financial planning is important if future conditions will be roughly the same as current conditions, such planning is critical when conditions are expected to change. The Twins management, for instance, did not make a 1993 decision to add 500 new seats behind home plate hurriedly. The incremental revenues could not be estimated by simply multiplying the additional seats by the ticket price per seat. Some of the seats would be sold to fans who had previously bought tickets in a different part of the stadium and would now move in closer for better seating. The incremental costs that needed to be considered included the costs of moving the dugouts and constructing the seats.

In the same vein, ticket prices cannot be raised simply to cover increases in player salaries. Team managers need to consider the economic climate in the team's primary market (Minnesota, North and South Dakota, and Iowa), the fact that most of the team's 81 home games are not sell-outs, and the fact that the club needs attendance of slightly over 2 million fans per year to break even. A ticket price increase could spell disaster for attendance.

During the planning process, managers attempt to agree on company goals and objectives and how to achieve them. Typically, goals are targets stated in abstract terms, while objectives are quantifiable targets for a specific period of time. Achievement of goals and objectives requires management to undertake complex activities and provide diverse resources. These, in turn, typically demand a formalized planning or budgeting process.

Planning should include qualitative narratives of goals, objectives, and means of accomplishment. However, if plans were *limited* to qualitative narratives, comparing actual results against expectations could involve only generalizations, and trying to measure how well the organization met its specified objectives would be impossible. Therefore, management translates qualitative narratives into a quantitative format, or budget.

The **budget** expresses an organization's self-imposed commitment to planned activities and resource acquisition and use (or deployment). "A budget is more than a forecast. A forecast is a prediction of what may happen and sometimes contains prescriptions for dealing with future events. A budget, on the other hand, involves a commitment to a forecast to make an agreed-on outcome happen."[1]

budget

This chapter discusses the behavioral aspects of budgeting and how budgeting relates to management's planning process. In addition, the sales and cost effects of a product's life cycle are addressed. Revenue variances are illustrated and the relationship between managerial control and the budgeting process is described.

PURPOSES OF BUDGETING

Budgeting is the process of devising a financial plan for future operations. Budgeting is a management task, not an accounting task. The accounting function simply assembles the information provided into a known and consistent format. Budgeting is an important part of an organization's planning and controlling processes; and as indicated in Exhibit 10–1 (page 496), the resulting budgets may serve many different roles.

budgeting

■ LEARNING OBJECTIVE 1
Understand the importance of the budgeting process.

Budgets can be used to indicate direction and priorities; measure individual, divisional, and corporate performance; encourage achievement and continuous improvement efforts; and identify areas of concern. The process itself can be performed in a variety of ways: top-down, bottom-up, or a combination of the two. The basics of the budgeting process are illustrated in the flow diagram in Exhibit 10-2 (page 497); the individual steps are discussed in the remainder of this chapter and in Chapter 11.

Like any other planning activity, budgeting helps managers focus on one direction chosen from many future alternatives. Management generally defines the chosen path using some accounting measure of financial performance, such as net income, earnings per share, or sales level in dollars or units. Such accounting-based measures provide specific quantitative criteria against which future performance (also recorded in accounting terms) can be compared. Budgets, then, are a type of standard, and variances from a budget can be computed.

Budgeting can also help identify potential problems in achieving specified goals and objectives. For example, assume the Minnesota Twins have 1996 objectives of generating $55 million of revenues and $2.5 million of net income. The budget might

[1]Neil C. Churchill, "Budget Choice: Planning vs. Control," *Harvard Business Review* (July-August 1984), p. 150.

■ **EXHIBIT 10–1**
Different Roles of Budgeting Process and Budgets

■ Planning—By linking objectives and resources, budgets serve as primary planning documents and project expected or pro forma results.
■ Motivation—Motivation of workers can be affected by several key elements of both the budgeting process and the budget's content, such as degree of participation and reasonableness of financial goals.
■ Evaluation—Considerable care must be exercised to ensure that performance evaluations are fair and productive; like motivation, this budget role is affected by elements such as degree of participation and reasonableness of financial goals.
■ Coordination—Coordination among the various interest or functional areas in an organization is essential in the budgeting process and budget preparation because of the financial interaction of those areas.
■ Communication—Communication must take place among the various interest or functional areas in an organization if coordination is to occur.
■ Education—Managers and staff will learn from their involvement in the budgeting process. A major educational component can be the discovery of changes in cost structure as cost behavior and cost drivers are analyzed.
■ Ritual—In some organizations, the budgeting process is simply a ritual that occurs periodically, in which all players merely go through the motions. While the ritual aspect creates financial and emotional costs for the participants, it delivers few real benefits.

SOURCE: Adapted from Stephen V. Senge, "A Curricular Model for Short-Term Budgeting," *Accounting Instructor's Report* (Fall 1994), p. 6.

indicate that, based on current ticket prices and player salaries, such a bottom line cannot be obtained. Managers could then brainstorm to find ways to increase revenues or reduce costs so that these objectives can be reached. By quantifying potential difficulties and making them visible, budgets can help stimulate managers to think of ways to overcome those difficulties.

A well-prepared budget can be an effective device to communicate objectives, constraints, and expectations to people throughout an organization. Such communication helps everyone understand exactly what is to be accomplished, how those accomplishments are to be achieved, and how resources are to be allocated. Decisions about resource allocations are made, in part, through a process of obtaining information, justifying requests, and negotiating compromises. Allowing managers to participate in the budgeting process motivates them and instills a feeling of teamwork. Employee participation is needed to effectively integrate necessary information from various sources as well as to obtain individual managerial commitment to the resulting budget.

The budget indicates the resource constraints under which managers must operate for the upcoming budget period. Thus, the budget becomes the basis for controlling activities and resource usage. Periodic budget-to-actual comparisons allow managers to determine how well they are doing and to assess how well they understand their operations.

While budgets are typically expressed in financial terms, the budgeting and planning processes are concerned with all organizational resources—raw materials, inventory, supplies, personnel, and facilities. These processes can be viewed from a long-term or a short-term perspective. Exhibit 10-3 on page 498 provides a checklist for the budgeting process.

■ **EXHIBIT 10–2**

The Budgeting Process

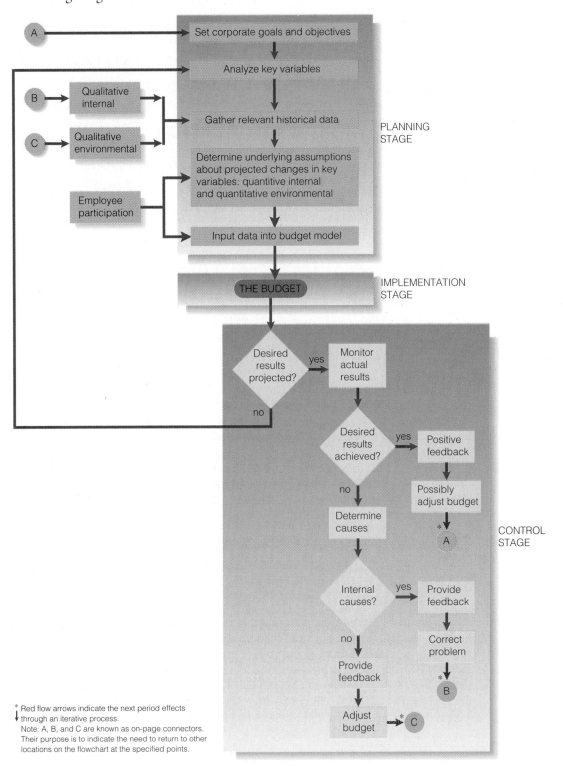

* Red flow arrows indicate the next period effects
↓ through an iterative process.
Note: A, B, and C are known as on-page connectors.
Their purpose is to indicate the need to return to other
locations on the flowchart at the specified points.

■ **EXHIBIT 10–3**
Checklist for a Successful Budgeting Process

Questions to ask about the budgeting process and the budget:

■ Is it realistic, accurate, and internally consistent?
■ Does it plan the best results achievable for the company that are consistent with acceptable risk and long-term health?
■ Does it contain the information most useful for management?
■ Is it consistent with a strategy that reassures employees that the company is moving in a good direction?
■ Does it facilitate goal setting and measurement at all levels?
■ Does it communicate strategy, plans, and required outputs?
■ Does it communicate operating plans, including support needs, across functions?
■ Will it be beaten?
■ Will it be approved?
■ Does it give every [organizational unit] the resources it needs to [accomplish what is needed]?

SOURCE: Robert G. Finney, "Budgeting: From Pain to Power," reprinted, by permission of publisher from *Management Review* (September 1993), p. 28. © 1993, American Management Association, New York. All rights reserved.

STRATEGIC AND TACTICAL PLANNING

strategic planning

■ **LEARNING OBJECTIVE 2**
Differentiate between strategic and tactical planning and relate these to the budgeting process.

When managers devise long-term plans (usually five years or more), they are engaged in **strategic planning**. This process is generally performed only by top-level management with the assistance of several key staff members. Strategic planning should be performed in all organizations, not just profit-making entities, as indicated in the accompanying News Note.

The result of the strategic planning process is a statement of long-range goals for the organization and of the strategies and policies that will help the organization achieve those goals. Strategy can be defined as follows:

Strategy is the art of creating value. It provides the intellectual frameworks, conceptual models, and governing ideas that allow a company's managers to identify opportunities for bringing value to customers and for delivering value at a profit. In this respect, strategy is the way a company defines its business and links together the only two resources that really matter in today's economy: knowledge and relationships or an organization's competencies and its customers.[2]

Expressing long-term goals first requires an acknowledgment of the organization's business. Sometimes, the obvious function is not the true function. For example, the management of the Minnesota Twins does not see its business as baseball; instead, it sees the Twins as part of the entertainment business. The city of Mississauga does not simply want to be a place for people to live and businesses to operate; it wants to be the "municipality of choice in the Greater Toronto Area." Xerox used to be viewed as a copier company; but after going head-to-head with Japanese competitors and los-

---

[2]Richard Normann and Rafael Ramirez, "From Value Chain to Value Constellation: Designing Interactive Strategy," *Harvard Business Review* (July-August 1993), p. 65.

Mississauga Has an Established Commitment to Strategic Planning

Less than 30 years ago, the City of Mississauga (Ontario, Canada) was a series of small communities, each with its own history and personality. Now, it is an urban center of more than 465,000 people.

The city's first official plan was approved in 1981. It set out in broad terms the location of industrial and residential growth, as well as greenbelt areas. The plan was reviewed in 1992 to provide draft guidelines for taking Mississauga to full development during the next 20 to 30 years. This plan defined the city's intention to become a major cultural center and to provide its residents with a broad range of opportunities in the performing and visual arts. The strategic plan also calls for increased naturalization of greenbelt areas to protect wildlife and ecological systems. To guide city staff in day-to-day operations, a management strategy was developed which focuses on a pay-as-you-go philosophy.

Capital and operating budgets are developed collectively by senior management for submission to the council. The team approach helps to balance service priorities—such as roads and transportation—with the cultural and recreational needs of the community. An executive information system developed in 1992 provides an ongoing overview of budgeted versus actual expenditures and revenue, and permits continuous monitoring and fine-tuning during the year. By controlling growth and balancing priorities, the city will be able to achieve its strategic plan without incurring any long-term debt and new initiatives will be developed to ensure that the city is providing the right level of services at acceptable cost.

SOURCE: Adapted from *The Corporation of the City of Mississauga 1992 Annual Report.*

---

ing, it has decided to refocus as a document company. Now, Xerox defines *document* in the broadest possible sense: "a social artifact structured for human comprehension, to facilitate the interpretation of information."[3] The company has chosen a strategy to position itself as a market leader for the near future when analog media (which generally capture information in hard-copy form) are replaced by digital media (which capture information in the 0s and 1s used by computers).

Strategic planning is not concerned with day-to-day operations, although the strategic plan is the foundation on which short-term planning is based. Managers engaging in strategic planning should identify **key variables**, or critical factors believed to be direct causes of the achievement of or failure to achieve organizational goals and objectives. Key variables can be internal or external. Exhibit 10–4 (page 500) provides the results of one study about the external factors considered most critical in determining the strategic plans of manufacturing companies. One conclusion from the study is that a "firm's long-term success is dependent on the integration of the forces in its environment into its own planning process so that the firm influences its own destiny instead of constantly reacting to environmental forces."[4] Internal key variables are under the control of management, while external key variables are normally noncontrollable.

key variables

After the key variables have been identified, information related to them can be gathered and appropriate assumptions about them made. While much of the information will be historical, the assumptions must focus on a vision for the future and

---

[3] Subrata N. Chakravarty, "Back in Focus," *Forbes* (June 6, 1994), p. 74.

[4] James F. Brown, Jr., "How U.S. Firms Conduct Strategic Planning," *Management Accounting* (February 1986), p. 55.

■ **EXHIBIT 10–4**
External Factors to Include in Strategic Plans

Organizational Characteristics

- Market share
- Quality of products
- Discretionary cash flow/gross capital investment

Market & Consumer Behavior

- Market segmentation
- Market size
- New market development
- Buyer loyalty

Industry Stucture

- Rate of technological change in products or processes
- Degrees of product differentiation
- Industry price/cost structure
- Economies of scale

Supplier

- Major changes in availability of raw materials

Social, Economic & Political

- GNP trend
- Interest rates
- Energy availability
- Government established and legally enforceable regulations

SOURCE: James F. Brown, Jr., "How U.S. Firms Conduct Strategic Planning," *Management Accounting* (February 1986), p. 55. Published by Institute of Management Accountants, Montvale, N.J.

on the *next* opportunity for competitive advantage. For instance, in 1987, Commerce Clearing House, with $53 million in earnings, had the third-best return on equity of 22 U.S. publishers. But the company ignored the trend away from print products and mainframe computer operations and, by 1992, showed a $64 million loss. Since then, the company has made a huge shift to electronic publishing in an effort to get its customers back.[5] "Companies that turn out products or services with a traditionally short life cycle—high-tech, retailing, fashion, entertainment—are particularly vulnerable when they fail to detect and bend with shifting consumer winds."[6]

tactical planning

   The process of determining the specific objectives and means by which strategic plans will be achieved is called **tactical** (or operational) **planning**. Although some tactical plans, such as corporate policy statements, exist for the long term and address repetitive situations, most tactical plans are short-term (one to eighteen months). Such short-term tactical plans are considered "single-use" plans and are developed to address a given set of circumstances or for a specific time frame.

   The annual budget is an example of a single use tactical plan. While a budget covers a twelve-month period, intermediate (quarterly and monthly) plans should also be included for the budget to work effectively. A well-prepared budget "translates the

[5]Patty de Llosa, "The Vision Thing," *Fortune* (November 14, 1994), p. 60.
[6]Kenneth Labich, "Why Companies Fail," *Fortune* (November 14, 1994), p. 64.

strategic plans of the organization and [its] implementation programs into period-oriented operational guides to company activities."[7] Exhibit 10–5 illustrates the relationships among strategic planning, tactical planning, and budgeting.

Both strategic and tactical planning require that information regarding the economy, technological developments, and available resources be incorporated into the setting of goals and objectives. In addition, two other important factors—the operating environment and the life cycle stages of the company's products—are of concern in the budgeting process.

OPERATING ENVIRONMENT

The operating environment of a firm consists of the market structure in which it exists, the government regulations under which it must act, and the influence of the laws of supply and demand.

Market Structure

The market structure in which a firm operates and the degree of competition it faces have significant impacts on that firm's ability to set strategic and tactical plans. There are four basic market structures: pure competition, monopolistic competition, monopoly, and oligopoly.

When **pure competition** exists, there are many firms, all with small market shares and all producing identical products. Market share may switch from one firm to another over time, but rarely will any firm be able to achieve a major market share

■ **LEARNING OBJECTIVE 3**
Understand the influence of the operating environment on managerial planning.

pure competition

■ **EXHIBIT 10–5**
Relationships Among Planning Processes

WHO?	WHAT?	HOW?	WHY?
Top management	Strategic planning	Statement of organizational mission, goals, and strategies; long range (5 years or more)	Establish a long-range vision of the organization and provide a sense of unity and commitment to specified purposes
Top and middle management	Tactical planning	Statement of organizational objectives and operational plans; short range (less than 18 months)	Provide direction for the achievement of strategic plans; state strategic plans in terms that can be acted on; furnish a basis against which results can be measured
Top, middle, and operational management	Budgeting	Quantitative and monetary statements that coordinate company activities for periods of 12 months or less	Allocate resources effectively and efficiently; indicate a commitment to objectives; provide a monetary control device

---

[7]Churchill, "Budget Choice," p. 151.

and sustain it for long periods. Thus, from the standpoint of strategy, maintenance of market share is a reasonable goal. In this situation, firms are aware that product prices are set by the interaction of market demand for and supply of the product, rather than by any individual firm.

monopolistic competition

When many firms offer slightly differentiated products and services, there is **monopolistic competition**. Since product differentiation is crucial, monopolistically competitive firms use advertising to create brand loyalty and consumer recognition. In such an environment, firms attempt to engage in strategies to build additional market share and, because the products and services differ, to have purchasers pay a premium price for products.

monopoly

A **monopoly** exists when there is only one seller of a product or provider of a service. The monopolistic firm has total control over its products, setting both market price and output level to maximize its profit. In the United States, federal antitrust laws restrict most monopolies; those that are allowed to exist are regulated and their prices controlled by various levels of government.

oligopoly

In an **oligopoly**, there are only a few firms, whose products and services may be differentiated or standardized. If the goods can be differentiated (such as spaghetti sauce or airline flights), oligopolistic firms spend large sums of money on advertising and product development to build market share. Because firms are interdependent, prices tend to be rigid, and price leadership is typical. Once price changes are announced by a dominant firm, others in the industry typically match the announced price. Price decreases are almost always matched immediately; occasionally, price increases are not followed, and the announcing firm is forced to return prices to previous levels to maintain market share.

At one time, most domestic companies were concerned only with competing within national boundaries. With the world becoming more accessible politically, economically, and technologically for international trade, domestic companies face new strategic opportunities and greater competitive pressures. The new opportunities involve access to more markets with vast numbers of new customers. The pressures come from the need to at least meet the selling prices charged and quality provided by international competitors, as well as from the greater risks involved in becoming equipped to sell effectively in global markets.

Government Regulations

Companies are also subject to domestic government regulations. These regulations generally seek to maintain a market environment in which healthy competitive forces supply consumers with the best-quality products at the lowest prices and afford providers a viable business community in which to succeed. Regulatory agencies monitor various business practices on a fairly continuous basis to detect activities believed to be detrimental to healthy commerce. Some of the U.S. laws affecting businesses are given in Exhibit 10-6. Each of these laws can affect an organization's business strategy in matters such as how it may legally obtain new business or reduce costs. There are also numerous international laws and treaties aimed at governing global operating activities.

Laws of Supply and Demand

Because consumer preferences are extremely important in determining what an organization sells, company management needs to engage in market research. Such research is designed to determine the factors that influence purchasers' rationales for buying certain products or services. Customers may buy for many reasons including

■ **EXHIBIT 10–6**

Some U.S. Laws Affecting the Business Operating Environment

- ■ **Sherman** (1890), **Clayton** (1914), **and Federal Trade Commission** (1914) **Acts**—designed to eliminate unfair trade practices, including antitrust activities, price discrimination (charging different prices for the same product to different groups of buyers when those prices do not reflect cost differences), and deceptive acts or practices in business
- ■ **Foreign Corrupt Practices Act** (1977)—enacted to prevent companies and individuals within companies from offering or giving bribes (directly or indirectly) to foreign officials to influence those individuals (or to cause them to use their influence) to obtain or retain business; excludes "grease" (or facilitating) payments to minor employees (such as payments made to customs officials to expedite the rapid processing of the goods on the dock)
- ■ **Occupational Safety and Health Act** (1970)—designed to protect the health and safety of employees while they are on the job; places on companies the duty to provide safe working conditions and requires that the workplace be free from recognized hazards that could cause death or serious injury to workers
- ■ **Civil Rights Act of 1964**—the cornerstone of laws preventing discrimination in employment on a variety of bases; makes it illegal to discriminate on the basis of race, religion, color, creed, sex, or national origin
- ■ **Equal Pay Act** (1963), **Pregnancy Discrimination Act** (1978), **and Age Discrimination in Employment Act** (1967)— designed to eliminate discrimination related to gender, discrimination against women of childbearing years, and discrimination against persons over 40 years old
- ■ **Consumer Product Safety Act** (1972)—designed to make manufacturers design and build safer products
- ■ **National Environmental Policy Act** (1970), **Clean Air** (1970) **and Water** (1972) **Acts, Nuclear Waste Policy Act** (1982), **and Endangered Species Act** (1973) (to list a few)—designed to address a variety of environmental problems

the features, quality, and reliability of the product, the service the company provides, and the company's ethical reputation. Most consumers, however, must also consider price in making a purchase, because they are trying to make efficient use of their scarce resources. If they think a product is priced too high, they will seek similar products at lower prices. If they don't find these, they may then seek alternatives.

It is to be expected that the volume of some products and services will react differently from others to a change in sales price. For any good or service, **price elasticity of demand** is a measure of the sensitivity of the sales volume to a change in unit price. It is computed as either the actual or expected percentage change in quantity demanded divided by the percentage change in price. A value of 0 reflects complete inelasticity or insensitivity of demand to a change in sales price. The closer the elasticity value is to 0, the more inelastic is the demand. Alternatively, products or services for which the elasticity measure exceeds 1 are regarded as having high price elasticity of demand. In such cases, a given percentage change in price yields an even larger percentage change in volume. Thus, a decrease in price will cause an increase in total revenues because the increase in volume will offset the unit price effect. Alternatively, a price increase will cause a decrease in total revenues because the decrease in volume will overwhelm the unit price effect. For all products, the price elasticity of demand depends on the existing price-to-volume relationship. As price changes are implemented, the price elasticity of demand moves to a new level; thus, computations are valid only for a given price-to-volume relationship.

price elasticity of demand

When product demand exceeds product supply, both buyers and sellers will bid the price up. In addition, the higher price often stimulates greater production, which in turn increases supply (unless production is constrained by cost factors). When demand is less than supply, buyers and sellers will bid the price down. This lower price should motivate lower production, which lowers supply. Therefore, price is consistently and circularly influenced by the relationship of supply to demand. As supply increases or decreases because of changing demands and demand increases or decreases because of changing prices, supply and demand reach a point at which they are equal. At this point, price will stabilize as long as other factors (such as new technology and changing consumer incomes) do not intervene. Companies attempting to engage in either strategic or tactical planning must be aware of the relationships of supply and demand as well as how those relationships are affected over a product's life cycle.

PRODUCT LIFE CYCLE

■ **LEARNING OBJECTIVE 4**
Explain how product life cycle stages affect sales and costs.

Products and services, like people, go through a series of life cycle stages. It is not easy to determine how "old" a product must be before it moves from one stage to another. Some products, such as Cabbage Patch dolls, come and go fairly quickly; others, such as Kool-Aid and Jell-O, have been changed minimally and manage to remain in the forefront of purchasing habits. Still other products (such as hula hoops and miniskirts) have been revitalized and have "come back from the dead" with renewed vigor. Services, too, change over time. For instance, 20 years ago, personal shopping and home health care services were in their infancy, and long-distance bus service was beginning to decline in importance. It is difficult, if not impossible, to predict what services will be available in 2010.

The stages of the product life cycle are development, introduction, growth, maturity, and harvest; relative sales levels for these stages are shown in Exhibit 10-7. Companies must be aware of the life cycle stage at which each of their products have arrived, because the stage may have a tremendous impact on costs, sales, and pricing strategies.

During the development stage, costs are high, but there are no corresponding offsetting revenues. High costs are also incurred during the introduction stage, but sales are just beginning; therefore, profits are still nonexistent or very limited. Unit costs tend to level off during the remaining three stages as cost standards are stabilized and production becomes routine. Total sales increase through growth, level off in maturity, and then decline during the harvest stage.

■ **EXHIBIT 10–7**
Product Life-Cycle

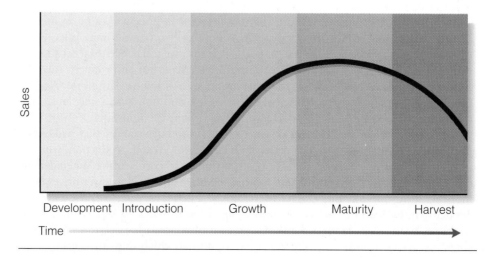

Development Stage

Once a product idea has been formulated, the market is researched to determine the features customers desire. As discussed in Chapter 6, it is at this time that target costing is useful. Engineers, designers, and suppliers should discuss the production process and the types of components to be used. It is often helpful to have suppliers participate in the design phase. Alternatively, the company can provide product specifications to the supplier, who can then draft a design for approval. At some companies in Japan, the research staffs of companies and their suppliers periodically hold joint meetings "to integrate the research and development efforts of the two groups, allow suppliers to provide inputs much earlier in the design process, and help ensure that target cost negotiations are more substantive."[8] Development should include a forecast of the selling price that the market will bear. Knowing this forecast allows managers to determine a target production cost.

If products are designed properly, they should require only a minimal number of engineering changes after being released to production. Each time an engineering change is made, one or more of the following problems occurs and creates additional costs: the operations flow document must be reprinted; workers must relearn tasks; machine dies or setups must be changed; and parts currently ordered or in stock may be made obsolete. As indicated in Exhibit 10–8 (page 506), if costs and time to market are not to be affected significantly, any design changes must be made early in the process.

Products need to be designed to use the fewest number of parts, and parts should be standardized to the greatest extent possible. Consumers may appreciate some degree of variety, but a company can end up with too much of a good thing; for example, "at one point, Nissan had 300 different ashtrays in its cars."[9] Changes can be made after original design, but any cost savings generated by such changes will be substantially less than if the changes had been made early in the design/development process.

Decisions made during the design stage are particularly important. They can affect product sales, design, costs, and quality for the remainder of the product's life cycle. Most studies have indicated that about 80 to 90 percent of a product's life cycle cost is determined by decisions made before production ever begins.

Introduction Stage

Product introduction is essentially a start-up phase. Sales are usually quite low, and selling prices often are set according to the market price of similar **substitute goods** or services, if such goods or services are available. Costs, however, can be quite substantial in the introduction phase. For example, in a 1990 survey, a grocery industry task force determined that on average, "manufacturers paid $5.1 million to get a new product or line extension on grocery store shelves nationwide. The cheapest [product introduction] studied cost $378,000; the most expensive, $21.2 million."[10] Costs incurred during this phase are typically related to product design, market research, advertising, and promotion.

substitute goods

---

[8]Robin Cooper, "Komatsu, Ltd. (A)," *Harvard Business School Case* No. 194-037, p. 3.

[9]Jacob M. Schlesinger, Michael Williams, and Craig Forman, "Japan Inc., Wracked by Recession, Takes Stock of Its Methods," *Wall Street Journal* (September 29, 1993), p. A4.

[10]Richard Gibson, "Marketing—Pinning Down Costs of Product Introductions," *Wall Street Journal* (November 26, 1990), p. B1.

■ **EXHIBIT 10–8**
Design Change Effects on Cost and Time to Market

IMPACT ON

If design changes are made:	ADDITIONAL COST	TIME TO MARKET
DURING DESIGN STAGE	Negligible	Negligible
DURING PROCESS PLANNING	Adds 50%	Adds 25%
DURING PRODUCTION	Adds 100%	Adds 100%

SOURCE: Industry reports; illustrated in "Moving Past the Assembly Line," by Otis Port, reprinted from *Business Week/Reinventing America 1992*, p. 180, by special permission, copyright © 1992 by McGraw-Hill, Inc.

Growth, Maturity, and Harvest Stages

The growth stage begins when the product first breaks even. During the growth stage, the product has been accepted by the market, and profits begin to rise. Product quality also may improve during this stage because competitors may have improved on original production designs. Prices are fairly stable during this period because many substitutes exist or because consumers have become "attached" to the product and are willing to pay a particular price for it rather than buy a substitute.

In the maturity stage, sales begin to stabilize or slowly decline, and firms often compete on the basis of selling price. Costs are often at their lowest level during this period, so profits may be high. Mattel's Barbie doll is in its maturity stage. Some products, like this one, seem to remain at this stage virtually forever.

The harvest (decline) stage reflects waning sales. For example, the Barney dinosaur product line grew and declined fairly quickly; Hasbro, the largest Barney licensee, had

Life Cycle Stage of Product Affects Budgeting Process

A product life cycle budgeting system improves the traditional process because the assumptions used in any budgeting system should depend on a product's life cycle stage—start-up, growth, maturity, or harvest. Most managers, however, budget as if all products were always in the maturity stage.

Budgeting has three main functions: planning, control, and motivation. For planning purposes, managers want the most realistic outcome. For motivational purposes, managers want the budget to be difficult yet attainable. For control purposes, a manager wants a budget to be the optimal one.

In the start-up and growth stages, planning is the most important budgetary function. Control ranks second. Motivation is the least important budget function during these stages because, for the product to survive, employees must be internally motivated.

Planning remains the most important function during product maturity, but motivation replaces control in second place. As the product matures, the process becomes standardized. Therefore, employees need more motivation because their job tasks do not provide it. The controls should have been formalized by this stage or the product probably would not have made it this far.

In the harvest stage, motivation is the most important function. The product is dying, so employees are shifted around or terminated. Employees, then, need a reason to keep on producing. Planning is now in second place but continues to be important. If the product is canceled too soon, the company loses potential future revenue. If the product is canceled too late, extra expenses are incurred for producing, storing, and disposing of obsolete goods. Control is basically unimportant at this point because there is now a relatively small product investment.

Managers who understand which function is most important to budgetary success in a particular stage can allocate company resources more efficiently.

SOURCE: Adapted from Alan B. Czyzewski and Rita P. Hull, "Improving Profitability with Life Cycle Costing," *Journal of Cost Management* (Summer 1991), p. 20ff. Reprinted with permission from the Journal of Cost Management for the Manufacturing Industry, © 1991, Warren, Gorham & Lamont, 31 St. James Avenue, Boston, Ma 02116. All rights reserved.

$130 million of Barney sales in 1993 and only $30 million in 1994.[11] During the decline stage, prices are often cut dramatically to stimulate business.

Cost and Price Changes Over Life

Customers are concerned with obtaining a high-quality product or service for a price they perceive to be reasonable. Product prices change, however, over the product life cycle. Producers of goods and providers of service should be concerned with maximizing profits over a product's or service's life cycle because, to be profitable, the product or service must generate revenues in excess of its total (not period) costs.

As indicated in the accompanying News Note, each stage of the product life cycle requires a different budgetary focus. Then, as activity takes place and plans are implemented, a monitoring system needs to be in place to provide feedback so that the control function can be operationalized.

---

[11]Harry Berkowitz, "Barney Ads Go Straight to Parents," *[New Orleans] Times-Picayune* (November 20, 1994), p. F–2.

PARTICIPATION IN BUDGETING

Once management has evaluated the operating environment and relevant product life cycles and decided on the organization's strategic plan, budgeting activity should begin for future periods. The budgeting process requires carefully integrating a complex set of facts and projections with human relationships and attitudes. Most budgeting literature notes that an "appropriate" budgeting system (including development, implementation, and control) can only be defined within the context of a specific organization's structure, goals and objectives, management leadership style, and employee attitudes.[12] In other words, no single system of budgeting is right for all organizations. However, it is recognized that there are two primary ways by which budgets can be derived: from the top down (imposed budgets) or from the bottom up (participatory budgets).

For decades, budgets in governmental and not-for-profit organizations, such as the city of Mississauga, have had the primary goals of monetary control and fiscal responsibility. Business budgets originally maintained the same focus and were prepared by top management with little or no input from operating personnel. Such **imposed budgets** were simply provided by managment to the operating personnel, who had to work within the budgeted figures and constraints. In such a budgeting environment, operating personnel may be given an opportunity to suggest changes to the budget, but such suggestions are not always seriously considered. As indicated in Exhibit 10–9, imposed budgets are effective and provide some distinct benefits under certain circumstances; but they involve disadvantages as well.

imposed budgets

Businesspeople soon recognized the disadvantages of imposed budgets and the dissatisfaction they caused. Thus, participation at various management levels was introduced. From the standpoint of operational managers, participation can be viewed on a spectrum. At one end is the right to comment on budgets before their implementation; at the other, the ultimate right to set budgets. Neither end of the spectrum is quite appropriate. Simply giving managers the right to comment on the handed-down budget still reflects an imposed budgeting system, while giving each individual manager the right to set his or her own budget ignores the fact that cooperation and communication among areas are essential to the functioning of a cohesive organization.

participatory budget

A **participatory budget** is generally defined as one that has been developed through a process of joint decision making by top management and operating personnel. The degree to which lower-level operating management is allowed to participate in budget development usually depends on two factors: top management's awareness of the advantages of the participation process and its confidence in those advantages. Both the advantages and disadvantages of participatory budgets are listed in Exhibit 10–10 (page 510).

budget slack

Managers may introduce **budget slack** (the intentional underestimation of revenues and/or overestimation of expenses) into the budgeting process. Slack, if it exists, is usually built into the budget during the participation process; it is not often found in imposed budgets. Having slack in the budget allows subordinate managers to achieve their objectives with less effort than if there were no slack. Budget slack

---

[12]Mary T. Soulier, "A Psychological Model of the Budgetary Process," *The Woman CPA* (January 1980), p. 3.

creates problems because of the significant interaction of budgeting factors. If sales are understated, for example, problems can arise in the production, purchasing, and personnel areas.

To reduce the possibility of slack, management may wish to consider basing the budget on activities rather than costs. Activity-based budgets require an analysis of cost drivers and a mapping of budget line items to activities performed. Activity-based budgets, as discussed in the News Note on page 511, allow the following questions to be answered:

- How well do the processes and activities each unit performs conform to its mission?
- Could resources devoted to low-value processes or activities be scaled back or eliminated?
- Can the company reduce costs by reengineering processes or activities?
- Could some activities be performed more effectively or efficiently outside the company?[13]

Since the functions of operating personnel are affected by the budget and these individuals must work under the budget guidelines, input from the operating level is often invaluable in the planning process. While there is no concrete evidence as to

---

■ EXHIBIT 10–9
Imposed Budgets

BEST TIMES TO USE

- In start-up organizations
- In extremely small businesses
- In times of economic crisis
- When operating managers lack budgetary skills or perspective
- When organizational units require precise coordination of efforts

ADVANTAGES OF IMPOSED BUDGETS

- Increase probability that organization's strategic plans will be incorporated in planned activities
- Enhance coordination among divisional plans and objectives
- Use top management's knowledge of overall resource availability
- Reduce the possibility of input from inexperienced or uninformed lower-level employees
- Reduce the time frame for the budgeting process

DISADVANTAGES OF IMPOSED BUDGETS

- May result in dissatisfaction, defensiveness, and low morale among individuals who must work under the budget
- Reduce the feeling of teamwork
- May limit the acceptance of the stated goals and objectives
- Limit the communication process among employees and management
- May create a view of the budget as a punitive device
- May result in unachievable budgets for international divisions if local operating and political environments are not adequately considered
- May stifle the initiative of lower-level managers

---

[13]Jeffrey A. Schmidt, "Is It Time to Replace Traditional Budgeting?" *Journal of Accountancy* (October 1992), p. 105.

■ **EXHIBIT 10–10**
Participatory Budgets

BEST TIMES TO USE

- In well-established organizations
- In extremely large businesses
- In times of economic affluence
- When operating managers have strong budgetary skills and perspectives
- When organizational units are quite autonomous

ADVANTAGES OF PARTICIPATORY BUDGETS

- Provide information from persons most familiar with the needs and constraints of organizational units
- Integrate knowledge that is diffused among various levels of management
- Lead to better morale and higher motivation
- Provide a means to develop fiscal responsibility and budgetary skills of employees
- Develop a high degree of acceptance of and commitment to organizational goals and objectives by operating management
- Are generally more realistic
- Allow organizational units to coordinate with one another
- Allow subordinate managers to develop operational plans that conform to organizational goals and objectives
- Include specific resource requirements
- Blend overview of top management with operating details
- Provide a social contract that expresses expectations of top management and subordinates

DISADVANTAGES OF PARTICIPATORY BUDGETS

- Require significantly more time
- May find that the effects of managerial participation are negated by top-management changes, creating a level of dissatisfaction with the process approximately equal to that occurring under imposed budgets
- May result in ambivalent or unqualified managers participating in the process and creating an unachievable budget
- May cause managers to introduce slack into the budget
- May support "empire building" by subordinates
- May require the budgeting process to begin earlier in the year when there is more uncertainty about the future year

how well participatory budgeting works in all circumstances, such participation by operating managers also seems to create a higher commitment to the budget's success. Additionally,

> [t]he more that a budgetary system can be used to encourage the flow of relevant information to decision makers, the greater is the system's ability to diminish uncertainty. Should participation release more information to the budget planner, then the uncertainty surrounding their projections will be diminished and their plans will be based more upon informed, rational judgments and less upon guesswork.[14]

---

[14]Lee D. Parker, "Participation in Budget Planning: The Prospects Surveyed," *Accounting and Business Research* (Spring 1979), pp. 123–37.

Activity-Based Budgeting Focuses on Work, Not Costs

A budget should be based on knowledge of how good the organization can be and should be. Developing an achievable budget is often difficult because most managers develop a budget on what they spend, not on what they do (activities) that consumes the budgeted costs.

Many organizations, such as Johnson & Johnson and Chrysler Corporation, are looking to their existing activity-based cost systems as the basis for reengineering their budgeting process. Unlike conventional budgeting that focuses on resource cost, the reengineered budget process should assume that the focus will center on activities and business processes. Activity-based budgeting (ABB) is a process of planning and controlling the expected activities of an organization. ABB links work (activity) with the strategic cost, time and quality objectives of the organization. ABB focuses on activities. Costs are determined after the activity workload is defined.

The following list compares traditional and activity-based budgeting:

TOP 10 WEAKNESSES OF TRADITIONAL BUDGETING	VS.	TOP 10 ADVANTAGES OF ACTIVITY-BASED BUDGETING
1. Does not provide a common language that supports common sense.		1. Uses a common (verb + noun) activity language.
2. Focuses on costs, not quality or time.		2. Focuses on activity cost, time, and quality.
3. Focuses on input (costs), not output.		3. Focuses on activity input and output.
4. Does not link to the strategic plan.		4. Strategic goals are linked to the activity's cost, time, and quality.
5. Does not identify levels of service.		5. Focuses on required versus discretionary activity output.
6. Does not identify root causes of costs.		6. Aids in identifying the cost drivers of activities and processes.
7. Focuses on functions, not processes.		7. Focuses on functional activities and business processes.
8. Focuses on cuts, not continuous improvement.		8. Focuses on the unending improvement of activity output.
9. Does not identify work or workload.		9. Focuses on activity and output.
10. Does not identify or quantify waste.		10. Quantifies non-value-added activity costs.

SOURCE: Tom Pryor, "The Budget Is Not the Best You Can Be," *Focus on ABM* (Winter 1993), pp. 1–2.

Thus, the budgeting process represents a continuum with imposed budgets on one end and participatory budgets on the other. Currently, most business budgets are prepared through a coordinated effort including input from operating personnel and revision by top management. In this manner, plans of managers at all levels can be considered. Top management first sets strategic objectives for lower-level management; then lower-level managers suggest and justify their operations' performance targets. Upper-level managers combine all component budgets, evaluate the overall results, and provide feedback on any needed changes to the lower-level managers.

Regardless of whether the process is top-down or bottom-up, management must review the completed budget before approving and implementing it. This process is necessary to determine (1) if the underlying assumptions on which the budget is based are reasonable and (2) if the budgeted results are acceptable and realistic. The budget may indicate that the results expected from the planned activities do not achieve the desired objectives. In this case, planned activities should be reconsidered and revised to more appropriately aim the company toward the desired outcomes expressed during the tactical planning stage (assuming they are not overly ambitious).

THE BUDGETING PROCESS

The budget is normally prepared on an annual basis and detailed first by quarters and, then, by months within those quarters. At a *minimum*, budget preparation should begin two to three months before the period to be covered, but management must keep two things in mind: (1) participatory budget development will take longer than an imposed budget process and (2) the larger and more complex the company is, the longer the budgeting process will take.

The evolution of electronic spreadsheets has dramatically affected the budgeting process. Computerized spreadsheets allow companies to quickly and inexpensively examine "what if" scenarios and adjust interrelated budgets to reflect environmental or internal changes. These spreadsheets are also helpful to a company's ability to maintain a continuous budget. Once the set of budget headings, budget formulas, and current twelve months of budget figures have been tested and entered on a spreadsheet, each new month's figures can be developed as the month just concluded is deleted.

continuous budget

Some companies use a **continuous** (or rolling) **budget,** an ongoing twelve-month budget that adds a new budget month (twelve months into the future) as each current month expires. As shown in Exhibit 10–11, at any point, management is working within the present one-month component of a full twelve-month annual budget. Continuous budgets make the planning process less sporadic and disruptive. Rather than "going into the budgeting period" at a specific point in time, managers are continuously involved in planning and budgeting. Continuous budgets also provide a

Working under imposed budgets is similar to living under a dictator. Lower level managers have no opportunity to integrate their experience and knowledge of conditions into the budget whose objectives those managers are expected to achieve.

longer-range focus, so that no surprises occur at year-end. Surprises within the budgeting process can also be minimized through the use of a detailed budget manual.

A good budget requires a substantial amount of time and effort from the persons engaged in preparing it. This process can be improved by the availability of an organizational **budget manual**, a detailed set of documents that provide information and guidelines about the budgetary process. The manual should include the following:

budget manual

■ LEARNING OBJECTIVE 6
Explain how a budget manual facilitates the budgeting process.

1. Statements of the budgeting purpose and its desired results,
2. A listing of specific budgetary activities to be performed,
3. A calendar of scheduled budgetary activities,
4. Sample budget forms, and
5. Original, revised, and approved budgets.

The *statements of budgeting purpose and desired results* communicate the reasons behind the process and should flow from general statements to specific details. An example of a general statement of budgeting purpose is: "The cash budget provides a basis for planning, reviewing, and controlling cash flows from and for various activities; this budget is essential to the preparation of a pro forma Statement of Cash Flows." Specific statements regarding the cash budget could include references to minimum desired cash balances and periods of high cash needs. These needs are taken into consideration when the cash budget portion of the total budget is prepared.

Budgetary activities should be listed by job rather than by a person's name because the responsibility for actions should be delegated to whomever is holding each specific job when the manual is implemented. This section should indicate who has the

■ EXHIBIT 10–11
Continuous Budget

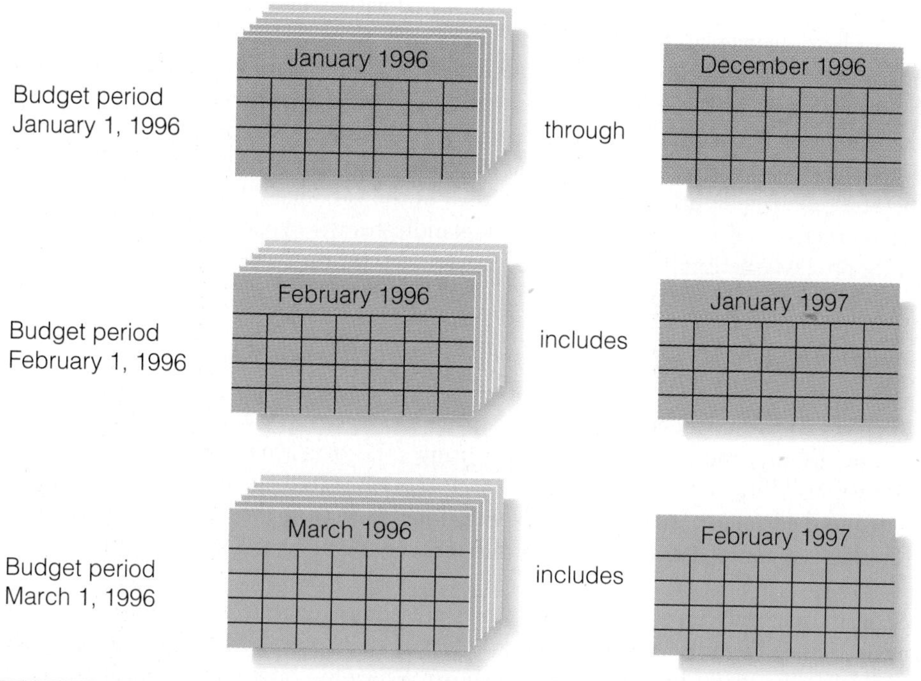

final authority for revising and approving the budget. Budget approval may be delegated to a budget committee or to one or several members of top management.

The *budget calendar* coordinates the budgetary process and should include a timetable for all budgetary activities. The budget timetable is unique to each organization. The larger the organization, the more time will be needed to gather information, coordinate that information, identify weak points in the process or the budget itself, and take corrective action. The calendar should also indicate control points for the upcoming periods, when budget-to-actual comparisons will be made, and when and how feedback will be provided to managers responsible for operations.

Sample forms provide a means for consistent presentation of budget information by all individuals, making summarizations of information easier, quicker, and more effective. The sample forms should be understandable and could include standardized worksheets that allow managers to update historical information to arrive at budgetary figures. This section of the manual may also provide standard cost tables for items on which the organization has specific guidelines or policies. For example, in estimating employee fringe benefit costs, the company rule of thumb may be 30 percent of base salary. Similarly, a company policy may set the meal per diem allowance for salespersons at $30; in estimating meal expenses for the future period, the sales manager would simply multiply total estimated travel days by $30.

The last section of the manual includes the *original and revised budgets*. It is helpful for future planning to understand how the revision process works and why changes were made. The final approved budget is composed of many individual budgets, serves as a control document for budget-to-actual comparisons, and is known as the master budget (discussed in Chapter 11).

BUDGET IMPLEMENTATION AND CONTROL

■ LEARNING
OBJECTIVE 7
Understand how the managerial function of control is related to budgeting.

After a budget is prepared and accepted, it is implemented, which means that the budget is considered a standard against which to measure performance. Managers operating under budget guidelines should be provided with copies of all appropriate budgets. These managers should also be informed that their performance will be evaluated by comparison of actual results against budgeted amounts. Such evaluations should generally be made by budget category for specific periods of time.

Once the budget is implemented, the control phase begins. Control includes making actual-to-budget comparisons, determining variances, providing feedback to operating managers, investigating the causes of the variances, and taking any necessary corrective action. This control process indicates the cyclical nature of the budgeting process (see Exhibit 10–12). Feedback (both positive and negative) is essential to the control process and must be provided in a timely manner to be useful.

Sales Price and Sales Volume Variances

■ LEARNING
OBJECTIVE 8
Explain why actual revenue from a product differs from budgeted revenue.

When actual-to-budget comparisons are made, managers are held accountable for the revenues (if any) and the costs in the operating areas over which they have authority and responsibility. Actual performance should be compared against budgeted performance to determine variances from expectations. In making such comparisons, however, management needs to be certain that it is considering results from a proper perspective.

For an operating area in which revenues are being generated (for example, ticket sales for the Twins or the Chevrolet Division of General Motors), comparisons should first be made on the revenue level to determine how closely projected rev-

■ **EXHIBIT 10–12**
Nature of the Budgeting Process

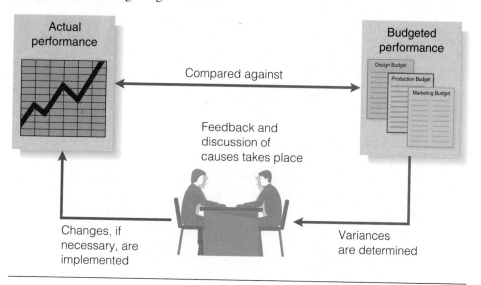

enues are being met. As discussed in Chapter 6, on standard costing, a total variance from standard can have both a price (or cost) and a quantity element. Thus, revenue variance calculations should be made for both of these elements.

Calculating the difference between actual and budgeted selling prices and multiplying this number by the actual number of units sold will provide the **sales price variance**. This variance indicates the portion of the total variance that is related to a change in selling price. A variance is also created by the difference between actual and budgeted sales volumes; multiplying this difference by the budgeted selling price yields the **sales volume variance**. The sales variance model is as follows:[15]

sales price variance

sales volume variance

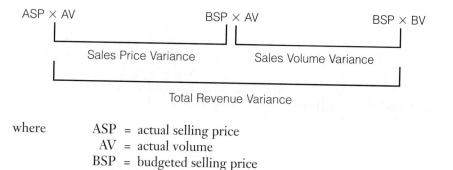

where   ASP = actual selling price
         AV = actual volume
         BSP = budgeted selling price
         BV = budgeted volume

---

[15]These computations assume the company sells a single product. If the company sells multiple products, another variance will exist called the sales mix variance. This variance explains the change in budgeted revenue caused by selling a mix of products different from the expected. Sales mix is discussed in Chapter 8 on cost-volume-profit analysis. Sales mix variance computations require information on the estimated percentage of total expected sales for each product. For the Twins, a sales mix variance would be necessary because of the different ticket prices offered.

To illustrate these computations, assume that the Colorado Miners (a fictitious minor-league baseball team) budgets 1996 ticket sales at $70,000 per home game, which represents the sale of an estimated 10,000 tickets at a selling price of $7. At July's first home game, actual gate ticket revenue was $66,000, creating a total unfavorable revenue variance of $4,000. To make a valid comparison, it is necessary to know that the $66,000 was composed of a volume of 12,000 tickets sold at a price of $5.50. Thus, the following variance calculations can be made:

$5.50 × 12,000	$7.00 × 12,000	$7.00 × 10,000
$66,000	$84,000	$70,000
$18,000 U	$14,000 F	
Sales Price Variance	Sales Volume Variance	
$4,000 U		
Total Revenue Variance		

Team management should be pleased with the increased volume but displeased with the reduced selling price. Discussions with managers might indicate that this game was a special promotional game in which everyone received a $1.50 discount for bringing a can of food for charity. If these people enjoyed themselves and will return for future games, this unfavorable revenue variance may be offset by positive variances in the future.

Analyzing Cost Variances

After revenue variances have been explained, managers can focus on analyzing cost variances. Costs should be analyzed in relation to the actual volume of sales rather than the budgeted volume of sales. Such analysis requires the use of flexible budgets and flexible budget formulas.

For example, assume that the Colorado Miners have a flexible budget formula for advertising expenses of $1,000 per game plus 6 percent of gate receipt revenues. The original advertising expense budget estimate for the first game in July would have been $5,200 [$1,000 + .06($7 × 10,000)]. However, since the game only achieved an actual revenue level of $66,000, the division should only expect advertising expenses of $4,960 [$1,000 + .06($66,000)]. If actual advertising expenses were $5,100, costs were not in conformity with expectations. The Miners should recognize a $140 ($5,100 − $4,960) unfavorable variance for advertising expense—although team managers may believe that the benefits to charity were worth the excess advertising cost. Comparing actual expenses with budgeted expenses that were calculated *at a different level of sales* (or ticket revenue) will not provide valid information on how well costs were controlled during a period.

In addition to determining whether costs were controlled, managers need to analyze the ways in which money was spent. Saving money and generating favorable cost variances is not necessarily good. For example, in 1994, USAir was losing $2 million per day, and some employees felt "pressure to keep planes flying. In one incident, a USAir maintenance supervisor said he had tried to save the company money by letting a plane fly even though a mandatory warning system was inoperative."[16]

---

[16]Douglas Frantz and Ralph Blumenthal, "USAir Safety Lapses Alleged," *[New Orleans] Times-Picayune* (November 13, 1994), p. A–6.

Spending analysis should focus on individual line items, not just totals, and on spending within categories. While failing to spend a budgeted amount is not necessarily good, spending money at the budgeted level may also be inappropriate. Often, money is spent simply because it is available for spending—not because there is a need for spending.

As with any variance computations, income statement actual-to-budget comparisons are made to determine why actual results differed from planned results. To determine the underlying reasons for variances requires that comparisons be made as early as possible. Delaying variance computations until the end of a period may impede a manager's ability to detect and, therefore, control the causes of variances. Providing useful variance computations requires that an effective and prompt variance reporting system be maintained.

Management should also consider the effects that current changes in conditions may have on future operations and on the types and extent of future budgetary variances. Will increased current sales mean reduced sales in later periods? Could a current selling price reduction spur product demand sufficiently to increase revenues to total projected levels? Does the increased cost of a raw material make the use of an alternative, higher-grade material more cost-beneficial? These are just some of the possible questions that management may need to consider when making actual-to-budget comparisons.

Exhibit 10–13 (page 518) lists some examples of budgeting problems with possible causes and managerial responses. This list is not intended to be comprehensive, and some factors may work together to cause budgeting problems. Once the causes of the deviations are known, management may wish to consider budget revisions. If actual results are favorable compared to the budget, management would still want to identify causes and prepare appropriate responses. For example, if sales were greater than budgeted, the company may want to increase advertising to take advantage of the popularity of an item. Lower costs (with equal or greater quality) would be investigated to determine if they should be incorporated into new standards.

Analyzing revenue variances for the Twins is quite difficult. Selling price per seat depends on the seat's location as well as whether promotion or group discounts were used. If the average ticket price is less than budgeted, increases in volume may not result in greater-than-budgeted revenues.

■ **EXHIBIT 10–13**

Instances and Causes of Budgetary Problems

BUDGETARY PROBLEM	POSSIBLE CAUSES (OR LACK OF CONSIDERATION GIVEN TO)	POSSIBLE MANAGEMENT RESPONSES
Sales significantly less than expected	Economic conditions weakened so product sales declined or made a lower selling price necessary; new product introduced by competitor	Revise budget estimates; consider innovative promotion alternatives; increase R&D expenditures
Direct materials costs significantly higher than expected	Inflation; used higher-grade materials; revised product components to reduce assembly time	Revise budget estimates; return to using original grade of material
Compensation costs higher than expected	Raised labor rates; minimum wage was increased; paid productivity bonuses to production personnel	Revise budget estimates; outsource; automate processes; (if the last cause) congratulate production personnel
Overhead costs higher than expected	Fringe benefits, insurance, or utility rates increased; incurred training costs to teach workers manufacturing teamwork concepts	Revise budget estimates; discover cost driver and brainstorm on how to reduce
Severe cash flow difficulties	Collection patterns declined; interest rates increased; money supply weakened; delayed new product launch to change production process to reduce manufacturing costs	Revise budget estimates; analyze credit and collection policies; encourage earlier design changes
Selling expenses higher than expected	Advertising rates increased; changed advertising media (such as substituted TV spots for print advertising); new product was developed more rapidly than expected, so promotion costs were incurred earlier	Seek cost drivers and study alternatives to more efficiently promote products and services; (if the last cause) congratulate R&D and design team
Interest costs higher than expected	Inflation; money supply tightened; obtained more debt financing to increase company's tax shield	Liquidate investments to reduce debt; issue capital stock
Production cannot keep up with demand	Shortages of critical direct materials or supplies; closed plant temporarily to install new safety equipment	Enter long-term partnership with qualified suppliers for mutual benefits

■■■ BUDGET REVISIONS AND
PERFORMANCE EVALUATIONS

■ **LEARNING OBJECTIVE 9**
Recognize why managers should use achievable budget targets.

It is not usually possible to make arrangements rapidly enough to revise the current month's budget. However, under certain circumstances, and if managers so desire, they can revise future months' budgets. If actual performance is substantially less than expected, the budget may or may not be adjusted, depending on the causes of the variances. If the causes are beyond the organization's control (such as when the Gulf War caused oil prices to increase dramatically), management may revise budget estimates upward to more realistically reflect costs. If the causes are internal (the sales staff simply is not selling the product, for example), management may leave the budget in its original form so that the problem is visible in the comparisons. If the variations are believed to be caused by special, non-random causes, these causes should be studied so that ways can be found to help the sales staff improve their processes. The causes should be viewed as opportunities for continuous improvement.

If actual performance is substantially better than expected, budget alterations may be made; however, management may not alter the budget so that the positive performance is highlighted through its comparison to the lower budget amounts. Regardless of whether the budget is revised, managers should commend those responsible and communicate the effects of the performance to departments affected by it. For example, if the sales force has been very effective and has sold significantly more product than expected (at the expected selling price), the production and purchasing areas must be made aware of the need to increase the number of units manufactured and the quantity of materials purchased.

One important reason that management must decide whether to revise is that the budget is often used as a benchmark against which actual results are compared. Management must communicate with the "owners" of the processes if budget revisions have been made. Although revised budgets may provide more accurate information, they also create a fluctuating benchmark against which process owners can compare their actual process statistics. Thus, if revised budgets are prepared, top management may want to compare actual results against both the original and revised budgets and then use multiple tools to assess the quality as well as the activity for the purpose of continuous improvement in the process and its results.

Because, as mentioned, operating managers may introduce slack into their budgets, top management may want to use a bonus system to encourage actual performance that exceeds budgeted performance. Operating managers can be rewarded with large bonuses for budgeting relatively high performance levels and achieving those levels. If performance is set at a low or minimal level, achievement of that performance level is either not rewarded or only minimally rewarded.

Modern management thinking is beginning to recognize that individuals working in groups should not receive personal credit or blame for the success or failure of the group's efforts. Because of the complex interdependencies of group interaction, group members should be empowered with the ownership of their processes for reasons of synergy, respect, *esprit de corps*, and trust. The group is both accountable and rewarded as a team.

Until a climate of trust and respect permeates the firm, budget slack and other "budget games" will be played simply because of human nature. **Games** can be defined as a series of organized behavior patterns conforming to a set of rules that promote a defined outcome. Budget games may be played by top or lower-level management; some of these games are described in Exhibit 10-14 (page 520). If managers are playing one or more of these games in the budgeting process, conflicts result and company performance suffers since many numbers are more sham, than real, projections. Company management often expects that good budgets will result simply because participation is allowed and encouraged. Good budgets, however, result only from having responsible individuals involved in the process and from creating an atmosphere of sound interpersonal relationships. In other words, good budgeting relies heavily on trust among the parties involved.

If budgets are to be used in effectively evaluating performance, they should be challenging but achievable. The advantages of using achievable budget targets include the following:

games

■ **EXHIBIT 10–14**
Budget Games

1. **The Dictator Game** This game is simply imposed budgeting. The budget is developed by top management and is handed down to lower levels with no room for discussion.

2. **The Father-Knows-Best Game** In this game, input is requested from lower-level managers, but either is not used or is changed with no reasons provided. This game allows people to believe at first that they are important to the process, but they recognize in the end that they are not.

3. **The Do-What-You-Want (And Fail) Game** In this game, lower-level managers submit their own budgets, which are then used for performance evaluation purposes. Unfortunately, individual managers are not informed of the "big picture." At year-end, they fail to measure up because their original budget figures were (a) too high and unachievable or (b) too low and not acceptable.

4. **The It's-Not-In-the-Budget Game** In this game, a manager submits a worthwhile project that is turned down because money is unavailable. Then, when the manager's performance level is low, he or she can be criticized for not justifying the project properly.

5. **The Cut-Everything-10% Game** This game is a favorite of all organizations. Rather than allowing managers to decide to cut certain expenditures and justify why others need to be raised, top management simply hands down a mandate to cut everything by 10%. Managers get to figure out how to play with what remains. A problem with this game, if played too often by top management, is that lower-level managers simply increase their budget requests by 10% and therefore are not disturbed by the reduction.

6. **The End-of-Year (or Spend-It-or-Lose-It) Game** Lower-level managers, recognizing that the end of the period is near, evaluate the remaining budget dollars per category and spend everything that is left. In this way, they can justify budget increases next year, because "I used everything I was budgeted for this year, and you know costs will increase." (The opposite of this game is played by top managers. Budget dollars that were not spent this period are lost, regardless of the reasons. This is a tough game when played with personnel budgets—a person not replaced is a position lost.)

7. **The It-Wasn't-My-Fault Game** The object of this game is for a manager to try to shift the blame for a failure to meet budget. This game probably allows for the most creativity. (Hint: The economy is always a good target because it's hard to prove or disprove what effect the economy actually had.)

8. **The Accounting Change Game** This game requires a high degree of understanding of accounting rules but can work wonders on income statements. Unfortunately, only one play is allowed for any given accounting change.

9. **The Sell-It-No-Matter-What Game** This game often involves the use of high-pressure tactics designed to move inventory. Managers who play this game are probably headed for a transfer and wanting to make a final name for themselves. They should be aware of CVP relationships; if the contribution margin is high and fixed costs are low, then increased volume will pad the bottom line substantially. But watch out for returns next period.

10. **The Build-a-Kingdom Game** This game allows managers to use budgets to create their own kingdoms. The larger the budget that can be obtained, the more "possessions" (equipment, personnel, etc.) the kingdom has. This game provides many opportunities to win friends by helping others maintain or increase their budget requests while extracting promises from them to reciprocate. However, these relationships can only work for a limited time before the kingdoms are in competition for the same budget dollars. Then war occurs.

1. Managers' commitment to achieving budget targets is increased because the managers will have little reason not to meet the targets.
2. Managers' confidence remains high; achievement of the target is perceived as successful performance.
3. Organizational control costs decrease because there is less necessity to apply the management-by-exception principle when targets are achieved.
4. The risk of managers' engaging in harmful short-term "income management" practices (such as delaying maintenance or shifting sales between years) is reduced.
5. Effective managers gain greater operating flexibility because they may be able to accumulate some additional resources based on good performance.
6. The organization is protected to some extent against the costs of optimistic projections, such as overproduction and warehousing.
7. Predictability of earnings is increased because the probability of target achievement is high.[17]

What degree of "achievability" must budgets have to yield these seven benefits? That depends on the organization's stage of life, its operating considerations (market structure, past performance, need for sales, types of products, and product life cycles), and its management personnel and their motivation levels.

Managers must engage in the budgeting process and judge performance with a realistic attitude. Budgets are not the "be-all, end-all" managerial accounting technique. As indicated in the News Note on the next page, if budgets are used improperly, they can cause serious organizational problems. If used properly, however, budgets can provide significant benefits.

BUDGETING IN AN INTERNATIONAL BUSINESS

Similar to many other business practices, the budgeting process and budget uses are unique to individual businesses. The budgeting process in a small, closely-held company may be informal and, potentially, imposed on lower-level managers by top management. As the organization becomes more complex, so does the budgeting process. Lower-level managerial participation in the budgeting process may be more important. When an organization reaches multinational status, participatory budgeting is not simply desired, it becomes necessary for the effort to be effective.

In a multinational environment, an organization faces an almost unlimited number of external variables that can affect the planning process. The effects of foreign currency exchange rates, interest rates, inflation, implications of prices for inventory transferred between international divisions of an organization, and risk may necessitate the preparation of separate budgets for each international market served in addition to a coordinated corporate-wide budget. Budget preparation must incorporate a thorough understanding of local market conditions including all known external forces and estimates of potential economic and market changes. Thus, each foreign operation's budget should also be supported by a comprehensive list of assumptions explaining how budget figures were derived.

Budgets are not only developed differently in different types of companies, but they are used differently. In small organizations, the budget may be used simply as a basis

■ **LEARNING OBJECTIVE 10**
Understand how budgeting in an international context differs from that in a domestic context.

---

[17]Kenneth A. Merchant, "How Challenging Should Profit Budget Targets Be?" *Management Accounting* (November 1990), pp. 46–48. Published by Institute of Management Accountants, Montvale, NJ.

Business Can't Be Managed Solely by the Budget

You have an inspiration. You sound out a couple of colleagues and customers, estimate costs, and take it to your boss. "I like it," he says. Then he utters the most dismal sentence in corporate life: "But it's not in the budget."

Budgets, forecasts, plans—whatever you call them, you cannot escape the annual ritual. For tracking where the money goes, budgets are dandy. They become iniquitous when they are made to do more—when the budget becomes management's main tool to gauge performance, or when it distorts long-term planning or blocks managers from shifting resources when they need to. Then the budget becomes an end in itself. "Making the numbers" becomes [management's] overriding goal.

The result can be madcap or maddening, depending. Managers, says A. T. Kearney's James Morehouse, "do incredibly stupid things" to make budgets, especially if incentive pay is at stake. They woo marginal customers. They cut prices too deeply. They overload distributors with goods—then take them back or shell out for costly promotions to sell them. Says David Nadler, president of Delta Consulting Group: "We once found a guy who made his sales budget by selling stuff to a dummy company. He put it in his basement and returned it the next year." And who hasn't endured a fourth-quarter spending freeze that cost more than it saved?

Then there's the manager whose problem is running *under* budget. Consultants swap tales of late autumn spending sprees as executives realize that a penny saved is a penny lost from next year's budget. Nadler had a client whose managers used to pay in December for consulting time that they did not want until the next year. Use-it-or-lose-it is still a fact of life at many companies.

Budgets can tell you who runs a tight ship, but a good admiral demands more: captains who know the difference between a reef and a tail wind, for example. 3M CEO Allen Jacobson told his division general managers in November 1989, "I never want to hear anyone put down a project because it isn't in the budget." But opportunities to toss out the budget won't work unless managers feel safe to act on the knowledge that the world is not on a fiscal year. Says Robert Hershock (a VP at 3M): "I've overrun budgets—overrun them pretty good sometimes. I was never criticized if I could justify it."

against which actual results are compared and not as a control or managerial performance evaluation mechanism. As the business expands, a role for budgeting as a control and coordination tool arises because of interactions among multiple departments or organizational units. Managerial and employee performance may then be gauged against the budget and resulting comparisons used in a reward system.

In many circumstances, it is difficult to determine the underlying causes of budget variations because of the effects of noncontrollable factors such as competitive maneuvers, economic conditions, and government regulations. In an international organization, the supporting list of assumptions are critical if the budget is to be used for control and evaluation purposes. Managers and employees should not be faulted for failing to achieve budget targets if the underlying causes reflect unforeseen, noncontrollable factors such as newly introduced government policies relating to import or export

Budgeting Purposes Are Not the Same Worldwide

Japanese planning and budgeting processes are very different from the typical American practice. Japanese companies develop a vision which is relatively permanent. They also develop a strategic plan which, again, is relatively brief and revised infrequently. More important, Japanese companies develop what they call a mid-term plan, which really is generated at only a very high level of the organization. It is relatively simple, containing such information as market share, sales, product costs, selling and administrative expenses, financing expenses, and inventory. It is revised periodically but never more than once a year.

The heart of Japanese companies' planning and budgeting is the six-month budget. Some companies tag onto it a rolling set of half-year projections that reach out several additional years. The six-month budget normally is prepared in no more than one month's time and often takes only two or three weeks.

The six-month budget is produced in a fashion similar to U.S. methods, with some top-down guidelines and a bottom-up estimate of achievable results. The finance and accounting staff plays a strong role in facilitation, working with senior management to communicate market realities and with line personnel to revise target costs. Even in the short two- to three-week cycle there may be several iterations of guideline delivery, budget preparation, and presentation.

The final budget is translated into target cost and productivity measures for the various groups. It is fair to say that the purpose to which Japanese companies put their plans and budgets is very different from U.S. companies. The primary purpose is to take a new look at the foreseeable future and to set short-run targets that are communicated clearly to the appropriate levels and groups of management so they can focus their efforts toward achieving them. Japanese companies spend virtually no time each month comparing actual results to budget and, more important, going through a lengthy, drawn-out process of explaining the causes of such variances. Rather, everyone is committed to achieving the targets that have been embodied into the six-month budgets.

Performance measurement and achievement of individual bonuses is another explanation for the different levels of detail generated by U.S. and Japanese companies in preparing annual budgets. In the United States, managers' bonuses and salaries are related directly to how well they achieve their individual plans. Japanese companies, on the other hand, place little emphasis on meeting budget when evaluating individual performance and therefore do not require as detailed a budget or plan.

SOURCE: Robert A. Howell and Michiharu Sakurai, "Management Accounting (and Other) Lessons from the Japanese," *Management Accounting* (December 1992), pp. 32-33. Published by Institute of Management Accountants, Montvale, NJ.

restrictions, exchange rate fluctuations, or market disturbances created by economic adjustments in a foreign country. Managers should, however, be held accountable for taking advantage of new opportunities created by these same factors.

The News Note above discusses the differences between the budgeting process and budget usage in Japan and in the United States. This excerpt highlights the fact that no single planning process is correct and that not only will differences exist among companies of different sizes, but that multinationals domiciled in different countries will also have different perspectives.

Budgeting for an international business requires detailed knowledge of numerous factors related to economic conditions in the organization's markets. Assumptions, such as those related to prices and costs, that are appropriate for one foreign market may need to be revised before budgeting for another market.

SITE ANALYSIS

The Twins organization has defined its goal as providing high-quality, consumer-oriented entertainment. In pursuit of that goal, management has sought to make the Twins one of the most affordable attractions in Minneapolis/St. Paul by pricing a lower-deck general admission ticket at approximately the cost of a movie. The budgeting process, however, needs to use an average ticket price that considers all possible seating, from luxury boxes to the new home-plate seats to the outfield. This wide differential in selling prices promotes an interesting budgeting scenario. As attendance increases, the average ticket price decreases, since more of the less expensive seats and possibly more discounted group tickets are being sold. Thus, the Twins may budget for an average ticket price of $9; and if the team is on a winning streak, club management may find that the average ticket price has fallen to $7.50.

In facing its quantitative, financial objectives, the Twins organization has had to develop new methods of decreasing costs and increasing revenue. A solution to the first objective was to have the team do all its own ticketing rather than using Ticketmaster or Ticketron so that no fees would have to be paid to outside entities. Unfortunately, this solution created a market perception problem: fans felt that tickets were not readily accessible. Thus, in recognition of its commitment to its customers, the organization installed ticket kiosks in grocery and discount stores around the metropolitan area. Using touchscreens, fans can view the available seating locations for a game and purchase tickets on the spot. This solution increased both revenues and customer satisfaction.

The Twins organization must continuously resell its product (sports entertainment) to current customers in addition to creating a desire for it in new customers. And while advertising may heavily influence sales, so do many uncontrollable factors, including player statistics, events such as the 1994–1995 labor strike, and records of other baseball teams. Gate ticket prices have essentially peaked, so volume and mix of ticket types are the primary considerations for this revenue source. Media revenue is negotiated and, again, is related to many external variables—including strikes. Concessions revenue is affected by stadium volume but is often unpredictable, as the relationship depends on the types of individuals at a game. For example, if the crowd were predominantly men, there might be more beer revenue; children, more souvenir revenue; conventioneers, more food revenue. Thus, the organization would have to determine whether it would be more profitable to sell full-price, home-plate tickets to men and forego some concession revenue (assuming that beer generates fewer sales dollars than souvenirs or food) or to sell discounted tickets to children or convention groups and increase the team's souvenir and food revenue.

The Twins organization has a unique budgeting situation in that the revenue choices it makes during the budgeting process affects its ability to estimate the amounts available for players' salaries. If revenues are underbudgeted, salaries may be set too low, making it difficult for the team to keep good players; if good players leave and the win-lose record declines, so does the revenue available to pay future salaries; and so on and so on. If revenues are overbudgeted, salaries may be set too high, making it difficult for the team to remain profitable. Thus, it is essential that the Twins' budget be set at a realistic and achievable level and that ongoing budget-to-actual comparisons be made to determine how well the team is performing monetarily. After all, baseball is not simply a game to the owners; it's a business.

SOURCE: Interview with Kevin Mather, Vice-President of Finance, Minnesota Twins (July 1994).

Discipline	Application
Accounting	Integrating budgets and standards into the accounting system is necessary for capturing and reporting variances for cost control purposes. Clarity in the budget manual is heightened by standardized accounting input.
Economics	Budgets assist managers in using resources effectively and efficiently to provide customers with goods and services at competitive prices. The budgeting process allows persons working within budget guidelines to analyze the allocation of limited resources (especially important in governmental budgeting circumstances). Flexible budgets reveal relationships between volume and costs. Achievability of budget targets is affected by total economic constraints of supply and demand.
Finance	The budgeting process emphasizes the necessity for integrating resource wants, needs, and availability among areas. Knowledge of the achievability (or lack thereof) of budget targets can help future assessment of performance.
Management	The budgeting process promotes awareness of resource scarcities; strengthens an organization's capacity to mobilize internal and external resources; promotes the "art of persuasion" ability in managers through justifying budget requests; forces choices as to goals and objectives; and creates interdisciplinary and interdepartmental discussion and cooperation.
Marketing	Knowledge of product life cycles can help an organization develop effective business strategies. The marketing staff can help assess achievability of budget sales targets, which will be affected by media promotion choices. The budget manual should provide guidelines on cost standards for various sales techniques. Participation in the budget process should motivate the sales staff to achieve budget targets.

CROSS-FUNCTIONAL APPLICATIONS STRATEGIES

CHAPTER SUMMARY

An organization is an open system that must successfully adapt to its environment to survive and prosper. The firm's adaptation process and business strategy are influenced by its operating environment, which includes market structure, government regulation, and supply-and-demand relationships. There are four basic market structures: pure competition, monopolistic competition, monopoly, and oligopoly. New global markets are providing sales opportunities, but these markets are also creating pricing and quality pressures for domestic firms. Numerous government regulations affect how business can be carried out.

The product life cycle also influences a firm's business strategy. The stage a product has reached in its life cycle significantly affects sales volume, price, and unit production cost. Both revenues and costs for a given product change as the product advances through development, introduction, growth, maturity, and harvest stages. Total revenues are nonexistent during the development stage and commence during introduction. They typically rise during growth, level off in maturity, and decline during harvest. Costs are characteristically high during development and introduction and tend to stabilize as production becomes routine. Rigorous product development and design efforts are usually worthwhile because 80 to 90 percent of a product's life cycle cost is determined by decisions made before production begins.

Budgets may be imposed or participatory, but in either case top management is responsible for assuring that the budget is attainable and acceptable. The common budget period is one fiscal year, segmented for quarterly and monthly periods. Continuous budgets may be used to ensure an ongoing one-year planning cycle.

A budget is the primary basis and justification for financial operations in a firm. Budget preparation is part of the tactical planning function. Implementing and administering a budget are parts of the coordination and control functions. A well-prepared budget provides the following benefits:

1. A detailed path for managers to follow to achieve organizational goals;
2. Improved planning and decision making;
3. An allocation of resources among departments;
4. A better understanding of key business variables;
5. A means of employee participation and influence;
6. A means to determine troublesome or hard-to-control cost areas;
7. A recognition of departmental interrelationships;
8. A means of responding more rapidly to changing economic conditions; and
9. A means by which managerial performance can be judged.

Budget manuals may be used to assure that procedures are standardized and understood by all parties involved in the process. When budgets are used for performance evaluation, care should be taken that the budget is achievable and that managers understand the process by which they will be evaluated.

Actual operating results should be compared against budget figures to measure how effectively and efficiently organizational goals were met. Sales price and sales volume variances should be calculated before expense comparisons are made. Expense comparisons should be made based on the actual level of sales volume achieved rather than on budgeted volume. Regardless of whether variances are unfavorable or favorable, feedback to operating personnel is an important part of the budget process. Additionally, managers should recognize that budget games may be played and should strive to create a climate of mutual trust and respect to minimize or eliminate this counterproductive behavior.

Zero-Based Budgeting

Traditional budgeting is often limited in its usefulness as a control tool because poor budgeting techniques are often used. One such technique involves beginning with the prior year's funding levels and treating these as given and essential to operations. Decisions are then made about whether and by what percentage to incrementally raise existing **appropriations**, which represent maximum allowable expenditures. Such an approach has often resulted in what is known as the "creeping commitment syndrome," in which activities are funded without systematic annual regard for priorities or alternative means for accomplishing objectives.

appropriations

To help eliminate the creeping commitment syndrome, **zero-based budgeting** (ZBB) was developed for the government. ZBB is a comprehensive budgeting process that systematically considers the priorities and alternatives for current and proposed activities relative to organizational objectives. Annual justification of programs and activities is required so that managers must rethink priorities within the context of agreed-upon objectives. Specifying that each operation be evaluated from a zero-cost base would be unrealistic and extreme, but ZBB does require that managers reevaluate all activities at the start of the budgeting process to make decisions about which activities should be continued, eliminated, or funded at a lower level. Differences between traditional budgeting and zero-based budgeting are shown in Exhibit 10–15.

zero-based budgeting

Zero-based budgeting is applicable in all organizations, especially in the support and service areas, where nonmonetary measures of performance are available. ZBB does not, however, provide measures of efficiency, and it is difficult to implement because of the significant amount of time and effort necessary to investigate the causes of prior costs and justify the purposes of budgeted costs.

■ LEARNING OBJECTIVE 11
(Appendix) Differentiate traditional budgeting from zero-based budgeting.

The ZBB process is based on organizational goals and objectives and involves three steps: (1) converting the company activities into decision packages; (2) ranking each decision package; and (3) allocating resources based on priorities. A decision package contains information about the activity: objectives and benefits, consequences of not funding, and necessary costs and staffing requirements. The decision packages are ranked and prioritized on the basis of need, costs, and benefits.

■ **EXHIBIT 10–15**
Differences Between Traditional Budgeting and ZBB

TRADITIONAL BUDGETING	ZERO-BASED BUDGETING
Starts with last year's funding appropriation	Starts with a minimal (or zero) figure for funding
Focuses on money	Focuses on goals and objectives
Does not systematically consider alternatives to current operations	Directly examines alternative approaches to achieving similar results
Produces a single level of appropriation for an activity	Produces alternative levels of funding based on availability of funds and desired results

Zero-based budgeting is a rigorous exercise that demands considerable time and effort, as well as wholehearted commitment by the organization's personnel to make it work. An organization lacking the time, effort, and commitment needed should not attempt ZBB. An organization that can supply these three ingredients can use ZBB to become more effective in planning for and controlling costs. One of the major benefits of zero-based budgeting is that, in using it, managers focus on identifying non-value-added activities and working to reduce items that cause money to be spent unnecessarily or ineffectively.

An organizaton considering ZBB should assess whether the benefits are worth the costs. Management may consider "zero-basing" certain segments of the company on a rotating basis over a period of years as an alternative to applying the approach to the entire firm annually.

GLOSSARY

Appropriation (p. 527)   a maximum allowable expenditure for a budget item (from appendix)

Budget (p. 495)   the quantitative expression of an organization's commitment to planned activities and resource acquisition and use

Budget manual (p. 513)   a detailed set of documents that provides information and guidelines about the budgetary process

Budget slack (p. 508)   the intentional underestimation of revenues and/or overestimation of expenses

Budgeting (p. 495)   the process of determining a financial plan for future operations

Continuous budget (p. 512)   an ongoing twelve-month budget that is created by the addition of a new budget month (twelve months into the future) as each current month expires

Games (p. 519)   a series of organized behavior patterns conforming to a set of rules that promote a defined outcome

Imposed budget (p. 507)   a budget that is prepared by top management with little or no input from operating personnel, who are simply informed of the budget goals and constraints

Key variable (p. 499)   a critical factor believed to be a direct cause of the achievement of or failure to achieve organizational goals and objectives; can be internal or external

Monopolistic competition (p. 502)   a market structure in which there are many firms offering slightly differentiated products and services

Monopoly (p. 502)   a market structure in which there is only one seller of a product or provider of a service

Oligopoly (p. 502)   a market structure in which there are only a few firms, whose products or services may be either differentiated or standardized

Participatory budget (p. 508)   a budget that has been developed through a process of joint decision making by top management and operating personnel

Price elasticity of demand (p. 503)   a relationship that reflects the percentage change in the quantity demanded relative to the percentage change in price

Pure competition (p. 501)   a market structure in which there are many firms, each with a small market share, producing identical products

Sales price variance (p. 515)   the difference between actual and budgeted selling prices multiplied by the actual number of units sold

Sales volume variance (p. 515)   the difference between actual and budgeted volumes multiplied by the budgeted selling price

Strategic planning (p. 498)   the process of developing a statement of long-range goals for the organization and defining the strategies and policies that will help the organization achieve those goals

Substitute good (p. 505)   a good that can be used in place of another to satisfy the same wants or needs

c. Severe cash flow difficulties

d. Overhead costs higher than expected

e. Production cannot keep up with demand

f. Selling expenses higher than expected

g. Direct materials costs higher than expected

h. Interest costs higher than expected

3. Increased labor contract rates or minimum wage

4. Recessionary economic conditions

5. Inflation

6. Declining collection patterns

7. Operations are at maximum capacity

8. Increased advertising rates

33. (LO 9; *Budget games*) Match the numbered descriptions on the right with the lettered names of budget games on the left.

a. It-Wasn't-My-Fault

b. It's-Not-in-the-Budget

c. The Accounting Change

d. Build-a-Kingdom

e. Sell-It-No-Matter-What

f. The Dictator

g. Father-Knows-Best

h. Cut-Everything-10%

i. Spend-It-or-Lose-It

j. Do-What-You-Want

1. An attempt to increase the bottom line without regard to reducing customer satisfaction and subsequent sales returns

2. Imposed budget with no room for discussion

3. Mandated across-the-board cuts; no opportunity given for managers to justify selected increases and decreases

4. Inputs by operating personnel are encouraged but subsequently ignored

5. Worthwhile projects are rejected, and managers are later blamed for low performance because the projects were not adequately justified

6. Changing accounting methods to influence calculated net income

7. Shifting blame for failure to achieve budget

8. Pushing for larger budgets to gain power

9. Withholding support information; allowing a subordinate manager to undertake budgetary projects that are probably destined to fail

10. Spending everything left at the end of a period so that next period's budget will not be reduced

■ COMMUNICATION ACTIVITIES

34. (LO 2, 7; *Budgets and organizational change*) *The giant accounting firm of Ernst & Young gutted its national legal department, firing 37 of its 66 attorneys, shortly after pushing out one of the best-known and enduring general counsels in corporate America.*

The swift dismantling of [the legal department] came as a shock to many in the New York firm's law group. When they arrived at work..., they were confronted by guards in plain clothes stationed to prevent the destruction of files and computer equipment.

[SOURCE: Lee Berton, "Ernst & Young Decimates Its Legal Department," *Wall Street Journal* (October 11, 1994), pp. B1, B7.]

a. Do you think the dismantling of the legal department at Ernst & Young was a spur-of-the-moment decision and that's why it took members of the legal department by surprise?

b. Why would it have been difficult for Ernst & Young's top managers to incorporate the dismantling of the legal department into the firm's formal budgets?

c. What were the behaviors Ernst & Young apparently expected of the fired individuals?

d. Describe the various types of experts and information that should be involved in a managerial decision to downsize.

35. (LO 1, 2, 7; *Benefits of successful planning*) Successful business organizations appear to be those that have clearly defined long-range goals and a well-planned strategy to reach those goals. These successful organizations understand their markets as well as the internal strengths and weaknesses of the organizations. These organizations take advantage of this knowledge to grow (through internal development or acquisitions) in a consistent and disciplined manner.

a. Discuss the need for long-range goals for business organizations.

b. Discuss how long-range goals are set.

c. Define the concepts of strategic planning and management control. Discuss how they relate to each other and contribute to progress toward the attainment of long-range goals.

(CMA adapted)

36. (LO1, 5, 7, 9; *Departmental budgeting*) SteelCo is a medium-sized company in the steel fabrication industry with six divisions located in different geographical sectors of the United States. Considerable autonomy in operational management is permitted in the divisions, due in part to the distance between corporate headquarters in Illinois and five of the six divisions. Corporate management establishes divisional budgets using prior year data adjusted for industry and economic changes expected for the coming year. Budgets are prepared by year and by quarter, with top management attempting to recognize problems unique to each division in the divisional budget-setting process. Once the year's divisional budgets are set by corporate management, they cannot be modified by division management.

The budget for calendar year 1997 projects total corporate net income before taxes of $3,750,000 for the year, including $937,500 for the first quarter. Results of first-quarter operations presented to corporate management in early April showed corporate net income of $865,000, which was $72,500 below the projected net income for the quarter. The Chicago Division operated at 4.5 percent above its projected divisional net income, while the other five divisions showed net incomes with variances ranging from 1.5 to 22 percent below budgeted net income.

Corporate managers are concerned with the first-quarter results because they believed strongly that differences between divisions had been recognized. An entire day in late November of last year had been spent presenting and explaining the corporate and divisional budgets to the division managers and their division controllers. A mid-April meeting of corporate and division management had generated unusual candor. All five out-of-state division managers cited reasons why first-quarter results in their respective divisions represented effective management and was the best that could be expected. Corporate management remained unconvinced and informed division managers that "results would be brought into line with the budget by the end of the second quarter."

a. Identify and explain the major disadvantages in the procedures employed by SteelCo's corporate management in preparing and implementing the divisional budgets.

b. Discuss the behavioral problems that may arise from requiring division managers to meet the quarterly budgeted net income figures as well as the annual budgeted net income.

c. Describe how you, as a high-level corporate manager at SteelCo, would attempt to evaluate the reasons offered by the divisional managers for their poor performance.

(CMA adapted)

37. (LO 1, 10; *International*) Your Canadian-based consumer electronics firm, CanadaExcel, is in the process of establishing a camcorder assembly plant in Malaysia. The manager of the Malaysian plant is to have responsibility for the following: sourcing materials (about 60 percent of materials will be acquired from outside the company and the other 40 percent will be acquired from internal plants located in Canada and Mexico); hiring, training, and supervising workers; controlling operating costs; meeting a production schedule that is based on projected sales; and maintaining production quality. Completed units will be shipped to internal marketing divisions located in North America.

Place yourself in the position of controller of CanadaExcel. It is your job to incorporate the operating plans for the Malaysian assembly plant into the company's formal budget. Describe, in general terms, what information you would need to acquire to develop the budget for the Malaysian operation and where you would expect to acquire such information. Further, describe any significant decisions that would be your responsibility to make in compiling the budget.

■ PROBLEMS

38. (LO 8; *Sales variances*) Thurgood Industries employs a budgeting system to aid in organizational planning and control. At the end of the period, actual results are compared against budgeted figures. The company's actual and budgeted data for 1995 appear below:

UNIT SALES	BUDGETED	ACTUAL
Product A	24,000	20,000
Product B	16,000	30,000

DOLLAR SALES		
Product A	$96,000	$85,000
Product B	48,000	75,000

COST OF SALES (ALL VARIABLE)		
Product A	$48,000	$50,000
Product B	32,000	60,000

a. Compute the budgeted gross margin for each product.

b. Compute the actual gross margin for each product.

    c. Compute the sales variances for each product.

    d. Why do the sales volume and price variances not explain the entire difference between budgeted and actual gross margin for both products?

39. (LO 8; *Sales variances*) Sports Products Inc. manufactures two products: basketballs and baseball gloves. For 1997, the firm budgeted the following:

	BASKETBALLS	**BASEBALL GLOVES**
Sales	$800,000	$1,200,000
Unit sales price	$40	$30

At the end of 1997, managers were informed of the following:

- Actual sales of basketballs were 21,000 units. The price variance for basketballs was $63,000 unfavorable.

- Actual sales of baseball gloves generated revenue of $1,120,000 and a volume variance of $240,000 unfavorable.

    a. Compute the budgeted sales volume for each product.

    b. Compute the volume variance for 1997 for basketballs.

    c. Compute the price variance for 1997 for baseball gloves.

    d. Summarize the difference between budgeted and actual sales for 1997.

  40. (LO 8; *Sales variances*) Sara Friez manages the marketing department at Holiday Ceramics Company. She is evaluated based on her ability to meet budgeted revenues. For May 1997, her revenue budget was as follows:

	PRICE PER UNIT	**UNIT SALES**
Jack-O-Lantern	$240	1,600
Santa Claus	130	2,150
American Flag	160	4,200

    The actual sales generated by the marketing department in May were as follows:

	PRICE PER UNIT	**TOTAL SALES DOLLARS**
Jack-O-Lantern	$230	$391,000
Santa Claus	140	282,800
American Flag	150	622,500

    a. For May 1997, compute the sales price variance for Holiday Ceramics Company for each product.

    b. For May 1997, compute the sales volume variance for Holiday Ceramics Company.

    c. Assuming that the variances you computed in parts a and b are controllable by Sara Friez, discuss what actions she may have taken to cause actual results to deviate from budgeted results.

    d. Describe circumstances in which it would be more appropriate to hold the manufacturing manager (rather than the marketing manager) responsible for sales variances.

 41. (LO 6, 7, 9; *Budget process revisions*) FarmMart is a divisionalized corporation in the agribusiness industry with its corporate headquarters in Omaha. The R&D Division is located in central Texas and is responsible for all of the corporation's seed, fertilizer, and insecticide research and development. The R&D is conducted primarily for the benefit of FarmMart's other operating divisions. The

R&D Division conducts contract research for outside firms when such research does not interfere with the division's regular work or does not represent work that is directly competitive with FarmMart's interests.

FarmMart's annual budget preparation begins approximately 5 months before the beginning of the fiscal year. Each division manager is responsible for developing the budget for his or her division within the guidelines provided by corporate headquarters. Once the annual budget procedure is completed and the budget is accepted and approved, the division managers have complete authority to operate within the limits prescribed by the budget.

The budget procedures apply to the R&D Division. However, because this division does work for other FarmMart divisions and for the corporate office, careful coordination between the R&D Division and the other units is needed to construct a good budget for the R&D Division. Further, the costs associated with the contract research require special consideration by FarmMart's management. In the past, there has been good cooperation that has resulted in sound budget practices.

R&D's management always has presented well-documented budgets for both the internal and external contract research. When the submitted budget has been changed, the revisions are the result of review, discussion, and agreement between R&D's management and corporate management.

Staff travel is a major item included in R&D's budget. Some 25 to 35 trips are made annually to corporate headquarters for meetings by R&D's employees. In addition, the division's technical staff make trips related to their research projects and are expected to attend professional meetings and seminars. These trips always have been detailed in a supporting schedule presented with the annual budget.

FarmMart's performance for the current year is considered reasonable in light of current and expected future poor economic conditions, but corporate management has become extremely cost conscious. Divisions have been directed to cut down on any unnecessary spending. A specific new directive has been issued stating that any travel in excess of $500 must now be approved in advance by corporate headquarters. In addition, once a division's total dollar amount budgeted for travel has been spent, no budget overruns would be allowed. This directive is effective immediately, and corporate management has indicated that it will continue to be in effect for at least the next two years.

The R&D manager is concerned because this directive appears to represent a change in budget policy. Now, travel that was thought already approved because it was included in the annual budget must be reapproved before each trip. In addition, some scheduled trips previously approved may have to be canceled because travel funds are likely to run out before the end of the year. R&D staff members already have had to make five special trips to corporate headquarters that were not included in the current year's budget.

The new directive will probably increase costs. The approval process may delay the purchase of airline tickets, thus reducing the opportunity to obtain the lowest fares. Further, there will be a major increase in paperwork for the R&D Division because virtually every trip exceeds the $500 limit.

a. The directive requiring the reapproval of all travel in excess of $500 could have far-reaching effects for FarmMart.

   1. Explain how this directive could affect the entire budget process, especially the validity of the annual budget.

2. Explain what effect this directive is likely to have on the care with which divisions prepare their annual travel budgets in the future.

b. Explain what effect the directive on reapproval of travel costs is likely to have on the morale and motivation of the division manager and research staff of the R&D Division.

c. If you were president of FarmMart, would you subject the R&D Division to the same budgetary restrictions as the other divisions? Why or why not?

(CMA adapted)

■ CASES

42. (LO 1, 5; *Budgets and organizational behavior*) Stark Manufacturing, a division of Davis Corporation, produces and sells a variety of leather goods to both wholesalers and retail outlets. Four months ago, Davis sent a team from the company's Internal Audit Department to Stark to perform a routine review of operations. A portion of the audit report presented to Davis on the operations of Stark is presented below.

OBSERVATION

Departmental budgets are not being utilized at Stark. Currently, the division does not have the automated systems capability to produce budget analyses at the departmental level. Traditionally, the plant has been controlled through a total plant concept rather than a departmental approach to cost control. Given present business conditions, this approach may no longer be the optimum control process. Increased competition in the marketplace, declining profits, deteriorating margins, and increased costs have combined to necessitate an aggressive approach to cost reduction. Based on experience at other Davis plants we believe that Stark would benefit from the development and use of departmental budgets for all functions.

RECOMMENDATION

We recommend that Stark establish a management objective to develop and utilize flexible departmental expense budgets for all departments. Resources and systems development efforts should be devoted to this objective as they become available. We suggest, as an interim step, that operating budgets be employed on a monthly basis. Operating targets for both direct labor and indirect labor expense should be established for each manufacturing department monthly. Departmental managers should track performance and explain deviations from targets as part of the regular agenda at the weekly production meetings.

PRELIMINARY MANAGEMENT RESPONSE

Stark will develop and utilize a flexible departmental budget system. In the interim, work has begun to establish daily, month-to-date, and annual targets for direct and indirect labor for the manufacturing departments. These targets include efficiency objectives, overtime objectives, and indirect labor usage objectives based on volume and product mix.

Prior to making the Preliminary Management Response presented in the audit report, the president of Stark announced to the departmental managers that the company was planning to accept the audit recommendation to implement a departmental budgeting system. The managers were asked for sugges-

tions on implementation procedures and were encouraged to raise any questions they might have about the budget system.

a. Describe the benefits, other than better cost control, that should accrue to Stark Manufacturing from the implementation of departmental budgeting.

b. Discuss the behavioral impact the introduction of departmental budgeting is likely to have on Stark Manufacturing's departmental managers and production workers.

c. Assume that you are the controller at Stark. What role would you expect the Accounting Department to play in the development of departmental budgets?

(CMA adapted)

43. (LO 7, 8; *Sales and cost variances*) (Note: Includes variances and sales mix) The Markley Division of Rosette Industries manufactures and sells patio chairs. The chairs are manufactured in two versions—a plastic model and a metal model of a lesser quality. The company uses its own sales force to sell the chairs to retail stores and to catalog outlets. Generally, customers purchase both the plastic and the metal versions.

The chairs are manufactured on two different assembly lines located in adjoining buildings. The division management and sales department occupy the third building on the property. The division management includes a division controller responsible for the divisional financial activities and the preparation of reports explaining the differences between actual and budgeted performance. The controller structures these reports such that the sales activities are distinguished from cost factors so that each can be analyzed separately.

The operating results for the first three months of the fiscal year as compared to the budget follow. The budget for the current year was based upon the assumption that Markley Division would maintain its present market share of the estimated total patio chair market (plastic and metal combined). A status report had been sent to corporate management toward the end of the second month indicating that divisional operating income for the first quarter would probably be about 45 percent below budget; this estimate was just about on target. The division's operating income was below budget even though industry volume for patio chairs increased by 10 percent more than was expected at the time the budget was developed.

	ACTUAL	BUDGET	FAVORABLE (UNFAVORABLE) RELATIVE TO THE BUDGET
Sales in units			
Plastic model	60,000	50,000	10,000
Metal model	20,000	25,000	(5,000)
Sales revenue			
Plastic model	$630,000	$500,000	$130,000
Metal model	300,000	375,000	(75,000)
Total sales	$930,000	$875,000	$ 55,000
Less variable costs			
Manufacturing (at standard)			
Plastic model	$480,000	$400,000	$(80,000)
Metal model	200,000	250,000	50,000
Selling			
Commissions	46,500	43,750	(2,750)
Bad debt allowance	9,300	8,750	(550)

Total variable costs (except variable manufacturing variances)	$735,800	$702,500	$(33,300)
Contribution margin (except variable manufacturing variances)	$194,200	$172,500	$ 21,700
Less other costs			
Variable manufacturing cost variances from standard	$ 49,600	$ 0	$(49,600)
Fixed manufacturing costs	49,200	48,000	(1,200)
Fixed selling & administrative costs	38,500	36,000	(2,500)
Allocation of corporate office costs	18,500	17,500	(1,000)
Total other costs	$155,800	$101,500	$(54,300)
Divisional operational income	$ 38,400	$ 71,000	$(32,600)

The manufacturing activities for the quarter resulted in the production of 55,000 plastic chairs and 22,500 metal chairs. The costs incurred by each manufacturing unit follow. The raw materials quantities are stated in terms of the equivalents of finished chairs; for example, although 55,000 plastic chairs were produced, the company purchased enough material for 60,000 chairs and used enough material to make 56,000 chairs.

	QUANTITY	PRICE	PLASTIC MODEL	METAL MODEL
Purchases				
Plastic	60,000	$5.65	$339,000	
Metal	30,000	$6.00		$180,000
Usage				
Plastic	56,000	$5.00	280,000	
Metal	23,000	$6.00		138,000
Direct labor				
9,300 hours @ $6.00 per hour			55,800	
5,600 hours @ $8.00 per hour				44,800
Manufacturing overhead				
Variable				
Supplies			43,000	18,000
Power			50,000	15,000
Employee benefits			19,000	12,000
Fixed				
Supervision			14,000	11,000
Depreciation			12,000	9,000
Property taxes & other items			1,900	1,300

The standard variable manufacturing costs per unit and the budgeted monthly fixed manufacturing costs established for the current year are presented next.

	PLASTIC MODEL	METAL MODEL
Raw material	$ 5.00	$ 6.00
Direct labor		
1/6 hour @ $6.00 per DLH	1.00	
1/4 hour @ $8.00 per DLH		2.00
Variable overhead		
1/6 hour @ $12.00 per DLH	2.00	
1/4 hour @ $8.00 per DLH		2.00
Standard variable manufacturing cost per unit	$ 8.00	$10.00

Budgeted fixed costs per month

Supervision	$4,500	$3,500
Depreciation	4,000	3,000
Property taxes & other fixed costs	600	400
Total budgeted fixed costs for month	$9,100	$6,900

a. Explain the variance in Markley Division's contribution margin attributable to sales activities by calculating the:

    1. sales price variance.

    2. sales mix variance. Hint: Compute as follows: (actual total units sold × {budgeted UCM − [(actual TCM − price variance) ÷ actual units sold]}).

    3. sales volume variance.

b. What portion of the sales volume variance, if any, can be attributed to a change in Markley Division's market share?

c. Analyze the variance in Markley Division's variable manufacturing costs ($49,600) in as much detail as the data permit.

d. Based upon your analyses prepared for parts a, b, and c:

    1. Identify the major cause of Markley Division's unfavorable profit performance.

    2. Did Markley's management attempt to correct this problem? Explain your answer.

    3. What other steps, if any, could Markley's management have taken to improve the division's operating income? Explain your answer.

(CMA)

■ ETHICS AND QUALITY DISCUSSIONS

44. *Business leaders feel current college accounting courses don't sufficiently teach students the skills they really need to be effective in business, according to a major report by a six-member joint committee of the 85,000-member Institute of Management Accountants and the 14,000-member Financial Executives Institute.*

    The report "attacks the entire fabric of accounting education," some panel members say. "Few college courses focus enough on business budgeting, cost accounting [what products really cost to produce] and how to manage working capital, which is what companies need. . . ."

    The report says most college accounting courses focus too much on auditing, nonprofit accounting and taxation. These courses help prepare students to work for major public accounting firms, but don't adequately prepare graduates to work for big companies, the report adds. Yet two-thirds of the 50,000 students who take undergraduate accounting courses every year eventually work for business, rather than for accounting firms.

    At Citgo Petroleum Corp., many recent college graduates who majored in accounting aren't up to snuff for jobs at the company, says Steven R. Berlin, senior vice president of finance at the Tulsa, Okla., oil concern and a member of the six-member panel. Consequently, in the last four years, Citgo has been hiring liberal-arts or business-school graduates for 50% of its 20 or more financial jobs each year, he says. Mr. Berlin says it takes an added two years of in-house training to show accounting graduates how to make budget decisions useful to Citgo, a unit of Petroleos de Venezuela SA.

[SOURCE: Lee Berton, "College Courses on Accounting Get Poor Grade," *Wall Street Journal* (August 12, 1994), pp. B1, B10. Reprinted by permission of The Wall Street Journal, © 1994 Dow Jones & Company, Inc. All Rights Reserved Worldwide.]

a. If an accounting department in a typical business college is to develop a quality-oriented, consumer-focused view of its curriculum, it must first identify its customers. In your view, who are the customers of an accounting department's curriculum? Explain.

b. Review the course offerings in accounting at your university. Does the curriculum appear to be similar to that described in the survey referrred to above? Explain.

c. Why would an accounting department have a natural bias to offer too many financial accounting courses and too few managerial/cost accounting courses? [Hint: one way to proceed is to examine the incentives of the accounting department.]

d. Assume that you accept the results of the survey and that your school's accounting department provides too little coverage in its courses for topics such as budgeting. What actions can you take to make your school's accounting department more sensitive to the needs of the business community?

45. *After nearly 26 years, two heart attacks and a stroke, Harry Ellis retired from his factory job in March, too sick to work anymore. He clung to one oasis of security—his medical insurance.*

Then, last summer, he learned he could lose that. Pirelli Armstrong Tire Corp. announced it was terminating health benefits for retirees, saying rising medical costs had become intolerable and jeopardized the company's future. Harry Ellis now fears his own future.

"When I worked here, I believed it straight out they'll take care of you for the rest of your life," said the 56-year-old former welder, his voice rising, his face flushed pink with anger beneath his pastel-print railroad cap. "I thought all I have to do is bury myself. Now I might not have nothing."

Ellis is not alone in his anger; he is at the center of one of the most rancorous labor-management disputes of the 1990's.

The debate reverberates in work places across America as more companies—heavyweights like General Motors, Unisys and Navistar, among them—slash or eliminate medical health insurance for more retirees. Faced with spiraling health care costs and growing numbers of retirees, companies argue their own financial health is at stake. Changes in accounting rules have forced them to subtract the projected cost of retiree health benefits from profits—a drain on the bottom line.

[SOURCE: Sharon Cohen, "Retirees Protest Loss of Medical Insurance," *Bryan-College Station Eagle* (December 4, 1994), pp. C1, C4.]

a. Why would companies such as Pirelli Armstrong Tire Corp. have initiated health care coverage for retirees?

b. How might the elimination of health care coverage for retired workers affect the quality of work at Pirelli Armstrong Tire Corp.?

c. Ask your accounting instructor to explain the new accounting rule referred to in the preceding article. Then discuss whether this new accounting rule is likely an important consideration for companies in the process of deciding whether to drop retiree health coverage.

d. What important ethical considerations are involved in company decisions to discontinue health care coverage for retired workers—after they have retired?

46. Many managers believe that if they do not spend all amounts in their budgets during a period, they will lose allocations in future periods and will receive little or no recognition for cost savings. The following figure indicates the results of a survey of IMA members about the motivating factors behind budgeting issues:

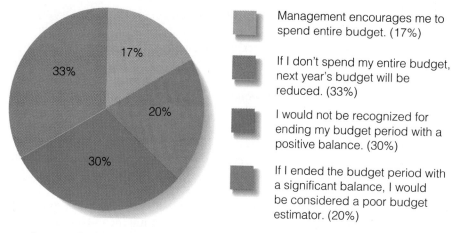

Management encourages me to spend entire budget. (17%)

If I don't spend my entire budget, next year's budget will be reduced. (33%)

I would not be recognized for ending my budget period with a positive balance. (30%)

If I ended the budget period with a significant balance, I would be considered a poor budget estimator. (20%)

[SOURCE: Gerald L. Finch and William Mihal, "Spend It or Lose It," *Management Accounting* (March 1989), p. 45. Published by Institute of Management Accountants, Montvale, NJ.]

Discuss the behavioral and ethical issues involved in a "spend it or lose it" attitude. Include in your discussion the issue of negotiating budget allocation requests before the beginning of the period.

47. Assume that you are a top manager in an advertising firm with eight regional locations. Kim Taylor is the manager in charge of the Denver office.

In 1996, Kim worked diligently with her staff to create an optimal 1997 budget for her office; she believed the amounts for revenues and expenses were as precisely forecasted as they could be. When you received her 1997 budget, you immediately increased her expected revenues 15 percent and reduced all expense categories by 10 percent. You informed her that you believed her office capable of dealing with both adjustments. Near the end of 1997, it was obvious that Kim's office would probably come in about 12 percent below the increased budget in regard to revenues and almost exactly equal to her original estimates in regard to costs.

Although 1997 has not ended, Kim needs to prepare the 1998 budget. She again elicits substantial information from her staff and prepares a detailed budget. Before sending it to you, however, she reduces revenues by 20 percent and increases costs by 15 percent in each category.

a. What justifications might you have had for changing Kim's 1997 budget? What ethical considerations are involved in your decision to change her budget without consulting her after asking for her input?

b. Why would Kim have sent a less accurate forecast for 1998 than she did for 1997? What ethical considerations are involved in her decision to make the budget misstatements?

c. Since advertising firms do not manufacture products, would Kim's understatement of her revenues have any effects on other offices of the firm?

48. Norton Company, a manufacturer of infant furniture and carriages, is in the initial stages of preparing the annual budget for 1997. Scott Ford has recently joined Norton's accounting staff and is interested to learn as much as possible about the company's budgeting process. During a recent lunch with Marge Atkins, sales manager, and Pete Granger, production manager, Ford initiated the following conversation:

Ford: "Since I'm new around here and am going to be involved with the preparation of the annual budget, I'd be interested to learn how the two of you estimate sales and production numbers."

Atkins: "We start out very methodically by looking at recent history, discussing what we know about current accounts, potential customers, and the general state of consumer spending. Then we add that usual dose of intuition to come up with the best forecast we can."

Granger: "I usually take the sales projections as the basis for my projections. Of course, we have to make an estimate of what this year's closing inventories will be, which is sometimes difficult."

Ford: "Why does that present a problem? There must have been an estimate of closing inventories in the budget for the current year."

Granger: "Those numbers aren't always reliable, since Marge makes some adjustments to the sales numbers before passing them on to me."

Ford: "What kind of adjustments?"

Atkins: "Well, we don't want to fall short of the sales projections, so we generally give ourselves a little breathing room by lowering the initial sales projection anywhere from 5 to 10 percent."

Granger: "So, you can see why this year's budget is not a very reliable starting point. We always have to adjust the projected production rates as the year progresses and, of course, this changes the ending inventory estimates. By the way, we make similar adjustments to expenses by adding at least 10 percent to the estimates. I think everyone around here does the same thing."

a. Marge Atkins and Pete Granger have described the use of budgetary slack.

   1. Explain why Atkins and Granger behave in this manner, and describe the benefits they expect to realize from the use of budgetary slack.

   2. Explain how the use of budgetary slack can adversely affect Atkins and Granger.

b. As a management accountant, Scott Ford believes that the behavior described by Marge Atkins and Pete Granger may be unethical and that he may have an obligation to not support this behavior. By citing the specific standards of competence, confidentiality, integrity, and/or objectivity from Statements on Management Accounting, "Standards of Ethical Conduct for Management Accountants," (Appendix A to text) explain why the use of budgetary slack can adversely affect Atkins and Granger.

(CMA)

▣ PROJECTS

49. Following is a list of typical questions that are raised and dealt with during the process of strategic planning. Assume that you and two or three of your classmates are part of top management in one of the following types of organizations: a major automotive manufacturer; a major charitable organization; a major pharmaceutical company; a major airline; a major advertising agency; or a major hospital chain. Obtain several current annual reports (if available) from a particular company of your choice, perform some library (or other) research, and do some creative thinking to prepare a research paper that answers these questions about that company.

   ■ What is the company's justification for existence?

   ■ In what environment will the company operate?
        Nature of the industry
        Nature of the competitive situation

Nature of the general economy
Political situation in markets served and potential markets

- What are the key variables to being successful in this industry?

- What product, product lines, and market should the company pursue?
    What is the company good at doing?
    What directions should the company take in relation to new products, new markets, development of existing products, and development of existing markets?

- What are the company's strengths and weaknesses?
    In organization
    In facilities
    In finance

- Where is the company now and where does it appear to be heading?
    What has the company accomplished?
    How does it stand financially, organizationally, and in its industry?
    Should it consider any acquisitions? Which ones and why?

- What assumptions should be made about the future with respect to sales, profit, growth, return on investment, and other factors?

[SOURCE: Questions adapted from Clarence B. Nickerson, *Accounting Handbook for Nonaccountants* (Boston: Cahners Books International, 1975), pp. 533-534. Used with permission of Cahners Publishing Company, a division of Reed Publishing (USA) Inc.]

50. Deregulation, the removal or scaling down of the regulatory authority and activities of the government, was advocated during the late 1970s and early 1980s. Many economists and politicians believed that consumers would benefit from freedom of choice, lower prices, and improved services if regulated industries were subjected to the vagaries of the competitive marketplace. Among the major segments of the U.S. economy affected were banking, communications, energy, and transportation.

As financial institutions and corporations were freed from regulatory restraints, managements of regulated industries had to change their ways; they could no longer be complacent, hiding behind the regulatory blankets that previously had provided order, equity, and antitrust immunity. With barriers relaxed, new entities emerged, seeking new opportunities and threatening the existence of many well-known companies. As competitive pressures intensified, the financial policies and strategies needed for success and survival in a deregulated environment centered on improving profitability and maintaining or expanding market share. Select an industry mentioned above, go to the library and find articles that deal with effects of deregulation on that industry, and then summarize your findings. Include discussions of how deregulation has affected:

a. the way prices are set in the industry.
b. the consumers of the products or services produced by the industry.
c. the profitability of firms in the industry.

Note: This project may be completed by teams. If so, a team should be composed of three membrs and each member should have individual responsibility for one of the three requirements.

(CMA adapted)

51. Assume that it is the first day of your managerial accounting class and your instructor has just been introduced. Following the introduction, the instructor indicates that it is time to prepare the "class budget" for the semester. The

instructor passes out the course syllabus that outlines the material (and a weekly work schedule) to be covered during the semester. The syllabus also contains the following information:

COURSE OBJECTIVES

We have three primary objectives. They are to gain a fundamental understanding of and the ability to communicate to others the (1) technical aspects of managerial accounting; (2) role of accountants in organizations; and (3) behavioral implications of accounting information.

USE OF CLASS TIME

PERFORMANCE EVALUATION

You immediately note that the last two categories are blank. The instructor indicates that he or she believes in a "participative" course plan. Your task is to complete the syllabus (course plan) and submit it to your instructor for approval. In completing the syllabus, be mindful of the course objectives and remember that you are helping to establish the standard by which you will be evaluated. [Note: It may be helpful to read "Classroom Participative Budgeting," by C. Douglas Poe in *Management Accounting* (May 1994), p. 61.]

THE MASTER BUDGET

LEARNING OBJECTIVES

1. Explain the purpose and preparation of a master budget.

2. Determine the starting point of a master budget and why this item is chosen.

3. Prepare the various component budgets of the master budget and relate them to one another.

4. Prepare a cash budget and understand why it is so important in the master budgeting process.

5. Develop the budgeted, (pro forma) financial statements.

People who fail to plan, have planned to fail.
George Hewell

Lloyd Manufacturing: Quality Affects the Budget Process

Located in Warren, Rhode Island, Lloyd Manufacturing was founded in 1938 to manufacture rubber threading and card cloth for the textile industry. A primary use for rubber thread was in the making of three-ply golf balls. But in the mid-1980s, a new method of making golf balls (two-ply molded) was introduced, and Lloyd's business dropped. The company took stock of its strengths and began to emphasize its ability to custom-formulate low-gauge, close tolerance calendered (rolled) rubber sheeting. Products include gaskets for electrical capacitors and intravenous bags, sound-deadening pads, door seals, and rubber straps for safety masks.

Because Lloyd's products are unique to customer specifications, revenue forecasts are difficult. Estimates are made by the salespeople using historical data combined with anticipated shifts in business. Sales forecasts are distributed to the manufacturing, technical, and administrative departments for use in assessing the manpower, capital, and other support requirements. Expenses are generally more easily projected: raw materials cost is a fairly stable percentage of sales dollars; labor cost per hour is set by the union; and many overhead costs are fixed. Lloyd's emphasis on quality and introduction of statistical process controls have had some budget impacts: forecasted revenues are on the rise; scrap and customer return costs can be budgeted at 3 percent and 1 percent, respectively, less than in the past; and capital expenditures are expected to increase as the company installs quality control instrumentation on equipment and makes facility renovations for better work flow. Most importantly, bottom line profit estimates are up. By recognizing the effects of quality improvements in the budget, Lloyd Manufacturing management can see that spending for prevention—rather than paying for failure—makes good business sense.

SOURCE: Information provided by Jeffrey Leyh, President, Lloyd Manufacturing Corporation, 1994.

Regardless of the type of endeavor in which you engage, it is necessary at some point to visualize the future, imagine what results you want to achieve, and determine the activities and resources required to achieve those results. If the process is complex, the means by which results are to be achieved should be written because of the human tendency to forget and the difficulty of mentally processing many facts and relationships at the same time. Written plans that are monetarily enumerated are called budgets. While budgeting is important for everyone, organizations (such as Lloyd Manufacturing, New York City, or the Girl Scouts) that have significant amounts of cash and other resources should prepare and use detailed budgets for both planning and control purposes.

Chapter 10 describes the managerial aspects of the budgeting and planning process. This chapter covers quantitative aspects of the process and the preparation of a master budget.

THE MASTER BUDGET

master budget

operating budgets

From an accounting standpoint, the budgeting process culminates in the preparation of a **master budget**, which is a comprehensive set of an organization's budgetary schedules and pro forma (projected) financial statements. The master budget is composed of both operating and financial budgets. **Operating budgets** are expressed in both units and dollars. When an operating budget is related to revenues, the units are those expected to be sold, and the dollars reflect selling prices. When an operating budget relates to expense items, the units are those expected to be used and the dollars reflect costs.

Monetary details from the operating budgets are aggregated in **financial budgets**, which reflect the funds to be generated or consumed during the budget period. Financial budgets include the company's cash and capital budgets as well as its pro forma financial statements. These budgets are the ultimate focal points for the firm's top management.

The master budget is prepared for a specific period and is static rather than flexible. It is static in that it is based on a single, most probable level of output demand. The selection of this level of output is discussed in the News Note on page 550. Expressing the budget on a single level of demand is necessary to facilitate the many time-consuming financial arrangements that must be made before beginning operations for the budget period. Such arrangements include hiring an adequate number of people, obtaining needed production and/or storage space, obtaining suppliers, and confirming prices, delivery schedules, and quality of resources.

The demand level of sales or service quantities selected for use in the preparation of the master budget affects all organizational components. It is essential that all the components interact in a coordinated manner. Exhibit 11–1 indicates the budgetary

financial budgets

■ LEARNING OBJECTIVE 1
Explain the purpose and preparation of a master budget.

■ LEARNING OBJECTIVE 2
Determine the starting point of a master budget and why this item is chosen.

■ **EXHIBIT 11–1**
The Budgetary Process in a Manufacturing Organization

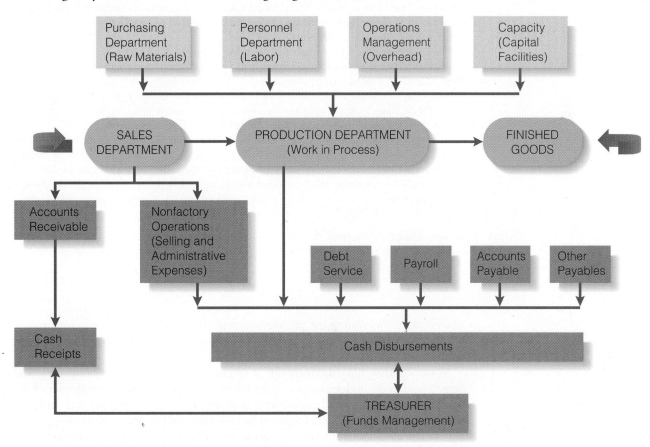

Don't Make Budget Targets Too Easy or Too Difficult

It is a basic axiom of management that budget targets should be set to be challenging but achievable. But to establish that target, management must first determine what "challenging but achievable" really means. Should profits be targeted at some easily obtainable goal, a realistic middle ground, or at a point so high that hope of attainment is slim?

There is no one right answer, given the number of purposes for which budgets are used: planning, coordination, control, motivation, and performance evaluation. Some may argue that planning purposes are served best with a best-guess budget, one that is as likely to be exceeded as missed. Others may propose that, for optimum motivation, budget targets should be highly challenging, with only a 25% to 40% chance of achievement.

There is one target-level choice, however, that serves the combination of purposes for which budgets are used quite well in the vast majority of organizational situations. Therefore, it provides an effective compromise. That choice is to set budget targets with a high probability of achievement—achievable by most managers 80% to 90% of the time—and then to supplement these targets with promises of extra incentives for performance exceeding the target level.

Only in a few organizational situations is it not desirable to set highly achievable profit budget targets. One exception is caused by organizational need. A company in grave difficulty may want to set less achievable budget targets as a signal to its managers that a certain higher level of performance is necessary for the corporation to survive or for the [organizational unit] to stave off divestment.

A second exception occurs when it is desirable to correct for [an organizational unit's] windfall gain. Sometimes when managers have been lucky in a prior period, perhaps earning large and mostly undeserved bonuses, a more challenging budget target can be set as an effective way of making compensation more fair across the multiyear period. Here, though, care must be taken to guard against unwarranted management turnover because current period expected compensation probably will fall below competitive market levels.

In virtually all other situations, it is desirable to set highly achievable profit budget targets while allowing the managers few excuses for not achieving the targets but providing them significant additional rewards for exceeding the targets. Setting targets that are highly achievable but not too easy takes considerable managerial skill. But when [upper-level managers] implement this combination of mechanisms effectively, they will ensure that all the purposes for which budgets are used are served well.

SOURCE: Kenneth A. Merchant, "How Challenging Should Profit Budget Targets Be?" *Management Accounting* (November 1990), pp. 46, 48. Published by Institute of Management Accountants, Montvale, NJ.

interrelationships among the primary departments of a manufacturing organization. A budget developed by one department is commonly an essential ingredient in developing another department's budget.

Assuming that top management is engaging in participatory budgeting, each department in the budgetary process either prepares its own budget or provides information for inclusion in a budget. As is true at Lloyd Manufacturing, the budgetary process begins with the Sales Department's estimates of the types, quantities, and timing of demand for the company's products. This information is needed by both Production and Accounts Receivable. The production manager combines sales estimates with information from Purchasing, Personnel, Operations, and Capital Facilities to determine the types, quantities, and timing of products to be manufactured. Accounts Receivable uses sales estimates, in conjunction with estimated collection patterns, to determine the amounts and timing of cash receipts. Cash receipts information is necessary for the treasurer to properly manage the organization's flow of funds. All areas create cash disbursements that must be matched with cash receipts so that cash is available when it is needed.

In Exhibit 11–1, note that certain information must flow back into the department from which it began. For example, the Sales Department must receive finished goods information to know if goods are in stock (or can be produced to order) before selling products. The treasurer must receive continual input on cash receipts and disbursements as well as provide output to various organizational units on the availability of funds so that proper funds management can be maintained.

Exhibit 11–2 presents an overview of the master budget and component budgets preparation sequence and component budgets, indicates the department responsible for each budget's preparation, and illustrates how the budgets relate to one another. While the flow of information is visible in Exhibit 11–2, the quantitative and monetary implications are not. The remainder of the chapter reflects these implications through the preparation of a master budget.

THE MASTER BUDGET ILLUSTRATED

■ LEARNING OBJECTIVE 3
Prepare the various component budget of the master budget and relate them to one another.

Scorpio Ltd. is used to illustrate the process of preparing a master budget for 1998. The company produces color-coded rubber gaskets for use in the automotive industry. The master budget is prepared for the entire year and then subdivided into quarterly and monthly periods. Scorpio Ltd.'s Marketing Division has estimated total sales for the year at 4,000,000 gaskets. While annual sales are detailed on a monthly basis, the Scorpio Ltd. illustration focuses only on the first-quarter budgets. The process of developing the master budget is the same regardless of whether the time frame is one year or one quarter.

The December 31, 1997, balance sheet presented in Exhibit 11–3 (page 553) provides the account balances needed to prepare the master budget. The December 31 balances are really estimates rather than actual figures because the budget process for 1998 must begin significantly before December 31, 1997. A company's budgetary time schedule depends on many factors, including its size and its degree of forecasting sophistication. Scorpio Ltd. starts its budgeting process in November when the sales forecast is received by management or the budget committee. The **budget committee** reviews and approves, or makes adjustments to, the master budget and/or the budgets submitted from operational managers. This committee is usually composed of top management and the chief financial officer.

budget committee

Sales Budget

The sales budget is prepared in terms of both units and sales dollars. The selling price set for 1998 is $.50 per gasket, and the price is the same for all sales territories and all customers. Monthly sales demand and revenue for the first five months of 1998 are shown in Exhibit 11–4 (page 554). Dollar sales figures are computed as sales quantities times product selling price. April and May information is given because it is needed later to determine production information for the March budget. The "Total for Quarter" column shows sales for only January, February, and March.

Production Budget

The production budget follows naturally from the sales budget and uses information regarding the type, quantity, and timing of units to be sold. Sales information is combined with information on beginning and ending inventories so that managers can schedule the necessary production.

■ **EXHIBIT 11–2**
The Master Budget: An Overview

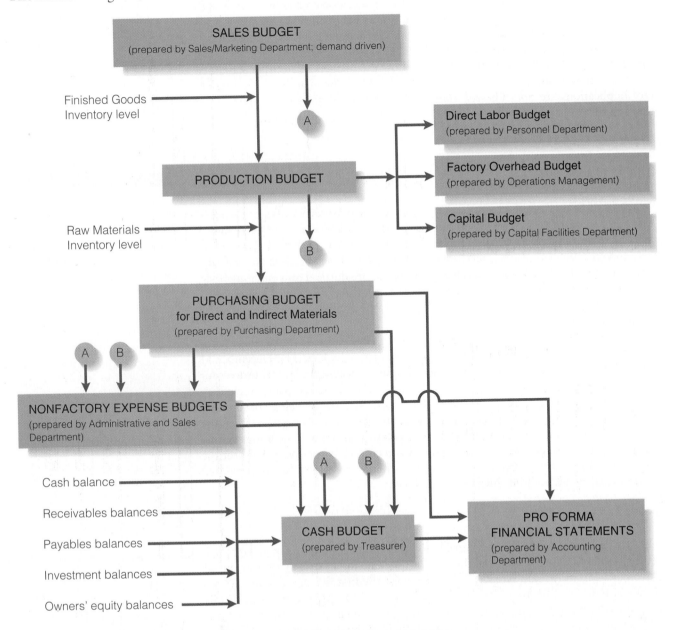

Note: The circled letters reflect a flow of information as an output of one area and an input of another.

■ **EXHIBIT 11–3**
Balance Sheet (Estimated) December 31, 1997

ASSETS

Current Assets		
Cash		$ 5,050
Accounts Receivable	$ 84,000	
Less Allowance for Uncollectibles	(1,200)	82,800
Inventories:		
Direct Materials	$ 8,758	
Finished Goods (30,800 units @ $.35)	10,780	19,538
Total Current Assets		$107,388
Plant Assets		
Property, Plant and Equipment	$540,000	
Less Accumulated Depreciation	(180,000)	360,000
TOTAL ASSETS		$467,388

LIABILITIES & STOCKHOLDERS' EQUITY

Current Liabilities		
Accounts Payable		$ 48,757
Dividends Payable (due 1/15/98)		15,000
Total Current Liabilities		$ 63,757
Stockholders' Equity		
Common Stock	$300,000	
Retained Earnings	103,631	403,631
TOTAL LIABILITIES AND STOCKHOLDERS' EQUITY		$467,388

Ending inventory policy (as to quantity of units) is generally specified by company management. Desired ending inventory is normally a function of the quantity and timing of demand in the upcoming period together with the firm's production capacity and speed. Before making a decision about how much inventory to keep on hand, managers should consider the high costs of stockpiling inventory. Management may stipulate that ending inventory be a given percentage of the next period's projected sales. Other alternatives include maintaining a constant amount of inventory, building up inventory levels for future high-demand periods, and keeping inventory levels near zero under a just-in-time system. The decision about ending inventory levels affects whether a firm has constant production with varying inventory levels or variable production with constant inventory levels. And, as indicated in the following quote, the size of the inventory is also directly related to cash flow.

■ **EXHIBIT 11–4**
Sales Budget (for Five Months and for the Quarter Ending March 31, 1998)

	JANUARY	FEBRUARY	MARCH	TOTAL FOR QUARTER	APRIL	MAY
Sales in units	440,000	410,000	387,000	1,237,000	360,000	390,000
Sales in dollars	$220,000	$205,000	$193,500	$ 618,500	$180,000	$195,000

Mismanagement of your company's inventory can create a financial hemorrhage that may cripple the business for life. Excessive inventory purchases, slow-moving inventory, and the inability to reorder in a timely fashion can all wreak havoc on your cash flow. Remember that inventory is "cash" sitting on your shelves without earning any interest. Actually, it may be one of your firm's larger expenditures, depending on the type of business and industry you are in.[1]

Demand for gaskets varies throughout the year, and Scorpio Ltd. carries very little inventory. Production time is short, so company management has a policy that Finished Goods Inventory need be only 7 percent of the next month's sales. Based on the ending inventory policy and the sales information from Exhibit 11–4, the production budget shown in Exhibit 11–5 is prepared.

The beginning inventory balance shown for January is the number of units on hand at December 31, 1997. This inventory figure is 30,800 units, which represents 7 percent of January's estimated 440,000 units of sales. March's ending inventory balance is 7 percent of April's estimated 360,000 units of sales. Scorpio Ltd. has no Work in Process Inventory because all units placed into production are fully completed each period.[2]

Purchases Budget

Direct materials are essential to production and must be purchased each period in sufficient quantities to meet production needs and to conform with the company's ending inventory policies. Scorpio Ltd.'s management has established that raw materials be 10 percent of the following month's production needs. This inventory level is slightly higher than that of the finished goods because the raw materials are petroleum-based and oil supplies affect both availability and price.

The purchases budget is first stated in whole units of finished products. It is subsequently converted to individual direct material component requirements. Production of a gasket requires two ounces of rubber. The quantity of coloring dye and its cost are insignificant, so the dye is treated as an indirect material. Unit material cost has been estimated by the purchasing agent to be $.10 per ounce. The whole-

---

■ **EXHIBIT 11–5**
Production Budget (for the Three Months and Quarter Ending March 31, 1998)

	JANUARY	FEBRUARY	MARCH	TOTAL
Sales in units (from Exhibit 11-4)	440,000	410,000	387,000	1,237,000
+ Desired ending inventory	28,700	27,090	25,200	25,200
Total needed	468,700	437,090	412,200	1,262,200
- Beginning inventory	(30,800)	(28,700)	(27,090)	(30,800)
Units to be produced	437,900	408,390	385,110	1,231,400

Note: April's production would be 360,000 + 27,300 - 25,200 = 362,100

---

[1]Leslie N. Masonson, ed., *Cash Management Performance Report* (Boston: Warren, Gorham & Lamont, January 1991), p. 1.

[2]Most manufacturing entities do not produce only whole units during the period. Normally, partially completed beginning and ending in-process inventories exist. Consideration of partially completed inventories is covered in Chapter 7, on process costing.

unit and component purchases budgets for each month of the first quarter of 1998 are shown in Exhibit 11–6. The beginning inventory for January is 10 percent of January production.

Given expected production, the Engineering and Personnel Departments can work together to determine the necessary labor requirements for the factory, sales force, and office staff. Labor requirements are stated in total number of people, and number of specific types of people (skilled laborers, sales people, clerical personnel), as well as production hours required of factory employees. Labor costs are computed based on items such as union labor contracts, minimum wage laws, fringe benefit costs, payroll taxes, and bonus arrangements. The various personnel amounts are shown, as appropriate, in either the direct labor budget, the manufacturing overhead budget, or the selling, general, and administrative costs budget.

Direct Labor Budget

The management of Scorpio Ltd. has reviewed the staffing requirements and has developed the direct labor cost estimates shown in Exhibit 11–7 (page 556) for the first quarter of 1998. Factory direct labor costs are based on the standard hours of labor needed to produce the number of units shown in the production budget. The average wage rate shown in the exhibit includes both the basic direct labor payroll rate and the payroll taxes and fringe benefits related to direct labor (since these items usually add between 25 and 30 percent to the base labor cost). All compensation is paid in the month in which it is incurred.

Overhead Budget

Overhead is another production cost that must be estimated by management. Exhibit 11–8 (page 556) presents Scorpio Ltd.'s monthly cost of each overhead item for the first quarter of 1998. The company has determined that machine hours are the best predictor of overhead costs.

At Lloyd Manufacturing, as at most companies, the annual sales projection is the starting point of creating a master budget. Development of the completed master budget requires the participation of numerous individuals who provide the details needed to quantify the interrelationships among organizational activities.

■ **EXHIBIT 11–6**

Purchases Budget (for the Three Months and Quarter Ending March 31, 1998)

	JANUARY	FEBRUARY	MARCH	TOTAL
Units to be produced (from Exhibit 11–5)	437,900	408,390	385,110	1,231,400
+ EI units	40,839	38,511	36,210	36,210
= Total whole unit quantites needed	478,739	446,901	421,320	1,267,610
− Beginning inventory units	(43,790)	(40,839)	(38,511)	(43,790)
= Purchases required in whole unit quantities	434,949	406,062	382,809	1,223,820
× Ounces per unit	× 2	× 2	× 2	× 2
Total ounces to be purchased	869,898	812,124	765,618	2,447,640
× Price per ounce	× $.10	× $.10	× $.10	× $.10
Total cost of rubber	$86,989.80	$81,212.40	$76,561.80	$ 244,764

Note: All dollar amounts will be rounded to the nearest whole dollar when used in computations later in the chapter.

■ **EXHIBIT 11–7**
Direct Labor Budget (for the Three Months and Quarter Ending March 31, 1998)

	JANUARY	FEBRUARY	MARCH	TOTAL
Units of production	437,900	408,390	385,110	1,231,400
× Standard hours per unit	.005	.005	.005	.005
Total hours allowed	2,189.5	2,041.95	1,925.55	6,157
× Average wage rate (including fringe benefits)	$10.00	$10.00	$10.00	$10.00
Direct labor cost (rounded)	$ 21,895	$ 20,420	$ 19,256	$ 61,570

In estimating overhead, all costs must be specified and mixed costs must be separated into their fixed (a) and variable (b) elements. Each overhead amount shown is calculated by use of the $y = a + bX$ formula for a mixed cost, in which X is the number of units of activity (in this case, machine hours). For example, February maintenance cost is the fixed amount of $2,600 plus ($5.80 times 160 estimated machine hours), or $2,600 + $928 = $3,528. Both total cost and cost net of depreciation are shown in the budget. The cost net of depreciation is the amount that is expected to be paid in cash during the month and will, therefore, affect the cash budget.

Selling, General, and Administrative (SG&A) Budget

Selling, general, and administrative expenses for each month can be predicted in the same manner as overhead costs. Exhibit 11–9 presents the SG&A budget. Note that sales figures rather than production levels are used as the measure of activity in preparing this budget. The company's sales force consists of a manager with a month-

■ **EXHIBIT 11–8**
Manufacturing Overhead Budget (for the Three Months and Quarter Ending March 31, 1998)

			JANUARY	FEBRUARY	MARCH	TOTAL
Estimated Machine Hours (X) (given)			180	160	150	490
	Value of					
	Fixed Cost	Variable Cost per Unit				
Factory Overhead Items:	**a**	**b**				
Depreciation	$14,000	$10.00	$15,800	$15,600	$15,500	$ 46,900
Indirect materials	—	.10	18	16	15	49
Indirect labor	7,000	.50	7,090	7,080	7,075	21,245
Utilities	3,000	1.60	3,288	3,256	3,240	9,784
Property taxes	5,000	—	5,000	5,000	5,000	15,000
Insurance	6,500	—	6,500	6,500	6,500	19,500
Maintenance	2,600	5.80	3,644	3,528	3,470	10,642
Total cost (y)	$38,100	$18.00	$41,340	$40,980	$40,800	$123,120
Total cost net of depreciation			$25,540	$25,380	$25,300	$ 76,220

■ **EXHIBIT 11–9**

Selling, General, and Administrative Budget (for the Three Months and Quarter Ending March 31, 1998)

			JANUARY	FEBRUARY	MARCH	TOTAL
Predicted Sales (from Exhibit 11–4)			$220,000	$205,000	$193,500	$618,500
	Value of					
	Fixed Cost	*Variable Cost per Unit*				
SG&A Items:	**a**	**b**				
Supplies	$ 350	$ .02	$ 4,750	$ 4,450	$ 4,220	$ 13,420
Depreciation	3,800	—	3,800	3,800	3,800	11,400
Utilities	200	—	200	200	200	600
Miscellaneous	500	—	500	500	500	1,500
Salaries:						
Sales manager	5,000		5,000	5,000	5,000	15,000
Salespeople	2,000	.10	24,000	22,500	21,350	67,850
General and administrative	18,000	--	18,000	18,000	18,000	54,000
Total cost (y)	$29,850	$.12	$ 56,250	$ 54,450	$ 53,070	$163,770
Total cost net of depreciation			$ 52,450	$ 50,650	$ 49,270	$152,370

ly salary of $5,000 and four salespeople who receive $500 per month plus a 10 percent commission on sales. General and administrative staff salaries total $18,000 per month.

Capital Budget

The budgets included in the master budget focus on the short-term or upcoming fiscal period. Managers, however, must also consider long-term needs in the area of plant and equipment purchases. The process of assessing such needs and budgeting for the expenditures is called **capital budgeting.**[3] The capital budget is prepared separately from the master budget, but since expenditures are involved, capital budgeting does affect the master budgeting process. As shown in Exhibit 11–10, Scorpio Ltd. managers have decided that only one capital purchase will be made in the first

capital budgeting

■ **EXHIBIT 11–10**

Capital Budget (for the Three Months and Quarter Ending March 31, 1998)

	JANUARY	FEBRUARY	MARCH	TOTAL
Acquisitions:				
Quality control instrument	$40,000	$0	$0	$40,000
Cash payments:				
Quality control instrument	$0	$40,000	$0	$40,000

[3]Chapter 14 covers the concepts and techniques of capital budgeting.

quarter of 1998. The company is planning to acquire a quality control instrument as an accessory for the plant's calender (rolling) machine. This instrument will cost $40,000 and will be purchased and placed into service at the beginning of January. The company will pay for the instrument at the end of February. Depreciation on this quality control instrument is included in the overhead calculation in Exhibit 11–8. No equipment will be sold or scrapped when the instrument is purchased.

Cash Budget

■ LEARNING
OBJECTIVE 4
Prepare a cash budget and
understand why it is so
important in the master
budgeting process.

After all the preceding budgets have been developed, a cash budget can be constructed. The cash budget may be the most important schedule prepared during the budgeting process because a company cannot survive without cash. "Market growth cannot materialize, expansion will stagnate, capital expansion programs cannot occur, and R&D programs cannot be achieved without adequate cash flow."[4]

The following model can be used to summarize cash receipts and disbursements in a manner that helps managers to devise appropriate financing measures to meet company needs.

CASH BUDGET MODEL

Beginning cash balance
+ Cash receipts from collections
= Cash available for disbursements exclusive of financing
− Cash needed for disbursements
= Cash excess or deficiency (a)
− Minimum desired cash balance
= Cash (needed) or available for investment or repayment
   Financing methods:
± Borrow money (repay loans)
± Issue (reacquire) capital stock
± Sell (acquire) investments or plant assets
± Receive (pay) interest or dividends
   Total impact (+ or −) of planned financing (b)
= Ending cash balance (c), where c = a ± b

Cash budgets can be used to predict seasonal variances in any potential cash flow. Such predictions can indicate a need for short-term borrowing and a potential schedule of repayments. The cash budget may also show the possibility of surplus cash, which can be used for funds management, such as for investment. Cash budgets can be used to measure the performance of the accounts receivable and accounts payable departments by comparing actual to scheduled collections, payments, and discounts taken.

Cash Receipts and Accounts Receivable   Once sales revenues have been determined, managers translate that information into actual cash receipts through the use of an expected collection pattern. This pattern considers the actual collection patterns experienced in recent past periods and management's judgment about changes that could disturb current collection patterns. For example, changes that could weaken current collection patterns include recessionary conditions, increases in interest rates, and less strict credit-granting practices.

---

[4]Cosmo S. Trapani, "Six Critical Areas in the Budgeting Process," *Management Accounting* (November 1982), p. 54.

In specifying collection patterns, managers should recognize that different types of customers pay in different ways. Any sizeable, unique category of clientele should be segregated. For example, in 1992, Wal-Mart paid invoices in an average of 29 days, while Kmart took 45.[5] Suppliers selling to these two companies would want to show separate collection patterns for receivables for each of these businesses. As indicated in the News Note on page 561, it is essential for companies to know their customers' payment patterns.

Scorpio Ltd. has two types of customers. Forty percent of the customers pay cash and receive a 2 percent discount. The remaining 60 percent of the customers purchase products on credit and have the following collection pattern: 30 percent in the month of sale and 69 percent in the month following the sale. One percent of credit sales are uncollectible. Scorpio Ltd.'s collection pattern is diagrammed in Exhibit 11–11.

Using the sales budget, information on December 1997 sales, and the collection pattern, management can estimate cash receipts from sales during the first three months of 1998. Management must have December sales information because collections for credit sales extend over two months, meaning that some collections from the $200,000 of December 1997 sales occur in January 1998. Projected monthly collections for the first quarter of 1998 are shown in Exhibit 11–12 (page 560). The individual calculations relate to the various collection patterns and related percentages presented in Exhibit 11–11. All amounts have been rounded to the nearest dollar.

The December collection amounts can be reconciled to the December 31, 1997, balance sheet (Exhibit 11–3), which indicated an Accounts Receivable balance of $84,000. This amount appears in the collection schedule as follows:

January collections of December sales	$82,800
Estimated uncollectibles from December sales	1,200
December 31, 1997, balance in Accounts Receivable	$84,000

January 1998 sales of $220,000 are used as an example of the collection calculations in Exhibit 11–12. Line A of the diagram in Exhibit 11–11 represents cash sales of 40 percent, or $88,000. These sales will be collected net of the 2 percent discount:

■ **EXHIBIT 11–11**
Collection Pattern for Sales

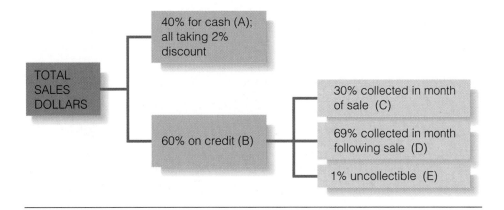

[5]George Stalk, Philip Evans, and Lawrence E. Shulman, "Competing on Capabilities," *Harvard Business Review* (March-April 1992), p. 63.

Sales to customers allowed discount (40% × $220,000)	$88,000	
Discount taken by customers (2% × $ 88,000)	(1,760)	
Net collections from customers allowed discount	$86,240	

The next three January calculations in Exhibit 11–12 represent customers who buy on credit (60 percent; line B in Exhibit 11–11) and who (1) pay within the month of the sale (line C), (2) pay in the month after the sale (line D), or (3) do not pay (line E):

Sales to customers on credit (60% × $220,000)	$132,000
Collections in month of sale (30% × $132,000)	39,600
Collections in month after sale (69% × $132,000)	91,080
Uncollectible from January credit sales (1% × $132,000)	1,320

The remaining amounts are computed in the same manner. Note that the collection in the month after the sale is 69 percent of the original credit sale, and uncollectibles are 1 percent of the original credit sales, not of the remaining balance.

Once the schedule of cash collections is prepared, the balances of the Accounts Receivable and Allowance for Uncollectibles accounts can be projected. The accounts for Scorpio Ltd. are shown at the top of page 562 and are used in preparing pro forma year-end 1998 financial statements. Note that the Allowance account balance indicates that Scorpio Ltd. has not written off any accounts receivable since December 1997. The company may still believe some of these accounts are collectible or may simply choose to write them off after the end of the first quarter of 1998.

■ **EXHIBIT 11–12**

Cash Collections (for the Three Months and Quarter Ending March 31, 1998)

	JANUARY	FEBRUARY	MARCH	TOTAL	DISCOUNT	UNCOLLECTIBLE
From:						
December 1997 Sales:						
$200,000 (60%) (69%)	$ 82,800			$ 82,800		
$200,000 (60%) (1%)						$1,200
January 1998 Sales:						
$220,000 (40%) (98%; 2%)	86,240 N			86,240	$1,760	
$220,000 (60%) (30%)	39,600			39,600		
$220,000 (60%) (69%)		$ 91,080		91,080		
$220,000 (60%) (1%)						1,320
February 1998 Sales:						
$205,000 (40%) (98%; 2%)		80,360 N		80,360	1,640	
$205,000 (60%) (30%)		36,900		36,900		
$205,000 (60%) (69%)			$ 84,870	84,870		
$205,000 (60%) (1%)						1,230
March 1998 Sales:						
$193,500 (40%) (98%; 2%)			75,852 N	75,852	1,548	
$193,500 (60%) (30%)			34,830	34,830		
$193,500 (60%) (1%)						1,161
Totals	$208,640	$208,340	$195,552	$612,532	$4,948	$4,911

Note: "N" stands for "Net of discount." The total amount of cash sales is the sum of the net of discount collection plus the amount shown on the same line in the discount column.

Slow Payments Can Mean Rapid Demise

A Dun & Bradstreet Corp. survey indicates that companies with 500 or more workers paid bills more slowly in the first quarter of 1994 than in the four years D&B has been tracking such behavior. The survey canvasses mostly small suppliers—recipients of late payments and the firms that can least afford delays. It often endangers cash flow just as an expanding economy should be creating opportunities.

Lawrence Winters, a D&B assistant vice president, says some large companies are routinely paying their bills as much as 90 days after receiving invoices, routinely due in 30 days. Not all warn vendors.

Smaller suppliers typically accept such terms "out of desperation to get business," Mr. Winters says. "They don't realize the implication of the decision until it hits them."

Earthly Elements Inc. didn't anticipate how much an overdue payment would hurt. When the maker of dried floral gifts and accessories landed a $10,000 order from a national home-shopping service in November 1993, founder Thomas Re says he threw a party. The order represented 20% of the start-up's $50,000 in orders for 1993.

But by the end of February 1994, Earthly Elements was no longer rejoicing. Mr. Re says fulfilling the order cost 25% more than expected, and then the payment was 30 days overdue. Faced with a worsening cash crunch, Mr. Re delayed paying his own bills and began to lay off employees. In March 1994, he closed shop. By the time the customer paid in April, "it was way too late" to revive the company.

SOURCE: Michael Selz, "Big Customers' Late Bills Choke Small Suppliers," *Wall Street Journal* (June 22, 1994), p. B1. Reprinted by permission of The Wall Street Journal, © 1994 Dow Jones & Company, Inc. All Rights Reserved Worldwide.

Sales dollars and cash collections per period are not the same amounts for most companies. To develop the cash budget, accrual-based sales figures cannot be used; companies must estimate the cash collection patterns for accounts receivable.

ACCOUNTS RECEIVABLE

12/31/97 Balance (Ex. 11–3)	84,000	January collections (Ex. 11–12)	208,640
January sales (Ex. 11–4)	220,000	January discounts	1,760
February sales (Ex. 11–4)	205,000	February collections (Ex. 11–12)	208,340
March sales (Ex. 11–4)	193,500	February discounts	1,640
		March collections (Ex. 11–12)	195,552
		March discounts	1,548
3/31/98 Balance	85,020		

ALLOWANCE FOR UNCOLLECTIBLES

12/31/97 Balance (Ex. 11–3)	1,200
January estimate (Ex. 11–12)	1,320
February estimate (Ex. 11–12)	1,230
March estimate (Ex. 11–12)	1,161
3/31/98 Balance	4,911

Cash Disbursements and Accounts Payable   Using the purchases information from Exhibit 11–6, management can prepare an estimated cash disbursements schedule for Accounts Payable. All purchases of direct materials are made on account by Scorpio Ltd. The company pays for 40 percent of each month's purchases in the month of purchase, taking a 2 percent cash discount. The remaining 60 percent of each month's purchases are paid in the month following the month of purchase; no discount is available for these payments.

Exhibit 11–13 presents the cash disbursements information related to purchases for the first quarter of 1998. The December 31, 1997, accounts payable balance of $48,757 (Exhibit 11–3) represents the 60 percent remaining payment required for December purchases. All amounts have been rounded to whole dollars.

■ **EXHIBIT 11–13**

Cash Disbursements—Accounts Payable (for the Three Months and Quarter Ending March 31, 1998)

	JANUARY	FEBRUARY	MARCH	TOTAL	DISCOUNT
Payment for purchases of:					
December 1997	$48,757			$48,757	
January 1998 (from Exhibit 11–6)					
$86,990 (40%) (98%; 2%)	34,100 N			34,100	$ 696
$86,990 (60%)		$52,194		52,194	
February 1998 (from Exhibit 11–6)					
$81,212 (40%) (98%; 2%)		31,835 N		31,835	650
$81,212 (60%)			$48,727	48,727	
March 1998 (from Exhibit 11–6)					
$76,562 (40%) (98%; 2%)			30,012 N	30,012	613
Totals	$82,857	$84,029	$78,739	245,625	$1,959

Note: "N" stands for "Net of discount." The total amount of gross purchases is the sum of the net of discount payment plus the amount shown on the same line in the discount column.

The accounts payable activity is summarized in the following account. The March 31 balance represents 60 percent of March purchases that will be paid during April.

ACCOUNTS PAYABLE

		12/31/97 Balance (Ex. 11–3)	48,757
January payments (Ex. 11–13)	82,857	January purchases (Ex. 11–6)	86,990
January discounts taken	696		
February payments (Ex. 11–13)	84,029	February purchases (Ex. 11–6)	81,212
February discounts taken	650		
March payments (Ex. 11–13)	78,739	March purchases (Ex. 11–6)	76,562
March discounts taken	613		
		3/31/98 Balance	45,937

Given the cash receipts and disbursements information for Scorpio Ltd., the company uses the cash budget model to prepare the cash budget shown in Exhibit 11–14. The company has established $5,000 as its desired minimum cash balance.

■ **EXHIBIT 11–14**

Cash Budget (for the Three Months and Quarter Ending March 31, 1998)

	JANUARY	FEBRUARY	MARCH	TOTAL
Beginning cash balance	$ 5,050	$ 5,048	$ 5,070	$ 5,050
Cash collections (Exhibit 11–12)	208,640	208,340	195,552	612,532
Cash available exclusive of financing	$213,690	$213,388	$200,622	$617,582
Disbursements:				
Accounts payable (Exhibit 11–13)	$ 82,857	$ 84,029	$ 78,739	$245,625
Direct labor (Exhibit 11–7)	21,895	20,420	19,256	61,571
Overhead (Exhibit 11–8)*	25,540	25,380	25,300	76,220
SG&A expenses (Exhibit 11–9)*	52,450	50,650	49,270	152,370
Total planned disbursements	$182,742	$180,479	$172,565	$535,786
Cash excess or (inadequacy) (a)	$ 30,948	$ 32,909	$ 28,057	$ 81,796
Minimum cash balance desired	5,000	5,000	5,000	5,000
Cash available or (needed)	$ 25,948	$ 27,909	$ 23,057	$ 76,796
Financing:				
Borrow (repay)	0	1,200	(1,200)	0
Issue (reacquire) stock	0	0	0	0
Liquidate (acquire) investments	(10,900)	10,900	(21,800)	(21,800)
Sell (pay for) plant assets (Exhibit 11–10)	0	(40,000)	0	(40,000)
Receive (pay) interest or dividends**	(15,000)	61	(12)	(14,951)
Total impact of planned financing (b)	$(25,900)	$(27,839)	$(23,012)	$(76,751)
Ending cash balance (a-b)	$ 5,048	$ 5,070	$ 5,045	$ 5,045

*These amounts are the net of depreciation figures.

**Dividends payable on the December 31, 1997, balance sheet were shown as being owed on January 15, 1998. Interest on investments is calculated assuming an 8% rate, and interest on borrowings is calculated assuming a 12% rate. Borrowings are made at the beginning of the month, and repayments or investments are made at the end of the month. For February, interest received is $73 ($10,900 × .08 × 1/12) and interest owed is $12 ($1,200 × .12 × 1/12). In March, interest owed is $12 ($1,200 × .12 × 1/12).

The primary reason for maintaining a minimum cash balance is the uncertainty associated with the budgeting process. If management had perfect certainty about cash inflows and outflows, there would be no need for this cash "cushion."

All borrowings by Scorpio Ltd. are assumed to take place in increments of $100 at the beginning of a month. All repayments and investments are made in $100 amounts and are assumed to occur at the end of a month. These assumptions are simplistic, since management would not actually borrow until the need for funds arose and would repay as quickly as possible so as to minimize interest expenditures. Interest on any company investments is assumed to be added to the company's bank account at the end of each month.

Exhibit 11–14 indicates that Scorpio Ltd. has $30,948 in excess cash available in January. This excess not only meets the specified $5,000 minimum balance and the dividend payment requirement from the December 1997 balance sheet, but also gives the firm an opportunity to invest $10,900. In February, Scorpio Ltd. expects to have enough cash to meet its desired minimum cash balance but not enough to pay for the machine purchased in January. The January investment must be liquidated and an additional $1,200 borrowed. Since the machine does not have to be paid for until the end of the month, the investment can continue to draw interest until that time. The borrowing has been assumed, however, to occur at the beginning of the month for consistency with the previously specified plan. Thus, Scorpio Ltd. earns interest on the investment but must pay interest on the borrowings for February. In March, there is enough cash available to meet budgeted disbursements, pay off the February borrowings, and make a $21,800 investment. Interest on borrowings and investments is calculated at the bottom of Exhibit 11–14. Changes in the interest rate will affect any future budget-to-actual comparisons.

Several things should be specially noted involving the total column in Exhibit 11–14. First, the beginning cash balance is not the total of the three months, but is the balance at January 1. Second, the monthly and quarterly minimum cash balance is $5,000, not $15,000. Last, the ending cash balance should be the same as what appears in the final month of the quarter. These figures (beginning, minimum, and ending cash balances) are the only ones that are not summed across the three-month information; all other figures are totals. These figures can be updated monthly; a spreadsheet program is very useful for this function.

Budgeted Financial Statements

■ LEARNING
OBJECTIVE 5
Develop the budgeted (pro forma) financial statements.

The final step in the budgeting process is the development of budgeted or pro forma financial statements for the period. These statements reflect the results that will be achieved if the estimates and assumptions used for all previous budgets actually occur. Such statements allow management to determine if the predicted results are acceptable for the period. If the predicted results are not acceptable, management has the opportunity to change and adjust items before beginning the period.

For example, if expected net income is not considered a reasonable amount, management may discuss raising selling prices or finding ways to decrease costs. Any specific changes considered by management may have related effects that must be included in the revised projections. For example, if selling prices are raised, volume may decrease. Alternatively, reductions in costs from using a lesser grade of materials could have an effect on spoilage during production or could cause a decline in demand. Computer spreadsheet programs are used to quickly and easily make the recalculations necessary from such changes in assumptions.

Cost of Goods Manufactured Schedule   Before an income statement can be drafted, management must prepare a Schedule of Cost of Goods Manufactured, which is necessary to determine Cost of Goods Sold.[6] Using information from previous budgets, Scorpio Ltd.'s accountant has prepared the budgeted cost of goods manufactured schedule shown in Exhibit 11–15. Since there were no beginning or ending work in process inventories, cost of goods manufactured is equal to the manufacturing costs of the period.

Income Statement   Scorpio Ltd.'s projected income statement for the first quarter of 1998 is shown in Exhibit 11–16 (page 566). This statement uses much of the information previously developed in determining the revenues and expenses for the period.

Balance Sheet   Upon completion of the income statement, Scorpio Ltd. accountants can prepare a pro forma March 31, 1998, balance sheet (Exhibit 11–17, page 567). The letters in parentheses after some of the items in Exhibit 11–17 refer to the calculations shown at the bottom of the exhibit.

Statement of Cash Flows   The information found on the income statement, balance sheet, and cash budget is used in preparing a statement of cash flows (SCF). This statement is a principal internal, as well as external, report. The SCF explains the change in the cash balance by reflecting the company's sources and uses of cash. Such knowledge is useful in judging the company's ability to handle fixed cash outflow commitments, adapt to adverse changes in business conditions, and undertake new

---

■ **EXHIBIT 11–15**
Pro Forma Cost of Good Manufactured Schedule for First Quarter 1998

Beginning work in process		$ 0
Cost of direct materials used:		
Beginning balance of direct materials inventory (Exhibit 11–3)	$ 8,758	
Purchases (Exhibit 11–6, net of $1,959 of discounts taken)	242,805	
Total direct materials available	$251,563	
Ending balance of direct materials inventory (Note A)	7,242	
Cost of direct materials used	$244,321	
Direct labor (Exhibit 11–7)	61,571	
Factory overhead (Exhibit 11–8)	123,120	429,012
Total costs to be accounted for		$429,012
Ending work in process inventory		0
Cost of goods manufactured		$429,012

Note A	
Ending balance (Exhibit 11–6) in units	36,210
Ounces of rubber per unit	× 2
Total ounces of rubber	72,420
Price per ounce	× $.10
Ending balance in dollars	$7,242

---

[6]Chapter 3 discusses the cost of goods manufactured schedule.

commitments. Further, because the cash flow statement identifies the relationships between net income and net cash flow from operations, it assists managers in judging the quality of the company's earnings.

While the cash budget is essential to current cash management, the budgeted SCF gives managers a more global view of cash flows by rearranging them into three distinct major activities: operating, investing, and financing. Such a rearrangement permits management to judge whether the specific anticipated flows are consistent with the company's strategic plans. In addition, the SCF incorporates a schedule or narrative about significant noncash transactions, such as an exchange of stock for land, that are ignored in the cash budget.

It is acceptable for external reporting to present the operating section of the statement of cash flows on either a direct or an indirect basis. The direct basis uses pure cash flow information—cash collections and cash disbursements for operating activi-

---

■ EXHIBIT 11–16
Pro Forma Income Statement for First Quarter 1998

Sales (Exhibit 11–4)			$618,500
Less: Sales discounts (Exhibit 11–12)			(4,948)
Net sales			$613,552
Cost of goods sold:			
Finished goods—12/31/97 (Exhibit 11–3)		$ 10,780	
Cost of goods manufactured (Exhibit 11–15)		429,012	
Cost of goods available for sale		$439,792	
Finished goods—3/31/98 (Note A)		(8,820)	(430,972)
Gross margin			$182,580
Expenses:			
Bad debts expense (Note B)		$ 3,711	
SG&A expenses (Exhibit 11–9)		163,770	(167,481)
Operating Income			$ 15,099
Net interest income (Exhibit 11–14)			49
Income before income taxes			$ 15,148
Income taxes (assumed rate of 30%)			4,544
Net income			$ 10,604

Note A:		
Beginning balance (Exhibit 11–5) in units		30,800
Production (Exhibit 11–5)		1,231,400
Units available for sale		1,262,200
Sales (Exhibit 11–4)		(1,237,000)
Ending balance in units		25,200
Costs per unit:		
Materials	$ .20	
Conversion (assumed)	.15	× $.35
Ending inventory in dollars		$ 8,820

Note B:	
Total sales	$618,500
× % credit sales	× .60
Credit sales	$371,100
× % estimated uncollectible	× .01
Estimated bad debts	$ 3,711

ties. The indirect basis begins the operating section with net income and makes reconciling adjustments to arrive at cash flow from operations. Exhibit 11–18 provides a statement of cash flows for Scorpio Ltd. using the information from the cash budget in Exhibit 11–14. Indirect presentation of the operating section appears at the bottom of Exhibit 11–18 and uses the information from the income statement in Exhibit 11–16 and the balance sheets in Exhibits 11–3 and 11–17.

It is interesting to note that Scorpio Ltd. generates a very high cash flow from operating activities but is only earning 1.7 percent on each sales dollar. However, both

---

■ **EXHIBIT 11–17**
Pro Forma Balance Sheet, March 31, 1998

ASSETS			
Current Assets			
Cash (Exhibit 11–14)			$ 5,045
Investments (Exhibit 11–14)			21,800
Accounts Receivable (p. 562)		$ 85,020	
Less Allowance for Uncollectibles (p. 562)		(4,911)	80,109
Inventories:			
Direct Materials (Exhibit 11–15, Note A)		$ 7,242	
Finished Goods (Exhibit 11–16, Note A)		8,820	16,062
Total Current Assets			$123,016
Plant Assets			
Property, Plant and Equipment (a)		$580,000	
Less Accumulated Depreciation (b)		(238,300)	341,700
TOTAL ASSETS			$464,716

LIABILITIES AND STOCKHOLDERS' EQUITY			
Current Liabilities			
Accounts Payable (p. 563)			$ 45,937
Income Taxes Payable (Exhibit 11–16)			4,544
Total Current Liabilities			$ 50,481
Stockholders' Equity			
Common Stock		$300,000	
Retained Earnings (c)		114,235	414,235
TOTAL LIABILITIES AND STOCKHOLDERS' EQUITY			$464,716

(a)	Beginning balance (Exhibit 11–3)	$540,000
	New instrument purchase (Exhibit 11–10)	40,000
	Ending balance	$580,000
(b)	Beginning balance (Exhibit 11–3)	$180,000
	Factory depreciation (Exhibit 11–8)	46,900
	SG&A depreciation (Exhibit 11–9)	11,400
	Ending balance	$238,300
(c)	Beginning balance (Exhibit 11–3)	$103,631
	Net income (Exhibit 11–16)	10,604
	Ending balance	$114,235

cash flow from operations and net income are necessary for long-run success in business. It appears that Scorpio Ltd. either is not charging enough for its products or is not controlling costs well.

CONCLUDING COMMENTS

Because of its fundamental importance in the budgeting process, demand must be predicted as accurately and with as many details as possible. Sales forecasts must indicate type and quantity of products to be sold, geographic locations of the sales, types of buyers, and points in time at which the sales are to be made. Such detail is necessary because different products require different production and distribution facilities; different customers have different credit terms and payment schedules; and different seasons or months may necessitate different shipping schedules or methods.

Estimated sales demand has a pervasive impact on the master budget. To arrive at a valid prediction, managers use all the information available and may combine sev-

■ **EXHIBIT 11–18**
Pro Forma Statement of Cash Flows for the First Quarter of 1998

Operating Activities:			
Cash collections:			
From sales		$612,532	
From interest		49	$612,581
Cash payments:			
For inventory:			
Direct materials	$245,625		
Direct labor	61,571		
Overhead	76,220	$383,416	
For non-factory costs		152,370	(535,786)
Net cash inflow from operating activities			$ 76,795
Investing Activities:			
Purchase of plant asset		$ (40,000)	
Short-term investment		(21,800)	
Net cash outflow from investing activities			(61,800)
Financing Activities:			
Issuance of short-term note payable		$ 1,200	
Repayment of short-term note payable		(1,200)	
Payment of dividends		(15,000)	
Net cash outflow from financing activities			(15,000)
Net decrease in cash			$ (5)

Alternative (Indirect) Basis

Operating Activities:			
Net income			$ 10,604
+ Depreciation expense ($46,900 + $11,400)			58,300
+ Decrease in net Accounts Receivable ($82,800 − $80,109)		$ 2,691	
+ Decrease in Inventories ($19,538 − $16,062)		3,476	
- Decrease in Accounts Payable ($48,757 − $45,937)		(2,820)	
+ Increase in Taxes Payable ($4,544 − $0)		4,544	7,891
Net cash inflow from operating activities			$ 76,795

The preparation of the master budget is extremely important to managerial planning functions. In addition, budgeted financial statements can help gain access to funds because they indicate to creditors that the company is aware of the timing and amounts of its loan requirements and repayments.

What Happens If ....?

The management accountant should take the initiative for making contingency planning an integral part of the planning and budgeting process. An effective response to a business reversal is not mere recognition of the problem. Rather, early warning signals should trigger implementation of a contingency plan that details the predetermined countermeasures required to avoid a crisis while maintaining the firm's financial integrity.

Preparation of a contingency plan starts with an analysis of the company's financial capacity for responding to and weathering various simulated adversities such as a sales decline caused by a general recession or a change in competitive position. These scenarios serve as the backdrop for designing the strategic maneuvers needed to ensure the firm's survival at various levels of financial distress. The principal components of these strategies are:

- An estimate of the uncommitted liquid [cash or near cash] reserves that would be readily available during a given emergency.

- A program for reducing both controllable cash outflows and the level of investment in current assets and fixed assets.

- A strategic plan that, in the event of a prolonged or irreparable misfortune, outlines the controlled liquidation of plant, equipment, or business units previously identified as expendable.

Developing a contingency plan, through the combined efforts of the management accountant and top-level management, forces the latter to examine the extent to which resources are available, the strong interdependence of planning and control, and the delicate interrelationship between financial reserves and budgeted cash outflows.

SOURCE: Arthur R. DeThomas, William B. Fredenberger, and Monojit Ghosal, "Turnarounds: Lessons for the Management Accountant," *Management Accounting* (July 1994), p. 25. Published by Institute of Management Accountants, Montvale, NJ.

eral estimation approaches. Combining prediction methods provides managers with corroboration of estimates, which reduces uncertainty. Some ways of estimating future demand are (1) asking sales personnel for a subjective consensus; (2) making simple extrapolations of past trends; (3) using market research; and (4) employing statistical and other mathematical models.

Sensitivity analysis is one modeling technique that can be used in assessing risk in the budgeting process. It is a means of determining the amount of change that must occur in one variable before a different decision would be made. In preparing the master budget, for example, the variable under consideration might be selling price, advertising expense, grade of materials used in production, machine hours available, or maintenance expenditures. The technique identifies an "error" range for each of the various estimated values over which the budget would still provide a reasonably acceptable forecast. Repetitive computer simulations can be run after one or more factors have been changed so that managers can review expected results under various circumstances.

After the master budget and all of its pro forma financial statements have been developed, they can and should be used for a variety of purposes. One common use of the master budget is to help the organization to obtain bank loans. Banks also need to be kept informed after loans have been obtained. Additionally, management can use master budgets to monitor performance by comparing budgeted figures to actual results. Variances, as they occur, should be investigated so that the underlying causes can be determined. Understanding the reasons for not meeting a budget can be useful in controlling future operations within the budget period, evaluating performance, and budgeting more accurately in the future. Finally, management should be aware that forecasted sales and profits may not materialize or, as with Earthly Elements (discussed in an earlier News Note), factors beyond the business's control may create problems. In such instances, it is essential that management have made contingency plans, as discussed in the News Note on the previous page.

SITE ANALYSIS

Planning for the future is an ongoing process at Lloyd Manufacturing because the company president Jeffrey Leyh wants the organization to be a viable competitor in the global economy. In making plans, management must analyze the elastomer product industry as well as competitors and their products, current and future company products, and personnel requirements. Forecasts of future operations are essential, since the company is incurring numerous costs for facility remodeling, research and development on new products, and business expansion. The large sums being spent for these activities must be justifiable in terms of projected increases in sales and profits. For example, in 1993, Lloyd acquired technology, equipment, and customer lists from Rainfair Inc. of Racine, Wisconsin. This purchase allowed Lloyd to expand into the graphic arts market and would not have been made without forecasted data on market potential and expected costs. Another planned acquisition is expected to cause budgeted sales to increase by approximately 10 percent.

The budgeting process at Lloyd Manufacturing is not highly sophisticated and uses no intricate computer programs or simulations, but it is fairly reliable. While monthly budget-to-actual comparisons are made, more emphasis is placed on annual budget targets. Selling prices of products vary greatly from product line to product line, so revenues are strongly affected by which products are sold during any particular period. Because many of the company's costs are fixed, monthly budget-to-actual variances generally are not significant. Since the company began its quality improvement efforts, some budget adjustments have had to be made. Supervisor salary budgets were reduced because decision making was pushed down to the worker level and three supervisor positions were eliminated. In addition, an incentive program based on safety, quality, and sales was introduced for all department heads. Thus, forecasts must be made of these factors before the incentive compensation is budgeted. Negotiations about the budget take place between the departments and management, but Lloyd Manufacturing finalizes its budget only after management and ownership agree on their expectations for the future.

SOURCE: Information provided by Jeffrey Leyh, President, Lloyd Manufacturing Corporation, 1994.

CROSS-FUNCTIONAL APPLICATIONS STRATEGIES

Discipline
Accounting

Applications
A master budget provides a basis against which actual accounting information can be compared and translates management plans into quantitative and monetary information. The budgetary process organizes management's plans according to the accountant's chart of accounts so that plans can conform to the way financial statement results will be presented, thus allowing accounting to assist managers in performance evaluation.

Economics	The master budgeting process enhances efforts to use resources in the most efficient and effective ways and is similar to the process existing in governmental units.
Finance	The cash budget helps indicate the need for and ability to repay borrowings so that advance arrangements can be made and can assist in developing dividend strategy. The pro forma financial statements provide information about potential future earnings that may affect stock prices or new issues of capital.
Management	The budgeting process enhances communication of authority, provides a basis for performance evaluation, and promotes teamwork. Expected production levels have hiring implications. The master budget indicates resource allocations among areas and serves as an organizational plan for the upcoming period.
Marketing	Market sales forecasts are generally the starting point for all budgets. Thus, the sales budget requires an astute assessment of market demand as the key variable on which the entire budgeting process is based; provides individual sales quotas for the budget period; and helps prioritize how marketing resources will be spent (advertising, sales expenses, trade shows) to generate the projected sales level. Input from the marketing area is critical because many expenditures, (such as sales salaries and commissions, advertising, promotions, inventory, delivery trucks) drive or are driven by sales volume and, thus, should be correlated with the desired sales volume.

CHAPTER SUMMARY

Planning is the process of setting goals and objectives and translating them into activities and resources required for their accomplishment within a specified time horizon. Budgeting is the quantifying of a company's financial plans and activities. Budgets facilitate communication, coordination, and teamwork. A master budget is a comprehensive set of projections (including pro forma financial statements) for a specific budget period. It is composed of operating and financial budgets and is usually detailed by quarters and months.

Sales demand is the proper starting point for the master budget. Once sales demand quantities are determined, managers forecast revenues, production, costs, and cash flows for the firm's activities for the upcoming period. These expectations reflect the firm's input and output of resources and are used in preparing the master budget. When budgeting, managers need to remember that the various organizational departments interact with each other and the budget for one department may form the basis of or have an effect on the budgets in other departments.

For example, the production department's production budget is predicated on sales demand provided by the sales department. The production budget then influences the purchasing department's budget as well as the treasurer's budgeting of cash flows and accounts payable management. Sales also affect cash flows and the selling, general, and administrative expense budget.

Pro forma financial statements help managers determine if their plans will provide the desired results, in terms of both net income and cash flow. Inadequate results should cause a reevaluation of the objectives that have been set, and appropriate changes should be made.

GLOSSARY

Budget committee (p. 551)   a group, usually composed of top management and the chief financial officer, that reviews and approves, or makes adjustments to, the master budget and/or the budgets submitted from operational managers

Capital budgeting (p. 557)   the process of making decisions and budgeting for expenditures in long-term plant and equipment items

Financial budget (p. 549)   a budget that reflects the funds to be generated or used during the budget period; includes the cash and capital budgets and the projected or pro forma financial statements

Master budget (p. 548)   the comprehensive set of all budgetary schedules and the pro forma financial statements of an organization

Operating budget (p. 548)   a budget that is expressed in both units and dollars

SOLUTION STRATEGIES

SALES BUDGET

   Units of sales
$\times$ Selling price per unit
= Dollars of sales

PRODUCTION BUDGET

   Units of sales
+ Units desired in ending inventory
− Units in beginning inventory
= Units to be produced

PURCHASES BUDGET

   Units to be produced
$\times$ Appropriate quantity measure per unit
= Units needed for production
+ Units desired in ending inventory
− Units in beginning inventory
= Units to be purchased

PERSONNEL COMPENSATION BUDGET

   Number of people or direct labor hours
$\times$ Salaries per month or wages per hour
= Cost of compensation

OVERHEAD BUDGET (EXCLUDING COMPENSATION)

   Predicted activity base
$\times$ VOH rate per unit of activity
= Total variable OH cost
+ Fixed OH cost
= Total OH cost

SELLING, GENERAL, AND ADMINISTRATIVE BUDGET (EXCLUDING COMPENSATION)

    Predicted sales dollars (or other variable measure)
× Variable SG&A rate per dollar (or other variable measure)
= Total variable SG&A cost
+ Fixed SG&A cost
= Total SG&A cost

SCHEDULE OF CASH COLLECTIONS (FOR SALES ON ACCOUNT)

    Dollars of credit sales for month
× Percent collection for month of sale
= Decrease in Accounts Receivable for current month's sales
− Sales discounts allowed and taken
= Receipts for current month's sales
+ Current month's cash receipts for prior months' sales
= Cash receipts for current month

SCHEDULE OF CASH PAYMENTS (FOR PURCHASES ON ACCOUNT)

    Units to be purchased
× Cost per unit
= Total cost of purchases
× Percent payment for current purchases
= Increase in Accounts Payable for current month's purchases
− Purchase discounts taken
= Cash payments for current month's purchases
+ Current month's cash payments for prior months' purchases
= Cash payments for inventory for current month

CASH BUDGET

    Beginning cash balance
+ Cash receipts
= Cash available for disbursements
− Cash needed for disbursements:
        Cash payments for Accounts Payable for month
        Cost of compensation
        Total OH cost less depreciation
        Total SG&A cost less depreciation
= Cash excess or deficiency ◄
− Minimum desired cash balance
= Cash needed or available for investment or financing

    Cash excess or deficiency ◄
+ Various financing amounts
= Ending cash balance

DEMONSTRATION PROBLEM

Our Miss Brooke, Inc.'s, September 30, 1996, balance sheet includes the following:

Cash	$ 30,000 debit
Accounts Receivable	100,800 debit
Allowance for Uncollectible Accounts	2,240 credit
Merchandise Inventory	21,000 debit

Our Miss Brooke's management has designated $30,000 as the firm's monthly minimum cash balance. Other information about the firm follows:

■ Revenues of $280,000 and $336,000 are expected for October and November, respectively. All goods are sold on account.
■ The collection pattern for Accounts Receivable is 55 percent in the month of sale, 44 percent in the month following the sale, and 1 percent uncollectible.
■ Cost of goods sold approximates 60 percent of sales revenues.
■ Management's desired ending balance of Merchandise Inventory is 10 percent of the current month's sales.
■ All Accounts Payable for inventory are paid in the month of purchase.
■ Other monthly expenses are $37,800, which includes $2,800 of depreciation but does not include bad debt expenses.
■ Borrowings or investments can only be made in $5,000 amounts at the end of a month. Interest will be paid at the rate of 10% per year; interest will be earned at the rate of 8% per year.

Required:

a. Forecast the October cash collections.
b. Forecast the October and November cost of purchases.
c. Prepare the cash budget for October including the effects of financing (borrowing or investing).

■ SOLUTION TO DEMONSTRATION PROBLEM

a.

	OCTOBER COLLECTIONS
From September ($100,800 − $2,240)	$ 98,560
From October ($280,000 × .55)	154,000
Total	$252,560

b.

	OCTOBER	NOVEMBER
Sales	$280,000	$336,000
	× .60	× .60
× Cost of goods	$168,000	$201,600
+ Desired ending balance	16,800	20,160
= Total needed	$184,800	$221,760
− Beginning balance	(21,000)	(16,800)
= Cost of purchases	$163,800	$204,960

c.

OCTOBER CASH BUDGET

Beginning cash balance		$ 30,000	
October collections		252,560	
Total cash available before financing		$282,560	
Disbursements:			
Purchases of merchandise	$163,800		
Other monthly expenses ($37,800 − $2,800)	35,000		
Total disbursements		(198,800)	
Cash excess (a)		$ 83,760	
Less: Minimum cash balance desired		(30,000)	$30,000
Cash available		$ 53,760	
Financing: Acquire investment (b)		(50,000)	3,760
Ending cash balance (c); (c = a − b)			$33,760

END-OF-CHAPTER MATERIALS

■ QUESTIONS

1. Why is it important to put organizational plans in written form?

2. How are operating and financial budgets different? How are they related?

3. Why is the master budget said to be a static budget? Why is it necessary for the master budget to be static?

4. Why must the beginning of the budget year balance sheet be estimated? Why is it needed in the master budget process?

5. Why is the sales budget the first of the operating budgets prepared?

6. Explain the purposes of the production budget. How is this budget influenced by the firm's inventory policies?

7. What are the primary inputs in the determination of the materials purchases budget?

8. What source documents would one likely use to compile the direct labor budget?

9. Why is it necessary to separate overhead costs into variable and fixed components to determine the budget for overhead costs?

10. Even though the capital budget is normally prepared outside the context of master budget preparation, how may it influence the preparation of the master budget?

11. Explain the importance of the cash budget to management.

12. How are cash collections from sales determined? What part do cash collections play in the budgeting process?

13. How does a firm's credit terms for credit sales affect the pattern for cash collections? Why would a firm give a discount for cash sales?

14. Why would a firm wish to maintain a minimum cash balance?

15. Why are pro forma statements included in the master budget?

16. Since a cash budget is included in the master budget, why is a budgeted statement of cash flows also included?

17. What is the relationship between the budgeted statement of cash flows and the budgeted balance sheet?

18. Give some examples of items included in the financing section of a statement of cash flows and their cash flow effects.

19. Why would it be desirable to prepare the master budget using a spreadsheet program that links the individual budgets?

20. List the schedules and statements that make up the master budget in the sequence in which they would normally be prepared. If two or more schedules can be prepared simultaneously, so indicate.

■ EXERCISES

21. (LO 3; *Production budget*) Rockland Industries has budgeted its second-quarter unit sales for 1997 as follows:

April	9,000
May	10,000
June	11,000

   The company desires an ending inventory equal to 8 percent of budgeted sales of the following month. July's sales are expected to be 12,000 units. Produce a second-quarter production budget by month and in total.

22. (LO 3; *Production budget*) West Electric has projected quarterly sales of electric motors for 1997 as follows:

1st quarter	200,000
2nd quarter	150,000
3rd quarter	250,000
4th quarter	180,000

   The firm expects to begin 1997 with 80,000 motors. Desired ending balances are to be 40 percent of the subsequent quarter's sales. Sales in the first quarter of 1998 are expected to be 220,000 motors.

   a. Prepare a production budget by quarter and in total for 1997.
   b. Explain how the firm might benefit by reducing the level of finished goods inventories carried.

23. (LO 3; *Purchases budget*) Flip Flop Flippers expects to sell 14,200 pairs of swim flippers during June. Two pounds of rubber are required to make each pair. The company has a beginning June inventory of 3,300 pairs of flippers and 12,800 pounds of rubber. The company wishes to end June with 8,200 pairs of flippers and 16,000 pounds of rubber. Because flippers can be made very quickly from heated rubber, the firm does not maintain any work in process inventory. How much rubber should Flip Flop budget to buy for June?

24. (LO 3; *Purchases budget*) Southern Metals expects to sell 74,000 units of its major product in November 1997. Each unit requires two pounds of material A and five pounds of material B. Material A costs $4.80 per pound, and material B costs $2.10 per pound. Expected beginning and ending inventories are as follows:

	NOVEMBER 1	NOVEMBER 30
Finished goods (units)	4,000	6,300
Material A (pounds)	4,000	4,900
Material B (pounds)	6,100	6,000

   a. How many pounds of material A does Southern Metals plan to purchase in November? What is the expected cost of those purchases?

b. How many pounds of material B does Southern Metals plan to purchase in November? What is the expected cost of those purchases?

c. Briefly describe how improved raw materials inventory management could reduce the level of raw materials inventories carried.

25. (LO 3; *Mixed overhead cost budget*) Mistell Industries wants to estimate the cost of manufacturing overhead in the master budget. Overhead is a mixed cost with the following flexible budget formula: $y = \$451{,}000 + \$14.25X$, where X represents machine hours. The fixed overhead includes $72,000 of depreciation.

a. Calculate the overhead cost assuming Mistell Industries plans to work 12,000 machine hours for the coming year.

b. Determine how much cash will be spent for overhead if the company works the 12,000 machine hours.

26. (LO 4; *Cash collections*) Luster Corp. is experiencing difficulty in estimating cash collections for the second quarter of 1996. Inspection of records and documents reveals the following sales information:

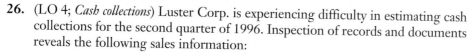

FEBRUARY	MARCH	APRIL	MAY	JUNE
$252,000	$232,000	$248,000	$292,000	$272,000

Analysis of past collection patterns helped management to develop the following information:

- 30 percent of each month's sales are for cash, with no discount.
- Of the credit sales, 50 percent are collected in the month of sale; customers paying during this time are given a 2 percent discount.
- 40 percent of credit sales are collected in the month following the sale.
- 10 percent of credit sales are collected in the second month after the sale.

Bad debts are negligible and should be ignored. Luster's balance in Accounts Receivable at April 1 is estimated at $98,840.

a. Prepare a schedule of cash received from sales for each month in the second quarter.

b. Calculate the balance in Accounts Receivable at the end of the second quarter.

27. (LO 4; *Cash collections*) Cumberland Mechanical's records revealed an accounts receivable balance of $194,000 at April 1, 1997. Analysis shows that $140,000 of this balance remains from March billings. April billings are expected to be $210,000. The company's pattern of collections is 30 percent in the month of billing for services, 40 percent in the month following the service, 29 percent in the second month following the service, and 1 percent uncollectible. No write-off of bad debts has been made for February or March billings.

a. What were the February billings?

b. What amount of the March billings is expected to be uncollectible?

c. What are the projected cash collections in April?

d. Prepare a brief oral report to Cumberland's managers describing how they might manipulate their credit policies to collect credit sales sooner.

e. What types of information should be gathered before making a decision to change a credit policy?

28. (LO 4; *Cash collections*) Millett, Inc., expects sales of $400,000, $300,000, and $360,000 for January, February, and March, respectively. Millett has determined the following collection profile from its sales, all of which are on account:

Current month's sales	22%
First month after sale	60%
Second month after sale	14%
Uncollectible	4%

A bank loan is due in March, so Millett's managers want to be sure that they have done a good job of predicting collections.

a. How much cash can Millett expect to collect in March?

b. Write a brief report to Millett managers describing actions they might take to reduce the level of uncollectible accounts.

29. (LO 4; *Cash payments*) Tillison Industrial Hose Co. is trying to budget the June 1996 cash payments for Accounts Payable. Management believes that, of a given month's purchases, 40 percent are paid in the month of purchase, and a 2 percent discount is given on one-half of what is paid in that month. The remaining 60 percent are paid in the following month. Expected unit purchases for May and June of 1997 are 91,200 and 68,300, respectively. The cost per unit is $3.80.

a. What are expected cash payments for purchases on account in June?

b. If Tillison expects a temporary cash shortage in June, what actions might managers take with respect to its creditors to address the cash shortage?

30. (LO 4; *Cash budget*) Darren Huitt Enterprises expects to begin 1997 with a cash balance of $10,000. Cash collections from sales and on account are expected to be $468,600. The firm wants to maintain a minimum cash balance of $4,000. Cash disbursements are projected as follows:

Payoff of notes payable	$ 13,000
Interest on notes payable	4,200
Purchase of computer system	14,800
Payments on account for operating costs and purchases	90,000
Direct labor payments	100,000
Overhead payments	127,000
Selling, general, and administrative payments	93,000

Prepare the 1997 cash budget in good form.

31. (LO 5; *Cost of goods manufactured schedule*) Johnson Electrical is trying to complete preparation of its 1997 master budget. The firm provides you with the following expected data:

Work in Process Inventory—January 1	$ 12,200
Work in Process Inventory—December 31	9,300
Direct Materials Inventory—January 1	3,300
Direct Materials Inventory—December 31	6,200
Purchases of direct materials from purchases budget	187,700
Direct labor—from personnel compensation budget	106,700
Factory overhead—from factory overhead budget	215,500

Prepare a pro forma cost of goods manufactured schedule.

■ COMMUNICATION ACTIVITIES

32. (LO 3; *Revenue and cost budgeting*) Over the past 20 years, the legal profession has been characterized by its fixation on hourly billing. Basing revenues on hours of time worked and materials consumed, law firms have had very predictable revenue streams. However, for their clients, the hourly billing system means very unpredictable costs and no guarantee of either the quality of the service or the outcome of litigation. Before the 1970s, most legal work performed in the United States was billed on a fixed fee basis.

The hourly-rate method emerged quite recently, with the rapid expansion of commercial law firms in the early 1970s. They needed a sense of internal budgeting as well as the ability to offer accountability to clients. Many firms began requiring lawyers to account for their time in 10 minute increments.

In the late 1980s, the method came under attack as consultants pointed out that hourly billing neither promotes efficiency nor recognizes expertise. Moreover, clients began to audit legal bills and some found instances of attorneys padding time sheets or spending too much time on matters.

[SOURCE: Amy Stevens, "Firms Try More Lucrative Ways of Charging for Legal Services," *Wall Street Journal* (November 25, 1994), pp. B1, B3. Reprinted by permission of The Wall Street Journal, © 1994 Dow Jones & Company, Inc. All Rights Reserved Worldwide.]

  a. How does billing based on time spent promote inefficiency?
  b. What budgeting advantage does a fixed fee billing arrangement offer clients?
  c. In general, how does a billing arrangement affect the ability of a supplier to predict revenues and a customer to predict costs?

33. (LO 4; *Planning and cash management*) In December 1994, Hayes Microcomputer Products, Inc., filed for bankruptcy.

Dennis C. Hayes, chief executive officer of the closely held concern, attributed the action to a "short-term cash shortage" brought on by rapidly growing demand amid a series of manufacturing snafus. In an interview, he said the company—whose assets and liabilities total more than $100 million each—remains solvent and expects to emerge from its reorganization in a matter of months.

Mr. Hayes said the company's problems began in April, when its broad expansion plan began to produce sharply higher demand for Hayes's modems and other computer products. Having surpassed the capacity of its own manufacturing facilities, Hayes laid plans to subcontract additional manufacturing and ordered semiconductors, enclosures and other materials that make up a modem.

But Hayes and its subcontractors weren't able to ramp up production fast enough, saddling Hayes with a huge materials backlog that ate into the company's cash flow. Many of the debts that piled up between April and July, and are owed primarily to vendors, remain on the books. It is these debts, whose exact value Mr. Hayes declined to disclose, that pushed Hayes to pursue bankruptcy protection under the U.S. Bankruptcy Code.

[SOURCE: Emory Thomas, Jr., "Modem Maker Hayes Files for Chapter 11," *Wall Street Journal* (November 17, 1994), p. A16. Reprinted by permission of The Wall Street Journal, © 1994 Dow Jones & Company, Inc. All Rights Reserved Worldwide.]

  a. Why does rapid growth cause cash shortages?
  b. Discuss actions Hayes might have taken in response to the sharply higher sales to avoid such a severe cash shortage.
  c. Comment on the adequacy of Hayes's planning in light of the fact that the company had a "broad expansion plan," yet ended up in bankruptcy.
  d. How could closer cooperation between internal finance specialists and operating managers have resulted in a better outcome for Hayes?

34. (LO 4; *Cash management*) Wilson Container, a privately held firm founded in 1994, specializes in the packaging of toys and games. The company's administrative offices are in Chicago, and the regional packaging plants are located in Seattle, Little Rock, Nashville, and Hartford. Wilson Container expects 1998 sales to exceed $25 million, and the company is forecasting its first profitable year.

Because of its rapid growth, Wilson Container has had ongoing requirements for additional working capital. The bank that participated in the initial financing of the company has continued to be supportive by arranging for additional long-range loans and extending a $3 million line of credit to the company. However, the bank is now reluctant to enter into a new loan agreement and has declined to increase the company's line of credit.

The board of directors of Wilson Container is concerned about the company's capital position and has recently hired Jim Tyler as treasurer of the company. Tyler has been directed to improve the company's working capital position. Since joining Wilson Container, Tyler has gathered the following information about the company's operations.

■ Based on sales data received from the regional plants, all invoices are prepared at the Chicago office during the last week of each month. All sales are made on a credit basis, and payment terms are net 30 days.

■ Customers' checks are sent to the Chicago office for processing and are deposited in the bank at 3 P.M. each afternoon. Approximately one and one-half days are required to process and deposit a check once it is received at the Chicago office.

■ The collection effort on past-due accounts is haphazard and consists entirely of phone calls made by the controller when time allows. The company does not charge interest on past-due accounts.

■ Wilson Container has a strict credit policy, but it is not applied evenly. Because sales are made from all five locations, credit is often approved and extended by the individual making the sale.

■ Each of Wilson Container's regional plants has its own bank account for disbursements, which include payroll, inventory purchases, and repair and maintenance of equipment. These accounts are replenished by wire transfer of funds from the Chicago office.

■ Because each plant controls its own disbursements, payment procedures are not standardized. Some locations take advantage of vendor discounts while others pay in 30 days.

■ Wilson Container has yet to develop inventory policies and procedures. Each plant does its own purchasing and maintains its own inventory records. New toys and games are continually being developed to keep up with changing tastes, and Wilson Container must keep pace. Therefore, new items are frequently added to inventories.

Wilson Container's board is concerned about the company's working capital position; however, board members do not wish to make a public offering to raise cash unless it becomes absolutely necessary.

a. Discuss how Jim Tyler could improve Wilson Container's working capital position by addressing the following areas of cash management:
   1. Acceleration of cash receipts
   2. Deceleration of cash disbursements
   3. Generation of cash

b. Describe how Wilson Container's cash management might differ between a period of high interest rates and a period of low interest rates.

(CMA)

■ PROBLEMS

35. (LO 3; *Production and purchases budgets*) L.A. Fabrics has budgeted monthly unit sales for the first quarter of 1998 as follows:

	JANUARY	FEBRUARY	MARCH	TOTAL
Sales in units	36,000	32,000	30,000	98,000

April's sales are expected to be 28,000 units.

The following are estimates of finished units and direct materials in pounds at various times:

	12/31/97	1/31/98	2/29/98	3/31/98
Finished units	9,000	8,000	7,500	7,000
Direct material M	6,750	6,000	5,625	5,250
Direct material N	4,500	4,000	3,750	3,500
Direct material O	9,000	8,000	7,500	7,000

The production process requires three pounds of material M, two pounds of material N, and four pounds of material O.

a. Prepare a monthly production and purchases budget for the first quarter of 1998.

b. The company is considering the installation of new production equipment before 1998. Such equipment would largely replace the current labor-intensive production system. Write a memo to corporate management explaining why new production equipment could affect the direct material budgets.

c. Who should be consulted to determine the new material requirements per unit, if the new production equipment is installed?

36. (LO 3; *Production purchases, direct labor and overhead budgets*) Quality Carpentry Tools Co. manufactures two products: saws and planes. Estimated production needs for a unit of each product follow:

	SAWS	PLANES
Steel (in pounds)	2	4
Wood (in board feet)	.5	.2
Direct labor (in hours)	2	4
Machine hours	.5	3

Overhead is applied to production at the rate of $16 per machine hour.
The estimated sales by product for 1998 are:

	SAWS	PLANES
Sales (in units)	40,000	15,000

The estimated beginning and required ending inventories for 1998 are:

	BEGINNING	ENDING
Steel (pounds)	2,000	1,400
Wood (board feet)	500	400
Saws (units)	400	320
Planes (units)	600	450

a. Prepare the following budgets: production, purchases, direct labor (hours only), overhead.

b. What evidence exists to support the argument that this company uses modern methods to manage inventories of materials and products?

37. (LO 3, 4; *Purchases and cash payments*) Brazilian Coffee Company expects to sell 200,000 one-pound bags of coffee in November and 240,000 one-pound bags of coffee in December. Each one-pound bag contains fifteen ounces of coffee and one ounce of additional ingredients, such as chicory. The company expects to begin November with the following inventories:

Finished goods	5,000 units
Unused bags	12,000 units
Coffee beans	14,000 pounds
Additional ingredients	1,100 pounds

Based on a recent study, the company has decided to carry 5 percent of the subsequent month's sales in finished goods as of November 30. Enough direct materials are also to be carried to produce 5 percent of the next month's sales. Bags cost $.14, coffee beans cost $1.52 per pound, and the additional ingredients cost $.20 per pound. Management normally pays for 60 percent of a month's purchases in the month of purchase and takes a 2 percent discount on those payments.

a. How many bags must be acquired during November?
b. How many pounds of coffee beans must be purchased during November?
c. How many pounds of additional ingredients should be acquired in November?
d. Calculate the dollar amount of November purchases.
e. Determine the cash payments in November for November purchases.
f. How would the adoption of modern production management tools such as JIT affect the purchase budget and the production budget?

38. (LO 3, 4; *Estimates of various amounts*) Potter Retail, Inc. expects its May 1998 Cost of Goods Sold to be $420,000. Included in this amount is $24,000 of fixed overhead. Total variable cost approximates 70 percent of sales. Potter's gross margin percentage averages 35 percent of sales, and net income averages 10 percent of sales. Depreciation is $7,000 per month. All other expenses and purchases are paid 60 percent in the month incurred and 40 percent in the following month. Potter purchases only enough goods to satisfy sales of any given month.

a. Estimate Potter's expected May sales.
b. Estimate Potter's expected variable selling, general, and administrative costs for May.
c. How much are Potter's total expected fixed costs for May?

d. Potter normally collects 70 percent of its sales in the month of sale and 30 percent in the following month. Estimate cash collections and cash payments in May related only to May transactions.

39. (LO 3, 4; *Multiple budgets*) North Shore Decorative Furniture Co. makes book stands. Sales quantities, sales dollars, and cash collections for the first quarter of 1998 are as follows:

	JANUARY	FEBRUARY	MARCH	TOTAL
Quantity (units)	6,400	5,200	7,400	19,000
Revenue	$73,600	$59,800	$85,100	$218,500
Collections	$76,200	$61,300	$81,100	$218,600

The December 31, 1997, estimated balance sheet contains the following balances: Cash, $18,320; Direct Materials Inventory, $8,230; Finished Goods Inventory, $23,200; and Accounts Payable, $5,800. The direct materials inventory balance represents 2,000 pounds of scrap iron and 3,200 bookstand bases. Finished Goods Inventory consists of 4,220 book stands.

Each book stand requires two pounds of scrap iron, which costs $2 per pound. Bookstand bases are purchased from a local lumber mill at a cost of $1.80 per unit. Beginning in 1998, management wants the ending balance of Direct Materials Inventory to equal 25 percent of the following month's production requirements. Management also wants the ending balance of Finished Goods Inventory to equal 20 percent of the next month's sales. Sales for April and May are expected to be 8,000 bookstands per month.

The payment pattern for purchases is 75 percent in the month of purchase with a 1 percent discount. The remainder is paid in the next month with no discount.

Direct labor is budgeted at $.70 per book stand and out-of-pocket plant overhead runs $24,000 per month plus $1.30 per bookstand. Total monthly out-of-pocket period costs run $13,600 plus 10 percent of sales revenue. All out-of-pocket costs are paid in the month of incurrence, with the exception of materials purchases, as discussed earlier.

Management wants a minimum cash balance of $15,000. The company has a policy of borrowing funds in multiples of $1,000 at the beginning of a month and repaying borrowed funds in multiples of $1,000 plus interest at the rate of 12 percent per year.

a. Prepare a monthly production budget for the first quarter of 1998.

b. Prepare a monthly direct materials purchases budget for the first quarter of 1998.

c. Prepare a monthly schedule of cash payments for purchases for the first quarter of 1998.

d. Prepare a combined payments schedule for factory overhead and period costs on a monthly basis for the first quarter of 1998.

e. Prepare a cash budget for each month and in total for the first quarter of 1998.

f. Assume that you are the staff accountant assigned to work on the materials purchasing budget. With whom are you likely to confirm the credit policies of the firm's vendors? Explain.

40. (LO 4; *Cash budget*) Smith's Wholesale Appliances' September 30, 1997, balance sheet follows:

ASSETS		LIABILITIES AND STOCKHOLDERS' EQUITY	
Cash	$ 40,000	Accounts payable	$272,000
Accounts receivable (net of $3,800 allowance for bad debts)	144,400		
Inventory	108,000		
Plant assets (net of $40,000 of accumulated depreciation)	320,000	Common stock	120,000
		Retained earnings	220,400
		Total liabilities and	
Total assets	$612,400	stockholders' equity	$612,400

Other information about the company follows:

- The company wants a minimum cash balance of $40,000.

- Revenues of $360,000 and $480,000 are expected for October and November 1997, respectively.

- The collection pattern is 60 percent in the month of sale, 38 percent in the next month, and 2 percent uncollectible.

- Cost of goods sold is 75 percent of sales.

- Purchases each month are 60 percent of the current month's sales and 40 percent of the following month's sales. All purchases are paid for in the month following the purchase.

- Other monthly expenses total $48,000. This amount includes $2,000 of depreciation but does not include bad debts expense.

a. Forecast the October cash collections.
b. Forecast the October 31 inventory balance.
c. Forecast the October 31 retained earnings balance.
d. Prepare the October cash budget, including the amount available for investment or to be borrowed during October.
e. Why would the firm want to maintain a minimum cash balance of $40,000? Who would set such a policy?

41. (LO 4; *Cash collections and payments*) Gags-N-Rags, which operates in the New York City area, is a wholesale distributor of joke books and humorous magazines. The company is preparing its budget for the first three months of 1998. At the end of 1997, the following balances are estimated:

Accounts Receivable	$188,280
Inventory	52,875
Accounts Payable	41,700
Other payables	7,120

Management has agreed on the following guidelines in preparing the budget:

COLLECTIONS

- Credit sales are billed on the last day of each month.

- Cash customers and credit customers who pay by the 10th of the month are allowed a 1 percent discount.

- 10 percent of sales are for cash. Of the credit sales, 10 percent are received within the discount period; another 40 percent are received during the rest of the month after billing; 40 percent are received in the second month after billing; and 10 percent are received in the third month after billing.

PAYMENTS

- 40 percent of purchases are paid for in the month of purchase. The rest are paid in the next month.

- Of the operating expenses incurred, 60 percent are paid in the month incurred and the remainder are paid in the next month.

OTHER OPERATING STATISTICS

- All sales are made at 200 percent of cost.

- Desired ending inventory is set at 75 percent of the following month's Cost of Goods Sold.

- Actual and projected sales are estimated at:

October	$122,000
November	128,000
December	133,000
January	141,000
February	139,000
March	124,000
April	127,000

- Selling, general, and administrative expenses are 10 percent of sales plus $6,000 monthly. Included in the monthly SG&A expenses are $1,500 of depreciation.

a. Determine total monthly cash receipts for the first quarter.
b. Determine monthly purchases for the first quarter.
c. Determine monthly cash disbursements for the first quarter.

42. (LO 4, 5; *Cash budget and pro forma income statement*) Billy's Fresh Fruit Stand purchases, wholesales and retails fresh fruits and vegetables. Company estimates reveal the following for the first three fiscal months of 1998:

	PURCHASES	SALES
June	$66,000	$102,000
July	58,000	92,000
August	79,600	116,000

Management expects that May 1998 purchases and sales will be $80,000 and $120,000, respectively. The company usually pays 60 percent of any month's purchases in the month of purchase and takes an average 2 percent discount. The remaining amount is paid in the following month with no discount. Other monthly payments for expenses run $24,000 plus 12 percent of sales. Depreciation is $4,000 per month. The company wishes to maintain a minimum cash balance of $28,000 and expects to start May with $36,000 cash.

All retail sales are for cash and all wholesale transactions are on credit. Overall, experience indicates the following expected collection pattern for sales:

25 percent in the month of sale, 60 percent in the month after the sale, and 15 percent in the second month after the sale. The company has no debt other than what is currently owed for purchases on account.

a. Calculate the July 31 balances for Accounts Receivable and Accounts Payable.

b. Calculate the cash collections expected in August.

c. Calculate the expected total cash disbursements in August.

d. Present a cash budget for August. Assume management wants no more cash on hand at August 31 than the minimum cash balance desired.

e. Prepare an income statement for August. Assume an average gross margin percentage of 40 percent. Ignore income taxes.

f. Explain how inventory management must be different for perishable commodities than for nonperishable commodities.

43. (LO 5; *Pro forma income statement*) The projected January 31, 1998, balance sheet for Ohio Rubber Co. follows (all dollar amounts are in thousands):

Cash	$ 16,000
Accounts receivable (net of allowance for uncollectible accounts of $4,000)	76,000
Inventory	32,000
Property, plant, and equipment (net)	70,000
Total assets	$194,000
Accounts payable	$165,000
Common stock	100,000
Retained earnings (deficit)	(71,000)
Total liabilities and stockholders' equity	$194,000

Additional information follows:

■ Sales are budgeted as follows:

February	$220,000
March	240,000

■ Collections are expected to be 60 percent in the month of sale, 38 percent in the next month, and 2 percent uncollectible.

■ The company's gross margin is projected at 25 percent of sales. Purchases each month are 75 percent of the next month's projected sales, and these are paid in full in the following month.

■ Other expenses for each month, paid in cash, are expected to be $31,000. Monthly depreciation is $10,000.

a. Prepare a pro forma income statement for February.

b. Prepare a pro forma balance sheet for February.

c. Describe any special problems this company may encounter because of its weak balance sheet. As a finance specialist, recommend actions the firm might take to improve the balance sheet.

44. (LO 2, 3, 4, 5; *Comprehensive*) Green Smoke makes an environmentally friendly artificial fireplace log. You have been asked to prepare the company's 1998 master budget and have been provided with the following:

a. The 12/31/97 estimated balance sheet data follow:

ASSETS

Cash		$ 4,330
Accounts Receivable		8,450
Direct Materials Inventory (2,046 pounds)		409
Finished Goods Inventory (1,200 logs)		2,808
Plant and Equipment	$220,000	
Less Accumulated Depreciation	(57,700)	162,300
Total assets		$178,297

LIABILITIES AND STOCKHOLDERS' EQUITY

Accounts Payable		$ 1,109
Note Payable		20,000
Total liabilities		$ 21,109
Common Stock	$100,000	
Retained Earnings	57,188	157,188
Total liabilities and stockholders' equity		$178,297

b. Each log requires the following standards for direct materials, labor, and overhead:

- 3.3 pounds of materials mix at $.20
  (.3 pound is discarded as waste) $.66

- 2 minutes of labor time; direct labor
  averages $14.40 per hour   .48

Each finished log requires three minutes of machine time. Variable overhead is applied at the rate of $12 per hour of machine time. Annual fixed production overhead of $42,000 is applied based on an expected annual production capacity of 70,000 logs. The total fixed factory overhead is comprised of the following:

Salaries	$26,000
Insurance	1,800
Fixed portion of utilities	5,300
Depreciation	8,900

Fixed overhead is incurred evenly throughout the year.
Direct labor and overhead (except depreciation) are paid in cash as incurred.

c. Expected sales in units for the first five months of 1998 are:

January	6,000
February	9,000
March	6,500
April	5,900
May	5,100

Green Smoke grants no discounts, and all sales are on credit at $6 per log. The company's collection pattern is 80 percent in the month of sale, 15 percent in the month following the sale, and 5 percent in the second month following the sale. The Accounts Receivable balance in the balance sheet data shown earlier represents amounts remaining due from November sales of $33,000 and December sales of $34,000.

d. Green Smoke completes all production each day. The desired ending balance of Direct Materials Inventory is 10 percent of the amount needed to satisfy the next month's production for finished goods. The desired ending balance in Finished Goods Inventory is 20 percent of the next month's sales.

e. Purchases are paid 70 percent in the month of purchase and 30 percent in the month following the purchase. No discounts are taken. The note payable has a 12 percent interest rate, and the interest is paid at the end of each month. The $20,000 balance of the principal on the note is due on March 31, 1998.

f. Green Smoke's minimum desired cash balance is $4,000. The firm may borrow at the beginning of a month and repay at the end of the month in $500 increments. Interest on these short-term loans, if any, is payable monthly. Investments and investment liquidations are made only in $500 amounts at the end of a month. Investments earn 1 percent per month, collected at month's end.

g. Period (SG&A) expenses, paid as incurred, are $9,000 per month plus 1 percent of revenue.

h. The company accrues income taxes at a 40 percent rate. A quarterly tax installment will be paid on April 15, 1998.

Prepare master budget schedules on a monthly basis for the first quarter of 1998 and pro forma financial statements as of the end of the first quarter. Round all numbers in schedules and pro forma statements to the nearest whole dollar.

■ CASES

45. (LO 4; *Cash budget*) CrossMan Corporation, a rapidly expanding crossbow distributor to retail outlets, is in the process of formulating plans for 1998. Joan Caldwell, director of marketing, has completed her 1998 forecast and is confident that sales estimates will be met or exceeded. The following sales figures show the growth expected and will provide the planning basis for other corporate departments.

MONTH	FORECASTED SALES	MONTH	FORECASTED SALES
January	$1,800,000	July	$3,000,000
February	2,000,000	August	3,000,000
March	1,800,000	September	3,200,000
April	2,200,000	October	3,200,000
May	2,500,000	November	3,000,000
June	2,800,000	December	3,400,000

George Brownell, assistant controller, has been given the responsibility for formulating the cash flow projection, a critical element during a period of rapid expansion. The following information will be used in preparing the cash analysis:

■ CrossMan has experienced an excellent record in accounts receivable collections and expects this trend to continue. The company collects 60 percent of billings in the month after sale and 40 percent in the second month after the sale. Uncollectible accounts are insignificant and should not be considered in the analysis.

■ The purchase of crossbows is CrossMan's largest expenditure; the cost of these items equals 50 percent of sales. The company receives 60 percent of the crossbows one month prior to sale and 40 percent during the month of sale.

■ Prior experience shows that 80 percent of accounts payable are paid by CrossMan one month after receipt of the purchased crossbows, and the remaining 20 percent are paid the second month after receipt.

■ Hourly wages, including fringe benefits, are a function of sales volume and are equal to 20 percent of the current month's sales. These wages are paid in the month incurred.

■ General and administrative expenses are projected to be $2,640,000 for 1998. The composition of the expenses is given next. All of these expenses are incurred uniformly throughout the year except the property taxes. Property taxes are paid in four equal installments in the last month of each quarter.

Salaries	$ 480,000
Promotion	660,000
Property taxes	240,000
Insurance	360,000
Utilities	300,000
Depreciation	600,000
Total	$2,640,000

■ Income tax payments are made by CrossMan in the first month of each quarter based on income for the prior quarter. CrossMan's income tax rate is 40 percent. CrossMan's net income for the first quarter of 1998 is projected to be $612,000.

■ CrossMan has a corporate policy of maintaining an end-of-month cash balance of $100,000. Cash is invested or borrowed monthly, as necessary, to maintain this balance.

■ CrossMan uses a calendar year reporting period.

a. Prepare a pro forma schedule of cash receipts and disbursements for CrossMan Corporation, by month, for the second quarter of 1998. Be sure that all receipts, disbursements, and borrowing/investing amounts are presented on a monthly basis. Ignore the interest expense and/or interest income associated with the borrowing/investing activities.

b. Discuss why cash budgeting is particularly important for a rapidly expanding company such as CrossMan Corporation.

c. Do monthly cash budgets ignore the pattern of cash flows within the month? Explain.

(CMA adapted)

46. (LO 1, 2, 5; *Sales and cost of goods sold budgets*) Watson Corporation manufactures and sells extended keyboard units to be used with microcomputers. Robin Halter, budget analyst, coordinated the preparation of the annual budget for the year ending August 31, 1998. The budget was based on the prior year's sales and production activity. The pro forma statements of income and cost of goods sold are as follows:

WATSON CORPORATION
PRO FORMA STATEMENT OF INCOME
FOR THE YEAR ENDING AUGUST 31, 1998
($000 OMITTED)

Net sales		$25,550
Cost of goods sold		(16,565)
Gross profit		$ 8,985
Operating expenses		
Marketing	$3,200	
General and administrative	2,000	(5,200)
Income from operations before income taxes		$ 3,785

WATSON CORPORATION
PRO FORMA STATEMENT OF COST OF GOODS SOLD
FOR THE YEAR ENDING AUGUST 31, 1998
($000 OMITTED)

Direct materials		
Materials inventory, 9/1/97	$ 1,200	
Materials purchased	11,400	
Materials available for use	$12,600	
Materials inventory, 8/31/98	(1,480)	
Direct materials used		$11,120
Direct labor		980
Factory overhead		
Indirect materials	$ 1,112	
General factory overhead	2,800	3,912
Cost of goods manufactured		$16,012
Finished goods inventory, 9/1/97		930
Cost of goods available for sale		$16,942
Finished goods inventory, 8/31/98		(377)
Cost of goods sold		$16,565

On December 10, 1997, Halter met with Walter Collins, vice-president of finance, to discuss the first quarter's results (the period September 1 to November 30, 1997). After their discussion, Collins directed Halter to reflect the following changes to the budget assumptions in revised pro forma statements.

■ The estimated production in units for the fiscal year should be revised from 140,000 to 145,000 units, with the balance of production being scheduled in equal segments over the last months of the year. The actual first quarter's production was 25,000 units.

■ The planned inventory for finished goods of 3,300 units at the end of the fiscal year remains unchanged and will be valued at the average manufacturing cost for the year. The finished goods inventory of 9,300 units on September 1, 1997, had dropped to 9,000 units by November 30, 1997.

■ Due to a new labor agreement, the labor rate will increase 8 percent effective June 1, 1998, the beginning of the fourth quarter, instead of the previously anticipated effective date of September 1, 1998, the beginning of the next fiscal year.

■ The assumptions remain unchanged for direct materials inventory at 16,000 units for beginning inventory and 18,500 units for ending inventory. Direct materials inventory is valued on a first-in, first-out basis. During the first quarter, direct materials for 27,500 units of output were purchased for $2,200,000. Although direct materials will be purchased evenly for the last nine months, the cost of the direct materials will increase by 5 percent on March 1, 1998, the beginning of the third quarter.

■ Indirect material costs will continue to be projected at 10 percent of the cost of direct materials consumed.

■ One-half of general factory overhead and all of the marketing and general and administrative expenses are considered fixed.

a. Based on the revised data presented, calculate Watson Corporation's projected sales for the year ending August 31, 1998, in (1) number of units to be sold and (2) dollar volume of net sales.

b. Prepare the pro forma statement of costs of goods sold for the year ending August 31, 1998.

c. In light of the fact that management is aware certain changes (price change for materials and rate increase for labor) are forthcoming, what actions might they take to exploit the changes?

d. For each budgetary change mentioned, identify the source or sources of information Walter Collins might have used to become aware of the change.

(CMA adapted)

47. (LO 4; *Cash budget*) Collegiate Management Education, Inc. (CME), is a non-profit organization that sponsors a wide variety of management seminars throughout the Southwest. In addition, it is heavily involved in research into improved methods of teaching and motivating college administrators. The seminar activity is largely supported by fees and the research program by membership dues.

CME operates on a calendar year basis and is in the process of finalizing the budget for 1998. The following information has been taken from approved plans, which are still tentative at this time:

SEMINAR PROGRAM

Revenue—The scheduled number of programs should produce $12,000,000 of revenue for the year. Each program is budgeted to produce the same amount of revenue as the others. The revenue is collected during the month the program is offered. The programs are scheduled during the basic academic year and are not held during June, July, August, and December. Twelve percent of the revenue is generated in each of the first five months of the year, and the remainder is distributed evenly during September, October, and November.

Direct expenses—The seminar expenses are made up of three types:

- Instructors' fees are paid at the rate of 70 percent of seminar revenue in the month following the seminar. The instructors are considered independent contractors and are not eligible for CME employee benefits.

- Facilities fees total $5,600,000 for the year. Fees are the same for all programs and are paid in the months the programs are given.

- Annual promotional costs of $1,000,000 are spent equally in all months except June and July when there is no promotional effort.

RESEARCH PROGRAM

Research grants—The research program has a large number of projects nearing completion. The other main research activity this year includes feasibility studies for new projects to be started in 1998. The total grant expense of $3,000,000 for 1998 is expected to be paid out at the rate of $500,000 per month during the first six months of the year.

SALARIES AND OTHER CME EXPENSES

Office lease—Annual amount of $240,000 paid monthly at the beginning of each month.

General administrative expenses—$1,500,000 annually or $125,000 per month. These are paid in cash as incurred.

Depreciation expense—$240,000 per year.

General CME promotion—Annual cost of $600,000, paid monthly.
Salaries and benefits—

NUMBER OF EMPLOYEES	ANNUAL CASH SALARY	TOTAL ANNUAL SALARIES
1	$50,000	$ 50,000
3	40,000	120,000
4	30,000	120,000
15	25,000	375,000
5	15,000	75,000
22	10,000	220,000
50		$960,000

Employee benefits amount to $240,000, or 25 percent of annual salaries. Except for the pension contribution, the benefits are paid as salaries are paid. The annual pension payment of $24,000, based on 2.5 percent of salaries, is due on April 15, 1998.

OTHER INFORMATION

Membership income—CME has 100,000 members, and each pays an annual fee of $100. The fee for the calendar year is invoiced in late June. The collection schedule is as follows: July, 60 percent; August, 30 percent; September, 5 percent; and October, 5 percent.

Capital expenditures—The capital expenditures program calls for a total of $510,000 in cash payments to be spread evenly over the first five months of 1998. Cash and temporary investments at January 1, 1998, are estimated at $750,000.

a. Prepare a budget of the annual cash receipts and disbursements for 1998.
b. Prepare a cash budget for CME, Inc. for January 1998.
c. Using the information developed in parts a and b, identify two important operating problems of CME, Inc.

(CMA)

48. (LO 2, 3; *Cost budgets*) The Mason Agency, a division of General Service Industries, offers consulting services to clients for a fee. The corporate management at General Service is pleased with the performance of the Mason Agency for the first nine months of the current year and has recommended that the division manager of the Mason Agency, Richard Howell, submit a revised forecast for the remaining quarter, as the division has exceeded the annual plan year-to-date by 20 percent of operating income. An unexpected increase in billed hour volume over the original plan is the main reason for this gain in income. The original operating budget for the first three quarters for the Mason Agency is as follows:

1998-1999 OPERATING BUDGET

	1st Quarter	2nd Quarter	3rd Quarter	Total
Revenue:				
Consulting fees				
Management consulting	$315,000	$315,000	$315,000	$ 945,000
EDP consulting	421,875	421,875	421,875	1,265,625
Total	$736,875	$736,875	$736,875	$2,210,625
Other revenue	10,000	10,000	10,000	30,000
Total	$746,875	$746,875	$746,875	$2,240,625

Expenses:

Consultant salaries	$386,750	$386,750	$386,750	$1,160,250
Travel and entertainment	45,625	45,625	45,625	136,875
General and administration	100,000	100,000	100,000	300,000
Depreciation	40,000	40,000	40,000	120,000
Corporate allocation	50,000	50,000	50,000	150,000
Total	$622,375	$622,375	$622,375	$1,867,125
Operating income	$124,500	$124,500	$124,500	$ 373,500

When comparing the actuals for the first three quarters against the original plan, Howell analyzed the variances. His revised forecast for the fourth quarter will reflect the following information:

■ The division currently has 25 consultants on staff—10 for management consulting and 15 for EDP consulting—and has hired 3 additional management consultants to start work at the beginning of the fourth quarter in order to meet the increased client demand.

■ The hourly billing rate for consulting revenues is acceptable in the market and will remain at $90 per hour for each management consultant and $75 per hour for each EDP consultant. However, owing to the favorable increase in billing hour volume, the hours for each consultant will be increased by 50 hours per quarter. New employees are as capable as current employees and will be billed at the current rates.

■ The budgeted annual salaries and actual annual salaries, paid monthly, are the same at $50,000 for a management consultant and 8 percent less for an EDP consultant. Corporate management has approved a merit increase of 10 percent at the beginning of the fourth quarter for all 25 existing consultants, while the new consultants will be compensated at the planned rate.

■ The planned salary expense includes a provision for employee fringe benefits amounting to 30 percent of the annual salaries; however, the improvement of some corporate-wide employee programs will increase the fringe benefit allocation to 40 percent.

■ The original plan assumes a fixed hourly rate for travel and other related expenses for each billing hour of consulting. These expenses are not reimbursed by the client, and the previously determined hourly rate has proved to be adequate to cover these costs.

■ Other revenues are derived from temporary rentals and interest income and remain unchanged for the fourth quarter.

■ General and administrative expenses have been favorable at 7 percent below the plan; this 7 percent savings on fourth-quarter expenses will be reflected in the revised plan.

■ Depreciation for office equipment and microcomputers will stay constant at the projected straight-line rate.

■ Because of the favorable experience for the first three quarters and the division's increased ability to absorb costs, the corporate management at General Service Industries has increased the corporate expense allocation by 50 percent.

a. Prepare a revised operating budget for the fourth quarter for the Mason Agency, which Richard Howell will present to General Service Industries. Be sure to furnish supporting calculations for all revised revenue and expense amounts.

b. Discuss the reasons why an organization would prepare a revised forecast.

(CMA adapted)

■ ETHICS AND QUALITY DISCUSSIONS

49. *[Southwest Airlines has been a leader in designing new and more efficient ways of contracting in the air carrier industry. Recently it] agreed to an unusual 10-year contract with its pilots union that provides no wage increases in the first five years.*

In lieu of wage increases during the first half of the apparently unprecedented agreement, Southwest's 2,000 pilots will be granted options to acquire as many as 1.4 million shares of the Dallas carrier's stock each year during the life of the contract.

During the second half of the contract, the pilots will receive the options plus three 3% wage increases. The pilots also can get additional compensation based on Southwest's profitability.

And the carrier is unique in the airline industry in that when Southwest employees are promised profit-sharing, they actually receive it; the airline has had an unbroken string of profitable years since 1973.

[SOURCE: Bridget O'Brian, "Southwest Agrees to Pilots Pact Offering No Wage Boost in First Five of 10 Years," *Wall Street Journal* (November 18, 1994), p. A2. Reprinted by permission of The Wall Street Journal, © 1994 Dow Jones & Company, Inc. All Rights Reserved Worldwide.]

a. How could the new wage agreement with its pilots provide Southwest Airlines with an edge in both competing and planning?

b. How would the new wage agreement likely affect the quality of services provided by Southwest Airlines? (Specifically address the provisions for profit sharing and stock option ownership.)

50. Ford Motor Co. recently negotiated a three-year price agreement with its major steel suppliers. The agreement calls for a price increase of 7 to 8 percent in the first year of the agreement. Because Ford was willing to make a multi-year agreement, the company is believed to have negotiated smaller price increases than Chrysler. Estimates indicate that Chrysler agreed to price increases in the 10 percent range.

The steelmakers' supply contracts with automakers cover about 50 percent of the flat-rolled steel produced in the United States. Steelmakers have invested heavily in specialized equipment that produces steel to the unique specifications of the automakers.

[SOURCE: Based on Erle Norton, "Steelmakers Near Supply Agreement With Ford That Raises Prices 7% to 8%," *Wall Street Journal* (November 9, 1994), pp. A2, A13. Reprinted by permission of The Wall Street Journal, © 1994 Dow Jones & Company, Inc. All Rights Reserved Worldwide.]

a. In terms of accuracy, how do multi-year price agreements facilitate planning and budgeting for both automakers and steel suppliers?

b. What are the risks associated with multi-year price agreements for automakers? For suppliers?

c. How can multi-year supply agreements be used to positively affect the quality of production processes?

51. Comet Company is in the process of acquiring a $10,000,000 bank loan that is vital to the continuation of the business. Comet submitted its 1995 pro forma financial statements to the bank two weeks ago. Caspari Pacioli, the loan officer, informed Comet's CFO that the pro formas would be a primary ingredient in determining whether the loan would be granted.

After the pro forma statements were submitted, Comet's CFO learned that a major customer (which accounts for 35 percent of annual sales) is being absorbed by a large national chain. Because the national chain has the capability of providing Comet's customer with products like those Comet now provides, Comet's CFO believes that the company will lose the customer.

Comet's sales manager believes that the lost sales can be replaced over the next two years. Loss of the customer will, however, most likely result in a poor cash flow situation, which could easily affect the scheduled bank loan repayment. The company president is concerned that if the bank is told of the situation at this time, the loan will not be made and Comet Company will be forced out of business. Comet's president reasons that, when the pro forma information was submitted, the expected figures were provided in good faith. Had the company known about the loss of the customer when the pro formas were prepared, other arrangements might have been made.

a. Does the company have a legal or a moral obligation to immediately inform the bank of what has occurred?

b. What are the implications of telling the bank's loan officer?

c. What are the implications of not telling the bank's loan officer?

d. What do you recommend, and why?

52. Although this chapter discusses budgeting largely in the context of internal management, budgeting is also important with respect to financial information that is published externally. In short, managers are very concerned with the effect of projected financial results on external investors and financial markets. Consider how one company reacts to large projected increases or decreases in reported earnings:

In the past decade, GE's earnings have risen every year, although net income fell in 1991 and 1993 because of accounting changes related to post-retirement benefits. The gains, ranging between 1.7% and 17%, have been fairly steady—especially for a company in a lot of cyclical businesses. As a result, GE almost seems able to override the business cycle.

How does GE do it? One undeniable explanation is the fundamental growth of its eight industrial businesses and 24 financial-services units. "We're the best company in the world," declares Dennis Dammerman, GE's chief financial officer.

But another way is "earnings management," the orchestrated timing of gains and losses to smooth out bumps and, especially, avoid a decline. Among big companies, GE is "certainly a relatively aggressive practitioner of earnings management," says Martin Sankey, a CS First Boston Inc. analyst.

To smooth out fluctuations, GE frequently offsets one-time gains from big asset sales with restructuring charges; that keeps earnings from rising so high that they can't be topped the following year. GE also times sales of some equity stakes and even acquisitions to produce profit gains

. . . A look at GE illustrates how analysts say one giant corporation manages earnings. They add that few companies have maneuvered so successfully for so long on so large a scale. GE's size and diversity give it an unusual array of opportunities, of course. Moreover, Chairman Jack Welch relentlessly monitors GE's profit growth.

[SOURCE: Randall Smith, Steven Lipin, and Amal Kumar Naj, "How General Electric Damps Fluctuations in Its Annual Earnings," *Wall Street Journal* (November 3, 1994), pp. A1, A11. Reprinted by permission of The Wall Street Journal, © 1994 Dow Jones & Company, Inc. All Rights Reserved Worldwide.]

a. Why would companies want to manage earnings?

b. Is the use of budgeting and forecasting tools to manage earnings an ethical behavior on the part of managers? Explain.

c. How can the management of earnings lead to the long-term loss of profits?

   d. Why do larger companies have greater opportunity than smaller companies to engage in earnings management?

■ PROJECTS

53. An interesting behavioral aspect of budgeting involves the actions taken by managers to improve profitability and efficiency. The clothing industry makes for an interesting case study.

   For many consumers—particularly women—finding the right clothing size is increasingly time-consuming. One important reason is that apparel companies, seeking to produce goods more efficiently and cheaply, are making fewer sizes and more one-size-fits-all items.

   Men are also having an increasingly difficult time finding correct sizes. Manufacturers now provide many items in just four sizes: small, medium, large, and extra-large. The fewer the alternatives, the less stock the retailer needs to carry to meet the needs of its customers.

   A significant additional problem in the industry is the lack of common definitions for size measurements. Not surprisingly, the reasons most frequently cited by customers in returning women's and children's clothing are size and fit.

   [SOURCE: Based on Teri Agins, "Go Figure: Same Shopper Wears Size 6, 8, 10, 12," *Wall Street Journal* (November 11, 1994), p. B1.]

   Some of the problems in the clothing industry can be attributed to lack of industry level plans and standards to coordinate the efforts of individual manufacturers. Divide your class into teams of four members each. Have each team (1) provide arguments as to why an industry-level planning process is necessary and (2) develop a written, industry-level plan to be adopted by individual companies that has the general goal of enhancing consumer satisfaction with U.S. clothing manufacturers.

54. *The nation's biggest charities logged a 4% increase in gifts for the second consecutive year in 1993, according to the Chronicle of Philanthropy's annual survey.*

   Groups that did well included museums, which had an average 47% gain, thanks often to gifts of appreciated property—not cash. Community foundations, which often benefit from bequests and big gifts, gained an average 32%. Youth groups gained an average 10%, public broadcasting rose 7% and human services increased 5%. United Way of America's 2,000 or so locals logged a small overall gain for the year. Gifts were flat to environmental, public-advocacy and religious groups. Performing-arts groups faired poorly, with an average decrease of 5%, the Washington-based Chronicle said.

   As for museum gains, more gifts of art were largely due to tax rules that let donors continue to take a full tax deduction on works of art and other property that had grown in value. But separately, the American Association of Museums . . . noted that gift-objects don't help cash flow.

   [SOURCE: Pamela Sebastian, "Donations to Top Charities Rise 4%; Property Gifts Put Museums in Lead," *Wall Street Journal* (November 1, 1994), p. A11. Reprinted by permission of The Wall Street Journal, © 1994 Dow Jones & Company, Inc. All Rights Reserved Worldwide.]

   Planning in charitable organizations, especially in terms of projecting revenues, is very different from planning in profit-oriented businesses. Research and prepare an oral report on the topic "Unique Characteristics of Budgeting Revenues in Charitable Organizations."

55. Prepare a personal cash flow budget for each month of the semester and the semester in total. In the event that you project an excess of expenditures over inflows, what alternatives do you have for covering your outflows? How can you increase your cash inflows?

IV

USING MANAGERIAL ACCOUNTING INFORMATION FOR CONTROLLING

12 CONTROLLING NONINVENTORY COSTS

LEARNING OBJECTIVES

1. Recognize why cost consciousness is of great importance to all members of an organization.

2. Differentiate between committed and discretionary costs.

3. Understand how the benefits from discretionary cost expenditures can be measured.

4. Determine when standards are applicable to discretionary costs.

5. Explain how a budget helps in controlling discretionary costs.

6. Calculate the cost of quality so that control can be exercised.

7. (Appendix) Understand how program budgeting is used for cost control in not-for-profit entities.

Take care of your pennies and the pounds will take care of themselves.
Scottish proverb

ON SITE

Ochsner Medical Foundation: Manage Costs Without Reducing Quality

Ochsner Clinic was formed in New Orleans, Louisiana, in January 1942 and, in 1944, the Alton Ochsner Medical Foundation (the Foundation) was established. Today, the Foundation owns and operates a medical complex that comprises, in part, an acute care hospital, clinic buildings, research facilities, a hotel, and a parking garage. One of Ochsner's basic and fundamental objectives is the provision of the highest quality of healthcare to patients and their families in its service area. As healthcare services become increasingly competitive, this objective faces new and greater challenges. For example, the healthcare industry has seen payment terms progress from the traditional fee-for-service-rendered to the more complex set-fee per covered life.

To succeed in this rapidly changing environment, hospitals are faced with the need to provide services in the most cost-effective manner. Cost control is extremely important at Ochsner, yet it must be implemented without affecting the quality of service given to Ochsner's patients and their families. Because wages and supplies comprise the majority of the organization's costs, all manpower needs and supply procurement and usage activities are subject to detailed scrutiny. Ochsner managers seek cost reduction answers in the most logical way possible. First, the various steps in patient treatment and in hospital support functions are analyzed to determine what activities are value-added in that they maintain the highest-quality patient services. Any activities seen to be non-value-added are targets for elimination.

SOURCES: Ochsner Medical Institutions *1992 Annual Report* and 1994 interview with Graham Cowie, Assistant Director of Finance, Ochsner Medical Institutions.

A ny business wanting to succeed must not only generate reasonable levels of revenues but also control the costs that are matched against those revenues. Hospitals are in a unique situation in that, in many respects, they are unable to control the revenues they receive, since the fee-for-service amounts are set by external parties. Cost control may be difficult because doctors are ethically bound to provide "appropriate" treatment, a mandate unconcerned with cost. In addition, hospitals often have a certain level of capacity (bed space, number of operating rooms, and so on) that commits the entity to a given level of cost. After making this commitment, the hospitals sometimes find that the size of the actual patient base has declined or expanded from the original estimate. Regardless of the difficulties involved, hospitals must attempt to control costs because these costs can no longer simply be "passed through" to customers by way of increased prices.

Previous chapters presented various ways to control costs. For example, control of direct materials and direct labor costs are typically linked to the development and implementation of a standard cost system. Additionally, just-in-time inventory techniques can significantly reduce the cost of warehousing and purchasing. This chapter focuses on three topics related to cost control. First, the **cost control system**, which covers all the formal and informal activities related to controlling costs, is discussed. This system is used to analyze and evaluate how well expenditures were managed during a period. Second, costs that are set by management at specific levels each period are considered. Often, these costs are difficult to control because their benefits are harder to measure than those provided by costs that are fixed from long-term commitments. Third, the use of flexible, rather than static, budgets to control costs is

cost control system

reviewed. The chapter appendix considers an alternative budgeting method (program budgeting) used in governmental and not-for-profit entities because of the unique nature of their output.

COST CONTROL SYSTEMS

A good control system should perform three functions: control before an event; control during an event; and control after an event. An event could be a period of time, the manufacture of a product, or the performance of a service. Exhibit 12–1 indicates the ways in which an effective cost control system can address each of these three functions.

Managers alone cannot control costs. An organization is composed of a group of individuals whose attitudes and efforts should be considered in determining how an organization's costs may be controlled. Cost control is a continual process that requires the support of *all* employees at *all* times. Thus, a good control system encompasses not only the functions shown in Exhibit 12–1 but also the ideas about cost consciousness shown in Exhibit 12–2 (page 602). **Cost consciousness** refers to a companywide employee attitude toward the topics of cost understanding, cost containment, cost avoidance, and cost reduction. Each of these topics is important at a different stage of the control system.

Cost Understanding

Control requires that a set of expectations exist. Thus, cost control is first exercised when a budget is prepared. Budgets can be properly prepared only when the reasons for periodic cost changes are understood. These documents allow expected costs to be compared with actuals. Knowing that variations occurred is good information, but cost control can be achieved only if managers understand why costs differed from the budgeted amounts.

■ **LEARNING OBJECTIVE 1**
Recognize why cost consciousness is of great importance to all members of an organization.

cost consciousness

■ **EXHIBIT 12–1**
Functions of an Effective Cost Control System

FUNCTION	REASON	COST CONTROL METHOD
Control before an event	Preventive; reflects planning	Budgets; standards; policies concerning approval for deviations; expressions of quantitative and qualitative objectives
Control during an event	Corrective; ensures that the event is being pursued according to plans; allows managers to correct problems as they occur	Periodic monitoring of on-going activities; comparison of activities and costs against budgets and standards; avoidance of excessive expenditures
Control after an event	Diagnostic; guides future actions	Feedback; variance analysis; responsibility reports (discussed in Chapter 15)

■ **EXHIBIT 12-2**
Cost Control System

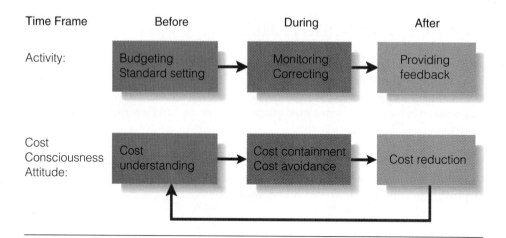

Cost changes due to cost behavior. Costs may change from previous periods or differ from budget expectations for many reasons. Some costs change because of their underlying behavior. Total variable or mixed cost increases or decreases with increases or decreases in activity level. If the current period's activity level differs from a prior period's activity level or the budgeted activity level, total actual variable or mixed cost will differ from that of the prior period or that in the budget. For example, Ochsner Hospital's laundry costs vary almost in direct proportion to the number of patients. A flexible budget can compensate for such differences by providing expected variable costs at any actual activity level. Managers can then make valid budget-to-actual cost comparisons to determine if total variable costs were properly controlled.

In addition to the reactions of variable costs to changes in activity levels, the following three factors can cause costs to differ from those of prior periods or the budget. In considering these factors, remember that an external *price* becomes an internal *cost* when a good or service is acquired.

Cost changes due to inflation/deflation. Fluctuations in the value of money are called general price-level changes. When the general price level changes, the prices of goods and services also change. General price-level changes affect almost all prices approximately equally and in the same direction, if all other factors are constant.

Cost changes due to supply/supplier cost adjustments. The relationship of the availability of a good or service to the demand for that item affects its selling price. If supply of an item is low but demand is high, the selling price of the item increases. The higher price often stimulates greater production, which, in turn, increases supply. In contrast, if demand falls but supply remains constant, the price falls. This lowered price should motivate lower production, which will lower supply. Therefore, price is consistently and circularly influenced by the relationship of supply to demand. Price changes for independent items are specific price-level changes, and these may move in the same or opposite direction as a general price-level change.

To illustrate, rental space in Hong Kong is among the most expensive in the world, already double that of Tokyo and New York. In the extremely crowded and desirable section of Hong Kong, one 30-square-foot store rents for HK$38,000 (≈US$4,918) per month; a 1,400-square-foot two-floor store rents for HK$850,000 (≈US$110,000) per month. Rents remain high because a growing number of retailers want space—a commodity that is limited in the primary shopping areas of the city.

But rents in other parts of Hong Kong are falling because of a lack of public transportation and of tenants.[1] Thus, the supply of retail sites and the demand for those sites can play a significant part in the cost of doing business in Hong Kong.

Specific price-level changes may also be caused by advances in technology. As a general rule, when the technology of producing a good or performing a service is advanced, the cost of the goods to producing firms declines. Assuming competitive market conditions, such cost declines are often passed along to consumers the form of lower selling prices. Consider the following: "You receive one of those little greeting cards that plays 'Happy Birthday' when you open it. Casually toss it into the trash, and you've just discarded more computer processing power than existed in the entire world before 1950."[2] This example simply demonstrates the basic interaction of increasing technology and decreasing selling prices and costs.

Of course, when suppliers incur additional production or performance costs, they typically pass such increases on to their customers as part of specific price–level changes. Such costs may be within or outside the control of the supplier. For example, an agreement in 1994 by General Motors to pay up to 12 percent more for steel may cause GM automobiles to increase in price.[3] The price of dynamic random-access memories (or DRAMs) increased after an explosion at the Japanese Sumitomo Chemical plant, which made a large portion of the world's supply of the plastic resin used to cover the DRAMs. The price of peanut butter rose significantly in 1990 after a drought-induced peanut shortage. Increased costs for employee health care benefits at a company are commonly passed along in the form of higher selling prices for that company's products or services.

The quantity of suppliers of a product or service can also affect selling prices. As the number of suppliers increases in a competitive environment, prices tend to fall. Likewise, a reduction in the number of suppliers will, all else remaining equal, cause prices to increase. A change in the number of *suppliers* is not the same as a change in the quantity of *supply*. If the supply of an item is large, one normally expects a low price; however, if there is only one supplier, the price can remain high because of supplier control. Consider that combating illnesses commonly requires the use of various medications. When drugs are first introduced under patent, the supply may be readily available, but the selling price is high, since there is only a single source. As patents expire and generics become available, selling prices decline because more suppliers can produce the item. For example, when the patents on Syntex Corp.'s antiarthritis drugs Naprosyn and Anaprox expired in December 1993, two-thirds of the prescriptions filled within a month were filled with generic versions and the price plummeted more than 80 percent.[4]

In some cases, all other factors are not equal, and the quantity of suppliers may not affect the selling price of a good or service. Firms may unethically conspire to engage in **price fixing** or setting an item's price at a specified level. Buyers must purchase the good or service at the specified price because no suppliers are offering the item at a lower price. Price fixing may be vertical or horizontal.

price fixing

[1]Craig S. Smith, "Shop Owners Struggle to Stay Open Amid Hong Kong's Pricey Real Estate," *Wall Street Journal* (April 19, 1994), p. C25.

[2]John Huey, "Waking Up to the New Economy," *Fortune* (June 27, 1994), p. 37.

[3]Erle Norton, "GM Agrees to Pay As Much As 12% More in Supply Pacts with Major Steelmakers," *Wall Street Journal* (December 8, 1994), p. A2.

[4]Elyse Tanouye, "Price Wars, Patent Expirations Promise Cheaper Drugs," *Wall Street Journal* (March 24, 1994), p. B1.

vertical price fixing

Vertical price fixing (also known as resale price maintenance) involves agreements by businesses and their distributors to control the prices at which products may be sold to consumers. In 1993, a 1985 U.S. policy that allowed manufacturers to fix retail prices with distributors was rescinded, making all vertical price fixing illegal.[5] Companies may set suggested retail selling prices for items, but any attempts to prohibit retailers from selling below those prices are considered antitrust activities.

horizontal price fixing

In **horizontal price fixing**, competitors attempt to regulate prices by agreeing on either a selling price or the quantity of goods that may be produced or offered for sale. Airlines, oil and credit card companies, the NCAA, and eight Ivy League schools and M.I.T. have all been accused of horizontal price fixing. In 1994, the United States and Canada filed the first joint criminal antitrust prosecution against several Japanese companies that controlled the thermal fax paper market; the Justice Department will collect almost $6.5 million in settlement.[6] And, as indicated in the accompanying News Note, there has been a crackdown on the practice of price fixing in the European Union.

Company personnel should seek to control cost increases from one period to the next and to eliminate unnecessary costs. For utility costs, it may be possible to effect some cost avoidance and reduction techniques, but it may not be possible to fully contain utility costs if the local power company increases rates.

Sometimes, cost increases are caused by increases in taxes or regulatory requirements. For example, paper manufacturers are continually faced with more stringent clean air, clean water, and safety legislation. Complying with these regulations increases costs for paper companies. The companies can (1) pass along the costs as price increases to maintain the same income level, (2) decrease other costs to maintain the same income level, or (3) experience a decline in net income. A recent study commissioned by the Independent Bankers Association of America and conducted by the accounting firm of Grant Thornton indicated that "complying with 13 of the most burdensome regulations costs community banks approximately 24 cents out of every dollar of net income before taxes . . . or an estimated $3.2 billion a year. If this figure is extrapolated to the entire banking industry, the number tops $11 billion."[7]

Cost changes due to quantity purchased. Firms are normally given quantity discounts, up to some maximum level, when bulk purchases are made. Therefore, a cost per unit may change because quantities are purchased in lot sizes different from those of previous periods or those projected. Ochsner, for example, is involved in a national group purchasing organization (GPO) of approximately 800 hospitals. Because the GPO negotiates contracts for the volume needed by all its affiliated hospitals, it can obtain substantial discounts from the prices that a single hospital could negotiate.

[5]Joe Davidson, "Rules Allowing Manufacturers to Fix Prices with Distributors Are Rescinded," *Wall Street Journal* (August 11, 1993), p. A3.

[6]Yi-Hsin Chang, "Two Firms to Pay Almost $6.5 Million to Settle Charges on Fax Paper Pricing," *Wall Street Journal* (July 15, 1994), p. C17.

[7]"IBAA Study Documents Cost of Burdensome Bank Regulations," *(Grant Thornton) Currency* (Spring 1993), p. 1.

NEWS NOTE

In the United States or European Union, Price Fixing Is Illegal

The European Union Commission fined 19 carton-board manufacturers a record total of 132 million European currency units ($164.9 million) for operating a "pernicious" cartel that fixed prices at secret meetings held in luxury Zurich hotels. (Carton board is a material used to produce folding boxes and other packaging material. The EU carton-board market totals about 2.5 billion ECUs a year, with annual consumption of more than three million tons.) The fines dwarfed the EU's previous record fine of 104 million ECUs, set earlier in 1994 in a case involving 14 producers of steel beams.

The alleged cartel was discovered in a series of surprise inspections in April 1991. According to the commission, [the cartel] operated from 1986 to 1991 and involved twice-yearly coordinated price increases of 6% to 10%. The price increases were "planned and programmed in advance in the most explicit detail," the commission said, and the companies agreed among themselves which would be the first to announce the new higher price.

Under EU law, the commission can fine companies as much as 10% of their yearly revenue for operating a cartel. The commission said several companies that acted as "ringleaders" received the highest fines, at 9% of their sales, while some companies had their fines reduced because they cooperated with the commission investigation.

SOURCE: Charles Goldsmith, "EU Fines 19 Carton-Board Companies Record $164.9 Million for Price Fixing," *Wall Street Journal* (July 14, 1994), p. A6. Reprinted by permission of The Wall Street Journal, ©1994 Dow Jones & Company, Inc. All Rights Reserved Worldwide.

While the preceding reasons indicate why costs change, they do not indicate what managers can do to contain the upward effects of the changes. Minimizing the upward trends means controlling costs. The next section discusses some concepts of cost containment.

Cost Containment

To the extent possible, managers should attempt to practice **cost containment** through minimizing period-by-period increases in per-unit variable and total fixed costs. Cost containment is generally not possible for changes resulting from inflation, tax and regulatory changes, and supply and demand adjustments, because these forces occur outside the organizational structure. Additionally, in most Western companies, adjustments to prices resulting from factors within the supply chain are not controlled by managers.

Japanese companies may not have the same view of supply-chain cost containment techniques. In some circumstances, there is a significant exchange of information among members of the supply chain and members of one organization may actually be involved in activities designed to reduce costs of another organization. For example, Citizen Watch Company has long set target cost reductions for external suppliers. If suppliers cannot meet the target, they are assisted by Citizen engineers in efforts to meet the target in the following year.[8]

cost containment

---

[8]Robin Cooper, *Citizen Watch Company, Ltd.* (Boston: Harvard Business School Case No. 194-033).

In the United States, some interorganizational arrangements of this kind do exist. For instance, an agreement between Baxter International (a hospital supply company) and BJC Health System allows Baxter access to BJC's hospital computer information data base. The information obtained is used by Baxter "to measure more precisely the types of procedures conducted and the exact amount of supplies needed."[9]

Increases in other types of costs are subject to cost containment activities and companies should look for ways to cap upward changes. The accompanying News Note addresses how Southwest Airlines works at containing costs.

Companies should be aware of the suppliers available for needed goods and services. New suppliers should be investigated to determine whether they can provide needed items in the quantity, quality, and time desired. Comparing costs and finding new sources of supply can increase buying power and reduce costs. Buying in bulk is not a new or unique idea, but it is often not applied on an extended basis for related companies or enterprises. In a corporation, one division can take the responsibility for obtaining a supplier contract for items (such as computer disks) that are necessary to all divisions. The savings resulting from buying a combined quantity appropriate for all divisions could offset the additional shipping costs to get the disks to the divisions.

If bids are used to select suppliers, the purchasing agent should remember that a bid is merely the first step in negotiating. A low bid is made to eliminate the competition from consideration. It is possible that, as a result of negotiations with the supplier, the goods or services can be provided at a cost lower than the bid amount or concessions (such as faster and more reliable delivery) can be obtained.

Reduced costs can often be obtained when long-term or single-source contracts are signed. Ochsner has several limited (one to three) source relationships in the areas of office and pharmaceutical supplies, food, and sutures. Most of these suppliers also provide just-in-time delivery. For instance, operating room (OR) supplies are ordered based on the next day's OR schedule. Two hours later, individual OR trays containing specified supplies for each operation are delivered by the vendor. By engaging in supplier relationships of this kind, Ochsner has not only introduced volume purchasing discounts but also effected timely delivery with total quality control.

A company may circumvent seasonal cost changes by postponing or advancing purchases of goods and services. However, such purchasing changes should not mean buying irresponsibly or incurring excessive carrying costs. The concepts of economic order quantities, safety stock levels, materials requirements planning, and the just-in-time philosophy should be considered in making purchases. These concepts are discussed in the next chapter.

Cost Avoidance and Reduction

Cost containment techniques can prove very effective if they can be implemented. In some instances, cost containment may not be possible but cost avoidance may be. **cost avoidance** **Cost avoidance** means finding acceptable alternatives to high-cost items and not spending money for unnecessary goods or services. Avoiding one cost may require that an alternative, lower cost be incurred. For example, many hospitals are practicing cost avoidance with regard to orthopedic implants. One survey found that over half the hospital respondents were using a consignment system for implants.

> Generally, consignment allows a hospital to have an implant device available for use, but it doesn't have to take title to the item—or pay for it—until it's actually been used in a proce-

---

[9]Thomas M. Burton, "Baxter Reaches Novel Supply Pact with Duke Hospital," *Wall Street Journal* (July 15, 1994), p. B2.

Cost Control Is One Reason Southwest Is Different

[Southwest Airlines began flying in 1971 and became profitable in 1973] and has remained profitable every year since—a record unmatched in the U.S. airline industry.

[One difference between Southwest and other airlines is its distribution system.] While most airlines rely on independent travel agents to write up to 90% of their tickets, Southwest has steadfastly refused to link up with the computer reservation systems the agents use. The result is that nearly half of all Southwest tickets are sold directly to passengers, with an annual savings to the airline of about $30 million.

Southwest also eschews the hub-and-spoke systems favored by other big carriers, preferring to fly frequently between pairs of cities not too far apart. The average Southwest flight is a mere 375 miles, the average fare a puny $58. The airline favors uncongested secondary airports such as Dallas' Love Field, Chicago's Midway, and Detroit City Airport. The airline flies only one type of aircraft, the 737, which leads to millions more in savings because flight-crew training and plane maintenance are vastly simplified.

Fierce cost controls are close to the heart of Southwest's profitability. Company Chairman Herb Kelleher personally approves every expenditure over $1,000—"not because I don't trust our people, but because I know if they know I'm watching, they'll be just that much more careful"—and he constantly monitors the key industry standard, cost per available seat mile, to make sure he stays a penny or two below the pack.

SOURCE: Kenneth Labich, "Is Herb Kelleher America's Best CEO?" *Fortune* (May 2, 1994), p. 47. ©1994 Time Inc. All rights reserved.

dure. As a result, a hospital doesn't have to tie up its money stocking implants [and it] avoids being saddled with implant systems that may become outdated or rendered useless if a surgeon who prefers that system suddenly leaves the hospital.[10]

Although suppliers may charge more for implants acquired on consignment, the hospitals employing this procedure believe that the additional purchase cost is much less than the potential carrying costs or costs of obsolescence that are associated with purchasing the implants.

Very closely related to the concept of cost avoidance is **cost reduction**, which means lowering current costs—especially those in excess of what is necessary. For example, it is not possible for a company to control increases in utility cost per kilowatt hour or to avoid using electricity, but it is possible for employees to reduce some of the organization's energy costs by using sound energy conservation techniques. It is also possible for companies to reduce costs by outsourcing or using specialist external providers of services rather than maintaining internal departments. Data processing activities are one prime candidate for outsourcing and, as indicated in the News Note on the next page, legal costs are another.

Sometimes money must be spent to generate cost savings. Installing a computer control box on a copier that records how many copies each employee makes is often an incentive for employees to control the number of copies they make. Some compa-

cost reduction

---

[10]Mary Wagner, "Common Buying Strategies Not Used to Acquire Implants," *Modern Healthcare* (March 23, 1992), p. 52.

Stanford Sets Up an LMO (Law Maintenance Organization)

What do you do when you have an $8 million budget and complete freedom to change the way a giant institution handles its legal costs? The new chief legal officer at Stanford University swiftly swept away the old way of doing business. Out the window went the billable-hour system, which rewarded law firms for spending more time. Out the door went two-thirds of his legal staff, to slash pay and benefits costs.

Michael Roster's first big move was to design a sort of health maintenance organization for legal needs—though he doesn't call it that. Instead of having to write a check every time Stanford is hit by a lawsuit and phones a lawyer, the university now pays a fixed fee each month for all the work performed by its outside attorneys. That includes everything from routine headaches such as employee contracts to specialized traumas such as First Amendment cases.

To find law firms willing to work for a flat fee rather than the traditional hourly rate, Mr. Roster sought bids from around the country. Some 14 big firms responded that they were interested in at least a piece of the unusual project. Seven firms said they would be willing to handle Stanford's entire legal load.

Their bids all undercut his own budget estimates by $1 million to $1.5 million, or 12% to 18%, Mr. Roster says. He selected three firms to share the work: Boston's Ropes & Gray and San Francisco's McCutchen, Doyle, Brown & Enersen and Pillsbury, Madison & Sutro.

Before Mr. Roster arrived at Stanford, its in-house legal department of 21 attorneys was the largest of any university, he says. As at many big companies, the legal staff had grown as more work was kept on site in an effort to control costs. Then the president of the university asked him to trim $500,000 from his budget.

Mr. Roster crunched some numbers. Benefits alone were chewing up $1 million annually, he says. Keeping lawyers supplied with books and reimbursing them for continuing education courses was another big line item. He decided the appropriate ratio would be about a third of the work done by his own staff and two-thirds by outside firms.

SOURCE: Amy Stevens, "Stanford's Legal Chief Overturns Status Quo and Sets Up 'Law HMO,'" *Wall Street Journal* (November 18, 1994), p. B10. Reprinted by permission of The Wall Street Journal, ©1994 Dow Jones & Company, Inc. All Rights Reserved Worldwide.

nies are also beginning to look outside for information about how and where to cut costs. Consulting firms, such as Fields & Associates (Burlingame, California), review files for duplicate payments and tax overpayments. Fields "recovered about $1 million for Intel Corp. in two years, in exchange for part of the savings."[11]

A starting point for determining appropriate cost reduction practices is to focus on the activities that are creating costs. As discussed in Chapter 5 on activity-based management, reducing or eliminating non-value-added activities will cause the associated costs to be reduced or eliminated. It is important to analyze activities so that those adding no value are uncovered and to recognize the amount of cost reduction that can occur when such activities are eliminated. Although many companies believe that eliminating jobs and labor are effective ways to reduce costs, the following quote provides a more appropriate viewpoint:

---

[11]Jeffrey A. Tannenbaum, "Entrepreneurs Thrive by Helping Big Firms Slash Costs," *Wall Street Journal* (November 10, 1993), p. B2.

Cutting staffs to cut costs is putting the cart before the horse. The only way to bring costs down is to restructure the work. This will then result in reducing the number of people needed to do the job, and far more drastically than even the most radical staff cutbacks could possibly do. Indeed, a cost crunch should always be used as an opportunity to re-think and to re-design operations.[12]

In fact, sometimes cutting costs by cutting people merely creates other problems. The people who are cut may have been performing a value-added activity; and by eliminating the people, a company may reduce its ability to do necessary and important tasks.

This point can be illustrated by the following example. After Carlson Travel Network reduced its travel agent work force by 17 percent, some of the remaining people had to perform unfamiliar tasks. One agent, who had previously handled only domestic trips, forgot to tell an international traveler that he needed a visa to enter Taiwan. He was denied entry and had to return home. His next ticket was upgraded to first class by Carlson, which also paid his incidental expenses on the first trip.[13] A few experiences such as this could become very expensive to an organization.

Use of temporary rather than full-time employees is another cost reduction technique. When temporaries (temps) are used, companies do not have to pay payroll taxes, fringe benefits, or Social Security. Thus, although temps often cost more per hour than full time workers, total cost may be reduced. If the amount of work in an area fluctuates substantially, temporaries can be hired for peak periods. Businesses are also hiring temps to work on special projects, provide expertise in a specific area, or fill in until the "right" full-time employee can be found for a particular position. Using temporary workers provides a flexible staffing "cushion" that helps insulate the jobs of permanent, core employees.

Companies are beginning to view their personnel needs from a **strategic staffing** perspective. This outlook requires departments to analyze their personnel needs by considering long-term objectives and determining a specific combination of permanent and temporary or highly-skilled and less-skilled employees that offer the best opportunity to meet those needs. However, as the News Note on the following page indicates, there may be differences in opinion about what the strategic staffing level should be.

strategic staffing

Companies can also reduce costs by using permanent part-time employees. The airline industry provides an excellent example of how part-time employees can be beneficial. Airlines often hire permanent part-time ground personnel because of the "bunching" nature of the airline schedule (early morning, mid-day, and early evening flights). Use of these part-timers has dramatically reduced airline fringe benefit costs.

Cost consciousness concepts must be implemented within the budgeting system. Although costs cannot be controlled *after* they have been incurred, future costs may be controlled based on information learned about past costs. Cost control should not cease at the end of a fiscal period or because costs were reduced or controlled during the current period.

On-the-job training is an important component in the process of instilling cost consciousness within an organization's quest for continuous improvement. Giving training to personnel throughout the firm is an effective investment in human resources because workers can apply the concepts and skills they are learning directly to the jobs they are doing.

---

[12]Peter Drucker, "Permanent Cost Cutting," *Wall Street Journal* (January 11, 1991), p. A8.

[13]Lucinda Harger, "Travel Agency Learns Service Firms' Perils in Slimming Down," *Wall Street Journal* (March 20, 1992), p. A1.

How Much Care Would You Want an Aide to Give You?

When hospital executives want cost-cutting advice, they increasingly turn to the consulting firm of APM Inc. But to many nurses, APM is an enemy.

At issue is one of APM's most frequent recommendations: that hospitals change their "nursing skills mix" to rely less on higher-paid and better-trained nurses and more on lower-paid aides to perform routine tasks. APM claims it can save money without affecting patient care; many nurses disagree.

"We view APM as the nemesis of health care," says Rose Ann DeMoro, president of the California Nurses Association. "They're out selling cost-savings models that have been used in the industrial sector. The problem is they look at the patient as a bunch of parts, rather than as a whole human being."

The showdown typifies the turmoil associated with hospitals' efficiency campaigns. Many of America's 5,300 hospitals say they must trim expenses as they lose business to outpatient services and cope with insurers' demands for discounts to hospitals' prices. But cost cutting can bring labor clashes and a hail of questions about whether patient care is at risk.

At many hospitals, 75% or more of patient care is provided by registered nurses, who have at least two to four years of training. They make appreciably more than licensed practical nurses, who generally have 12 to 14 months of training, and often make double the pay of unlicensed aides or orderlies.

Because of the cost differentials, APM advises hospitals to redesign work teams to rely more on lower-paid aides for simple duties, like making beds. This workplace re-engineering can mean big savings. In California, hospitals can save as much as $25,000 a year for each nurse's job converted to an aide's job.

More controversy may lie ahead as some hospitals try to expand the work that lower-paid aides can perform. Among those tasks are drawing blood, gathering data for medical charts or bandaging incisions after surgery—duties that nurses may not want to leave in the hands of less-trained personnel.

SOURCE: George Anders, "Nurses Decry Cost-Cutting Plan that Uses Aides to Do More Jobs," *Wall Street Journal* (January 20, 1994), p. B1. Reprinted by permission of The Wall Street Journal, ©1994 Dow Jones & Company, Inc. All Rights Reserved Worldwide.

Organizations can adopt a five-step method of implementing a cost control system. First, they must understand the types of costs they incur. This understanding will provide insight into how changes in activity (either volume or type) will affect the behavior of those costs. Second, a cost consciousness attitude must be communicated to all employees. Management-level employees are extremely important in cost reduction programs. These individuals provide important input on cost reduction measures, and their attitudes set the tone for the entire department or organization. Third, employees must be motivated by education and incentives to embrace cost consciousness concepts. Employees often do not mind engaging in cost control efforts if such efforts will provide them some benefit, either monetary or at performance review time. Managers must also be flexible enough to accept changes from the current method of operation. Fourth, reports must be generated that indicate actual results, budget-to-actual comparisons, and variances. These reports must be evaluated by management to improve future performance. And fifth, the cost control system should be viewed as a long-run process, not a short-run solution. "To be successful, organizations must avoid the illusion of short-term, highly simplified cost-cutting procedures. Instead, they must carefully evaluate proposed solutions to insure that they are practical, workable, and measure changes based on realities, not illusions."[14]

Following these five steps will provide an atmosphere conducive to controlling costs to the fullest extent possible as well as deriving the most benefit from the costs that are incurred. All costs incurred should have been subjected to appropriate value-added/non-value-added and cost-benefit analyses. However, distinct approaches should exist in the cost control system for addressing committed and discretionary costs.

COMMITTED FIXED COSTS

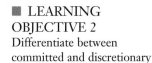

■ **LEARNING OBJECTIVE 2**
Differentiate between committed and discretionary costs.

Managers are charged with planning and controlling the types and amounts of costs needed to conduct business activities. Many activities required for the achievement of business objectives involve fixed costs. All fixed costs (and the activities that create them) can be categorized as either committed or discretionary. The difference between the two categories is primarily the time period for which management binds itself to the activity and the cost.

committed costs

The costs associated with the basic plant assets and personnel structure that an organization must have to operate are known as **committed costs**. The amount of committed costs is normally dictated by long-run management decisions involving the desired level of operations. Committed costs include depreciation, lease rentals, and property taxes. Such costs cannot easily be reduced even during periods of temporarily diminished activity.

One method of controlling committed costs involves comparing the expected benefits of having plant assets (or human resources) with the expected costs of such investments. Managers must decide what activities are needed to attain company objectives and what (and how many) assets are needed to support those activities.

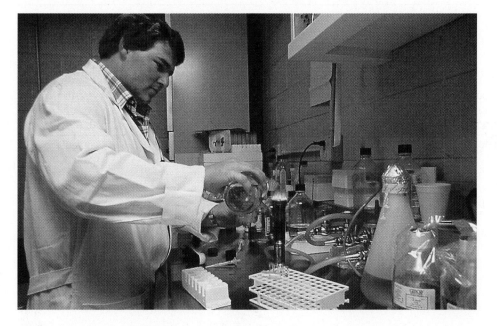

At Ochsner, investments in fixed assets must continually be made to assure the availability of new technology. The costs of and benefits to be provided by new equipment are assessed relative to Ochsner's goal of providing high quality care at a reasonable cost.

---

[14]Mark D. Lutchen, "Cost-Cutting Illusions," *Today's CPA* (May/June 1989), p. 46.

Once the assets are acquired, managers are committed to both the activities and their related costs for the long run. However, regardless of how good an asset investment appears to be on the surface, managers need to understand how committed fixed costs could affect income in the event of changes in operations.

Assume that the managers of the Epstein Clinic are considering an investment of $1,000,000 in patient room furniture. The furniture will be depreciated at the rate of $200,000 per year. The clinic's cost relationships indicate that variable costs are 45 percent of revenues, giving a contribution margin of 55 percent. Exhibit 12–3 illustrates the potential effects of this long-term commitment on net income under three conditions: maintenance of current revenues, a 20 percent increase in revenues, and a 20 percent decrease in revenues.

Note that the $200,000 increase in depreciation expense affects the income statement more significantly when sales decline than when sales increase. This effect is caused by the operating leverage factor discussed in Chapter 8. Companies that have fairly high contribution margins can withstand large increases in fixed costs as long as revenues increase. However, these same companies feel the effects of decreases in revenue more strongly because the margin available to cover fixed costs erodes so rapidly. As the magnitude of committed fixed costs increases, so does the risk of incurring an operating loss in the event of a downturn in demand. Therefore, managers must be extremely careful about the level of fixed costs to which they commit the organization.

A second method of controlling committed costs involves comparing actual and expected results from plant asset investments. During this process, managers are able to see and evaluate the accuracy of their cost and revenue predictions relative to the investment. This comparison is called a post-investment audit and is discussed in Chapter 14.

Although some companies are attempting to become "virtual" organizations that outsource almost all activities, most organizations cannot operate without some basic

■ **EXHIBIT 12–3**
Risk Related to Committed Costs

	CURRENT LEVEL OF OPERATIONS	**(a) CURRENT LEVEL OF REVENUES AND INCREASE IN DEPRECIATION**	**(b) INCREASE IN REVENUES OF 20% AND INCREASE IN DEPRECIATION**	**(c) DECREASE IN REVENUES OF 20% AND INCREASE IN DEPRECIATION**
Revenues	$5,000,000	$5,000,000	$6,000,000	$4,000,000
Variable costs (45%)	(2,250,000)	(2,250,000)	(2,700,000)	(1,800,000)
Contribution margin	$2,750,000	$2,750,000	$3,300,000	$2,200,000
Fixed costs	(2,400,000)	(2,600,000)	(2,600,000)	(2,600,000)
Net income	$ 350,000	$ 150,000	$ 700,000	$ (400,000)

Each change from the original income level to the new income level is explained as the change in the contribution margin minus the increase in fixed costs:

$$\text{Change to (a)} = \text{Increase in CM} - \text{Increase in FC} = \$0 - \$200{,}000 = \$(200{,}000)$$

$$\text{Change to (b)} = \text{Increase in CM} - \text{Increase in FC} = \$550{,}000 - \$200{,}000 = \$350{,}000$$

$$\text{Change to (c)} = \text{Decrease in CM} - \text{Increase in FC} = \$(550{,}000) - \$200{,}000 = \$(750{,}000)$$

levels of plant and human assets. Considerable control can be exercised over the process of determining how management wishes to define *basic* and what funds will be committed to those levels. The benefits from committed costs can generally be predicted and are commonly compared with actual results in the future.

DISCRETIONARY COSTS

In contrast to a committed cost, a **discretionary cost** is one "that a decision maker must periodically review to determine that it continues to be in accord with ongoing policies."[15] A discretionary fixed cost is a fixed cost that reflects a management decision to fund an activity at a specified amount for a specified period of time. Discretionary costs relate to company activities that are important but are viewed as optional. Discretionary cost activities are usually service-oriented and include employee travel, repairs and maintenance, advertising, research and development, and employee training and development. There is no "correct" amount at which to set funding for discretionary costs, and there are no specific activities whose costs are always considered discretionary (or discretionary fixed) in all organizations. In the event of cash flow shortages or forecasted operating losses, discretionary costs may be more easily reduced than committed costs. For instance, companies may decide that they can provide employee training as well and less expensively by using videotapes rather than live presentations.

Discretionary costs, then, relate to relatively unstructured activities that vary in type and magnitude from day to day and whose benefits are often not measurable in monetary terms. For example, in 1993, Frito-Lay decided to spend $100 million to market and promote Doritos Tortilla Thins.[16] How did the company know that this advertising campaign would create a demand for the product? Similarly, the accounting firm of Coopers & Lybrand spent $1.7 million for a one minute advertisement during the 1993 Super Bowl.[17] How did C&L know if this ad generated any new clients? Expenditures of this magnitude require that management have some idea of the benefits that are expected, but measuring results is often difficult. Management can employ market research in trying to gain knowledge of the effectiveness of advertising and other promotional tools.

Just as discretionary cost activities vary, the quality of performance may also vary according to the tasks involved and the skill levels of the persons performing them. Because of these two factors—varying activities and varying quality levels—discretionary costs are not usually susceptible to the precise measures available to plan and control variable production costs or the cost/benefit evaluation techniques available to control committed fixed costs. Since the benefits of discretionary cost activities cannot be assessed definitively, these activities are often among the first to be cut when profits are lagging. Thus, proper planning for discretionary activities and costs

discretionary cost

■ LEARNING
OBJECTIVE 2
Differentiate between committed and discretionary costs.

---

[15]Institute of Management Accountants (formerly National Association of Accountants), *Statements on Management Accounting Number 2: Management Accounting Terminology* (Montvale, N.J.: National Association of Accountants, June 1, 1983), p. 35.

[16]Eleena de Lisser, "Frito-Lay Plans $100 Million Pitch for New Doritos," *Wall Street Journal* (March 25, 1993), p. C13.

[17]Mark Landler, "Super Bowl '93: The Bodies Are Already Piled Up," *Business Week* (January 25, 1993), p. 65.

may be more important than subsequent control measures. Control after the planning stage is often restricted to monitoring expenditures to assure conformity with budget classifications and preventing managers from overspending their budgeted amounts.

Budgeting Discretionary Costs

Budgets are described in Chapters 10 and 11 as both planning and controlling devices. Budgets serve to officially communicate a manager's authority to spend up to a maximum amount (appropriation) or rate for each budget item. Budget appropriations serve as a basis for comparison with actual costs. Accumulated expenditures in each budgetary category are periodically compared with appropriated amounts to determine whether funds have been under- or overexpended.

Before top management can budget amounts for discretionary cost activities, company goals must be translated into specific objectives and policies that will lead to organizational success. Management should then decide which discretionary activities will help accomplish the chosen objectives and to what degree. Funding levels should be set only after discretionary cost activities have been prioritized and cash flow and income expectations for the coming period have been reviewed. Management tends to be more generous in making discretionary cost appropriations during periods of strong economic outlook for the organization than in periods of weak economic outlook.

Management does not generally know the optimal amount for a discretionary cost activity, so discretionary cost appropriations are generally based on three factors: an activity's perceived significance to the achievement of objectives and goals; the upcoming period's expected level of operations; and managerial negotiations in the budgetary process. For some discretionary costs, managers are expected to spend the full amount of their appropriations within the specified time frame. For others, a "less is better" adage is appropriate.

Consider, for example, the difference between machine maintenance on the one hand and executive travel and entertainment on the other. Top management would probably not consider the money saved by foregoing preventive maintenance to be a positive measure of cost control. In fact, spending (with supervisory approval) more than originally appropriated in this area might be necessary or even commendable—assuming that positive results are indicated. However, spending less than budgeted on travel and entertainment (while achieving the desired results) would probably be considered positive performance.

Managers may often view discretionary activities and costs as though they were committed. A discretionary expenditure may be budgeted on an annual basis as a function of planned volume of company sales. Once this appropriation has been justified, management's intention may be that it is not to be reduced within that year regardless of whether actual sales are less than planned sales. A manager who states that a particular activity's cost will not be reduced during a period has chosen to view that activity and cost as committed for that period. However, such a statement does not change the underlying discretionary nature of the item. In such circumstances, top management must have a high degree of faith in the ability of lower-level management to perform the specified tasks in an efficient manner.

■ LEARNING
OBJECTIVE 3
Understand how the benefits from discretionary cost expenditures can be measured.

Measuring Benefits from Discretionary Costs

The amounts spent on discretionary activities are the inputs to a process that should provide some desired output. Unfortunately, as mentioned, the value of the output produced by most discretionary cost activities is difficult to determine on a monetary basis. Nevertheless, managers compare input costs and output results to assess whether there is a reasonable cost/benefit relationship between the two. Managers use this cost/benefit relationship to judge how efficiently costs were used and how effectively they achieved their purposes. These relationships can be seen in the following model:

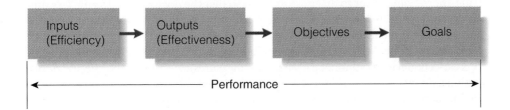

The degree to which comparing output to input reveals a satisfactory relationship reflects the **efficiency** of an activity. Thus, efficiency is a yield concept and is usually measured by a ratio of output to input. For instance, one measure of automobile efficiency is the number of miles the car travels per gallon of gas consumed. The higher the number of miles per gallon, the greater the efficiency. In contrast, comparing actual output results for a particular period to desired output results indicates the **effectiveness** of an activity, which is a measure of how well the firm's objectives and goals were achieved.

efficiency

effectiveness

Determination of both efficiency and effectiveness requires a valid measure of output. When such a measure is available, efficiency and effectiveness can be assessed as follows:

ACTUAL RESULT	COMPARED WITH	DESIRED RESULT
Efficiency $= \dfrac{\text{Actual Output}}{\text{Actual Input}}$		$\dfrac{\text{Planned Output}}{\text{Planned Input}}$
or		
Efficiency $= \dfrac{\text{Actual Input}}{\text{Actual Output}}$		$\dfrac{\text{Planned Input}}{\text{Planned Output}}$
Effectiveness $= \dfrac{\text{Actual Output}}{\text{Planned Output}}$		Preestablished Standard

Efficiency can only be reasonably determined when both input and output can be measured quantitatively and matched in the same period and when there is a credible causal relationship between them. Effectiveness does not require the consideration of input. Efficiency or effectiveness may be stated in either monetary or nonmonetary terms. Managers should avoid making expenditures for discretionary activities that may be conducted efficiently, but for which the results are of dubious effectiveness.

For several reasons, many discretionary costs cannot be closely tied to outcomes. First, several years may pass before the output of a discretionary activity is noticeable. Consider, for example, how much time might elapse between the incurrence of costs for research and development and the materialization of the benefits of these expenditures. Second, it is frequently almost impossible to be certain that a cause-and-effect relationship exists between a discretionary cost input and a particular output. For instance, assume that patients at the Epstein Clinic have been complaining about the time they spend waiting to see a doctor. Each doctor at the clinic paid $500 to attend a time-management seminar in hopes of reducing complaints by at least 90 percent. The month after the seminar, patient complaints about waiting are down by 72 percent. While the clinic has been 80 percent ($.72 \div .90$) effective in achieving its goal of reducing complaints, it cannot be presumed that the training was totally responsible. Perhaps the nature of patients' illnesses in the month after the seminar made the patients easier to diagnose or treat, so that the doctors could spend less time with each one. In such cases, effectiveness can only be subjectively assessed, and efficiency is very difficult to measure.

Because of these difficulties, managers must be willing to spend the time necessary to creatively devise nonmonetary surrogate measures to estimate the success of discretionary expenditures. Exhibit 12–4 presents some surrogate measures that can be used to determine the effectiveness of various types of discretionary costs. Some of these surrogates can be documented and gathered quickly and easily; others are abstract, and measurement requires a longer time horizon. As discussed in Chapter 16, surrogates are often what is needed to measure and evaluate performance.

In summary, attempts to ensure the efficiency of discretionary costs in achieving their desired results are tenuous at best, and the effectiveness of discretionary costs can only be inferred from the relationship of actual output to desired output. Since many discretionary costs result in benefits that must be measured on a nondefinitive

■ **EXHIBIT 12–4**
Nonmonetary Measures of Outputs from Discretionary Costs

DISCRETIONARY COST ACTIVITY	SURROGATE MEASURE OF RESULTS
Executive training seminar on leadership	Reduction in subordinate complaints Increased productivity of department Decrease in staff absenteeism
Research and development	Number of patents applied for Number of engineering changes issued for cost reduction purposes
Guest lecturers at a university	Increased enrollments in related courses Length of coverage of lecture in various news media Quantity of positive feedback about lecture
Special programming on public television	Number of new subscribers Number of calls about program Change in market share for periods of program Decrease in subscriber "gifts" in station's inventory
Charitable contribution to local shelter for homeless	Number of letters received from sponsors Positive employee feedback Decrease in homeless persons in the city
Employee health club	Decrease in health insurance claims Improved employee morale Decrease in number of sick days

and nonmonetary basis, it is difficult to exercise control of these costs during or after the occurrence of the activities. Therefore, planning may be more important than subsequent control.

CONTROLLING DISCRETIONARY COSTS

Control of discretionary costs is often limited to a monitoring function. Management compares actual discretionary expenditures with standard or budgeted amounts to determine variances in attempts to understand the cause-and-effect relationships of discretionary activities.

Control Using Engineered Costs

Some discretionary activities are repetitive enough to allow the development of standards similar to those for manufacturing costs. Such activities result in **engineered costs**, which are costs that have been found to bear observable and known relationships to a quantifiable activity base. Such costs may be treated as either variable or fixed. Discretionary cost activities that can fit into the engineered cost category are usually geared to a performance measure related to work accomplished.

For example, quality control may be considered an engineered cost. Taken as a whole, quality control inspections may be similar enough to allow management to develop a standard inspection time. If a company can hire quality control inspectors on an hourly basis, the company can determine how many inspectors to hire and can compare actual cost against a standard cost each month. The activity base of this engineered cost is the number of inspections performed.

Budget appropriations for engineered costs are based on the static master budget level. However, control can be exerted through the use of flexible budgets if the expected level of activity is not achieved.

Assume that the Epstein Clinic has determined that processing insurance forms can be treated as an engineered cost. Clinic management, in a cost reduction effort, has

■ LEARNING OBJECTIVE 4
Determine when standards are applicable to discretionary costs.

engineered costs

A hotel manager can establish a time standard for room check-in. That standard in conjunction with an average wage rate provides an engineered cost that can be used to determine the efficiency of the check-in process—and the possibility of the need for additional registration clerks.

decided to contract with part-time, experienced secretarial personnel to perform all such processing tasks. Through statistical analysis, clinic management has found that the time required to process each of the most common forms averages slightly less than 15 minutes. Thus, one secretary should be able to process approximately four forms per hour. From this information, managers can estimate how much processing costs should be, based on a particular level of activity. Therefore, the managers have a basis against which to compare actual costs.

For March, the clinic predicts that 3,200 forms will be needed, so 800 processing hours should be provided. If the standard hourly rate for secretaries is $10, the cost budgeted for March will be $8,000. In March, 3,320 forms are processed at a cost of $8,788 for 845 actual hours. Based on the model for variance analysis presented in Chapter 6, the following calculations can be made:

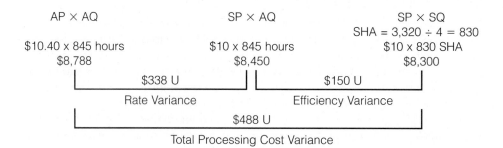

This analysis is meaningful only if the clinic is willing and able to hire personnel to provide the exact number of processing hours needed. If the clinic had to employ only full-time salaried employees, analyzing processing costs in this manner would not be very useful. In this instance, processing becomes a discretionary fixed cost, and the Epstein Clinic may prefer to use the following type of fixed overhead variance analysis:

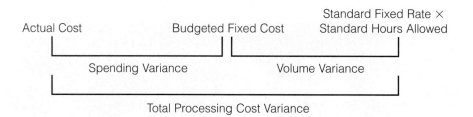

In a third type of analysis, it is assumed that part-time help will be needed in addition to the full-time staffing and the flexible budget is used as the center column measure in the following diagram. Assume the following facts: (1) there are four full-time secretaries, each earning $1,600 per month and working 160 hours per month; (2) the standard hourly rate for part-time help is $10; (3) the standard quantity of work is four forms per hour; (4) 3,320 forms were processed during the month; and (5) actual payroll for 785 total hours was $6,400 for full-time secretaries and $1,595 for part-time secretaries (145 hours hired × $11 per hour). The Epstein Clinic prepares a flexible budget for its fixed secretarial cost at $6,400 (4 × $1,600) based on a normal processing volume of 2,560 forms and $10 per hour for part-time workers. Actual total payroll for the month is $7,995. The following variances can be computed:

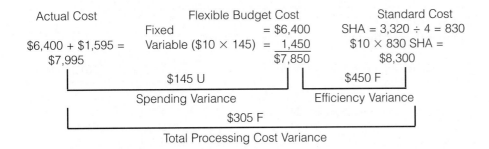

The $145 unfavorable spending variance was incurred because part-time employees had to be hired at $1 more than standard (145 hours × $11). The $450 favorable efficiency variance reflects the above-normal productivity [(830 standard hours allowed − 785 actual hours) × $10 standard cost per hour]. To determine the implications of these figures, clinic management would need to know which employees did and did not process four forms per hour. Management can compare an individual's productivity to ascertain if it is within preestablished control limits. If productivity is outside those limits, management should seek the causes and work with the employee to improve the system.

The method of variance analysis and, thus, cost control must be appropriate to the cost category and management information needs. Regardless of the variance levels or the explanations provided, managers should always consider whether the activity itself and, therefore, the cost incurrence was sufficiently justified.

Control Using the Budget

Once discretionary cost appropriations have been made, monetary control is effected through the use of budget-to-actual comparisons. Discretionary costs are treated the same as all other costs in the budget. Actual and expected results are compared, and explanations should be provided for variances. Variances can often be explained with reference to the various cost consciousness attitudes. The following illustration (which includes two discretionary cost activities) provides a budget-to-actual comparison that demonstrates employee cost consciousness.

The Epstein Clinic prepared the condensed budget shown in Exhibit 12–5 (page 620) for the first quarter of 1996. Kay Poston, the accountant for the clinic, estimated that 15,625 patients with an average billing of $80 each would be treated during that period. Expenses were estimated on the basis of the last quarter charges for 1995 and included expected increases, such as personnel raises.

In the budget, salaries and fringe benefits are fixed for the physicians and certain employees. Reference books, subscriptions, dues, and the like are discretionary expenditures and are budgeted at 7 percent of revenues. The clinic manager has the option of purchasing whatever quantity of insurance she desires. Purchasing no insurance, or only a minimal amount of insurance, means that the doctors would assume more personal risk of loss. Thus, because the amount of insurance purchased is based on managerial choice, insurance cost is discretionary. Its cost is budgeted at $90,000 per quarter plus 2 percent of patient service revenues. Supplies and utility costs are variable. Supplies are budgeted at 15 percent of patient service revenues, and utility costs at $25.50 per hour that the clinic is open. The clinic operates 40 hours per week, and there are 13 weeks in the budget quarter. Wages and fringe benefits are given for the 15 staff members who are paid by the hour; these costs are totally variable at an average of $18 per hour per person. Mailings and other costs, such as taxes, are fully variable; depreciation is fixed.

■ **LEARNING OBJECTIVE 5**
Explain how a budget helps in controlling discretionary costs.

■ **EXHIBIT 12–5**

Epstein Clinic Budget—First Quarter 1996

Patient service revenues (15,625 @ $80)		$1,250,000
Expenses:		
Salaries and fringe benefits	$243,000	
Reference books, subscriptions, dues, etc.	87,500	
Insurance	115,000	
Supplies	187,500	
Utilities	13,260	
Wages and fringe benefits	140,400	
Rent	123,000	
Mailing, advertising, etc.	71,340	
Depreciation	144,000	(1,125,000)
Income before taxes		$ 125,000
Taxes (30%)		(37,500)
Net income		$ 87,500

Exhibit 12–6 provides the actual revenue and expense data collected by Kay Poston during the first quarter of 1996. Epstein Clinic acquired several new patients in late February, requiring the clinic to remain open and fully staffed 10 additional hours at time-and-a-half overtime pay.

After reviewing the actual results, Marc Epstein, the clinic's chief physician, requested a budget-to-actual comparison from Ms. Poston and explanations for the cost differentials. Dr. Epstein believed that costs had been well controlled, since income was higher than budgeted. Ms. Poston's comparison is presented in Exhibit 12–7, and she provided the following explanations for the variances. Each explanation is preceded by the related budget item number from Exhibit 12–7.

1. One doctor retired and was replaced with a new doctor whose salary is higher by $48,000 per year ($12,000 per quarter). The increase is justified because of the new doctor's expertise in an area previously unavailable at the clinic and because of the patient base the person brings the clinic. *Comment: This explanation reflects an understanding of supply and demand relationships and their effects on costs. (An alternative justification could have been inflationary trends in salaries.)*

■ **EXHIBIT 12–6**

Epstein Clinic Actual Results—First Quarter 1996

Patient service revenues (16,000 @ $80)		$1,280,000
Expenses:		
Salaries and fringe benefits	$255,000	
Reference books, subscriptions, dues, etc.	80,000	
Insurance	121,400	
Supplies	190,000	
Utilities	15,100	
Wages and fringe benefits	144,450	
Rent	120,000	
Mailing, advertising, etc.	75,800	
Depreciation	144,000	(1,145,750)
Income before taxes		$ 134,250
Taxes (30%)		(40,275)
Net income		$ 93,975

■ **EXHIBIT 12–7**

Epstein Clinic Flexible Budget-to-Actual Comparison—First Quarter 1996

	BUDGET ITEM NUMBER	ORIGINAL BUDGET	BUDGET BASED ON ACTUAL RESULTS	ACTUAL	VARIANCE (U) OR F
Patient revenues		$1,250,000	$1,280,000	$1,280,000	$ 0
Expenses:					
Salaries and					
fringe benefits	(1)	$ 243,000	$ 243,000	$ 255,000	(12,000)
Reference books, etc.	(2)	87,500	89,600	80,000	9,600
Insurance	(3)	115,000	115,600	121,400	(5,800)
Supplies	(4)	187,500	192,000	190,000	2,000
Utilities	(5)	13,260	13,515	15,100	(1,585)
Wages and fringe benefits	(6)	140,400	143,100	144,450	(1,350)
Rent	(7)	123,000	123,000	120,000	3,000
Mailing, advertising, etc.	(8)	71,340	73,052	75,800	(2,748)
Depreciation	(9)	144,000	144,000	144,000	0
Total expenses		$1,125,000	$1,136,867	$1,145,750	$(8,883)
Income before taxes		$ 125,000	$ 143,133	$ 134,250	
Taxes		(37,500)	(42,940)	(40,275)	
Net income		$ 87,500	$ 100,193	$ 93,975	

2. The decrease in the category that includes reference books occurred because the clinic acquired fewer reference publications during this period than expected (no major revisions were made to the present publications). The clinic also signed several long-term subscriptions contracts at reduced rates and payments needed to be made only for the current period. *Comment: This cost adjustment represents a cost reduction that provides the same results for fewer dollars of expenditure.*

3. The increase in insurance costs occurred because malpractice insurance companies raised their rates because of numerous lawsuits by patients. However, the Epstein Clinic joined with several other clinics and hospitals to form a consortium to work with one insurance provider. *Comment: The increase in rates by the insurance companies reflects an understanding of supply and demand relationships and their effects on costs; the Epstein Clinic's response to that increase represents cost reduction techniques. Had Epstein Clinic not joined the consortium, its insurance costs would have increased by an additional $3,500.*

4. Supply costs were less than expected because of the nature of the illnesses and the types of patients treated by the clinic during this quarter.

5. The utility cost increase was caused by three factors: the additional 10 hours of operation; an increase in local utility rates; and the use of a fax machine that the clinic purchased in January. *Comment: This explanation reflects an understanding of the nature of variable costs. Since the clinic had more hours of operations and used more equipment, more utility costs were incurred. The increase in utility rates could have been caused by inflation.*

6. The increase in wages was caused by two factors: 10 additional operating hours and time-and-a-half pay for overtime. The clinic had a total of 530 hours of operation:

15 people × 530 hours × $18 per hour	$143,100
15 people × 10 hours of overtime × $9	1,350
Total wages cost	$144,450

Comment: Each of these increases reflects the nature of variable costs. Had the clinic known overtime would be needed, those costs could have been budgeted.

7. The rent decrease resulted from a lease renegotiation. The city in which Epstein Clinic operates had excess rental properties, and landlords were willing to decrease rents to maintain tenants. *Comment: This factor reflects supply and demand relationships.*

8. Mailing and other costs in this category increased in part because of an increase in postal rates. The costs would have increased more except that the clinic was able to fax some of its paperwork rather than using express mail services, as it previously had done. *Comment: This change represents avoidance of higher-priced services.*

9. Depreciation was unchanged. Since the cost of the fax machine was immaterial, the clinic expensed it as part of the mailing category.

Note that the variance computations in Exhibit 12–7 are based on a comparison of actual revenues and costs against a flexible budget reflecting actual patient service revenues. Managers should always analyze variances using an equitable basis of comparison. Comparisons between the original (static) budget and actual results for the variable cost items would not have been useful for control purposes, because total variable costs automatically rise with increases in activity. Cost control should be judged on the basis of what costs should have been for the level of activity actually achieved.[18]

If, however, management wants to consider total variances from *plans*, actual results should be compared with the original (rather than the flexible) budget. Such comparisons are usually made when revenues (in units or dollars) are lower than expected. The comparisons give managers a perspective on the magnitude of the deviations between expected and actual results.

Another possible comparison of expected and actual results can be based on actual activity and after-the-fact information about the new factors influencing costs. This comparison would require that formulas be developed to show the relationships between costs and various causal factors. Regression analysis could then be used to calculate the dependent variables for control purposes. While this method is extremely useful for controlling costs, comparisons based on master or flexible budgets are more commonly employed in practice because they require less preparation time and cost.

CONTROLLING QUALITY COSTS

■ **LEARNING OBJECTIVE 6**
Calculate the cost of quality so that control can be exercised.

One often mentioned discretionary cost category is that of quality assurance and quality control. However, with the current competitive business emphasis on total quality management, it is unlikely that quality costs can be reduced in the short term without harming the long term profitability potential of an organization.

Chapter 3 indicated that two types of costs comprise the total quality cost of an entity: (1) cost of quality compliance or assurance and (2) cost of noncompliance or quality failure. Compliance costs are incurred with the intention of eliminating the present costs of failure and avoiding such costs in the future; thus, they are proactive on management's part. These costs are composed of prevention and appraisal costs. Costs of noncompliance are considered failure costs and result from production or service imperfections. The costs in this category are equal to all internal failure costs (such as scrap and rework) plus all external failure costs (such as product returns due to quality problems, warranty costs, and complaint department costs). Expenditures made for either prevention or appraisal reduce the amount of failure costs. The accompanying News Note indicates that, after failure problems, General Motors is now willing to spend money for prevention.

---

[18]Revenue variances are discussed in Chapter 10.

Quality Up Front Could Have Saved Lives

Doug Worden was taking a left turn off a highway in his 1977 model GM C-K pickup when he was sideswiped on the driver's side and the truck caught on fire. "To get out, even on the passenger side, I had to go through the fire," Worden of Puyallup, Washington, said. Worden was burned over 55 percent of his body and spent painful weeks getting skin grafts.

Worden settled a lawsuit against General Motors in June 1994. However, . . . [in December 1994, a public hearing was scheduled to determine if the trucks should be recalled] when Transportation Secretary Federico Pena announced that the government would drop the case. In return, GM will spend $51 million on auto safety and research programs.

Pena said if the Department of Transportation fought GM in court it could have taken years to resolve, while the millions GM spent on auto safety programs would "save lives immediately."

At issue are GM's sidesaddle gas tanks on model years 1973 to 1987—two 20-gallon tanks mounted on each side outside the truck's frame. About 9 million of the trucks were manufactured before GM brought the gas tank back inside the frame; 5 million are still on the road.

In October 1994, Pena acknowledged the trucks meet federal crash-safety standards, but he said the law requires that they be safe in real-world conditions as well. He blamed the fuel tank design for 150 deaths.

The National Highway Traffic Safety Administration asked GM to recall the trucks in 1993. The automaker refused.

SOURCE: Associated Press, "GM Will Spend $51 Million on Safety, Research," *(New Orleans) Times-Picayune* (December 6, 1994), p. D-2.

Historically, quality costs have not been given separate recognition in the accounting system. In most instances, the cost of quality is "buried" in a variety of general ledger accounts, including Work in Process Inventory and Finished Goods Inventory (for rework, scrap, preventive maintenance, and other overhead costs), marketing and advertising expenses (to recall products, improve image after poor products were made available to customers, or obtain customer survey information), personnel costs (for training), and engineering department costs (for engineering change orders and redesign).

In trying to control the cost of quality, an organization must first be able to calculate its total cost of quality. Quality costs should be measured to the extent possible and practical and the benefits of those costs estimated. Such calculations are likely to use estimates rather than actual figures, but this is preferred to not making any calculations. Exhibit 12–8 (page 624) provides formulas for calculating the total cost of quality for a company using the basic categories of prevention, appraisal, and failure.

To illustrate these computations, consider the following July 1996 operating information for the Lee Company, which makes some of the medical equipment used by Epstein Clinic:

Defective units (D)	1,000	Units reworked (Y)	600
Profit for good unit (P_1)	$25	Profit for defective unit (P_2)	$15
Cost to rework defective unit (r)	$5	Defective units returned (D_r)	100
Cost of return (w)	$8	Prevention cost (K)	$25,000
Appraisal cost (A)	$4,400		

■ **EXHIBIT 12–8**
Formulas for Calculating Total Quality Cost

CALCULATING LOST PROFITS

Profit Lost by Selling Units as Defects = (Total Defective Units − Number of
Units Reworked) × (Profit for Good Unit - Profit for Defective Unit)

$$Z = (D − Y) (P_1 − P_2)$$

CALCULATING TOTAL COSTS OF FAILURE

Rework Cost = Number of Units Reworked × Cost to Rework Defective Unit

$$R = (Y) (r)$$

Cost of Processing Customer Returns = Number of Defective Units Returned ×
Cost of a Return

$$W = (D_r) (w)$$

Total Failure Cost = Rework Cost + Profit Lost by Selling Units as Defects
+ Cost of Processing Customer Returns

$$F = Z + R + W$$

CALCULATING THE TOTAL QUALITY COST

Total Quality Cost = Defect Control Cost + Failure Cost

$$T = \text{Prevention Cost} + \text{Appraisal Cost} + \text{Failure Cost}$$

$$T = K + A + F$$

Prevention and appraisal costs are total estimated amounts; no formulas are required. As the
cost of prevention rises, the number of defective units should decline. Additionally, as the
cost of prevention rises, the cost of appraisal should decline; however, appraisal cost can
never become zero.

SOURCE: James T. Godfrey and William R. Pasewark, "Controlling Quality Costs," *Management
Accounting* (March 1988), p. 50. Published by Institute of Management Accountants, Montvale, NJ.

Substituting these values into the formulas provided in Exhibit 12-8 yields the following results:

$$
\begin{aligned}
Z &= (D − Y) (P_1 − P_2) = (1,000 − 600) (\$25 − \$15) = \$4,000 \\
R &= (Y) (r) = (600) (\$5) = \$3,000 \\
W &= (D_r) (w) = (100) (\$8) = \$800 \\
F &= Z + R + W = \$4,000 + \$3,000 + \$800 = \$7,800 \text{ total failure cost} \\
T &= K + A + F = \$25,000 + \$4,400 + \$7,800 \\
  &= \$37,200 \text{ total quality cost}
\end{aligned}
$$

Of the total quality cost of $37,200, Lee Company managers will seek the causes of
the $7,800 total failure cost and work to eliminate them. The results of the analysis
may affect the planned amounts of prevention and appraisal costs for future periods.

High quality affords a company the ability to improve current profits—either by
controlling failure costs, by selling additional product, or, if the market will bear, by
charging higher prices. Because management should be more interested in long-run
business objectives than short-run profits, it is essential that control also be exercised
over prevention and appraisal costs. Theoretically, if prevention and appraisal costs

were prudently incurred, failure costs would be reduced to zero. However, it is highly unlikely that any organization can afford to spend enough on prevention to assure 100 percent quality 100 percent of the time. Managers should evaluate the cost/benefit relationships among expenditures in this discretionary area and calculate measures of effectiveness and efficiency. When quality is increased through greater attention to prevention and appraisal activities, overall costs should decline, and productivity should increase. Lower costs and greater productivity support lower prices, which, in turn, often stimulate demand. The result is greater market share—meaning that surrogate measures such as fewer customer returns can be translated into monetary measures of profit increases.

SITE ANALYSIS

The price of health care is under heavy scrutiny by patients, insurance companies, and the government. It is imperative for organizations such as Ochsner Hospital to examine their operations to find effective ways to reduce costs (or at least hold them constant).

The provision of medical services has changed in recent years from a fee-for-service basis to a managed-care environment composed of various health maintenance organizations (HMOs) that generate revenue on a fixed-fee-per-patient (or "capitated business") basis. Ochsner recognized this reality in the mid-1980s and formed its own HMO (the Ochsner Health Plan). Adopting this plan created many committed costs in that the hospital had to expand its facilities to include a network of convenient neighborhood clinics, which are served by a medical staff of over 350 physicians.

When hospitals select a level of capacity for their primary care facilities, they create a "domino effect" on committed fixed costs. For instance, each operating room requires a given number of recovery rooms which require a given number of beds and a given number of staff, and so on and so on. Should the capacity level selected be an inappropriate one, the hospital's finances will suffer. Too much capacity will create too many uncovered costs; too little capacity will restrict revenues. Thus, Ochsner must assess multiple cost issues when making commitments to add capacity.

In the past few years, Ochsner has implemented numerous cost control procedures to deal with the deteriorating bottom line common to all health care providers. For example, all new and replacement staff positions must be justified to the hospital executive committee. Need is then assessed on the basis of issues such as current patient volume, department overtime, and potential for use of "temps" from external agencies or other internal departments. Ochsner has been gradually introducing a "paperless" system for purchasing, receiving, and payables and is eyeing electronic billing as a means to avoid key-punching costs for invoices. The hospital's Quality Assessment Department has been active for some years; its function is to review the average length of hospital stays so as to avoid costly and unnecessary hospital visits by patients.

A movement to use more disposable medical supplies has occurred at Ochsner. This change may seem illogical since reusables are often less expensive than non-reusable throwaways. However, estimates of storage and resterilization costs were made and compared with estimates for the potential failure costs of selecting the wrong instrument, desterilizing the instrument after selecting it, and inaccurately estimating the number of times an instrument can be used. Then the cost of disposing of medical waste was put into the equation. Ochsner decided it was more economical and safer to take the more expensive prevention route—just-in-time deliveries of throwaways. While controlling costs is a priority at Ochsner, it is not the number-one priority: that priority is high-quality patient care.

SOURCE: Interview with Graham Cowie, Assistant Director of Finance, Ochsner Medical Institutions, 1994.

Discipline	Applications
Accounting	Cost control requires analysis of budget expenditures by category and amount. Accountants can use value analysis performed for activity-based costing to determine excess spending. Accounting should formally assist managers in their control efforts before, during, and after production.
Economics	Analysis can help explain profitability of different types of customers and sizes of orders. Cost understanding requires knowledge of supply and demand relationships. Cost understanding requires a recognition of the trade-offs and relationship between efficiency and effectiveness. Cost consciousness is essential to providing goods and services to customers at competitive prices and quality.
Finance	Capital expenditures for technology can be justified by other cost reductions, and increases in income and cash flow. Cost control requires budget preparation for proper planning and comparison.
Management	Cost control requires justification of budget expenditures and focuses on controlling the cause of a cost (the underlying activity) rather than the result (the cost itself). Instilling cost consciousness in all workers helps managers to achieve their objectives of maintaining a profitable organization, providing jobs in a community, paying bills promptly, and paying dividends to shareholders.
Marketing	Cost control creates a focus on product "benchmarking" and on comparisons of product costs with costs in other organizations. Lower costs result in lower selling prices, which will typically increase market share. Cost understanding can help focus on cost effects of product "clutter" strategies—those designed to significantly increase product variety or expand product lines.

CROSS-FUNCTIONAL APPLICATIONS STRATEGIES

CHAPTER SUMMARY

Cost control is essential to an organization's long-run success. An effective cost control system encompasses efforts before, during, and after a cost is incurred. Regardless of the type of cost involved, managers and other employees must exercise attitudes of cost consciousness to provide the best means of cost control. Cost consciousness reflects employees' predisposition toward cost understanding, cost containment, cost avoidance, and cost reduction.

Two types of costs are committed and discretionary costs. Committed fixed costs are the long-run costs of establishing and maintaining the basic plant assets and permanent organizational personnel required to operate at a level desired by top management. Careful consideration must be given to the selection of that activity level because the choice binds the company to a specified level of fixed costs for the long run.

People and organizations engage in activities to produce results, and those activities create costs. Comparing actual output with actual input reflects efficiency, while comparing actual output with desired results reflects effectiveness. Efficiency plus effectiveness indicates performance. Measuring the output generated by cost inputs, however, is not always easy. Measurement difficulty is most frequently encountered with discretionary costs.

Most discretionary costs are appropriated annually for the conduct of service-type activities that managers may consider optional in the short run. The outputs of discretionary activities are often nonmonetary and qualitative in nature. The efficiency and effectiveness of these activities are difficult to measure. Surrogate measures of output can be useful in estimating the success of discretionary activities and costs. Discretionary activities should be planned to achieve results that fit within an overall management philosophy.

Some discretionary costs may be treated as engineered costs because they are routine and structured enough to allow for the computation of standards. Engineered cost standards can be used to determine the appropriate amount of planned expenditures to achieve a given result. One aspect of control over engineered costs involves performing variance analysis similar to that used for variable factory overhead.

Budgeting is a primary tool in planning and controlling discretionary activities and costs. Budget appropriations provide both authorization for spending and the bases against which actual costs are compared. Care must be taken that appropriate levels of activity are used for budget-to-actual comparisons, so that cost control can be effective.

Prevention and appraisal costs are incurred to enhance quality and reduce failure costs. Quality costs should be retrievable and reportable so that managers can evaluate the efficiency and effectiveness of the company's quality efforts.

APPENDIX

Program Budgeting

The problem of controlling discretionary costs has been particularly acute in governmental and other not-for-profit entities. In addition, activities performed by these organizations produce results that are often difficult to measure in monetary terms or take several years to be measurable, though the related activities must be funded annually. Traditional budgeting often takes the current year's spending levels as givens in setting the budget for the next year. Additions to the budget each year may lead to nonprioritized and ever-increasing spending levels (the creeping commitment syndrome). **Program budgeting** is useful for cost control purposes in certain types of organizations. In program budgeting, resource inputs are related to service outputs so that managers can focus on the relevant cost/benefit relationships.

Program budgeting starts by defining objectives in terms of output results rather than quantity of input activities. For instance, an input measure of an executive development program might be a statement of the target number of courses each person must complete by year-end. An output measure might state the objective in terms of expected improvement rates on executive annual performance evaluations. Once output results have been defined in some measurable terms, effectiveness can be measured. Program budgeting involves a thorough analysis of alternative activities for achieving a firm's objectives. This analysis includes projecting both quantitative and qualitative costs and benefits for each alternative and selecting those alternatives that, in the judgment of top management, yield a satisfactory result at a reasonable cost. These choices are then translated into budget appropriations to be acted on by the managers responsible for the related programs.

Program budgeting requires the use of detailed surrogate measures of output. These measures call for answers to the following questions:

1. When should results be measured? Since many not-for-profit programs are effective only after some time has passed, it may be necessary to employ different mea-

■ **LEARNING OBJECTIVE 7**
(Appendix) Understand how program budgeting is used for cost control in not-for-profit entities.

program budgeting

sures at different times to determine effectiveness. When should these measurements initially be made, and how often should they be made thereafter?

2. What results should be chosen as output measures? Many not-for-profit programs have multiple results. For example, reading programs for the adult illiterate can affect unemployment and crime statistics, welfare spending, and so on. Should these results be ranked in importance, or should all results be given equal weight?

3. What actually caused the result? Is there really a cause-and-effect relationship between the observed result and the not-for-profit program? For example, did an adult literacy program cause a decrease in unemployment statistics, or did that decrease result from an unrelated job placement program?

4. Did the program actually affect the target population? An adult literacy program may have been aimed at the unemployed. If most of the persons who attended the program already had jobs, the program did not affect the target group. However, it could still be considered effective if the participants increased their job skills and employment level.

Program budgeting can be useful not only in government and not-for-profit organizations but also for service activities in for-profit businesses. Program budgeting can help managers evaluate and control discretionary activities and costs, avoid excessive cost expenditures, and assure that expenditures are used for programs and activities that generate the most beneficial results.

GLOSSARY

Committed cost (p. 611)   the cost of the basic plant assets and personnel structure that an organization must have to operate

Cost avoidance (p. 606)   a process of finding acceptable alternatives to high-cost items and not spending money for unnecessary goods or services

Cost consciousness (p. 601)   a companywide employee attitude toward cost understanding, cost containment, cost avoidance, and cost reduction

Cost containment (p. 605)   the process of attempting, to the extent possible, to minimize period-by-period increases in per-unit variable and total fixed costs

Cost control system (p. 600)   a logical structure of formal and informal activities designed to influence costs and to enable management to analyze and evaluate how well expenditures were managed during a period

Cost reduction (p. 607)   a process of lowering current costs, especially those in excess of necessary costs

Discretionary cost (p. 613)   an optional cost that a decision maker must periodically review to determine whether it continues to be in accord with ongoing policies

Effectiveness (p. 615)   a measure of how well the firm's objectives and goals were achieved; it involves comparing actual output results with desired results

Efficiency (p. 615)   the degree to which the relationship between output and input is satisfactory

Engineered cost (p. 617)   a cost that has been found to bear an observable and known relationship to a quantifiable activity base

Horizontal price fixing (p. 604)   a practice by which competitors attempt to regulate prices through an agreement or conspiracy

Price fixing (p. 603)   a practice by which firms conspire to set a product's price at a specified level

Program budgeting (p. 627)   an approach to budgeting that relates resource inputs to service outputs and thereby focuses on the relationship of benefits to cost expenditures (from appendix)

Strategic staffing (p. 609)   a practice in which organizations analyze their personnel needs by considering long-term objectives and determine a specific combination of permanent and temporary or highly-skilled and less-skilled employees that offer the best opportunity to meet those needs

Vertical price fixing (p. 604)   a practice of collusion between a producing business and its distributors to control the prices at which the business's products may be sold to consumers

SOLUTION STRATEGIES

Efficiency (relationship of input and output):

Actual yield ratio   =   Actual output ÷ Actual input
or
Actual input ÷ Actual output

Desired yield ratio =   Planned output ÷ Planned input
or
Planned input ÷ Planned output

Effectiveness (actual output compared with desired output)

Efficiency + Effectiveness = Performance

COST VARIANCES

Comparison of actual costs with budgeted costs—allows management to assess discrepancies from the original plan

Comparison of actual costs with budgeted costs at actual activity level—allows management to determine how well costs were controlled; uses a flexible budget

Variance analysis using standards for discretionary costs—allows management to compute variances for routine, structured discretionary costs

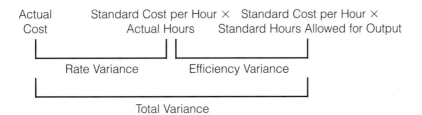

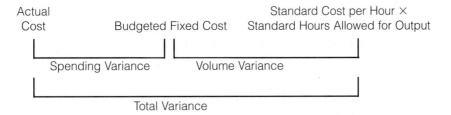

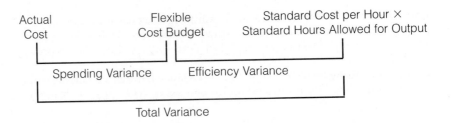

END OF CHAPTER MATERIALS

■ QUESTIONS

1. In a cost control system, at what points in time can control over an activity be exerted?

2. Explain the meaning and significance of cost consciousness.

3. What primary factors may cause costs to change from one period to another?

4. What is price fixing? What is the difference between horizontal and vertical price fixing? Are these practices legal in the United States? Explain.

5. Since committed costs are in place for the long run, how can they be controlled?

6. How do discretionary and committed costs differ? Does management's attitude toward a cost affect whether it is classified as discretionary or committed?

7. If a manager having responsibility for a discretionary cost spends less than is budgeted for that cost, should that manager be praised? Discuss the rationale for your answer.

8. Define *efficiency* and *effectiveness* and distinguish one from the other.

9. Management performance is evaluated by how efficiently and effectively the company's goals are achieved. Describe the links from inputs to goals by which management performance can be described and measured.

10. Why is it often difficult to measure the output of activities funded by discretionary costs?

11. What are surrogate (nonmonetary) output measures? Explain their use in connection with discretionary costs.

12. Explain why it is often difficult to measure the efficiency of discretionary costs. How can discretionary cost effectiveness be measured?

13. What is an engineered cost? How can engineered costs be used in controlling some discretionary costs?

14. Of what importance is budgeting in the control of discretionary costs?

15. Why is the budget that is used for planning purposes not necessarily the best budget to use for evaluating cost control?

16. What two types of costs comprise a firm's total quality cost? What are the two subtypes within each type? Given the tradeoffs between the two main types of quality costs, is quality ever free? Explain.

17. Why is it difficult to determine the amount of quality cost a firm has incurred by examining accounting records?

18. (Appendix) What is program budgeting? How does it differ from traditional budgeting?

■ **EXERCISES**

19. (LO 1, 2, 3, 4; *Terminology*) Match the numbered items on the right with the lettered items on the left.

a. Discretionary cost	**1.** A cost that bears a known and observable relationship to an activity base
b. Committed cost	**2.** An attitude regarding cost understanding, cost containment, and cost reduction
c. Engineered cost	**3.** A measure of input-output yield
d. Cost containment	**4.** An optional cost incurred to fund an activity for a specified period
e. Cost consciousness	**5.** A process of holding unit variable costs and total fixed costs at prior-period levels
f. Efficiency	**6.** A cost incurred to provide physical or organizational capacity
g. Effectiveness	**7.** A logical structure of activities designed to analyze and evaluate how well expenditures were managed during a period
h. Cost avoidance	**8.** A process of finding acceptable alternatives for high priced items and not buying unnecessary goods or services
i. Cost reduction	**9.** A process of lowering current costs
j. Cost control system	**10.** An assessment of how well a firm's goals and objectives were achieved

20. (LO1; *Cost consciousness*) An accounting firm hires temporary staff to work on certain audit engagements and tax work during the tax season. The firm compensates these employees at $25 per hour with no fringe benefits. However, if a temporary employee works more than 1,600 hours in a year, that employee is given a 10 percent bonus above normal compensation for all hours over 1,600.

Each permanent staff member receives $36,000 annually, to which fringe benefits of 24 percent are added.

a. Is the practice of hiring part-time staff an example of cost containment, cost avoidance, or cost reduction? Explain.

b. At what level of hours of work should the firm hire permanent staff rather than part-time employees?

21. (LO 1; *Cost consciousness*) Below are various actions taken by management teams to control costs. For each item listed, indicate whether the action indicates an application of cost understanding, cost containment, cost avoidance, or cost reduction.

a. A company canceled its contract with an external firm that it used for training in computerized manufacturing methods. At the same time, the firm created an in-house training department. Even though the in-house training will be more expensive, management believes the extra cost is justified because of the added flexibility in scheduling training sessions.

b. A municipality, faced with a 13 percent increase in health insurance premiums, raised the deductible on its coverage, and was able to keep health insurance costs at the prior year's level.

c. Anticipating a rise in raw material prices, a manufacturing firm signed a contract to acquire a year's supply of materials at the current prices.

d. Because beef by-product costs had been rising over the past year, a dog food manufacturer increased the proportion of pork by-products relative to the content of beef by-products in the input mix of its dog food.

e. Because a small foreign country offered a 10-year income tax "holiday" for new businesses, a U.S. leather-goods manufacturer relocated its production facilities to that country.

f. Because it had suffered large losses caused by currency fluctuations, a U.S. importer instituted a practice of hedging its currency transaction risk.

g. After the new union contract was signed, wage rates for highly-skilled workers rose by 18 percent. As a result, a tool-and-die maker elected to automate three of its higher-volume production processes. This decision resulted in a cost savings of $1,400,000 over a period of 5 years.

22. (LO 2; *Committed vs. discretionary costs*) Indicate whether each of the following discriptions best relates to committed (C) costs or discretionary (D) costs. Explain the rationale for your choice.

a. Temporary reductions in this cost can usually be made without impairing the firm's long-range capacity or profitability.

b. Control is first provided over this cost during the capital budgeting process.

c. This cost is primarily affected by long-range decisions regarding desired capacity levels.

d. Examples of this cost include property taxes, depreciation, and lease rentals.

e. This cost often provides benefits that are not monetarily measurable.

f. Examples of this cost include research and development, quality control, and advertising.

g. This cost cannot be easily reduced, even during temporary slowdowns in activity.

h. Outcomes often cannot be demonstrated to be closely correlated with this cost.

i. This cost usually relates to service activities.

j. No "correct" amount at which to set funding levels usually exists for this cost.

23. (LO 2; *Committed vs. discretionary costs*) Following is a list of specific discretionary and committed costs.

1. Property taxes
2. Marketing research
3. Quality control
4. Equipment depreciation
5. Insurance on equipment
6. Research and development
7. Secretarial pool
8. Executive training
9. Advertising
10. Interest expense
11. Preventive maintenance
12. Legal staff salaries
13. Employee safety training
14. Charitable contributions

Answer the following questions.

a. Is each cost ordinarily classified as committed (C) or discretionary (D)?

b. What is a monetary or nonmonetary surrogate measure of output for any item you designated as discretionary (D)?

c. Which costs could be classified as either committed or discretionary, depending on management attitude?

24. (LO 3; *Efficiency vs. effectiveness*) Captain Fischer has a fleet of deep-sea fishing excursion vessels operating out of Plymouth, Massachusetts. He is considering outfitting an older vessel with the more efficient of two diesel engines he has in his shop. These engines have been used in vessels similar to the one in which he intends to make the installation. Records show that engine A ran 22,500 miles and consumed 2,500 gallons of fuel and engine B ran 19,950 miles and consumed 2,100 gallons of fuel. Diesel fuel is expected to cost $1.32 per gallon next year. The refitted boat is expected to run 12,100 miles next year.

    a. Which engine has demonstrated the most efficiency?
    b. How much will be spent next year on diesel fuel if engine A is installed? Round your answer to the nearest dollar.
    c. How much will be spent next year on diesel fuel if engine B is installed? Round your answer to the nearest dollar.
    d. How much savings will there be if the more efficient engine is installed?

25. (LO 3; *Efficiency vs. effectiveness*) Ottawa Community Hospital administration has concluded that the number of original letters dictated is a good measure of output for its secretarial pool. The hospital included $114,000 for the pool in its 1998 budget. Lena Swanson, chief administrator of the hospital, estimated that 10,000 letters would be dictated in 1998.

    Review of the actual 1998 results showed that 9,800 letters were dictated to the pool and typed. The payroll for the secretarial pool was $109,760. Another 500 letters were dictated and sent to an external agency at an additional cost of $7,500.

    a. What were the secretarial pool's planned and actual degrees of efficiency? What was the hosiptal's degree of efficiency in having letters processed?
    b. What was the secretarial pool's degree of effectiveness?

26. (LO 3; *Efficiency vs. effectiveness*) The Dallas County director of motor vehicle licenses, Frank Garza, was granted a $3,000,000 budget for salaries in that department for the 1998 fiscal year. Garza estimated that each motor vehicle license issued should require 15 minutes to prepare, input, and review. The county expected to issue 1,200,000 motor vehicle licenses during the year. The director can hire part-time employees during periods of peak activity.

    Early in the 1999 fiscal year it was determined that actual payroll in the prior year was $3,120,000 and that 1,320,000 licenses had been issued.

    a. Was the department efficient? Present the basis for your answer.
    b. Was the department effective? Discuss your answer.
    c. What areas of expertise would Mr. Garza likely consult in developing the standard of one license for each 15 minutes of labor time?

27. (LO 3; *Surrogate measures of output*) The management control system at the Nevada Noose, a hotel and gaming casino, is based on the concept of management by objectives. This means that there are performance objectives established for each major area of operation for the budget year. Following are some of the major objectives that were established for the budget year 1996. For each objective, identify a surrogate measure of performance.

    a. Increase volume of customer traffic at the gaming tables.
    b. Decrease the labor content per beverage served to customers.
    c. Increase the length of stay per hotel guest.
    d. Attract more out-of-state visitors and reduce the number of in-state visitors.
    e. Increase convention business.
    f. Increase the quality of room-cleaning services.

g. Increase the relative amount of gaming revenue generated by the slot machines.

28. (LO 4; *Engineered cost variances*) Luther Motors is instituting a quality control inspection program. Management estimates that each inspector should make an average of five inspections per hour. Retired production workers are well acquainted with the company's products and are expected to do well as quality control inspectors. A standard hourly rate of $15 has been established for these part-time inspectors.

    In the first month of the program, 5,120 inspections were made, and the inspectors were paid $15,872 for 1,024 hours.

    a. Analyze variances for quality control labor.
    b. If Luther could hire three full-time inspectors, each to work 200 hours monthly at a salary of $3,500, and use the part-time inspectors for the needed extra inspections, how much better or worse off would the company be than with the current system?

29. (LO 4; *Engineered cost variances*) Wilson Courier Service employs three drivers who are paid an average of $9 per hour for regular time and $13.50 for overtime. A pickup and delivery requires, on average, one hour of driver time. Drivers are paid for a 40-hour week because they must be on call all day. One driver stands by for after-hour deliveries.

    During one week in July, the company made 112 daytime deliveries and 9 after-hour deliveries. The payroll for drivers for that week was $1,116. The employees worked 120 hours regular time and 8 hours overtime.

    Analyze the labor costs for the week.

30. (LO 6; *Cost of quality*) Blue Water Racing Sails, Inc., manufactures custom-made sails for racing sailboats. Below are selected cost data taken from records of the company for 1997 and 1998:

DEFECT PREVENTION COSTS	1997	1998
Quality training	$16,000	$19,000
Quality technology	12,000	16,000
Quality production design	8,000	18,000

EXTERNAL FAILURE COSTS		
Warranty handling	$30,000	$20,000
Customer reimbursements	22,000	14,400
Customer returns handling	14,000	8,000

    a. Compute the percentage change from 1997 to 1998 in the two main quality cost categories.
    b. Write a brief explanation for the pattern of change in the two categories.

31. (LO 6; *Cost of quality*) Custom Home Drapes manufactures window coverings to customer specifications from a wide array of available materials. The company is evaluating its quality control costs for 1996 and preparing plans and budgets for 1997. The 1996 quality costs incurred in the Draperies Division follow:

Prevention	$ 400,000
Appraisal	100,000
Internal failure costs	300,000
External failure costs	200,000
Total	$1,000,000

a. Which categories of failure costs would be affected by a decision to spend $300,000 on a new computer-controlled machine to "lay out" and cut material (the machine would replace a manual cutting system)? Explain.

b. The CEO of Custom Home Drapes is trying to quantify all of the benefits and costs that would be associated with the acquisition of the machine referred to in part a. What could each of the following experts add to the CEO's understanding of benefits and costs associated with the machine?

   1. Electrical engineer

   2. Mechanical engineer

   3. Production supervisor

   4. Marketing director

   5. Cost accountant

c. Assume that the firm can reduce projected external failure costs for 1997 by 50 percent from 1996 levels by either spending $80,000 more on appraisal or spending $120,000 more on prevention. Why might the firm rationally opt to spend the $120,000 on prevention rather than the $80,000 on appraisal?

32. (LO 6; *Cost of quality*) Gunther Water Systems manufactures sprinkler heads for irrigation systems. The company is interested in evaluating its quality control efforts for 1997. Accordingly, it has gathered the following information from 1997 records:

Defective units	10,000
Units reworked	9,000
Defective units returned	200
Appraisal costs	$16,000
Prevention costs	$24,000
Cost per unit for rework	$8
Cost per unit for customer returns	$12
Profit per good unit produced and sold	$15
Profit per defective unit sold	$5

a. Compute profits lost from selling defective units in 1997.
b. Compute total failure cost for 1997.
c. Compute the total cost of quality for 1997.
d. Why would the company elect not to rework 1,000 defective units?

■ COMMUNICATION ACTIVITIES

33. (LO 1; *Cost control*) *Recently, the California State University system placed a purchase order (PO) for a book published by a small New Canaan, Conn., company, The Information Economics Press. The following is a copy of the letter the press sent back to the California procurement officer. It illustrates some of the joys of doing business with government organizations.*
Mr. M. J. Whitson
California State University
Los Alamitos, CA 90720
Attn: Charleen Wood,
Procurement and Support
Services Officer

   We have your eight page PO#940809 for one copy of our book "The Politics of Information Management." We are unable to fill your $49 order for the following reasons:

■ *In the Purchase Order Terms and Conditions you wish us to waive any infringement of our copyrighted materials by officers, agents and employees of the California State University. We cannot agree to make available a valuable Copyright for the price of a book.*

■ *You will withhold all payments or make a 38% withholding in order to file a year-end 1099 form. We are unable to handle the paperwork of a separate 1099 for every book we sell. That would double our paperwork.*

■ *You are requiring us to file a Vendor Data Record (form 204) which is largely identical with your Vendor Information form. Filing both forms takes excessive amounts of time.*

■ *We are a small business, and therefore you require that we submit a copy of the OSMB Small Business Certification. We do not have an OSMB Certification and we do not know where to get one.*

■ *Your attachment to form 204 specifies that I obtain a determination with regard to my being classified either as resident or non-resident subject to California tax withholdings, to be reclaimed by filing at year-end California tax returns. We do not plan to make any tax filings in California.*

■ *Your contract rider contains a Privacy Statement on unspecified disclosures that makes us liable for penalties of up to $20,000.*

■ *As a condition of our filling out the order you are asking us to post statements notifying all employees of compliance with Code Section 8355 and certifying as to our adopting a four point Drug-Free Awareness program that complies with California law. Deviations are punishable as perjury under the laws of the State of California. Please note our firm has only two employees, who do not take even an aspirin.*

■ *Your Minority/Women Business Enterprise Self Certification Form 962 requires detailed statistics on ethnic characteristics of our firm, defining each ethnic group according to their stated geographic origins. To assist in making such distinctions you provide a check-list of ethnic identity of the owners of this firm, leaving us by default with only one open choice, Caucasian, which you do not define. My husband and I do not know of any ancestors who may have ever been in the proximity of the Caucasian mountains, and therefore we are unable to comply with your requirement to identify our ethnic origin according to your geographic rules.*

We therefore suggest that you purchase our book at a bookstore.

Mona Frankel

Publisher

[SOURCE: Mona Frankel, "Just Go to the Bookstore and Buy One," *Wall Street Journal* (October 18, 1994), p. A20. Reprinted by permission of The Wall Street Journal, ©1994 Dow Jones & Company, Inc. All Rights Reserved Worldwide.]

a. What cost control strategy was the author of the preceding letter employing in her decision to reject the book order? Explain.

b. What appears to be the source of most of the complexity associated with the purchase order? Explain.

c. What does the letter suggest about the opportunity for improved cost control in the California State University purchasing system? Explain.

34. (LO 1, 5; *Causes of changes in cost*) *When the going gets tough, Americans go to the library. They go to scan the help-wanted ads. They go to borrow books they can no longer afford to buy. If they have no home, they go to warm up, wash up, doze off, and get treated with a dignity hardly any place else accords them. They go, but more and more often*

the library is closed. People want to use library books to train themselves for new careers; they want to use typewriters to type resumes so that they may search for jobs. In small towns, libraries serve as a place to pick up the latest romance novel and gossip. Rural libraries are often the only source of information and culture in small counties. The public libraries are the people's universities.

[SOURCE: Jonathan Tilove, "Budgets Dwindle When Libraries Are Needed Most," *(New Orleans) Times-Picayune* (February 10, 1991), p. A-10.]

a. Organizations (especially governmental agencies) cannot find money for specific activities when money does not exist. Using the factors discussed in the chapter as a guide, provide some explanations of the problems facing city libraries.

b. Assume you are a local politician seeking reelection. Your city is faced with library cuts and/or closures. Discuss some ways in which the benefits of keeping the libraries open can be measured against the continuously rising costs.

35. (LO 1; *Cost control and financial records*) Turbo Propulsion is a medium-sized manufacturing plant in a capital-intensive industry. The corporation's profitability is very low at the moment. As a result, investment funds are limited and hiring is restricted. These consequences of the corporation's problems have placed a strain on the plant's repair and maintenance program. The result has been a reduction in work efficiency and cost control effectiveness in the repair and maintenance area.

The assistant controller proposes the installation of a maintenance work order system to overcome these problems. This system would require a work order to be prepared for each repair request and for each regular maintenance activity. The maintenance superintendent would record the estimated time to complete a job and send one copy of the work order to the department in which the work was to be done. The work order would also serve as a cost sheet for a job. The actual cost of the parts and supplies used on the job as well as the actual labor costs incurred in completing the job would be recorded directly on the work order. A copy of the completed work order would be the basis of the charge to the department in which the repair or maintenance activity occurred.

The maintenance superintendent opposes the program on the grounds that the added paperwork will be costly and nonproductive. The superintendent states that the departmental clerk who now schedules repairs and maintenance activities is doing a good job without all the extra forms the new system would require. The real problem, in the superintendent's opinion, is that the department is understaffed.

a. Discuss how such a maintenance work order system would aid in cost control.
b. Explain how a maintenance work order system might assist the maintenance superintendent in getting authorization to hire more mechanics.

(CMA)

36. (LO 6; *Managing quality costs*) Following are data for two firms in the toy industry. The data pertain to quality costs, by category, as a percentage of sales dollars for 1998. The firms are of similar size in terms of both assets and sales.

	FIRM 1	FIRM 2
Training and prevention costs	5%	1%
Appraisal and evaluation costs	3%	2%
Internal failure costs	2%	3%

	1%	5%
External failure costs		
Total costs	$\overline{11}\%$	$\overline{11}\%$

a. Are the two firms equally successful in controlling quality costs?

b. Which firm is more likely to have adopted a total quality management philosophy? Explain.

37. (LO 6; *Quality costs in different industries*) For a benchmark, assume that the typical U.S. firm incurs quality costs in the following proportions:

Prevention	25%
Appraisal	25%
Internal failure	25%
External failure	25%
Total quality costs	100%

Explain why each of the following firms might have a spending pattern for quality costs that differs from the benchmark.

a. Architectural firm

b. Hair salon

c. Heavy equipment manufacturer

d. Health maintenance organization

■ PROBLEMS

38. (LO 1; *Type of cost consciousness*) After assuming the position of U.S. Postmaster General in July 1992, Marvin Runyon was faced with eliminating a projected $2 billion operating deficit. Following are actions that Runyon proposed to take to reduce or eliminate the deficit.

■ Institute a freeze on new real estate and other construction projects. The postal service had intended to spend $579 million on such projects in a single fiscal year.

■ Outline a plan to reduce the size of the postal service's administrative bureaucracy.

■ Spend $7 million on a new logo to upgrade the image of the postal service.

■ Outline numerous initiatives to increase quality of services.

[SOURCE: Facts based on Associated Press, "Postal Service Told to Trim Costs," *(New Orleans) Times-Picayune* (July 15, 1992), p. A-4; and Bill McAllister, "New Eagle Adds to Woes of Postal Service," *(New Orleans) Times-Picayune* (April 7, 1994), p. A-14.

a. For each action, indicate whether it represents cost understanding, cost containment, cost avoidance, or cost reduction.

b. Runyon was also successful in increasing the postal rate for first-class mail. However, one of Runyon's concerns in controlling costs was to maintain the high volume of business in consideration of the high level of fixed costs the postal service incurs. Discuss why maintaining a high volume of business is an effective way to deal with fixed costs and evaluate the likely effect of a price increase on volume.

39. (LO 1; *Cost consciousness*) Temporary or part-time employees are sometimes used in the following ways.

a. To make desserts for restaurants

b. To serve as security guards

c. To write articles for monthly magazines
d. To tailor men's suits for department stores
e. To sell clothing in department stores during the Christmas season
f. To conduct classes as substitute teachers in the absence of the regular teachers
g. To teach evening courses at universities
h. To work as medical doctors in the emergency rooms of hospitals
i. To prepare tax returns for CPA firms
j. To draw house plans for construction companies
k. To do legal research for law firms

For each way listed, suggest potential advantages and disadvantages of using temporary or part-time employees from the perspective of both the employer and the end user of the product or service.

40. (LO 4; *Committed vs. discretionary cost*) Champion Sports Products is concerned about proper staffing in the expansion of its purchasing department. Analysis shows that the historical average time needed to prepare a purchase order is 30 minutes. Management believes that the predicted number of purchase orders is highly correlated with the predicted sales for any future year. The average revenue for the past three years is $12,000,000, and the average number of purchase orders in those years is 40,000. The cost of a full-time purchasing staff member is $32,000 annually. Full-time employees work 8 hours per day, 5 days per week, 50 weeks annually. Part-time purchasing staff can be hired at $14 per hour. Budgeted revenue for 1998 is $12,600,000.

a. How many purchase orders are predicted for 1998?
b. If only part-timers were used, what would it cost to staff the department for 1998?
c. If only full-timers were used, what would it cost to staff the department for 1998?
d. Assume that management wants to have eight full-time employees and to staff the remaining hours needed with part-timers. What would the staff costs be?

41. (LO 3; *Efficiency vs. effectiveness*) The health care industry has recently found itself in a new era that is characterized by cost competition. As a result of the new emphasis on cost management, many existing practices are being revised or dropped. Following are changes that have been made by specific health care providers. For each change mentioned, indicate whether the change is intended to control cost through increased efficiency or increased effectiveness. Also indicate whether the change represents cost understanding, cost containment, cost avoidance, or cost reduction. Discuss your justification for each answer.

a. Before entering the hospital for chemotherapy, a patient's health care provider required her to drink more than two quarts of water at home. By doing so, a day's stay in the hospital for hydration was avoided.
b. By administering an antibiotic within two hours of each operation, a hospital reduced the post-operation infection rate from 1.8 percent of patients to .4 percent of patients.
c. Some surgeons have started removing the drainage tubes from heart-bypass patients 24 hours after the operation rather than 48 hours after the operation. The change reduces the length of the typical hospital stay.
d. Doctors at a major hospital tightened scheduling requirements for blood analysis so that results were obtained on the same day that the blood was drawn. The change allowed many patients to be dismissed immediately.

e. A hospital began a practice of paying about $130 per average dose of a new antinausea drug to be administered to chemotherapy patients. The drug allowed vomiting to be controlled much faster and the patient to be more comfortable and dismissed a day earlier.

[SOURCE: Facts based on Ron Winslow, "Health-Care Providers Try Industrial Tactics to Reduce Their Costs," *Wall Street Journal* (November 3, 1993), p. A1, A5.]

42. (LO 3, 4, 5; *Efficiency vs. effectiveness; variance analysis*) Hanson Bridge Construction Co. budgeted $280,000 for its bid department to make bids on potential bridge-building contracts in 1998. The company expected to issue 400 bids in 1998. When 1998 activity was analyzed in early 1999, the following statistics were ascertained:

Actual bids prepared	440
Actual bid department expenses	$292,000

a. Was the bid department effective? Present calculations.
b. Was the bid department efficient? Present calculations.
c. Did the bid department stay within its budget? If not, discuss what bid department personnel might have done before overspending the budget.
d. Prepare a variance analysis of the bid department costs.

43. (LO 3, 4, 5; *Cost control*) Silicon Valley Electronics' top management observed that the EDP department was justifying ever-larger budget requests on the basis of ever-larger usage by the company's various departments. User departments are not charged for EDP services and state that EDP personnel are "always very generous in recommending ways the EDP department can be of greater service."

Operating statistics for the EDP department for 1997 follow.

- Budget—$107,500 based on 2,150 hours of run time; of this amount, $75,250 relates to fixed costs

- Actual—$43,700 variable cost (incurred for 2,300 hours of run time); $75,250 fixed cost

a. Did the EDP department operate within its approved budget? Present calculations.
b. Calculate the department's effectiveness and comment.
c. Was the department efficient in using its variable costs? Fixed costs?
d. Calculate variable and fixed cost variances.
e. Devise an hourly rate scheme to charge EDP users for the cost of operating the EDP department. Do you think charging for EDP services will slow expansion of the EDP department budget? Explain.

44. (LO 1, 3; *Output measures*) A large industrial company recently spent $11 million to build a 100,000-square-foot fitness center. The center includes racquetball courts, Nautilus exercise equipment, and a conference and training center for 264 people. The company has 2,500 employees who can use the center.

The following information is also available:

- Health care costs for the employees typically average $2,000 per employee per year.

- The average loss per year to employee illness is $17 million for this company.

- Joining a comparable fitness center would cost an employee $4,000 for the sign-up fee and annual dues of approximately $1,000.

- An estimated 85 percent of the employees will use the center; 40 precent of these will use it more than three times per week.

- Statistics have shown that people who exercise reduce their health care costs by half.

- The health club will continue to be maintained at a nominal annual cost to the company.

a. Justify the expenditure made to construct this health club. Any assumptions you make should be stated and be consistent with the data.

b. If you wanted more information on the effect of exercise on worker productivity, where would you go (or what sources would you use) to obtain such data?

45. (LO 6; *Cost of quality*) Ride-On Bicycle Company has gathered the following information pertaining to quality costs of production for November 1997:

Total defective units	400
Number of units reworked	280
Number of bicycles returned	45
Total prevention cost	$8,000
Total appraisal cost	$9,200
Per unit profit for defective units	$10
Per unit profit for good units	$25
Cost per unit to rework defective units	$11
Cost per unit to handle returned units	$16

a. Determine the total cost to rework.
b. Determine the profit lost from not reworking all defective units.
c. Determine the cost of processing customer returns.
d. Calculate the total failure costs.
e. Calculate the total quality cost.

46. (LO 6; *Cost of quality*) Water Toys Co. just completed its first year of operations. The company manufactures water skis. The firm produced 6,000 pairs of skis during the year. Of these, 600 pairs were so defective that they could not be economically reworked and sold through regular channels, and 5,400 pairs were eventually sold through regular market channels. At year end, there was no inventory of finished goods. For this first year, the firm spent $36,000 on prevention costs and $18,000 on quality appraisal. There were no customer returns. An income statement for the year follows.

Sales (regular channel)	$324,000	
(scrap)	15,000	$339,000
Cost of Goods Sold		
Original production costs	$240,000	
Rework costs	33,000	
Quality appraisal and prevention	54,000	(327,000)
Gross margin		$ 12,000
Selling and administrative expenses (all fixed)		(80,000)
Net income (loss)		$ (68,000)

a. Compute the total profits that Water Toys Co. lost in its first year of operations by selling defective units as scrap rather than selling the units through regular channels.

b. Compute the total failure costs incurred by Water Toys Co. in its first year.

    c. Compute total quality costs incurred by Water Toys Co. in its first year.

    d. What evidence indicates that the firm is dedicated to manufacturing and selling high-quality products?

    e. Water Toys Co. sold 600 defective units as scrap because that they could not be economically reworked. In a typical manufacturing firm, who would make judgments about whether a given defective unit of product should be reworked or sold as scrap? Who would he or she seek advice from in making that decision?

47. (LO 6; *Cost of quality*) Shakespeare Block and Line manufactures block-and-tackle systems that are used in theaters to move props, raise and lower curtains, and so forth. The company has been innovative in developing equipment for specialized applications and is the recognized industry leader in product quality. In recent months, top managers have become more interested in trying to quantify the costs of quality in the company. As an initial effort, the company identified the following quality costs, by category, for 1997:

PREVENTION COSTS

Quality training	$30,000
Quality technology	90,000
Quality participation	62,000

APPRAISAL COSTS

Quality inspections	$38,000
Test equipment	24,000
Procedure verifications	19,000

INTERNAL FAILURE COSTS

Scrap and waste	$13,500
Waste disposal	5,100

EXTERNAL FAILURE COSTS

Warranty handling	$18,200
Customer reimbursements and returns	9,100

    Managers were also aware that in 1997, 150 of the 5,000 units produced had to be sold as scrap. These 150 units were sold for $80 less per unit than "good" systems. Also, the company incurred rework costs amounting to $5,500 to sell 90 other units through regular market channels.

    a. Find Shakespeare's 1997 expense for lost profits from scrapping the 150 units.

    b. Determine total failure costs for 1997.

    c. Determine total quality costs for 1997.

    d. Assume that the company is considering expanding its existing full 7–year warranty to a full 10-year warranty in 1998. How would such a change likely be reflected in quality costs? Who would make such a decision?

48. (LO 7; *Appendix*) Indicate whether each item in the following list describes traditional budgeting (T) or program budgeting (P). After identifying the appropriate type of budgeting, discuss how the other budgeting method differs.

    a. It is especially useful in government and not-for-profit entities and for service activities in for-profit firms.

b. It begins with amounts budgeted in the prior year and builds on those numbers based on expansion of resources to fund greater input activity.

c. It begins by defining objectives in terms of output results rather than quantity of input activities.

d. It is concerned with alternative approaches to achieving similar results.

e. It treats the prior year's funding levels as given and essential to operations.

f. It requires the use of surrogate measures of output.

g. It focuses on budgeted monetary levels rather than on goals, objectives, and outputs.

h. It is particularly well suited to budgeting for discretionary cost expenditures.

i. It requires an analysis of alternative activities for achieving a firm's objectives.

j. It is concerned with choosing the particular results that should be used as output measures.

■ CASES

49. (LO 1; *Governmental cost control*) According to recent news reports, the Pentagon has spent large amounts on items that may be considered unneeded and obsolete. Some examples of the stockpiled items in the arsenal follow.

■ 150,000 tons of tannin, used in tanning cavalry saddles and knapsacks—enough, in the words of one top Pentagon official, "to refight the Civil War"

■ 1.5 million pounds of quartz, a needed component for radios which have since become antiques

■ 3.3 million ounces of quinine, an anti-malaria compound supplanted years ago by superior medicines

■ 22 million pounds of mica, used in camp stoves and radio vacuum tubes—artifacts from earlier in this century.

[SOURCE: Facts from Mark Thompson, "Pentagon Stockpile Rife with Relics," *(New Orleans) Times Picayune* (February 23, 1992), p. A-18.]

a. Assume that you are the head of the area responsible for each of the above items. Defend your rationale for the use of funds.

b. Assume that you are the head of the General Accounting Office. Discuss your reply to part a.

c. What type of cost consciousness ideas would you suggest to the Pentagon, and how would these ideas help? What would be the deterrents to implementation?

50. (LO 5; *Budgeting and cost control*) Wagner Company employs flexible budgeting techniques to evaluate the performance of its activities. The selling expense flexible budgets for three representative monthly activity levels are as follows:

REPRESENTATIVE MONTHLY FLEXIBLE BUDGETS—SELLING EXPENSES

	Unit Sales Volume		
	400,000	425,000	450,000
Dollar sales volume	$10,000,000	$10,625,000	$11,250,000
Number of orders	4,000	4,250	4,500
Number of salespersons	75	75	75
Monthly expenses:			
Advertising and promotion	$ 1,200,000	$ 1,200,000	$ 1,200,000

Administrative salaries	57,000	57,000	57,000
Sales salaries	75,000	75,000	75,000
Sales commissions	200,000	212,500	225,000
Salesperson travel	170,000	175,000	180,000
Sales office expense	490,000	498,750	507,500
Shipping expense	675,000	712,500	750,000
Total expenses	$ 2,867,000	$ 2,930,750	$ 2,994,500

The following assumptions were used to develop the selling expense flexible budgets:

■ The average size of Wagner's sales force during the year was expected to be 75 people.

■ Salespersons are paid a monthly salary plus a commission on gross dollar sales.

■ The travel costs have both a fixed and a variable element. The variable portion tends to fluctuate with gross dollars of sales.

■ Sales office expense is a mixed cost, with the variable portion related to the number of orders processed.

■ Shipping expense is a mixed cost, with the variable portion related to the number of units sold.

A sales force of 80 persons generated a total of 4,300 orders, resulting in a sales volume of 420,000 units during November. The gross dollar sales amounted to $10.9 million. Selling expenses incurred for November were as follows:

Advertising and promotion	$1,350,000
Administrative salaries	57,000
Sales salaries	80,000
Sales commissions	218,000
Salesperson travel	185,000
Sales office expense	497,200
Shipping expense	730,000
Total expenses	$3,117,200

a. Explain why the selling expense flexible budget just presented would not be appropriate for evaluating Wagner's November selling expenses, and indicate how the flexible budget would have to be revised.

b. Determine the budgeted variable cost per salesperson and variable cost per sales order for Wagner Company.

c. Prepare a selling expense report for November that Wagner Company can use to evaluate its control over selling expenses. The report should have a line for each selling expense item showing the appropriate budgeted amount, the actual selling expense, and the monthly dollar variation.

d. Determine the actual variable cost per sales order for Wagner Company.

e. Comment on the effectiveness and efficiency of the salespersons during November.

(CMA adapted)

51. (LO 1, 3, 4, 5; *Analyzing cost control*) The financial results for the Continuing Education Department of BusEd Corporation for November 1997 are presented in the schedule at the end of the case. Mary Ross, president of BusEd, is pleased with the final results but has observed that the revenue and most of the costs and expenses of this department exceeded the budgeted amounts. Barry Stein, vice-

president of the Continuing Education Department, has been requested to provide an explanation of any amount that exceeded the budget by 5 percent or more.

Stein has accumulated the following facts to assist in his analysis of the November results:

- The budget for calendar year 1997 was finalized in December 1996, and at that time, a full program of continuing education courses was scheduled to be held in Chicago during the first week of November 1997. The courses were scheduled so that eight courses would be run on each of the five days during the week. The budget assumed that there would be 425 participants in the program and 1,000 participant days for the week.

- BusEd charges a flat fee of $150 per day of course instruction, so the fee for a three-day course would be $450. BusEd grants a 10 percent discount to persons who subscribe to its publications. The 10 percent discount is also granted to second and subsequent registrants for the same course from the same organization. However, only one discount per registration is allowed. Historically, 70 percent of the participant day registrations are at the full fee of $150 per day, and 30 percent of the participant day registrations receive the discounted fee of $135 per day. These percentages were used in developing the November 1997 budgeted revenue.

- The following estimates were used to develop the budgeted figures for course-related expenses.

Food charges per participant day (lunch/coffee breaks)	$ 27
Course materials per participant	8
Instructor fee per day	1,000

- A total of 530 individuals participated in the Chicago courses in November 1997, accounting for 1,280 participant days. This number included 20 persons who took a new, two-day course on pension accounting that was not on the original schedule; thus, on two of the days, nine courses were offered, and an additional instructor was hired to cover the new course. The breakdown of the course registration was as follows:

Full fee registrations	704
Discounted fees	
Current periodical subscribers	128
New periodical subscribers	128
Second registrations from the same organization	320
Total participant day registrations	1,280

- A combined promotional mailing was used to advertise the Chicago program and a program in Cincinnati that was scheduled for December 1997. The incremental costs of the combined promotional price were $5,000, but none of the promotional expenses ($20,000) budgeted for the Cincinnati program in December will have to be incurred. This earlier-than-normal promotion for the Cincinnati program has resulted in early registration fees collected in November as follows (in terms of participant days):

Full fee registrations	140
Discounted registrations	60
Total participant day registrations	200

■ BusEd continually updates and adds new courses, and includes $2,000 in each monthly budget for this purpose. The additional amount spent on course development during November was for an unscheduled course that will be offered in February for the first time.

Barry Stein has prepared the following quantitative analysis of the November 1997 variances:

BUSED CORPORATION
STATEMENT OF OPERATIONS
CONTINUING EDUCATION DEPARTMENT

	Budget	Actual	Favorable/ (Unfavorable) Dollars	Favorable/ (Unfavorable) Percent
Revenue				
Course fees	$145,500	$212,460	$ 66,960	46.0
Expenses				
Food charges	$ 27,000	$ 32,000	$ (5,000)	(18.5)
Course materials	3,400	4,770	(1,370)	(40.3)
Instructor fees	40,000	42,000	(2,000)	(5.0)
Instructor travel	9,600	9,885	(285)	(3.0)
Staff salaries & benefits	12,000	12,250	(250)	(2.1)
Staff travel	2,500	2,400	100	4.0
Promotion	20,000	25,000	(5,000)	(25.0)
Course development	2,000	5,000	(3,000)	(150.0)
Total expenses	$116,500	$133,305	$(16,805)	(14.4)
Revenue over expenses	$ 29,000	$ 79,155	$ 50,155	172.9

BUSED CORPORATION
ANALYSIS OF NOVEMBER 1997 VARIANCES

Budgeted revenue		$145,500
Variances:		
Quantity variance [(1,280 − 1,000) × $145.50]	$40,740 F	
Mix variance [($143.25 − $145.50) × 1,280]	2,880 U	
Timing difference ($145.50 × 200)	29,100 F	66,960 F
Actual revenue		$212,460
Budgeted expenses		$116,500
Quantity variances		
Food charges [(1,000 − 1,280) × $27]	$ 7,560 U	
Course materials [(425 − 530) × $8]	840 U	
Instructor fees (2 × $1,000)	2,000 U	10,400 U
Price variances		
Food charges [($27 − $25) × 1,280]	$ 2,560 F	
Course materials [($8 − $9) × 530]	530 U	2,030 F
Timing differences		
Promotion	$ 5,000 U	
Course development	3,000 U	8,000 U
Variances not analyzed (5% or less)		
Instructor travel	$ 285 U	
Staff salaries and benefits	250 U	
Staff travel	100 F	435 U
Actual expenses		$133,305

After reviewing Barry Stein's quantitative analysis of the November variances, prepare a memorandum addressed to Mary Ross explaining the following:

a. The cause of the revenue mix variance
b. The implication of the revenue mix variance
c. The cause of the revenue timing difference
d. The significance of the revenue timing difference
e. The primary cause of the unfavorable total expense variance
f. How the favorable food price variance was determined
g. The impact of the promotion timing difference on future revenues and expenses
h. Whether or not the course development variance has an unfavorable impact on the company

(CMA)

■ ETHICS AND QUALITY DISCUSSIONS

52. As chairman of United Airlines, Stephen Wolf initiated a $20 million project to repaint all of the firm's airplanes as part of a movement to create more of a global image for the firm. At present, about one-third of United's 540+ planes have been painted in the new colors: midnight-blue belly, dark gray upper fuselage, and two-tone tail. Not anticipated by Mr. Wolf were the following consequences of the new colors:

- Air-traffic control personnel complain that, because of the dark-blue belly, they can't see the planes in cloudy weather or at night.

- Thirty additional workers had to be hired to wash the planes and apply a special sealant to keep the colors from fading.

- The dark paint absorbs heat and causes additional fuel costs to be incurred to cool the cabins.

- Many customers complain that the new look is too austere.

[SOURCE: Based on Carl Quintanilla, "United Airlines Goes for the Stealth Look," *Wall Street Journal* (November 12, 1994), p. A1, A4.]

a. Evaluate the new United Airlines' paint scheme in terms of its impact on (1) cost control, (2) quality control, and (3) revenue generation.
b. On what basis could a $20 million expenditure for a new corporate color scheme be justified? Can you think of any other instances in which the same or a similar type of change has occurred? If so, discuss.

53. *The National League of Cities reported that 85% of all U.S. municipalities raised fees and taxes, or imposed new ones, during 1990. These amounted to another $10 billion annually. Even with all that new cash, 61% of city governments claimed they wouldn't have enough money in the kitty to pay their bills during 1991.*

   But state and local governments can be made to work. There are alternatives to the bulimic spend-and-trim cycles that have plagued them for decades. Look behind the headlines about fiscal crises and rising taxes, and you'll find a growing number of officials quietly embracing concepts that have transformed American industry over the past decade—quality, teamwork, outsourcing, and yes, customer service.

[SOURCE: Ronald Henkoff, "Some Hope for Troubled Cities," *Fortune* (September 9, 1991), p. 121. © 1991 Time Inc. All rights reserved.]

    a. How does the concept of civil service for employees mesh with and/or conflict with the concept of quality management?

    b. Have you seen instances in your city or state in which fees or taxes were increased with no increase in service? Explain.

    c. Have you seen instances in your city or state in which fees or taxes were increased with equitable increases in service? Explain.

    d. Have there been instances in your city or state in which fees or taxes were reduced because of some governmental program? If so, describe the situation.

    e. How do the incentives for workers in private industry to provide high-quality products and services differ from the incentives of government workers in this regard?

54. The most popular air traffic route in the United States may be the flight between the Pentagon and Andrews Air Force Base, a distance of about 14 miles. According to the *Washington Post*, top military officials made this flight 238 times in 1993. According to the Post's calculations, the average cost per flight is between $1,000 and $3,000. By car, the trip takes about 25 minutes which, using taxi rates, amounts to $22. Using these estimates, if all trips were made by taxi, the total cost of the trips would have been approximately $5,236 for 1993.

    "It's an issue of efficiency," stated a secretary of former Secretary of Defense, Les Aspin. "The amount of time it takes to go by ground is sometimes prohibitive. . ."

[SOURCE: Associated Press, "Thousands Spent on 14-Mile Flights," *(New Orleans) Times-Picayune* (May 2, 1994), p. A-3.]

    a. Evaluate the argument that air transportation is used in the name of efficiency.

    b. Could the use of air transportation be better justified on the grounds of effectiveness? Explain.

    c. Could the use of air transportation be defended on the basis of quality considerations? Explain.

55. Assume that you are in charge of a social service agency that provides counseling services to welfare families. The agency's costs have been increasing with no corresponding increase in funding. In an effort to reduce some costs, you implement the following ideas:

    ■ Counselors are empowered to make their own decisions about the legitimacy of all welfare claims.

    ■ To emphasize the concept of "doing it right the first time," counselors are told not to review processed claims at a later date.

    ■ To discourage "out-of-control" conditions, an upper and lower control limit of 5 minutes is set on a standard 15 minute time for consultations.

    Discuss the ethics as well as the positive and negative effects of each of the ideas listed.

56. In 1991, Alcoa went through a major reorganization by reducing many senior management positions and splitting the company into more autonomous organizational units. However, while profits are up, so are customer complaints. "Customer rejections at Alcoa's main can-sheet plant are running 25% above [those in 1991], with customer satisfaction at one point falling below 50%. Virtually all of the unit's largest customers have complained of poor quality, and Alcoa has missed deliveries for the first time in years."

[SOURCE: Dana Milbank, "Restructured Alcoa Seeks to Juggle Cost and Quality," *Wall Street Journal* (August 24, 1992), p. B4.]

a. Alcoa has been pointed to as an example of how cost reductions can lower quality. What kinds of costs could be reduced in an organization that would almost automatically lower product/service quality? Why?

b. If quality improvements create cost reductions, why could cost reductions not create quality improvements?

c. Are there instances in which cost reductions would create quality improvements? Explain.

57. *For Caesar O'Neal, a nausea-free day is priceless. But for the hospital treating the 6-foot-8-inch University of Florida football player for liver cancer, the price of delivering that relief is becoming troublesome.*

Mr. O'Neal has been getting massive chemotherapy, including a round last fall that left him vomiting so much that he nearly quit treatment. After that crisis, doctors gave him Zofran, a powerful antinausea drug. Now chemotherapy isn't so frightening, Mr. O'Neal says as he sits on his bed sipping Gatorade. Instead of suffering anguish after each treatment, he can enjoy small pleasures such as video games, big meals or chats with relatives.

But Zofran is one of the most expensive drugs around—and a hot issue as hospitals and drug makers clash over the cost of medications. A standard 32-milligram dose of Zofran—less than a single teardrop—costs hospitals $143. Factor in expenses for stocking it and having nurses administer it intravenously, and each use of Zofran can turn into a $300 patient charge. By weight, gem-quality diamonds are cheaper.

Many doctors and nurses, however, think they can slash Zofran costs without making patients feel worse. "We may be overusing the drug," says Robert Benjamin, an oncologist who treats Mr. O'Neal at the University of Texas M.D. Anderson Cancer Center in Houston. He and other doctors around the U.S. think Glaxo's official package inserts, though approved by the Food and Drug Administration, overstate the Zofran dose that many patients need.

M.D. Anderson is seeking to trim its spending on costly antinausea drugs such as Zofran by 10% this year. Other teaching hospitals, in Boston, New York and Chicago, are looking for cuts of 25% to 50%—mostly by drafting new treatment standards that lean on doctors to shrink dosages or try less costly substitutes.

[SOURCE: George Anders, "Costly Medicine Meets its Match: Hospitals Just Use Lower Doses," *Wall Street Journal* (August 1, 1994), pp. A1, A6. Reprinted by permission of The Wall Street Journal, ©1994 Dow Jones & Company, Inc. All Rights Reserved Worldwide.]

a. What cost control strategy are health administrators attempting to employ for Zofran?

b. What are the ethical considerations in cutting drug costs by cutting doses and by switching to less costly substitutes?

c. What is the ethical responsibility of the pharmaceutical manufacturer in setting the prescribed doses for medicines it develops?

58. In 1992, American, Russian, and British investors combined their resources to open a GM car dealership in Russia. The dealership has offices in Moscow, St. Petersburg, and Kiev and is expected to expand to as many as 50 other major Russian cities.

Mark Thimmig manages the operations in Moscow. Following are some of the major changes with which Thimmig has had to cope in the brief time Trinity Motors has been in operation.

■ Value-added taxes on car imports to Russia have increased from zero percent to 166 percent. This means that Trinity Motors now pays about $30,000 per car in duties and taxes.

- Price hikes caused by the increase in taxes have caused sales volume to decline about 50 percent.

- Russian gangsters have organized to import cars into Russia without paying taxes; many of these cars are stolen.

- New Russian consumer protection laws require Trinity Motors to replace defective cars within 20 days. However, it takes 30 days to ship a car from the United States to Russia.

[SOURCE: Facts based on Adi Ignatius, "GM Dealer Hits Rough Road in Russia," *Wall Street Journal* (June 28, 1994), p. A15.]

a. The high import fees instituted in Russia are intended to protect the domestic auto manufacturing plants. What is the likely effect of such duties on the quality of manufacturing operations in Russia?

b. What is the likely effect of the new consumer protection laws on the warranties that will be offered by foreign auto makers?

c. How do high import duties and taxes affect the incentives to import cars illegally?

d. Does the Russian government bear any ethical obligation to foreign businesses in structuring its systems of taxation and import fees? Defend your position.

■ PROJECTS

59. *Last month May Oquendo had breast surgery at Johns Hopkins Medical Center at 7:30 in the morning. At noon, she was discharged from the hospital and went home.*

Such are the frontiers of outpatient surgery. Procedures such as partial mastectomies, gall-bladder removals, heart catheterizations and even hysterectomies are being done without an overnight hospital stay. More than half of the operations done in 1992 were on an outpatient basis, up from 21% in 1982, according to the American Hospital Association.

Rapid advances in surgical techniques and anesthesia make certain operations much faster and less drastic than they used to be, doctors say. Besides, quick turnarounds are an important way for hospitals to hold down costs. . . .

In some cases, technology has advanced so far that once-major surgery has been transformed into a few minutes' work. Cataract operations, for example, can be done by laser in as little as 30 minutes, with patients needing minimal recovery time. That contrasts with long hospitalizations in the pre-laser era, when patients were immobilized for a week or more after surgery.

[SOURCE: George Anders, "More Patients Get Quick Surgery and Go Home," *Wall Street Journal* (August 11, 1994), pp. B1, B4. Reprinted by permission of The Wall Street Journal, ©1994 Dow Jones & Company, Inc. All Rights Reserved Worldwide.]

Advances in technology have dramatically affected cost control efforts in the medical field. Select another industry and conduct a library search on how technology has affected costs and cost control strategies. Write a report on your findings.

60. *The lonely nights finally over, U.S. hoteliers are gleefully lighting up their no-vacancy signs: Guests are showing up in droves, and profits are rising handsomely even if nationwide room rates aren't.*

Chastened by their spendthrift ways in the 1980s, hoteliers have discovered that cost-cutting measures can feed profits—even without substantial room-rate increases.

While hotel operators are quick to cite operating-cost controls as the primary reason for their improved fortunes, the biggest boost to earnings has come from restructuring debt.

"Roughly half of the turnaround in the industry over the last four years is attributable to a decline in capital charges," says Roger Cline, Arthur Andersen & Co.'s worldwide director of hospitality consulting services. "We thought much of the improvement would come from improved efficiencies and operations, but only a small percentage came from that."

[SOURCE: Pauline Yoshihashi, "Long Restless Night Is Ending for Hotel Companies," *Wall Street Journal* (November 2, 1994), p. B4. Reprinted by permission of The Wall Street Journal, ©1994 Dow Jones & Company, Inc. All Rights Reserved Worldwide.]

Divide your class into teams of five members. Each team member should be assigned to research one prominent publicly-traded company in the hotel/motel industry. Obtain copies of financial statements for each company over the period 1988 through 1994. [Note: Many university libraries have these types of records on computerized data bases.] For each firm in each year, compute the following ratios: cost of services to sales, interest cost to sales, all other expenses to sales, and net income to sales. Plot each ratio for each firm over the seven-year period and then write a brief report describing for each firm the principal sources of improvement in profitability based on the ratios your team computed.

13 CONTROLLING INVENTORY AND PRODUCTION COSTS

Inventory stored in a high-rise warehouse is less likely to be reduced, since it is out of sight and out of mind. However, if this inventory is placed on the floor in less space than is adequate, corrective action to reduce the inventory is likely to occur.

Mark DeLuzio, "The Tools of Just-in-Time," *Journal of Cost Management* (Summer 1993)

LEARNING OBJECTIVES

1. Understand why managers use ABC inventory control systems.

2. Explain the three costs associated with inventory.

3. Discuss the buyer-supplier relationship.

4. Calculate and use economic order quantity and order point.

5. Understand why a company carries safety stock and how the appropriate amount is estimated.

6. Differentiate between the economic order quantity model and material requirements planning.

7. Evaluate the workings of the push and pull systems of production control.

8. Explain the JIT philosophy and how it affects production.

9. Explain how the traditional accounting system would change if a JIT inventory system were adopted.

10. Explain the impact of flexible manufacturing systems on production and on satisfying customers.

11. (Appendix) Prepare journal entries under a backflush costing system.

ON SITE

Marcopolo, S.A.: Making Buses for the World in Brazil

Walking into Marcopolo, S.A.'s factory in Caxias do Sul, in southern Brazil, is like walking into a museum for modern industrial art. The walls and machinery are painted pastel colors; the high ceilings and highly polished concrete floors give the place an airy feeling. [However,] Marcopolo (1993 revenues, $206 million) is not some New Age high-tech firm but a producer of a basic industrial product: buses. The 45-year-old company makes and finishes bus bodies and assembles them on chassis made by Mercedes, Scania, and other big automotive companies. Hertz and National buy Marcopolo's buses to use as airport shuttles. Other customers include private and municipal bus lines in 40 countries. Half of Marcopolo's production is exported.

Paulo Bellini, Marcopolo's president, was one of seven young mechanics who pooled their savings to found Marcopolo in 1949. At first blush the venture seemed foolhardy. There was no Brazilian auto industry to speak of at the time, and none of the partners had any experience with motor vehicles. [But] Bellini and his partners knew they could build buses if they could find customers.

Their first order came from a local commuter line. "It was all trial and error at first," recalls Bellini. "Everything was handmade." That first bus took 90 days to construct. Even by the mid-1950s the little company was producing just two buses a month. [Demand grew through 1982 when] the Latin debt crisis hit, and demand for buses plummeted.

To replace Marcopolo's lost Brazilian orders, Bellini sent the company's salesmen to Latin America, the Middle East and other export markets. Now Marcopolo was an international company, and had to produce to demanding international standards. To raise Marcopolo's levels of quality and efficiency, in 1986 Bellini and a production chief, Cloud Gomes, went to Japan on a research expedition. They saw about a dozen factories and sat through hours of presentations on production teams, just-in-time inventory systems and other elements of efficient Japanese manufacturing.

"We taped everything and sat up in our rooms listening to the lectures again every night," Gomes recalls. "When we got home we looked at each other and said, 'Let's do it.'" "It" meant making Marcopolo over in a Japanese image.

SOURCE: Joel Millman, "Evolving to Perfection," reprinted by permission of *Forbes* (November 7, 1994), pp. 298-299. © Forbes, Inc., 1994.

L ike Marcopolo, many companies around the world have begun concentrating on ways to improve productivity, use available technology, and increase efficiency. These efforts are often directed at reducing the costs of producing and carrying inventory. Very often, Japanese companies have been the role models for change.

Aside from the amount spent on plant assets, the amount spent on inventory can be the largest investment made by a company, especially in retail companies. Unfortunately, until it is sold, inventory provides no return to the organization. This chapter deals with several techniques that minimize organizational investment in inventory: economic order quantity (EOQ), order point, and safety stock; material requirements planning (MRP); just-in-time (JIT) systems; and flexible manufacturing systems (FMS) and computer-integrated manufacturing (CIM).

MANAGING INVENTORY

Management needs to control its significant investment in inventory in a way that maximizes attention to the most important inventory items and minimizes attention to the least important items. Unit cost is commonly a factor in the degree of control that is maintained over an inventory item. As the unit cost increases, internal controls (such as access to inventory) are typically tightened, and a perpetual inventory system is more often used. Recognition of the appropriate cost/benefit relationships may result in an **ABC analysis** of inventory, which separates inventory into three groups based on annual cost-to-volume usage.[1]

Items having the highest dollar volume are referred to as A items, while C items represent the lowest dollar volume. All other inventory items are designated as B items. Exhibit 13–1 provides the results of a typical ABC inventory analysis: 20 percent of the inventory items account for 80 percent of the total inventory cost; an additional 30 percent of the items, taken together with the first 20 percent, account for 90 percent of the cost; and the remaining 50 percent of the items account for the remaining 10 percent of the cost.

■ **LEARNING OBJECTIVE 1**
Understand why managers use ABC inventory control systems.

ABC analysis

■ **EXHIBIT 13–1**
ABC Inventory Analysis

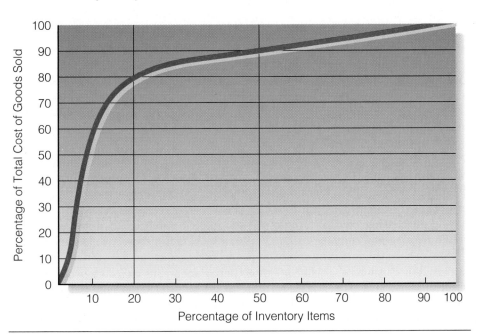

---

[1]ABC inventory analysis should not be confused with activity-based costing (also ABC), which is covered in depth in Chapter 5.

Once inventory items are categorized as A, B or C, management can determine the best inventory control method for the items within each category. A-type inventory should require a perpetual inventory system. Such items are likely candidates for purchasing techniques that minimize the funds tied up in inventory investment. The highest-level control procedures should be assigned to these items. Such a treatment reflects the financial accounting concept of materiality.

Controls on C-type inventory items are normally minimal because of the immateriality of the inventory cost. C-category items may justify only periodic inventory procedures and may use either a two-bin or a red-line system. Under a **two-bin system**, two containers (or stacks) of inventory are available for production needs. When it is necessary to begin using materials from the second bin, a purchase order is placed to refill the first bin. Having the additional container or stack of inventory on hand is considered reasonable because the dollar amount of investment for C-category items is insignificant. In a **red-line system**, a red line is painted inside an inventory container at a designated order point. When enough inventory has been used so that the line becomes visible, a purchase order is issued for replenishment. Both the two-bin and red-line systems require that estimates of production needs and receipt-times from suppliers be fairly accurate.

For B-type items, the inventory system (perpetual or periodic) and the level of internal control depend on management judgment. Such judgment will be based on how crucial the item is to the production process, how quickly suppliers respond to orders, and whether the estimated benefits of increased controls are greater than the costs. Advances in technology, such as computers and bar coding, have made it easier and more cost-beneficial to institute additional controls over inventory.

two-bin system

red-line system

COSTS ASSOCIATED WITH INVENTORY

■ LEARNING
OBJECTIVE 2
Explain the three costs
associated with inventory.

Most organizations engaging in a conversion process use both intangible and tangible inputs. For example, direct labor and other types of services are nonphysical and are supplied and consumed simultaneously. In constrast, raw materials are tangible and may be stockpiled for later use. Likewise, outputs of a manufacturing process may be stored until sold. The potential for physical items to be placed in or withdrawn from storage creates opportunities for managers to improve organizational effectiveness and efficiency relative to the quantities in which such items are purchased, produced, and stored.

Good inventory management relies largely on cost-minimizing strategies. As indicated in Exhibit 13–2, there are three basic costs associated with inventory: (1) purchasing or production; (2) ordering or setup; and (3) carrying or not carrying goods in stock.

The **purchasing cost** of inventory is the quoted purchase price minus any discounts allowed plus shipping cost and insurance charges incurred while the items are in transit. In a manufacturing company, production cost includes costs associated with buying direct materials, paying for direct labor, incurring traceable overhead, and absorbing allocated fixed overhead. Purchasing or production cost is recorded in Merchandise Inventory, Raw Materials Inventory, Work in Process Inventory, or Finished Goods Inventory.

The incremental, variable costs associated with preparing, receiving, and paying for an order are **ordering costs**. These costs include the cost of forms and a variety of clerical costs. Ordering costs are traditionally expensed as incurred. Under an activity-based costing system, however, these costs can be traced to the items ordered as an additional direct cost. Retailers incur ordering costs for all their merchandise invento-

purchasing cost

ordering costs

■ EXHIBIT 13–2
Categories of Inventory Costs

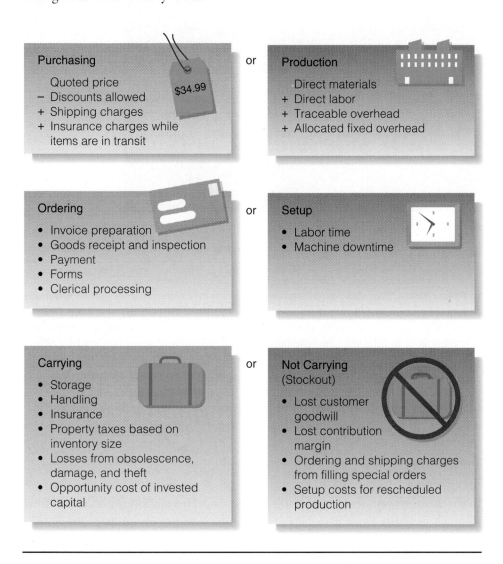

Purchasing

    Quoted price
− Discounts allowed
+ Shipping charges
+ Insurance charges while
   items are in transit

$34.99

or

Production

    Direct materials
+ Direct labor
+ Traceable overhead
+ Allocated fixed overhead

Ordering

• Invoice preparation
• Goods receipt and inspection
• Payment
• Forms
• Clerical processing

or

Setup

• Labor time
• Machine downtime

Carrying

• Storage
• Handling
• Insurance
• Property taxes based on
  inventory size
• Losses from obsolescence,
  damage, and theft
• Opportunity cost of invested
  capital

or

Not Carrying
(Stockout)

• Lost customer
  goodwill
• Lost contribution
  margin
• Ordering and shipping charges
  from filling special orders
• Setup costs for rescheduled
  production

---

ry. Manufacturers incur ordering costs for raw material purchases. If a manufacturer produces rather than orders a part, direct and indirect **setup costs** (rather than ordering costs) are created as equipment is readied for each new production run.

    Inventory **carrying costs** consist of storage, handling, insurance charges, and property taxes based on inventory size. Because inventory is one of many organizational investments, it should be expected to earn a rate of return similar to other investments.[2] Thus, carrying cost should include an opportunity cost for the amount invested in inventory. One additional opportunity cost that is often ignored is any possible loss that might result from inventory obsolescence or damage. Carrying costs can be estimated by use of information from various budgets, special studies, or other

setup costs

carrying costs

---

[2]The rate of return expected should be the weighted average cost of capital, which is discussed in Chapter 14.

Retail stores often buy in large amounts to obtain quantity discounts. To be certain that the purchases were wise, however, managers should compare the discounts with the costs of warehousing and insuring the inventory.

analytical techniques. One estimate of annual carrying cost is between 20 and 30 percent of inventory value.[3]

stockout

While excess inventory generates costs, so can an absence of inventory. When a company does not have inventory available upon customer request, a **stockout** occurs. Stockout cost is not easily determinable nor is it generally recorded. It is an opportunity cost that includes lost customer goodwill, lost contribution margin from not being able to fill a sale, and the ordering and shipping charges incurred for filling special orders.

All of the costs associated with inventory should be considered when purchasing decisions are made—and purchases should be made in reasonable quantities. The economic order quantity model is one technique that is often used to determine reasonable quantity. It is discussed later in this chapter.

SUPPLIERS AND QUANTITIES

■ ■ LEARNING OBJECTIVE 3
Discuss the buyer-supplier relationship.

In purchasing inventory, a purchasing manager needs to make three decisions: from whom, how much, and when. Each of these decisions depends in part on the relationship an organization has with its suppliers. Traditionally, the buyer-supplier relationship was viewed as adversarial; however, many companies are now viewing this relationship as a more cooperative, integrated partnership.

What Supplier?

Traditionally, deciding "from whom to buy" was based primarily on price. A company found several firms that could provide the desired item and chose the firm offering the lowest price. However, the lowest-cost supplier in the short run is not necessarily the best supplier for the long run. The partnership approach views purchase cost in relation to quality and reliability, while taking a long-run perspective of supply-chain management. Thus, purchases are made from suppliers offering the most appropriate quality at the best overall price and delivering in the most reliable manner.

---

[3]Leslie N. Masonson, ed., "The Inventory Cardiogram: Unlocking an Overlooked Cash Flow Generator," *Cash Management Performance Report* (January 1991), p. 1.

Moving from the adversarial to the partnership view of buyer-supplier relations takes time, effort, and trust on the part of both entities. Changes must be made relative to contract agreements, quality, delivery, and ability to openly communicate information.

The optimal partnership would have only a single vendor for each purchased item. Having single suppliers, however, does create the risk of not having alternative sources (especially for critical products or materials) in the event of vendor production strikes, unfair pricing, or shipment delays. Thus, it is often more feasible and realistic to reduce the number of vendors to a limited group. Vendors are selected on a combination of quality, reliability, and price factors. Working with fewer vendors on a long-term basis provides the opportunity to develop better communications, assure quality and service (including delivery), obtain quantity discounts, and reduce operating costs.

However, multiple suppliers may be a necessity for companies manufacturing goods internationally. Such companies may be either required by law or impelled by the need to reduce costs (especially tariffs), or prompted by a desire to help sustain a local economy to use some proportion of products and components made by local suppliers. Quality and reliability should be equally important in choosing international suppliers as in choosing domestic ones.

Long-term contracts are often signed with the chosen suppliers that specify exclusive purchasing arrangements for a fixed period of time and under specified conditions—usually associated with quality and reliability factors. An agreed-upon purchase price is set, but should allow for some flexibility in the event of cost or efficiency changes. For example, if the cost of input ingredients for a product increases for all purchasers, upward adjustments might be made to the negotiated price. On the other hand, companies may expect suppliers to become more efficient so that costs will decrease as experience in the relationship is gained.

In adversarial buyer-supplier relationships, quality control efforts are essential; this is not necessarily true in buyer-supplier partnerships. Relative to quality in buyer-supplier relationships, Karoru Ishikawa (president of Musashi Institute of Technology and professor emeritus at Tokyo University) says there are three stages:

> In the first stage, the manufacturer checks the entire lot that is brought in by the supplier. In the second stage, the manufacturer only sample-checks. In the final stage, the manufacturer accepts everything without checking the quality. Only in the third stage may it be said that a truly worthwhile relationship has been established.[4]

To achieve that third stage, companies have begun certifying vendors as to quality. People from various organizational areas must decide on the factors by which the vendor will be rated and must then weigh these factors as to relative importance. Evaluations should be discussed with the vendors so they will understand their strong and weak points and how they compare with their competitors. Vendors should be monitored after selection to assure continued compliance. Once vendors have been certified, buyers can spend less time performing quality inspections for defective products and more time on assuring quality in their own processes and improving their service to customers.

In the traditional system, buyers would order large quantities of goods to obtain quantity discounts or to maximize usage of truck or other shipping container volumes. In contrast, in buyer-supplier partnership arrangements, order size is often considerably reduced and frequency of delivery increased. Ford, for example, has

---

[4]Masaaki Imai, *Kaizen* (New York: McGraw-Hill, 1986), p. 213.

some deliveries made every two hours![5] To comply with the need for frequent deliveries, it is desirable for vendors to be located close to the company, which helps to minimize both delivery time and shipping cost. Alternatively, overnight delivery services can be used. These services have recognized the critical nature of prompt delivery and have risen in importance in the business world. Managers of both buying and supplying companies are becoming well-versed in analyzing the cost/benefit relationship involved in using such services. Long-term supplier contracts are negotiated, and then delivery reliability is monitored. Generally, suppliers missing a certain number of scheduled deliveries by more than a specified amount of time are dismissed.

If a buyer-supplier partnership is to work and be beneficial to both parties, there must be an open exchange of information. Each party needs to understand the other's processes. The parties normally do this through site visits and discussion. In addition, suppliers are often asked for cost and profit information that would, under the traditional adversarial relationship, be considered "privileged." For example, Scott Paper requires its suppliers to open their accounting records and explain their cost structures: what costs represent materials, labor, marketing, and so on. By doing this, Scott can justify the elimination of certain cost categories, such as marketing, since the partnership arrangement makes them unnecessary.[6] Suppliers whose processes are inefficient or who are pursuing excessive profit margins create additional costs for the purchasing company and, thus, make that company less competitive.

To build truly productive relationships, purchasing firms should help suppliers improve their processes to achieve reduced costs, as indicated in the accompanying News Note. Purchasing firms should also solicit information from suppliers about cost reduction possibilities related to new or existing products. Such an interchange of information and ideas requires that the partnership be built on a foundation of trust.

■ LEARNING
OBJECTIVE 4
Calculate and use economic
order quantity and order point.

**economic order quantity
(EOQ)**

What Quantity?

After the supplier is selected, the firm must decide how many units to buy at a time. The objective is to buy in the most economical quantity possible, which requires consideration of the ordering and carrying costs of inventory. One tool used in this decision process is the **economic order quantity (EOQ)** model. The EOQ model provides an estimate of the number of units per order that would provide the optimal balance between ordering and carrying costs. The EOQ formula is:[7]

**economic production run
(EPR)**

---

[5]David N. Burt, "Managing Suppliers Up to Speed," *Harvard Business Review* (July-August 1989), p. 128.

[6]Myron Magnet, "The New Golden Rule of Business," *Fortune* (February 21, 1994), p. 62.

[7]In a manufacturing company, managers are concerned with "how many units to produce" in addition to "how many units (of a raw material) to buy." The EOQ formula can be modified to yield the appropriate number of units to manufacture in an **economic production run (EPR).** The EPR quantity minimizes the total costs of setting up a production run and carrying a unit in stock for one year. In the EPR formula, the terms of the EOQ equation are simply defined as manufacturing costs rather than purchasing costs:

$$EPR = \sqrt{\frac{2QS}{C}}$$

where   EPR = economic production run
       Q = estimated quantity produced per year in units
       S = estimated cost of setting up a production run
       C = estimated cost of carrying one unit in stock for one year

Just Returning the Favor

NEWS NOTE

In the early 1930s, Henry Ford opened his factories to the Toyodas, then in the spinning and weaving business, and showed them the secrets of mass production, the assembly line and interchangeable parts. In late 1991, Shoichiro Toyoda, the Toyota chairman, announced it was time for the Japanese to return the favor [to others].

Here's how the supplier counseling works: Toyota assigns a team of engineers to a supplier factory and shows management and workers how to smooth process flows, shrink lead times and whittle down inventory. Toyota staffers push and monitor them for as long as it takes.

In the case of Garden State Tanning, an automotive leather supplier, for example, Toyota consultants were on-site for nearly two years. The results speak for themselves. In January 1992, when Toyota first arrived, Garden State had 140 days of inventory stockpiled. Today, it has just nine. In early 1990 one cut hide in 100 was defective; today it's one in 2,000.

Toyota has a very clear reason for aiding Garden State. In late 1991 demand for the Lexus exploded. Garden State, the supplier of leather for Lexus seats and consoles, couldn't cope. Rather than just dropping them as a supplier, as a typical U.S. carmaker might have done, however, Toyota stuck with them, demanding change. As a result, Garden State has maintained its near-total hold on Lexus leather.

The true finesse of Toyota's consulting is that it allows the supplier to remain in control of the changes. Says Garden State Chairman Sean Traynor: "Toyota didn't ask us to level our 100-year-old tanning plant and replace it with some robotic, postmodern, glistening gem. They just helped us figure out how to make the production process more efficient inside these old walls."

SOURCE: James Bamford, "Driving America to Tiers," *Financial World* (November 8, 1994), pp. 24–25. Excerpted from Financial World, 1328 Broadway, New York, NY 10001. © copyrighted 1994 by Financial World Partners. All rights reserved.

$$EOQ = \sqrt{\frac{2QO}{C}}$$

where   EOQ = economic order quantity in units
        Q = estimated quantity used per year in units
        O = estimated cost of placing *one* order
        C = estimated cost to carry *one* unit in stock for one year

The EOQ formula does not include purchase cost, since that amount relates to "from whom to buy" rather than "how many to buy." Purchase cost does not affect ordering and carrying costs, except to the extent that opportunity cost is calculated on the basis of cost.

Assume that Marcopolo purchases water pumps for its buses. The purchasing manager, Luis Guillen, has found several suppliers who can continuously provide pumps of the proper quality at a cost of $200 each. Exhibit 13–3 (page 662) provides information for use in calculating economic order quantity. The exhibit uses a flexible budget to show the total costs of purchasing 4,200 pumps per year in various order sizes.

The EOQ model assumes that orders are filled exactly when needed; so when the order arrives, the inventory on hand is zero units. Thus, the average inventory size is

■ **EXHIBIT 13–3**

Yearly Purchasing Cost for Water Pumps

Quantity needed per year (Q) = 4,200
Cost of ordering (O)   = $30 per order
Cost of carrying (C)   = $10 per unit

Size of order	50	100	150	200	300
Average inventory	25	50	75	100	150
Number of orders	84	42	28	21	14
Annual ordering cost	$2,520	$1,260	$ 840	$ 630	$ 420
Annual carrying cost	250	500	750	1,000	1,500
Total annual cost	$2,770	$1,760	$1,590	$1,630	$1,920

half of the order size. The frequency with which orders must be placed depends on how many units are ordered each time. The total number of orders equals the total annual quantity of units needed divided by the size of the order.

Based on total costs, Exhibit 13–3 indicates that Marcopolo's most economical order size is between 150 and 200 units. The formula yields a value of 159 units for the economic order quantity:

$$EOQ = \sqrt{\frac{2QO}{C}} = \sqrt{\frac{2(4{,}200)\,(30)}{10}} = 159 \text{ (rounded)}$$

The total annual cost to place and carry orders of 159 units is $1,587, calculated as follows:

Average inventory (159 ÷ 2)	79.5
Number of orders (4,200 ÷ 159)	26.4 (rounded)
Cost of ordering (26.4 × $30)	$ 792
Cost of carrying (79.5 × $10)	795
Total cost	$1,587

Note again that this total cost does not include the $200 purchase cost per unit.

The EOQ formula contains estimated values and may produce answers that are unrealistic. For example, it is impossible to place 4/10 of an order. And suppose Marcopolo's supplier only sells water pumps in boxes of 10. In that case, Marcopolo will need to order 150 or 160 units at a time. In most instances, small errors in estimating costs or rounding results do not create major impacts on total cost. If the cost of ordering quantities close to the EOQ level is not significantly different from the cost of ordering at the EOQ level, some leeway is available in choosing the order size. Other factors, such as cash availability and storage space constraints, should also be considered.

As order size increases, the number of orders and the total annual ordering costs decline. At the same time, the total annual cost of carrying inventory increases because more units are being held in inventory at any given point. Conversely, reducing order size reduces carrying costs but increases annual ordering costs.

Companies are currently decreasing their order costs dramatically by using techniques such as open purchase orders and electronic data interchange. For example,

R. J. Reynolds Tobacco Co. estimates that "purchase orders that previously cost between $75 and $125 to process now cost 93 cents."[8]

Another development in this area involves estimates of carrying costs, which are increasing. Companies are using higher estimates of these costs in part because they are more aware of the high cost of non-value-added activities, such as move time and storage time for purchased-but-unneeded units. As carrying costs rise, the economic order quantity falls. For example, if Marcopolo's ordering and carrying costs were reversed and estimated at $10 and $30, respectively, the EOQ would be 53 pumps.

When to Order?

While the EOQ model indicates how many units to order, managers are also concerned with the **order point**—the inventory level that triggers the placement of an order. Order point is based on usage (the amount of inventory used or sold each day), **lead time** (the time from order placement to order arrival), and **safety stock** (a quantity of inventory carried for protection against stockouts). The size of the safety stock for a particular item should be based on how crucial the item is to the business, the item's purchase cost, and the amount of uncertainty related to both usage and lead time. The optimal safety stock is the quantity that balances the cost of carrying with the cost of not carrying safety stock units.

When companies can project a constant figure for both usage and lead time, the order point is calculated as follows:

$$\text{Order Point} = (\text{Daily Usage} \times \text{Lead Time}) + \text{Safety Stock}$$

Assume that Marcopolo uses 15 water pumps per day and the company's supplier can deliver pumps in three days. If no safety stock is carried, pumps should be reordered when 45 units (15 × 3) are in inventory, and the order should arrive precisely when the inventory reaches zero.

However, companies often experience excess usage or excess lead time. In such cases, safety stock provides an inventory cushion. Although Marcopolo's average daily usage may be 15 pumps, the company occasionally might use a greater quantity but never more than 19 in one day. A simple way to estimate safety stock is as follows:

$$
\begin{aligned}
\text{Safety stock} &= (\text{Maximum usage - Normal usage}) \times \text{Lead time} \\
&= (19 - 15) \times 3 \\
&= 12 \text{ pumps}
\end{aligned}
$$

Using this estimate, Marcopolo would reorder pumps when 57 pumps (45 original order point + 12 safety stock) were on hand.

Problems with the EOQ Model

Mathematical determination of economic order quantity and optimal quantity of safety stock will help a company control its investment in inventory. However, such models are only as valid as the estimates used in the formulas. For example, projecting costs such as lost customer goodwill may be extremely difficult. In some cases, the degree of inaccuracy may not be important; in other cases, however, it may be critical.

order point

lead time

safety stock

■ LEARNING
OBJECTIVE 5
Understand why a company carries safety stock and how the appropriate amount is estimated.

---

[8]Andy Kessler, "Fire Your Purchasing Managers," *Forbes ASAP* (October 10, 1994), p. 33.

The basic EOQ model determines what quantity of inventory to order. But, there are at least three major problems associated with this model. First, identifying all the relevant inventory costs (especially carrying costs) is very difficult. Second, the model does not provide any direction for managers attempting to control the individual types of purchasing and carrying costs. By considering only trade-offs between total purchasing and total carrying costs, the EOQ model fails to lead managers to consider inventory management alternatives that might simultaneously reduce cost in both categories. Third, relationships among inventory items are ignored. For example, Marcopolo might require eight lug nuts to install a wheel rim on a bus. If the EOQs for wheel rims and lug nuts are computed independently, this interrelationship could be overlooked. Marcopolo might find that, at a time when one thousand wheel rims are on hand, there are only three thousand lug nuts. Computer techniques known as MRP and MRP II overcome this deficiency in the EOQ model by integrating interrelationships of units into the ordering process.

MATERIALS REQUIREMENTS PLANNING

materials requirements planning (MRP)

■ LEARNING OBJECTIVE 6
Differentiate between the economic order quantity model and material requirements planning.

Materials requirements planning (MRP), is a computer simulation system that was developed to answer the questions of what, how many, and when items are needed. MRP coordinates the future production output requirements with individual future production input needs using a master production schedule (MPS).

The MPS is developed from budgeted sales information and is essentially equivalent to the production budget shown in Chapter 11, although the MPS has significantly more detail regarding time horizons. Once projected sales and production for a product have been estimated, the MRP computer model accesses the product's bill of materials to determine all production components. Quantities needed are compared with current inventory balances. If purchases are necessary, the estimated lead time for each purchase is obtained from supplier information contained in an internal data base. The model then generates a time-sequenced schedule for purchases and production component needs.

bottlenecks

The MPS is integrated with the operations flow documents to project the work load for each work center that would result from the master schedule. The work load is compared with the work center's capacity to determine whether meeting the master schedule is feasible. Potential **bottlenecks**, or resource constraints, are identified so that changes in input factors (such as the quantity of a particular component) can be made. Then the MRP program is run again. This process is reiterated until the schedule compensates for all potential bottlenecks in the production system.

manufacturing resource planning (MRP II)

A variation of the MRP system is **manufacturing resource planning (MRP II)** . This fully integrated system plans production jobs using the usual MRP method and also calculates resource needs such as labor and machine hours. MRP II involves the manufacturing, marketing, and finance areas in determining the master production schedule. While manufacturing is primarily responsible for carrying out the master production schedule, it is essential that appropriate levels of resource and sales support be available to make the plan work.

push systems

The MRP models extend, rather than eliminate, the economic order quantity concept. EOQ indicates the most economical quantity to order at one time, and MRP indicates which items of inventory to order at what points in time. The EOQ and MRP models are considered **push systems** of production control because they may cause inventory to be purchased or produced that is not currently needed. Such inventory must be stored until needed by other work centers. Exhibit 13–4 depicts

■ **EXHIBIT 13–4**

Push System of Production Control

Purchases and production are constantly pushed down into storage locations until need arises.

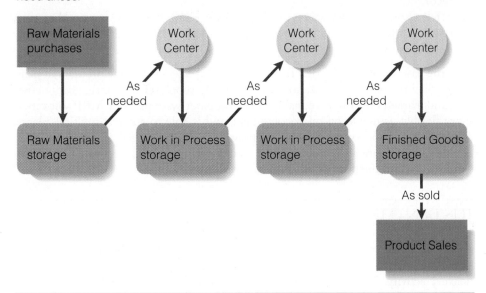

the relationship of inventory to production processes in such traditional production environments.

Many firms have achieved the significant benefits of reduced inventories, improved labor and space utilization, better communications, and streamlined scheduling by using MRP and MRP II. In addition, companies report better customer service because of the elimination of erratic production and back orders. But MRP and MRP II also have their problems, some of which are caused by less-than-realistic underlying assumptions. These assumptions are not unique to MRP/MRP II and can also cause difficulties when they are used in other decision-making situations. The following are five "problem" assumptions:

1. The bill of materials and operations flow documents are assumed to be complete and totally accurate. If they are not, even small inconsistencies or distortions in quantities or labor times may become cumulatively significant over time.

2. MRP assumes that there are no bottleneck operations in the factory even though most production processes have bottlenecks. (The MRP system is run successively until all bottlenecks are eliminated in the computer model—but that does not *necessarily* eliminate them in the workplace.) This assumption often results in unrealistic schedules and the model tends to compensate by building excess lead time and higher inventories into the system.

3. MRP is based on the EOQ model, which employs fixed estimates for annual usage, carrying and ordering costs, and lead time. These estimates may be imprecise, and actual cost factors may be quite volatile. For example, carrying cost is often simply estimated as the direct financing cost of holding inventory. This type of estimate fails to include indirect costs such as additional space requirements, higher obsolescence, and so on. One source estimates that if the financing cost of holding inventory "is 10%, then a more accurate estimate of the total cost may be

20 to 25%."[9] Such a significant understatement in carrying cost may cause firms to purchase in much larger quantities than are cost-beneficial.

4. Current inventory levels are assumed to be the amounts reflected by the accounting records. These records can be incorrect for a variety of reasons, such as shortages from theft, breakage, or deterioration or from human errors in counting or recording.

5. MRP assumes that the system will be in effect and used at all times. Managers, however, often use less formalized systems to achieve objectives and may not fully implement MRP.

In the past, many MRP/MRP II systems focused only on a single production plant rather than the entire organization (including any supply-chain management activities) and worked only on large main-frame computer systems. New MRP software is more flexible, is usable on microcomputers, and is able to support multiple plants, production systems, organizational relationships, and languages. In addition, many companies today are also attempting to reduce inventory levels and order quantities through the introduction of just-in-time inventory systems.

JUST-IN-TIME SYSTEMS

■ **LEARNING OBJECTIVE 8**
Explain the JIT philosophy and how it affects production.

As an earlier chapter pointed out, just-in-time (JIT) is a philosophy about when to do something. The *when* is "as needed" and the *something* is a production, purchasing, or delivery activity. The basic elements of the JIT philosophy are outlined in Exhibit 13–5. Regardless of the type of organization (retail, service, or manufacturing) in which it exists, a just-in-time system has three primary goals:

■ Eliminating any production process or operation that does not add value to the product/service,
■ Continuously improving production/performance efficiency, and
■ Reducing the total cost of production/performance while increasing quality.

■ **EXHIBIT 13–5**
Elements of JIT Philosophy

■ Inventory is a liability, not an asset; eliminate it to the extent possible.
■ Storage space is directly related to inventories; eliminate it in response to the elimination of inventories.
■ Long lead times cause inventory build-up; keep lead times as short as possible by using frequent deliveries.
■ Creative thinking doesn't cost anything; use it to find ways to reduce costs before making expenditures for additional resources.
■ Quality is essential at all times; work to eliminate defects and scrap.
■ Suppliers are essential to operations; establish and cultivate good relationships with them, including the use of long-term contracts.
■ Employees often have the best knowledge of ways to improve operations; listen to them.
■ Employees generally have more talents than are being used; train them to be multiskilled and increase their productivity.
■ Ways to improve operations are always available; constantly look for them, being certain to make fundamental changes rather than superficial ones.

---

[9]Robert A. Howell and Stephen R. Soucy, "The New Manufacturing Environment: Major Trends for Management Accounting," *Management Accounting* (July 1987), p. 22.

The Big Box Theory

You've heard of the "big bang theory"; now hear about the "big box theory." The big box is our factory. We put costs into the box and out come products. For too long we have been analyzing the individual costs within the box and forgetting about the number of products coming out. We played games like building inventory to lower our unit costs, but the product stayed in the box. We appeared to be very efficient in labor and machine utilization, but what good is it if the product stays in the box?

We also soon realized our box was not big enough to hold all the products we produced. So we built other boxes, called warehouses, to store them in. Most companies became very efficient at producing products with low unit costs. Unfortunately, the products sat in the warehouses.

While we were filling up the boxes with products we did not need, we were simultaneously missing our customer delivery promise dates. The factory was very efficient with long production runs but the wrong product was being produced.

SOURCE: John F. Towey, ed., "What is JIT and FMS?" *Management Accounting* (May 1988), p. 71. Published by Institute of Management Accountants, Montvale, NJ.

For example, a company using a **JIT manufacturing system** attempts to acquire components and produce inventory units only as they are needed, minimize product defects, and reduce lead/setup times for acquisition and production.

JIT manufacturing system

Production was traditionally dictated by the need to smooth operating activity over time, which allowed a company to maintain a steady work force and generate continuous machine use. However, as discussed in the accompanying News Note, smooth production often tends to build buffer stocks of inventory and components. This process creates a "just-in-case," rather than just-in-time, scenario.

In traditional systems, the various types of inventory (raw materials, components, supplies, and work in process) were generally maintained at high enough levels to cover up inefficiencies in acquisition and/or production. Exhibit 13–6 (page 668) depicts these inefficiencies or problems as "rocks" in a stream of "water" representing inventory. The traditional philosophy is that the water level (inventory) should be kept high enough for the rocks (problems) to be deeply submerged, so that there will be "smooth sailing" in production activity. This technique is intended to solve the original problems, but it creates a new one. By covering up the problems, the excess inventory adds to the difficulty of making corrections. The JIT manufacturing philosophy is to lower the inventory level, expose the problems, and eliminate them to the extent possible. The shallower stream will then flow more smoothly and rapidly than the deep river.

Just-in-time manufacturing has many names, including zero-inventory production system (ZIPS), MAN (material as needed), and **kanban** (the Japanese word for card). The JIT system originated in Japan from the use of cards to control the flow of materials between work centers. In a JIT system, products are not produced until customers have demanded them and, thus, no manufacturing activity occurs unless the resulting product is needed by the next work center in the production line. These factors make JIT a pull, rather than a push, system of production control.

kanban

■ **EXHIBIT 13–6**

Traditional and JIT Production Philosophies

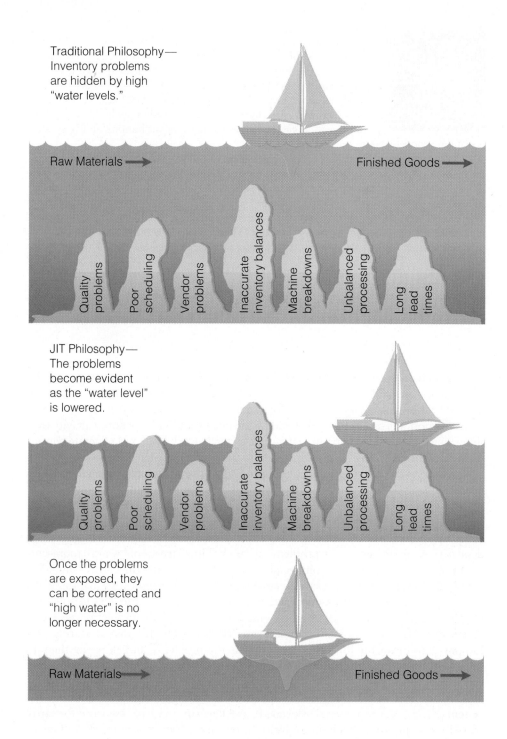

SOURCE: Reprinted with permission of Ernst & Young. © Ernst & Young, 1987.

In a **pull system** of production, parts are delivered or manufactured only as they are needed by the work center for which they are intended. There are almost no storage areas to which work can be "pushed" when it is completed but not needed to meet current sales orders or production demands. Exhibit 13–7 illustrates a pull system of production, and the News Note on page 670 discusses how JIT works at Motorola.

JIT depends on accurate market data, since a tight linkage is required between sales and production volume. Forecasted sales demand is the controlling production force. Once demand is estimated, the production schedule is set for an extended period (such as a month), and schedule changes should be minimal. Level scheduling creates a constant rate of use for component materials, labor, equipment, materials handling, maintenance, and support functions. Additionally, high-quality production processes are mandatory so that defects can be avoided. Slack time in the schedule is not treated as idle time. If workers are not needed for production activities, time is used for employee training, machine maintenance, and workplace organization.

A just-in-time system cannot be implemented overnight; it took Toyota over 20 years to develop its system and realize significant benefits from it. While JIT techniques are becoming better known and can be more quickly and easily implemented, the most impressive benefits are normally reached only after the system has been operational for 5 to 10 years. Exhibit 13–8 on page 670 details some of the improvements experienced by Oregon Cutting Systems over a 4-year period after implementation of a just-in-time program.

Any company that aims to achieve the JIT goals must change the majority of its organizational functions. Companies must investigate the partnership-type purchasing arrangements discussed earlier in the chapter. Manufacturers must address product design, product processing, plant layout considerations, and employee empowerment. Product design is discussed in Chapter 10; each of the remaining topics are discussed in the following sections.

pull system

■ LEARNING
OBJECTIVE 7
Evaluate the workings of the push and pull systems of production control.

■ **EXHIBIT 13–7**
Pull System of Production Control

Product sales dictate total production. Purchases and production are pulled through the system on an as-needed basis.

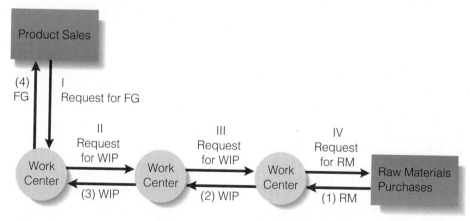

→   Information flow that creates (pulls) demand at each successive operation

←   Physical production flow in which raw materials (RM) and work in process (WIP) flow successively through work centers until completed (FG)

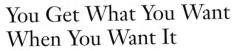

NEWS NOTE

You Get What You Want When You Want It

[At the Boynton Beach, Florida, plant where Motorola makes pagers,] orders for the pocket-size gizmos stream in from resellers and Motorola salesmen, typically via an 800 line or E-mail. As the salesman spells out what the customer wants—"one Sizzling Yellow pager that goes ding-dong, five in Bimini Blue that beep, ten in Vibra Pink that play a little arpeggio," and so on—the data are digitized and flow to the assembly line. So-called pick-and-place robots select the proper components, but humans assemble the pagers. Often the order is complete within 80 minutes and, depending on where the customer lives, he can have his pagers that same day or the day after.

Motorola thinks of the process not as manufacturing but as rapidly translating data from customers into products; its aim is to do so even faster. Says Sherita Ceasar, director of manufacturing: "Our vision is simultaneous manufacturing, to make the pager even as the customer talks. We're getting close."

SOURCE: Gene Bylinsky, "The Digital Factory," *Fortune* (November 14, 1994), pp. 93,94. © 1994 Time Inc. All rights reserved.

Product Processing

In making processing improvements, one primary JIT consideration is to reduce machine setup time. Reducing setup time allows processing to shift more rapidly among different types of units and, thus, makes the manufacturing process more flexible. A company may need to incur some costs (possibly for new equipment or training) to reduce setup time. Such increased costs have been found to be more than recovered by the savings derived from reducing downtime, work in process inventory, and materials handling, as well as increasing safety and ease of operation.

■ **EXHIBIT 13–8**

Productivity Increases from JIT at Oregon Cutting Systems

- Cut die change time from 6.5 hours to 1 minute and 40 seconds
- Cut space requirements 40%
- Cut lead times from 21 days to 3 days
- Reduced floor space required for manufacturing 30% to 40%
- Reduced setup time for a punch press from 3 hours to 4.5 minutes
- Reduced defects 80% with no increases in quality costs
- Reduced scrap, sort, and rework 50%
- Reduced work in process 85%
- Reduced manufacturing costs 35%
- Improved shipping productivity 90%
- Improved order turnaround time from 10-14 days with a 75% order fill rate to 1-2 days with a 97% order fill rate
- Reduced product flow distance 94%
- Reduced lot sizes between 75% and 90%

SOURCE: Jack C. Bailes and Ilene K. Kleinsorge, "Cutting Waste with JIT," *Management Accounting* (May 1992), p. 29. Published by Institute of Management Accountants, Montvale, NJ.

Another essential part of JIT product processing is implementing the highest quality standards and focusing on a goal of zero defects. High quality is essential because inferior quality causes additional costs for downtime, rework, scrap, warranty work, and lost customer goodwill. Under JIT systems, quality is determined on a continual basis rather than at quality control checkpoints. Companies using such systems achieve continuous quality first by ensuring vendor product quality and then by ensuring quality in the conversion processes.

Quality in manufacturing can be partially obtained through the use of modern production equipment, which often relies on computerized technology to schedule,

Adopting JIT allowed Marcopolo to have the flexibility, quality, and cycle time to meet customer demands for variations in styles, colors, and amenities of buses. The company works with Mercedes-Benz, Volvo, and Scania to produce buses not only for South American countries, but also for Greece, Kuwait, Nigeria, and the United States.

control, and monitor production processes. Some elements of the production system may be designed to be self-checking—such as the poka-yoke techniques discussed in Chapter 2. In the most integrated systems, sophisticated computer programs monitor each process in the production stream and develop statistical data on the reliability of both components and processes. The data are then available for use in programs that design new products and processes and that evaluate the reliability of components obtained from each internal and external supplier. In the event that defective products are made, they should be promptly discovered and the problem that created them identified and corrected.

Often, the traditional cost accounting system buries quality control costs and costs of scrap in the standard cost of production. For instance, adding excess materials or labor time into the standard quantities creates a "buried" cost of quality. Such costs are often 10 to 30 percent of total production cost. Consider a company making a $10 product that has quality control and scrap costs of 10 percent, or $1 per unit. If that company's annual cost of goods sold is $10,000,000, its quality control and scrap costs are $1,000,000! When quality is controlled on an ongoing basis, costs of obtaining high quality may be significantly reduced. It is less costly in many manufacturing situations to avoid mistakes than to correct them.

Plant Layout

In an effective JIT system, the physical plant is arranged in a way that is conducive to the flow of goods and the organization of workers. Equipment is placed in a rational arrangement according to the materials flow. Such a layout reduces material handling cost and the lead time required to get work in process from one point to another. Streamlined design allows people to see problems—such as excess inventory, product defects, equipment malfunctions, and out-of-place tools—more easily.

One way to minimize cycle time through the plant is to establish linear or U-shaped groupings of workers or machines, commonly referred to as **manufacturing cells**. These cells improve materials handling and flow, increase machine utilization rates, maximize communication among workers, and result in better quality control. A 1994 study by the National Association of Manufacturers in Washington estimates that almost 40 percent of plants with fewer than 100 employees and 74 percent of

manufacturing cells

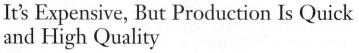

NEWS NOTE

It's Expensive, But Production Is Quick and High Quality

[When Howard Lind and Avi Telyas bought Bayside Controls, Inc., they quickly] scrapped the old assembly line, in which 35 factory workers had toiled at various stages of production to manufacture a single part. Bayside adopted so-called cell manufacturing, where small, self-contained "cells" of employees make a product from start to finish. Mr. Lind says the company was able to speed up production and introduce custom-made gearheads, which help motors operate more smoothly.

At Bayside, four production cells now make precision gearheads. Each production cell measures, cuts, assembles and cleans new gearheads. Since switching to the cell system five years ago, Bayside has seen its average production time for a gearhead shrink to two days from six weeks. The company saves money by keeping inventories of finished parts and raw materials to a minimum. The cell system also empowers factory employees. They monitor their own productivity and cells compete for quality and production awards.

[But] cell manufacturing is extremely capital intensive. Bayside spent about $5 million on equipment. Increased sales ultimately would force Bayside to install a fifth production cell at a cost of between $800,000 and $1 million, Mr. Lind says. To justify that expense, he continues, annual sales would have to jump more than $2 million.

SOURCE: Stephanie N. Mehta, "Cell Manufacturing Gains Acceptance at Smaller Plants," *Wall Street Journal* (September 15, 1994), p. B2. Reprinted by permission of The Wall Street Journal, © 1994 Dow Jones & Company, Inc. All Rights Reserved Worldwide.

larger plants use some sort of cell manufacturing.[10] The accompanying News Note discusses the use of cell manufacturing at a small gear-parts plant in Port Washington, New York.

Manufacturing cells create an opportunity for workers to be cross-trained and thereby broaden their skills and deepen their workplace involvement. Training workers to be multiskilled is valid even in nonmanufacturing companies. For instance, USAA—a San Antonio, Texas, insurance and financial services company—consolidated its departments and trained its salespeople to handle every aspect of processing insurance policies after installing a huge network of automated equipment. The cost of training in such situations can be substantial, and workers often resent change. In the long run, however, employers have a more viable work force and workers seem to be more satisfied with their jobs. Additionally, companies may find that workers, when they know more about the process as a whole, are better able to provide helpful suggestions about process improvement.

Employee Empowerment

An underlying feature of a just-in-time system and its emphasis on cross-training is the concept of employee empowerment. Employees can only be empowered if they have the abilities, tools, and training to perform tasks well, are involved in organiza-

---

[10]Stephanie N. Mehta, "Cell Manufacturing Gains Acceptance at Smaller Plants," *Wall Street Journal* (September 15, 1994), p. B2.

tional planning, and can trust and be trusted by management. Given these factors, employees will be able to commit themselves to the pursuit of organizational goals and objectives.But before any employee empowerment can take place, the organization must be willing to invest resources in people and training activities.

Any business should recognize that the first condition of hiring and placement is to put the right people in the right jobs. Employees placed in jobs for which they do not have the appropriate skills are destined to fail. If workers do not have the necessary abilities when they are hired, the organization is responsible for making certain that they can acquire these abilities through training.

Training should not be limited to giving people basic competencies but should be an on-going process designed to increase employees' knowledge and capabilities. Such training will improve both job quality and employee self-esteem. Employees who learn more are better able to perform their current tasks, analyze those tasks and suggest methods of improvement, acquire new skills, and participate to a greater degree in organizational planning.

The organization must also provide employees with the necessary tools (including equipment, information, and authority) to perform their jobs in a manner consistent with organizational objectives. Employees who use improperly maintained or ineffective equipment, who do not have the necessary information to investigate and correct problems, or who cannot effect solutions to identified problems are not empowered in their jobs.

At a minimum, involvement in organizational planning requires that employees be told of, and agree with, the business's basic strategy. However, true empowerment means that the company has flattened the organizational structure and pushed decision-making authority and responsibility down to the lowest reasonable level. Flatter structures are more flexible and allow decisions to be made rapidly in response to need. Where such structures exist, feedback must be provided to employees about their involvement and the impact of their decisions.

For empowerment to work effectively in an organization, there must be an atmosphere of trust among all employees at all levels. This element of empowerment is critical and often difficult to obtain, because many American organizations currently operate in "an atmosphere of mistrust" between managers and subordinates.[11] This mistrust creates a wide variety of fears: fear of making mistakes, fear of retaliation (including job loss), fear of being viewed as a troublemaker, fear of risk taking, fear of speaking out, and, very importantly, fear of change. Employees' fears can be eliminated only through development of mutual trust, which will allow the fears and their underlying causes to be confronted, analyzed, and resolved.

Overall, the just-in-time philosophy is more than a cost-cutting endeavor. It requires good human resource management and a dedication to teamwork. Exhibit 13–9 on the next page provides an action plan for implementing a JIT system.

It is important to note that just-in-time systems may not be appropriate for all types of companies. As indicated in the News Note on page 675, retail toy companies experienced some disadvantages in the use of JIT. Furthermore, companies whose raw materials or components are critical to processing activities may be unable to afford the potential stockout cost of maintaining minimal inventories. Finally, when there are unexpected occurrences (such as the rail strike of 1991), companies using a just-in-time system may face business closure or limited production for some time—even

---

[11]Jack Hagan, *Management of Quality* (Milwaukee: ASQC Quality Press and Business One Irwin, 1994), p. 72.

■ **EXHIBIT 13–9**

Seven Steps to Implement a JIT System

1. Determine how well products, materials, or services are delivered now.
2. Determine how customers define superior service, and set priorities accordingly.
3. Establish specific priorities for distribution (and possibly purchasing) functions to meet customer needs.
4. Collaborate with and educate managers and employees to refine objectives and to prepare for implementation of JIT.
5. Execute a pilot implementation project and evaluate its results.
6. Refine the JIT delivery program and execute it companywide.
7. Monitor progress, adjust objectives over time, and always strive for excellence.

SOURCE: Gene R. Tyndall, "Just-in-Time Logistics: Added Value for Manufacturing Cost Management," *Journal of Cost Management* (Spring 1989), pp. 57-59. Reprinted with permission from The Journal of Cost Management for the Manufacturing Industry, © 1989, Warren, Gorham & Lamont, 31 St. James Avenue, Boston, MA 02116. All rights reserved.

if they have arranged for alternative means of transport.[12] In addition, manufacturers have found that JIT has made their inventory purchases more volatile as they try to adjust quickly to changing sales conditions.[13]

ACCOUNTING IMPLICATIONS OF JIT

■ **LEARNING OBJECTIVE 9**

Explain how the traditional accounting system would change if a JIT inventory system were adopted.

There are significant accounting implications for companies adopting a just-in-time inventory system. A primary accounting impact occurs in the area of variance analysis. Because a traditional standard cost accounting system is primarily historical in nature, its main goal is variance reporting. Once reported, variances can be analyzed and similar problems can be avoided in the future.

Variances Under JIT

Variance reporting and analysis essentially disappear in JIT systems. Since most variances first appear in a *physical* (rather than financial) fashion, JIT mandates that variances be recognized on the spot so that causes can be ascertained and, if possible, promptly removed. JIT workers are trained and expected to monitor quality and efficiency continually *while production occurs* rather than only at the end of production. Therefore, the number and monetary significance of end-of-period variances that have not already been addressed should be limited.

Under a JIT system, long-term price agreements have been made with vendors, so material price variances should be minimal. The JIT accounting system should be designed so that no one can prepare a purchase order for an amount greater than the

---

[12]While General Motors operated normally for one day, a spokeswoman indicated that the company expected the rail strike to affect 70 percent to 80 percent of its assembly plants by the second day and all plants within one week. [Daniel Machalaba, "Railroads Stop Moving Freight Due to Walkout," *Wall Street Journal* (April 18, 1991), p. A2.]

[13]Vivian Brownstein, "Business Regains Its Courage," *Fortune* (May 18, 1992), p. 22.

Just-In-Time Isn't for Everybody

These days, retailers order in trickles and then, before ordering more, track sales with computers linked to cash-register scanners via satellite. In the jargon of the trade, this is called "just-in-time" because shipments are timed to replace products just as they are sold off the shelf. Just-in-time was first championed in retailing by the likes of Toys "R" Us Inc., Wal-Mart Stores Inc. and Home Depot Inc., which sought to reduce inventory carrying costs and the likelihood of stocking warehouses full of duds.

But retailers and manufacturers alike are beginning to realize that just-in-time inventory control can have a serious downside: It doesn't give them enough time to take advantage of surprise hits. This risk is a special problem in toys, which are greatly subject to fad buying, especially during the relatively short Christmas season. Just-in-time helped create a near panic [at Christmas in 1993] as parents scrambled to find Power Rangers and other toys in short supply.

"Just-in-time is great for Crest toothpaste, not toys," says Howard Davidowitz, chairman of Davidowitz & Associates, a retail consulting firm. David Million, president of the Toy Manufacturers Association, agrees. "The problem with just-in-time is you don't get solid readings on big Christmas items until late September or October. By then, it's too late to get any significant shipments." On average, it takes three months to make, ship and stock a product on the shelf, he says. But Power Rangers figures, which can be bent in 22 different places, compared with five for an average action figure, take longer to make.

The flinty inventory-control practices became vogue about [1990] . . . on the heels of high-wire acts during the 1980s that led to the bankruptcy of several toy manufacturers. Among them: Coleco Industries Inc, then the maker of Cabbage Patch Kids, and Worlds of Wonder Inc., creator of Teddy Ruxpin. Excess inventory contributed to their downfalls. Watching the carnage, retailers—many of whom had to sell those toys at a loss—became cautious, too, and smarter. They began placing orders based on what they needed and not on what they thought they might be able to sell. The new approach worked: Just-in-time slashed costs and generated big profits.

Today, retailers, as a group, stand by just-in-time. [But now], with several big toy retailers having failed in recent years, the remaining chains have grown in clout—and in confidence that they can compel manufacturers to ship products on short notice. "No longer can we be just vendors to them; we must and are becoming partners," says Alan Hassenfeld, chairman of Hasbro, the nation's largest toy maker. [However,] manufacturers say they could have sold more toys this Christmas without the retailers' tough inventory controls.

SOURCE: Joseph Pereira, "Toy Industry Finds It's Harder and Harder to Pick the Winners," *Wall Street Journal* (December 21, 1993), pp. A1, A5. Reprinted by permission of The Wall Street Journal, © 1993 Dow Jones & Company, Inc. All Rights Reserved Worldwide.

Toy stores have found that just-in-time purchasing is sometimes not in their best interest. When toys become popular, children want them *immediately*—and production of things such as Power Rangers require significant cycle time.

designated price without management approval.[14] In this way, the variance amount and its cause are known in advance, providing an opportunity to eliminate the excess expenditure before it occurs. Calls can be made to the vendor to negotiate the price or other vendors can be contacted for quotes.

The ongoing use of specified vendors also gives a company the ability to control material quality. Since raw material quality is expected to be better controlled, material usage variances caused by substandard materials should be rare. If usage standards

---

[14]This procedure can be implemented under a traditional standard cost system as well as under JIT. It is, however, less common in the traditional standard cost system; it is a requirement under JIT.

are accurate, there should be virtually no favorable material usage variance during production. Unfavorable usage of materials should be promptly detected because of ongoing machine or human observation of processing. When an unfavorable variance occurs, the JIT production system is stopped and the error causing the unfavorable material usage is corrected.

One type of usage variance is caused not by errors but by engineering changes (ENCs) in the product specifications. A JIT system has two comparison standards: an annual standard and a current standard. Design modifications change the current standard, but not the annual one. If the current, but not the annual, standard is changed, the cost effects of making engineering changes after a product has been put into production can be determined. A material usage variance caused by an ENC is illustrated in Exhibit 13–10. In the illustration, the portion of the total usage variance caused by the engineering change ($9,600 U) is shown separately from the portion created by inefficiency ($1,160 U). It is also possible to have ENC variances for the labor and overhead or conversion cost categories.

Labor variances in a just-in-time system should be minimal if standard rates and times have been set appropriately. Labor time standards should be carefully evaluated after the implementation of a JIT production system. If the plant is not entirely automated, redesigning the physical layout and minimizing any non-value-added labor activities should decrease the direct labor time component. If the plant is entire-

---

■ **EXHIBIT 13–10**

Material Variances Under a JIT System

Annual standard:	6 pounds of material A @ $4.40	$26.40	
	3 pounds of material B @ $5.20	15.60	
		$42.00	

Current standard:	5 pounds of material A @ $4.40	$22.00	
	4 pounds of material B @ $5.20	20.80	
		$42.80	

Production during month: 12,000 units

Usage during month:	60,500 pounds of material A @ $4.40		$266,200
	47,800 pounds of material B @ $5.20		248,560
	Total cost of materials used		$514,760

Material usage variance:
12,000 × 5 × $4.40	$264,000
12,000 × 4 × $5.20	249,600
Material cost at current standard	$513,600
Actual material cost	(514,760)
Material usage variance	$ 1,160 U

Engineering change variance for materials:
12,000 × 6 × $4.40	$316,800
12,000 × 3 × $5.20	187,200
Material cost at annual standard	$504,000
Material cost at current standard	(513,600)
ENC variance (materials)	$ 9,600 U

ly automated, all workers will be classified as indirect labor and, thus, there could be no direct labor variances.

Another accounting change that may occur in a JIT system is the use of a conversion category, rather than separate labor and overhead categories, for purposes of cost control. This category becomes more useful as factories automate and reduce direct labor cost. A standard departmental or manufacturing cell conversion cost per unit of product (or per hour of production time per department) may be calculated rather than separate standards for labor and overhead. The denominator for the cost per unit is practical capacity in either hours or units.[15] For example, if time were used as the base, the conversion cost for a day's production would be equal to the number of units produced times the standard number of production hours allowed times the standard cost per hour. Variances would be determined by comparison of actual cost with the designated standard.

A JIT system can have a major impact on inventory accounting as well as on variances. Companies employing JIT production processes no longer need a separate inventory account for raw materials, because materials are acquired only as production occurs. Instead, a Raw and In Process (RIP) Inventory account is used.

Backflush Costing

Accounting in a JIT system focuses on the plant's output (**throughput**) to the customer.[16] Because each area depends on the previous area, any problems will quickly stop the production process. Daily accounting for the individual costs of production is no longer necessary; all costs should be at standard, since variations are observed and corrected almost immediately.

Further, since costs are more easily traced to their related output in a JIT system, fewer costs are arbitrarily allocated to products. Costs are incurred in specified cells on a per-hour or per-unit basis. Energy costs are direct to production in a comprehensive JIT system because there should be a minimum of downtime by machines or unplanned idle time for workers. Virtually the only costs that are allocated are those associated with the structure (building depreciation, rent, taxes, and insurance). Machinery depreciation may be considered direct if products are bar coded and time is clocked as products are worked on.

Backflush costing is a streamlined cost accounting method that speeds up, simplifies, and reduces accounting effort in an environment that minimizes inventory balances, requires few allocations, uses standard costs, and has minimal variances from standard. During the period, this costing method records purchases of raw materials and accumulates actual conversion costs. Then, either at completion of production or upon the sale of goods, an entry is made to allocate total production costs incurred to Cost of Goods Sold and to Finished Goods Inventory using standard costs. Backflush costing system journal entries are illustrated in the appendix to this chapter.

throughput

backflush costing

---

[15]Practical capacity is the appropriate measure of activity because the goal of JIT is virtually continuous processing. In a highly automated plant, practical capacity is set closer to theoretical capacity than in a traditional plant. However, it may still be unreasonable to set the denominator at the theoretical level because, even under a JIT system, work stoppages occur, for a variety of reasons.

[16]A company may wish to measure the output of each manufacturing cell or work center rather than throughput. While this practice may reveal problems in a given area, it does not correlate with the JIT philosophy emphasizing a team approach, plantwide attitude, and total cost picture.

Implementation of a just-in-time system can cause significant cost reductions and productivity improvements. But even within a single company, not all inventories need to be managed according to a just-in-time philosophy. The costs and benefits of any inventory control system must be evaluated before management installs the system.

FLEXIBLE MANUFACTURING SYSTEMS AND COMPUTER INTEGRATED MANUFACTURING

■ **LEARNING OBJECTIVE 10**
Explain the impact of flexible manufacturing systems on production and on satisfying customers.

Automated equipment and cellular plant layout, coupled with computer hardware, software, and new manufacturing systems and philosophies such as JIT and activity-based management, have allowed many manufacturers to change their basic manufacturing philosophy. Traditionally, most manufacturing firms employed long production runs to make thousands of identical models of the same products; this process was encouraged by the idea of economies of scale. After each run, the machines would be stopped, and a slow and expensive setup would be made for the next massive production run. Now, an entirely new generation of manufacturing known as the flexible manufacturing system (FMS) is being developed.

computer integrated manufacturing (CIM)

As discussed in Chapter 2, an FMS is a network of robots and material conveyance devices monitored and controlled by computers. The system is characterized by rapid production and prompt responsiveness to changes in production needs. Two or more FMSs connected by a host computer and an information networking system are generally referred to as **computer integrated manufacturing (CIM)**. Exhibit 13–11 contrasts a traditional manufacturing system with an FMS. While an FMS is typically associated with short-volume production runs, many companies (such as Cummins Engine) have also begun to use CIM for high-volume lines.

As mentioned, companies using an FMS or CIM are able to quickly and inexpensively stop producing one item and start producing another. This ability to make quick and inexpensive production changes and to operate at great speed permits a company to build a large assortment of products. Thus, the company can offer its customers a wide variety of high-quality products while minimizing product costs. The system can operate in a "lights-out" (or fully automated) environment and never tire. The accompanying News Note discusses Toshiba's flexible manufacturing system in Ome, Japan.

The FMS works so fast that moving products along and out of the way of other products is sometimes a problem. Japan's Nissan Motor Company's new FMS facility on Kyushu Island is replacing the time-honored conveyor belt with a convoy of little yellow intelligent motor-driven dollies that "tote cars at variable speeds down the assembly line sending out a stream of computer-controlled signals to coach both robots and workers along the way."[17]

The need for direct labor is diminished in such a technology-intensive environment. The workers who remain in a company employing an FMS must be more highly trained than workers in traditional systems and will find themselves handling a greater variety of tasks than the narrowly specialized workers of earlier manufacturing eras. The manufacturing cells are managed by empowered employees who have greater authority and responsibility than in the past. This increase in control is necessary because production and production scheduling changes happen so rapidly on the shop floor. An FMS relies on immediate decisions by persons who "live there" and have a grasp of the underlying facts and conditions.

---

[17]Clay Chandler and Joseph B. White, "It's Hello Dollies at Nissan's New 'Dream Factory,'" *Wall Street Journal* (July 6, 1992), p. 1.

Flexible Systems Mean Frequent Changes

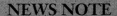

Flexibility is an explicit goal at Toshiba, whose $35.5 billion in sales in 1991 came from products as diverse as appliances and computers, light bulbs and power plants. Okay, so the slogan "synchronize production in proportion to customer demand" probably made a few hearts leap when Toshiba workers first heard it in 1985. The idea, explains Toshiba President Fumio Sato, is to push Toshiba's two dozen factories to adapt faster to markets. Says Sato: "Customers wanted choices. They wanted a washing machine or a TV set that was precisely right for their needs. We needed variety, not mass production."

Sato hammered home his theme in an almost nonstop series of factory visits. The key to variety: finding ways to make money from ever shorter production runs. Sato urged managers to reduce setup times, shrink lead time, and learn to make more products with the same equipment and people. He says: "Every time I go to a plant I tell the people, 'Smaller lot!'"

[Toshiba's computer factory in Ome is referred to as] an "intelligent works" because a snazzy computer network links office, engineering, and factory operations, providing just-in-time information as well as just-in-time parts. Ome workers assemble nine different word processors on the same line and, on an adjacent one, 20 varieties of laptop computers. Usually they make a batch of 20 before changing models, but Toshiba can afford lot sizes as small as 10.

Workers have been trained to make each model but don't need to rely on memory. A laptop at every post displays a drawing and instructions, which change when the model does. Product life-cycles for low-end computers are measured in months these days, so the flexible lines allow the company to guard against running short of a hot model or overproducing one whose sales have slowed.

When it comes to hardware for flexible manufacturing, the Japanese lead is, if anything, widening. Okuma Corp. which makes the world's broadest machine-tool product line sells 14 flexible manufacturing systems in Japan for every one it exports to America. Though U.S. purchases of industrial robots are at record highs, Japan has already installed 390,000 to America's 45,000.

SOURCE: Thomas A. Stewart, "Brace for Japan's Hot New Strategy," *Fortune* (September 21, 1992), pp. 64, 74.

■ **EXHIBIT 13–11**

Comparison of Traditional Manufacturing and FMS

FACTOR	TRADITIONAL MANUFACTURING	FMS
Information requirements	Batch-based	On-line, real-time
Product variety	Low	Basically unlimited
Response time to market needs	Slow	Rapid
Worker tasks	Specialized	Diverse
Production runs	Long	Short
Lot sizes	Massive	Small
Basis of performance rewards	Individual	Team
Setups	Slow and expensive	Fast and inexpensive
Product life cycle expectations	Long	Short
Work area control	Centralized	Decentralized
Technology	Labor-intensive	Technology-intensive
Worker knowledge of technology	Low to medium	Highly trained

SITE ANALYSIS

[After Marcopolo began operations, it wasn't long before] bigger and better financed competitors arrived on Marcopolo's turf. Unable to compete on price or delivery time, Marcopolo concentrated on custom service. Bellini: "We could make special seats, give the customer a bigger or smaller luggage rack, or fruit racks for buses in farm towns. Leather seats or plastic. Whatever the customer wanted."

[Thus, the company had a customer service attitude similar to that of Japanese companies from the start. After deciding to be "made over" in an image even closer to Japanese models, Marcopolo management began an education and reformation process focused on production.] From 1987 to 1990 Gomes and Bellini held seminars for their workers extolling Japanese manufacturing methods. Marcopolo became obsessive about every aspect of its business, from the cleanliness of its factory floors to the mental health of its workers. Today each production team posts a running tab of days without accident or other work stoppage—the record is 1,605—but also for such things as how many liters-per-bus of paint is being consumed.

Inventory controls are intense. From the moment a contract is signed, it is codified on a computer; parts are ordered and shipped according to a tight production schedule. The progress of every window is carefully charted, from the ordering of the glass panels, to installation into metal frames, to final installation on the bus. The same for seats, railings, accordion doors and fiberglass dashboards.

Pastel-colored carts labeled, in English, "Just in Time" rumble along the polished concrete floors containing parts stacked in the order of that day's assembly. Gomes says the average time between parts procurement and installation has been cut from two weeks to three days for most of the roughly 100,000 items in normal use. He would like to cut the time to hours.

[From 1989 to 1994,] Marcopolo's inflation-adjusted earnings [rose] on average 18% annually. The drive to internationalize Marcopolo continues. Bellini is expanding a small factory in Portugal, and is working on a manufacturing joint venture with a Latin American partner. "Evolving to perfection is our goal," says Bellini. "And we will."

SOURCE: Joel Millman, "Evolving to Perfection," reprinted by permission of *Forbes* (November 7, 1994), p. 299. © Forbes, Inc., 1994.

CROSS-FUNCTIONAL APPLICATIONS STRATEGIES

Discipline	Applications
Accounting	With ABC analysis, the use of different inventory techniques for the different categories of inventory can minimize record keeping. Under JIT, raw materials are combined with work in process to form one inventory known as RIP. The number and magnitude of variances from standard are minimized under JIT, and taking inventory should be streamlined.
Economics	The EOQ model involves a trade-off between inventory carrying costs and ordering costs, with the objective being to minimize the sum of these costs. JIT can make companies more "recession-proof" by reducing their need to cut production in response to declining sales. Implementing JIT and advanced production management systems helps companies lower costs and increase quality.
Finance	Strong production and inventory management reduces costs and the investment in inventory, resulting in improved financial ratios. Lower costs and higher quality enhance operating results and make it easier to obtain additional financing for expansion.

Management	Managers can perform more efficiently and effectively with tools such as MRP, JIT, and ABC analysis. Better use of workers and other resources permits management to better serve customers, owners, and the public. Managers may want to implement better communication channels with their customers and help them set up their own JIT inventory systems which, in turn, would help managers better understand their role in the value chain.
Marketing	Higher quality and lower costs and prices contribute to a stronger market position and competitive advantages. Shorter lead times mean faster servicing of sales orders. Sales personnel need to inform managers of the delivery delays customers would consider acceptable for various products. To help determine ABC inventory analysis in a retail company, sales people must assess customer buying preferences. Sales forecasts are critical to determine needed delivery dates and allow decreases in inventory levels.

CHAPTER SUMMARY

Classifying inventory into ABC categories allows management to establish controls over inventory items that are related to the cost and volume of those items. Two-bin and red-line systems are acceptable for inventory items in the C category because of the limited financial investment they involve.

Costs associated with inventory can be significant for any company, and sound business practices seek to limit the amount of those costs. Inventory costs include the costs of purchasing, ordering, carrying, and not carrying inventory. The economic order quantity (EOQ) model determines the purchase order size that minimizes, in total, the costs of ordering and carrying inventory. (This model can also be adapted to find the most economical production run.)

The EOQ model ignores relationships among product components. To overcome this shortcoming, material requirements planning (MRP) can be used to generate master production and time-sequenced purchasing schedules. Manufacturing resource planning (MRP II) implements MRP on a companywide basis and includes top management input. MRP is a push system of production control dictated by delivery lead times and EOQ (or EPR) requirements. Purchased and produced goods must be stored until needed.

In contrast, a pull system of production control (such as just-in-time manufacturing) involves the purchase and/or production of inventory only as needs arise. Storage is eliminated except for a minimal level of safety stock.

The JIT philosophy can be applied to some extent in any company having inventories. JIT requires that purchases be made in small quantities and that deliveries be frequent. Production lot sizes are minimized so that many different products can be made on a daily basis. Products are designed for quality, and component parts are standardized to the extent possible. Machine setup time is reduced so that production runs can be easily shifted between products. To eliminate the need for or buildup of buffer inventories between operations, plant layout emphasizes manufacturing cells, and the operating capabilities of all factory equipment are considered.

Instituting a JIT system has accounting implications. JIT implementation may allow the use of a merged raw materials and work in process inventory (RIP) classification because raw materials are acquired only as needed in production. A conversion cost category may take the place of direct labor and overhead. Backflush costing techniques may be used; these eliminate the need for many journal entries to trace production costs through the process. In addition, more costs may be directly traceable to production under a JIT system. Variances from standards should be negligible under JIT; variances should be recognized earlier in the process so that causes may be found and corrective action taken quickly.

A special type of just-in-time company is one that engages in flexible manufacturing. Flexible manufacturing systems are so fast and versatile that products can be tailored to customer requests with only an insignificant delay in production time in most instances.

APPENDIX

Journal Entries for Backflush Costing

■ LEARNING
OBJECTIVE 11
(Appendix) Prepare journal
entries under a backflush costing
system.

Exhibit 13–12 provides information on a product of the Arnold Company. This information is used to illustrate the journal entries for backflush costing. The company has a long-term contract with its supplier for raw materials at $75 per unit, so there is no material price variance. Arnold's JIT inventory system has minimum inventories that remain constant from period to period. Beginning inventories for April are assumed to be zero.

Three alternatives are possible to the entries in Exhibit 13–12. First, if Arnold's production time were extremely short, the company might not journalize raw material purchases until completion of production. In that case, entries (1) and (3) from Exhibit 13–12 can be combined as follows:

Raw and In Process Inventory	30,000	
Finished Goods Inventory	5,180,000	
Accounts Payable		1,530,000
Conversion Costs		3,680,000

If goods were immediately shipped to customers on completion, Arnold could use a second alternative, in which entries (3) and (4) (a) from Exhibit 13–12 to complete and sell the goods can be combined in the following manner:

Finished Goods Inventory	51,800	
Cost of Goods Sold	5,128,200	
Raw and In Process Inventory		1,500,000
Conversion Costs		3,680,000

The third alternative reflects the ultimate JIT system, in which only one entry is made to replace entries (1), (3), and (4) (a) in Exhibit 13–12. For Arnold, this entry would be:

Raw and In Process Inventory (minimal overpurchases)	30,000	
Finished Goods Inventory (minimal overproduction)	51,800	
Cost of Goods Sold	5,128,200	
Accounts Payable		1,530,000
Conversion Costs		3,680,000

■ **EXHIBIT 13–12**
Backflush Costing

Arnold Company's standard production cost per unit:

Direct materials	$ 75
Conversion	184
Total cost	$259

No beginning inventories exist.

(1) Purchased $1,530,000 of direct materials in April:

Raw and In Process Inventory	1,530,000	
Accounts Payable		1,530,000
Purchased materials at standard cost under a long-term agreement with supplier.		

(2) Incurred $3,687,000 of conversion costs in April:

Conversion Costs	3,687,000	
Various accounts		3,687,000
Record conversion costs. Various accounts include wages payable for direct and indirect labor, accumulated depreciation, supplies, etc.		

(3) Completed 20,000 units of production in April:

Finished Goods Inventory (20,000 × $259)	5,180,000	
Raw and In Process Inventory (20,000 × $75)		1,500,000
Conversion Costs (20,000 × $184)		3,680,000

(4) Sold 19,800 units on account in April for $420:

(a) Cost of Goods Sold (19,800 × $259)	5,128,200	
Finished Goods Inventory		5,128,200
(b) Accounts Receivable (19,800 × $420)	8,316,000	
Sales		8,316,000

Ending balances:

Raw and In Process Inventory ($1,530,000 − $1,500,000)	$30,000
Finished Goods Inventory ($5,180,000 − $5,128,200)	$51,800

In addition, there are underapplied conversion costs of $7,000 ($3,687,000 − $3,680,000).

Note that in all cases, entry (2) is not affected. All conversion cost must be recorded as incurred (or accrued at the end of a period) because of their effect on a variety of accounts.

GLOSSARY

ABC analysis (p. 655)   an inventory control method that separates items into three groups based on annual cost-to-volume usage; items having the highest dollar volume are referred to as A items, while C items represent the lowest dollar volume

Backflush costing (p. 677)   a costing system that focuses on output and works backward through the system to allocate costs to cost of goods sold and inventory accounts

Bottleneck (p. 664)   a resource whose ability to process is less than the need for processing

Carrying cost (p. 657)   the variable cost of keeping one unit of inventory in stock for one year; consists of storage, handling, insurance charges, property taxes based on inventory size, possible losses from obsolescence or the like, and opportunity cost

Computer integrated manufacturing (CIM) (p. 678)   a production system in which two or more flexible manufacturing systems are connected by a host computer and an information network

Economic order quantity (EOQ) (p. 660)   an estimate of the least costly quantity of units per order that would provide the optimal balance between ordering and carrying costs

Economic production run (EPR) (p. 660)   an estimate of the least costly quantity of units to produce on a production run to provide the optimal balance between setup and carrying costs

Just-in-time (JIT) manufacturing system (p. 667)   a production system with the goals of acquiring components and producing inventory units only as they are needed, minimizing product defects, and reducing lead and setup times for acquisition and production

Kanban (p. 667)   the Japanese word for card; another name for just-in-time manufacturing which originated in Japan from the use of cards to control the flow of materials or units between work centers

Lead time (p. 663)   the time from the placement of an order to the arrival of the goods

Manufacturing cell (p. 671)   a linear or U-shaped grouping of workers and/or machines

Manufacturing resource planning (MRP II) (p. 664)   a fully integrated computer simulation system that involves the functional areas of marketing, finance, and manufacturing in planning the master production schedule using the MRP method; also can calculate resource needs such as labor and machine hours

Material requirements planning (MRP) (p. 664)   a computer simulation system that helps companies plan by coordinating future production output requirements with individual future production input needs using a master production schedule

Order point (p. 663)   the inventory level that triggers the placement of an order

Ordering cost (p. 656)   the variable costs associated with preparing, receiving, and paying for an order

Pull system (p. 669)   a production system in which parts are delivered or manufactured only as they are needed

Purchasing cost (p. 656)   the quoted purchase price of an item minus any discounts allowed plus shipping charges

Push system (p. 664)   a production system in which work centers may produce inventory that is not currently needed because of lead time or economic order (or production) quantity requirements; the excess inventory is stored until it is needed

Red-line system (p. 656)   an inventory system in which a single container (or stack) of inventory is available for production needs and a red line is painted on the inventory container (or on the wall, for a stack) at a point deemed to be the reorder point

Safety stock (p. 663)   the quantity of inventory kept on hand by a company to compensate for potential fluctuations in usage or unusual delays in lead time

Setup cost (p. 657)   the direct and indirect labor cost of getting equipment ready for a new production run

Stockout (p. 658)   a condition in which a company does not have inventory available when customers request it or when it is needed for production

Throughput (p. 677)   a plant's output to customers during a single period

Two-bin system (p. 656)   an inventory system in which two containers or stacks of inventory are available for production needs; when production begins to use materials in the second bin, a purchase order is placed to refill the first bin

SOLUTION STRATEGIES

ECONOMIC ORDER QUANTITY

$$EOQ = \sqrt{\frac{2QO}{C}}$$

where   EOQ = economic order quantity in units
            Q = estimated quantity used per year in units
            O = estimated cost of placing one order
            C = estimated cost to carry one unit in stock for one year

ECONOMIC PRODUCTION RUN

$$EPR = \sqrt{\frac{2QS}{C}}$$

where   EPR = economic production run
            Q = estimated quantity produced per year in units
            S = estimated cost of setting up a production run
            C = estimated cost of carrying one unit in stock for one year

ORDER POINT

Order Point = (Daily Usage $\times$ Lead Time) + Safety Stock

BACKFLUSH ACCOUNTING   (from appendix)

Upon purchase of direct materials:

Raw and In Process Inventory (at standard cost)	XX	
Accounts Payable (at actual cost)		XX

A material price variance account will be debited (if actual is greater than standard) or credited (if actual is less than standard) for the difference.

Upon incurrence of conversion costs:

Conversion Costs (at actual cost)	XX	
Various accounts (at actual cost)		XX

Upon completion of units:

Finished Goods Inventory (at standard cost)	XX	
Raw and In Process Inventory (at standard cost)		XX
Conversion Costs (at standard cost)		XX

Upon sale of units:

Cost of Goods Sold (at standard cost)	XX	
Finished Goods Inventory (at standard cost)		XX
Accounts Receivable (at selling price)	XX	
Sales (at selling price)		XX

DEMONSTRATION PROBLEM

Theresa Vuong owns a large office supply store in a university section of Gainesville, Florida. She wonders how many highlighters to order at a time, when to place an order, and how many highlighters she should maintain as a safety stock. Upon analysis, she determines the following information:

Annual sales in units	10,400
Number of days the store is open	260
Average lead time to receive an order, in days	3
Cost per order	$4
Cost of carrying one unit for one year	$.10
Maximum lead time, in days	5
Maximum daily sales in units	50

Required:

   a. Determine the economic order quantity.
   b. Determine the safety stock.
   c. Determine the reorder point.
   d. Determine the total ordering cost using the economic order quantity.
   e. Determine the total carrying cost using the economic order quantity.

SOLUTION TO DEMONSTRATION PROBLEM

a. $\text{EOQ} = \sqrt{\dfrac{2\,(10{,}400)\,(\$4)}{\$.10}} = 912$ (rounded)

b. Safety stock = (Maximum lead time − Average lead time) (Maximum daily usage − Average daily usage)
Average daily usage = 10,400 ÷ 260 = 40 units
Safety stock = (5 − 3) (50 − 40) = 20 units

c. Reorder point = (Average daily usage × Average lead time) + Safety stock
Reorder point = (40 × 3) + 20 = 140 units

d. Total ordering cost = Cost per order × Number of orders
Number of orders = 10,400 ÷ 912 = 11.4 orders
Total ordering cost = $4 × 11.4 = $45.60

e. Total carrying cost = Average inventory × Carrying cost per unit
Average inventory = (EOQ ÷ 2) + Safety stock = [(912 ÷ 2) + 20] = 476
Total carrying cost = 476 × $.10 = $47.60

END-OF-CHAPTER MATERIALS

■ QUESTIONS

1. In an ABC analysis of inventory, what are the characteristics of the items that would be placed in each category?

2. List four costs included in each of the following categories: ordering inventory, carrying inventory, and not carrying inventory. How does incurring costs in one of these categories affect the costs in the other categories?

3. Describe some major considerations in deciding "from whom to buy." How have the considerations changed over time?

4. In buyer-supplier relationships, why is it desirable for the supplier to be located geographically close to the buyer?

5. Why is the purchasing cost of an item not included in the economic order quantity formula?

6. Assuming that all costs in the EOQ formula could be determined with absolute precision, discuss some reasons that a company might not buy at the economic order quantity amount.

7. Although MRP is based on EOQ and safety stock models, it overcomes an inherent deficiency in those models. What is this deficiency, and how does MRP overcome it?

8. Why is MRP said to be a push system?

9. What significant benefits have many firms achieved using MRP? Discuss some of the problems associated with using MRP.

10. It is recognized that MRP does not, in fact, eliminate bottlenecks. How are bottlenecks treated in an MRP system?

11. Why is it said that JIT views inventory as a liability rather than as an asset?

12. What are the primary goals of the JIT philosophy, and how does JIT attempt to achieve these goals?

13. Discuss the differences between push and pull inventory systems.

14. What are manufacturing cells, and what are their benefits?

15. What is empowerment, and why does it frequently accompany the adoption of JIT?

16. "Philosophically, JIT is aimed at minimizing time, space, and energy." Discuss what you think the person making this statement meant.

17. How can JIT be used by nonmanufacturers?

18. Are MRP and JIT systems compatible? Explain your answer.

19. Why do traditional variance analysis and reporting virtually disappear when a JIT system is adopted?

20. What is an engineering change variance? How is it measured? Why is it computed?

21. What is backflush accounting? What are its advantages?

22. What is FMS manufacturing? What is CIM? Why are such systems so expensive to install?

■ **EXERCISES**

23. (LO 1, 2, 6, 7; *Terminology*) Match the numbered items on the right to the lettered items on the left:

a. Push system

b. ABC analysis

c. MRP

1. Generates an interrelated purchase order and production schedule

2. Time from placing an order to receiving the goods

3. U-shaped grouping of workers or machines

d. Lead time

e. Bottleneck

f. Two-bin system

g. Pull system

h. Setup cost

i. Kanban

j. Manufacturing cell

4. Any resource whose ability to process is less than the need for processing

5. Segregates inventory into three groups based on cost and volume

6. Inventory is acquired/produced no sooner than it is needed/sold

7. Inventory is produced and stored before it is sold

8. Direct and indirect labor costs of getting equipment ready for a production run

9. A system in which usage of materials from a second bin causes a purchase order to be issued

10. A system using cards to control the flow of materials or units between work centers

24. (LO 1; *ABC inventory*) Following is a list of techniques used to control inventories.

a. Perpetual inventory system
b. Daily inventory counts
c. Monthly inventory counts
d. Annual inventory count
e. Limited access to storage areas
f. Open-access display areas
g. Red-line system
h. Two-bin system
i. Specific identification inventory method
j. Weighted-average cost flow
k. Rigorous, in-depth demand estimation (EOQ, lead time, order point, safety stock)

For each of the preceding items, indicate whether it would most likely be used for A-, B-, or C-type inventory items. More than one type of inventory item may be indicated for a given technique.

25. (LO 2; *Types of costs*) Classify each of the following items as a cost of ordering (O), carrying (C), or not carrying (N) inventory. Use N/A for items not fitting any of the categories.

a. Contribution margin lost on a sale because of a stockout
b. Spoilage of products in storage
c. Opportunity cost of capital invested in inventory
d. Inventory storage cost
e. Wages of staff in purchasing agent's office
f. Long-distance calls to vendor to get prices
g. Property tax based on inventory value
h. Freight-out on sales of inventory
i. Purchase order forms, receiving report forms, disbursement voucher forms
j. Insurance on warehouse and its inventory contents
k. Extra freight on rush orders necessitated by stockouts
l. Freight-in on purchases
m. Postage to send purchase orders
n. Handling costs for products on hand
o. Purchase price of products

26. (LO 2; *Carrying costs*) Determine the carrying costs for an item costing $6.50, given the following per-unit cost information:

Shipping cost	$.02
Storage cost	.15
Handling cost	.04
Production labor cost	.65
Insurance	.06
Import taxes (per unit)	.09

27. (LO 4; *EOQ*) A company wants to determine its EOQ for a high-volume part and supplies you with the following information:

Quantity used per year, in units	12,000
Per-unit cost	$8.50
Cost of each order	$6.00
Annual cost of stocking one unit	$.50

Determine the EOQ.

28. (LO 4; *EPR*) Rows a through e below represent five independent situations, each with a missing item of data.

	EPR	(Q) QUANTITY USED PER YEAR	(S) SETUP COST	(C) CARRYING COST
a.	?	8,100	$ 1	$2
b.	40	?	$ 2	$4
c.	100	1,000	$15	?
d.	20	400	$ 5	?
e.	30	150	?	$3

Provide the missing numbers.

29. (LO 2, 4; *EOQ, carrying costs*) The following information was determined by examination of financial records of Smithfield Customer Computers. The data pertain to a computer chip.

Annual demand in units	75,000
Ordering cost per order	$10.25
Carrying cost per unit	$.65

  a. Determine the EOQ.
  b. Now assume that an error was made in estimating the ordering costs. It has been determined that the true cost of ordering is $7.25 rather than $10.25. Compute the new EOQ.
  c. Compute the total costs of ordering and carrying inventory based on the EOQs computed in parts a and b.
  d. Discuss how using an incorrect ordering cost affected Smithfield's total inventory cost.
  e. Why is it important to involve an expert from the Finance staff or Treasury staff when attempting to compute carrying cost?

30. (LO 4; *EOQ and related components*) Huxton Toy Company manufactures toy wagons. Among the parts needed to manufacture each wagon are two axles and four wheels. These parts are purchased from external vendors. The annual demand, ordering costs, and carrying costs for each follow.

COMPONENT	ORDERING COST	CARRYING COST	DEMAND
Axles	$10	$ .50	4,000
Wheels	18	3.00	8,000

a. Compute the EOQ for each component.

b. Compute the average inventory level for each component assuming that no safety stock is carried.

c. Write a memo to management discussing any problems you perceive in managing the inventories of these two components. Also, suggest solutions to any problems you identify.

31. (LO 4; *EOQ, order point*) Heinrick Bauer is a Pennsylvania farmer who raises pheasants. His birds eat approximately 7,300 pounds of feed per year. On the average, 18 days pass from the time he places an order until the feed is delivered. It costs Heinrick $8 to place each order and the annual carrying cost is $.48 per pound.

a. What is Heinrick's EOQ?

b Assuming he holds no safety stock, calculate Heinrick's order point.

c. Assuming the lead time varies by three days, calculate a safety stock.

d. Assuming the average daily consumption per bird varies 10 percent, calculate a safety stock.

e. Using the information calculated in parts c and d, determine a conservative order point.

32. (LO 9; *JIT variances*) A JIT system is in use at Beltway Electronics Co. The following standards are related to two materials that are used to make one unit of the company's final product:

Annual material standards:	
8 pounds of material A @ $3.75	$30.00
12 pounds of material B @ $4.90	58.80
	$88.80
Current material standards:	
10 pounds of material A @ $3.75	$37.50
10 pounds of material B @ $4.90	49.00
	$86.50

The current material standards differ from the original because of an engineering change made near the end of March. During April, the company produced 2,000 units of its final product and used 21,000 pounds of material A and 19,500 pounds of material B. All material is acquired at the standard cost per pound.

a. Calculate the material usage variance and the ENC materials variance.

b. Explain the effect of the engineering change on product cost.

c. Who would typically be responsible for effecting an engineering change to a product?

33. (LO 11; *Appendix*) Bolson Company produces a variety of rubber-based consumer goods. The company uses a JIT inventory system. The following transactions occurred during July 1997:

■ Raw materials of $186,000 were purchased on account.

■ Conversion costs of $282,000 were incurred.

■ Conversion costs of $281,880 were applied to production.

- The cost of goods manufactured during July was $468,000.
- July sales were $644,000 on account, with the cost of sales being $460,000.

Beginning of July balances were: Raw and In Process Inventory, $6,000; Finished Goods Inventory, $12,000.

a. Journalize the previous transactions using backflush costing.
b. Determine the July balances in the inventory accounts.

■ COMMUNICATION ACTIVITIES

34. (LO 2, 5; *Inventory management*) John Holster, controller for ProCorp, Inc., has been examining all phases of ProCorp's manufacturing operations in order to reduce costs and improve efficiency. The reason for urgency is that the company's sales force has been complaining about lost sales caused by product stockouts, and the production people are unhappy about downtime caused by shortages of raw materials. Holster believes the company may be losing as much as $220,000 in revenue as a result of these problems.

ProCorp manufactures only one product: boomerangs (tradename, Boomers). The single raw material used in making Boomers is plastic, with each Boomer requiring 8 ounces of red plastic. ProCorp expects to manufacture 300,000 Boomers this year with a steady demand through the entire year. The ordering costs for clerical processing are $30 per order of plastic. There is a three-day delay between placement of an order and receipt of the inventory. The carrying costs for storage, handling, insurance, and interest are $.72 per Boomer unit per year.

a. Discuss the general benefits of a well-managed inventory policy.
b. By using the economic order quantity formula, ProCorp, Inc., determined that the optimal economic order quantity is 2,500 pounds of plastic, which will produce 5,000 units.

  1. Discuss how an increase in each of the following components will affect the economic order quantity: annual sales demand; ordering costs; and carrying costs for storage, handling, insurance, and interest.

  2. Determine the number of times ProCorp will order plastic during the year.

c. ProCorp, Inc., while reviewing its safety stock policy, has determined that an appropriate safety stock is 1,250 pounds of plastic, which will produce 2,500 units.

  1. Describe the factors that affect an appropriate safety stock level.
  2. List the effects of maintaining an appropriate safety stock level on ProCorp's short-term and long-term profitability.
  3. Identify the effect that a well-implemented just-in-time inventory procedure will have on safety stock level, and explain why it will have this effect.

(CMA adapted)

35. (LO 3, 8; *Small supplier/large customer relationships*) *The restructuring of General Motors Corp., International Business Machines Corp. and other huge firms to improve their competitiveness has scared tens of thousands of small concerns that count on the giants for much of their business. Suddenly, some of these companies are reducing orders or canceling them. Others are placing tough new conditions on suppliers, including cutting prices and requiring costly measures to increase speed and quality.*

Large suppliers commonly have the resources and broad customer bases to absorb such changes. But the rising unpredictability of large customers can threaten the survival of a smaller firm. As a result, small suppliers are "re-evaluating doing business with the Fortune 500," says Alexander

Guthrie, president and co-owner of Davis Electric Wallingford Corp., a small maker of wire, cable and fiberoptic machinery. "You cannot rely on these major customers for consistent business any more."

The co-owner of a small aerospace-industry supplier that derives two-thirds of its sales from Boeing Co. says his firm also is seeking to diversify its customer base. Pressure from Boeing to reduce prices "has gotten worse in the past couple of years," he says, requesting anonymity. "They haven't learned to cut costs internally so they're beating up on the vendors." To cope, "we're looking for new customers wherever we can," he says.

[SOURCE: Michael Selz, "Some Suppliers Rethink Their Reliance on Big Business," *Wall Street Journal* (March 29, 1993), p. B2. Reprinted by permission of The Wall Street Journal, © 1993 Dow Jones & Company, Inc. All Rights Reserved Worldwide.]

a. Why do large customers have so much influence on the success of small supplier firms?

b. Why would large firms wish to purchase parts and materials from smaller firms rather than larger firms?

c. How might the adoption of JIT by a large customer increase the usual problems experienced by a small supplier?

d. From a supplier's perspective, what are the relative advantages and disadvantages of having a diversified set of customers versus having a dominant customer.

36. (LO 4, 8; *Technology changes and inventory management*) A plant manager and her controller were discussing the plant's inventory control policies one day. The controller suggested that the plant's ordering policies needed revising. The controller argued that the revision was needed because of new technology that had been put in place in the plant's purchasing department. Among the changes were: (1) installation of computerized inventory tracking; (2) installation of electronic data interchange capabilities, which would allow communications with the plant's major suppliers; and (3) installation of in-house facilities for electronic fund transfers.

a. As technology changes, why should managers update ordering policies for inventory?

b. What would be the likely impact of the changes in this plant on the EOQ of material inputs?

c. What experts should be invited to provide input into the design of new policies for ordering materials?

37. (LO 8; *Implementing JIT*) [*Successfully implementing JIT requires certain conditions be met. Consider the case of] Allen-Edmonds Shoe Corp., a 71-year old maker of pricey shoes. Three years ago, the Port Washington, Wis., company tried just-in-time methods to speed production, boost customer satisfaction and save money. The result? "It really flopped miserably," says John Stollenwerk, the company's president and biggest shareholder. The manufacturer lost $1 million on the project—and in 1991, resumed doing some things the old way.*

"It's somewhat difficult for a small company to achieve some of the just-in-time gains of large companies," says Thomas W. Bruett, a partner at Ernst & Young who advised Allen-Edmonds on production techniques.

Like owners of other small, old-line manufacturing firms, Mr. Stollenwerk also had difficulty persuading some of his 325 production workers to accept change. At the outset, Mr. Stollenwerk thought just-in-time concepts could stem his firm's loss of business from retailers unwilling to wait as many as eight weeks for their shoe orders. He sought to slice overall production time by as much as 87%, to five days.

[However, problems plagued the company from the start. To achieve the teamwork and quality focus that JIT demanded, the company dropped its piecework pay plan and adopted an hourly pay plan. But the culture wasn't ripe for such a change:] As productivity plummeted, Allen-Edmonds workers complained about co-workers slacking off. Jacqueline Summers, who makes $9

to $10 an hour, stitching wingtips and other pieces, says she observed "more breaks, more laughing, more giggling." A stitcher must pay attention, she insists, because "you see the same shoe all day long in a nine-hour day, and your eyes can eventually cross."

[Also,] it wasn't easy to get suppliers to go along with just-in-time strategy of matching delivery to need. Suppliers of leather soles did agree to make deliveries weekly, rather than monthly, to Allen-Edmonds.

But European tanneries supplying calf-skin hides refused to cooperate. They stuck with their practice of processing huge quantities of hides at once and wouldn't handle small batches to meet the weekly needs of a small customer.

[SOURCE: Barbara Marsh, "Allen-Edmonds Shoe Tries 'Just-in-Time' Production," *Wall Street Journal* (March 4, 1994), p. B2. Reprinted by permission of The Wall Street Journal, © 1994 Dow Jones & Company, Inc. All Rights Reserved Worldwide.]

a. Why might the implementation of JIT be more difficult in a small firm than in a large firm?

b. How does the "culture" of a firm influence its potential to successfully implement JIT?

c. Describe any recommendations for changes that you might have made to Allen-Edmonds in advance of the company's attempt to implement JIT.

38. Select a company in your area or one about whose production processes you can find substantial information. Assume that you have been hired as a consultant to provide a plan for successfully implementing JIT in one of the company's plants. Prepare a broad, written plan for implementing JIT, being certain to address the following items: internal and external communications; possible engineering changes needed for new production arrangements and their impacts; number, quality, and location of suppliers and any changes needed in supplier arrangements; behavioral implications; and length of time horizon for system implementation.

39. (LO 8; *Implementing JIT in Japan vs. the United States*) Experts believe that we are far behind the Japanese in JIT for demographic and cultural reasons, and cannot possibly achieve JIT in the near future. Demographic differences can be related to the geographical vastness of the United States in comparison with Japan, an island which is only two hundred miles across. Cultural differences between the two countries include the fact that the Japanese culture has high regard for dependability, concern for quality, cooperative behavior, and respect for authority. This work ethic carries over into the typical six-day work week. Obvious difficulties exist in translating a system that works for such a culture to the American worker, who puts in a five-day work week in anticipation of two days off for private pursuits.

[SOURCE: Adapted from Michael A. Muchnik, Margaret F. Shipley, and Hugh M. Shane, "Why JIT Can't Bear Fruit in American Plants," *Business Forum* (Summer 1990), p. 13.]

a. Do you believe the basic premises stated by these authors? Discuss the reasoning behind your answer.

b. Which aspects of JIT might be more difficult to implement in the United States than in Japan?

c. Do you think that the cited circumstances may be relevant for some businesses but not others? Why or why not? If so, to what businesses might they relate?

d. Assume that you believe the cited circumstances to be true and you are the manager of a medium-sized manufacturer that wants to implement a JIT system. How would you go about trying to reduce the effects of the problems just mentioned?

40. (LO 8; *Objectives of JIT*) The management at Megafilters, Inc., has been discussing the possible implementation of a just-in-time (JIT) production system at its Illinois plant, where oil filters and air filters for heavy construction equipment and large, off-the-road vehicles are manufactured. The Metal Stamping Department at the Illinois plant has already instituted a JIT system for controlling raw materials inventory, but the remainder of the plant is still discussing how to proceed with the implementation of this concept. Some of the other department managers have grown increasingly cautious about the JIT process after hearing about the problems that have arisen in the Metal Stamping Department.

Robert Goertz, manager of the Illinois plant, is a strong proponent of the JIT production system and recently made the following statement at a meeting of all departmental managers. "Just-in-time is often referred to as a management philosophy of doing business rather than a technique for improving efficiency on the plant floor. We will all have to make many changes in the way we think about our employees, our suppliers, and our customers if we are going to be successful in using just-in-time procedures. Rather than dwelling on some of the negative things you have heard from the Metal Stamping Department, I want each of you to prepare a list of things we can do to make a smooth transition to the just-in-time philosophy of management for the rest of the plant."

a. The just-in-time management philosophy emphasizes objectives for the general improvement of a production system. Describe several important objectives of this philosophy.

b. Discuss several actions that Megafilters, Inc., can take to ease the transition to a just-in-time production system at the Illinois plant.

c. For the JIT production system to be successful, Megafilters, Inc., must establish appropriate relationships with its vendors, employees, and customers. Describe each of these three relationships.

d. Who (or what functions) in the firm would be involved in developing new arrangements with (1) vendors, (2) employees, and (3) customers?

(CMA adapted)

41. (LO 8; *Engineering changes*) *Ford Motor Co. said it is halting production of its new line of compact sedans for one week because of a fuel-leakage problem with 28,500 of the cars built so far.*

Production at [Ford's] Kansas City, Mo., assembly plant, [is being stopped] because [the company] wants to rush replacement fuel-tank assemblies to dealers and customers. Of the 28,500 affected cars, nearly 8,000 have been delivered to U.S. and Canadian customers, Ford said. The shutdown will cost Ford production of 6,400 cars. Ford hopes to recoup its lost production through additional overtime shifts at the Kansas City plant. The latest problem stems from a tricky weld near the fuel tank's filler pipe, Ford said. When the weld is improperly made, fuel can leak from the reinforcement on the fuel tank. . . . Ford said it learned of the problem from its customers.

[SOURCE: Oscar Suris, "Ford Is Halting The Production Of a New Line," *Wall Street Journal* (October 18, 1994), p. A4. Reprinted by permission of The Wall Street Journal, © 1994 Dow Jones & Company, Inc. All Rights Reserved Worldwide.]

a. This story indicates one reason for making engineering changes. What are some other possible reasons for such changes?

b. Why would Ford elect to shut down assembly operations to correct the production flaw?

c. In what ways might a firm learn of the existence of production flaws? Why would a firm prefer to learn of such flaws from some source other than customers?

■ PROBLEMS

42. (LO 1; *ABC inventory analysis*) The following 20 items, along with unit costs and volumes of sales last year, are part of an ABC analysis of Gulf Coast Dive Shop:

ITEMS		UNIT COST	VOLUME SOLD
Flippers (pair):	Men's	$ 3.00	320
	Women's	2.50	210
	Children's	1.80	66
Masks:	Men's	4.00	280
	Women's	3.40	172
	Children's	2.80	40
Weight belts:	Men's	1.80	63
	Women's	1.70	46
	Children's	1.20	12
Snorkels		1.20	420
Air tanks		36.00	42
Meters and connections		2.00	36
Wet suits:	Men's	60.00	170
	Women's	52.00	102
	Children's	42.00	12
Weights:	Large	2.00	160
	Medium	1.50	180
	Small	1.25	64
Underwater watches		25.00	32
Ear plugs		.25	120

a. Rearrange the items in descending order of magnitude according to the product of cost times volume. Use these headings: Items; Unit Cost; Volume Sold; and Cost × Volume.

b. Classify the items in three groups: A items (to include 20 percent of the total volume sold); B items (to include the next 30 percent of the total volume sold); and C items (to include the final 50 percent of the volume sold).

c. Recommend three techniques to control each group.

43. (LO 2; *Identification of carrying, ordering costs*) Lugwell Wheel Corp. has been evaluating its policies with respect to control of the costs of flat metal, one of the firm's major component materials. The firm's controller has gathered the following financial data, which may be pertinent to controlling costs associated with the flat metal:

ORDERING COSTS

Annual salary of purchasing department manager	$62,500
Depreciation of equipment in purchasing department	$44,300
Cost per order for purchasing department supplies	$.90
Typical phone expense per order placed	$4.20
Monthly expense for heat and light in purchasing department	$900

CARRYING COSTS

Annual depreciation on material storage building	$25,000
Annual inventory insurance premium (per dollar of inventory value)	$.11
Annual property tax on material storage building	$3,700
Obsolescence cost, per dollar of average annual inventory	$.12
Annual salary of security officer assigned to the material storage building	$38,000

a. Which of the ordering costs would Lugwell Wheel Corp.'s controller take into account in using the EOQ model? Explain.

b. Which of the carrying costs would Lugwell Wheel Corp.'s controller take into account in using the EOQ model? Explain.

44. (LO 4; *EOQ*) One contractor's requirement for cement amounts to 80,000 bags per year. No shortages are allowed. Cement costs $4 a bag, holding cost is $6 per unit per year, and it costs $24 to process a purchase order. The lead time is 30 days. The company works 365 days per year.

a. Find the EOQ.

b. Calculate the total cost of ordering and carrying inventory for a period of one year.

c. Determine the order point.

d. How does total inventory cost change if the firm orders in a lot size of 4,000 units rather than the EOQ?

e. Why might the company prefer to order in a lot size of 4,000 units rather than the EOQ?

45. (LO 4; *EOQ*) The Hotel Supply Company sells a number of products to various hotel chains in the Midwest. One of the products is a bathroom cleaning compound that is purchased and then sold in one-gallon containers. Each gallon is purchased for $15 and sold for $20.

After a number of years, it has been determined that the demand for the cleaning compound is constant at 2,000 gallons per month. The product requires a three-day lead time for ordering; the carrying cost is $.12 per gallon per year, and the ordering cost is $10. The company requires a safety stock of 500 gallons.

a. Calculate the EOQ.

b. Calculate the number of orders that must be placed per year.

c. Calculate the total cost of ordering and carrying the inventory for a period of one year.

d. Prepare an oral report discussing the problems that firms might have in applying the EOQ formula to their inventory situation.

46. (LO 4; *EOQ, order point*) Each of the following independent cases has a missing amount.

	CASE A	CASE B	CASE C	CASE D	CASE E
Order point	400	(b)	120	300	500
Daily usage	20	30	(c)	15	(e)
Lead time (days)	12	10	7	(d)	5
Safety stock	(a)	60	50	30	60

Supply the missing amounts for the lettered spaces.

47. (LO 8; *JIT features*) Items a through j below describe features of just-in-time systems. The categories D, U, and T, described below, also relate to JIT systems. Indicate by letter which of the three categories applies to each item. More than one category may apply to an item.

D—desired intermediate result of using JIT
U—ultimate goal of JIT
T—technique associated with JIT

   a. Reducing setup costs
   b. Reducing total cost of producing and carrying inventory
   c. Using a focused factory arrangement in which a supplier provides a limited number of unique products
   d. Designing products to minimize design changes after production starts
   e. Monitoring quality on a continuous basis
   f. Using manufacturing cells
   g. Minimizing inventory stored
   h. Using backflush accounting
   i. Involving all workers to control quality
   j. Pulling purchases and production through the system based on sales demand

48. (LO 8, 9; *Changes from implementing JIT*) The table below gives symbols for areas where changes occur as a result of the implementation of JIT. Categorize items a through s in the list that follows the table by associating the appropriate symbol with each item.

SYMBOL	AREA OF CHANGE RELATED TO USE OF JIT
PSR&D	Purchasing, Supplier Relationships, and Distribution
PD	Product Design
PP	Production Processing
PL	Plant Layout
JP	JIT Philosophy
AI	Accounting Implications of JIT

   a. Management recognizes that employees often know best how to improve operations.
   b. A single RIP account replaces two inventory accounts.
   c. A focused factory arrangement is used with a supplier providing a limited number of specialized products.
   d. The ideal is one vendor for each part or raw material.
   e. Setup time is reduced.
   f. Layout is intended to minimize throughput time.
   g. Long-term contracts are negotiated.
   h. Physical arrangement is conducive to a worker's handling a greater number of tasks.
   i. Inventory is viewed as a liability.
   j. A single conversion account combines direct labor and overhead.
   k. Fewer costs need to be arbitrarily allocated.
   l. Workers and machines monitor quality during processing.
   m. U-shaped groupings of workers and machines are used.
   n. Many setup tasks are performed while machines are running.
   o. Layout makes the use of visual controls more effective.
   p. The plan is to use fewest number of parts (reduce product complexity).
   q. Creative thinking doesn't cost anything.
   r. As many parts as possible are standardized.
   s. Careful design minimizes the number of subsequent changes.

49. (LO 9; *JIT variances*) Jonie Bend uses a JIT system in her manufacturing firm which makes a variety of canned food products. One such product is canned rice and beans. The current and annual standard for rice and beans per 16-ounce can of rice and beans follows:

Annual material standards:

6 ounces of rice @ $.02	$.12
6 ounces of beans @ $.03	.18
	$.30

Current material standards:

5 ounces of rice @ $.02	$.10
7 ounces of beans @ $.03	.21
	$.31

The changes in the standards are due to a nutritional (engineering) change just effected. Production during May is 50,000 cans of rice and beans. Raw materials are all purchased at standard costs and include 16,562 pounds of rice and 21,250 pounds of beans.

a. Calculate the material usage variance for each component.
b. Calculate the engineering change variance for each component.
c. Why would a company implement an engineering change that increases the standard production cost?

50. (LO 11; *Appendix*) Feminine Footwear has the following standard cost per pair of its famous leather shoes:

Direct materials	$11.20
Conversion	8.80
Total	$20.00

The company had no beginning inventories on April 1. During April, the following occurred:

- Purchased $450,000 of direct materials on account at standard cost.
- Incurred $353,900 of actual conversion costs.
- Completed 40,000 pairs of shoes.
- Sold 39,800 pairs of shoes on account for $36 per pair.

Using backflush costing, journalize these events.

51. (LO 11; *Appendix*) Henrietta Manufacturing has implemented a just-in-time system for production of its one-half-inch plastic pipe. Inventories of raw materials and work in process are very small, so Henrietta uses a Raw and In Process (RIP) Inventory account. In addition, the company has become highly automated and includes labor and overhead in a single conversion category. Production standards for 1997 for 100 yards of pipe are:

Direct material, 100 pounds @ $2.00	$200
Conversion, 4 machine hours @ $35	140
Total	$340

The conversion cost of $35 per machine hour was estimated on the basis of 500,000 machine hours for the year and $17,500,000 of conversion costs. 1997 activities are as follows:

1. Direct material purchased and placed into production amounted to 12,452,000 pounds. All except 8,000 pounds were purchased at standard. The other 8,000 pounds were purchased at a cost of $2.06 per pound when the regular vendor was unable to meet demand. All purchases are on account. The accounts payable were paid within the period.

2. From January 1 to February 28, Henrietta made 2,080,000 yards of pipe. Conversion costs for this period were $2,918,000. Of this amount, $321,000 was for depreciation. The remaining costs were either paid in cash ($103,000) or acquired on account. The accounts payable were paid within the period.

3. Conversion costs were applied to the RIP Inventory account from January 1 to February 28.

4. Total production for the remainder of 1997 was 10,320,000 yards of pipe. Conversion costs from March through December were $14,432,000. Of this amount, $4,000,000 was depreciation, $9,325,000 was cash, and $1,107,000 was on account. The accounts payable were paid within the period.

5. Standard costs for conversion costs were applied to the RIP Inventory account for the period of March through December 1997.

Prepare the journal entries to record the events just presented.

■ CASES

52. (LO 8; *JIT, special orders*) Systrack Systems produces a private brand of compact disc player. The company makes only one type of player. It is sold through various distribution organizations, which resell the players under their own brand names. The quality of Systrack Systems' product is high, equal to that of nationally branded competitors.

The compact disc industry is highly concentrated, with three major players holding the lion's share of the market. A half-dozen other suppliers, such as Systrack Systems, hold small and about equal market shares. All three of the major suppliers have high-quality products. Consumers are aware of this, leading to a tendency for them to see all brands, including private brands, as about the same. As a result, price competition is intense; and the introduction of new technology as soon as possible is a very important element of marketing strategy.

Systrack Systems has significant experience in the production of compact disc players, having produced an average of 500,000 units per year over the past three years. During manufacturing, compact disc players go through three major processes: cutting, assembly, and finishing. Historically, the manufacturing costs of producing one compact disc player are as follows:

Direct material	$ 80
Direct labor	60
Variable overhead	40
Fixed overhead	20
Total manufacturing costs	$200

At present, Systrack Systems operates at 80 percent of production capacity. The product is sold at $300 in the market.

Andrea Chicoine, president of Systrack Systems, is very interested in converting the company's conventional accounting system to an activity-based costing system and also introducing just-in-time measures into her manufacturing system. Chicoine has asked her controller, John Russ, to submit a comparison of the manufacturing costs under the present system and a just-in-time system to meet a special 100,000-unit order at a price of $220 per unit. The company has the capacity to meet the special order at no increase in fixed costs. According to Russ's report, if a JIT system is implemented, the following manufacturing costs will be incurred and manufacturing overhead will be allocated based on an activity-based costing system:

Direct material	$ 80
Direct labor	70
Variable overhead	30
Fixed overhead	10
Total manufacturing costs	$190

A JIT manufacturing system requires the establishment of manufacturing cells in the plant. The company has to adopt the philosophy of total quality control (TQC). No scrap or waste is allowed. Inventory levels should be zero (because JIT is a demand pull approach). Workers in each cell are trained to perform various tasks within the cell. Therefore, idle time is not permissible. Finally, each cell is considered a separate unit.

Under an activity-based costing system, manufacturing overhead costs are applied to products based on cost drivers and not on departmental overhead rates. Plant layout should be changed, and manufacturing cells should be developed. Many costs that are considered indirect costs under the current system will be considered direct costs that are easy to trace to the final product and are measured precisely. A JIT system considers direct labor costs as fixed costs, not variable costs, as under conventional accounting systems. This is legitimate because workers are trained to perform various jobs within a given work cell. Chicoine is convinced that a JIT manufacturing system would allow the company to more accurately determine product costs.

[SOURCE: Adapted from Nabil Hassan, Herbert E. Brown, and Paula M. Saunders, "Management Accounting Case Study: Systrack Systems," *Management Accounting Campus Report* (Spring 1991). Copyright © 1991 IMA (formerly NAA).]

a. Should the special order be accepted or rejected under the conventional system? Under the JIT system? Show computations.

b. If the cost activities described in the case will result in different cost estimates and different contribution margins, which cost accounting system is preferable for pricing this special order? Explain.

53. (LO 8; *Benefits of adopting JIT*) AgriCorp is a manufacturer of farm equipment that is sold by a network of distributors throughout the United States. A majority of the distributors are also repair centers for AgriCorp equipment and depend on AgriCorp's Service Division to provide a timely supply of spare parts.

In an effort to reduce the inventory costs incurred by the Service Division, Richard Bachman, division manager, implemented a just-in-time inventory program on June 1, 1997, the beginning of the company's fiscal year. After JIT had been in place for a year, Bachman asked the division controller, Janice Grady, to determine the effect the program had on the Service Division's financial performance. Grady has been able to document the following results of JIT implementation.

■ The Service Division's average inventory declined from $550,000 to $150,000.

■ Projected annual insurance costs of $80,000 declined 60 percent because of the lower average inventory.

■ A leased 8,000 square foot warehouse, previously used for raw material storage, was not used at all during the year. The division paid $11,200 annual rent for the warehouse and was able to sublet three-quarters of the building to several tenants at $2.50 per square foot, while the balance of the space remained idle.

■ Two warehouse employees whose services were no longer needed were transferred on June 1, 1997, to the Purchasing Department to assist in the coordination of the JIT program. The annual salary expense for these two employees totaled $38,000 and continued to be charged to the indirect labor portion of fixed overhead.

■ Despite the use of overtime to manufacture 7,500 spare parts, lost sales caused by stockouts totaled 3,800 spare parts. The overtime premium incurred amounted to $5.60 per part manufactured. The use of overtime to fill spare parts orders was immaterial prior to June 1, 1997.

Prior to the decision to implement the JIT inventory program, AgriCorp's Service Division had completed its 1997-1998 fiscal budget. The division's pro forma income statement, without any adjustments for JIT inventory, is presented next. AgriCorp's borrowing rate related to inventory is 9 percent after income taxes. All AgriCorp budgets are prepared using an effective tax rate of 40 percent.

AGRICORP SERVICE DIVISION
PRO FORMA INCOME STATEMENT
FOR THE YEAR ENDING MAY 31, 1998

Sales (280,000 spare parts)		$6,160,000
Cost of goods sold		
Variable	$2,660,000	
Fixed	1,120,000	(3,780,000)
Gross profit		$2,380,000
Selling and administrative expense		
Variable	$ 700,000	
Fixed	555,000	(1,255,000)
Operating income		$1,125,000
Other income		75,000
Income before interest and taxes		$1,200,000
Interest expense		(150,000)
Income before income taxes		$1,050,000
Income taxes		(420,000)
Net income		$ 630,000

a. Calculate the after-tax cash savings (loss) for AgriCorp's Service Division that resulted during the 1997-1998 fiscal year from the adoption of the JIT program.

b. Identify and explain the factors, other than financial, that should be considered before a company implements a JIT program.

(CMA)

■ ETHICS AND QUALITY DISCUSSION

54. *Daewoo Group, Korea's fourth-largest conglomerate, has spent most of the past few years trying to shed its image as a debt-strapped producer of cut-rate cars, electronic equipment and home appliances. Through enhanced engineering, it has largely succeeded. But rather than aiming at developed-country markets, which had gobbled up Korean goods in the early 1980s but have*

turned away from them because of allegedly poor quality and after-sales service, Daewoo is concentrating on the Third World. [In 1993], Chairman Kim Woo Choong committed some $8 billion to make and sell Daewoo goods in Eastern Europe, Central Asia and Latin America, where Daewoo hoped to tap new consumers and cheap labor.

[SOURCE: Steve Glain, "Daewoo Group Shifts Its Markets in the Third World," *Wall Street Journal* (October 11, 1993), pp. A1, A10. Reprinted by permission of The Wall Street Journal, © 1993 Dow Jones & Company, Inc. All Rights Reserved Worldwide.]

a. Express your opinion on whether the quality of Daewoo's products will be affected by the choice to compete primarily in Third World countries rather than the more developed countries.

b. Why would Daewoo believe that its chances for competitive success are better in Third World countries?

c. If you were a consumer in a Third World market, how would you react to the news of Daewoo's new strategy?

55. *Although federal law allows food to contain small traces of bugs, molds and other substances, officials acknowledge that the shard of glass found in a jar of baby food, the maggot in a bag of frozen green beans or caustic cleaner in chicken broth should be taken seriously.*

While soda companies in June [1993] were busy assuring the public about the safety precautions in their processing plants, authorities received three legitimate reports of foreign objects in soda cans and bottles.

In Connecticut, a metal and plastic piece from a filling machine was found in a can of caffeine-free Coca-Cola. In Florida, a screw was found in a can of Diet Pepsi. And in Massachusetts, Coca-Cola initiated a recall after it discovered a defect that caused the plastic bottle cap liners to fall into bottles during production, posing a choking hazard.

[SOURCE: Anthony Giorgianni, "Objects in Food More Common Than Syringes in Soda," *(New Orleans) Times-Picayune* (August 18, 1993), p. E-6. © 1993, The Hartford Courant. Reprinted with permission.]

a. What do the preceding examples of food contamination suggest about the importance of suppliers (such as those that supply containers or production machinery) to providing product quality?

b. In the food industry, in your opinion, which is more important to the financial prospects of a firm—actual quality of the product as measured by some objective scale—or quality as subjectively perceived by the consumer? Explain.

c. What are the ethical considerations in determining the quality of products offered by the food industry?

56. Shelby Lessons is the production manager for the Demure Company, located in a small town in Mississippi. Demure is the only major employer in the county, which has substantial unemployment.

Shelby is in the process of trying to introduce manufacturing cells in the company. Of the 150 employees at Demure, approximately 80 percent have little formal education and have worked for the company for 15 years or more. Some— but not all—of these employees are close to retirement.

In talking with the employees, Shelby determines that most would require substantial training before they would be able to change from performing their current single-task production jobs to handling multifunctional tasks.

A neighboring county has a vocational-technical school that is educating many young people in the use of the new types of multitask equipment that could be used at Demure. Shelby has discussed the company's plans with the head of the vo-tech school, who has indicated that the school could easily provide a cadre of 150 well-trained employees within the next 10 months—approximately the time it will take the equipment to arrive and be installed.

Shelby is excited to hear this, because Demure would not have to pay for training and would be able to hire new graduates at a slightly lower hourly wage because of their "lack of experience." Her only difficulty is trying to determine how to remove the older work force from the plant. She decides to institute a rigorous training program that would be intolerable for most of the less-educated employees.

a. Discuss the business sense of hiring graduates with the necessary skills rather than paying for on-location training.

b. Discuss the ethics of the plan to "remove" the current work force.

c. Why should Shelby and Demure be concerned about the welfare of the current work force if it makes good business sense to hire the graduates of the vo-tech school?

57. Two potential impediments to the implementation of JIT and other quality-oriented production systems that require employee participation are labor relations laws (such as the National Labor Relations Act) and union contracts. In the case of labor unions, union officials are often suspicious of management actions taken in the name of quality improvement because employers have frequently used such quality initiatives as an excuse to fire employees. This historical context of quality improvement has caused present-day mistrust between employees and managers. Naturally, implementation of genuine quality-enhancing programs are met with suspicion by employees.

Even so, labor and management are trying to cooperate in some firms for the sake of their mutual survival. For example, Levi Strauss recently worked out an agreement with its labor union that allows the union to sign up an additional 10,000 of the company's employees. In exchange the union has agreed to certain changes to make the company more efficient. For example, in its Harlingen, Texas, plant, the company will be restructuring the production line of 320 people into teams of 15 or more workers.

Some employees feel the new agreement begins a new age of trust and cooperation between their union and their employer; other workers are more suspicious of the new cozy relationship between management and the union.

[SOURCE: Adapted from Josh Lemieux, "Hopes Set on Levi Strauss, Union Pact," *Bryan-College Station Eagle* (October 16, 1994), p. C3.]

a. Why might unionization constrain the successful implementation of quality-oriented programs in manufacturing plants?

b. What are the ethical obligations of management to workers in implementing quality programs?

c. What ethical obligations do employees bear in implementing new programs devised by managers?

■ PROJECTS

58. Find out if any company in your area has recently adopted JIT. If so, discuss with a representative of the company the benefits that the company expected to derive from the system and the benefits that the company has actually realized thus far. Also ask the representative to discuss the implementation plan, including any major problems that were encountered.

59. (*Implementing JIT*) You have been employed for two years by the Wm. Pickering Dental Tools Company. The president, Bill Pickering, has called you into his office to ask you to prepare a brief report on what JIT manufacturing is about.

The company has been experiencing increased difficulty in meeting competitors' prices and quality in recent years and Pickering has heard that JIT manufacturing should be considered.

a. Prepare a brief report describing JIT in such situations.

b. After reading your report, Mr. Pickering asks you to prepare another report recommending ways in which the firm can implement JIT. Choose several members of your class to act as a team and prepare this report for presentation to the other class members.

60. Select a large publicly-traded company that has adopted JIT. It is common for companies to adopt JIT and other quality-oriented programs and philosophies simultaneously. Identify the date on which the company began to adopt such initiatives. Obtain copies of the public financial statements of this company several years prior to and several years subsequent to the adoption date. Write a report that answers the following questions:

a. How has the adoption affected apparent profitability of the company?

b. How has the adoption affected the level of inventories of finished goods carried by the company?

c. How has the adoption affected the level of raw and in-process inventories carried by the company?

d. Identify one (or more) of the firm's suppliers that is also publicly traded. To investigate the effects of the customer's adoption of JIT, answer the preceding three questions for the supplier firm.

61. Read and prepare reports on two books: *The Goal* by Eliyahu M. Goldratt, and *The Race* by Jeff Cox and Robert Fox.

14 CAPITAL ASSET SELECTION AND CAPITAL BUDGETING

Which of you, intending to build a tower, sitteth not down first and counteth the cost.

Luke 14:28, c. A.D. 80

LEARNING OBJECTIVES

1. Understand how managers choose capital budgeting projects.

2. Recognize why most capital budgeting methods use cash flows.

3. Differentiate among payback period, the net present value method, profitability index, and internal rate of return.

4. Understand how the underlying assumptions and limitations of each capital project evaluation method affect its use.

5. Show how taxes and depreciation methods affect cash flows.

6. Explain why managers occasionally need to quantify qualitative information in making capital budgeting decisions.

7. Understand how and why management should conduct a post-investment audit of a capital project.

8. (Appendix 1) Use the time value of money concept.

9. (Appendix 2) Determine the accounting rate of return for a project.

First Bank Systems: Investing in Technology a Necessity

[First Bank Systems, Inc. is a regional bank holding company that is headquartered in Minneapolis and primarily serves Minnesota, Colorado, Montana, North and South Dakota, and Wisconsin. The bank has grown substantially in size through acquisition but found itself slightly out-of-date relative to equipment.] "Our DDA [demand deposit account] system was circa 1960. Our installment loan system was circa 1959. Our basic customer information system was 1964. We had an on-line savings system that was 20 years old, and we had an archaic lobby system," said Philip G. Heasley, vice chairman and president of the retail product group. [So] First Bank has invested $250 million in technology to upgrade or replace virtually every [management information] system.

All of First Bank's 181 branches now use Hogan Systems Inc.'s software for deposit accounting. The bank has gone from a handful of personal computers at banking offices—personnel previously used "dumb" terminals connected to a mainframe—to more than 8,000 PCs bankwide.

First Bank's automatic teller machine (ATM) network has expanded rapidly, from about 100 to more than 1,000. The bank is installing a new customer information file system that officials say will be up and running by early 1995. And imaging technology has been installed at the mortgage company.

To house the new technology, the bank opened an operations center and consolidated its customer phone centers into two locations.

"At the same time, we built a mailing capability" linked to a customer data base that runs profitability models, said Heasley. First Bank now generates about 2.2 million pieces of direct mail each month.

"The technology allows us to do a lot of stratifying of the customer base," Chairman and Chief Executive John Grundhofer said, adding that the bank is segmenting its customers into demographic categories.

SOURCE: Jeffrey Zack, "Technology Gives First Bank's Grundhofer a Cost-Cutting Edge," *American Banker's Management Strategies* (May 9, 1994), p. 8A.

W hy did First Bank spend millions of dollars to invest in technology? According to Philip Heasley, the investment was necessary for one reason: "Technology is helping us be more productive. That's good for our customers, our employees and, ultimately, our shareholders."[1] But how did the bank decide what type of deposit accounting software to select, which ATM machines to purchase, and whether the mailing capability was a reasonable expenditure? Such choices illustrate just a few of the kinds of capital budgeting decisions that managers must make.

One of the most important and basic tasks managers face is choosing the investments that the firm will make. Investments are made in short-term working capital assets (such as inventory) and in long-term **capital assets**, which are used to generate revenues or cost savings. Capital assets provide production, distribution, or service capabilities lasting more than one year. Capital assets may be tangible, such as machinery and buildings, or intangible, such as capital leases and patents. In 1994, it was estimated that companies would spend $634 billion on investments in buildings and equipment, an increase of more than 8 percent over 1993's $586 billion.[2]

The computers purchased by First Bank are tangible assets that make employees' jobs easier and customer service faster. For example, the new technology gave the

capital assets

[1]"Technology at the Heart of Integration," *(First Bank's) Direction* (November 1993), p. 12.

[2]"Companies Upgrading in Spite of Interest Rise," *Austin American Statesman* (June 10, 1994), p. F1.

bank the ability to develop a market-segmented data base of customers who might be candidates for home equity loans. A mail campaign was directed at these individuals; and when customers called in, the technology allowed employees to take applications over the phone and let customers know immediately whether they qualified for the loans. The data base and the rapid response time would not have been possible under the previous information system.

Capital asset acquisition decisions involve long-term commitments of large amounts of money. Managers typically find that the availability of projects that meet investment criteria exceeds the availability of resources. Making the most economically beneficial investments within resource constraints is critical to the organization's long-range well-being. Capital budgeting techniques are designed to enhance mangement's success in making capital investment decisions.

This chapter presents four basic methods used to analyze capital projects: payback period, net present value, profitability index, and internal rate of return. Also covered in the chapter are some complexities of acquiring automated equipment, the need to include qualitative information in decision making, and the desirability of post-investment audits. Appendix 1 discusses some basic concepts about the time value of money, and Appendix 2 discusses the accounting rate of return.

THE INVESTMENT DECISION

Capital budgeting is the process of evaluating long-range investment proposals for the purpose of allocating limited resources effectively and efficiently. The future activities, referred to as **projects**, typically include the purchase, installation, and operation of a capital asset. However, capital investment decisions are not restricted to purchases of fixed assets and construction of buildings. Any decision that will involve long-term assets, such as expanding a plant or instituting cost reduction efforts, is an investment decision.

Management must identify the investments that will best support the firm as it works to fulfill its goals and objectives. This process requires answers to the following four basic questions.

capital budgeting

projects

■ LEARNING
OBJECTIVE 1
Understand how managers choose capital budgeting projects.

Is the Activity Worth the Required Investment?

Companies acquire assets that have value relative to specific organizational activities. For example, banks acquire security systems because they are important in safeguarding funds. Before making decisions to acquire assets, company management must be certain that the activity for which the assets will be needed is worth the required investment.

Management initially measures an activity's worth by monetary cost/benefit analysis. If an activity's financial benefits exceed its costs, the activity is, to that extent, considered worthwhile. In some cases, however, benefits cannot be measured in terms of money. In other cases, it is known in advance that the financial benefits will not exceed the costs. An activity meeting either of these criteria may still be judged worthwhile for some qualitative reasons.

For instance, a bank may decide to invest in an ATM for a college campus. Bank management may not be able to measure the monetary benefits of the ATM objectively but may believe it is worth the cost because it provides access to a large market segment. Another example is a rural hospital that invests in a kidney dialysis machine although there are only a few kidney patients in the area. Hospital administrators may believe the goodwill generated by such an acquisition justifies the cost. If an activity is deemed worthwhile, the question of cost may become secondary.

Providing customers the opportunity to transact banking business is essential to First Bank's operations. Bank management recognized that this activity could be provided by the installation of automatic teller machines rather than incurring costs for full-scale branch offices throughout its operating area.

Which Assets Can Be Used for the Activity?

Determining the assets for conducting the intended activity is closely related to determining the activity's worth. Management must have an idea of how much the needed assets will cost to determine if the activity should be pursued. Thus, managers should gather both monetary and nonmonetary information about each available and suitable asset. As shown in Exhibit 14–1, this information includes initial cost, estimated life and salvage value, raw material and labor requirements, operating costs (both fixed and variable), output capability, service availability and cost, maintenance expectations, and revenues to be generated (if any).

Of the Suitable Assets, Which Are the Best Investments?

Using all available information, management should select the best asset from all the candidates (or the best asset from each of the different groups) and exclude all others

■ **EXHIBIT 14–1**
Capital Investment Information

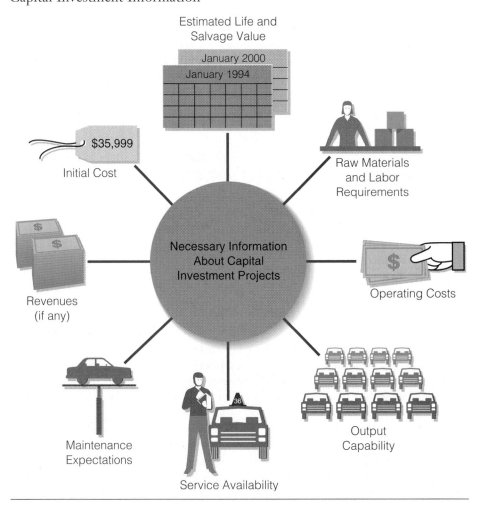

from consideration. Deciding which assets are the best investments requires the use of one or more of the evaluation techniques discussed later in the chapter.

In judging the acceptability of capital projects, managers should recognize that there are two types of capital budgeting decisions: screening and preference. A **screening decision** indicates whether a capital project is desirable based on some previously established minimum criterion or criteria. If the project does not meet the minimum standards, it is excluded from further consideration. Once unacceptable projects have been screened out, a **preference decision** is made in which the remaining projects are ranked based on their contributions to the achievement of company objectives.

Many companies set up ranking categories such as those shown in Exhibit 14–2. Projects are first screened and placed into an appropriate category. Within each category, projects are ranked according to some established criterion or criteria. Resources are then allocated to projects in a top-to-bottom fashion. Management's goal should be to fund those projects that, within budget constraints, will maximize shareholder wealth over the long run.

A company may use one set of techniques to screen projects as to acceptability and another set to rank the projects in order of preference. The method of choosing tech-

screening decision

preference decision

■ **EXHIBIT 14–2**
Ranking Categories for Capital Projects

CATEGORY 1—REQUIRED BY LEGISLATION

Includes items such as pollution control equipment that has been mandated by law. Most companies can ill afford the fines or penalties that can be assessed if the required equipment is not installed; however, these capital acquisitions may not meet the company's minimum established criteria.

CATEGORY 2—ESSENTIAL TO OPERATIONS

Includes capital assets without which the primary functions of the organization could not continue. This category could include purchases of new capital assets or replacements of broken or no longer usable assets. For example, the purchase of a kiln for a ceramics manufacturer would fall into this category.

CATEGORY 3—NONESSENTIAL BUT INCOME GENERATING

Includes capital assets that would improve organizational operations by providing cost savings or supplements to revenue. Robots in an automobile manufacturing plant would be included in this group.

CATEGORY 4—OPTIONAL IMPROVEMENTS

Includes capital assets that do not provide any cost savings or additional revenue but would make operations run more smoothly or make working conditions better. The purchase of computer hardware or software that is faster than that currently being used and the installation of a microwave oven in the employees' lounge would be included here.

CATEGORY 5—MISCELLANEOUS

Includes "pet projects" that might be requested. Such acquisitions may benefit a single individual and not the whole organization. The projects may not even be related to organizational objectives. The installation of new carpeting in a manager's office might be an example. Items in this category will normally be chosen only when the organization has substantial unencumbered resources at its disposal.

niques to be used for screening and ranking varies among companies. Additionally, most large companies have committees to discuss, evaluate, and approve capital projects. In small companies, the owner-managers may simply decide on capital projects.

Which of the "Best Investments" Should the Company Choose?

Although many worthwhile investments exist, resources at any given time are limited. Therefore, after choosing the best asset for each activity, management must decide which activities and assets to fund. Investment projects may be classified as mutually exclusive, independent, or mutually inclusive.

mutually exclusive projects

Mutually exclusive projects are alternative projects that perform the same basic task. When one project is selected from the group, all others will be rejected, as they would provide unneeded or redundant capability. Asset replacement decisions are mutually exclusive projects. If the company keeps the old asset, it will not buy the new one; if the new one is purchased, the old one will be sold. The accompanying News Note discusses decisions at some airlines to repair rather than replace.

independent projects

Other potential investments are **independent projects** in that they have no specific bearing on one another. For instance, acquiring a microcomputer system is not related to purchasing an automated teller machine. Each project is analyzed and accepted or rejected on its own merits. While limited resources may preclude the acquisition of all acceptable projects, the projects are not mutually exclusive.

mutually inclusive projects

Management may be considering certain investments that are all related to a primary project, or are **mutually inclusive**. In this situation, if the primary project is chosen, all related projects are also selected. Alternatively, rejection of the primary project requires rejection of the other related projects. For instance, when First Bank selected the Integrated Banking Application (IBA)/Hogan as the primary information system, that choice dictated the acquisition and installation of miles of cable and wire to network the system to all First Bank locations.

Exhibit 14–3 shows a typical investment decision process. To assure that capital funds are invested in the best projects available, managers must carefully evaluate all projects and decide which ones represent the most effective and efficient use of resources—a difficult determination. The evaluation process should consider and rank projects based on business activity priorities, project risk, and project cash flows.

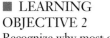

CASH FLOWS

LEARNING OBJECTIVE 2
Recognize why most capital budgeting methods use cash flows.

Every investment is expected to earn some type of return. The amount of the return allows analysts to equate an investment in a bank (a savings account or a certificate of deposit), an investment in marketable securities (bonds or stocks), and an investment in an operating asset. In each case, money is spent and money (cash interest, cash dividends, or cash generated from use) is hopefully returned. Information on the cash generated from asset use is *not* available from the income statement because it reflects accrual-based revenues and expenses—not all of which may currently be in cash.

cash flows

Cash flows are cash receipts and cash disbursements that arise from the purchase, operation, and disposition of capital assets. Cash receipts include project revenues that have been earned and collected, savings generated by reduced project operating costs, and inflows from the asset's sale and release of working capital at the end of the asset's useful life. Cash disbursements include expenditures to acquire the asset, additional working capital investments, and amounts paid for related operating costs.

Interest is a cash flow created by the method of financing a project and should not be considered in project evaluation. The funding of projects is a financing, not an

It's Cheaper, But Is It Less Expensive?

Hundreds of old U.S. jetliners are battling repeated breakdowns and excessive wear, but some of these aging planes aren't heading for the hangar. Instead, they will be flying for another decade or more, raising serious questions about maintenance and inspection procedures. Pummeled by years of losses, airlines of every size are holding back on new-jet purchases and stretching the use of their planes years beyond what manufacturers originally intended. Carriers such as Northwest Airlines Corp. and USAir Group Inc. are planning to let some planes fly to their 30th birthdays or longer.

[In a 1993 report, the General Accounting Office] criticized the Federal Aviation Administration for problems in tracking the nation's aging fleet, and for gaps in surveillance. Among maintenance difficulties facing the airlines: meeting new federal noise standards. In these tough financial times for airlines, replacing an elderly fleet of 90, 50 or even 30 jetliners with new planes is out of the question. The economics of spending $2 million to $3 million to quiet the engines on a 25-year-old plane seems more logical than buying a new one for $35 million.

That, at least, is the thinking at USAir and Northwest. "At a point in time when we are capital-constrained," quieting the engines and continuing to fly the planes seems to be the best way to meet the noise requirements, says Bruce Aubin, USAir's senior vice president, maintenance operations. USAir is retrofitting 24 of its 72 DC-9s—the total fleet's average age is 21.6 years—and says it will decide what to do with the rest soon. Mr. Aubin says the refitted planes will have to fly for several or more years to pay for the improvements.

Northwest says it plans to spend about $3 million per plane for hushkits and for spruced-up interiors. The carrier figures it will spend another $3 million for each jetliner over the next 15 years to replace various systems. Such expenditures will save it $1.4 billion in today's dollars compared with the cost of 100 new jets.

Still, Northwest's DC-9s encountered 218 unscheduled landings; 80 aborted takeoffs; 65 incidents of emergency descent or loss of cabin pressurization; 126 landing-gear malfunctions or false warnings of such problems; 36 complications with wing-slats and indicators; and 74 major engine shutdowns, flameouts or other problems, according to reports filed between January 1992 and August 1994.

Further, mechanics found, repaired and reported 580 occurrences of cracking, corrosion and other age-related problems in the period. By contrast, Northwest's fleet of 50 Airbus Industrie A-320s, with an average age of 2.6 years, had only 29 incidents of cracking and corrosion.

Some are skeptical about the economics of quieting and refurbishing old jets. "To even contemplate a return on investment, you have to commit to fly for another 10 to 15 years," says Bob Baker, executive vice president of operations at American Airlines, which has yet to decide if it will fly older jets into the next century. He adds that "for a company that is capital-starved, it may be a way to stay in business. But that's a short-term view. The long-term view would be that that's financial foolery."

SOURCE: Jeff Cole and Susan Carey, "Airlines Are Keeping Aging Planes Aloft, Testing Repair Rules," *Wall Street Journal* (November 3, 1994), pp. A1, A15. Reprinted by permission of The Wall Street Journal, © 1994 Dow Jones & Company, Inc. All Rights Reserved Worldwide.

investing, decision, and cash flows of the two types of decisions should not be combined. A **financing decision** is a judgment regarding what method of raising funds will be used to make an acquisition. Financing is based on the entity's ability to issue and service debt and equity securities. In contrast, **investing decisions** are judgments

financing decision

investing decision

■ **EXHIBIT 14–3**

Typical Investment Decision Process

Activity—Provide capability to calculate monetary statistics for life insurance policies (premium payments, cash surrender values, loan values, and so on) for insurance company staff of 25 persons

1. Is the activity worth an investment?
   Yes; this decision is based on the fact that such computational ability is essential to operating an insurance company.
2. Which assets can be used for the activity?

   Available: Desk calculators, stand-alone microcomputers, an LAN (local-area network). of microcomputers, microcomputers on-line with the company's preexisting mainframe
   Infeasible: Desk calculators, because of the time required by staff to look up required information.
   Feasible: Various types of stand-alone microcomputers to purchase (assume asset options A through H); various LAN configurations to purchase (assume options K through P); various on-line to mainframe micros to purchase (assume options X through Z); leasing arrangements for each option above (assume options 1 through 17); current office equipment.
   Gather all relevant quantitative and qualitative information on feasible assets (A–H; K–P; X–Z; current equipment).

3. Which assets are the best investments?
   Compare all relevant information and choose the best asset candidate from the purchase group (assume asset M) and the lease group (assume asset 11).
4. Which investment should the company make?
   Compare the best asset candidate from the purchase group with the best candidate from the lease group; this represents a mutually exclusive project decision. The best candidate is found to be the purchase of asset M. Compare the costs and benefits of purchasing asset M with those of keeping currently owned equipment; this is a mutually exclusive project relating to a replacement decision. The best choice is to sell the currently owned office equipment and purchase a LAN of 25 asset M microcomputers.

about which assets will be acquired by an entity to achieve its stated objectives. Company management must justify the acquisition and use of an asset before justifying the method of financing that asset.

Cash flows from a capital project are received and paid at different times in a project's life. Some cash flows occur at the beginning of a period (for example, a payment on a leased asset) and some at the end (for example, a payment on a mortgaged asset). Although many cash flows occur during the period, analysts simplify reality by assuming that flows occur either at the beginning or the end of the period during which they actually occur. Assumed end-of-period cash flows include inflows provided by contribution margins from product sales and outflows for repair expenditures and property taxes on the capital asset.

A distinction must be made between cash flows representing a return *of* capital and those representing a return *on* capital. A **return of capital** is simply recovery of the original investment, while a **return on capital** represents income. The return on capital is computed for each investment period and is equal to the interest included in the receipt or payment. An investment makes a company better off only when, over the life of the investment, it produces cash inflows greater than the investment made plus the cost of the capital used to acquire it.

return of capital
return on capital

The calculation of cash flows is illustrated by the following example. Minehead National Bank is considering the purchase of a coin-sorting machine. Basic data about the asset appear in Exhibit 14–4. This detailed information can be simplified into two basic cash flows: a net negative flow representing the initial expenditure for the acquisition and a net positive flow representing the net annual labor and energy cost savings from the use of the machine less the annual repair and maintenance costs. The savings provided by the sorter are not truly *new* cash inflows into the bank (as would occur with the sale of a product, for example). The savings do, however, represent a decrease in cash outflows—an equally beneficial situation.

Note that depreciation is excluded in these cash flow computations. Depreciation is not a cash flow item; it is important in capital budgeting only to the extent that it reduces the amount of taxable income. Income taxes and the related depreciation effect are important elements in capital budgeting analysis, but add unnecessary complexities at this point. These elements are discussed later in the chapter.

One helpful tool for analyzing cash flows is a **timeline**, which illustrates the timing of expected cash receipts and payments. On a timeline, cash inflows are shown as positive amounts and cash outflows are shown as negative amounts.

timeline

The following timeline represents the cash flows from Minehead National's potential equipment purchase. Although individual cash flows can be shown in a timeline, it is easier to use net cash flows. Thus, only two types of cash flows are shown below: the net negative flow for the acquisition and the net positive flow produced each year by the savings. The equal annual cash flows are called an **annuity**.

annuity

TIME:	t0	t1	t2	t3	t4	t5	t6	t7	t8
AMOUNT:	−$60,000	+$9,200	+$9,200	+$9,200	+$9,200	+$9,200	+$9,200	+$9,200	+$9,200

On a timeline, the acquisition date represents time point 0. Each year thereafter is represented as a full time period. Periods only serve to separate the times at which

---

■ **EXHIBIT 14–4**
Coin Sorter Acquisition Decision

Purchase price of coin sorter: $62,000 (10% cash discount)
Installation costs: $8,000
Sales price of old coin sorter: $3,800

Purchase price of new coin sorter	$(62,000)
Less discount (10%)	6,200
Cash cost of new coin sorter	$(55,800)
Installation costs	(8,000)
Total cash outflows for new coin sorter	$(63,800)
Less sales price of old coin sorter	3,800
Net actual cash outflow for new coin sorter	$(60,000)

Annual labor and energy savings generated by new coin sorter: $9,500
Annual repairs and maintenance: $300

Savings per year	$ 9,500
Less repairs and maintenance	(300)
Net actual cash inflow (benefit) from new coin sorter	$ 9,200

Life of new coin sorter: 8 years; no salvage value

flows occur. Nothing is presumed to happen *during* a period. Thus, for example, the net savings provided by the machine each year are shown as occurring at the end of, rather than during, the time period. A less conservative assumption would show the cash flows occurring at the beginning of the period.

PAYBACK PERIOD

payback period

■ LEARNING
OBJECTIVE 3
Differentiate among payback period, the net present value method, profitability index, and internal rate of return.

The information on the timing of net cash flows is an input to a simple and often-used capital budgeting analysis technique called **payback period**. This method provides a measure of the time it will take a project's cash inflows to equal the original investment. At the end of the payback period, a company has recouped its investment.

In one sense, payback period measures a dimension of project risk by focusing on timing of cash flows. The assumption is that the longer it takes to recover the initial investment, the greater is the project's risk, because cash flows in the more distant future are more uncertain than near-team cash flows. Another reason for concern about long payback periods relates to capital reinvestment. The faster capital is returned from an investment, the more rapidly it can be invested in other projects.

When a project provides an annuity cash inflow, the payback period equals the investment cost divided by the amount of the projected annuity inflow. The payback period for Minehead National's coin sorter is approximately 6 ½ years ($60,000 ÷ $9,200).

To determine the payback period for a project having unequal cash inflows, it is necessary to accumulate the projected cash flows until the original investment is recovered. For instance, consider a project costing $58,000 and providing the following cash flows over its life:

YEAR	AMOUNT
1	$12,000
2	18,000
3	22,000
4	24,000
5	16,000
6	5,000

A yearly cumulative total of the above inflows is prepared:

YEAR	AMOUNT	CUMULATIVE TOTAL
1	$12,000	$ 12,000
2	18,000	30,000
3	22,000	52,000
4	24,000	76,000
5	16,000	92,000
6	5,000	97,000

At the end of the first three years, $52,000 has been received, and $6,000 more is needed to recover the original $58,000 investment. If the $24,000 inflow in the fourth year is assumed to occur evenly throughout the year, it should take 25 percent ($6,000 ÷ $24,000) of the fourth year to recover the rest of the original investment, giving a payback period for this project of three years and three months.

Company management typically sets a maximum acceptable payback period as part of its evaluation of capital projects. Most companies use payback period as only one of several ways of judging an investment project—usually as a screening technique.

Normally, after being found acceptable in terms of payback period, a project is subjected to evaluation by another capital budgeting technique. This second evaluation is performed because the payback period method ignores three important considerations: inflows occurring after the payback period has been reached; the company's desired rate of return; and the time value of money. These issues are incorporated into the decision process by use of discounted future cash flow values.

DISCOUNTED CASH FLOW METHODS

Money has a time value because interest is paid or received on funds.[3] For example, $1,000 received today has greater value than the same sum received one year from today because that money can be invested at an interest rate that will cause it to accumulate to more than $1,000 by the end of one year. This fact encourages the use of discounted cash flow techniques in most capital budgeting situations.

    Discounting future cash flows means reducing them to their present values by removing the portion representing interest. This "imputed" interest amount is based on two considerations: the timing of receipts or payments and the assumed interest rate. After discounting, all future values are stated in a common base of current dollars. Thus, managers can view all project amounts in terms of their **present values (PVs).** Cash flows occurring at the beginning of a project are already stated at their present values and do not need to be discounted.

discounting

present values (PVs)

    Since current expenditures (such as initial project investment) are undiscounted in the capital budgeting process, it is extremely important for managers to obtain the best possible information about these cash flows. Next, the amounts and timing of future cash inflows and outflows must be carefully estimated. Managers need to consider all future cash flows—those that are obvious and those that might be hidden, as indicated in the News Note on page 716. Companies installing computer systems, for example, find that the most expensive costs are those that are not readily apparent: supplies, support, training, maintenance, and opportunity costs.

    To appropriately discount the future cash flows, managers must estimate the rate of return on capital required by the company. This rate of return is called the **discount rate** and is used to determine the imputed interest portion of future cash receipts and expenditures. The discount rate should equal or exceed the company's **cost of capital (COC),** which is the weighted average rate for the costs of the various sources of funds (debt and stock) that comprise a firm's capital structure.[4] For example, a company with a COC of 10 percent pays an annual average of 10 percent on each capital dollar to finance investment projects. To determine if a capital project is a worthwhile investment, this company should generally use a *minimum* rate of 10 percent to discount the project's future cash flows.

discount rate

cost of capital (COC)

---

[3]Time value of money and present value computations are reviewed in Appendix 1 of this chapter. These concepts are essential to your understanding of the rest of the chapter; be certain they are clear to you before continuing.

[4]Some managers believe the discount rate should reflect the opportunity cost of capital, which is the highest rate of return that could be earned by using capital for the most attractive alternative project available. Using the opportunity cost of capital to discount project cash flows reflects the benefits that could have been realized from the foregone opportunity. Use of this rate has theoretical merit, but its application is generally not feasible. Therefore, most companies use the overall cost of capital as the discount rate. The computations involved in calculating the cost of capital are covered in finance textbooks and are beyond the scope of this text.

In Evaluating Projects, Make Sure All Costs Are Considered

When Jefferson Parish bought an 18-acre abandoned barrel factory in 1991 for $800,000, some officials boasted the parish pulled off the real estate deal of the century. Two years later, critics say the deal has gone sour. Since buying the sprawling 1930s vintage factory for storage space, the parish has spent an additional $800,000 on the property. That includes $335,000 on engineering fees and $226,000 to remove hazardous materials from the site.

Despite all the money spent on it, most of the complex is not being used because its roof and walls are riddled with asbestos. The parish plans to seek bids to remove and replace the roof and walls and renovate 10,000 square feet of office space—a job that is expected to cost about $1.6 million.

[One estimate of the complex's worth after renovation is $5+ million,] nearly $2 million more than the parish will spend. . . . [The complex] will allow the parish to consolidate all of its sewerage and drainage operations. It will also provide space for the parish's central garage. A shortage of storage space [currently] forces the parish to keep much of its equipment outdoors, reducing its life.

SOURCE: Kim Chatelain, "Jeff Factory Purchase Has Problems," *[New Orleans] Times-Picayune* (July 31, 1993), p. A1. © The Times-Picayune Publishing Company.

Three discounted cash flow techniques are the net present value method, the profitability index, and the internal rate of return. These methods are discussed and illustrated in the following subsections.

Net Present Value Method

net present value method

The **net present value method** uses discounted cash flows to determine if the rate of return on a project is equal to, higher than, or lower than the desired rate of return. While the cost of capital is generally the minimum desired rate of return, that rate may not be used to discount cash flows from all projects. Different types of projects may be viewed differently by management; and the COC rate may be adjusted up or down to yield a discount rate that helps to compensate for dissimilar underlying factors in investment projects.

For instance, managers in multinational organizations may calculate all domestic projects at the COC rate but use a higher rate for international investments. The higher rate might help to compensate for the greater risks involved in those projects, such as foreign exchange fluctuations and potential political intervention. Managers may also raise or lower the COC rate to compensate for qualitative factors. For instance, an investment in high-technology equipment that would provide a strategic advantage over competitors might be discounted at a rate lower than the COC. This lower rate would provide higher present values for the cash flows and make it easier for such a project to be selected as a viable candidate for funding.

net present value (NPV)

In the net present value method, each cash flow is discounted based on the rate of return specified by the company. A project's **net present value (NPV)** is the difference between the present values of all its cash inflows and cash outflows.

The possible purchase of a mobile automatic teller machine (ATM) by Minehead National Bank is used to illustrate the computation of net present value. The traveling ATM (nicknamed Adam) is a security-intensive vehicle that can be driven to various sites in Minehead National's service area for special events such as football games, concerts, and parades. Since Minehead's service area is a popular tourist destination, the majority of people using Adam will be from out of town and will be charged a processing fee for usage. Additionally, Adam will provide a higher degree of service for Minehead National's own customers because it will offer them increased access to ATM services. Further, the investment will mean Minehead does not have to expend funds to place permanent ATMs at locations that only experience high traffic at certain times. Exhibit 14–5 on the next page presents information and net present value calculations, assuming an 8 percent discount rate, related to Minehead National's prospective investment in Adam.

The ATM's net present value to Minehead National is a positive $124,750. NPV represents the net cash benefit or cost to a company acquiring and using the investment asset. Applying this criterion, whenever the NPV is zero or greater, the project is acceptable on a quantitative basis. If the NPV is zero, the actual rate of return on the project is equal to the desired rate of return. If NPV is positive, the actual rate is greater than the desired rate. If NPV is negative, the actual rate is less than the desired rate of return. If all estimates are correct, the ATM being considered by Minehead National Bank will provide a return of over 8 percent. The exact rate of return is not determined by the net present value method unless the NPV happens to be exactly equal to zero.

Had Minehead National Bank used any rate other than 8 percent in conjunction with the same basic facts, a different net present value would have resulted. For example, if the bank had set 12 percent as the discount rate, a negative $197,308 NPV would have resulted for the project, as shown in Exhibit 14–6 at the bottom of page 719. This exhibit also gives net present values at other selected discount rates.

As Exhibit 14–6 indicates, the NPV is sensitive to the assumptions made. Net present value is a function of several factors. First, changing the discount rate while holding the amounts and timing of cash flows constant affects the NPV. Increasing the discount rate causes the NPV to decrease; decreasing the discount rate causes the

In determining the feasibility of an investment in an amusement park, estimates of the future cash flows from ticket, concession, and souvenir sales were compared with estimates of costs for park operations, maintenance, and working capital requirements (such as inventory). These cash inflows and outflows were then discounted to their present values using Knott's Berry Farm owners' desired rate of return.

NPV to increase.[5] Second, any changes in the estimated amounts or timing of cash inflows and outflows affect the net present value of a project. The effects on the NPV of cash flow changes depend on the nature of the changes themselves. For example,

---

■ **EXHIBIT 14–5**
Purchase of Mobile ATM

Discount rate: 8%

CASH OUTFLOWS:

Cost of machinery (now)	$1,700,000
Cost of maintenance (end of 3rd year)	10,000
Cost of maintenance (end of 7th year)	16,000

CASH INFLOWS:

Fees generated per transaction	$1.00	
Cash costs per transaction	− .20	
Cash contribution margin per transaction	$ .80	
Number of estimated transactions per year	× 300,000	
Total cash contribution margin per year for 10 years		$240,000
Salvage value (end of 10th year)		500,000

TIMELINE

t0	t1	t2	t3	t4	t5	t6	t7
−$1,700,000	+$240,000	+$240,000	+$240,000	+$240,000	+$240,000	+$240,000	+$240,000
			−$ 10,000				−$ 16,000

t8	t9	t10
+$240,000	+$240,000	+$240,000
		+$500,000

NPV CALCULATION #1:

Period	Item		Present Value
t 0	Cost: −$1,700,000 × 1.000		−$1,700,000
t 1	Contribution margin: +$240,000 × .9259 [8%; year 1]	+	222,216
t 2	Contribution margin: +$240,000 × .8573 [8%; year 2]	+	205,752
t 3	Contribution margin − Maintenance:		
	(+$240,000 − $10,000) × .7938 [8%; year 3]	+	182,574
t 4	Contribution margin: +$240,000 × .7350 [8%; year 4]	+	176,400
t 5	Contribution margin: +$240,000 × .6806 [8%; year 5]	+	163,344
t 6	Contribution margin: +$240,000 × .6302 [8%; year 6]	+	151,248
t 7	Contribution margin − Maintenance:		
	(+$240,000 − $16,000) × .5835 [8%; year 7]	+	130,704
t 8	Contribution margin: +$240,000 × .5403 [8%; year 8]	+	129,672
t 9	Contribution margin: +$240,000 × .5003 [8%; year 9]	+	120,072
t10	Contribution margin + Salvage:		
	(+$240,000 + $500,000) × .4632 [8%; year 10]	+	342,768
	Net present value	+	$ 124,750

(Exhibit 14–5 continued on next page)

---

[5]As the interest rate is increased, fewer dollars of investment are needed to obtain the same ultimate outcome over the same time period, because more interest is earned.

(Exhibit 14-5 continued)

ALTERNATIVELY

NPV CALCULATION #2:

Cost: −$1,700,000 × 1.000	− $1,700,000
Contribution margin: +$240,000 × 6.7101 [8%; 10 year annuity]	+ 1,610,424
Maintenance: −$10,000 × .7938 [8%; year 3]	− 7,938
Maintenance: −$16,000 × .5835 [8%; year 7]	− 9,336
Salvage: +$500,000 × .4632 [8%; year 10]	+ 231,600
Net present value	+ $ 124,750

Note: The factors used to compute the net present values are obtained from the present value tables provided in Appendix C at the end of the text. The first NPV computation uses the net cash flows for each period; the second shows each individual cash flow. NPVs for lump-sum cash flows use a factor from Table 1 (PV of $1) for 8 percent and the appropriate number of years designated for the cash flow. For example, the first maintenance cost amount uses the factor for the third period, while salvage value uses the factor for the tenth period. In the second NPV calculation, the annuities for each period use factors from Table 2 in Appendix B. For example, the contribution margin cash flow uses the Table 2 factor at 8 percent for 10 periods.

decreasing the estimate of cash outflows causes NPV to increase; reducing the stream of the cash inflows causes NPV to decrease. When amounts and timing of cash flows change in conjunction with one another, it is impossible to predict the effects of the changes without calculating the results.

While the net present value method does not provide the actual rate of return on a project, it does provide information on how the actual rate compares with the desired rate. This information allows managers to eliminate from consideration any projects on which the rates of return are less than the desired rate.

■ EXHIBIT 14–6
ATM Purchase NPVs from Alternative Discount Rates

Using a 12% discount rate and factors from Tables 1 and 2 in Appendix B

Cost: −$1,700,000 × 1.000	− $1,700,000
Contribution margin: +$240,000 × 5.6502 [12%; 10 year annuity]	+ 1,356,048
Maintenance: −$10,000 × .7118 [12%; year 3]	− 7,118
Maintenance: −$16,000 × .4524 [12%; year 7]	− 7,238
Salvage: +$500,000 × .3220 [12%; year 10]	+ 161,000
Net present value	− $ 197,308

For various other discount rates:

DISCOUNT RATE	NET PRESENT VALUE*
5%	+ $440,149
7%	+ $221,736
10%	− $ 48,270
14%	− $326,430

*To indicate your understanding of the NPV method, you may want to prove these computations.

The NPV method can be used to select the best project when choosing among investments that can perform the same task or achieve the same objective. However, when making investment comparisons, managers must use the same project life span for all projects under consideration. This is necessary because the funds released from a shorter-lived project can be used for another investment, which will generate additional dollars of revenues and create additional dollars of costs.[6]

Additionally, NPV should not be used to compare independent investment projects that do not have approximately the same original asset cost. Such comparisons favor projects having higher net present values over those with lower net present values without regard to the capital invested in the project. Logically, companies should invest in projects that produce the highest return per investment dollar.

Profitability Index

profitability index (PI)

Projects with different costs can be compared by use of a variation of the NPV method known as the **profitability index (PI).** The profitability index is a ratio that compares the present value of net cash inflows with the present value of the net investment. The PI is calculated as follows:

$$PI = \frac{\text{Present Value of Net Future Cash Inflows}}{\text{Present Value of Investment}}$$

The PI for Minehead National Bank's ATM is 1.07, calculated as \$1,824,750 divided by \$1,700,000. The present value of the net future cash inflows is equal to the net present value of \$124,750 plus the investment cost of \$1,700,000.

Although firms sometimes make decisions on a least-cost (rather than most-profit) basis, the general rule for project acceptability when the profitability index is used is that the PI should be equal to or greater than 1.00. Such a PI indicates that the present value of the expected net cash inflows is equal to or greater than the investment cost. Thus, Minehead National would consider the ATM a viable purchase.

The present value of the net future cash inflows represents an output measure of the project's worth. This amount equals the cash benefit provided by the project, or the present value of future cash inflows minus the present value of future cash outflows. The present value of the investment represents an input measure of the project's cost. By relating these two measures, the profitability index gauges the firm's efficiency at using its capital. The higher the index, the more efficient are the firm's capital investments.

In some instances, the NPV and PI methods provide different conclusions as to the relative ranking of projects. For example, the NPV of Project A may be higher than the NPV of Project B, but the PI for Project B may be greater than that for Project A. In such a case, either of two conditions must exist for the PI to provide better information than the NPV.

First, the projects must be mutually exclusive. Accepting one project must require rejecting the other. This condition would be met if, for example, Minehead National were considering the purchase of five ATMs from either AT&T or NCR.

---

[6]If the alternative projects' lives are not equal, they are treated for computational purposes as if they were. For example, if Minehead could purchase the ATM (which has a 10-year life) or lease the ATM for five years, managers could compare the two alternatives either by using only five years of cash flows on the purchase alternative or by assuming that another ATM would be leased for five years at the end of the first lease term. For the latter assumption, managers would make appropriate estimates relating to any cash flows that varied from those of the first five-year period. Computer packages are available to quickly do "what if" (or sensitivity) analysis for such scenarios.

Alternatively, the availability of investment funds must be limited. If Minehead National's total capital budget is $1,800,000, buying the mobile ATM would preclude buying a $1,050,000 corporate plane. But buying the ATM would leave $100,000 that the bank could invest in another capital asset. In this case, the ATM and any alternative projects should be considered as "packaged" investments, and the benefits of each package should be determined and compared.

Like the net present value method, the profitability index does not indicate an investment's expected rate of return. This measure is provided by the project's internal rate of return.

Internal Rate of Return

A project's **internal rate of return (IRR)** is its expected rate of return. The IRR is the discount rate at which the present value of the net future cash inflows minus the present value of the investment equals zero (NPV = 0). This relationship is shown in the following formula:

internal rate of return (IRR)

$$\text{NPV} = -\text{Investment} + \text{PV of cash inflows} - \text{PV of other cash outflows}$$
$$0 = -\text{Investment} + [\text{Cash inflows (PV factor)}] - [\text{Cash outflows (PV factor)}]$$

In evaluating a capital project, managers have information about the investment amount, cash inflows, and cash outflows. Thus, the only missing items in the formula are the present value factors.

When all cash flows after time period 0 comprise an annuity, the NPV formula can be restated as follows:

$$\text{NPV} = -\text{Investment} + \text{PV of annuity}$$
$$0 = -\text{Investment} + (\text{Annuity cash flow} \times \text{PV factor})$$

Determining the internal rate of return involves substituting known amounts (investment and annuity) into the formula, rearranging terms, and solving for the unknown (the present value factor):

$$\text{NPV} = -\text{Investment} + (\text{Annuity} \times \text{PV Factor})$$
$$0 = -\text{Investment} + (\text{Annuity} \times \text{PV Factor})$$
$$\text{Investment} = (\text{Annuity} \times \text{PV Factor})$$
$$\text{Investment} \div \text{Annuity} = \text{PV Factor}$$

The solution yields a present value factor for the number of annuity periods of project life at the internal rate of return. Looking up this factor in an appropriate PV table provides the internal rate of return.

To illustrate, consider the coin sorter described in Exhibit 14–4. The project will cost $60,000 and produce annual net cash inflows of $9,200 for eight years. These values are substituted into the NPV equation, which then is solved for the present value factor.

$$\text{NPV} = -\text{Investment} + (\text{Annuity} \times \text{PV Factor})$$
$$0 = -\$60,000 + (\$9,200 \times \text{PV Factor})$$
$$+\$60,000 = (\$9,200 \times \text{PV Factor})$$
$$+\$60,000 \div \$9,200 = \text{PV Factor}$$
$$6.5217 = \text{PV Factor}$$

The table of present values of an ordinary annuity (Table 2, Appendix C) will provide the internal rate of return. In the table, find the row representing the project's life (in this case, eight periods). Look across the row for the present value factor yielded by the equation, 6.5217. The IRR (or its approximation) is the rate at the top of the column containing the factor. The 6.5217 factor on row 8 falls between the PV factors for 4 percent (6.7327) and 5 percent (6.4632). Interpolation, a computer program, or a programmable calculator gives 4.78 percent as the IRR for this project, if all assumed project information holds true.[7]

When a project does not have equal annual cash flows, finding the IRR involves an iterative trial-and-error process. An initial estimate is made of a rate believed to be close to the IRR, and the NPV is computed. If the resulting NPV is negative, a lower rate is estimated, and the NPV is computed again. If the NPV is positive, a higher rate is tried. This process is continued until the net present value equals zero, at which time the internal rate of return has been found.

Exhibit 14–7 uses data given in Exhibit 14–5 for the Minehead National ATM purchase to demonstrate this process. The ATM investment was previously shown to have an expected rate of return of more than 8 percent (since discounting at that rate resulted in a positive NPV) but less than 12 percent (as shown in Exhibit 14–6). Exhibit 14–7 indicates a first estimate of 9 percent as the IRR for this project, but the NPV is still positive at this discount rate. A second estimate of 9.5 percent is made, resulting in a negative NPV. Thus, the internal rate of return falls between 9 percent and 9.5 percent.

■ EXHIBIT 14–7
Trial-and-Error Determination of IRR for Mobile ATM Purchase

If the initial IRR estimate is 9%, all present value factors are at a 9% rate and the NPV calculation is:

NPV = −Investment + (PV of cash inflows) − (PV of other cash outflows)
  = −$ 1,700,000 + ($240,000 × PV of an annuity factor for 10 periods) +
    ($500,000 X PV of $1 factor at end of 10 periods) − ($10,000 × PV of
    $1 factor at end of 3 periods) − ($16,000 × PV of $1 factor at end of
    7 periods)
  = −$ 1,700,000 + ($240,000 × 6.4177) + ($500,000 × .4224) − ($10,000 × .7722) −
    ($16,000 × .5470)
  = −$ 1,700,000 + $1,540,248 + $211,200 − $7,722 − $8,752
  = + $34,974

Since 9% yields a positive NPV, a higher rate should be tried. The present value factors for a 9.5% rate are attempted next:

NPV = −$ 1,700,000 + ($240,000 × 6.2788) + ($500,000 × .4035) − ($10,000 × .7617) −
    ($16,000 × .5298)
  = −$ 1,700,000 + $1,506,912 + $201,750 − $7,617 − $8,477
  = −$ 7,432

The IRR is between 9% and 9.5%.

---

[7]Interpolation is the process of finding a term between two other terms in a series. The difference in the NPVs at 4 percent and 5 percent is $2,479 [$1,941 − (−$538)]. The interpolation process gives the following computation: Actual rate = 4% + [($1,941 ÷ $2,479)(1.0)]= 4% + (.78)(1.0)= 4.78% (rounded). The 1.0 represents the 1 percent difference between the 4 percent and 5 percent rates.

Once the IRR on a project is known, it is compared with the company's discount rate or a preestablished hurdle rate. A company's **hurdle rate** is the rate of return deemed by management to be the lowest acceptable return on investment. This rate should be at least equal to the cost of capital. It is typically the discount rate used in computing net present value amounts.

hurdle rate

If a project's IRR is equal to or greater than the hurdle rate, the project is considered an acceptable investment. The higher the internal rate of return, the more financially attractive is the investment proposal. In choosing among alternative investments, however, managers cannot look solely at the internal rates of return on projects. The rate does not reflect the dollars involved. An investor would normally rather have a 10 percent return on $1,000 than a 100 percent return on $10!

ASSUMPTIONS AND LIMITATIONS OF METHODS

Each capital budgeting technique has its own underlying assumptions and limitations; these are summarized in Exhibit 14–8 (page 724). To derive the most success from the capital budgeting process, managers should understand the basic similarities and differences of the various methods and use several techniques to evaluate a project.

■ LEARNING OBJECTIVE 4
Understand how the underlying assumptions and limitations of each capital project evaluation method affect its use.

All of the methods share two limitations: (1) they do not consider management preferences about the pattern of cash flows, and (2) they use a single, deterministic measure of cash flow amounts rather than ranges of cash flow values based on probabilities. Management can compensate for the first limitation by subjectively favoring projects whose cash flow profiles better suit organizational preferences, assuming other project factors are equal. The second limitation can be overcome by use of probability estimates of cash flows. These estimates can be input into a computer program to determine a distribution of cash flows for each method under various conditions of uncertainty. As indicated in the News Note on page 726, "fuzzy logic" techniques represent a new way to use computers in this area.

Considering the various assumptions, benefits, and drawbacks of each of the capital budgeting techniques, the results from a 1990 survey shown on page 725 in Exhibit 14–9 are interesting. The same techniques are used worldwide to evaluate the cost/benefit relationships provided by capital projects.

The previous examples of capital budgeting analysis have all ignored one major influence—taxation and its effects on cash flows. This topic is covered in the following section.

THE EFFECT OF TAXATION ON CASH FLOWS

Income taxes are a significant aspect of the business world. Tax planning is a central part of management planning and overall business profitability. Managers should give thorough consideration to the tax implications of all company decisions. In evaluating capital projects, managers should use after-tax cash flows to determine the projects' acceptability. Like interest on debt, depreciation on capital assets is deductible in computing taxable income. As taxable income decreases, so do the taxes that must be paid; thus, cash flow is affected.

■ LEARNING OBJECTIVE 5
Show how taxes and depreciation methods affect cash flows.

Continuously profitable businesses generally find it advantageous to claim depreciation deductions as rapidly as permitted by tax law. As noted earlier, depreciation expense is not a cash flow item. Companies neither pay nor receive any funds for depreciation. However, by reducing the amount of taxable income, depreciation expense becomes a **tax shield** for revenues. The amount of the tax shield depends on

tax shield

■ **EXHIBIT 14–8**
Selected Assumptions and Limitations of Capital Budgeting Methods

ASSUMPTIONS	LIMITATIONS
Payback	
■ Speed of investment recovery is the key consideration ■ Timing and size of cash flows are accurately predicted ■ Risk (uncertainty) is lower for a shorter payback project	■ Ignores cash flows after payback ■ Basic method treats cash flows and project life deterministically without explicit consideration of probabilities ■ Ignores time value of money ■ Cash flow pattern preferences are not explicitly recognized
Net Present Value	
■ Discount rate used is valid ■ Timing and size of cash flows are accurately predicted ■ Life of project is accurately predicted ■ If the shorter-lived of two projects is selected, the proceeds of that project will continue to earn the discount rate of return through the theoretical completion of the longer-lived project	■ Basic method treats cash flows and project life deterministically without explicit consideration of probabilities ■ NPV does not measure expected rates of return on projects being compared ■ Cash flow pattern preferences are not explicitly recognized ■ IRR of project is not reflected
Profitability Index	
■ Same as NPV ■ Size of PV of net inflows relative to size of PV of investment measures efficient use of capital	■ Same as NPV ■ Gives a relative answer but does not reflect dollars of NPV
Internal Rate of Return	
■ Hurdle rate used is valid ■ Timing and size of cash flows are accurately predicted ■ Life of project is accurately predicted ■ If the shorter-lived of two projects is selected, the proceeds of that project will continue to earn the IRR through the theoretical completion of the longer-lived project	■ Projects are ranked for funding based on IRR rather than dollar size ■ Does not reflect dollars of NPV ■ Basic method treats cash flows and project life deterministically without explicit consideration of probabilities ■ Cash flow pattern preferences are not explicitly recognized ■ It is possible to calculate multiple rates of return on the same project
Accounting Rate of Return	
(presented in Appendix 2 to this chapter)	
■ Effect on company accounting earnings relative to average investment in a project is a key consideration ■ Size and timing of investment cost, project life, salvage value, and increases in earnings can be accurately predicted	■ Does not consider cash flows ■ Does not consider time value of money ■ Treats earnings and project life deterministically without explicit consideration of probabilities

■ **EXHIBIT 14–9**

Criteria Used for Investment Justification

Qualitative Factors   *(Percentage of Total Respondents)*

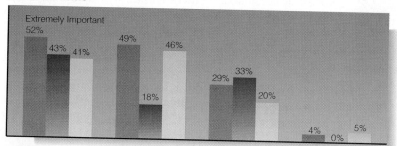

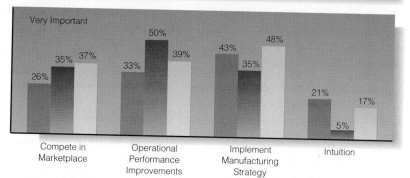

Percentage of total respondents who listed specific qualitative factors as (1) extremely important (2) very important.

Quantitative Factors

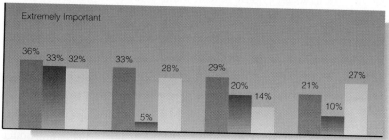

Percentage of total respondents who listed specific qualitative factors as (1) extremely important (2) very important.

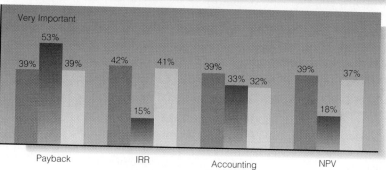

Korea

Japan

U.S.A.

SOURCE: Il-Woon Kim and Ja Song, "U.S., Korea, & Japan: Accounting Practices in Three Countries," *Management Accounting* (August 1990), p. 27. Published by Institute of Management Accountants, Montvale, NJ.

NEWS NOTE

Fuzzy Logic Systems Help Clear Up Uncertainties

The only certainty in business is uncertainty, but managers must make daily decisions on a variety of issues in the face of this uncertainty. Assumptions are combined with historical information, and the resulting data may be analyzed using spreadsheet software. Generally, though, only one assumption per unknown is permitted in spreadsheet models—and most capital budgeting decisions have multiple unknowns.

An alternative to traditional spreadsheet analysis exists in the form of software packages that are based on "fuzzy logic" or "fuzzy set theory." Although fuzzy logic was developed in the United States, the Japanese have been using it since about 1988 to improve the way uncertainties are managed in the engineering and production of electronics. And fuzzy logic software applications are being introduced daily to help improve decision making.

Fuzzy set theory is premised on the assumption that 99.9% of human reasoning is imprecise. Thus, it would seem natural for people to use technologies based on fuzzy set theory for decision making.

With traditional NPV calculations, one value is assigned to each type of cash inflow and outflow included in the model, and all other possible amounts are disregarded. Therefore, the resulting NPV is simply a single estimate of the true discounted present value of this project.

This limitation has been partially overcome by use of sensitivity analysis, in which both best- and worst-case scenarios are prepared with two additional combinations of cash flow numbers. However, if a 10-year project contains 30 variables, each having a range of 20 possible annual outcomes, there are actually 6,000 possible outcome combinations. Making a decision based on three of 6,000 possible outcomes overlooks a lot of useful information.

Fuzzy system software allows each dollar amount within the range of possible outcomes to be assigned a "degree of belief" value ranging from 0 (impossible) to 1 (absolute certainty). The software is then run, and a graph is composed illustrating the range of possibilities of the beliefs about outcomes. Such information can improve both the timeliness and the quality of many management accounting decisions.

SOURCE: Adapted from Peter C. Brewer, Amy W. Gatian, and James M. Reeve, "Managing Uncertainty," *Management Accounting* (October 1993), pp. 39–45. Published by Institute of Management Accountants, Montvale, NJ.

tax benefit

the asset's cost, life, and the depreciation method chosen. The tax shield produces a **tax benefit** equal to the depreciation amount multiplied by the tax rate.

The concepts of tax shield and tax benefit are illustrated on the following income statements. The tax rate is assumed to be 35 percent.

	No Depreciation Deduction		Depreciation Deduction	
	Income Statement		*Income Statement*	
Sales		$1,100,000	Sales	$1,100,000
Cost of goods sold		(450,000)	Cost of goods sold	(450,000)
Gross margin		$ 650,000	Gross margin	$ 650,000
Expenses other than depreciation		(150,000)	Expenses other than depreciation	(150,000)
Depreciation expense		0 ⟷	Depreciation expense	(200,000)
Income before taxes		$ 500,000	Income before taxes	$ 300,000
Tax expense (35%)		(175,000) ⟷	Tax expense (35%)	(105,000)
Net income		$ 325,000	Net income	$ 195,000

TIME	CASH FLOW	10% DISCOUNT FACTOR	PRESENT VALUE
0	$(63,000)	1.0000	$(63,000)
1	25,800	.9091	23,455
2	24,000	.8265	19,836
3	22,714	.7513	17,065
4	21,796	.6830	14,887
5	21,140	.6209	13,126
6	20,671	.5645	11,669
7	26,328	.5132	13,512
		NPV	$ 50,550

Since the NPV is positive, the satellite transmission system will earn a rate higher than the 10 percent discount rate.

The PI for the investment is determined as follows:

PI = Present Value of Net Future Cash Inflows ÷ Present Value of Investment
  = (NPV + Investment) ÷ Present Value of Investment
  = ($50,550 + $63,000) ÷ $63,000
  = $113,550 ÷ $63,000
  = 1.80

This result exceeds 1.00 and, thus, indicates that the investment earns more than the discount rate.

The internal rate of return for the system must exceed 10 percent because there is a positive $50,550 NPV. Because the cash flows are not even each year, a trial-and-error approach to determining the IRR must be used. The following schedule shows that use of an estimated rate of 20 percent results in a fairly large NPV. Thus, the actual rate is above 20 percent.

TIME	CASH FLOW	20% DISCOUNT FACTOR	PRESENT VALUE
0	$(63,000)	1.0000	$(63,000)
1	25,800	.8333	21,499
2	24,000	.6944	16,666
3	22,714	.5787	13,145
4	21,796	.4823	10,512
5	21,140	.4019	8,496
6	20,671	.3349	6,923
7	26,328	.2791	7,348
		NPV	$ 21,589

A programmable calculator indicates that the IRR is 32.25 percent.

The after-tax payback period is found as follows:

YEAR	CASH INFLOWS	CUMULATIVE TOTAL
1	$25,800	$ 25,800
2	24,000	49,800
3	22,714	72,514
4	21,796	94,310
5	21,140	115,450
6	20,671	136,121
7	26,328	162,449

It should take the first two years plus approximately 58 percent of the third year [($63,000 − $49,800) ÷ $22,714] to recover the initial $63,000. The payback period, then, is approximately two years and seven months, which is shorter than the minimum payback period required.

Based solely on quantitative investment criteria, each of the previous techniques indicates that purchasing the satellite transmission system is a viable investment for Minehead National Bank. If the bank has limited funds available, this project should be compared with all acceptable alternative uses of funds to determine which investment or investments would provide the best return to the bank and the most efficient use of resources. Additionally, Minehead National Bank should consider all important qualitative factors, such as customer service issues, before making its investment decision.

HIGH-TECH INVESTMENTS AND QUALITATIVE CONSIDERATIONS

■ **LEARNING OBJECTIVE 6**
Explain why managers occasionally need to quantify qualitative information in making capital budgeting decisions.

One area of business investment in which uncertainty is extremely prevalent is that of high-technology equipment. Some of the most pressing investment decisions currently facing American companies are those related to the purchase of automated and robotic equipment. One estimate is that less than 15 percent of the factory machinery in the United States was computer-controlled as of 1993. The proportion is somewhat higher in Japan, and the difference between the two countries is becoming wider.[8] Thus, in many instances, the decision is more a question of "how much" and "when" than "whether."

High-technology equipment generally requires massive monetary investment. Justification of such equipment must include the numerous advantages from these investments, including significantly reduced labor costs, increased quality and quantity of production, shortened processing time, and increased utility and maintenance costs. Thus, as indicated in the accompanying News Note, significant thought should be given to the investment's tangible benefits (such as increased throughput) and intangible benefits (such as increased customer satisfaction with the quality of products). The grid shown in Exhibit 14–11 (page 732) identifies some of the quantifiable and nonquantifiable benefits of high-tech capital equipment and their association with the short-term (financial) and long-term (strategic) objectives of the organization.

Possible Reasons for Not Investing

Almost all businesses have now automated their office equipment and customer service activities. The 1990s will be a decade of substantially increased investment in factory automation. Companies have been slow to invest in automated factory equipment for several reasons. One reason has been a desire to minimize worker displacement and the corresponding increases in unemployment. A second concern has been morale problems for employees who retain their jobs after some degree of automation has occurred. These employees often feel guilty because they kept their jobs and feel uneasy about learning new skills. Third, after some companies have installed automated equipment, management found that the equipment did not work correctly, was difficult to integrate with nonautomated equipment, or did not do as good a job as humans, or that the operators did not have the appropriate education and training to operate such equipment effectively. A fourth concern is that automat-

---

[8]Edward Faltermayer, "Invest or Die," *Fortune* (February 22, 1993), p. 50.

Assess All Costs and Benefits

The main issue in the economic evaluation of capital equipment that promotes quality is the measurement of the costs and benefits generated from these investments. Traditional accounting systems furnish many of the tangible costs such as repairs and scrap. However, they do not provide any way to measure intangible costs of low quality. Thus, intangible costs must be estimated. These costs, often referred to as hidden quality costs, may be significant and their assessment imperative in spite of the difficulties inherent in this task.

Investment in capital equipment that promotes quality helps reduce both internal failure and external failure costs. The reduction in internal failure costs provides a quantifiable addition to the contribution margin. The reduction in external failure costs also affects sales volume and other intangible factors such as customers' trust and loyalty.

Some of the major costs and benefits of investment in in-line [quality] measurement systems and preventive activities for reducing variation are listed below.

Major costs are:

- Acquisition costs: equipment cost plus costs to transport and install equipment;
- Change in working capital;
- Other costs: training, initial programming, programming labor, maintenance, measurement labor, and process inspection.

Benefits are classified as quantifiable benefits and other benefits. Among the quantifiable benefits are:

- Quicker response to variation problems: The rapid response due to the knowledge base gained from solved problems leads to reduced average cost of manufacturing process problems.
- Reduced production costs: Lower scrap and repair costs result from the early in-process identification of defects.
- Reduced work-in-process and other inventories: Better process control and more stable processes lead to fewer [defects] and lower parts inventory. Less work-in-process results in [less obsolescence from] engineering changes.
- Shorter launch time: Quicker problem solving leads to faster process stabilization, which reduces the average launch time. The shorter launch time reduces the cost of introducing new models.
- Higher uptime and throughput: A stable process allows more uptime that leads to higher production and sales. More uptime also reduces costs due to less overtime and other plant costs.
- Higher quality of supplier parts: The early in-process detection of defects provides quick feedback to supplier of parts for quality improvement.

Other benefits include:

- Lower fatigue and injury-related costs: A controlled and stable process implies fewer crisis situations, so workers remain more alert physically and mentally.
- Higher employee morale: Morale is higher because employees are more involved in monitoring the manufacturing process, which gives them a sense of empowerment.
- Higher customer satisfaction: Customers are satisfied because the finished product is of high quality.

SOURCE: Alahassane Diallo, Zafar U. Khan, and Curtis F. Vail, "Measuring the Cost of Investment in Quality Equipment," *Management Accounting* (August 1994), pp. 34-35. Published by Institute of Management Accountants, Montvale, NJ.

■ **EXHIBIT 14–11**

Characteristics of High-Technology Capital Projects

	QUANTIFIABLE	NON-QUANTIFIABLE
FINANCIAL (shorter-term)	■ Material cost reduction ■ Labor savings ■ Inventory reduction ■ Scrap/waste reduction ■ Increased capacity	■ Setup reduction ■ Elimination of non-value-added activities (moves; inspections) ■ Reduced manufacturing leadtime ■ Reduced administration cycle time ■ Increased plant safety
STRATEGIC (longer-term)	■ Increased flexibility ■ Improved quality ■ Increased market share due to new product/innovation ■ Price premiums due to shorter leadtimes	■ Improved employee morale ■ Improved work environment ■ Ability to attract better employees ■ Better skilled employees ■ Perceived technology leadership by customer ■ Regulatory requirements met

SOURCE: Chris Koepfer, "To Buy or Not to Buy—A New Look at Justifying Capital Equipment," *Modern Machine Shop* (November 1992), p. 72. Used by permission of Modern Machine Shop, Copyright 1992, Gardner Publications Inc., Cincinnati, Ohio USA.

ed equipment is computer-driven. Some senior managers still do not regard computers as competitive assets, because they do not or will not recognize some of the less tangible factors that add to its value as a competitive asset. But probably the most significant reason for not acquiring automated equipment is that it is often difficult, using traditional analyses, to justify the extensive capital investment required.

This mindset is illustrated in the following example. Japan's Yamazaki Manufacturing Company spent $18 million to install a flexible manufacturing system. The number of machines went from 68 to 18; production floor space declined from 103,000 square feet to 30,000; and average processing (throughput) time was reduced from 35 to 1.5 days. But the total savings after two years was only $6.9 million, and $3.9 million of that amount came from a one-time inventory reduction. "Even if the system continued to produce annual labor savings of $1.5 million for 20 years, the project's return would be less than 10% per year."[9] Most American companies would not consider 10 percent to be a reasonable rate of return in spite of the huge savings in fixed assets and time. Additionally, the investment's payback period would extend far beyond the norms set by most firms.

Considerations in High-Tech Investment Analysis

Managers making decisions about investments in automated equipment or equipment that enhances product or process quality should make their capital budgeting analyses carefully. First, the discount or hurdle rate used should be chosen very thought-

---

[9]Robert S. Kaplan, "Must CIM Be Justified by Faith Alone?" *Harvard Business Review* (March-April 1986), p. 87.

Projects Are Evaluated Better in "Bundles"

When Caterpillar embarked on its $1.5 billion worldwide plant modernization program, management realized that the traditional use of IRR or NPV on a project-by-project basis would be too narrow to analyze complex capital investments in synergistic manufacturing plants with just-in-time delivery schedules. To analyze the initial investments in these strategic projects and subsequently track their results, Caterpillar developed a concept called "bundling." At Caterpillar, a bundle is defined as a homogeneous segment of work or product that has common elements. The common elements of a bundle may be size of components, type of components, processes, or location.

A bundle may be a manufacturing process, a commodity, or a new product. A manufacturing bundle is a factory area or minifactory that could be managed on its own. Examples of manufacturing bundles at Caterpillar are a flexible machining and robotic welding system, an assembly line, an integrated heat treating system, and an integrated press shop. Examples of commodity bundles are gears or axles. An axle factory bundle might include gear line and integrated heat treat, wheel and drum line, axle machining line, and axle assembly area. A new product bundle would include all the R&D and new equipment required to produce a new product line.

Focusing on bundles rather than on individual machines or other components of bundles has two main advantages. First, cost and benefits can be identified more easily with bundles than with individual machines or other components in the bundles. For example, it is much easier to relate the benefits of lower work-in-process inventory or reduced throughput time to the axle factory bundle mentioned above than to individual machines in the bundle. Monitoring bundles avoids the arbitrary allocation of costs and benefits to individual components of bundles. Thus, the full impact of the related costs and benefits of capital projects is captured.

Second, bundle monitoring focuses on the strategic marketing and manufacturing goals of the firm. Top management is more interested in the performance of strategic bundles, such as an axle factory bundle, than in the performance of individual machines or other components within the bundle. Bundling encourages the proper evaluation of projects in the context of the total plant plan.

SOURCE: James A. Hendricks, Robert C. Bastian, and Thomas L. Sexton, "Bundle Monitoring of Strategic Projects," *Management Accounting* (February 1992), pp. 31–35. Published by Institute of Management Accountants, Montvale, NJ.

fully. Although interest rates are fairly low at this time, managers often still set hurdle or discount rates between 12 and 18 percent. Such high rates severely penalize capital investments (such as flexible manufacturing systems) that require high initial investments and may take many years to achieve payback.

Second, both the quantitative and qualitative benefits to be provided by all capital expenditures need to be considered, especially high-tech ones. Often, justification of high-tech investments has required a "leap of faith" because of the difficulty of quantifying some of the new key elements of such investment projects.[10] In making investment decisions, management has often assigned a zero dollar value to benefits such

---

[10]Thornton Parker and Theodore Lettes, "Is Accounting Standing in the Way of Flexible Computer-integrated Manufacturing?" *Management Accounting* (January 1991), p. 34.

as quality improvements, shortened delivery time, and improved competitive position because of the difficulty in determining their worth. Some managers do attempt to quantify these qualitative factors in their analyses. The following quote from a professor at England's University of Manchester Institute of Science and Technology discusses such quantification:

> One of the biggest difficulties encountered [in investment justification is that] some of the benefits of advanced manufacturing technology are often considered intangible and—by implication—unquantifiable. But there is no such thing as an intangible benefit: Every benefit that can be identified can be redefined, quantified, and included in an investment appraisal.
>
> Quantifying every benefit is important because it overcomes the main excuse managers have for making investments without an evaluation. More importantly, if some benefits fail to be quantified, the project cannot be correctly reflected in the company's cost system.[11]

A third item to consider in regard to high-tech investments is that such projects are not "free-standing." As discussed in the accompanying News Note, many high-tech investments are interrelated, integrated parts of a whole and should not be viewed as individual projects. The benefits of the "bundled" project are greater than the benefits that would accrue from the individual elements. Consider that after General Motors made a multibillion-dollar investment in robots in the 1980s, the company failed to reengineer factories so the robots could be used to their full potential to produce "different models and innovative designs by the car lot. [Instead, the company simply] wound up using the robots as an inflexible substitute for labor."[12]

Finally, consideration should be given to the opportunity cost of *not* acquiring automated equipment. As indicated in the accompanying News Note regarding a moving "baseline," the opportunity cost of nonautomation refers to the competitive disadvantage a company will experience when its competitors acquire such equipment and experience the qualitative benefits mentioned earlier.

Just six attendants oversee operations in Allen-Bradley's $15 million World Contactor Facility in Milwaukee. The automated assembly line can produce 600 motor starters an hour with up to 999 variations, all with consistent quality. Justifying this expenditure required an analysis of competitive benefits as well as sales figures. Courtesy of Allen-Bradley, a Rockwell International company.

Illustration of High-Tech Investment Analysis

In making capital budgeting decisions, managers should quantify all benefits and costs that can be quantified with any reasonable degree of accuracy. Managers can also attempt to quantify the qualitative benefits using probabilities. The probabilities can be included in calculations of the investment's net present value or internal rate of return. Alternatively, management can simply make subjective evaluations of nonquantifiable items to make certain that those items are properly weighted in the decision model. Exhibit 14–12 (page 736) provides data on a computer system being con-

[11]P. L. Primrose, "Is Anything Really Wrong with Cost Management?" *Journal of Cost Management* (Spring 1992), p. 48. Reprinted with permission from The Journal of Cost Management for the Manufacturing Industry, © 1992, Warren, Gorham & Lamont, 31 St. James Avenue, Boston, MA 02116. All rights reserved.

[12]Rob Norton, "A New Tool to Help Managers," *Fortune* (May 30, 1994), p. 140.

Capital Budgeting Analysis Requires a Moving Baseline

Present value capital expenditure analysis is calculated by summing the present value of future cash returns, discounted at the minimum rate of return. One major fallacy with this procedure is [that it] evaluates cash flows against present industry and firm conditions and assumes that those conditions will remain constant throughout the projected life of the asset or project. Clearly this is not the case. If new equipment is not purchased, present equipment will not continue to produce at a constant level while requiring equivalent maintenance and repair costs. If innovative projects are not initiated by the firm, competitors will initiate similar projects that will change the competitive nature of the industry.

When companies compare numbers generated by net future cash flow with existing conditions, new technology sometimes seems to cost too much for the relatively small labor and material savings the technology affords. Often these projects appear to be associated with only minor improvements in cash flow. However, if a competitor invests in the new technology, the comparison cannot be made with the status quo. Instead, the company must assume that its own cash flow will decline. Indeed, financial justification does not prevent the forecasting of a loss of market share or a decline in profit margins as a result of falling behind in competitive technology.

To assess new technology as it relates to the business environment, a firm must thoroughly evaluate its competitors. Firms such as Caterpillar have realized this requirement and have implemented new systems of competitive cost analysis. These systems emphasize:

- An understanding of the economic conditions and how the competition might react to the environment;
- The financial performance of the competition; and
- The costs of the competition.

SOURCE: David H. Sinason, "A Dynamic Model for Present Value Capital Expenditure Analysis," *Journal of Cost Management* (Spring 1991), p. 40–41. Reprinted with permission from The Journal of Cost Management for the Manufacturing Industry, © 1991, Warren, Gorham & Lamont, 31 St. James Avenue, Boston, MA 02116. All rights reserved.

sidered by Minehead National Bank. The system costs $690,000. Management has set 10 percent as the discount rate to be used and requires a payback period no greater than two-thirds the life of the investment project. Based on these criteria, part A of the exhibit indicates that the system is not an acceptable acquisition. However, Minehead National's marketing vice-president estimates that customer goodwill will increase because of the quickness with which transactions can be processed and loan approvals can be made. A value of $50,000 per year is placed on that intangible benefit. This amount is added to the annual cash flow, and a new net present value and payback period are computed in part B of the exhibit. When an estimated value for the qualitative goodwill benefit is included, the computer system meets Minehead National's selection criteria.

The "hottest" high-tech investments being made by manufacturers are flexible manufacturing systems (FMSs) that use computer-controlled robots to produce numerous high-quality, customized products at very low per-unit costs. The keys to customization are small lot sizes, rapid setup, and a great deal of information; the ability to be flexible is useful only if a company understands its customers and sales market. Salespeople working for companies that have FMSs will soon be able to ask cus-

■ **EXHIBIT 14–12**

Computer System Acquisition

Cost: $690,000
Annual maintenance: $200,000
Life: 5 years

Efficiency: 3 time as efficient as manual system
Manual equivalent of system: 6 operators
Annual salary per operator: $60,000

Part A—Traditional Capital Budgeting Technique

Annual net cash flows of system:

Maintenance	− $200,000
Labor savings ($60,000 × 6)	+ 360,000
Net cash flow	+ $160,000

NPV @ 10% = −$690,000 + ($160,000 × 3.7908) = − $83,472
Payback period = ($690,000 ÷ $160,000) = 4.3 years

Part B—Adjustment for Qualitative Value Added

Estimated value of customer goodwill from increased speed of response time ($50,000 per year) raises "cash flow" to $210,000 annually

NPV @ 10% = −$690,000 + ($210,000 × 3.7908) = + $106,068
Payback period = ($690,000 ÷ $210,000) = 3.3 years

tomers what they want rather than telling them what the company has available. FMSs are not inexpensive, but the investment can pay for itself through increased sales at higher prices as well as lower costs.

Regardless of the type of investment project under consideration, selection of and investment in a project should not end the capital budgeting process. At some point (or points) in time, management should perform a post-investment audit or review of the project.

POST-INVESTMENT AUDIT

post-investment audit

■ **LEARNING OBJECTIVE 7**
Understand how and why management should conduct a post-investment audit of a capital project.

After a capital investment has been made, information on actual project results can be gathered and compared against expected results. This comparison is referred to as a **post-investment audit**. This process is intended "to accomplish at least four primary objectives: serve as an important financial control mechanism, provide information for future capital expenditure decisions, remove certain psychological and/or political impediments usually associated with asset control and abandonment, and have a psychological impact on those proposing capital investments."[13]

[13]Lawrence A. Gordon and Mary D. Myers, "Postauditing Capital Projects," *Management Accounting* (January 1991), p. 39.

Management should make the decision about when to have the post-investment audit. In cases where significant learning or training is necessary, start-up costs of the first year may not be appropriate indicators of future costs. Such projects should be given a chance to stabilize before the project audit is made. Once the project is stabilized, actual information about the costs and benefits of the project can be gathered and extrapolated to future periods. Such extrapolations allow the cash flows for the full life of the asset to be considered. Actual-to-expected cash flow comparisons should be made using the technique or techniques originally used to determine project acceptance, but such comparisons are not enough. Management should take action to find the causes of any adverse differences and the means, if possible, of remedying them.

As the size of capital expenditures increases, post-investment audits become more crucial. Although an audit cannot change a past investment decision, it can be used to pinpoint areas of operations that are not in line with expectations so that problems can be corrected before they get out of hand. Also, an audit will help managers evaluate the accuracy of the original cost/benefit predictions. Project sponsors may have been biased in favor of their projects. As a result, their forecasts of future revenues, cost savings, or expenses may have been overly optimistic. Individuals who provided unrealistic estimates should be required to explain all major differences. Furthermore, knowing that post-investment audits will be made may cause project sponsors to provide more realistic cash flow forecasts for capital requests in the future.

Performing a post-investment audit is not easy, for several reasons. First, actual information may be in a form different from that of the original estimates. Second, some project benefits may be difficult to quantify. Third, project returns vary considerably over time, so results gathered at one point in time may not be representative of the project. But regardless of the difficulties involved, post-investment audits provide managers with information that can help them to make better capital investment decisions in the future.

SITE ANALYSIS

When First Bank decided to invest in technology and replace its old management information system, an analyst with Merrill Lynch & Co. in New York commented that the move brought First Bank "out of the dark ages." But this investment was simply one of many in which the bank engages on a continual basis. During the process of making the five-year strategic and the one-year operating plans at First Bank, managers voice their desires and concerns about what capital assets should be acquired, how much should be spent in various business lines (retail services, commercial lending, and so forth), and what the competition is doing or is expected to do.

Capital investment projects at the company are analyzed on the basis of internal rates of return and payback periods, but the primary decision criterion for all capital acquisitions is a shareholder value model based on net present values of cash flows. The model uses sensitivity analysis to provide ranges of present value answers by varying the possibilities in the underlying assumptions about costs and benefits.

The number of people involved in the analysis process depends on the size of the investment. Project managers must be able to articulate their assumptions and assign some level of probability or expectation to them. In addition, managers are expected to develop estimates of values for the nonquantitative benefits that may arise from the project so that these benefits can be included in the present value model. In the end, however, First Bank always looks to its competition and quantifies what the competitive disad-

vantage would be of *not* investing in a particular capital asset. After all, capital investments provide ways of differentiating First Bank from other banks—and that enhances profitability.

SOURCES: Jeffrey Zack, "Technology Gives First Bank's Grundhofer a Cost-Cutting Edge," *American Banker's Management Strategies* (May 9, 1994), p. 1; and interview with Andrew Cecere, senior vice president of management accounting, First Bank Systems, 1994.

CROSS-FUNCTIONAL APPLICATIONS STRATEGIES

Discipline	Applications
Accounting	Accountants can help provide the financial data needed for capital project analysis and for post-investment audits. Accountants can help management find ways to meaningfully quantify qualitative investment factors.
Economics	Economics is concerned with maximizing the use of scarce resources, such as those available for capital investments. Investment projects involve cost reductions, revenue generation, or some combination of both and hence are designed to enhance the profit potential of the firm. Capital investments are important for economic growth and, therefore, play an important part in the viability of the domestic economy.
Finance	The finance officer is responsible for determining which capital projects are the most beneficial to the entity; allocating resources most efficiently; determining methods of financing for projects once they are deemed acceptable; and understanding the impact of capital investments on cash flows, taxes, and profitability.
Management	Managers must recognize, and integrate into their decision-making process, the impacts of replacing human workers with machines; must be able to select the activities that are best suited for investment and the assets to best achieve target goals; and must work with accounting and finance personnel to analyze the costs and benefits of various projects.
Marketing	Significant market research input about estimated sales volumes must be gathered when investments are to be made in equipment needed to make new products or to protect market share by making higher-quality, lower cost products. While marketing may have impressive "ideas" for new products, presenting these ideas to management requires more than sales volume and market share predictions—it requires showing that customer needs can be met in a way that makes the firm profitable.

CHAPTER SUMMARY

Capital budgeting is the process of evaluating long-range projects involving the acquisition, operation, and disposition of one or more capital assets. Management should select investment projects that will help the organization to achieve its objectives, provide a reasonable rate of return on invested capital, and help maximize shareholder wealth. The company must determine whether the activities in which it wishes to engage are worth an investment and which assets can be used for those activities. Then decisions must be made about the best investments to accept from all the ones available.

The most common capital budgeting evaluation techniques are payback period, net present value (NPV), profitability index (PI), and internal rate of return (IRR). NPV, PI, and IRR are discounted cash flow methods. The minimum rate at which the discount rate should be set is the cost of capital, but setting this rate requires management judgment based on the amount of capital employed and the risk involved.

Depreciation expense and changes in tax rates affect after-tax cash flows. Depreciation expense, although not a cash flow, provides a tax shield for revenues. For the best results, discounted cash flow methods should use after-tax cash flows. The tax rates and allowable depreciation methods used in analyzing an investment may not be the ones in effect when the project is implemented. Such changes can cause the actual NPV and IRR amounts to differ significantly from those originally estimated on the project.

Each capital project evaluation technique is based on certain assumptions and, therefore, has certain limitations. To compensate for these limitations, many managers subject capital projects to more than one evaluation technique.

Installation of high-technology equipment is one type of capital investment currently being considered by many company managers. Such equipment can significantly reduce labor cost, increase quality and quantity of production, and shorten throughput time. However, investments of this type are often not justifiable under traditional capital budgeting evaluation techniques because the payback period is long and many of the benefits are nonquantifiable.

After a capital project is accepted and implemented, a post-investment audit should be undertaken to compare actual with expected results. The audit will help managers identify and correct any problems that may exist, evaluate the accuracy of estimates used for the original investment decision, and help improve the forecasts of future investment projects.

APPENDIX 1

Time Value of Money

The time value of money can be discussed in relation to its future or its present value. **Future value (FV)** refers to the amount to which a sum of money invested at a specified interest rate will grow over a specified number of time periods. Present value (PV) is the amount that a future cash flow is worth currently, given a specified rate of interest. Thus, future and present values depend on three things: (1) amount of the cash flow, (2) rate of interest, and (3) timing of the cash flow. Only present values are discussed in this appendix, since they are most relevant to the types of management decisions discussed in this text.

In computing future and present values, simple or compound interest may be used. **Simple interest** is calculated as a percentage of the original investment, or principal amount only.[14] With **compound interest**, interest earned in prior periods is added to the original investment so that, in each successive period, interest is earned on both principal and interest. The time from one interest computation to the next is called the **compounding period**. The more often interest is compounded, the higher is the

future value (FV)
■ LEARNING
OBJECTIVE 8
(Appendix 1) Use the time value of money concept.

simple interest
compound interest

compounding period

---

[14]Interest can be earned or owed, received or paid. To simplify the discussion, the topic of interest is viewed only from the inflow standpoint.

actual rate of interest being received relative to the stated rate. The following discussion assumes compound interest, since most transactions use this method.

Interest rates are typically stated for an annual period. If compounding occurs more often, the annual interest rate must be divided by the number of compounding periods per year to get the interest rate per compounding period. The number of years multiplied by the number of compounding periods per year provides the total number of interest periods. For example, if 14 percent interest is to be received each year for five years and the compounding period is semiannual, the rate per compounding period is 7 percent (14% ÷ 2), and the total number of interest periods is 10 (5 years × 2).

Present Value of a Single Cash Flow

Assume that Bob Glover knows that Minehead National Bank pays interest at 4 percent per year compounded semiannually. Bob wants to have $1,126 in three years and wants to know what amount to invest now. A table of factors for the present value of $1 (Table 1 in Appendix C at the end of the text) for a variety of i and n values can be used to solve this problem:

$$PV = FV \text{ (PV factor at i for n)}$$

where
$$PV = \text{present value of a future amount}$$
$$FV = \text{future value of a current investment}$$
$$i = \text{interest rate per compounding period}$$
$$n = \text{total number of compounding periods}$$

The PV factor is obtained from Table 1 using the known interest rate of 2 percent and the six discount periods. Substituting known values into the formula gives the following:

$$PV = \$1,126 \text{ (.8880)} = \$1,000 \text{ (rounded)}$$

The rate of return used in present value computations is called the discount rate. In capital budgeting, future value amounts normally need to be converted to present values. The process of discounting is merely the reverse of the process of compounding.

Present Value of an Annuity

ordinary annuity

annuity due

rent

An annuity is a series of equal cash flows. In an **ordinary annuity** (such as bond interest), the first cash flow occurs at the end of the first period. In contrast, the cash flows from an **annuity due** occur at the beginning of a period. A lease payment made at the beginning of the month for the upcoming month is one cash flow of an annuity due. Each equal cash flow of an annuity is called a **rent**.

To illustrate the computation of the present value of an annuity, consider the following situation. Minehead National Bank is planning to give the local university a charitable contribution of $5,000 at the end of each of the next five years. The university would prefer to have the money now to invest in a project that will earn 6 percent compounded annually. Minehead National Bank management is willing to give the university a lump sum amount now, but refuses to give the entire $25,000. University administrators need to know what amount represents a current equivalent of the $5,000 per year cash flow in the future. The following diagram presents the situation:

Time in Years	0	1	2	3	4	5
Future Value		$5,000	$5,000	$5,000	$5,000	$5,000
Present Value		? (using the desired 6 percent interest rate)				

The present value of each single cash flow can be found by use of 6 percent discount factors from Table 1 as follows:

PV of first receipt	= $5,000 (.9434)	$ 4,717
PV of second receipt	= $5,000 (.8900)	4,450
PV of third receipt	= $5,000 (.8396)	4,198
PV of fourth receipt	= $5,000 (.7921)	3,960
PV of fifth receipt	= $5,000 (.7473)	3,737
Total present value		$21,062

The present value factor for an ordinary annuity can be determined by addition of the present value factors for all periods having a future cash flow. Alternatively, Table 2 in Appendix C provides factors for the present value of an ordinary annuity at various interest rates and time periods. From this table, the factor of 4.2124 can be obtained. Multiplying by $5,000 yields the same result as above.

If this had been an annuity due problem, the ordinary annuity PV factors could have been converted to annuity due PV factors. Using one less time period and adding 1.000 to the annuity factor given would achieve this conversion. For example, assume that Minehead National Bank wanted to give the university $5,000 per year for five years, beginning immediately. The following timeline reflects the cash outflows, and the calculation for the present value (using 6 percent and four periods) is also given.

Time in Years	0	1	2	3	4
Future Value	$5,000	$5,000	$5,000	$5,000	$5,000
Present Value	? (assuming a 6 percent interest rate)				

PV = $5,000 (4.4651) = $22,326

APPENDIX 2

The **accounting rate of return (ARR)** measures the expected rate of earnings on the average capital investment over a project's life. This evaluation method uses the projected net income amount shown on accrual-based financial statements and is a return on investment formula for a single project. It is the one evaluation technique that is not based on cash flows. The formula to compute the accounting rate of return is:

$$ARR = \frac{\text{Average Annual Income from Project}}{\text{Average Investment in Project}}$$

Project investment includes original cost and project support costs, such as those needed for working capital items (for example, inventory). Investment, salvage value,

accounting rate of return (ARR)

■ LEARNING OBJECTIVE 9
(Appendix 2) Determine the accounting rate of return for a project.

and working capital released at the end of the project's life are summed and divided by two to obtain the average investment.[15]

To illustrate the computation of the accounting rate of return, consider information for a piece of equipment being analyzed by Minehead National Bank. Data on the potential investment are as follows:

Beginning investment:	
Initial cost of equipment	$200,000
Additional working capital needed for the project	70,000
Return at end of project:	
Salvage value of equipment at the end of 10 years	20,000
Working capital released at the end of 10 years	70,000
Return over life of project:	
Average incremental company profits after taxes	44,000

Solving the formula for the accounting rate of return gives:

$$ARR = \frac{\$44,000}{(\$270,000 + \$90,000) \div 2} = \frac{\$44,000}{\$180,000} = 24.4\%$$

The project's 24.4 percent ARR can be compared with a preestablished hurdle rate set by management. This hurdle rate will most likely not be the same as the desired discount rate, since the data used in calculating the accounting rate of return are not cash flow data. Management may set the ARR hurdle rate at a higher level than the discount rate because the method does not account for the time value of money. In addition, the 24.4 percent accounting rate of return for this project should be compared with ARRs on other investment projects being considered by Minehead National Bank to determine which projects have the highest accounting rates of return.

GLOSSARY

Accounting rate of return (ARR) (p. 741)   the rate of accounting earnings obtained on the average capital investment over a project's life (from appendix)

Annuity (p. 713)   a series of equal cash flows occurring at equal time intervals

Annuity due (p. 740)   an annuity in which each cash flow occurs at the beginning of the period (from appendix)

Capital asset (p. 706)   an asset used to generate revenues or cost savings by providing production, distribution, or service capabilities for more than one year

Capital budgeting (p. 707)   a process for evaluating proposed long-range projects or courses of future activity for the purpose of allocating limited resources to desirable projects

Cash flow (p. 710)   the receipt or disbursement of cash

Compound interest (p. 739)   interest calculated on the basis of principal plus interest already earned (from appendix)

Compounding period (p. 739)   the time from one interest computation to the next (from appendix)

Cost of capital (COC) (p. 715)   the weighted average rate that reflects the costs of the various sources of funds making up a firm's debt and equity structure

---

[15]Sometimes initial cost rather than average investment is used as the denominator in the ARR equation. This form of the equation ignores the return of funds at the end of the project's life and is less

Discount rate (p. 715)   the rate of return on capital investments required by the company; the rate of return used in present value computations

Discounting (p. 715)   the process of removing the portion of a future cash flow that represents interest, thereby reducing that flow to a present value amount

Financing decision (p. 711)   a judgment regarding how funds will be obtained to make an acquisition

Future value (FV) (p. 739)   the amount to which one or more sums of money invested at a specified interest rate will grow over a specified number of time periods (from appendix)

Hurdle rate (p. 723)   the rate of return deemed by management to be the lowest acceptable return on investment

Independent project (p. 710)   an investment project that has no specific bearing on any other investment project

Internal rate of return (IRR) (p. 721)   the discount rate at which the present value of the cash inflows minus the present value of the cash outflows equals zero

Investing decision (p. 711)   a judgment regarding which assets an entity will acquire to achieve its stated objectives

Mutually exclusive projects (p. 710)   a set of proposed investments for which there is a group of available candidates that all perform essentially the same function or meet the same objective; from this group, one is chosen and all others are rejected

Mutually inclusive projects (p. 710)   a set of proposed investments that are all related to a primary project; when the primary project is chosen, all related investments are also selected

Net present value (NPV) (p. 716)   the difference between the present values of all the cash inflows and cash outflows of an investment project

Net present value method (p. 716)   an investment evaluation technique that uses discounted cash flows to determine if the rate of return on a project is equal to, higher than, or lower than the desired rate of return

Ordinary annuity (p. 740)   an annuity in which each cash flow occurs at the end of the period (from appendix)

Payback period (p. 714)   the time required to recoup the original investment in a project through its cash flows

Post-investment audit (p. 736)   a procedure in which management compares actual project results against the results expected at the inception of the project

Preference decision (p. 709)   a judgment regarding how projects are to be ranked based on their impact on the achievement of company objectives

Present value (PV) (p. 715)   the amount that a future cash flow is worth currently, given a specified rate of interest

Profitability index (PI) (p. 720)   a ratio that compares the present value of net cash inflows with the present value of the net investment

Project (p. 707)   a course of future investment activity; typically includes the purchase, installation, and operation of a capital asset

Rent (p. 740)   each equal cash flow of an annuity (from appendix)

Return of capital (p. 712)   recovery of the original investment

Return on capital (p. 712)   income; equals the discount rate times the investment amount

Screening decision (p. 709)   a judgment regarding the desirability of a capital project based on some previously established minimum criterion or criteria

Simple interest (p. 739)   interest calculated as a percentage of the original investment, or principal amount, only (from appendix)

Tax benefit (of depreciation) (p. 726)   the depreciation provided by a capital investment multiplied by the tax rate

Tax shield (of depreciation) (p. 723)   the amount of the reduction of taxable income provided by depreciation expense

Timeline (p. 713)   a visual tool that illustrates the timing of expected cash receipts and payments; used for analyzing cash flows of a capital investment proposal

SOLUTION STRATEGIES

- Prepare a timeline to illustrate all moments in time when cash flows are expected to occur.
- Use the cost of capital rate as the discount rate to determine PVs.

PAYBACK PERIOD

1. For projects with equal annual cash flows:

$$\text{Payback period} = \text{Investment} \div \text{Annuity amount}$$

2. For projects with unequal annual cash flows:
   Sum the annual cash flows until investment is reached to find payback period.

If payback period is equal to or less than a preestablished maximum number of years, the project is acceptable.

NET PRESENT VALUE

$$
\begin{aligned}
&\quad \text{Current investment (always valued at a factor of 1.0000)} \\
&+\ \text{PV of future cash inflows or cost savings} \\
&-\ \underline{\text{PV of future cash outflows}} \\
&=\ \text{NPV}
\end{aligned}
$$

If NPV is equal to or greater than zero, the project is returning a rate equal to or greater than the discount rate. The project is acceptable.

PROFITABILITY INDEX

$$
\begin{aligned}
&+\ \text{PV of future cash inflows or cost savings} \\
&-\ \underline{\text{PV of future cash outflows}} \\
&=\ \text{PV of net future cash inflows} \\
&\qquad \text{PI} = (\text{PV of net future cash inflows}) \div \text{PV of investment}
\end{aligned}
$$

If PI is 1.00 or greater, the project is returning a rate equal to or greater than the discount rate. The project is acceptable.

INTERNAL RATE OF RETURN

1. For projects with equal annual cash flows:

$$\text{PV factor} = \text{Investment} \div \text{Annuity amount}$$

In a table, find the PV factor (or the one closest to it) on the row for the appropriate number of periods. The percentage at the top of the column where this factor is found will approximate the IRR.

2. For projects with unequal annual cash flows:
   Estimate the rate provided by the project; compute the NPV. If the NPV is positive (negative), try a higher (lower) rate. Repeat this process until the NPV is zero.

Compare IRR with the discount rate or preestablished hurdle rate. If the IRR is equal to or greater than that rate, the project is acceptable.

ACCOUNTING RATE OF RETURN

$$ARR = \frac{\text{Average Annual Income from Project}}{\text{Average Investment in Project}}$$

$$\text{Average Investment} = \frac{\text{Investment + Salvage}}{2}$$

Compare calculated ARR to hurdle ARR. If calculated ARR is equal to or greater, the project is acceptable.

TAX BENEFIT OF DEPRECIATION

$$\text{Tax benefit of depreciation} = \text{Depreciation amount} \times \text{Tax rate}$$

BASIC CONCEPTS OF CAPITAL BUDGETING TECHNIQUES

	NPV	PI	IRR	PAYBACK	ARR
Uses time value of money?	Yes	Yes	Yes	No	No
Provides a rate of return?	No	No	Yes	No	Yes
Uses cash flows?	Yes	Yes	Yes	Yes	No
Considers returns throughout life of project?	Yes	Yes	Yes	No	Yes
Discount rate used in calculation?	Yes	Yes	No*	No	No

*Discount rate is not used in the calculation, but it may be used as the hurdle rate.

DEMONSTRATION PROBLEM

The Consumer Products Company is considering an investment in a new product line. The company produces a variety of consumer products from various plastic materials. The new product under consideration is a high-tech frisbee-boomerang.

To make the product, the company would need to acquire additional production and marketing equipment with an investment of $1,000,000. The equipment would have an expected life of six years, at which time it would have no market value. The company would also need to invest $200,000 in additional working capital (primarily to support an increase in Accounts Receivable).

Over the six-year life of the equipment, the company projects the following sales volume:

	SALES VOLUME
Year 1	200,000 units
Year 2	300,000 units
Year 3	400,000 units
Year 4	300,000 units
Year 5	200,000 units
Year 6	200,000 units

The company projects the sales price for the new product to be $2.75 for all years and estimates all variable costs would be $1.30 per unit. Fixed cash expenses are projected at $125,000 per year. For tax purposes, the original cost of the equipment would be depreciated at the following rates (consistent with cost recovery rules in the tax code):

Year 1	15%
Year 2	22%
Year 3	21%
Year 4	21%
Year 5	21%
Year 6	0%
Total	100%

For financial accounting purposes, the equipment would be depreciated based on the straight-line method over six years.

The company's marginal tax rate is expected to remain at the current rate of 40 percent over the life of the equipment. The company uses a hurdle rate of 8 percent (its cost of capital) to evaluate projects of this type.

Required:
a. Compute the after-tax NPV of the proposed project. Based on the NPV, is the project acceptable?
b. Compute the profitability index.
c. Compute the payback period for the proposed project.
d. Without computing the IRR, determine whether the IRR is greater than the discount rate.

■ SOLUTION TO DEMONSTRATION PROBLEM

a. Compute the net income and tax expense for each year:

	YEAR 1	YEAR 2	YEAR 3	YEAR 4	YEAR 5	YEAR 6
Sales	$550,000	$825,000	$1,100,000	$825,000	$550,000	$550,000
Variable costs	(260,000)	(390,000)	(520,000)	(390,000)	(260,000)	(260,000)
CM	$290,000	$435,000	$ 580,000	$435,000	$290,000	$290,000
Cash FC	(125,000)	(125,000)	(125,000)	(125,000)	(125,000)	(125,000)
Depreciation	(150,000)	(220,000)	(210,000)	(210,000)	(210,000)	0
Pretax income	$ 15,000	$ 90,000	$ 245,000	$100,000	$(45,000)	$165,000
Taxes	(6,000)	(36,000)	(98,000)	(40,000)	18,000	(66,000)
Net income	$ 9,000	$ 54,000	$ 147,000	$ 60,000	$(27,000)	$ 99,000

Items to note:

- ■ The investment in working capital is not depreciable.
- ■ The pretax loss in year 5 results in a tax refund.
- ■ The investment in working capital is not deductible for tax purposes.
- ■ The relevant depreciation is the amount for tax purposes rather than the financial accounting amount.

Convert the NI for each year to a net annual cash flow after tax (CFAT):

	YEAR 1	YEAR 2	YEAR 3	YEAR 4	YEAR 5	YEAR 6
NI	$ 9,000	$ 54,000	$147,000	$ 60,000	$ (27,000)	$99,000
Add depreciation	150,000	220,000	210,000	210,000	210,000	0
CFAT	$159,000	$274,000	$357,000	$270,000	$183,000	$99,000

Using present value tables, compute the NPV of the project:

CASH FLOW DESCRIPTION	TIME	CFAT* AMOUNT	DISCOUNT FACTOR	PRESENT VALUE
Required investment	t0	$(1,200,000)	1.0000	$ (1,200,000)
Net cash flow	t1	159,000	.9259	147,218
Net cash flow	t2	274,000	.8573	234,900
Net cash flow	t3	357,000	.7938	283,387
Net cash flow	t4	270,000	.7350	198,450
Net cash flow	t5	183,000	.6806	124,550
Net cash flow	t6	99,000	.6302	62,390
Return of working capital**	t6	200,000	.6302	126,040
		Net present value		$ (23,065)

*CFAT = Cash flow after taxes
**Working capital is returned at the end of the project's life.
Because the NPV is less than zero, the project is unacceptable.

b. The profitability index is:

$$\frac{(\$147,218 + \$234,900 + \$283,387 + \$198,450 + \$124,550 + \$62,390 + \$126,040)}{\$1,200,000} = .98$$

c. The payback period is:

	CASH FLOW	REMAINING COST TO RECAPTURE
Original cost		$1,200,000
Year 1 cash flow	$159,000	1,041,000
Year 2 cash flow	274,000	767,000
Year 3 cash flow	357,000	410,000
Year 4 cash flow	270,000	140,000

After year 4, there is $140,000 of investment remaining to be recaptured. The fifth-year cash flow of $183,000 is assumed to flow evenly throughout the year. Therefore, it will take 76.5 percent ($140,000 ÷ $183,000) of the fifth year to completely recapture the original investment. Thus, the payback period would be 4.765 years or approximately 4 years and 9 months.

d. The IRR must be less than 8 percent because an 8 percent discount rate causes the NPV to be less than zero. The IRR, when used as the discount rate, would cause the NPV to be exactly zero.

END-OF-CHAPTER MATERIALS

■ QUESTIONS

1. What is a capital asset? How is it distinguished from other assets?

2. What is the objective of capital budgeting? Why is this objective an important business consideration?

3. Discuss some reasons why managers might use different techniques to screen projects and to evaluate project preferences.

4. In the capital budgeting context, what are mutually exclusive projects? Give three examples.

5. In the capital budgeting context, what are independent projects? Give three examples.

6. Of the five capital budgeting techniques discussed in the chapter, which ones consider the time value of money? How does discounting account for the time value of money?

7. Why do the capital budgeting methods that consider the time value of money consider only cash flows rather than accrual-based accounting numbers?

8. What is the distinction between a return on capital and a return of capital?

9. What is a timeline, and how does it aid the evaluation of capital projects?

10. What is the difference between an annuity and an ordinary cash flow?

11. What does the payback period of a project represent? Why is the payback method commonly used in conjunction with other methods rather than as a stand-alone evaluation measure?

12. How is an interest rate selected for discounting the cash flows associated with a project?

13. When using the NPV method, how does one determine if the actual rate of return on a project is greater than or less than the discount rate?

14. If a project's net present value is zero, what can be said about the internal rate of return on the project? Discuss the reasoning behind your answer.

15. Relative to the NPV method, what is the primary strength of the profitability index method of evaluating capital projects?

16. In general, how does one estimate the internal rate of return on a potential project?

17. What are the major weaknesses of the internal rate of return method of project evaluation?

18. NPV, PI, and IRR can all be used as criteria in accept/reject decisions regarding capital projects. What type of value for each of these measures indicate that a project is acceptable?

19. How does depreciation expense, which is an accounting expense rather than a cash flow, become relevant in the capital budgeting analysis when the effects of income taxes are considered?

20. Why will an accelerated method of depreciation usually produce a higher present value for the tax shield than the straight-line method?

21. If all other factors are equal, which of the following changes will increase the present value of the depreciation tax shield?

    a. An increase in the tax rate

    b. An increase in the discount rate

    c. An increase in the rate of depreciation

22. Why are high-technology projects often rejected when evaluation relies on traditional capital budgeting techniques?

23. Why is it important to perform a post-investment audit?

24. (Appendix 1) What factors affect the present value of a sum of $1 to be received at some point in the future?

25. (Appendix 2) Which method of evaluating capital projects uses accrual accounting information rather than cash flows? How does net income differ from net cash flows?

26. (Appendix 2) What characteristic of the accounting rate of return method makes it unique among the techniques discussed?

■ EXERCISES

27. (LO 2, 3, 4; *Payback*) The city manager of Lincoln is considering two mutually exclusive investment proposals for the town's water utility. Both proposals, A and B, promise cash inflows of $40,000 per year based on an investment of $120,000. Expected useful lives are as follows:

PROPOSAL	LIFE
A	3.5 years
B	4.5 years

    a. Compute the payback period for each alternative. Based on the payback criterion, which of the alternatives is preferred?

    b. How does this problem demonstrate a need to use a second evaluation technique when the payback technique is used?

28. (LO 2, 3, 4; *Payback*) The manager of a major division of MetroCorp is considering two mutually exclusive projects for the company's manufacturing operations. The two proposals, Z and T, promise the following cash inflows:

YEAR	PROPOSAL Z	PROPOSAL T
1	$ 40,000	$120,000
2	80,000	80,000
3	120,000	40,000
4	20,000	20,000

An initial investment of $240,000 is required for both projects.

    a. Using the payback method, evaluate the projects.

    b. What weakness of the payback method is evident in this problem? Explain.

29. (LO 2, 3, 8; *NPV; timeline*) A lumber supply company is considering the purchase of some building equipment costing $100,000. The equipment is expected to have a life of five years with no salvage value. Cash inflows are expected to be $50,000 per year for the first two years, and $20,000 per year for the last three years. Assuming the company uses a discount rate of 10 percent to evaluate capital projects, prepare a timeline showing all cash flows, and compute the net present value of the equipment investment.

30. (LO 2, 3, 8; *NPV; timeline*) An individual is faced with two investment alternatives. In one case, she can invest $100,000 with an expected return of $12,000
per year for the next six years. At the end of the sixth year, the investment can
be sold for $100,000. Alternatively, she can purchase some equipment for
$100,000 that will provide her with revenues of $30,000 a year for four years and
$10,000 a year for two more years.

a. Prepare a timeline for each project showing all cash flows associated with
each project.

b. Assuming her discount rate is 12 percent, compute the net present value of
the alternative investments.

c. Is either investment acceptable? Explain. Which investment is preferred?
Explain.

31. (LO 2, 3, 8; *NPV*) Joney Wilson is examining an investment in an annuity contract that would pay him $12,000 per year for the next eight years. If Joney's dis-
count rate is 12 percent, what is the most that he would be willing to pay for this
investment?

32. (LO 2, 3, 8; *NPV*) Toby Wilkes is considering the purchase of a machine costing $513,000 to manufacture brass and wooden end tables. According to his
market research, Mr. Wilkes estimates that no more than 70,000 of these tables
can be produced and sold during the life of the machine. Mr. Wilkes is sure that
he can sell all of the tables at $48 each and estimates the following costs associ-
ated with each table:

Direct labor	$ 8
Direct materials	4
Other out-of-pocket costs	3
Commissions and royalties	21
Total	$36

Mr. Wilkes provides you with the following schedule of unit sales (all sales are
for cash) and states that he plans to produce the tables according to the same
schedule:

YEAR	SALES IN UNITS
1	7,000
2	14,000
3	21,000
4	23,000
5	5,000
Total	70,000

At the end of the five years, the machine will have no salvage value.

a. Using a discount rate of 12 percent, determine the NPV of the machine
investment.

b. Assume that Mr. Wilkes is uncertain about the life of the machine. What
types of experts could he consult to gain assurance that the life of the
machine is sufficiently long to produce 70,000 units? Explain.

33. (LO 2, 3, 8; *NPV, payback*) Lawler Custom Frames recently purchased a new
computerized machine to cut glass. The machine required an initial investment
of $7,000, and the company estimated that, over the machine's five-year life, it
would generate net additional annual cash inflows of $2,200.

   a. What is the net present value of the investment in the machine if the company's discount rate is 11 percent?
   b. What is the expected payback period?
   c. If the company determined that the investment in the new machine generated a net present value of $1,447 (rounded to the nearest dollar), what was the company's discount rate?
   d. In the typical large corporation, who would be responsible for setting the discount rate? Explain.

34. (LO 2, 3, 8; *NPV, payback*) Managers of Cow Hop Junction, a regional fast food chain, are evaluating the feasibility of purchasing rights to serve Lim-N-Aid, a popular soft drink. The rights would give the firm exclusive license to market Lim-N-Aid in a four-state area for a period of six years. According to estimates by the company's marketing staff, the license would increase net annual cash receipts by $630,000 in each of the six years.

   a. Assuming the company's cost of capital is 8 percent, what is the most it would pay for the marketing rights?
   b. Based on your answer in part a, compute the payback period.

35. (LO 2, 3, 8; *NPV, PI, payback*) Donni Samson is considering two alternative investments for her idle cash. Project A would require an initial investment of $25,000 and project B would require an investment of $40,000. Cash inflows available from each project follow:

YEAR	PROJECT A	PROJECT B
1	$ 3,000	$ 4,800
2	3,000	4,800
3	3,000	4,800
4	3,250	4,400
5	28,250	44,400

Ms. Samson's discount rate is 11 percent.

   a. Compute the net present value of each project.
   b. Compute the profitability index of each project.
   c. Which of the two projects is preferred? Discuss.

36. (LO 2, 3, 8; *PI*) The City Bus Authority is considering replacing a bus with a new one that will last 10 years, cost $80,000, and have no salvage value. A $12,000 trade-in can be obtained on the old bus. The City Bus Authority uses a 10 percent required rate of return. Annual operating costs will be reduced by $9,000 if the new bus is acquired.

   a. Compute the profitability index. Does this indicate that the purchase of the new bus is acceptable?
   b. Should the City Bus Authority buy the new bus? Discuss other points that the City Bus Authority should consider.
   c. Assume that you are the controller of the City Bus Authority. Describe the role you may have played in determining that a new bus would reduce operating costs by $9,000.

37. (LO 2, 3, 8; *IRR*) A food products company plans to buy a new vending machine at a fully-installed cost of $55,475. The company estimates that the machine will have a life of six years. Net annual cash inflows are estimated to be $12,000. No salvage is expected at the end of the sixth year.

a. Calculate the internal rate of return for this project.

b. If the company's cost of capital is 10 percent, is this an acceptable investment? Explain.

38. (LO 2, 3, 6, 8; *IRR*) Texas Food Processing Company is considering the purchase of a new machine to steam vegetables. One machine has an initial cost of $90,000. By using it, the company could save $15,000 annually for 10 years over what it would spend using the current manual methods. No salvage value is expected on the machine at the end of its useful life. The firm's cost of capital and discount rate are 12 percent.

a. Calculate the internal rate of return for the machine. Does this indicate that the machine is an acceptable investment?

b. Should the company purchase the machine? Discuss other points that the company should consider.

39. (LO 2, 3, 5, 8; *Depreciation effects*) Technical Solutions is a software firm specializing in applications related to manufacturing technology. The firm is presently considering an investment in a new mainframe computer to aid in management of its software development. The computer would cost $1,500,000 and have an expected life of eight years. For tax purposes, the computer can be depreciated using the straight-line method over eight years. Alternatively, it can be depreciated over five years at a rate of 15 percent in year 1, 22 percent in year 2, and 21 percent in years 3 through 5. No salvage value is recognized under either method. The company's cost of capital is 10 percent, and its tax rate is 35 percent.

a. Compute the present value of the depreciation tax shield if the company uses the straight-line depreciation method.

b. Compute the present value of the depreciation tax shield if the company uses the alternative method.

c. If the company expected its annual tax rate to rise over the eight-year life of the computer, would it be more likely to choose straight line depreciation or the alternative method? Explain.

d. If you were the president of Technical Solutions, and you had doubts about the assumptions made with regard to tax rate or depreciation method, what experts would you consult to resolve such doubts? Explain.

40. (LO 8; *Appendix 1*) On January 1, 1997, LorenCo invested some funds in a note that will mature on December 31, 1999. The controller determined that the firm would earn 12 percent interest (compounded annually) on this investment. If the maturity value of the investment is $18,000, how much did the company invest?

41. (LO 8; *Appendix 1*) Jesse Moore recently purchased a new car. He paid $4,000 down and financed the balance on an installment credit plan. According to the credit agreement, Jesse agreed to pay $300 per month for a period of 48 months. If the credit agreement was based on a monthly interest rate of 1 percent, what was the cost of the car?

42. (LO 2, 3, 9; *Appendix 2; payback*) The accounting firm of Dutton, Honey & Dauterive is considering an investment in 100 new personal notebook computers with internal modems and CD ROM drives. The cost of the new computers would be $300,000, and they would have an expected life of five years. The company would depreciate the computers using the straight-line method. At the end of their lives, the computers would have no market value. The computers would reduce the company's annual labor costs by $69,000.

    a. Compute the accounting rate of return on the computer investment. (Ignore income taxes.)

    b. Compute the payback period for the investment.

43. (LO 2, 3, 8, 9; *All methods; Appendix 2*) Lawn and Garden Supply Co. is considering purchasing a new fertilizer blender. The equipment would cost $300,000 and produce annual cost savings of $50,000. The equipment is expected to last 10 years and have no salvage value. The company's discount rate is 10 percent. Answer the following questions relative to this investment.

    a. What is the net present value?

    b. What is the profitability index?

    c. What is the internal rate of return?

    d. What is the payback period?

    e. What is the accounting rate of return? (Ignore income taxes.)

44. (LO 2, 3, 5, 7, 8, 9; *After-tax amounts; payback; Appendix 2*) Herb's Retail Flowers is evaluating the purchase of an integrated, computerized point-of-sale and inventory management system. The company purchasing agent advised the owner, Herb Tarlick, that the system would generate $13,000 of cash savings each year for four years. At the end of that time, the system would have no salvage value because of technological obsolescence. The purchasing agent also estimated that cash operating and maintenance costs would be $1,500 annually. The company's tax rate (combined state and federal) is expected to be 40 percent during the life of the asset, and the company uses straight-line depreciation. The initial cost of the system would be $36,000.

    a. Determine the annual after-tax cash flows from the project.

    b. Determine the after-tax payback period for the project.

    c. Determine the after-tax accounting rate of return for the project.

45. (LO 2, 3, 5, 6, 9; *After-tax amounts; payback; Appendix 2*) Bassett Livestock Auction operates an auction market for cattle. The company is considering the purchase of a new computerized scale to weigh cattle. The equipment selected would cost $150,000 and would have a life of eight years and an estimated salvage value of $20,000. The company depreciates assets on a straight-line basis, and its tax rate is 30 percent. Additional business generated by installation of the new scale would increase annual net cash inflows on a before-tax basis by $40,000. Annual cash maintenance costs would amount to $4,000. The company requires that the cost of investment be recouped in less than five years and that the investment produce an accounting rate of return of at least 16 percent.

    a. Compute the after-tax payback period and the after-tax accounting rate of return for this piece of equipment.

    b. Quantitatively, is this piece of equipment an acceptable investment? Why or why not?

    c. Regardless of your answer to part b, what other factors relating to this purchase should be considered?

■ COMMUNICATION ACTIVITIES

46. (LO 1, 6; *Governmental investment*) *For years, travelers [in Ainsworth, Nebraska,] were greeted by a billboard that said, only half in jest, "Welcome to Ainsworth, the Middle of Nowhere." So when a gust of wind blew the sign down last spring, it seemed like an omen of change.*

    While Ainsworth is far from the nearest interstate, it and many other tiny towns find themselves located right on the information superhighway. For the rest of the nation, the multimedia, megabit future may still be mostly hype and hope, but small-town America is starting to get an inkling of what it means, as the new technology blurs distinctions between rural and urban areas.

Ainsworth's public library boasts a two-way video-conferencing unit. Sidney Salzman, the town's 67-year-old mayor, says when state officials installed the system two years ago, he figured it would be an electronic gadget gathering dust. But by now, just about everybody in town has tried it—including him. Local ministers, hospital officials, a lawyer and insurance agent use it regularly. The Over-50 Club even squeezed in front of the set to discuss their arthritis with the staff of a nursing school in far-off Omaha.

"With this thing," the mayor marvels, "we're just another suburb of Chicago."

[SOURCE: Bill Richards, "Many Rural Regions Are Growing Again; A Reason: Technology," *Wall Street Journal* (November 21, 1994), pp. A1, A5. Reprinted by permission of The Wall Street Journal, © 1994 Dow Jones & Company, Inc. All Rights Reserved Worldwide.]

   a. Describe important differences in how businesses and government evaluate potential capital projects.

   b. Why would it be more difficult for government to quantify the benefits of technology investments than it would be for business to do so?

   c. How does business benefit from governmental investment in technology?

47. (LO 1, 6; *Timing of new investment*) Clewash Linen Supply Company provides laundered items to various commercial and service establishments in a large city. Clewash is scheduled to acquire new cleaning equipment in mid-1997 that should provide some operating efficiencies. The new equipment would enable Clewash to increase the volume of laundry it handles without any increase in labor costs. In addition, the estimated maintenance costs in terms of pounds of laundry would be reduced slightly with the new equipment.

The new equipment was justified not only on the basis of reduced cost but also on the basis of an expected increase in demand starting in late 1997. However, since the original forecast was prepared, several potential new customers have either delayed or discontinued their own expansion plans in the market area that is serviced by Clewash. The most recent forecast indicates that no great increase in demand can be expected until late 1998 or early 1999.

Identify and explain the factors that Clewash Linen Supply Company should consider in deciding whether to delay the investment in the new cleaning equipment. In the presentation of your response, distinguish between those factors that tend to indicate that the investment should be made as scheduled versus those that tend to indicate that the investment should be delayed.

(CMA)

48. (LO 7; *Post-investment audit*) Dickson, Inc., has formal policies and procedures to screen and ultimately approve capital projects. Proposed capital projects are classified as one of the following types:

- Expansion requiring new plant and equipment.
- Expansion by replacement of present equipment with more productive equipment.
- Replacement of old equipment with new equipment of similar quality.

All expansion projects and replacement projects that will cost more than $50,000 must be submitted to the top management capital investment committee for approval. The investment committee evaluates proposed projects considering the costs and benefits outlined in the supporting proposal and the long-range effects on the company.

The projected revenue and/or expense effects of the projects, once operational, are included in the proposal. Once a project is accepted, the committee approves an expenditure budget for the project from its inception until it becomes operational. The expenditures required each year for the expansions or replacements are also incorporated into Dickson's annual budget procedure. The budgeted revenue and/or cost effects of the projects, for the periods in which they become operational, are incorporated into the five-year forecast.

Dickson, Inc., does not have a procedure for evaluating projects once they have been implemented and become operational. The vice-president of finance has recommended that Dickson establish a post-investment audit program to evaluate its capital expenditure projects.

a. Discuss the benefits a company could derive from a post-investment audit program for capital expenditure projects.

b. Discuss the practical difficulties in collecting and accumulating information that would be used to evaluate a capital project once it becomes operational.

(CMA)

49. (LO 1, 6; *Investment in training*) *Bruce McCloud, a research assistant from Boston, recently flew to Italy with colleagues to present a paper on Lyme disease. On his way home, he took a weeklong vacation in Egypt.*

Just three years ago, Mr. McCloud was 35 years old, poor, unemployed and living with his mother in a bad part of town. His life changed when he enrolled in a nine-month biotechnology training program with Jobs for Youth Inc. Upon finishing, he landed a laboratory job at New England Medical Center at a yearly salary of $27,000.

This story may look good to proponents of job training, but here's the catch: Jobs for Youth, a Boston-based employment training agency with a $1.5 million budget, spent $10,000 to put Mr. McCloud through its biotech program. In the past three years, the program has graduated 70 people, all at about the same cost.

How best to get people off welfare and into the work force has lately become the subject of heated debate. President Clinton's welfare-reform bill, which lingers in committee in Congress, proposes about $7.7 billion in new funding over the next five years to help get the five million current welfare recipients off the dole. That's a little more than $1,000 a person. But if Jobs for Youth is any indication, it costs far more than that to train unskilled people for meaningful jobs.

Indeed, many federally funded job-training programs currently spend $2,000 to $4,000 a person, last two to three months—and aim to qualify people for jobs with salaries of $10,000 to $15,000 a year.

[SOURCE: Joseph Pereira, "Good Job Training Comes at a Price, Program Shows," *Wall Street Journal* (August 5, 1994), pp. B1, B4. Reprinted by permission of The Wall Street Journal, © 1994 Dow Jones & Company, Inc. All Rights Reserved Worldwide.]

a. In general, who benefits from public job training programs? Who bears the cost of public job-training programs?

b. Write an essay either attacking or defending the expenditure of $10,000 of public funds to train a welfare recipient. Use quantitative estimates to support your arguments.

■ PROBLEMS

50. (LO 2, 3, 8; *Timeline; payback; NPV*) Realistic Taxi Company is considering the purchase of a new car to replace one it has been leasing. The new car would cost $10,000, last eight years, and have no salvage value. Annual incremental operating costs on the new car are expected as follows:

YEAR	AMOUNT
1	$2,700
2	2,800
3	3,000
4	4,000
5	4,000
6	4,100
7	4,200
8	4,500

The annual lease rental cost is $6,000. Realistic uses a 10 percent discount rate.

a. Construct a timeline for the purchase of the car.
b. Determine the payback period.
c. Calculate the net present value of the project.

51. (LO 2, 3, 6, 8; *NPV*) Minnesota Steelworks manufactures running gears for various types of automobile trailers. One of its main manufacturing processes involves bending sheet metal into various shapes. At the current time, this process is performed manually by a staff of 10 workers. The company is considering mechanizing this process with a computer-driven bending machine. The machine would cost $1,200,000 and would be operated by a single person. It would have an estimated life of 10 years and a salvage value of $50,000 at the end of its life. Following are estimates of the annual labor savings as well as the additional costs associated with the operation of the new machine:

Annual labor cost savings (10 workers)	$260,000
Wages of bending machine operator	50,000
Annual maintenance costs	22,000
Annual property taxes	14,000
Annual insurance costs	14,000

a. Assuming the company's cost of capital is 12 percent, compute the net present value of the investment in the computer-driven bending machine. Ignore taxes.
b. Based on the NPV, should the company invest in the new machine?
c. What other factors should the company consider in evaluating this investment?
d. Why would you want the personnel director involved in this capital budgeting decision?

52. (LO 2, 3, 6, 8; *NPV; alternative financing and operating arrangements*) The Electrical Wholesale Supply Co. sells electrical supplies and products throughout the Rocky Mountain states. The company maintains one central warehouse of merchandise to supply demand companywide. Because of increased customer demand and weather patterns, the company has found it necessary to acquire an additional warehousing facility. The owner of one warehouse has offered to lease space to the company under two alternative arrangements.

Under the first arrangement, the company would be required to pay $100,000 per year for a 20-year lease agreement. The owner would provide all insurance, maintenance, and other such costs. Under the second alternative, the company would assume total management of the facility and would pay $800,000 in advance for a 20-year lease. This alternative would also require the company to pay an estimated $20,000 in annual operating expenses.

a. Assuming the company's cost of capital is 8 percent and using the net present value method, determine which lease option would be the most appealing to the company.

b. What other factors might the company consider in selecting the lease arrangement?

53. (LO 2, 3, 4, 8; *NPV; uncertainty*) Atlanta Industrial is a midsize manufacturing company with a total market value of approximately $100,000,000. The president of the company, Joanna Mills, is considering investing in an expansion project.

    Ms. Mills admits that there is a great deal of uncertainty about the net present value of this project because the net present value is highly correlated with the future state of the economy. She has prepared estimates for the three possible states:

STATE OF THE ECONOMY	RESULTING NPV	PROBABILITY OF OCCURRENCE
Great	$15,000,000	.5
Normal	7,500,000	.4
Poor	(60,000,000)	.1

a. Determine an overall expected NPV based on the preceding data. Is the project acceptable?

b. If an alternative project were available that had the same expected overall NPV but was not dependent on the state of the economy, would Atlanta Industrial prefer the alternative project? Explain.

c. What other techniques could the company use to deal with the uncertainty inherent in this investment?

54. (LO 2, 3, 4, 8; *NPV; uncertainty*) The Stone Mountain Road Co. supplies materials to construction companies to build roads and bridges. The company has been searching for a location at which to "mine" gravel for a new major interstate road project.

    The owner of one location is willing to allow the company to mine all the gravel it needs for the road project, provided the firm reclaims the land (which essentially involves building a road and a small lake and planting trees) after the road project is completed. The firm would also be required to post a $2,000,000 damage deposit, which would be refunded (without interest) at the end of the reclamation. The road project is expected to last three years, and the reclamation of the mining location would require an additional year. To evaluate the feasibility of this offer, the company has estimated cash expenses and cash income under a pessimistic and an optimistic scenario:

	PESSIMISTIC	OPTIMISTIC
Costs to relocate mining equipment	$ 200,000	$ 200,000
Damage deposit	2,000,000	2,000,000
Year 1 gravel sales	4,000,000	4,400,000
Year 2 gravel sales	4,000,000	4,400,000
Year 3 gravel sales	6,000,000	7,000,000
Costs of reclamation (year 4)	1,000,000	700,000
Annual fixed cash expenses	800,000	800,000
Annual variable expenses	75% of sales	70% of sales

The annual fixed and variable expenses would be incurred only in years 1 through 3, when the mine is operational.

a. Assuming the company's cost of capital is 11 percent, compute the net present value under both alternatives. Ignore taxes.

b. Suppose the company estimates that the probability of the pessimistic scenario's occurring is .3 and the probability of the optimistic scenario's occurring is .7. What should the company do?

55. (LO 2, 3, 4, 8; *NPV; payback; uncertainty*) The Zulch County Zoo is considering the acquisition of an exotic snake collection. The collection and needed equipment could be purchased for $800,000 and would have an expected life of 15 years with no salvage value. The annual cash cost of maintaining the snakes is estimated at $72,000. The manager of the zoo is uncertain as to how much the new collection would increase annual cash revenues.

a. Assuming the zoo's cost of capital is 9 percent, compute the minimum amount by which cash receipts would need to increase to induce the manager to purchase the snake collection. If the zoo admission price is $12 per person, how many new admissions must the zoo attract annually?

b. Based on your answer in part a, compute the payback period for the new investment.

c. Besides the executive manager, what other experts might have provided input into the determination of the costs associated with the proposed snake collection? Explain.

56. (LO 2, 3, 8; *NPV; IRR; financing decision*) George Lewis is trying to decide whether to pay $600,000 to buy the land and building where his business is located or to continue to rent it for $96,000 annually. The present owner assures George that he can continue to rent for the next 20 years. If George buys the property, he will incur property taxes of $4,000 and maintenance costs of $2,000 annually. At the end of 20 years, the property would have such an uncertain salvage value that George wishes to ignore it in his calculations. George's cost of capital (which he uses to discount cash flows) is 13 percent.

a. Should George continue to rent or buy? Base your answer on the net present value of the property.

b. Based on your answer to part a, what is the profitability index of the investment?

c. What is the internal rate of return on the investment?

57. (LO 2, 3, 6, 8; *PI*) Laura-Leigh Corp. has $400,000 available for commitment to capital projects. All projects listed below have cleared the company's screening criteria. Now the company must reduce the list to the *most* acceptable projects.

PROJECTS	REQUIRED INVESTMENT	NPV
A	$110,000	$ 12,000
B	50,000	24,000
C	220,000	120,000
D	200,000	112,000
E	20,000	10,000
F	80,000	16,000
G	30,000	8,000
H	100,000	28,000
I	400,000	170,000

a. From a purely quantitative perspective, which projects should be accepted?

b. What factors might cause the list of projects actually selected to differ from the list you identified for part a?

58. (LO 2, 3, 8; *NPV; PI; payback*) Jill Grayson is the division manager of the Metalworks Division of the Aluminum Siding and Awning Company. One of Jill's assistants, Jack Hawk, has heard about a new machine on the market that could replace one of their existing machines. Jack has suggested to Jill that the new machine be purchased because it would allow the division to save $250,000 per year in the costs of applying vinyl to the aluminum siding. Jack has asked Jill to look at the following information, which summarizes his analysis:

Old machine:
Original cost new	$750,000
Present book value	500,000
Annual cash operating costs	500,000
Market value now	100,000
Market value in 5 years	0
Remaining useful life	5 years

New machine:
Cost	$900,000
Annual cash operating costs	250,000
Market value in 5 years	0
Useful life	5 years

Jill tells Jack that they cannot make such a decision by looking at operating cost savings alone; both costs and benefits of the new machine must be considered.

a. Assume that the cost of capital in this company is 10 percent, which is the rate to be used in a discounted cash flow analysis. Compute the net present value and profitability index of investing in the new machine. Ignore taxes. Should the machine be purchased? Why or why not?

b. Compute the payback period for the investment in the new machine. Ignore taxes.

59. (LO 2, 3, 5, 8; *NPV; depreciation methods*) Ted Wright, president of Wright Works, asked his accountant to evaluate a proposal to buy a new press that would cost $104,000. The purchase would be made at the beginning of the company's fiscal year. The press would have an estimated life of eight years and no salvage value at the end of its life. Wright's accountant estimated that the press would save $38,000 annually in operating costs. The firm uses a discount rate of 8 percent and has a tax rate of 32 percent.

a. Using straight-line depreciation, calculate the net present value of the press.

b. Mr. Wright asks how much the NPV would differ if the sum-of-the-years-digits (SYD) depreciation method were used. Assume for this problem that the SYD method is acceptable for tax purposes in the fiscal year of the purchase and recompute the net present value. (Round all calculations to the nearest dollar.)

c. Which NPV is higher, that computed in part a or part b? Why?

d. Referring to your answer in part a, what discount rate would cause the NPV to equal 0? What is this discount rate called?

60. (LO 2, 3, 5, 8; *After-tax amounts; NPV*) Hubert Drew manages the U.S. division of South-of-the-Border Fruit Company. Mr. Drew is presently contemplating

an investment in a new fruit processing technology. The new technology is superior to existing technology because it reduces waste and spoilage. However, several years of experience will be required to fully understand and utilize the technology. Following are financial characteristics of the investment.

Initial cost	$2,500,000
Net annual increase in cash revenues:	
Year 1	250,000
Year 2	500,000
Year 3	650,000
Year 4	2,000,000
Year 5	1,800,000

The technology will have a five-year life with no salvage value. The company's cost of capital is 10 percent and its income tax rate is 35 percent. All assets are depreciated by the straight-line method.

a. Compute the after-tax NPV of the potential investment.

b. Based on the NPV, will Mr. Drew invest in the project?

c. Assume Mr. Drew is evaluated based on the amount of pretax profit his division generates. Compute the effect of the new investment on the divisional profit for years 1 through 3.

d. Based on your computations in part c, will Mr. Drew want to invest in the new project? Explain.

61. (LO 2, 3, 5, 8; *After-tax amounts; NPV; PI; payback*) Ornamental Glassworks is considering adding a new product line. The line would consist of glass Christmas ornaments and would require the following investment:

Production equipment	$ 600,000
Working capital	300,000
Marketing equipment and displays	150,000
Total	$1,050,000

The production and marketing equipment, as well as the marketing displays, would have an expected life of 10 years. All equipment and displays would be depreciated over this 10-year period by the straight-line method (no salvage value would be recognized in computing depreciation deductions). At the end of 10 years, it is expected the equipment and displays could be sold for a total of $25,000. Following are the expected operating cash receipts and cash expenses by year for the proposed product line:

	CASH RECEIPTS	CASH EXPENSES
Year 1	$120,000	$150,000
Year 2	240,000	150,000
Year 3	300,000	155,000
Year 4	360,000	205,000
Year 5	450,000	200,000
Years 6–10	540,000	245,000

The company's tax rate is 35 percent, and its cost of capital is 7 percent.

a. Compute the after-tax net present value and profitability index for the proposed investment.

b. Compute the after-tax payback for the proposed investment.

c. Based on the NPV and PI, should the investment be made?

d. Assume you are an expert in U.S. income taxation. Why would your knowledge be useful in this capital budgeting decision?

62. (LO 2, 3, 5, 6, 8; *After-tax amounts; IRR; payback*) The Armadillo Hide Company manufactures high-quality products from armadillo skins. Currently the company relies on a system of carts and pallets to move materials among work stations. The company is now considering the installation of a robotic conveyor system to move the materials. Some of the financial characteristics of the proposed investment follow:

Required initial investment	$1,800,000
Net annual savings in cash operating costs	310,000
Annual depreciation expense	120,000
Expected salvage value	0
Expected life	15 years

The company's combined state and federal income tax rate is 36 percent.

a. To the nearest whole percentage point, compute the internal rate of return on the investment in the conveyor system.

b. If its cost of capital is 11 percent, should the company invest in the conveyor system? Are there any qualitative factors that might need to be considered?

c. Compute the after-tax payback period for the investment.

63. (LO 6, 9; *Appendix 2*) Sally's Salon is a tanning business that operates 25 tanning booths. Sally is presently considering the installation of computer-controlled tanning equipment. The major benefit of the computer-controlled machinery is that it consumes less electricity and requires less maintenance and oversight. Furthermore, the equipment can be centrally monitored. The installation of 10 computer-controlled machines would allow the firm to scrap 10 existing tanning machines that have no market value. The following financial information summarizes the prospective investment:

Initial cost of the equipment and software	$140,000
Annual depreciation	28,000
Annual labor savings	32,000
Expected salvage value in 5 years	0
Expected life of the computerized machines	5 years

a. Compute the accounting rate of return on this investment. If Sally requires that projects generate an accounting rate of return of 12 percent or greater, is the project acceptable from a quantitative perspective?

b. Based on your knowledge of computerized equipment, do you think Sally has captured all of the relevant costs and benefits associated with the installation of the computerized equipment? Explain.

64. (LO 2, 3, 8, 9; *Comprehensive; Appendix 2*) The management of Fairfax Manufacturing Company is evaluating a proposal to purchase a new drill press as a replacement for a less efficient piece of similar equipment, which would then be sold. The cost of the new drill press, including delivery and installation, is $87,500. If the equipment is purchased, Fairfax will incur $2,500 of costs to remove the present equipment and revamp service facilities. The present equipment has a book value of $25,000 and a remaining useful life of 10 years. The present market value is also $25,000.

Management has provided you with the following comparisons:

	PRESENT EQUIPMENT	NEW EQUIPMENT
Annual production in units	200,000	250,000
Revenue from each unit	$.15	$.15
Annual costs:		
Labor	$15,000	$12,500
Depreciation (10% of asset book value or cost)	2,500	8,750
Other cash operating costs	24,000	10,000

The company uses a 14 percent discount rate in evaluating capital projects and expects the cost of capital projects to be recouped within five years.

Both the existing and new equipment are expected to have a negligible salvage value at the end of ten years.

a. Determine the net present value of the new equipment.
b. Determine the payback period for the new equipment.
c. Determine the accounting rate of return for the new equipment. Assume that 14 percent is also the company's hurdle rate.

65. (LO 2, 3, 8 9; *Comprehensive; Appendix 2*) Oklahoma Grain Co. is considering purchasing a new 150-foot elevator leg for $600,000. The equipment is expected to have a 10-year life and a salvage value of $60,000. The firm currently has a similar piece of equipment. If the new leg is purchased, the firm will sell its old equipment for $40,000. The new leg will save $100,000 in annual operating costs.

Company management has the following policies regarding acceptability of capital projects: (1) the pre-tax rate of return must equal or exceed a discount rate of 11 percent; (2) the accounting rate of return must equal or exceed a hurdle rate of 16 percent; and (3) the payback period cannot be longer than 5.5 years.

a. Prepare a timeline for this project.
b. Compute the net present value.
c. Compute the profitability index.
d. Compute the internal rate of return to the nearest whole percent.
e. Compute the payback period.
f. Compute the accounting rate of return using the following additional information:

1. The $40,000 received from selling the old equipment equals the old leg's book value, so there is no accounting gain or loss on the sale.
2. The project will produce average annual accounting profits of $61,400.

g. For each of the methods, discuss whether your computations showed the project to be quantitatively acceptable.

■ CASES

66. (LO 1, 6, 7; *Making capital investments*) *When Bill Clinton appointed Federico Peña transportation secretary, he described the former Denver mayor as a "doer" who could do for his country what he did for his city. Peña's biggest legacy is the new Denver International Airport, one of the most ambitious—and controversial—public projects in decades. It rises, pryamidlike, on windswept prairie 23 miles northeast of the city. Peña describes it as an airport for the 21st century, a high-tech hub that will draw business from around the world and help keep Denver prosperous. "This is a visionary project," he says, adding that cities with "efficient international airports" will be clear winners in the global marketplace.*

Excited by such prospects, voters approved the project in 1989 by a 2-to-1 margin. But now reality has set in. When selling the project to voters, planners at one point forecast up to 36 weekly flights to Europe by 1993; [as of mid-1993,] there were four. The number of passengers departing from Denver was to rise from 16 million in 1985 to some 26 million by 1995. [The 1992] figure: about the same as in 1985. . . .

Finances have also been unpredictable. Voters approved an airport that would cost around $2 billion, with six runways (and space for six more) and some 120 gates, according to Ted Hackworth, head of the city council's finance committee. Now, it's $3.7 billion he says, citing the latest bond prospectus. For that, Denver gets an airport with five runways and 88 gates, 20 fewer than Stapleton [the existing Denver airport].

The final irony, after all the cost and inconvenience, is that the new airport may lose money. Stapleton last year produced revenues of some $164 million; Denver International will need at least $350 million to break even.

The airport finally opened in early 1995. Because of the extraordinary cost of the airport that airlines have been forced to bear, initial cost of round trip tickets in and out of Denver have been increased by $40.

[SOURCES: Annetta Miller with Seema Nayyar, "Build It and Hope They'll Come," *Newsweek* (June 7, 1993), pp. 41, 44 © 1993, Newsweek, Inc., all rights reserved, reprinted by permission; and Martin Zimmermand, "Airport's Off Ground with Few Hitches," *Dallas Morning News* (March 1, 1995), pp. 1D-2D.]

a. 1. Denver residents hoped that the new airport would bring substantial new business to the area. Why may the cost overruns in building the airport cause businesses to locate elsewhere?

2. Why would the city of Denver perceive an efficient airport as being the key variable in its future growth?

b. One of the biggest problems experienced in building the new airport has been the baggage-handling system:

The $3.7 billion airport, with the latest in high-tech systems, is suffering from the most basic of problems: If it opened as scheduled . . . , passengers would be guaranteed of losing their luggage.

The [luggage conveyance] system relies on more than 100 computers and 56 laser scanners to move 3,600 luggage "telecars" down 21 miles of track. Working properly, it should be able to handle 34,000 bags an hour without human intervention, officials say.[Note: When the airport actually opened in early 1995, the new baggage system worked only for outbound flights and only for flights of United Airlines.]

[SOURCE: J. Lynn Lunsford and Terry Maxon, "Denver Airport Faces Rocky Start," *Dallas Morning News* (March 2, 1994), pp. 1A, 7A.]

1. Why would Denver Airport managers be reluctant to simply scrap the computerized luggage conveyance system and replace it with more traditional technology—a manual conveyance system?

2. How might delaying the opening of the airport, because of the unworkable system, affect the future competitive position of the Denver Airport?

c. The article cited in part b indicates that the annual per-passenger cost of using the Denver Airport will be slightly more than $15. This is about three times the per-passenger cost of Stapleton Airport and a major competitor, Dallas-Fort Worth Airport. The Denver Airport is obviously counting on this cost differential to narrow over the longer run. What factors likely cause the cost differential, and why would it be expected to narrow over time?

d. Why will it be very important to conduct a post-investment audit of this project?

67. (LO 2, 3, 4, 6, 8; *NPV*) Da Limo is a limousine service operating in Chicago. The owner is considering the purchase of five new white stretch limos at a cost of $75,000 each. Each limo will have a useful life of five years and a salvage value of $15,000. Estimated revenues and operating costs for each limo are as follows:

RENTAL FEES

First two years: $150 per hour; 20 hours per week for 52 weeks
Next three years: $100 per hour; 15 hours per week for 52 weeks

OPERATING COSTS

Driver's annual salary: $12,000 (increases $1,000 each year)
Uniform: $200 (at the beginning of the first, third, and fifth years)
Annual insurance: $5,000 each year; annual rate decreases for age are offset by annual increases in premium rates (paid at the beginning of each year)
Annual fees for personalized license plate and inspection: $100 (paid at the beginning of each year)
Annual gas and oil: $36,850 (increases 10% each year of use)
Annual repairs and maintenance: $10,000 (increases 10% each year of use)
Major repairs at the end of the third year: $2,000
Tires at end of second and fourth years: $400

Ignore income taxes in answering the following questions.

a. Determine the net cash flows for each year of the five-year period.
b. Assuming a 14 percent discount rate, what is the net present value? Is the purchase quantitatively acceptable?
c. Assuming a 16 percent discount rate, what is the net present value? Is the purchase quantitatively acceptable?
d. What other factors should be Da Limo's owner consider before acquiring the limos, assuming a positive net present value?

68. (LO 2, 3; *Investment financing*) The board of directors of Miami Hospital is attempting to decide whether to purchase or lease a CAT scanner. The cost of the equipment is $500,000, and its estimated useful life is seven years. The lease period is only five years, so the lease would have to be renewed for the additional two years. The renewal rate is 10 percent of the original lease rate of $100,000 per year.

All costs of operating the CAT scanner are the same under both alternatives. Therefore, they are not relevant to this decision. In addition, all revenues (except those generated by Medicare reimbursements) are the same under both alternatives. Medicare reimbursement is based on either the amount of depreciation or the amount of lease payment. Medicare patients are assumed to use the CAT scanner 30 percent of the time, and Medicare will reimburse that percentage of equipment cost. Equipment cost is defined in the Medicare reimbursement policy as annual straight-line depreciation or out-of-pocket lease payments. Miami Hospital has a discount rate of 8 percent.

a. Assume that the CAT scanner will have no salvage value if it is purchased. Lease payments and Medicare reimbursements occur at the end of each year. What is the net present value of the purchase alternative? The lease alternative? Should the board purchase or lease the CAT scanner?
b. Assume that the CAT scanner will have no salvage value if it is purchased. Lease payments are made at the beginning of the year, and Medicare reimbursements occur at the end of the year. What is the net present value of each alternative? Should the board purchase or lease the CAT scanner?

c. Assume that the CAT scanner will have a 5 percent salvage value if it is purchased. Lease payments and Medicare reimbursements occur at the end of each year. What is the net present value of each alternative? Should the board purchase or lease the CAT scanner?

d. Assume that the CAT scanner will have a 5 percent salvage value if it is purchased. Lease payments are made at the beginning of the year, and Medicare reimbursements occur at the end of the year. What is the net present value of each alternative? Should the board purchase or lease the CAT scanner?

69. (LO 2, 3, 6; *Investment financing*) HMG Corporation is a for-profit health care provider that operates three hospitals. One of these hospitals, Metrohealth, plans to acquire new X-ray equipment. Management has already decided the equipment will be cost beneficial and will enhance the technology available in the outpatient diagnostic laboratory. Before Metrohealth prepares the requisition to corporate headquarters for the purchase, Paul Monden, Metrohealth's controller, has to prepare an analysis to compare financing alternatives.

The equipment is a Supraimage X-ray 400 machine priced at $1,000,000, including shipping and installation; it would be delivered January 2, 1998. Under the tax regulations, this machine qualifies as "qualified technological equipment" with a five-year recovery period. It will be depreciated over five years for tax purposes using the double-declining balance method, with a switch to straight-line at a point in time to maximize the depreciation deduction. The machine will have no salvage value at the end of five years. The three financing alternatives Metrohealth is considering are described next.

■ Finance Internally

   HMG Corporation would provide Metrohealth with the funds to purchase the equipment. The supplier would be paid on the day of delivery.

■ Finance with a Bank Loan

   Metrohealth could obtain a bank loan to finance 90 percent of the equipment cost at 10 percent annual interest, with five annual payments of $237,420 each due at the end of each year, with the first payment due on December 31, 1998. The loan amortization schedule is presented next. Metrohealth would provide the remaining $100,000, which would be paid upon delivery.

YEAR	BEGINNING BALANCE	PAYMENT	INTEREST	PRINCIPAL REDUCTION
1	$900,000	$237,420	$90,000	$147,420
2	752,580	237,420	75,258	162,162
3	590,418	237,420	59,042	178,378
4	412,040	237,420	41,204	196,216
5	215,824	237,420	21,596	215,824

■ Lease from a Lessor

   The equipment could be leased from MedLeasing, with an initial payment of $50,000 due on equipment delivery and five annual payments of $220,000 each, commencing on December 31, 1998. At the option of the lessee, the equipment can be purchased at the fair market value at lease termination (the lessor is currently estimating a 30 percent salvage value). The lease satisfies the requirements to be an operating lease for both FASB and income tax purposes. This means that all lease payments are deductible for tax purposes each year. Because of expected technological changes in medical equipment, Metrohealth would not plan to purchase the X-ray equipment at the end of the lease commitment.

Both HMG Corporation and Metrohealth have an effective income tax rate of 40 percent, an incremental borrowing rate of 10 percent, and an after-tax corporate hurdle rate of 12 percent. Income taxes are paid at the end of the year.

a. Prepare a present value analysis as of January 1, 1998, of the expected after-tax cash flows for each of the three financing alternatives available to Metrohealth to acquire the new X-ray equipment. As part of your present value analysis, (1) justify the discount rates you used and (2) identify the financing alternative most advantageous to Metrohealth.

b. Discuss the qualitative factors Paul Monden should include for management consideration before a final decision is made regarding the financing of this new equipment.

(CMA)

■ ETHICS AND QUALITY DISCUSSIONS

70. *Eleven years since the first car crossed the Luling Bridge [in Louisiana], the span is already undergoing full resurfacing, to the tune of $700,000.*

The cable support system that makes the bridge an architectural wonder is the source of frustration for engineers assigned to unlock the mysteries of the bridge, one of fewer than 10 like it across the country.

Almost as soon as the bridge opened, officials rushed to keep pace with the rapidly deteriorating asphalt-epoxy surface, used because the design could not support heavier concrete.

"I'm not sure anybody knows what failed—if it was the material or the construction or exactly what caused it," said Joseph Smith, bridge maintenance engineer for the state Department of Transportation and Development in Baton Rouge.

Because there are so few bridges like it, Smith said, "I'm not sure if anybody will know.

[SOURCE: Rhonda Bell, "Engineers Baffled by Hale Boggs," *(New Orleans) Times-Picayune* (December 31, 1994), p. B-3. © The Times-Picayune Publishing Corporation.]

a. What message does this news article convey about the relationship between new technology and quality?

b. How might the state have used this new technology to build the bridge while avoiding the failure of the bridge surface?

71. *Conoco's new fitness center cost the company $3 million. Tenneco's two-story 100,000-square-foot facility in Houston cost $11 million. Pepsico, Inc.'s $2 million fitness and health complex is located at its New York headquarters. [Since health and fitness programs are expensive] and intangible benefits can be hard to measure, how does a company know if it is in its best interest to establish and/or continue these programs? Is the company actually benefitting from having more healthy and fit employees, or is it simply incurring hefty expenses and low, if any, short-term returns on investments?*

[The following statistics indicate the benefits provided by such programs.]

1. *The average claim for nonexercising women at Tenneco was $1,535.83, more than double the $639.07 average claim for those who exercise. For men, the average claim for nonexercisers was $1,003.87, compared with $561.68 for those who exercise. The company also observed that a high proportion of excellent business performers also are the exercisers, while a great number of lower performers are nonexercisers. The reason may be that fitness requires discipline. Exercisers said that their "high" feeling from a good workout resulted in positive work attitude and fewer work frustrations.*

2. *Lockheed Missiles and Space Co. estimates that in five years it saved $1 million in life insurance costs through its wellness program. Absenteeism for exercisers was 60% lower than for nonexercisers. It also reports that turnover rate is 13% lower among regular exercisers.*

3. *Dallas school teachers who enrolled in a fitness program took an average of three fewer sick days per year, a savings of almost a half-million dollars a year in substitute teachers' pay.*

The evidence accumulated thus far strongly indicates that fitness programs pay off not only in monetary terms—such as savings in health insurance, life insurance, and sick pay—but also in intangible ways such as productivity, morale, retention, and recruiting.

[SOURCE: Otto H. Chang and Cynthia Boyle, "Fitness Programs: Hefty Expense or Wise Investment," *Management Accounting* (January 1989), pp. 45–47. Published by Institute of Management Accountants, Montvale, NJ.]

a. As extensively as possible, describe the types of business costs and benefits that could be affected by exercise facilities.

b. How could an exercise facility affect the quality of a company's products?

c. Assume that exercise offers the benefits consistent with those described above. Instead of providing exercise facilities for employees, would it be ethical for employers to hire only individuals who are actively involved with private exercise programs? Discuss.

72. Heidi Swenson, the plant manager of the St. Paul plant of the Nordtvedt Manufacturing Company, has submitted a capital budgeting proposal for a new CAD/CAM system for her plant. She is excited about the acquisition, as it almost perfectly meets the plant's needs and she has received approval from the home office. However, reading the local newspaper this morning, Heidi is surprised to discover that Nordtvedt's purchasing agent happens to be the sister of the vendor of the CAD/CAM system.

Nordtvedt Manufacturing has a strict policy that prohibits purchasing from relatives. If this relationship comes to light, the purchasing agent could be fired, and Heidi might not get the system that is best, in her judgment, for the plant. Since the purchasing agent is married, her name is different from her brother's, and it is unlikely that a connection will be made. Heidi is concerned about what to do—abide by the policy or acquire the necessary system at the reasonable price quoted by the vendor.

a. Why would a company have a policy of this nature?

b. What are the ethical conflicts in this situation?

c. What are the potential risks for Heidi? For the company?

d. What do you recommend, and why?

73. The Fore Corporation has operations in over two dozen countries. Fore's headquarters are in Chicago, and company executives frequently travel to visit Fore's foreign and domestic operations.

Fore owns two business jets with international range and six smaller aircraft for shorter flights. Company policy is to assign aircraft to trips based on cost minimization, but practice is to assign aircraft based on organizational rank of the traveler. Fore offers its aircraft for short-term lease or for charter by other organizations whenever Fore employees do not plan to use the aircraft. Fore surveys the market often to keep its lease and charter rates competitive.

William Earle, Fore's vice-president of finance, claims that a third business jet can be justified financially. However, some people in the controller's office think the real reason for a third business jet is because people outranking Earle keep the two business jets busy. Thus, Earle usually must travel in the smaller aircraft.

The third business jet would cost $11 million. A capital expenditure of this magnitude requires a formal proposal with projected cash flows and net present value computations using Fore's minimum required rate of return. If Fore's president and finance committee approve the proposal, it would be submitted to the full board. The board has final approval on capital expenditures exceeding $5 million and has established a policy of rejecting any discretionary proposal that has a negative net present value.

Earle asked Rachel Arnett, assistant corporate controller, to prepare a proposal on a third business jet. Arnett gathered the following information:

- Acquisition cost of the jet, including instrumentation and interior furnishings
- Operating cost of the jet for company use
- Projected avoidable commercial airfare and other avoidable costs from company use of the plane
- Projected value of executive time saved by using the third business jet
- Projected contribution margin from incremental lease and charter activity
- Estimated resale value of the jet
- Estimated income tax effects of the proposal

When Earle reviewed Arnett's completed proposal and saw the large negative net present value figure, he returned the proposal to Arnett and insisted she had made an error in her calculations.

Feeling some pressure, Arnett checked her computations and found no errors. However, Earle's message was clear. Arnett discarded her projections and estimates and replaced them with figures that had a remote chance of actually occurring but were more favorable to the proposal. For example, she used first-class airfares to refigure the avoidable commercial airfare costs, even though the company policy is to fly coach. She found revising the proposal to be distressing.

The revised proposal still had a negative net present value. Earle's anger was evident as he told Arnett to revise the proposal again, and to start with a $100,000 positive net present value and work backward to compute supporting estimates and projections.

a. Explain whether Rachel Arnett's revision of the proposal was in violation of the Standards of Ethical Conduct for Management Accountants. (Refer to Appendix A of the text.)
b. Was William Earle in violation of the Standards of Ethical Conduct for Management Accountants by telling Arnett specifically to revise the proposal? Explain your answer.
c. What elements of the projection and estimation process would be compromised in preparing an analysis for which a preconceived result is sought?
d. Identify specific controls over the capital budgeting process that Fore Corporation could implement to prevent unethical behavior on the part of the vice-president of finance.

(CMA)

74. Andy Vickers was reprimanded by the home office for recommending a pollution abatement project because the project did not meet the standard financial criterion of a 10 percent rate of return. However, Andy had concluded that the $60,000 piece of equipment was necessary to prevent small amounts of arsenic from seeping into the city's water system. No EPA warnings had been issued to the company.

a. Discuss the company requirement of a 10 percent rate of return on all projects.
b. What might be the ultimate consequence to Vickers's company if it fails to prevent arsenic seepage into the groundwater system?
c. How should (or can) Vickers justify the purchase of the equipment to the home office?

■ **PROJECTS**

75. Invite to class the executive at your university who is responsible for computer systems on the campus. Ask the individual to explain to the class the answers to the following questions:

  a. What factors are considered in evaluating the need for new computer systems?
  b. How are new computer systems financially justified?
  c. How is a selection made among competing computer vendors?

76. Conduct a library search on the Economic Recovery Tax Act of 1981. Write a report answering the following questions:

  a. Why was the tax act passed?
  b. Why was the cost recovery period for capital assets substantially reduced under the act?
  c. Was the act successful in stimulating new investment in the United States?

77. Assume that you are employed by a large wholesaler of automobile replacement parts. Your firm provides parts to over 3,000 retailers in the United States, Canada, Mexico, Europe, and Asia. The firm is now considering the acquisition of a new parts management system that would allow major retailers to have an on-line link to the firm for their inventory purchasing and inventory management. The system is compatible with the point-of-sale inventory management systems used by many retailers. Some major benefits of the system include a faster response to orders from retailers, reduction in travel costs for sales people, and reduction in paper costs and other transaction costs associated with sales orders.

  Divide your class into four groups (groups may be formed based on the natural interests of the students): management, marketing, finance, and accounting. Have each group prepare a five minute oral presentation which outlines the contribution that each functional area could make to the evaluation of the proposed inventory management system. After each group has made its presentation, discuss areas of redundancy and any gaps in coverage of relevant areas.

15 RESPONSIBILITY ACCOUNTING AND TRANSFER PRICING IN DECENTRALIZED OPERATIONS

"*We cannot succeed if we persist in our use of the traditional command and control system of management where many thousands of people believe their only responsibility is to do what they are told to do.*"

Paul O'Neill, Alcoa, 1991

LEARNING OBJECTIVES

1. Discuss when decentralized operations are appropriate.

2. Relate responsibility accounting to decentralization.

3. Differentiate among the four types of responsibility centers.

4. Discuss the concept and effects of suboptimization.

5. Understand how and why transfer prices for products are used internally in organizations.

6. Understand how and why transfer prices for services are used internally in organizations.

7. Understand how and why transfer prices are used in multinational enterprises.

ON SITE | ABB Asea Brown Boveri: Decentralized and Determined

[ABB, a $28 billion-in-sales company, was created by the 1988 merger of two engineering firms: Sweden's ASEA and Switzerland's Brown Boveri. To this basic duo, president and CEO Percy Barnevik added 70 more companies in Europe and the United States, making ABB] a global electrical equipment giant that is bigger than Westinghouse and can go head to head with GE. It is a world leader in high-speed trains, robotics, and environmental control.

To make this monster dance, Barnevik . . . created a corps of just 250 global managers to lead 210,000 employees. Says a senior executive at Mitsubishi Heavy Industries: "They're as aggressive as we are. I mean this as a compliment. They are sort of super-Japanese."

ABB isn't Japanese, nor is it Swiss nor Swedish. It is a multinational without a national identity. The company's 13 top managers hold frequent meetings in different countries. Since they share no common first language, they speak only English, a foreign tongue to all but one.

[When the Iron Curtain collapsed,] Barnevik saw a one-time chance to expand his conglomerate. Now ABB Asea Brown Boveri is the most important investor in the former Warsaw Pact countries. Through shrewdly managed acquisitions, it controls 58 companies with 20,000 employees in 16 Eastern countries. Most of these—from turbine makers in Poland to a full-scale power plant assembler in Russia—have already been integrated into the parent company's global production network.

Barnevik follows a simple formula. First, he rarely buys whole companies, preferring potentially profitable divisions among the detritus of the huge, usually bankrupt, socialist enterprises. Once the jewels are identified, ABB negotiators begin devising a business plan while still talking terms. Then they look for local managers. Often this means bypassing older command bureaucrats in favor of younger people, whom ABB finds more adaptable—and hungrier. ABB has already trained more than 5,800 Eastern Europeans.

ABB refuses to accept a minority position. Once in control, it divides the company into profit centers, installs a Western accounting system, starts English lessons for middle managers so they can communicate with headquarters in Zurich, and puts in new testing devices to help raise quality to Western levels. Says Barnevik: "My experience is that within two years you can restore a typical Eastern European company to profitability. But you have to believe in the people."

SOURCES: Carla Rapoport, "A Tough Swede Invades the U.S.," *Fortune* (June 29, 1992), p. 76, © 1992 Time Inc., all rights reserved; and Paul Hofheinz, "Yes, You Can Win in Eastern Europe," *Fortune* (May 16, 1994), PP. 110–112, © 1994 Time Inc., all rights reserved.

Many large companies expand over the years until their corporate structures are so cumbersome that they hinder, rather than help, achievement of organizational goals and objectives. In such cases, top managers often decide to change those structures so the companies can more effectively use their resources and their employees' talents. However, there was never a need to regain effectiveness at ABB Asea Brown Boveri, because Percy Barnevik did not give his young company a chance to develop any degree of stagnation. Decentralization was one of his top priorities from the beginning. In 1991, Barnevik made an odd, but telling, statement about the company: "ABB is an organization with three internal contradictions. We want to be global and local, big and small, radically decentralized with centralized reporting and control."[1] He resolves these seeming inconsistencies by providing his managers with "well-defined sets of responsibilities, clear accountability, and maximum degrees of freedom to execute."[2]

Each organization's structure evolves as its goals, technology, and employees change. For many companies, the progression goes from highly centralized to highly decentralized. The degree of centralization reflects a chain of command, authority and responsibility relationships, and decision-making capabilities. This chapter discusses the extent to which top managers delegate authority to subordinate managers and the reporting systems that can be used to communicate managerial responsibility. In addition, since many decentralized organizations exchange goods and services internally, the concept of transfer pricing among organizational units is discussed.

DECENTRALIZATION

The degree to which authority is retained by top management **(centralization)** or released from top management and passed to lower managerial levels **(decentralization)** can be viewed in terms of a continuum. In a completely centralized firm, a single individual (usually the company owner or president) performs all decision making and retains full authority and responsibility for that organization's activities. In contrast, a purely decentralized organization has virtually no central authority, and each subunit acts as a totally independent entity. Either of these extremes represents a clearly undesirable arrangement. In the totally centralized company, the single individual may not have enough expertise or information to make decisions in all areas. In the totally decentralized firm, subunits may act in ways that are not consistent with the goals of the total organization. Factors associated with pure centralization and pure decentralization are presented in Exhibit 15–1 on page 774. Most businesses (regardless of nationality) fall somewhere between the extremes at a point dictated by practical necessity or, as with ABB, by management design.

While almost every organization is decentralized to some degree, quantifying the extent of decentralization may not be possible. Some subunits may have more autonomy than others. In addition to top management philosophy, decentralization depends on the type of organizational units. For example, a unit, segment, or division that operates in a turbulent environment and must respond quickly to new and unanticipated problems is likely to be a prime candidate for decentralization. For instance, ABB is expanding operations in Russia in spite of political turmoil. "We can't wait for the region to stabilize," says Barnevik. "We want to create a home market there now."[3]

As indicated in the News Note on page 775, top management must also consider the subunit managers' personalities and perceived abilities. Managers in decentralized environments must be goal-oriented, assertive, decisive, and creative. While these employee traits are always desirable, they are essential for decentralized company managers. Managers in decentralized companies must also be willing to accept the authority delegated by top management and to be judged based on the outcomes of the decisions that they make. Some subunit managers may be either reluctant or

centralization
decentralization

■ LEARNING
OBJECTIVE 1
Discuss when decentralized
operations are appropriate.

---

[1]William Taylor, "The Logic of Global Business: An Interview with ABB's Percy Barnevik," *Harvard Business Review* (March-April 1991), p. 95.

[2]Ibid., p. 99.

[3]Paul Hofheinz, "Yes, You Can Win in Eastern Europe," *Fortune* (May 16, 1994), p. 112.

unable to accept this authority or responsibility. Therefore, a company may allow some units to be highly decentralized, while others are only minimally decentralized. Since managerial behaviors change and managers are replaced, supervisors should periodically reassess their decisions about a unit's extent of decentralization.

Decentralization does not necessarily mean that a unit manager has the authority to make all decisions concerning that unit. Top management selectively determines what types of authority to delegate and what types to withhold. For example, ABB wants decentralization with centralized reporting and control. It has achieved this goal in part by establishing coordinated accounting methods and by retaining certain functions at headquarters. Treasury and legal work are provided by headquarters through freestanding service centers whose output is charged to the various decentralized companies. In addition, purchasing is somewhat consolidated in that many supplies for ABB's worldwide business units are bought by a single center in Mannheim, Germany.

Like any management technique, decentralization has advantages and disadvantages. These pros and cons are summarized in Exhibit 15–2 and discussed in the following sections.

Advantages of Decentralization

Decentralization has many personnel advantages. Managers have both the need and the opportunity to develop their leadership qualities, creative problem-solving abili-

■ **EXHIBIT 15–1**
Continuum of Centralization in Organizational Structures

FACTOR	CONTINUUM	
	Pure Centralization	Pure Decentralization
Age of firm	Young ⟶	Mature
Size of firm	Small ⟶	Large
Stage of product development	Stable ⟶	Growing
Growth rate of firm	Slow ⟶	Rapid
Expected impact of incorrect decisions on profits	High ⟶	Low
Top management's confidence in subordinates	Low ⟶	High
Historical degree of control in firm	Tight ⟶	Moderate or loose
Use of technology	Low ⟶	High
Rate of change in the firm's market	Slow ⟶	Rapid

Style Relates to Both Who You Are and Where You're From

When Stig Eriksson and Peter Williams report that most people are delighted to be given greater responsibility and power, with more independence from their boss, they might seem to be stating the obvious. But the two European managers of 3M, the diversified US multinational, have also found that others "are uncomfortable, and need to be coached," as Williams puts it.

The type of response depends partly on the person's character and experience, but also often on their nationality, adds Eriksson. People from relatively authoritarian cultures such as Germany, France and Italy, tend to be unsettled by being allowed considerable autonomy and can take longer to get used to it.

Eriksson and Williams, who are at the heart of a radical reorganisation of the 21,000-person European operations of 3M, have experienced both types of reaction from their staff this year. The reorganisation has transferred most business responsibility from separate country subsidiaries to a network of 19 pan-European divisions—what 3M calls "European Business Centres."

SOURCE: Christopher Lorenz, "Facing Up to Responsibility," *[London] Financial Times* (December 15, 1993), p. 11.

ties, and decision-making skills. Decentralized units provide excellent settings for training personnel and for screening aspiring managers for promotion. Managers can be judged on job performance and on the results of their units relative to units headed by other managers; such comparisons can encourage a healthy level of organizational competition. Decentralization also often leads to greater job satisfaction for managers because it provides for job enrichment and gives a feeling of increased importance to the organization. Employees are given more challenging and responsible work that provides greater opportunities for advancement.

In addition to the personnel benefits, decentralization is generally more effective than centralization in accomplishing organizational goals and objectives. The decen-

---

■ **EXHIBIT 15–2**

Advantages and Disadvantages of Decentralization

ADVANTAGES

- Helps top management recognize and develop managerial talent
- Allows managerial performance to be comparatively evaluated
- Often leads to greater job satisfaction
- Makes the accomplishment of organizational goals and objectives easier
- Allows the use of management by exception

DISADVANTAGES

- May result in a lack of goal congruence or suboptimization
- Requires more effective communication abilities
- May create personnel difficulties upon introduction
- Can be extremely expensive

tralized unit manager has more knowledge of the local operating environment than top management which means (1) reduction in decision-making time, (2) minimization of difficulties resulting from attempts to communicate problems and instructions through an organizational chain of command, and (3) quicker perceptions of environmental changes. Thus, the manager of a decentralized unit not only is in closest contact with daily operations but also is charged with making decisions about those operations.

A decentralized structure also allows implementation of the management by exception principle. Top management, when reviewing divisional reports, can address issues that are out of the ordinary rather than dealing with operations that are proceeding according to plans.

Disadvantages of Decentralization

goal congruence

Not all aspects of a decentralized structure are positive. For instance, authority and responsibility for making decisions may be divided among too many individuals, which can result in a lack of goal congruence among the organizational units. (**Goal congruence** exists when the personal and organizational goals of decision makers throughout a firm are consistent and mutually supportive.) In a decentralized company, unit managers are essentially competing with one another since the results of unit activities are compared. Unit managers may make decisions that positively affect their own units but are detrimental to other organizational units or to the whole company. This process results in suboptimization, which is discussed later in the chapter.

A decentralized organization requires more effective methods of communicating plans, activities, and achievements because decision making is removed from the central office. Top management has delegated the authority to make decisions to unit managers but still retains the ultimate responsibility (to corporate ownership) for the effects of those decisions. Thus, to determine if operations are progressing toward established goals, top management must be continuously aware of events occurring at

As all parts of the former Soviet bloc move toward becoming true free-market economies, businesses see expanded production and sales market opportunities. Companies expanding to such highly unstable overseas locations must recognize that only decentralization will allow managers to react to local situations in a timely and informed manner.

lower levels. If decentralization gets totally out of control, top management must also be willing to step in and take action. To illustrate, operating control at the various Daewoo companies in Korea was given to individual company presidents. But Chairman Kim Woo-Choong took over Daewoo Shipbuilding after labor costs had risen tenfold in ten years and employees had been receiving free haircuts that cost the company $60 a month (including lost time) for every employee. One of the chairman's first acts in making the near-bankrupt company profitable again was to remove the barbershops, which saved $8 million per year.[4]

Some employees may be disrupted when top management attempts to introduce decentralization policies. Employees may be asked to do too much too soon or without enough training. Furthermore, some top managers have difficulty relinquishing control or are unwilling or unable to delegate effectively. Others, like Rupert Murdoch, the billionaire chairman of News Corp., may believe that "micromanaging" is the only way to get things accomplished. As indicated in the accompanying News Note on the next page, some of his employees do not agree.

A final disadvantage of decentralization is that it may be extremely expensive. In a large company, it is unlikely that all subordinate managers have equally good decision-making skills. Thus, the first cost is for training lower-level managers to make better decisions. Second, there is the potential cost of poor decisions. Decentralization implies the willingness of top management to let subordinates make some mistakes, but says ABB's Barnevik, "You have to accept a fair share of mistakes. I tell my people that if we make 100 decisions and 70 turn out to be right, that's good enough. I'd rather be roughly right and fast than exactly right and slow."[5] This philosophy is reiterated in the following quote:

> Decentralization of authority in itself has ethical consequences. It absolutely requires trust and latitude for error. The inability to monitor the performance—especially when measurement of results is the only surveillance—of executives assigned to tasks their superiors cannot know in detail results inexorably in delegation. The leaders of a corporation are accustomed to reliance upon the business acumen of . . . managers, whose results they watch with a practiced eye. Those concerned with the maintenance of the ethical standards of the corporation are dependent just as much on the ethical judgment and moral character of the managers to whom authority is delegated. Beyond keeping our fingers crossed, what do we do?[6]

Decentralization can also create a duplication of activities that can be quite expensive in terms of both time and money. To illustrate, the head of a Du Pont division remarked, "We don't want to have 25 divisions working with 25 consultants, each one getting $100,000 from the company."[7]

Another cost of decentralization relates to developing and operating a more sophisticated planning and reporting system. Since top management delegates decision-making authority but retains ultimate responsibility for decision outcomes, a reporting system must be implemented that will provide top management with the ability to measure the overall accountability of the subunits. This reporting system is known as a responsibility accounting system.

---

[4]Laxmi Nakarmi, "At Daewoo, a 'Revolution' at the Top," *Business Week* (February 18, 1991), pp. 68–69.

[5]Taylor, "The Logic of Global Business," p. 101.

[6]Kenneth R. Andrews, ed., *Ethics in Practice: Managing the Moral Corporation* (Boston: Harvard Business School Press, 1989), p. 7.

[7]Richard Koenig, "Du Pont to Abolish Executive Committee, in Bid to Push More Authority into Ranks," *Wall Street Journal* (October 1, 1990), p. B6.

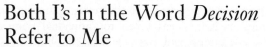

Both I's in the Word *Decision* Refer to Me

[On a single day, Rupert Murdoch would negotiate severance pay for failed talk-show host Chevy Chase,] mull a proposal from Ticket-Master to exchange guns for sports tickets at the local Fox TV station, review the next day's lead editorial for the New York Post, and discuss new sports programming in Asia.

Call it micromanagement, on a global scale. It is a style that hasn't always won fans for the Australian. Some company insiders resent his meddling; scores of journalists have quit over the years because of the way he uses his newspapers to express his personal views. Others say his autocratic rule can be capricious, as he sours suddenly on projects he had only recently championed. And though he relies on a fiercely loyal cadre of lieutenants, he can't seem to tolerate a strong No. 2.

"The atmosphere is sort of like a monarchy," says Greg Nathanson, a former head of Fox's TV stations. "Everybody works for the king, and nothing else matters."

Yet Mr. Murdoch says this is what it takes to manage on a global scale. In an era when the sun never sets on many multinational companies, Mr. Murdoch has fashioned his own antidote to global sprawl: He focuses intensely on one business at a time, yet he drops in on his other holdings at a moment's notice to take command of minor, even trivial, decisions. "If you're going to get into a business," Mr. Murdoch says, "you should get as close to it as possible, even run it yourself for a period."

"You must accept the fact that you work for someone who is in and out of your business," says one News Corp. executive. "Occasionally he's going to dial you up and it isn't always about your priority for that day or that week." Managers say they are sometimes paralyzed in decision-making as they wait to hear from him first.

SOURCE: Meg Cox, "How Do You Tame a Global Company? Murdoch Does It Alone," *Wall Street Journal* (February 14, 1994), pp. A1, A6. Reprinted by permission of The Wall Street Journal, © 1994 Dow Jones & Company, Inc. All Rights Reserved Worldwide.

RESPONSIBILITY ACCOUNTING SYSTEMS

responsibility accounting

Responsibility accounting refers to an accounting system that provides information to top management about the performance of an organizational subunit. As decentralization became more prevalent in the business environment, responsibility accounting systems evolved from the increased need to communicate operating results through the managerial hierarchy.

responsibility reports

■ LEARNING OBJECTIVE 2
Relate responsibility accounting to decentralization.

A responsibility accounting system produces **responsibility reports** to assist each successively higher level of management in evaluating the performances of its subordinate managers and their respective organizational units. These reports reflect the revenues and/or costs under the control of a specific unit manager. Any revenues or costs that are not under the control of a specific unit manager should not be shown on his or her responsibility reports. Much of the information communicated on these reports is monetary, although some nonmonetary data may be included.

The number of responsibility reports issued at a specific point in time for a decentralized unit depends on how much influence that unit's manager has on the unit's day-to-day operations and costs. If a manager strongly influences all operations and costs of a unit, one report will suffice for both the manager and the unit. Normally, however, some costs are not controlled (or are only partially or indirectly controlled) by the unit manager. In such instances, the responsibility report takes one of two forms. First, a single report can be issued that shows all costs incurred in the unit, separately classified as either controllable or uncontrollable by the manager. Alternatively, separate reports can be prepared for the manager and for the unit. The manager's report would include only costs under his or her control, while the unit's report would include all costs.

A responsibility accounting system is the lynch pin in making decentralization work effectively. The responsibility reports about unit performance are primarily tailored to fit the planning, controlling, and decision-making needs of subordinate managers. Top managers review these reports to evaluate the efficiency and effectiveness of each unit and each manager.

One purpose of a responsibility accounting system is to "secure control at the point where costs are incurred instead of assigning them all to products and processes remote from the point of incurrence."[8] This purpose agrees with the concepts of standard costing and activity-based costing. In standard costing, variances are traced to the person (or machine) responsible for the variance (for example, the material purchase price variance can generally be traced to the purchasing agent). Activity-based costing attempts to trace as many costs as possible to the activities that caused the costs rather than using highly aggregated allocation techniques.

Control procedures are implemented for the following three reasons:

- Managers attempt to cause actual operating results to conform to planned results. This conformity is known as effectiveness.
- Managers attempt to cause, at a minimum, the standard output to be produced from the actual input costs incurred. This conformity is known as efficiency.
- Managers need to ensure, to the extent possible, a reasonable utilization of plant and equipment. Utilization is primarily affected by product or service demand. At higher volumes of activity or utilization, fixed capacity costs can be spread over more units, resulting in a lower unit cost. Utilization is even an appropriate concept in service businesses. For instance, bank credit card operations require substantial investments in technology and marketing. According to the general manager of Bank of New York's credit-card operation, "In effect, you're running a factory, and the more volume you can push through your fixed costs, the better the profits are."[9] (BNY, though, selectively targets potential customers and does not send credit card applications to everyone—regardless of how much volume that might generate.)

Responsibility accounting implies that subordinate managers accept the authority given to them by top management and helps them in conducting the control functions shown in Exhibit 15–3 (page 780). Budgets are used to officially communicate output expectations (sales, production, and so forth) and, through budget appropriations, to delegate the authority to spend. Ideally, subunit managers negotiate budgets and standards for their units with top management for the coming year. Involvement in the budgeting process is essential for motivating those whose performance will be evaluated on budget-to-actual comparisons.

The responsibility accounting system should be designed so that actual data are captured in conformity with budgetary accounts. During the year, the accounting sys-

[8]W. W. Cooper and Yuji Ijiri, eds., *Kohler's Dictionary for Accountants* (Englewood Cliffs, N.J.: Prentice-Hall, 1983), p. 435.

[9]Douglas R. Sease and Robert Guenther, "Big Banks Are Plagued by a Gradual Erosion of Key Profit Centers," *Wall Street Journal* (August 1, 1990), p. A14.

tem records and summarizes data for each organizational unit. Operating reports comparing actual account balances with budgeted, standard, or target amounts are prepared periodically and issued to managers. Because of day-to-day contact with operations, managers should be aware of any significant variances before they are reported, identify variance causes, and attempt to correct causes of the problems. Top managers, on the other hand, may not know about operational variances until they receive responsibility reports. By the time top management receives the reports, problems causing the variances should have been corrected, or subordinate managers should be able to explain why the problems were not or could not have been resolved.

The responsibility reports received by top management may compare actual performance against the master budget. Such a comparison can be viewed as yielding an overall performance evaluation, since the master budget reflects management's expectations about sales prices, volume, and mix, as well as costs. However, using the budget for comparison may be inappropriate in some cases. For example, if the budget has an allowance for scrap built into the materials usage estimate, comparing results

■ **EXHIBIT 15–3**
Basic Steps in a Control Process

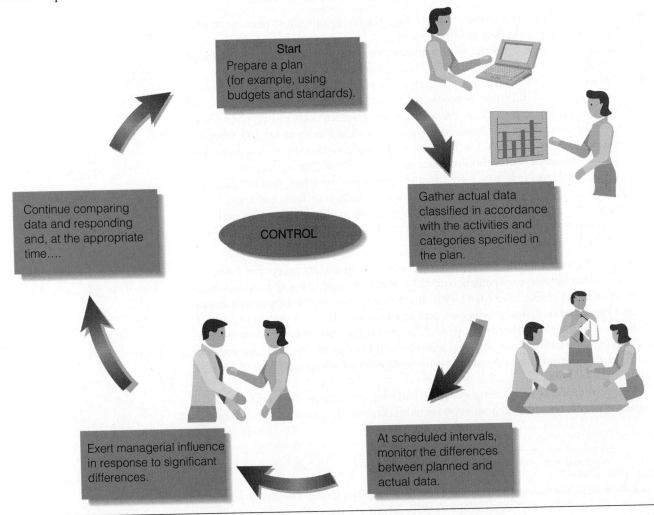

with the budget figure fails to support a focus on total quality. In such a case, a positive variance relative to the budget should not necessarily be judged as favorable performance if significant scrap still is being produced. Establishing a target goal of zero scrap would mean that any variance would be identified as unfavorable.

Perhaps a more appropriate form of responsibility report is that associated with the flexible budget. This report form compares actual information about controllable items (revenues and/or costs) both with the master budget and with amounts based on the achieved activity level. This secondary comparison is more useful for control purposes, since both operating results and budget figures are based on the same level of activity.

Regardless of the comparisons provided, responsibility reports reflect the upward flow of information from operational units to top management. These reports indicate the broadening scope of managerial responsibility. Managers receive detailed information on the performance of their immediate areas of control and summary information on all other organizational units for which they are responsible. Summarizing results causes a pyramiding of information. Reports for the lowest-level units are highly detailed, while reports are less specific at the top of the organization. Upper-level managers desiring information more specific than that provided in summary reports can review the responsibility reports prepared for their subordinates.

Exhibit 15–4 (page 782) illustrates the January set of performance reports for the Pump Division of Karlsson-Andersson, a fictional Swiss conglomerate. All information is shown in the home office currency of Swiss francs (SwF). The Cutting and Assembly Department's actual costs are compared with those in the flexible budget. Data for Cutting and Assembly are then aggregated with data of other departments under the control of the production vice-president. These combined data are shown in the middle section of Exhibit 15–4. In a like manner, the total costs of the production vice-president's area of responsibility are combined with other costs for which the company president is responsible and are shown in the top section of Exhibit 15–4.

Variances should be individually itemized in lower-level performance reports so that the manager under whose supervision those variances occurred has the detail needed to take appropriate corrective action. Under the management by exception principle, major deviations from expectations are highlighted in the subordinate manager's reporting section to assist upper-level managers in making decisions about when to become involved in subordinates' operations. If no significant deviations exist, top management is free to devote its attention to other matters. In addition, such detailed variance analysis alerts operating managers to items they may need to explain to superiors.

In addition to the monetary information shown in Exhibit 15–4, many responsibility accounting systems are now providing information on critical nonmonetary measures of the period's activity. Some examples are shown in Exhibit 15–5 (page 783). Many of these measures are equally useful for manufacturing and service organizations and can be used along with basic financial measurements in judging performance.

The performance reports of each management layer are reviewed and evaluated by all successive layers of management. Managers are likely to be more careful and alert in controlling operations knowing that the reports generated by the responsibility accounting system reveal financial accomplishments and problems. Thus, in addition to providing a means for control, responsibility reports can motivate managers to influence operations in ways that will reflect positive performance.

The focus of responsibility accounting is people. The people emphasized are the managers responsible for an organizational unit such as a department, division, or geographic region. The subunit under the control of a manager is called a responsibility center.

■ **EXHIBIT 15–4**
Pump Division January 1996 Performance Reports

PRESIDENT'S PERFORMANCE REPORT

	Actual Results	Flexible Budget	Variance Over (Under)
Administrative Office—President	SwF 267,200	SwF 264,000	SwF 3,200
Financial Vice-President	313,200	316,600	(3,400)
Production Vice-President	1,105,200	1,103,800	1,400
Sales Vice-President	368,800	366,000	2,800
Totals	SwF 2,054,400	SwF 2,050,400	SwF 4,000

PRODUCTION VICE-PRESIDENT'S PERFORMANCE REPORT

	Actual Results	Flexible Budget	Variance Over (Under)
Administrative Office—VP	SwF 243,000	SwF 240,000	SwF 3,000
Inspect, Polish and Package	112,600	113,400	(800)
Finishing	168,000	169,600	(1,600)
Cutting and Assembly	581,600	580,800	800
Totals	SwF 1,105,200	SwF 1,103,800	SwF 1,400

CUTTING AND ASSEMBLY MANAGER'S PERFORMANCE REPORT

	Actual Results	Flexible Budget	Variance Over (Under)
Direct Materials	SwF 163,400	SwF 166,400	SwF (3,000)
Direct Labor	255,200	253,000	2,200
Supplies	24,600	23,400	1,200
Indirect Labor	59,600	58,600	1,000
Power	50,200	52,200	(2,000)
Repairs and Maintenance	17,200	16,200	1,000
Other	11,400	11,000	400
Totals	SwF 581,600	SwF 580,800	SwF 800

TYPES OF RESPONSIBILITY CENTERS

responsibility centers

■ **LEARNING OBJECTIVE 3**
Differentiate among the four types of responsibility centers.

Responsibility accounting systems identify, measure, and report on the performance of people who control the activities of **responsibility centers.** There are four classifications of responsibility centers, based on the manager's scope of authority and type of financial responsibility: cost, revenue, profit, and investment. These centers are illustrated in Exhibit 15–6 (page 784) and discussed in the following sections.

Cost Centers

cost center

In a **cost center,** the manager has the authority only to incur costs and is specifically evaluated on the basis of how well costs are controlled. In many cost centers, no revenues are generated because the unit does not engage in any revenue-producing activity. For example, the placement center in a university may be a cost center, since it does not charge for the use of its services but does incur costs.

■ **EXHIBIT 15–5**

Nonmonetary Information for Responsibility Reports

- Departmental/divisional throughput
- Number of defects (by product, product line, supplier)
- Number of orders backlogged (by date, quantity, cost, and selling price)
- Number of customer complaints (by type and product); method of complaint resolution
- Percentage of orders delivered on time
- Manufacturing (or service) cycle efficiency
- Percentage of reduction in non-value-added time from previous period (broken down by idle time, storage time, quality control inspection time)
- Number of employee suggestions considered significant and practical
- Number of employee suggestions implemented
- Number of unplanned production interruptions
- Number of schedule changes
- Number of engineering change orders; percentage change from previous period
- Number of safety violations; percentage change from previous period
- Number of days of employee absences; percentage change from previous period

In other instances, revenues may be associated with a particular subunit, but they either are not under the manager's control or are not effectively measurable. The first type of situation exists in a governmental agency that is provided a specific proration of sales tax dollars but has no authority to levy or collect the related taxes. The second situation could exist in engineered and discretionary cost centers in which the outputs (revenues or benefits generated from the cost inputs) are not easily measured.[10] In these situations, revenues should not be included in the manager's responsibility accounting report. As discussed in the News Note on page 785, a person's performance should be judged only in relation to his or her specific duties and responsibilities.

In the traditional manufacturing environment, a standard costing system is generally used, and variances are reported and analyzed. In such an environment, the highest priority in a cost center is often the minimization of unfavorable cost variances. Top management may often concentrate only on the unfavorable variances occurring in a cost center and ignore the efficient performance indicated by favorable variances. For example, referring back to Exhibit 15–4, the production vice-president of the Pump Division of Karlsson-Andersson might focus only on the unfavorable materials and power variances for the Cutting and Assembly Department while disregarding the favorable variances for the other costs of production. Significant favorable variances should not be ignored if the management by exception principle is to be applied appropriately. Using this principle, all variances (both favorable and unfavorable) that fall outside the preestablished limits for normal deviations should be investigated.

Individual departments in a large retail store may be treated as cost or revenue centers by the store manager, while the store itself may be treated as a profit or investment center by corporate headquarters. Such designations reflect the degree of control a manager has over selling prices, costs, and/or plant assets.

[10]Engineered and discretionary costs are discussed in Chapter 12.

■ **EXHIBIT 15–6**

Types of Responsibility Centers

Cost center—manager is responsible for cost containment.

Revenue center—manager is responsible for revenue generation.

Profit center—manager is responsible for profit (both revenue generation and cost containment).

Investment center—manager is responsible for return on asset base.

In the Karlsson-Andersson example, Darrel Reeves, the manager of the Cutting and Assembly Department, should have determined the causes of the variances before filing the report. For instance, it is possible that substandard materials were purchased and caused excessive usage. If this is the case, the purchasing agent, not Mr. Reeves, should be held accountable for the variance. Other possible causes for the unfavorable material variance include increased material prices, excess waste, or some combination of all these causes. Only additional inquiry or investigation can determine whether that variance could have been controlled by Mr. Reeves. Similarly, the power variance may have resulted from an increase in utility costs.

The favorable direct labor variance should also be analyzed. Mr. Reeves may have used inexperienced personnel who were being paid lower rates. Such a situation might explain both the favorable direct labor variance and, to some extent, the unfavorable direct material variance (because the workers were less skilled and may have overused materials). Alternatively, the people working in the Cutting and Assembly Department could simply have been very efficient this period. In this case, Reeves would compliment and reward the efficient employees and might also consider incorporating the improvement as a revised time standard.

Performance Measurements Must Correlate with Jobs

Measuring individual processes with overall gross indicators is analogous to measuring a professional baseball player on his team's overall performance. It isn't fair to say that a player is no good because his team has a losing record. It is fair, however, to measure that player on RBIs, batting average, or on base percentage because he can influence those measures directly. In the manufacturing process, it is not fair to measure a line foreman on cost of production as a percentage of sales because he cannot control sales price, sales volume, or many elements of cost. It is fair to measure that foreman on utility usage, cycle time, and schedule attainment, which he can control and influence directly.

SOURCE: Mark E. Beischel and K. Richard Smith, "Linking the Shop Floor to the Top Floor," *Management Accounting* (October 1991), p. 26. Published by Institute of Management Accountants, Montvale, NJ.

Revenue Centers

A **revenue center** is strictly defined as an organizational unit whose manager is accountable only for the generation of revenues and has no control over setting selling prices or budgeting costs. In many retail stores, the individual sales departments are considered independent units and managers are evaluated based on the total revenues generated by their departments. Departmental managers, though, may not be given the authority to change selling prices to affect volume, and they often do not participate in the budgeting process related to departmental costs. In general, however, few pure revenue centers exist.

revenue center

Managers of "revenue centers" are typically responsible for revenues but also are involved in planning and control related to some (but not necessarily all) of the center's costs. Thus, this organizational unit is more appropriate termed a "revenue and limited cost center." For example, a sales manager who is responsible for the sales revenues generated in her territory may additionally be accountable for controlling the mileage and other travel-related expenses of her sales staff. She may not, however, be able to influence the types of cars her sales staff obtain, because cars are acquired on a fleetwide basis by top management.

Salaries, if directly traceable, are often a cost responsibility of a "revenue center" manager. This situation reflects the traditional retail environment in which each sales clerk is assigned to a specific department and is only allowed to check out customers who want to purchase that department's merchandise. Most stores have found such a checkout situation detrimental to business, because customers are forced to wait for the appropriate clerk. Clerks in many stores are now allowed to assist all customers with all types of merchandise. Such a change in policy converts what was a traceable departmental cost into an indirect cost. Stores carrying high-cost, high-selling-price merchandise normally retain the traditional system. Managers of such departments are thus able to trace sales salaries as a direct departmental cost. If the departmental manager has control over the salaries paid (or hours worked by hourly-wage employees), the manager should be held accountable for such costs.

In analyzing variances from budget, managers in a revenue center need to consider three possible causes: sales price differences, sales mix differences, and volume differences. The effects of sales price differences and volume differences were discussed in Chapter 11. The model presented in that chapter is expanded below to illustrate the effect of a difference in product sales mix from that which was budgeted.

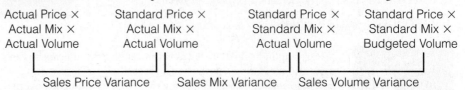

Exhibit 15–7 presents the revenue statistics and variance computations for the Canadian Engine Division of Karlsson-Andersson for May 1996. Inspection of the results reveals that (1) prices increased (except for turbine engines), causing an overall favorable price variance; (2) the actual mix included more of the lower-priced engines (gas and electric) than the standard mix, causing an overall unfavorable mix variance; and (3) the number of units sold (6,100) was greater than the number of units budgeted (6,000), causing a favorable volume variance. The Canadian Engine Division's manager is to be commended for good performance.

■ EXHIBIT 15–7
Variances for a Revenue Center

BUDGET	UNIT PRICE	UNITS	REVENUE	STANDARD MIX FOR BUDGETED VOLUME	
Gas engines (G)	C$1400	3,000	C$4,200,000	3,000 ÷ 6,000 =	50.0%
Turbine engines (T)	1,600	2,000	3,200,000	2,000 ÷ 6,000 =	33.3%
Electric engines (E)	1,100	1,000	1,100,000	1,000 ÷ 6,000 =	16.7%
Totals		6,000	C$8,500,000		100.0%

ACTUAL MIX FOR ACTUAL VOLUME

Gas engines	C$1,500	3,200	C$4,800,000	
Turbine engines	1,600	1,800	2,880,000	
Electric engines	1,200	1,100	1,320,000	
Totals		6,100	C$9,000,000	

STANDARD MIX FOR ACTUAL VOLUME

Gas engines	(6,100 × .500) = 3,050
Turbine engines	(6,100 × .333) = 2,031
Electric engines	(6,100 × .167) = 1,019

Actual Price × Actual Mix × Actual Volume	Standard Price × Actual Mix × Actual Volume	Standard Price × Standard Mix × Actual Volume	Standard Price × Standard Mix × Budgeted Volume
G $1,500 (3,200) = $4,800,000	$1,400 (3,200) = $4,480,000	$1,400 (3,050) = $4,270,000	$1,400 (3,000) = $ 4,200,000
T $1,600 (1,800) = 2,880,000	$1,600 (1,800) = 2,880,000	$1,600 (2,031) = 3,249,600	$1,600 (2,000) = 3,200,000
E $1,200 (1,100) = 1,320,000	$1,100 (1,100) = 1,210,000	$1,100 (1,019) = 1,120,900	$1,100 (1,000) = 1,100,000
C$9,000,000	C$8,570,000	C$8,640,500	C$ 8,500,000

C$430,000 F — Sales Price Variance

C$70,500 U — Sales Mix Variance

C$140,500 F — Sales Volume Variance

C$500,000 F — Total Revenue Variance

Profit Centers

In **profit centers**, managers are responsible for generating revenues and for planning and controlling all expenses. A profit center manager's goal is to maximize the center's net income. Profit centers should be independent organizational units whose managers have the authority to obtain resources at the most economical prices and to sell products at prices that will maximize revenue. If managers do not have complete authority to buy and sell at objectively determined costs and prices, it is difficult to make a meaningful evaluation of the profit center.

Profit centers are not always manufacturing divisions or branches of retail stores. Banks may view each department (checking and savings accounts, loans, and credit cards) as a profit center, and a university may view certain educational divisions as profit centers (undergraduate education, non-degree-seeking night school, and law school).

To illustrate the variance computations for a profit center, assume that Karlsson-Andersson uses 18-wheelers to deliver products in the United States and each truck is considered a profit center. The budgeted and actual revenues and expenses for "Big Mack," a truck for which Jayne Lindesmith is responsible, are shown in Exhibit 15–8. The profit center should be judged on the $67,250 of profit center income, but Lindesmith should be judged on the controllable margin of $96,500. Lindesmith should point out that her delivery revenues were greater than budgeted because she drove more miles than budgeted. Thus, using the master budget as a basis for comparison, it is natural that unfavorable variances would exist for all of the variable costs.

The comparison of actual results to a flexible budget at the actual activity level shown in Exhibit 15–9 (page 788) provides better information for assessing cost control within the profit center. Lindesmith did a good job controlling the costs of her profit center; the problem area relates to the noncontrollable fixed overhead. She should investigate the causes for the $2,250 unfavorable variance. Then she and her manager can discuss any ideas she may have for addressing those causes. It is also possible that the budgeted figure for the noncontrollable fixed overhead is inappropriate because of cost increases for some or all of the items composing that fixed overhead pool.

profit centers

■ **EXHIBIT 15–8**
Profit Center Master Budget Comparisons for June 1996

	MASTER BUDGET	**ACTUAL**	**VARIANCE**
Delivery revenues	$180,000	$186,000	$6,000 F
Variable costs:			
Direct labor	$ 4,500	$ 4,600	$ 100 U
Gas and oil	37,800	39,050	1,250 U
Variable overhead	7,740	7,850	110 U
Total	$ 50,040	$ 51,500	$1,460 U
Contribution margin	$129,960	$134,500	$4,540 F
Fixed overhead—controllable	38,400	38,000	400 F
Controllable segment margin	$ 91,560	$ 96,500	$4,940 F
Fixed overhead—not controllable			
by profit center manager	27,000	29,250	2,250 U
Profit center income	$ 64,560	$ 67,250	$2,690 F

■ **EXHIBIT 15–9**
Profit Center Flexible Budget Comparisons for June 1996

	FLEXIBLE BUDGET	ACTUAL	VARIANCE
Delivery revenues	$186,000	$186,000	$ 0
Variable costs:			
Direct labor	$ 4,650	$ 4,600	$ 50 F
Gas and oil	39,060	39,050	10 F
Variable overhead	7,998	7,850	148 F
Total	$ 51,708	$ 51,500	$ 208 F
Contribution margin	$134,292	$134,500	$ 208 F
Fixed overhead—controllable	38,400	38,000	400 F
Controllable segment margin	$ 95,892	$ 96,500	$ 608 F
Fixed overhead—not controllable			
by profit center manager	27,000	29,250	2,250 U
Profit center income	$ 68,892	$ 67,250	$1,642 U

Investment Centers

investment center

An **investment center** is an organizational unit in which the manager is responsible for generating revenues, planning and controlling costs, and acquiring, using, and disposing of plant assets. The manager performs each of these activities with the aim of earning the highest feasible rate of return on the investment base. As in ABB Asea Boveri Brown, many investment centers are independent, freestanding divisions or subsidiaries of a firm. This independence allows investment center managers the opportunity to make decisions about all matters affecting their organizational units and to be judged on the outcomes of those decisions. Says Barnevik:

> Separate companies allow you to create real balance sheets with *real* responsibility for cash flow and dividends. With real balance sheets, managers inherit results from year to year through changes in equity. Separate companies also create more effective tools to recruit and motivate managers. People can aspire to meaningful career ladders in companies small enough to understand and be committed to.[11]

Assume that Eberhard Works (a subsidiary of Karlsson-Andersson) is an investment center headed by Heinrich von Koerber. The 1996 income statement for the company (in Deutsche marks) is as follows:

Sales	DM3,226,400
Variable expenses	1,800,000
Contribution margin	DM1,426,400
Fixed expenses	980,000
Net income	DM 446,400

Von Koerber has the authority to set selling prices, incur costs, and acquire and dispose of plant assets. The plant has an asset base of DM4,960,000; and thus, the rate of return on assets for the year was 9 percent (DM446,000 ÷ DM4,960,000). In evaluating the performance of Eberhard Works, top management would compare this rate of return with the rates desired by Karlsson-Andersson's management and with the rates of other investment centers in the company. Rate of return and other performance measures for responsibility centers are treated in Chapter 16.

---

[11]Taylor, "The Logic of Global Business," p. 99.

SUBOPTIMIZATION

■ **LEARNING OBJECTIVE 4**
Discuss the concept and effects of suboptimization.

Because of their closeness to daily divisional activities, responsibility center managers should have more current and detailed knowledge about sales prices, costs, and other market information than does top management. Managers of profit and investment centers are encouraged, to the extent possible, to operate those subunits as separate economic entities while making certain that they exist to achieve the same organizational goals.

Regardless of size, type of ownership, or product or service being sold, one goal for any business is to generate profits. For other organizations, such as charities and governmental entities, the ultimate financial goal may be to break even. The ultimate goal will be achieved through the monitoring of organizational **critical success factors**—those items that are so important that, ignoring them, the organization would cease to exist. Most organizations would consider quality, customer service, efficiency, cost control, and responsiveness to change as five critical success factors. If all of these factors are managed properly, the organization should be financially successful. If they are not, sooner or later the organization will fail. All members of the organization—especially managers—should work toward the same objectives if the critical success factors are to be satisfied. Losing sight of the overall organizational goals while working to achieve a separate responsibility center's conflicting goal will result in suboptimization.

critical success factors

Suboptimization exists when individual managers pursue goals and objectives that are in their own and/or their segments' particular interests rather than in the company's best interest. Because managers of profit and investment centers have great flexibility in regard to financial decisions, these managers must remember that their operations are integral parts of the entire corporate structure. Thus, actions of these organizational units should be in the best long-run interest of both the unit and its parent organization. Unit managers should be aware of and accept the need for goal congruence throughout the organization.

suboptimzation

For suboptimization to be constrained, top management must be aware of it and must develop ways to avoid it. One way managers can limit suboptimization is by communicating corporate goals to all organizational units. Exhibit 15–10 (page 790) depicts other ways of limiting suboptimization as stairsteps to the achievement of corporate goals. These steps are in no hierarchical order. If any steps are missing, however, the climb toward corporate goals and objectives becomes more difficult for divisional managers.

Companies may define their organizational units in various ways based on management accountability for one or more income-producing factors—costs, revenues, and/or assets. To properly evaluate the accomplishments of segments and their managers, a company must often set a "price" at which to transfer goods or services between segments. Such prices can help measure a "selling" segment's revenue and a "buying" segment's costs.

TRANSFER PRICING

Responsibility centers often provide goods or services to other company segments. These transfers require that a transfer price (or charge-back system) be established to account for the flow of these goods or services within the company. A **transfer price** is an *internal* charge established for the exchange of goods or services between organizational units of the same company. Internal company transfers should be presented

transfer price

■ **LEARNING OBJECTIVE 5**
Understand how and why transfer prices for products are used internally in organizations.

on external financial statements at the producing segment's costs. Thus, if transfers are "sold" at an amount other than cost, the intersegment profit, expense, and/or revenue accounts must be eliminated.

Intracompany transfers should be made only if they are in the best interest of the whole organization. If both the buying and selling managers have the authority to negotiate the transfer price, the following general rules define the upper and lower limits of the transfer pricing model:[12]

■ **EXHIBIT 15–10**
Performance Measures to Limit Suboptimization

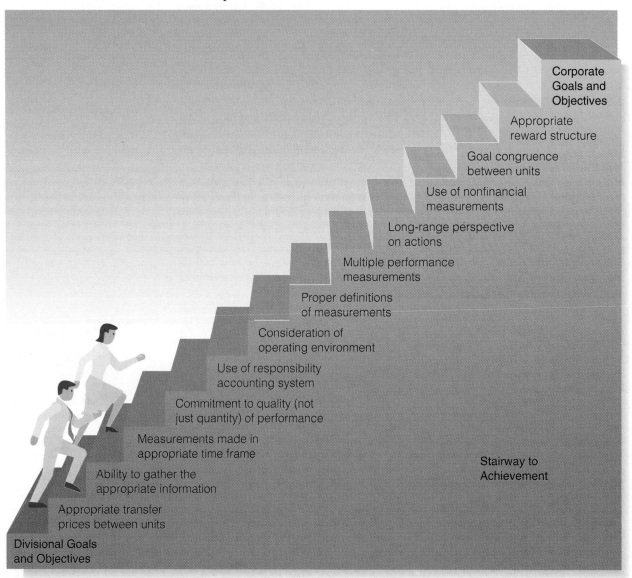

Corporate Goals and Objectives

Appropriate reward structure

Goal congruence between units

Use of nonfinancial measurements

Long-range perspective on actions

Multiple performance measurements

Proper definitions of measurements

Consideration of operating environment

Use of responsibility accounting system

Commitment to quality (not just quantity) of performance

Measurements made in appropriate time frame

Ability to gather the appropriate information

Appropriate transfer prices between units

Stairway to Achievement

Divisional Goals and Objectives

---

[12]These rules are more difficult to implement when the selling division is in a captive relationship and is not able to sell its products outside the corporate entity. In such situations, opportunity cost must be estimated to give the selling division an incentive to transfer products.

- The maximum transfer price should be no greater than the lowest market price at which the buying segment can acquire the goods or services externally.
- The minimum transfer price should be no less than the sum of the selling segment's incremental production costs plus the opportunity cost of the facilities used. (Incremental cost refers to the additional cost of producing a contemplated quantity of output, which generally means variable costs of production.)

The difference between this model's upper and lower limits is the corporate "profit" (or savings) generated by producing internally rather than buying externally. The transfer price acts to "divide the corporate profit" between the buying and selling segments. From the company's perspective, any transfer price set between these two limits is generally considered appropriate.

To illustrate use of this model, assume that product #76 is made by division A of XYZ Company. Product #76 has per unit incremental production and opportunity costs of $8 and $5, respectively. If division A were to transfer product #76 to division B, the minimum transfer price would be $13. The same product is available from external suppliers for $11. XYZ Company management has two choices. First, it can have division A stop making product #76 and, instead, have division B buy it from the external suppliers. This decision is reasonable since, compared with those suppliers, division A does not appear to be cost-efficient in its production activities. Stopping production would release the facilities for other, more profitable purposes. Or management could insist that division A improve its efficiency and reduce the cost of making product #76. Either choice would benefit the company as a whole.

After the transfer price range limits have been determined, management may consider understandability in choosing a price within the range. Managers should be able to comprehend how a transfer price was set and how it will affect their divisions' profits. Most transfer prices are cost-based or market-based, or are set through a process of negotiation.

Assume that the Republic Division (managed by Mr. Lew) of Karlsson-Andersson manufactures high-voltage switching gears for use in the Power Plant Equipment

Diversified and multinational companies often sell components between divisions. Divisional managers need to understand and agree on how the transfer prices will be determined.

Division (managed by Ms. Randall). The managers are attempting to establish a transfer price for the switching gears. Republic Division data (shown in Exhibit 15–11) are used to illustrate various transfer pricing approaches. Note that Republic Division is capable of supplying all external and internal production needs.

Cost-Based Transfer Prices

Because of its emphasis on cost, the cost-based method of establishing a transfer price would seem to be logical and appropriate. There are, however, numerous ways to compute cost. Product cost is defined in Chapter 3 as including direct materials, direct labor, variable production overhead, and fixed production overhead. This definition reflects the concept of absorption, or full, costing. In contrast, variable costing includes in product cost only those cost components that change in relationship to volume (direct materials, direct labor, and variable production overhead). Variable costing treats fixed production overhead as a period expense. If cost is to be used as the basis for setting a transfer price, the term *cost* must first be agreed on by the managers engaging in the intracompany transfer.

The absorption cost for the switching gears is $179 ($80 DM + $24 DL + $36 VOH + $39 FOH). A transfer price equal to absorption cost provides a contribution toward covering the selling division's fixed production overhead. Such a transfer price does not produce the same amount of income that would be generated if the transferring division sold the goods externally, but it does provide for coverage of all production costs.

A transfer price for switching gears based on variable cost is either $140 or $144. The difference depends on whether variable cost is defined as variable production cost or total variable cost. Using either of these costs as the transfer price will not give Mr. Lew much incentive to transfer the switching gears internally. Fixed costs of Republic Division are not being reduced by selling internally and no contribution margin is being generated by the transfers to help cover these fixed expenses.

■ **EXHIBIT 15–11**
Switching Gear Data

Standard unit production cost:		
Direct materials (DM)	$80	
Direct labor (DL)	24	
Variable overhead (VOH)	36	
Variable selling and administrative	4	
Total variable costs		$144
Fixed overhead cost (FOH)*	$39	
Fixed selling and administrative costs*	5	44
Total costs		$188
Normal mark-up on variable cost (50%)		72
List selling price		$260

Budgeted annual production: 400,000 units
Budgeted sales to outside entities 150,000 units
Budgeted intracompany transfers: 250,000 units

*Fixed costs are allocated to all units produced based on budgeted annual production.

One final difficulty with using a cost-based transfer price is whether to use an actual or standard cost. If actual costs are used, inefficiencies in production may not be corrected, since their costs will simply be covered by the buying division. But, if standard costs are used, and savings are effected over standard costs, the buying division will be "paying" more than actual cost for the goods.

Market-Based Transfer Prices

To eliminate the problems of defining *cost*, some companies simply use a market price approach to setting transfer prices. Market price is believed to be an objective measure of value and simulates the selling price that would exist if the segments were independent companies. If a selling division is operating efficiently relative to its competition, it should ordinarily be able to show a profit when transferring products or services at market prices. An efficiently operating buying division should not be troubled by a market-based transfer price. After all, that is what would have to be paid for the goods or services if the alternative of buying internally did not exist.

Still, several problems may exist with using market prices for intracompany transfers. The first problem is that transfers may involve products that have no exact counterparts in the external market. Second, market price may not be entirely appropriate because of internal cost savings arising from reductions in bad debts, packaging, advertising, and delivery expenditures. Third, difficulties can arise in setting a transfer price when the market is depressed because of a temporary reduction in demand for the product. Should the current depressed price be used as the transfer price, or should the expected long-run market price be used? Last, a question exists as to what is the "right" market price to use. Different prices are quoted and different discounts and credit terms are allowed to different buyers. Thus, it may not be possible to determine the most appropriate market price to charge.

Negotiated Transfer Prices

Because of the problems associated with both cost-based and market-based prices, a **negotiated transfer price** is often set through a process of bargaining between the selling and buying unit managers. Such a price is normally below the external sales price of the selling unit, above that unit's incremental costs including any opportunity cost, and below the market purchase price for the buying unit. A negotiated price meeting these specifications falls within the range limits of the transfer pricing model.

A negotiated transfer price for the Republic Division of Karlsson-Andersson would be less than the $260 list selling price or the Power Plant Equipment Division's buying price, if lower. The price would also be set greater than the $144 incremental variable cost. If some of the variable selling cost could be eliminated, the incremental cost would even be less. If Republic Division could not sell any additional switching gears externally nor downsize its facilities, there would be no opportunity cost involved. Otherwise, an opportunity cost would have to be determined. This could increase total cost to as much as the $260 list selling price (if all units could be sold externally).

Authority to negotiate a transfer price implies that division managers have the autonomy to sell or buy products externally if internal negotiations fail. To encourage cooperation between the transferring divisions, top management may consider allowing each party to set a different transfer price.

negotiated transfer price

Dual Pricing

dual pricing arrangements

Since a transfer price is used to satisfy internal managerial objectives, **dual pricing arrangements** can be used that allow different transfer prices for the selling and the buying segments. The selling division records the transfer of goods or services at a market or negotiated market price, which provides a "profit" for that division. The buying division records the transfer at a cost-based amount, which provides a minimal cost for that division. Dual transfer pricing gives managers the most relevant information for decision making and performance evaluation.

Choosing the Appropriate Transfer Price

The final determination of which method to set transfer prices to use should reflect the circumstances of the organizational units, as well as corporate goals. No one method is best in all instances. Exhibit 15–12 provides the results of a transfer pricing survey of 143 large industrial companies and indicates that multiple definitions of transfer prices are employed at individual firms. Also, transfer prices are not permanent; they are frequently revised in relation to changes in costs, supply, demand, competitive forces, and other factors. Such cost adjustments can encourage efficient use of divisional resources by stimulating internal consumption during downturns in demand and rationing consumption during peak demand times.

■ **EXHIBIT 15–12**
Survey of Transfer Pricing Methods

	DOMESTIC TRANSFERS		INTERNATIONAL TRANSFERS	
PRICING METHODS	# of Firms	% of Total	# of Firms	% of Total
Cost-based methods:				
Actual or standard variable production cost	8	3.6	2	1.3
Actual full production cost	20	9.0	6	3.8
Standard full production cost	34	15.2	11	7.0
Actual variable production cost plus a lump-sum subsidy	2	0.9	2	1.3
Full production cost (actual or standard) plus a markup	37	16.6	42	26.7
Other	2	0.9	2	1.3
Subtotal for cost-based	103	46.2	65	41.4
Market-based methods:				
Market price	56	25.1	41	26.1
Market price less selling expenses	17	7.6	19	12.1
Other	9	4.0	12	7.7
Subtotal for market-based	82	36.7	72	45.9
Negotiated price	37	16.6	20	12.7
Other methods	1	0.5	0	0.0
Total—all methods	223*	100.0	157*	100.0

*Many firms use more than one domestic or international transfer price.

SOURCE: Roger W. Tang, "Transfer Pricing in the 1990s," Management Accounting (February 1992), p. 24. Published by Insitutute of Management Accountants, Montvale, NJ.

Regardless of what method is used, a thoughtfully set transfer price will provide the following advantages:

- An appropriate basis for the calculation and evaluation of segment performance.
- The rational acquisition or use of goods and services between corporate divisions.
- The flexibility to respond to changes in demand or market conditions.
- A means of motivating managers in decentralized operations.

Setting a reasonable transfer price is not an easy task. Everyone involved in the process must be aware of the positive and negative aspects of each type of transfer price and be responsive to suggestions of change if the need is indicated.

TRANSFER PRICES FOR SERVICE DEPARTMENTS

Setting transfer prices for products moving between organizational units is a well-established practice. Instituting transfer prices for services is a less common, but effective, technique for some types of service departments. If management is considering setting a transfer price for a service department, the questions in Exhibit 15–13 (on page 796) should first be answered. The exhibit also presents some suggestions as to how the transfer price should be set. All the questions should be considered simultaneously and the suggestions combined to form a reasonable transfer price.

A department planning to use transfer prices for services must decide on a capacity level for use in price development. This decision is equivalent to that made in setting a predetermined overhead rate. For example, a service department may use expected capacity or practical capacity. If expected capacity is chosen, the transfer price per unit of service will be higher than if practical capacity is chosen. If the service department uses expected capacity and performs more services than expected, a favorable volume variance will arise.[13] Users, though, will not necessarily benefit from reduced charges because the transfer price is not normally changed unless departmental costs change. Use of practical capacity will, on the other hand, produce a lower price. It might also encourage more internal services use and generate ideas as to how to use the additional capacity. In addition, if the practical capacity level is not achieved, an unfavorable volume variance is noted, and the opportunity cost of underutilization is clearly identifiable.

In developing transfer prices for services, common costs must be allocated to the various departments equitably, and the underlying reason for cost incurrence must be determined. Transfer prices are useful when service departments provide distinct, measurable benefits to other areas or provide services having a specific cause-and-effect relationship. Transfer prices in these circumstances can provide certain advantages (see Exhibit 15–14, page 797) to the organization in both the revenue-producing and service departments.

First, transfer prices can encourage more involvement between the user and service departments. Users are more likely to suggest ways for the service department to improve its performance, since improved performance could result in lower transfer prices. Service departments are more likely to interact with users to find out the specific types of services that are needed and to eliminate or reduce those that are not cost beneficial.

Second, use of a transfer price for services should cause managers to be more cost conscious. Managers of user departments should attempt to eliminate wasteful usage.

■ LEARNING OBJECTIVE 6
Understand how and why transfer prices for services are used internally in organizations.

---

[13]Volume variances are covered in Chapter 6.

For example, if an MIS Department charged other departments for the number of reports received, managers would be less likely to request reports simply to be "on the receiving list," as sometimes occurs. For managers of the service departments, cost consciousness is directed at monitoring the cost to provide services. If excessive costs are incurred, a reasonable transfer price may not cover costs or a high transfer price may not be justifiable to users.

Last, transfer prices can provide information useful in evaluating managerial performance. Responsibility reports for user departments show a service department cost related to the quantity of actual services used. User department managers should be able to justify what services were used during the period. Transfer prices allow service departments to be treated as "money-making" operations rather than simply cost-generating operations. Responsibility reports of these departments indicate the transfer prices charged and the costs of providing services. Thus, these managers can be held accountable for cost control and profitability. The cost effectiveness of the provider department can then be determined and compared with the cost of outsourcing.

■ EXHIBIT 15–13
Setting a Transfer Price for Services

	IF RESPONSE IS:	
QUESTIONS	YES	NO
Is the service department to be considered a "money maker"?	Set transfer price using market-based, negotiated, or dual pricing.	Set transfer price using cost-based prices.
Does a user department have significant control over the quantity and quality of service used?	Use a base that reflects total quantity of activity of service department.	Transfer prices are not particularly useful.
Do opportunities exist to use external services rather than internal services?	Use a base that reflects the typical manner in which external purchases are made.	Set transfer price by negotiation or upper level management; use a base that reflects quantity of activity of service department.
Is there a reasonable alternative (or surrogate) measure of service benefits provided to users?	Use a base representing total volume of alternative measure produced by service department.	Transfer prices are not particularly useful.
Are the services provided of a recurring or similar nature?	Use a fixed price based on a single factor of use for each service use.	Use a price that reflects degree of use, constrained by whether user can bear
Are the services performed typically expensive?	Use market-based or negotiated prices, constrained by whether user can bear the cost. The base may be more complex than typical.	Use cost-based or negotiated prices. The base should be easy to understand and to compute.

Data processing, secretarial pools, and accounting departments all provide necessary services to an organization. Using transfer prices to "sell" services to user departments makes service providers control costs and respond to user needs more effectively.

Although transfer prices for services can be effective tools, they do have certain disadvantages. First, there can be, and often is, disagreement among unit managers as to how the transfer price should be set. Second, implementing transfer prices in the accounting system requires additional organizational costs and employee time. Third, transfer prices may not work equally well for all types of service departments. Service

■ **EXHIBIT 15–14**

Advantages of Transfer Pricing for Services

	USER DEPARTMENTS	PROVIDER DEPARTMENTS
User involvement	Because they are being charged for services, user departments may suggest ways in which provider departments can improve services.	Because they are charging for the services they are providing, provider departments may become more aware of the needs of their users and seek to develop services that are more beneficial to user departments.
Cost consciousness	Because they are being charged for services, user departments may restrict usage to those services that are necessary and cost beneficial.	Because they are charging for the services they are providing, provider departments must be able to justify the prices charged and, thus, may maintain more control over costs.
Performance evaluations	Because control over amount of services used exists, user departments can include costs in performance evaluations.	Because transfer prices can generate "revenues" for their departments, provider department managers have more ways to evaluate departmental performance (a cost center can be viewed as a profit center).

departments that do not provide measurable benefits or cannot show a distinct cause-and-effect relationship between cost incurrence and service use by other departments should not use transfer prices. Finally, depending on how the transfer price is set, a transfer price may cause dysfunctional behavior among the organizational units; for example, certain services may be underutilized or overutilized. A company should weigh the advantages and disadvantages of using transfer prices before deciding whether a transfer pricing system would enhance organizational effectiveness and efficiency.

TRANSFER PRICING IN MULTINATIONAL SETTINGS

■ **LEARNING OBJECTIVE 7**
Undestand how and why transfer prices are used in multinational enterprises.

Because of the differences in tax systems, customs duties, freight and insurance costs, import/export regulations, and foreign exchange controls, setting transfer prices for products and services becomes extremely difficult when the company is engaged in multinational operations. In addition, as shown in Exhibit 15–15, the internal and external objectives of transfer pricing in multinational enterprises (MNEs) differ.

Because of these differences, there is no simple way to determine transfer prices in MNEs. Multinational companies may use one transfer price when a product is sent to or received from one country and a totally different transfer price for the same product when it is sent to or received from another. However, some guidelines as to transfer pricing should be set by the company and followed on a consistent basis. For example, a company should not price transfers to nondomestic subsidiaries in a way that would send the majority of costs to a subsidiary in the country with the highest tax rate *unless that pricing method was reasonable and equitable to all subsidiaries.* The general test of reasonableness is that transfer prices should reflect unbiased, or "arm's length," transactions.

As indicated in the accompanying News Note, multinational entity transfer prices are now being carefully scrutinized by tax authorities in both the home and host countries because such prices determine which country taxes the income from the

■ **EXHIBIT 15–15**
Multinational Company Transfer Pricing Objectives

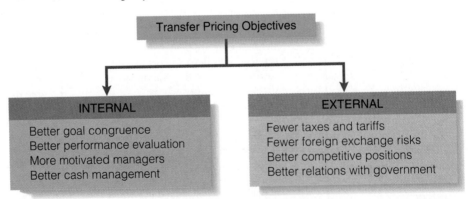

SOURCE: Wagdy M. Abdallah, "Guidelines for CEOs in Transfer Pricing Policies," *Management Accounting* (September 1988), p. 61. Published by Institute of Management Accountants, Montvale, NJ.

The United States Isn't Alone In Concerns about Transfer Pricing

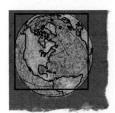

International tax planning may be complicated, but its rewards can be significant. Consider the case of Wind River Systems, a $25-million software developer in Alameda, Calif., whose success owes plenty to the way the company has managed its international tax liabilities over the past five years.

With operations around the world—three wholly owned subsidiaries in Europe, majority ownership in a joint venture in Japan, and distribution agreements with independent contractors in other nations—Wind River faces corporate tax rates that can be much higher than those for companies that operate only in the United States. So it has devised a "transfer-pricing" strategy that minimizes its global tax rates, bringing them to an average of less than 35%, compared with a worst-case scenario of almost 50%.

The goal of transfer pricing is to set international prices so that more profits are realized in those countries that have lower tax rates. So does it make sense to *lose* money on all ventures based overseas and declare all profits in the States, thus paying the lowest possible overall tax bill? Don't even think of it. Just as the IRS pays strict attention to the profits that foreign companies with U.S. operations declare for U.S. tax purposes, foreign governments closely examine the tax statements of U.S. businesses and their overseas subsidiaries. Companies that appear to transfer price too aggressively run the risk of costly audits.

Another caveat: while your transfer-pricing strategy needn't be set in stone for eternity, you cannot be tweaking it constantly to accommodate recent financial results. "If one of our foreign subsidiaries had a particularly good year," explains Dale Wilde, Wind River's chief financial officer, "I couldn't charge that subsidiary more for our software products so that it would recognize less profit, thus minimizing its taxes. That country's tax authority would come down on us in a second." The United Kingdom, France, and the Netherlands are among the nations that are more aggressive about auditing foreign companies' transfer-pricing policies.

SOURCE: Jill Andresky Fraser, "Controlling Global Taxes," *Inc.* (August 1993), p. 35. Reprinted by permission of Inc. Magazine. © 1993 by Goldhirsh Group, Inc.

transfer. The United States Congress is concerned about both U.S. multinationals operating in low-tax countries and foreign companies operating in the United States. Congress believes that, in both situations, companies could avoid paying U.S. corporate income taxes by using misleading or inaccurate transfer pricing. Thus, the Internal Revenue Service (IRS) may be quick to investigate U.S. subsidiaries that operate in low-tax countries or areas (such as Ireland, Singapore, and Puerto Rico) and suddenly show unusually high profits. If foreign companies charge their U.S. subsidiaries higher prices than what they would charge subsidiaries in their home country, U.S. taxable income (and thus the tax base) will decline—which may also bring about an IRS review.

The IRS will discuss and preapprove some advance transfer pricing agreements, which should help MNEs to set "reasonable" transfer prices. This process is extremely expensive, with a $500,000 minimum cost to receive an advance determination ruling that is valid for three years.[14] But the cost may be worthwhile considering the

---

[14]Susan C. Borkowski, "Section 482, Revenue Procedure 91-22, and the Realities of Multinational Transfer Pricing," *International Tax Journal* (Spring 1992), p. 63.

quantity of documentation required to justify transfer prices and potential penalties for lack of documentation. Additionally, the IRS can assess a 20 percent penalty for a "substantial valuation misstatement" (or a 40 percent penalty for a "gross valuation misstatement") of income.

As mentioned in Chapter 2, transfers among nations are becoming easier because of trade arrangements such as the European Union, the North American Free Trade Zone, and the General Agreement on Tariffs and Trade and its World Trade Organization. These arrangements should help reduce the significance of transfer price manipulations through (among other features) the harmonization of tax structures and reductions in import/export fees, tariffs, and capital movement restrictions.

Multinational companies must be able to determine the effectiveness of their transfer pricing policies:

> [In this determination,] two criteria can be used: (a) does the system achieve economic decisions that positively affect MNE performance, including international capital investment decisions, output level decisions for both intermediate and final products, and product pricing decisions for external customers? and (b) do subsidiary managers feel that they are being fairly evaluated and rewarded for their divisional contributions to the MNE as a whole?[15]

If the answers to both of these questions are yes, then the company appears to have a transfer pricing system that appropriately coordinates underlying considerations, minimizes internal and external goal conflicts, and balances short- and long-range perspectives of the multinational company.

SITE ANALYSIS

Percy Barnevik, 52, the rangy Swede with a Stanford MBA, has forged a competitive powerhouse out of Asea Brown Boveri by taking the concept of leanness to extremes. He turned ABB into 5,000 profit centers, each with its own balance sheet, then shrank headquarters drastically. His now famous cut-then-cut-again style reduced his Zurich corporate staff from 4,000 to 200. "We dislike headquarters," he says. "They cost a lot of money, and they disturb the people who are doing the real business." His formula? Cut the staff to 10% of its original size, let it run for a couple of years, then go back and cut it again by farming out every administrative chore that you can get done for less money outside.

Barnevik [also has a master organizational matrix that] gives all employees a country manager and a business sector manager. The country managers run traditional, national companies with local boards of directors, including eminent outsiders. ABB has about 100 such managers, most of them citizens of the country in which they work. Of more exalted rank are 65 global managers, who are organized into eight segments: transportation, process automation and engineering, environmental devices, financial services, electrical equipment (mainly motors and robots), and three electric power businesses: generation, transmission, and distribution. [Each area has a leader who is responsible for optimizing that business area globally. The leader plans and implements a global strategy, makes certain that the various global factories have similar cost and quality standards, allocates export markets to the various factories, rotates people among the units, and builds a culture of trust and communication.]

Barnevik is well aware that the once popular management by matrix is in disfavor in U.S. business schools and has been abandoned by most multinational companies. But he says he uses a loose, decentralized version of it—the two bosses are not always equal—

[15]Wagdy M. Abdallah, "Guidelines for CEOs in Transfer Pricing Policies," *Management Accounting* (September 1988), p. 61. Published by Institute of Management Accountants, Montvale, NJ.

that is particularly suited to an organization composed of many nationalities. ABB executives say the value of the company's matrix system extends beyond the swapping of technology and products. For example, the power transformer business segment consists of 31 factories in 16 countries. Barnevik wants each of these businesses to be run locally with intense global coordination. So every month the business segment headquarters in Mannheim, Germany, tells all the factories how all the others are doing according to dozens of measurements. If one factory is lagging, solutions to common problems can be discussed and worked out across borders.

As Barnevik says, "Nobody believes in decentralization more than I. For the last few years I have purposely gone overboard on it. Otherwise, we could never get people out of their protective nesting systems that are inherent in big companies."

SOURCES: Paul Hofheinz, "Europe's Tough New Managers," *Fortune* (September 6, 1993), p. 114, © 1993 Time Inc., all rights reserved; Carla Rapoport, "A Tough Swede Invades the U.S.," *Fortune* (June 29, 1992), pp. 78, 79, © 1992 Time Inc., all rights reserved; and Rich Karlgaard, "ASAP Interview: Percy Barnevik," *Forbes ASAP* (December 5, 1994), p. 68.

Discipline	Applications
Accounting	Accountants help managers in developing the degree of detail provided in responsibility reports. Responsibility accounting provides accurate, prompt information for performance evaluations and can provide nonmonetary and nontraditional measures of operations..
Economics	Addressing critical success factors can help management to determine resource allocations and reward systems. Economists can provide the understanding of the economic diversities among foreign subsidiaries that is necessary to develop appropriate performance measures.
Finance	Responsibility reporting is essential to determining the financial needs and resource requirements of individual operations.
Management	Decentralization allows for the personal development of managers and allows the managers closest to decision making situations to make those decisions promptly. Responsibility reports emphasize management by exception. Management should attempt to institute policies that limit suboptimization in decentralized units. Use of transfer prices for service departments can make those departments profit or investment centers rather than cost centers and provide more performance measurements.
Marketing	Decentralization allows quicker decisions about pricing, product line development, advertising, and so on. Responsibility reports provide detailed information about marketing area costs.

CROSS-FUNCTIONAL APPLICATIONS STRATEGIES

CHAPTER SUMMARY

Centralization refers to a concentration of management control at high organizational levels, while decentralization refers to the downward delegation of decision-making authority to subunit managers. Thus, a decentralized organization is composed of operational units led by managers who have some autonomy in decision making. The degree to which a company is decentralized depends on top management philosophy and the unit managers' abilities to perform independently. Decentralization provides the opportunity for managers to develop leadership qualities, creative problem-solving abilities, and decision-making skills. It also lets the individual most closely in tune with the operational unit and its immediate environment make the decisions for that unit and reduces the time spent in communicating and making decisions.

In a decentralized structure, subunit managers are evaluated in part by use of responsibility reports. Responsibility reports reflect the upward flow of information from each decentralized unit to the top of the organization. Managers receive information regarding the activities under their immediate control and under the control of their direct subordinates. The information is successively aggregated, and the reports allow the application of the management by exception principle.

Responsibility centers are classified as cost, revenue, profit, or investment centers. Each classification reflects the degree of authority managers have for financial items within their subunits. The type of responsibility center also affects the kind of performance measurements that can be used for the center and its manager.

Transfer prices are intracompany charges for goods or services exchanged between segments of a company. Product transfer prices are typically cost-based, market-based, or negotiated. A dual pricing system that assigns different transfer prices to the buying and selling units may also be used. Management should promote a transfer pricing system that is in the best interest of the whole company, motivates managers to strive for segment effectiveness and efficiency, and is practical.

Setting transfer prices in multinational enterprises is a complex process because of the differences that exist in tax structures, import/export regulations, customs duties, and other factors associated with international subsidiaries and divisions. A valid transfer price for a multinational firm is one that achieves economic benefit for the entire company and generates support from the domestic and international managers utilizing the system.

GLOSSARY

Centralization (p. 773)   an organizational structure in which top management makes most decisions and controls most activities of the organizational units from the company's central headquarters

Cost center (p. 782)   an organizational unit in which the manager has the authority only to incur costs and is specifically evaluated on the basis of how well costs are controlled

Critical success factor (p. 789)   an item that is so important to an organization that, ignoring it, the organization would fail; quality, customer service, efficiency, cost control, and responsiveness to change are five primary critical success factors

Decentralization (p. 773)   an organizational structure in which top management grants subordinate managers a significant degree of autonomy and independence in operating and making decisions for their organizational units

Dual pricing arrangement (p. 794)   a transfer price method that allows a selling division to record the transfer of goods or services at a market-based or negotiated price and a buying division to record the transfer at a cost-based amount

Goal congruence (p. 776)   a condition that exists when the personal and organizational goals of decision makers throughout a firm are consistent and mutually supportive

Investment center (p. 788)   an organizational unit in which the manager is responsible for generating revenues, planning and controlling costs, and acquiring, disposing of, and using plant assets to earn the highest feasible rate of return on the investment base

Negotiated transfer price (p. 793)   an intracompany charge for goods or services that has been set through a process of negotiation between the selling and purchasing unit managers

Profit center (p. 787)   an organizational unit in which the manager is responsible for generating revenues and planning and controlling all expenses

Responsibility accounting (p. 778)   an accounting system that provides information to top management about segment or subunit performance

Responsibility center (p. 782)   the cost object under the control of a manager; in the case of a decentralized company, the cost object is an organizational unit such as a division, department, or geographical region

Responsibility report (p. 778)   a report that reflects the revenues and/or costs under the control of a specific unit manager

Revenue center (p. 785)   an organizational unit in which the manager is responsible only for the generation of revenues and has no control over setting selling prices or budgeting costs

Suboptimization (p. 789)   a situation in which a unit manager makes decisions that positively affect his or her own unit, but are detrimental to other organizational units or to the company as a whole

Transfer price (p. 789)   an internal charge established for the exchange of goods or services between organizational units of the same company

SOLUTION STRATEGIES

REVENUE VARIANCES

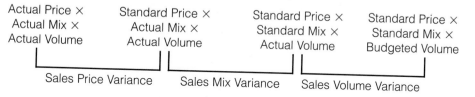

TRANSFER PRICES (COST-BASED, MARKET-BASED, NEGOTIATED, DUAL)

Assuming both managers have the authority to negotiate transfer price:

Upper Limit: Lowest price available from external suppliers

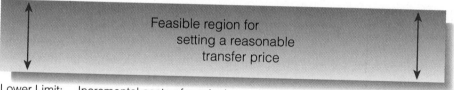

Lower Limit: Incremental costs of producing and selling the transferred goods or services plus the opportunity cost for the facilities used

DEMONSTRATION PROBLEM

Geld Vogel Company of Sweden makes duck callers. The firm's annual revenue is SKr14,000,000. (SKr is the symbol for the krona, the currency unit in Sweden.) Bjorn Petersen, the firm's controller, devised a new budgetary system. Annual budget figures are divided into 12 equal monthly amounts for monthly performance evaluations. Elka Hansen, vice-president of production, was distressed when she reviewed the following responsibility report for the Forming and Polishing Department for March 1997:

FORMING AND POLISHING DEPARTMENT—RESPONSIBILITY REPORT
FOR THE MONTH ENDED MARCH 31, 1997

	Actual	Budget	Variance Over (Under)
Volume in units	3,822	3,600	222
Variable production costs:			
Direct materials	SKr 119,250	SKr 115,200	SKr 4,050
Direct labor	140,650	133,200	7,450
Variable overhead	168,170	159,840	8,330
Total	SKr 428,070	SKr 408,240	SKr 19,830
Fixed production costs:			
Depreciation	SKr 7,200	SKr 7,200	SKr 0
Indirect labor	15,840	16,000	(160)
Insurance	1,150	1,150	0
Taxes	1,440	1,440	0
Other	4,930	4,460	470
Total	SKr 30,560	SKr 30,250	SKr 310
Corporate costs:			
Quality assurance staff	SKr 17,890	SKr 11,520	SKr 6,370
Selling and administrative	19,560	17,280	2,280
Total	SKr 37,450	SKr 28,800	SKr 8,650
Total costs	SKr 496,080	SKr 467,290	SKr 28,790

Required:

a. Discuss the weaknesses in the report.

b. Revise the report to reduce or eliminate the weaknesses.

c. Variances greater than 10 percent of budget are considered to be significant enough to be investigated. Identify these.

(CMA adapted)

■ SOLUTION TO DEMONSTRATION PROBLEM

a. There are two major deficiencies in the report:

1. Responsibility reports for a cost center should compare actual costs with flexible budget costs. The report presented compares actual costs with static budget costs (which were estimated for 3,600 units, while actual production was 3,822 units). Costs measured at two different activity levels are not comparable for control or evaluation purposes.

2. The report presented includes corporate costs that are not within the control of the Forming and Polishing Department manager. Some of the fixed production costs probably also are not controllable by the manager of this cost

center, although the problem does not provide enough information to address this concern.

b.   **FORMING AND POLISHING DEPARTMENT—RESPONSIBILITY REPORT**
FOR THE MONTH ENDED MARCH 31, 1997

Volume in units	Actual (3,822)		Budget (3,822)		Variance
	Per unit	Total	Per unit	Total	Over (Under)
Variable production costs:					
Direct materials	SKr 31.20	SKr 119,250	SKr 32.00	SKr 122,304	SKr (3,054)
Direct labor	36.80	140,650	37.00	141,414	(764)
Variable overhead	44.00	168,170	44.40	169,697	(1,527)
Total	SKr 112.00	SKr 428,070	SKr 113.40	SKr 433,415	SKr (5,345)
Fixed production costs:					
Depreciation		SKr 7,200		SKr 7,200	SKr 0
Indirect labor		15,840		16,000	(160)
Insurance		1,150		1,150	0
Taxes		1,440		1,440	0
Other		4,930		4,460	470
Total		SKr 30,560		SKr 30,250	SKr 310
Total production costs		SKr 458,630		SKr 463,665	SKr (5,035)

c.   Only the "other" cost category reflects a variance exceeding 10 percent of budget. Note that the revised report provides a more realistic and a more favorable view of performance than does the original report.

END-OF-CHAPTER MATERIALS

■ QUESTIONS

1. How does decision-making authority differ between centrally organized and decentralized companies?

2. Would a very young company or a large mature company be more likely to employ decentralized management? Explain.

3. Why do the personality traits of subunit managers affect the success of efforts to decentralize decision making?

4. Some organizational activities are more likely to be decentralized than others. What activities are most likely to be decentralized? Least likely?

5. Top managers at Global Manufacturing Company are pondering the possibility of decentralizing control of all foreign operating divisions. The firm has traditionally maintained very tight central control over these operations. What major costs of decentralization should Global's top managers consider in making their decision?

6. What is a responsibility accounting system? What is its role in a decentralized firm?

7. Why is a segment manager's performance evaluated separately from the segment's performance?

8. Describe the four types of responsibility centers. For each type, provide some criteria on which you think performance could be measured.

9. What is meant by the term variance, and how are variances used by managers in controlling an organization?

10. How is the philosophy of management by exception employed in responsibility accounting systems?

11. Describe why suboptimization may occur in decentralized firms.

12. Is managerial performance always evaluated solely on financial measures? Explain.

13. What is a transfer price? What role does a transfer price play in a decentralized company?

14. What are the high and low limits of transfer prices, and why do these limits exist?

15. A company is considering use of a cost-based transfer price. What argument favors the use of standard, rather than actual, cost?

16. What practical problems may interfere with the use of a market-based transfer price?

17. What is dual pricing? What is the intended effect of dual pricing on the reported performance of each division affected by the dual price?

18. How can service departments use transfer prices and what advantages do transfer prices have over cost allocation methods such as those discussed in Appendix 2, Chapter 4?

19. Explain why determining transfer prices may be more complex in a multinational setting than in a domestic setting.

20. Why do state, federal, and foreign taxing authorities scrutinize transfer price determination in multinational companies?

■ EXERCISES

21. (LO 1, 3, 4, 5; *Terminology*) Match each of the lettered items on the left with the number of the appropriate item on the right.

    a. Centralized organization

    b. Dual pricing arrangement

    c. Suboptimization

    d. Goal congruence

    e. Responsibility center

    f. Decentralized organization

    g. Cost center

    h. Investment center

    1. A company in which decisions are generally made by division managers

    2. A unit whose manager is primarily responsible for generating revenues, controlling costs, and managing assets

    3. A unit whose manager is primarily responsible for controlling operating costs

    4. A condition in which decisions made were not in the best interest of the entire firm

    5. A method of exchanging goods at different amounts for the buying and selling divisions

    6. A condition in which organizational and personal goals are consistent

    7. A unit whose manager is responsible for revenue generation and operating cost control

    8. A unit whose manager is primarily responsible for revenue generation

i. Profit center

j. Revenue center

9. The organizational cost object under the control of a manager

10. A company in which decisions are generally made by top management

22. (LO 1; *Centralized vs. decentralized control*) Each of the following independent descriptions characterizes some trait of an organization. For each description, indicate whether the firm would be more likely to adopt a centralized (C) or decentralized (D) control structure and why you made this selection.

   a. A bad decision would have disastrous consequences for the company.
   b. The firm is growing very rapidly.
   c. The firm has just been established.
   d. The entrepreneurial CEO is the firm's founder and wants to maintain involvement in all aspects of the business.
   e. The firm's operations span the globe. Many of the foreign divisions have operations that are very sensitive to volatility in local economic conditions.
   f. Top management expresses sincere doubts about the capability of lower-level managers to make sound economic decisions.

23. (LO 1; *Decentralization advantages and disadvantages*) Indicate whether each of the following might be a potential advantage (A) of decentralization, a disadvantage (D) of decentralization, or neither (N).

   a. Promotion of goal congruence
   b. Support of training in decision making
   c. Development of leadership qualities
   d. Complication of communication process
   e. Cost of developing planning and reporting system
   f. Placement of decision maker closer (in time and place) to problem
   g. Speed of decisions
   h. Use of management by exception principle by top management
   i. Greater job satisfaction
   j. Delegation of ultimate responsibility

24. (LO 2, 3; *Cost variances*) The Tool and Die Department of Metro Manufacturing is structured as a cost center. Below are selected budget and actual costs of the department for 1997:

	PLANNING BUDGET	ACTUAL	FLEXIBLE BUDGET
Professional labor	$900,000	$925,000	$1,000,317
Supplies	14,000	15,200	16,200
Materials	114,000	119,350	117,200
Energy	26,000	29,300	32,100
Quality control	172,600	172,000	195,100
Depreciation	250,000	250,000	250,000
Software amortization	90,000	103,000	90,000

   Metro has a policy of investigating any variance that differs from the "expected amount" for the actual level of operations by 5 percent or more.

   a. Which budget amount, planning or flexible, reflects the expected level of cost occurrence for the actual level of operations? Why?
   b. Based on your answer in part a, compute variances for each cost category.
   c. Which variances would be further investigated?
   d. Which favorable variances, if any, might be of great concern to management? Explain.

25. (LO 2, 3; *Revenue variances*) Calloway Industries produces and sells a stainless steel surgical knife. The Marketing Department is evaluated based on a comparison of achieved revenues with budgeted revenues. For 1996, the company projected sales to be 400,000 units at an average price of $22. The company actually sold 425,000 knives at an average price of $19.50.

a. Compute the sales price and volume variances for 1996.

b. The president of Calloway is curious as to why you didn't compute a sales mix variance. Write a brief memo to her explaining why a sales mix variance is inappropriate for her company.

c. Based on your computations in part (a), can you determine whether profits were above or below the budgeted level? Explain.

26. (LO 2, 3; *Revenue variances*) The Sales Department of the Dive Shop is responsible for sales of two principal products: snorkels and masks. For July 1997, the Sales Department's actual and budgeted sales were as follows:

	SNORKELS		MASKS	
	Dollars	*Units*	*Dollars*	*Units*
Budgeted sales	$20,000	4,000	$80,000	4,000
Actual sales	18,000	3,000	69,000	3,000

a. For July 1997, compute the sales price variance for the Sales Department.

b. Compute the sales volume variance for July 1997.

c. Compute the sales mix variance for July 1997.

d. Explain why you would expect a relatively minor sales mix variance for this company even when substantial variances may arise for sales volume and price.

27. (LO 2, 3; *Revenue variances*) Longhorn Leather Products Inc. manufactures two products: women's purses and baseball gloves. For 1997, the firm budgeted the following:

	PURSES	BASEBALL GLOVES
Sales	$800,000	$1,800,000
Unit sales price	$40	$30

At the end of 1997, managers were informed that total actual sales amounted to 70,000 units and totaled $2,700,000. Purse sales for the year amounted to 30,000 units at an average price of $35.

a. Compute the total revenue variance for 1997.

b. Compute the sales price variance for 1997.

c. Compute the sales mix variance for 1997.

d. Compute the sales volume variance for 1997.

28. (LO 2, 3; *Profit center variances*) Southern Mountain Inns evaluates its inns and innkeepers based on a comparison of actual profit with budgeted profit. A budgeted 1997 income statement for the Little Rock Inn follows:

Revenues		$2,650,000
Cost of services provided:		
Direct labor	$265,000	
Supplies	53,000	
Variable overhead	318,000	(636,000)
Contribution margin		$2,014,000
Fixed overhead—controllable		(320,000)
Controllable segment margin		$1,694,000
Fixed overhead—not controllable		
by segment manager		(1,220,000)
Profit center income		$ 474,000

For 1997, actual revenues generated were $2,900,000. Actual variable costs were: direct labor, 12 percent of revenues; supplies, 3 percent of revenues; variable overhead, 14 percent of revenues. Controllable fixed costs amounted to $330,000 and other fixed overhead costs amounted to $1,425,000.

a. Prepare an actual income statement for 1997.
b. Compute revenue and cost variances for 1997.
c. Evaluate the performance of the manager of the Little Rock Inn for 1997.
d. Evaluate the performance of the Little Rock Inn for 1997.

29. (LO 5; *Transfer pricing*) The Cast Products Division, an autonomous segment (profit center) of Global Motors, is considering what price to charge for transfers of water pumps to the Engine Division of the company. The following data on production cost per water pump have been gathered:

Direct materials	$18.40
Direct labor	4.20
Variable overhead	12.60
Fixed overhead	10.80
Total	$46.00

The Cast Products Division sells the water pumps to external buyers for $63. Managers of the Engine Division have received external offers to provide comparable water pumps ranging from $55 at one company to $73 at another.

a. Determine the upper and lower limits for the transfer price between the Cast Products Division and the Engine Division.
b. What is the transfer price if it is equal to full production cost?
c. What is the transfer price if it is equal to variable production cost?
d. Why would the Cast Products Division be reluctant to transfer goods at a price equal to variable production cost?

30. (LO 5; *Transfer pricing*) EL Corporation has several operating divisions. The E Division manufactures motors for ceiling fans and other appliances. The L Division manufactures ceiling fans and several other products that require the motor produced by E Division. E Division sells 90 percent of its output externally and transfers the other 10 percent to L Division. The EL Corporation makes all internal transfers at market price. E Division's revenue and cost structure follows:

Sales price per motor	$75
Variable manufacturing cost	37
Fixed manufacturing cost	14
Variable selling and administrative cost	2
Fixed selling and administrative cost	5

Both per-unit fixed cost computations are based on an expected capacity of 200,000 units.

a. What is the variable cost of producing and selling a fan motor from E Division's perspective?

b. What is the variable cost of a fan motor from the perspective of L Division?

c. Under what circumstances would it be desirable for L Division to know the true variable cost of an electric fan motor?

31. (LO 5; *Transfer pricing*) Among other products, Home Products Division of PlastiCorp produces small plastic cases. Forty percent of its output is sold to the Tool Division of PlastiCorp. All other output is sold to external parties. All internal transfers occur at a fixed price of $1.25 per unit. Home Products Division's 1997 expected results are shown below.

	INTERNAL	EXTERNAL
Sales (150,000 units)	$75,000	$135,000
Costs:		
Variable	(30,000)	(45,000)
Fixed	(36,000)	(54,000)
Gross profit	$ 9,000	$ 36,000

Home Products Division has received an external offer that would enable it to sell, at $1.40 per unit, all the units now scheduled to be sold internally. To accommodate this sale, Tool Division would have to purchase its units externally for $1.70 per unit.

a. By what amount will Home Products Division's gross profit change if it accepts the offer from the external party?

b. By what amount will Tool Division's gross profit change if Home Products Division accepts the offer from the external party?

c. Assume Home Products Division negotiates a transfer price of $1.40 per unit with Tool Division. However, the additional gross profit (relative to the normal internal sales price) generated for Home Products Division by this transfer price will be split between Home Products Division and Tool Division. What will be the actual transfer price for each unit after this sharing of profit takes place?

d. How could a dual pricing system be used to provide incentive for an internal transfer in this situation?

32. (LO 5; *Transfer pricing*) Sound Division produces one type of speaker set that is sold to Stereo Division at the market price of $80. Sound Division does not sell any of these speakers externally. Annual production and sales are 40,000 sets. The cost of production for Sound Division is shown below:

Variable production costs	$44
General fixed overhead ($12 per hour;	
1 hour for production time)	12
Direct fixed overhead ($320,000 ÷ 40,000)	8
Unit cost	$64
Variable shipping expenses	4
Total unit cost	$68

General fixed overhead is composed of some allocated production costs relating to the building and the production activities. Discontinuation of production of this speaker type would save Sound Division $40,000 in annual direct fixed overhead.

   a. Determine the incremental cost of producing the speaker set.

   b. Assume Sound Division is operating at full capacity. What is the appropriate unit cost to be used to set a minimum transfer price for selling speaker sets to Stereo Division?

33. (LO 6; *Transfer pricing for services*) Indicate whether each of the following statements constitutes a potential advantage (A) of using transfer prices for service department costs, a potential disadvantage (D) of using transfer prices for service department costs, or neither (N). Provide rationale for your answer.

   a. Can make a service department into a profit center
   b. May reduce goal congruence
   c. Can make users and providers more cost conscious
   d. May increase desire to waste resources
   e. Can increase disagreements about how transfer prices should be set
   f. Can put all service departments on an equal footing
   g. Can cause certain services to be underutilized or overutilized
   h. Can improve ability to evaluate performance
   i. Can increase communication about what additional services are needed and which can be reduced or eliminated
   j. Requires additional cost and employee time commitment

34. (LO 6; *Transfer pricing for services*) The MIS operation of Bolsa Engineering is in the process of developing a transfer price for its services. Capacity is defined by the computer operation as minutes of computer time. Expected capacity for next year (1998) is 700,000 minutes, and practical capacity is 900,000 minutes. Costs of the computer area for 1998 are expected to total $560,000.

   a. What is the transfer price if it is based on expected capacity?
   b. What is the transfer price if it is based on practical capacity?
   c. Assume the actual cost of operating the computer area in 1998 is$595,000. What is the total variance of that department? What are some possible causes of that variance?

■ COMMUNICATION ACTIVITIES

35. (LO 2, 3; *Performance report*) Golf course maintenance at the Westlake Country Club is managed by the greenskeeper and treated as a cost center. Performance measurement is based on a comparison of the budgeted amounts with the actual expenses for the year. The following statement has been prepared by the bookkeeper of the club.

WESTLAKE COUNTRY CLUB
GOLF COURSE MAINTENANCE EXPENSES
FOR THE YEAR ENDED DECEMBER 31, 1997

	Budgeted Amount	Actual Expense	Variance
Payroll and payroll taxes	$54,000	$54,500	$ (500)
Sand and gravel	300	500	(200)
Topsoil	1,000	800	200
Fertilizer	5,000	8,500	(3,500)
Fungicide	1,000	1,400	(400)

Grass seed	800	300	500
Parts	2,500	1,800	700
Petroleum products	1,800	3,100	(1,300)
Golf equipment	500	100	400
Uniforms	300	0	300
Training	300	0	300
Equipment rental	2,500	250	2,250
Utilities	3,000	5,100	(2,100)
Depreciation	5,000	5,000	0
Total	$78,000	$81,350	$(3,350)

The budget for the golf course is prepared by the greens committee and Mr. Jim Wallace, the greenskeeper. The budget is approved by the board of directors of the club and is used in evaluating the performance of Mr. Wallace at the end of the year. As a part of this evaluation, the following conversation occurred between Mr. Driver, the president of the club, and Mr. Wallace:

Mr. Driver: Jim, you should realize that the golf course budget represents the best judgments of the greens committee and the board of directors as to how resources should be used on the golf course. It is my opinion that differences between each budgeted amount and the expense incurred should be minor if you operate the course as directed by the committee with the approval of the board. The only items on this report where I view the differences as insignificant are payroll and depreciation. In many areas, such as fertilizer, petroleum products, and utilities, you significantly exceeded the budgeted amounts. To cover up these excesses, you failed to carry out our wishes concerning golf equipment and uniforms, and I can't explain the problem with equipment rental. I have received several complaints from our members about the condition of our markers and ball washers and the appearance of the employees on the course. I now see how this is reflected in this report. Besides that, we have had many complaints as to the condition of the course.

Mr. Wallace: My understanding has been that I am to run the golf course and try to remain within the total budget. I can explain all of the differences that show up on this report. The cost of fertilizer, fungicide, petroleum products, and utilities went up significantly this year. Because of this, we only put out a minimum of fertilizer. It was either this or incur a significant budget overrun. The late summer was very dry, which required excessive pumping, and this added to the increased utility cost.

Mr. Driver: Jim, you're telling me that the budget did not allow for any price increases, but I know this is not the case.

Mr. Wallace: I know price increases were built into the budget, but they in no way covered the actual increases for the year. No one could have anticipated the short supply of fertilizer and fungicide that existed this year.

Mr. Driver: You should have limited your expenditures for these items to the amounts in the budget, and you should have bought the new uniforms and golf equipment and started some of the reseeding that was included in your budget.

Mr. Wallace: In my opinion, I did the best job possible to maintain the course, given the economic and weather conditions during the year. These things cannot be anticipated in preparing a budget. I must use my professional judgment in some of these matters. In addition, concerning the depreciation, I have nothing to do with it! It just shows up at the end of each year.

Mr. Driver: I am not sure that helps the situation.

a. Explain how Mr. Driver and Mr. Wallace differ in the way that they interpret the budget and in the way they believe Mr. Wallace's performance is to be evaluated.

b. Prepare a report suggesting how the differences you identified in part a can be reconciled.

c. Do you see any problems with the treatment of depreciation in the budget? Explain.

d. Who should evaluate Mr. Wallace's performance: the greens committee or the board of directors? Explain.

36. (LO 2, 3, 4; *Cost center performance*) The Advertising Department of Ace Wholesale Sporting Goods is evaluated as a cost center. The fiscal year for the company ends on July 30, and divisional managers are evaluated on their ability to "live" within their budgets. For the last several years, the Advertising Department has run out of office supplies in June, and the advertising manager has made a vigorous attempt to control the volume of mail leaving the department.

   Later in the budget year, office equipment is not repaired, photo supplies run short, the signing of advertising and printing contracts is deferred, and all travel is eliminated. Because of these shortages, sales personnel and manufacturer's representatives frequently complain of inadequate service during this period. Several employees in the Advertising Department have observed that this condition is being encountered earlier each year. Some employees have been known to stockpile office supplies during the year so that they can function at the year's end.

   a. Describe the probable causes of the problems in the Advertising Department.

   b. Write a memo to the Advertising Department manager suggesting several means by which some of these problems can be corrected.

   c. How could advice from an expert in human behavior be used to deal with the games that are being played with the budget?

37. (LO 4, 5; *Transfer pricing*) Two of the divisions of International Tractor Company are the Engine Division and the Crane Division. The Engine Division produces motors that are used by both the Crane Division and a variety of external industrial customers.

   For external sales, sales orders are generally produced in 50-unit lots. Based on this typical lot size, the cost per motor is as follows:

Variable production cost	$2,100
Fixed manufacturing overhead cost	900
Variable selling expense	300
Fixed selling expense	420
Fixed general and administrative expense	640
Total unit cost	$4,360

   Engine Division normally earns a profit margin of 20 percent by setting the external selling price at $5,232. Because a significant number of sales are being made internally, Engine Division managers have decided that $5,232 is the appropriate price to use for all future transfers to the Crane Division. Previous transfers have been based on full cost plus a stipulated per-unit profit.

   When the managers in Crane Division heard of this change in the transfer price, they became very upset since the change will have a major negative impact on Crane's net income. Because of competition, corporate management has asked Engine Division to lower its sales prices, and the change in transfer price will cause Engine Division's profit margin to be only 15 percent on internal sales. At the same time, Crane Division management has asked to be allowed to buy motors externally. Bill Bird, Crane's president, has gathered the following price information in order to help the two divisional managers negotiate an equitable transfer price:

Current external sales price	$5,232
Total variable production cost plus 20% profit margin ($2,100 × 1.2)	2,520
Total production cost plus 20% profit margin ($3,000 × 1.2)	3,600
Bid price from external supplier (if motors are purchased in 50-unit lots)	4,640

a. Discuss advantages and disadvantages of each of the above transfer prices to the selling and buying divisions and to International Tractor Company. Explain what circumstances would make each of the alternative prices the most appropriate choice.

b. If Engine Division can sell all of its production externally at $5,232 each, what is the appropriate transfer price and why?

38. (LO 4, 5; *Transfer pricing*) AmerElectric is a decentralized company with divisions throughout the United States. Each division has its own sales force and production facilities and is operated autonomously as either a profit or an investment center. Switch Division has just been awarded a contract for a product that uses a component manufactured by Wire Division as well as by outside suppliers. Switch Division uses a cost figure of $3.80 for the component in preparing the bid for the new product. This cost figure was supplied by Wire Division in response to Switch Division's request for the average variable cost of the component.

Wire Division has an active sales force that is continually soliciting new customers. Its regular selling price for the component needed by Switch Division for the new product is $6.50. Sales of the component are expected to increase. Wire Division management has the following costs associated with the component:

Standard variable manufacturing cost	$3.20
Standard variable selling and distribution expense	.60
Standard fixed manufacturing cost	1.20
Total	$5.00

The two divisions have been unable to agree on a transfer price for the component. Corporate management has never established a transfer price because no interdivisional transactions have ever occurred. The following suggestions have been made for the transfer price.

- Regular selling price
- Regular selling price less variable selling and distribution expenses
- Standard manufacturing cost plus 15% percent
- Standard variable manufacturing cost plus 20 percent

a. Compute each of the suggested transfer prices.

b. Discuss the effect each of the transfer prices might have on Wire Division management's attitude toward intracompany business.

c. Is the negotiation of a price between Switch Division and Wire Division a satisfactory method of solving the transfer price problem? Explain your answer.

d. Should the corporate management of AmerElectric become involved in this transfer controversy? Explain your answer.

(CMA adapted)

39. (LO 6; *Service department pricing*) Klein Corp. is a diversified manufacturing company with corporate headquarters in Kansas City. The three operating divisions are the Aerospace Division, the Ceramic Products Division, and the Glass Products Division. Much of the manufacturing activity of the Aerospace Division is related to work performed for the government space program under negotiated contracts.

Klein Corp. headquarters provides general administrative support and computer services to each of the three operating divisions. The computer services are provided through a computer time-sharing arrangement whereby the central processing unit (CPU) is located in Kansas City and the divisions have remote terminals that are connected to the CPU by telephone lines. One standard from the Cost Accounting Standards Board provides that the cost of general administration may be allocated to negotiated defense contracts. Further, the standards provide that, in situations in which computer services are provided by corporate headquarters, the actual costs (fixed and variable) of operating the computer department may be allocated to another division based on a reasonable measure of computer usage.

The general managers of the three divisions are evaluated based on the before-tax performance of the divisions. The November 1997 performance evaluation reports (in millions of dollars) for each division are presented below.

	AEROSPACE DIVISION	CERAMIC PRODUCTS DIVISION	GLASS PRODUCTS DIVISION
Sales	$23.0	$15.0	$55.0
Cost of goods sold	13.0	7.0	38.0
Gross profit	$10.0	$ 8.0	$17.0
Selling and administrative:			
Division selling and administrative costs	$ 5.0	$ 5.0	$ 8.0
Corporate general administrative costs	1.0	—	—
Corporate computing	1.0	—	—
Total	$ 7.0	$ 5.0	$ 8.0
Profit before taxes	$ 3.0	$ 3.0	$ 9.0

If they are not charged for computing services, the operating divisions may not make the most cost-effective use of the resources of the Computer Systems Department of Klein Corp.

Outline and discuss a method for charging the operating divisions for use of computer services that would promote cost consciousness on the part of the operating divisions and operating efficiency by the Computer Systems Department.

(CMA adapted)

■ **PROBLEMS**

40. (LO 2; *Responsibility reports*) International Engineering Corp. was suffering from a decline in profit because of competitive pressures. One of its responses to declining profitability was to establish a responsibility accounting system. One of the several responsibility centers established was the Civil Engineering Division. This division is treated as a cost center for control purposes. In the first year (1997) after responsibility accounting was put in place, the responsibility report for the Civil Engineering Division contained the following comparisons:

	BUDGETED	ACTUAL	VARIANCE
Variable costs:			
Professional labor	$1,000,000	$ 940,000	$60,000 F
Travel	50,000	40,000	10,000 F
Supplies	100,000	90,000	10,000 F
Fixed costs:			
Professional labor	400,000	405,000	5,000 U
Facilities cost	250,000	265,000	15,000 U
Insurance	80,000	78,000	2,000 F
Totals	$1,880,000	$1,818,000	$62,000 F

For 1997, the Civil Engineering Division projected it would generate $2,000,000 of revenues; it actually generated $1,800,000.

a. What are the major weaknesses in the preceding responsibility report?

b. Recast the responsibility report in a more meaningful format for cost control evaluation.

c. International Engineering Corp. utilizes a management by exception philosophy. Using the report prepared in part b, which costs are likely to receive additional evaluation? Explain.

d. In most organizations, who would you expect to be involved in establishing policies on which variances should be investigated? Explain.

41. (LO 2, 4; *Performance report*) On January 1, 1997, fast-tracker Buddy Bluegill was promoted to the production manager position in Salmon Company. The firm purchases raw fish, cooks and processes the fish, and then cans the fish in single-portion containers. The canned fish is sold to several wholesalers that specialize in providing food to school lunch programs in the Northwest region of the United States and certain areas in Canada. All processing is conducted in the firm's single (highly automated) plant in Seattle, Washington. Performance of the production manager is evaluated on the basis of a comparison of actual costs with standard costs. Only costs that are controllable by the production manager are included in the comparison (all are variable). The cost of fish is noncontrollable. Standard costs per pound of canned fish for 1997 were set as follows:

Direct labor	$.50
Repairs	.10
Maintenance	.60
Indirect labor	.10
Power	.20

For 1997, the company purchased 2,500,000 pounds of fish and canned 1,500,000 pounds. There were no beginning or ending inventories of raw, in-process, or canned fish. Actual 1997 costs were:

Direct labor	$600,000
Repairs	160,000
Maintenance	650,000
Indirect labor	155,000
Power	315,000

a. Prepare a performance report for Buddy Bluegill for 1997.
b. Evaluate Buddy Bluegill's performance based on your report.
c. Buddy feels that his 1997 performance is so good that he should be considered for immediate promotion to the position of vice-president of operations. Do you agree? Defend your answer.
d. Should additional performance measures (other than standard cost variances) be added to evaluate the production manager's performance? If so, identify the measures you would recommend.

42. (LO 2, 3; *Cost center performance*) Sandi Hughes is a production supervisor at the North Carolina plant of U.S. Steelworks. As plant production supervisor, Ms. Hughes is evaluated based on her ability to meet standard production costs. At the North Carolina plant, the firm manufactures steel bridge guards. The standard costs to produce a one-foot section of bridge guard are given below:

Metal		$12.00
Galvanizing ($10 per gallon)		2.00
Direct labor ($15 per hour)		3.00
Overhead		
Welding supplies	$ .90	
Utilities	1.10	
Indirect labor	.80	
Machine maintenance/repairs	.40	
Equipment depreciation	2.20	
Miscellaneous	.80	6.20
Total		$23.20

In October 1997, the North Carolina plant produced 35,000 feet of bridge guards. During October, the plant incurred the following costs:

Metal		$507,500
Galvanizing ($9.40 per gallon)		65,800
Direct labor ($14.90 per hour)		104,300
Overhead		
Welding supplies	$34,900	
Utilities	38,300	
Indirect labor	25,500	
Machine maintenance and repairs	21,200	
Equipment depreciation	77,000	
Miscellaneous	29,500	226,400
Total		$904,000

a. For October 1997, compute the variance for each production cost category in the North Carolina plant.
b. Based on the variances computed in part a, evaluate the performance of Sandi Hughes. Which variances might deserve closer scrutiny by top management? Explain.

43. (LO 2, 3; *Revenue center performance*) Debra Subwitz manages the Retail Marketing Department at Kansas Electrical Supply. She is evaluated based on her ability to meet budgeted revenues. For May 1997, Ms. Subwitz's revenue budget was as follows:

	PRICE PER UNIT	UNIT SALES
Floor lamps	$107	960
Hanging lamps	55	2,800
Ceiling fixtures	75	4,240

The actual sales generated by Ms. Subwitz's department in May were as follows:

	PRICE PER UNIT	TOTAL SALES IN DOLLARS
Floor lamps	$115	$ 93,150
Hanging lamps	50	207,000
Ceiling fixtures	78	315,900

a. For May 1997, compute the sales price variance in the Retail Marketing Department at Kansas Electrical Supply.

b. For May 1997, compute the sales mix variance in the Retail Marketing Department at Kansas Electrical Supply.

c. For May 1997, compute the sales volume variance in the Retail Marketing Department at Kansas Electrical Supply.

d. Based on your answers to parts a, b, and c, evaluate the performance of Ms. Subwitz.

e. Assume you are Ms. Subwitz's supervisor. Why might you want to consider giving her the authority to set the salary and commission structure for the salespersons?

44. (LO 2, 3; *Profit center performance*) Sara Simon, the head of the accounting department at Big State U., has felt increasing pressure to raise external monies to compensate for dwindling state financial support. Accordingly, in early January 1997, she conceived the idea of offering a three-day accounting workshop in income taxation for local CPAs. She asked Mel Johnson, a tenured tax professor, to supervise the planning for the seminar which was to be held in late March 1997. In early February, Professor Johnson presented Simon with the following budgetary plan:

Revenues ($800 per participant)		$80,000
Expenses:		
Speakers ($1,000 each)	$10,000	
Rent on facilities	7,200	
Advertising	4,200	
Meals and lodging	36,000	
Departmental overhead allocation	7,000	64,400
Profit		$15,600

Explanations of budget items: The facilities rent of $7,200 is a fixed rental which is to be paid to a local hotel for use of its meeting rooms. The advertising is also a fixed budgeted cost. Meal expense is budgeted at $10 per person per meal (a total of nine meals are to be provided for each participant); lodging is budgeted at the rate of $90 per participant per night. The departmental overhead includes a specific charge for supplies costing $20 for each participant as well as a general allocation of $5,000 for use of departmental secretarial resources.

After reviewing the budget, Simon gave Johnson approval to proceed with the seminar.

a. Recast the income statement above in a segment income statement format.
b. Assume the actual financial results of the seminar were as follows:

Revenues (120 participants)		$77,000
Expenses:		
Speakers ($1,500 each)	$15,500	
Rent on facilities	8,400	
Advertising	5,800	
Meals and lodging	43,200	
Departmental overhead allocation	7,400	(80,300)
Loss		$ (3,300)

Explanation of actual results: Because signups were running below expectations, the seminar fee was reduced from $800 to $600 for late enrollees, and advertising expense was increased. In budgeting for the speakers, Professor Johnson neglected to include airfare, which averaged $500 per speaker. Because the number of participants was larger than expected, a larger meeting room had to be rented from the local hotel.

Recast the actual results in a segment income format.

c. Compute variances between the budgeted segment income statement and the actual segment income statement. Identify and discuss the factors that are primarily responsible for the difference between the budgeted profit and the actual loss on the tax seminar.
d. Evaluate Professor Johnson's management of the tax seminar.

45. (LO 5; *Transfer prices*) International Marine Products' North American operations are organized into two divisions: North and South. North Division sells a component that could be used by South Division in making one of the company's principal products. South Division has obtained three per-unit price quotations from external suppliers for the component: $162, $136, and $146. Examination of North Division's accounting records pertaining to the production of the component reveals the following costs: direct materials, $56; direct labor, $44; variable overhead, $18; and fixed overhead, $30.

a. What savings (or profits) would be available to International Marine Products if South Division bought the component internally rather than externally?
b. What would the transfer price be if the two divisions agreed to split the total company savings evenly between them?
c. Assuming dual transfer pricing is used, set the maximum realistic price for North Division and the minimum realistic price for South Division.

46. (LO 4, 5; *Transfer pricing*) The Controls Division of the Electric Motors Corporation manufactures a starter with the following standard costs:

Direct materials	$ 10
Direct labor	60
Overhead	30
Total unit cost	$100

The standard direct labor rate is $30 per hour, and overhead is assigned at 50 percent of the direct labor rate. Normal direct labor hours are 20,000, and the overhead rate is $5 variable and $10 fixed per direct labor hour.

The starters sell for $150, and the Controls Division is currently operating at a level of about 16,000 direct labor hours for the year. All transfers in Electric Motors Corporation are made at market price. The divisional managers are permitted to negotiate a transfer price if it is mutually agreed upon.

The Motor Division currently purchases 2,000 starters annually from the Controls Division at the market price. The divisional manager of the Motor Division indicates that she can purchase the starters from a foreign supplier for $130. Since she is free to select a supplier, she has indicated that she would like to negotiate a new transfer price with the Controls Division. The manager of the Controls Division indicates that he believes that the foreign supplier is attempting to "buy in" by selling the starters at what he considers an excessively low price.

a. From the viewpoint of the firm, should the Motor Division purchase the starters internally or externally? Show calculations and explain.

b. From the viewpoint of the Motor Division, should the starters be purchased internally or externally? Show calculations and explain.

c. Assume that the Controls Division is presently operating at capacity and could sell the starters that it now sells to the Motor Division to external buyers at its usual price. From the viewpoint of the firm, should the Motor Division purchase the starters internally or externally? Show calculations and explain.

d. If you were the marketing manager of the Motor Division, what concerns might you have regarding the decision to buy internally or externally?

47. (LO 4, 5; *Calculate income using transfer pricing*) Common Scents Ltd. manufactures a line of perfume. The manufacturing process is a series of mixing operations involving the addition of certain aromatic and coloring ingredients. The finished products are packaged in company-produced glass bottles and packed in cases containing six bottles.

Management feels that the sale of its product is heavily influenced by the appearance of the bottle and has, therefore, devoted considerable managerial effort to the bottle production process. This has resulted in the development of certain unique processes in which management takes considerable pride.

The two areas (perfume production and bottle manufacturing) have evolved almost independently over the years; in fact, rivalry has developed between management personnel about which division is more important to Common Scents. This attitude was probably intensified when the bottle manufacturing plant was purchased intact 10 years ago. No real interchange of management personnel or ideas (except at the top corporate level) has taken place.

Since the Bottle Division was acquired, its entire production has been absorbed by the Perfume Division. Each area is considered a separate profit center and evaluated as such. As the new corporate controller, you are responsible for the definition of a proper transfer price to use in assigning revenues to the bottle production profit center and in charging costs to the packaging profit center. At your request, the general manager of the Bottle Division has asked certain other bottle manufacturers to quote a price for the quantity and sizes demanded by the Perfume Division. These competitive prices for cases of six bottles each are as follows:

VOLUME	TOTAL PRICE	PRICE PER CASE
2,000,000 cases	$ 8,000,000	$4.00
4,000,000 cases	14,000,000	3.50
6,000,000 cases	20,000,000	3.33

A cost analysis of the internal bottle plant indicates that it can produce bottles at these costs:

VOLUME	TOTAL PRICE	PRICE PER CASE
2,000,000 cases	$ 6,400,000	$3.20
4,000,000 cases	10,400,000	2.60
6,000,000 cases	14,400,000	2.40

The above analysis represents fixed costs of $2,400,000 and variable costs of $2 per case.

These figures have given rise to considerable corporate discussion about the proper value to use in the transfer of bottles to the Perfume Division. This interest is heightened because a significant portion of a division manager's income is an incentive bonus based on profit center results.

The Perfume Division has the following costs in addition to the bottle costs:

VOLUME	TOTAL COST	COST PER CASE
2,000,000 cases	$32,800,000	$16.40
4,000,000 cases	64,800,000	16.20
6,000,000 cases	96,780,000	16.13

Market Research has furnished you with the following price-demand relationships for the finished product:

SALES VOLUME	TOTAL SALES REVENUE	SALES PRICE PER CASE
2,000,000 cases	$ 51,000,000	$25.50
4,000,000 cases	91,200,000	22.80
6,000,000 cases	127,800,000	21.30

a. Common Scents has used market-based transfer prices in the past. Using the current market prices and costs, and assuming a volume of 6,000,000 cases, calculate the income for the Bottle Division, the Perfume Division, and Common Scents Ltd.

b. Six million cases is the most profitable volume for which of the following: the Bottle Division, the Perfume Division, or Common Scents Ltd.? Explain your answer.

c. Place yourself in the position of president of Common Scents Ltd. and answer the following question posed by the controller: "Why have we structured the bottle operation as a separate division?"

(CMA adapted)

48. (LO 4, 5; *Evaluating transfer pricing policy*) Lansing Floor Coverings Inc. operates with 25 profit centers. Company policy requires all transfers between corporate units to be made at fair market price. Tile Division has been asked to produce 10,000 standard tiles for Retail Outlet Division. This order represents 10 percent of the division's capacity, stated in terms of machine hours. Tile Division has quoted a $3.50 price per tile, but Retail Outlet Division has found an exter-

nal company that will make the tiles for $2.80 each. Since corporate policy states that external market prices must be used, Tile Division will be required to sell the units at $2.80. Tile Division's total variable cost for this specific type of tile is $2.20.

a. What amount of contribution margin will Tile Division earn at the originally quoted price? At the externally quoted price?

b. What effect does the use of the externally quoted price have on Lansing Floor Covering's net income?

c. Some of the time that would be required to produce Retail Outlet Division's order could be used instead to produce a special order for an outside company. Discuss how Tile Division management should make the choice between producing the order for Retail Outlet Division and producing the outside company's order. What factors should be considered?

d. Should market price always be used to set a transfer price between organizational units? If so, discuss why. If not, discuss why not and when it is appropriate.

49. (LO 5; *Transfer prices*) Industrial Solutions Inc. has several regional divisions, which often purchase from each other. The company is fully decentralized, with divisions buying from and selling to each other or to outside markets. Conveyor Systems Division purchases most of its needs for hydraulic pumps from Hydraulic Division. The managers of these two divisions are currently negotiating a transfer price for the hydraulic pumps for next year. Hydraulic Division prepared the following cost information for negotiating purposes:

Direct material cost	$120
Direct labor cost	40
Variable overhead cost	30
Fixed production overhead cost	50
Fixed selling expense	30
Fixed administrative expense	20
Total	$290

Hydraulic Division is currently operating at 70 percent of its capacity. It is the policy of the division to target a net income to sales ratio of 20 percent.

The current market price for hydraulic pumps is $260 each. Recently, there has been a drop in price for such products because of industry advances in production technology.

Consider each of the following independently:

a. If Hydraulic Division desires to achieve its goal of a net income to sales ratio of 20 percent, what should the transfer price of pumps be?

b. If Hydraulic Division wants to maximize its income, what transfer price would you recommend it offer to the Conveyor Systems Division?

c. What is the price that you believe should be charged by Hydraulic Division if overall company profit is to be maximized? Why?

(CMA adapted)

50. (LO 6; *Service department transfer pricing and cost allocation*) Tanner & Associates, CPAs, has three revenue departments: Auditing and Accounting (A&A), Tax, and Consulting. In addition, the company has two support departments: administration and EDP. Administration costs are allocated to the three revenue departments on the basis of number of employees. The EDP department's fixed

costs are allocated to revenue departments on the basis of the peak hours of monthly service each revenue department expects to use. EDP's variable costs are assigned to the revenue departments at a transfer price of $40 per hour of actual service. Following are the direct costs and the allocation bases associated with each of the departments:

| | DIRECT COSTS | ALLOCATION BASES | | |
DEPARTMENT	(BEFORE TRANSFER COSTS)	Number of Employees	Peak Hours	EDP Hours Used
Administration	$450,000	4	30	290
EDP—Fixed	300,000	2	N/A	N/A
EDP—Variable	90,000	2	N/A	N/A
A&A	200,000	10	80	1,220
Tax	255,000	5	240	650
Consulting	340,000	3	25	190

a. Was the variable EDP transfer price of $40 adequate? Explain.

b. Allocate the Administration costs to A&A, Tax, and Consulting using the direct method of service department cost allocation. (See Appendix 2, Chapter 4.)

c. What are the total costs of the revenue-producing departments after allocation of all service department costs?

d. For what purposes are service department costs allocated to revenue-producing departments?

■ **CASES**

51. (LO 2; *Responsibility accounting*) Family Resorts, Inc., is a holding company for several vacation hotels in the northeast and mid-Atlantic states. The firm originally purchased several old inns, restored the buildings, and upgraded the recreational facilities. The inns have been well received by vacationing families, as many services are provided that accommodate children and afford parents time for themselves. Since the completion of the restorations 10 years ago, the company has been profitable.

Family Resorts has just concluded its annual meeting of regional and district managers. This meeting is held each November to review the results of the previous season and to help the managers prepare for the upcoming year. Prior to the meeting, the managers have submitted proposed budgets for their districts or regions as appropriate. These budgets have been reviewed and consolidated into an annual operating budget for the entire company. The 1997 budget has been presented at the meeting and accepted by the managers.

To evaluate the performance of its managers, Family Resorts uses responsibility accounting. Therefore, the preparation of the budget is given close attention at headquarters. If major changes need to be made to the budgets submitted by the managers, all affected parties are consulted before the changes are incorporated. The following are two pages from the budget booklet that all managers received at the meeting.

FAMILY RESORTS, INC.
RESPONSIBILITY SUMMARY
($000 OMITTED)

Reporting Unit: Family Resorts	
Responsible Person: President	
Mid-Atlantic Region	$605
New England Region	365
Unallocated costs	(160)
Income before taxes	$810
Reporting Unit: New England Region	
Responsible Person: Regional Manager	
Vermont	$200
New Hampshire	140
Maine	105
Unallocated costs	(80)
Total contribution	$365
Reporting Unit: Maine District	
Responsible Person: District Manager	
Harbor Inn	$ 80
Camden Country Inn	60
Unallocated costs	(35)
Total contribution	$105
Reporting Unit: Harbor Inn	
Responsible Person: Innkeeper	
Revenue	$600
Controllable costs	(455)
Allocated costs	(65)
Total contribution	$ 80

The budget for Family Resorts, Inc., follows.

FAMILY RESORTS, INC.
CONDENSED OPERATING BUDGET—MAINE DISTRICT
FOR THE YEAR ENDING DECEMBER 31, 1997
($000 OMITTED)

	Family Resorts	Mid-Atlantic	New Engl.	Not Allc.[1]	Vermt.	New Hamp.	Maine	Not Allc.[2]	Harbor	Camden Cnty.
Net sales	$7,900	$4,200	$3,700		$1,400	$1,200	$1,100		$600	$500
Cost of sales	4,530	2,310	2,220		840	720	660		360	300
Gross margin	$3,370	$1,890	$1,480		$ 560	$ 480	$ 440		$240	$200
Controllable expenses										
Supervisory expenses	$ 240	$ 130	$ 110		$ 35	$ 30	$ 45	$10	$ 20	$ 15
Training expenses	160	80	80		30	25	25		15	10
Advertising expenses	500	280	220	$ 50	55	60	55	15	20	20
Repairs and maintenance	480	225	255		90	85	80		40	40
Total controllable expenses	$1,380	$ 715	$ 665	$ 50	$ 210	$ 200	$ 205	$25	$ 95	$ 85
Controllable contribution	$1,990	$1,175	$ 815	$ (50)	$ 350	$ 280	$ 235	$(25)	$145	$115

Expenses controlled by others										
Depreciation	$ 520	$ 300	$ 220	$ 30	$ 70	$ 60	$ 60	$ 10	$ 30	$ 20
Property taxes	200	120	80		30	30	20		10	10
Insurance	300	150	150		50	50	50		25	25
Total expenses controlled by others	$1,020	$ 570	$ 450	$ 30	$ 150	$ 140	$ 130	$ 10	$ 65	$ 55
Total contribution	$ 970	$ 605	$ 365	$(80)	$ 200	$ 140	$ 105	$ (35)	$ 80	$ 60
Unallocated costs[3]	160									
Income before taxes	$ 810									

[1]Unallocated expenses include a regional advertising campaign and equipment used by the regional manager.

[2]Unallocated expenses include a portion of the district manager's salary, district promotion costs, and district manager's car.

[3]Unallocated costs include taxes on undeveloped real estate, headquarters expense, legal, and audit fees.

a. Responsibility accounting has been used effectively by many companies, both large and small.

   1. Define responsibility accounting.

   2. Discuss the benefits that accrue to a company using responsibility accounting.

   3. Describe the advantages of responsibility accounting for the managers of a firm.

b. The budget of Family Resorts, Inc. was accepted by the regional and district managers. Based on the facts presented, evaluate the budget process employed by Family Resorts by addressing the following:

   1. What features of the budget preparation process are likely to result in the managers' adopting and supporting the budget process?

   2. What recommendations, if any, could be made to the budget preparers to improve the budget process? Explain your answer.

(CMA)

52. (LO 2, 4; *Responsibility accounting and segment reporting*) Pittsburgh-Walsh Company (PWC) is a manufacturing company whose product line consists of lighting fixtures and electronic timing devices. The Lighting Fixtures Division assembles units for the upscale and midrange markets. The Electronic Timing Devices Division manufactures instrument panels that allow electronic systems to be activated and deactivated at scheduled times for both efficiency and safety purposes. Both divisions operate out of the same manufacturing facilities and share production equipment.

PWC's budget for the year ending December 31, 1997, was prepared on a business segment basis under the following guidelines:

■ Variable expenses are directly assigned to the incurring division.

■ Fixed overhead expenses are directly assigned to the incurring division.

■ Common fixed expenses are allocated to the divisions on the basis of units produced, which bears a close relationship to direct labor. Included in common fixed expenses are costs of the corporate staff, legal expenses, taxes, staff marketing, and advertising.

■ The production plan is for 8,000 upscale fixtures, 22,000 midrange fixtures, and 20,000 electronic timing devices.

PITTSBURGH–WALSH COMPANY
BUDGET FOR THE YEAR ENDING DECEMBER 31, 1997
(AMOUNTS IN THOUSANDS)

| | Lighting Fixtures | | Electronic Timing | |
	Upscale	Midrange	Devices	Totals
Sales	$1,440	$770	$800	$3,010
Variable expenses				
Cost of goods sold	(720)	(439)	(320)	(1,479)
Selling and administrative	(170)	(60)	(60)	(290)
Contribution margin	$ 550	$271	$420	$1,241
Fixed overhead expenses	(140)	(80)	(80)	(300)
Segment margin	$ 410	$191	$340	$ 941
Common fixed expenses				
Overhead	(48)	(132)	(120)	(300)
Selling and administrative	(11)	(31)	(28)	(70)
Net income (loss)	$ 351	$ 28	$192	$ 571

PWC established a bonus plan for division management that requires meeting the budget's planned net income by product line, with a bonus increment if the division exceeds the planned product line net income by 10 percent or more.

Shortly before the year began, the CEO, Jack Parkow, suffered a heart attack and retired. After reviewing the 1997 budget, the new CEO, Joe Kelly, decided to close the lighting fixtures midrange product line by the end of the first quarter and use the available production capacity to increase the remaining two product lines. The marketing staff advised that electronic timing devices could grow by 40 percent with increased direct sales support. Increases above that level and increasing sales of upscale lighting fixtures would require expanded advertising expenditures to increase consumer awareness of PWC as an electronics and upscale lighting fixture company. Kelly approved the increased sales support and advertising expenditures to achieve the revised plan. Kelly advised the divisions that for bonus purposes, the original product line net income objectives must be met, but he did allow the Lighting Fixtures Division to combine the net income objectives for both product lines for bonus purposes.

Prior to the close of the fiscal year, the division controllers were furnished with preliminary actual data for review and adjustment, as appropriate. These following preliminary year-end data reflect the revised units of production amounting to 12,000 upscale fixtures, 4,000 midrange fixtures, and 30,000 electronic timing devices.

PITTSBURGH–WALSH COMPANY
PRELIMINARY ACTUALS FOR THE YEAR
ENDING DECEMBER 31, 1997
(AMOUNTS IN THOUSANDS)

| | Lighting Fixtures | | Electronic Timing | |
	Upscale	Midrange	Devices	Totals
Sales	$2,160	$140	$1,200	$3,500
Variable expenses				
Cost of goods sold	(1,080)	(80)	(480)	(1,640)
Selling and administrative	(260)	(11)	(96)	(367)
Contribution margin	$ 820	$ 49	$ 624	$1,493
Fixed overhead expenses	(140)	(14)	(80)	(234)
Segment margin	$ 680	$ 35	$ 544	$1,259
Common fixed expenses				
Overhead	(78)	(27)	(195)	(300)
Selling and administrative	(60)	(20)	(150)	(230)
Net income (loss)	$ 542	$(12)	$ 199	$ 729

The controller of the Lighting Fixtures Division, anticipating a similar bonus plan for 1998, is contemplating deferring some revenues into the next year on the pretext that the sales are not yet final and accruing, in the current year, expenditures that will be applicable to the first quarter of 1998. The corporation would meet its annual plan, and the division would exceed the 10 percent incremental bonus plateau in the year 1997 despite the deferred revenues and accrued expenses contemplated.

a. 1. Outline the benefits that an organization realizes from segment reporting.

   2. Evaluate segment reporting on a variable cost basis versus an absorption cost basis. (See Chapter 8.)

b. 1. Segment reporting can be developed based on different criteria. What criteria must be present for division management to accept being evaluated on a segment basis?

   2. Why would the managers of the Electronic Timing Devices Division be unhappy with the current reporting, and how should the reporting be revised to gain their acceptance?

c. Are the adjustments contemplated by the controller of the Lighting Fixtures Division unethical? Explain.

(CMA)

■ ETHICS AND QUALITY DISCUSSIONS

53. *The notion of individual responsibility is much more prevalent in the United States than in Japan. Japanese people have more of a group orientation in the workplace. Nobuhiko Kawamoto, president of Honda Motor Co., perceived the lack of individual responsibility as a structural problem in his company: "We do too many things in groups," Mr. Kawamoto says. "We've lost a sense of responsibility, the feeling that every individual has his own specific duties."*

    Indicative of the groupthink mentality at Honda was the office arrangement for top executives. Rather than private offices, top managers were located in a single office on the 10th floor of the headquarters building. One executive could talk to another simply by rolling his chair a few feet.

Now, Mr. Kawamoto has established a new structure to instill a sense of personal responsibility for Honda's operations:

. . . senior executives will get direct line responsibilities and be held accountable. If these men think that they need private offices to fulfill their new obligations, "they can have them," Mr. Kawamoto says. He's sure he will want one before long. . . . Mr. Kawamoto also plans to give more responsibility to individual product designers. And product-development time will be shortened.

[SOURCE: Clay Chandler and Paul Ingrassia, "Just As U.S. Firms Try Japanese Management, Honda Is Centralizing," *Wall Street Journal* (April 11, 1991), pp. A1, A10. Reprinted by permission of The Wall Street Journal, © 1991 Dow Jones & Company, Inc. All Rights Reserved Worldwide.]

a. How may establishing personal responsibility for organizational success improve the quality of organizational operations?

b. How may establishing personal responsibility for organizational success diminish the quality of organizational operations?

c. Will Mr. Kawamoto also need to provide for changes in the accounting system to establish individual responsibility for the success of each product line? Explain.

54. The New Mexico Division is one of several divisions of U.S. Travel Industries. The divisional manager has a high degree of autonomy in operating the division. New Mexico Division's management staff consists of a division controller, a division sales manager, and a division production manager, all reporting to the division manager. The division manager reports to the executive vice-president at corporate headquarters, while the division controller has a functional reporting relationship to the corporate controller.

The members of the management staff of the New Mexico Division have developed good working relationships with each other over the past several years. Regularly scheduled staff meetings are held, and most of the management process is carried out through daily contact among the members of the staff.

An important staff meeting is held each September. At the meeting, management makes decisions required to finalize the annual budget to be submitted to corporate headquarters for the coming calendar year. The fourth-quarter plans are finalized, and the current year's forecasted results are reviewed prior to completion of the budget for the coming year.

For the first time in recent years, the budgeted amounts of the New Mexico Division for the coming year (1997) show no growth and lower profits than the forecast for the current year. A review of the coming year's plans has not uncovered any alternatives that could improve the sales and profits. This unusual situation is of concern to the division manager because he has developed the reputation for producing growing profits. In addition, growth and profits affect the division manager's performance evaluation and annual bonus.

During the meeting in September 1996, the division manager stated that he would like to see some of the profits shifted from 1996 to 1997. He has heard that another company shifted profits. He believes the following actions were used to accomplish this objective:

- Shipments made to customers in the last two weeks of December were not billed until January.
- The sales force was instructed to encourage customers to specify January delivery rather than December wherever possible.
- Abnormally generous amounts were used to establish accruals for warranties, bad debts, and other expenses.

- Purchased raw materials for which title had passed and that were in transit at the end of December were recorded as purchased in December. However, the raw materials were not included in the year-end inventory.
- Sales on account for the last day of December were not recorded until the first business day of January.
- The cleaning and painting of the exterior of the plant was rescheduled to be completed in the current year rather than in the coming year as planned.

The dollar amounts involved in these actions were material and would be material for the New Mexico Division if similar actions were taken. The division manager asked the division controller if profits would be shifted from 1996 to 1997 if actions similar to these were carried out at the New Mexico Division.

a. For each of the enumerated items, indicate whether there would be a shift of profit from 1996 to 1997.

b. How could the described manipulations of the responsibility accounting system adversely affect the quality of work performed in the division?

c. Comment on the ethics of accelerating or delaying transactions in order to manipulate the level of reported profit by a division.

55. A large American corporation participates in a highly competitive industry. To meet this competition and achieve profit goals, the company has chosen the decentralized form of organization. Each manager of a decentralized profit center is measured on the basis of profit contribution, market penetration, and return on investment. Failure to meet the objectives established by corporate management for these measures is unacceptable and usually results in demotion or dismissal of a profit center manager.

An anonymous survey of managers in the company has revealed that the managers feel pressure to compromise their personal ethical standards to achieve corporate objectives. For example, at certain plant locations there is pressure to reduce quality control to a level that cannot assure that all unsafe products will be rejected. Also, sales personnel are encouraged to use questionable sales tactics to obtain orders, including gifts and other incentives to purchasing agents.

The chief executive officer is disturbed by the survey findings. In his opinion, such behavior cannot be condoned by the company. He concludes that the company should do something about this problem.

a. Discuss what might be causing the ethical problems described.

b. Outline a program that could be instituted by the company to help reduce the pressures on managers to compromise personal ethical standards in their work.

(CMA)

56. *The big winners in Washington's revolving-door sweepstakes these days are former tax collectors.*

Foreign corporations, including a virtual who's who of Japanese industry, are snapping up former Internal Revenue Service and Treasury Department officials to help fight the government's efforts to collect billions of dollars in additional taxes from them.

The hiring spree has outraged some members of Congress, who say the IRS is now outgunned by some of its most skilled and experienced former employees. "This has an odor about it," says Republican Sen. Jesse Helms of North Carolina, who has been a loud critic of government officials who leave office to represent foreign—and particularly Japanese—clients. The former tax collectors, he says, ought to be "embarrassed."

At issue are a series of so-called "transfer pricing" cases in which the government is trying to collect more than $12 billion in additional taxes from more than 30 companies, a substantial number of which are Japanese.

[SOURCE: Jill Abramson, "Ex-Tax Collectors Help Foreign Firms Fight U.S. Efforts to Get More Funds," *Wall Street Journal* (October 18, 1991), pp. A16. Reprinted by permission of The Wall Street Journal, © 1991 Dow Jones & Company, Inc. All Rights Reserved Worldwide.]

   a. Comment on the ethics of former federal employees' working for foreign companies and using their knowledge of the U.S. Treasury in behalf of their new employers.

   b. Should the U.S. government pass legislation prohibiting foreign firms from hiring former Treasury employees or other legislation to curtail this practice? Discuss.

57. Quigley and Wigley are partners in an accounting firm. Quigley runs the tax practice and is both a CPA and a CMA. Wigley is in charge of the management consulting area; his background is in information systems and statistics. Quigley and Wigley used to be good friends; but since his divorce, Quigley believes that everyone is "out to take him" for everything possible. In addition to their salaries, Quigley and Wigley receive (1) a bonus based on the profits of their respective practice areas and (2) a share of total profits after expenses. The tax practice has consistently shown higher profits than the consulting area, although consulting revenues are growing and costs are remaining fairly constant.

Recently, Wigley asked for some help regarding several of his client engagements in tax matters. Quigley also needed some computer assistance from Wigley's area. Therefore, they agreed to establish a transfer price for such assistance. The transfer price was to be the cost of service provided. At the end of the year, the tax area showed a very large profit while the consulting area's increase was not so substantial, even though several new clients had been acquired. Quigley spent his bonus on a trip to the Cote d'Azur and felt much better when he returned after three weeks. He hoped the following year would be even more profitable since he was using absorption (full) cost as the basis for transferring his assistance to consulting and Wigley was using variable cost as the basis for transferring his assistance to tax.

   a. Do you think it is necessary to inform the uninformed about the differences in how things can be defined in accounting? You do not need to limit this discussion to cost-based transfer prices.

   b. Is Quigley being unethical in the distribution of profits with Wigley? Discuss.

   c. Is Quigley being illegal in the distribution of profits with Wigley? Discuss.

   d. The assistance being rendered between the two areas is similar to a product, since both areas produce revenues. Suggest an equitable way to determine a transfer price for the firm, and discuss how your transfer price would affect the bonuses earned by Quigley and Wigley.

58. The Gordon Company has several plants, one of which produces military equipment for the federal government. Many of the contracts are negotiated by use of cost plus a specified markup. Some of the other plants have been only marginally profitable, and the home office has engaged a consultant, Mr. Shifty, to meet with top management. At the meeting, Shifty observes that the company isn't using some of the more "creative" accounting techniques to shift costs toward the plant serving the federal government and away from the marginally profitable plants. He notes that "transfer pricing and service department allocations involve a lot of subjectivity, and there is plenty of room to stack the deck and let the taxpayer foot the bill. Taxpayers will never know, and even if the government suspects, it can't prove motive if we document the procedures with contrived business jargon." One of the staff states that "this would be a way to get back some of those exorbitant income taxes we have had to pay all these years." The company president ends the meeting and asks for some time to consider the matter.

a. What is the purpose of setting transfer prices and making service department allocations?

b. Can or should transfer prices and service department allocations be used to shift income from one plant to another? If so, under what conditions?

c. Do you think that what the consultant is suggesting is legal? Ethical? Ever been done? Discuss your reasoning for each answer.

■ PROJECTS

59. To understand the importance of transfer pricing in multinational companies, it is helpful to know the nature and extent of intracompany transfers. Conduct a library search on multinational transfers and transfer pricing. Based on this search, write a report documenting the kinds of services, technology, and products that are the subject of intracompany transfers. Also discuss any findings on the factors that affect the selection of the transfer pricing scheme.

60. Assume that the company you work for has just purchased a fleet of cars from a major automobile producer. The cars are to be made available to the six autonomous divisions in your company for business use by a variety of personnel. Each division has authority to either use these automobiles or make outside arrangements for its transportation needs. Your job is to determine an effective transfer pricing scheme under the two conditions below.

a. Demand from the divisions far exceeds the size of the fleet. Thus, you need to devise a transfer pricing scheme that will ration the cars to the divisions. The pricing scheme you develop should allow for recovery of all costs to acquire and operate the fleet.

b. The divisions demonstrate little interest in using the central fleet. Accordingly, you need to devise a transfer pricing scheme that will encourage the divisions to use the fleet rather than autos acquired from outside the firm. In this case, all costs of operating the fleet must be covered, but it is not necessary for the original cost of the autos to be fully recovered.

61. You are involved in the development of a new health food business which is to compete in major metropolitan areas in North America. The business will open 100 retail stores per year for the next several years. Your job is to develop a responsibility accounting system to evaluate performance of the store managers in each retail store. The firm will centralize the financing, purchasing, and accounting functions to obtain economies of scale. Nearly all other decisions will be made locally.

Your primary concern is with identifying the most important issues to be considered in the design of the responsibility accounting system. You are not concerned with operational details. For example, one major issue might be behavioral issues (such as manipulating accounting measures) that could occur within the control system.

You are to prepare a written report of these major issues to present to your business colleagues. You might consider working with two or three other class members as a team. Each team should devise its own method for apportioning the work among team members. If teams are used, one report that integrates the work of all members should be prepared for each team.

MEASURING AND REWARDING PERFORMANCE

LEARNING OBJECTIVES

1. Discuss the need for multiple performance measures.

2. Compare and contrast return on investment and residual income.

3. Explain why nonfinancial measures are important to evaluating performance.

4. Relate activity-based costing concepts to performance measurement.

5. Identify some reasons why it is more difficult to measure performance in multinational firms than in solely domestic companies.

6. Discuss how employee rewards (including compensation) and performance should be related.

7. Explain how expatriate reward systems may differ from those of domestic operations.

Not everything that counts can be counted, and not everything that can be counted counts.
Albert Einstein

ON SITE — Southwire Company: Assessing Excellence Requires Performance Measures

Southwire Company, founded in 1950 [and headquartered in Carrollton, Georgia], is the nation's largest wire maker, with an annual revenue of $1.3 billion. Southwire employs 5,000 persons at 17 facilities around the world.

Like many large companies, Southwire has a quality process, Quality Through Business Excellence. The company has developed a corporate vision and philosophy as a basis for the quality process. Southwire sees itself in the future as a world-class organization in which teamwork continuously improves its people, profitability, and product and service quality. [The company] has adopted the following corporate philosophy:

- ■ To design, produce, and market products and services that exceed customer expectations.
- ■ To create an environment in which personal involvement leads to individual satisfaction and continuous improvement.
- ■ To achieve long-term prosperity and success as a profitable business competing in the world marketplace.

Southwire identified three success factors for business excellence—people, product and service quality, and profits. To achieve business excellence, the company's people must be involved. Product and service quality means superior product performance, 100% on-time delivery, and low-cost production. Profits mean prosperity, not only for ownership but also for employees.

How will Southwire measure its performance in its drive to achieve business excellence? To discover how well the company is doing, Southwire developed key indicators for business excellence. It uses turnover, safety, education, and STAR process participation as measures of employee involvement. [STAR refers to suggestions, thoughts, and recommendations.] Product and service quality is indicated by data on customer complaints, service level, scrap/recycle levels, and process improvement. Profits are measured by comparing actual data to plans, return on assets (ROA), market share, and value added per person.

SOURCE: Gilda M. Agacer, Donald W. Baker, and Les Miles, "Implementing the Quality Process at Southwire Company," *Management Accounting* (November 1994), pp. 59-60. Published by Institute of Management Accountants, Montvale, NJ.

Businesses have traditionally measured performance according to a single dimension and in short-run financial terms. However, financial measures do not necessarily indicate how well an organizational unit is performing in a customer-driven, global marketplace. To highlight the essential nature of items such as quality and lead time, many firms, such as Southwire Company, have chosen to supplement traditional financial performance measures with additional qualitative and nonmonetary quantitative measures. Thus, the success equation becomes multidimensional rather than one-dimensional and balances short-run with long-run considerations.

This chapter covers two related sets of topics. First, performance measurement is discussed in the context of conventional monetary indicators such as cash flows, return on investment, and residual income. The more innovative performance measures that are needed by world-class, customer-driven companies such as Southwire are also addressed. Second, a variety of employee rewards that might be used by a company seeking to balance short-run and long-run interests are presented.

MEASURING ORGANIZATIONAL AND EMPLOYEE PERFORMANCE

As indicated in previous chapters, people must have benchmarks against which to compare their accomplishments in order to evaluate performance. A benchmark can be monetary (such as a standard cost or a budget appropriation) or nonmonetary (such as zero defect production or size of market share). Whatever measures are used, the following four general rules for performance measurement are appropriate:

1. Measures that assess progress toward organizational goals and objectives should be established.
2. Persons being evaluated should have had some input in developing the performance measurements and should be aware of them.
3. Persons being evaluated should have the appropriate skills and be provided the necessary equipment, information, and authority to be successful under the measurement system.
4. Feedback relative to performance should be provided in a timely and useful manner.

Need for Multiple Measures

Organizations have a variety of goals and objectives, and it is unlikely that a single measure or even several measures of the same type will effectively assess organizational progress toward all of those goals and objectives. A primary goal is, by necessity, to be financially solvent. If the organization is profit-oriented, this goal is satisfied by generating a net income considered by the owners to be satisfactory relative to the assets invested. Since the definition of "satisfactory earnings" may change over time and may differ with different types of businesses, owners and managers may select some relevant financial performance measures in addition to net income or profits for evaluation purposes. For example, cash flow measures are often critical to businesses, as indicated by the following statistic: "Of the 60,432 businesses that failed in 1990, more than 60% blamed their demise on economic factors linked to cash flow."[1]

Although financial measures provide necessary indications of performance, they do not address some of the new issues of competitive reality essential to business survival in a global economy. Many companies have established goals of customer satisfaction, zero defects, minimal lead time to market, and environmental social responsibility. Such goals are not measured directly by periodic income, but companies producing inferior goods, delivering late, abusing the environment, or, in general, making customers dissatisfied will lose market share and eventually be forced out of business. Nonfinancial performance measures can be developed that indicate progress (or lack thereof) toward achievement of the important, long-run critical success factors of world-class companies.

The News Note on page 836 addresses one critical nonfinancial performance measure—speed—and its effect on the bottom line. Nonfinancial indicators are, in effect, surrogate measures of financial performance. If cycle time is reduced, costs are reduced and profits will increase. Thus, supplementing traditional financial performance measures with innovative nonfinancial ones can provide information on why financial performance was better or worse than in the past or compared with budget.

■ LEARNING OBJECTIVE 1
Discuss the need for multiple performance measures.

---

[1]Shelly Branch, "Go with the Flow—Or Else," *Black Enterprise* (November 1991), p. 77.

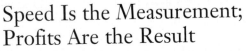

Speed Is the Measurement;
Profits Are the Result

Time is money. Time waits for no man. The unforgiving minute. These aren't just clichés. Increasingly, they are corporate strategy. Just as strategic planning drove corporate thinking a decade ago and Total Quality Management later became a mantra, speed is today's big thing.

In the manufacturing revolution of the past decade, U.S. companies adopted Japanese just-in-time techniques. Parts are delivered just before assembly, and products are shipped out almost as fast as they roll off the line. But today, the drive to speed up pervades entire companies, service and manufacturing alike, in everything they do—from receiving orders to making and delivering products to answering customers' questions.

Many companies haven't much choice. Michael Porter, Harvard Business School's competitiveness guru, says speed has become crucial to getting ahead internationally. "It's gone from a game of resources to a game of rate-of-progress," he says.

Beyond the obvious advantage of delivering a product faster than the competition can, many businesses are finding that focusing on speed also helps cut costs and raise quality.

Boosting speed is basic to corporate re-engineering, the trendy technique of using technology to reorganize operations. A survey by International Data Corp., of Framingham, Mass., found that of 200 big companies that were re-engineering, 28% said shortening cycle times of various processes was their primary goal; 23% viewed reducing costs as No. 1.

"You can only cut costs so far," says Paul Johnson, who ran the survey. "Cycle time helps differentiate you."

At Bell Helicopter, Lloyd Shoppa, executive vice president, says the Textron Inc. unit has reduced its normal lead time for building helicopters to 12 months from 24 months since 1991. Pushing for speed, Mr. Shoppa says, gave Bell crucial help in winning a $113 million Army contract for helicopter trainers.

SOURCE: William M. Bulkeley, "The Latest Big Thing at Many Companies Is Speed, Speed, Speed," *Wall Street Journal* (December 23, 1994), p. A1. Reprinted by permission of The Wall Street Journal, © 1994 Dow Jones & Company, Inc. All Rights Reserved Worldwide.

Exhibit 16–1 illustrates a "balanced scorecard" that ultimately links all aspects of performance to the company's strategies. The balanced scorecard provides a comprehensive set of financial and nonfinancial measures that encompass both internal and external perspectives.

Think of the balanced scorecard as the dials and indicators in an airplane cockpit. For the complex task of navigating and flying an airplane, pilots need detailed information about many aspects of the flight. They need information on fuel, air speed, altitude, bearing, destination, and other indicators that summarize the current and predicted environment. Reliance on one instrument can be fatal. Similarly, the complexity of managing an organization today requires that managers be able to view performance in several areas simultaneously.[2]

Various interrelated categories of performance measures are provided for an illustrative company in a later section of the chapter.

---

[2]Robert S. Kaplan and David P. Norton, "The Balanced Scorecard—Measures that Drive Performance," *Harvard Business Review* (January–February 1992), p. 72.

Awareness of and Participation in Performance Measures

Regardless of what performance measures are selected, they must be set at levels that
will encourage employees to do their best. Such a notion obviously means that indi-

■ **EXHIBIT 16–1**
Performance Measurement "Balanced Scorecard"

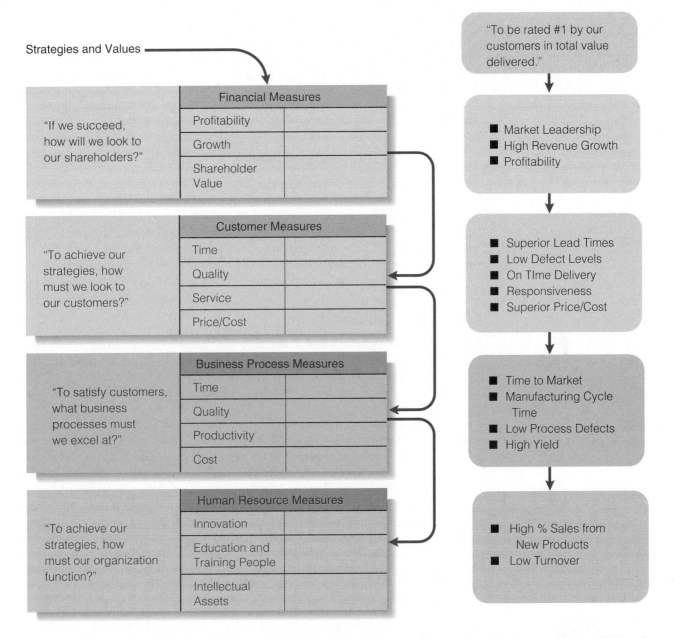

SOURCE: Lawrence S. Maisel, "Performance Measurement: The Balanced Scorecard Approach," *Journal of Cost Management* (Summer 1992), p. 50.
Reprinted with permission from The Journal of Cost Management for the Manufacturing Industry, © 1992, Warren, Gorham & Lamont, 31 St.
James Avenue, Boston, MA 02116. All right reserved.

viduals who will be evaluated by those measures must know about them. Communication of information is essential in any performance measurement process. Individuals must know and understand the performance measures to be used so that they can make a conscious choice to perform or not perform in a manner consistent with the measurement system. Withholding information about measures will keep employees from performing at their highest level of potential, will be frustrating for them, and will not support feelings of mutual respect and cooperation.

Participation in devising performance measures captures the attention of those persons being evaluated and results in a "social contract" between participants and evaluators. Individuals demonstrate a mutual respect for each other's ability to contribute effectively to the development process. Employee involvement in a performance measurement system is critical because that "management attempts to bolster productivity will plateau without employee support, which is the key to achieving maximum productivity."[3]

Performance measures should also promote harmonious operations among organizational units. The effects of suboptimization can then be minimized because all employees will be working toward the same goals.

Appropriate Tools for Performance

Managers must place individuals in the appropriate jobs because employees who are put in jobs for which they are unsuited are destined to fail. Assuming employees possess basic competencies, they must be given the appropriate tools—including equipment, information, authority, training, and support—to perform their jobs in a manner consistent with the measurement process. Competent individuals or teams of workers having the necessary job tools can be held responsible for their performance. If these tools are unavailable, people cannot be expected to accomplish their tasks.

Need for Feedback

Employee performance should be *monitored* and feedback provided on a continuous, ongoing basis. Positive feedback encourages employees to continue favorable behaviors, while negative feedback creates awareness of problems so that employees can respond with different behaviors. Positive reinforcement is discussed in the accompanying News Note.

Performance measurement and evaluation, on the other hand, should take place at one or more specified and known points in time. Waiting to provide feedback until some future "measurement point" allows employees no opportunity for early adjustment. Performance measurement typically relies on information generated during the management control process. A wide variety of nonfinancial performance measures can be used at all organizational levels: schedule attainment percentage, machine downtime percentage, number of defects, or the proportion of personnel retained during a period. For lower-level employees, financial measurement often focuses on aspects such as achievement of budget objectives and/or variances from budget or standard. For managerial-level employees, financial performance measurement is affected by their levels of authority and responsibility.

---

[3]Dan J. Seidner and Glenn Kieckhaefer, "Using Performance Measurement Systems to Create Gainsharing Programs," *(Grant Thornton) Manufacturing Issues* (Summer 1990), p. 8.

Praise Pays

NEWS NOTE

"When you're asking your employees to do more work than they ever had to before, there's only one way high performance will happen day after day," says Bob Nelson, a vice president at Blanchard Training and Development Inc. in San Diego. What's the secret? Hint: It's not dangling more money or cracking the whip.

"What gets people to excel on a daily basis, to stay late, to work weekends in a pinch, is when you regularly communicate to them that you value what they do," says Nelson. "Study after study demonstrates that's what employees want most."

Sound like hooey to you? Many managers think that in today's tough times, employees should be glad to have *any* job. And maybe they are, but will they really bust their rears on that score alone? "To consistently enjoy that level of performance, you've got to give them more than a paycheck," says Nelson.

"Everybody needs acknowledgment for working hard," he adds. "Give this recognition freely and sincerely, and amazing things start occurring in the workplace."

SOURCE: Robert McGarvey, "Bonus Points," *Entrepreneur* (July 1994), pp. 74, 77. Reprinted with permission from Entrepreneur magazine.

FINANCIAL PERFORMANCE MEASUREMENTS FOR MANAGERS

Attempts to use financial measures to evaluate higher-level managerial performance must consider the type of responsibility center over which the manager has control. If a manager is responsible for only one monetary item (such as in cost or revenue centers), performance measurements are limited to those relevant to that single monetary measure. Alternatively, profit and investment center managers are responsible for their centers' revenues and expenses. Given this greater accountability, a greater number of financial measures can be used to evaluate performance.

Divisional Profits

The segment margin of a profit center or income of an investment center is a frequently used measure of divisional performance.[4] This amount is compared with the center's budgeted segment margin or income as well as the associated revenue and expense amounts to determine where objectives were exceeded or were not achieved. However, as with any other accounting income–based amounts, the individual components used to derive the segment margin are subject to manipulations such as the following:

■ Sales transactions can be shifted between periods.

---

[4]The term *segment margin* is defined in Chapter 15 as segment sales minus (direct variable expenses plus avoidable fixed expenses). Thus, the margin would include neither unavoidable fixed costs nor allocated common costs.

- If a cost flow method other than FIFO is being used, inventory purchases can be accelerated or deferred at the end of a period to change Cost of Goods Sold.
- If actual overhead is allocated to inventory, an increase in production will cause cost per unit to decline because of the nature of fixed costs.
- Replacement of workers who have resigned or been terminated can be deferred to minimize salary expense for the period.
- Routine maintenance, advertising, or other discretionary costs can be delayed or eliminated to reduce expenses.
- Depreciation methods may be changed.

Any of these adjustments can cause reported segment margin to conform to budget expectations, but such tactics normally are not in the center's long-run best interest. Unfortunately, as indicated in the accompanying News Note, income manipulation sometimes seems to be a part of a manager's job.

Divisional segment margin or income is a short-term measure. Most reward systems (promotion, pay raises, bonuses, and so on) are based on annual performance. However, a year may be too short an interval for evaluating the quality of a manager's decisions.

Cash Flow

Use of accrual-based segment margin or income as a performance measure may divert management's attention from two critical issues—the size and direction of cash inflows and outflows. Profit and investment center managers know that continuous liquidity is essential for their entities to succeed. Thus, another valid performance measure is cash flow. The Statement of Cash Flows (SCF) highlights the cash impacts of the three primary categories of business activities (operating, investing, and financing). A cash-based portrayal of operations helps managers to judge an entity's ability to meet current fixed cash outflow commitments, undertake new commitments, and adapt to adverse changes in business conditions. Also, by identifying relationships between segment margin (or net income) and net cash flow from operations, the cash flow statement assists managers in judging the quality of the entity's earnings.

Like segment margin and income, cash flow can be manipulated and relates to the short-run rather than the long-run. But, as pointed out earlier, adequate cash flow is essential to business success. Inadequate cash flow may indicate poor judgment and decision making on the part of the entity's manager. A variety of financial ratios that use cash flow information (such as the current ratio, acid test ratio, and number of days' collections in accounts receivable) can help managers conduct their functions efficiently and effectively.

Return on Investment

return on investment (ROI)

■ LEARNING
OBJECTIVE 2
Compare and contrast return on investment and residual income.

Because they are responsible for generating revenues, controlling costs, and acquiring, using, and disposing of assets, investment center managers can be evaluated using return on investment. **Return on investment (ROI)** is a ratio that relates income generated by an entity to the resources (or the asset base) used to produce that income. The return on investment formula is:

$$ROI = \frac{Income}{Assets\ Invested}$$

Ethics of Income Manipulation

NEWS NOTE

Casual observers of the financial reporting process may assume that time, laws, regulation, and professional standards have restricted accounting practices to those which are moral, ethical, fair, and precise. But most managers and their accountants know otherwise— that managing short-term earnings can be part of a manager's job.

It seems many managers are convinced that if a practice is not explicitly prohibited or is only a slight deviation from rules, it is an ethical practice regardless of who might be affected either by the practice or the information that flows from it. This means that anyone who uses information on short-term earnings is vulnerable to misinterpretation, manipulation, or deliberate deception.

The essence of a moral or ethical approach to management is achieving a balance between individual interests and obligations to those who have a stake in what happens to the corporation (or what happens to a division or group within the corporation). These stakeholders include not only people who work in the firm, but customers, suppliers, creditors, shareholders, and investors as well.

Managers who take unproductive actions to boost short-term earnings may be acting totally within the laws and rules. Also they may be acting in the best interest of the corporation. But, if they fail to consider the adverse effects of their actions on other stakeholders, we may conclude that they are acting unethically.

SOURCE: William J. Bruns, Jr. and Kenneth A. Merchant, "The Dangerous Morality of Managing Earnings," *Management Accounting* (August 1990), pp. 22–23. Published by Institute of Management Accountants, Montvale, NJ.

Before the ROI formula can be used effectively, the numerator and denominator must be specifically defined. Exhibit 16–2 (page 842) presents several questions relative to these definitions and the answers to and rationale for each, assuming that the entity being measured is an investment center. (The answers would be different if ROI were being calculated for an entire company.) The ROI formula can be used to evaluate individual investment centers as well as to make intracompany, intercompany, and industry comparisons if managers making these comparisons are aware of and allow for any differences in the entities' characteristics and accounting methods.

Exhibit 16–3 (page 843) uses data for the Winston Wire Corporation to illustrate ROI computations. The company has divisions located in Portland, Santa Fe, and Edmonton. All of the divisions are operated as separate investment centers.

To provide useful information about individual factors that compose the rate of return, the ROI formula can be restated in terms of profit margin and asset turnover. **Profit margin** is the ratio of income to sales; it indicates what proportion of each sales dollar is *not* used for expenses and so becomes profit. **Asset turnover** (sales divided by assets) shows the sales dollars generated by each dollar of assets and measures asset productivity. The ROI formula restated in terms of profit margin and asset turnover is called the **Du Pont model**:

profit margin
asset turnover

Du Pont model

$$ROI = \text{Profit Margin} \times \text{Asset Turnover}$$
$$= \frac{\text{Income}}{\text{Sales}} \times \frac{\text{Sales}}{\text{Assets}}$$

As with the original ROI formula, terms must be specifically defined before the formula can be used for comparative or evaluative purposes. This model provides refined information about organizational improvement opportunities. Profit margin can be used to indicate management's efficiency as shown in the relation between sales and expenses. Asset turnover can be used to judge the effectiveness of asset use relative to revenue production.

Calculations based on the Winston Wire Corporation information are given in Exhibit 16–4 (page 844). Segment margin and total historical cost asset valuation are used as the income and asset base definitions. Thus, these computations provide the same answers as those given in Exhibit 16–3.

While Portland enjoys the highest profit margin and a strong turnover, Santa Fe has the highest turnover. To some extent, rapid turnover rates indicate that inventory is not being stockpiled. Thus, the Portland and Edmonton managers might inves-

■ **EXHIBIT 16–2**

ROI Definitional Questions and Answers

QUESTION	PREFERABLE ANSWER	RATIONALE
Is income defined as segment margin or operating income?	Segment margin	This amount includes only elements controllable by the investment center manager.
Is income defined on a before-tax or after-tax basis?	Before-tax basis	Investment centers are not taxed separately; if they were, the tax would probably be a different amount.
Is income defined on a before-interest or after-interest basis?	Before-interest basis	Interest rates are generally negotiated based on the company's (not the investment center's) credit-worthiness; if the center had to borrow funds as an independent entity, the rate might be different.
Should assets be defined as ■ total assets utilized; ■ total assets available for use; or ■ net assets (equity)?	Total assets available for use	The investment center manager is responsible for *all* assets, even idle ones.
Should plant assets be included in the asset denominator at: ■ original cost; ■ depreciated book value; or ■ current values?	Current values	These values measure the opportunity cost of using the assets.
Should beginning, ending, or average assets be used?	Average assets	Periodic income relates to assets used during the entire period.

tigate the reasons for Santa Fe's rapid throughput to determine if they can obtain the same level of performance.

Based on the proportions of accumulated depreciation to plant assets, Santa Fe appears to be the center with the newest assets. The Edmonton center seems to have fairly old plant assets, because the relationship of accumulated depreciation to historical cost (shown in Exhibit 16–3) is high. Perhaps because they are old, Edmonton's plant assets are not generating substantial sales dollars relative to the asset base. Edmonton's manager might consider purchasing more modern facilities to generate more sales dollars and greater profits. Such an acquisition could, however, cause ROI to decline, since the asset base would be increased. Return on investment computations encourage managers to retain and use old plant assets (especially when accumulated depreciation is excluded from the asset base) to keep the rates high as long as those assets are effective in keeping revenues up and expenses down. However, to avoid distorting results, calculations in these illustrations use original asset cost rather than net book values.

ROI is affected by decisions involving sales prices, volume and mix of products sold, expenses, and capital asset acquisitions and dispositions. Return on investment may be increased through various management actions including: (1) raising sales prices, if demand will not be impaired; (2) decreasing expenses; and (3) decreasing dollars invested in assets, especially if those assets are no longer productive. Thus, actions to improve performance should be taken only after all the interrelationships

■ **EXHIBIT 16–3**
Winston Wire Corporation

	PORTLAND	SANTA FE	EDMONTON	TOTAL
Revenues	$4,800,000	$645,000	$1,012,000	$6,457,000
Direct costs:				
Variable	(1,680,000)	(258,000)	(466,000)	(2,404,000)
Fixed (avoidable)	(825,000)	(90,000)	(176,000)	(1,091,000)
Segment margin	$2,295,000	$297,000	$ 370,000	$2,962,000
Unavoidable fixed				
and allocated costs	(558,000)	(75,000)	(117,000)	(750,000)
Operating income	$1,737,000	$222,000	$ 253,000	$2,212,000
Taxes (35%)	(607,950)	(77,700)	(88,550)	(774,200)
Net income	$1,129,050	$144,300	$ 164,450	$1,437,800
Current assets	$ 73,000	$ 30,000	$ 50,000	
Plant assets	9,268,000	731,000	6,915,000	
Total asset cost	$9,341,000	$761,000	$6,965,000	
Accumulated depreciation	(1,849,000)	(94,000)	(4,838,000)	
Asset book value	$7,492,000	$667,000	$2,127,000	
Liabilities	3,195,000	244,000	900,000	
Net assets	$4,297,000	$423,000	$1,227,000	
ROI:				
Segment margin	$2,295,000	$297,000	$ 370,000	
÷ Assets invested*	÷ $9,341,000	÷ $761,000	÷ $6,965,000	
= Return on investment	24.6%	39.0%	5.3%	

* While use of current values would have been preferable, Winston Wire Corporation found these values difficult to obtain and had more confidence in the original cost of the assets used.

■ **EXHIBIT 16–4**

Winston Wire Corporation ROI Components

PORTLAND INVESTMENT CENTER:

ROI = (Income ÷ Sales) × (Sales ÷ Assets)
      = ($2,295,000 ÷ $4,800,000) × ($4,800,000 ÷ $9,341,000)
      = .478 × .514 = 24.6%

SANTA FE INVESTMENT CENTER:

ROI = (Income ÷ Sales) × (Sales ÷ Assets)
      = ($297,000 ÷ $645,000) × ($645,000 ÷ $761,000)
      = .460 × .848 = 39.0%

EDMONTON INVESTMENT CENTER:

ROI = (Income ÷ Sales) × (Sales ÷ Assets)
      = ($370,000 ÷ $1,012,000) × ($1,012,000 ÷ $6,965,000)
      = .366 × .145 = 5.3%

that determine ROI have been considered. A change in one of the component elements can affect many of the others. For instance, a selling price increase can reduce sales volume if demand is elastic with respect to price.

Assessments of whether profit margin, asset turnover, and return on investment are favorable or unfavorable can only be made by comparison of actual results for each component with some valid basis. Bases of comparison include expected results, prior results, and results of other similar entities. Many companies establish target rates of return either for the company or for each division. These rates are based on the nature of the industry or market in which the company or division operates. Favorable results should mean rewards for investment center managers.

Unfavorable rates of return should be viewed as managerial opportunities for improvement. Factors used in the computation should be analyzed for more detailed information. For example, if asset turnover is low, additional analyses can be made of inventory turnover, accounts receivable turnover, machine capacity level experienced, and other rate-of-utilization measures. Such efforts should help indicate the causes of the problems so that adjustments can be made. Another measure related to return on investment is the amount of residual income of an investment center.

Residual Income

residual income (RI)

■ **LEARNING OBJECTIVE 2**

Compare and contrast return on investment and residual income.

Residual income (**RI**) is the profit earned that exceeds an amount "charged" for funds committed to an investment center. The amount charged for funds is equal to a management-specified target rate of return multiplied by the assets used by the division. The rate can be changed periodically to reflect market rate fluctuations or to compensate for risk. The residual income computation is:

$$\text{Residual Income} = \text{Income} - (\text{Target Rate} \times \text{Asset Base})$$

Perhaps the most significant advantage of residual income over return on investment is that residual income is concerned with a dollar figure rather than a percentage. It is always to a company's advantage to obtain new assets if they will earn a dollar amount of return greater than the dollar amount required by the rate charged for the additional investment. Expansion (or additional investments in assets) can occur in an investment center as long as positive residual income is expected on the additional investment.

Residual income can be calculated for each investment center of Winston Wire Corporation. The company has established 14 percent as the target rate of return on total assets invested and continues to define income as segment margin. Calculations are shown in Exhibit 16–5. The Portland and Santa Fe investment centers show positive residual incomes, meaning that these responsibility centers are earning above what top management considers a reasonable charge for funds. The Edmonton investment center's residual income is negative, which indicates that income is being significantly underproduced relative to the asset investment. Edmonton's manager should be apprised of the situation so that he or she can take steps to discover the cause of and correct this unsatisfactory result.

Limitations of Return on Investment and Residual Income

When used to measure investment center performance, return on investment and residual income have certain limitations (see Exhibit 16-6, p. 846) that must be considered by managers. Suboptimization, item 3 in the exhibit, is particularly troubling.

The Portland Division of Winston Wire is used to illustrate the effects of suboptimization. As indicated in Exhibit 16–3, the Portland Division has revenues of $4,800,000, segment expenses of $2,505,000, an asset base of $9,341,000, and an ROI of 24.6 percent. Assume that this division has an opportunity to increase its segment margin by $255,000 from sales of a new product. Product introduction will require an additional capital investment of $1,500,000. Considered separately, this project would result in a ROI of 17 percent ($255,000 ÷ $1,500,000). However, if Portland Division accepts this opportunity, total divisional ROI will drop, as follows:

Financial performance measures, including cash flow, are common in most organizations. Two problems with such measures are that they can be manipulated and are short-run focused. Alternatively, companies that are not financially solvent will not survive.

$$\begin{aligned}
\text{ROI} &= (\text{Original segment margin} + \text{New segment margin}) \div (\text{Original assets} \\
&\quad + \text{New assets}) \\
&= (\$2,295,000 + \$255,000) \div (\$9,341,000 + \$1,500,000) \\
&= \$2,550,000 \div \$10,841,000 \\
&= 23.5\%
\end{aligned}$$

If top management evaluates investment centers' managers on the ROIs of their divisions, the Portland Division manager will choose not to accept this investment opportunity.

■ **EXHIBIT 16–5**
Winston Wire Corporation Residual Income

Residual Income = Income − (Target Rate × Asset Base)

Portland:
RI = $2,295,000 − [.14 ($9,341,000)] = $2,295,000 − $1,307,740 = $987,260

Santa Fe:
RI = $297,000 − [.14 ($761,000)] = $297,000 − $106,540 = $190,460

Edmonton:
RI = $370,000 − [.14 ($6,965,000)] = $370,000 − $975,100 = $(605,100)

■ **EXHIBIT 16–6**
Limitations of ROI and RI

1. Problems related to income

- Income can be manipulated on a short-run basis.
- Because income depends on accounting methods selected, all investment centers must use the same methods if comparisons are to be made.
- Accrual-based income reflects neither the cash flow patterns nor the time value of money and these performance dimensions are generally important.

2. Problems related to the asset base

- Some asset investment values are difficult to measure and/or assign to investment centers, while some other values are not capitalized (such as research and development).
- Current managers may be evaluated on decisions over which they had no control, such as decisions by previous managers to acquire some of the assets included in the division's investment base.
- Inflation causes investment book values to be understated unless they are price-level adjusted.

3. ROI and RI reflect investment center performance without regard to companywide objectives, which can result in suboptimization.

Assume, though, that Winston Wire Corporation has established a target rate of return of 14 percent on investment dollars. The decision by the Portland manager to reject the new opportunity suboptimizes the companywide returns. This project should be accepted because it provides a return higher than the firm's target rate. Top management should be made aware of such opportunities, be informed of the effects acceptance will have on both divisional and companywide performance measurements, and be willing to reward such acceptance based on its impact on company performance.[5]

■ **LEARNING OBJECTIVE 3**
Explain why nonfinancial measures are important to evaluating performance.

NONFINANCIAL PERFORMANCE MEASURES

Customarily, performance evaluations have been conducted based almost solely on financial results. But top management, in maintaining such a narrow focus, is similar to a baseball player who, in hopes of playing well, concentrates solely on the scoreboard. Both the game score and financial measures reflect the *results of past decisions*. Success also requires that considerable attention be placed on steps to effectively compete—whether in the baseball stadium or the global marketplace. A baseball player must focus on hitting, fielding, and pitching. A company must focus on performing well in activities such as customer service, product development, manufacturing, marketing, and delivery. For a company to improve, its performance measurements must specifically track the causes and occurrences of these activities.

A progressively designed performance measurement system, then, should encompass both financial and nonfinancial measures, especially those that track factors nec-

---

[5]Capital budgeting techniques such as the internal rate of return and net present value (Chapter 14) can be used in conjunction with evaluating ROI. These techniques can indicate situations in which corporate performance will benefit to the perceived detriment of divisional performance.

essary for world-class status. Nonfinancial performance measures (NFPM) include statistics for activities such as on-time delivery, manufacturing cycle time, setup time, defect rate, number of unplanned production interruptions, and customer returns. NFPMs have two distinct advantages over financial performance measures:

■ Nonfinancial indicators directly measure an entity's performance in the activities that create shareholder wealth, such as manufacturing and delivering quality goods and services and providing service for the customer. . . .

■ Because they measure productive activity directly, nonfinancial measures may better predict the direction of future cash flows. For example, the long-term financial viability of some industries rests largely on their ability to keep promises of improved product quality at a competitive price.[6]

The "performance pyramid" depicted in Exhibit 16–7 indicates some financial and nonfinancial measures needed at various organizational levels and for various purposes. Also included are measures that can help in assessing both short-term and long-term organizational considerations.

■ **EXHIBIT 16–7**

The Performance Pyramid

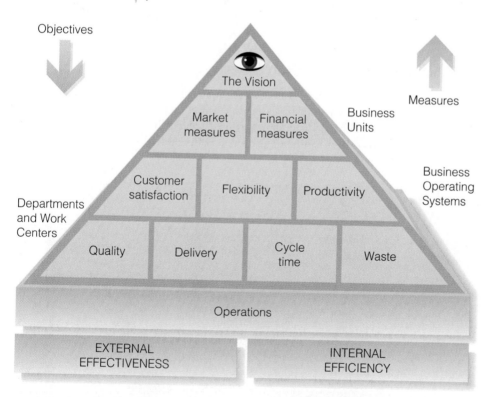

SOURCE: Adapted from C. J. McNair, Richard L. Lynch, and Kelvin F. Cross, "Do Financial and Nonfinancial Measures of Performance Have to Agree?" *Management Accounting* (November 1990), p. 30, Figure 1. Published by Institute of Management Accountants, Montvale, NJ.

---

[6]Institute of Management Accountants (formerly National Association of Accountants), *Statements on Management Accounting Number 4D: Measuring Entity Performance* (Montvale, N.J.: NAA, January 3, 1986), p. 12.

Selection of Nonfinancial Measures

The set of nonfinancial performance measures that can be used is quite large because it is limited only by the imaginations of the persons establishing the system. Before establishing the measurement system, though, management should strive to identify the firm's critical success factors. A company's critical success factors may include quality, customer satisfaction, manufacturing efficiency and effectiveness, technical excellence, and rapid response to market demands.

For each success factor chosen, management should target a few attributes of each relevant NFPM for continuous improvement. These attributes should include both short-run and long-run measures to properly steer organizational activities. For instance, a short-range success measure for quality is the number of customer complaints in the current period. A long-range success measure for quality is the number of patents obtained to improve the quality of the company's products.

The nonfinancial measures selected for the performance evaluation system can be qualitative or quantitative. Qualitative measures are often subjective; for example, simple low-to-high rankings may be assigned for job skills, such as knowledge, quality of work, and need for supervision. Although such measures provide useful information, performance should also be compared against a quantifiable standard.

Quantitative performance measures are more effective in creating employee receptiveness and compliance because such measures provide a defined target at which to aim. These measures must be systematically captured and compared with predetermined standards to assess performance.

Establishment of Comparison Bases

After performance measures have been chosen, managers should establish acceptable performance levels by providing bases against which actual statistical data can be compared. These benchmarks can be developed internally (such as from another well-performing division) or can be determined from external sources (such as other

The duplication process for CD-ROMs is highly mechanized and requires a "clean room." Duplicated disks are mechanically inspected for quality. West Publishing assesses performance for this process by determining the proportion of unacceptable disks to the total produced—using zero defects as the goal.

companies, regardless of whether they are within the company's industry). Exhibit 16–8 presents some companies that have been designated as appropriate targets for benchmarking in various nonfinancial performance areas.

In each area in which a performance measurement is to be made, an employee must agree (1) to accept specific responsibility for performance and (2) to being evaluated. A system for monitoring and reporting comparative performance levels should be established at appropriate intervals, as shown in Exhibit 16–9 (page 851). The exhibit reflects a responsibility hierarchy of performance standards, with the broader issues addressed by higher levels of management and the more immediate issues addressed by lower-level employees. Note also that the lower-level measures are monitored more frequently (continuously, daily, or weekly), while the upper-level measures are investigated less frequently (monthly, quarterly, and annually). Measures addressed by middle-level employees (in Exhibit 16–9, the plant manager) are intermediate linkages between the lower-level and upper-level performance measures and require monitoring at intermediate points in time (weekly, monthly, and annually).

A general model for measuring the relative success of an activity compares a numerator representing number of successes with a logical and valid denominator representing total activity volume. For example, delivery success could be measured as follows:

$$\frac{\text{Number of On-Time Deliveries}}{\text{Total Deliveries Made}} = \text{Delivery Success Rate}$$

Assume a division made 3,000 deliveries during a period, of which 2,700 were on time. Its delivery success rate is 90 percent (2,700 ÷ 3,000). If a competitive benchmark for on-time delivery success has been set at 92 percent, success will be evaluated as close to, but slightly below, the mark.

In contrast, management may prefer that a failure rate be measured. This approach is used when performance is expected to be perfect or nearly so. The failure rate indi-

---

■ **EXHIBIT 16–8**
Who Are the World-Class Companies?

Benchmarking Methods: AT&T, Digital Equipment, Ford, IBM, Motorola,
   Texas Instruments, Xerox
Billing and Collection: American Express, MCI, Fidelity Investments
Customer Satisfaction: L. L. Bean, Federal Express, GE Plastics, Xerox
Distribution and Logistics: L. L. Bean, Wal-Mart
Employee Empowerment: Corning, Dow, Milliken, Toledo Scale
Equipment Maintenance: Disney
Flexible Manufacturing: Allen-Bradley, Baldor, Motorola
Health-Care Programs: Allied-Signal, Coors
Marketing: Procter & Gamble
Product Development: Beckman Instruments, Calcamp, Cincinnati Milacron, DEC,
   Hewlett-Packard, 3M, Motorola, NCR
Quality Methods: AT&T, IBM, Motorola, Westinghouse, Xerox
Quick Shop Floor Changes: Dana, GM Lansing, Johnson Controls
Supplier Management: Bose, Ford, Levi Strauss, 3M, Motorola, Xerox
Worker Training: Disney, General Electric, Federal Express, Ford, Square D

SOURCE: "America's World-Class Champs," Reprinted from November 30, 1993, issue of *Business Week* by special permission, copyright © 1993 by McGraw-Hill, Inc.

cates the degree to which perfect performance did *not* occur. For example, suppose that the firm in the example above has established a total quality perspective and, therefore, expects no late deliveries. Since success is defined as total quality, the benchmark is 100 percent on-time deliveries and 0 percent late deliveries. The general model can be adapted and a new rate (based on the same information as above) calculated as follows:

$$\frac{\text{Number of Late Deliveries}}{\text{Total Deliveries Made}} = \text{Delivery Failure Rate}$$

The firm's delivery failure rate is 10 percent (300 ÷ 3,000). The company was obviously unsuccessful in achieving its performance goal of zero late deliveries. However, if this failure rate is less than the prior period's, it can be concluded that improvement is occurring. Analysis of the types and causes of the 300 late deliveries should allow management to contemplate actions to eliminate or minimize the root causes of these problems in the process of continual improvement.

Throughput

synchronous management

All endeavors undertaken to help an organization achieve its goals are considered to be **synchronous management** techniques. "Synchronous management's strategic objective is to simultaneously increase throughput, while reducing inventory and operating expenses."[7] Throughput is a valuable, nonfinancial indicator of performance that is gaining wide acceptability. Throughput refers to the number of good units produced and sold by an organization within a time period. An important aspect of this definition is that the company must sell the units and not simply produce them for inventory stockpiles. A primary goal of a profit-oriented organization is to make money, and inventory must be sold for profits to be achieved. Throughput can also refer to the number of services requested, performed, and delivered in a period.

One useful way to measure performance is to determine the extent to which the company is meeting its goal of making money by having rapid and high-quality throughput. Throughput, as mentioned, simply reflects how many good units are produced and sold for each available processing hour. Throughput can also be viewed as a set of component elements (as the Du Pont model, presented earlier, includes components of return on investment). Components of throughput include manufacturing cycle efficiency, process productivity, and process quality yield.[8]

$$\begin{array}{c} \text{Manufacturing} \\ \text{Cycle Efficiency} \end{array} \times \begin{array}{c} \text{Process} \\ \text{Productivity} \end{array} \times \begin{array}{c} \text{Process} \\ \text{Quality Yield} \end{array} = \text{Throughput}$$

or

$$\frac{\text{Value-added}}{\text{Total Time}} \times \frac{\text{Total Units}}{\text{Value-added Processing Time}} \times \frac{\text{Good Units}}{\text{Total Units}} = \frac{\text{Good Units}}{\text{Total Time}}$$

---

[7]Victor Lippa, "Measuring Performance with Synchronous Management," *Management Accounting* (February 1990), p. 54.

[8]This expanded throughput formula has been adapted from an article by Carole Cheatham, "Measuring and Improving Throughput," *Journal of Accountancy* (March 1990), pp. 89–91. One assumption that must be made in regard to this model is that the quantity labeled "throughput" is sold. Another assumption is that units started are always completed before the end of the measurement period.

The manufacturing cycle efficiency (as defined in Chapter 5) is the proportion of total processing time from beginning to completion of production or service performance that is value-added. This time relates to activities that increase the product's worth to the customer. For instance, assume that the Edmonton Division of Winston Wire Company worked a total of 10,000 hours in April 1997 making Product Q458. Of these hours, only 2,000 were considered value-added; thus, the division had a manufacturing cycle efficiency of 20 percent.

■ **EXHIBIT 16–9**

Performance Measurement Factors and Timetables

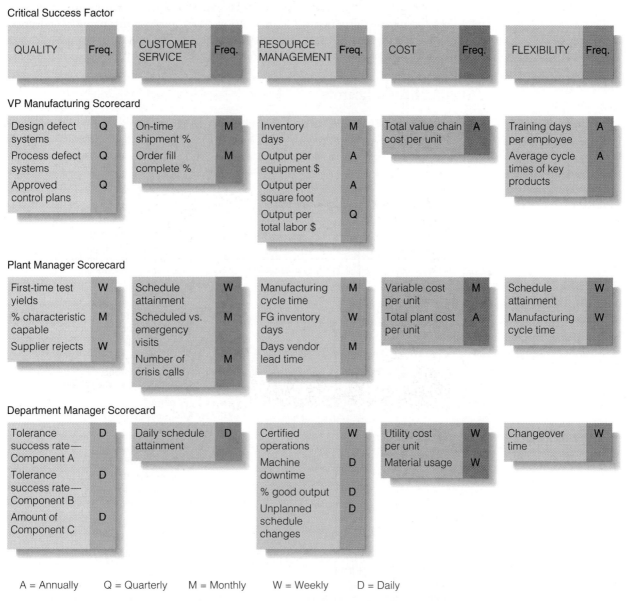

A = Annually   Q = Quarterly   M = Monthly   W = Weekly   D = Daily

SOURCE: Adapted from Mark E. Beischel and K. Richard Smith, "Linking the Shop Floor to the Top Floor," *Management Accounting* (October 1991), p. 28. Published by Institute of Management Accountants, Montvale, NJ.

process productivity

Total units started, completed, and sold during the period are divided by the value-added processing time to determine **process productivity**. Edmonton produced 15,000 units in April's 2,000 hours of value-added processing time and all units were sold. Thus, the division had a process productivity rate of 7.5 (meaning that 7.5 units could be produced in each value-added processing hour.)

process quality yield

But not all units started, completed, and sold during the period are necessarily good units—some may be defective. The proportion of good units produced is the **process quality yield**. Thus, if only 13,800 of the 15,000 units produced by Edmonton in April were good units, the division had a 92 percent process quality yield for the period. This measure reflects the quality of the production process.

The total product Q458 throughput for Edmonton Division in April was 1.38 (.20 × 7.5 × .92); that is, the division produced and sold only 1.38 good units for every hour of total actual processing time—quite a difference from the 7.5 units indicated as process productivity! The division could increase throughput by decreasing non-value-added activities, increasing total production and sales of units, decreasing the per-unit processing time, or increasing process quality yield.

Quality Indicators

A world-class company that is seeking growth and profitability will do well to systematically measure quality and assess its organizational cost of quality (COQ). Such

■ **EXHIBIT 16–10**
Cost of Quality Measurements

COQ CLASSIFICATIONS	MEASURE	OPERATIONAL COST DRIVERS	VA OR NVA
■ Prevention	Prevention cost[*] / Total COQ	Investment in reducing overall COQ operations	VA
■ Appraisal	Number of inspections	Setup frequency / Tight tolerance operations / Complex design	NVA
■ Internal failure	Number of pieces rejected	Machine reliability / Tooling age or condition / Design error / Operator error	NVA
■ External failure	Number of customer complaints	Order entry errors / Incorrect assembly instructions / Product failure / Operator error	NVA

[*]Ideally, the formula should equal 1. Prevention costs are, by definition, all value-added costs. As non-value-added costs included in the denominator are eliminated, total COQ is composed of only value-added costs. Therefore, the formula ideally ends up equaling 1 (value-added costs ÷ value-added costs), which is the target measurement.

SOURCE: Michael R. Ostrenga, "Return on Investment through the Cost of Quality," *Journal of Cost Management* (Summer 1991), p. 43. Reprinted with permission from The Journal of Cost Management for the Manufacturing Industry, © 1991, Warren, Gorham & Lamont, 31 St. James Avenue, Boston, MA 02116. All Rights Reserved.

measures should focus on and be related to actions that add value to products and services for the customer. Exhibit 16–10 presents several examples of quality indicators for each of the four quality classifications as well as their cost drivers and value-added status.

The only value-added COQ category presented in Exhibit 16–10 is prevention. Because quality cannot be inspected into products, appraisal costs add no customer value. Internal and external failures add no value for anyone; they simply create unnecessary correction costs that make total costs higher for both the company and the customer. These failure costs are the result of poor quality.

A firm can drive down the costs of appraisal, internal failure, and external failure by investing in prevention. Many prevention measures involve one-time costs that improve quality now and long into the future. Some prevention measures are fairly inexpensive. Such measures are often suggested by the employees engaged in the process. Suggestion programs can be effective in pointing out opportunities for continuous improvement that will benefit employees, customers, and the firm and its owners.

Recently, Ernst & Young and the American Quality Foundation collaborated to survey management practices in more than 500 organizations in Canada, Germany, Japan, and the United States. This international quality study indicated (as shown in Exhibit 16–11) that most companies use quality information to evaluate business per-

■ **EXHIBIT 16–11**

Frequency of Use of Quality Information to Evaluate Business Performance

	Less than Annually or Not at All	Annually	Quarterly	Monthly or More Frequently
Canada	14%	7%	28%	51%
Germany	9%	24%	12%	55%
Japan	2%	10%	18%	70%
United States	18%	11%	16%	55%

SOURCE: Ernst & Young and American Quality Foundation, *International Quality Study* (New York: Ernst & Young and American Quality Foundation, 1991), p. 16. Reprinted with permission of Ernst & Young. © Ernst & Young 1991.

formance at least monthly. Note that, while 18 percent of U.S. businesses rarely (if ever) review quality information, absence of such review is almost unheard of in Japan. "Until the reporting of quality results achieves parity with traditional financial and operating reporting, the link between quality, performance, and profit cannot be fully realized."[9]

ACTIVITY-BASED COSTING AND PERFORMANCE MEASUREMENT

■ LEARNING
OBJECTIVE 4
Relate activity-based costing concepts to performance measurement.

Choosing appropriate nonfinancial performance measures can significantly help a company focus on activities that create costs. By controlling those activities, the company can more effectively control costs and improve processes.

Activity-based costing is concerned with reducing non-value-added activities to increase throughput. Traditional performance measurements in accounting are filled with factors that contribute to non-value-added activities. Material and labor standards often include factors for waste and idle time. Predetermined overhead rates are based on estimates of expected capacity usage rather than full capacity usage. Inventories are produced to meet budget expectations rather than sales demand. Detailed explanations of how to treat spoiled and defective unit costs are provided in organizational accounting procedures. Exhibit 16–12 provides some traditional performance indicators and some potential suboptimizing results they may create.

If companies are to move toward world-class operations, non-value-added activities must be removed from performance evaluation measurements and value-added activities must be substituted. For example, when a performance measurement is the cost of defective units produced during a period, the original assumption is that management is expecting defects to occur and will accept some stated or understood defect cost. Instead, when the performance benchmark is zero defects, the assumption is that no defects are to occur. It seems reasonable that managers would strive harder to eliminate defects under the second measurement than under the first.

Because activity-based costing focuses on actions that add value from a customer's viewpoint, this accounting method stresses external performance measurements. Customers define good performance as performance that equals or exceeds their expectations as to quality, cost, and delivery. Companies that cannot measure up will find themselves without customers and without a need for financial measures of performance. In this regard, nonfinancial measures are more effective because they can be designed to monitor the characteristics desired by external parties rather than internal financial goals.

Knowing that performance is to be judged according to some external criteria of success should cause companies to begin implementing concepts such as just-in-time inventory and total quality management. The common themes of these concepts are to make the organization, its products, and its processes better and to lower costs to provide better value.

Although some performance measurements, such as zero defects, can be implemented anywhere, companies operating in a multinational environment face more complex issues than do companies operating only in a domestic setting. Thus, multinational companies need to consider some additional factors relative to performance measurement and evaluation.

---

[9]Ernst & Young and American Quality Foundation, *International Quality Study* (New York: Ernst & Young and American Quality Foundation, 1991), p. 17.

■ **EXHIBIT 16–12**

Traditional Performance Measurements and Results

MEASUREMENT	ACTION	RESULT
Purchase price variance	Purchasing increases order quantity to get lower price and ignores quality and speed of delivery	Excess inventory; increased carrying cost; suppliers with the best quality and delivery are overlooked
Machine utilization percentage	Supervisor requires employees to produce more than daily unit requirements to maximize machine utilization percentage	Excess inventory; wrong inventory
Scrap built into standard cost	Supervisor takes no action if there is no variance (from the lax standard)	Inflated standard; scrap threshold built in
Overhead rate based on expected capacity	Supervisor overproduces WIP or FG to have a favorable fixed overhead volume variance	Excess inventory
Cost center reporting	Management focus is on cost centers instead of activities	Missed cost reduction opportunities because common activities among cost centers are overlooked

SOURCE: Charles Porter, *Cost Management in the New Manufacturing Environment* (Coopers & Lybrand presentation, Directory XAT8803A).

PERFORMANCE EVALUATION IN MULTINATIONAL SETTINGS

Operating overseas business units is more complex than operating domestic units. In attempting to compare multinational organizational units, differences among cultures and economies are as important as differences in accounting standards and reporting practices. In Japan, for instance, a company president views shareholders as inconsequential. When the head of a large Japanese conglomerate was asked "whether stockmarket movements would ever affect his business decisions, he answered in a single word: 'Never!'"[10] This type of attitude allows Japanese companies to concentrate on long-run, rather than short-run, business decisions. Such a concept is unheard of in the United States, where top management is often removed by stockholders for making decisions that appear not to currently maximize shareholder value.

The investment base needed to create a given type of organizational unit may differ substantially in different countries. For example, because of the exchange rate and legal costs, it is significantly more expensive for a company to open a Japanese subsidiary than an Indonesian one. If performance measures are based on a concept such

■ LEARNING OBJECTIVE 5
Identify some reasons why it is more difficult to measure performance in multinational firms than in solely domestic companies.

[10]Alan S. Blinder, "Doing It Their Way," *Business Edge* (October 1992), p. 27.

as residual income, the Japanese unit will be placed at a distinct disadvantage because of its large investment base. However, the parent company may believe that the possibility of future joint ventures with Japanese organizations—which the parent has specified as a primary corporate goal—justifies the larger investment. The company may wish to handle the discrepancy in investment bases by assigning a lower target rate to compute residual income for the Japanese subsidiary. Such a differential is appropriate because of the lower political, financial, and economic risks.

Income comparisons between multinational units may be invalid because of important differences in trade tariffs, income tax rates, currency fluctuations, and possible restrictions on the transfer of goods or currency. Income earned by a multinational unit may also be affected by conditions totally outside its control, such as government protection of local companies, government aid in some countries, and varying wage rates resulting from differing standards of living, levels of industrial development, or quantities of socialized services. If the multinational subunit adopts the local country's accounting practices, differences in international standards can make income comparisons among units difficult and inconvenient even after the statements have been translated to a single currency basis.

The diverse economic, legal/political, and tax structures of countries have affected the development and practice of accounting. The International Accounting Standards Committee is working to achieve harmonization of accounting standards. However, many of the standards issued to date by this organization reflect compromise positions, allow for a significant number of alternatives, and rely on voluntary compliance. Additionally, as discussed in Chapter 15, managers may be able to transfer goods between segments at prices that minimize profits or tariffs in locations where taxes are high by shifting profits or cost values to more advantageous climates. These transfers must, of course, be made within the constraints of moral and social responsibility.

Given all these difficulties in monitoring the performance of their nondomestic investment centers, companies should use multiple measures that consider both the short-run and the long-run. Firms should establish flexible systems of measuring profit performance for those units. Such systems should recognize that differences in sales volume, accounting standards, economic conditions, and risk may be outside the control of an international subunit's manager. In such cases nonfinancial, qualitative factors may become significantly more useful. Performance evaluations can include measures such as market share increases, quality improvements (defect reductions), establishment of just-in-time inventory systems with the related reduction in working capital, and new product development. The use of measures that limit suboptimization of resources is vital to the proper management of multinational responsibility centers. No single system is appropriate for all companies or, perhaps, even for all responsibility centers within the same company. The measurement of performance is the measurement of people. Since each person is unique and has multiple facets, the performance measurement system must reflect those individual differences. Once the measurement system is established, people are generally concerned about the way in which that system will affect their personal rewards or compensation.

RELATING COMPENSATION AND PERFORMANCE

■ LEARNING OBJECTIVE 6
Discuss how employee rewards (including compensation) and performance should be related.

A company should compensate employees in a manner that motivates them to act in ways that result in the company's effectively and efficiently achieving its goals. A rational compensation plan ties its component elements—organizational goals, performance measurements, and employee rewards—together in a cohesive package. The relations and interactions among these elements are shown in Exhibit 16–13.

In this model, strategic organizational goals are determined by the board of directors (the governing body representing stockholder interests) and top management. From these strategic goals, the organization's critical success factors are identified and operational targets are defined. For example, operational targets could include specified annual net income, unit sales of a specific product, quality measures, customer service measures, or costs.

The board of directors and top management must also decide on a **compensation strategy** for the organization. This strategy should provide a foundation for the compensation plan by addressing the role compensation should play in the organization. The compensation strategy should be made known to everyone, from the board of directors to the lowest-level worker.

In an era of cost competitiveness, automatic cost-of-living adjustments and annual pay raises are being reduced or eliminated. Compensation plans need to encourage greater levels of employee performance and loyalty while lowering overall costs and raising profits. Plans of this kind reflect a pay-for-performance strategy that encourages behavior essential to achieving organizational goals and maximizing stockholder value.

compensation strategy

■ **EXHIBIT 16–13**
Plan-Performance-Reward Model

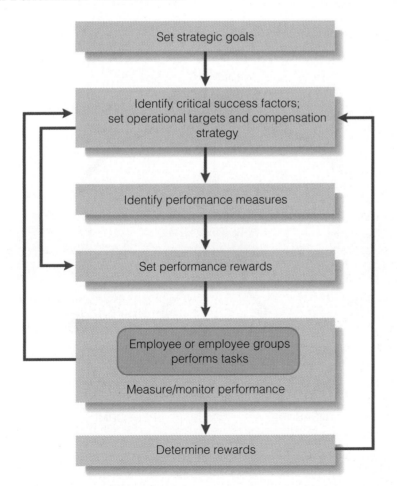

Pay-for-Performance Plans

Recall that what gets measured gets employees' attention—especially when compensation is involved. Therefore, in structuring a pay-for-performance plan, it is crucial that the defined performance measures be highly correlated with the organization's operational targets. Otherwise, suboptimization may occur and workers can earn incentive pay even though broader organizational objectives are not achieved.

Tying an organization's pay-for-performance plan to goals established in the strategic planning phase is the first step to motivating employees to focus on productivity improvement. The entire package of decisions regarding performance measurements can be referred to as a performance management system (depicted in Exhibit 16–14). When employees meet improvement objectives with results, rewards follow, and corporate results such as growth in market share, faster throughput, and greater profits can be expected. Reevaluating the performance measurement linkages with the satisfaction of corporate goals completes the cycle. Traditionally, performance measures have focused on short-run profits without giving adequate attention to long-run performance. Pay-for-performance criteria should encourage employees to adopt a long-run perspective.

This set of activities assures ongoing production of the high-quality products for which a company becomes known around the world as well as a unique and value-

■ **EXHIBIT 16–14**
Performance Management System

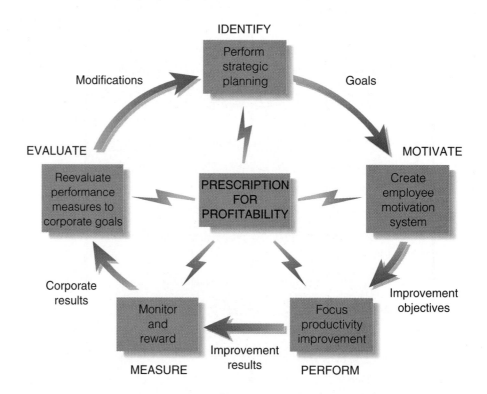

SOURCE: Dan J. Seidner and Glenn Kieckhaefer, "Using Performance Measurement Systems to Create Gainsharing Programs," *(Grant Thornton) Manufacturing Issues* (Summer 1990), p. 9. © Grant Thornton 1990.

based corporate culture for employees. Product consistency, use of standards, and employee reward and empowerment systems are important components of total quality management.

Since many companies have shifted from evaluating workers by observing their inputs to evaluating them based on their outputs, new problems have been created in the pay-for-performance relationship. Earlier chapters have stressed the importance of evaluating managers and workers only on the basis of controllable factors. Regrettably, most performance measures tend to capture results that are a function of both controllable and noncontrollable factors.

Actual performance results from worker effort, worker skill, and random effects. Random effects include performance measurement error, problems or efficiencies created by co-workers or adjacent work stations, illness, and weather-related production problems. Once an actual performance has been measured, it is impossible (in many instances) to determine the contributions of the controllable and noncontrollable factors to the achieved performance. Consequently, the worker bears the risk that a less-than-desirable outcome may result from an uncontrollable cause. Management should seek to identify performance measures that minimize this risk.

At the basic worker level, performance measures should be specific and should usually focus on cost and/or quality control. At higher organizational levels, the critical success factors under a manager's control and responsibility become more important. Performance measures should, by necessity, be less specific, focus on a longer time horizon, and be more concerned with organizational longevity than with short-run cost control or income. This type of thinking has resulted in shifts in compensation plans to include shares of corporate common stock. When employees become stockholders in their employing company, they tend to develop the same perspective as other stockholders: long-run wealth maximization. This situation is especially true at the CEO level—so much so that a significant number of large firms (such as Campbell Soup, Eastman Kodak, Xerox, Union Carbide, Hershey Foods, Continental Trust, and Chrysler) have recently begun to either require or encourage executives to purchase and retain stock in the company. As indicated in Exhibit 16–15 on page 860, a recent survey found that stock ownership by chief executives seems to enhance corporate profits.

In an empowered employee environment, management and workers need to agree on what performance is required, how it will be measured, and how compensation will relate to accomplishments. If teams are used in the organization, compensation elements should be developed for both individual and group endeavors.

Inclusion of Subjective Performance Measures

Because output is influenced somewhat by noncontrollable factors, one school of thought advocates basing compensation on subjectively assessed intangible measures rather than the more objective performance-related measures. Subjective measures could include items such as leadership skills, flexibility, attitude, ability to work well with colleagues, professional pride, and enthusiasm. The News Note on page 861 discusses a subjective method of rewarding employees.

By including subjective measures in the compensation system, management can blend less quantifiable but potentially more important long-range aspects of job performance (such as leadership, responsiveness, pride in work, cooperativeness, and enthusiasm) with more quantifiable but shorter-range considerations. For example, one study conducted by William M. Mercer, Inc. on executive compensation practices at 1,400 companies found that 35 percent of those companies used customer satisfaction in the compensation formula (and another 33 percent planned to do so); on-time product and service delivery was used in 33 percent of the companies (and was being considered by an additional 24 percent).[11] These measures are often used in conjunction with internal financial measures such as cash flow trends.

Compensation Packages

Conventionally, the compensation system has been based primarily on current monetary incentives. Middle managers are paid salaries with the opportunity for raises based on some measure of performance, usually accounting-related, such as segment income, divisional return on investment, or residual income. Lower-level workers are compensated through wages (usually specified by union contract or tied to the minimum wage law) based on the number of hours worked or production level achieved;

■ EXHIBIT 16–15
Profit Benefits When Executives Own Stock

Companies in which chief executives own a relatively large amount of company stock typically have greater stock-price performance, according to a survey by Hay Group.

INDUSTRY	AVERAGE PERCENT SHARES OWNED BY CEO	ANNUALIZED TOTAL RETURN TO SHAREHOLDERS (1989-1991)
CHEMICAL		
High-ownership companies	.84%	21.20%
Low-ownership companies	.63	-.40
RETAIL		
High-ownership companies	3.53%	48.46%
Low-ownership companies	1.51	7.28
PHARMACEUTICALS		
High-ownership companies	1.21%	57.00%
Low-ownership companies	.12	27.00
INSURANCE		
High-ownership companies	2.65%	24.18%
Low-ownership companies	1.79	11.15

Notes: Average percent shares of company owned is the number of shares owned by the chief executive, plus stock options exercisable within 60 days, as a percent of the shares outstanding of the company. The shareholder return is the annualized compound growth rate of a stock purchase, including dividends paid out as cash.

SOURCE: Hay Group, "The More You Own, the More You Earn," *Wall Street Journal* (April 21, 1993), p. R9. Reprinted by permission of The Wall Street Journal, © 1993 Dow Jones & Company, Inc. All Rights Reserved Worldwide.

---

[11]"Incentive Pay Plans Emphasize Nonfinancial Measures," *Journal of Accountancy* (May 1993), pp. 17–18.

Kerrygold's Case against Pay for Performance

[In 1990], Kerrygold, the [British] dairy product company, abandoned its performance related pay [PRP] structure. After 15 years, the system had degenerated to becoming automatic, with almost no effort made by managers to appraise and monitor staff in a way which distinguished the performers from the rest.

Says Dennis Gwilt, Kerrygold's personnel controller, "During the Eighties we were a fast-expanding company which grew to 2,500 employees by 1985. Then we started to get rid of workers as we retreated to our core business. We now have around 380 employees and new management. This meant everything going under the microscope, and we found performance related pay wasn't working. The managers were going for an easy life and rewarding everyone. This in turn led to expectations, which meant the managers became entrapped.

"We now have a far more informal system which considers and rewards aspects like attitude and enthusiasm which could never be picked up in the more formal system. Certainly, our present subjective system is open to accusations of favouritism and the rest, but it's not a very large scheme and the same people are not rewarded every year."

The moral of the Kerrygold story appears to be that not only does the recession change everything, but that managers must keep standards under constant review, particularly during periods of rapid expansion. But, ultimately, Kerrygold's experiences also support the results of [a 1993] study by the London Business School into performance related pay, which found that a third of managers in companies currently operating PRP schemes felt the schemes had done little to boost performance. Those same managers identified professional pride as the greatest motivator, and criticized PRP for serving simply to demotivate those who did not receive a bonus.

SOURCE: Hugh Thompson, "The Paying Game," *Intercity* (July/August 1994), p. 17.

current or year-end bonuses may be given when performance is above some specified quantitative measure. If provided, worker performance bonuses usually amount to a fairly small sum or percentage of wages. Significant incentive pay is usually limited to top management (and possibly the sales force)—regardless of the levels of employees who may have contributed to increased profits. This type of traditional compensation system provides little motivation for employees who are not top managers to improve organizational performance.

As with performance measures, an employee's organizational level and current compensation should affect the types of rewards chosen. Individuals at different levels of employment typically view monetary rewards differently because of the relationship of pay to standard of living. Using relative pay scales is essential to recognizing the value of this difference. At lower employee levels, more incentives should be monetary and short-term; at higher levels, more incentives should be nonmonetary and long-term. The system should, though, include some nonmonetary and long-term incentives for lower-level employees and some monetary and short-term incentives for top management. Such a two-faceted compensation system provides lower-paid people with tangible rewards (more money) that directly enhance their lifestyles but also provides rewards (such as stock options) that cause them to take a long-run "ownership" view of the organization. In turn, top managers, who are well paid by most standards, would receive more rewards (such as stock and stock options) that should cause them to be more concerned about the organization's long-term well-being rather than short-term personal gains.

Another consideration in designing compensation packages is to balance the incentives provided for both groups (or teams) and individuals. In automated production systems, workers function more by indirectly monitoring and controlling machinery and are, therefore, less directly involved in hands-on production. Additionally, evolving organizational and managerial philosophies, such as total quality management and implementation of quality circles, have stressed group performance and the performance of work in teams.

Incentive plans for small groups and individuals are often virtually interchangeable. As the group grows larger, incentives must be in place for both the group and the individual. Group incentives are necessary to encourage cooperation among workers. However, if *only* group incentives are offered, the incentive compensation system may be ineffective because the reward for individual effort goes to the group. The larger the group size, the smaller the individual's share of the group reward becomes. Eventually, individual workers will be encouraged to "free-ride" on the group. This situation occurs when individuals perceive their proportional shares of the group reward as insufficient to compensate for their efforts.

Besides various forms of monetary compensation, workers may also be motivated by nonfinancial factors. Although all employees value and require money to satisfy basic human needs, other human needs are not necessarily fulfilled with monetary wealth. Employees desire some compensation that is not monetary in nature but satisfies the higher-order social needs of humans. For example, workers and managers are typically more productive in environments in which they think their efforts are appreciated. Simple gestures such as compliments and small awards can be used by superiors to formally recognize contributions of subordinates. Allowing subordinates to participate in decisions affecting their own welfare and the welfare of the firm also contributes to making employment socially fulfilling. Such efforts provide assurance to employees that they are serving a productive role in the firm and that superiors are attentive to and appreciative of employee contributions. These attitudes are illustrat-

Transportation and child care costs in London are lower than in many large cities, but housing can be substantially more expensive. Costs affecting the standard of living must be reviewed in determining the appropriate compensation package to offer an expatriate.

ed by a recent survey of 1,000 Americans about compensation issues by the Employee Benefit Research Institute and the Gallup Organization. The results indicated, among other things, that:

- Employees value employer-paid pension benefits and company stock more than an increase in their current paychecks.
- Sixty-four percent of employees prefer having input into company decisions over having a share of company ownership.
- Fifty-six percent of employees would not sell company stock, if they owned any, at twice the current market price to an outside investor attempting a takeover.[12]

Finally, the concept of job security, which is so prevalent in Japanese companies, is a powerful incentive. For example, while A. T. Cross & Co. (makers of Cross pens and mechanical pencils) does offer a modest profit-sharing plan and comparable wages, CEO Brad Boss believes the company's high quality standards result in part from employee loyalty. "The company has never had a layoff. When new, more efficient production technology is introduced, workers are retained and generally promoted."[13]

There is, however, a downside to the concept of job security as indicated in the News Note on page 864. In Japan, because of the existence of a lifetime employment system, companies have been known to retain middle-aged employees and pay them *not* to work; these "window sitters" (as they are termed) are often bored with their situations.

Compensation Differentials

A contemporary debate in the financial press involves perceptions that the disparity between the pay of ordinary workers and the pay of top managers is too large. Plato argued that no one should earn more than five times the pay earned by the lowest-paid worker. In the early 1900s, J. P. Morgan took the position that the differential should be no more than twenty times. In general, neither Plato's nor Morgan's compensation relationships have held true in the United States, where CEOs' compensation relative to that of lower-level employees has well exceeded those limits. A recent study indicated that companies in Britain, Canada, France, Germany, Japan, and Italy were all well within at least Morgan's guidelines.[14] The News Note on page 865 discusses protests nevertheless occurring in the United Kingdom over that country's gap in pay structures.

Salary differentials between workers and CEOs are often created by a type of self-fulfilling prophecy on the part of the board of directors. It is a common practice for a company's board of directors to survey a group of similar organizations to determine the "average" compensation for an executive. If the company's executive appears to be underpaid, the board will increase his or her compensation. Thus, the next time the survey is performed, the average will be increased—regardless of managerial performance. Such indiscreet consumption of organizational resources can cause common stock prices to decline and can undermine the stockholder value maximization goal.

Care must also be taken that a company's compensation strategy does not result in suppressing creativity, innovation, risk taking, and proactive assumption and conduct

---

[12]"FYI—What Do Workers Want?" *Inc.* (June 1994), p. 12.

[13]Louis S. Richman, "What America Makes Best," *Fortune* (*The New American Century*, 1991), p. 81.

[14]Amanda Bennett, "Managers' Incomes Aren't Worlds Apart," *Wall Street Journal* (October 12, 1992), p. B1.

Window Sitters Clip Toenails

In his last 10 years with Mitsubishi Corp., Yasuhiko Ushiba got lots of experience—twiddling his thumbs.

Posted in a "planning promotion group," he was given no assignments by the giant trading company. When he tried proposing projects, the plans were thrown back in his face. So Mr. Ushiba hung out at the zoo and took in triple features at adult movie theaters. All the while his paychecks—about $85,000 a year—kept sailing in.

"The message from management was, you can stay here if you want to, but we're not going to give you any work to do," says the 55-year-old Mr. Ushiba, who eventually quit to start a consulting company. "What could be worse for a person than being ignored?"

Mr. Ushiba had been shown the "window seat," as the Japanese say of unneeded middle-aged workers who have been shunted aside. Sitting by the window is a form of welfare under Japan's lifetime-employment system, which often leaves senior employees on the payroll with little or nothing to do. With the average age of Japan's population rising, and the economy still in the tank, there is now more window sitting than ever. Fuji Bank's research arm figures Japanese offices and factories are carrying the equivalent of one million redundant employees. Sign of the times: One secretary recently wrote to a magazine to complain about an office colleague who kills time by clipping his toenails.

Traditionally, companies dole out window seats as a way of supporting employees until they retire, typically at age 60. Getting branded a window sitter is a big loss of face, but a dead-end job beats the bread line. These days, though, more and more strapped businesses are using mind-numbingly dull jobs to humiliate aging workers into quitting. A lot of window sitters are therefore hard at work camouflaging their idleness.

SOURCE: Yumiko Ono, "Unneeded Workers in Japan Are Bored, and Very Well Paid," *Wall Street Journal* (April 20, 1993), p. A1. Reprinted by permission of The Wall Street Journal, © 1993 Dow Jones & Company, Inc. All Rights Reserved Worldwide.

of job responsibilities. If monetary rewards can be withheld when failure occurs, employees who are otherwise industrious and cooperative might avoid taking actions or making proposals that could fail. Fear of failure can be reduced if management creates an atmosphere of employee empowerment in which failure is accepted as part of the progression toward continuous improvement.

Organizational compensation packages must be developed that blend organizational goals with monetary and nonmonetary employee rewards. Only if there is a perception of equity across the contributions and entitlements of labor, management, and capital will the organization be capable of achieving the efficiency to compete in global markets.

GLOBAL COMPENSATION

expatriate

With international operations increasing, plans that compensate **expatriate** employees and managers on a fair and equitable basis must be developed. Expatriates are parent company and third-country nationals assigned to a foreign subsidiary or foreign nationals assigned to the parent company. Placing employees in foreign countries requires careful consideration of compensation. What is thought to be a fair and rea-

Tensions Mount Over Surge in Executive Pay

NEWS NOTE

A public outcry in the United Kingdom over rising pay for executives has prompted Prime Minister John Major to weigh measures to rein in remuneration for British corporate chiefs.

The controversy, which has aggravated simmering class tensions [in London], was ignited [in November 1994] when British Gas PLC boosted the salary for Chief Executive Officer Cedric Brown by 76%. The increase in base salary, to £475,000 ($742,000) from £270,000, would be no big deal in the U.S., where Walt Disney Co.'s Michael D. Eisner received $203 million in salary and other compensation [in 1993]. The British Gas executive's new salary isn't even out of line with the average salary of £479,000 for the highest-paid executives of the 50 largest United Kingdom companies.

But the raise, coming just after the utility increased its rates and at a time when the company is holding annual pay increases for workers to 3%, provoked protest from trade units, shareholder groups and politicians.

The union-backed Labor Research Survey found that average boardroom pay rose 19% [in 1993], while workers were held to increases under 5%. In 1992, boardroom pay climbed 16%, compared with 4% for the average worker. Hay Management Consultants says U.K. company directors received a median total cash increase of 11% in the year ended July 1994.

Sir Bryan Nicholson, president of the Confederation of British Industry, said in a speech [in November 1994] that executives "have a clear responsibility, moral and political, to set an example on pay discipline. We cannot be satisfied with a situation in which pay increases for the management and the board run ahead of those awarded to the work force in general."

SOURCE: Dana Milbank, "Tensions Over Surge in Executive Pay Spur U.K.'s Major to Consider Limits," *Wall Street Journal* (December 8, 1994), p. A15. Reprinted by permission of The Wall Street Journal, © 1994 Dow Jones & Company, Inc. All Rights Reserved Worldwide.

■ LEARNING OBJECTIVE 7
Explain how expatriate reward systems may differ from those of domestic operations.

sonable compensation package in one setting may not be fair and reasonable in another. To illustrate, in a recent survey of 45 multinational organizations, 100 percent of the respondents concluded that differing pay levels, benefits, and perks were the biggest problems in developing an international work force.[15]

Expatriates' compensation packages must reflect labor market factors, cost-of-living considerations, and currency fluctuations as well as tax consequences. Since expatriates have a variety of financial requirements, these individuals may be paid in the currency of the country where they have been relocated or in their home currency or a combination of both. An expatriate's base salary and fringe benefits should typically reflect what he or she would have been paid domestically. This base should then be adjusted for reasonable cost-of-living factors. These factors may be obvious (such as the need for transportation, shelter, clothing, and groceries similar to those that would have been obtained in the home country or the need to be compensated for a spouse's loss of employment), or they may be less apparent (such as a need to hire someone in the home country to care for young children or to manage an investment portfolio). Price-level adjustment clauses are often included in the compensation

[15]Organizational Resources Counselors Inc., "Global Headaches," cited in *Wall Street Journal* (April 21, 1993), p. R5.

How Am I Paid?

As more American companies emerge as global marketers and man-ufacturers, they are discovering a crying need for more sophisticated global compensation systems.

Some companies, for instance, are tying their peripatetic man-agers' pay to their own home countries, and some to the new coun-tries where they reside. Still others struggle to come up with a truly global standard for pay—a task complicated by a host of factors ranging from fluctuating currencies to cultural differences in how pay is perceived. Europeans and Japanese, for example, often are leery of stock and stock options because such compensation tools aren't widely used outside the U.S.

At the root of the movement toward a global-style pay system is cost. Expatriate packages based on American salaries and needs increasingly are seen as too expensive for international managers. With salaries and standards of living varying drastically from country to country, companies must grapple with the issue of fairness. Employers want to find ways of making transfers attractive without paying people too much more—or too much less—than their new colleagues overseas.

Fairness, indeed, is a major issue in virtually every attempt at global pay programs—espe-cially when two people doing the same job are on radically different pay standards based partly on their home-country pay. Yet plans that try to treat everyone equally also run into problems—[often, because they are too complex to be understandable].

SOURCE: Amanda Bennett, "What's an Expatriate?" *Wall Street Journal* (April 21, 1993), p. R5. Reprinted by permission of The Wall Street Journal, © 1993 Dow Jones & Company, Inc. All Rights Reserved Worldwide.

arrangement to mitigate any local currency inflation or deflation. Regardless of the currency makeup of the pay package, the fringe benefit portion related to retirement must be tied to the home country and should be paid in that currency.

Income taxes are important in expatriates' compensation packages because such individuals may be required to pay taxes in the local country, the home country, or both. Some countries (such as the United States and Great Britain) exempt expatri-ates from taxation on a specified amount of income earned in a foreign country. If a tax treaty exists and local taxes are paid on the balance of the nonexempt income of an expatriate, those taxes may be credited against the expatriate's home-nation income taxes.

As indicated in the accompanying News Note, all of these issues are important in developing compensation packages for expatriates. However the package is ultimate-ly structured, an ethical company will assure itself that the system is as fair as possi-ble to all employees involved and that it is cost-beneficial and not an administrative nightmare.

In conclusion, tying the compensation system to performance measurement is essential because everyone in business recognizes that what gets measured and rewarded is what gets accomplished. Businesses must focus their reward structures to motivate employees to succeed at all activities that will create shareholder and per-sonal value. In this highly competitive age, the new paradigm of success is to provide high-quality products and services at a reasonable price while generating a reasonable profit margin.

In Southwire's drive to quality, the management accounting team partici-pates actively in the company's planning process. The process starts with developing a five-year plan in three areas—people, profits, and product and service quality. Plans for the company's employees include training, certifica-tion, involvement, teamwork, and recognition. The company believes strongly that profits are the result of focus on customers, reduced cycle time, and sound financial management. Product and service quality results from system enhancements, the STAR process, and establishing accurate measurements. [The STAR process recognizes employees for their ideas with stars to be placed on their hard hats—similar to the ones given for tackles, or other notable achievements on the field, to some football players to be placed on their helmets.]

[One of the company's primary nonfinancial performance measures is cycle and error time reduction.] Employees have a goal of obtaining at least three or more stars per year. More than 20,000 stars were issued companywide in 1994. Every plant selects its star of the month; from this group is selected the star of the quarter. At the end of the year a star of the year is chosen from among the four quarterly stars. The criteria for selection as star of the year include evaluation of the star's contribution to cost savings and to boosting employees' morale. [For example, one 1992 star submitted by the Starkville, Mississippi, plant] involved the setting of the take-up on an operator's machine. The operator adjusted the setting, reducing downtime and scrap and preventing the lowering of production. The adjustment also cut the average wire breaks more than 50%.

The scrap program [at the Starkville plant has become] the foundation for other pro-grams such as usage, standard scrap, production, and production analysis. Because *scrap percent* is one of Southwire's key indicators, the scrap program plays an important role in the company's quality process. Through the scrap program, a plant is able to identify and isolate high-scrap-producing areas and problems early in the process to prevent costly waste. The program involves analyzing scrap on a daily basis and breaking it down by departments, machines, and product lines.

SOURCES: Gilda M. Agacer, Donald W. Baker, and Les Miles, "Implementing the Quality Process at Southwire Company," *Management Accounting* (November 1994), pp. 61–62, published by Institute of Management Accountants, Montvale, NJ; and interview with Tommy Gable, Director of Quality, 1994.

Discipline	Applications
Accounting	Accountants should systematically provide financial and nonfinan-cial measures for performance evaluations as well as prompt and accurate information to assist managers in establishing and main-taining an effective compensation system.
Economics	Economists can help assess adequacy of performance measures to guide the efficient and effective allocation of scarce resources; then they can advise management on an optimal compensation approach for long-run success. Their understanding of the eco-nomic diversity among foreign subsidiaries will help economists provide information to management in developing appropriate per-formance measures and rational compensation methods.
Finance	Finance personnel can track and evaluate monetary measures such as profitability, return on investment, residual income, and cash flow for entity valuation purposes. They can also advise management on appropriate executive compensation measures and worthiness of plans for employee acquisition of company equity stock.

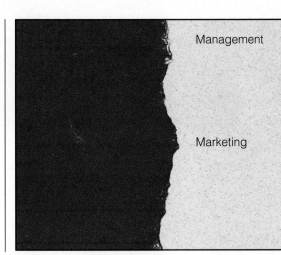

Management   Managers need to understand the limitations of short-run, single-dimension performance measures; know how to develop a balanced set of performance measures that include both monetary and nonmonetary measurements and that address both short-term and long-term considerations; and devise a compensation approach that promotes the creation of long-run stockholder wealth and the realization of organizational goals.

Marketing   Marketing personnel need to understand the importance of monetary measures such as ROI in setting prices and in deciding which markets to pursue; need to know the significance of nonmonetary measures such as measures of quality to maintenance and growth of market share; and should help management establish and maintain a strategic compensation plan that will motivate employees to cause the firm to win over competition in the marketplace.

CHAPTER SUMMARY

Performance measures should assess progress toward goals and objectives and should be accepted by the persons being evaluated. Using multiple measures of the firm's critical success factors is more effective than using a single performance measure. Divisional profits and cash flow are frequently used performance measures.

Two other significant financial measures of performance are return on investment and residual income. Return on investment is computed as segment margin (or net income) divided by invested assets. Residual income is the amount of segment margin (or net income) in excess of an amount calculated by use of a preestablished interest charge on the asset base. Both ROI and RI provide important information about the efficiency and effectiveness of managers. Neither should be used alone, however, and their inherent limitations (including the fact that they can be manipulated because of their basis in accounting) should be taken into account.

Financial measures can be effectively coupled with nonfinancial measures to provide a more complete and useful picture of performance. One useful nonfinancial measure is throughput—the nondefective goods or services started, finished, and sold by an organization during a period. When throughput is increased, the company goal of making money is enhanced. Various quality measures have also gained prominence as companies begin to compete more heavily in the global marketplace. These measures focus on activities that add value for the customer.

Performance measures may be more difficult to establish for multinational units than for domestic units because of differences in taxes, tariffs, currency exchange rates, and transfer restrictions. Top management may wish to consider extending the use of qualitative performance measures because of such differences.

Customarily, compensation systems have often been based solely on individual performance and short-run financial results. Because of operational changes and shifts in managerial philosophies, performance measurements and their related rewards now encompass group success, nonfinancial performance attributes, and long-run considerations. Companies also need to recognize that some top managers' compensation grossly exceeds pay to ordinary workers. Such excesses can be counterproductive, causing a demoralizing effect within the firm and, ultimately, failure to maximize long-term stockholder wealth. Thus, it is important that the compensation strategy and system are in harmony with the performance measurement system and that together they serve to assure fairness, effectiveness, and efficiency in an organization.

GLOSSARY

Asset turnover (p. 841)   a ratio that measures asset productivity and shows the number of sales dollars generated by each dollar of assets during a specific period

Compensation strategy (p. 857)   a foundation for the compensation plan that addresses the role compensation should play in the organization

Du Pont model (p. 841)   a model that indicates the return on investment as it is affected by profit margin and asset turnover

Expatriate (p. 864)   a parent company or third-country national assigned to a foreign subsidiary or a foreign national assigned to the parent company

Process productivity (p. 852)   the total units produced during a period using value-added processing time

Process quality yield (p. 852)   the proportion of good units that resulted from the activities expended

Profit margin (p. 841)   the ratio of income to sales

Residual income (RI) (p. 844)   the profit earned that exceeds an amount "charged" for funds committed to a responsibility center

Return on investment (ROI) (p. 840)   a ratio that relates income generated by the investment center to the resources (or asset base) used to produce that income

Synchronous management (p. 850)   all endeavors that help an organization achieve its goals

SOLUTION STRATEGIES

PERFORMANCE MEASUREMENTS FOR RESPONSIBILITY CENTERS

- **Profit Center**

  Budgeted divisional profits
  − Actual divisional profits
  = Variances (consider materiality)

  Cash inflows
  − Cash outflows
  = Net cash flow (adequate for operations?)

- **Investment Center**

  Budgeted investment center profits
  − Actual investment center profits
  = Variances (consider materiality)

  Cash inflows
  − Cash outflows
  = Net cash flow (adequate for operations?)

  Return on Investment = Income ÷ Assets Invested (high enough rate?)

  Du Pont model:
  ROI = Profit Margin × Asset Turnover
      = (Income ÷ Sales) × (Sales ÷ Assets)
        (high enough rate?)

  Residual Income = Income − (Target Rate × Asset Base)

  or

$$\text{Residual Income} = \text{Asset Base} \times (\text{ROI} - \text{Target Rate})$$
(positive or negative? high enough amount?)

MEASURING THROUGHPUT

$$\begin{matrix} \text{Manufacturing} & & \text{Process} & & \text{Process} \\ \text{Cycle Efficiency} & \times & \text{Productivity} & \times & \text{Quality Yield} \end{matrix} = \text{Throughput}$$

or

$$\frac{\text{Processing Time}}{\text{Total Time}} \times \frac{\text{Total Units}}{\text{Value-added Processing Time}} \times \frac{\text{Good Units}}{\text{Total Units}} = \frac{\text{Good Units}}{\text{Total Time}}$$

DESIGNING A REWARD SYSTEM

It is impossible to design a generic incentive model that would be effective across a variety of firms. However, affirmative answers to the following questions provide guidance as to the applicability of a proposed incentive and reward plan for a particular organization.

1. Will the organizational objectives be achieved if the proposed compensation structure is implemented?
2. Is the proposed structure consistent with the organizational design, culture, and management philosophy?
3. Are there reasonable and objective performance measures that are good surrogates for the organizational objectives?
4. Are factors beyond employee/group control minimized under the performance measures of the proposed compensation structure?
5. Are there minimal opportunities for employees to manipulate the performance measurements tied to the proposed compensation structure?
6. In light of the interests of managers, workers, and stockholders, is the proposed reward structure fair and does it encourage and promote ethical behavior?
7. Is the proposed reward structure arranged to take advantage of potential employee/employer tax benefits?
8. Does the proposed reward structure promote harmony between employee groups?
9. Is there an adequate balance between group and individual incentives?

DEMONSTRATION PROBLEM

One of several operating divisions of the Metal Products Company is the Automotive Components Division. Automotive Components produces various automobile parts (such as bumpers, fenders, axles, and drive shafts) and sells them to car manufacturers. The division and its management are evaluated by senior corporate executives based on investment center concepts. The following information pertains to operations of the Automotive Components Division for 1997:

Total revenues	$21,250,000
Direct variable costs	8,750,000
Direct fixed costs	7,500,000
Allocated corporate costs	3,938,000

	BOOK VALUES		CURRENT MARKET VALUES	
	12/31/96	*12/31/97*	*12/31/96*	*12/31/97*
Current assets	$ 1,250,000	$ 1,800,000		
Fixed assets	10,250,000	11,700,000		
Accumulated Depreciation	(1,250,000)	(1,750,000)		
Total assets	$10,250,000	$11,750,000	$9,500,000	$10,500,000
Liabilities	$ 3,000,000	$ 3,500,000		

Required:

1. For the 1997 operations of the Automotive Components Division, compute the segment margin and operating income.
2. Based on operating income and the book value of average total assets, compute the profit margin, asset turnover, and ROI.
3. Compute the ROI based on segment income and average current asset value.
4. Based on operating income and the book value of average net assets, compute the residual income. Assume the target rate of return is 12 percent.

■ SOLUTION TO DEMONSTRATION PROBLEM

1.

Total revenue	$21,250,000
Direct variable costs	(8,750,000)
Direct fixed costs	(7,500,000)
Segment margin	$ 5,000,000
Allocated costs	(3,938,000)
Operating income	$ 1,062,000

2. Profit margin $= \dfrac{\$1,062,000}{\$21,250,000} = 5\%$

Asset turnover $= \dfrac{\$21,250,000}{(\$10,250,000 + \$11,750,000) \div 2} = 1.93$

ROI $= .05 \times 1.93 = 9.65\%$

3. ROI $= \dfrac{\$5,000,000}{(\$9,500,000 + \$10,500,000) \div 2} = 50\%$

4. First determine the value of net assets:

	12/31/96	12/31/97
Total assets	$10,250,000	$11,750,000
Less liabilities	(3,000,000)	(3,500,000)
Net assets	$ 7,250,000	$ 8,250,000

Next determine target return and subtract from operating income:

Operating income	$1,062,500
Target return [($7,250,000 + $8,250,000) ÷ 2] × .12	(930,000)
Residual income	$ 132,500

END-OF-CHAPTER MATERIALS

■ QUESTIONS

1. What basic rules should be observed in selecting benchmarks for evaluating managers' performance?

2. Should performance measures be financial, nonfinancial, or both? Justify your answer.

3. What is the message conveyed by the phrase "managers devote their attention to activities that get measured"?

4. How can feedback, both positive and negative, be used to improve managerial performance?

5. Why must the process of designing performance measures take into account the possibility of manipulation?

6. What are the two primary financial requirements for the success of a profit or investment center?

7. What is the major difference between a profit center and an investment center? How does this difference create a need for different financial performance measures in these two types of centers?

8. Discuss the most appropriate definition of the term *assets invested* in computing return on investment.

9. What is the Du Pont model? What are its component ratios and how are they calculated?

10. What is residual income and how is it used to measure divisional performance? How is it similar to and different from the return on investment measure?

11. Describe the circumstances in which use of ROI would likely create a suboptimization problem. Under what circumstances would use of this measure be less likely to create a suboptimization problem?

12. List two quantitative but nonfinancial measures that could be used to evaluate the quality of the performance of the outpatient care division of a major public hospital. Why would these measures be useful?

13. Modular Office Systems manufactures movable partitions for commercial offices. Recently, the company has become much more concerned about reducing the number of flaws in its completed products. Identify some performance measures that the company could use to monitor the effectiveness of its efforts to improve product quality.

14. What is a performance benchmark and what is its role in the use of nonfinancial performance measures? If number of product defects is the performance measure, what is a reasonable benchmark for a manufacturing firm practicing TQM?

15. What is captured by a throughput measure? Why is throughput defined on the basis of goods sold rather than goods produced?

16. Why is prevention the only value-added cost of quality category?

17. How can activity-based costing concepts be used in designing performance measures?

18. Why is the design of performance measures a more complex task in multinational companies than in single-country operations?

19. To be effective, why must firms link the compensation system to the performance measurement structure?

20. Why does a worker bear some risk when performance is evaluated based on a measure of achieved level of output?

21. Why is it desirable to have chief executives (as well as other managers) own stock in their companies?

22. Why are many companies using group pay incentives as well as individual pay incentives?

23. What special considerations bear on designing pay plans for expatriates?

■ EXERCISES

24. (LO 2, 3, 6, 7; *Terminology*) Match the definitions on the right with the terms on the left. Definitions may be used more than once or not at all.

a. Throughput	**1.** A parent-company worker in a foreign subsidiary
b. Return on investment	
c. Synchronous management	**2.** A measure of asset productivity
d. Residual income	**3.** A method of computing ROI as the product of two separate ratios
e. Compensation strategy	
f. Expatriate	**4.** All endeavors that help an organization achieve its goals
g. Du Pont model	
h. Asset turnover	**5.** Profit margin multiplied by asset turnover
i. Profit margin	
j. Process quality yield	**6.** Profits that exceed a normal return on assets
	7. Ratio of income to sales
	8. Ratio of good units to total units
	9. A plan for determining the role of compensation in an organization
	10. Total output completed and sold

25. (LO 2; *ROI*) Beufort Mfg. is made up of three autonomous divisions. Data for each division for the year 1996 follow:

DIVISION	1	2	3
Segment income	$ 25,000	$ 150,000	$ 200,000
Asset investment	100,000	1,000,000	2,000,000

Compute the return on investment in each division.

26. (LO 2; *ROI*) The managers of Marquette Ltd. are trying to calculate return on invested assets. The following information is available:

Average assets invested	$1,800,000
Revenues	7,200,000
Expenses	6,552,000

a. Calculate profit margin.
b. Calculate asset turnover.
c. Calculate return on investment using your answers to parts a and b.

27. (LO 2; *ROI*) Your managerial accounting class has been assigned a case, but the teacher has only provided partial information. You have been told that a division of Granite Manufacturing Co. has an ROI of 12.5 percent, average total assets of $1,700,000, and total direct expenses of $637,500. You have been asked to do the following:

a. Determine segment income.
b. Determine total revenues.
c. Determine asset turnover.
d. Determine profit margin.
e. Prove that ROI is 12.5 percent from the amounts calculated in parts a to d.

28. (LO 2; *ROI*) Cathy Alizondo owns an office complex in a small Mississippi town. She is uncertain whether she is doing well or poorly in her business and asks you to make some calculations that will help her understand her business's financial condition. The following information is available:

Assets, January 1, 1996	$140,000
Assets, December 31, 1996	182,000
1996 revenues	48,500
1996 expenses	30,000

Cathy has estimated that her variable expenses are 30 percent of total revenues; the remaining expenses are fixed.

a. Compute average assets for the year.
b. Compute the 1996 profit margin.
c. Compute the 1996 asset turnover.
d. Compute the 1996 return on investment.
e. Cathy thinks she can increase her revenues in 1997 by $15,000 above 1996 levels if she spends another $2,000 on advertising. Assuming Cathy is correct and that average assets in 1997 will be $200,000, what will be her expected return on investment for 1997? (Assume that the cost structure in 1997 will be the same as for 1996 except for the changes noted.)

29. (LO 2; *RI*) East and West Divisions of Panther Gear Co. reported the following data for 1997 (in thousands):

	EAST DIVISION	WEST DIVISION
Segment income	$ 20,000	$ 34,000
Investment	100,000	200,000

a. Assuming the firm charges each division 12 percent of the capital invested, determine the residual income for each division.
b. Based on the preceding information, which division is more successful? Explain.

30. (LO 2; *RI*) Universe Enterprises operates with two investment centers. Following is some financial information about each of these investment centers:

	CATALINA DIVISION	PACER DIVISION
Sales	$4,800,000	$ 8,400,000
Total variable costs	1,200,000	5,460,000
Total fixed cost	2,800,000	1,250,000
Average assets invested	4,000,000	10,000,000

a. What is each division's residual income if Universe has established a 14 percent target rate of return on invested assets?

    b. Which division is more successful? Explain.

    c. What would be each division's residual income if its sales increased by 10 percent and no other changes occurred? Which division would be more successful if such a sales change occurred? Explain.

    d. Explain why the answers to parts b and c differed or did not differ.

31. (LO 2; *ROI, RI*) Munson Management Services Co. relies on a residual income measure to evaluate the performance of certain segment managers. The target rate of return for all segments is 16 percent. One segment, Accounting Systems, generated segment income of $1,800,000 for the year just ended. For the same period, its residual income was $520,000.

    a. Compute the amount of average assets employed by Accounting Systems.

    b. Compute the return on investment for Accounting Systems.

32. (LO 2; *ROI, RI*) Fill in the missing numbers in the following three independent cases.

	CASE 1	CASE 2	CASE 3
Revenue	$220,000	e	$200,000
Expenses	a	$ 425,000	$175,000
Segment income	$ 55,000	$ 75,000	i
Average total assets	b	$1,000,000	$100,000
Asset turnover	2	f	j
Profit margin	25%	g	12.5%
Actual ROI	c	7.5%	k
Residual income	d	h	$ 5,000
Target return	25%	12%	l

33. (LO 2; *ROI, RI*) Stealth Technology Corporation has a target rate of return of 20 percent. Laser Division is analyzing a new investment that promises to generate an ROI of 25 percent and a residual income of $20,000.

    a. What is the acquisition cost of the investment that Laser Division is considering?

    b. What is the estimated segment income from the new project?

34. (LO 2; *ROI, RI*) Home Supply Co. has a target rate of return of 10 percent for its Paint Division. For 1996, the division generated sales of $8,000,000 on average assets of $4,000,000. The Paint Division's variable costs were 55 percent of sales, and direct fixed costs were $3,200,000. For 1996, compute the division's:

    a. Profit margin

    b. Asset turnover

    c. Return on investment

    d. Residual income

35. (LO 3; *Throughput*) The Milwaukee Wave is a chain of microbreweries. The company evaluates its store managers on the basis of both financial and nonfinancial performance measures. One of the nonfinancial measures used is throughput. The following data pertain to the company's store in Atlanta. The unit of measurement is gallons.

Units started into production	360,000
Total good units completed	270,000
Total hours of value-added processing time	180,000
Total hours	240,000

a. What was the manufacturing cycle efficiency?
b. What was the process productivity of the store?
c. What was the process quality yield of the store?
d. What was the total throughput per hour?

36. (LO 3; *Nonfinancial performance measures*) For each of the following nonfinancial performance measures, indicate whether the measure captures performance in terms of quality (Q), customer service (CS), resource management (RM), or flexibility (F) and discuss the rationale for your answer.

   a. First-time-through rejection rate
   b. Percent on-time shipments
   c. Manufacturing cycle time
   d. Percent good output
   e. Percent of units meeting design tolerance
   f. Output per labor dollar
   g. Number of crisis calls
   h. Changeover time
   i. Machine downtime
   j. Supplier rejects

37. (LO 6; *Pay plan and suboptimization*) Stella Clark is a division manager of Cal-Tex Hydraulics. She is presently evaluating a potential revenue-generating investment that has the following characteristics:

Initial cost	$2,000,000
Net annual increase in divisional income before consideration of depreciation:	
Year 1	200,000
Year 2	300,000
Year 3	380,000
Year 4	1,600,000
Year 5	1,600,000

   The project would have a five-year life with no salvage value. All assets are depreciated according to the straight-line method. Stella is evaluated and compensated based on the amount of pretax profit her division generates. More precisely, she receives an annual salary of $100,000 plus a bonus equal to 6 percent of divisional segment income. Stella anticipates that without the above project her division will generate $2,000,000 in divisional pretax profit.

   a. Compute the effect of the new investment on the level of divisional pretax profits for years 1 through 5.
   b. Determine the effect of the new project on Stella's compensation for each of the five years.
   c. Based on your computations in part b, will Stella be hesitant to invest in the new project? Explain.
   d. Would upper management likely view the new investment favorably? Explain.
   e. How could Stella's compensation system be changed to provide more incentive for her to invest in the new project?

■ COMMUNICATION ACTIVITIES

38. (LO 1, 5; *Performance evaluation*) *Ben & Jerry's Homemade Inc., citing declining sales in the super-premium ice-cream market, said it expects to post a fourth-quarter loss of between $700,000 and $900,000, or 10 cents to 13 cents a share, on as much as a 5% drop in sales.*

 The loss will be the first by Ben & Jerry's since it went public in 1985. Once a high-flier known for its off-beat marketing, soaring sales, and social awareness, the company is making a painful transition to more-traditional business tactics as its high-priced ice-cream niche has gotten hurt by less expensive, lower-fat premium brands.

 The plant and sales woes are sure to put immediate pressure on the company's new chief executive.

[SOURCE: Steve Stecklow, "Ben & Jerry's Expects First Loss in Fourth Quarter," *Wall Street Journal* (December 20, 1994), p. B4. Reprinted by permission of The Wall Street Journal, © 1994 Dow Jones & Company, Inc. All Rights Reserved Worldwide.]

 a. Ben & Jerry's is switching from being an owner-managed firm to being under the control of an outside manager. Describe concerns that you would have coming into Ben & Jerry's as the new CEO.

 b. Discuss how the switch to professional management will cause Ben & Jerry's performance evaluation system to change.

 c. Why would owners of Ben & Jerry's want to turn over control of their company to a professional manager?

 d. As an owner of Ben & Jerry's, what types of performance incentives would you want to include in the new manager's contract?

39. (LO 2; *Performance measures*) For the past three years, the highest divisional ROI within Angleton Corporation has been generated by Atlantic Division, a very high-tech manufacturing division. The segment income and ROI for each year appear below:

	1994	1995	1996
Segment income	$200,000	$195,000	$193,500
ROI	20%	23%	27%

 a. Why do you think Atlantic Division has been so successful as measured by its ROI?

 b. As controller of Angleton Corporation, what change or changes would you recommend to control the continued escalation in the ROI?

40. (LO 2; *ROI*) Explain how each of the following items will affect the asset turnover ratio of a corporate division if asset amounts are determined by their net book values.

 a. A new labor contract is negotiated that reduces labor costs by 10 percent.

 b. Unused assets are carried on the books. These assets could be sold.

 c. Obsolete inventory is carried on the books.

 d. Uncollectible accounts receivable are maintained on the books.

 e. The rate of depreciation on plant and equipment is increased.

 f. Fixed costs allocated to the division drop by 4 percent.

41. (LO 6; *Incentive pay plan*) Shareholders of H. J. Heinz Co. were scheduled to vote at their September 1994 meeting on a new executive incentive plan. Under the proposed stock-option plan, Heinz would reserve a certain number of shares to be used to fulfill stock options exercised by eligible managers and employees. However, at least one shareholder opposed the issuance of stock options to employees and managers.

According to the proxy statement for the shareholder meeting, the unidentified shareholder asked stockholders to vote against the plan because stock options often result in "a ticket to gamble on a mostly rising stock market." In contrast, the company argued in the proxy statement that stock options create incentives for managers to take actions that enhance the value of the stock.

[SOURCE: Based on Matt Murray, "Heinz's CEO Receives 32% Pay Cut as a Result of Lackluster Fiscal 1994," *Wall Street Journal* (August 10, 1994), p. B4.]

a. Is the incentive provided by owning a stock option different from the incentive provided by owning the actual stock for an employee or a manager? Discuss. [Hint: If you are unfamiliar with stock options, before you answer this question conduct a brief library review of articles that discuss them.]

b. Why might stockholders prefer to issue stock options rather than stock to motivate employees?

c. As a corporate manager, what functional group in the corporation would you expect to be experts on stocks and stock options? Explain.

42. (LO 2; *Defining performance measures*) The Institute of Management Accountants issued Statement on Management Accounting 4D, "Measuring Entity Performance," to help management accountants deal with the issues associated with measuring entity performance. Managers can use these measures to evaluate their own performance or the performance of subordinates, to identify and correct problems, and to discover opportunities. To assist management in measuring achievement, a number of performance measures are available. To present a more complete picture of performance, it is strongly recommended that several of these performance measures be utilized and that they be combined with nonfinancial measures such as market share, new product development, and human resource utilization. Five commonly used performance measures that are derived from the traditional historical accounting system are:

- Gross profit margin (percentage)
- Cash flows
- Return on the investment in assets
- Residual income
- Total asset turnover

For each of the five performance measures just identified,

a. Describe how the measure is calculated.

b. Describe the information provided by the measure.

c. Explain the limitations of this information.

(CMA)

43. (LO 7; *Foreign managers*) *As the great wall of China tumbles, more big U.S. corporations are scurrying to find bosses for their booming operations there.*

The catch: Few local managers in that land of 1.2 billion boast Western business experience. And expatriates, wary about harsh living conditions in parts of China, seek lavish compensation packages to move there.

A senior U.S. executive relocating to China can command an expatriate package that typically includes a hardship allowance ranging between 20% and 35% of base salary, free housing, "frequent rest and relaxation" trips to Hong Kong and a chauffeur-driven car.

[SOURCE: Joann S. Lublin and Craig S. Smith, "U.S. Companies Struggle with Scarcity of Executives to Run Outposts in China," *Wall Street Journal* (August 23, 1994), pp. B1, B8. Reprinted by permission of The Wall Street Journal, © 1994 Dow Jones & Company, Inc. All Rights Reserved Worldwide.]

a. Discuss why an executive could command significantly more income for living and working in China than in the United States.

b. One of the problems U.S. firms have with hiring Chinese managers is that the Chinese have no loyalty to the companies and tend to job-hop. Discuss actions that a U.S. firm might take to hire Chinese managers and induce them to stay with the company.

c. Describe the characteristics that executives should have if they are to live and work effectively in China.

■ PROBLEMS

44. (LO 2; *ROI*) Sterling Steel Company manufactures various pieces of steel production equipment. Corporate management has examined industry-level data and determined the following industry norms for producers of material handling systems:

Asset turnover	1.6
Profit margin	8%

The actual 1997 results for the company's Material Handling Division are summarized below:

Total assets at year end 1996	$ 9,600,000
Total assets at year end 1997	12,800,000
Sales	13,440,000
Operating expenses	12,499,200

a. For 1997, how did the Material Handling Division perform relative to industry norms?

b. Where, as indicated by the performance measures, should divisional managers focus their efforts to improve performance in the Material Handling Division?

45. (LO 2; *ROI*) Omana, Eastside, and RiverRun are three companies that operate in the retail clothing industry. Some information on each of these companies for 1996 follows:

	OMANA	EASTSIDE	RIVERRUN
Average total assets	$2,100,000	$1,800,000	$2,400,000
Revenues	4,200,000	5,400,000	4,800,000
Expenses	3,780,000	5,076,000	4,140,000

a. For each company, calculate profit margin, asset turnover, and return on investment.

b. Based on the computations in part a, which company appears strongest? Which company appears weakest?

c. Is there any indication of how any of the companies could improve its performance?

46. (LO 2; *ROI*) The 1996 income statement for the Langtry Division of Wellfleet Corp. follows:

Sales	$3,200,000
Variable expenses	(1,600,000)
Contribution margin	$1,600,000
Fixed expenses	(800,000)
Segment income	$ 800,000

Assets at the beginning of 1996 for Langtry Division were $3,600,000. Because of various capital investments during the year, the division ended 1996 with $4,400,000 of assets. Overall, Wellfleet Corp. experienced a 15 percent return on investment for 1996. It is company policy to award year-end bonuses to the managers whose divisions show the highest ROIs.

The chief operating officer of Langtry is investigating a new product line of glassware for the division. The new line is expected to show the following approximate annual results: sales, $400,000; variable expenses, $200,000; and fixed expenses, $100,000. The glassware would require a $620,000 average first year investment in plant assets.

a. What was Langtry's 1996 ROI?

b. What is the expected ROI on the new product line?

c. If Langtry had invested in the new product line in 1996 and the expected results had occurred, what would have been the division's ROI?

d. Is the Langtry Division manager likely to want to add the new product line? Would the president of Wellfleet Corp. want Langtry to add the new product line? Discuss the rationale of each of the individuals.

47. (LO 2; *ROI*) The numbers (1–9) in the following table identify missing data for three divisions of Elm Creek Industries.

	PACKAGE DIVISION	TRANSPORT DIVISION	STORAGE DIVISION
Sales	$2,000,000	$16,000,000	$8,000,000
Segment income	$ 400,000	(4)	$1,000,000
Profit margin	(1)	15%	(7)
Asset turnover	(2)	1.4	(8)
Average assets	(3)	(5)	$4,000,000
Return on investment	10%	(6)	(9)

a. Determine the values for each of the missing items.

b. Identify the area where each division's performance is weakest and strongest relative to the other divisions.

48. (LO 2; *ROI, RI*) Stolzer Wholesaling sells a broad line of clothing to specialty retail and department stores. For 1997, the company's Canadian Division had the following performance targets:

Asset turnover	1.5 times
Profit margin	8%

Actual information concerning the performance of the Canadian Division in 1997 follows:

Total assets at year-end 1996	C$2,400,000
Total assets at year-end 1997	3,600,000
Sales for 1997	6,000,000
Operating expenses for 1997	5,640,000

a. For 1997, what was the Canadian Division's target objective for ROI? Show calculations.

b. For 1997, did the Canadian Division achieve its target objectives for ROI, asset turnover, and profit margin?

c. Where, as indicated by the performance measures, are the areas that are most in need of improved performance?

d. If the company has an overall target return of 13 percent, what was the Canadian Division's residual income for 1997?

49. (LO 2; *Transaction effects on ROI, RI*) The following are a number of transactions affecting a specific division within a multiple-division company. Indicate whether each described transaction would increase (IN), decrease (D), have no effect (N) on, or have an indeterminate effect (I) on each of the following measures: asset turnover, profit margin, ROI, and RI for the present fiscal year. Each transaction is independent.

a. The division writes down an inventory of obsolete finished goods through the cost of goods sold expense account. The journal entry is:

Cost of Goods Sold	40,000	
Finished Goods Inventory		40,000

b. A special overseas order is accepted. The sales price for this order is well below the normal sales price but is sufficient to cover all costs traceable to this order.

c. A piece of equipment is sold for $70,000. The equipment's original cost was $400,000. At the time of sale, the book value of the equipment was $60,000. The sale of the equipment has no effect on product sales.

d. The division fires its research and development manager. The manager will not be replaced during the current fiscal year.

e. The company raises its target rate of return for this division from 12 percent to 14 percent.

f. At midyear, the divisional manager decides to increase scheduled annual production by 2,000 units. This decision has no effect on scheduled sales.

g. Also at midyear, the division manager spends an additional $150,000 on advertising. Sales immediately increase thereafter.

h. The divisional manager replaces a labor-intense operation with machine technology. This action has no effect on sales, but total annual expenses of the operation are expected to decline by 12 percent.

50. (LO 2; *Decisions based on ROI*) Sally is a division manager of Woodland Furniture Co. Her performance as a division manager is evaluated primarily on one measure: divisional segment income divided by gross book value of total divisional assets. For existing operations in Sally's division, projections for 1996 follow:

Sales	$20,000,000
Expenses	(17,500,000)
Segment income	$ 2,500,000

The gross book value of total assets for existing operations is $12,500,000.

At this moment, Sally is evaluating an investment in a new product line that would, according to her projections, increase 1996 segment income by $200,000. The cost of the investment has not yet been determined.

a. Ignoring the new investment, what is Sally's projected ROI for 1996?

b. In light of your answer in part a, what is the maximum amount that Sally would be willing to invest in the new product line?

c. Assuming the new product line would require an investment of $1,100,000, what would be the revised projected ROI for Sally's division in 1996 if the investment were made?

d. If the new product line requires an investment of $1,100,000, will Sally invest in the new product line? If the cost were only $750,000, would she invest in the product line? Explain.

51. (LO 2; *Decisions based on ROI, RI*) The Canadian Yacht Company evaluates the performance of its two division managers using an ROI formula. For the forthcoming period, divisional estimates of relevant measures are:

	PLEASURE	COMMERCIAL	TOTAL COMPANY
Sales	$12,000,000	$48,000,000	$60,000,000
Expenses	10,800,000	42,000,000	52,800,000
Divisional assets	10,000,000	30,000,000	40,000,000

The managers of both operating divisions have the authority to make decisions regarding new investments. The manager of Pleasure Crafts is contemplating an investment in an additional asset that would generate an ROI of 14 percent, and the manager of Commercial Crafts is considering an investment in an additional asset that would generate an ROI of 18 percent.

a. Compute the projected ROI for each division disregarding the contemplated new investments.

b. Based on your answer in part a, which of the managers is likely to actually invest in the asset under consideration?

c. Are the outcomes of the investment decisions in part b likely to be consistent with overall corporate goals? Explain.

d. If the company evaluated the division managers' performance using a residual income measure with a target return of 17 percent, would the outcomes of the investment decisions be different from those described in part b? Explain.

52. (LO 1; *Evaluating cash flow*) Major Currency, the controller of Texoma Meat Products, has become increasingly disillusioned with the company's system of evaluating the performance of profit centers and their managers. The present system focuses on a comparison of budgeted to actual income from operations. Major's concern with the current system is the ease with which the measure "income from operations" can be manipulated by profit center managers. The basic business of Texoma Meat Products consists of purchasing live hogs and cattle, slaughtering the animals, and then selling the various meat products and by-products to regional wholesalers and large retail chains. Most sales are made on credit, and all live animals are purchased for cash. The profit centers consist of geographical segments of Texoma Meat Products, and all profit center segments conduct both production and sales activities within their geographical territories. Following is a typical quarterly income statement for a profit center, which appears in the responsibility report for the profit center:

Sales	$5,000,000
Cost of goods sold	(3,000,000)
Gross profit	$2,000,000
Selling and administrative expenses	(1,500,000)
Income from operations	$ 500,000

Major has suggested to top management that the company replace the accrual income evaluation measure "income from operations" with a measure called "cash flow from operations." He says that this measure will be less susceptible to manipulation by profit center managers. To defend his position, he compiles a cash flow income statement for the same profit center:

Cash receipts from customers	$4,400,000
Cash payments for production labor, livestock, and overhead	(3,200,000)
Cash payments for selling and administrative activities	(800,000)
Cash flow from operations	$ 400,000

a. If Major is correct about profit center managers' manipulating the income measure, where are manipulations likely taking place?

b. Is the proposed cash flow measure less subject to manipulation than the income measure? Explain.

c. Could manipulation be reduced if both cash flow and income measures were utilized? Explain.

d. Do the cash and income measures reveal different information about profit center performance? Explain.

e. Could the existing income statement be used more effectively in evaluating performance? Explain.

53. (LO 3; *Throughput*) Custom Storage Systems has historically evaluated divisional performance exclusively on financial measures. Top managers have become increasingly concerned with this approach to performance evaluation and are now actively seeking alternative measures. Specifically, they wish to focus on activities that generate value for customers. One promising measure is throughput. To experiment with the annual throughput measure, management has gathered the following historical information on one of its larger operating divisions:

Units started into production	200,000
Total good units completed	130,000
Total hours of value-added processing time	80,000
Total hours of division time	120,000

a. What is the manufacturing cycle efficiency?

b. What is the process productivity of the division?

c. What is the process quality yield of the division?

d. Based on your answers to parts a, b, and c, what is the total throughput per hour?

e. Which of the previous measures (part a, b, or c) reflects the possible existence of a production bottleneck?

f. Which of the previous measures (part a, b, or c) reflects potentially poor quality in the production process as measured by the number of defective units?

■ **CASES**

54. (LO 2; *ROI; new investment evaluation*) Raddington Industries produces tool and die machinery for manufacturers. The company expanded vertically in 1993 by acquiring one of its suppliers of alloy steel plates, Reigis Steel Company. In order to manage the two separate businesses, the operations of Reigis are reported separately as an investment center.

Raddington monitors its divisions on the basis of both unit contribution and return on average investment (ROI), with investment defined as average operating assets employed. Management bonuses are determined based on ROI. All investments in operating assets are expected to earn a minimum return of 11 percent before income taxes.

Reigis's cost of goods sold is considered to be entirely variable, while the division's administrative expenses are not dependent on volume. Selling expenses are a mixed cost with 40 percent attributed to sales volume. Reigis's ROI has ranged from 11.8 percent to 14.7 percent since 1993. During the fiscal year ended November 30, 1997, Reigis contemplated a capital acquisition with an estimated ROI of 11.5 percent; however, division management decided that the investment would decrease Reigis's overall ROI.

The 1997 operating statement for Reigis follows. The division's operating assets employed were $15,750,000 at November 30, 1997, a 5 percent increase over the 1996 year-end balance.

REIGIS STEEL DIVISION
OPERATING STATEMENT
FOR THE YEAR ENDED NOVEMBER 30, 1997
($000 OMITTED)

Sales revenue		$25,000
Less expenses		
Cost of goods sold	$16,500	
Administrative expenses	3,955	
Selling expenses	2,700	(23,155)
Operating income before taxes		$ 1,845

a. Calculate the unit contribution for Reigis Steel Division if 1,484,000 units were produced and sold during the year ended November 30, 1997.

b. Calculate the following performance measures for 1997 for the Reigis Steel Division:

   1. Pretax return on average investment on operating assets employed (ROI)

   2. Residual income calculated on the basis of average operating assets employed

c. Explain why the management of the Reigis Steel Division would have been more likely to accept the contemplated capital acquisition if residual income rather than ROI was used as a performance measure.

d. The Reigis Steel Division is a separate investment center within Raddington Industries. Identify several items that Reigis should control if it is to be evaluated fairly by either the ROI or residual income performance measure.

(CMA)

55. (LO 2, 6; *Performance and compensation*) Northstar Offroad Co. (NOC), a subsidiary of Allston Automotive, manufactures go-carts and other recreational vehicles. Family recreational centers that feature go-cart tracks, miniature golf,

batting cages, and arcade games have increased in popularity. As a result, NOC has been receiving some pressure from Allston Automotive top management to diversify into some of these other recreational areas. Recreational Leasing Inc. (RLI), one of the largest firms that leases arcade games to family recreation centers, is looking for a friendly buyer. Allston Automotive management believes that RLI's assets could be acquired for an investment of $3.2 million and has strongly urged Bill Grieco, division manager of NOC, to consider acquiring RLI.

Grieco has reviewed RLI's financial statements with his controller, Marie Donnelly, and they believe that the acquisition may not be in NOC's best interests. "If we decide not to do this, the Allston Automotive people are not going to be happy," said Grieco. "If we could convince them to base our bonuses on something other than return on investment, maybe this acquisition would look more attractive. How would we do if the bonuses were based on residual income using the company's 15% cost of capital?"

Allston Automotive has traditionally evaluated all of its divisions on the basis of return on investment, which is defined as the ratio of operating income to total assets; the desired rate of return for each division is 20%. The management team of any division reporting an annual increase in the return on investment is automatically eligible for a bonus. The management of divisions reporting a decline in the return on investment must provide convincing explanations for the decline to be eligible for a bonus, and this bonus is limited to 50% of the bonus paid to divisions reporting an increase.

Presented below are condensed financial statements for both NOC and RLI for the fiscal year ended May 31, 1997.

	NOC	RLI
Sales revenue	$10,500,000	
Leasing revenue		$2,800,000
Variable expenses	(7,000,000)	(1,000,000)
Fixed expenses	(1,500,000)	(1,200,000)
Operating income	$ 2,000,000	$ 600,000
Current assets	$ 2,300,000	$1,900,000
Long-term assets	5,700,000	1,100,000
Total assets	$ 8,000,000	$3,000,000
Current liabilities	$ 1,400,000	$ 850,000
Long-term liabilities	3,800,000	1,200,000
Shareholders' equity	2,800,000	950,000
Total liabilities and shareholders' equity	$ 8,000,000	$3,000,000

a. Under the present bonus system how would the acquisition of RLI affect Grieco's bonus expectations?

b. If Grieco's suggestion to use residual income as the evaluation criterion is accepted, how would acquisition of RLI affect Grieco's bonus expectations?

c. Given the present bonus arrangement, is it fair for Allston Automotive management to expect Grieco to acquire RLI?

d. Is the present bonus system consistent with Allston Automotive's goal of expansion of NOC into new recreational products?

(CMA)

56. (LO 6; *Performance and compensation*) Gulfland Chemical Corp is a multinational firm that markets a variety of chemicals for industrial uses. One of the many autonomous divisions is the North America Petro-Chemical Division (NAPCD). The manager of NAPCD, Karyn Kravitz, was recently overheard discussing a vexing problem with her controller, William Michaels. The topic of discussion was whether the division should replace its existing chemical-handling equipment with newer technology that is safer, more efficient, and cheaper to operate.

According to an analysis by Mr. Michaels, the cost savings over the life of the new technology would pay for the initial cost of the technology several times over. However, Ms. Kravitz remained reluctant to invest. Her most fundamental concern involved the disposition of the old processing equipment. Because the existing equipment has been in use for only two years, it has a very high book value relative to its current market value. Ms. Kravitz noted that if the new technology were not purchased, the division would expect a segment income of $4,000,000 for the year. However, if the new technology were purchased, the old equipment would have to be sold, and the division could probably sell it for only $1.2 million. This equipment had an original cost of $8 million, and $1.5 million in depreciation has been recorded. Thus a book loss of $5.3 million ($6.5 − $1.2) would be recorded on the sale.

Ms. Kravitz' boss, Jim Heitz, is the president of the Western Chemical Group, and his compensation is based almost exclusively on the amount of ROI generated by his group, which includes NAPCD. After thoroughly analyzing the facts, Ms. Kravitz concluded, "The people in the Western Chemical Group will swallow their dentures if we book a $5.3 million loss."

a. Why is Ms. Kravitz concerned about the book loss on disposal of the old technology in her division?

b. What weaknesses in Western Chemical Group's performance pay plan are apparently causing Ms. Kravitz to avoid an investment that meets all of the normal criteria for acceptability (ignoring the ROI effect)?

■ ETHICS AND QUALITY DISCUSSIONS

57. Refer to the News Note entitled "Speed Is the Measurement; Profits Are the Result" on page 836 in the chapter.

a. Discuss how the continual search for ways to speed up processing can aid companies' efforts to improve quality and reduce costs.

b. Describe performance measures that manufacturing companies might use to evaluate their improvement in the area of "speed of product delivery."

58. We often think that a performance evaluation system can be devised for a given position that will be appropriate for any individual who might be selected to fill that position. However, a recent survey has indicated substantial differences within the U.S. population in terms of motivating factors. Further, many people in the current work force have been through traumas such as downsizing that have caused them to be less loyal to their employers than their predecessors (and also less trusting of their employers).

Another alarming finding of the study is that the American work force is experiencing significant problems in dealing with diversity. For example, the study found:

■ Employees under age 25 are no more likely than older employees to indicate a preference for working with employees of other races or ethnicities.

- Half of all respondents indicated a preference for working with other employees of the same race, sex, gender, and level of education.

- Employees of all types indicated that minorities were less likely to advance in the organization than other worker groups.

- One-fifth of minority workers indicated that they had been discriminated against in the workplace.

- Women were more than twice as likely as men to rate their job advancement opportunities as poor or only fair.

- Nonfinancial employee benefits were more likely than pay to be highly correlated with job satisfaction.

[SOURCE: Based on Sue Shellenbarger, "Work-Force Study Finds Loyalty Is Weak, Divisions of Race and Gender Are Deep," *Wall Street Journal* (September 3, 1993), pp. B1, B2.]

a. Does the lack of progress in achieving widespread acceptance of worker diversity have implications for the quality of work in American businesses? Discuss.

b. What actions might managers take to encourage greater acceptance of diversity?

59. *Bobbie Pilkington, a United Air Lines flight attendant from Chicago, went five years without a pay raise while watching [the value of] her new shares of stock plunge right along with the company's 71 percent drop in profits.*

UAL chairman Stephen Wolf had no such problems. Despite the company's poor performance, he earned $18.3 million [in 1990], or about 610 times more than Pilkington and 1,272 times more than a newly hired flight attendant.

[SOURCE: Mary Kane, "CEO Pay, Perks Foster Resentment," *[New Orleans] Times-Picayune* [November 3, 1991], p. F1. © Newhouse News Service.]

a. Plato said that the highest-paid worker should earn no more than five times what the lowest-paid worker earns. Do you agree with Plato? Justify your answer.

b. Should corporate executives have their compensation packages (total cash and noncash elements) tied in some way to company performance? If so, why? If not, why not?

c. Discuss the ethics of allowing corporate executives to be paid extremely well when the companies for which they work are laying off employees, deferring payments to creditors, and not declaring dividends to stockholders.

d. Many companies use "golden parachutes"—substantial payments made to executives when they leave the firm involuntarily (and sometimes when they leave voluntarily). Assume that you are the CEO of a company that has just been taken over by another company. The new company's board of directors has decided to replace you because your company has not been performing at what the directors believe is a "reasonable" level. Discuss why you would have wanted a golden parachute in place prior to the takeover and why the stockholders might have disagreed with that desire.

60. Nason Corporation manufactures and distributes a line of toys for children. As a consequence, the corporation has large seasonal variations in sales. The company issues quarterly financial statements, and first-quarter earnings were down from the same period last year.

During a visit to the Preschool and Infant Division, Nason's president expressed dissatisfaction with the division's first-quarter performance. As a result, John Kraft, division manager, felt pressure to report higher earnings in the second quarter. Kraft was aware that Nason Corporation uses the LIFO inventory method, so he had the purchasing manager postpone several large inventory orders scheduled for delivery in the second quarter. Kraft knew that the use of older inventory costs during the second quarter would cause a decline in the cost of goods sold and thus increase earnings.

During a review of the preliminary second-quarter income statement, Donna Jensen, division controller, noticed that the cost of goods sold was low relative to sales. Jensen analyzed the inventory account and discovered that the scheduled second-quarter material purchases had been delayed until the third quarter. Jensen prepared a revised income statement using current replacement costs to calculate cost of goods sold and submitted the income statement to John Kraft, her superior, for review. Kraft was not pleased with these results and insisted that the second-quarter income statement remain unchanged. Jensen tried to explain to Kraft that the interim inventory should reflect the expected cost of the replacement of the liquidated layers when the inventory is expected to be replaced before the end of the year. Kraft did not relent and told Jensen to issue the income statement using LIFO costs. Jensen is concerned about Kraft's response and is contemplating what her next action should be.

a. Determine whether the actions of John Kraft are ethical and explain your position.

b. Recommend a course of action that Donna Jensen should take in proceeding to resolve this situation.

(CMA)

61. In a survey published in 1990, 649 managers responded to a questionnaire and provided their opinion as to the ethical acceptability of manipulating accounting earnings to achieve higher managerial compensation. One of the questions dealt with the acceptability of changing a sales practice to pull some of next year's sales into the current year so that reported current earnings can be pushed up. The results of the survey indicated that about 43 percent of the respondents felt this practice was ethically acceptable, 44 percent felt the practice was ethically questionable, and 13 percent felt the practice was ethically unacceptable.

Other results of the survey indicate that the managers considered large manipulations more unethical than small manipulations and income-increasing manipulations more ethically unacceptable than income-decreasing manipulations.

[SOURCE: Based on William J. Bruns and Kenneth A. Merchant, "The Dangerous Morality of Managing Earnings," *Management Accounting* (August 1990), pp. 22–25.]

a. If managers can manipulate earnings to effect changes in their pay, is this a signal of a weakness in the pay-for-performance plan? Explain.

b. In your view, does the amount of a manipulation partly determine the extent to which the manipulation is ethically acceptable?

c. Describe any circumstances in which you believe manipulation would be ethically acceptable.

■ PROJECTS

62. *Donald Hudgens thinks ConAgra Inc.'s chairman and chief executive officer, Philip B. Fletcher, has it too easy.*

"Maybe I'm naive," says Mr. Hudgens, a retired railroad chemist. "I've never had a high-powered job." Still, he contends that ConAgra's CEO should be working harder for his millions.

As a consequence, ConAgra shareholders will vote . . . on Mr. Hudgens' proposal that the company revise a special long-term incentive plan directors approved for Mr. Fletcher [in 1993]. Under that plan, the chairman would receive 50,000 ConAgra common shares for every percentage point over 10% the company's per-share earnings rise during the next four fiscal years.

For example, if earnings grow at a compound annual rate of 14%, as they did [in 1993] Mr. Fletcher would get 200,000 shares of stock—that is, four percentage points times 50,000 shares. The payout would occur in July 1998. At ConAgra's current price, every 50,000 shares would be valued at $1.6 million.

"They'll do it [exceed 10%] in spite of any incentive award," Mr. Hudgens says. He has some statistical support. . . . ConAgra's per-share earnings have grown at a 15.4% compounded annual rate; ConAgra's longtime internal goal is for per-share earnings [growth] to exceed 14% a year, on average.

Thus, Mr. Hudgens wants ConAgra to compare its performance with that of other food companies [instead of its own growth targets] and he has drawn up a list of 13 [competitors]. . . . Moreover, per-share growth must come from continuing operations, the 54 year-old shareholder says.

ConAgra, the nation's largest independent food company, opposes Mr. Hudgens' suggestion. Initially, the company said it wouldn't allow shareholders to consider it at all, only to have the Securities and Exchange Commission disagree.

[SOURCE: Richard Gibson, "ConAgra Holder Is Seeking Changes in Incentive Plan," *Wall Street Journal* (September 6, 1994), p. B5. Reprinted by permission of The Wall Street Journal, © 1994 Dow Jones & Company, Inc. All Rights Reserved Worldwide.]

Divide your class into teams to debate whether ConAgra should change its incentive compensation scheme. Teams should be assigned to argue either for change or for the status quo. Team members should use concepts from the chapter to support the positions they take.

63. The text discusses the importance of delivering both positive and negative feedback to employees. The method of delivering such feedback is often as important as the nature of the feedback in terms of its impact on the affected employee. Invite a high-level manager from a local firm to address your class on methods he or she uses to deliver feedback to employees. Use the methods as a basis for a class discussion about desirable and undesirable ways to give feedback.

64. For the fiscal year ending September 30, 1994, Mesa Air's CEO Larry Risley earned $153,000 in salary and a cash bonus of $2.4 million. The amount of the bonus was believed by many to be much too large, given the company's size and recent performance. Consider, for example, the following points:

- The share price of Mesa Air's stock declined from a high of about $22.50 in early 1993 to well under $10 by late 1994.

- The pay of AMR (American Airlines) chairman, Robert L. Crandall, for 1994 was about $1 million.

- Net income for Mesa Air in fiscal 1994 was $27.6 million.

- Net income for Mesa Air in fiscal 1993 was $26.3 million and Mr. Risley's bonus was only about one-third of its 1994 level.

- Mr. Risley sold 100,000 shares of stock in 1993 several weeks before announcing disappointing earnings. The 100,000 shares represented about one-half of Mr. Risley's Mesa Air holdings.

[SOURCE: Adapted from Bridget O'Brian, "Mesa Air's Fortunes Sink, But Its CEO Is Flying High," *Wall Street Journal* (February 2, 1995), p. B4. Reprinted by permission of The Wall Street Journal, © 1995 Dow Jones & Company, Inc. All Rights Reserved Worldwide.]

Your task is to redesign a compensation system for Mr. Risley. In doing so, you are to specifically consider the following:

a. The role of common stock share price.
b. Whether the performance benchmarks should be industry-related or simply the past or expected performance measures of Mesa Air.
c. Whether any bonus should be in cash, stock, or stock options.
d. What specific performance dimensions should be captured—financial and nonfinancial.

THE MANAGEMENT ACCOUNTING PROFESSION

Management accountants may work in manufacturing, retail, or service companies or in government or not-for-profit enterprises. But, regardless of where they work, management accountants are essential members of the management team. As they gain experience and advance in their careers, management accountants must diversify their knowledge base and provide strategic, rather than repetitive, information. The following description is appropriate:

> Management accounting is a specialized discipline that goes far beyond the bounds of traditional accounting. Its objective is to provide management with dynamic information both for making operating decisions and for developing blueprints for business success. Using all manner of financial and nonfinancial information, the management accountant monitors and assesses real-time performance and helps businesses prepare for future needs by facilitating better decision making within the organization.[1]

In providing their services to organizations, management accountants recognize that their discipline, like that of public accounting, is a professional one. Professions around the world are generally characterized by certain features, including an organization of members, a process of certification or licensing, a set of standards or guidelines as foundation for practice, and a code of ethics. The profession of management accounting adheres to these commonalties.

MANAGEMENT ACCOUNTING ORGANIZATIONS AND CERTIFICATIONS

In the United States, over 11,000 management accountants are members of a private-sector body called the Institute of Management Accountants (IMA). *Management Accounting* is a monthly journal published by the IMA; it contains articles on topics important to today's business, governmental, and service organizations.

The IMA's Certificate in Management Accounting (CMA) is a professional designation that recognizes the successful completion of a two-day examination, acceptable work experience, and the satisfaction of certain continuing education requirements. The exam consists of four parts (Economics, Finance, and Management; Financial Accounting and Reporting; Management Reporting, Analysis, and Behavioral Issues;

---

[1]Society of Management Accountants of Canada, *Fact Sheet: Certified Management Accountants* (Hamilton, Ontario: Society of Management Accountants of Canada, October 1993).

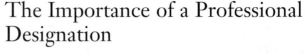

The Importance of a Professional Designation

A professional designation is a highly valued personal asset. Once acquired, a member has a choice—live off the principal value, probably for a short period of time or increase the equity value of the designation.

Being a professional in today's markets is competitive. There is no certainty of employment and standing still in career development is an invitation to redundancy.

Individually and collectively, we have a lot to gain in ensuring that equity growth underpins our professional designation. That equity growth is our competitive advantage. Like any other asset with value, it means we must ensure our reputation, our uniqueness, our investment, and our legal standing.

We believe that CMA designation is the starting point of a successful career, not the destination. Once the designation is earned, the skill base and knowledge surrounding it should be constantly updated and improved. In the same way that total quality is a process of continuous improvement in an organization, professionalism should be seen as a life-long process of continuous improvement . . . .

SOURCE: Doug Dodds, "A Professional Designation: The CMA's Competitive Edge," *CMA Magazine* (February 1995), p. 2. Reprinted from an article by Doug Dodds, CMA, FCMA appearing in CMA Magazine (February 1995 issue) with permission of the Society of Management Accountants of Canada.

and Decision Analysis and Information Systems). Questions on the exam are multiple choice, discussion, and mathematical problems.

The corresponding Canadian organization is the Society of Management Accountants. The Society publishes *CMA Magazine*, which is printed in both English and French, and contains articles on topical areas such as quality, performance evaluation, information support systems, and management styles. The organization is composed of 29,000 members, of whom 26,000 are CMAs and 3,000 are professional program students. The Canadian CMA program differs from the American one in that there are two exams (an entrance and a comprehensive final). Between taking these two examinations, the aspiring CMA must obtain practical experience while participating in a demanding professional program that concentrates on management theory and practice, professionalism, ethics, and emerging management accounting issues. The accompanying News Note discusses the importance of the CMA designation, but the benefits are equally applicable to *any* professional designation including the CPA (Certified Public Accountant), CA (Chartered Accountant), CFP (Certified Financial Planner), and CLU (Certified Life Underwriter).

MANAGEMENT ACCOUNTING STANDARDS

Cost Accounting Standards Board (CASB)

Financial accounting standards are established by the Financial Accounting Standards Board (FASB), a private-sector body. In the United States, no similar board exists to define *universal* management accounting standards. However, a public-sector board called the **Cost Accounting Standards Board (CASB)** was established in 1970 by the U.S. Congress to promulgate uniform cost accounting standards for all negotiated federal government contracts in excess of $500,000. Twenty cost accounting standards

■ **EXHIBIT A–1**
Standards of Ethical Conduct for Management Accountants

COMPETENCE

Management accountants have a responsibility to:

- Maintain an appropriate level of professional competence by on-going development of their knowledge and skills.
- Perform their professional duties in accordance with relevant laws, regulations, and technical standards.
- Prepare complete and clear reports and recommendations after appropriate analyses of relevant and reliable information.

CONFIDENTIALITY

Management accountants have a responsibility to:

- Refrain from disclosing confidential information acquired in the course of their work except when authorized, unless legally obligated to do so.
- Inform subordinates as appropriate regarding the confidentiality of information acquired in the course of their work and monitor their activities to assure the maintenance of that confidentiality.
- Refrain from using or appearing to use confidential information acquired in the course of their work for unethical or illegal advantage either personally or through third parties.

INTEGRITY

Management accountants have a responsibility to:

- Avoid actual or apparent conflicts of interest and advise all appropriate parties of any potential conflict.
- Refrain from engaging in any activity that would prejudice their ability to carry out their duties ethically.
- Refuse any gift, favor, or hospitality that would influence or would appear to influence their actions.
- Refrain from either actively or passively subverting the attainment of the organization's legitimate and ethical objectives.
- Recognize and communicate professional limitations or other constraints that would preclude responsible judgment or successful performance of an activity.
- Communicate unfavorable as well as favorable information and professional judgments or opinions.
- Refrain from engaging in or supporting any activity that would discredit the profession.

OBJECTIVITY

Management accountants have a responsibility to:

- Communicate information fairly and objectively.
- Disclose fully all relevant information that could reasonably be expected to influence an intended user's understanding of the reports, comments, and recommendations presented.

SOURCE: Institute of Management Accountants (formerly National Association of Accountants), *Statements on Management Accounting No. 1B: Objectives of Management Accounting* (New York, N.Y., June 17, 1982). Copyright by Institute of Management Accountants (formerly National Association of Accountants), Montvale, NJ.

NEWS NOTE

The Small Ethical Decisions Help You Make the Big Ones

When the body of moral principles that govern your day-to-day life conflicts with the ethical practices of your company, clearing a path through the tangle can be slow, arduous work. Even though all ethical decisions deserve in-depth consideration, often there's no time for it.

There is a way to prepare yourself for making complex ethical judgments on the spot. It sounds corny, but the best way to meet these big challenges is to practice on the small ones you face every day. If you've been at a job for more than a week, you know the sorts of routine compromises that go with your professional territory. With just this information, you are well equipped to begin to establish where you feel comfortable drawing the line between personal standards and professional duty. . . . Where ethical behavior is concerned, definitely sweat the small stuff—it's what will help you deal with tougher, more ambiguous situations later in your career.

Some things are out of the individual's control, however. Fundamentally, it's the chair, the chief executive, and the senior officers who set the underlying ethical tone for the company. They show what counts through hundreds of small actions that are highly visible to everyone else.

If the everyday compromises you are asked to make in a company seem to consistently clash with your own sense of propriety, look hard at your bosses. If they aren't the sort of people whose ethics you respect, then you're bound for a head-on collusion.

SOURCE: Nancy K. Austin, "Ethics: Personal vs. Professional," *Working Woman* (September 1992), pp. 28, 32. First appeared in Working Woman in September 1992. Written by Nancy Austin. Reprinted with the permission of Working Woman magazine. Copyright © 1992 by Working Woman magazine.

■ **EXHIBIT A–2**

Code of Professional Ethics for the Society of Management Accountants of Ontario

All members shall adhere to the following "Code of Professional Ethics" of the Society:

i. A Member shall act at all times with:
   1. responsibility for and fidelity to public needs;
   2. fairness and loyalty to his associates, clients and employers; and
   3. competence through devotion to high ideals of personal honour and professional integrity.
ii. A Member shall
   1. maintain at all times independence of thought and action;
   2. not express his opinion on financial statements without first assessing his relationship with his client to determine whether he might expect his opinion to be considered independent, objective and unbiased by one who has knowledge of all the facts; and
   3. when preparing financial statements or expressing an opinion on financial statements which are intended to inform management only, disclose all material facts known to him in order not to make such financial statements misleading, acquire sufficient information to warrant an expression of opinion and report all material misstatements or departures from generally accepted accounting principles.

iii.   A Member shall

1. not disclose or use any confidential information concerning the affairs of his employer or client unless acting in the course of his duties or except when such information is required to be disclosed in the course of any defence of himself or any associate or employee in any lawsuit or other legal proceeding or against alleged professional misconduct by order of lawful authority of the Board or any committee of the Society in proper exercise of their duties but only to the extent necessary for such purpose;

2. inform his employer or client of any business connections or interests of which his employer or client would reasonably expect to be informed;

3. not, in the course of exercising his duties on behalf of his employer or client, hold, receive, bargain for or acquire any fee, remuneration or benefit without his employer's or client's knowledge and consent; and

4. take all reasonable steps, in arranging any engagement as a consultant, to establish a clear understanding of the scope and objectives of the work before it is commenced and will furnish the client with an estimate of cost, preferably before the engagement is commenced, but in any event as soon as possible thereafter.

iv.   A Member shall

1. conduct himself toward other Members with courtesy and good faith;

2. not commit an act discreditable to the profession;

3. not engage in or counsel any business or occupation which, in the opinion of the Society, is incompatible with the professional ethics of a management accountant;

4. not accept any engagement to review the work of another Member for the same employer except with the knowledge of that Member, or except where the connection of that Member with the work has been terminated, unless the Member reviews the work of others as a normal part of his responsibilities;

5. not attempt to gain an advantage over other Members by paying or accepting a commission in securing management accounting work;

6. uphold the principle of adequate compensation for management accounting work; and

7. not act maliciously or in any other way which may adversely reflect on the public or professional reputation or business of another Member.

v.   A Member shall

1. at all times maintain the standards of competence expressed by the academic and experience requirements for admission to the Society and for continuation as a Member;

2. disseminate the knowledge upon which the profession of management accounting is based to others within the profession and generally promote the advancement of the profession;

3. undertake only such work as he is competent to perform by virtue of his training and experience and will, where it would be in the best interests of an employer or client, engage, or advise the employer or client to engage, other specialists;

4. expose before the proper tribunals of the Society any incompetent, unethical, illegal or unfair conduct or practice of a Member which involves the reputation, dignity or honour of the Society; and

5. endeavour to ensure that a professional partnership or company, with which such Member is associated as a partner, principal, director or officer, abides by the Code of Professional Ethics and the rules of professional conduct established by the Society.

SOURCE: Society of Management Accountants of Ontario, *Code of Professional Ethics* (Ontario, Canada: Society of Management Accountants of Ontario, June 1991).

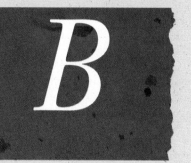

B USING THE ETHICAL DISCUSSION QUESTIONS

There are few more difficult issues facing business graduates or people in the business world today than those pertaining to ethical dilemmas. Some of these situations are specifically covered by professional codes of conduct; others reflect the differences among what is ethical, what is legal, and what is professionally accepted. Most traditional coverage of ethics in accounting course focuses on the teachings of the various professional codes of ethics. While teaching about codes of ethics is important, it can be greatly enhanced by presenting cases involving questionable breaches of proper conduct in the myriad of everyday business transactions. By covering such situations, college faculty have an opportunity to make a significant contribution to their students' success and well-being in the area of day-to-day ethics.

The text provides a series of end of chapter situations that can be used to give the student practice in recognizing ethical issues and an opportunity to develop appropriate responses. Some of the questions address what appear to be fairly innocuous issues (price setting for a price bid); other address mainstream environmental and ethical matters (the handling of environmentally destructive waste materials). Both types of situations, however, have important underlying ethical conflicts and require a logical thought process to arrive at the most ethical solution rather than simply *rationalizing* any solution chosen. Students need to recognize that it may be easy to make an unethical decision when the stakes are not very high; however, when the stakes increase, the pattern of unethical decision making may already be in place. If the minor ethical decisions can be analyzed and resolved ethically, the major decisions are more likely to be addressed in a thoughtful and ethical manner.

It is important that students be prepared, while they are in school, for ethical conflicts with which they may be confronted in the workplace. An essential part of such preparation is obtaining the *ability* to recognize ethical problems before they become realities and learning how, when, and to whom to respond to such problems. The purpose of managerial accounting is not to provide a philosophy lecture, but students should be made aware of at least some of the major existing ethical theories and problem-solving models before being asked to analyze and resolve ethical conflict situations. Thus, the following information may be useful to both the faculty member teaching this course as well as the students taking it.

Ethics can be viewed and taught at two levels: (1) as a set of general theories and (2) as a set of specific principles.

ETHICAL THEORIES

Viewing ethics as a set of general theories allows people to learn the background used in developing specific principles and, therefore, be able to develop their own principles or guidelines when confronted with unique situations in which the existing principles seem to have no relevance. This type of teaching is usually performed in philosophy courses, but some of the basic theories can be briefly defined and illustrated at this point.

Utilitarianism. This theory holds that the primary method of determining what is right or ethical is the usefulness of an action or a policy in producing other actions or experiences that people value. It emphasizes the consequences that an action has on all the people directly and/or indirectly affected by that action. Utilitarianism reflects a societal viewpoint of the "greatest good for the greatest number." While this theory may provide extremely valid ethical decisions, it is highly unworkable in its theoretical state in practice. This model would require determining *all* possible solutions to a dilemma, determining *all* possible stakeholders for each solution, determining *all* the costs and benefits of *each* solution to *each* stakeholder, summing such costs and benefits, and choosing the decision that maximizes the benefits of the most stakeholders. Thus, when utilitarianism is applied as a model of ethical decision making, certain shortcuts are normally taken, such as considering only certain types of stakeholders or solutions within a certain type of framework. When such shortcuts are taken, however, the decision maker should occasionally review them to make sure that such simplifications have not automatically ignored important constituencies, reference points, interests, or values. (Utilitarianism is a type of cost-benefit analysis.)

Categorical Imperatives. This set of rules requires that a person act on the premise that whatever he or she does would become a universal law. Categorical imperatives form the basis of duties that are considered inherently right. Because actions are determined to be inherently right or wrong (regardless of the positive or negative consequences), the decision maker is responsible for behavior, nor for consequences. Thus, the model emphasizes treating all persons equally and as the person acting would like to be treated. Additionally, the model emphasizes respect for individuals and their freedoms. (Categorical imperatives reflect a basic "Do unto others as you would have them do unto you" concept.)

The theory of rights asserts that people have some fundamental rights that must be respected in all types of decisions and is a variation of duty-based analysis. Rights advocates suggest that there are liberty rights and welfare rights for all persons. Liberty rights basically have been embedded in the U.S. Constitution and include:

- the right of free consent (people should be treated only as they knowingly and willingly consent to be treated)
- the right to privacy (outside the work environment)
- the right to freedom of conscience
- the right to free speech
- the right to due process

Welfare rights reflect the right of all people to some minimum standard of living; these rights typically have fallen into the realm of governmental or corporate social responsibilities.

The theory of justice requires that people make decisions based on equity, fairness, and impartiality. While the theory of justice requires that people who are similar must be treated in a similar manner, it allows people who are different in a *relevant* way to be treated differently. The relevant ways affecting when people can be treated differently cannot relate to arbitrary characteristics; the differences must be related to the task that is to be performed or differences in people's needs. In using the theory of justice, a decision maker must be careful to make certain that the characteristic(s) on which he or she is making the distinction is(are) relevant and not discriminatory.

(While these are not the only ethical theories that exist, they do provide a foundation from which to begin ethical discussions.)

ETHICS AS A SET OF PRINCIPLES

Teaching ethics as a set of specific principles provides individuals with a means to answer concrete, problem-oriented situations. This method is typically how ethics are treated in an auditing course or in discussions of codes of ethics.

It is important to point out to students the difference between ethics and legality. Ethics can be viewed as a nonjurisdictional system of moral rights. It represents the moral rights that people have regardless of where or when they live, whether these rights are recognized or not. Legality merely refers to what is permissible under the law in a particular society. Sometimes society may condone an act as legal because of the surrounding circumstances even though the act itself may be viewed as unethical. (For example, it is unethical to kill another human being, but society may make it legal to do so under certain situations.) Legitimizing a "wrong" act because of circumstances does not make that act any more moral.

In making ethical decisions, a person must first have the sensitivity to recognize that an ethical dilemma exists and exert the self-control to attempt to resolve it. This resolution may cause conflict at the personal, organizational, or societal level. All feasible alternatives should be considered along with their influencing factors such as values, laws, resources constraints, pressures, and cultural mores. *Once all ramifications are considered and the decision maker selects an alternative using whatever theories or processes he or she chooses, the decision maker must also be willing to accept the outcomes from and responsibility for that choice.* An individual acts as an autonomous agent when he or she acts on the basis of principles that have been consciously evaluated and accepted by the individual as the correct principles to direct behavior; individuals cannot be considered autonomous when they act based on principles that have been imposed from the outside (through peer pressure or by some authority) or that have been internalized as a matter or mere habit.

The making of ethical choices is not a science; it is subjective and cannot be resolved from a societal point of view. Different individuals will always have different viewpoints as to what is ethical and what is the proper decision for an ethical dilemma. The challenge is to create a means for students to foresee potential problems, recognize they have an obligation to derive internal and personal criteria by which to resolve such dilemmas, and accept personal, organizational, societal, and legal determinations as to the ethical or unethical nature of solutions chosen when (or if) those solutions are made public.

C

PRESENT AND FUTURE VALUE TABLES

TABLE 1 PRESENT VALUE OF $1

Period	1.00%	2.00%	3.00%	4.00%	5.00%	6.00%	7.00%	8.00%	9.00%	9.50%	10.00%	10.50%	11.00%
1	0.9901	0.9804	0.9709	0.9615	0.9524	0.9434	0.9346	0.9259	0.9174	0.9132	0.9091	0.9050	0.9009
2	0.9803	0.9612	0.9426	0.9246	0.9070	0.8900	0.8734	0.8573	0.8417	0.8340	0.8265	0.8190	0.8116
3	0.9706	0.9423	0.9151	0.8890	0.8638	0.8396	0.8163	0.7938	0.7722	0.7617	0.7513	0.7412	0.7312
4	0.9610	0.9239	0.8885	0.8548	0.8227	0.7921	0.7629	0.7350	0.7084	0.6956	0.6830	0.6707	0.6587
5	0.9515	0.9057	0.8626	0.8219	0.7835	0.7473	0.7130	0.6806	0.6499	0.6352	0.6209	0.6070	0.5935
6	0.9421	0.8880	0.8375	0.7903	0.7462	0.7050	0.6663	0.6302	0.5963	0.5801	0.5645	0.5493	0.5346
7	0.9327	0.8706	0.8131	0.7599	0.7107	0.6651	0.6228	0.5835	0.5470	0.5298	0.5132	0.4971	0.4817
8	0.9235	0.8535	0.7894	0.7307	0.6768	0.6274	0.5820	0.5403	0.5019	0.4838	0.4665	0.4499	0.4339
9	0.9143	0.8368	0.7664	0.7026	0.6446	0.5919	0.5439	0.5003	0.4604	0.4419	0.4241	0.4071	0.3909
10	0.9053	0.8204	0.7441	0.6756	0.6139	0.5584	0.5084	0.4632	0.4224	0.4035	0.3855	0.3685	0.3522
11	0.8963	0.8043	0.7224	0.6496	0.5847	0.5268	0.4751	0.4289	0.3875	0.3685	0.3505	0.3334	0.3173
12	0.8875	0.7885	0.7014	0.6246	0.5568	0.4970	0.4440	0.3971	0.3555	0.3365	0.3186	0.3018	0.2858
13	0.8787	0.7730	0.6810	0.6006	0.5303	0.4688	0.4150	0.3677	0.3262	0.3073	0.2897	0.2731	0.2575
14	0.8700	0.7579	0.6611	0.5775	0.5051	0.4423	0.3878	0.3405	0.2993	0.2807	0.2633	0.2471	0.2320
15	0.8614	0.7430	0.6419	0.5553	0.4810	0.4173	0.3625	0.3152	0.2745	0.2563	0.2394	0.2237	0.2090
16	0.8528	0.7285	0.6232	0.5339	0.4581	0.3937	0.3387	0.2919	0.2519	0.2341	0.2176	0.2024	0.1883
17	0.8444	0.7142	0.6050	0.5134	0.4363	0.3714	0.3166	0.2703	0.2311	0.2138	0.1978	0.1832	0.1696
18	0.8360	0.7002	0.5874	0.4936	0.4155	0.3503	0.2959	0.2503	0.2120	0.1952	0.1799	0.1658	0.1528
19	0.8277	0.6864	0.5703	0.4746	0.3957	0.3305	0.2765	0.2317	0.1945	0.1783	0.1635	0.1500	0.1377
20	0.8195	0.6730	0.5537	0.4564	0.3769	0.3118	0.2584	0.2146	0.1784	0.1628	0.1486	0.1358	0.1240
21	0.8114	0.6598	0.5376	0.4388	0.3589	0.2942	0.2415	0.1987	0.1637	0.1487	0.1351	0.1229	0.1117
22	0.8034	0.6468	0.5219	0.4220	0.3419	0.2775	0.2257	0.1839	0.1502	0.1358	0.1229	0.1112	0.1007
23	0.7954	0.6342	0.5067	0.4057	0.3256	0.2618	0.2110	0.1703	0.1378	0.1240	0.1117	0.1006	0.0907
24	0.7876	0.6217	0.4919	0.3901	0.3101	0.2470	0.1972	0.1577	0.1264	0.1133	0.1015	0.0911	0.0817
25	0.7798	0.6095	0.4776	0.3751	0.2953	0.2330	0.1843	0.1460	0.1160	0.1034	0.0923	0.0824	0.0736
26	0.7721	0.5976	0.4637	0.3607	0.2812	0.2198	0.1722	0.1352	0.1064	0.0945	0.0839	0.0746	0.0663
27	0.7644	0.5859	0.4502	0.3468	0.2679	0.2074	0.1609	0.1252	0.0976	0.0863	0.0763	0.0675	0.0597
28	0.7568	0.5744	0.4371	0.3335	0.2551	0.1956	0.1504	0.1159	0.0896	0.0788	0.0693	0.0611	0.0538
29	0.7493	0.5631	0.4244	0.3207	0.2430	0.1846	0.1406	0.1073	0.0822	0.0719	0.0630	0.0553	0.0485
30	0.7419	0.5521	0.4120	0.3083	0.2314	0.1741	0.1314	0.0994	0.0754	0.0657	0.0573	0.0500	0.0437
31	0.7346	0.5413	0.4000	0.2965	0.2204	0.1643	0.1228	0.0920	0.0692	0.0600	0.0521	0.0453	0.0394
32	0.7273	0.5306	0.3883	0.2851	0.2099	0.1550	0.1147	0.0852	0.0634	0.0058	0.0474	0.0410	0.0355
33	0.7201	0.5202	0.3770	0.2741	0.1999	0.1462	0.1072	0.0789	0.0582	0.0500	0.0431	0.0371	0.0319
34	0.7130	0.5100	0.3660	0.2636	0.1904	0.1379	0.1002	0.0731	0.0534	0.0457	0.0391	0.0336	0.0288
35	0.7059	0.5000	0.3554	0.2534	0.1813	0.1301	0.0937	0.0676	0.0490	0.0417	0.0356	0.0304	0.0259
36	0.6989	0.4902	0.3450	0.2437	0.1727	0.1227	0.0875	0.0626	0.0449	0.0381	0.0324	0.0275	0.0234
37	0.6920	0.4806	0.3350	0.2343	0.1644	0.1158	0.0818	0.0580	0.0412	0.0348	0.0294	0.0249	0.0210
38	0.6852	0.4712	0.3252	0.2253	0.1566	0.1092	0.0765	0.0537	0.0378	0.0318	0.0267	0.0225	0.0190
39	0.6784	0.4620	0.3158	0.2166	0.1492	0.1031	0.0715	0.0497	0.0347	0.0290	0.0243	0.0204	0.0171
40	0.6717	0.4529	0.3066	0.2083	0.1421	0.0972	0.0668	0.0460	0.0318	0.0265	0.0221	0.0184	0.0154
41	0.6650	0.4440	0.2976	0.2003	0.1353	0.0917	0.0624	0.0426	0.0292	0.0242	0.0201	0.0167	0.0139
42	0.6584	0.4353	0.2890	0.1926	0.1288	0.0865	0.0583	0.0395	0.0268	0.0221	0.0183	0.0151	0.0125
43	0.6519	0.4268	0.2805	0.1852	0.1227	0.0816	0.0545	0.0365	0.0246	0.0202	0.0166	0.0137	0.0113
44	0.6455	0.4184	0.2724	0.1781	0.1169	0.0770	0.0510	0.0338	0.0226	0.0184	0.0151	0.0124	0.0101
45	0.6391	0.4102	0.2644	0.1712	0.1113	0.0727	0.0476	0.0313	0.0207	0.0168	0.0137	0.0112	0.0091
46	0.6327	0.4022	0.2567	0.1646	0.1060	0.0685	0.0445	0.0290	0.0190	0.0154	0.0125	0.0101	0.0082
47	0.6265	0.3943	0.2493	0.1583	0.1010	0.0647	0.0416	0.0269	0.0174	0.0141	0.0113	0.0092	0.0074
48	0.6203	0.3865	0.2420	0.1522	0.0961	0.0610	0.0389	0.0249	0.0160	0.0128	0.0103	0.0083	0.0067
49	0.6141	0.3790	0.2350	0.1463	0.0916	0.0576	0.0363	0.0230	0.0147	0.0117	0.0094	0.0075	0.0060
50	0.6080	0.3715	0.2281	0.1407	0.0872	0.0543	0.0340	0.0213	0.0135	0.0107	0.0085	0.0068	0.0054

11.50%	12.00%	12.50%	13.00%	13.50%	14.00%	14.50%	15.00%	15.50%	16.00%	17.00%	18.00%	19.00%	20.00%
0.8969	0.8929	0.8889	0.8850	0.8811	0.8772	0.8734	0.8696	0.8658	0.8621	0.8547	0.8475	0.8403	0.8333
0.8044	0.7972	0.7901	0.7832	0.7763	0.7695	0.7628	0.7561	0.7496	0.7432	0.7305	0.7182	0.7062	0.6944
0.7214	0.7118	0.7023	0.6931	0.6839	0.6750	0.6662	0.6575	0.6490	0.6407	0.6244	0.6086	0.5934	0.5787
0.6470	0.6355	0.6243	0.6133	0.6026	0.5921	0.5818	0.5718	0.5619	0.5523	0.5337	0.5158	0.4987	0.4823
0.5803	0.5674	0.5549	0.5428	0.5309	0.5194	0.5081	0.4972	0.4865	0.4761	0.4561	0.4371	0.4191	0.4019
0.5204	0.5066	0.4933	0.4803	0.4678	0.4556	0.4438	0.4323	0.4212	0.4104	0.3898	0.3704	0.3521	0.3349
0.4667	0.4524	0.4385	0.4251	0.4121	0.3996	0.3876	0.3759	0.3647	0.3538	0.3332	0.3139	0.2959	0.2791
0.4186	0.4039	0.3897	0.3762	0.3631	0.3506	0.3385	0.3269	0.3158	0.3050	0.2848	0.2660	0.2487	0.2326
0.3754	0.3606	0.3464	0.3329	0.3199	0.3075	0.2956	0.2843	0.2734	0.2630	0.2434	0.2255	0.2090	0.1938
0.3367	0.3220	0.3080	0.2946	0.2819	0.2697	0.2582	0.2472	0.2367	0.2267	0.2080	0.1911	0.1756	0.1615
0.3020	0.2875	0.2737	0.2607	0.2483	0.2366	0.2255	0.2149	0.2049	0.1954	0.1778	0.1619	0.1476	0.1346
0.2708	0.2567	0.2433	0.2307	0.2188	0.2076	0.1969	0.1869	0.1774	0.1685	0.1520	0.1372	0.1240	0.1122
0.2429	0.2292	0.2163	0.2042	0.1928	0.1821	0.1720	0.1625	0.1536	0.1452	0.1299	0.1163	0.1042	0.0935
0.2179	0.2046	0.1923	0.1807	0.1699	0.1597	0.1502	0.1413	0.1330	0.1252	0.1110	0.0986	0.0876	0.0779
0.1954	0.1827	0.1709	0.1599	0.1496	0.1401	0.1312	0.1229	0.1152	0.1079	0.0949	0.0835	0.0736	0.0649
0.1752	0.1631	0.1519	0.1415	0.1319	0.1229	0.1146	0.1069	0.0997	0.0930	0.0811	0.0708	0.0618	0.0541
0.1572	0.1456	0.1350	0.1252	0.1162	0.1078	0.1001	0.0929	0.0863	0.0802	0.0693	0.0600	0.0520	0.0451
0.1410	0.1300	0.1200	0.1108	0.1024	0.0946	0.0874	0.0808	0.0747	0.0691	0.0593	0.0508	0.0437	0.0376
0.1264	0.1161	0.1067	0.0981	0.0902	0.0830	0.0763	0.0703	0.0647	0.0596	0.0506	0.0431	0.0367	0.0313
0.1134	0.1037	0.0948	0.0868	0.0795	0.0728	0.0667	0.0611	0.0560	0.0514	0.0433	0.0365	0.0308	0.0261
0.1017	0.0926	0.0843	0.0768	0.0700	0.0638	0.0582	0.0531	0.0485	0.0443	0.0370	0.0309	0.0259	0.0217
0.0912	0.0826	0.0749	0.0680	0.0617	0.0560	0.0509	0.0462	0.0420	0.0382	0.0316	0.0262	0.0218	0.0181
0.0818	0.0738	0.0666	0.0601	0.0543	0.0491	0.0444	0.0402	0.0364	0.0329	0.0270	0.0222	0.0183	0.0151
0.0734	0.0659	0.0592	0.0532	0.0479	0.0431	0.0388	0.0349	0.0315	0.0284	0.0231	0.0188	0.0154	0.0126
0.0658	0.0588	0.0526	0.0471	0.0422	0.0378	0.0339	0.0304	0.0273	0.0245	0.0197	0.0160	0.0129	0.0105
0.0590	0.0525	0.0468	0.0417	0.0372	0.0332	0.0296	0.0264	0.0236	0.0211	0.0169	0.0135	0.0109	0.0087
0.0529	0.0469	0.0416	0.0369	0.0327	0.0291	0.0258	0.0230	0.0204	0.0182	0.0144	0.0115	0.0091	0.0073
0.0475	0.0419	0.0370	0.0326	0.0289	0.0255	0.0226	0.0200	0.0177	0.0157	0.0123	0.0097	0.0077	0.0061
0.0426	0.0374	0.0329	0.0289	0.0254	0.0224	0.0197	0.0174	0.0153	0.0135	0.0105	0.0082	0.0064	0.0051
0.0382	0.0334	0.0292	0.0256	0.0224	0.0196	0.0172	0.0151	0.0133	0.0117	0.0090	0.0070	0.0054	0.0042
0.0342	0.0298	0.0260	0.0226	0.0197	0.0172	0.0150	0.0131	0.0115	0.0100	0.0077	0.0059	0.0046	0.0035
0.0307	0.0266	0.0231	0.0200	0.0174	0.0151	0.0131	0.0114	0.0099	0.0087	0.0066	0.0050	0.0038	0.0029
0.0275	0.0238	0.0205	0.0177	0.0153	0.0133	0.0115	0.0099	0.0086	0.0075	0.0056	0.0043	0.0032	0.0024
0.0247	0.0212	0.0182	0.0157	0.0135	0.0116	0.0100	0.0088	0.0075	0.0064	0.0048	0.0036	0.0027	0.0020
0.0222	0.0189	0.0162	0.0139	0.0119	0.0102	0.0088	0.0075	0.0065	0.0056	0.0041	0.0031	0.0023	0.0017
0.0199	0.0169	0.0144	0.0123	0.0105	0.0089	0.0076	0.0065	0.0056	0.0048	0.0035	0.0026	0.0019	0.0014
0.0178	0.0151	0.0128	0.0109	0.0092	0.0078	0.0067	0.0057	0.0048	0.0041	0.0030	0.0022	0.0016	0.0012
0.0160	0.0135	0.0114	0.0096	0.0081	0.0069	0.0058	0.0049	0.0042	0.0036	0.0026	0.0019	0.0014	0.0010
0.0143	0.0120	0.0101	0.0085	0.0072	0.0060	0.0051	0.0043	0.0036	0.0031	0.0022	0.0016	0.0011	0.0008
0.0129	0.0108	0.0090	0.0075	0.0063	0.0053	0.0044	0.0037	0.0031	0.0026	0.0019	0.0013	0.0010	0.0007
0.0115	0.0096	0.0080	0.0067	0.0056	0.0046	0.0039	0.0033	0.0027	0.0023	0.0016	0.0011	0.0008	0.0006
0.0103	0.0086	0.0077	0.0059	0.0049	0.0041	0.0034	0.0028	0.0024	0.0020	0.0014	0.0010	0.0007	0.0005
0.0093	0.0077	0.0063	0.0052	0.0043	0.0036	0.0030	0.0025	0.0020	0.0017	0.0012	0.0008	0.0006	0.0004
0.0083	0.0068	0.0056	0.0046	0.0038	0.0031	0.0026	0.0021	0.0018	0.0015	0.0010	0.0007	0.0005	0.0004
0.0075	0.0061	0.0050	0.0041	0.0034	0.0028	0.0023	0.0019	0.0015	0.0013	0.0009	0.0006	0.0005	0.0003
0.0067	0.0054	0.0044	0.0036	0.0030	0.0024	0.0020	0.0016	0.0013	0.0011	0.0007	0.0005	0.0003	0.0002
0.0060	0.0049	0.0039	0.0032	0.0026	0.0021	0.0017	0.0014	0.0011	0.0009	0.0006	0.0004	0.0003	0.0002
0.0054	0.0043	0.0035	0.0028	0.0023	0.0019	0.0015	0.0012	0.0010	0.0008	0.0005	0.0004	0.0003	0.0002
0.0048	0.0039	0.0031	0.0025	0.0020	0.0016	0.0013	0.0011	0.0009	0.0007	0.0005	0.0004	0.0002	0.0002
0.0043	0.0035	0.0028	0.0022	0.0018	0.0014	0.0012	0.0009	0.0007	0.0006	0.0004	0.0003	0.0002	0.0001

TABLE 2   PRESENT VALUE OF AN ORDINARY ANNUITY OF $1

Period	1.00%	2.00%	3.00%	4.00%	5.00%	6.00%	7.00%	8.00%	9.00%	9.50%	10.00%	10.50%	11.00%
1	0.9901	0.9804	0.9709	0.9615	0.0524	0.9434	0.9346	0.9259	0.9174	0.9132	0.9091	0.9050	0.9009
2	1.9704	1.9416	1.9135	1.8861	1.8594	1.8334	1.8080	1.7833	1.7591	1.7473	1.7355	1.7240	1.7125
3	2.9410	2.8839	2.8286	2.7751	2.7233	2.6730	2.6243	2.5771	2.5313	2.5089	2.4869	2.4651	2.4437
4	3.9020	3.8077	3.7171	3.6299	3.5460	3.4651	3.3872	3.3121	3.2397	3.2045	3.1699	3.1359	3.1025
5	4.8534	4.7135	4.5797	4.4518	4.3295	4.2124	4.1002	3.9927	3.8897	3.8397	3.7908	3.7429	3.6959
6	5.7955	5.6014	5.4172	5.2421	5.0757	4.9173	4.7665	4.6229	4.4859	4.4198	4.3553	4.2922	4.2305
7	6.7282	6.4720	6.2303	6.0021	5.7864	5.5824	5.3893	5.2064	5.0330	4.9496	4.8684	4.7893	4.7122
8	7.6517	7.3255	7.0197	6.7327	6.4632	6.2098	5.9713	5.7466	5.5348	5.4334	5.3349	5.2392	5.1461
9	8.5660	8.1622	7.7861	7.4353	7.1078	6.8017	6.5152	6.2469	5.9953	5.8753	5.7590	5.6463	5.5371
10	9.4713	8.9826	8.5302	8.1109	7.7217	7.3601	7.0236	6.7101	6.4177	6.2788	6.1446	6.0148	5.8892
11	10.3676	9.7869	9.2526	8.7605	8.3064	7.8869	7.4987	7.1390	6.8052	6.6473	6.4951	6.3482	6.2065
12	11.2551	10.5753	9.9540	9.3851	8.8633	8.3838	7.9427	7.5361	7.1607	6.9838	6.8137	6.6500	6.4924
13	12.1337	11.3484	10.6350	9.9857	9.3936	8.8527	8.3577	7.9038	7.4869	7.2912	7.1034	6.9230	6.7499
14	13.0037	12.1063	11.2961	10.5631	9.8986	9.2950	8.7455	8.2442	7.7862	7.5719	7.3667	7.1702	6.9819
15	13.8651	12.8493	11.9379	11.1184	10.3797	9.7123	9.1079	8.5595	8.0607	7.8282	7.6061	7.3938	7.1909
16	14.7179	13.5777	12.5611	11.6523	10.8378	10.1059	9.4467	8.8514	8.3126	8.0623	7.8237	7.5962	7.3792
17	15.5623	14.2919	13.1661	12.1657	11.2741	10.4773	9.7632	9.1216	8.5436	8.2760	8.0216	7.7794	7.5488
18	16.3983	14.9920	13.7535	12.6593	11.6896	10.8276	10.0591	9.3719	8.7556	8.4713	8.2014	7.9452	7.7016
19	17.2260	15.6785	14.3238	13.1339	12.0853	11.1581	10.3356	9.6036	8.9501	8.6496	8.3649	8.0952	7.8393
20	18.0456	16.3514	14.8775	13.5903	12.4622	11.4699	10.5940	9.8182	9.1286	8.8124	8.5136	8.2309	7.9633
21	18.8570	17.0112	15.4150	14.0292	12.8212	11.7641	10.8355	10.0168	9.2922	8.9611	8.6487	8.3538	8.0751
22	19.6604	17.6581	15.9369	14.4511	13.1630	12.0416	11.0612	10.2007	9.4424	9.0969	8.7715	8.4649	8.1757
23	20.4558	18.2922	16.4436	14.8568	13.4886	12.3034	11.2722	10.3711	9.5802	9.2209	8.8832	8.5656	8.2664
24	21.2434	18.9139	16.9355	15.2470	13.7986	12.5504	11.4693	10.5288	9.7066	9.3342	8.9847	8.6566	8.3481
25	22.0232	19.5235	17.4132	15.6221	14.0939	12.7834	11.6536	10.6748	9.8226	9.4376	9.0770	8.7390	8.4217
26	22.7952	20.1210	17.8768	15.9828	14.3752	13.0032	11.8258	10.8100	9.9290	9.5320	9.1610	8.8136	8.4881
27	23.5596	20.7069	18.3270	16.3296	14.6430	13.2105	11.9867	10.9352	10.0266	9.6183	9.2372	8.8811	8.5478
28	24.3164	21.2813	18.7641	16.6631	14.8981	13.4062	12.1371	11.0511	10.1161	9.6971	9.3066	8.9422	8.6016
29	25.0658	21.8444	19.1885	16.9837	15.1411	13.5907	12.2777	11.1584	10.1983	9.7690	9.3696	8.9974	8.6501
30	25.8077	22.3965	19.6004	17.2920	15.3725	13.7648	12.4090	11.2578	10.2737	9.8347	9.4269	9.0474	8.6938
31	26.5423	22.9377	20.0004	17.5885	15.5928	13.9291	12.5318	11.3498	10.3428	9.8947	9.4790	9.0927	8.7332
32	27.2696	23.4683	20.3888	17.8736	15.8027	14.0840	12.6466	11.4350	10.4062	9.9495	9.5264	9.1337	8.7686
33	27.9897	23.9886	20.7658	18.1477	16.0026	14.2302	12.7538	11.5139	10.4664	9.9996	9.5694	9.1707	8.8005
34	28.7027	24.4986	21.1318	18.4112	16.1929	14.3681	12.8540	11.5869	10.5178	10.0453	9.6086	9.2043	8.8293
35	29.4086	24.9986	21.4872	18.6646	16.3742	14.4983	12.9477	11.6546	10.5668	10.0870	9.6442	9.2347	8.8552
36	30.1075	25.4888	21.8323	18.9083	16.5469	14.6210	13.0352	11.7172	10.6118	10.1251	9.6765	9.2621	8.8786
37	30.7995	25.9695	22.1672	19.1426	16.7113	14.7368	13.1170	11.7752	10.6530	10.1599	9.7059	9.2870	8.8996
38	31.4847	26.4406	22.4925	19.3679	16.8679	14.8460	13.1935	11.8289	10.6908	10.1917	9.7327	9.3095	8.9186
39	32.1630	26.9026	22.8082	19.5845	17.0170	14.9491	13.2649	11.8786	10.7255	10.2207	9.7570	9.3299	8.9357
40	32.8347	27.3555	23.1148	19.7928	17.1591	15.0463	13.3317	11.9246	10.7574	10.2473	9.7791	9.3483	8.9511
41	33.4997	27.7995	23.4124	19.9931	17.2944	15.1380	13.3941	11.9672	10.7866	10.2715	9.7991	9.3650	8.9649
42	34.1581	28.2348	23.7014	20.1856	17.4232	15.2245	13.4525	12.0067	10.8134	10.2936	9.8174	9.3801	8.9774
43	34.8100	28.6616	23.9819	20.3708	17.5459	15.3062	13.5070	12.0432	10.8380	10.3138	9.8340	9.3937	8.9887
44	35.4555	29.0800	24.2543	20.5488	17.6628	15.3832	13.5579	12.0771	10.8605	10.3322	9.8491	9.4061	8.9988
45	36.0945	29.4902	24.5187	20.7200	17.7741	15.4558	13.6055	12.1084	10.8812	10.3490	9.8628	9.4163	9.0079
46	36.7272	29.8923	24.7755	20.8847	17.8801	15.5244	13.6500	12.1374	10.9002	10.3644	9.8753	9.4274	9.0161
47	37.3537	30.2866	25.0247	21.0429	17.9810	15.5890	13.6916	12.1643	10.9176	10.3785	9.8866	9.4366	9.0236
48	37.9740	30.6731	25.2667	21.1951	18.0772	15.6500	13.7305	12.1891	10.9336	10.3913	9.8969	9.4449	9.0302
49	38.5881	31.0521	25.5017	21.3415	18.1687	15.7076	13.7668	12.2122	10.9482	10.4030	9.9063	9.4524	9.0362
50	39.1961	31.4236	25.7298	21.4822	18.2559	15.7619	13.8008	12.2335	10.9617	10.4137	9.9148	9.4591	9.0417

11.50%	12.00%	12.50%	13.00%	13.50%	14.00%	14.50%	15.00%	15.50%	16.00%	17.00%	18.00%	19.00%	20.00%
0.8969	0.8929	0.8889	0.8850	0.8811	0.8772	0.8734	0.8696	0.8658	0.8621	0.8547	0.8475	0.8403	0.8333
1.7012	1.6901	1.6790	1.6681	1.6573	1.6467	1.6361	1.6257	1.6154	1.6052	1.5852	1.5656	1.5465	1.5278
2.4226	2.4018	2.3813	2.3612	2.3413	2.3216	2.3023	2.2832	2.2644	2.2459	2.2096	2.1743	2.1399	2.1065
3.0696	3.0374	3.0056	2.9745	2.9438	2.9137	2.8841	2.8850	2.8263	2.7982	2.7432	2.6901	2.6386	2.5887
3.6499	3.6048	3.5606	3.5172	3.4747	3.4331	3.3922	3.3522	3.3129	3.2743	3.1994	3.1272	3.0576	2.9906
4.1703	4.1114	4.0538	3.9976	3.9425	3.8887	3.8360	3.7845	3.7341	3.6847	3.5892	3.4976	3.4098	3.3255
4.6370	4.5638	4.4923	4.4226	4.3546	4.2883	4.2236	4.1604	4.0988	4.0386	3.9224	3.8115	3.7057	3.6046
5.0556	4.9676	4.8821	4.7988	4.7177	4.6389	4.5621	4.4873	4.4145	4.3436	4.2072	4.0776	3.9544	3.8372
5.4311	5.3283	5.2285	5.1317	5.0377	4.9464	4.8577	4.7716	4.6879	4.6065	4.4506	4.3030	4.1633	4.0310
5.7678	5.6502	5.5364	5.4262	5.3195	5.2161	5.1159	5.0188	4.9246	4.8332	4.6586	4.4941	4.3389	4.1925
6.0698	5.9377	5.8102	5.6869	5.5679	5.4527	5.3414	5.2337	5.1295	5.0286	4.8364	4.6560	4.4865	4.3271
6.3406	6.1944	6.0535	5.9177	5.7867	5.6603	5.5383	5.4206	5.3069	5.1971	4.9884	4.7932	4.6105	4.4392
6.5835	6.4236	6.2698	6.1218	5.9794	5.8424	5.7103	5.5832	5.4606	5.3423	5.1183	4.9095	4.7147	4.5327
6.8013	6.6282	6.4620	6.3025	6.1493	6.0021	5.8606	5.7245	5.5936	5.4675	5.2293	5.0081	4.8023	4.6106
6.9967	6.8109	6.6329	6.4624	6.2989	6.1422	5.9918	5.8474	5.7087	5.5755	5.3242	5.0916	4.8759	4.6755
7.1719	6.9740	6.7848	6.6039	6.4308	6.2651	6.1063	5.9542	5.8084	5.6685	5.4053	5.1624	4.9377	4.7296
7.3291	7.1196	6.9198	6.7291	6.5469	6.3729	6.2064	6.0472	5.8947	5.7487	5.4746	5.2223	4.9897	4.7746
7.4700	7.2497	7.0398	6.8399	6.6493	6.4674	6.2938	6.1280	5.9695	5.8179	5.5339	5.2732	5.0333	4.8122
7.5964	7.3658	7.1465	6.9380	6.7395	6.5504	6.3701	6.1982	6.0342	5.8775	5.5845	5.3162	5.0700	4.8435
7.7098	7.4694	7.2414	7.0248	6.8189	6.6231	6.4368	6.2593	6.0902	5.9288	5.6278	5.3528	5.1009	4.8696
7.8115	7.5620	7.3257	7.1016	6.8889	6.6870	6.4950	6.3125	6.1387	5.9731	5.6648	5.3837	5.1268	4.8913
7.9027	7.6447	7.4006	7.1695	6.9506	6.7429	6.5459	6.3587	6.1807	6.0113	5.6964	5.4099	5.1486	4.9094
7.9845	7.7184	7.4672	7.2297	7.0049	6.7921	6.5903	6.3988	6.2170	6.0443	5.7234	5.4321	5.1669	4.9245
8.0578	7.7843	7.5264	7.2829	7.0528	6.8351	6.6291	6.4338	6.2485	6.0726	5.7465	5.4510	5.1822	4.9371
8.1236	7.8431	7.5790	7.3300	7.0950	6.8729	6.6629	6.4642	6.2758	6.0971	5.7662	5.4669	5.1952	4.9476
8.1826	7.8957	7.6258	7.3717	7.1321	6.9061	6.6925	6.4906	6.2994	6.1182	5.7831	5.4804	5.2060	4.9563
8.2355	7.9426	7.6674	7.4086	7.1649	6.9352	6.7184	6.5135	6.3198	6.1364	5.7975	5.4919	5.2151	4.9636
8.2830	7.9844	7.7043	7.4412	7.1937	6.9607	6.7409	6.5335	6.3375	6.1520	5.8099	5.5016	5.2228	4.9697
8.3255	8.0218	7.7372	7.4701	7.2191	6.9830	6.7606	6.5509	6.3528	6.1656	5.8204	5.5098	5.2292	4.9747
8.3637	8.0552	7.7664	7.4957	7.2415	7.0027	6.7779	6.5660	6.3661	6.1772	5.8294	5.5168	5.2347	4.9789
8.3980	8.0850	7.7923	7.5183	7.2613	7.0199	6.7929	6.5791	6.3776	6.1872	5.8371	5.5227	5.2392	4.9825
8.4287	8.1116	7.8154	7.5383	7.2786	7.0350	6.8060	6.5905	6.3875	6.1959	5.8437	5.5277	5.2430	4.9854
8.4562	8.1354	7.8359	7.5560	7.2940	7.0482	6.8175	6.6005	6.3961	6.2034	5.8493	5.5320	5.2463	4.9878
8.4809	8.1566	7.8542	7.5717	7.3075	7.0599	6.8275	6.6091	6.4035	6.2098	5.8541	5.5356	5.2490	4.9898
8.5030	8.1755	7.8704	7.5856	7.3193	7.0701	6.8362	6.6166	6.4100	6.2153	5.8582	5.5386	5.2512	4.9930
8.5229	8.1924	7.8848	7.5979	7.3298	7.0790	6.8439	6.6231	6.4156	6.2201	5.8617	5.5412	5.2531	4.9930
8.5407	8.2075	7.8976	7.6087	7.3390	7.0868	6.8505	6.6288	6.4204	6.2242	5.8647	5.5434	5.2547	4.9941
8.5567	8.2210	7.9090	7.6183	7.3472	7.0937	6.8564	6.6338	6.4246	6.2278	5.8673	5.5453	5.2561	4.9951
8.5710	8.2330	7.9191	7.6268	7.3543	7.0998	6.8615	6.6381	6.4282	6.2309	5.8695	5.5468	5.2572	4.9959
8.5839	8.2438	7.9281	7.6344	7.3607	7.1050	6.8659	6.6418	6.4314	6.2335	5.8713	5.5482	5.2582	4.9966
8.5954	8.2534	7.9361	7.6410	7.3662	7.1097	6.8698	6.6450	6.4341	6.2358	5.8729	5.5493	5.2590	4.9972
8.6058	8.2619	7.9432	7.6469	7.3711	7.1138	6.8732	6.6479	6.4364	6.2377	5.8743	5.5502	5.2596	4.9976
8.6150	8.2696	7.9495	7.6522	7.3754	7.1173	6.8761	6.6503	6.4385	6.2394	5.8755	5.5511	5.2602	4.9980
8.6233	8.2764	7.9551	7.6568	7.3792	7.1205	6.8787	6.6524	6.4402	6.2409	5.8765	5.5517	5.2607	4.9984
8.6308	8.2825	7.9601	7.6609	7.3826	7.1232	6.8810	6.6543	6.4418	6.2421	5.8773	5.5523	5.2611	4.9986
8.6375	8.2880	7.9645	7.6645	7.3855	7.1256	6.8830	6.6559	6.4431	6.2432	5.8781	5.5528	5.2614	4.9989
8.6435	8.2928	7.9685	7.6677	7.3881	7.1277	6.8847	6.6573	6.4442	6.2442	5.8787	5.5532	5.2617	4.9991
8.6489	8.2972	7.9720	7.6705	7.3904	7.1296	6.8862	6.6585	6.4452	6.2450	5.8792	5.5536	5.2619	4.9992
8.6537	8.3010	7.9751	7.6730	7.3925	7.1312	6.8875	6.6596	6.4461	6.2457	5.8797	5.5539	5.2621	4.9993
8.6580	8.3045	7.9779	7.6752	7.3942	7.1327	6.8886	6.6605	6.4468	6.2463	5.8801	5.5541	5.2623	4.9995

TABLE 3 FUTURE VALUE OF $1

Period	3.00%	4.00%	5.00%	6.00%	7.00%	8.00%	9.00%	10.00%	11.00%	12.00%	13.00%	14.00%	15.00%
1	1.0300	1.0400	1.0500	1.0600	1.0700	1.0800	1.0900	1.1000	1.1100	1.1200	1.1300	1.1400	1.1500
2	1.0609	1.0816	1.1025	1.1236	1.1449	1.1664	1.1881	1.2100	1.2321	1.2544	1.2769	1.2996	1.3225
3	1.0927	1.1249	1.1576	1.1910	1.2250	1.2597	1.2950	1.3310	1.3676	1.4049	1.4429	1.4815	1.5209
4	1.1255	1.1699	1.2155	1.2625	1.3108	1.3605	1.4116	1.4641	1.5181	1.5735	1.6305	1.6890	1.7490
5	1.1593	1.2167	1.2763	1.3382	1.4026	1.4693	1.5386	1.6105	1.6851	1.7623	1.8424	1.9254	2.0114
6	1.1941	1.2653	1.3401	1.4185	1.5007	1.5869	1.6771	1.7716	1.8704	1.9738	2.0820	2.1950	2.3131
7	1.2299	1.3159	1.4071	1.5036	1.6058	1.7138	1.8280	1.9487	2.0762	2.2107	2.3526	2.5023	2.6600
8	1.2668	1.3686	1.4775	1.5938	1.7182	1.8509	1.9926	2.1436	2.3045	2.4760	2.6584	2.8526	3.0590
9	1.3048	1.4233	1.5513	1.6895	1.8385	1.9990	2.1719	2.3579	2.5580	2.7731	3.0040	3.2519	3.5179
10	1.3439	1.4802	1.6289	1.7908	1.9672	2.1589	2.3674	2.5937	2.8394	3.1058	3.3946	3.7072	4.0456
11	1.3842	1.5395	1.7103	1.8983	2.1049	2.3316	2.5804	2.8531	3.1518	3.4785	3.8359	4.2262	4.6524
12	1.4258	1.6010	1.7959	2.0122	2.2522	2.5182	2.8127	3.1384	3.4985	3.8960	4.3345	4.8179	5.3503
13	1.4685	1.6651	1.8856	2.1329	2.4098	2.7196	3.0658	3.4523	3.8833	4.3635	4.8980	5.4924	6.1528
14	1.5126	1.7317	1.9799	2.2609	2.5785	2.9372	3.3417	3.7975	4.3104	4.8871	5.5348	6.2613	7.0757
15	1.5580	1.8009	2.0789	2.3966	2.7590	3.1722	3.6425	4.1772	4.7846	5.4736	6.2543	7.1379	8.1371
16	1.6047	1.8730	2.1829	2.5404	2.9522	3.4259	3.9703	4.5950	5.3109	6.1304	7.0673	8.1372	9.3576
17	1.6528	1.9479	2.2920	2.6928	3.1588	3.7000	4.3276	5.0545	5.8951	6.8660	7.9861	9.2765	10.7613
18	1.7024	2.0258	2.4066	2.8543	3.3799	3.9960	4.7171	5.5599	6.5436	7.6900	9.0243	10.5752	12.3755
19	1.7535	2.1068	2.5270	3.0256	3.6165	4.3157	5.1417	6.1159	7.2633	8.6128	10.1974	12.0557	14.2318
20	1.8061	2.1911	2.6533	3.2071	3.8697	4.6610	5.6044	6.7275	8.0623	9.6463	11.5231	13.7435	16.3665

TABLE 4 FUTURE VALUE OF AN ORDINARY ANNUITY OF $1

Period	3.00%	4.00%	5.00%	6.00%	7.00%	8.00%	9.00%	10.00%	11.00%	12.00%	13.00%	14.00%	15.00%
1	1.0000	1.0000	1.0000	1.0000	1.0000	1.0000	1.0000	1.0000	1.0000	1.0000	1.0000	1.0000	1.0000
2	2.0300	2.0400	2.0500	2.0600	2.0700	2.0800	2.0900	2.1000	2.1100	2.1200	2.1300	2.1400	2.1500
3	3.0909	3.1216	3.1525	3.1836	3.2149	3.2464	3.2781	3.3100	3.3421	3.3744	3.4069	3.4396	3.4725
4	4.1836	4.2465	4.3101	4.3746	4.4399	4.5061	4.5731	4.6410	4.7097	4.7793	4.8498	4.9211	4.9934
5	5.3091	5.4163	5.5256	5.6371	5.7507	5.8666	5.9847	6.1051	6.2278	6.3528	6.4803	6.6101	6.7424
6	6.4684	6.6330	6.8019	6.9753	7.1533	7.3359	7.5233	7.7156	7.9129	8.1152	8.3227	8.5355	7.7537
7	7.6625	7.8983	8.1420	8.3938	8.6540	8.9228	9.2004	9.4872	9.7833	10.0890	10.4047	10.7305	11.0668
8	8.8923	9.2142	9.5491	9.8975	10.2598	10.6366	11.0285	11.4359	11.8594	12.2997	12.7573	13.2328	13.7268
9	10.1591	10.5828	11.0266	11.4913	11.9780	12.4876	13.0210	13.5795	14.1640	14.7757	15.4157	16.0853	16.7858
10	11.4639	12.0061	12.5779	13.1808	13.8164	14.4866	15.1929	15.9374	16.7220	17.5487	18.4197	19.3373	20.3037
11	12.8078	13.4864	14.2068	14.9716	15.7836	16.6455	17.5603	18.5312	19.5614	20.6546	21.8143	23.0445	24.3493
12	14.1920	15.0258	15.9171	16.8699	17.8885	18.9771	20.1407	21.3843	22.7132	24.1331	25.6502	27.2707	29.0017
13	15.6178	16.6268	17.7130	18.8821	20.1406	21.4953	22.9534	24.5227	26.2116	28.0291	29.9847	32.0887	34.3519
14	17.0863	18.2919	19.5986	21.0151	22.5505	24.2149	26.0192	27.9750	30.0949	32.3926	34.8827	37.5811	40.5047
15	18.5989	20.0236	21.5786	23.2760	25.1290	27.1521	29.3609	31.7725	34.4054	37.2797	40.4175	43.8424	47.5804
16	20.1569	21.8245	23.6575	25.6725	27.8881	30.3243	33.0034	35.9497	39.1899	42.7533	46.6717	50.9804	55.7175
17	21.7616	23.6975	25.8404	28.2129	30.8402	33.7502	36.9737	40.5447	44.5008	48.8837	53.7391	59.1176	65.0751
18	23.4144	25.6454	28.1324	30.9057	33.9990	37.4502	41.3013	45.5992	50.3959	55.7497	61.7251	68.3941	75.8364
19	25.1169	27.6712	30.5390	33.7600	37.3790	41.4463	46.0185	51.1591	56.9395	63.4397	70.7494	78.9692	88.2118
20	26.8704	29.7781	33.0660	36.7856	40.9955	45.7620	51.1601	57.2750	64.2028	72.0524	80.9468	91.0249	102.4436

GLOSSARY

ABC analysis an inventory control method that separates items into three groups based on annual cost-to-volume usage; items having the highest dollar volume are referred to as A items, while C items represent the lowest dollar volume

absorption costing a cost accumulation method that treats the costs of all manufacturing components (direct material, direct labor, variable overhead, and fixed overhead) as inventoriable, or product, costs; also known as full costing

accounting rate of return (ARR) the rate of accounting earnings obtained on the average capital investment over a project's life

activity a repetitive action, movement, or work sequence performed to fulfill a business function

activity-based costing an accounting information system that identifies the various activities performed in an organization and collects costs on the basis of the underlying nature and extent of those activities

activity-based management a discipline that focuses on how the activities performed during the production/performance process can improve the value received by a customer and the profit achieved by providing this value

activity center a segment of the production or service process for which management wants a separate report of the costs of activities performed

activity driver a measure of the demands placed on activities and, thus, the resources consumed by products and services; often indicates an activity's output

actual cost system a method of accumulating product or service costs that uses actual direct material, actual direct labor, and actual overhead costs

administrative department an organizational unit that performs management activities that benefit the entire organization

allocate assign based on the use of a cost predictor or an arbitrary method

annuity a series of equal cash flows occurring at equal time intervals

annuity due an annuity in which each cash flow occurs at the beginning of the period

applied overhead the amount of overhead assigned to Work in Process Inventory as a result of the occurrence of the activity that was used to develop the application rate; the result of multiplying the quantity of actual activity by the predetermined rate

appraisal cost a quality control cost incurred for monitoring or inspection; compensates for mistakes not eliminated through prevention

appropriation a maximum allowable expenditure for a budget item

asset turnover a ratio that measures asset productivity and shows the number of sales dollars generated by each dollar of assets during a specific period

authority the right (usually by virtue of position or rank) to use resources to accomplish a task or achieve an objective

backflush costing a costing system that focuses on output and works backward through the system to allocate costs to cost of goods sold and inventory accounts

Baldrige Award an award program administered by the U.S. Department of Commerce to recognize quality achievements by U.S. businesses

bar code a group of lines and spaces arranged in a special machine-readable pattern

batch-level cost a cost that is created by a group of similar things being made, handled, or processed at a single time

benchmarking the process of investigating, comparing, and evaluating the company's products, processes, and/or services against those of companies believed to be the "best in class" so that the investigating company can imitate, and possibly improve on, their techniques

benefits-provided ranking a listing of service departments in an order that begins with the one providing the most service to all other organizational areas; the ranking ends with the service department that provides the least service to all but the revenue-producing areas

bill of materials a document that contains information about product material components, their specifications (including quality), and the quantities needed for production

bottleneck a resource whose ability to process is less than the need for processing

breakeven graph a graphical depiction of the relationships among revenues, variable costs, fixed costs, and profits (or losses)

breakeven point (BEP) the level of activity, in units or dollars, at which total revenues equal total costs

budget the quantitative expression of an organization's commitment to planned activities and resource acquisition and use

budget committee a group, usually composed of top management and the chief financial officer, that reviews and approves, or makes adjustments to, the master budget and/or the budgets submitted from operational managers

budget manual a detailed set of documents that provides information and guidelines about the budgetary process

budget slack the intentional underestimation of revenues and/or overestimation of expenses

budgeting the process of determining a financial plan for future operations

business process reengineering (BPR) process innovation and redesign aimed at finding and implementing radical changes in how things are made or how tasks are performed to achieve substantial cost, service, or time reductions

business-value-added activity an activity that is necessary for the operation of a business but for which a customer would not want to pay

capacity a measure of production volume or of some other cost driver related to plant production capability during a period

capital asset an asset used to generate revenues or cost savings by providing production, distribution, or service capabilities for more than one year

capital budgeting the process of making decisions and budgeting for expenditures in long-term plant and equipment items; a process for evaluating proposed long-range projects or courses of future activity for the purpose of allocating limited resources to desirable projects

carrying cost the variable cost of keeping one unit of inventory in stock for one year; consists of storage, handling, insurance charges, property taxes based on inventory size, possible losses from obsolescence or the like, and opportunity cost

cash flow the receipt or disbursement of cash

centralization an organizational structure in which top management makes most decisions and controls most activities of the organizational units from the company's central headquarters

Certified Management Accountant an American or Canadian professional designation in the area of management accounting that recognizes the successful completion of an examination, acceptable work experience, and continuing education requirements

committed cost the cost of the basic plant assets and personnel structure that an organization must have to operate

compensation strategy a foundation for the compensation plan that addresses the role compensation should play in the organization

compound interest interest calculated on the basis of principal plus interest already earned

compounding period the time from one interest computation to the next

computer integrated manufacturing (CIM) a production system in which two or more flexible manufacturing systems are connected by a host computer and an information network

constraint a restriction on the ability to reach an objective

continuous budget an ongoing twelve-month budget that is created by the addition of a new budget month (twelve months into the future) as each current month expires

continuous improvement the process of making small, but ongoing, positive adjustments in the status quo

contribution margin (CM) selling price per unit minus all variable production, selling, and administrative costs per unit; the amount that contributes to the coverage of fixed costs and the generation of profits

contribution margin ratio (CM%) contribution margin divided by revenue; indicates what proportion of selling price remains after variable costs have been covered

control chart a graphical presentation of the results of a specified activity; indicates the upper and lower control limits and the results that are out of control

controller the person who supervises operations of the accounting system, but does not handle or negotiate changes in actual resources

controlling the exerting of managerial influence on operations so that they will conform to plans

conversion the process of changing raw materials and supplies into a different form

conversion cost the sum of direct labor and factory overhead costs; the cost incurred in changing direct materials or supplies into finished products or services

correlation a statistical measure of the strength of relationship between two variables

cost a monetary measure of the resources given up to acquire a good or a service

cost accounting an area of management accounting that focuses on determining the cost of making products or performing services

Cost Accounting Standards Board (CASB) a U.S. public-sector board with the power to promulgate uniform cost accounting standards for government contractors and federal agencies; established in 1970, terminated in 1980, and reestablished in 1988

cost avoidance a process of finding acceptable alternatives to high-cost items and not spending money for unnecessary goods or services

cost behavior the manner in which a cost responds to a change in a related level of activity

cost center an organizational unit in which the manager has the authority only to incur costs and is specifically evaluated on the basis of how well costs are controlled

cost consciousness a companywide employee attitude toward cost understanding, cost containment, cost avoidance, and cost reduction

cost containment the process of attempting, to the extent possible, to minimize period-by-period increases in per-unit variable and total fixed costs

cost control system a logical structure of formal and informal activities designed to influence costs and to enable management to analyze and evaluate how well expenditures were managed during a period

cost driver a factor that has a direct cause-effect relationship with a cost

cost object anything to which costs attach or are related

cost of capital (COC) the weighted average rate that reflects the costs of the various sources of funds making up a firm's debt and equity structure

cost of goods manufactured (CGM) the total cost of the goods that were completed and transferred to Finished Goods Inventory during the period

cost pool a grouping of all costs that are associated with the same activity or cost driver

cost reduction a process of lowering current costs, especially those in excess of necessary costs

cost table a database that provides information about how using different input resources, manufacturing processes, and product designs will affect product costs

cost-volume-profit (CVP) analysis a process of examining the relationships among revenues, costs, volume, and profits for a relevant range of activity and for a particular time frame

critical success factor an item that is so important to an organization that, ignoring it, the organization would fail; quality, customer service, efficiency, cost control, and responsiveness to change are five primary critical success factors

customer a generic term for the recipient or beneficiary of a process's output; can be internal or external

cycle time the time from when a customer places an order to the time that product or service is delivered or, using a full life-cycle approach, the time from the conceptualization of a product or service to the time the product or service is delivered to the customer

decentralization the downward delegation by top management of authority and decision making to the individuals who are closest to internal processes and customers; an organizational structure in which top management grants subordinate managers a significant degree of autonomy and independence in operating and making decisions for their organizational units

decision making the process of choosing among the alternative solutions available for a particular course of action

degree of operating leverage (DOL) a measure of how a percentage change in sales will affect profits; calculated at a specified sales level as contribution margin divided by income before tax

Deming Prize Japan's premier quality award

dependent variable an unknown variable that is to be predicted by use of one or more independent variables

design for manufacturability the process of reducing the number of parts in a product, using standard (rather than special order) parts when possible, and simplifying the assembly process

direct cost a cost that is clearly, conveniently, and economically traceable to a particular cost object

direct labor the time spent by individuals who work specifically on manufacturing a product or performing a service and whose efforts are conveniently and economically traceable to that product or service; can also be viewed as the cost of the direct labor time

direct material a readily identifiable, physical part of a product that is conveniently and economically traceable to that product

direct method (of service department cost allocation) a method that uses a specific base to assign service department costs directly to revenue-producing departments with no intermediate cost allocations

discount rate the rate of return on capital investments required by the company; the rate of return used in present value computations

discounting the process of removing a portion of the future cash flow that represents interest, thereby reducing that flow to a present value amount

discretionary cost an optional cost that a decision maker must periodically review to determine whether it continues to be in accord with ongoing policies

distribution cost any cost incurred to fill an order for a product or service; includes all money spent on warehousing, delivering, and/or shipping products and services to customers

dual pricing arrangement a transfer price method that allows a selling division to record the transfer of goods or services at a market-based or negotiated price and a buying division to record the transfer at a cost-based amount

dumping selling products abroad at lower prices than those charged in the home country or in other national markets

Du Pont model a model that indicates the return on investment as it is affected by profit margin and asset turnover

economic order quantity (EOQ) an estimate of the least costly quantity of units per order that would provide the optimal balance between ordering and carrying costs

economic production run (EPR) an estimate of the least costly quantity of units to produce in a production run to provide the optimal balance between setup and carrying costs

effectiveness the successful accomplishment of a task; a measure of how well the firm's objectives and goals were achieved; it involves comparing actual output results with desired results

efficiency the performance of a task to produce the best outcome at the lowest cost from the resources used; the degree to which the relationship between output and input is satisfactory

electronic data interchange (EDI) the almost instantaneous computer-to-computer transfer of information

employee time sheet (time ticket) a source document that indicates, for each employee, what jobs were worked on and for what amount of time

empowerment the process of giving workers the training and authority they need to manage their own jobs

engineered cost a cost that has been found to bear an observable and known relationship to a quantifiable activity base

equivalent units of production (EUP) an approximation of the number of whole units of output that could have been produced during a period from the actual effort expended during that period

ethical standard a moral code of conduct for an individual

European Community (EC) an economic alliance originally created in 1957 as the European Economic Community by France, Germany, Italy, Belgium, the Netherlands, and Luxembourg and later joined by the United Kingdom, Ireland, Denmark, Spain, Portugal, and Greece; has eliminated virtually all barriers to the flow of capital, labor, goods, and services among member nations; under the terms of the Maastricht Treaty (1993), the EC became the European Union

European Union (EU) see European Community

expatriate a parent company or third-country national assigned to a foreign subsidiary or a foreign national assigned to the parent company

expected capacity a short-run concept representing the anticipated level of activity for the upcoming year

expected standard a standard that reflects what is actually expected to occur in a future period

facility-level cost see *organizational-level cost*

failure cost a quality control cost associated with goods or services that have been found not to conform or perform in accordance with the required standards, as well as all related costs (such as that of the complaint department); may be internal or external

feasible solution an answer to a linear programming problem that does not violate any of the problem constraints

FIFO method a method of process costing that computes an average cost per equivalent unit of production using only current period production and current cost information; units and costs in beginning inventory are accounted for separately

financial budget a budget that reflects the funds to be generated or used during the budget period; includes the cash and capital budgets and the projected or pro forma financial statements

financing decision a judgment regarding how funds will be obtained to make an acquisition

fixed cost a cost that remains constant in total within a speci-

fied range of activity

fixed overhead spending variance the difference between actual and budgeted fixed overhead

flexible budget a series of financial plans that detail the individual variable and fixed cost factors comprising total cost and present those costs at different levels of activity according to cost behavior

flexible manufacturing system (FMS) a production system in which a single factory manufactures numerous variations of products through the use of computer-controlled robots

Foreign Corrupt Practices Act (FCPA) a law designed to prevent U.S. companies from offering or giving bribes (directly or indirectly) to foreign officials for the purpose of influencing those officials (or causing them to use their influence) to help the companies obtain or retain business

functional classification a grouping of costs incurred for the same basic purpose

future value (FV) the amount to which one or more sums of money invested at a specified interest rate will grow over a specified number of time periods

game a series of organized behavior patterns conforming to a set of rules that promote a defined outcome

General Agreement on Tariffs and Trades (GATT) a treaty among many nations setting standards for tariffs and trade for signees

global economy an economy characterized by the international trade of goods and services, the international movement of labor, and international flows of capital and information

globalization a changeover in market focus from competition among national or local suppliers to competition among international suppliers

goal a desired result or condition, contemplated in qualitative terms

goal congruence a condition that exists when the personal and organizational goals of decision makers throughout a firm are consistent and mutually supportive

grease payment a facilitating payment to a minor employee

high-low method a technique for separating mixed costs that uses actual observations of a total cost at the highest and lowest levels of activity and calculates the change in both activity and cost; the levels chosen must be within the relevant range

horizontal price fixing a practice by which competitors attempt to regulate prices through an agreement or conspiracy

hurdle rate the rate of return deemed by management to be the lowest acceptable return on investment

idle time the time spent waiting at a production operation for processing or the time spent in storage

imposed budget a budget that is prepared by top management with little or no input from operating personnel, who are simply informed of the budget goals and constraints

incremental analysis a decision making or computational process that focuses only on factors that change from one course of action or decision to another

incremental cost the additional cost of producing and/or selling a contemplated quantity of output

incremental revenue the additional revenue resulting from a contemplated sale of a quantity of output

independent project an investment project that has no specific bearing on any other investment project

independent variable a variable that, when changed, will cause consistent, observable changes in another variable; a variable used as the basis of predicting the value of a dependent variable

indirect cost a cost that cannot be clearly traced to a particular cost object; a common cost; a cost that must be allocated to a cost object

innovation a dramatic improvement in the status quo caused by radical new ideas, technological breakthroughs, or large investments in new technology or equipment

inspection time the time taken to perform quality control

Institute of Management Accountants a United States organization composed of individuals interested in the field of management accounting; was previously the National Association of Accountants; coordinates the American Certified Management Accountant program through its affiliate organization (the Institute of Certified Management Accountants)

internal rate of return (IRR) the discount rate at which the present value of the cash inflows minus the present value of the cash outflows equals zero

inventoriable cost see *product cost*

investing decision a judgment regarding which assets an entity will acquire to achieve its stated objectives

investment center an organizational unit in which the manager is responsible for generating revenues, planning and controlling costs, and acquiring, disposing of, and using plant assets to earn the highest feasible rate of return on the investment base

ISO 9000 a set of standards established by the international community to define the minimum acceptable quality for processes that generate products and services offered in international trade

job a single unit or group of like units identifiable as being produced to distinct customer specifications

job order costing the product costing system used by entities that produce tailor-made goods or services in limited quantities that conform to specifications designated by the purchaser of those goods or services

job order cost sheet a source document that provides virtually all the financial information about a particular job; the set of all job order cost sheets for uncompleted jobs provides supporting information about Work in Process Inventory

joint cost the cost incurred, up to the split-off point, for material, labor, and overhead in a joint process

joint process a process in which one product cannot be manufactured without others' being produced

just-in-time (JIT) a philosophy about when to do something; the *when* is "as needed" and the *something* is a production, purchasing, or delivery activity

just-in-time (JIT) manufacturing system a production system with the goals of acquiring components and producing inventory units only as they are needed, minimizing product defects, and reducing lead and setup times for acquisition and production

kaizen costing a costing technique to reflect continuous efforts to reduce product costs, improve product quality, and/or improve the production process after manufacturing activities have begun

kanban the Japanese word for card; another name for just-in-time manufacturing which originated in Japan from the use of cards to control the flow of materials or units between work centers

key variable a critical factor believed to be a direct cause of the achievement of or failure to achieve organizational goals and objectives; can be internal or external

labor efficiency variance the difference between the number of actual direct labor hours worked and the standard hours allowed for the actual output multiplied by the standard labor rate per hour

labor rate variance the difference between the total actual direct labor wages for the period and the standard rate multiplied by all hours worked during the period

lead time the time from the placement of an order to the arrival of the goods

least-squares regression analysis a statistical technique for mathematically determining the cost line of a mixed cost that best fits the data set by considering all representative data points; allows the user to investigate the relationship between or among dependent and independent variables

linear programming a method used to solve problems with one objective and multiple limiting factors; finds the optimal allocation of scarce resources when the objective and the restrictions on achieving that objective can be stated as linear equations

line employee a person who is directly responsible for achieving an organization's goals and objectives

long-term variable cost a cost that has traditionally been viewed as fixed, but which will actually react to some significant change in activity; a step fixed cost

make-or-buy decision a decision based on comparing the cost of internally manufacturing a product component with the cost of purchasing it from outside suppliers or from another division and, thus, attempting to assess the best uses of available facilities

Malcolm Baldrige National Quality Award   see *Baldrige Award*

management accounting   the process of identification, measurement, accumulation, analysis, preparation, interpretation, and communication of financial information used by management to plan, evaluate, and control within an organization and to assure appropriate use of and accountability for its resources

management by exception   a technique in which managers set upper and lower limits of tolerance for deviations and investigate only deviations that fall outside those tolerance ranges

manufacturing cell   a linear or U-shaped grouping of workers and/or machines

manufacturing cycle efficiency (MCE)   value-added processing time divided by total cycle time; provides a measure of processing efficiency

manufacturing resource planning (MRP II)   a fully integrated computer simulation system that involves the functional areas of marketing, finance, and manufacturing in planning the master production schedule using the MRP method; also can calculate resource needs such as labor and machine hours

margin of safety   the excess of the budgeted or actual sales of a company over its breakeven point; can be calculated in units or sales dollars, or as a percentage

mass customization   relatively low-cost mass production of products to the unique specifications of individual customers; requires the use of flexible manufacturing systems

master budget   the comprehensive set of all budgetary schedules and the pro forma financial statements of an organization

material price variance   the amount of money spent under (favorable) or over (unfavorable) the standard total price for a given quantity of materials; may be calculated for quantity purchased or quantity used

material quantity variance   the cost saved (favorable) or expended (unfavorable) because of the difference between the actual quantity of material used and the standard quantity of material allowed for the goods produced during the period

material requirements planning (MRP)   a computer simulation system that helps companies plan by coordinating future production output requirements with individual future production input needs using a master production schedule

materials requisition   a source document that indicates the types and quantities of materials to be placed into production or used in performing a service; causes materials and their costs to be released from the raw materials warehouse and sent to Work in Process Inventory

matrix structure   an organizational structure in which functional departments and project teams exist simultaneously, so that the resulting lines of authority resemble a grid

method of neglect   a method of treating spoiled units in the equivalent units schedule as if they did not exist

mixed cost   a cost that has both a variable and a fixed component; it does not fluctuate in direct proportion to changes in activity, nor does it remain constant with changes in activity

monopolistic competition   a market structure in which there are many firms offering slightly differentiated products and services

monopoly   a market structure in which there is only one seller of a product or provider of a service

move time   see *transfer time*

mutually exclusive projects   a set of proposed investments for which there is a group of available candidates that all perform essentially the same function or meet the same objective; from this group, one is chosen and all others are rejected

mutually inclusive projects   a set of proposed investments that are all related to a primary project; when the primary project is chosen, all related investments are also selected

negotiated transfer price   an intracompany charge for goods or services that has been set through a process of negotiation between the selling and purchasing unit managers

net present value (NPV)   the difference between the present values of all the cash inflows and cash outflows of an investment project

net present value method   an investment evaluation technique that uses discounted cash flows to determine if the rate of return on a project is equal to, higher than, or lower than the desired rate of return

non-value-added activity   an activity that increases the time spent on a product or service but does not increase its worth to the customer

normal capacity   a firm's long-run average activity (over five to ten years) which considers historical and estimated future production levels as well as cyclical and seasonal fluctuations

normal cost system   a method of accumulating product or service costs that uses actual direct material and direct labor costs but assigns overhead costs to Work in Process Inventory through using a predetermined overhead rate

North American Free Trade Agreement (NAFTA)   an agreement among Canada, Mexico, and the United States establishing the North American Free Trade Zone, with a resulting reduction in trade barriers

objective   a target that can be expressed in quantitative terms to be achieved during a preestablished period or by a specified date

objective function   a mathematical equation that states the maximization or minimization goal of a linear programming problem

oligopoly   a market structure in which there are only a few firms, whose products or services may be either differentiated or standardized

operating budget   a budget that is expressed in both units and dollars

operating leverage a factor that reflects the relationship of a company's variable and fixed costs; measures the change in profits expected to result from a specified percentage change in sales

operations flow document a listing of all tasks necessary to make a unit of product or perform a service and the time allowed for each operation

opportunity cost the benefit foregone when one course of action is chosen over another

optimal solution the solution to a linear programming problem that provides the best answer to the allocation problem without violating any problem constraints

order point the inventory level that triggers the placement of an order

ordering cost the variable costs associated with preparing, receiving, and paying for an order

ordinary annuity an annuity in which each cash flow occurs at the end of the period

organization chart an illustration of the functions, divisions, and positions in a company and how they are related

organizational-level cost a cost incurred to support ongoing operations and provide available facilities

outlier a nonrepresentative point that either falls outside the relevant range or is a distortion of typical cost-volume relationships within the relevant range

outsource use a source external to the company to provide a service or manufacture a needed product or component

overapplied overhead the excess of overhead applied to Work in Process Inventory above the actual overhead incurred for a period

overhead the indirect or supporting costs of converting materials or supplies into finished products or services

Pareto principle a rule which states that the greatest effects in human endeavors are traceable to a small number of causes (the *vital few*), while the majority of causes (the *trivial many*) collectively yield only a small impact; this relationship is often referred to as the 20:80 rule

participatory budget a budget that has been developed through a process of joint decision making by top management and operating personnel

payback period the time required to recoup the original investment in a project through its cash flows

performance evaluation the process of determining the degree of success in accomplishing a task; relates to both effectiveness and efficiency

period cost any cost other than those associated with making or acquiring inventory

planning the process of translating goals and objectives into the specific activities and resources required to achieve those goals and objectives

post-investment audit a procedure in which management compares actual project results against the results expected at the inception of the project

practical capacity the activity level of a firm that could be achieved during normal working hours given unused capacity and ongoing, regular operating interruptions, such as holidays, downtime, and start-up time

practical standard a standard that allows for normal, unavoidable time problems or delays, such as machine downtime and worker breaks; can be reached or slightly exceeded approximately 60 to 70 percent of the time with reasonable effort by workers

predetermined overhead rate a budgeted constant charge per unit of activity used to assign overhead costs to production or services

predictor an activity measure that changes in a consistent, observable manner with changes in another item

preference decision a judgment regarding how projects are to be ranked based on their impact on the achievement of company objectives

present value (PV) the amount that a future cash flow is worth currently, given a specified rate of interest

prevention cost a quality control cost incurred to improve quality by preventing defects from occurring

price elasticity of demand a relationship that reflects the percentage change in the quantity demanded relative to the percentage change in price

price fixing a practice by which firms conspire to set a product's price at a specified level

price variance the difference between what was paid and what should have been paid for inputs during the period

prime cost the sum of direct material and direct labor costs

process benchmarking benchmarking in which the quality of internal processes are assessed by comparing them with similar processes of firms identified as having the highest-quality processes globally; also involves subsequent efforts to emulate and improve on the quality achievements of the benchmark firms

process costing a method of accumulating and assigning costs to units of production in companies that make large quantities of homogeneous products

process costing system the product costing system used by entities that produce large quantities of homogeneous goods in continuous mass production; costs are accumulated for each cost component in each department and assigned to all units that flow through the department

processing time the time taken to perform the functions necessary to manufacture a product

process-level cost a cost created by the need to implement or support a specific process

process map a flowchart or diagram that indicates every step in making a product or providing a service

process productivity the total units produced during a period using value-added processing time

process quality yield the proportion of good units that resulted from the activities expended

product complexity an assessment about the number of components in a product or the number of processes or operations through which a product flows

product contribution margin revenue minus total variable production costs

product cost any cost associated with making or acquiring inventory; also called inventoriable cost

product-level cost a cost that is caused by the development, production, or acquisition of a type of product

product margin the excess of a product's revenues over both its direct variable expenses and avoidable fixed expenses; the amount remaining to cover unavoidable direct fixed expenses and common costs and then to provide profits

product variety the number of different types of products produced (or services rendered) by a firm

production and cost report a document used in a process costing system; details all manufacturing quantities and costs, shows the computation of cost per EUP, and indicates the cost assignment to goods completed during the period and to those remaining in ending Work in Process Inventory

profitability index (PI) a ratio that compares the present value of net cash inflows with the present value of the net investment

profit center an organizational unit in which the manager is responsible for generating revenues and planning and controlling all expenses

profit margin the ratio of income to sales

profit-volume (PV) graph a graphical presentation of the profit or loss associated with each level of sales

program budgeting an approach to budgeting that relates resource inputs to service outputs and thereby focuses on the relationship of benefits to cost expenditures

project a future investment activity; typically includes the purchase, installation, and operation of a capital asset

pull system a production system in which parts are delivered or manufactured only as they are needed

purchasing cost the quoted purchase price of any item minus any discounts allowed plus shipping charges

pure competition a market structure in which there are many firms, each with a small market share, producing identical products

push system a production system in which work centers may produce inventory that is not currently needed because of lead time or economic order (or production) quantity requirements; the excess inventory is stored until it is needed

quality circle an intradepartmental or interdepartmental team of empowered workers who meet to identify and solve quality-related problems

quantity variance the difference between the quantity of actual inputs and the standard quantity of inputs for the actual output of the period multiplied by a standard price or rate

red-line system an inventory system in which a single container (or stack) of inventory is available for production needs and a red line is painted on the inventory container (or on the wall, for a stack) at a point deemed to be the reorder point

regression line a line representing the cost formula for a set of cost observations which has been fit to those observations in a mathematically determined manner

relevant cost a cost that is pertinent to or logically associated with a specific problem or decision and that differs between alternatives

relevant costing a process that allows managers to focus on pertinent facts and disregard extraneous information by comparing, to the extent possible and practical, the differential, incremental revenues and incremental costs of alternative decisions

relevant information information that is logically related to the decision under consideration, is important to a decision maker, and has a connection to or bearing on some future endeavor; information that is useful to managers in fulfilling their organizational functions

relevant range the specified range of activity over which a variable cost remains constant per unit or a fixed cost remains fixed in total

rent each equal cash flow of an annuity

residual income (RI) the profit earned that exceeds an amount "charged" for funds committed to a responsibility center

responsibility the obligation to accomplish a task or achieve an objective

responsibility accounting an accounting system that provides information to top management about segment or subunit performance

responsibility center the cost object under the control of a manager; in the case of a decentralized company, the cost object is an organizational unit such as a division, department, or geographical region

responsibility report a report that reflects the revenues and/or costs under the control of a specific unit manager

results benchmarking benchmarking in which an end product or service is examined; the focus is on product/service specifications and performance results

return of capital recovery of the original investment

return on capital income; equals the discount rate times an investment amount

return on investment (ROI) a ratio that relates income generated by an investment center to the resources (or asset base) used to produce that income

revenue center an organizational unit in which the manager is responsible only for the generation of revenues and has no control over setting selling prices or budgeting costs

routing document see *operations flow document*

safety stock the quantity of inventory kept on hand by a company to compensate for potential fluctuations in usage or unusual delays in lead time

sales mix the relative combination of quantities of sales of the various products that make up the total sales of a company

sales price variance the difference between actual and budgeted selling prices multiplied by the actual number of units sold

sales volume variance the difference between actual and budgeted volumes multiplied by the budgeted selling price

scarce resource an item that is essential to production activity but that is available only in a limited quantity

screening decision a judgment regarding the desirability of a capital project based on some previously established minimum criterion or criteria

service department an organizational unit that performs one or more functional support or assistance tasks for other internal units

service time the time taken to perform all necessary service functions for a customer

setup cost the direct and indirect labor cost of getting equipment ready for a new production run

simple interest interest calculated as a percentage of the original investment, or principal amount, only

simple regression a method in which only one independent variable is used to predict a dependent variable in least-squares regression

simplex method an iterative technique used to solve multi-variable, multiconstraint linear programming problems; usually requires the aid of a computer

simultaneous (concurrent) engineering an integrated approach in which all primary functions and personnel contributing to a product's origination and production are involved continuously from the beginning of a project

Society of Management Accountants of Canada the professional body representing an influential and diverse group of over 26,000 Certified Management Accountants; this body produces numerous publications that address business management issues

special order pricing the process of setting a sales price for manufacturing or service jobs that are outside the company's normal production or service realm

split-off point the point at which the outputs of a joint process are first identifiable as individual products

staff employee a person who is responsible for providing advice, guidance, and service to line personnel

standard a benchmark or norm against which actual results may be compared

standard cost a budgeted or estimated cost to manufacture a single unit of product or perform a single service

standard cost card a document that summarizes the direct material and direct labor standard quantities and prices as well as the overhead allocation bases and rates needed to complete one unit of product

standard cost system a product costing system that uses norms for direct material and direct labor quantities and/or costs and a predetermined rate as the standard for overhead; these standards are used to measure inventories and to compare with actual costs to determine deviations; a system in which standards are developed and used for planning and control purposes; a system in which both standard and actual costs are recorded in the accounting records

standard quantity allowed a measure of quantity that translates the actual output achieved into the standard input quantity that should have been used to achieve that output

Statements on Management Accounting (SMAs) nonbinding guidelines for cost and management accounting issued by the Institute of Management Accountants

statistical process control (SPC) any technique that is used to analyze whether processes are in or out of control; based on the theory that a process varies naturally over time but that uncommon variations also occur and are typically the points at which the process produces errors, which may be defective or spoiled goods or poor service

step cost a variable or fixed cost that shifts upward or downward when activity changes by a certain interval or step

step method (of service department cost allocation) a method in which service department costs are assigned to cost objects by use of a specific base after the most important interrelationships of the service departments and the revenue-producing departments have been considered

stockout a condition in which a company does not have inventory available when customers request it or when it is needed for production

strategic cost management (SCM) the managerial use of cost information for the purposes of setting and communicating organizational strategies; establishing, implementing, and monitoring the success of methods to accomplish the strategies; and assessing the level of success in meeting the promulgated strategies

strategic planning the process of developing a statement of long-range goals for an organization and defining the strategies and policies that will help the organization achieve those goals

strategic staffing a practice in which organizations analyze their personnel needs by considering long-term objectives and determine a specific combination of permanent and temporary or highly-skilled and less-skilled employees that offer the best opportunity to meet those needs

suboptimization a situation in which a unit manager makes decisions that positively affect his or her own unit, but are detrimental to other organizational units or to the company as a whole

substitute good a good that can be used in place of another to satisfy the same wants or needs

sunk cost the historical or past cost associated with the acquisition of an asset or a resource; it has no future recovery value

synchronous management all endeavors that help an organization achieve its goals

tactical planning the process of determining the specific objectives and means by which strategic plans will be achieved; also called operational planning

target costing a Japanese method of determining the maximum allowable cost of a product before it is designed, engineered, or produced by subtracting an acceptable profit margin rate from a forecasted selling price

tax benefit (of depreciation) the depreciation provided by a capital investment multiplied by the tax rate

tax shield (of depreciation) the amount of the reduction of taxable income provided by depreciation expense

theoretical capacity the estimated maximum potential production activity of a firm for a specific time

theoretical standard a standard that allows for no inefficiency of any type and, therefore, is sometimes also called a perfection or theoretical standard

throughput a plant's output to customers during a single period

timeline a visual tool that illustrates the timing of expected cash receipts and payments; used for analyzing cash flows of a capital investment proposal

total contribution margin revenue minus all variable costs regardless of the area (production or nonproduction) of incurrence

total cost to account for the balance in Work in Process Inventory at the beginning of the period plus all current costs for direct material, direct labor, and factory overhead

total quality management (TQM) a philosophy for organizational management and organizational change that seeks ever-increasing quality or continuous improvement

total units to account for the total units that were worked on in a department during the period; consists of beginning inventory units plus units started

total variance the difference between total actual cost incurred and total standard cost applied for the output produced during the period; can also be designated by cost components (direct material, direct labor, variable factory overhead, and fixed factory overhead)

transfer price an internal charge established for the exchange of goods or services between organizational units of the same company

transfer time the time it takes to move products or components from one place to another

treasurer the person who generally handles the actual resources in an organization but who does not have access to the accounting records

two-bin system an inventory system in which two containers or stacks of inventory are available for production needs; when production begins to use materials in the second bin, a purchase order is placed to refill the first bin

underapplied overhead the excess of actual overhead above the overhead applied to Work in Process Inventory for a period

unit-level cost a cost created by the production or acquisition of a single unit of product or the delivery of a single unit of service

units started and completed the total units completed during the period minus the units in beginning inventory; alternatively, units started minus units in ending inventory

value-added activity an activity that increases the worth of a product or service to the customer and for which the customer is willing to pay

value chain the linked set of value-creating activities beginning with the basic raw material sources and concluding with delivery of the ultimate end-use product to the final consumer

value chart a visual representation of the value-added and non-value-added activities and the time spent in all of these activities from the beginning to the end of a process

variable cost a cost that varies in total in direct proportion to changes in activity

variable costing a cost accumulation method that includes only variable production costs (direct material, direct labor, and variable overhead) as product or inventoriable costs and treats fixed overhead as a period cost; also known as direct costing

variable overhead efficiency variance the difference between budgeted variable overhead at actual input activity and budgeted variable overhead at standard input activity allowed

variable overhead spending variance the difference between actual variable overhead and budgeted variable overhead based on actual input

variance any difference between actual and standard (or budgeted) costs or quantities

variance analysis the process of categorizing the nature (favorable or unfavorable) of the differences between standard and actual costs and seeking the reasons for those differences

vertical price fixing a practice of collusion between a producing business and its distributors to control the prices at which the business's products may be sold to consumers

volume variance the difference between budgeted and applied fixed overhead

weighted average method a method of process costing that computes an average cost per equivalent unit of production; combines beginning inventory units with current production and beginning inventory costs with current costs to compute that average

work in process goods or services that have been started, but are not yet complete

zero-based budgeting a comprehensive budgeting process that systematically considers the priorities and alternatives for current and proposed activities in relation to organizational objectives

AUTHOR INDEX

ORGANIZATION INDEX

SUBJECT INDEX

U

Underapplied overhead, 148, 149
Unexpired cost, 15, 85
Unit costs, 87, 133, 200
Unit-level cost, 200
Units started and completed, 325

V

Value-added activity, 196, 834
Value chain, 13, 15, 45, 50, 68, 70
Value chart, 196, 197, 199
Value-to-price relationship, 69
Variable cost (see also Cost behavior), 85, 87, 138
Variable costing
 advantages, 374, 378
 comparison with absorption costing, 371
 defined, 371
 effects on accounting records, 380
 model, 373
Variable overhead (see also Overhead, variable)
 efficiency variance, 268, 269
 spending variance, 268, 269
Variance (see also Direct material variances; Direct labor variances; Management by exception; Overhead variances), 145, 251, 261
 analysis, 145, 271, 781, 785
 causes, 519
 conversion cost, 276, 277
 disposal at year-end, 149, 285
 price, 263
 quantity, 263
 responsibility for, 271, 781
 total, 263
Vertical price fixing, 604
Virtual company, 450, 612, 613
Volume variance (see also Fixed overhead volume variance), 270, 274

W

Wages (for factory labor), 93
Waste, 285, 443, 444
Weighted average cost of capital, 657
Weighted average method, 316, 320–327
Work in process, 11, 12, 15
Work in Process Inventory, 106, 134, 144, 147, 261, 285, 316, 326
Work teams, 44
World-class companies, 849

Z

Zero-base budgeting (see Budgeting, zero-base)
Zero-defects (see Continuous improvement; Quality; Just-in-time)
Zero inventory production systems (ZIPS) (see Just-in-time)
Zero volume inventory (see Just-in-time)

Photo Credits

vii: Courtesy of Rubbermaid. **viii:** Courtesy of Motorola. **ix,** top: Courtesy of Jubilations, Inc. **ix,** bottom: © Michael Newman/PhotoEdit. **x:** © Tom Hollyman/Photo Researchers, Inc. **xi:** Courtesy of Levi Strauss & Co. (Canada) Inc. **xii:** Courtesy of Marguerite's Cakes and Cecily Raiborn. **xiii:** Courtesy of DeBourgh Manufacturing Co. **xiv:** Courtesy of Gillette Company. **xv,** top: Courtesy of the Minnesota Twins. **xv,** bottom: Courtesy of Lloyd Manufacturing. **xvi:** Courtesy of Ochsner Medical Institutions. **xvii:** Courtesy of Marcopolo S/A. **xviii:** Courtesy of First Bank Systems. **xix:** Courtesy of ABB Asea Brown Boveri. **xx:** Courtesy of Southwire Company. **1:** Greg Pease/Tony Stone Images. **3:** Courtesy of Rubbermaid. **9:** Courtesy of Rubbermaid. **15:** Courtesy of Rubbermaid. **20:** Courtesy of Rubbermaid. **43:** Courtesy of Motorola. **52:** Courtesy of L.L. Bean Inc. **56:** Courtesy of the National Institute of Standards and Technology, U.S. Department of Commerce. **66:** Courtesy of Cecily Raiborn. **83:** Courtesy of Jubilations, Inc. **86:** Michael Siluk. **92:** Courtesy of Welch Foods Inc. **96:** © Julie Houck/Stock Boston. **100:** Courtesy of Sally Corporation. **129:** © Michael Newman/PhotoEdit. **132:** © Michael Newman/PhotoEdit. **134:** © Tony Freeman/PhotoEdit. **146:** Courtesy of Cecily Raiborn. **151:** Courtesy of Masco Corporation. **191:** © Tom Hollyman/Photo Researchers, Inc. **199:** © Tom McHugh/Photo Researchers, Inc. **200:** © Stacy Pick/Stock Boston. **215:** Bob Daemmrich/Stock Boston. **247:** Courtesy of Hewlett Packard. **249:** Courtesy of Levi Strauss & Co. (Canada) Inc. **257:** © Dennis Bud Gray/Stock Boston. **258:** Courtesy of Levi Strauss & Co. (Canada) Inc. **276:** © Dorothy Littell/Stock Boston. **315:** Courtesy of Marguerite's Cakes and Cecily Raiborn. **321:** © John Coletti/Stock Boston. **329:** Courtesy of Marguerite's Cakes and Cecily Raiborn. **336:** Courtesy of Senco Products, Inc. **367:** © Bill Pogue/Tony Stone Images. **369:** Courtesy of DeBourgh Manufacturing Co. **379:** Courtesy of DeBourgh Manufacturing Co. **386:** Courtesy of DeBourgh Manufacturing Co. **397:** © Dave Bartruff/Stock Boston. **405:** Courtesy of DeBourgh Manufacturing Co. **437:** Courtesy of The Gillette Company. **440:** © Bill Gillette/Stock Boston. **445:** Courtesy of The Gillette Company. **463:** © Larry Mulvehill/Photo Researchers, Inc. **493:** Courtesy of Minnesota Twins. **512:** © Lou Jones/Image Bank. **517:** Courtesy of Minnesota Twins. **524:** © Greg Pease/Tony Stone Images. **547:** Courtesy of Lloyd Manufacturing. **555:** Courtesy of Lloyd Manufacturing. **561:** © Felicia Martinez/PhotoEdit. **568:** © Andrew Sachs/Tony Stone Images. **597:** © Stacy Pick/Stock Boston. **599:** Courtesy of Ochsner Medical Institutions. **604:** © Bill Gallery/Stock Boston. **611:** Courtesy of Ochsner Medical Institutions. **617:** © Richard Pasley/Stock Boston. **653:** Courtesy of Marcopolo S/A. **658:** © Herb Snitzer/Stock Boston. **671:** Courtesy of Marcopolo S/A. **675:** © Michael Newman/PhotoEdit. **705:** Courtesy of First Bank Systems. **708:** Courtesy of First Bank Systems. **717:** © Lionel Delivigne/Stock Boston. **734:** Courtesy of Allen-Bradley Co. Inc. **771:** Courtesy of ABB Asea Brown Boveri. **776:** © Bill Bachman/PhotoEdit. **783:** Mark Richards/PhotoEdit. **791:** © Frank Herholdt/Tony Stone Images. **797:** © Stacy Pick/Stock Boston. **833:** Courtesy of Southwire Company. **845:** © Murray Alcosser/Image Bank. **848:** Courtesy of West Publishing Company. **859:** © Steve Skjold/PhotoEdit. **862:** © Robert Brenner/PhotoEdit.

GREENLAND
(DEN.)

ALASKA
(U.S.)

CANADA

UNITED
STATES

ATLANTIC

OCEAN

BAHAMAS

MEXICO   CUBA   DOMINICAN REP.
                                                   PUERTO RICO
HAWAII   HAITI   ST. KITTS
(U.S.)   ANTIGUA
                          BELIZE   VIRGIN ISLANDS DOMINICA
PACIFIC   GUATEMALA HONDURAS   ST. LUCIA BARBADOS
                 EL SALVADOR NICARAGUA ST. VINCENT GRENADA
                      COSTA RICA   TRINIDAD & TOBAGO GUYANA
                                                            SURINAME
                          PANAMA   VENEZUELA   FR. GUYANA

GA
GUINEA-B

S

OCEAN   COLOMBIA

                               ECUADOR

            NAURU   PERU
                 KIRIBATI
SOLOMON   TUVALU   TOKELAU   BRAZIL
ISLANDS   WEST.   AM.
           SAMOA SAMOA
VANUATU   FIJI
                             COOK   BOLIVIA
      TONGA NIUE IS.   PARAGUAY
NEW   (N.Z.) (N.Z.) FRENCH
CALEDONIA   POLYNESIA

A

                    PITCAIRN
                    (U.K.)

                                                    ARGENTINA
NEW   CHILE   URUGUAY
ZEALAND

                                            FALKLAND IS.
                                            (U.K.)

Tactical planning (p. 500)   the process of determining the specific objectives and means by which strategic plans will be achieved; also called operational planning

Zero-based budgeting (p. 527)   a comprehensive budgeting process that systematically considers the priorities and alternatives for current and proposed activities in relation to organizational objectives (from appendix)

SOLUTION STRATEGIES

BUDGET MANUAL

Should include:

1. Statements of the budgetary purpose and its desired results;
2. A listing of specific budgetary activities to be performed;
3. a calendar of scheduled budgetary activities;
4. sample budgetary forms; and
5. Original, revised, and approved budgets.

REVENUE VARIANCES

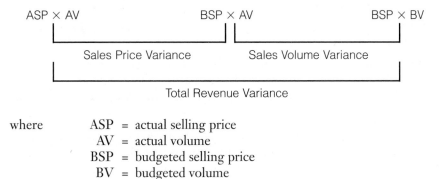

where   ASP = actual selling price
          AV = actual volume
          BSP = budgeted selling price
          BV = budgeted volume

END-OF-CHAPTER MATERIALS

■ QUESTIONS

1. Why is budgeting important? Discuss the reasons why it may be more important in some organizations than in others.

2. Briefly describe the budgeting process. Which steps do you consider the most critical?

3. Explain how strategic and tactical planning differ.

4. How are strategic and tactical planning related to budgeting? Present a model that depicts the relationship.

5. What are key variables, and how do they affect the process of planning?

6. What are the four primary market structures? Describe how each market type would affect strategy for a given product.

7. How do government regulations affect planning processes in the business organizations in your country?

8. Assume that a given product has a price elasticity of demand of 5. What does this suggest about the sensitivity of demand for this product to a change in its price?

9. Why must companies be aware of where their products are in their life cycles?

10. Why are decisions made during the development stage of a product so important?

11. Why do most organizations use participatory budgets? Discuss the disadvantages of using such budgets.

12. Define *budget slack*. Why does it occur, and what might be done to reduce or eliminate it?

13. Explain the following statement: "Good budgeting relies on trust."

14. What is a continuous budget? Why would a company use a continuous budget?

15. List the sections of a budget manual and briefly explain the role of each section.

16. Explain how managerial control is related to budgeting.

17. What does the sales price variance measure? What does the sales volume variance measure? Collectively, what do the sales price and sales volume variances explain?

18. Why should cost variances be based on actual volume of sales rather than budgeted volume of sales?

19. If a given manager fails to achieve his or her budget target, does this necessarily indicate that the manager has performed poorly? Explain.

20. Is it ever appropriate for managers to revise budgets once they have been set? Explain.

21. Why is it necessary to make budgets achievable so that managers who must work under the budgets will not play budget games?

22. Describe important external variables that affect the planning process in firms that operate globally.

23. (*Appendix*) What is zero-based budgeting? Why do you think it began in the governmental sector rather than in the business sector?

■ EXERCISES

24. (LO 1, 2, 5, 8; *Terminology*) Match the numbered item on the right with the lettered term on the left.

a. Key variable	**1.** A financial plan developed through joint decision making by top managers and operating personnel
b. Sales price variance	**2.** A quantitative expression of commitment to planned activities and resource acquisition and use
c. Budgeting	**3.** A difference between actual and budgeted revenues caused by selling a different number of units than budgeted
d. Sales volume variance	**4.** A financial plan prepared by top managers with little or no input from operating personnel
e. Imposed budget	**5.** A critical causal factor in achievement of organizational goals and objectives
f. Budget	**6.** A difference between budgeted and

actual sales caused by a difference between actual and budgeted sales price

g. Participatory budget

7. The process of developing a quantitative plan in financial terms to satisfy company goals and objectives

25. (LO 2, 3, 5, 11; *Terminology*) Match the numbered item on the right with the lettered term on the left.

a. Tactical planning

1. A market structure in which there is only one seller of a product or service

b. Budget slack

2. The development of long-term goals, strategies, and policies

c. Monopoly

3. A market structure in which there are only a few sellers of a product or service

d. Strategic planning

4. The development of specific short-term objectives and the means by which strategic plans will be achieved

e. Oligopoly

5. The intentional underestimation of revenues or overestimation of expenses in a budget

f. Appropriation (appendix)

6. A process that systematically (re)considers current or proposed activities in light of priorities and alternatives for achievement of organizational goals and objectives

g. Zero-based budgeting (appendix)

7. Maximum allowable expenditure for an item in the budget

26. (LO 5; *Imposed vs. participatory budgets*) Indicate whether each of the following is an advantage of imposed budgets (AI), an advantage of a participatory budget (AP), or neither (N).

a. Develop fiscal responsibility and budgetary skills of operating personnel
b. Blend overview of top management with operating details
c. Reduce budgeting to entering data into a computer program
d. Increase chances that strategic plans will be incorporated into planned activities
e. Allow operating managers to completely take over the budgeting process
f. Incorporate top management's knowledge of overall resource availability
g. Produce more realistic budgets
h. Improve morale and motivation
i. Encourage operating managers to establish the long-run company goals
j. Incorporate inputs from persons most familiar with the needs and constraints of organizational units

27. (LO 4; *Product life cycle*) Below are characteristics of various stages of the product life cycle. For each characteristic, indicate which stage of the product life cycle is being described—development, introduction, growth, maturity, or harvest.

a. Prices are often cut dramatically to stimulate business.
b. No revenues are generated.
c. Expenditures are incurred for market research.
d. Sales have peaked and are declining.
e. The product reaches the breakeven point.

    f. Sales begin to stabilize or slowly decline.

    g. Profits begin to rise.

    h. Costs reach their lowest (per unit) level.

    i. Some 80 to 90 percent of a product's life cycle costs are determined.

    j. Revenues are just starting to be generated, but profits are very limited or nonexistent.

28. (LO 8; *Sales variances*) Macklin Company planned 1996 sales of 400,000 units at a $40 unit selling price. In early 1997, the company president asked why budgeted revenue had not been achieved. Investigation revealed the following:

Actual sales volume	412,000
Actual average sales price	$38

    Analyze the facts given and provide an explanation for the president.

29. (LO 8; *Sales variances*) The manager of a dairy has been asked by the company owner why sales of milk are below budget. Review of the budget reveals that revenue was expected to be $42,000, based on expected sales of 420,000 gallons at $.10 per gallon. Inspection of the records shows that 430,000 gallons were actually sold at $.09 per gallon. Analyze sales and explain what happened.

30. (LO 8; *Sales variances*) Jacqueline Hess delivers two-day marketing seminars for sales executives. Each program normally brings Jacqueline a $4,000 fee. Last year she presented 30 seminars, and she budgeted a 20 percent increase in programs for the current year. At the end of the current year, she is disappointed that her actual revenue is only $136,500. She presented 39 programs during the year.

    a. What was Ms. Hess's expected revenue for the current year?

    b. Explain why she did not achieve the budgeted revenue.

31. (LO 8; *Budget-to-actual comparison*) Photo Genic does wedding photography on weekends. He has been charging $225 for a complete album, and his costs have averaged $78 each. He believes he can book 30 weddings in 1997, and on that basis he prepares the following budget:

Revenue (30 × $225)	$6,750
Costs (all variable) (30 × $78)	2,340
Projected profits	$4,410

    In 1998, Photo is contemplating his results for 1997 and is disappointed that his profits are only $4,256. He asks your help in understanding the shortfall. Review of his journal shows that his fee averaged $218 per wedding and that his costs averaged $85. He photographed 32 weddings in 1997. Explain to Photo why he made less than he budgeted. (Hint: Analyze costs using the model for analyzing revenues that is presented in this chapter.)

32. (LO 8; *Causes of budgeting errors*) Some budgeting errors are listed below on the left; possible causes of these errors are listed on the right. Match the errors with the causes. More than one numbered cause may be appropriately matched with each error, and a cause may be used more than once.

a. Compensation costs higher than expected	**1.** Shortages in supply of critical direct materials
b. Sales volume less than expected	**2.** Increased rates for fringe benefits, insurance, or utilities